FEDERAL COURTS

CASES, COMMENTS, AND QUESTIONS

Sixth Edition

By

Martin H. Redish

*Louis and Harriet Ancel Professor of Law
and Public Policy
Northwestern University*

Suzanna Sherry

*Herman O. Loewenstein Professor of Law
Vanderbilt University*

AMERICAN CASEBOOK SERIES®

THOMSON
™
WEST

Mat #40393349

COPYRIGHT © 1983, 1989, 1994 WEST PUBLISHING CO.
© West, a Thomson business, 1998, 2002
© 2007 Thomson/West
    610 Opperman Drive
    P.O. Box 64526
    St. Paul, MN 55164–0526
    1–800–328–9352
Printed in the United States of America

ISBN–13: 978–0–314–16270–0
ISBN–10: 0–314–16270–4

 TEXT IS PRINTED ON 10% POST
CONSUMER RECYCLED PAPER

*To our children, Jessica and Elisa Redish, and
Hannah and Joshua Edelman*

*

Preface to the Sixth Edition

This edition reflects the jurisprudence of the last years of the Rehnquist Court and the first year of the Roberts Court, a time of exciting transitions. The Supreme Court has continued to refine and change doctrines of federal jurisdiction, including doctrines regarding state sovereign immunity, habeas corpus, federal question jurisdiction, supplemental jurisdiction, and others. We have included a number of new Supreme Court cases as principal cases, and have added many others to the notes. This edition also includes the latest federal courts scholarship. Throughout, we have maintained the core pedagogic structure and values that have characterized this book since its very first edition.

As always, we have been assisted in the preparation of this edition by many people. Excellent research assistance was provided by Vanderbilt students Christopher Champion, Laura Gary, Ty Shaffer, Catherine Tennant, and Benjamin Wickert, and Northwestern student Daniel Greenfield. We also thank our families for their unwavering support.

MARTIN H. REDISH
SUZANNA SHERRY

Chicago, IL
Nashville, TN
July 2006

*

Preface to the Fifth Edition

In this edition, we have updated the coverage to include recent judicial decisions and legal scholarship, while still maintaining the basic pedagogic structure of earlier editions. In the five years since the last edition, the Supreme Court has significantly expanded the reach of the Eleventh Amendment, interpreted the new federal habeas corpus legislation, and clarified or modified a variety of other doctrines. Federal courts scholarship has kept pace, addressing both the changing doctrines and the underlying theory. This new edition brings the casebook up to date on all of these exciting developments.

Many people contributed valuable assistance to this edition. Joshua Knapp (Vanderbilt class of 2003) provided excellent research assistance. And we are, as always, grateful for the love and support of our families.

MARTIN H. REDISH
SUZANNA SHERRY

Chicago, IL
Nashville, TN
May 13, 2002

*

Preface to the Fourth Edition

By combining a casebook that has been in use for over 15 years with the new perspectives of an experienced teacher and scholar of Federal Courts, we hope to bring to this edition the best of both worlds. In many ways the book follows the original pedagogic structure, one that is designed to reflect both the nature of the issues faced in current federal court litigation and that pervade modern scholarship. However, in certain instances we have added new chapters or sections which are intended either to reflect recent doctrinal developments or to focus more sharply some of the underlying theoretical issues that are implicated by the subject.

As is always the case, the book could not have been possible without the assistance of numerous individuals. We would especially like to thank our secretaries, Marti Blake at Minnesota and Sang Kim and Rob Steiner at Northwestern, for their tireless work in typing the manuscript. We would also like to thank our research assistants, Betsey Buckheit at Minnesota and Larry Katz, Daniel Polsby and Eli Rohlman at Northwestern, for their very valuable efforts. Finally, we would like to thank our families for their willingness to put up with us.

MARTIN H. REDISH
SUZANNA SHERRY

Chicago, Il
Minneapolis, MN
March 23, 1998

*

Preface to the Third Edition

This edition differs from the previous two in two important ways. First, it has benefitted from the addition of an experienced teacher and scholar of Federal Jurisdiction as a co-author. Second, it has added a completely new chapter dealing with the substantive scope of federal civil rights law under 42 U.S.C. § 1983, a subject ultimately related to the civil rights jurisdictional issues already covered in the book. The book's substantive scope was expanded without sacrificing either the detailed theoretical and doctrinal coverage of traditional areas of Federal Jurisdiction or its relatively compact size.

As is usually the case, the authors owe a debt of gratitude to those who provided valuable assistance in the preparation of this volume. We would like to thank Devri Glick of the class of 1995 at Northwestern and Ellen Kohler and John Cyran at the University of Colorado for their important research assistance. We would also like to thank Patricia Franklin at Northwestern and Carol Gillaspy at Colorado for their more-than-efficient secretarial assistance. Finally, we would both like to thank our families for being who they are.

MARTIN H. REDISH
GENE R. NICHOL

June, 1994

*

Preface to the Second Edition

This edition basically follows the same pedagogical structure employed in the first edition. However, several new sections and chapters have expanded the book's substantive scope, and of course all chapters have been updated, in terms of both judicial decisions and legal scholarship.

This edition has benefited substantially from the many valuable comments and suggestions I have received from Federal Jurisdiction teachers who have taught from the first edition. These include Patti Alleva, George Brown, Ron Collins, Stephen Gillers, Larry Marshall, Gene Nichol, Keith Rosenn and David Skover.

In addition, the diligent efforts of my research assistants have substantially improved the final product. They include Larry Allberg and Stephen Rothchild at Northwestern and Karen Calhoun and William Odle at the University of Michigan, where I have spent the last year as a visiting professor. The book would not have been produced without the hard work of my secretaries, Patricia Franklin at Northwestern and Jeanne Vestevich at Michigan. Finally, the moral and financial support of Northwestern University School of Law is gratefully acknowledged.

Indirect contributions to this book have also been made by the important people in my personal life. As ever, my wife, Caren, and my daughter, Jessica, remain the focus of my existence; their support continues to be essential to all of my scholarly efforts. A special thanks goes to my brother Joe, a pretty fair academic in his own right, without whose life-long friendship, encouragement and sibling rivalry this book no doubt would not have been written. A final word of thanks goes to my colleague and close friend, Phil Postlewaite, who has always been available to share the joys and frustrations of academic life. Perhaps more importantly, he remains, beyond question, the finest person with whom to share an afternoon in the Wrigley Field bleachers.

MARTIN H. REDISH

Chicago, Illinois
September, 1988

*

Preface to the First Edition

This book is designed for use solely in a classroom setting. The emphasis is therefore on cases, questions and notes that are designed to stimulate both the individual student's thought processes and class discussion of the material. Thus, the student should not expect that many of the questions following excerpted cases will lend themselves to easy or specific answers. In order to avoid undue frustration, the student should view the questions primarily as a means of guiding his or her personal analysis of the case and of providing a basis for in-class examination of the relevant issues.

The book would not have been possible without the aid I received from numerous sources. Initially, I should note the invaluable research services made available by the Northwestern University School of Law, which provided me with more than adequate physical and moral support. An important part of this support came in the form of the diligent work of my research assistants, all present or past law students at Northwestern: James Bowe, Yvette Ehr, Jeffrey Lillien, Mark Litvak and Karen Zulauf. In addition, Martha Koning, my secretary, deserves special thanks for her never-ending hard work and efficiency in typing the manuscript. Finally, my wife and daughter have made it all worthwhile.

Martin H. Redish

Northwestern University
School of Law
February, 1983

*

Summary of Contents

*

Table of Contents

Table of Cases

The principal cases are in bold type. Cases cited or discussed in the text are roman type. References are to pages. Cases cited in principal cases and within other quoted materials are not included.

*

FEDERAL COURTS

CASES, COMMENTS, AND QUESTIONS

Sixth Edition

*

Chapter 1

ISSUES IN JUDICIAL REVIEW

§ 1. THE INSTITUTION OF JUDICIAL REVIEW

In Marbury v. Madison, Chief Justice John Marshall established for American society the principle of judicial review—the power of the judiciary to invalidate acts of the majoritarian branches of the federal government found to be in conflict with the United States Constitution. In a number of ways, this decision and its progeny are concerned with issues of substantive constitutional law and theory. But the decision is also fundamentally intertwined with issues of federal jurisdiction, for that entire subject matter—and the material concerned in the first three chapters of this book in particular—are shaped in an important sense by an overriding theory of the role of the federal judiciary in a constitutional democracy.

Examine Article III of the Constitution, the judicial article. Note that under section 1, the judges of the federal courts are appointed (not elected) for life, and that their salaries cannot be reduced. Obviously, these protections are designed to insulate the federal judiciary, at least to some degree, from the influences and pressures of the political process. Yet the basic premise of our democratic society is, of course, some level of majoritarian rule, primarily through the decisionmaking of the representative branches of government. Exercise by the unrepresentative judiciary of the authority to invalidate the actions of the majoritarian branches presented at least a *prima facie* tension with the fundamental tenet of democratic theory.

Thus, in reading *Marbury* and the notes that follow, it is necessary to ask yourself the following questions: How does Chief Justice Marshall rationalize the judicial review power? How persuasive is his analysis? Are there alternative rationales that more cogently support the doctrine? In the sections following *Marbury,* keep in mind this basic question: In what manner should doctrines of federal jurisdiction be structured so that the federal judiciary will perform its proper role within the constitutional democratic structure?

1

MARBURY v. MADISON

Supreme Court of the United States, 1803.
5 U.S. (1 Cranch) 137.

At the last term, * * * William Marbury, Dennis Ramsay, Robert Townsend Hooe, and William Harper, by their counsel, Charles Lee, esq. late attorney general of the United States, severally moved the court for a rule to James Madison, secretary of state of the United States, to show cause why a mandamus should not issue commanding him to cause to be delivered to them respectively their several commissions as justices of the peace in the district of Columbia. This motion was supported by affidavits of the following facts; that notice of this motion had been given to Mr. Madison; that Mr. Adams, the late president of the United States, nominated the applicants to the senate for their advice and consent to be appointed justices of the peace of the district of Columbia; that the senate advised and consented to the appointments; that commissions in due form were signed by the said president appointing them justices, & c. and that the seal of the United States was in due form affixed to the said commissions by the secretary of state; that the applicants have requested Mr. Madison to deliver them their said commissions, who has not complied with that request; and that their said commissions are withheld from them; that the applicants have made application to Mr. Madison as secretary of state of the United States at his office, for information whether the commissions were signed and sealed as aforesaid; that explicit and satisfactory information has not been given in answer to that enquiry, either by the secretary of state or any officer in the department of state; that application has been made to the secretary of the Senate for a certificate of the nomination of the applicants, and of the advice and consent of the senate, who has declined giving such a certificate; whereupon a rule was laid to show cause on the 4th day of this term. * * *

* * *

Opinion of the court [delivered by Chief Justice Marshall].

At the last term on the affidavits then read and filed with the clerk, a rule was granted in this case, requiring the secretary of state to show cause why a mandamus should not issue, directing him to deliver to William Marbury his commission as a justice of the peace for the county of Washington, in the district of Columbia.

No cause has been shown, and the present motion is for a mandamus. The peculiar delicacy of this case, the novelty of some of its circumstances, and the real difficulty attending the points which occur in it, require a complete exposition of the principles, on which the opinion to be given by the court, is founded.

* * *

In the order in which the court has viewed this subject, the following questions have been considered and decided.

1st. Has the applicant a right to the commission he demands?

2dly. If he has a right, and that right has been violated, do the laws of his country afford him a remedy?

3dly. If they do afford him a remedy, is it a *mandamus* issuing from this court?

The first object of enquiry is,

1st. Has the applicant a right to the commission he demands?

His right originates in an act of congress passed in February 1801, concerning the district of Columbia.

* * *

It appears, from the affidavits, that in compliance with this law, a commission for William Marbury as a justice of peace for the county of Washington, was signed by John Adams, then president of the United States; after which the seal of the United States was affixed to it; but the commission has never reached the person for whom it was made out.

In order to determine whether he is entitled to this commission, it becomes necessary to enquire whether he has been appointed to the office. For if he has been appointed, the law continues him in office for five years, and he is entitled to the possession of those evidences of office, which, being completed, became his property.

* * *

It is * * * decidedly the opinion of the court, that when a commission has been signed by the President, the appointment is made; and that the commission is complete, when the seal of the United States has been affixed to it by the secretary of state.

Where an officer is removeable at the will of the executive, the circumstance which completes his appointment is of no concern; because the act is at any time revocable; and the commission may be arrested, if still in the office. But when the officer is not removeable at the will of the executive, the appointment is not revocable, and cannot be annulled. It has conferred legal rights which cannot be resumed.

The discretion of the executive is to be exercised until the appointment has been made. But having once made the appointment, his power over the office is terminated in all cases, where, by law, the officer is not removeable by him. The right to the office is *then* in the person appointed, and he has the absolute, unconditional, power of accepting or rejecting it.

Mr. Marbury, then, since his commission was signed by the President, and sealed by the secretary of state, was appointed; and as the law creating the office, gave the officer a right to hold for five years, independent of the executive, the appointment was not revocable; but vested in the officer legal rights, which are protected by the laws of his country.

To withhold his commission, therefore, is an act deemed by the court not warranted by law, but violative of a vested legal right.

This brings us to the second enquiry; which is,

2dly. If he has a right, and that right has been violated, do the laws of his country afford him a remedy?

The very essence of civil liberty certainly consists in the right of every individual to claim the protection of the laws, whenever he receives an injury. One of the first duties of government is to afford that protection. In Great Britain the king himself is sued in the respectful form of a petition, and he never fails to comply with the judgment of his court.

* * *

The government of the United States has been emphatically termed a government of laws, and not of men. It will certainly cease to deserve this high appellation, if the laws furnish no remedy for the violation of a vested legal right.

If this obloquy is to be cast on the jurisprudence of our country, it must arise from the peculiar character of the case.

It behooves us then to enquire whether there be in its composition any ingredient which shall exempt it from legal investigation, or exclude the injured party from legal redress. In pursuing this enquiry the first question which presents itself, is, whether this can be arranged with the class of cases which come under the description of *damnum absque injuria*—a loss without an injury.

This description of cases never has been considered, and it is believed never can be considered, as comprehending offices of trust, of honor or of profit. The office of justice of peace in the district of Columbia is such an office; it is therefore worthy of the attention and guardianship of the laws. It has received that attention and guardianship. It has been created by special act of congress, and has been secured, so far as the laws can give security to the person appointed to fill it, for five years. It is not then on account of the worthlessness of the thing pursued, that the injured party can be alleged to be without remedy.

Is it in the nature of the transaction? Is the act of delivering or withholding a commission to be considered as a mere political act, belonging to the executive department alone, for the performance of which, entire confidence is placed by our constitution in the supreme executive; and for any misconduct respecting which, the injured individual has no remedy.

That there may be such cases is not to be questioned; but that every act of duty, to be performed in any of the great departments of government, constitutes such a case, is not to be admitted.

* * *

The conclusion from this reasoning is, that where the heads of departments are the political or confidential agents of the executive, merely to execute the will of the President, or rather to act in cases in which the executive possesses a constitutional or legal discretion, nothing can be more perfectly clear than that their acts are only politically examinable. But where a specific duty is assigned by law, and individual rights depend upon the performance of that duty, it seems equally clear that the individual who considers himself injured, has a right to resort to the laws of his country for a remedy.

If this be the rule, let us enquire how it applies to the case under the consideration of the court.

That question has been discussed, and the opinion is, that the latest point of time which can be taken as that at which the appointment was complete, and evidenced, was when, after the signature of the president, the seal of the United States was affixed to the commission.

It is then the opinion of the court,

1st. That by signing the commission of Mr. Marbury, the president of the United States appointed him a justice of peace, for the county of Washington in the district of Columbia; and that the seal of the United States, affixed thereto by the secretary of state, is conclusive testimony of the verity of the signature, and of the completion of the appointment; and that the appointment conferred on him a legal right to the office for the space of five years.

2dly. That, having this legal title to the office, he has a consequent right to the commission; a refusal to deliver which, is a plain violation of that right, for which the laws of his country afford him a remedy.

It remains to be enquired whether,

3dly. He is entitled to the remedy for which he applies. This depends on,

1st. The nature of the writ applied for, and,

2dly. The power of this court.

1st. The nature of the writ.

* * *

It is true that the mandamus, now moved for, is not for the performance of an act expressly enjoined by statute.

It is to deliver a commission; on which subject the acts of Congress are silent. This difference is not considered as affecting the case. It has already been stated that the applicant has, to that commission, a vested legal right, of which the executive cannot deprive him. He has been appointed to an office, from which he is not removable at the will of the executive; and being so appointed, he has a right to the commission which the secretary has received from the president for his use. The act of congress does not indeed order the secretary of state to send it to him, but it is placed in his hands for the person entitled to it; and cannot be more lawfully withheld by him, than by any other person.

* * *

This, then, is a plain case for a mandamus, either to deliver the commission, or a copy of it from the record; and it only remains to be enquired,

Whether it can issue from this court.

The act to establish the judicial courts of the United States authorizes the supreme court "to issue writs of mandamus, in cases warranted by the principles and usages of law, to any courts appointed, or persons holding office, under the authority of the United States."

The secretary of state, being a person holding an office under the authority of the United States, is precisely within the letter of the description; and if this court is not authorized to issue a writ of mandamus to such an officer, it must be because the law is unconstitutional, and therefore absolutely incapable of conferring the authority, and assigning the duties which its words purport to confer and assign.

The constitution vests the whole judicial power of the United States in one supreme court, and such inferior courts as congress shall, from time to time, ordain and establish. This power is expressly extended to all cases arising under the laws of the United States; and consequently, in some form, may be exercised over the present case; because the right claimed is given by a law of the United States.

In the distribution of this power it is declared that "the supreme court shall have original jurisdiction in all cases affecting ambassadors, other public ministers and consuls, and those in which a state shall be a party. In all other cases, the supreme court shall have appellate jurisdiction."

It has been insisted, at the bar, that as the original grant of jurisdiction, to the supreme and inferior courts, is general, and the clause, assigning original jurisdiction to the supreme court, contains no negative or restrictive words; the power remains to the legislature, to assign original jurisdiction to that court in other cases than those specified in the article which has been recited; provided those cases belong to the judicial power of the United States.

If it had been intended to leave it in the discretion of the legislature to apportion the judicial power between the supreme and inferior courts according to the will of that body, it would certainly have been useless to have proceeded further than to have defined the judicial power, and the tribunals in which it should be vested. The subsequent part of the section is mere surplusage, is entirely without meaning, if such is to be the construction. If congress remains at liberty to give this court appellate jurisdiction, where the constitution has declared their jurisdiction shall be original; and original jurisdiction where the constitution has declared it shall be appellate; the distribution of jurisdiction, made in the constitution, is form without substance.

Affirmative words are often, in their operation, negative of other objects than those affirmed; and in this case, a negative or exclusive sense must be given to them or they have no operation at all.

It cannot be presumed that any clause in the constitution is intended to be without effect; and therefore such a construction is inadmissible, unless the words require it.

When an instrument organizing fundamentally a judicial system, divides it into one supreme, and so many inferior courts as the legislature may ordain and establish; then enumerates its powers, and proceeds so far to distribute them, as to define the jurisdiction of the supreme court by declaring the cases in which it shall take original jurisdiction, and that in others it shall take appellate jurisdiction; the plain import of the words seems to be, that in one class of cases its jurisdiction is original, and not appellate; in the other it is appellate, and not original. If any other construction would render the clause inoperative, that is an additional reason for rejecting such other construction, and for adhering to their obvious meaning.

To enable this court then to issue a mandamus, it must be shown to be an exercise of appellate jurisdiction, or to be necessary to enable them to exercise appellate jurisdiction.

It has been stated at the bar that the appellate jurisdiction may be exercised in a variety of forms, and that if it be the will of the legislature that a mandamus should be used for that purpose, that will must be obeyed. This is true, yet the jurisdiction must be appellate, not original.

It is the essential criterion of appellate jurisdiction, that it revises and corrects the proceedings in a cause already instituted, and does not create that cause. Although, therefore, a mandamus may be directed to courts, yet to issue such a writ to an officer for the delivery of a paper, is in effect the same as to sustain an original action for that paper, and therefore seems not to belong to appellate, but to original jurisdiction. Neither is it necessary in such a case as this, to enable the court to exercise its appellate jurisdiction.

The authority, therefore, given to the supreme court, by the act establishing the judicial courts of the United States, to issue writs of mandamus to public officers, appears not to be warranted by the constitution; and it becomes necessary to enquire whether a jurisdiction, so conferred, can be exercised.

The question, whether an act, repugnant to the constitution, can become the law of the land, is a question deeply interesting to the United States; but, happily, not of an intricacy proportioned to its interest. It seems only necessary to recognise certain principles, supposed to have been long and well established, to decide it.

That the people have an original right to establish, for their future government, such principles as, in their opinion, shall most conduce to their own happiness, is the basis, on which the whole American fabric has been erected. The exercise of this original right is a very great exertion; nor can it, nor ought it to be frequently repeated. The principles, therefore, so established, are deemed fundamental. And as the authority, from which they proceed, is supreme, and can seldom act, they are designed to be permanent.

This original and supreme will organizes the government, and assigns, to different departments, their respective powers. It may either stop here; or establish certain limits not to be transcended by those departments.

The government of the United States is of the latter description. The powers of the legislature are defined, and limited; and that those limits may not be mistaken, or forgotten, the constitution is written. To what purpose are powers limited, and to what purpose is that limitation committed to writing, if these limits may, at any time, be passed by those intended to be restrained? The distinction, between a government with limited and unlimited powers, is abolished, if those limits do not confine the persons on whom they are imposed, and if acts prohibited and acts allowed, are of equal obligation. It is a proposition too plain to be contested, that the constitution controls any legislative act repugnant to it; or, that the legislature may alter the constitution by an ordinary act.

Between these alternatives there is no middle ground. The constitution is either a superior, paramount law, unchangeable by ordinary means, or it is on a level with ordinary legislative acts, and like other acts, is alterable when the legislature shall please to alter it.

If the former part of the alternative be true, then a legislative act contrary to the constitution is not law: if the latter part be true, then written constitutions are absurd attempts, on the part of the people, to limit a power, in its own nature illimitable.

Certainly all those who have framed written constitutions contemplate them as forming the fundamental and paramount law of the nation, and consequently the theory of every such government must be, that an act of the legislature, repugnant to the constitution, is void.

This theory is essentially attached to a written constitution, and is consequently to be considered, by this court, as one of the fundamental principles of our society. It is not therefore to be lost sight of in the further consideration of this subject.

If an act of the legislature, repugnant to the constitution, is void, does it, notwithstanding its invalidity, bind the courts, and oblige them to give it effect? Or, in other words, though it be not law, does it constitute a rule as operative as if it was a law? This would be to overthrow in fact what was established in theory; and would seem, at first view, an absurdity too gross to be insisted on. It shall, however, receive a more attentive consideration.

It is emphatically the province and duty of the judicial department to say what the law is. Those who apply the rule to particular cases, must of necessity expound and interpret that rule. If two laws conflict with each other, the courts must decide on the operation of each.

So if a law be in opposition to the constitution; if both the law and the constitution apply to a particular case, so that the court must either decide that case conformably to the law, disregarding the constitution; or conformably to the constitution, disregarding the law; the court must determine which of these conflicting rules governs the case. This is of the very essence of judicial duty.

If then the courts are to regard the constitution; and the constitution is superior to any ordinary act of the legislature; the constitution, and not such ordinary act, must govern the case to which they both apply.

Those then who controvert the principle that the constitution is to be considered, in court, as a paramount law, are reduced to the necessity of maintaining that courts must close their eyes on the constitution, and see only the law.

This doctrine would subvert the very foundation of all written constitutions. It would declare that an act, which, according to the principles and theory of our government, is entirely void; is yet, in practice, completely obligatory. It would declare, that if the legislature shall do what is expressly forbidden, such act, notwithstanding the express prohibition, is in reality effectual. It would be giving to the legislature a practical and real omnipotence, with the same breath which professes to restrict their powers within narrow limits. It is prescribing limits, and declaring that those limits may be passed at pleasure.

That it thus reduces to nothing what we have deemed the greatest improvement on political institutions—a written constitution—would of itself be sufficient, in America, where written constitutions have been viewed with so much reverence, for rejecting the construction. But the peculiar expressions of the constitution of the United States furnish additional arguments in favour of its rejection.

The judicial power of the United States is extended to all cases arising under the constitution.

Could it be the intention of those who gave this power, to say that, in using it, the constitution should not be looked into? That a case arising under the constitution should be decided without examining the instrument under which it arises?

This is too extravagant to be maintained.

In some cases then, the constitution must be looked into by the judges. And if they can open it at all, what part of it are they forbidden to read, or to obey?

There are many other parts of the constitution which serve to illustrate this subject.

It is declared that "no tax or duty shall be laid on articles exported from any state." Suppose a duty on the export of cotton, of tobacco, or of flour; and a suit instituted to recover it. Ought judgment to be rendered in such a case? ought the judges to close their eyes on the constitution, and only see the law.

The constitution declares that "no bill of attainder or *ex post facto* law shall be passed."

If, however, such a bill should be passed and a person should be prosecuted under it; must the court condemn to death those victims whom the constitution endeavours to preserve?

"No person," says the constitution, "shall be convicted of treason unless on the testimony of two witnesses to the same overt act, or on confession in open court."

Here the language of the constitution is addressed especially to the courts. It prescribes, directly for them, a rule of evidence not to be departed from. If the legislature should change that rule, and declare *one* witness, or a confession *out* of court, sufficient for conviction, must the constitutional principle yield to the legislative act?

From these, and many other selections which might be made, it is apparent, that the framers of the constitution contemplated that instrument, as a rule for the government of *courts*, as well as of the legislature.

Why otherwise does it direct the judges to take an oath to support it? This oath certainly applies, in an especial manner, to their conduct in their official character. How immoral to impose it on them, if they were to be used as the instruments, and the knowing instruments, for violating what they swear to support!

The oath of office, too, imposed by the legislature, is completely demonstrative of the legislative opinion on this subject. It is in these words, "I do solemnly swear that I will administer justice without respect to persons, and do equal right to the poor and to the rich; and that I will faithfully and impartially discharge all the duties incumbent on me as according to the best of my abilities and understanding, agreeably to *the constitution*, and laws of the United States."

Why does a judge swear to discharge his duties agreeably to the constitution of the United States, if that constitution forms no rule for his government? if it is closed upon him, and cannot be inspected by him?

If such be the real state of things, this is worse than solemn mockery. To prescribe, or to take this oath, becomes equally a crime.

It is also not entirely unworthy of observation, that in declaring what shall be the *supreme* law of the land, the *constitution* itself is first mentioned; and not the laws of the United States generally, but those only which shall be made in *pursuance* of the constitution, have that rank.

Thus, the particular phraseology of the constitution of the United States confirms and strengthens the principle, supposed to be essential to all written constitutions, that a law repugnant to the constitution is void; and that *courts*, as well as other departments, are bound by that instrument.

The rule must be discharged.

Notes

1. The political context of *Marbury* was well described in Van Alstyne, *A Critical Guide to Marbury v. Madison*, 1969 Duke L.J. 1, 3–5:

On January 20, 1801, President John Adams offered the name of John Marshall for approval by the Senate as the fourth Chief Justice of the United States. The President's action followed the resignation of Oliver Ellsworth (who resigned as the third Chief Justice for reasons of health), and an unsuccessful overture to John Jay (the first Chief Justice) who declined the President's appointment on grounds of age and the necessity of sitting on the circuit courts. Marshall was forty-five years old, with twelve years practice but no prior judicial experience, and he was serving as Adams' secretary of state at the time of his appointment to the Court. The Senate approved the appointment and Marshall took the oath of office on February 4, 1801. A strong Federalist, Marshall was already at political odds with Thomas Jefferson who was about to take office as President, and his relationship with Jefferson became more antagonistic as subsequent events began to unfold.

In the presidential election of 1800, Jefferson had received a popular majority over Adams, but Federalist strength among the electors resulted in an electoral-vote tie between Jefferson and Aaron Burr. The election was therefore committed to the House of Representatives. Before the House acted on the presidency, however, the Federalist holdover Congress took a number of actions in an effort to preserve vestiges of party influence during the next administration. Two of these actions had a direct bearing on the federal judiciary.

On February 13, 1801, just nine days after Marshall took office as Chief Justice and four days before Jefferson was declared president by the House, the Federalist Congress adopted the Circuit Courts Act. This act altered the federal judiciary by relieving Supreme Court Justices of circuit duty, reducing the number of Supreme Court Justices from six to five (reportedly to keep Jefferson from appointing a replacement for Mr. Justice Cushing who was ill), and establishing six new circuit courts with sixteen judges all of whom were to be appointed by Adams and quickly approved by Congress before Jefferson took office. On March 2, 1801, two days before the government passed to Jefferson and the Republicans, Senate confirmation of all judicial posts was completed. Virtually all of the appointees were Federalists.

The Circuit Court Act itself, however, was not the immediate source of the legal issue subsequently reviewed in Marbury v. Madison. Rather, that issue arose from still another post-election Federalist effort to secure control of certain offices during the anticipated Jefferson administration. Pursuant to an act passed on February 27, 1801, Adams appointed forty-two justices of the peace for the District of Columbia and Alexandria, each to serve for a five-year term as provided by the Act itself. These appointees were all confirmed by the Senate on March 3, 1801, just one day before the national government changed hands. The commissions for these posts were made out in John Marshall's office, as Marshall was still serving as holdover Secretary of State although he had also been Chief Justice for nearly a month, but by midnight of March 3, at least four commissions had not yet been delivered.

Immediately upon assuming office, Jefferson ordered his new Secretary of State, James Madison, to hold up all commissions which had not yet been delivered. One of these was that of William Marbury.

On December 21, 1801, Marbury filed suit in the Supreme Court seeking a writ of mandamus to compel Madison to deliver his commission which, he claimed, Madison had no right to withhold. Marbury was represented by Charles Lee who had served as Attorney General under Adams. Madison received notice, but declined to acknowledge the propriety of the suit even by appearing through counsel. The order to show cause was issued by the Court and the case was set down for argument on the law for the next term. Thus the stage was already set for several important and politically incendiary issues: (1) Was the Secretary of State answerable in court for the conduct of his office? (2) Could the Court countermand a presidential decision respecting subordinate appointments? (3) By what means could any such judicial decision possibly be enforced?

The issue of judicial review came to independent prominence the next year, in 1802, while Marbury's case was still pending, when the Republican Congress debated its own authority to repeal the Circuit Courts Act. There was some apprehension that the Federalist-dominated Supreme Court might presume to declare the proposed act of repeal unconstitutional.

Early in 1802, however, the new Congress overcame its doubts respecting its own authority and that of the Court, and repealed the Circuit Courts Act. To gain time to strengthen Republican control of the national government, Congress also eliminated part of the 1802 Term of the Supreme Court, thus postponing a test of the Repeal Act's constitutionality, of judicial review itself, and of Marbury's case as well. All three matters awaited the Court's determination in 1803.

Professor Van Alstyne notes that "the Chief Justice had personal knowledge [of the facts] because of his previous involvement in the controversy while serving as Secretary of State." Id. at 1–2. For other historical accounts, see B. Ackerman, The Failure of the Founding Fathers 116–98 (2005); Hobson, *John Marshall, the Mandamus Case, and the Judiciary Crisis, 1801–1803*, 72 Geo.Wash.L.Rev. 289 (2003); O'Fallon, *Marbury*, 44 Stan.L.Rev. 219 (1992).

2.   Professor Akhil Amar argues that Chief Justice Marshall misinterpreted the mandamus clause of section 13 of the Judiciary Act, thus creating a conflict with the language of Article III that did not exist. Amar suggests that "the mandamus clause is best read as simply giving the Court remedial authority—for both original and appellate cases after jurisdiction * * * has been independently established. Strictly speaking, the * * * clause does not add to or 'confer' either original or appellate jurisdiction—it specifies a

possible consequence of, rather than a basis for, jurisdiction." Amar, *Marbury, Section 13, and the Original Jurisdiction of the Supreme Court*, 56 U.Chi.L.Rev. 443, 456 (1989). See also Van Alstyne, supra, 1969 Duke L.J. at 15. For recent defenses of Marshall's interpretation of section 13, see Edward A. Hartnett, *Not The King's Bench*, 20 Constit. Commentary 283 (2003); James E. Pfander, Marbury, *Original Jurisdiction, and the Supreme Court's Supervisory Powers*, 101 Colum.L.Rev. 1515 (2001). For background on the Judiciary Act, see G. Casper, Separating Power: Essays on the Founding Period 132–52 (1997).

3.   Can you articulate Chief Justice Marshall's reasoning in developing the concept of judicial review? Do you agree "that Marshall's arguments concerning the relationship between the actions of the other branches of the federal government and the Constitution can be subdivided into a series of assertions, none of which inexorably leads to the conclusion which Marshall draws from them"? J. Nowak & R. Rotunda, Constitutional Law 7 (4th ed. 1991). Cf. L. Hand, The Bill of Rights 1–11 (1958). Consider Van Alstyne, supra, 1969 Duke L.J. at 23, where it is argued that Marshall "blurs the distinction between *ordinary* judicial review and substantive *constitutional* review. [He] implies, wrongly, that substantive constitutional review is as customary and necessary as ordinary judicial review * * *. From the proposition that the judicial department must necessarily say what the law 'is', i.e., how a statute is to be interpreted, he derives the corollary that therefore the judicial department must also say what is 'law' in some sense beyond that of determining merely whether a purported statute is in fact an authentic legislative act, duly adopted and properly enrolled. It does not necessarily follow, however, that the powers of statutory interpretation, reconciliation, and procedural review embrace the power of substantive constitutional review." For a thoughtful modern defense of judicial review as a matter of constitutional interpretation, see John Harrison, *The Constitutional Origins and Implications of Judicial Review*, 84 Va.L.Rev. 333 (1998).

4.   Justice Frankfurter has asserted that Marshall's "conclusion in Marbury v. Madison has been deemed by great English speaking courts an indispensable, implied characteristic of a written constitution." Frankfurter, *John Marshall and the Judicial Function*, 69 Harv.L.Rev. 217, 219 (1955). Do you concur in this judgment? Cf. Van Alstyne, supra, 1969 Duke L.J. at 17: "That the Constitution is a 'written' one yields little or nothing as to whether acts of Congress may be given the force of positive law notwithstanding the opinion of judges, the executive, a minority or majority of the population or even of Congress itself * * * that such Acts are repugnant to the Constitution. That this is so is clear enough simply from the fact that even in Marshall's time (and to a great extent today), a number of nations maintained written constitutions and yet gave national legislative acts the full force of positive law without providing any constitutional check to guarantee the compatibility of those acts with their constitutions."

5.   One commentator has suggested that the holding in *Marbury* put the Supreme Court "in the delightful position * * * of rejecting and assuming power in a single breath." R. McCloskey, The American Supreme Court 42 (1960). What does this statement mean? Do you agree with it? Cf. G. Haskins & H. Johnson, II The History of the Supreme Court of the United States—Foundations of Power: John Marshall, 1801–15, 185 (1981) ("From

a political standpoint, Marshall's opinion has been considered as both expedient and tendentious"). For an analysis of Marshall's approach to the problem of separating law and politics, see Nelson, *The Eighteenth–Century Background of John Marshall's Constitutional Jurisprudence*, 76 Mich. L.Rev. 893, 932–42 (1978).

6. The Constitution, of course, says nothing directly on the issue of judicial review. There is debate among scholars as to whether the framers assumed or intended that such review would be exercised. Two commentators describe the nuances of the historical context:

> The principle of judicial review of legislative acts had been forming since at least the time of the Constitutional Convention. Forerunners of the principle undoubtedly can be found in colonial experience with enforcement of charters, in judicial nullification of legislation through interpretation, and in political correction by the English Privy Council of acts emanating from an inferior level of government, but the actual practice of judicial invalidation of acts of a coordinate branch of government did not arise until after the Revolution. * * *

> [By the latter part of the eighteenth century,] the judiciary had begun to evolve as a more distinct entity and to separate itself from its supportive role to the executive, with the result that legal issues were tending to be separated from political issues and to be decided in what we would call a 'legal' way, in accordance with more or less fixed norms or principles; other more controversial types of issues were being resolved by the executive and the legislature. This emerging distinction was not easy for many to grasp, since in the colonial period the courts— to some extent as handmaidens of political power—had performed innumerable executive, administrative, and even legislative tasks. No doubt those earlier functions help to explain why judicial review, when it began to appear in the 1780s seemed to be a political act that did not express, or was not responsive to, the will of the people. Even deeper-lying sentiments were present. The dread of royal power still lay heavily in the minds of those who had framed the Constitution, and it was to limit and check excessive exercise of power in the government that men had turned to popularly chosen legislative bodies. Yet it was not long before conservative opinion began to be alarmed by what were viewed as legislative excesses, reminiscent of magisterial decrees of the pre-Revolutionary period, because the legislatures were enacting laws to which the people at large had never given their full and unqualified assent. Because the acts of legislatures could thus arguably be subject to scrutiny, a certain mistrust developed that had the effect of benefiting the judiciary. * * *

> Against this background, it should not be startling that beginning in the 1780s courts began to hold unconstitutional legislative acts of a coordinate branch of government. G. Haskins & H. Johnson, supra at 186, 188–89.

For other historical accounts of the place of judicial review in the American founding, see J. Goebel, I The History of the Supreme Court of the United States—Antecedents and Beginnings to 1801 (1971); R. Berger, Congress v. The Supreme Court (1969); W. Crosskey, Politics and the Constitution in the

History of the United States (1953); Barnett, *The Original Meaning of the Judicial Power*, 12 S.Ct.Econ.Rev. 115 (2004). For discussions of the exercise of judicial review prior to *Marbury*, see Treanor, *Judicial Review Before Marbury*, 58 Stan.L.Rev. 455 (2005); Hamburger, *Law and Judicial Duty*, 72 Geo.Wash.L.Rev. 1 (2003); Sherry, *The Founders' Unwritten Constitution*, 54 U.Chi.L.Rev. 1127 (1987). On the history of judicial review generally, see S. Snowiss, Judicial Review and the Law of the Constitution (1990); Ruger, *A Question Which Convulses a Nation: The Early Republic's Greatest Debate About the Judicial Review Power*, 117 Harv.L.Rev. 826 (2004); Nelson, *Changing Conceptions of Judicial Review: The Evolution of Constitutional Theory in the States, 1790–1860*, 120 U.Pa.L.Rev. 1166 (1972); Van Alstyne, supra, 1969 Duke L.J. at 38–45.

In Federalist No. 78, Hamilton wrote: "The complete independence of the courts of justice is peculiarly essential in a limited Constitution. By a limited Constitution, I understand one which contains certain specified exceptions to the Legislative authority; such, for instance, as that it shall pass no bills of attainder, no *ex post facto* laws, and the like. Limitations of this kind can be preserved in practice no other way than through the medium of courts of justice; whose duty it must be to declare all acts contrary to the manifest tenor of the Constitution void. Without this, all the reservations of particular rights or privileges would amount to nothing."

To what extent should the conclusion about the framers' understanding or assumptions about the existence of judicial review be relevant to our modern conclusion about use of the concept? If relevant, should it be determinative? Cf. A. Bickel, The Least Dangerous Branch 15–16 (1962):

> [I]t is as clear as such matters can be that the Framers of the Constitution specifically, if tacitly, expected that the federal courts would assume a power—of whatever exact dimensions—to pass on the constitutionality of actions of the Congress and the President, as well as the several states. Moreover, not even a colorable showing of decisive historical evidence to the contrary can be made * * *.

> * * * But Holmes * * * told us that it is 'revolting to have no better reason for a rule of law than that so it was laid down in the time of Henry IV. It is still more revolting if the grounds upon which it was laid down have vanished long since, and the rule simply persists from blind imitation of the past.' * * *. Judicial review is a present instrument of government. It represents a choice that men have made, and ultimately we must justify it as a choice in our own time.

For a contrary view about the relevance of the framers' intent, see R. Berger, supra at 208–09. For a critical analysis of Berger's position, see Bice, *An Essay Review of Congress v. The Supreme Court*, 44 S.Cal.L.Rev. 499 (1971).

7. Is the concept of constitutional judicial review consistent with a democratic system of government? What are the competing arguments? Consider E. Rostow, The Sovereign Prerogative: The Supreme Court and the Quest for Law 149 (1962): "It is a grave oversimplification to contend that no society can be democratic unless its legislature has sovereign powers. The social quality of democracy cannot be defined by so rigid a formula * * *. The purpose of the Constitution is to assure the people a free and democratic

society. The final aim of that society is as much freedom as possible for the individual human beings * * *. The separation of powers under the Constitution serves the end of democracy by limiting the roles of the several branches of government and protecting the citizen, and the various parts of the state itself, against encroachments from any source."

To what extent is there even a conflict between judicial review and majoritarianism? A number of scholars have suggested the "countermajoritarian difficulty" with judicial review is exaggerated, if it exists at all. These scholars argue that the courts are not much more countermajoritarian than the legislative and executive branches, that "majoritarianism" is not an accurate description of our constitutional regime, and that in any case we should consider the system as a whole rather than its individual parts when we evaluate its democratic legitimacy. See D. Farber & S. Sherry, Desperately Seeking Certainty: The Misguided Quest for Constitutional Foundations (2002); Markovits, *Democratic Disobedience*, 114 Yale L.J. 1897 (2005); Croley, *The Majoritarian Difficulty: Elective Judiciaries and the Rule of Law*, 62 U.Chi.L.Rev. 689 (1995); Friedman, *Dialogue and Judicial Review*, 91 Mich.L.Rev. 577 (1993); Graber, *The Nonmajoritarian Difficulty: Legislative Deference to the Judiciary*, 7 Stud. in Am.Pol.Dev. 35 (1993); Winter, *An Upside/Down View of the Countermajoritarian Difficulty*, 69 Tex.L.Rev. 1881 (1991); Chemerinsky, *Foreword: The Vanishing Constitution*, 103 Harv. L.Rev. 43 (1989).

8. How broad is the power to which Chief Justice Marshall laid claim in *Marbury*? Some scholars have suggested that *Marbury* established only some form of "departmentalism" rather than judicial supremacy. See, e.g., K. Whittington, Constitutional Construction (1999) ("each branch, or department, of government has an equal authority to interpret the Constitution in the context of conducting its duties" and is "supreme within its own interpretive sphere"); Johnsen, *Functional Departmentalism and Nonjudicial Interpretation: Who Determines Constitutional Meaning*, 67 L. & Contemp.Probs. 105 (2004); Paulsen, *The Most Dangerous Branch: Executive Power to Say What the Law Is*, 83 Geo.L.J. 217 (1994); Engdahl, *John Marshall's "Jeffersonian" Concept of Judicial Review,* 42 Duke L.J. 279, 280 (1992). President Lincoln, in his first inaugural address, argued that " * * * the candid citizen must confess that if the policy of the Government upon vital questions affecting the whole people is to be irrevocably fixed by decisions of the Supreme Court, the instant they are made in ordinary litigation between parties in personal actions the people will have ceased to be their own rulers, having to that extent practically resigned their Government into the hands of that eminent tribunal." March 4, 1861, First Inaugural Address [6 Messages and Papers of the Presidents (Richardson ed. 1897) p. 5–10].

In Cooper v. Aaron, 358 U.S. 1 (1958), however, the United States Supreme Court answered an Arkansas challenge to judicial desegregation decisions by declaring that "the federal judiciary is supreme in the exposition of the law of the Constitution, and that principle [is] * * * a permanent and indispensable feature of our constitutional system." Id. at 18. The Court has recently reaffirmed this view of its own role: "No doubt the political branches have a role in interpreting and applying the Constitution, but ever since *Marbury* this Court has remained the ultimate expositor of the constitutional text." United States v. Morrison, 529 U.S. 598 (2000).

Professor Edward White has argued that *both* "judicial supremacy and departmental discretion [are] foundational principles" laid down by *Marbury*:

> [T]he "constitutional journey" of *Marbury v. Madison* is a narrative in which the two principles of *Marbury* have been consistently understood, while their relationship has been differently interpreted. In some periods of American history the judicial supremacy principle has been thought to require more or less constant constitutional scrutiny of activities of other branches of government by the Supreme Court, resulting in narrow definitions of the departmental discretion principle. In other times the judicial supremacy principle has been thought, because of its tendency to produce judicial sovereignty, to require comparatively broad definitions of the departmental discretion principle. In still other times the two principles seem at equipoise, as if a tacit understanding exists as to what constitutes the appropriate range of judicial supremacy. G. Edward White, *The Constitutional Journey of* Marbury v. Madison, 89 Va.L.Rev. 1463, 1469 (2003).

Much of what follows in this book depends on how broadly one reads the judicial role. Think about these different positions as you study the ebb and flow of federal court jurisdiction.

§ 2. STANDING

BENNETT v. SPEAR

Supreme Court of the United States, 1997.
520 U.S. 154.

JUSTICE SCALIA delivered the opinion of the Court.

This is a challenge to a biological opinion issued by the Fish and Wildlife Service in accordance with the Endangered Species Act of 1973 (ESA), concerning the operation of the Klamath Irrigation Project by the Bureau of Reclamation, and the project's impact on two varieties of endangered fish. The question for decision is whether the petitioners, who have competing economic and other interests in Klamath Project water, have standing to seek judicial review of the biological opinion under the citizen-suit provision of the ESA, and the Administrative Procedure Act (APA).

I

The ESA requires the Secretary of the Interior to promulgate regulations listing those species of animals that are "threatened" or "endangered" under specified criteria, and to designate their "critical habitat." The ESA further requires each federal agency to "insure that any action authorized, funded, or carried out by such agency ... is not likely to jeopardize the continued existence of any endangered species or threatened species or result in the destruction or adverse modification of habitat of such species which is determined by the Secretary ... to be critical." If an agency determines that action it proposes to take may adversely affect a listed species, it must engage in formal consultation with the Fish and Wildlife Service, as delegate of the Secretary; after which the Service must provide the agency with a written statement (the Biological Opinion) explaining how the proposed action will affect the species or its habitat. If the Service concludes that the proposed action will "jeopardize the continued existence of any [listed] species or result in the destruction or adverse modification of [critical habitat]," the Biological Opinion must outline any "reasonable and prudent alternatives" that the Service believes will avoid that consequence. Additionally, if the Biological Opinion concludes that the agency action will not result in jeopardy or adverse habitat modification, or if it offers reasonable and prudent alternatives to avoid that consequence, the Service must provide the agency with a written statement (known as the "Incidental Take Statement") specifying the "impact of such incidental taking on the species," any "reasonable and prudent measures that the [Service] considers necessary or appropriate to minimize such impact," and setting forth "the terms and conditions ... that must be complied with by the Federal agency ... to implement [those measures]."

The Klamath Project, one of the oldest federal reclamation schemes, is a series of lakes, rivers, dams and irrigation canals in northern California and southern Oregon. The project was undertaken by the Secretary of the Interior pursuant to the Reclamation Act of 1902, and is administered by the Bureau of Reclamation, which is under the Secretary's jurisdiction. In 1992, the Bureau notified the Service that operation of the project might affect the Lost River Sucker (Deltistes luxatus) and Shortnose Sucker (Chasmistes brevirostris), species of fish that were listed as endangered in 1988. After formal consultation with the Bureau * * * the Service issued a Biological Opinion which concluded that the " 'long-term operation of the Klamath Project was likely to jeopardize the continued existence of the Lost River and shortnose suckers.' " The Biological Opinion identified "reasonable and prudent alternatives" the Service believed would avoid jeopardy, which included the maintenance of minimum water levels on Clear Lake and Gerber reservoirs. The Bureau later notified the Service that it intended to operate the project in compliance with the Biological Opinion.

Petitioners, two Oregon irrigation districts that receive Klamath Project water and the operators of two ranches within those districts, filed the present action against the director and regional director of the Service and the Secretary of the Interior. Neither the Bureau nor any of its officials is named as defendant. The complaint asserts that the Bureau "has been following essentially the same procedures for storing and releasing water from Clear Lake and Gerber reservoirs throughout the twentieth century;" that "[t]here is no scientifically or commercially available evidence indicating that the populations of endangered suckers in Clear Lake and Gerber reservoirs have declined, are declining, or will decline as a result" of the Bureau's operation of the Klamath Project;

that "[t]here is no commercially or scientifically available evidence indicating that the restrictions on lake levels imposed in the Biological Opinion will have any beneficial effect on the ... populations of suckers in Clear Lake and Gerber reservoirs;" and that the Bureau nonetheless "will abide by the restrictions imposed by the Biological Opinion."

Petitioners' complaint included three claims for relief that are relevant here. The first and second claims allege that the Service's jeopardy determination with respect to Clear Lake and Gerber reservoirs, and the ensuing imposition of minimum water levels, violated § 7 of the ESA, 16 U.S.C. § 1536. The third claim is that the imposition of minimum water elevations constituted an implicit determination of critical habitat for the suckers, which violated § 4 of the ESA, 16 U.S.C. § 1533(b)(2), because it failed to take into consideration the designation's economic impact. Each of the claims also states that the relevant action violated the APA's prohibition of agency action that is "arbitrary, capricious, an abuse of discretion, or otherwise not in accordance with law." 5 U.S.C. § 706(2)(A).

The complaint asserts that petitioners' use of the reservoirs and related waterways for "recreational, aesthetic and commercial purposes, as well as for their primary sources of irrigation water" will be "irreparably damaged" by the actions complained of, and that the restrictions on water delivery "recommended" by the Biological Opinion "adversely affect plaintiffs by substantially reducing the quantity of available irrigation water." In essence, petitioners claim a competing interest in the water the Biological Opinion declares necessary for the preservation of the suckers.

The District Court dismissed the complaint for lack of jurisdiction. It concluded that petitioners did not have standing because their "recreational, aesthetic, and commercial interests ... do not fall within the zone of interests sought to be protected by ESA." The Court of Appeals for the Ninth Circuit affirmed. * * * We granted certiorari.

In this Court, petitioners raise two questions: first, whether the prudential standing rule known as the "zone of interests" test applies to claims brought under the citizen-suit provision of the ESA; and second, if so, whether petitioners have standing under that test notwithstanding that the interests they seek to vindicate are economic rather than environmental. In this Court, the Government * * * advances three * * * grounds for affirmance: (1) that petitioners fail to meet the standing requirements imposed by Article III of the Constitution; (2) that the ESA's citizen-suit provision does not authorize judicial review of the types of claims advanced by petitioners; and (3) that judicial review is unavailable under the APA because the Biological Opinion does not constitute final agency action.

II

We first turn to the question the Court of Appeals found dispositive: whether petitioners lack standing by virtue of the zone-of-interests test.

Although petitioners contend that their claims lie both under the ESA and the APA, we look first at the ESA because it may permit petitioners to recover their litigation costs, and because the APA by its terms independently authorizes review only when "there is no other adequate remedy in a court."

The question of standing "involves both constitutional limitations on federal-court jurisdiction and prudential limitations on its exercise." Warth v. Seldin, 422 U.S. 490, 498 (1975). To satisfy the "case" or "controversy" requirement of Article III, which is the "irreducible constitutional minimum" of standing, a plaintiff must, generally speaking, demonstrate that he has suffered "injury in fact," that the injury is "fairly traceable" to the actions of the defendant, and that the injury will likely be redressed by a favorable decision. Lujan v. Defenders of Wildlife, 504 U.S. 555, 560–561 (1992); Valley Forge Christian College v. Americans United for Separation of Church and State, Inc., 454 U.S. 464, 471–472 (1982). In addition to the immutable requirements of Article III, "the federal judiciary has also adhered to a set of prudential principles that bear on the question of standing." Id., at 474–475. Like their constitutional counterparts, these "judicially self-imposed limits on the exercise of federal jurisdiction," Allen v. Wright, 468 U.S. 737, 751 (1984), are "founded in concern about the proper—and properly limited—role of the courts in a democratic society," Warth, supra, at 498; but unlike their constitutional counterparts, they can be modified or abrogated by Congress, see 422 U.S., at 501. Numbered among these prudential requirements is the doctrine of particular concern in this case: that a plaintiff's grievance must arguably fall within the zone of interests protected or regulated by the statutory provision or constitutional guarantee invoked in the suit. See Allen; Valley Forge.

The "zone of interests" formulation was first employed in Association of Data Processing Service Organizations, Inc. v. Camp, 397 U.S. 150 (1970). There, certain data processors sought to invalidate a ruling by the Comptroller of the Currency authorizing national banks to sell data processing services on the ground that it violated, inter alia, § 4 of the Bank Service Corporation Act of 1962, which prohibited bank service corporations from engaging in "any activity other than the performance of bank services for banks." The Court of Appeals had held that the banks' data-processing competitors were without standing to challenge the alleged violation of § 4. In reversing, we stated the applicable prudential standing requirement to be "whether the interest sought to be protected by the complainant is arguably within the zone of interests to be protected or regulated by the statute or constitutional guarantee in question." Data Processing, supra, at 153. Data Processing, and its companion case, Barlow v. Collins, 397 U.S. 159 (1970), applied the zone-of-interests test to suits under the APA, but later cases have applied it also in suits not involving review of federal administrative action, and have specifically listed it among other prudential standing requirements of general application, see, e.g., Allen; Valley Forge. We have made clear, however, that the breadth of the zone of interests varies according to the provisions of law at issue, so that what comes within the zone of interests of a statute for purposes of obtaining judicial review of administrative action under the " 'generous review provisions' " of the APA may not do so for other purposes.

Congress legislates against the background of our prudential standing doctrine, which applies unless it is expressly negated. The first question in the present case is whether the ESA's citizen-suit provision, set forth in pertinent part in the margin,[2] negates the zone-of-interests test (or, perhaps more accurately, expands the zone of interests). We think it does. The first operative portion of the provision says that "any person may commence a civil suit"—an authorization of remarkable breadth when compared with the language Congress ordinarily uses. Even in some other environmental statutes, Congress has used more restrictive formulations, such as "[any person] having an interest which is or may be adversely affected," 33 U.S.C. § 1365(g) (Clean Water Act); see also 30 U.S.C. § 1270(a) (Surface Mining Control and Reclamation Act) (same); "[a]ny person suffering legal wrong," 15 U.S.C. § 797(b)(5) (Energy Supply and Environmental Coordination Act); or "any person having a valid legal interest which is or may be adversely affected ... whenever such action constitutes a case or controversy," 42 U.S.C. § 9124(a) (Ocean Thermal Energy Conversion Act). And in contexts other than the environment, Congress has often been even more restrictive. In statutes concerning unfair trade practices and other commercial matters, for example, it has authorized suit only by "[a]ny person injured in his business or property," 7 U.S.C. § 2305(c); see also 15 U.S.C. § 72 (same), or only by "competitors, customers, or subsequent purchasers," § 298(b).

Our readiness to take the term "any person" at face value is greatly augmented by two interrelated considerations: that the overall subject matter of this legislation is the environment (a matter in which it is common to think all persons have an interest) and that the obvious purpose of the particular provision in question is to encourage enforcement by so-called "private attorneys general"—evidenced by its elimination of the usual amount-in-controversy and diversity-of-citizenship requirements, its provision for recovery of the costs of litigation (including even expert witness fees), and its reservation to the Government of a right of first refusal to pursue the action initially and a right to

---

2. "(1) Except as provided in paragraph (2) of this subsection any person may commence a civil suit on his own behalf

to enjoin any person, including the United States and any other governmental instrumentality or agency (to the extent permitted by the eleventh amendment to the Constitution), who is alleged to be in violation of any provision of this chapter or regulation issued under the authority thereof; or

"(C) against the Secretary where there is alleged a failure of the Secretary to perform any act or duty under section 1533 of this title which is not discretionary with the Secretary. The district courts shall have jurisdiction, without regard to the amount in controversy or the citizenship of the parties, to enforce any such provision or regulation, or to order the Secretary to perform such act or duty, as the case may be...."

* * *   * * *

intervene later. Given these factors, we think the conclusion of expanded standing follows *a fortiori* from our decision in Trafficante v. Metropolitan Life Ins. Co., 409 U.S. 205 (1972), which held that standing was expanded to the full extent permitted under Article III by a provision of the Civil Rights Act of 1968 that authorized "[a]ny person who claims to have been injured by a discriminatory housing practice" to sue for violations of the Act. There also we relied on textual evidence of a statutory scheme to rely on private litigation to ensure compliance with the Act. See id., at 210–211. The statutory language here is even clearer, and the subject of the legislation makes the intent to permit enforcement by everyman even more plausible.

It is true that the plaintiffs here are seeking to prevent application of environmental restrictions rather than to implement them. But the "any person" formulation applies to all the causes of action authorized by § 1540(g)—not only to actions against private violators of environmental restrictions, and not only to actions against the Secretary asserting underenforcement under § 1533, but also to actions against the Secretary asserting overenforcement under § 1533. As we shall discuss below, the citizen-suit provision does favor environmentalists in that it covers all private violations of the Act but not all failures of the Secretary to meet his administrative responsibilities; but there is no textual basis for saying that its expansion of standing requirements applies to environmentalists alone. The Court of Appeals therefore erred in concluding that petitioners lacked standing under the zone-of-interests test to bring their claims under the ESA's citizen-suit provision.

III

The Government advances several alternative grounds upon which it contends we may affirm the dismissal of petitioners' suit. Because the District Court and the Court of Appeals found the zone-of-interests ground to be dispositive, these alternative grounds were not reached below. A respondent is entitled, however, to defend the judgment on any ground supported by the record. The asserted grounds were raised below, and have been fully briefed and argued here; we deem it an appropriate exercise of our discretion to consider them now rather than leave them for disposition on remand.

A

The Government's first contention is that petitioners' complaint fails to satisfy the standing requirements imposed by the "case" or "controversy" provision of Article III. This "irreducible constitutional minimum" of standing requires: (1) that the plaintiff have suffered an "injury in fact"—an invasion of a judicially cognizable interest which is (a) concrete and particularized and (b) actual or imminent, not conjectural or hypothetical; (2) that there be a causal connection between the injury and the conduct complained of—the injury must be fairly traceable to the challenged action of the defendant, and not the result of the independent action of some third party not before the court; and (3) that it be likely, as opposed to merely speculative, that the injury will be redressed by a favorable decision. *Defenders of Wildlife*, 504 U.S., at 560–561.

Petitioners allege, among other things, that they currently receive irrigation water from Clear Lake, that the Bureau "will abide by the restrictions imposed by the Biological Opinion," and that "[t]he restrictions on lake levels imposed in the Biological Opinion adversely affect [petitioners] by substantially reducing the quantity of available irrigation water." The Government contends, first, that these allegations fail to satisfy the "injury in fact" element of Article III standing because they demonstrate only a diminution in the *aggregate* amount of available water, and do not necessarily establish (absent information concerning the Bureau's water allocation practices) that the *petitioners* will receive less water. This contention overlooks, however, the proposition that each element of Article III standing "must be supported in the same way as any other matter on which the plaintiff bears the burden of proof, i.e., with the manner and degree of evidence required at the successive stages of the litigation." *Defenders of Wildlife*, supra, at 561. Thus, while a plaintiff must "set forth" by affidavit or other evidence "specific facts," to survive a motion for summary judgment, Fed. Rule Civ. Proc. 56(e), and must ultimately support any contested facts with evidence adduced at trial, "[a]t the pleading stage, general factual allegations of injury resulting from the defendant's conduct may suffice, for on a motion to dismiss we 'presum[e] that general allegations embrace those specific facts that are necessary to support the claim.' "*Defenders of Wildlife*, supra, at 561 (quoting Lujan v. National Wildlife Federation, 497 U.S. 871, 889 (1990)). Given petitioners' allegation that the amount of available water will be reduced and that they will be adversely affected thereby, it is easy to presume specific facts under which petitioners will be injured—for example, the Bureau's distribution of the reduction pro rata among its customers. The complaint alleges the requisite injury in fact.

The Government also contests compliance with the second and third Article III standing requirements, contending that any injury suffered by petitioners is neither "fairly traceable" to the Service's Biological Opinion, nor "redressable" by a favorable judicial ruling, because the "action agency" (the Bureau) retains ultimate responsibility for determining whether and how a proposed action shall go forward. "If the petitioners have suffered injury," the Government contends, "the proximate cause of their harm is an (as yet unidentified) decision by the Bureau regarding the volume of water allocated to petitioners, not the biological opinion itself." This wrongly equates injury "fairly traceable" to the defendant with injury as to which the defendant's actions are the very last step in the chain of causation. While, as we have said, it does not suffice if the injury complained of is " 'th[e] result [of] the *independent* action of some third party not before the court,' " *Defenders of Wildlife*, supra, at 560–61 (emphasis added) (quoting Simon v. Eastern Ky. Welfare Rights Organization, 426 U.S. 26, 41–42 (1976)), that does not exclude injury produced by determinative or coercive effect upon the action of someone else.

By the Government's own account, while the Service's Biological Opinion theoretically serves an "advisory function," in reality it has a powerful coercive effect on the action agency:

Bio opinion has powerful effect

> "The statutory scheme ... presupposes that the biological opinion will play a central role in the action agency's decisionmaking process, and that it will typically be based on an administrative record that is fully adequate for the action agency's decision insofar as ESA issues are concerned.... [A] federal agency that chooses to deviate from the recommendations contained in a biological opinion bears the burden of 'articulat[ing] in its administrative record its reasons for disagreeing with the conclusions of a biological opinion.' In the government's experience, action agencies very rarely choose to engage in conduct that the Service has concluded is likely to jeopardize the continued existence of a listed species." Brief for Respondents 20–21.

What this concession omits to say, moreover, is that the action agency must not only articulate its reasons for disagreement (which ordinarily requires species and habitat investigations that are not within the action agency's expertise), but that it runs a substantial risk if its (inexpert) reasons turn out to be wrong. * * * The action agency is technically free to disregard the Biological Opinion and proceed with its proposed action, but it does so at its own peril (and that of its employees), for "any person" who knowingly "takes" an endangered or threatened species is subject to substantial civil and criminal penalties, including imprisonment.

conseq's of disobeying Bio op.

The Service itself is, to put it mildly, keenly aware of the virtually determinative effect of its biological opinions. * * * Given all of this, and given petitioners' allegation that the Bureau had, until issuance of the Biological Opinion, operated the Klamath Project in the same manner throughout the twentieth century, it is not difficult to conclude that petitioners have met their burden—which is relatively modest at this stage of the litigation—of alleging that their injury is "fairly traceable" to the Service's Biological Opinion and that it will "likely" be redressed—i.e., the Bureau will not impose such water level restrictions—if the Biological Opinion is set aside.

B

Next, the Government contends that the ESA's citizen-suit provision does not authorize judicial review of petitioners' claims.

* * *

Viewed in the context of the entire statute, § 1540(g)(1)(A)'s reference to any "violation" of the ESA cannot be interpreted to include the Secretary's maladministration of the Act. Petitioners' claims are not subject to judicial review under § 1540(g)(1)(A).

IV

The foregoing analysis establishes that the principal statute invoked by petitioners, the ESA, does authorize review of their § 1533 claim, but does not support their claims based upon the Secretary's alleged failure to comply with § 1536. To complete our task, we must therefore inquire whether these § 1536 claims may nonetheless be brought under the Administrative Procedure Act, which authorizes a court to "set aside agency action, findings, and conclusions found to be ... arbitrary, capricious, an abuse of discretion, or otherwise not in accordance with law," 5 U.S.C. § 706.

ARB & CAPRICOUS

A

No one contends (and it would not be maintainable) that the causes of action against the Secretary set forth in the ESA's citizen-suit provision are exclusive, supplanting those provided by the APA. The APA, by its terms, provides a right to judicial review of all "final agency action for which there is no other adequate remedy in a court," 5 U.S.C. § 704, and applies universally "except to the extent that—(1) statutes preclude judicial review; or (2) agency action is committed to agency discretion by law," § 701(a). Nothing in the ESA's citizen-suit provision expressly precludes review under the APA, nor do we detect anything in the statutory scheme suggesting a purpose to do so. And any contention that the relevant provision of 16 U.S.C. § 1536(a)(2) is discretionary would fly in the face of its text, which uses the imperative "shall."

In determining whether the petitioners have standing under the zone-of-interests test to bring their APA claims, we look not to the terms of the ESA's citizen-suit provision, but to the substantive provisions of the ESA, the alleged violations of which serve as the gravamen of the complaint. See *National Wildlife Federation*, 497 U.S., at 886. The classic formulation of the zone-of-interests test is set forth in *Data Processing*, 397 U.S., at 153: "whether the interest sought to be protected by the complainant is arguably within the zone of interests to be protected or regulated by the statute or constitutional guarantee in question." The Court of Appeals concluded that this test was not met here, since petitioners are neither directly regulated by the ESA nor seek to vindicate its overarching purpose of species preservation. That conclusion was error.

Whether a plaintiff's interest is "arguably ... protected ... by the statute" within the meaning of the zone-of-interests test is to be determined not by reference to the overall purpose of the Act in question (here, species preservation), but by reference to the particular provision of law upon which the plaintiff relies. It is difficult to understand how the Ninth Circuit could have failed to see this from our cases. In *Data Processing* itself, for example, we did not require that the plaintiffs' suit vindicate the overall purpose of the Bank Service Corporation Act of 1962, but found it sufficient that their commercial interest was sought to be protected by the anti-competition limitation contained in § 4 of the

ZOI = provision NOT overall purpose

Act—the specific provision which they alleged had been violated. See *Data Processing*, supra, at 155–56. As we said with the utmost clarity in *National Wildlife Federation*, "the plaintiff must establish that the injury he complains of ... falls within the 'zone of interests' sought to be protected *by the statutory provision whose violation forms the legal basis for his complaint.*" *National Wildlife Federation*, supra, at 883 (emphasis added).

In the claims that we have found not to be covered by the ESA's citizen-suit provision, petitioners allege a violation of § 7 of the ESA, 16 U.S.C. § 1536, which requires, inter alia, that each agency "use the best scientific and commercial data available," § 1536(a)(2). Petitioners contend that the available scientific and commercial data show that the continued operation of the Klamath Project will not have a detrimental impact on the endangered suckers, that the imposition of minimum lake levels is not necessary to protect the fish, and that by issuing a Biological Opinion which makes unsubstantiated findings to the contrary the defendants have acted arbitrarily and in violation of § 1536(a)(2). The obvious purpose of the requirement that each agency "use the best scientific and commercial data available" is to ensure that the ESA not be implemented haphazardly, on the basis of speculation or surmise. While this no doubt serves to advance the ESA's overall goal of species preservation, we think it readily apparent that another objective (if not indeed the primary one) is to avoid needless economic dislocation produced by agency officials zealously but unintelligently pursuing their environmental objectives. That economic consequences are an explicit concern of the Act is evidenced by § 1536(h), which provides exemption from § 1536(a)(2)'s no-jeopardy mandate where there are no reasonable and prudent alternatives to the agency action and the benefits of the agency action clearly outweigh the benefits of any alternatives. We believe the "best scientific and commercial data" provision is similarly intended, at least in part, to prevent uneconomic (because erroneous) jeopardy determinations. Petitioners' claim that they are victims of such a mistake is plainly within the zone of interests that the provision protects.

* * *

The Court of Appeals erred in affirming the District Court's dismissal of petitioners' claims for lack of jurisdiction. Petitioners' complaint alleges facts sufficient to meet the requirements of Article III standing, and none of their ESA claims is precluded by the zone-of-interests test. Petitioners' § 1533 claim is reviewable under the ESA's citizen-suit provision, and petitioners' remaining claims are reviewable under the APA.

The judgment of the Court of Appeals is reversed, and the case is remanded for further proceedings consistent with this opinion.

It is so ordered.

Notes

1. What are the justifications for imposing an injury requirement? Consider Brilmayer, *The Jurisprudence of Article III: Perspectives on the "Case or Controversy" Requirement*, 93 Harv.L.Rev. 297 (1979). Professor Brilmayer points to "three interrelated policies" behind the constitutional requirement of "case or controversy," which in turn leads to the constitutional branch of the standing requirement:

> [T]he smooth allocation of power among courts over time; the unfairness of holding later litigants to an adverse judgment in which they may not have been properly represented; and the importance of placing control over political processes in the hands of the people most closely involved. Id. at 302.

As to the first reason, she argues:

> Given that opinions about the proper scope of constitutional protections are bound to differ, and given that a decision settles the matter for a while at least, it is obviously important who is vested with the responsibility for making the initial decision and, thus, at what point the issue is considered ready for decision. To allow a court to settle any matter it wished to address would give precedence to the preferences of earlier courts, who are able to tie the hands of the subsequent ones.

> * * *

> Allowing issues to be resolved at a faster rate would have one of two undesirable results: inflexibility from over-commitment to outmoded standards * * * or an erosion of the stare decisis doctrine through a high rate of overruling. Id. at 304–305.

Do you understand the asserted connection between the constitutional requirement of standing and the impact on stare decisis? What about Brilmayer's second point: In what way is a future litigant "held" to an earlier decision? Why is it necessarily more unfair to hold a future litigant to a decision in which an "affected" plaintiff was involved than one brought by a plaintiff simply interested in the outcome of the case? Professor Brilmayer's obvious assumption is that the former will take the case more seriously than will the latter. Do you think this is necessarily true?

2. To what extent does an "injury-in-fact" requirement foster principles of separation of powers? See generally Scalia, *The Doctrine of Standing as an Essential Element of the Separation of Powers*, 17 Suffolk U.L.Rev. 881, 881 (1983). Justice Scalia argues that the standing requirement avoids "an overjudicialization of the processes of self-governance":

> [T]he law of standing roughly restricts courts to their traditional undemocratic role of protecting individuals and minorities against impositions of the majority, and excludes them from the even more undemocratic role of prescribing how the other two branches should function in order to serve the interests *of the majority itself*. Id. at 894.

See also Bellia, *Article III and the Cause of Action,* 89 Iowa L.Rev. 777 (2004); Driesen, *Standing for Nothing: The Paradox of Demanding Concrete Context for Formalist Adjudication,* 89 Cornell L.Rev. 808 (2004); Hartnett, *The Standing of the United States: How Criminal Prosecutions Show That Standing Doctrine is Looking for Answers in All the Wrong Places,* 97 Mich.L.Rev. 2239 (1999); Pushaw, *Justiciability and Separation of Powers: A Neo–Federalist Approach,* 81 Cornell L.Rev. 393 (1996).

3. The injury determination has hardly proven to be simple and straightforward. Extensive discussions of the injury analysis appear in Nichol, *Injury and the Disintegration of Article III,* 74 Cal.L.Rev. 1915 (1986) (injury analysis conflates two inquiries—the actuality of the proffered harm and the judicial cognizability of the interests asserted); Fletcher, *The Structure of Standing,* 98 Yale L.J. 221, 232 (1988) (injury determination is "based on [a] normative judgment about what ought to constitute a judicially cognizable in the particular context"); and Sunstein, *Standing and the Privatization of Public Law,* 88 Colum.L.Rev. 1432 (1988) (injury determination rooted in inappropriate private rights model). The Court has also had some difficulty applying the "injury in fact" test. See Clinton v. New York, 524 U.S. 417 (1998); FEC v. Akins, 524 U.S. 11 (1998).

4. Do you understand the relationship between the constitutional and prudential strands of the standing doctrine? Why should there be any prudential limitations on standing? If the Court denies standing in a case that satisfies the "irreducible constitutional minimum," is that consistent with Article III?

If standing is, at base, a constitutional doctrine, must it be a threshold question in every case? In Steel Co. v. Citizens for a Better Environment, 523 U.S. 83 (1998), the Court rejected the previously common lower court doctrine of "hypothetical jurisdiction:" courts had sometimes presumed jurisdiction and proceeded directly to the merits if they found both that the jurisdictional question was much more difficult than the merits and that the party challenging jurisdiction would prevail on the merits anyway.

In Ruhrgas AG v. Marathon Oil Co., 526 U.S. 574 (1999), however, the Supreme Court further refined the *Steel Co.* rule. In *Ruhrgas,* the Court permitted a district court (in a case removed from state court) to dismiss a case for lack of personal jurisdiction without first deciding whether it had subject matter jurisdiction. Justice Ginsburg's opinion for a unanimous Court held that although ordinarily a federal court should resolve subject matter jurisdiction issues before personal jurisdiction issues, where "a district court has before it a straightforward personal jurisdiction issue presenting no complex questions of state law, and the alleged defect in subject matter jurisdiction raises a difficult and novel question, the district court does not abuse its discretion by turning directly to personal jurisdiction." See also Ortiz v. Fibreboard Corp., 527 U.S. 815 (1999) (permitting court to resolve question of class certification before turning to whether class members have standing); Vermont Agency of Natural Resources v. United States ex rel. Stevens, 529 U.S. 765 (2000) (resolving question of whether particular statute reaches states as defendants before determining whether suit is barred by eleventh amendment immunity). Are *Ruhrgas, Ortiz,* and

Stevens consistent with *Steel Co.*? See generally Steinman, *After* Steel Co.: *"Hypothetical Jurisdiction" in the Federal Appellate Courts*, 58 Wash. & Lee L.Rev. 855 (2001); Friedenthal, *The Crack in the* Steel *Case*, 68 Geo. Wash.L.Rev. 258 (2000); Idleman, *The Demise of Hypothetical Jurisdiction in the Federal Courts*, 52 Vand.L.Rev. 235 (1999).

5. How should a court determine whether a particular plaintiff falls within the scope of the "zone of interests" standard? In National Credit Union Administration v. First National Bank & Trust Co., 522 U.S. 479 (1998), a divided Court held that banks had standing to challenge agency regulations allegedly relaxing statutory restrictions on credit unions. The banks claimed that the regulations allowed credit unions to compete more directly with banks. The majority opinion canvassed the prior "zone of interests" cases under the Administrative Procedure Act and concluded that to fall within the "zone of interests," plaintiffs need not show a congressional intent to benefit them, but only that the statute "arguably" protects their interests. By limiting credit union membership, the statute at issue arguably protected the interests of credit union competitors. Interestingly, the majority opinion, authored by Justice Thomas, did not cite *Bennett*.

Justice O'Connor, joined by Justices Stevens, Souter, and Breyer, dissented. They would have focused on whether the statutory provision that was allegedly violated by the agency regulation "was intended to protect [the banks'] commercial interest." According to the dissent, the majority so broadened the "zone of interests" test that it would necessarily be satisfied any time a party could show "injury in fact caused by an alleged violation of [a] statute." The dissent did cite *Bennett*, noting that the Court had found standing in that case only by concluding that protecting against overzealous enforcement, to the detriment of economic interests, was one intended purpose of the provision at issue.

6. The Court recently applied its prudential rules to deny standing in an unusual situation. In Elk Grove Unified School Dist. v. Newdow, 542 U.S. 1 (2004), a divorced father sought to challenge the mandatory recitation of the Pledge of Allegiance in his daughter's school. (He alleged that the words "under God" in the Pledge violated the Establishment Clause.) His ex-wife did not object to the Pledge, claimed that the daughter did not object, and indeed believed it to be in the daughter's best interests not to be a party to the suit. While he and his ex-wife shared custody of their daughter, a state court had explicitly held that if the parents disagreed, the mother had final authority to make decisions regarding the daughter. For that reason, a state court enjoined Newdow from proceeding in the federal lawsuit as his daughter's "next friend," that is, on her behalf. He therefore brought the suit alleging the violation of his own right to expose his daughter to his religious beliefs (atheism) without interference by the state. Although the Ninth Circuit found some support in California state law for the proposition that the recitation of the Pledge interfered with Newdow's right to instruct his daughter in his religious views, the Supreme Court suggested that Newdow's claim was "more ambitious" than the claims in the California cases. The Court therefore relied on prudential considerations to hold that Newdow did not have standing:

In our view, it is improper for the federal courts to entertain a claim by a plaintiff whose standing to sue is founded on family law rights that are in dispute when prosecution of the lawsuit may have an adverse effect on the person who is the source of the plaintiff's claimed standing. When hard questions of domestic relations are sure to affect the outcome, the prudent course is for the federal court to stay its hand rather than to reach out to resolve a weighty question of constitutional law. There is a vast difference between Newdow's right to communicate with his child—which both California law and the First Amendment recognize—and his claimed right to shield his daughter from influences to which she is exposed in school despite the terms of the custody order. We conclude that, having been deprived under California law of the right to sue as next friend, Newdow lacks prudential standing to bring this suit in federal court. 542 U.S. at 17–18.

Does *Newdow* apply established precedent on prudential limitations? Does it create a workable standard for future cases? Do you think that the Court was influenced by a desire to avoid both the California domestic relations question and the Establishment Clause question on the merits?

7.   For commentary on *Bennett*, see Stearns, *From* Lujan *to* Laidlaw: *A Preliminary Model of Environmental Standing*, 11 Duke Envtl L. & Pol'y F. 321 (2001); Kalen, *Standing on Its Last Legs:* Bennett v. Spear *and the Past and Future of Standing in Environmental Cases*, 13 J.Land Use & Envtl.L. 1 (1997); Buzbee, *Expanding the Zone, Tilting the Field: Zone of Interests and Article III Standing Analysis After* Bennett v. Spear, 49 Admin.L.Rev. 763 (1997).

THE STANDING DOCTRINE OVER TIME

In *Bennett*, the Court construed the allegations in the complaint quite generously, and also applied what seemed to be a fairly relaxed constitutional standard. Compare the Court's approach in *Bennett* with the approach taken in the following two cases, both of which are cited and discussed in *Bennett* itself:

WARTH v. SELDIN, 422 U.S. 490, 95 S.Ct. 2197, 45 L.Ed.2d 343 (1975). In *Warth*, the Supreme Court denied standing to a variety of plaintiffs who sought to challenge a town's zoning restrictions. Penfield, New York, a small town adjacent to the larger metropolis of Rochester, enacted a zoning ordinance which was alleged to have the effect of excluding persons of low and moderate income from Penfield.

Four different groups of plaintiffs challenged the zoning ordinance. As to all four, the Court carefully noted that an inquiry into standing differs from consideration on the merits:

One further preliminary matter requires discussion. For purposes of ruling on a motion to dismiss for want of standing, both the trial and reviewing courts must accept as true all material allegations of the complaint, and must construe the complaint in favor of the complaining party. At the same time, it is within the trial court's power to allow or to require the plaintiff to supply, by amendment to the complaint or by affidavits, further particularized allegations of fact deemed supportive of plaintiff's standing. If, after this opportunity, the plaintiff's standing does not adequately appear from all materials of record, the complaint must be dismissed. Id. at 501–02.

One set of plaintiffs was a group of taxpayers who lived and owned property in Rochester. They alleged that "because of Penfield's exclusionary practices, the city of Rochester had been forced to impose higher tax rates on them * * *." Id. at 496. The Court found a number of problems with this group of plaintiffs. First, Justice Powell's majority opinion suggested, the alleged injury was merely "conjectural;" moreover, "the line of causation between Penfield's actions and such injury is not apparent from the complaint. Whatever may occur in Penfield, the injury complained of—increases in taxation—results only from the decisions made by the appropriate Rochester authorities, who are not parties to this case." Id. at 509. More importantly, however, the Court suggested that even if the Rochester taxpayers could establish that Penfield's zoning practices did result in higher taxes, they "did not, even if they could, assert any personal right under the Constitution or any statute to be free of action by a neighboring municipality that may have some incidental adverse effect on Rochester." Id. "In short," the Court concluded, "the claim of these petitioners falls squarely within the prudential standing rule that normally bars litigants from asserting the rights or legal interests of others in order to obtain relief from injury to themselves." Id.

Another set of plaintiffs included current residents of Pennfield, who argued that the town's zoning practices deprived them "of the benefits of living in a racially and ethnically integrated community." Id. at 512. The Court held that these plaintiffs did not present a judicially cognizable injury. It distinguished Trafficante v. Metropolitan Life Ins. Co., 409 U.S. 205 (1972), in which plaintiffs had prevailed on a similar claim brought under the 1968 Civil Rights Act. The Court noted that although "Congress may create a statutory right or entitlement the alleged deprivation of which can confer standing to sue even where the plaintiff would have suffered no judicially cognizable injury in the absence of a statute," "[n]o such statute is applicable here." Id. at 514.

The Court also denied standing to two other groups of plaintiffs: low-income individuals who alleged that as a result of the zoning practices, they could not find affordable housing in Penfield (where they wished to live), and a group of builders, who alleged that as a result of the zoning practices they had been prohibited from building particular, specified, low-income housing projects. The Court first denied standing to the low-income individuals:

> We may assume, as petitioners allege, that respondents' actions have contributed, perhaps substantially, to the cost of housing in Penfield. But there remains the question whether petitioners' inability to locate suitable housing in Penfield reasonably can be said to have resulted, in any concretely demonstrable way, from respondents' alleged constitutional and statutory infractions. Petitioners

must allege facts from which it reasonably could be inferred that, absent the respondents' restrictive zoning practices, there is a substantial probability that they would have been able to purchase or lease in Penfield and that, if the court affords the relief requested, the asserted inability of petitioners will be removed.

We find the record devoid of the necessary allegations. As the Court of Appeals noted, none of these petitioners has a present interest in any Penfield property; none is himself subject to the ordinance's strictures; and none has even been denied a variance or permit by respondent officials. Instead, petitioners claim that respondents' enforcement of the ordinance against third parties—developers, builders, and the like—has had the consequence of precluding the construction of housing suitable to their needs at prices they might be able to afford. The fact that the harm to petitioners may have resulted indirectly does not in itself preclude standing. When a governmental prohibition or restriction imposed on one party causes specific harm to a third party, harm that a constitutional provision or statute was intended to prevent, the indirectness of the injury does not necessarily deprive the person harmed of standing to vindicate his rights. But it may make it substantially more difficult to meet the minimum requirement of Art. III: to establish that, in fact, the asserted injury was the consequence of the defendants' actions, or that prospective relief will remove the harm.

Here, by their own admission, realization of petitioners' desire to live in Penfield always has depended on the efforts and willingness of third parties to build low-and moderate-cost housing. The record specifically refers to only two such efforts: that of Penfield Better Homes Corp., in late 1969, to obtain the rezoning of certain land in Penfield to allow the construction of subsidized cooperative townhouses that could be purchased by persons of moderate income; and a similar effort by O'Brien Homes, Inc., in late 1971. But the record is devoid of any indication that these projects, or other like projects, would have satisfied petitioners' needs at prices they could afford, or that, were the court to remove the obstructions attributable to respondents, such relief would benefit petitioners. Indeed, petitioners' descriptions of their individual financial situations and housing needs suggest precisely the contrary—that their inability to reside in Penfield is the consequence of the economics of the area housing market, rather than of respondents' assertedly illegal acts. In short, the facts alleged fail to support an actionable causal relationship between Penfield's zoning practices and petitioners' asserted injury. Id. at 504–07.

The Court then considered the claims of Home Builders, an association of builders. After noting that an association generally has standing to raise the claims of its members, the Court denied standing to the association. First, the Court held, the association did not have standing to claim damages on behalf of its members, because any right to damages was not held in common but rather accrued to each individual builder. Second, the Court found that the association did not have standing to seek an injunction against the enforcement of the zoning ordinance:

> Home Builders' prayer for prospective relief fails for a different reason. It can have standing as the representative of its members only if it has alleged facts sufficient to make out a case or controversy had the members themselves brought suit. No such allegations were made. The complaint refers to no specific project of any of its members that is currently precluded either by the ordinance or by respondents' action in enforcing it. There is no averment that any member has applied to respondents for a building permit or a variance with respect to any current project. Indeed, there is no indication that respondents have delayed or thwarted any project currently proposed by Home Builders' members, or that any of its members has taken advantage of the remedial processes available under the ordinance. In short, insofar as the complaint seeks prospective relief, Home Builders has failed to show the existence of any injury to its members of sufficient immediacy and ripeness to warrant judicial intervention. Id. at 516.

The Court also denied standing to another group of low-income housing developers, Housing Council, on the same grounds.

Justices Douglas, Brennan, White, and Marshall dissented. Justice Brennan criticized the majority for unnecessarily constricting existing standing doctrines: "While the Court gives lip service to the principle, oft repeated in recent years, that 'standing in no way depends on the merits of the plaintiff's contention that particular conduct is illegal,' in fact the opinion, which tosses out of court almost every conceivable kind of plaintiff who could be injured by the activity claimed to be unconstitutional, can be explained only by an indefensible hostility to the claim on the merits." Id. at 520. Justice Brennan's primary criticism was that the Court should have considered together the claims of the low-income individuals and the builders:

*[handwritten margin note: DISSENT * only exp for tossing out every claim = hostility to MERITS]*

> Indeed, one glaring defect of the Court's opinion is that it views each set of plaintiffs as if it were prosecuting a separate lawsuit, refusing to recognize that the interests are intertwined, and that the standing of any one group must take into account its position vis-à-vis the others. For example, the Court says that the low-income minority plaintiffs have not alleged facts sufficient to show that but for the exclusionary practices claimed, they would be able to reside in Penfield. The Court then intimates that such a causal relationship could be shown only if "the initial focus [is] on a particular project." Later, the Court objects to the ability of the Housing Council to prosecute the suit on behalf of its member, Penfield Better Homes Corp., *despite* the fact that Better Homes *had* displayed an interest in a particular project, because that project was no longer live. Thus, we must suppose that even if the low-income plaintiffs had alleged a desire to live in the Better Homes project, that allegation would be

insufficient because it appears that that particular project might never be built. The rights of low-income minority plaintiffs who desire to live in a locality, then, seem to turn on the willingness of a third party to litigate the legality of preclusion of a particular project, despite the fact that the third party may have no economic incentive to incur the costs of litigation with regard to one project, and despite the fact that the low-income minority plaintiffs' interest is *not* to live in a particular project but to live somewhere in the town in a dwelling they can afford. Id. at 521–22.

Justice Brennan also argued that the majority was essentially requiring the plaintiffs to prove their claims on the merits in order to obtain standing.

LUJAN v. DEFENDERS OF WILDLIFE, 504 U.S. 555 (1992). In *Lujan*, the Supreme Court denied standing to a wildlife organization which sought to challenge a ruling by the Secretary of the Interior that limited the applicability of the Endangered Species Act to actions within the United States or on the high seas. The ESA requires that "[e]ach federal agency * * *, in consultation with * * * the Secretary of the Interior, insure that any action authorized, funded or carried out by such agency * * * is not likely to jeopardize the continued existence of any endangered species * * *." From 1978 to 1986, the Department of Interior interpreted the ESA requirements to apply to federal agency actions in foreign nations. A regulation issued by the departments of Interior and Commerce in 1986 limited the geographical scope of statute's consultation standards. That regulation was challenged in *Lujan*.

The majority opinion, written by Justice Scalia, focused initially on the affidavits of two of Defenders' members. One affiant indicated that she had travelled to Egypt and " 'observed the traditional habitat of the endangered Nile crocodile * * * and intend[s] to do so again,' " and that she "will suffer harm in fact as a result of [the] American role . . . in overseeing the rehabilitation the Aswan High Dam on the Nile * * *." Id. at 563. The other averred that she had " 'observed the habitat' of 'endangered species such as the Asian elephant and the leopard' " in Sri Lanka at what is now the site of the Mahaweli Project funded by the Agency for International Development [AID]. Id. The Endangered Species Act grants standing to "any person" alleging a violation "of any provision of this chapter." 16 U.S.C. § 1540(g).

Justice Scalia concluded that the plaintiffs had demonstrated neither injury nor redressability. Deriding the litigants' allegations as "fantasy," "remarkable," and the product of a "Linnean leap," id. at 567 & n.3, he determined that no imminent loss was threatened: "the affiants' profession of an 'inten[t]' to return to the places they had visited before—where they will presumably, this time, be deprived of the opportunity to observe animals of the endangered species—is simply not enough." Id. at 564,. Redressability was also deemed lacking (although here Justice Scalia wrote only for a plurality), in part because "the agencies generally support only a fraction of the funding" for foreign projects. Id. at 571. The plaintiffs had "produced nothing to indicate that the projects they have named will either be suspended, or do less harm to listed species, if that fraction is eliminated." Id.

Notes

1. Consider *Bennett*, *Warth*, and *Lujan* together. Is the Court applying the same test for standing in all three cases? How would the *Warth* plaintiffs have fared under Justice Scalia's approach in *Bennett*? To what extent is the Court in these cases influenced by its views on the merits? By a desire to avoid deciding the merits?

The Court clarified the relationship between *Bennett* and *Lujan* in Friends of the Earth, Inc. v. Laidlaw Environmental Services, 528 U.S. 167 (2000). In that case, plaintiffs sued a polluter under the Clean Water Act. By the time of trial, the defendant had ceased its illegal conduct. The district court held that the plaintiffs had standing, and imposed a light civil penalty (payable to the government under the statute) because there had been "no demonstrated proof of harm to the environment" from the defendant's violations. The Court of Appeals vacated the case as moot. The Supreme Court, after holding the case not moot [see infra p. 75], addressed the standing question.

The Court held that plaintiffs had demonstrated the requisite injury: "[t]he relevant showing for purposes of Article III standing * * * is not injury to the environment but injury to the plaintiff." This requirement was satisfied by affidavits from members of the plaintiff organization attesting to individual aesthetic and recreational harms. One member testified that he could no longer fish and swim downriver from the defendant's facility because of his concerns about the defendant's discharges into the river. Another testified that she no longer picnicked, walked, or birdwatched in the area for the same reason. Distinguishing *Lujan*, Justice Ginsburg's majority opinion found these to be more than the "general averments" and "conclusory allegations" found inadequate in *Lujan*. "Nor can affiants' conditional statements—that they would use the nearby North Tyger River for recreation if Laidlaw were not discharging pollutants into it—be equated with the speculative 'some day' intentions to visit endangered species halfway around the world that we held insufficient" in *Lujan*.

Are you persuaded by the Court's distinction between *Lujan* and *Laidlaw*? How would you advise members of environmental groups to proceed in future litigation?

Laidlaw also addressed the question whether plaintiffs had standing to seek civil penalties payable to the government. The Court concluded that they did, because such a sanction—even though the plaintiffs received no monetary benefit from it—"effectively abate[d] the conduct and prevent[ed] its recurrence."

2. Village of Arlington Heights v. Metropolitan Housing Development Corp., 429 U.S. 252 (1977): Respondent Metropolitan, a nonprofit developer, conditionally contracted to purchase a tract of land within the boundaries of the Village for the purpose of building racially integrated low-and moderate-income housing. One of the conditions was that rezoning be obtained, which

was denied by the Village Plan Commission. Metropolitan and individual minority group members then sued for injunctive and declaratory relief, alleging that the denial was racially discriminatory. The Court found that Metropolitan had standing, because if the barrier of the Village's actions were removed, it could build the project, and because it "has expended thousands of dollars on the plans * * * and on the studies submitted to the Village in support of the petition for rezoning. Unless rezoning is granted, many of these plans and studies will be worthless * * *." Id. at 262. Moreover, the Court, citing Metropolitan's nonprofit nature, noted its "interest in making suitable low-cost housing available in areas where such housing is scarce", something more than "mere abstract concern about a problem of general interest." Id. at 263. The Court concluded that it need not decide whether Metropolitan could assert the constitutional rights of its prospective tenants, since an individual black plaintiff had established standing. "The complaint alleged that he seeks and would qualify for the housing", and he testified at trial that if it was built, "he would probably move there, since it is closer to his job." Id. at 264. "Unlike the individual plaintiffs in *Warth*, [this plaintiff] has adequately averred an 'actionable causal relationship' between Arlington Heights' zoning practices and his asserted injury." Id. at 264. Do you see a legitimate distinction between the individual plaintiffs in *Warth* and in *Arlington Heights*?

Suppose that an exclusive suburb, separately incorporated, passed a statute prohibiting blacks from purchasing housing in the locale. Assume further that the suburb is composed entirely of ten-acre privately-owned parcels, each valued in excess of $2 million. The facts, as developed, indicate that no one in the suburb has present plans to sell. How would plaintiffs achieve standing in such a case? Must they not only be black, but also be able to prove capacity and willingness to buy a $2 million home? See Nichol, *Rethinking Standing,* 72 Cal.L.Rev. 68, 81–82 (1984).

3. In Regents of the University of California v. Bakke, 438 U.S. 265, 280, n. 14 (1978), a substantial question arose concerning whether Alan Bakke could prove that he would have been admitted to medical school absent the affirmative action program he contested. The Court skirted the standing issue, however, by declaring that the university's decision not to permit Bakke to compete for all 100 places was the relevant injury. Could the plaintiffs in *Warth* have made an analogous claim? In Northeastern Florida Chapter of the Associated General Contractors of America v. City of Jacksonville, 508 U.S. 656, 666 (1993), contractors challenged a municipal minority set-aside program in the awarding of construction contracts. The court below had denied standing since the plaintiffs had not alleged that any particular project would have been awarded to them if the set-aside program did not exist. The Supreme Court reversed, finding injury in the imposition of a barrier making it more difficult to obtain contracts rather than "the ultimate inability to obtain the benefit." The Supreme Court reaffirmed and clarified the principle of *Northeastern Contractors* in Adarand Constructors, Inc. v. Pena, 515 U.S. 200 (1995), allowing a disappointed bidder to challenge a federal affirmative action set-aside program. The Court found that the plaintiff had "made an adequate showing that sometime in the relatively near future it will bid on another government contract" subject to the set-aside. Id. at 211.

4. Scholarly commentary on *Lujan* is extensive. See generally Sunstein, *What's Standing After* Lujan? *Of Citizen Suits, "Injuries", and Article III,* 91 Mich.L.Rev. 163 (1992); Nichol, *Justice Scalia, Standing, and Public Law Litigation,* 42 Duke L.J. 1141 (1993); Pierce, Lujan v. Defenders of Wildlife: *Standing as a Judicially Imposed Limit on Legislative Power,* 42 Duke L.J. 1170 (1993); Breger, *Defending* Defenders: *Remarks on Nichol and Pierce,* 42 Duke L.J. 1202 (1993). Krent & Shenkman, *Of Citizen Suits and Citizen Sunstein,* 91 Mich.L.Rev. 1793 (1993); Sunstein, *Article II Revisionism,* 92 Mich.L.Rev. 131 (1993); Abate & Myers, *Broadening the Scope of Environmental Standing: Procedural and Informational Injury-in-Fact after* Lujan v. Defenders of Wildlife, 12 U.C.L.A.J.Env.Law & Pol'y 345 (1994); Feld, *Saving the Citizen Suit: The Effect of* Lujan v. Defenders of Wildlife *and the Role of Citizen Suits in Environmental Enforcement,* 19 Colum.J.Env.L. 141 (1994); Gatchel, *Informational and Procedural Standing after* Lujan v. Defenders of Wildlife, 11 J.Land Use & Envtl.L. 75 (1995); Farber, *Stretching the Margins: The Geographic Nexus in Environmental Law,* 48 Stan.L.Rev. 1247 (1996); Kelso & Kelso, *Standing to Sue: Transformations in Supreme Court Methodology, Doctrine and Results,* 28 U.Tol.L.Rev. 93 (1996); Pierce, *Is Standing Law or Politics?* 77 N.Car.L.Rev. 1741 (1999). For a social choice analysis of standing generally, see Stearns, *Standing Back From the Forest: Justiciability and Social Choice,* 83 Cal. L.Rev. 1309 (1993); Stearns, *Standing and Social Choice: Historical Evidence,* 144 U.Pa.L.Rev. 309 (1995).

STATUTORY STANDING

In Trafficante v. Metropolitan Life Ins. Co., 409 U.S. 205 (1972) the tenants of an apartment complex filed complaints with the Secretary of Housing and Urban Development pursuant to section 810(a) of the Civil Rights Act of 1968, claiming that their landlord discriminated against non-whites and that, as a result, the tenants lost social and economic benefits. The Supreme Court held that the tenants had standing within the statutory definition of "person aggrieved". Justice White concurred, expressing the view that "absent the Civil Rights Act of 1968, I would have great difficulty in concluding that petitioners' complaint in this case presented a case or controversy within the jurisdiction of the District Court under Article III of the Constitution. But with the statute purporting to give all those who are authorized to complain to the agency the right also to sue in Court, I would sustain the statute insofar as it extends standing to those in the position of the petitioners in this case." 409 U.S. at 212. In Linda R.S. v. Richard D., 410 U.S. 614, 617 n. 3 (1973), the Supreme Court explained its view of the power to grant standing by statute further by ruling that "Congress may create a statutory right of entitlement the alleged deprivation of which can confer standing to sue even where the plaintiff would have suffered no judicially cognizable injury in the absence of a statute."

These rulings seemed to suggest that as long as a plaintiff came within the terms of a statutory grant of jurisdiction, Article III posed no effective barrier to access. In Gollust v. Mendell, however, 501 U.S. 115, 125 (1991), the Supreme Court expressed "serious constitutional doubt" whether Congress may create standing in the absence of a "distinct and palpable injury". The "doubt" expressed in *Gollust* was made concrete in Lujan v. Defenders of Wildlife, 504 U.S. 555 (1992).

In *Lujan* [also discussed supra pp. 34–35], Justice Scalia's majority opinion first suggested that the plaintiffs lacked constitutional standing, and then addressed the statutory standing issue:

> The Court of Appeals found that respondents had standing for an additional reason: because they had suffered a "procedural injury". The so-called "citizen suit" provision of the ESA provides * * * that "any person" may commence a civil suit on his own behalf * * * to enjoin any person * * * who is in violation of any provision of this chapter. The court held that, because sec. 7(a)(2) requires interagency consultation, the citizen-suit provision creates a "procedural right" to consultation in all "persons"—so that anyone can file suit in federal court to challenge the Secretary's * * * failure to follow the assertively correct consultative procedure, notwithstanding their inability to allege any discrete injury flowing from that failure * * *. [T]he court held that the injury-in-fact requirement had been satisfied by congressional conferral upon all persons of an abstract, self-contained, non-instrumental "right" to have the Executive observe the procedures required by law. We reject this view. 504 U.S. at 571–73.

* * *

To be sure, our generalized-grievance cases have typically involved Government violation of procedures assertedly ordained by the Constitution rather than the Congress. But there is absolutely no basis for making the Article III inquiry turn on the source of the asserted right. Whether the courts were to act on their own, or at the invitation of Congress, in ignoring the concrete injury requirement described in our cases, they would be discarding a principle fundamental to the separate and distinct constitutional role of the Third Branch—one of the essential elements that identifies those "Cases" and "Controversies" that are the business of the courts rather than of the political branches. "The province of the court," as Chief Justice Marshall said in Marbury v. Madison, "is, solely, to decide on the rights of individuals." Vindicating the *public* interest (including the public interest in government observance of the Constitution and laws) is the function of Congress and the Chief Executive. The question presented here is whether the public interest in proper administration of the laws (specifically, in agencies' observance of a particular, statutorily prescribed procedure) can be converted into an individual right by a statute that denominates it as such, and that permits all citizens (or, for that matter, a subclass of citizens who suffer no distinctive concrete harm) to sue. If the concrete injury requirement has the separation-of-powers significance we have always said, the answer must be obvious: To permit Congress to convert the undifferentiated public interest in executive officers' compliance with the law into an "individual right" vindicable in the courts is to permit Congress to transfer from the President to the courts the Chief Executive's most important constitutional duty, to "take Care that the Laws be faithfully executed," Art. II, § 3. It would enable the courts, with the permission of Congress, "to assume a position of authority over the governmental acts of another and co-equal department," to become "virtually continuing monitors of the wisdom and soundness of Executive action. We have always rejected that vision of our role:"

> "When Congress passes an Act empowering administrative agencies to carry on governmental activities, the power of those agencies is circumscribed by the authority granted. This permits the courts to participate in law enforcement entrusted to administrative bodies only to the extent necessary to protect justifiable individual rights against administrative action fairly beyond the granted powers.... This is very far from assuming that the courts are charged more than administrators or legislators with the protection of the rights of the people. Congress and the Executive supervise the acts of administrative agents.... But under Article III, Congress established courts to adjudicate cases and controversies as to claims of infringement of individual rights whether by unlawful action of private persons or by the exertion of unauthorized administrative power." Stark v. Wickard, 321 U.S. 288, 309–310 (1944).

"Individual rights," within the meaning of this passage, do not mean public rights that have been legislatively pronounced to belong to each individual who forms part of the public.

Nothing in this contradicts the principle that "the ... injury required by Art. III may exist solely by virtue of 'statutes creating legal rights, the invasion of which creates standing.' " *Warth*, 422 U.S., at 500 (quoting Linda R.S. v. Richard D., 410 U.S. 614, 617 n. 3 (1973)). Both of the cases used by *Linda R.S.* as an illustration of that principle involved Congress's elevating to the status of legally cognizable injuries concrete, *de facto* injuries that were previously inadequate in law (namely, injury to an individual's personal interest in living in a racially integrated community, see Trafficante v. Metropolitan Life Ins. Co., 409 U.S. 205, 208–212 (1972), and injury to a company's interest in marketing its product free from competition, see Hardin v. Kentucky Utilities Co., 390 U.S. 1, 6 (1968)). As we said in *Sierra Club*, "[Statutory] broadening [of] the categories of injury that may be alleged in support of standing is a different matter from abandoning the requirement that the party seeking review must himself have suffered an injury." Whether or not the principle set forth in *Warth* can be extended beyond that distinction, it is clear that in suits against the government, at least, the concrete injury requirement must remain. 504 U.S. at 576–78.

More recently, however, the Court seems to have deferred more to congressional determinations of injury. In Federal Election Comm'n v. Akins, 524 U.S. 11 (1998), the Court upheld a broad congressional grant of standing. Over Justice Scalia's dissenting warning that the case would give Congress virtually unlimited power, the Court held that individual voters could challenge the FEC's determination that a particular organization was not a political committee and thus did not have to disclose certain information. The Court found that the inability to obtain information constituted a sufficient injury in fact to satisfy the constitutional requirements, and that the relevant statute granted standing to any "aggrieved" person. Does *Akins* conflict with *Lujan*? Can it be limited to "informational" cases? See Sunstein, *Informational Regulation and Informational Standing:* Akins *and* Beyond, 147 U.Pa.L.Rev. 613 (1999).

THIRD PARTY STANDING

The *Warth* plaintiffs who were taxpayers of the City of Rochester were denied standing, at least in part, because their claim was that "Penfield's zoning ordinance and practices violate the constitutional and statutory rights of third parties, namely, persons of low and moderate income who are said to be excluded from Penfield." Should a litigant be allowed to assert the interests of third parties not directly involved in the litigation?

While it is traditionally held that "one to whom application of a statute is constitutional will not be heard to attack the statute on the ground that impliedly it might also be taken as applying to other persons or other situations in which its application might be unconstitutional," United States v. Raines, 362 U.S. 17, 21 (1960), several exceptions to this precept have been recognized.

1. **Overbreadth.** The classic illustration of such a practice is the so-called first amendment "overbreadth doctrine," under which an individual who would in fact fall within the terms of a narrowly and properly drawn statute may challenge a law on the grounds that it unconstitutionally reaches others whose activity is protected by the first amendment. In Broadrick v. Oklahoma, 413 U.S. 601 (1973), the Supreme Court found the overbreadth doctrine to be "strong medicine", and therefore imposed severe restrictions on its use. The Court reasoned that the doctrine's value "attenuates as the otherwise unprotected behavior that it forbids the State to sanction moves from 'pure speech' toward conduct and that conduct—even if expressive—falls within the scope of otherwise valid criminal laws that reflect legitimate state interest in maintaining comprehensive controls over harmful, constitutionally unprotected conduct * * *. To put the matter another way, particularly where conduct and not merely speech is involved, we believe that the overbreadth of a statute must not only be real, but substantial as well, judged in relation to the statute's plainly legitimate sweep." 413 U.S. at 615.

In New York v. Ferber, 458 U.S. 747 (1982), the Court abandoned its speech-conduct dichotomy, and imposed *Broadrick*'s "substantiality" requirement on all first amendment overbreadth challenges. The case concerned an overbreadth attack on a New York statute that prohibited the knowing promotion of a sexual performance by a child under the age of sixteen by distributing material that depicts such a performance. The Court held that the "substantiality" requirement applied, even though pure speech was involved, because

> the extent of deterrence of protected speech can be expected to decrease with the declining reach of the regulation. This observation appears equally applicable to the publication of books and films as it is to activities, such as picketing or participation in election campaigns, which have previously been categorized as involving conduct

plus speech. We see no appreciable difference between the position of a publisher or bookseller in doubt as to the reach of New York's child pornography law and the situation faced by the Oklahoma state employees with respect to that state's restriction on partisan political activity. Indeed, it could reasonably be argued that the bookseller, with an economic incentive to sell materials that may fall within the statute's scope, may be less likely to be deterred than the employee who wishes to engage in political campaign activity. 458 U.S. at 772.

Do you agree that "the extent of deterrence of protected speech can be expected to decrease with the declining reach of the regulation"? See Redish, *The Warren Court, the Burger Court and the First Amendment Overbreadth Doctrine,* 78 Nw.U.L.Rev. 1031, 1063–69 (1983).

The Court expounded upon the overbreadth doctrine in Los Angeles Police Department v. United Reporting Publishing Corp., 528 U.S. 32 (1999). In that case, the Court refused to consider a facial challenge to a state statute that limited the information individuals were permitted to obtain from police departments. The Court held that a commercial distributor of such information—which was now prevented from obtaining it—had no standing to challenge the law on the basis of its effect on others. According to the Court, this was unlike traditional overbreadth situations because allowing the statute to remain on the books did not chill other speech.

Professor Henry Monaghan has challenged the traditional view that the overbreadth doctrine constitutes a procedural departure from standing requirements. Monaghan, *Overbreadth,* 1981 Sup.Ct.Rev. 1. He contends that "[u]nder 'conventional' standing principles, a litigant has always had the right to be judged in accordance with a constitutionally valid rule of law," and that, as a general matter, "a litigant could make a facial challenge to the constitutional sufficiency of the rule actually applied to him, irrespective of the privileged character of his own activity." Id. at 13. Under Professor Monaghan's analysis, the overbreadth doctrine is simply a substantive first amendment principle, and indeed is not necessarily limited to the first amendment context. Id. at 37–38. Professor Richard Fallon makes a related argument, suggesting that the Court's willingness to consider facial—as opposed to as-applied—challenges is a function of the underlying substantive law rather than a separate standing doctrine. Fallon, *As-Applied and Facial Challenges and Third–Party Standing,* 113 Harv.L.Rev. 1321 (2000). See also Fallon, *Making Sense of Overbreadth,* 100 Yale L.J. 853 (1991). For a broader philosophical discussion of the relationship between constitutional rules and third-party standing, see Adler, *Rights Against Rules: The Moral Structure of American Constitutional Law,* 97 Mich.L.Rev. 1 (1998); Adler, *Personal Rights and Rule Dependence: Can the Two Co–Exist?* 6 Legal Theory 337 (2000).

2. **Beyond Overbreadth.** Exceptions to the prohibition against third-party standing have also been recognized in areas other than first

amendment overbreadth. In Barrows v. Jackson, 346 U.S. 249 (1953), the Supreme Court held that a white seller had standing to assert the rights of a black purchaser against a racially restrictive covenant, because otherwise "it would be difficult if not impossible for the persons whose rights are asserted to present their grievance before any court." Id. at 257. The plaintiff had in fact been sued for damages for failure to comply with the terms of the covenant, but apparently the Court nevertheless deemed the case to involve third-party standing.

The Court summarized its third-party standing guidelines in Caplin & Drysdale, Chartered v. United States, 491 U.S. 617, 623 n. 3 (1989), as follows:

> When a person or entity seeks standing to advance the constitutional rights of others, we ask two questions: first, has the litigant suffered injury in fact, adequate to satisfy article III's case or controversy requirement; and second, do prudential considerations which we have identified in our prior cases point to permitting the litigant to advance the claim. [The prudential inquiry explores] three factors: the relationship of the litigant to the person whose rights are being asserted; the ability of the person to advance his own rights; and the impact of the litigation on third party interests.

More recently, the Court has stated the standard in the form of a two-part test: "First, we have asked whether the party asserting the right has a 'close' relationship with the person who possesses the right. * * * Second, we have considered whether there is a 'hindrance' to the possessor's ability to protect his own interests." Kowalski v. Tesmer, 543 U.S. 125, 130 (2004).

In Bush v. Gore, 531 U.S. 98 (2000), the Court held that a Florida Supreme Court decision ordering a manual recount of contested presidential ballots discriminated against some Florida voters in violation of the Equal Protection Clause. No Florida voter was a party to the suit: the Equal Protection challenge was brought by candidate George W. Bush. The Court did not discuss the issue of standing. Was Bush's challenge an appropriate instance of third-party standing? If the Equal Protection violation did not occur until the Florida Supreme Court ruling itself—in a suit brought by Al Gore against the Florida Secretary of State, who was responsible for certifying the presidential vote—who, if anyone, should have had standing to bring the case to the United States Supreme Court? See Chemerinsky, Bush v. Gore *Was Not Justiciable*, 76 Notre Dame L.Rev. 1093 (2001).

For other Supreme Court cases on third party standing, see Miller v. Albright, 523 U.S. (1998); Campbell v. Louisiana, 523 U.S. 392 (1998); Whitmore v. Arkansas, 495 U.S. 149 (1990). See generally Monaghan, *Third Party Standing,* 84 Colum.L.Rev. 277 (1984).

TAXPAYER STANDING

The Supreme Court has had particular difficulty applying the requirement of injury in fact to what might be called psychological or ideological injuries. Is the "case or controversy" requirement satisfied when a plaintiff alleges that his only injury is that the government is spending taxpayers' money in an unconstitutional fashion? The Court has considered the issue a number of times.

FROTHINGHAM v. MELLON, 262 U.S. 447 (1923). The case challenged the constitutionality of the Act of November 23, 1921, c. 135, 42 Stat. 224, commonly called the Maternity Act, which, among other things, provided for appropriations, to be apportioned among participating states, for the purpose of reducing maternal and infant mortality and protecting the health of mothers and infants. It was alleged "that the act is a usurpation of power not granted to Congress by the Constitution— an attempted exercise of the power of local self-government reserved to the States by the Tenth Amendment * * *." Id. at 479. Plaintiff was a taxpayer who contended "that the effect of the appropriations complained of will be to increase the burden of future taxation and thereby take her property without due process of law." Id. at 485. The Court found that plaintiff lacked standing:

> The administration of any statute, likely to produce additional taxation to be imposed upon a vast number of taxpayers, the extent of whose several liability is indefinite and constantly changing, is essentially a matter of public and not of individual concern. If one taxpayer may champion and litigate such a cause, then every other taxpayer may do the same, not only in respect of the statute here under review, but also in respect of every other appropriation act and statute whose administration requires the outlay of public money, and whose validity may be questioned. The bare suggestion of such a result, with its attendant inconveniences, goes far to sustain the conclusion which we have reached, that a suit of this character cannot be maintained.

> * * * The party who invokes the power must be able to show, not only that the statute is invalid, but that he has sustained or is immediately in danger of sustaining some direct injury as the result of its enforcement, and not merely that he suffers in some indefinite way in common with people generally. Id. at 487–88.

The Court rationalized its conclusion in separation-of-powers terms:

> The functions of government under our system are apportioned. To the legislative department has been committed the duty of making laws, to the executive the duty of executing them, and to the judiciary the duty of interpreting and applying them in cases properly brought before the courts. The general rule is that neither department may invade the province of the other and neither may control, direct, or restrain the action of the other. * * * We have no power per se to review and annul acts of Congress on the ground that they are unconstitutional. That question may be considered only when the justification for some direct injury suffered or threatened, presenting a justiciable issue, is made to rest upon such an act. Then the power exercised is that of ascertaining and declaring the

law applicable to the controversy. It amounts to little more than the negative power to disregard an unconstitutional enactment, which otherwise would stand in the way of the enforcement of a legal right. * * * If a case for preventive relief be presented, the court enjoins, in effect, not the execution of the statute, but the acts of the official, the statute notwithstanding. Here the parties plaintiff have no such case. Looking through forms of words to the substance of their complaint, it is merely that officials of the executive department of the government are executing and will execute an act of Congress asserted to be unconstitutional; and this we are asked to prevent. To do so would be not to decide a judicial controversy, but to assume a position of authority over the governmental acts of another and co-equal department, an authority which plainly we do not possess. Id. at 488–89.

The Court distinguished taxpayer suits brought against municipalities:

The interest of a taxpayer of a municipality in the application of its moneys is direct and immediate and the remedy by injunction to prevent their misuse is not inappropriate. * * * But the relation of a taxpayer of the United States to the federal government is very different. His interest in the moneys of the treasury—partly realized from taxation and partly from other sources—is shared with millions of others, is comparatively minute and indeterminable; and the effect upon future taxation, of any payment out of the funds, so remote, fluctuating and uncertain, that no basis is afforded for an appeal to the preventive powers of a court of equity. Id. at 486–87.

The door to "citizens' suits" was similarly closed in EX PARTE LEVITT, 302 U.S. 633 (1937). In *Levitt* the plaintiff, suing as a "citizen and member of the bar" of the Supreme Court, was denied standing to contest the appointment of Justice Black as contrary to Article I, section 6 of the Constitution. Describing mere citizen status as "insufficient to support standing," the Court indicated that a plaintiff "must show that he has sustained * * * a direct injury as the result of that action and it is not sufficient that he has merely a generalized interest common to all members of the public." 302 U.S. at 634.

Taxpayer standing took a different turn, however, in FLAST v. COHEN, 392 U.S. 83 (1968). Faced with a first amendment challenge to the use of federal funds to support instructional activities and materials in religious schools, the Court in *Flast* for the first time unequivocally recognized taxpayer status, without more, as a basis for standing. Sweeping aside any claimed Article III barrier to taxpayer standing, Chief Justice Warren's opinion established a two-pronged test allegedly designed to determine whether a sufficient "nexus" could be demonstrated between the plaintiff's status as a taxpayer and the constitutional violation alleged. Accordingly, the plaintiffs were required to allege that the statute challenged was an exercise of the congressional spending power and that the expenditure violated a specific constitutional limitation on the authority to spend. 392 U.S. at 102–103. Since the plaintiffs in *Flast* contested a federal spending program, and since the establishment clause was deemed to be a specific rather than a general limitation, standing was granted. Determination of the exact parameters of the ruling was left to subsequent cases.

VALLEY FORGE CHRISTIAN COLLEGE v. AMERICANS UNITED FOR SEPARATION OF CHURCH AND STATE, INC.

Supreme Court of the United States, 1982.
454 U.S. 464.

JUSTICE REHNQUIST delivered the opinion of the Court.

I

Article IV, Section 3, Clause 2 of the Constitution vests Congress with the "Power to dispose of and make all needful Rules and Regulations respecting the * * * Property belonging to the United States." Shortly after the termination of hostilities in the Second World War, Congress enacted the Federal Property and Administrative Services Act of 1949, 63 Stat. 377, 40 U.S.C. § 471 *et seq.* (1976 ed. and Supp. III). The Act was designed, in part, to provide "an economical and efficient system for * * * the disposal of surplus property." 63 Stat. 378, 40 U.S.C. § 471. In furtherance of this policy, federal agencies are directed to maintain adequate inventories of the property under their control and to identify excess property for transfer to other agencies able to use it. See 63 Stat. 384, 40 U.S.C. § 483(b), (c). Property that has outlived its usefulness to the federal government is declared "surplus" and may be transferred to private or other public entities. See generally 63 Stat. 385, as amended, 40 U.S.C. § 484.

The Act authorizes the Secretary of Health, Education, and Welfare (now the Secretary of Education) to assume responsibility for disposing of surplus real property "for school, classroom, or other educational use." 63 Stat. 387, as amended, 40 U.S.C. § 484(k)(1). Subject to the disapproval of the Administrator of General Services, the Secretary may sell or lease the property to nonprofit, tax exempt educational institutions for consideration that takes into account "any benefit which has accrued or may accrue to the United States" from the transferee's use of the property. 63 Stat. 387, 40 U.S.C. § 484(k)(1)(A), (C). By regulation, the Secretary has provided for the computation of a "public benefit allowance," which discounts the transfer price of the property "on the basis of benefits to the United States from the use of such property for educational purposes." 34 CFR § 12.9(a) (1980).

The property which spawned this litigation was acquired by the Department of the Army in 1942, as part of a larger tract of approximately 181 acres of land northwest of Philadelphia. The Army built on that land the Valley Forge General Hospital, and for 30 years thereafter, that hospital provided medical care for members of the Armed Forces. In April 1973, as part of a plan to reduce the number of military installations in the United States, the Secretary of Defense proposed to close the hospital, and the General Services Administration declared it to be "surplus property."

The Department of Health, Education, and Welfare (HEW) eventually assumed responsibility for disposing of portions of the property, and in August 1976, it conveyed a 77–acre tract to petitioner, the Valley Forge Christian College. * * * The deed from HEW conveyed the land in fee simple with certain conditions subsequent, which required petitioner to use the property for 30 years solely for the educational purposes described in petitioner's application. In that description, petitioner stated its intention to conduct "a program of education * * * meeting the accrediting standards of the State of Pennsylvania, The American Association of Bible Colleges, the Division of Education of the General Council of the Assemblies of God and the Veterans Administration."

Petitioner is a nonprofit educational institution operating under the supervision of a religious order known as the Assemblies of God. By its own description, petitioner's purpose is "to offer systematic training on the collegiate level to men and women for Christian service as either ministers or laymen."

In September 1976, respondents Americans United for Separation of Church and State, Inc. (Americans United), and four of its employees, learned of the conveyance through a news release. Two months later, they brought suit in the United States District Court for the Eastern District of Pennsylvania to challenge the conveyance on the ground that it violated the Establishment Clause of the First Amendment. * * * In its amended complaint, Americans United described itself as a nonprofit organization composed of 90,000 "taxpayer members." The complaint asserted that each member "would be deprived of the fair and constitutional use of his (her) tax dollar for constitutional purposes in violation of his (her) rights under the First Amendment of the United States Constitution." Respondents sought a declaration that the conveyance was null and void, and an order compelling petitioner to transfer the property back to the United States.

On petitioner's motion, the District Court granted summary judgment and dismissed the complaint. * * * The court found that respondents lacked standing to sue as taxpayers under Flast v. Cohen, 392 U.S. 83 (1968), and had "failed to allege that they have suffered any actual or concrete injury beyond a generalized grievance common to all taxpayers."

Respondents appealed to the Court of Appeals for the Third Circuit, which reversed the judgment of the District Court by a divided vote. All members of the court agreed that respondents lacked standing as taxpayers to challenge the conveyance under Flast v. Cohen, supra, since that case extended standing to taxpayers *qua* taxpayers only to challenge congressional exercises of the power to tax and spend conferred by Art. I, § 8, of the Constitution, and this conveyance was authorized by legislation enacted under the authority of the Property Clause, Art. IV, § 3, cl.

2. Notwithstanding this significant factual difference from *Flast,* the majority of the Court of Appeals found that respondents also had standing merely as "citizens," claiming " 'injury in fact' to their shared individuated right to a government that 'shall make no law respecting the establishment of religion.' " In the majority's view, this "citizen standing" was sufficient to satisfy the "case or controversy" requirement of Art. III.

Because of the unusually broad and novel view of standing to litigate a substantive question in the federal courts adopted by the Court of Appeals, we granted certiorari, 450 U.S. 909, and we now reverse.

* * *

III

The injury alleged by respondents in their amended complaint is the "depriv[ation] of the fair and constitutional use of [their] tax dollar." * * * As a result, our discussion must begin with Frothingham v. Mellon, 262 U.S. 447 (1923).

Following the decision in *Frothingham,* the Court confirmed that the expenditure of public funds in an allegedly unconstitutional manner is not an injury sufficient to confer standing, even though the plaintiff contributes to the public coffers as a taxpayer. In Doremus v. Board of Education, 342 U.S. 429 (1952), plaintiffs brought suit as citizens and taxpayers, claiming that a New Jersey law which authorized public school teachers in the classroom to read passages from the Bible violated the Establishment Clause of the First Amendment. The Court dismissed the appeal for lack of standing * * *. In short, the Court found that plaintiffs' grievance was "not a direct dollars-and-cents injury but is a religious difference."

* * *

Unlike the plaintiffs in *Flast,* respondents fail the first prong of the test for taxpayer standing. Their claim is deficient in two respects. First, the source of their complaint is not a congressional action, but a decision by HEW to transfer a parcel of federal property. *Flast* limited taxpayer standing to challenges directed "only [at] exercises of congressional power."

Second, and perhaps redundantly, the property transfer about which respondents complain was not an exercise of authority conferred by the taxing and spending clause of Art. I, § 8. The authorizing legislation, the Federal Property and Administrative Services Act of 1949, was an evident exercise of Congress' power under the Property Clause, Art. IV, § 3, cl. 2.

Any doubt that once might have existed concerning the rigor with which the *Flast* exception to the *Frothingham* principle ought to be applied should have been erased by this Court's recent decisions in United States v. Richardson, 418 U.S. 166 (1974), and Schlesinger v.

Reservists Committee to Stop the War, 418 U.S. 208 (1974). In *Richardson*, the question was whether the plaintiff had standing as a federal taxpayer to argue that legislation which permitted the Central Intelligence Agency to withhold from the public detailed information about its expenditures violated the Accounts Clause of the Constitution. We rejected plaintiff's claim of standing because "his challenge [was] not addressed to the taxing or spending power, but to the statutes regulating the CIA." 418 U.S., at 175. The "mere recital" of those claims "demonstrate[d] how far he [fell] short of the standing criteria of *Flast* and how neatly he [fell] within the *Frothingham* holding left undisturbed."

The claim in *Schlesinger* was marred by the same deficiency. Plaintiffs in that case argued that the Incompatibility Clause of Art. I prevented certain Members of Congress from holding commissions in the Armed Forces Reserve. We summarily rejected their assertion of standing as taxpayers because they "did not challenge an enactment under Art. I, § 8, but rather the action of the Executive Branch in permitting Members of Congress to maintain their Reserve status."

Respondents, therefore, are plainly without standing to sue as taxpayers. The Court of Appeals apparently reached the same conclusion. It remains to be seen whether respondents have alleged any other basis for standing to bring this suit.

IV

Although the Court of Appeals properly doubted respondents' ability to establish standing solely on the basis of their taxpayer status, it considered their allegations of taxpayer injury to be "essentially an assumed role."

> "Plaintiffs have no reason to expect, nor perhaps do they care about, any personal tax saving that might result should they prevail. The crux of the interest at stake, the plaintiffs argue, is found in the Establishment Clause, not in the supposed loss of money as such. As a matter of primary identity, therefore, the plaintiffs are not so much taxpayers as separationists * * *."

In the court's view, respondents had established standing by virtue of an " 'injury in fact' to their shared individuated right to a government that 'shall make no law respecting the establishment of religion.' " Ibid. The court distinguished this "injury" from "the question of 'citizen standing' as such." Although citizens generally could not establish standing simply by claiming an interest in governmental observance of the Constitution, respondents had "set forth instead a particular and concrete injury" to a "personal constitutional right."

The Court of Appeals was surely correct in recognizing that the Art. III requirements of standing are not satisfied by "the abstract injury in nonobservance of the Constitution asserted by * * * citizens." Schlesinger v. Reservists Committee to Stop the War, 418 U.S., at 223, n. 13. This Court repeatedly has rejected claims of standing predicated on " 'the right, possessed by every citizen, to require that the Government be administered according to law * * *.' " Fairchild v. Hughes, 258 U.S. 126, 129 * * * Such claims amount to little more than attempts "to employ a federal court as a forum in which to air * * * generalized grievances about the conduct of government." Flast v. Cohen, 392 U.S., at 106.

In finding that respondents had alleged something more than "the generalized interest of all citizens in constitutional governance," *Schlesinger,* supra, 418 U.S., at 217, the Court of Appeals relied on factual differences which we do not think amount to legal distinctions. The court decided that respondents' claim differed from those in *Schlesinger* and *Richardson,* which were predicated, respectively, on the Incompatibility and Accounts Clauses, because "it is at the very least arguable that the Establishment Clause creates in each citizen a 'personal constitutional right' to a government that does not establish religion." The court found it unnecessary to determine whether this "arguable" proposition was correct, since it judged the mere allegation of a legal right sufficient to confer standing.

This reasoning process merely disguises, we think with a rather thin veil, the inconsistency of the court's results with our decisions in *Schlesinger* and *Richardson.* The plaintiffs in those cases plainly asserted a "personal right" to have the government act in accordance with their views of the Constitution; indeed, we see no barrier to the *assertion* of such claims with respect to any constitutional provision. But assertion of a right to a particular kind of government conduct, which the government has violated by acting differently, cannot alone satisfy the requirements of Art. III without draining those requirements of meaning.

Nor can *Schlesinger* and *Richardson* be distinguished on the ground that the Incompatibility and Accounts Clauses are in some way less "fundamental" than the Establishment Clause. Each establishes a norm of conduct which the federal government is bound to honor—to no greater or lesser extent than any other inscribed in the Constitution. To the extent the Court of Appeals relied on a view of standing under which the Art. III burdens diminish as the "importance" of the claim on the merits increases, we reject that notion. The requirement of standing "focuses on the party seeking to get his complaint before a federal court and not on the issues he wishes to have adjudicated." Flast v. Cohen, supra, 392 U.S., at 99. Moreover, we know of no principled basis on which to create a hierarchy of constitutional values or a complementary "sliding scale" of standing which might permit respondents to invoke the judicial power of the United States. "The proposition that all constitutional provisions are enforceable by any citizen simply because citizens are the ultimate beneficiaries of those provisions has no boundaries." Schlesinger v. Reservists Committee to Stop the War, supra, 418 U.S., at 227.

The complaint in this case shares a common deficiency with those in *Schlesinger* and *Richardson.* Although they claim that the Constitution has been violated, they claim nothing else. They fail to identify any personal injury suffered by the plaintiffs *as a consequence* of the alleged constitutional error, other than the psychological consequence presumably produced by observation of conduct with which one disagrees. That is not an injury sufficient to confer standing under Art. III, even though the disagreement is phrased in constitutional terms. It is evident that respondents are firmly committed to the constitutional principle of separation of church and State, but standing is not measured by the intensity of the litigant's interest or the fervor of his advocacy. "[T]hat concrete adverseness which sharpens the presentation of issues," Baker v. Carr, 369 U.S., at 204, is the anticipated consequence of proceedings commenced by one who has been injured in fact; it is not a permissible substitute for the showing of injury itself.

In reaching this conclusion, we do not retreat from our earlier holdings that standing may be predicated on noneconomic injury. * * * We simply cannot see that respondents have alleged an *injury* of *any* kind, economic or otherwise, sufficient to confer standing. Respondents complain of a transfer of property located in Chester County, Pennsylvania. The named plaintiffs reside in Maryland and Virginia; their organizational headquarters are located in Washington, D.C. They learned of the transfer through a news release. Their claim that the government has violated the Establishment Clause does not provide a special license to roam the country in search of governmental wrongdoing and to reveal their discoveries in federal court. The federal courts were simply not constituted as ombudsmen of the general welfare.

V

The Court of Appeals in this case ignored unambiguous limitations on taxpayer and citizen standing. It appears to have done so out of the conviction that enforcement of the Establishment Clause demands special exceptions from the requirement that a plaintiff allege " 'distinct and palpable injury to himself,' * * * that is likely to be redressed if the requested relief is granted." Gladstone, Realtors v. Village of Bellwood, 441 U.S., at 100 (quoting Warth v. Seldin, 422 U.S., at 501). The court derived precedential comfort from Flast v. Cohen, supra: "The underlying justification for according standing in *Flast* it seems, was the implicit recognition that the Establishment Clause does create in every citizen a personal constitutional right, such that any citizen, including taxpayers, may contest under that clause the constitutionality of federal expenditures." The concurring opinion was even more direct. In its view, "statutes alleged to violate the Establishment Clause may not have an individual impact sufficient to confer standing in the traditional sense." To satisfy "the need for an available plaintiff," and thereby to assure a basis for judicial review, respondents should be granted standing because, "as a practical matter, no one is better suited to bring this lawsuit and thus vindicate the freedoms embodied in the Establishment Clause".

Implicit in the foregoing is the philosophy that the business of the federal courts is correcting constitutional errors, and that "cases and controversies'' are at best merely convenient vehicles for doing so and at worst nuisances that may be dispensed with when they become obstacles to that transcendent endeavor. This philosophy has no place in our constitutional scheme. It does not become more palatable when the underlying merits concern the Establishment Clause. Respondents' claim of standing implicitly rests on the presumption that violations of the Establishment Clause typically will not cause injury sufficient to confer standing under the "traditional" view of Art. III. But "[t]he assumption that if respondents have no standing to sue, no one would have standing, is not a reason to find standing." Schlesinger v. Reservists Committee to Stop the War, 418 U.S., at 227. This view would convert standing into a requirement that must be observed only when satisfied. Moreover, we are unwilling to assume that injured parties are nonexistent simply because they have not joined respondents in their suit. The law of averages is not a substitute for standing.

Were we to accept respondents' claim of standing in this case, there would be no principled basis for confining our exception to litigants relying on the Establishment Clause. Ultimately, that exception derives from the idea that the judicial power requires nothing more for its invocation than important issues and able litigants. The existence of injured parties who might not wish to bring suit becomes irrelevant. Because we are unwilling to countenance such a departure from the limits on judicial power contained in Art. III, the judgment of the Court of Appeals is reversed.

It is so ordered.

JUSTICE BRENNAN, with whom JUSTICE MARSHALL and JUSTICE BLACKMUN join, dissenting.

* * *

The opinion of the Court is a stark example of this unfortunate trend of resolving cases at the "threshold" while obscuring the nature of the underlying rights and interests at stake. The Court waxes eloquent on the blend of prudential and constitutional considerations that combine to create our misguided "standing" jurisprudence. *But not one word is said about the Establishment Clause right that the plaintiff seeks to enforce.* And despite its pat recitation of our standing decisions, the opinion utterly fails, except by the sheerest form of *ipse dixit*, to explain why this case is unlike Flast v. Cohen, 392 U.S. 83 (1968), and is controlled instead by Frothingham v. Mellon, 262 U.S. 447 (1923).

Notes

1. Justice Harlan dissented in *Flast*. He argued that the *Flast* plaintiffs, just like the plaintiff in *Frothingham*, "sought to complain, not as taxpayers, but as 'private attorneys-general.'" 392 U.S. at 119. He reasoned that although the *constitutional* requirements for standing are met by such ideological (or "non-Hohfeldian") plaintiffs, prudential considerations should bar most such suits. He worried that "unrestricted public actions" in these

sorts of cases would "go far toward the final transformation of this Court into the Council of Revision" proposed by James Madison and rejected by the drafters of the Constitution. Id. at 130. Madison's proposal would have given the Supreme Court the authority to consider—and to veto—any law proposed by Congress. See D. Farber & S. Sherry, A History of the American Constitution 66–75 (1990).

Was Justice Harlan right? Are there relevant differences between ideological plaintiffs and those with more concrete injuries? See Jaffe, *The Citizen as Litigant in Public Actions: The Non–Hohfeldian or Ideological Plaintiff*, 116 U.Pa.L.Rev. 1033 (1968); Fletcher, *The Structure of Standing*, 98 Yale L.J. 221 (1988). Even if there are such differences, if ideological plaintiffs satisfy the constitutional requirements, should federal courts refuse to entertain such suits for prudential reasons?

Consider Brilmayer, *The Jurisprudence of Article III: Perspectives on the "Case or Controversy" Requirement,* 93 Harv.L.Rev. 297 (1979). Professor Brilmayer views with great skepticism the concept of a purely "ideological" plaintiff: "Isn't a traditional plaintiff better able vividly to illustrate the adverse effects of the complained-of activity? Isn't there a danger that by seeking to change the law too rapidly an ideological plaintiff will take greater risks by framing the issues in a broader, more controversial, manner?" Id. at 309. Do you think these concerns are valid? If so, are they sufficient to reject the concept of an ideological plaintiff?

Professor Mark Tushnet responds to Professor Brilmayer's arguments in Tushnet, *The Sociology of Article III: A Response to Professor Brilmayer,* 93 Harv.L.Rev. 1698, 1708 (1980): "Professor Brilmayer's approach bears little relation to the real world of public interest litigation." Pointing to the experience of the NAACP as a public interest litigant, Professor Tushnet urges "a barebones rule allowing standing when the litigant or the attorneys are part of an institution with a continuing concern for the relevant substantive law, and are capable of generating an adequate record." Id. at 1709. In response to Brilmayer's concerns, Tushnet asserts that they are "purely evidentiary and irrelevant to whether the nominal litigant should have standing. Auxiliary devices can ensure an adequate record and fully address this problem. Second, and more important, a public interest litigant will rarely fail to present a sufficiently concrete case. The lore of public interest litigation is replete with tales of trying to find the 'best' plaintiff, that is, the one on whom the legal rule to be challenged operates in the most heart-rending way." Id. at 1713–14. In response, Professor Brilmayer contends: "If cases involving real people are more likely to succeed on the merits, if such people are virtually always available and if the experienced lawyer seeks them out, then objections to requiring the presence of a traditional plaintiff seem perversely designed to procure for inexperienced litigating institutions the option of acting irresponsibly." Brilmayer, *A Reply,* 93 Harv.L.Rev. 1727, 1728 (1980). Can you tell which of them gets the better of the argument? In light of the last points made by each, can an argument be made that it doesn't matter?

Professor Larry Yackle adds another observation to this debate. He suggests that plaintiffs with more tangible injuries are not always willing to pursue lawsuits, because "[t]hey are discouraged by the costs and other burdens associated with lawsuits, which often outweigh any personal bene-fits that litigation might bring." L. Yackle, Reclaiming the Federal Courts 69 (1994). Ideological litigants are not discouraged by these costs, because they are responding to "psychological and ideological stimuli." Id. Thus, Yackle argues, "the litigants that a more generous standing doctrine would empow-er are not isolated individual dilettantes out for a frolic at the courthouse, but serious, sophisticated, and committed organizations that use litigation as an instrument for restraining governmental power regarding some of the most sensitive aspects of human life." Id.

Is this a sufficient response to Professor Brilmayer? Are litigants who "respond to psychological and ideological stimuli" likely to make the best plaintiffs? How might their conduct of the lawsuit differ from plaintiffs with other, more tangible injuries? Even if an ideological plaintiff's advocacy is impeccable, is there something illegitimate about creating binding precedent in a case in which the plaintiff has no tangible interest? See Peters, *Adjudication as Representation*, 97 Colum.L.Rev. 312, 420–30 (1997).

Professor Edward Hartnett argues that Harlan was right on two counts: generalized ideological grievances *are* injuries in fact, but as a prudential matter the Court should not adjudicate such cases unless Congress clearly creates a cause of action. Hartnett, *The Standing of the United States: How Criminal Prosecutions Show that Standing Doctrine is Looking for Answers in All the Wrong Places*, 97 Mich.L.Rev. 2239 (1999). Would adoption of such a position change the results in *Flast*? In *Valley Forge*? In *Lujan v. Defenders Wildlife* [discussed supra pp. 34–35 and 38–39]? Does requiring a prior congressional authorization of private attorneys general respond to Professor Brilmayer's concerns?

2. Justice Harlan also criticized the majority's two-part test for taxpay-er standing. He argued that the two criteria devised by the Court "are not in any sense a measurement of any plaintiff's interest in the outcome of any suit." 392 U.S. at 121. He complained that the Court, instead of analyzing the circumstances under which ideological plaintiffs should be permitted to bring suit, simply arbitrarily "deemed" certain plaintiffs to be non-ideologi-cal. Is he correct? Is there any connection between the *Flast* test and the concreteness of the plaintiff's injury?

3. Did the distinction the Court drew in *Flast* lead inevitably to the result in *Valley Forge*? Notice that the dissent in *Valley Forge* does not seem to argue that the plaintiffs in that case satisfied the *Flast* test. Might that be because they did not satisfy it, since the challenged congressional action was authorized not by the taxing and spending clause but by the surplus property clause? Consider how, with hindsight, you might rewrite *Flast* (1) to meet Justice Harlan's objections, and (2) to create standing in *Valley Forge*. Should the *Flast* Court have focused on the taxing and spending clause, or on the establishment clause?

4. Consider a case that falls somewhere between *Flast* and *Valley Forge*. In Freedom From Religion Foundation, Inc. v. Chao, 433 F.3d 989 (7th Cir.2006), plaintiffs challenged as violative of the Establishment Clause "the use of money appropriated by Congress under Article I, section 8, to fund conferences that various executive-branch agencies hold to promote President Bush's 'Faith–Based and Community Initiatives,'" a program

created by a series of executive orders. Thus, as the court noted, the challenged expenditures were not "pursuant to specific congressional grant programs," but simply "the general 'program' of appropriating some money to executive-branch departments without strings attached." Should plaintiffs have standing?

5. By what principle can the Court hold as it has in cases such as Davis v. Passman, 442 U.S. 228 (1979), that the due process clause confers a right to be free from sex discrimination and still assert, as it does in *Valley Forge*, that the establishment clause does not confer a right to be free from the intermingling of church and state? The Court suggests that the difference lies in the "personal" as opposed to the "generalized" nature of the interest asserted. The Constitution, at least since *Marbury*, has been held to create legally protected interests. Doesn't the entire Constitution create legally protected interests? Does the particularized harm standard effectively create a "hierarchy" of constitutional rights? See, Nichol, *Rethinking Standing*, 72 Cal.L.Rev. 68, 84–87 (1984); Segall, *Standing Between the Court and the Commentators: A Necessity Rationale for Public Actions*, 54 U.Pitt.L.Rev. 351 (1993); Bandes, *The Idea of a Case*, 42 Stan.L.Rev. 227, 230 (1990) ("unstated acceptance of the private rights model leads to a refusal to recognize * * * collective rights and collective harms.") But see Marshall & Flood, *Establishment Clause Standing: The Not Very Revolutionary Decision at Valley Forge*, 11 Hofstra L.Rev. 63 (1982) (defending *Valley Forge* on narrower grounds as reflecting the lack of a plaintiff with personal interest).

6. The Court has also considered the question of legislator standing. In Raines v. Byrd, 521 U.S. 811 (1997), the Court ruled that individual federal legislators did not have standing to challenge the line-item veto. Despite a provision in the line-item veto statute itself purportedly granting federal legislators standing, the Court held that the legislators suffered no individualized injury and thus did not meet Article III standing requirements. The Court distinguished Coleman v. Miller, 307 U.S. 433 (1939), in which the Court had held that state legislators had standing to challenge a state statute. In *Coleman*, the plaintiff legislators would have prevailed in the challenged vote had the lieutenant governor not cast an allegedly illegal vote. At most, the Court said, *Coleman* stands for the proposition that "legislators whose votes would have been sufficient to defeat (or enact) a specific legislative act have standing to sue * * * on the ground that their votes have been completely nullified." 521 U.S. at 823. Since plaintiffs in *Raines* were in a substantial minority in voting against the line-item veto, they did not fit under *Coleman* as so characterized. For a thorough discussion of *Raines*, see Devins & Fitts, *The Triumph of Timing:* Raines v. Byrd *and the Modern Supreme Court's Attempt to Control Constitutional Confrontations*, 86 Geo. L.J. 351 (1997).

ALLEN v. WRIGHT

Supreme Court of the United States, 1984.
468 U.S. 737.

JUSTICE O'CONNOR delivered the opinion of the Court.

Parents of black public school children allege in this nationwide class action that the Internal Revenue Service (IRS) has not adopted sufficient standards and procedures to fulfill its obligation to deny tax-exempt status to racially discriminatory private schools. They assert that the IRS thereby harms them directly and interferes with the ability of their children to receive an education in desegregated public schools. The issue before us is whether plaintiffs have standing to bring this suit. We hold that they do not.

I

The Internal Revenue Service denies tax-exempt status under §§ 501(a) and (c)(3) of the Internal Revenue Code, 26 U.S.C. §§ 501(a) and (c)(3)—and hence eligibility to receive charitable contributions deductible from income taxes under §§ 170(a)(1) and (c)(2) of the Code, 26 U.S.C. §§ 170(a)(1) and (c)(2)—to racially discriminatory private schools. Rev.Rul. 71–447, 1971–2 Cum.Bull. 230. The IRS policy requires that a school applying for tax-exempt status show that it "admits the students of any race to all the rights, privileges, programs, and activities generally accorded or made available to students at that school and that the school does not discriminate on the basis of race in administration of its educational policies, admissions policies, scholarship and loan programs, and athletic and other school-administered programs." Ibid. To carry out this policy, the IRS has established guidelines and procedures for determining whether a particular school is in fact racially nondiscriminatory. Rev.Proc. 75–50, 1975–2 Cum.Bull. 587. Failure to comply with the guidelines "will ordinarily result in the proposed revocation of" tax-exempt status. Id., § 4.08, p. 589.

The guidelines provide that "[a] school must show affirmatively both that it has adopted a racially nondiscriminatory policy as to students that is made known to the general public and that since the adoption of that policy it has operated in a bona fide manner in accordance therewith." Id., § 2.02. The school must state its nondiscrimination policy in its organizational charter, id., § 4.01, pp. 587–588, and in all of its brochures, catalogues, and other advertisements to prospective students, id., § 4.02, p. 588. The school must make its nondiscrimination policy known to the entire community served by the school and must publicly disavow any contrary representations made on its behalf once it becomes aware of them. Id., § 4.03. The school must have nondiscriminatory policies concerning all programs and facilities, id., § 4.04, p. 589, including scholarships and loans, id., § 4.05, and the school must annually certify, under penalty of perjury, compliance with these requirements, id., § 4.07.

The IRS rules require a school applying for tax-exempt status to give a breakdown along racial lines of its student body and its faculty and administrative staff, id., § 5.01–1, as well as of scholarships and loans awarded, id., § 5.01–2. They also require the applicant school to state the year of its organization, id., § 5.01–5, and to list "incorporators, founders, board members, and donors of land or buildings," id., § 5.01–3, and state whether any of the organizations among these have an objective of maintaining segregated public or private school education, id., § 5.01–4. The rules further provide that, once given an exemption, a school must keep specified records to document the extent of compliance with the IRS guidelines. Id., § 7, p. 590. Finally, the rules announce that any information concerning discrimination at a tax-exempt school is officially welcomed. Id., § 6.

In 1976 respondents challenged these guidelines and procedures in a suit filed in Federal District Court against the Secretary of the Treasury and the Commissioner of Internal Revenue. The plaintiffs named in the complaint are parents of black children who, at the time the complaint was filed, were attending public schools in seven States in school districts undergoing desegregation. They brought this nationwide class action "on behalf of themselves and their children, and * * * on behalf of all other parents of black children attending public school systems undergoing, or which may in the future undergo, desegregation pursuant to court order [or] HEW regulations and guidelines, under state law, or voluntarily." * * * They estimated that the class they seek to represent includes several million persons.

Respondents allege in their complaint that many racially segregated private schools were created or expanded in their communities at the time the public schools were undergoing desegregation. * * * According to the complaint, many such private schools, including 17 schools or school systems identified by name in the complaint (perhaps some 30 schools in all), receive tax exemptions either directly or through the tax-exempt status of "umbrella" organizations that operate or support the schools. * * * Respondents allege that, despite the IRS policy of denying tax-exempt status to racially discriminatory private schools and despite the IRS guidelines and procedures for implementing that policy, some of the tax-exempt racially segregated private schools created or expanded in desegregating districts in fact have racially discriminatory policies. Id., at 17–18 (IRS permits "schools to receive tax exemptions merely on the basis of adopting and certifying—but not implementing—a policy of nondiscrimination") * * *.[11] Respondents allege that the IRS grant of

11. The complaint generally uses the phrase "racially segregated school" to mean simply that no or few minority students attend the school, irrespective of the school's maintenance of racially discriminatory policies or practices. Although the complaint, on its face, alleges that granting tax-exempt status to any "racially segregated" school in a desegregating public school district is unlawful, it is clear that respondents premise their allegation of illegality on discrimination, not on segregation alone.

The nub of respondent's complaint is that current IRS guidelines and procedures are inadequate to detect false certifications of nondiscrimination policies. This allegation would be superfluous if respondents were claiming that racial segregation even without racial discrimination made the grant of tax-exempt status unlawful. Moreover, re-

spondents have noticeably refrained from asserting that the IRS violates the law when it grants a tax exemption to a nondiscriminatory private school that happens to have few minority students. Indeed, respondents' brief in this Court makes a point of noting that their complaint alleges not only segregation but discrimination, and it repeatedly states that the challenged Government conduct is the granting of tax exemptions to racially discriminatory private schools, ("Respondents alleged that the federal petitioners are continuing to grant tax-exempt status to racially discriminatory private schools * * * ");

Since respondents' entire argument is built on the assertion that their rights are violated by IRS grants of tax-exempt status to some number of unidentified racially dis-

tax exemptions to such racially discriminatory schools is unlawful.[12]

Respondents allege that the challenged Government conduct harms them in two ways. The challenged conduct

(a) constitutes tangible federal financial aid and other support for racially segregated educational institutions, and

(b) fosters and encourages the organization, operation and expansion of institutions providing racially segregated educational opportunities for white children avoiding attendance in desegregating public school districts and thereby interferes with the efforts of federal courts, HEW and local school authorities to desegregate public school districts which have been operating racially dual school systems.

injuries alleged

Thus, respondents do not allege that their children have been the victims of discriminatory exclusion from the schools whose tax exemptions they challenge as unlawful. Indeed, they have not alleged at any stage of this litigation that their children have ever applied or would ever apply to any private school. See Wright v. Regan, 656 F.2d 820, 827 (1981) ("Plaintiffs * * * maintain they have no interest whatever in enrolling their children in a private school"). Rather, respondents claim a direct injury from the mere fact of the challenged Government conduct and, as indicated by the restriction of the plaintiff class to parents of children in desegregating school districts, injury to their children's opportunity to receive a desegregated education.[13] The latter injury is traceable to the IRS grant of tax exemptions to racially discriminatory schools, respondents allege, chiefly because contributions to such schools are deductible from income taxes under §§ 170(a)(1) and (c)(2) of the Internal Revenue Code and the "deductions facilitate the raising of funds to organize new schools and expand existing schools in order to accommodate white students avoiding attendance in desegregating public school districts."[14]

criminatory private schools in desegregating districts, we resolve the ambiguity in respondents' complaint by reading it as making that assertion.

Contrary to Justice Brennan's statement, * * * the complaint does not allege that each desegregating district in which they reside contains one or more racially discriminatory private schools unlawfully receiving a tax exemption.

12. The complaint alleges that the challenged IRS conduct violates several laws: § 501(c)(3) of the Internal Revenue Code, 26 U.S.C. § 501(c)(3); Title VI of the Civil Rights Act of 1964, 78 Stat. 252, 42 U.S.C. § 2000d et seq.; Rev.Stat. § 1977, 42 U.S.C. § 1981; and the Fifth and Fourteenth Amendments to the United States Constitution.

Last Term, in Bob Jones University v. United States, 461 U.S. 574 (1983), the Court

concluded that racially discriminatory private schools do not qualify for a tax exemption under § 501(c)(3) of the Internal Revenue Code.

13. Respondents did not allege in their 1976 complaint that their children were currently attending racially segregated schools. In 1979, during argument before the District Court, counsel for respondents stated that his clients' children "do go to desegregated schools * * *."

14. Several additional tax benefits accrue to an organization receiving a tax exemption under § 501(c)(3) of the Code. Such an organization is exempt not only from income taxes but also from federal social security taxes, 26 U.S.C. § 3121(b)(8)(B), and from federal unemployment taxes, 26 U.S.C. § 3306(c)(8). Moreover, contributions to the organization are deductible not only from income taxes,

Respondents request only prospective relief. They ask for a declaratory judgment that the challenged IRS tax-exemption practices are unlawful. They also ask for an injunction requiring the IRS to deny tax exemptions to a considerably broader class of private schools than the class of racially discriminatory private schools. Under the requested injunction, the IRS would have to deny tax-exempt status to all private schools

which have insubstantial or nonexistent minority enrollments, which are located in or serve desegregating public school districts, and which either—

(1) were established or expanded at or about the time the public school districts in which they are located or which they serve were desegregating;

(2) have been determined in adversary judicial or administrative proceedings to be racially segregated; or

(3) cannot demonstrate that they do not provide racially segregated educational opportunities for white children avoiding attendance in desegregating public school systems * * *.

Finally, respondents ask for an order directing the IRS to replace its 1975 guidelines with standards consistent with the requested injunction.

In May 1977 the District Court permitted intervention as a defendant by petitioner Allen, the head of one of the private school systems identified in the complaint. Thereafter, progress in the lawsuit was stalled for several years. During this period, the Internal Revenue Service reviewed its challenged policies and proposed new Revenue Procedures to tighten requirements for eligibility for tax-exempt status for private schools.[15] In 1979, however, Congress blocked any strengthening of the IRS guidelines at least until October 1980.[16] The District Court

---

26 U.S.C. § 170(a)(1) and (c)(2), but also from federal estate taxes, 26 U.S.C. § 2055(a)(2), and from federal gift taxes, 26 U.S.C. § 2522(a)(2).

15. The first proposal was made on August 22, 1978. It placed the burden of proving good faith operation on a nondiscriminatory basis, evaluated according to specified factors, on any private school that had an insignificant number of minority students and that had been formed or substantially expanded at a time the public schools in its community were undergoing desegregation. The second proposal was made on February 9, 1979, after public comment and hearings. It afforded private schools "greater flexibility" in proving nondiscriminatory operation, permitting satisfaction of this proof requirement by a showing that the school has "undertaken actions or programs reasonably designed to attract minority students on a continuing basis."

16. Treasury, Postal Service, and General Government Appropriations Act of 1980, §§ 103 and 615, 93 Stat. 562, 577. Section 615 of the Act, known as the Dornan Amendment, specifically forbade the use of funds to carry out the IRS's proposed Revenue Procedures. Section 103 of the Act, known as the Ashbrook Amendment, more generally forbade the use of funds to make the requirements for tax-exempt status of private schools more stringent than those in effect prior to the IRS's proposal of its new Revenue Procedures.

These provisions expired on October 1, 1980, but Congress maintained its interest in IRS policies regarding tax exemptions for racially discriminatory private schools. The Dornan and Ashbrook Amendments were reinstated for the period December 16, 1980, through September 30, 1981. H.J.Res. 644, Pub.L. 96–536, § 101(a)(1) and (4), 94 Stat. 3166, as amended by Supplemental Appropriations and Rescission Act of 1981,

thereupon considered and granted the defendants' motion to dismiss the complaint, concluding that respondents lack standing, that the judicial task proposed by respondents is inappropriately intrusive for a federal court, and that awarding the requested relief would be contrary to the will of Congress expressed in the 1979 ban on strengthening IRS guidelines.

The United States Court of Appeals for the District of Columbia reversed, concluding that respondents have standing to maintain this lawsuit. The court acknowledged that Simon v. Eastern Kentucky Welfare Rights Org., 426 U.S. 26 (1976), "suggests that litigation concerning tax liability is a matter between taxpayer and IRS, with the door barely ajar for third party challenges." The court concluded, however, that the *Simon* case is inapposite because respondents claim no injury dependent on taxpayers' actions: "[t]hey claim indifference as to the course private schools would take."[17] Instead, the court observed, "[t]he sole injury [respondents] claim is the denigration they suffer as black parents and schoolchildren when their government graces with tax-exempt status educational institutions in their communities that treat members of their race as persons of lesser worth." The court held this denigration injury enough to give respondents standing * * *.

We granted certiorari, and now reverse.

II

A

Article III of the Constitution confines the federal courts to adjudicating actual "cases" and "controversies." As the Court explained in Valley Forge Christian College v. Americans United for Separation of Church and State, Inc., 454 U.S. 464, 471–476 (1982), the "case or controversy" requirement defines with respect to the Judicial Branch the idea of separation of powers on which the Federal Government is founded. The several doctrines that have grown up to elaborate that requirement are "founded in concern about the proper—and properly limited—role of the courts in a democratic society." Warth v. Seldin, 422 U.S. 490, 498 (1975).

> All of the doctrines that cluster about Article III—not only standing but mootness, ripeness, political question, and the like—relate in part, and in different though overlapping ways, to an idea, which is more than an intuition but less than a rigorous and explicit theory, about the constitutional and prudential limits to the powers of an unelected, unrepresentative judiciary in our kind of government.

§ 401, 95 Stat. 95. For fiscal year 1982, Congress specifically denied funding for carrying out not only administrative actions but also court orders entered after the date of the IRS's proposal of its first revised Revenue Procedure. No such spending restrictions are currently in force.

17. Indeed, the Court of Appeals observed that respondents "do not dispute that it is 'speculative,' within the *Eastern Kentucky* frame, whether any private school would welcome blacks in order to retain tax exemption or would relinquish exemption to retain current practices."

Vander Jagt v. O'Neill, 699 F.2d 1166, 1178–1179 (1982) (Bork, J., concurring).

The case-or-controversy doctrines state fundamental limits on federal judicial power in our system of government.

The Art. III doctrine that requires a litigant to have "standing" to invoke the power of a federal court is perhaps the most important of these doctrines. "In essence the question of standing is whether the litigant is entitled to have the court decide the merits of the dispute or of particular issues." Warth v. Seldin, supra, 422 U.S., at 498. Standing doctrine embraces several judicially self-imposed limits on the exercise of federal jurisdiction, such as the general prohibition on a litigant's raising another person's legal rights, the rule barring adjudication of generalized grievances more appropriately addressed in the representative branches, and the requirement that a plaintiff's complaint fall within the zone of interests protected by the law invoked. * * * The requirement of standing, however, has a core component derived directly from the Constitution. A plaintiff must allege personal injury fairly traceable to the defendant's allegedly unlawful conduct and likely to be redressed by the requested relief.

Like the prudential component, the constitutional component of standing doctrine incorporates concepts concededly not susceptible of precise definition. The injury alleged must be, for example, " 'distinct and palpable,' " Gladstone, Realtors v. Village of Bellwood, 441 U.S. 91, 100 (1979) (quoting Warth v. Seldin, supra, 422 U.S., at 501), and not "abstract" or "conjectural" or "hypothetical," City of Los Angeles v. Lyons, 461 U.S. 95, 101–102 (1983); O'Shea v. Littleton, 414 U.S. 488, 494 (1974). The injury must be "fairly" traceable to the challenged action, and relief from the injury must be "likely" to follow from a favorable decision. See Simon v. Eastern Kentucky Welfare Rights Org., 426 U.S., at 38, 41. These terms cannot be defined so as to make application of the constitutional standing requirement a mechanical exercise.

The absence of precise definitions, however, as this Court's extensive body of case law on standing illustrates, see generally *Valley Forge,* supra, 454 U.S., at 471–476, hardly leaves courts at sea in applying the law of standing. Like most legal notions, the standing concepts have gained considerable definition from developing case law. In many cases the standing question can be answered chiefly by comparing the allegations of the particular complaint to those made in prior standing cases. See, e.g., City of Los Angeles v. Lyons, supra, 461 U.S., at 102–105. More important, the law of Art. III standing is built on a single basic idea—the idea of separation of powers. It is this fact which makes possible the gradual clarification of the law through judicial application. Of course, both federal and state courts have long experience in applying and elaborating in numerous contexts the pervasive and fundamental notion of separation of powers.

Determining standing in a particular case may be facilitated by clarifying principles or even clean rules developed in prior cases. Typically, however, the standing inquiry requires careful judicial examination of a complaint's allegations to ascertain whether the particular plaintiff is entitled to an adjudication of the particular claims asserted. Is the injury too abstract, or otherwise not appropriate, to be considered judicially cognizable? Is the line of causation between the illegal conduct and injury too attenuated? Is the prospect of obtaining relief from the injury as a result of a favorable ruling too speculative? These questions and any others relevant to the standing inquiry must be answered by reference to the Art. III notion that federal courts may exercise power only "in the last resort, and as a necessity," Chicago & Grand Trunk R. Co. v. Wellman, 143 U.S. 339, 345 (1892), and only when adjudication is "consistent with a system of separated powers and [the dispute is one] traditionally thought to be capable of resolution through the judicial process," Flast v. Cohen, 392 U.S. 83, 97 (1968). See *Valley Forge,* 454 U.S., at 472–473.

B

Respondents allege two injuries in their complaint to support their standing to bring this lawsuit. First, they say that they are harmed directly by the mere fact of Government financial aid to discriminatory private schools. Second, they say that the federal tax exemptions to racially discriminatory private schools in their communities impair their ability to have their public schools desegregated. * * *

We conclude that neither suffices to support respondents' standing. The first fails under clear precedents of this Court because it does not constitute judicially cognizable injury. The second fails because the alleged injury is not fairly traceable to the assertedly unlawful conduct of the IRS.[19]

1

Respondents' first claim of injury can be interpreted in two ways. It might be a claim simply to have the Government avoid the violation of law alleged in respondents' complaint. Alternatively, it might be a claim of stigmatic injury, or denigration, suffered by all members of a racial

---

19. The "fairly traceable" and "redressability" components of the constitutional standing inquiry were initially articulated by this Court as "two facets of a single causation requirement." C. Wright, Law of Federal Courts § 13, p. 68, n. 43 (4th ed. 1983). To the extent there is a difference, it is that the former examines the causal connection between the assertedly unlawful conduct and the alleged injury, whereas the latter examines the causal connection between the alleged injury and the judicial relief requested. Cases such as this, in which the relief requested goes well beyond the violation of law alleged, illustrate why it is important to keep the inquiries separate if the "redressability" component is to focus on the requested relief. Even if the relief respondents request might have a substantial effect on the desegregation of public schools, whatever deficiencies exist in the opportunities for desegregated education for respondents' children might not be traceable to IRS violations of law— grants of tax exemptions to racially discriminatory schools in respondents' communities.

group when the Government discriminates on the basis of race.[20] Under neither interpretation is this claim of injury judicially cognizable.

This Court has repeatedly held that an asserted right to have the Government act in accordance with law is not sufficient, standing alone, to confer jurisdiction on a federal court. In Schlesinger v. Reservists Committee to Stop the War, 418 U.S. 208 (1974), for example, the Court rejected a claim of citizen standing to challenge Armed Forces Reserve commissions held by Members of Congress as violating the Incompatibility Clause of Art. I, § 6, cl. 2, of the Constitution. As citizens, the Court held, plaintiffs alleged nothing but "the abstract injury in nonobservance of the Constitution * * *." More recently, in *Valley Forge,* supra, we rejected a claim of standing to challenge a Government conveyance of property to a religious institution. Insofar as the plaintiffs relied simply on " 'their shared individuated right' " to a Government that made no law respecting an establishment of religion, id., 454 U.S., at 482 (quoting Americans United v. U.S. Dept. of HEW, 619 F.2d 252, 261 (C.A.3 1980)), we held that plaintiffs had not alleged a judicially cognizable injury. "[A]ssertion of a right to a particular kind of Government conduct, which the Government has violated by acting differently, cannot alone satisfy the requirements of Art. III without draining those requirements of meaning." 454 U.S., at 483. Respondents here have no standing to complain simply that their Government is violating the law.

Neither do they have standing to litigate their claims based on the stigmatizing injury often caused by racial discrimination. There can be no doubt that this sort of noneconomic injury is one of the most serious consequences of discriminatory government action and is sufficient in some circumstances to support standing. See Heckler v. Mathews, 465 U.S. 728, 739–740 (1984). Our cases make clear, however, that such injury accords a basis for standing only to "those persons who are personally denied equal treatment" by the challenged discriminatory conduct.

In Moose Lodge No. 107 v. Irvis, 407 U.S. 163 (1972), the Court held that the plaintiff had no standing to challenge a club's racially discriminatory membership policies because he had never applied for membership. In O'Shea v. Littleton, 414 U.S. 488 (1974), the Court held that the plaintiffs had no standing to challenge racial discrimination in the administration of their city's criminal justice system because they had not alleged that they had been or would likely be subject to the challenged practices. The Court denied standing on similar facts in Rizzo v. Goode, 423 U.S. 362 (1976). In each of those cases, the plaintiffs alleged official racial discrimination comparable to that alleged by respondents here. Yet standing was denied in each case because the plaintiffs were not personally subject to the challenged discrimination.

---

20. We assume, *arguendo,* that the asserted stigmatic injury may be caused by the Government's grant of tax exemptions to racially discriminatory schools even if the Government is granting those exemptions without knowing or believing that the schools in fact discriminate. That is, we assume, without deciding, that the challenged Government tax exemptions are the equivalent of Government discrimination.

Insofar as their first claim of injury is concerned, respondents are in exactly the same position: unlike the appellee in Heckler v. Mathews, supra, 465 U.S., at 740–741, n. 9, they do not allege a stigmatic injury suffered as a direct result of having personally been denied equal treatment.

The consequences of recognizing respondents' standing on the basis of their first claim of injury illustrate why our cases plainly hold that such injury is not judicially cognizable. If the abstract stigmatic injury were cognizable, standing would extend nationwide to all members of the particular racial groups against which the Government was alleged to be discriminating by its grant of a tax exemption to a racially discriminatory school, regardless of the location of that school. All such persons could claim the same sort of abstract stigmatic injury respondents assert in their first claim of injury. A black person in Hawaii could challenge the grant of a tax exemption to a racially discriminatory school in Maine. Recognition of standing in such circumstances would transform the federal courts into "no more than a vehicle for the vindication of the value interests of concerned bystanders." United States v. SCRAP, 412 U.S. 669, 687 (1973). Constitutional limits on the role of the federal courts preclude such a transformation.

2

It is in their complaint's second claim of injury that respondents allege harm to a concrete, personal interest that can support standing in some circumstances. The injury they identify—their children's diminished ability to receive an education in a racially integrated school—is, beyond any doubt, not only judicially cognizable but, as shown by cases from Brown v. Board of Education, 347 U.S. 483 (1954), to Bob Jones University v. United States, 461 U.S. 574 (1983), one of the most serious injuries recognized in our legal system. Despite the constitutional importance of curing the injury alleged by respondents, however, the federal judiciary may not redress it unless standing requirements are met. In this case, respondents' second claim of injury cannot support standing because the injury alleged is not fairly traceable to the Government conduct respondents challenge as unlawful.[22]

---

22. Respondents' stigmatic injury, though not sufficient for standing in the abstract form in which their complaint asserts it, is judicially cognizable to the extent that respondents are personally subject to discriminatory treatment. See Heckler v. Mathews, 465 U.S. 728, 739–740 (1984). The stigmatic injury thus requires identification of some concrete interest with respect to which respondents are personally subject to discriminatory treatment. That interest must independently satisfy the causation requirement of standing doctrine.

In Heckler v. Mathews, for example, the named plaintiff (appellee) was being denied monetary benefits allegedly on a discriminatory basis. We specifically pointed out that the causation component of standing doctrine was satisfied with respect to the claimed benefits. In distinguishing the case from Simon v. Eastern Kentucky Welfare Rights Org., 426 U.S. 26 (1976), we said: "there can be no doubt about the direct causal relationship between the Government's alleged deprivation of appellee's right to equal protection and the personal injury appellee has suffered—denial of Social Security benefits solely on the basis of his gender." 465 U.S., at 741, n. 9.

In this litigation, respondents identify only one interest that they allege is being dis-

The illegal conduct challenged by respondents is the IRS's grant of tax exemptions to some racially discriminatory schools. The line of causation between that conduct and desegregation of respondents' schools is attenuated at best. From the perspective of the IRS, the injury to respondents is highly indirect and "results from the independent action of some third party not before the court," Simon v. Eastern Kentucky Welfare Rights Org., 426 U.S., at 42. As the Court pointed out in Warth v. Seldin, 422 U.S., at 505, "the indirectness of the injury * * * may make it substantially more difficult to meet the minimum requirement of Article III * * *."

The diminished ability of respondents' children to receive a desegregated education would be fairly traceable to unlawful IRS grants of tax exemptions only if there were enough racially discriminatory private schools receiving tax exemptions in respondents' communities for withdrawal of those exemptions to make an appreciable difference in public-school integration. Respondents have made no such allegation. It is, first, uncertain how many racially discriminatory private schools are in fact receiving tax exemptions.[23] Moreover, it is entirely speculative * * * whether withdrawal of a tax exemption from any particular school would lead the school to change its policies. It is just as speculative whether any given parent of a child attending such a private school would decide to transfer the child to public school as a result of any changes in educational or financial policy made by the private school once it was threatened with loss of tax-exempt status. It is also pure speculation whether, in a particular community, a large enough number of the numerous relevant school officials and parents would reach decisions that collectively would have a significant impact on the racial composition of the public schools.

The links in the chain of causation between the challenged Government conduct and the asserted injury are far too weak for the chain as a whole to sustain respondents' standing. In Simon v. Eastern Kentucky Welfare Rights Org., supra, the Court held that standing to challenge a Government grant of a tax exemption to hospitals could not be founded on the asserted connection between the grant of tax-exempt status and the hospitals' policy concerning the provision of medical services to indigents.[24] The causal connection depended on the decisions hospitals

criminatorily impaired—their interest in desegregated public-school education. Respondents' asserted stigmatic injury, therefore, is sufficient to support their standing in this litigation only if their school-desegregation injury independently meets the causation requirement of standing doctrine.

23. Indeed, contrary to the suggestion of Justice Brennan's dissent, * * * of the schools identified in respondents' complaint, none of those alleged to be directly receiving a tax exemption is alleged to be racially discriminatory, and only four schools * * * are alleged to have discriminatory policies that deprive them of direct

tax exemptions yet operate under the umbrella of a tax-exempt organization. These allegations constitute an insufficient basis for the only claim made by respondents—a claim for a change in the IRS regulations and practices. Cf. Wright v. Miller, 480 F.Supp. 790, 796 (DC 1979) ("it is purely speculative whether, in the final analysis, any fewer schools would be granted tax exemptions under plaintiffs' system than under the current IRS system").

24. Simon v. Eastern Kentucky Welfare Rights Org., supra, framed its standing discussion in terms of the redressability of the alleged injury. The relief requested by the

would make in response to withdrawal of tax-exempt status, and those decisions were sufficiently uncertain to break the chain of causation between the plaintiffs' injury and the challenged Government action. See also Warth v. Seldin, supra. The chain of causation is even weaker in this case. It involves numerous third parties (officials of racially discriminatory schools receiving tax exemptions and the parents of children attending such schools) who may not even exist in respondents' communities and whose independent decisions may not collectively have a significant effect on the ability of public-school students to receive a desegregated education.

The idea of separation of powers that underlies standing doctrine explains why our cases preclude the conclusion that respondents' alleged injury "fairly can be traced to the challenged action" of the IRS. Simon v. Eastern Kentucky Welfare Rights Org., supra, at 41, 96 S.Ct., at 1926. That conclusion would pave the way generally for suits challenging, not specifically identifiable Government violations of law, but the particular programs agencies establish to carry out their legal obligations. Such suits, even when premised on allegations of several instances of violations of law, are rarely if ever appropriate for federal-court adjudication.

* * *

Case-or-controversy considerations, the Court observed in O'Shea v. Littleton, supra, 414 U.S., at 499, "obviously shade into those determining whether the complaint states a sound basis for equitable relief." The latter set of considerations should therefore inform our judgment about whether respondents have standing. Most relevant to this case is the principle articulated in Rizzo v. Goode, supra, 423 U.S., at 378–379,:

> When a plaintiff seeks to enjoin the activity of a government agency, even within a unitary court system, his case must contend with 'the well-established rule that the Government has traditionally been granted the widest latitude in the "dispatch of its own internal affairs," Cafeteria Workers v. McElroy, 367 U.S. 886, 896 (1961),' quoted in Sampson v. Murray, 415 U.S. 61, 83 (1974).

When transported into the Art. III context, that principle, grounded as it is in the idea of separation of powers, counsels against recognizing standing in a case brought, not to enforce specific legal obligations whose violation works a direct harm, but to seek a restructuring of the apparatus established by the Executive Branch to fulfill its legal duties. The Constitution, after all, assigns to the Executive Branch, and not to the Judicial Branch, the duty to "take Care that the Laws be faithfully executed." U.S. Const., Art. II, § 3. We could not recognize respondents' standing in this case without running afoul of that structural principle.[26]

* * *

plaintiffs, however, was simply the cessation of the allegedly illegal conduct. In those circumstances, as the opinion for the Court in *Simon* itself illustrates, see id., 426 U.S., at 40–46, the "redressability" analysis is identical to the "fairly traceable" analysis. See n. 19, supra.

26. We disagree with Justice Stevens' suggestions that separation of powers merely underly standing requirements, have no

III

"The necessity that the plaintiff who seeks to invoke judicial power stand to profit in some personal interest remains an Art. III requirement." Simon v. Eastern Kentucky Welfare Rights Org., 426 U.S., at 39. Respondents have not met this fundamental requirement. The judgment of the Court of Appeals is accordingly reversed, and the injunction issued by that court is vacated.

JUSTICE MARSHALL took no part in the decision of the case.

JUSTICE BRENNAN, dissenting.

Once again, the Court "uses 'standing to slam the courthouse door against plaintiffs who are entitled to full consideration of their claims on the merits.'" Valley Forge Christian College v. Americans United for Separation of Church and State, Inc., 454 U.S. 464, 490 (1982) (Brennan, J., dissenting) (quoting Barlow v. Collins, 397 U.S. 159, 178 (1970) (Brennan, J., concurring in the result and dissenting)). And once again, the Court does so by "wax[ing] eloquent" on considerations that provide little justification for the decision at hand. This time, however, the Court focuses on "the idea of separation of powers," * * * as if the mere incantation of that phrase provides an obvious solution to the difficult questions presented by these cases.

One could hardly dispute the proposition that Article III of the Constitution, by limiting the judicial power to "cases" or "controversies," embodies the notion that each branch of our National Government must confine its actions to those that are consistent with our scheme of separated powers. But simply stating that unremarkable truism provides little, if any, illumination of the standing inquiry that must be undertaken by a federal court faced with a particular action filed by particular plaintiffs.

The Court's attempt to obscure the standing question must be seen, therefore, as no more than a cover for its failure to recognize the nature of the specific claims raised by the respondents in these cases. By relying on generalities concerning our tripartite system of government, the Court is able to conclude that the respondents lack standing to maintain this action without acknowledging the precise nature of the injuries they have alleged. In so doing, the Court displays a startling insensitivity to the historical role played by the federal courts in eradicating race discrimination from our nation's schools—a role that has played a prominent part in this Court's decisions from Brown v. Board of Education, 347 U.S. 483 (1954), through Bob Jones University v. United

role to play in giving meaning to those requirements, and should be considered only under a distinct justiciability analysis. * * * Moreover, our analysis of this case does not rest on the more general proposition that no consequence of the allocation of administrative enforcement resources is judicially cognizable. * * * Rather, we rely on separation of powers principles to interpret the "fairly traceable" component of the standing requirement.

States, 461 U.S. 574 (1983). Because I cannot join in such misguided decisionmaking, I dissent.

* * *

III

More than one commentator has noted that the causation component of the Court's standing inquiry is no more than a poor disguise for the Court's view of the merits of the underlying claims.[10] The Court today does nothing to avoid that criticism. What is most disturbing about today's decision, therefore, is not the standing analysis applied, but the indifference evidenced by the Court to the detrimental effects that racially segregated schools, supported by tax-exempt status from the Federal Government, have on the respondents' attempt to obtain an education in a racially integrated school system. I cannot join such indifference, and would give the respondents a chance to prove their case on the merits.

Notes

1. Is *Allen* consistent with *Bennett*?

2. Consider the following argument: The Court's decision in *Allen* confuses the standing issue with the substantive merits of the plaintiffs' case. As a result, the Court gives inadequate attention to *both* the standing *and* the substantive issues in the case. For an argument that it is not possible to examine standing in isolation from the merits, see Sunstein, *Standing Injuries*, 1993 Sup.Ct.Rev. 37.

Professor Sunstein argues that Northeastern Florida Chapter of the Associated General Contractors v. Jacksonville [supra p. 36], provides a way to approach standing that would change the result in *Allen*. In that case, the Court granted standing to disappointed bidders challenging an affirmative action set-aside even though they could not show they would have received the contract in the absence of the set-aside program. The Court held that being deprived of the opportunity to compete for public contracts on an equal basis was a sufficient injury. Professor Sunstein suggests that the plaintiffs in *Allen* could similarly have argued that they were deprived of "the opportunity to have a desegregation process unaffected by unlawful incentives for white flight," 1993 Sup.Ct.Rev. at 50, even if they could not show any actual effect on any particular child. Thus the standing issue, according to Professor Sunstein, depends on how the Court characterizes the substantive right.

3. In not finding any injury to plaintiffs traceable to the IRS' actions, did the Court implicitly assume certain facts that were the subject of

---

10. See, *e.g.,* L. Tribe, American Constitutional Law § 3–21 (1978); Chayes, Foreword: Public Law Litigation and the Burger Court, 96 Harv.L.Rev. 1, 14–22 (1982); Nichol, Causation as a Standing Requirement: The Unprincipled Use of Judicial Restraint, 69 Ky.L.J. 185 (1980–1981); Tushnet, The New Law of Standing: A Plea for Abandonment, 62 Cornell L.Rev. 663 (1977).

dispute? See *The Supreme Court, 1983 Term*, 98 Harv.L.Rev. 236, 241 (1984):

> The majority's finding that neither prong of the causality requirement was met was based on an assumption that the IRS's program of subsidies has no effect on the behavior of the private segregated schools and the students who attend them, and that the plaintiffs could not, as a matter of law, plead facts sufficient to support a reasonable inference to the contrary. Such an assumption seems strained at best. The Court is implicitly saying that there is no way to allege that the withdrawal of a tax subsidy from producers (and consumers) will diminish the supply of (and demand for) the subsidized product—here, education at discriminatory private schools. This implication is absurd on its face. Perhaps such allegations could not later be substantiated in a courtroom, but that is a matter that goes to the merits, not to standing.

4. Consider the Court's reliance on separation-of-powers principles to support its refusal to "trace" plaintiffs' alleged injury to the IRS' action. Exactly what is the separation-of-powers argument? Is it persuasive? Cf. 98 Harv.L.Rev. 236, 241–42 (1984): "The Court in *Wright* wholly failed to move beyond generalities regarding separation of powers doctrine and specify the institutional issues that underlie the decision." Note that the Court contends that the separation-of-powers principle "counsels against recognizing standing in a case brought, not to enforce specific legal obligations whose violation works a direct harm, but to seek a restructuring of the apparatus established by the Executive Branch to fulfill its legal duties" because "[t]he Constitution * * * assigns to the Executive Branch, and not to the Judicial Branch, the duty 'to take care that the Laws be faithfully executed.' " Does the standing issue really have anything to do with the Court's point? Would the Court's concern be just as valid, even if the plaintiffs were clearly affected directly by the IRS' practices? Are separation-of-powers concerns greater because the plaintiffs' injury is deemed remote?

See also Nichol, *Abusing Standing: A Comment on* Allen v. Wright, 133 U.Pa.L.Rev. 635, 646 (1985):

> Suppose that the *Allen* plaintiffs had presented a perfect case of causation: the Secretary of the Treasury testified that the IRS procedures were promulgated solely to foster and encourage private discriminatory schools for the purpose of defeating desegregation efforts, and the private schools acknowledged that they could not exist but for the IRS policy. Would the relief requested intrude any less into the workings of the executive branch? The answer is no, and the reason it is no is that the causation requirement has nothing to do with separation of powers. The nature and extent of the interference with a coequal branch of government would not vary.

Do you agree? See also Adams, *Causation, Constitutional Principles, and the Jurisprudential Legacy of the Warren Court*, 59 Wash. & Lee L.Rev. 1173, 1191 (2002) ("*Allen* illustrates how the use of rigid notions of causation, purportedly to serve articulated structural principles, can ultimately frustrate progressive and minority group interests").

5. The Court applied *Allen* in the context of redistricting challenges in United States v. Hays, 515 U.S. 737 (1995). The plaintiffs did not live in the majority-minority district created by the challenged Louisiana statute. Nevertheless, they claimed that the creation of that district affected all Louisiana voters, because their own district might have been drawn differently had the majority-minority district not been racially gerrymandered. The Court rejected this claim, holding that voters outside the challenged district did not have standing because they had not been " 'personally * * * denied equal treatment.' " Id. at 744, quoting *Allen*. See also Shaw v. Hunt, 517 U.S. 899 (1996) and Bush v. Vera, 517 U.S. 952 (1996) (only residents of challenged districts have standing). For arguments that even voters who live in a majority-minority district should not have standing, see Issacharoff & Karlan, *Standing and Misunderstanding in Voting Rights Law*, 111 Harv.L.Rev. 2276 (1998); Karlan, *All Over the Map: The Supreme Court's Voting Rights Trilogy*, 1993 Sup.Ct.Rev. 245; see also Dow, *The Equal Protection Clause and the Legislative Redistricting Cases—Some Notes Concerning the Standing of White Plaintiffs*, 81 Minn.L.Rev. 1123 (1997). For a contrary argument, see Ely, *Standing to Challenge Pro–Minority Gerrymanders*, 111 Harv.L.Rev. 576 (1997).

§ 3. MOOTNESS

DEFUNIS v. ODEGAARD

Supreme Court of the United States, 1974.
416 U.S. 312.

PER CURIAM.

In 1971 the petitioner Marco DeFunis, Jr., applied for admission as a first-year student at the University of Washington Law School, a state-operated institution. The size of the incoming first-year class was to be limited to 150 persons, and the Law School received some 1,600 applications for these 150 places. DeFunis was eventually notified that he had been denied admission. He thereupon commenced this suit in a Washington trial court, contending that the procedures and criteria employed by the Law School Admissions Committee invidiously discriminated against him on account of his race in violation of the Equal Protection Clause of the Fourteenth Amendment to the United States Constitution.

DeFunis brought the suit on behalf of himself alone, and not as the representative of any class, against the various respondents, who are officers, faculty members, and members of the Board of Regents of the University of Washington. He asked the trial court to issue a mandatory injunction commanding the respondents to admit him as a member of the first-year class entering in September 1971, on the ground that the Law School admissions policy had resulted in the unconstitutional denial of his application for admission. The trial court agreed with his claim and granted the requested relief. DeFunis was, accordingly, admitted to the Law School and began his legal studies there in the fall of 1971. On appeal, the Washington Supreme Court reversed the judgment of the trial court and held that the Law School admissions policy did not violate the Constitution. By this time DeFunis was in his second year at the Law School.

He then petitioned this Court for a writ of certiorari, and Mr. Justice Douglas, as Circuit Justice, stayed the judgment of the Washington Supreme Court pending the "final disposition of the case by this Court." By virtue of this stay, DeFunis has remained in law school, and was in the first term of his third and final year when this Court first considered his certiorari petition in the fall of 1973. Because of our concern that DeFunis' third-year standing in the Law School might have rendered this case moot, we requested the parties to brief the question of mootness before we acted on the petition. In response, both sides contended that the case was not moot. The respondents indicated that, if the decision of the Washington Supreme Court were permitted to stand, the petitioner could complete the term for which he was then enrolled but would have to apply to the faculty for permission to continue in the school before he could register for another term.[2]

We granted the petition for certiorari on November 19, 1973.

In response to questions raised from the bench during the oral argument, counsel for the petitioner has informed the Court that De-Funis has now registered "for his final quarter in law school." Counsel for the respondents have made clear that the Law School will not in any way seek to abrogate this registration. In light of DeFunis' recent registration for the last quarter of his final law school year, and the Law School's assurance that his registration is fully effective, the insistent question again arises whether this case is not moot, and to that question we now turn.

The starting point for analysis is the familiar proposition that "federal courts are without power to decide questions that cannot affect the rights of litigants in the case before them." North Carolina v. Rice, 404 U.S. 244, 246 (1971). The inability of the federal judiciary "to review moot cases derives from the requirement of Art. III of the Constitution under which the exercise of judicial power depends upon the existence of a case or controversy." Liner v. Jafco, Inc., 375 U.S. 301, 306 n. 3 (1964). Although as a matter of Washington state law it appears that this case would be saved from mootness by "the great public interest in the continuing issues raised by this appeal," the fact remains that under Art. III "[e]ven in cases arising in the state courts, the question of mootness is a federal one which a federal court must resolve before it assumes jurisdiction." North Carolina v. Rice, supra, at 246.

The respondents have represented that, without regard to the ultimate resolution of the issues in this case, DeFunis will remain a student

---

2. By contrast, in their response to the petition for certiorari, the respondents had stated that DeFunis "will complete his third year [of law school] and be awarded his J.D. degree at the end of the 1973–74 academic year regardless of the outcome of this appeal."

in the Law School for the duration of any term in which he has already enrolled. Since he has now registered for his final term, it is evident that he will be given an opportunity to complete all academic and other requirements for graduation, and, if he does so, will receive his diploma regardless of any decision this Court might reach on the merits of this case. In short, all parties agree that DeFunis is now entitled to complete his legal studies at the University of Washington and to receive his degree from that institution. A determination by this Court of the legal issues tendered by the parties is no longer necessary to compel that result and could not serve to prevent it. DeFunis did not cast his suit as a class action, and the only remedy he requested was an injunction commanding his admission to the Law School. He was not only accorded that remedy, but he now has also been irrevocably admitted to the final term of the final year of the Law School course. The controversy between the parties has thus clearly ceased to be "definite and concrete" and no longer "touch[es] the legal relations of parties having adverse legal interests." Aetna Life Ins. Co. v. Haworth, 300 U.S. 227, 240–241 (1937).

It matters not that these circumstances partially stem from a policy decision on the part of the respondent Law School authorities. The respondents, through their counsel, the Attorney General of the State, have professionally represented that in no event will the status of DeFunis now be affected by any view this Court might express on the merits of this controversy. And it has been the settled practice of the Court, in contexts no less significant, fully to accept representations such as these as parameters for decision.

There is a line of decisions in this Court standing for the proposition that the "voluntary cessation of allegedly illegal conduct does not deprive the tribunal of power to hear and determine the case, i.e., does not make the case moot." United States v. W. T. Grant Co., 345 U.S. 629, 632 (1953) * * *. These decisions and the doctrine they reflect would be quite relevant if the question of mootness here had arisen by reason of a unilateral change in the *admissions procedures* of the Law School. For it was the admissions procedures that were the target of this litigation, and a voluntary cessation of the admissions practices complained of could make this case moot only if it could be said with assurance "that 'there is no reasonable expectation that the wrong will be repeated.'" United States v. W. T. Grant Co., supra, at 633. Otherwise, "[t]he defendant is free to return to his old ways," id., at 632, and this fact would be enough to prevent mootness because of the "public interest in having the legality of the practices settled." Ibid. But mootness in the present case depends not at all upon a "voluntary cessation" of the admissions practices that were the subject of this litigation. It depends, instead, upon the simple fact that DeFunis is now in the final quarter of the final year of his course of study, and the settled and unchallenged policy of the Law School to permit him to complete the term for which he is now enrolled.

It might also be suggested that this case presents a question that is "capable of repetition, yet evading review," Southern Pacific Terminal

Co. v. ICC, 219 U.S. 498, 515 (1911); Roe v. Wade, 410 U.S. 113, 125 (1973), and is thus amenable to federal adjudication even though it might otherwise be considered moot. But DeFunis will never again be required to run the gantlet of the Law School's admission process, and so the question is certainly not "capable of repetition" so far as he is concerned. Moreover, just because this particular case did not reach the Court until the eve of the petitioner's graduation from law school, it hardly follows that the issue he raises will in the future evade review. If the admissions procedures of the Law School remain unchanged, there is no reason to suppose that a subsequent case attacking those procedures will not come with relative speed to this Court, now that the Supreme Court of Washington has spoken. This case, therefore, in no way presents the exceptional situation in which the *Southern Pacific Terminal* doctrine might permit a departure from "[t]he usual rule in federal cases * * * that an actual controversy must exist at stages of appellate or certiorari review, and not simply at the date the action is initiated." Roe v. Wade, supra, at 125.

Because the petitioner will complete his law school studies at the end of the term for which he has now registered regardless of any decision this Court might reach on the merits of this litigation, we conclude that the Court cannot, consistently with the limitations of Art. III of the Constitution, consider the substantive constitutional issues tendered by the parties.[5] Accordingly, the judgment of the Supreme Court of Washington is vacated, and the cause is remanded for such proceedings as by that court may be deemed appropriate.

Mr. Justice Brennan, with whom Mr. Justice Douglas, Mr. Justice White, and Mr. Justice Marshall concur, dissenting.

I respectfully dissent. Many weeks of the school term remain, and petitioner may not receive his degree despite respondents' assurances that petitioner will be allowed to complete this term's schooling regardless of our decision. Any number of unexpected events—illness, economic necessity, even academic failure—might prevent his graduation at the end of the term. Were that misfortune to befall, and were petitioner required to register for yet another term, the prospect that he would again face the hurdle of the admissions policy is real, not fanciful; for respondents warn that "Mr. DeFunis would have to take some appropriate action to request continued admission for the remainder of his law school education, and *some discretionary action by the University on such request would have to be taken.*" Thus, respondents' assurances have not dissipated the possibility that petitioner might once again have to run the gantlet of the University's allegedly unlawful admissions policy. The Court therefore proceeds on an erroneous premise in resting its moot-

---

5. It is suggested in dissent that "[a]ny number of unexpected events—illness, economic necessity, even academic failure— might prevent his graduation at the end of the term." * * * "But such speculative contingencies afford no basis for our passing on the substantive issues [the petitioner] would have us decide," Hall v. Beals, 396 U.S. 45, 49 (1969), in the absence of "evidence that this is a prospect of 'immediacy and reality.'" Golden v. Zwickler, 394 U.S. 103, 109 (1969); Maryland Casualty Co. v. Pacific Coal & Oil Co., 312 U.S. 270, 273 (1941).

ness holding on a supposed inability to render any judgment that may affect one way or the other petitioner's completion of his law studies. For surely if we were to reverse the Washington Supreme Court, we could insure that, if for some reason petitioner did not graduate this spring, he would be entitled to re-enrollment at a later time on the same basis as others who have not faced the hurdle of the University's allegedly unlawful admissions policy.

In these circumstances, and because the University's position implies no concession that its admissions policy is unlawful, this controversy falls squarely within the Court's long line of decisions holding that the "[m]ere voluntary cessation of allegedly illegal conduct does not moot a case." United States v. Phosphate Export Assn., 393 U.S. 199, 203 (1968) * * *. Since respondents' voluntary representation to this Court is only that they will permit petitioner to complete this term's studies, respondents have not borne the "heavy burden," United States v. Phosphate Export Assn., supra, 393 U.S. at 203, of demonstrating that there was not even a "mere possibility" that petitioner would once again be subject to the challenged admissions policy.

I can thus find no justification for the Court's straining to rid itself of this dispute. While we must be vigilant to require that litigants maintain a personal stake in the outcome of a controversy to assure that "the questions will be framed with the necessary specificity, that the issues will be contested with the necessary adverseness and that the litigation will be pursued with the necessary vigor to assure that the constitutional challenge will be made in a form traditionally thought to be capable of judicial resolution," Flast v. Cohen, 392 U.S. 83, 106 (1968), there is no want of an adversary contest in this case. Indeed, the Court concedes that, if petitioner has lost his stake in this controversy, he did so only when he registered for the spring term. But petitioner took that action only after the case had been fully litigated in the state courts, briefs had been filed in this Court, and oral argument had been heard. The case is thus ripe for decision on a fully developed factual record with sharply defined and fully canvassed legal issues.

Moreover, in endeavoring to dispose of this case as moot, the Court clearly disserves the public interest. The constitutional issues which are avoided today concern vast numbers of people, organizations, and colleges and universities, as evidenced by the filing of twenty-six *amicus curiae* briefs. Few constitutional questions in recent history have stirred as much debate, and they will not disappear. They must inevitably return to the federal courts and ultimately again to this Court. Because avoidance of repetitious litigation serves the public interest, that inevitability counsels against mootness determinations, as here, not compelled by the record. Although the Court should, of course, avoid unnecessary decisions of constitutional questions, we should not transform principles of avoidance of constitutional decisions into devices for sidestepping resolution of difficult cases. Cf. Cohens v. Virginia, 6 Wheat. 264, 404–405 (1821) (Marshall, C.J.).

[The dissenting opinion of JUSTICE DOUGLAS is omitted.]

Notes

1.   What is the rationale for the mootness doctrine? See generally Note, *The Mootness Doctrine in the Supreme Court*, 88 Harv.L.Rev. 373 (1974). Should it be deemed to be a constitutionally dictated doctrine, or simply one of judicial prudence? Do you agree with Professor Wright that "[i]t is easy to understand * * * why moot cases are held to be beyond the judicial power. There is no case or controversy once the matter has been resolved"? C. Wright, Law of Federal Courts 55 (4th ed. 1983). If so, is the generally recognized exception for cases presenting issues "capable of repetition, yet evading review," Southern Pacific Terminal Co. v. Interstate Commerce Commission, 219 U.S. 498, 515 (1911), constitutional? Does the fact that the issue is likely to arise in subsequent cases, but be difficult to review, make the present, moot case any more of a "case or controversy"? Professor Evan Tsen Lee argues that the Court should view mootness as a prudential doctrine, and should decide technically moot cases whenever it would "serve the public interest" by "clarifying critically important areas of law." Lee, *Deconstitutionalizing Justiciability: The Example of Mootness*, 105 Harv. L.Rev. 603, 608 (1992). Recall that one of the most famous applications of the "capable of repetition yet evading review" exception is Roe v. Wade, 410 U.S. 113 (1973), in which the Court struck down anti-abortion laws. Might Lee's approach explain the Court's actual use of the "capable of repetition" doctrine? Why doesn't the *DeFunis* case fit the exception? For an argument that the Court has been too generous in making exceptions to the mootness doctrine, and has thus fostered "unnecessary constitutional rulings" on the merits, see Healy, *The Rise of Unnecessary Constitutional Rulings*, 83 N.Car.L.Rev. 847 (2005).

2.   In the "voluntary cessation" line of cases, mentioned in *DeFunis*, the Court held that a defendant could not deprive the courts of jurisdiction by voluntarily ceasing the challenged conduct, because that conduct might recur. In Super Tire Engineering Co. v. McCorkle, 416 U.S 115 (1974), decided seven days prior to *DeFunis*, the Court held not to be moot a case challenging the availability of state public assistance to workers engaged in a strike, though the strike ended before the case was tried. The Court reasoned that the dispute did not depend on "the distant contingencies of another strike," but on the effect that the known availability of public assistance would continue to have on the collective-bargaining relationship. *Super Tire* is not mentioned in *DeFunis*. Do the two decisions conflict?

3.   In a voluntary cessation case, who should bear the burden of proof on the likelihood of recurrence, and what level of likelihood should satisfy it? The Court has vacillated on the level of proof necessary to defeat mootness in a circumstance of voluntary cessation. In the 1970s, it was relatively easy for a defendant to moot a case by ceasing the challenged activity, because in order to avoid mootness the plaintiff was required to demonstrate a reasonable expectation of recurrence. See County of Los Angeles v. Davis, 440 U.S.

625 (1979); Securities and Exchange Commission v. Medical Committee for Human Rights, 404 U.S. 403 (1972).

More recently, however, the Court held that the party asserting mootness bears the burden of demonstrating that it is "absolutely clear" that the behavior will not recur. Friends of the Earth Inc. v. Laidlaw Environmental Services, 528 U.S. 167, 189 (2000). Note that the *Laidlaw* standard is different from the one used to determine if a plaintiff has standing to sue a defendant who is currently complying with the law. In order to initiate a lawsuit, a plaintiff must show that prior wrongful behavior is likely to recur; but if the defendant changes its behavior and complies with the law in the middle of the lawsuit, the suit will continue unless the defendant shows that its conduct will not recur. As the Court noted in *Laidlaw*, this difference means that "there are circumstances in which the prospect that a defendant will engage in (or resume) harmful conduct may be too speculative to support standing, but not too speculative to overcome mootness." Id. at 190. Why should the standards be different? Are there concerns present in determining mootness that are not present in determining standing? Why not simply deem a voluntary cessation case moot unless and until the defendant resumes the practice a second time?

4. Consider the following case: The defendant, in addition to disputing the plaintiff's substantive claims, also challenged the district court's exercise of personal jurisdiction. The district court agreed and dismissed the suit. Plaintiff appealed. During the pendency of the appeal, the parties settled all their substantive disagreements. The settlement agreement included a provision that if the Court of Appeals upheld the district court and found that the court lacked personal jurisdiction over the defendant, the plaintiff would pay the defendant $10,000. Has the case now become moot? See Gator.com Corp. v. L.L. Bean, Inc., 398 F.3d 1125 (9th Cir.2005) (en banc).

5. When a case is ruled moot after judgment has been entered by a state tribunal, what is the proper disposition by the United States Supreme Court? In *DeFunis,* the Court vacated the judgment of the Washington Supreme Court and remanded the case "for such proceedings as by that court may be deemed appropriate." If no case or controversy exists at the United States Supreme Court level, however, is a decision to vacate the state determination below appropriate?

The Court addressed this issue in ASARCO, Inc. v. Kadish, 490 U.S. 605, 621 n. 1 (1989):

> The Court's treatment of cases that become moot on review from the lower federal courts as distinct from state courts is illuminating. * * * In the former situation, the settled disposition * * * is for this court to "vacate the judgment below and remand with a direction to dismiss." The power to make that disposition is predicated on our "supervisory power over the judgments of the lower federal courts" which is a "broad one". In the latter situation, on review of state judgments, the same judgment is not made. Traditionally, where the entire case has become moot, the Court vacated the judgment below and remanded for such further proceedings as the state court might deem appropriate, as in DeFunis v. Odegaard * * * since the state courts, not bound by Article III, were free to dispose of the case in a variety of ways, including the

reinstatement of the judgment. More recently, however, the regular practice in the latter situation has been to dismiss the case and leave the judgment of the state court undisturbed, which evinces a proper recognition that in the absence of any live case or controversy, we lack jurisdiction and thus power to disturb the state court's judgment.

The Court has recently confirmed that it has jurisdiction to vacate moot cases. See U.S. Bancorp Mortgage Company v. Bonner Mall Partnership, 513 U.S. 18 (1994). In considering whether to vacate or leave undisturbed a judgment below, should the Court take into account what caused the case to become moot? Compare *U.S. Bancorp* (mootness by reason of settlement does not justify vacatur) with Anderson v. Green, 513 U.S. 557 (1995)(loss of justiciability that is not the result of voluntary action by the party seeking vacatur does justify vacatur). Should a lower federal court vacate its own prior judgment after subsequent settlement? See Fisch, *Rewriting History: The Propriety of Eradicating Prior Decisional Law Through Settlement and Vacatur*, 76 Cornell L.Rev. 589 (1991).

6. What should happen if the conduct of the *prevailing* party below makes the case moot? In Erie v. Pap's A.M., 529 U.S. 277 (2000), a lower court struck down a city's ban on nude dancing. In the Supreme Court, the plaintiff—an owner of a nude dancing establishment—asserted that he had ceased to operate his establishment and that at age 72, he had no intention of going back into business. He therefore argued that the case was moot. The Court first held that the plaintiff's assertion did not satisfy the *Laidlaw* standard: "Several Members of this Court can attest, however, that the 'advanced age' of Pap's owner (72) does not make it 'absolutely clear' that a life of quiet retirement is his only reasonable expectation."

The Court went on to hold, however, that this was "not a run of the mill voluntary cessation case," since "the plaintiff * * * having prevailed below, now seeks to have the case declared moot." The Court held that the defendant city still had "an ongoing injury because it is barred from enforcing the public nudity provisions of its ordinance." Does this mean that if DeFunis had prevailed in the Washington Supreme Court—and had graduated by the time the case reached the U.S. Supreme Court—that the case would not have been moot? Note that in City News & Novelty, Inc. v. City of Waukesha, 531 U.S. 278 (2001), the Court distinguished *Pap's* on the ground that in *City News* the plaintiff (the party seeking to avoid mootness) "left the fray a loser, not a winner," leaving the city with no "ongoing injury." How can mootness depend on who prevails below, if there is no longer any dispute between the parties?

As Justice Scalia pointed out in his concurring opinion in *Pap's*, the city's dilemma arose because of the intersection of various doctrines: although the Court will usually vacate a judgment that becomes moot by the unilateral action of the prevailing party (*Anderson*), it cannot do so if the judgment was issued by a state court (*ASARCO*). Unlike the majority, Justice Scalia would have held the case moot. Is that the right answer to the dilemma? If it is the lower court's order that creates the injury to the city, what *is* the appropriate judicial response? Could the city have simply tried to enforce the ordinance against someone else, and appealed the predictable adverse judgment? Should it have to?

Can the discussion in *Pap's* be reconciled with the statement in another recent case that "an interest that is merely a 'byproduct' of the suit itself cannot give rise to a cognizable injury in fact for Article III standing purposes"? Vermont Agency of Natural Resources v. United States ex rel. Stevens, 529 U.S. 765 (2000). Is this another example of the distinction between standing and mootness? Does the distinction make sense?

7. **Mootness in Criminal Prosecutions.** In Sibron v. New York, 392 U.S. 40 (1968) the defendants challenged the admissibility of evidence seized from them during a search. Although they had already served their six-month sentences, the Court ruled that a challenge to the legality of their convictions was not moot. The " * * * obvious fact of life [is] that most criminal convictions do in fact entail adverse collateral legal consequences. The mere possibility that this will be the case is enough to preserve a case from ending * * * in mootness." 392 U.S. at 55. In Carafas v. LaVallee, 391 U.S. 234, 237–38 (1968), the Court explained, in a similar fashion, that "in consequence" of a conviction the challenger "cannot engage in certain businesses; * * * serve as an official of a labor union * * *; cannot vote in New York State; * * * serve as a juror." Thus, "the case is not moot." As a general matter, however, a challenge to the length of a particular sentence, as opposed to the validity of the conviction itself, is moot after the sentence has been served. See North Carolina v. Rice, 404 U.S. 244 (1971). See also Spencer v. Kemna, 523 U.S. 1 (1998) (challenge to parole revocation moot after completion of underlying sentence).

8. **Mootness in Class Actions.** Sosna v. Iowa, 419 U.S. 393 (1975): Plaintiff filed a class action in federal district court challenging Iowa's one-year residency requirement for obtaining a divorce. The district court certified the case as a class action, but ruled against the plaintiff on the merits. When the case reached the Supreme Court, plaintiff had already satisfied the Iowa residency requirement and had obtained a divorce. The Court found the case not to be moot, because a "case" remained for the certified class. "[B]ecause of the passage of time," said the Court, "no single challenger will remain subject to [the law's] restrictions for the period necessary to see such a lawsuit to its conclusion." Id. at 400. A finding of mootness

> would permit a significant class of federal claims to remain unredressed for want of a spokesman who could retain a personal adversary position throughout the course of the litigation. Such a consideration would not itself justify any relaxation of the provision of Art. III which limits our jurisdiction to "cases and controversies," but it is a factor supporting the result we reach if consistent with Art. III. 419 U.S. at 401, n. 9.

While there must exist a live controversy at the time of Supreme Court review, the "controversy may exist * * * between a named defendant and a member of the class represented by the named plaintiff, even though the claim of the named plaintiff has become moot." Id. at 402. The Court limited its holding by stating: "In cases in which the alleged harm would not dissipate during the normal time required for resolution of the controversy, the general principles of Art. III jurisdiction require that the plaintiff's personal stake in the litigation continue throughout the entirety of the litigation." Id. Does this limitation make sense? Cf. Rohr, *Fighting for the*

Rights of Others: The Troubled Law of Third–Party Standing and Mootness in the Federal Courts, 35 U.Miami L.Rev. 393, 445–46 (1981). In such a case, can the named plaintiff be considered to be an adequate representative of the class, as required by Rule 23(a)(4) of the Federal Rules of Civil Procedure? See Zeidman v. J. Ray McDermott & Co., Inc., 651 F.2d 1030, 1044 (5th Cir.1981). Cf. Franks v. Bowman Transportation Co., Inc., 424 U.S. 747 (1976); Dunn v. Blumstein, 405 U.S. 330 (1972); Roe v. Wade, 410 U.S. 113 (1973). Should the approach used in *Sosna* apply when the trial court has *denied* class certification, rather than granted it? See United States Parole Commission v. Geraghty, 445 U.S. 388 (1980). There the Court noted that "[a]lthough one might argue that *Sosna* contains at least an implication that the critical factor for Art. III purposes is the timing of class certification, other cases, applying a 'relation back' approach, clearly demonstrate that timing is not crucial." Id. at 398. The Court held that an action brought on behalf of a class is not rendered moot when the named plaintiff's substantive claim expires, even though class certification was denied, since the proposed representative still retains the sufficient "personal stake". Rohr, supra, 35 U.Miami L.Rev. at 447–48. On the general issue, see Greenstein, *Bridging the Mootness Gap in Federal Court Class Actions,* 35 Stan.L.Rev. 897 (1983).

§ 4. RIPENESS

UNITED PUBLIC WORKERS OF AMERICA v. MITCHELL, 330 U.S. 75 (1947): The union challenged the constitutionality of the Hatch Act, which declared unlawful specified political activities of federal employees. They sought both declaratory and injunctive relief. None of the plaintiffs (with the exception of one, whose case was now moot) had actually violated the act's provisions or been charged under its terms. The Court therefore found the case to lack the requisite ripeness:

> The affidavits [of plaintiffs] * * * declare a desire to act contrary to the rule against political activity but not that the rule has been violated * * *.

* * *

As is well known, the federal courts established pursuant to Article III of the Constitution do not render advisory opinions. For adjudication of constitutional issues, "concrete legal issues, presented in actual cases, not abstractions," are requisite. This is as true of declaratory judgments as any other field. These appellants seem clearly to seek advisory opinions upon broad claims of rights protected by the First, Fifth, Ninth and Tenth Amendments to the Constitution * * *. [T]he facts of [plaintiffs'] personal interest in their civil rights, of the general threat of possible interference with those rights by the Civil Service Commission under its rules, if specified things are done by appellants, does not make a justiciable case or controversy. Appellants want to engage in "political management and political campaigns," to persuade others to follow appellants' views by discussion, speeches, articles and other acts reasonably designed to secure the selection of appellants' political choices. Such generality of objection is really an attack on the political expediency of the Hatch Act, not the presentation of legal issues. It is beyond the competence of courts to render such a decision.

> The power of courts, and ultimately of this Court, to pass upon the constitutionality of acts of Congress arises only when the interests of litigants require the use of this judicial authority for their protection against actual interference. A hypothetical threat is not enough. We can only speculate as to the kinds of political activity the appellants desire to engage in or as to the contents of their proposed public statements or the circumstances of their publication. 330 U.S. at 88–90.

What would the plaintiffs have to have done in order to render the case ripe for adjudication? Does requiring such action on their part prior to adjudication make sense?

ADLER v. BOARD OF EDUCATION, 342 U.S. 485 (1952): The Court upheld a provision of New York's civil service law and a provision of the state's education law regulating the employment as teachers of those advocating the overthrow of the government by force and violence. The plaintiffs sought declaratory judgment and injunction against the laws in state court. Justice Frankfurter dissented on the grounds that the case was not ripe for adjudication:

> We are asked to pass on a scheme to counteract what are currently called "subversive" influences in the public school system of New York. The scheme is formulated partly in statutes and partly in administrative regulations, but all of it is still an unfinished blueprint. We are asked to adjudicate claims against its constitutionality before the scheme has been put into operation, before the limits that it imposes upon free inquiry and association, the scope of scrutiny that it sanctions, and the procedural safeguards that will be found to be implied for its enforcement have been authoritatively defined. I think we should adhere to the teachings of this Court's history to avoid constitutional adjudications on merely abstract or speculative issues and to base them on the concreteness afforded by an actual, present, defined controversy, appropriate for judicial judgment, between adversaries immediately affected by it. 342 U.S. at 497–498.

Frankfurter concluded:

> The allegations in the present action fall short of those found insufficient in the *Mitchell* case. These teachers do not allege that they have engaged in proscribed conduct or that they have any intention to do so. They do not suggest that they have been, or are, deterred from supporting causes or from joining organizations for fear of the [statute's] interdict, except to say generally that the system complained of will have this effect on teachers as a group. They do not assert that they are threatened with action under the law, or that steps are imminent whereby they would incur the hazard of punishment for conduct innocent at the time, or under standards too vague to satisfy due process of law. They merely allege that the statutes and Rules permit such action against some teach-

ers. Since we rightly refused in the *Mitchell* case to hear government employees whose conduct was much more intimately affected by the law there attacked than are the claims of plaintiffs here, this suit is wanting in the necessary basis for our review.

The majority failed to deal with the ripeness issue.

PACIFIC GAS & ELECTRIC COMPANY v. STATE ENERGY RESOURCES CONSERVATION & DEVELOPMENT COMMISSION

Supreme Court of the United States, 1983.
461 U.S. 190.

JUSTICE WHITE delivered the opinion of the Court.

* * *

This case emerges from the intersection of the federal government's efforts to ensure that nuclear power is safe with the exercise of the historic state authority over the generation and sale of electricity. At issue is whether provisions in the 1976 amendments to California's Warren–Alquist Act, Cal.Pub.Res.Code §§ 25524.1(b) and 25524.2 (West 1977), which condition the construction of nuclear plants on findings by the State Energy Resources Conservation and Development Commission that adequate storage facilities and means of disposal are available for nuclear waste, are preempted by the Atomic Energy Act of 1954, 42 U.S.C. § 2011, et seq.

I

A nuclear reactor must be periodically refueled and the "spent fuel" removed. This spent fuel is intensely radioactive and must be carefully stored. The general practice is to store the fuel in a water-filled pool at the reactor site. For many years, it was assumed that this fuel would be reprocessed; accordingly, the storage pools were designed as short-term holding facilities with limited storage capacities. As expectations for reprocessing remained unfulfilled, the spent fuel accumulated in the storage pools, creating the risk that nuclear reactors would have to be shutdown. This could occur if there were insufficient room in the pool to store spent fuel and also if there were not enough space to hold the entire fuel core when certain inspections or emergencies required unloading of the reactor. * * *

The California laws at issue here are responses to these concerns. In 1974, California adopted the Warren–Alquist State Energy Resources Conservation and Development Act, Cal.Pub.Res.Code §§ 25000–25986 (West 1977 and Supp.1981). The Act requires that a utility seeking to build in California any electric power generating plant, including a nuclear power plant, must apply for certification to the State Energy Resources and Conservation Commission (Energy Commission). The Warren–Alquist Act was amended in 1976 to provide additional state regulation of new nuclear power plant construction.

Two sections of these amendments are before us. Section 25524.1(b) provides that before additional nuclear plants may be built, the Energy Commission must determine on a case-by-case basis that there will be "adequate capacity" for storage of a plant's spent fuel rods "at the time such nuclear facility requires such * * * storage." The law also requires that each utility provide continuous, on-site, "full core reserve storage capacity" in order to permit storage of the entire reactor core if it must be removed to permit repairs of the reactor. In short, § 25524.1(b) addresses the interim storage of spent fuel.

Section 25524.2 deals with the long-term solution to nuclear wastes. This section imposes a moratorium on the certification of new nuclear plants until the Energy Commission "finds that there has been developed and that the United States through its authorized agency has approved and there exists a demonstrated technology or means for the disposal of high-level nuclear waste." "Disposal" is defined as a "method for the permanent and terminal disposition of high-level nuclear waste * * *" Cal.Pub.Res.Code § 25524.2(a), (c). Such a finding must be reported to the state legislature, which may nullify it.

In 1978, petitioners Pacific Gas and Electric Company and Southern California Edison Company filed this action in the United States District Court, requesting a declaration that numerous provisions of the Warren–Alquist Act, including the two sections challenged here, are invalid under the Supremacy Clause because they are preempted by the Atomic Energy Act. The District Court held that petitioners had standing to challenge §§ 25524.1(b) and 25524.2, that the issues presented by these two statutes are ripe for adjudication, and that the two provisions are void because they are preempted by and in conflict with the Atomic Energy Act.

The Court of Appeals for the Ninth Circuit affirmed the District Court's ruling that the petitioners have standing to challenge the California statutes, and also agreed that the challenge to § 25524.2 is ripe for review. It concluded, however, that the challenge to § 25524.1(b) was not ripe "because we cannot know whether the Energy Commission will ever find a nuclear plant's storage capacity to be inadequate * * *". On the merits, the court held that the nuclear moratorium provisions of § 25524.2 were not preempted because §§ 271 and 274(k) of the Atomic Energy Act, 42 U.S.C. §§ 2018 and 2021(k), constitute a Congressional authorization for states to regulate nuclear power plants "for purposes other than protection against radiation hazards."

We granted certiorari limited to the questions of whether §§ 25524.1(b) and 25524.2 are ripe for judicial review, and whether they are preempted by the Atomic Energy Act.

II

We agree that the challenge to § 25524.2 *is* ripe for judicial review, but that the questions concerning § 25524.1(b) are not. The basic rationale of the ripeness doctrine "is to prevent the courts, through avoidance of premature adjudication, from entangling themselves in abstract disagreements over administrative polices, and also to protect the agencies from judicial interference until an administrative decision has been formalized and its effects felt in a concrete way by the challenging parties." Abbott Laboratories v. Gardner, 387 U.S. 136, 148–149 (1967). In *Abbott Laboratories,* which remains our leading discussion of the doctrine, we indicated that the question of ripeness turns on "the fitness of the issues for judicial decision" and "the hardship to the parties of withholding court consideration."

Both of these factors counsel in favor of finding the challenge to the waste disposal regulations in § 25524.2 ripe for adjudication. The question of preemption is predominantly legal, and although it would be useful to have the benefit of California's interpretation of what constitutes a demonstrated technology or means for the disposal of high-level nuclear waste, resolution of the preemption issue need not await that development. Moreover, postponement of decision would likely work substantial hardship on the utilities. As the Court of Appeals cogently reasoned, for the utilities to proceed in hopes that, when the time for certification came, either the required findings would be made or the law would be struck down, requires the expenditures of millions of dollars over a number of years, without any certainty of recovery if certification were denied. The construction of new nuclear facilities requires considerable advance planning—on the order of 12 to 14 years. Thus, as in the Rail Reorganization Act Cases, 419 U.S. 102, 144 (1974), "decisions to be made now or in the short future may be affected" by whether we act. "One does not have to await the consummation of threatened injury to obtain preventive relief. If the injury is certainly impending, that is enough." Id., at 143, quoting Pennsylvania v. West Virginia, 262 U.S. 553, 593 (1923). To require the industry to proceed without knowing whether the moratorium is valid would impose a palpable and considerable hardship on the utilities, and may ultimately work harm on the citizens of California. Moreover, if petitioners are correct that § 25524.2 is void because it hinders the commercial development of atomic energy, "delayed resolution would frustrate one of the key purposes of the [Atomic Energy] Act." Duke Power Co. v. Carolina Environmental Study Group, Inc., 438 U.S. 59, 82 (1978). For these reasons, the issue of whether § 25524.2 is preempted by federal law should be decided now.[15]

---

15. Respondents also contend that the waste disposal provision question is not ripe for review because even if the law is invalid, petitioners' injury—being prevented as a practical matter from building new nuclear power plants—will not be fully redressed inasmuch as other sections of the Warren–Alquist Act, not before the Court, also prevent such construction. Respondents also suggest that this lack of redressability rises to the level of an Article III concern. Both arguments are predicated entirely upon a statement in petitioners' reply brief in support of the petition for certiorari that "un-less and until the California certification system statutes are reviewed and at least largely invalidated, petitioners will not again undertake to build nuclear power plants in California." Respondents attempt to draw entirely too much from this statement. The California certification provisions do not impose a moratorium on new construction; in the main, they require that information be gathered on a variety of issues and be considered by the Energy Commission. It is unreasonable to presume that these informational requirements will

Questions concerning the constitutionality of the interim storage provision, § 25524.1(b), however, are not ripe for review. While the waste disposal statute operates on a statewide basis, the Energy Commission is directed to make determinations under § 25524.1(b) on a case-by-case basis. As the Court of Appeals explained, because "we cannot know whether the Energy Commission will ever find a nuclear plant's storage capacity to be inadequate," judicial consideration of this provision should await further developments.[16] Furthermore, because we hold today that § 25524.2 is not preempted by federal law, there is little likelihood that industry behavior would be uniquely affected by whatever uncertainty surrounds the interim storage provisions. In these circumstances, a court should not stretch to reach an early, and perhaps premature, decision respecting § 25524.1(b).

* * *

[The opinion of JUSTICE BLACKMUN, joined by JUSTICE STEVENS, concurring in part and concurring in the judgment, on other grounds, is omitted.]

Notes

1. A case must be ripe at the time of review. Anderson v. Green, 513 U.S. 557 (1995), involved a challenge to a California welfare program. The program required a federal waiver to take effect. At the time the lower courts invalidated the program, the federal Secretary of Health and Human Services had granted a waiver. While the case was pending before the Supreme Court, the Court of Appeals invalidated the waiver in a separate proceeding. That decision was not appealed. Thus, at the time of the Supreme Court decision, no waiver was in effect, and the state conceded that

---

exert the same chilling effect on new construction as would a moratorium. The Ninth Circuit concurs.

"[A] delay in adjudication will not cause any undue hardship for the parties. The certification scheme, in general, does not have an 'immediate and substantial impact' on the utilities. Gardner v. Toilet Goods Association, 387 U.S. 167, 171 (1967); neither [Pacific Gas & Electric] nor [So.Calif. Edison] has a notice of intention or application for certification pending, and the threat that procedural burdens might someday be imposed or that certification might someday be denied for failure to meet Energy Commission standards is remote at best."

Respondents' "fears" that petitioners will not seek to pursue the nuclear option, notwithstanding a favorable decision in this litigation, appear greatly exaggerated.

16. The Court of Appeals noted that the draft report by the State Energy Commission's Nuclear Fuel Cycle Committee, which recommended requiring all nuclear plants to provide a specified amount of storage space, see Nuclear Fuel Cycle Committee, Status of Nuclear Fuel Reprocessing, Spent Fuel Storage and High–Level Waste Disposal 113 (ERCDC Draft Report Jan. 11, 1978), does not necessarily render the provision ripe. The Committee report is only an indication of the views of two of five members of the Energy Commission in 1978. Not only may views change in the future, but the report itself cautions that it does not represent final agency action. Indeed, the full Commission's decision on Jan. 25, 1978, did not adopt this report or the committee's recommendations regarding on-site storage. Finally, the recently enacted Nuclear Waste Disposal Act of 1982, P.L. 97–425, 96 Stat. 2201 (1982), authorizes the NRC to license technology for the on-site storage of spent fuel, § 133, and directs the Secretary of Energy to provide up to 1,900 metric tons of capacity for the storage of spent fuel, § 135; these provisions might influence the State Commission's ultimate findings.

even if it prevailed in the Supreme Court, the program would not take effect. The Court dismissed the case on ripeness grounds, noting that " 'ripeness is peculiarly a question of timing,' and 'it is the situation now rather than the situation at the time of the [decision under review] that must govern.' " Id. at 559, quoting Regional Rail Reorganization Act Cases, 419 U.S. 102 (1974).

2. The Supreme Court applied its ripeness doctrine to a fifth and fourteenth amendment takings question in Suitum v. Tahoe Regional Planning Agency, 520 U.S. 725 (1997). In *Suitum*, the plaintiff's land had been declared ineligible for development and she had been denied permission to build on it. In return, she had been given certain transferable development rights, which could be used on other properties. She sued in federal court, alleging a taking of her land in violation of the fifth and fourteenth amendments. The courts below had held the case unripe because plaintiff had never tried to sell her transferable development rights and therefore could not know their value. The Supreme Court unanimously reversed, holding that the act of declaring her land ineligible for development constituted a sufficient final decision by the planning agency to make the case ripe. The appropriate valuation of the transferable development rights was simply an issue of fact that could be decided at trial. For other recent ripeness cases in the Supreme Court, see National Park Hospitality Ass'n v. Dept. of Interior, 538 U.S. 803 (2003); Palazzolo v. Rhode Island, 533 U.S. 606 (2001); Ohio Forestry Assoc. v. Sierra Club, 523 U.S. 726 (1998); Texas v. United States, 523 U.S. 296 (1998).

3. To what extent is the ripeness standard based in the "case-or-controversy" requirement of Article III? See Nichol, *Ripeness and the Constitution*, 54 U.Chi.L.Rev. 153 (1987).

§ 5. THE POLITICAL QUESTION DOCTRINE

POWELL v. McCORMACK

Supreme Court of the United States, 1969.
395 U.S. 486.

CHIEF JUSTICE WARREN delivered the opinion of the Court.

In November 1966, petitioner Adam Clayton Powell, Jr., was duly elected from the 18th Congressional District of New York to serve in the United States House of Representatives for the 90th Congress. However, pursuant to a House resolution, he was not permitted to take his seat. Powell (and some of the voters of his district) then filed suit in Federal District Court, claiming that the House could exclude him only if it found he failed to meet the standing requirements of age, citizenship, and residence contained in Art. I, § 2, of the Constitution—requirements the House specifically found Powell met—and thus had excluded him unconstitutionally. The District Court dismissed petitioners' complaint "for want of jurisdiction of the subject matter." A panel of the Court of Appeals affirmed the dismissal, although on somewhat different grounds, each judge filing a separate opinion. We have determined that it was error to dismiss the complaint and that petitioner Powell is entitled to a

declaratory judgment that he was unlawfully excluded from the 90th *HOLDING*
Congress.

I.

FACTS.

During the 89th Congress, a Special Subcommittee on Contracts of the Committee on House Administration conducted an investigation into the expenditures of the Committee on Education and Labor, of which petitioner Adam Clayton Powell, Jr., was chairman. The Special Subcommittee issued a report concluding that Powell and certain staff employees had deceived the House authorities as to travel expenses. The report also indicated there was strong evidence that certain illegal salary payments had been made to Powell's wife at his direction. No formal action was taken during the 89th Congress. However, prior to the organization of the 90th Congress, the Democratic members-elect met in caucus and voted to remove Powell as chairman of the Committee on Education and Labor.

When the 90th Congress met to organize in January 1967, Powell was asked to step aside while the oath was administered to the other members-elect. Following the administration of the oath to the remaining members, the House discussed the procedure to be followed in determining whether Powell was eligible to take his seat. After some debate, by a vote of 363 to 65 the House adopted House Resolution No. 1, which provided that the Speaker appoint a Select Committee to determine Powell's eligibility. Although the resolution prohibited Powell from taking his seat until the House acted on the Select Committee's report, it did provide that he should receive all the pay and allowances due a member during the period.

so what were damages?

* * *

* * * The Committee recommended that Powell be sworn and seated as a member of the 90th Congress but that he be censured by the House, fined $40,000 and be deprived of his seniority.

The report was presented to the House on March 1, 1967, and the House debated the Select Committee's proposed resolution. At the conclusion of the debate, by a vote of 222 of 202 the House rejected a motion to bring the resolution to a vote. An amendment to the resolution was then offered; it called for the exclusion of Powell and a declaration that his seat was vacant. The Speaker ruled that a majority vote of the House would be sufficient to pass the resolution if it were so amended. 113 Cong.Rec. 5020. After further debate, the amendment was adopted by a vote of 248 to 176. Then the House adopted by a vote of 307 to 116 House Resolution No. 278 in its amended form, thereby excluding Powell and directing that the Speaker notify the Governor of New York that the seat was vacant.

Powell and 13 voters of the 18th Congressional District of New York subsequently instituted this suit in the United States District Court for the District of Columbia. Five members of the House of Representatives were named as defendants individually and "as representatives of a class of citizens who are presently serving * * * as members of the House of Representatives." John W. McCormack was named in his official capacity as Speaker, and the Clerk of the House of Representatives, the Sergeant at Arms and the Doorkeeper were named individually and in their official capacities. The complaint alleged that House Resolution No. 278 violated the Constitution, specifically Art. I, § 2, cl. 1, because the resolution was inconsistent with the mandate that the members of the House shall be elected by the people of each State, and Art. I, § 2, cl. 2, which, petitioners alleged, sets forth the exclusive qualifications for membership.

* * *

Respondents press upon us a variety of arguments to support the court below; they will be considered in the following order. (1) Events occurring subsequent to the grant of certiorari have rendered this litigation moot. (2) The Speech or Debate Clause of the Constitution, Art. I, § 6, insulates respondents' action from judicial review. (3) The decision to exclude petitioner Powell is supported by the power granted to the House of Representatives to expel a member. (4) This Court lacks subject matter jurisdiction over petitioners' action. (5) Even if subject matter jurisdiction is present, this litigation is not justiciable either under the general criteria established by this Court or because a political question is involved.

* * *

IV.

Exclusion or Expulsion.

The resolution excluding petitioner Powell was adopted by a vote in excess of two-thirds of the 434 Members of Congress—307 to 116. Article I, § 5, grants the House authority to expel a member "with the Concurrence of two thirds."[27] Respondents assert that the House may expel a member for any reason whatsoever and that, since a two-thirds vote was obtained, the procedure by which Powell was denied his seat in the 90th Congress should be regarded as an expulsion, not an exclusion.

Although respondents repeatedly urge this Court not to speculate as to the reasons for Powell's exclusion, their attempt to equate exclusion with expulsion would require a similar speculation that the House would have voted to expel Powell had it been faced with that question. Powell had not been seated at the time House Resolution No. 278 was debated and passed. After a motion to bring the Select Committee's proposed

---

27. Powell was "excluded" from the 90th Congress, i.e., he was not administered the oath of office and was prevented from taking his seat. If he had been allowed to take the oath and subsequently had been required to surrender his seat, the House's action would have constituted an "expulsion." Since we conclude that Powell was excluded from the 90th Congress, we express no view on what limitations may exist on Congress' power to expel or otherwise punish a member once he has been seated.

resolution to an immediate vote had been defeated, an amendment was offered which mandated Powell's exclusion. Mr. Celler, chairman of the Select Committee, then posed a parliamentary inquiry to determine whether a two-thirds vote was necessary to pass the resolution if so amended "in the sense that it might amount to an expulsion." The Speaker replied that "action by a majority vote would be in accordance with the rules." Had the amendment been regarded as an attempt to expel Powell, a two-thirds vote would have been constitutionally required. The Speaker ruled that the House was voting to exclude Powell, and we will not speculate what the result might have been if Powell had been seated and expulsion proceedings subsequently instituted.

Nor is the distinction between exclusion and expulsion merely one of form. The misconduct for which Powell was charged occurred prior to the convening of the 90th Congress. On several occasions the House has debated whether a member can be expelled for actions taken during a prior Congress and the House's own manual of procedure applicable in the 90th Congress states that "both Houses have distrusted their power to punish in such cases." * * * Members of the House having expressed a belief that such strictures apply to its own power to expel, we will not assume that two-thirds of its members would have expelled Powell for his prior conduct had the Speaker announced that House Resolution No. 278 was for expulsion rather than exclusion.

* * *

* * * We need express no opinion as to the accuracy of Congressman Eckhardt's prediction that expulsion proceedings would have produced a different result. However, the House's own views of the extent of its power to expel combined with the Congressman's analysis counsel that exclusion and expulsion are not fungible proceedings. The Speaker ruled that House Resolution No. 278 contemplated an exclusion proceeding. We must reject respondents' suggestion that we overrule the Speaker and hold that, although the House manifested an intent to exclude Powell, its action should be tested by whatever standards may govern an expulsion.

V.

SUBJECT MATTER JURISDICTION.

As we pointed out in Baker v. Carr, 369 U.S. 186, 198 (1962), there is a significant difference between determining whether a federal court has "jurisdiction of the subject matter" and determining whether a cause over which a court has subject matter jurisdiction is "justiciable." The District Court determined that "to decide this case on the merits * * * would constitute a clear violation of the doctrine of separation of powers" and then dismissed the complaint "for want of jurisdiction of the subject matter." However, as the Court of Appeals correctly recognized, the doctrine of separation of powers is more properly considered in determining whether the case is "justiciable." We agree with the unanimous conclusion of the Court of Appeals that the District Court had jurisdiction over the subject matter of this case. However, for reasons set forth in Part VI, infra, we disagree with the Court of Appeals' conclusion that this case is not justiciable.

* * *

VI.

JUSTICIABILITY.

Having concluded that the Court of Appeals correctly ruled that the District Court had jurisdiction over the subject matter, we turn to the question whether the case is justiciable. Two determinations must be made in this regard. First, we must decide whether the claim presented and the relief sought are of the type which admit of judicial resolution. Second, we must determine whether the structure of the Federal Government renders the issue presented a "political question"—that is, a question which is not justiciable in federal court because of the separation of powers provided by the Constitution.

* * *

B. Political Question Doctrine.

1. Textually Demonstrable Constitutional Commitment.

Respondents maintain that even if this case is otherwise justiciable, it presents only a political question. It is well established that the federal courts will not adjudicate political questions. See, e.g., Coleman v. Miller, 307 U.S. 433 (1939); Oetjen v. Central Leather Co., 246 U.S. 297 (1918). In Baker v. Carr, supra, we noted that political questions are not justiciable primarily because of the separation of powers within the Federal Government. After reviewing our decisions in this area, we concluded that on the surface of any case held to involve a political question was at least one of the following formulations:

> "a textually demonstrable constitutional commitment of the issue to a co-ordinate political department; or a lack of judicially discoverable and manageable standards for resolving it; or the impossibility of deciding without an initial policy determination of a kind clearly for nonjudicial discretion; or the impossibility of a court's undertaking independent resolution without expressing lack of the respect due co-ordinate branches of government; or an unusual need for unquestioning adherence to a political decision already made; or the potentiality of embarrassment from multifarious pronouncements by various departments on one question." 369 U.S., at 217.

Respondents' first contention is that this case presents a political question because under Art. I, § 5, there has been a "textually demonstrable constitutional commitment" to the House of the "adjudicatory power" to determine Powell's qualifications. Thus it is argued that the House, and the House alone, has power to determine who is qualified to be a member.

In order to determine whether there has been a textual commitment to a coordinate department of the Government, we must interpret the Constitution. In other words, we must first determine what power the Constitution confers upon the House through Art. I, § 5, before we can determine to what extent, if any, the exercise of that power is subject to judicial review. Respondents maintain that the House has broad power under § 5, and, they argue, the House may determine which are the qualifications necessary for membership. On the other hand, petitioners allege that the Constitution provides that an elected representative may be denied his seat only if the House finds he does not meet one of the standing qualifications expressly prescribed by the Constitution.

If examination of § 5 disclosed that the Constitution gives the House judicially unreviewable power to set qualifications for membership and to judge whether prospective members meet those qualifications, further review of the House determination might well be barred by the political question doctrine. On the other hand, if the Constitution gives the House power to judge only whether elected members possess the three standing qualifications set forth in the Constitution, further consideration would be necessary to determine whether any of the other formulations of the political question doctrine are "inextricable from the case at bar."[42] Baker v. Carr, supra, at 217.

In other words, whether there is a "textually demonstrable constitutional commitment of the issue to a coordinate political department" of government and what is the scope of such commitment are questions we must resolve for the first time in this case. For, as we pointed out in Baker v. Carr, supra, "[d]eciding whether a matter has in any measure been committed by the Constitution to another branch of government, or whether the action of that branch exceeds whatever authority has been committed, is itself a delicate exercise in constitutional interpretation, and is a responsibility of this Court as ultimate interpreter of the Constitution." Id., at 211.

In order to determine the scope of any "textual commitment" under Art. I, § 5, we necessarily must determine the meaning of the phrase to "be the Judge of the Qualifications of its own Members." Petitioners argue that the records of the debates during the Constitutional Convention; available commentary from the post-Convention, pre-ratification period; and early congressional applications of Art. I, § 5, support their construction of the section. Respondents insist, however, that a careful examination of the pre-Convention practices of the English Parliament and American colonial assemblies demonstrates that by 1787, a legislature's power to judge the qualifications of its members was generally understood to encompass exclusion or expulsion on the ground that an individual's character or past conduct rendered him unfit to serve. When the Constitution and the debates over its adoption are thus viewed in

42. Consistent with this interpretation, federal courts might still be barred by the political question doctrine from reviewing the House's factual determination that a member did not meet one of the standing qualifications. This is an issue not presented in this case and we express no view as to its resolution.

historical perspective, argue respondents, it becomes clear that the "qualifications" expressly set forth in the Constitution were not meant to limit the long-recognized legislative power to exclude or expel at will, but merely to establish "standing incapacities," which could be altered only by a constitutional amendment. Our examination of the relevant historical materials leads us to the conclusion that petitioners are correct and that the Constitution leaves the House without authority to *exclude* any person, duly elected by his constituents, who meets all the requirements for membership expressly prescribed in the Constitution.

[The Court here canvassed the historical record in support of its conclusion.]

d. *Conclusion.*

Had the intent of the Framers emerged from these materials with less clarity, we would nevertheless have been compelled to resolve any ambiguity in favor of a narrow construction of the scope of Congress' power to exclude members-elect. A fundamental principle of our representative democracy is, in Hamilton's words, "that the people should choose whom they please to govern them." 2 Elliot's Debates 257. As Madison pointed out at the Convention, this principle is undermined as much by limiting whom the people can select as by limiting the franchise itself. In apparent agreement with this basic philosophy, the Convention adopted his suggestion limiting the power to expel. To allow essentially that same power to be exercised under the guise of judging qualifications, would be to ignore Madison's warning, borne out in the Wilkes case and some of Congress' own post-Civil War exclusion cases, against "vesting an improper & dangerous power in the Legislature." 2 Farrand 249. Moreover, it would effectively nullify the Convention's decision to require a two-thirds vote for expulsion. Unquestionably, Congress has an interest in preserving its institutional integrity, but in most cases that interest can be sufficiently safeguarded by the exercise of its power to punish its members for disorderly behavior and, in extreme cases, to expel a member with the concurrence of two-thirds. In short, both the intention of the Framers, to the extent it can be determined, and an examination of the basic principles of our democratic system persuade us that the Constitution does not vest in the Congress a discretionary power to deny membership by a majority vote.

For these reasons, we have concluded that Art. I, s 5, is at most a "textually demonstrable commitment" to Congress to judge only the qualifications expressly set forth in the Constitution. Therefore, the "textual commitment" formulation of the political question doctrine does not bar federal courts from adjudicating petitioners' claims.

2. *Other Considerations.*

Respondents' alternate contention is that the case presents a political question because judicial resolution of petitioners' claim would produce a "potentially embarrassing confrontation between coordinate branches" of the Federal Government. But, as our interpretation of Art. I, § 5, discloses, a determination of petitioner Powell's right to sit would require no more than an interpretation of the Constitution. Such a determination falls within the traditional role accorded courts to interpret the law, and does not involve a "lack of the respect due [a] coordinate [branch] of government," nor does it involve an "initial policy determination of a kind clearly for nonjudicial discretion." Baker v. Carr, 369 U.S. 186. Our system of government requires that federal courts on occasion interpret the Constitution in a manner at variance with the construction given the document by another branch. The alleged conflict that such an adjudication may cause cannot justify the courts' avoiding their constitutional responsibility.

Nor are any of the other formulations of a political question "inextricable from the case at bar." Baker v. Carr, supra, at 217. Petitioners seek a determination that the House was without power to exclude Powell from the 90th Congress, which, we have seen, requires an interpretation of the Constitution—a determination for which clearly there are "judicially ... manageable standards." Finally, a judicial resolution of petitioners' claim will not result in "multifarious pronouncements by various departments on one question." For, as we noted in Baker v. Carr, supra, at 211, it is the responsibility of this Court to act as the ultimate interpreter of the Constitution. Marbury v. Madison, 1 Cranch (5 U.S.) 137 (1803). Thus, we conclude that petitioners' claim is not barred by the political question doctrine, and, having determined that the claim is otherwise generally justiciable, we hold that the case is justiciable.

* * *

Further, analysis of the "textual commitment" under Art. I, § 5 (see Part VI, B (1)), has demonstrated that in judging the qualifications of its members Congress is limited to the standing qualifications prescribed in the Constitution. Respondents concede that Powell met these. Thus, there is no need to remand this case to determine whether he was entitled to be seated in the 90th Congress. Therefore, we hold that, since Adam Clayton Powell, Jr., was duly elected by the voters of the 18th Congressional District of New York and was not ineligible to serve under any provision of the Constitution, the House was without power to exclude him from its membership.

Petitioners seek additional forms of equitable relief, including mandamus for the release of petitioner Powell's back pay. The propriety of such remedies, however, is more appropriately considered in the first instance by the courts below. Therefore, as to respondents McCormack, Albert, Ford, Celler, and Moore, the judgment of the Court of Appeals for the District of Columbia Circuit is affirmed. As to respondents Jennings, Johnson, and Miller, the judgment of the Court of Appeals for the District of Columbia Circuit is reversed and the case is remanded to the United States District Court for the District of Columbia with instructions to enter a declaratory judgment and for further proceedings consistent with this opinion.

It is so ordered.

Notes

1. Does the political question doctrine represent a wise exercise of judicial restraint, or is it an abdication of judicial responsibility? Consider Wechsler, *Toward Neutral Principles of Constitutional Law*, 73 Harv.L.Rev. 1, 7–8, 9 (1959):

> [A]ll the doctrine can defensibly imply is that the courts are called upon to judge whether the Constitution has committed to another agency of government the autonomous determination of the issue raised, a finding that itself requires an interpretation.

> * * *

> [T]he only proper judgment that may lead to an abstention from decision is that the Constitution has committed the determination of the issue to another agency of government than the courts. Difficult as it may be to make that judgment wisely, whatever factors may be rightly weighed in situations where the answer is not clear, what is involved is in itself an act of constitutional interpretation, to be made and judged by standards that should govern the interpretive process generally. That, I submit, is *toto caelo* different from a broad discretion to abstain or intervene.

Do you understand the distinction Professor Wechsler is attempting to draw? Why does he believe that the form of the doctrine he describes is preferable to "a broad discretion to abstain or intervene"? Do you agree?

Professor Scharpf has described Professor Wechsler's approach as the "classical" version of the political question doctrine. According to Scharpf, supporters of the classical position "insist, as did John Marshall in Marbury v. Madison, that the power of judicial review rests ultimately upon the constitutional *duty* of the judiciary 'to say what the law is'—that is, to exercise its independent judgment in finding, interpreting and applying the law (including the law of the Constitution) whenever the decision of a case and controversy should depend on it. To acknowledge that the courts might be free to disregard this duty by treating a 'political' determination as conclusive of some questions of law would destroy the assumption of a judicial duty which is fundamental for the classical theory. This difficulty would disappear, however, if it could be shown that in those instances in which the courts do in fact defer without inquiry to a decision by the political departments, this deference is itself compelled by the constitutional allocation of competence to decide." Scharpf, *Judicial Review and the Political Question: A Functional Analysis*, 75 Yale L.J. 517, 518 (1966) (emphasis in original). Professor Scharpf questions whether the "classical" theory can adequately explain all of the political question cases. Id. at 540–42.

Compare with Wechsler's position that taken in Bickel, *The Supreme Court, 1960 Term—Foreword: The Passive Virtues*, 75 Harv.L.Rev. 40, 46 (1961): "There is something different about [the political question doctrine], in kind, not in degree, from the general 'interpretive process'; something greatly more flexible, something of prudence, not construction and not principle. And it is something that cannot exist within the four corners of Marbury v. Madison." Professor Bickel also included this analysis of the doctrine:

> Such is the basis of the political-question doctrine: the court's sense of lack of capacity, compounded in unequal parts of the strangeness of the issue and the suspicion that it will have to yield more often and more substantially to expediency than to principle; the sheer momentousness of it, which unbalances judgment and prevents one from subsuming the normal calculations of probabilities; the anxiety not so much that judicial judgment will be ignored, as that perhaps it should be but won't; finally and in sum ("in a mature democracy"), the inner vulnerability of an institution which is electorally irresponsible and has no earth to draw strength from. Id. at 75.

Unlike Professor Wechsler, Professor Bickel views a broad political question doctrine as consistent with a "principled" approach to constitutional interpretation: "[I]t is quite plain that some questions are held to be political pursuant to a decision on principle that there ought to be discretion free of principled rules." Id. Do you agree? Cf. Gunther, *The Subtle Vices of the "Passive Virtues"—A Comment on Principle and Expediency in Judicial Review*, 64 Colum.L.Rev. 1 (1964).

Do you think there ought to be a prudential element to the political question doctrine? Professor Scharpf has suggested three conceivable rationales for a "prudential" version of the doctrine, but concludes that none can explain it. One is the "opportunistic" theory, which focuses on "the Court's instincts for political survival, instincts which would persuade it to avoid the decision of 'prickly issues' and 'contentious questions' touching the 'hypersensitive nerve of public opinion.' " Scharpf, supra, 75 Yale L.J. at 549. A second is the "cognitive" rationale, or the absence of judicially usable principles and standards. Id. at 555–56. Finally, Professor Scharpf recognizes a "normative" rationale for the "prudential" version of the doctrine. As an illustration, he cites Jaffe, *Standing to Secure Judicial Review: Public Actions*, 74 Harv.L.Rev. 1265, 1303 (1961), in which it is suggested that many political questions "are of the sort for which we do not choose, or have not been able as yet to establish, strongly guiding rules. We may believe that the job is better done without rules, or that even though there are applicable rules, these rules should be only among the numerous relevant considerations." Scharpf concludes that all these theories are too general, and cannot account for "the empirical finding that the Supreme Court will decide on the merits the overwhelming majority of all cases which it accepts for decision * * *." Id. at 566.

Professor Tushnet takes a different approach in explaining the demise of any prudential approach to the political question doctrine. He suggests that Bickel's position is inconsistent with modern constitutional jurisprudence: "Bickel thought that the political question doctrine 'resists being domesticated.' By this he meant that applying the doctrine inevitably required the courts to respond to prudential concerns that could not be reduced to rules, criteria, or even standards." Tushnet, *Law and Prudence in the Law of Justiciability: The Transformation and Disappearance of the Political Question Doctrine*, 80 N.Car.L.Rev. 1203, 1204 (2002). Professor Tushnet argues that Baker itself "doctrinalized" the political question doctrine, minimizing its prudential elements, and that the rise of judicial supremacy further distanced constitutional jurisprudence from Bickel's views.

Regardless of its contours, is the political question doctrine justifiable? The following argument is made in Redish, *Judicial Review and the Political Question,* 79 Nw.U.L.Rev. 1031, 1059–60 (1985):

> Once we make the initial assumption that judicial review plays a legitimate role in a constitutional democracy, we must abandon the political question doctrine, in all of its manifestations. The inherent implication of the doctrine's application is that one or both of the political branches may continue conduct that is unconstitutional, without any examination or supervision by the judicial branch. The moral cost of such a result, both to society in general and the Supreme Court in particular, far outweighs whatever benefits are thought to derive from the judicial abdication of the review function.

> This does not mean that the Court, in reaching its constitutional decisions, should not, in certain cases, take into account the comparative expertise that the political branches may have in deciding whether certain actions are essential, or the institutional limitations on the judiciary's power to supervise day-to-day operations of the government, particularly when emergency actions may be called for. But in each case, if the Court is to perform the essential function of protector against a lawless government, the Court must draw the final constitutional calculus. If in certain instances the Court abdicates this responsibility, it becomes logically difficult to distinguish the majority of cases, in which the Court deems the exercise of its review power legitimate; a large number of *prima facie* incursions of liberty by the political branches could conceivably be justified on some notion of expertise.

Professor Nagel reaches quite a different conclusion in *Political Law, Legalistic Politics: A Recent History of the Political Question Doctrine,* 56 U.Chi.L.Rev. 643 (1989). Nagel argues that "the political question doctrine is largely incomprehensible to the Court and to the academy * * * because the idea of law is now largely incomprehensible." Both "constitutional content and judicial function are now political * * *." Id. at 668. For another suggested reformulation of the political question doctrine, see Choper, *The Political Question Doctrine: Suggested Criteria,* 54 Duke L.J. 1457 (2005).

2. Does a "political question" doctrine actually exist? Consider Henkin, *Is There a "Political Question" Doctrine?* 85 Yale L.J. 597, 598–600, 601 (1976): "One needs no special doctrine to describe the ordinary respect of the courts for the political domain. If a political question is one which the Constitution commits to the political branches, our political life is full of them. The courts may sometimes have occasion to decide whether a question was in fact constitutionally committed to the political branches, but that, too, needs no special doctrine suggesting a quality of 'nonjusticiability' with connotations that the courts must dismiss for lack of jurisdiction and authority without reaching the merits * * *. Failure to maintain the distinction between the ordinary respect of the courts for the substantive decisions of the political branches, and extraordinary deference to those branches' determination that what they have done is constitutional, has aggravated

confusion and controversy as to whether, and why, and when, such extraordinary judicial deference is called for * * *. The cases which are supposed to have established the political question doctrine required no such extraordinary abstention from judicial review; they called only for the ordinary respect by the courts for the political domain. Having reviewed, the Court refused to invalidate the challenged actions because they were within the constitutional authority of President or Congress." For more recent discussion of this issue, see Fallon, *Judicially Manageable Standards and Constitutional Meaning*, 119 Harv.L.Rev. 1274 (2006); Seidman, *The Secret Life of the Political Question Doctrine*, 37 J. Marshall L.Rev. 441 (2004); Weinberg, *Political Questions and the Guarantee Clause*, 65 U.Colo.L.Rev. 887 (1994); Simard, *Standing Alone: Do We Still Need the Political Question Doctrine?* 100 Dick.L.Rev. 303 (1996).

3. The holding in *Baker* that challenges to apportionment did not present a political question led to a long series of cases in which the Supreme Court held that both state legislatures and state congressional districts must adhere to the principle of one person, one vote. A related series of cases restrict racial gerrymandering—that is, the creation of "majority minority" districts to ensure minority representation. A third line of cases deals with challenges to political gerrymandering: the drawing of district lines in order to advantage or disadvantage candidates of one or the other political party. The seminal case is Davis v. Bandemer, 478 U.S. 109 (1986), in which the Court held such claims justiciable, but could not agree on a standard for evaluating them.

In 2004, the Court once again confronted a political gerrymandering claim in Vieth v. Jubelirer, 541 U.S. 267 (2004). The Court rejected the challenge but again could not agree on the reasoning. Four Justices—Chief Justice Rehnquist and Justices Scalia, O'Connor, and Thomas—would have concluded that political gerrymandering claims were not justiciable because no judicially discernible and manageable standards exist for adjudicating them. These Justices would therefore have overruled *Davis*. Four Justices—Stevens, Souter, Ginsburg, and Breyer—would have held the challenged districting scheme unconstitutional, but each proposed a different standard for determining the constitutionality of such schemes. Finally, Justice Kennedy believed that while no judicially manageable standard had yet been proposed, one might ultimately be found. He therefore voted to reject the plaintiffs' challenge (making five votes to affirm the district court's dismissal of the case), but refused to conclude that political gerrymandering always raises a non-justiciable political question.

What should lower courts make of the multiple opinions in *Vieth*? Should they dismiss all political gerrymandering challenges unless the plaintiffs propose a judicially manageable standard? How should courts determine whether a particular standard is either judicially manageable, or, more important, constitutionally correct? Do these questions suggest that perhaps the Rehnquist plurality was right to argue that political gerrymandering claims are non-justiciable, or is it the Court's failure to agree on a rationale that creates the problem? For a thorough and interesting analysis of *Vieth* and the judicially manageable standards generally, see Fallon, *Judicially Manageable Standards and Constitutional Meaning*, 119 Harv.L.Rev. 1274, 1277 (2006) (arguing that "[j]udicially manageable standards * * * are far more often the products or outputs of constitutional adjudication than inherent elements of the Constitution's meaning'').

In a rerun of *Vieth*, a similarly divided Court again rejected a claim of partisan political gerrymandering in League of United Latin American Citizens v. Perry, 548 U.S. ___, 126 S.Ct. 2594 (2006). As in *Vieth*, a majority declined to "revisit the justiciability holding" of *Davis*, but none of the plaintiffs' suggested standards for measuring the fairness of the redistricting plan satisfied five Justices.

NIXON v. UNITED STATES

Supreme Court of the United States, 1993.
506 U.S. 224.

CHIEF JUSTICE REHNQUIST delivered the opinion of the Court.

Petitioner Walter L. Nixon, Jr., asks this court to decide whether Senate Rule XI, which allows a committee of Senators to hear evidence against an individual who has been impeached and to report that evidence to the full Senate, violates the Impeachment Trial Clause, Art. I, § 3, cl. 6. That Clause provides that the "Senate shall have the sole Power to try all Impeachments." But before we reach the merits of such a claim, we must decide whether it is "justiciable," that is, whether it is a claim that may be resolved by the courts. We conclude that it is not.

Nixon, a former Chief Judge of the United States District Court for the Southern District of Mississippi, was convicted by a jury of two counts of making false statements before a federal grand jury and sentenced to prison. The grand jury investigation stemmed from reports that Nixon had accepted a gratuity from a Mississippi businessman in exchange for asking a local district attorney to halt the prosecution of the businessman's son. Because Nixon refused to resign from his office as a United States District Judge, he continued to collect his judicial salary while serving out his prison sentence.

On May 10, 1989, the House of Representatives adopted three articles of impeachment for high crimes and misdemeanors. The first two articles charged Nixon with giving false testimony before the grand jury and the third article charged him with bringing disrepute on the Federal Judiciary.

After the House presented the articles to the Senate, the Senate voted to invoke its own Impeachment Rule XI, under which the presiding officer appoints a committee of Senators to "receive evidence and take testimony." Senate Impeachment Rule XI, reprinted in Senate Manual, S.Doc. No. 101–1, 101st Cong., 1st Sess., 186 (1989).[1] The Senate

---

1. Specifically, Rule XI provides:

"[I]n the trial of any impeachment the Presiding Officer of the Senate, if the Senate so orders, shall appoint a committee of Senators to receive evidence and take testimony at such times and places as the committee may determine, and for such purpose the committee so appointed and the chairman thereof, to be elected by the committee, shall (unless otherwise ordered by the Senate) exercise all the powers and functions conferred upon the

committee held four days of hearings, during which 10 witnesses, including Nixon, testified. Pursuant to Rule XI, the committee presented the full Senate with a complete transcript of the proceeding and a report stating the uncontested facts and summarizing the evidence on the contested facts. Nixon and the House impeachment managers submitted extensive final briefs to the full Senate and delivered arguments from the Senate floor during the three hours set aside for oral argument in front of that body. Nixon himself gave a personal appeal, and several Senators posed questions directly to both parties. The Senate voted by more than the constitutionally required two-thirds majority to convict Nixon on the first two articles. The presiding officer then entered judgment removing Nixon from his office as United States District Judge.

Nixon thereafter commenced the present suit, arguing that Senate Rule XI violates the constitutional grant of authority to the Senate to "try" all impeachments because it prohibits the whole Senate from taking part in the evidentiary hearings. See Art. I, § 3, cl. 6. Nixon sought a declaratory judgment that his impeachment conviction was void and that his judicial salary and privileges should be reinstated. The District Court held that his claim was nonjusticiable and the Court of Appeals for the District of Columbia Circuit agreed.

A controversy is nonjusticiable—*i.e.,* involves a political question—where there is "a textually demonstrable constitutional commitment of the issue to a coordinate political department; or a lack of judicially discoverable and manageable standards for resolving it * * *." Baker v. Carr. But the courts must, in the first instance, interpret the text in question and determine whether and to what extent the issue is textually committed. See ibid.; Powell v. McCormack. As the discussion that follows makes clear, the concept of a textual commitment to a coordinate political department is not completely separate from the concept of a lack of judicially discoverable and manageable standards for resolving it; the lack of judicially manageable standards may strengthen the conclusion that there is a textually demonstrable commitment to a coordinate branch.

In this case, we must examine Art. I, § 3, cl. 6, to determine the scope of authority conferred upon the Senate by the Framers regarding impeachment. It provides:

Senate and the Presiding Officer of the Senate, respectively, under the rules of procedure and practice in the Senate when sitting on impeachment trials.

"Unless otherwise ordered by the Senate, the rules of procedure and practice in the Senate when sitting on impeachment trials shall govern the procedure and practice of the committee so appointed. The committee so appointed shall report to the Senate in writing a certified copy of the transcript of the proceedings and testimony had and given before such committee, and such report shall be received by the Senate and the evidence so received and the testimony so taken shall be considered to all intents and purposes, subject to the right of the Senate to determine competency, relevancy, and materiality, as having been received and taken before the Senate, but nothing herein shall prevent the Senate from sending for any witness and hearing his testimony in open Senate, or by order of the Senate having the entire trial in open Senate."

"The Senate shall have the sole Power to try all Impeachments. When sitting for that Purpose, they shall be on Oath or Affirmation. When the President of the United States is tried, the Chief Justice shall preside: And no Person shall be convicted without the Concurrence of two thirds of the Members present."

The language and structure of this Clause are revealing. The first sentence is a grant of authority to the Senate, and the word "sole" indicates that this authority is reposed in the Senate and nowhere else. The next two sentences specify requirements to which the Senate proceedings shall conform: the Senate shall be on oath or affirmation, a two-thirds vote is required to convict, and when the President is tried the Chief Justice shall preside.

Petitioner argues that the word "try" in the first sentence imposes by implication an additional requirement on the Senate in that the proceedings must be in the nature of a judicial trial. From there petitioner goes on to argue that this limitation precludes the Senate from delegating to a select committee the task of hearing the testimony of witnesses, as was done pursuant to Senate Rule XI. " '[T]ry' means more than simply 'vote on' or 'review' or 'judge.' In 1787 and today, trying a case means hearing the evidence, not scanning a cold record." Petitioner concludes from this that courts may review whether or not the Senate "tried" him before convicting him.

There are several difficulties with this position which lead us ultimately to reject it. The word "try," both in 1787 and later, has considerably broader meanings than those to which petitioner would limit it. Older dictionaries define try as "[t]o examine" or "[t]o examine as a judge." See 2 S. Johnson, A Dictionary of the English Language (1785). In more modern usage the term has various meanings. For example, try can mean "to examine or investigate judicially," "to conduct the trial of," or "to put to the test by experiment, investigation, or trial." Webster's Third New International Dictionary 2457 (1971). Petitioner submits that "try," as contained in T. Sheridan, Dictionary of the English Language (1796), means "to examine as a judge; to bring before a judicial tribunal." Based on the variety of definitions, however, we cannot say that the Framers used the word "try" as an implied limitation on the method by which the Senate might proceed in trying impeachments. "As a rule the Constitution speaks in general terms, leaving Congress to deal with subsidiary matters of detail as the public interests and changing conditions may require * * *." Dillon v. Gloss, 256 U.S. 368, 376 (1921).

The conclusion that the use of the word "try" in the first sentence of the Impeachment Trial Clause lacks sufficient precision to afford any judicially manageable standard of review of the Senate's actions is fortified by the existence of the three very specific requirements that the Constitution does impose on the Senate when trying impeachments: the members must be under oath, a two-thirds vote is required to convict, and the Chief Justice presides when the President is tried. These

limitations are quite precise, and their nature suggests that the Framers did not intend to impose additional limitations on the form of the Senate proceedings by the use of the word "try" in the first sentence.

Petitioner devotes only two pages in his brief to negating the significance of the word "sole" in the first sentence of Clause 6. As noted above, that sentence provides that "[t]he Senate shall have the sole Power to try all Impeachments." We think that the word "sole" is of considerable significance. Indeed, the word "sole" appears only one other time in the Constitution—with respect to the House of Representatives' "*sole* Power of Impeachment." Art. I, § 2, cl. 5 (emphasis added). The common sense meaning of the word "sole" is that the Senate alone shall have authority to determine whether an individual should be acquitted or convicted. The dictionary definition bears this out. "Sole" is defined as "having no companion," "solitary," "being the only one," and "functioning * * * independently and without assistance or interference." Webster's Third New International Dictionary 2168 (1971). If the courts may review the actions of the Senate in order to determine whether that body "tried" an impeached official, it is difficult to see how the Senate would be "functioning * * * independently and without assistance or interference."

* * *

The history and contemporary understanding of the impeachment provisions support our reading of the constitutional language. The parties do not offer evidence of a single word in the history of the Constitutional Convention or in contemporary commentary that even alludes to the possibility of judicial review in the context of the impeachment powers. This silence is quite meaningful in light of the several explicit references to the availability of judicial review as a check on the Legislature's power with respect to bills of attainder, *ex post facto* laws, and statutes. See The Federalist No. 78, p. 524 (J. Cooke ed. 1961) ("Limitations * * * can be preserved in practice no other way than through the medium of the courts of justice").

The Framers labored over the question of where the impeachment power should lie. Significantly, in at least two considered scenarios the power was placed with the Federal Judiciary. See 1 Farrand 21–22 (Virginia Plan); id., at 244 (New Jersey Plan). Indeed, Madison and the Committee of Detail proposed that the Supreme Court should have the power to determine impeachments. See 2 id., at 551 (Madison); id., at 178–179, 186 (Committee of Detail). Despite these proposals, the Convention ultimately decided that the Senate would have "the sole Power to Try all Impeachments." Art. I, § 3, cl. 6. According to Alexander Hamilton, the Senate was the "most fit depositary of this important trust" because its members are representatives of the people. See The Federalist No. 65, p. 440 (J. Cooke ed. 1961). The Supreme Court was not the proper body because the Framers "doubted whether the members of that tribunal would, at all times, be endowed with so eminent a portion of fortitude as would be called for in the execution of so difficult a task" or whether the Court "would possess the degree of credit and authority" to carry out its judgment if it conflicted with the accusation brought by the Legislature—the people's representative. See id., at 441. In addition, the Framers believed the Court was too small in number: "The awful discretion, which a court of impeachments must necessarily have, to doom to honor or to infamy the most confidential and the most distinguished characters of the community, forbids the commitment of the trust to a small number of persons." Id., at 441–442.

There are two additional reasons why the Judiciary, and the Supreme Court in particular, were not chosen to have any role in impeachments. First, the Framers recognized that most likely there would be two sets of proceedings for individuals who commit impeachable offenses—the impeachment trial and a separate criminal trial. In fact, the Constitution explicitly provides for two separate proceedings. See Art. I, § 3, cl. 7. The Framers deliberately separated the two forums to avoid raising the specter of bias and to ensure independent judgments:

> "Would it be proper that the persons, who had disposed of his fame and his most valuable rights as a citizen in one trial, should in another trial, for the same offence, be also the disposers of his life and his fortune? Would there not be the greatest reason to apprehend, that error in the first sentence would be the parent of error in the second sentence? That the strong bias of one decision would be apt to overrule the influence of any new lights, which might be brought to vary the complexion of another decision?" The Federalist No. 65, p. 442 (J. Cooke ed. 1961).

Certainly judicial review of the Senate's "trial" would introduce the same risk of bias as would participation in the trial itself.

Second, judicial review would be inconsistent with the Framers' insistence that our system be one of checks and balances. In our constitutional system, impeachment was designed to be the *only* check on the Judicial Branch by the Legislature. On the topic of judicial accountability, Hamilton wrote:

> "The precautions for their responsibility are comprised in the article respecting impeachments. They are liable to be impeached for mal-conduct by the house of representatives, and tried by the senate, and if convicted, may be dismissed from office and disqualified for holding any other. This is the only provision on the point, which is consistent with the necessary independence of the judicial character, and is the only one which we find in our own constitution in respect to our own judges." Id., No. 79, pp. 532–533 (emphasis added).

Judicial involvement in impeachment proceedings, even if only for purposes of judicial review, is counterintuitive because it would eviscerate the "important constitutional check" placed on the Judiciary by the Framers. See id., No. 81, p. 545. Nixon's argument would place final reviewing authority with respect to impeachments in the hands of the same body that the impeachment process is meant to regulate.

Nevertheless, Nixon argues that judicial review is necessary in order to place a check on the Legislature. Nixon fears that if the Senate is given unreviewable authority to interpret the Impeachment Trial Clause, there is a grave risk that the Senate will usurp judicial power. The Framers anticipated this objection and created two constitutional safeguards to keep the Senate in check. The first safeguard is that the whole of the impeachment power is divided between the two legislative bodies, with the House given the right to accuse and the Senate given the right to judge. Id., No. 66, p. 446. This split of authority "avoids the inconvenience of making the same persons both accusers and judges; and guards against the danger of persecution from the prevalency of a factious spirit in either of those branches." The second safeguard is the two-thirds supermajority vote requirement. Hamilton explained that "[a]s the concurrence of two-thirds of the senate will be requisite to a condemnation, the security to innocence, from this additional circumstance, will be as complete as itself can desire." Ibid.

In addition to the textual commitment argument, we are persuaded that the lack of finality and the difficulty of fashioning relief counsel against justiciability. See Baker v. Carr, 369 U.S., at 210. We agree with the Court of Appeals that opening the door of judicial review to the procedures used by the Senate in trying impeachments would "expose the political life of the country to months, or perhaps years, of chaos." This lack of finality would manifest itself most dramatically if the President were impeached. The legitimacy of any successor, and hence his effectiveness, would be impaired severely, not merely while the judicial process was running its course, but during any retrial that a differently constituted Senate might conduct if its first judgment of conviction were invalidated. Equally uncertain is the question of what relief a court may give other than simply setting aside the judgment of conviction. Could it order the reinstatement of a convicted federal judge, or order Congress to create an additional judgeship if the seat had been filled in the interim?

Petitioner finally contends that a holding of nonjusticiability cannot be reconciled with our opinion in Powell v. McCormack, 395 U.S. 486 (1969). The relevant issue in *Powell* was whether courts could review the House of Representatives' conclusion that Powell was "unqualified" to sit as a Member because he had been accused of misappropriating public funds and abusing the process of the New York courts. We stated that the question of justiciability turned on whether the Constitution committed authority to the House to judge its members' qualifications, and if so, the extent of that commitment. Article I, § 5 provides that "Each House shall be the Judge of the Elections, Returns and Qualifications of its own Members." In turn, Art. I, § 2 specifies three requirements for membership in the House: The candidate must be at least 25 years of age, a citizen of the United States for no less than seven years, and an inhabitant of the State he is chosen to represent. We held that, in light of the three requirements specified in the Constitution, the word "qualifications"—of which the House was to be the Judge—was of a precise, limited nature. Id., at 522; see also The Federalist No. 60, p. 409 (J. Cooke ed. 1961) ("The qualifications of the persons who may choose or be chosen, as has been remarked upon another occasion, are defined and fixed in the constitution; and are *unalterable by the legislature.*") (emphasis added) (quoted in *Powell,* supra, 395 U.S., at 539).

Our conclusion in *Powell* was based on the fixed meaning of "[q]ualifications" set forth in Art. I, § 2. The claim by the House that its power to "be the Judge of the Elections, Returns and Qualifications of its own Members" was a textual commitment of unreviewable authority was defeated by the existence of this separate provision specifying the only qualifications which might be imposed for House membership. The decision as to whether a member satisfied these qualifications *was* placed with the House, but the decision as to what these qualifications consisted of was not.

In the case before us, there is no separate provision of the Constitution which could be defeated by allowing the Senate final authority to determine the meaning of the word "try" in the Impeachment Trial Clause. We agree with Nixon that courts possess power to review either legislative or executive action that transgresses identifiable textual limits. As we have made clear, "whether the action of [either the Legislative or Executive Branch] exceeds whatever authority has been committed, is itself a delicate exercise in constitutional interpretation, and is a responsibility of this Court as ultimate interpreter of the Constitution." Baker v. Carr, supra. But we conclude, after exercising that delicate responsibility, that the word "try" in the Impeachment Clause does not provide an identifiable textual limit on the authority which is committed to the Senate.

For the foregoing reasons, the judgment of the Court of Appeals is

Affirmed.

[The concurring opinion of JUSTICE STEVENS and the opinions of JUSTICES WHITE and SOUTER, concurring in the judgment, are omitted.]

Notes

1. Are all aspects of impeachment properly characterized as political questions? Would the political question doctrine bar judicial review of an impeachment case if the Senate chose to "try" a federal official by coin toss? What if an impeached President claimed that the conduct for which he was impeached did not constitute "treason, bribery, or other high crimes and misdemeanors" (as specified in Art. II, § 4)? Is that claim closer to the claim in *Nixon* or the claim in *Powell?* For discussions of the correctness of the *Nixon* decision, see Redish, *Judicial Discipline, Judicial Independence, and the Constitution: A Textual and Structural Analysis,* 72 U.S.C.L.Rev. 873 (1999); Gerhardt, *Rediscovering Nonjusticiability: Judicial Review of Impeachments After* Nixon, 44 Duke L.J. 231 (1994); Brown, *When Political Questions Affect Individual Rights: The Other* Nixon v. United States, 1993 Sup.Ct.Rev. 125.

2. Justice Souter wrote in concurrence that though the *Nixon* case presented a political question, in other impeachment cases, judicial interference "might well be appropriate". 506 U.S. at 254. Is a case-by-case political question analysis distinguishable from review on the merits?

3. Do challenges to the appointment of presidential electors raise a political question? Consider Bush v. Gore, 531 U.S. 98 (2000). In that case, the Florida Supreme Court had interpreted Florida statutory law to require a recount of certain disputed presidential ballots. The United States Supreme Court reversed, holding that the recount violated the Equal Protection Clause. (For a discussion of the appropriate remedy for such a violation, see Chapter Eighteen.) Without mentioning the political question doctrine, Justice Breyer, in dissent, suggested that the Court should not have decided the case, but instead left the resolution of the dispute to Congress:

> The Constitution and federal statutes themselves make clear that restraint is appropriate. They set forth a road map of how to resolve disputes about electors, even after an election as close as this one. That road map foresees resolution of electoral disputes by *state* courts. See 3 U.S.C. § 5 (providing that, where a "State shall have provided, by laws enacted prior to [election day], for its final determination of any controversy or contest concerning the appointment of ... electors ... by *judicial* or other methods," the subsequently chosen electors enter a safe harbor free from congressional challenge). But it nowhere provides for involvement by the United States Supreme Court.
>
> To the contrary, the Twelfth Amendment commits to Congress the authority and responsibility to count electoral votes. A federal statute, the Electoral Count Act, enacted after the close 1876 Hayes–Tilden Presidential election, specifies that, after States have tried to resolve disputes (through "judicial" or other means), Congress is the body primarily authorized to resolve remaining disputes. See Electoral Count Act of 1887, 24 Stat. 373, 3 U.S.C. §§ 5, 6, and 15.
>
> The legislative history of the Act makes clear its intent to commit the power to resolve such disputes to Congress, rather than the courts:
>
> "The two Houses are, by the Constitution, authorized to make the count of electoral votes. They can only count legal votes, and in doing so must determine, from the best evidence to be had, what are legal votes.... The power to determine rests with the two Houses, and there is no other constitutional tribunal." H. Rep. No. 1638, 49th Cong., 1st Sess., 2 (1886) (report submitted by Rep. Caldwell, Select Committee on the Election of President and Vice–President).

The Member of Congress who introduced the Act added:

> "The power to judge of the legality of the votes is a necessary consequent of the power to count. The existence of this power is of absolute necessity to the preservation of the Government. The interests of all the States in their relations to each other in the Federal Union demand that the ultimate tribunal to decide upon the election of President should be a constituent body, in which the States in their federal relationships and the people in their sovereign capacity should be represented." 18 Cong. Rec. 30 (1886).

"Under the Constitution who else could decide? Who is nearer to the State in determining a question of vital importance to the whole union of States than the constituent body upon whom the Constitution has devolved the duty to count the vote?" *Id.*, at 31.

The Act goes on to set out rules for the congressional determination of disputes about those votes. If, for example, a state submits a single slate of electors, Congress must count those votes unless both Houses agree that the votes "have not been . . . regularly given." 3 U.S.C. § 15. If, as occurred in 1876, one or more states submits two sets of electors, then Congress must determine whether a slate has entered the safe harbor of § 5, in which case its votes will have "conclusive" effect. *Ibid.* If, as also occurred in 1876, there is controversy about "which of two or more of such State authorities . . . is the lawful tribunal" authorized to appoint electors, then each House shall determine separately which votes are "supported by the decision of such State so authorized by its law." *Ibid.* If the two Houses of Congress agree, the votes they have approved will be counted. If they disagree, then "the votes of the electors whose appointment shall have been certified by the executive of the State, under the seal thereof, shall be counted." *Ibid.*

Given this detailed, comprehensive scheme for counting electoral votes, there is no reason to believe that federal law either foresees or requires resolution of such a political issue by this Court. Nor, for that matter, is there any reason to that think the Constitution's Framers would have reached a different conclusion. Madison, at least, believed that allowing the judiciary to choose the presidential electors "was out of the question." Madison, July 25, 1787 (reprinted in 5 Elliot's Debates on the Federal Constitution 363 (2d ed. 1876)).

The decision by both the Constitution's Framers and the 1886 Congress to minimize this Court's role in resolving close federal presidential elections is as wise as it is clear. However awkward or difficult it may be for Congress to resolve difficult electoral disputes, Congress, being a political body, expresses the people's will far more accurately than does an unelected Court. And the people's will is what elections are about.

* * *

* * * Those who caution judicial restraint in resolving political disputes have described the quintessential case for that restraint as a case marked, among other things, by the "strangeness of the issue," its "intractability to principled resolution," its "sheer momentousness, . . . which tends to unbalance judicial judgment," and "the inner vulnerability, the self-doubt of an institution which is electorally irresponsible and has no earth to draw strength from." Those characteristics mark this case.

* * * And, above all, in this highly politicized matter, the appearance of a split decision runs the risk of undermining the public's confidence in the Court itself. That confidence is a public treasure. It has been built slowly over many years, some of which were marked by a Civil War and the tragedy of segregation. It is a vitally necessary ingredient of any successful effort to protect basic liberty and, indeed, the rule of law itself. We run no risk of returning to the days when a President (responding to this Court's efforts to protect the Cherokee Indians) might have said, "John Marshall has made his decision; now let him enforce it!" Loth, Chief Justice John Marshall and The Growth of the American Republic 365 (1948). But we do risk a self-inflicted wound—a wound that may harm not just the Court, but the Nation.

I fear that in order to bring this agonizingly long election process to a definitive conclusion, we have not adequately attended to that necessary "check upon our own exercise of power," "our own sense of self-restraint." United States v. Butler, 297 U.S. 1, 79 (1936) (Stone, J., dissenting). Justice Brandeis once said of the Court, "The most important thing we do is not doing." What it does today, the Court should have left undone. I would repair the damage done as best we now can, by permitting the Florida recount to continue under uniform standards.

Of what relevance is the existence of a federal statute? If the Twelfth Amendment commits the judging of electoral counts to Congress, does it matter whether Congress has specified how disputes are to be resolved? Perhaps Justice Breyer is suggesting that the statute and its history simply bolster the conclusion that resolving election disputes is not within the role of the Court. Or perhaps he is suggesting that the Court should be more willing to stay out of politicized disputes if Congress has established an alternative mechanism for resolving them. Which argument is more persuasive?

Compare Justice Breyer's discussion of why the Court should not decide this case with the multi-factor test for identifying political questions, applied by the Court in *Powell* and *Nixon*. Which test works better? Which accords better with the underlying theory of judicial review in a constitutional democracy? How would *Bush v. Gore* come out under the standard test? Why might the Court be eager to decide this particular electoral dispute? For another argument in favor of Justice Breyer's position, see Chemerinsky, Bush v. Gore *Was Not Justiciable*, 76 Notre Dame L.Rev. 1093 (2001).

Is the progression from *Baker* to *Bush* inevitable, as the Court became more willing to control the American electoral process? For one carefully argued affirmative answer (and criticism), see R. Hasen, The Supreme Court and Election Law: Judging Equality from *Baker v. Carr* to *Bush v. Gore* (2003). Another commentator has suggested that *Bush v. Gore* was predictable as the result of a clash between the political question doctrine, which limits courts' authority, and the Court's own view of its "superior competency vis-a-vis Congress and the Executive to decide all constitutional questions." Barkow, *More Supreme Than Court? The Fall of the Political Question Doctrine and the Rise of Judicial Supremacy*, 102 Colum.L.Rev. 237, 242 (2002). Professor Barkow goes on to conclude that "[i]t is hardly surprising that the Court has opted for the course that aggrandizes its own power." Id. See also Tushnet, *Law and Prudence in the Law of Justiciability: The Transformation and Disappearance of the Political Question Doctrine*, 80 N.Car.L.Rev. 1203 (2002); Soifer, *Courting Anarchy*, 82 B.U.L.Rev. 699 (2002).

Chapter 2

CONGRESSIONAL POWER TO CONTROL FEDERAL JURISDICTION

§ 1. CONGRESSIONAL POWER TO REGULATE LOWER FEDERAL COURT JURISDICTION

SHELDON v. SILL

Supreme Court of the United States, 1850.
49 U.S. (8 How.) 441.

This was an appeal from the Circuit Court of the United States for the District of Michigan, sitting in equity.

The appellee was the complainant in the court below. The bill was filed to procure satisfaction of a bond, executed by the appellant, Thomas C. Sheldon, and secured by a mortgage on lands in Michigan, executed by him and Eleanor his wife, the other appellant. The bond and mortgage were dated on the 1st of November, 1838, and were given by the appellants, then, and ever since, citizens of the State of Michigan, to Eurotas P. Hastings, President of the Bank of Michigan, in trust for the President, Directors, and Company of the Bank of Michigan.

The said Hastings was then and ever since has been a citizen of the State of Michigan, and the Bank of Michigan was a body corporate in the same State.

On the 3d day of January, A. D. 1839, Hastings, President of said bank, under the authority and direction of the Board of Directors, "sold, assigned, and transferred, by deed duly executed under the seal of the bank, and under his own seal, the said bond and mortgage, and the moneys secured thereby, and the estate thereby created," to said Sill, the complainant below, who was then and still is a citizen of New York.

* * *

Mr. Justice Grier delivered the opinion of the court.

106

The only question which it will be necessary to notice in this case is, whether the Circuit Court had jurisdiction.   *Issue*

Sill, the complainant below, a citizen of New York, filed his bill in the Circuit Court of the United States for Michigan, against Sheldon, claiming to recover the amount of a bond and mortgage, which had been assigned to him by Hastings, the President of the Bank of Michigan.

Sheldon, in his answer, among other things, pleaded that "the bond and mortgage in controversy, having been originally given by a citizen of Michigan to another citizen of the same State, and the complainant being assignee of them, the Circuit Court had no jurisdiction."   *No Div.*

The eleventh section of the Judiciary Act, which defines the jurisdiction of the Circuit Courts, restrains them from taking "cognizance of any suit to recover the contents of any promissory note or other chose in action, in favor of an assignee, unless a suit might have been prosecuted in such court to recover the contents, if no assignment had been made, except in cases of foreign bills of exchange."

The third article of the Constitution declares that "the judicial power of the United States shall be vested in one Supreme Court, and such inferior courts as the Congress may, from time to time, ordain and establish." The second section of the same article enumerates the cases and controversies of which the judicial power shall have cognizance, and, among others, it specifies "controversies between citizens of different States."

It has been alleged, that this restriction of the Judiciary Act, with regard to assignees of choses in action, is in conflict with this provision of the Constitution, and therefore void.

It must be admitted, that if the Constitution had ordained and established the inferior courts, and distributed to them their respective powers, they could not be restricted or divested by Congress. But as it has made no such distribution, one of two consequences must result,—   *1 & 2 results*
either that each inferior court created by Congress must exercise all the judicial powers not given to the Supreme Court, or that Congress, having the power to establish the courts, must define their respective jurisdictions. The first of these inferences has never been asserted, and could not be defended with any show of reason, and if not, the latter would seem to follow as a necessary consequence. And it would seem to follow, also, that, having a right to prescribe, Congress may withhold from any court of its creation jurisdiction of any of the enumerated controversies.   *Congress defines*
Courts created by statute can have no jurisdiction but such as the statute confers. No one of them can assert a just claim to jurisdiction exclusively conferred on another, or withheld from all.

The Constitution has defined the limits of the judicial power of the United States, but has not prescribed how much of it shall be exercised by the Circuit Court; consequently, the statute which does prescribe the limits of their jurisdiction, cannot be in conflict with the Constitution, unless it confers powers not enumerated therein.   *Const. as ceiling for jurisdiction*

Such has been the doctrine held by this court since its first establishment. To enumerate all the cases in which it has been either directly advanced or tacitly assumed would be tedious and unnecessary.

In the case of Turner v. Bank of North America, 4 Dall. at 10, it was contended, as in this case, that, as it was a controversy between citizens of different States, the Constitution gave the plaintiff a right to sue in the Circuit Court, notwithstanding he was an assignee within the restriction of the eleventh section of the Judiciary Act. But the court said,—"The political truth is, that the disposal of the judicial power (except in a few specified instances) belongs to Congress: and Congress is not bound to enlarge the jurisdiction of the Federal courts to every subject, in every form which the Constitution might warrant." This decision was made in 1799; since that time, the same doctrine has been frequently asserted by this court, as may be seen in McIntire v. Wood, 7 Cranch, 506; Kendall v. United States, 12 Peters, 616; Cary v. Curtis, 3 Howard, 245.

The only remaining inquiry is, whether the complainant in this case is the assignee of a "chose in action," within the meaning of the statute. The term "chose in action" is one of comprehensive import. It includes the infinite variety of contracts, covenants, and promises, which confer on one party a right to recover a personal chattel or a sum of money from another, by action.

* * *

The complainant in this case is the purchaser and assignee of a sum of money, a debt, a chose in action, not of a tract of land. He seeks to recover by this action a debt assigned to him. He is therefore the "assignee of a chose in action," within the letter and spirit of the act of Congress under consideration, and cannot support this action in the Circuit Court of the United States, where his assignor could not.

The judgment of the Circuit Court must therefore be reversed, for want of jurisdiction.

* * *

Notes

1. Consider the history of Article III described in Redish & Woods, *Congressional Power to Control the Jurisdiction of Lower Federal Courts: A Critical Review and a New Synthesis,* 124 U.Pa.L.Rev. 45, 52–55 (1975):

From the beginning of the debates in the Constitutional Convention regarding article III, the framers agreed that at least one national tribunal, a supreme court, would be necessary to exercise the judicial power of the new nation. However, the proposal for the creation of national tribunals inferior to the "one supreme court," met strong opposition among various factions of the Convention.

Several proposals were introduced concerning inferior federal courts. Edmund Randolph of Virginia proposed the mandatory establishment of lower federal courts, as did Charles Pinckney of South Carolina. William Patterson of New Jersey presented a proposal providing for no inferior courts and Alexander Hamilton of New York suggested that Congress be given the power to create such courts for the determination of all matters of general concern. A proposal for the establishment of only lower courts of admiralty was introduced by John Blair of Virginia. The Patterson and Randolph plans were referred to the Committee of the Whole.

The Randolph plan, providing for "one supreme tribunal, and * * * one or more inferior tribunals," was adopted by the Committee of the Whole with little discussion. Many of the delegates, however, remained fervently opposed to federal trial courts, believing that all litigation should be left to the state courts. The day following its passage, John Rutledge of South Carolina moved to reconsider the Randolph plan. In support of his motion he urged that

many wanted all lit in mal cts.

State Tribunals might and ought to be left in all cases to decide in the first instance, the right of appeal to the supreme national tribunal being sufficient to secure the national rights & uniformity of Judgments: that it was * * * creating unnecessary obstacles to their adoption of the new system.

Sherman of Connecticut agreed, emphasizing the great and unnecessary expense in setting up a parallel system of courts.

James Madison objected, arguing that appellate review would inadequately remedy biased trials in state courts. Additionally, he contended that the sheer number of appeals from the state courts to the "supreme bar" would be totally unmanageable: "[I]nferior [federal] tribunals * * * dispersed throughout the Republic with *final* jurisdiction in *many* cases" were needed, he believed, to insure the future of the nation. "An effective Judiciary establishment commensurate to the legislative authority [is] essential. A Government without a proper Executive & Judiciary would be the mere trunk of a body without arms or legs to act or move."

Madisonian compromise

The opponents of such courts believed them to be unnecessary, however, because state trial courts would be available as forums to hear the assertion of federal rights, making the creation of federal trial courts an expensive repetition. Rutledge was of the opinion that the right of appeal from state courts to the Supreme Court was sufficient to protect national interests and that federal trial courts would constitute an "unnecessary encroachment" on state court jurisdiction and state sovereignty. Rutledge's motion for reconsideration and elimination of the clause mandating establishment of lower federal courts carried the Convention, five states to four with two divided.

lower cts unnece.

Madison and James Wilson subsequently offered a compromise solution. While the Randolph plan had mandated Congress to create lower federal courts, Madison and Wilson moved to give Congress the option to create or not create such courts. This distinction caused four states to change their position toward inferior federal courts and the compromise motion carried, eight states to two with only one divided. The Madisonian Compromise had been struck.

The course of events that culminated in this "Great Compromise" has been interpreted by some to mean that not only the very existence of lower courts but also the scope of their jurisdiction was to be in Congress' discretion: "[I]t seems to be a necessary inference from the express decision that the creation of inferior federal courts was to rest in the discretion of Congress that the scope of their jurisdiction, once created, was also to be discretionary."

Arguing from Congress' discretionary power over the creation of the lower federal courts, some commentators have thus maintained that Congress has the authority to grant, withhold, or remove after vestment the jurisdiction of the lower federal courts over particular matters. They argue that if the lower courts need not have been established in the first instance, they may be abolished at any time by Congress and that, since they can be abolished, they can effectively be "abolished" to a lesser extent by removing or denying jurisdiction over particular cases. In other words, the greater power of total abolition logically includes the lesser power of removing certain areas from their jurisdiction.

2. The following argument was made in Rotunda, *Congressional Power to Restrict the Jurisdiction of the Lower Federal Courts and the Problem of School Busing*, 64 Geo.L.J. 839, 842–43 (1976):

The "lesser power" to carve out narrow exceptions to the lower federal courts' jurisdiction is really a greater power. The framers could justifiably leave Congress with the unrestricted discretion to determine whether to create any lower courts, for this power is a limited one; in exercising it, Congress would be forced to balance the advantages of having no lower federal courts with the disadvantages. An independent political check operates in such circumstances to assure that the congressional judgment will likely be a proper one. This independent political check, not judicial review, operates to prevent Congress from abusing its discretion. Congressional enactment of a narrow, nonneutral, interstitial limitation of the lower courts' jurisdiction, however, may achieve what the Congress perceives to be practical benefits without the burdens; the independent political check will not operate effectively, and consequently there is a greater need for judicial review.

The Constitution can safely be read to grant Congress broad power to create or abolish the lower federal courts because practical considerations make it unlikely that Congress would have failed to create some lower courts or would ever attempt to abolish all lower courts. A government in the process of nation-building would find it difficult to rely entirely on state courts to enforce its laws: the government would prefer that its laws be sympathetically interpreted by its own judges, and it would desire the greater likelihood of uniformity of decision that a system of lower federal courts would bring. State courts still would be available for the enforcement of federal laws, but unless Congress provided broad appellate review in the Supreme Court, there would be 50 different and possibly inconsistent resolutions of federal issues.

Is this argument persuasive?

3. Could Congress constitutionally enact a statute prohibiting the lower federal courts from considering any first amendment challenges to

federal legislation? Could it constitutionally prohibit *all* courts from considering such challenges? Consider Hart, *The Power of Congress to Limit the Jurisdiction of Federal Courts: An Exercise in Dialectic*, 66 Harv.L.Rev. 1362, 1372 (1953): "[A] necessary postulate of constitutional government * * * [is] that a court must always be available to pass on claims of constitutional right to judicial process, and to provide such process if the claim is sustained." Do you agree? Why? Could Congress persuasively contend that an exclusion of judicial jurisdiction to consider first amendment challenges to federal legislation does not mean that first amendment rights will go unprotected, since Congress itself can and will consider conceivable First Amendment problems before enacting the legislation in question? In answering, consider the relevance of the special protections of federal judicial independence provided for in Article III, section 1. Federal judges appointed under that provision have life tenure during good behavior and their salaries cannot be reduced. "While controversy existed at the time of the Constitution's framing over whether a system of lower courts should be created, there was apparently no significant disagreement that if inferior federal courts were created they should be independent of the other burdens of the federal government. The framers sought to protect this independence by the constitutional guarantee of salary and tenure." Redish, *Federal Judicial Independence: Constitutional and Political Perspectives*, 46 Mercer L.Rev. 697, 700 (1995). What function do these independence protections serve? Reconsider Marbury v. Madison [supra p. 2], and the role of judicial independence in performing the judicial review function.

4. In light of the logic of the Court in *Sheldon v. Sill*, could Congress constitutionally prohibit all African–Americans and Jews from gaining access to federal court?

5. The view expressed in *Sheldon v. Sill* about the power of Congress to limit lower federal court jurisdiction is widely accepted law today. See, e.g., International Science & Technology Institute, Inc. v. Inacom Communications, Inc., 106 F.3d 1146 (4th Cir.1997). But see Young, *A Critical Reassessment of the Case Law Bearing on Congress's Power to Restrict the Jurisdiction of the Lower Federal Courts*, 54 Md.L.Rev. 132 (1995) (arguing that "the relevant Supreme Court cases offer less support for complete congressional power than courts and commentators have assumed."). Nevertheless, several theories have been proposed which question Congress' power in the area. The first was that of Justice Story, who construed the words, "shall be vested" in Article III, section 1 of the Constitution to mean that the entire federal judicial power (as described in Article III, section 2) had to be vested in *some* federal court. See Martin v. Hunter's Lessee, 14 U.S. (1 Wheat.) 304 (1816). He emphasized the extremely limited nature of the original jurisdiction of the Supreme Court [see Article III, section 2], and concluded that, in light of Article III's "shall be vested" directive, "Congress are bound to create some inferior courts, in which to vest all that jurisdiction which, under the constitution, is *exclusively* vested in the United States, and of which the supreme court cannot take original cognizance." Id. at 331. For "[i]f congress may lawfully omit to establish inferior courts, it might follow, that in some of the enumerated cases the judicial power could nowhere exist * * * It would seem, therefore, to follow, that congress are bound to create some inferior courts, in which to vest all that jurisdiction which, under the

constitution, is *exclusively* vested in the United States, and of which the supreme court cannot take original cognizance." Id. at 330–331. See also J. Story, Commentaries on the Constitution of the United States 1584–90 (1833).

With rare exception (see Eisentrager v. Forrestal, 174 F.2d 961 (D.C.Cir. 1949), *reversed on other grounds sub nom.* Johnson v. Eisentrager, 339 U.S. 763 (1950)), Justice Story's theory has not received favorable reaction in the courts. What, if anything, is wrong with his logic? In answering, consider carefully the excerpt from Redish & Woods, supra. Does Justice Story take into account the history described there in fashioning his theory?

Professor Michael Collins makes a historical argument in support of parts of Story's theory. Collins, *Article III Cases, State Court Duties, and the Madisonian Compromise*, 1995 Wisc.L.Rev. 39. Professor Collins suggests that the framers assumed that state courts would be constitutionally disabled from adjudicating certain federal issues, and that Congress was required to create inferior federal courts to hear those cases. He explains the Madisonian "compromise"—which, as he notes, did not receive much attention at the time—as a compromise between those who wanted separate federal courts and those who wanted Congress to constitute state courts as inferior federal courts. He also suggests that the "compromise" did more than apparently make the establishment of lower courts discretionary: it also clarified that *Congress* would be authorized to appoint lower federal tribunals, which had not been clear under the original, mandatory language. That clarification, Professor Collins suggests, may have made the existence of lower federal courts more palatable to those who voted against the original mandatory language.

For the view that "Story's argument in *Martin* deserves to be taken very seriously indeed," see Amar, *A Neo–Federalist View of Article III: Separating the Two Tiers of Federal Jurisdiction*, 65 B.U.L.Rev. 205, 272 (1985).

6.   Another theory rejecting Congress' unlimited power to limit lower federal court jurisdiction appears in Eisenberg, *Congressional Authority to Restrict Lower Federal Court Jurisdiction*, 83 Yale L.J. 498 (1974). Professor Eisenberg accepts the traditional historical analysis of Congress' power under Article III, but suggests that

> [i]f, because of changing circumstances, the framers' aspirations for the national judiciary cannot be fulfilled today without lower federal courts, then there is a conflict between the * * * view of the decision to leave creation of lower courts to Congress' whim and the constitutional definition of the judiciary's role. Id. at 504.

According to Eisenberg, the framers envisioned two roles for the federal judiciary: to provide a check on the other branches of the federal government, and to achieve uniformity of decisions in questions of national concern. Originally, these functions could be performed by the Supreme Court, and the framers therefore did not find a need to require the creation of lower federal courts. However, because of the enormous increase in the judiciary's workload, Eisenberg states, the Supreme Court today cannot perform those functions. Therefore, he concludes, Congress cannot abolish the lower courts.

However, he would allow Congress to enact neutral, or "housekeeping" statutes, designed to avoid case overloads. Id. at 516.

How compelling is Professor Eisenberg's reasoning? Is he doing something more than merely providing a "contemporary" interpretation of a constitutional provision, as is commonly done with such provisions as the due process or commerce clauses? In answering examine the language of Article III closely. Does it lend itself to Professor Eisenberg's interpretation?

7. **Professor Hart's "Dialogue".** The article that to date has probably had the greatest scholarly impact on the issue of congressional power to control federal jurisdiction is Professor Henry Hart's *The Power of Congress to Limit the Jurisdiction of Federal Courts: An Exercise in Dialectic*, 66 Harv.L.Rev. 1362 (1953), commonly referred to as the "Dialogue" because the entire article takes the form of an exchange between two scholars, Q. and A. Questions by the inquisitive but somewhat naive Q. are answered in varying degrees of detail and clarity by A.

While the article is quite extensive in both scope and length, its most important themes are captured in several of the exchanges between Q. and A. at various points. It begins with an exchange concerning congressional power over inferior federal court jurisdiction:

Q. Does the Constitution give people any right to proceed or be proceeded against, in the first instance, in a federal rather than a state court?

A. It's hard to see how the answer can be anything but no in view of cases like Sheldon v. Sill and Lauf v. E. G. Shinner & Co., and in view of the language and history of the Constitution itself. Congress seems to have plenary power to limit federal jurisdiction when the consequence is merely to force proceedings to be brought, if at all, in a state court.

The following exchange then takes place:

Q. But suppose the state court disclaims any jurisdiction?

A. If federal rights are involved, perhaps the state courts are under a constitutional obligation to vindicate them.

Id. at 1363–64.

Later A. asserts that "a necessary postulate of constitutional government [is] that a court must always be available to pass on claims of constitutional right to judicial process, and to provide such process if the claim is sustained." Id. at 1372. In light of A.'s opening response, however, he apparently doesn't believe that that court has to be federal. But A. notes "that the difficulty involved in asserting any judicial control in the face of a total denial of jurisdiction doesn't exist if Congress gives jurisdiction but puts strings on it." Id. He thus draws a distinction between would-be federal court plaintiffs where Congress has *denied* federal court jurisdiction and federal court defendants where Congress has granted the federal courts enforcement powers but limited their authority to inquire into the legitimacy of the laws they are enforcing.

In the middle portion of the Dialogue, Hart turns his attention to what Q. refers to as "the sixty-four dollar question": "What happens if the Government is hurting people and not simply refusing to help them?

Suppose Congress authorizes a program of direct action by Government officials against private persons or private property. Suppose, further, that it not only dispenses with judicial enforcement but either limits the jurisdiction of the federal courts to inquire into what the officials do or denies it altogether." A. responds that

> the answer to this one is easy, isn't it—so long as there is any applicable grant of general jurisdiction?
>
> Obviously, the answer is that the validity of the jurisdictional limitation depends on the validity of the program itself, or the particular part of it in question.
>
> If the court finds that what is being done is invalid, its duty is simply to declare the jurisdictional limitation invalid also, and then proceed under the general grant of jurisdiction. Id. at 1386, 1387.

The general grant of jurisdiction that A. mentions refers to statutes conferring jurisdiction on the federal courts in broad classes of cases, as opposed to grants of jurisdiction for cases arising under specific federal statutes. Examples are the general federal question statute, 28 U.S.C.A. § 1331, giving the federal courts jurisdiction of cases arising "under the Constitution, laws, or treaties of the United States" [see Chapter Thirteen], and the federal habeas corpus provision, 28 U.S.C.A. §§ 2254, 2255 [see Chapter Twelve].

However, at the close of the Dialogue, when Q. presses A. for an answer to the question, what happens if Congress repeals those general grants of jurisdiction, A. responds:

> I've given all the important answers to that question, haven't I?

* * *

> The state courts. In the scheme of the Constitution, they are the primary guarantors of constitutional rights, and in many cases they may be the ultimate ones. Id. at 1401.
>
> Though A. acknowledges that Congress has the power to regulate state court jurisdiction in federal matters, he asserts that "Congress can't do it unconstitutionally. The state courts always have a general jurisdiction to fall back on. And the Supremacy Clause binds them to exercise that jurisdiction in accordance with the Constitution." Id. at 1401.

Consider the following questions about Professor Hart's thesis:

a. If, as Hart suggests at both the outset and closing of his article, state courts are fully competent to protect federal constitutional rights against invasion by Congress or federal officers, what is the logic behind the conclusion in the middle portion of his article that the validity of a limit on *federal* court jurisdiction (note not on *state* jurisdiction) depends on the validity of the substantive program under attack? What do you suppose is the source of a federal court's authority to disregard an express limitation on its jurisdiction? Is it the Constitution? How could it be, as long as state courts remain open? Is it congressional intent? How could it be, given that Congress has expressly indicated its desire that the federal court *not* exercise jurisdiction?

b.   Why do you suppose Hart believes the existence of a general grant of jurisdiction is a prerequisite to the power of a federal court to review legislation, despite the presence of an express congressional limitation on its power to engage in such review? Assuming he is correct in believing he needs such a general grant, is he correct in thinking he has one, when Congress has imposed a specific limit on federal court jurisdiction? Consider Redish & Woods, supra at 65: "When Congress limits lower federal court jurisdiction over a particular matter, it necessarily is suspending all available general grants of jurisdiction with respect to that particular matter. In other words, the so-called, 'general' grant of jurisdiction is no longer 'general.' It has, in effect, been amended by subsequent legislation (that is, by the limitation in question) so as to be 'general' for all cases *except* the type described in the limitation itself. This must be true, or the limitation Congress has imposed is no limitation at all."

8.   **Professor Sager's Thesis.** Another important contribution to the debate is Sager, *The Supreme Court 1980 Term, Foreword: Constitutional Limitations on Congress' Authority to Regulate the Jurisdiction of the Federal Courts*, 95 Harv.L.Rev. 17 (1981). Professor Sager basically asserts two postulates: (1) in light of Article III's requirement that judges of Article III courts retain protections of salary and tenure, Congress must leave at least one Article III court (*either* the Supreme Court *or* a lower federal court) available to review assertions of federal constitutional right, and (2) Congress may not constitutionally limit lower federal court or Supreme Court jurisdiction selectively (i.e. remove jurisdiction to hear specific substantive issues or a substantive category of cases, such as those arising under the first amendment).

Consider Sager's first postulate. Does the language of Article III's salary and tenure provision support Sager's conclusion? If so, can it logically be limited in its application to cases involving the assertion of a federal constitutional right, as Sager suggests, rather than applying across the board to *any* issue of federal law? In further support of his conclusion, Sager cites "the firm commitment to federal judicial supervision of the states reflected in the history and logic of the Constitution." Id. at 45. He notes the framers' concern that the states might attempt to disrupt federal control, and therefore concluded that the federal judiciary should be available to assure federal supremacy. Does this fact support Sager's conclusion that Congress may not choose to entrust state courts with the final say as to the meaning of federal law, even if Congress so desires? Also, does this fact support Sager's conclusion that the requirement of an Article III court applies only in cases asserting a federal constitutional right, rather than in all cases involving an issue of federal law?

In support of his second postulate, Sager asserts that Congress cannot employ its power to regulate federal court jurisdiction in a manner that will reach an unconstitutional result. He further argues:

> If Congress enacts a selective jurisdictional limitation for cases that concern state conduct, it will be issuing an open, unambiguous invitation to state and local officials to engage in conduct that the Supreme Court has explicitly held unconstitutional * * * In effect, Congress would be painting a target on constitutionally protected rights.

> If, on the other hand, Congress removes slices of federal jurisdiction in order to insulate *federal* conduct from disfavored constitutional challenges, its role in the attack on judicially recognized rights will have changed from accessory to perpetrator. Congress will be insulating its own unconstitutional conduct, not merely "encouraging" others'. Id. at 69.

Do you agree that if Congress selectively limits federal court jurisdiction only in cases involving a particular constitutional right, Congress is necessarily impinging upon or violating that right? Reconsider the discussion of the Madisonian Compromise and of Professor Hart's Dialogue. What about the state courts?

For a critical discussion of Sager's theory, see Redish, *Constitutional Limitations on Congressional Power to Control Federal Jurisdiction: A Reaction to Professor Sager*, 77 Nw.U.L.Rev. 143, 151 (1982). There it is argued as to Sager's first postulate:

> Surely the framers were aware, when they inserted the salary and tenure provision, of the broad power which they were vesting in Congress to regulate federal jurisdiction. Therefore, if there exists any way in which the salary and tenure provision may be reconciled with the undisputed existence of this broad congressional discretion, such an interpretation must be adopted.

> * * *

> [T]he salary and tenure provision means only that *if and when* Congress employs judges of the federal courts as interpreters and enforcers of federal law, it may not interfere with their independence.

> This reading of the salary and tenure provision is consistent with a traditional separation-of-powers analysis of article III. * * * The final balance struck is a form of *quid pro quo*: If Congress desires the stamp of legitimacy which article III courts provide, it cannot simultaneously undermine that legitimacy by impeding the independence of those courts.

> None of this, however, requires that for all assertions of constitutional right an article III federal court must be available.

For the expression of another criticism of Sager's salary-and-tenure protection theory, see Gunther, *Congressional Power to Curtail Federal Court Jurisdiction: An Opinionated Guide to the Ongoing Debate*, 36 Stan. L.Rev. 895, 915 (1984). See also Berger, *Inculcation of Judicial Usurpation: A Comment on Lawrence Sager's Court Stripping Polemic*, 44 Ohio. St.L.J. 611 (1983).

On the general issue of congressional power to control federal jurisdiction, Professor Gunther states:

> [I]n this area, as in others, it is useful—and often difficult—to bear in mind the distinction between constitutionality and wisdom. A good many commentators (including myself) take a rather broad view of congressional power over the jurisdiction of federal courts in terms of sheer legal authority. Very few (and I am not one of those) support jurisdiction-stripping measures as a matter of desirability and effective-

ness. The oft-heard admonition about the distinction between constitutionality and wisdom bears special emphasis in this context, for some of the scholarly commentary (and many of the comments in the media and in the political arena) tend to obscure the distinction; too often perceptions of what the Constitution authorizes tend to be confused with what sound constitutional statesmanship admonishes. 36 Stan.L.Rev. at 898.

9. The history of the drafting of Article III was reexamined in Clinton, *A Mandatory View of Federal Court Jurisdiction: A Guided Quest for the Original Understanding of Article III,* 132 U.Pa.L.Rev. 741 (1984). The conclusion of Professor Clinton's historical analysis is "that the framers, by providing that '[t]he judicial Power of the United States, *shall be vested* in one supreme Court and in such inferior Courts as the Congress may from time to time ordain and establish,' intended to mandate that Congress allocate to the federal judiciary as a whole each and every type of case or controversy defined as part of the judicial power of the United States by section 2, clause 1 of Article III, excluding, possibly, only those cases that Congress deemed to be so trivial that they would pose an unnecessary burden on both the federal judiciary and on the parties forced to litigate in federal court." Id. at 749–50. See also Clinton, *A Mandatory View of Federal Court Jurisdiction: Early Implementation of and Departures from the Constitutional Plan,* 86 Colum.L.Rev. 1515 (1986).

For an argument that "reliance on the Framers' intent to resolve issues of federal courts law is misguided" and that "reliance on an originalist approach to interpreting Article III unnecessarily limits the constitutional debate," see Wells & Larson, *Original Intent and Article III,* 70 Tul.L.Rev. 75 (1995).

10. One commentator has suggested the following interpretation of Article III's approach to federal court jurisdiction: "[T]he judicial power of the United States must, as an absolute minimum, comprehend the subject matter jurisdiction to decide finally all cases involving federal questions, admiralty, or public ambassadors. * * * [T]he judicial power may—but need not—extend to cases in the six other, party-defined, jurisdictional categories." Amar, *A Neo–Federalist View of Article III: Separating the Two Tiers of Federal Jurisdiction,* 65 B.U.L.Rev. 205, 229 (1985). Professor Amar supports this dichotomy by an examination of the text of Article III, section 2:

> Nine specific—and overlapping—categories of cases are spelled out in the section 2 menu, but these categories are not all of equal importance. The judicial power must extend to "all" cases in the first three categories, not so with the final six enumerated categories, where the word "all" is nowhere to be found. The implication of the text, while perhaps not unambiguous, is strong: although the judicial power must extend to all cases in the first three categories, it may, but need not, extend to all cases in the last six. The choice concerning the precise scope of federal jurisdiction in the latter set of cases seems to be given to Congress * * *. Id. at 240.

Professor Amar does not suggest that under his construction of Article III, his dichotomy necessarily limits Congress' power to control *lower* federal court jurisdiction. Rather, he contends that the power to adjudicate cases falling within the first category of his dichotomy must be retained by *some* Article III court—either a lower court or the Supreme Court. He reaches this conclusion, despite Article III's explicit extension of power to Congress to make exceptions to the Supreme Court's appellate jurisdiction [discussed in detail, infra at pp. 159–70] and explicit reference to Congress' power to choose not to create lower federal courts.

Is Professor Amar engaging in understatement when he concedes that the text is "perhaps not unambiguous" in support of his suggested dichotomy in Article III categories of cases for purposes of congressional control of federal jurisdiction? Recall the generally accepted view of the framers' compromise, resulting in the drafting of Article III. Recall also the language of Article III, section 1, stating that there shall be such lower federal courts "as the Congress may from time to time ordain and establish." Is there any basis in either that history or that language to support the dichotomy urged by Professor Amar? If the framers had, in fact, intended such a dichotomy, would it have made sense for them to do so in so cryptic and indirect a manner as prefacing only certain categories of cases described in section 2 with the word "all," while leaving the language of section 1 concerning Congress' power to control federal court jurisdiction totally unlimited? Is it reasonable to suppose that the framers were such poor draftsmen? Is it reasonable to accept Professor Amar's construction of the framers' intent, when there exists no evidence in all of the framers' debates on congressional power over federal court jurisdiction, as extensive as they were, to support his suggested interpretation?

Professor Amar expounded further on his thesis in Amar, *The Two–Tiered Structure of the Judiciary Act of 1789,* 138 U.Pa.L.Rev. 1499 (1990). See also Meltzer, *The History and Structure of Article III,* 138 U.Pa.L.Rev. 1569 (1990), and Casto, *An Orthodox View of the Two–Tiered Analysis of Congressional Control Over Federal Jurisdiction,* 7 Const.Comm. 89 (1990). Consider the following criticism of Amar's theory:

> We can see how far Professor Amar's "two-tier" thesis departs from article III's text, viewed as a whole, by imagining what would have happened had Congress chosen to exercise its article III authority— conceded by Professor Amar—not to create lower federal courts. If no lower federal courts existed, and Congress at some point chose to exercise its authority under the exceptions clause to take cases within Amar's first tier out of the Supreme Court's appellate jurisdiction, Professor Amar's thesis breaks down.

Redish, *Text, Structure, and Common Sense in the Interpretation of Article III,* 138 U.Pa.L.Rev. 1633, 1637–38 (1990). For the view that Amar's theory suffers from a "serious methodological difficulty," see Harrison, *The Power of Congress to Limit the Jurisdiction of Federal Courts and the Text of Article III,* 64 U.Chi.L.Rev. 203 (1997). For a defense of Amar's theory, see Pushaw, *Congressional Power Over Federal Court Jurisdiction: A Defense of the Neo–Federalist Interpretation of Article III,* 1997 B.Y.U. L. Rev. 847.

Professor Michael Collins argues that "the debates over the 1789 Judiciary Act reveal a widely voiced understanding that state courts were constitutionally disabled from hearing certain Article III matters in the first instance—such as federal criminal prosecutions and various admiralty matters—and that Congress could not empower state courts to hear them." Collins, *The Federal Courts, The First Congress, and the Non–Settlement of 1789*, 91 Va.L.Rev. 1515, 1515–16 (2005). Is there anything in the body of the Constitution that inherently precludes the state courts from adjudicating *any* federal case? Examine the Supremacy Clause, Article VI, clause 2. If Congress enacted a substantive federal criminal statute and expressly required the state courts to adjudicate suits arising under that law, could the state courts constitutionally refuse to adjudicate those suits? If the answer is no because of their obligations under the Supremacy Clause, then how could it ever be unconstitutional for state courts to adjudicate those federal suits? What if the first Congress chose *not* to create lower federal courts in the first place? Under Professor Collins's theory, would it necessarily follow that *no court* could adjudicate federal crimes or admiralty actions? Is that a tenable conclusion? On the general issue, see Barham, Note, *Congress Gave and Congress Hath Taken Away: Jurisdiction Withdrawal and the Constitution*, 62 Wash. & Lee L.Rev. 1139 (2005).

11.   Professor Barry Friedman has developed a theory "in which the contours of federal jurisdiction are resolved as the result of an interactive process between Congress and the Court on the appropriate uses and bounds of the federal judicial power." Friedman, *A Different Dialogue: The Supreme Court, Congress and Federal Jurisdiction*, 85 Nw.U.L.Rev. 1, 2–3 (1990). He believes that this "dialogue approach" fosters a more "sensible system of separation of powers" than the traditional "congressional control" model, because "[i]t is hard to accept a model of federal jurisdiction in which the judiciary serves docilely at the whim of the majoritarian branches, enforcing rights when those branches wish, but otherwise not at all. Acceptance of this model requires more faith in the political branches than is warranted by the facts or was envisioned by the Framers." Id. at 60.

Friedman's approach is criticized in Amar, Taking Article III Seriously: A Reply to Professor Friedman, 85 Nw.U.L.Rev. 442 (1991); Tushnet, *The Law, Politics, and Theory of Federal Courts: A Comment*, 85 Nw.U.L.Rev. 454 (1991); and Wells, *Congress's Paramount Role in Setting the Scope of Federal Jurisdiction*, 85 Nw.U.L.Rev. 465 (1991). Are Professor Friedman's concerns about the traditional view of congressional power warranted? What about limits derived from due process? What about the state courts? In answering these questions, consider the relevance of the three cases that follow.

12.   For the defense of "a comprehensive interpretation of Article III that reaffirms the traditional view" of broad congressional power to regulate federal court jurisdiction, see Velasso, *Congressional Control Over Federal Court Jurisdiction: A Defense of the Traditional View*, 46 Catholic L.Rev. 671 (1997). See also Harrison, *The Power of Congress to Limit the Jurisdiction of Federal Courts and the Text of Article III*, 64 U.Chi.L.Rev. 203 (1997), defending "the traditional view that Congress's authority is substantial."

LOCKERTY v. PHILLIPS

Supreme Court of the United States, 1943.
319 U.S. 182.

MR. CHIEF JUSTICE STONE delivered the opinion of the Court.

The question for our decision is whether the jurisdiction of the district court below to enjoin the enforcement of price regulations prescribed by the Administrator under the Emergency Price Control Act of 1942, 56 Stat. 23, was validly withdrawn by § 204(d) of the Act. Appellants brought this suit in the district court for the District of New Jersey for an injunction restraining appellee, the United States Attorney for that district, from the prosecution of pending and prospective criminal proceedings against appellants for violation of §§ 4(a) and 205 (b) of the Act, and of Maximum Price Regulation No. 169. In view of the provisions of § 204(d) of the Act, the district court of three judges, 28 U.S.C. § 380a, dismissed the suit for want of jurisdiction to entertain it.

The amended bill of complaint alleges that appellants are established merchants owning valuable wholesale meat businesses, in the course of which they purchase meat from packers and sell it at wholesale to retail dealers; that Maximum Price Regulation No. 169, promulgated by the Price Administrator under the purported authority of § 2(a) of the Act, as originally issued and as revised, fixed maximum wholesale prices for specified cuts of beef; that in fixing such prices the Administrator had failed to give due consideration to the various factors affecting the cost of production and distribution of meat in the industry as a whole; that the Administrator had failed to fix or regulate the price of livestock; that the conditions in the industry—including the quantity of meat available to packers for distribution to wholesalers, the packers' expectation of profit and the effect of these conditions upon the prices of meat sold by packers to wholesalers—are such that appellants are and will be unable to obtain a supply of meat from packers which they can resell to retail dealers within the prices fixed by Regulation No. 169; that enforcement of the Regulation will preclude appellants' continuance in business as meat wholesalers; that the Act as thus applied to appellants is a denial of due process in violation of the Fifth Amendment of the Constitution, and involves an unconstitutional delegation of legislative power to the Administrator; that appellee threatens to prosecute appellants for each sale of meat at a price greater than that fixed by the Regulation, and to subject them to the fine and imprisonment prescribed by §§ 4 and 205(b) of the Act for violations of the Act or of price regulations prescribed by the Administrator under the Act; and that such enforcement by repeated prosecutions of appellants will irreparably injure them in their business and property.

Section 203(a) sets up a procedure whereby any person subject to any provision of any regulation, order or price schedule promulgated under the Act may within sixty days "file a protest specifically setting forth objections to any such provision and affidavits or other written evidence in support of such objections." He may also protest later on grounds arising after the expiration of the original sixty days. The subsection directs that within a specified time "the Administrator shall either grant or deny such protest in whole or in part, notice such protest for hearing, or provide an opportunity to present further evidence in connection therewith. In the event that the Administrator denies any such protest in whole or in part, he shall inform the protestant of the grounds upon which such decision is based, and of any economic data and other facts of which the Administrator has taken official notice."

By § 204(a), "Any person who is aggrieved by the denial or partial denial of his protest may, within thirty days after such denial, file a complaint with the Emergency Court of Appeals [consisting of three Federal District or Circuit Judges] created pursuant to subsection (c), specifying his objections and praying that the regulation, order, or price schedule protested be enjoined or set aside in whole or in part." Subsection (b) provides that no regulation, order, or price schedule, shall be enjoined "unless the complainant establishes to the satisfaction of the court that the regulation, order, or price schedule is not in accordance with law, or is arbitrary or capricious." Under subsections (b) and (d), decisions of the Emergency Court may, by writ of certiorari, be brought for review to the Supreme Court, which is required to advance the cause on its docket and to expedite the disposition of it.

Although by following the procedure prescribed by these provisions of the Act appellants could have raised and obtained review of the questions presented by their bill of complaint, they did not protest the price regulation which they challenge and they took no proceedings for review of it by the Emergency Court. * * *

* * * Section 204(d) declares: "The Emergency Court of Appeals, and the Supreme Court upon review of judgments and orders of the Emergency Court of Appeals, shall have exclusive jurisdiction to determine the validity of any regulation or order issued under section 2, of any price schedule effective in accordance with the provisions of section 206, and of any provision of any such regulation, order, or price schedule. Except as provided in this section, no court, Federal, State, or Territorial, shall have jurisdiction or power to consider the validity of any such regulation, order, or price schedule, or to stay, restrain, enjoin, or set aside, in whole or in part, any provision of this Act authorizing the issuance of such regulations or orders, or making effective any such price schedule, or any provision of any such regulation, order, or price schedule, or to restrain or enjoin the enforcement of any such provision."

By this statute Congress has seen fit to confer on the Emergency Court (and on the Supreme Court upon review of decisions of the Emergency Court) equity jurisdiction to restrain the enforcement of price orders under the Emergency Price Control Act. At the same time it has withdrawn that jurisdiction from every other federal and state court. There is nothing in the Constitution which requires Congress to confer equity jurisdiction on any particular inferior federal court. All federal courts, other than the Supreme Court, derive their jurisdiction wholly from the exercise of the authority to "ordain and establish" inferior courts, conferred on Congress by Article III, § 1, of the Constitution. Article III left Congress free to establish inferior federal courts or not as it thought appropriate. It could have declined to create any such courts, leaving suitors to the remedies afforded by state courts, with such appellate review by this Court as Congress might prescribe. * * * The Congressional power to ordain and establish inferior courts includes the power "of investing them with jurisdiction either limited, concurrent, or exclusive, and of withholding jurisdiction from them in the exact degrees and character which to Congress may seem proper for the public good." Cary v. Curtis, 3 How. 236, 245; Lauf v. E. G. Shinner & Co., 303 U.S. 323, 330 * * *. In the light of the explicit language of the Constitution and our decisions, it is plain that Congress has power to provide that the equity jurisdiction to restrain enforcement of the Act, or of regulations promulgated under it, be restricted to the Emergency Court, and, upon review of its decisions, to this Court. Nor can we doubt the authority of Congress to require that a plaintiff seeking such equitable relief resort to the Emergency Court only after pursuing the prescribed administrative procedure.

Appellants argue that the command of § 204(d) that "no court, Federal, State, or Territorial, shall have jurisdiction or power to ... restrain, enjoin, or set aside ... any provision of this Act" extends beyond the mere denial of equitable relief by way of injunction, and withholds from all courts authority to pass upon the constitutionality of any provision of the Act or of any order or regulation under it. They insist that the phrase "set aside" is to be read broadly, as meaning that no court can declare unconstitutional any such provision, and that consequently the effect of the statute is to deny to those aggrieved, by statute or regulation, their day in court to challenge its constitutionality. But the statute expressly excepts from this command those remedies afforded by § 204, including that of subsection (b), which gives to complainants a right to an injunction whenever they establish to the satisfaction of the Emergency Court that the regulation, order, or price schedule is "not in accordance with law, or is arbitrary or capricious." A construction of the statute which would deny all opportunity for judicial determination of an asserted constitutional right is not to be favored. The present Act has at least saved to the Emergency Court, and, upon review of its decisions, to this Court, authority to determine whether any regulation, order, or price schedule promulgated under the Act is "not in accordance with law, or is arbitrary or capricious." We think it plain that orders and regulations involving an unconstitutional application of the statute are "not in accordance with law" within the meaning of this clause, and that the constitutional validity of the Act, and of orders and regulations under it, may be determined upon the prescribed review in the Emergency Court.

Appellants also contend that the review in the Emergency Court is inadequate to protect their constitutional rights, and that § 204 is therefore unconstitutional, because § 204 (c) prohibits all interlocutory relief by that court. We need not pass upon the constitutionality of this restriction. For in any event, the separability clause of § 303 of the Act would require us to give effect to the other provisions of § 204, including that withholding from the district courts authority to enjoin enforcement of the Act—a provision which as we have seen is subject to no unconstitutional infirmity.

Since appellants seek only an injunction which the district court is without authority to give, their bill of complaint was rightly dismissed. We have no occasion to determine now whether, or to what extent, appellants may challenge the constitutionality of the Act or the Regulation in courts other than the Emergency Court, either by way of defense to a criminal prosecution or in a civil suit brought for some other purpose than to restrain enforcement of the Act or regulations issued under it.

[handwritten margin note: Issue left unanswered]

Notes

[handwritten note: took away jurisi. from every ct. but 1 to hear particular challenge]

[handwritten note: took away jurisdiction created by assignment / diversity]

[handwritten check mark]

1. How does the congressional restriction on federal court jurisdiction involved in *Lockerty* differ from that involved in Sheldon v. Sill? Should this distinction have made a difference? *[handwritten: No]*

2. After *Lockerty* was decided, if you were the lawyer for someone in the plaintiff's position, where would you attempt to challenge the constitutionality of the absence of interlocutory relief? *[handwritten: ALJ]*

3. Would the case have been decided differently if Congress had limited federal court jurisdiction the way it did in the Emergency Price Control Act, but had not created the Emergency Court of Appeals? *[handwritten: No sup. ct. couldt hear challenge]* *[handwritten: Sep. of powers / due proc. problem]*

YAKUS v. UNITED STATES

Supreme Court of the United States, 1944.
321 U.S. 414.

Opinion of the Court by Mr. Chief Justice Stone, announced by Mr. Justice Roberts.

* * *

Petitioners in both of these cases were tried and convicted by the District Court for Massachusetts upon several counts of indictments charging violation of §§ 4(a) and 205(b) of the [Emergency Price Control] Act by the willful sale of wholesale cuts of beef at prices above the maximum prices prescribed by §§ 1364.451–1364.455 of Revised Maximum Price Regulation No. 169, 7 Fed.Reg. 10381 *et seq.* Petitioners have not availed themselves of the procedure set up by §§ 203 and 204 by which any person subject to a maximum price regulation may test its validity by protest to and hearing before the Administrator, whose determination may be reviewed on complaint to the Emergency Court of Appeals and by this Court on certiorari, see Lockerty v. Phillips, 319

U.S. 182. When the indictments were found the 60 days' period allowed by the statute for filing protests had expired.

In the course of the trial the District Court overruled or denied offers of proof, motions and requests for rulings, raising various questions as to the validity of the Act and Regulation, including those presented by the petitions for certiorari. In particular petitioners offered evidence, which the District Court excluded as irrelevant, for the purpose of showing that the Regulation did not conform to the standards prescribed by the Act and that it deprived petitioners of property without the due process of law guaranteed by the Fifth Amendment. They specifically raised the question reserved in Lockerty v. Phillips, supra, whether the validity of a regulation may be challenged in defense of a prosecution for its violation although it had not been tested by the prescribed administrative procedure and complaint to the Emergency Court of Appeals. The District Court convicted petitioners upon verdicts of guilty. The Circuit Court of Appeals for the First Circuit affirmed, and we granted certiorari, * * *.

* * *

We consider * * * the question whether the procedure which Congress has established for determining the validity of the Administrator's regulations is exclusive so as to preclude the defense of invalidity of the Regulation in this criminal prosecution for its violation under §§ 4(a) and 205(b). * * *

* * *

In Lockerty v. Phillips, supra, we held that [the Act's] provisions conferred on the Emergency Court of Appeals, subject to review by this Court, exclusive equity jurisdiction to restrain enforcement of price regulations of the Administrator and that they withdrew such jurisdiction from all other courts. This was accomplished by the exercise of the constitutional power of Congress to prescribe the jurisdiction of inferior federal courts, and the jurisdiction of all state courts to determine federal questions, and to vest that jurisdiction in a single court, the Emergency Court of Appeals.

The considerations which led us to that conclusion with respect to the equity jurisdiction of the district court, lead to the like conclusion as to its power to consider the validity of a price regulation as a defense to a criminal prosecution for its violation. The provisions of § 204(d), conferring upon the Emergency Court of Appeals and this Court "exclusive jurisdiction to determine the validity of any regulation or order," coupled with the provision that "no court, Federal, State or Territorial, shall have jurisdiction or power to consider the validity of any such regulation," are broad enough in terms to deprive the district court of power to consider the validity of the Administrator's regulation or order as a defense to a criminal prosecution for its violation.

* * *

We come to the question whether the provisions of the Act, so construed as to deprive petitioners of opportunity to attack the Regulation in a prosecution for its violation, deprive them of the due process of law guaranteed by the Fifth Amendment. * * *

Due process? violation.

* * *

Petitioners assert that they have been denied that opportunity because the sixty days' period allowed for filing a protest is insufficient for that purpose; because the procedure before the Administrator is inadequate to ensure due process; because the statute precludes any interlocutory injunction staying enforcement of a price regulation before final adjudication of its validity; because the trial of the issue of validity of a regulation is excluded from the criminal trial for its violation; and because in any case there is nothing in the statute to prevent their conviction for violation of a regulation before they could secure a ruling on its validity. A sufficient answer to all these contentions is that petitioners have failed to seek the administrative remedy and the statutory review which were open to them and that they have not shown that had they done so any of the consequences which they apprehend would have ensued to any extent whatever, or if they should, that the statute withholds judicial remedies adequate to protect petitioners' rights.

Holding

* * * In the absence of any proceeding before the Administrator we cannot assume that he would fail in the performance of any duty imposed on him by the Constitution and laws of the United States, or that he would deny due process to petitioners by "loading the record against them" or denying such hearing as the Constitution prescribes. * * * Only if we could say in advance of resort to the statutory procedure that it is incapable of affording due process to petitioners could we conclude that they have shown any legal excuse for their failure to resort to it or that their constitutional rights have been or will be infringed. * * * But upon a full examination of the provisions of the statute it is evident that the authorized procedure is not incapable of affording the protection to petitioners' rights required by due process.

* * *

The Emergency Court has power to review all questions of law, including the question whether the Administrator's determination is supported by evidence, and any question of the denial of due process or any procedural error appropriately raised in the course of the proceedings. No reason is advanced why petitioners could not, throughout the statutory proceeding, raise and preserve any due process objection to the statute, the regulations, or the procedure, and secure its full judicial review by the Emergency Court of Appeals and this Court.

In the circumstances of this case we find no denial of due process in the statutory prohibition of a temporary stay or injunction. * * *

The petitioners are not confronted with the choice of abandoning their businesses or subjecting themselves to the penalties of the Act before they have sought and secured a determination of the Regulation's validity. It is true that if the Administrator denies a protest no stay or injunction may become effective before the final decision of the Emergency Court or of this Court if review here is sought. It is also true that the process of reaching a final decision may be time-consuming. But while courts have no power to suspend or ameliorate the operation of a regulation during the pendency of proceedings to determine its validity, we cannot say that the Administrator has no such power or assume that he would not exercise it in an appropriate case.

* * *

In any event, we are unable to say that the denial of interlocutory relief pending a judicial determination of the validity of the regulation would, in the special circumstances of this case, involve a denial of constitutional right. If the alternatives, as Congress could have concluded, were wartime inflation or the imposition on individuals of the burden of complying with a price regulation while its validity is being determined, Congress could constitutionally make the choice in favor of the protection of the public interest from the dangers of inflation. * * *

* * *

No procedural principle is more familiar to this Court than that a constitutional right may be forfeited in criminal as well as civil cases by the failure to make timely assertion of the right before a tribunal having jurisdiction to determine it. * * *

* * *

We have no occasion to decide whether one charged with criminal violation of a duly promulgated price regulation may defend on the ground that the regulation is unconstitutional on its face. Nor do we consider whether one who is forced to trial and convicted of violation of a regulation, while diligently seeking determination of its validity by the statutory procedure, may thus be deprived of the defense that the regulation is invalid. There is no contention that the present regulation is void on its face, petitioners have taken no step to challenge its validity by the procedure which was open to them and it does not appear that they have been deprived of the opportunity to do so. Even though the statute should be deemed to require it, any ruling at the criminal trial which would preclude the accused from showing that he had had no opportunity to establish the invalidity of the regulation by resort to the statutory procedure, would be reviewable on appeal on constitutional grounds. It will be time enough to decide questions not involved in this case when they are brought to us for decision, as they may be, whether they arise in the Emergency Court of Appeals or in the district court upon a criminal trial.

* * *

Mr. Justice Rutledge, dissenting:

I agree with the Court's conclusions upon the substantive issues. But I am unable to believe that the trial afforded the petitioners conformed to constitutional requirements. The matter is of such importance as requires a statement of the reasons for dissent.

* * *

I have no difficulty with the provision which confers jurisdiction upon the Emergency Court of Appeals to determine the validity of price regulations or, if that had been all, with the mandate which makes its jurisdiction in that respect exclusive. Equally clear is the power of Congress to deprive the other federal courts of jurisdiction to issue stay orders, restraining orders, injunctions or other relief to prevent the operation of price regulations or to set them aside. So much may be rested on Congress' plenary authority to define and control the jurisdiction of the federal courts. Constitution, Article III, § 2; Lockerty v. Phillips, 319 U.S. 182. It may be taken too, for the purposes of this case, that Congress' power to channel enforcement of federal authority through the federal courts sustains the like prohibitions it has placed on the state courts. Without more, the statute's provisions would seem to be unquestionably within the Congressional power.

Congress however was not content to create a single national tribunal, give it exclusive jurisdiction to determine all cases arising under the statute, and deny jurisdiction over them to all other courts. It provided for enforcement by civil and criminal proceedings in the federal district courts and in the state courts throughout the country.

This, too, it could do, though only if adequate proceedings, in the constitutional sense, were authorized. And I agree that the enforcing jurisdiction would not be made inadequate merely by the fact that no stay order or other relief could be had pending the outcome of litigation.
* * *

The crux of this case comes, as I see it, in the question whether Congress can confer jurisdiction upon federal and state courts in the enforcement proceedings, more particularly the criminal suit, and at the same time deny them "jurisdiction or power to consider the validity" of the regulations for which enforcement is thus sought. This question which the Court now says "presents no novel constitutional issue" was expressly and carefully reserved in Lockerty v. Phillips, supra. The prohibition is the statute's most novel feature. In combination with others it gives the procedure a culminating summary touch and presents questions different from those arising from the other features.

* * *

It is one thing for Congress to withhold jurisdiction. It is entirely another to confer it and direct that it be exercised in a manner inconsistent with constitutional requirements or, what in some instances may be the same thing, without regard to them. Once it is held that Congress can require the courts criminally to enforce unconstitutional laws or statutes, including regulations, or to do so without regard for their validity, the way will have been found to circumvent the supreme law and, what is more, to make the courts parties to doing so. This Congress cannot do. There are limits to the judicial power. Congress may impose others. And in some matters Congress or the President has final say under the Constitution. But whenever the judicial power is called into play, it is responsible directly to the fundamental law and no other authority can intervene to force or authorize the judicial body to disregard it. The problem therefore is not solely one of individual right or due process of law. It is equally one of the separation and independence of the powers of government and of the constitutional integrity of the judicial process, more especially in criminal trials.

* * *

If I understand it, the argument to sustain the conviction, in its broadest form, rests upon the proposition that Congress, by providing in one proceeding a constitutionally adequate mode for deciding upon the validity of a law or regulation, and requiring this to be followed within a limited time, can cut off all other right to question it and make that determination, or the failure to secure it in time, conclusive for all purposes and in all other proceedings. The proposition cannot be accepted in that broad form. To do so would mean, for instance, that if in this case a regulation had prescribed one maximum price for sales by merchants of one race or religion and a lower one for distributors of another, the judicial power of the United States would have to be exercised to convict the latter for selling at the formers' price, if they had not availed themselves of the limited review afforded by this Act. It hardly would be consistent with accepted ideas of due process or equal protection for any court to impose penalty or restraint in such a case. And I cannot imagine this Court as sustaining such a conviction or any other as imposing it.

* * *

[The dissenting opinion of JUSTICE ROBERTS is omitted.]

Notes

1. In what way did the issue concerning congressional power over federal jurisdiction in *Yakus* differ from that in *Lockerty*?

2. How do you suppose the majority would have decided *Yakus* if Congress had limited federal court authority to consider an attack on the law's validity as a defense to a criminal prosecution but had not created the Emergency Court of Appeals?

3. What was Justice Rutledge's problem with the majority's opinion? What was the constitutional source of his concern?

4. How far apart are the majority and Justice Rutledge? Did the majority dispute Rutledge's premise? If not, about what did they disagree?

5. In a case decided the same day, Bowles v. Willingham, 321 U.S. 503 (1944), the Court upheld a limitation of the power of a lower court to inquire into the validity of the regulation in a civil action brought by the Adminis-

trator to enjoin a state court action brought to restrain issuance of an order by the Administrator. This time, Justice Rutledge concurred with the majority. 321 U.S. at 521. He explained his distinction of *Bowles* from *Yakus* in the following passage:

> Different considerations, in part, determine this question from those controlling when enforcement is by criminal sanction. The constitutional limitations specially applicable to criminal trials fall to one side. Those relating to due process of law in civil proceedings, including whatever matters affecting discrimination are applicable under the Fifth Amendment, and to the independence of the judicial power under Article III, in relation to civil proceedings, remain applicable. Since in these cases the rights involved are rights of property, not of personal liberty or life as in criminal proceedings, the consequences, though serious, are not of the same moment under our system, as appears from the fact they are not secured by the same procedural protections in trial. It is in this respect perhaps that our basic law, following the common law, most clearly places the rights to life and to liberty above those of property. 321 U.S. at 525.

However, he believed that "Congress can do this, subject * * * to the following limitations or reservations, which I think should be stated explicitly: (1) The order or regulation must not be invalid on its face; (2) the previous opportunity must be adequate for the purpose prescribed, in the constitutional sense; and (3) what is a corollary of the second limitation or implicit in it, the circumstances and nature of the substantive problem dealt with by the legislation must be such that they justify both the creation of the special remedy and the requirement that it be followed to the exclusion of others normally available." Id. at 526.

In light of Justice Rutledge's reasoning in his *Yakus* dissent, do his suggested distinctions between the situations in *Yakus* and *Bowles* hold up?

BATTAGLIA v. GENERAL MOTORS CORP., 169 F.2d 254 (2d Cir.1948), cert. denied, 335 U.S. 887 (1948): Under the Fair Labor Standards Acts of 1938, 29 U.S.C. §§ 201–219, covered employees are guaranteed time-and-a-half compensation for any work over and above a forty-hour work week. The Act provides for liability for unpaid overtime, as well as for payment of liquidated damages. In several decisions in the mid–1940's, the Supreme Court interpreted the phrase, "work week" to include such activities as the time required for underground travel to and from the mines, activities which neither unions nor employers had apparently considered to be part of the forty-hour work week.

In response to these decisions Congress passed the Portal–to–Portal Act of 1947, 29 U.S.C. §§ 216, 251–262. Sections 252(a) and 252(b) provided that an employer was not liable under the Fair Labor Standards Act for failure to compensate under the Supreme Court's construction of "work week." Section 252(d) provided in relevant part:

No court can hear case

No court of the United States, of any State, Territory, or possession of the United States, or of the District of Columbia, shall have jurisdiction of any action or proceeding, whether instituted prior to or on or after May 14, 1947, to enforce liability or impose punishment for or on account of the failure of the employer to pay minimum wages or overtime compensation under the Fair Labor Standards Act of 1938 * * * to the extent that such action or proceeding seeks to enforce any liability or impose any punishment with respect to an activity which was not compensable under subsections (a) and (b) or this section.

The case involved four separate suits brought in federal district court against General Motors on behalf of its employees to recover overtime pay in accordance with the Fair Labor Standards Act, as it had been interpreted by the Supreme Court. In ruling on the constitutionality of the Portal–to–Portal Act, Judge Chase, speaking for the court, stated:

Congress has this power, but it can't exercise that power in a way that would interfere with individual rights

A few of the district court decisions sustaining the Portal–to–Portal Act have done so on the ground that since jurisdiction of federal courts other than the Supreme Court is conferred by Congress, it may at the will of Congress be taken away in whole or in part. * * * [T]hese district court decisions would, in effect, sustain subdivision (d) * * * regardless of whether subdivisions (a) and (b) were valid. We think, however, that the exercise by Congress of its control over jurisdiction is subject to compliance with at least the requirements of the Fifth Amendment. That is to say, while Congress has the undoubted power to give, withhold, and restrict the jurisdiction of courts other than the Supreme Court, it must not so exercise that power as to deprive any person of law or to take private property without just compensation. * * * Thus, regardless of whether subdivision (d) * * * had an independent end in itself, if one of its effects would be to deprive the appellants of property without due process or just compensation, it would be invalid. 169 F.2d at 257.

The court then considered and rejected the constitutional challenge on the merits.

BARTLETT v. BOWEN

United States Court of Appeals, District of Columbia Circuit, 1987.
816 F.2d 695.

Before EDWARDS and BORK, CIRCUIT JUDGES, and WRIGHT, SENIOR CIRCUIT JUDGE.

EDWARDS, CIRCUIT JUDGE: Appellant Mary Bartlett, plaintiff below, brought suit in the District Court on behalf of her sister, the deceased Josephine Neuman. She challenged the constitutionality of Part A of the Medicare Act on the ground that its partial bar to payment of benefits burdened the free exercise of her sister's Christian Science faith. The

District Court dismissed the complaint for lack of subject matter jurisdiction because the claim failed to meet the $1,000 amount in controversy required by the Medicare Act for judicial review of benefit decisions. On appeal, appellant argues that the jurisdictional provisions of the Medicare Act do not preclude judicial review of her constitutional claim. In the alternative, she maintains that these provisions deny her due process and equal protection of the law if they do bar review.

Claim: Judicial review is not precluded

Upon careful review of the Medicare Act and its legislative history, and pursuant to the guidance given by the Supreme Court in Johnson v. Robison, 415 U.S. 361 (1974), we find that Congress did not intend to bar judicial review of constitutional challenges to the underlying Act. Because we find that Congress did not intend the provisions to preclude review of appellant's claim, we normally should have no need to reach her constitutional arguments. However, because the dissenting opinion has suggested that Congress may foreclose *all* judicial review of the constitutionality of a federal statute, we have addressed this issue. We believe that there would be a clear violation of due process if Congress did in fact preclude any opportunity for an aggrieved claimant to obtain judicial review of one of its enactments.

HELD

I. BACKGROUND

Josephine Neuman, a Christian Science practitioner, suffered a terminal illness and required skilled nursing care. In February, 1976, she entered Lynn House of the Potomac, a Christian Science facility, where she received such care. In May, 1976, during the same spell of illness, Neuman left Lynn House and entered the Washington Home for Incurables, a non-Christian Science facility, where she remained, except for a week's treatment at Georgetown University Hospital, until her death in July, 1978.

Before she died, Neuman claimed and received $377 in Medicare benefits for the post-hospital extended care provided by Lynn House under Part A of the Medicare Act. See 42 U.S.C. § 1395x(y)(1) (1982). After Neuman's death, Mary Bartlett, executrix of Neuman's estate, filed a Medicare claim of $286 for the post-hospital extended care Neuman had received at the Washington Home. The Social Security Administration denied that claim initially and upon reconsideration relying on 42 U.S.C. § 1395x(y)(2)(B) (1982), which bars payment of Part A benefits for extended care in a skilled nursing facility unaffiliated with Christian Science to anyone who has, during the same spell of illness, already received such benefits for extended care in a Christian Science skilled nursing facility. An administrative law judge ("ALJ") upheld the denial on appeal, and the Appeals Council of the Social Security Administration adopted the ALJ's decision as the final decision of the Secretary of Health and Human Services (the "Secretary").

Claim Denied

Bartlett does not dispute the Secretary's reading of the Medicare Act's provision. Her claim is that the Medicare Act's bar to payment penalizes Neuman's estate solely on account of Neuman's Christian

Argument

Science faith in contravention of the free exercise clause of the First Amendment. The then-Secretary recognized that she had no authority to rule on constitutional challenges to the Act, and thus she denied Bartlett's claim without addressing the merits of her constitutional challenge.

Having exhausted her administrative remedies, Bartlett brought this action in the United States District Court for the District of Columbia in February, 1982. She reasserts her claim that the Christian Science provisions of the Medicare Act burden Neuman's right to free exercise of religion under the First Amendment and deny her equal protection of the law under the Fifth Amendment. Bartlett further contends that the provision defining "spell of illness" also violates Neuman's rights to equal protection and due process under the Fifth Amendment.

The Secretary moved to dismiss Bartlett's action for lack of subject matter jurisdiction based on two jurisdictional provisions of the Medicare Act, 42 U.S.C. §§ 405(h)[4] and 1395ff(b)(2) (1982).[5] Section 405(h), incorporated from the Social Security Act into the Medicare Act by 42 U.S.C. § 1395ii (1982), denies federal question and mandamus jurisdiction over any claim "arising under" the Medicare Act. Section 1395ff(b)(2) bars "judicial review" of any "determination" of "the amount of benefits under part A" of the Medicare Act that has become a "final decision" of the Secretary, if the "amount in controversy" is less than $1,000. The District Court initially denied the Secretary's motion because "[t]he legislative history [of § 1395ff] is devoid of 'clear and convincing' evidence of a congressional purpose to preclude judicial review of substantial constitutional claims," and noted that "if plaintiff were precluded from all judicial review of her claim in this case, the most serious constitutional questions would be present." The court held in the alternative that it had independent federal question jurisdiction over Bartlett's claim, notwithstanding § 405(h). After Heckler v. Ringer, 466 U.S.

---

4. 42 U.S.C. § 405(h) provides:

(h) Finality of Secretary's decision

The findings and decision of the Secretary after a hearing shall be binding upon all individuals who were parties to such hearing. No findings of fact or decision of the Secretary shall be reviewed by any person, tribunal, or governmental agency except as herein provided. No action against the United States, the Secretary, or any officer or employee thereof shall be brought under sections 1331 or 1346 of title 28 to recover on any claim arising under this subchapter.

5. 42 U.S.C. § 1395ff(b) provides:

(b) Appeal by individuals

(1) Any individual dissatisfied with any determination under subsection (a) of this section as to—

. . .

(C) the amount of benefits under part A (including a determination where such amount is determined to be zero)

shall be entitled to a hearing thereon by the Secretary to the same extent as is provided in section 405(b) of this title and to judicial review of the Secretary's final decision after such hearing as is provided in section 405(g) of this title.

(2) Notwithstanding the provisions of subparagraph (C) of paragraph (1) of this subsection, a hearing shall not be available to an individual by reason of such subparagraph (C) if the amount in controversy is less than $100, nor shall judicial review be available to an individual by reason of such subparagraph (C) if the amount in controversy is less than $1,000.

602 (1984), was decided, however, the Secretary renewed the motion to dismiss and the court granted it, finding the Supreme Court's opinion in that case to be conclusive on the jurisdictional issues. On appeal, Bartlett claims that §§ 405(h) and 1395ff(b)(2) do not preclude judicial review of her claim and that if they do, they violate her rights to equal protection and due process of law.

II. CONGRESS' INTENT IN §§ 405(H) AND 1395FF(B)(2)

We begin with the general "presumption that Congress intends judicial review of administrative action."[9] It is axiomatic that this presumption can be overcome only by "clear and convincing evidence" that Congress intended to restrict access to judicial review.[10] Thus, the party seeking to read a legislative scheme to preclude review bears the burden of demonstrating Congress' intent to do so.

Courts have applied this "clear and convincing" standard in a particularly rigorous fashion when constitutional rights form the basis of the action over which judicial review is sought. As this court has explained:

> When [a] plaintiff seeks to invoke the aid of the judicial branch on constitutional grounds, the Supreme Court and this court have both indicated that only the clearest evocation of congressional intent to proscribe judicial review of constitutional claims will suffice to overcome the presumption that the Congress would not wish to court the constitutional dangers inherent in denying a forum in which to argue that government action has injured interests that are protected by the Constitution.[13]

Indeed, it has become something of a time-honored tradition for the Supreme Court and lower federal courts to find that Congress did not intend to preclude altogether judicial review of constitutional claims in light of the serious due process concerns that such preclusion would raise.[14] These cases recognize and seek to accommodate the venerable line of Supreme Court cases that casts doubt on the constitutionality of congressional preclusion of judicial review of constitutional claims.[15] This

---

9. Bowen v. Michigan Academy of Family Physicians, 106 S.Ct. 2133, 2135 (1986).

10. See Robison, 415 U.S. at 373–74; Abbott Laboratories v. Gardner, 387 U.S. 136, 141 (1967).

13. Ungar v. Smith, 667 F.2d 188, 193 (D.C.Cir.1981).

14. See, e.g., Bowen v. Michigan Academy of Family Physicians, 106 S.Ct. at 2141 & n. 12; Robison, 415 U.S. at 366; Cardenas v. Smith, 733 F.2d 909, 919 (D.C.Cir.1984); Ungar v. Smith, 667 F.2d at 193.

The dissent finds "dispositive" the Supreme Court's recent opinion in Commodity Futures Trading Comm'n v. Schor, 106 S.Ct. 3245 (1986), which has no relevance

to the instant case except that it concerns an unrelated situation in which the Court *rejected* an interpretation of a statute offered to avoid constitutional infirmity. In that case, however, the proposed interpretation was manifestly at war with the general purpose underlying the statute, while we reach exactly the opposite conclusion regarding our interpretation of § 1395ff.

15. See Califano v. Sanders, 430 U.S. 99, 109 (1977); Oestereich, 393 U.S. at 243 n. 6 (Harlan, J., concurring); St. Joseph Stock Yards Co. v. United States, 298 U.S. 38, 84 (1936) (Brandeis, J., concurring); Crowell v. Benson, 285 U.S. 22, 60 (1932); Martin v. Hunter's Lessee, 14 U.S. (1 Wheat.) 304, 330–33 (1816); see also M. Redish, Federal Jurisdiction: Tensions in

foreboding line of Supreme Court cases and the ominous warnings of scholarly commentators have moved modern courts to apply the "clear and convincing" standard to congressional enactments in part to avoid the constitutional morass, as we do here.

Applying this demanding standard with a careful eye on potential constitutional infirmity, we nonetheless find that Congress *did* intend to preclude *independent* federal jurisdiction over Bartlett's claim by enacting 42 U.S.C. § 405(h) and incorporating it into the Medicare Act in § 1395ii. Section 405(h) proscribes independent federal question or mandamus jurisdiction for any action "to recover on any claim arising under [the Medicare Act]." * * *

When we turn to the Act's judicial review provision in § 1395ff, however, we reach a different conclusion regarding congressional intent as to preclusion of judicial review of administrative action. * * *

* * *

We hold * * * that challenges to the constitutionality of the Medicare Act itself may be reviewed in federal court consistent with congressional intent as expressed in § 1395ff. * * *

* * *

III. CONSTITUTIONAL ISSUES

Even if we had found, as the dissent insists, that Congress *did* intend to preclude judicial review of appellant's claim, our analysis would not end there, because such a conclusion would raise the "serious constitutional questions" that the Court avoided in *Robison*. If we were to credit Congress with an intention to foreclose all judicial review under the Medicare Act, the appellant here would have no judicial forum whatsoever (in either a federal or state court) in which to pursue her constitutional claim. Indeed, because the Secretary has no authority to consider constitutional questions, the appellant would have *no forum at all* for the pursuit of her claims. We would thus be faced with a situation in which Congress has enacted legislation and simultaneously declared that legislation to be immune from any constitutional challenge by the plaintiff.

In our view, a statutory provision precluding *all* judicial review of constitutional issues removes from the courts an essential judicial function under our implied constitutional mandate of separation of powers, and deprives an individual of an independent forum for the adjudication of a claim of constitutional right. We have little doubt that such a "limitation on the jurisdiction of *both* state and federal courts to review

the Allocation of Judicial Power 7–34 (1980) [hereinafter Redish] (maintaining that due process limits Congress' power to deny a judicial forum for the litigation of constitutional claims); Sager, *The Supreme Court, 1980 Term—Foreword: Constitutional Limi-* tations on Congress' Authority to Regulate the Jurisdiction of the Federal Courts, 95 Harv.L.Rev. 17 (1981) (same); Taylor, *Limiting Federal Court Jurisdiction: The Unconstitutionality of Current Legislative Proposals*, 65 Judicature 199 (1981) (same).

the constitutionality of federal legislation ... would be [an] unconstitutional" infringement of due process.[32]

Due Process Violation

Because we have found that Congress did not intend to preclude judicial review in the case before us, we should have no occasion to consider whether it would be constitutional for Congress to enact legislation and preclude the judiciary from hearing challenges to the constitutionality of that legislation. Unfortunately, the dissenting opinion has pursued this issue and we feel constrained to respond because of the great significance of the question.

Review because of Dissent

The dissenting opinion, which purports to avoid the "serious constitutional questions" alluded to in *Robison,* relies on an extraordinary and wholly unprecedented application of the notion of sovereign immunity to uphold the Act's preclusion of all judicial review. We note, first, that the dissent finds no relevant support for the novel proposition that it advances. * * *

Second, we note that, in relying on an unprecedented notion of sovereign immunity, the dissent has effectively decided the precise constitutional issue that it claims to have avoided. To say that Congress may, as it sees fit, insist on immunity as a way to foreclose all judicial review on the constitutionality of a congressional enactment, is to decide that there is no infringement of due process. We absolutely disagree with this contention.

Moreover, we note that the dissent's hesitancy to address directly the constitutional issue may well stem from a misunderstanding of what that issue is. The dissent characterizes the limits of Congress' power over federal jurisdiction as a "complex" and "profound" question, citing authorities with a variety of viewpoints. And yet the complexities of the issue arise from the potential problems created if, for example, Congress wished to deny any *federal* forum for a federal claim, leaving only a state forum. It is on *this* problem that the dissent's authorities focus their efforts, asking whether Article III places any limits on Congress' plenary power over federal jurisdiction. The question we ask is whether *due process* places any limits on Congress' power, and we conclude, narrowly and rather uncontroversially, that it does and that these limits are broached when Congress denies *any* forum—federal, state or agency—for the resolution of a federal constitutional claim.

ISSUE

In his renowned "Dialogue," which the dissent cites as supporting its argument, the late Professor Henry M. Hart considered the bearing of sovereign immunity and asserted that "no democratic government can be immune to the claims of justice and legal right.... And where constitutional rights are at stake the courts are properly astute, in construing statutes, to avoid the conclusion that Congress intended to use the privilege of immunity, or of withdrawing jurisdiction, in order to defeat them."[34] Because we believe that this view is so firmly rooted in

32. Redish, supra note 15, at 27 (emphasis in original).

34. P. Bator, P. Mishkin, D. Shapiro & H. Wechsler, Hart and Wechsler's The Fed-

our constitutional tradition of separation of powers, we cannot ignore the contrary views advanced in the dissenting opinion.

A. The Due Process Right to Have the Scope of Constitutional Rights Determined By an Independent Judicial Body

In considering the constitutional issue, it is important to recall that, in the entire history of the United States, the Supreme Court has never once held that Congress may foreclose all judicial review of the constitutionality of a congressional enactment. Quite the contrary, on the few occasions when this issue has been considered, courts have declined to find an intention on the part of Congress to preclude all judicial review of constitutional claims. Less than one year ago, the Supreme Court adopted just such an analysis to conclude that Congress did not intend to bar judicial review of the method by which Medicare Part B awards are computed.[35] The Court recognized the constitutional dangers it averted by its holding, noting that "[o]ur disposition avoids the 'serious constitutional question' that would arise if we construed § 1395ii to deny a judicial forum for constitutional claims arising under Part B of the Medicare program."[36] The Court went on to endorse Professor Gunther's unequivocal conclusion that "all agree that Congress cannot bar all remedies for enforcing federal constitutional rights."[37]

Under our constitutional scheme, there are admittedly some difficult questions concerning Congress' Article III power to limit federal court jurisdiction.[38] However, most scholars agree that "under the due process clause of the fifth amendment Congress may not exercise Article III power over the jurisdiction of the [federal] courts in order to deprive a party of a right created by the Constitution."[39] Professor Hart, on the other hand, while not disagreeing with this proposition, has suggested that Congress might be free to limit federal court jurisdiction so long as some alternative forum was available:

> It's hard, for me at least, to read into Article III any guarantee to a civil litigant of a hearing in a federal constitutional court (outside the original jurisdiction of the Supreme Court), if Congress chooses to provide some alternative procedure. The alternative procedure may be unconstitutional. But, if so, it seems to me it must be

eral Courts and the Federal System 336 (2d ed. 1973).

35. Bowen v. Michigan Academy of Family Physicians, 106 S.Ct. 2133 (1986).

36. Id. at 2141 n. 12 (citing Weinberger v. Salfi, 422 U.S. at 762 (citing Johnson v. Robison, 415 U.S. 361, 366–67 (1974); Yakus v. United States, 321 U.S. 414, 433–44 (1944); St. Joseph Stock Yards Co. v. United States, 298 U.S. 38, 84 (1936) (Brandeis, J., concurring))).

37. Id. (quoting Gunther, Congressional Power to Curtail Federal Court Jurisdiction: An Opinionated Guide to the Ongoing Debate, 36 Stan.L.Rev. 895, 921 n. 113

(1984)). Other scholars have also agreed with Professor Gunther. See Redish, supra note 15, at 25 ("Courts have long recognized a due process right to have the scope of constitutional rights determined by an independent judicial body." (footnote omitted)).

38. See note 37 supra. See also L. Tribe, American Constitutional Law 33–47 (1978); C. Wright, Law of Federal Courts 32–39 (4th ed. 1983).

39. See, e.g., Nowak [Rotunda & Young, Constitutional Law], at 41 (footnote omitted).

because of some other constitutional provision, such as the due process clause.

On the other hand, if Congress directs an Article III court to decide a case, I can easily read into Article III a limitation on the power of Congress to tell the court *how* to decide it.[40]

* * *

[An] example of constitutional limitations on congressional power over the jurisdiction of the courts is Battaglia v. General Motors, 169 F.2d 254 (2d Cir.1948). In the mid–1940s, the Supreme Court ruled that certain incidental activities by workers were compensable under the Fair Labor Standards Act. Congress thereafter passed the Portal–to–Portal Act of 1947, 29 U.S.C. §§ 251–262 (1982), amending the statute to make the disputed work noncompensable and withdrawing the jurisdiction of the courts to hear cases under the old statute. The court in *Battaglia* held that the statutory amendment did not constitute an unconstitutional taking of property because the claimants had no vested rights to overtime pay under the old statute. However, what is noteworthy about *Battaglia* is that, "[b]y considering and rejecting [the plaintiffs'] constitutional claim, [the] court of appeals explicitly recognized that congressional power over the jurisdiction of the courts is limited by the due process clause."[43] The court thus considered both the constitutionality of the jurisdictional provision and the merits of plaintiffs' underlying claim. As the court noted, "regardless of whether [the deprivation of jurisdiction] had an independent end in itself, if one of its effects would be to deprive the appellant of property without due process or just compensation, it would be invalid."

The foregoing cases and authorities suggest that, "to the extent that the provisions of Article III are inconsistent with the due process clause of the fifth amendment, those provisions of Article III must be considered modified by the amendment."[45] This proposition is admittedly controversial insofar as it suggests that there must be some *federal* judicial forum for the enforcement of federal constitutional rights.[46] However, "[s]ince restrictions on federal courts ordinarily leave state courts as available forums, curtailments of federal jurisdiction do not typically require confrontation of the difficult and unsettled problem of access to *some* judicial forum."[47] In other words, courts and legal scholars routinely assume that there is a due process right to have the scope of constitutional rights determined by some independent judicial body—and the Supreme Court has never held or hinted otherwise. On the contrary, although it is undisputed that Congress has some leeway to

---

40. Hart & Wechsler, supra note 34, at 337 (emphasis in original).

43. Nowak [Rotunda & Young] at 43.

45. Redish, supra note 15, at 25. * * *

46. See generally Gunther, *Congressional Power to Curtail Federal Jurisdiction: An Opinionated Guide to the Ongoing Debate,*

26 Stan.L.Rev. 895 (1984). See also discussion and citation of authorities in W. Lockhart, Y. Kamisar & J. Choper, Constitutional Law 57–61 (5th ed. 1980).

47. G. Gunther, Constitutional Law 51 n. 6 (11th ed. 1985) (emphasis in original).

affect the jurisdiction of the lower federal courts, Congress may not deny to a person attacking a statute "the independent judgment of a court on the ultimate question of constitutionality." St. Joseph Stock Yards Co. v. United States, 298 U.S. at 84 (Brandeis, J., concurring).

Although there is no definitive answer to the question whether there are constitutional restraints when Congress seeks to limit the jurisdiction of all *federal* courts, we need not address that question here. This arguably hard question is not posed in a case such as this one where Congress has effectively foreclosed *all* judicial review of Bartlett's constitutional claim under the Medicare Act. We think it obvious that a statute that would have the effect of precluding any sort of review in an independent judicial forum * * * fails the test in *Battaglia*. We also believe that such a congressional enactment would be flatly inconsistent with the doctrine of separation of powers implicit in our constitutional scheme.

Since Marbury v. Madison, 5 U.S. (1 Cranch) 137 (1803), the Supreme Court has interpreted the Constitution to give to the judiciary an important, albeit limited, role in the structure of the government. First, federal courts fulfill their role *only* by adjudicating cases or controversies before them. Second, when faced with a proper case or controversy, courts, both state and federal, must apply all applicable laws in rendering their decisions. Third, courts have a duty to uphold the Constitution. Fourth, a law contrary to the Constitution may not be enforced. Last, a final judgment by a court is binding and must be enforced. So, once a case or controversy reaches the courts, the courts, in essence, become the final arbiter as to the constitutionality of government actions.

The delicate balance implicit in the doctrine of separation of powers would be destroyed if Congress were allowed not only to legislate, but also to judge the constitutionality of its own actions. We have no doubt that Congress may and, indeed, should, consider the constitutionality of any legislation that it passes. Moreover, we recognize that the courts may occasionally defer to the judgment of Congress with respect to the constitutionality of certain legislation. Further, the courts arguably may, in their discretion, elect to avoid certain "political" questions that appear to be better left for resolution in the legislative or executive branch. However, it is quite another matter to suggest that Congress may, as it sees fit, act to bar all courts from considering the constitutionality of a legislative act. * * *

It should be emphasized that this case involves a statute enacted by Congress that appellant claims infringes her right to the free exercise of religion. Congress has given appellant a right to benefits that seemingly varies depending upon whether or not she uses a Christian Science facility. This is a potentially serious infringement of appellant's free exercise of her religion. Whether Congress can impose such a statutory restriction is a question for the judiciary. It makes absolutely no sense to us, under any meaningful system of separation of powers, to allow the legislative branch to pass such a law and then avoid judicial review of a broad category of constitutional challenges by individuals injured by the law. We suspect that the dissent recognizes the folly of such a view; this may explain why the dissenting opinion seeks to rest not on a direct analysis of the constitutionality of the statute but on an absolutely unprecedented use of sovereign immunity.

B.   Sovereign Immunity

In order to avoid the obvious constitutional difficulties that might be posed with a finding that Congress has foreclosed all judicial review, the dissent seeks solace in a novel concept of sovereign immunity. It would be pointless for us to attempt to parse the limits of the dissent's thesis—all that need be understood is that, insofar as the dissent's thesis purports to claim that Congress may foreclose *all* judicial review of the constitutionality of a legislative enactment, it finds no support in the case law of the Supreme Court.

* * *

* * * The dissent cites a string of authorities unrelated to each other or to the instant case in an effort to demonstrate that the bar of sovereign immunity is not automatically defeated by the assertion of a constitutional claim. The dissent claims that the majority opinion requires the doctrine of sovereign immunity to disappear in all litigation against the Government where a constitutional challenge is made. But the dissent has set up a straw man here, as that is not our contention. Ours is the much narrower claim that sovereign immunity may not be invoked when its effect is to preclude *any* judicial review of a challenge to the constitutionality of congressional legislation.

* * *

The dissent attempts to support its position by analogy to *state* sovereign immunity doctrine. In doing so, it ignores the fact that the Eleventh Amendment deals only with federal *jurisdiction* to hear suits against the states, *not* with the states' immunity from suit in any forum. In many Eleventh Amendment cases, the state courts are available to hear the claims raised; only the availability of a federal forum is at issue. Moreover, the dissent conveniently ignores the doctrine of *Ex parte Young,* 209 U.S. 123 (1908), which mitigated the potential harshness of the Eleventh Amendment bar by permitting state officials to be sued for injunctive relief on federal claims in federal court. Thus, *Ex parte Young* prevents the Eleventh Amendment from denying any forum for constitutional claims. Prospective relief is always available in federal court. Indeed, the doctrine of *Ex parte Young* has been invoked to protect plaintiffs' rights to receive public benefits. It is plain that the Eleventh Amendment offers little analogous support for the dissent's contentions.

Finally, the dissent cites several cases holding suits for damages against the United States for the unconstitutional actions of executive officials barred by sovereign immunity. These cases offer no support for the contention that sovereign immunity likewise immunizes the legislative branch from judicial review. While we concede that the sovereign may not be sued for damages without its consent, that immunity does not also entail that courts may not review legislative enactments without Congress' consent. Judicial review has been with us since *Marbury v. Madison*, and no one has ever before suggested that it is discretionary on Congress' part. The dissent has conflated the sovereign's immunity from suit for damages with its purported ability to immunize its enactments from judicial review. The only people who have standing to challenge the Medicare provisions at issue in this case are those with claims for benefits. This posture cannot eliminate the availability of judicial review without also violating the claimants' right to due process of law and raising serious concerns about separation of powers.

* * * The dissent maintains that even if due process might require a forum for a constitutional claim when the Government is acting *coercively,* it requires no such forum when the Government has merely denied a claimant *benefits.* But *Robison,* in which the Supreme Court expressed its concern about "serious constitutional questions," was itself a benefits case—a fact that makes hash out of the dissent's much belabored distinction.

The dissent's sovereign immunity theory in effect concludes that the doctrine of sovereign immunity trumps every other aspect of the Constitution. According to the dissent, neither the delicate balance of power struck by the framers among the three branches of government nor the constitutional guarantee of due process limits the Government's assertion of immunity. Such an extreme position simply cannot be maintained. If we follow the reasoning of the dissent to its logical conclusion, Congress would have the power to enact, for example, a welfare law authorizing benefits to be available to white claimants only and to immunize that enactment from judicial scrutiny by including a provision precluding judicial review of benefits claims. We have difficulty understanding how such a law could ever be thought to be beyond judicial scrutiny because of sovereign immunity. To preclude judicial review in such a situation would be just as unconstitutional as the underlying governmental action. Any theory that would allow such a statute to stand untouched by the judicial branch flagrantly ignores the concept of separation of powers and the guarantee of due process. We see no evidence that *any* court, including the Supreme Court, would subscribe to the dissent's theory in such a case.

* * *

Bork, Circuit Judge, dissenting:

* * *

* * * Appellant contends that the statute should be read not to deny jurisdiction and, that if it is so read, the bar of judicial review is unconstitutional. The majority agrees with both of those positions. I agree with neither. My conclusion rests upon Supreme Court precedents,

which, it must be said, are not free of ambiguity, at least as to the constitutional issue. Since the issue is important in litigation about social insurance benefits programs, it is to be hoped that the Court will soon revisit and clarify this area of law.

* * *

* * * Judicial review is provided and limited in sections 1395ff(b)(1) and (2). * * * [I]t is clear that sections 1395ff(b)(1) and (2) waive sovereign immunity as to claims of $1000 and up and expressly assert sovereign immunity as to claims under $1000. That means Congress has asserted sovereign immunity as to Bartlett's claim, and the only question before us is whether Congress may constitutionally do so. There seems no doubt Congress may.

Once it is recognized that sovereign immunity is present, a solid body of doctrine comes into play. * * *

These principles of sovereign immunity suffuse every aspect of the present case—from the issue of statutory construction to that of constitutional power—and lead to the conclusion that the district court was without jurisdiction to entertain Bartlett's suit.

* * *

This case presents difficulties only because the Supreme Court appears to have said inconsistent things about benefits legislation that withholds judicial review of claims such as Bartlett's. On the one hand, the Court in *Bowen v. City of New York*, in which a constitutional claim was made, characterized statutory provisions indistinguishable from the provisions involved here as a waiver of sovereign immunity. That necessarily means that the United States could not have been sued if there had been no waiver. In cases such as United States v. Mottaz, 106 S.Ct. 2224, 2229 (1986), moreover, the Court continues to adhere to the rule, even where a constitutional claim is asserted, that "[w]hen the United States consents to be sued, the terms of its waiver of sovereign immunity define the extent of the court's jurisdiction." If we take these statements seriously, as we must, and if there were nothing to the contrary in the case law, then it would be obvious that the district court had no jurisdiction to entertain Bartlett's suit. On the other hand, this clear rule may have been cast into doubt by the Court's remark in *Robison* that a construction of a statute that "bars federal courts from deciding the constitutionality of veterans' benefits legislation ... would, of course, raise serious questions concerning the constitutionality" of the statute. 415 U.S. at 366. Though the government drew the doctrine of sovereign immunity to the Court's attention, *Robison* said nothing on the subject and did not mention the cases cited on the point.

This situation leaves lower courts in a quandary. *Robison*'s statement about questions of constitutionality must be taken as seriously intended, and yet it is not easy to accept the result of doing so. Should *Robison*'s statement be taken as a silent overturning of the doctrine of sovereign immunity for all constitutional challenges to benefits legislation? If so, much more would seem logically to follow. Benefits claims constitute the category of cases in which sovereign immunity is most readily upheld. Should *Robison,* therefore, be read to eliminate sovereign immunity for all constitutional claims against both federal and state legislation and executive action? These conclusions, though startling, would seem to follow logically. Lower courts, however, do not usually infer silent overruling when the Supreme Court gives no explicit indication that it has addressed an issue and that such overruling is intended. I think it safer for lower court judges to continue to respect established doctrine, particularly when that doctrine is as old and solidly rooted as sovereign immunity. In addition, the cases cited by the *Robison* Court for its aside about constitutionality do not address at all the subject of sovereign immunity. Under these circumstances, the implication of a momentous yet tacit change in the law seems much too tenuous to be acted upon.

* * *

Robison, it is to be stressed, merely stated that there was a serious question of constitutionality. It did not purport to answer the question. In the light of other Supreme Court decisions, I think it may also be said, with respect, that *Robison* raised the question in a context in which it does not belong. * * *

* * *

Bartlett is seeking a benefit from the government, not resisting a government or private enforcement action. There is a line of Supreme Court decisions that permits denial of jurisdiction in cases of the former type, whatever the rule may be as to those of the latter variety. Drawing upon case law, Professor Hart's *Dialectic,* * * * concluded that congressional withdrawal of jurisdiction is least troublesome and questionable in "the cases of plaintiffs complaining about governmental decisions which do not involve the direct coercion of private persons." Hart & Wechsler at 346. The group of cases he indicated

> includes problems with respect to plaintiffs who are *neither* (a) trying to avoid becoming defendants, or (b) complaining about a governmental decision concerning a judicially enforceable duty of another private person, or (c) complaining about extrajudicial governmental coercion of themselves. For example, a plaintiff seeking review of a government contracting officer's decision which he had agreed in the contract should be final. United States v. Moorman, 338 U.S. 457 (1950). *Or a plaintiff seeking some statutory benefit from the government.*

Hart & Wechsler at 346–47 (emphasis added). This last category is the one into which Bartlett falls. Her claim to Medicare Part A benefits addresses neither present nor future governmental coercion against her nor governmental interference with the legal duty of a private person running in her favor. * * *

Professor Davis has come to a similar conclusion: "Upholding unreviewability of questions of law, jurisdiction, and procedure is easiest in the batch of cases involving denial of government bounties or benefits...." 4 K. Davis, Administrative Law Treatise § 28.18, at 98 (1st ed. 1958). * * *

Professors Hart's and Davis's categorization accurately reflect the line drawn by the Supreme Court for many years. It has always been true that the United States could not be sued without its consent. This has nothing to do with the question of congressional power to remove the jurisdiction of federal courts when enforcement powers are brought to bear. * * *

* * *

* * * If sovereign immunity is abandoned as to constitutionally-based benefit claims, it would seem impossible to support immunity anywhere. The Tucker Act's waiver of immunity as to constitutional claims would be made superfluous. These upheavals in established doctrine are too much to draw from a remark in *Robison.* I think it safer for an inferior court to proceed on the premise that the law of sovereign immunity remains what it always has been and that it therefore deprives the district court of jurisdiction over Bartlett's suit.

III.

A word should be said about the majority opinion. The majority reads the jurisdictional statute involved here as containing an unstated exception for constitutional challenges to the Medicare Act. I have sufficiently explained why this construction of the statute is not "fairly possible," as the Supreme Court states that a construction must be if it is employed to avoid deciding a constitutional issue. Having purchased the right to avoid the constitutional issue at an unacceptably high price in the deformation of the statute, however, the majority then unaccountably casts its purchase away by going on to decide the constitutional issue *Robison* avoided. Resolution of that question—the power of Congress to remove jurisdiction over constitutional issues in any and all types of cases—is utterly unnecessary under either the majority's rationale or my own.

Despite the majority's purported resolution of the issue of Congress' plenary power over jurisdiction, * * * I express no opinion on that subject other than to note that it is far more complex than the majority's cursory disposition of it would suggest. Scholars are sharply divided on the subject and the literature is voluminous. Among the articles that conclude Congress has some degree of power to remove jurisdiction to hear constitutional defenses in enforcement cases are: Anderson, *The Power of Congress to Limit the Appellate Jurisdiction of the Supreme Court,* 1981 Det.C.L.Rev. 753; Graglia, *The Power of Congress to Limit Supreme Court Jurisdiction,* 7 Harv.J.L. & Pub. Pol'y 23 (1984); Van Alstyne, *A Critical Guide to Ex Parte McCardle,* 15 Ariz.L.Rev. 229 (1973); Wechsler, *The Courts and the Constitution,* 65 Colum.L.Rev. 1001

(1965). Among those reaching generally the opposite conclusion are: Ratner, *Congressional Power over the Appellate Jurisdiction of the Supreme Court,* 109 U.Pa.L.Rev. 157 (1960); Rotunda, *Congressional Power to Restrict the Jurisdiction of the Lower Federal Courts and the Problem of School Busing,* 64 Geo.L.J. 839 (1976); Sager, *The Supreme Court, 1980 Term—Foreword: Constitutional Limitations on Congress' Authority to Regulate the Jurisdiction of the Federal Courts,* 95 Harv.L.Rev. 17 (1981).[14] It seems to me rash, to put it no higher, to offer a quick answer to this profound question in a case that does not require or, given the majority's statutory construction, even touch upon it.[15]

It may be that the doctrine of sovereign immunity will change in the way the majority desires; it may be that the remark in *Robison* about the constitutional difficulties that would be presented if a benefits statute denied review of its own constitutionality presages a radical transformation of what had seemed settled doctrine. As Justice Frankfurter said in dissent in Larson v. Domestic & Foreign Commerce Corp., 337 U.S. 682, 709 (1949):

> The course of decisions concerning sovereign immunity is a good illustration of the conflicting considerations that often struggle for mastery in the judicial process, at least implicitly. In varying degrees, at different times, the momentum of the historic doctrine is arrested or deflected by an unexpressed feeling that governmental immunity runs counter to prevailing notions of reason and justice. Legal concepts are then found available to give effect to this feeling. . . .

Perhaps that is beginning to happen with respect to sovereign immunity in this field.

The implications of such a development should be recognized, however, before the next step is taken. It must be remembered that here Congress has not merely failed to articulate a waiver of sovereign immunity, it has affirmatively stated that there shall be no judicial review of the Secretary's denial of claims under $1000. To rule that this denial of review is unconstitutional is to decide the question of ultimate power * * *, for if Congress may not prevent review of claims for government benefits, it certainly may not take the more drastic action of barring constitutional challenges to a statute by a defendant against whom the statute is sought to be enforced. If a step so momentous is to

---

14. In order to realize just how complex the issue is and how enormous the literature has become, see Gunther, *Congressional Power to Curtail Federal Court Jurisdiction: An Opinionated Guide to the Ongoing Debate,* 36 Stan.L.Rev. 895, 896 n. 3 (1984).

15. The majority may be moved to state a position on this subject because of its expressed concern that application of the doctrine of sovereign immunity might permit abhorrent welfare legislation. The truth is, however, that constitutional doctrines cannot be framed to guard against every hypothetical evil. Much must be left to the wisdom and integrity of elected representatives. Were it otherwise, courts would long ago have had to abandon not only sovereign immunity but a variety of doctrines of justiciability, such as standing, political question, and the requirement of a case or controversy, that regularly operate to keep courts from constitutional issues. That sovereign immunity does so is not, of itself, sufficient ground to jettison the doctrine.

be taken, it should not be taken by an inferior court, particularly in a case where the court majority's statutory construction makes the step superfluous. If, on the other hand, the concept of sovereign immunity retains enough vitality to bar a claim for benefits, a decision to that effect has no implications as to congressional power to remove constitutional jurisdiction in enforcement actions.

* * * For the reasons given, I think it best to conclude, pending further clarification from the Supreme Court, that sovereign immunity denied the district court jurisdiction to entertain Bartlett's claim.

Notes

1. In what ways did the congressional limitations on judicial jurisdiction challenged in *Battaglia* and considered in *Bartlett* differ from the limits involved in Sheldon v. Sill and Lockerty v. Phillips?

2. The issue presented in *Battaglia* never reached the Supreme Court. No lower court that considered the question found for the plaintiffs on the merits of their substantive constitutional claim. See, e.g., Thomas v. Carnegie–Illinois Steel Corp., 174 F.2d 711 (3d Cir.1949).

3. What could Congress have done to satisfy the *Battaglia* court's due process concern? Would the court have accepted a statute which had vested full and exclusive power to review the constitutionality of the act in an administrative tribunal, whose members were selected by the President and served at his discretion?

4. If we accept the *Battaglia* court's premise that due process requires the availability of some forum (and perhaps a judicial forum) to adjudicate constitutional rights, does the court's conclusion that the limit on *federal* court power is therefore unconstitutional necessarily follow? Can you fashion an argument that in a case, such as *Battaglia*, where Congress has closed off *all* judicial fora, it is the limit on *state* court jurisdiction, rather than on federal court jurisdiction, which should fall initially? Are you persuaded by the argument you fashioned?

5. In *Bartlett,* do you understand Judge Bork's "sovereign immunity" theory? Is it persuasive? What is the majority's response?

6. The majority in *Bartlett* suggests that "[t]he delicate balance implicit in the doctrine of separation of powers would be destroyed" if Congress could judge the constitutionality of its own actions. Do you agree?

7. In his dissent, Judge Bork notes that "Bartlett is seeking a benefit from the government, not resisting a government or private enforcement action." Should that fact *ever* make a difference? If so, should it make a difference in this case, in light of the fact that Bartlett was presenting equal protection and religious freedom challenges?

8. Section 102(c) of the National Security Act of 1947 authorizes the Director of the Central Intelligence Agency, "in his discretion," to terminate the employment of any CIA employees "whenever he shall deem such termination necessary or advisable in the interests of the United States." 50 U.S.C. § 403(c). In Webster v. Doe, 486 U.S. 592 (1988), the Supreme Court

held that while judicial review of the Director's decisions has been precluded by the provision of the Administrative Procedure Act excluding judicial review where such review has been prohibited by statute or where the decision was committed to agency discretion by law, 5 U.S.C. §§ 701(a)(1), 701(a)(2), Congress had not intended to preclude review of constitutional attacks on the Director's decisions. In reaching this conclusion concerning congressional intent, the Court emphasized "that where Congress intends to preclude judicial review of constitutional claims its intent to do so must be clear." 486 U.S. at 603. The Court acknowledged that it "require[d] this heightened showing in part to avoid the 'serious constitutional question' that would arise if a federal statute were construed to deny any judicial forum for a colorable constitutional claim." Id.

In dissent, Justice Scalia argued:

> What could possibly be the basis for [the Court's] fear? Surely not some general principle that *all* constitutional violations must be remediable in the courts. The very text of the Constitution refutes that principle, since it provides that "[e]ach House shall be the Judge of the Elections, Returns and Qualifications of its own Member," Art. I, § 5 * * *. Even apart from the strict text of the Constitution, we have found some constitutional claims to be beyond judicial review because they involve "political questions." * * * In sum, it is simply untenable that there must be a judicial remedy for every constitutional violation. Members of Congress and the supervising officers of the Executive Branch take the same oath to uphold the Constitution that we do, and sometimes they are left to perform that oath unreviewed, as we always are.

486 U.S. at 612–13.

How persuasive is Justice Scalia's reasoning?

Justice Scalia further noted that in Webster v. Doe, "the denial of all judicial review is not at issue here, but merely the denial of review in United States district courts." Id. at 611.

Professor Richard Fallon has provided a carefully nuanced response to Justice Scalia's arguments. Fallon, *Some Confusions About Due Process, Judicial Review, and Constitutional Remedies*, 93 Colum.L.Rev. 309 (1993). Fallon suggests that the jurisdictional question of whether there is a constitutional right to judicial review in any given case depends on an analysis of the underlying substantive law. Where the constitution mandates "individually effective remedies," then it also requires judicial review. Id. at 370.

9. The Court has continued to hold that Congress may close off all review of statutory claims, and has also continued to intimate that it may not close off federal review of constitutional claims. In Dalton v. Specter, 511 U.S. 462 (1994), plaintiffs challenged implementation of the Defense Base Closure and Realignment Act of 1990, which set up a complex procedure for determining which military bases should be closed. The procedure culminated in a decision by the President to accept or reject, in its entirety, the report of a special commission on base closing. Plaintiffs claimed that procedural defects tainted early parts of the process, and thus that the President's ultimate approval could not be in compliance with the Act. The Supreme Court first held that the President's acts were not reviewable under the

Administrative Procedure Act, following Franklin v. Massachusetts, 505 U.S. 788 (1992). The Court then addressed plaintiffs' claim that in failing to comply with the statute, the President had acted unconstitutionally. The Court held that actions in excess of statutory authority are distinguishable from unconstitutional actions, and that plaintiffs' claims fell in the former category.

In concluding that Congress had authority to close off all judicial review of statutory claims, the Court several times referred to the "exception identified in *Franklin* for review of constitutional claims." Although this suggests that Congress may not preclude review of constitutional claims, neither *Franklin* nor *Dalton* raised the question directly since the Court found in each case that plaintiffs had raised only statutory claims against the President. The Court reaffirmed the strong presumption against interpreting a statute to preclude judicial review of constitutional claims in Demore v. Kim, 538 U.S. 510 (2003). For further discussion of *Dalton*, see Alexander & Lee, *Is There Such a Thing as Extraconstitutionality? The Puzzling Case of* Dalton v. Specter, 27 Ariz.St.L.J. 845 (1995).

The Court again avoided the question of whether Congress may close off judicial review of constitutional claims in Hamdan v. Rumsfeld, 548 U.S. __, 126 S.Ct. 2749 (2006). Hamdan, an alleged enemy combatant held at Guantanamo, invoked Supreme Court review of a lower court denial of a habeas petition he had filed in 2004. The federal government argued that the subsequently enacted Detainee Treatment Act of 2005 had stripped most federal courts—including the Supreme Court—of jurisdiction. The Court rejected the argument on statutory grounds, concluding that the 2005 Act did not apply to habeas petitions pending at the time of its enactment. The Court therefore did not reach Hamdan's argument that the statute "raise[d] grave questions about Congress' authority to impinge upon this Court's appellate jurisdiction, particularly in habeas cases." For further discussion of the Supreme Court's habeas jurisdiction, see infra pp. 159–66.

10.   On July 22, 2004, the House of Representatives passed the Marriage Protection Act of 2004, which would strip the federal courts of jurisdiction over cases challenging the constitutionality of the 1996 Defense of Marriage Act. H.R. 3313, 108th Cong. (2004). Is this restriction on federal court jurisdiction constitutional? What if Congress excluded all judicial review, state or federal, to review the constitutionality of the statute? Compare Gerhardt, *The Constitutional Limits to Court–Stripping*, 9 Lewis & Clark L.Rev. 347 (2005), with Redish, *Same-Sex Marriage, the Constitution, and Congressional Power to Control Federal Jurisdiction: Be Careful What You Wish For*, 9 Lewis & Clark L.Rev. 363 (2005). See also Weiman, Comment, *Jurisdiction Stripping, Constitutional Supremacy, and the Implications of* Ex Parte Young, 153 U.Pa.L.Rev. 1677 (2005). In addition to the Marriage Protection Act, the 108th Congress also considered legislation that would preclude federal judicial review of the pledge of allegiance (the Pledge Protection Act of 2004). See Hooper, *Jurisdiction-Stripping: The Pledge Protection Act of 2004*, 42 Harv.J.Legis. 511 (2005) (arguing that "the Act is both unconstitutional and ill-advised").

11.   If Congress cannot preclude all judicial review of constitutional claims, what implications does this have for *federal* jurisdiction? In his

dissent in *Webster*, Justice Scalia argued that "if there is any truth to the proposition that judicial cognizance of constitutional claims cannot be eliminated, it is, at most, that they cannot be eliminated from state courts, and from this Court's appellate jurisdiction over cases from state courts * * * involving such claims." 486 U.S. at 611–12. In this context, consider the following case.

TARBLE'S CASE

Supreme Court of the United States, 1871.
80 U.S. (13 Wall.) 397.

Error to the Supreme Court of Wisconsin.

This was a proceeding on *habeas corpus* for the discharge of one Edward Tarble, held in the custody of a recruiting officer of the United States as an enlisted soldier, on the alleged ground that he was a minor, under the age of eighteen years at the time of his enlistment, and that he enlisted without the consent of his father.

The writ was issued on the 10th of August, 1869, by a court commissioner of Dane County, Wisconsin, an officer authorized by the laws of that State to issue the writ of *habeas corpus* upon the petition of parties imprisoned or restrained of their liberty, or of persons on their behalf. It was issued in this case upon the petition of the father of Tarble, in which he alleged that his son, who had enlisted under the name of Frank Brown, was confined and restrained of his liberty by Lieutenant Stone, of the United States army, in the city of Madison, in that State and county; that the cause of his confinement and restraint was that he had, on the 20th of the preceding July, enlisted, and been mustered into the military service of the United States; that he was under the age of eighteen years at the time of such enlistment; that the same was made without the knowledge, consent, or approval of the petitioner; and was therefore, as the petitioner was advised and believed, illegal; and that the petitioner was lawfully entitled to the custody, care, and services of his son.

The writ was directed to the officer thus named, commanding him to have Tarble, together with the cause of his imprisonment and detention, before the commissioner, at the latter's office, in the city of Madison, immediately after the receipt of the writ.

The officer thereupon produced Tarble before the commissioner and made a return in writing to the writ, protesting that the commissioner had no jurisdiction in the premises, and stating, as the authority and cause for the detention of the prisoner, that he, the officer, was a first lieutenant in the army of the United States, and by due authority was detailed as a recruiting officer at the city of Madison, in the State of Wisconsin, and as such officer had the custody and command of all soldiers recruited for the army at that city; that on the 27th of July preceding, the prisoner, under the name of Frank Brown, was regularly enlisted as a soldier in the army of the United States for the period of five years, unless sooner discharged by proper authority; that he then duly took the oath required in such case by law and the regulations of the army, in which oath he declared that he was of the age of twenty-one years, and thereby procured his enlistment, and was on the same day duly mustered into the service of the United States; that subsequently he deserted the service, and being retaken was then in custody and confinement under charges of desertion, awaiting trial by the proper military authorities.

To this return the petitioner filed a reply, denying, on information and belief, that the prisoner was ever duly or lawfully enlisted or mustered as a soldier into the army of the United States, or that he had declared on oath that he was of the age of twenty-one years, and alleging that the prisoner was at the time of his enlistment under the age of eighteen years, and on information and belief that he was enticed into the enlistment, which was without the knowledge, consent, or approval of the petitioner; that the only oath taken by the prisoner at the time of his enlistment was an oath of allegiance; and that the petitioner was advised and believed that the prisoner was not, and never had been, a deserter from the military service of the United States.

On the 12th of August, to which day the hearing of the petition was adjourned, the commissioner proceeded to take the testimony of different witnesses produced before him, which related principally to the enlistment of the prisoner, the declarations which he made as to his age, and the oath he took at the time, his alleged desertion, the charges against him, his actual age, and the absence of any consent to the enlistment on the part of his father.

The commissioner, after argument, held that the prisoner was illegally imprisoned and detained by Lieutenant Stone, and commanded that officer forthwith to discharge him from custody.

Afterwards, in September of the same year, that officer applied to the Supreme Court of the State for a *certiorari*, setting forth in his application the proceedings before the commissioner and his ruling thereon. The *certiorari* was allowed, and in obedience to it the proceedings had before the commissioner were returned to the Supreme Court. These proceedings consisted of the petition for the writ, the return of the officer, the reply of the petitioner, and the testimony, documentary and parol, produced before the commissioner.

Upon these proceedings the case was duly argued before the Supreme Court, and in April, 1870, that tribunal pronounced its judgment, affirming the order of the commissioner discharging the prisoner. This judgment was now before this court for examination on writ of error prosecuted by the United States.

* * *

MR. JUSTICE FIELD, after stating the case, delivered the opinion of the court, as follows:

The important question is presented by this case, whether a State court commissioner has jurisdiction, upon *habeas corpus*, to inquire into the validity of the enlistment of soldiers into the military service of the United States, and to discharge them from such service when, in his judgment, their enlistment has not been made in conformity with the laws of the United States. The question presented may be more generally stated thus: Whether any judicial officer of a State has jurisdiction to issue a writ of *habeas corpus*, or to continue proceedings under the writ when issued, for the discharge of a person held under the authority, or claim and color of the authority, of the United States, by an officer of that government. For it is evident, if such jurisdiction may be exercised by any judicial officer of a State, it may be exercised by the court commissioner within the county for which he is appointed; and if it may be exercised with reference to soldiers detained in the military service of the United States, whose enlistment is alleged to have been illegally made, it may be exercised with reference to persons employed in any other department of the public service when their illegal detention is asserted. It may be exercised in all cases where parties are held under the authority of the United States, whenever the invalidity of the exercise of that authority is affirmed. The jurisdiction, if it exist at all, can only be limited in its application by the legislative power of the State. It may even reach to parties imprisoned under sentence of the National courts, after regular indictment, trial, and conviction, for offences against the laws of the United States. As we read the opinion of the Supreme Court of Wisconsin in this case, this is the claim of authority asserted by that tribunal for itself and for the judicial officers of that State. It does, indeed, disclaim any right of either to interfere with parties in custody, under judicial sentence, when the National court pronouncing sentence had jurisdiction to try and punish the offenders, but it asserts, at the same time, for itself and for each of those officers, the right to determine, upon *habeas corpus*, in all cases, whether that court ever had such jurisdiction. In the case of Booth, which subsequently came before this court, it not only sustained the action of one of its justices in discharging a prisoner held in custody by a marshal of the United States, under a warrant of commitment for an offence against the laws of the United States, issued by a commissioner of the United States; but it discharged the same prisoner when subsequently confined under sentence of the District Court of the United States for the same offence, after indictment, trial, and conviction, on the ground that, in its judgment, the act of Congress creating the offence was unconstitutional; and in order that its decision in that respect should be final and conclusive, directed its clerk to refuse obedience to the writ of error issued by this court, under the act of Congress, to bring up the decision for review.

It is evident, as said by this court when the case of Booth was finally brought before it, if the power asserted by that State court existed, no offence against the laws of the United States could be punished by their own tribunals, without the permission and according to the judgment of the courts of the State in which the parties happen to be imprisoned; that if that power existed in that State court, it belonged equally to every other State court in the Union where a prisoner was within its territorial limits; and, as the different State courts could not always agree, it would often happen that an act, which was admitted to be an offence and justly punishable in one State, would be regarded as innocent, and even praiseworthy in another, and no one could suppose that a government, which had hitherto lasted for seventy years, "enforcing its laws by its own tribunals, and preserving the union of the States, could have lasted a single year, or fulfilled the trusts committed to it, if offences against its laws could not have been punished without the consent of the State in which the culprit was found."

The decision of this court in the two cases which grew out of the arrest of Booth, that of Ableman v. Booth, and that of The United States v. Booth,* disposes alike of the claim of jurisdiction by a State court, or by a State judge, to interfere with the authority of the United States, whether that authority be exercised by a Federal officer or be exercised by a Federal tribunal. In the first of these cases Booth had been arrested and committed to the custody of a marshal of the United States by a commissioner appointed by the District Court of the United States, upon a charge of having aided and abetted the escape of a fugitive slave. Whilst thus in custody a justice of the Supreme Court of Wisconsin issued a writ of *habeas corpus* directed to the marshal, requiring him to produce the body of Booth with the cause of his imprisonment. The marshal made a return, stating that he held the prisoner upon the warrant of the commissioner, a copy of which he annexed to and returned with the writ. To this return Booth demurred as insufficient in law to justify his detention, and, upon the hearing which followed, the justice held his detention illegal, and ordered his discharge. The marshal thereupon applied for and obtained a *certiorari*, and had the proceedings removed to the Supreme Court of the State, where, after argument, the order of the justice discharging the prisoner from custody was affirmed. The decision proceeded upon the ground that the act of Congress respecting fugitive slaves was unconstitutional and void.

In the second case, Booth had been indicted for the offence with which he was charged before the commissioner, and from which the State judge had discharged him, and had been tried and convicted in the District Court of the United States for the District of Wisconsin, and been sentenced to pay a fine of $1000, and to be imprisoned for one month. Whilst in imprisonment, in execution of this sentence, application was made by Booth to the Supreme Court of the State, for a writ of *habeas corpus*, alleging in his application that his imprisonment was illegal, by reason of the unconstitutionality of the fugitive slave law, and that the District Court had no jurisdiction to try or punish him for the matter charged against him. The court granted the application, and issued the writ, to which the sheriff, to whom the prisoner had been committed by the marshal, returned that he held the prisoner by virtue of the proceedings and sentence of the District Court, a copy of which was annexed to his return. Upon demurrer to this return, the court

* 21 Howard, 506.

adjudged the imprisonment of Booth to be illegal, and ordered him to be discharged from custody, and he was accordingly set at liberty.

For a review in this court of the judgments in both of these cases, writs of error were prosecuted. No return, however, was made to the writs, the clerk of the Supreme Court of Wisconsin having been directed by that court to refuse obedience to them; but copies of the records were filed by the Attorney-General, and it was ordered by this court that they should be received with the same effect and legal operation as if returned by the clerk. The cases were afterwards heard and considered together, and the decision of both was announced in the same opinion. In that opinion the Chief Justice details the facts of the two cases at length, and comments upon the character of the jurisdiction asserted by the State judge and the State court; by the State judge to supervise and annul the proceedings of a commissioner of the United States, and to discharge a prisoner committed by him for an offence against the laws of the United States; and by the State court to supervise and annul the proceedings and judgment of a District Court of the United States, and to discharge a prisoner who had been indicted, tried, and found guilty of an offence against the laws of the United States and sentenced to imprisonment by that court.

And in answer to this assumption of judicial power by the judges and by the Supreme Court of Wisconsin thus made, the Chief Justice said as follows: If they "possess the jurisdiction they claim, they must derive it either from the United States or the State. It certainly has not been conferred on them by the United States; and it is equally clear it was not in the power of the State to confer it, even if it had attempted to do so; for no State can authorize one of its judges or courts to exercise judicial power, by *habeas corpus* or otherwise, within the jurisdiction of another and independent government. And although the State of Wisconsin is sovereign within its territorial limits to a certain extent, yet that sovereignty is limited and restricted by the Constitution of the United States. And the powers of the General government and of the State, although both exist and are exercised within the same territorial limits, are yet separate and distinct sovereignties, acting separately and independently of each other, within their respective spheres. And the sphere of action appropriated to the United States, is as far beyond the reach of the judicial process issued by a State judge or a State court, as if the line of division was traced by landmarks and monuments visible to the eye. And the State of Wisconsin had no more power to authorize these proceedings of its judges and courts, than it would have had if the prisoner had been confined in Michigan, or in any other State of the Union, for an offence against the laws of the State in which he was imprisoned."

It is in the consideration of this distinct and independent character of the government of the United States, from that of the government of the several States, that the solution of the question presented in this case, and in similar cases, must be found. There are within the territorial limits of each State two governments, restricted in their spheres of action, but independent of each other, and supreme within their respective spheres. Each has its separate departments; each has its distinct laws, and each has its own tribunals for their enforcement. Neither government can intrude within the jurisdiction, or authorize any interference therein by its judicial officers with the action of the other. The two governments in each State stand in their respective spheres of action in the same independent relation to each other, except in one particular, that they would if their authority embraced distinct territories. That particular consists in the supremacy of the authority of the United States when any conflict arises between the two governments. The Constitution and the laws passed in pursuance of it, are declared by the Constitution itself to be the supreme law of the land, and the judges of every State are bound thereby, "anything in the constitution or laws of any State to the contrary notwithstanding." Whenever, therefore, any conflict arises between the enactments of the two sovereignties, or in the enforcement of their asserted authorities, those of the National government must have supremacy until the validity of the different enactments and authorities can be finally determined by the tribunals of the United States. This temporary supremacy until judicial decision by the National tribunals, and the ultimate determination of the conflict by such decision, are essential to the preservation of order and peace, and the avoidance of forcible collision between the two governments. "The Constitution," as said by Mr. Chief Justice Taney, "was not framed merely to guard the States against danger from abroad, but chiefly to secure union and harmony at home; and to accomplish this end it was deemed necessary, when the Constitution was framed, that many of the rights of sovereignty which the States then possessed should be ceded to the General government; and that in the sphere of action assigned to it, it should be supreme and strong enough to execute its own laws by its own tribunals, without interruption from a State, or from State authorities." And the judicial power conferred extends to all cases arising under the Constitution, and thus embraces every legislative act of Congress, whether passed in pursuance of it, or in disregard of its provisions. The Constitution is under the view of the tribunals of the United States when any act of Congress is brought before them for consideration.

Such being the distinct and independent character of the two governments, within their respective spheres of action, it follows that neither can intrude with its judicial process into the domain of the other, except so far as such intrusion may be necessary on the part of the National government to preserve its rightful supremacy in cases of conflict of authority. In their laws, and mode of enforcement, neither is responsible to the other. How their respective laws shall be enacted; how they shall be carried into execution; and in what tribunals, or by what officers; and how much discretion, or whether any at all shall be vested in their officers, are matters subject to their own control, and in the regulation of which neither can interfere with the other.

Now, among the powers assigned to the National government, is the power "to raise and support armies," and the power "to provide for the government and regulation of the land and naval forces." The execution of these powers falls within the line of its duties; and its control over the subject is plenary and exclusive. It can determine, without question from any State authority, how the armies shall be raised, whether by voluntary enlistment or forced draft, the age at which the soldier shall be received, and the period for which he shall be taken, the compensation he shall be allowed, and the service to which he shall be assigned. And it can provide the rules for the government and regulation of the forces after they are raised, define what shall constitute military offences, and prescribe their punishment. No interference with the execution of this power of the National government in the formation, organization, and government of its armies by any State officials could be permitted without greatly impairing the efficiency, if it did not utterly destroy, this branch of the public service. Probably in every county and city in the several States there are one or more officers authorized by law to issue writs of *habeas corpus* on behalf of persons alleged to be illegally restrained of their liberty; and if soldiers could be taken from the army of the United States, and the validity of their enlistment inquired into by any one of these officers, such proceeding could be taken by all of them, and no movement could be made by the National troops without their commanders being subjected to constant annoyance and embarrassment from this source. The experience of the late rebellion has shown us that, in times of great popular excitement, there may be found in every State large numbers ready and anxious to embarrass the operations of the government, and easily persuaded to believe every step taken for the enforcement of its authority illegal and void. Power to issue writs of *habeas corpus* for the discharge of soldiers in the military service, in the hands of parties thus disposed, might be used, and often would be used, to the great detriment of the public service. In many exigencies the measures of the National government might in this way be entirely bereft of their efficacy and value. An appeal in such cases to this court, to correct the erroneous action of these officers, would afford no adequate remedy. Proceedings on *habeas corpus* are summary, and the delay incident to bringing the decision of a State officer, through the highest tribunal of the State, to this court for review, would necessarily occupy years, and in the meantime, where the soldier was discharged, the mischief would be accomplished. It is manifest that the powers of the National government could not be exercised with energy and efficiency at all times, if its acts could be interfered with and controlled for any period by officers or tribunals of another sovereignty.

It is true similar embarrassment might sometimes be occasioned, though in a less degree, by the exercise of the authority to issue the writ possessed by judicial officers of the United States, but the ability to provide a speedy remedy for any inconvenience following from this source would always exist with the National legislature.

State judges and State courts, authorized by laws of their States to issue writs of *habeas corpus*, have undoubtedly a right to issue the writ in any case where a party is alleged to be illegally confined within their limits, (unless) it appear upon his application that he is confined under the authority, or claim and color of the authority, of the United States, by an officer of that government. If such fact appear upon the application the writ should be refused. If it do not appear, the judge or court issuing the writ has a right to inquire into the cause of imprisonment, and ascertain by what authority the person is held within the limits of the State; and it is the duty of the marshal, or other officer having the custody of the prisoner, to give, by a proper return information in this respect. His return should be sufficient, in its detail of facts, to show distinctly that the imprisonment is under the authority, or claim and color of the authority, of the United States, and to exclude the suspicion of imposition or oppression on his part. * * *

Writ Should be refused

" * * * But, after the return is made, and the State judge or court judicially apprised that the party is in custody under the authority of the United States, they can proceed no further. They then know that the prisoner is within the dominion and jurisdiction of another government, and that neither the writ of *habeas corpus* nor any other process issued under State authority can pass over the line of division between the two sovereignties. He is then within the dominion and exclusive jurisdiction of the United States. If he has committed an offence against their laws, their tribunals alone can punish him. If he is wrongfully imprisoned, their judicial tribunals can release him and afford him redress." [The quotation is from Chief Justice Taney's previously cited opinion in *Booth*].

exclusive jurisdiction of US

Some attempt has been made in adjudications, to which our attention has been called, to limit the decision of this court in Ableman v. Booth, and The United States v. Booth, to cases where a prisoner is held in custody under undisputed lawful authority of the United States, as distinguished from his imprisonment under claim and color of such authority. But it is evident that the decision does not admit of any such limitation. * * *

This limitation upon the power of State tribunals and State officers furnishes no just ground to apprehend that the liberty of the citizen will thereby be endangered. The United States are as much interested in protecting the citizen from illegal restraint under their authority, as the several States are to protect him from the like restraint under their authority, and are no more likely to tolerate any oppression. Their courts and judicial officers are clothed with the power to issue the writ of *habeas corpus* in all cases, where a party is illegally restrained of his liberty by an officer of the United States, whether such illegality consist in the character of the process, the authority of the officer, or the invalidity of the law under which he is held. And there is no just reason to believe that they will exhibit any hesitation to exert their power, when it is properly invoked. Certainly there can be no ground for supposing that their action will be less prompt and efficient in such cases than would be that of State tribunals and State officers.

* * *

Judgment reversed.

THE CHIEF JUSTICE, dissenting.

I cannot concur in the opinion just read. I have no doubt of the right of a State court to inquire into the jurisdiction of a Federal court upon *habeas corpus*, and to discharge when satisfied that the petitioner for the writ is restrained of liberty by the sentence of a court without jurisdiction. If it errs in deciding the question of jurisdiction, the error must be corrected in the mode prescribed by the 25th section of the Judiciary Act; not by denial of the right to make inquiry.

I have still less doubt, if possible, that a writ of *habeas corpus* may issue from a State court to inquire into the validity of imprisonment or detention, without the sentence of any court whatever, by an officer of the United States. The State court may err; and if it does, the error may be corrected here. The mode has been prescribed and should be followed.

To deny the right of State courts to issue the writ, or, what amounts to the same thing, to concede the right to issue and to deny the right to adjudicate, is to deny the right to protect the citizen by *habeas corpus* against arbitrary imprisonment in a large class of cases; and, I am thoroughly persuaded, was never within the contemplation of the Convention which framed, or the people who adopted, the Constitution. That instrument expressly declares that "the privilege of the writ of *habeas corpus* shall not be suspended, unless when, in case of rebellion or invasion, the public safety may require it."

Notes

1. What relevance does Tarble's Case have to Professor Hart's Dialogue? If we assume that due process requires the availability of an independent forum for the adjudication of constitutional rights, what potential problems are created by *Tarble* when Congress closes off lower federal court jurisdiction to review the assertion of constitutional rights? Consider the following argument:

> While the Supreme Court's opinion in [*Tarble*] may leave much to be desired, [it can be] rework[ed] * * * into simply an inference of congressional intent to exclude state court power in the face of congressional silence * * * because, were Congress actually to consider the question, it likely would not want state courts—who will lack expertise in interpretation of federal law, who will inherently lack uniformity, and who may be hostile to federal interests—to have the authority to impair the operation of federal programs by directly controlling the actions of federal officers. To be sure, if Congress wishes state courts to have such authority, it may say so. But unless and until it does so, the courts should interpret congressional silence to exclude the exercise of state court authority.

> *Tarble's Case* thus can serve, in a certain sense, as a limiting force on Congress's exercise of its authority to close off lower federal court jurisdiction. For if we accept that due process requires some independent forum to enforce constitutional rights, Congress cannot remove

from the federal courts authority to protect constitutional rights, unless it simultaneously and *affirmatively* removes the bar of *Tarble's Case* to state court action. Otherwise, the result would be that *both* the federal courts *and* the state courts would be closed, and the due process right to an independent forum would be denied.

Redish, *Constitutional Limitations on Congressional Power to Control Federal Jurisdiction: A Reaction to Professor Sager,* 77 Nw.U.L.Rev. 143, 158–59 (1982).

Consider also the following response by Professor Bator to an earlier articulation of the same theory:

Why should the dubious tail of Tarble's Case wag such a large dog? Tarble's Case can be criticized as wrong (at least in theory) even on its facts—that is, even where Congress *has* provided a full and adequate remedy in federal court, why should it be presumed that a state court should not "interfere" with federal officials? Why then should we compound the error by reading the meandering and poorly reasoned Tarble opinion as creating a generic barrier to state-court actions to control the acts of federal officials even when there exists no remedy in federal court? Is there anything in the constitutional plan which would justify the notion that state courts of general jurisdiction were deemed by the Framers as presumptively *incapable* of passing on the legality of official action by federal officers—this at a time when it was a more than plausible possibility that lower federal courts would not be created at all?

P. Bator, P. Mishkin, D. Shapiro & H. Wechsler, Hart and Wechsler's The Federal Courts and the Federal System Supplement 120 (1981).

For another attack on *Tarble*, see Arnold, *The Power of State Courts to Enjoin Federal Officers,* 73 Yale L.J. 1385 (1964). Does it make sense today to judge *congressional* intent in the face of congressional silence on the basis of the *framers'* assumptions? Is the philosophy of judicial federalism today the same as it was then? Could a valid argument be fashioned that even if it is such a departure, the rule of *Tarble* is justified as reflecting the significant alteration in the state-federal balance in general and the role of state courts in particular after the Civil War? Consider Amsterdam, *Criminal Prosecutions Affecting Federally Guaranteed Civil Rights: Federal Removal and Habeas Corpus Jurisdiction to Abort State Court Trial,* 113 U.Pa.L.Rev. 793 (1965): "[After the Civil War] [t]he assumption was abandoned that the state courts were the normal place for enforcement of federal law save in rare and narrow instances where they affirmatively demonstrated themselves unfit or unfair." Id. at 828. See also *Developments in the Law: Section 1983 and Federalism,* 90 Harv.L.Rev. 1133, 1152–53 (1977) (noting that because of "the unreliable behavior of the state courts during the war and their evident susceptibility to local pressures, the courts that the Republicans turned to were the federal trial courts.").

Professor Sager has suggested that little turns on the outcome of this argument, because "*Tarble's* yea or *Tarble's* nay, federal immunity from state coercive relief is within Congress' control, subject to presumptions that could run in either direction and that will matter relatively little once they are clearly announced." Sager, *The Supreme Court, 1980 Term—Foreword:*

Constitutional Limitations on Congress' Authority to Regulate the Jurisdiction of the Federal Courts, 95 Harv.L.Rev. 17, 82 (1981). What do you think he means? Is he right? For a response, see Redish, supra, 77 Nw.U.L.Rev. at 159. For a recent defense of *Tarble*, including historical evidence, see Collins, *Article III Cases, State Court Duties, and the Madisonian Compromise*, 1995 Wisc.L.Rev. 39.

2.   What do you suppose the Court in *Tarble* contemplated would happen to its limit on state court jurisdiction if Congress closed off the federal courts? What *should* happen?

3.   *Tarble* itself dealt only with the issue of a state court's power to issue writs of habeas corpus to federal officers. In McClung v. Silliman, 19 U.S. (6 Wheat.) 598 (1821), the Supreme Court had held that state courts lacked the power to issue writs of mandamus to federal officers, and lower courts have continued to apply this doctrine. See Armand Schmoll, Inc. v. Federal Reserve Bank of New York, 286 N.Y. 503, 37 N.E.2d 225 (1941), *certiorari denied* 315 U.S. 818 (1942). One commentator concludes that "there is no good reason to predict that *McClung* will not govern whenever a plaintiff makes the mistake of labeling his papers 'mandamus.'" Arnold, supra, 73 Yale L.J. at 1392.

Somewhat less settled is the issue of a state court's power to enjoin federal officers. Compare Kennedy v. Bruce, 298 F.2d 860 (5th Cir.1962); Alabama ex rel. Gallion v. Rogers, 187 F.Supp. 848 (M.D.Ala.1960), *affirmed per curiam sub nom.* Dinkens v. Attorney General, 285 F.2d 430 (5th Cir.1961), *cert. denied* 366 U.S. 913; Alabama ex rel. Patterson v. Jones, 189 F.Supp. 61 (M.D.Ala.1960); Pennsylvania Turnpike Commission v. McGinnes, 179 F.Supp. 578 (E.D.Pa.1959), *affirmed per curiam* 278 F.2d 330 (3d Cir.), *cert. denied* 364 U.S. 820 (state courts lack power to enjoin federal officers) with Lewis Pub. Co. v. Wyman, 152 Fed. 200, 205 (C.C.E.D.Mo. 1907) (state courts can enjoin federal officers). See Wheeldin v. Wheeler, 373 U.S. 647, 664 n. 13 (1963) (Brennan, J., dissenting). One commentator has seriously questioned the extension of *Tarble* to injunctions. See Arnold, supra. Given the reasoning of the Court in *Tarble*, does it make sense to limit the holding to habeas corpus?

4.   The federal officer removal statute, 28 U.S.C. § 1442, provides in relevant part:

> (a) A civil action or criminal prosecution commenced in a State court against any of the following persons may be removed by them to the district court of the United States for the district and division embracing the place wherein it is pending:
>
> > (1) Any officer of the United States or any agency thereof, or person acting under him, for any act under color of such office or on account of any right, title or authority claimed under any Act of Congress for the apprehension or punishment of criminals or the collection of the revenue.

Could it be persuasively argued that the availability of federal officer removal obviates any need for the *Tarble* rule? What, if any, are likely to be the differences between the two? Would this statute be relevant to the question of whether the rule of *Tarble* should fall if Congress has closed the federal courts?

5.   Despite the questions that have been raised about *Tarble* by a few commentators, at least in its original context of habeas corpus the decision is universally followed in the courts. See Huff v. United States, 437 F.Supp. 564, 568 (W.D.Mo.1977); Thomas v. Levi, 422 F.Supp. 1027, 1033 (E.D.Pa. 1976); Quillar v. United States, 272 F.Supp. 55, 56 (W.D.Mo.1967). Additionally, state courts have on occasion recognized *Tarble's* continued vitality. See e.g., State v. Theoharopoulos, 72 Wis.2d 327, 240 N.W.2d 635, 639 (1976).

§ 2.   CONGRESSIONAL POWER TO REGULATE SUPREME COURT APPELLATE JURISDICTION

EX PARTE McCARDLE

Supreme Court of the United States, 1868.
74 U.S. (7 Wall.) 506.

The case was this:

The Constitution of the United States ordains as follows:

"§ 1. The judicial power of the United States shall be vested *in one Supreme Court*, and in such inferior courts as the Congress may from time to time ordain and establish."

"§ 2. The judicial power shall extend to all cases in law or equity arising *under this Constitution, the laws of the United States*," & c.

And in these last cases the Constitution ordains that,

"The Supreme Court shall have appellate jurisdiction, both as to law and fact, *with such exceptions, and under such regulations, as the Congress shall make.*"

With these constitutional provisions in existence, Congress, on the 5th February, 1867, by "An act to amend an act to establish the judicial courts of the United States, approved September 24, 1789," provided that the several courts of the United States, and the several justices and judges of such courts, within their respective jurisdiction, in addition to the authority already conferred by law, should have power to grant writs of *habeas corpus* in all cases where any person may be restrained of his or her liberty in violation of the Constitution, or of any treaty or law of the United States. And that, from the final decision of any judge, justice, or court inferior to the Circuit Court, appeal might be taken to the Circuit Court of the United States for the district in which the cause was heard, and *from the judgment of the said Circuit Court to the Supreme Court of the United States*.

This statute being in force, one McCardle, alleging unlawful restraint by military force, preferred a petition in the court below, for the writ of *habeas corpus*.

The writ was issued, and a return was made by the military commander, admitting the restraint but denying that it was unlawful.

It appeared that the petitioner was not in the military service of the United States, but was held in custody by military authority for trial before a military commission, upon charges founded upon the publication of articles alleged to be incendiary and libellous, in a newspaper of which he was editor. The custody was alleged to be under the authority of certain acts of Congress.

Upon the hearing, the petitioner was remanded to the military custody; but, upon his prayer, an appeal was allowed him to this court, and upon filing the usual appeal-bond, for costs, he was admitted to bail upon recognizance, with sureties, conditioned for his future appearance in the Circuit Court, to abide by and perform the final judgment of this court. The appeal was taken under the above-mentioned act of February 5, 1867.

A motion to dismiss this appeal was made at the last term, and, after argument, was denied.

Subsequently, on the 2d, 3d, 4th, and 9th March, the case was argued very thoroughly and ably upon the merits, and was taken under advisement. While it was thus held, and before conference in regard to the decision proper to be made, an act was passed by Congress,[†] returned with objections by the President, and, on the 27th March, repassed by the constitutional majority, the second section of which was as follows:

> "*And be it further enacted*, That so much of the act approved February 5, 1867, entitled 'An act to amend an act to establish the judicial courts of the United States, approved September 24, 1789,' as authorized an appeal from the judgment of the Circuit Court to the Supreme Court of the United States, or the exercise of any such jurisdiction by said Supreme Court, on appeal which have been, or may hereafter be taken, be, and the same is hereby repealed."

* * *

THE CHIEF JUSTICE delivered the opinion of the court.

The first question necessarily is that of jurisdiction; for, if the act of March, 1868, takes away the jurisdiction defined by the act of February, 1867, it is useless, if not improper, to enter into any discussion of other questions.

It is quite true, as was argued by the counsel for the petitioner, that the appellate jurisdiction of this court is not derived from acts of Congress. It is, strictly speaking, conferred by the Constitution. But it is conferred "with such exceptions and under such regulations as Congress shall make."

It is unnecessary to consider whether, if Congress had made no exceptions and no regulations, this court might not have exercised

† Act of March 27, 1868, 15 Stat. at Large, 44.

general appellate jurisdiction under rules prescribed by itself. For among the earliest acts of the first Congress, at its first session, was the act of September 24th, 1789, to establish the judicial courts of the United States. That act provided for the organization of this court, and prescribed regulations for the exercise of its jurisdiction.

The source of that jurisdiction, and the limitations of it by the Constitution and by statute, have been on several occasions subjects of consideration here. In the case of Durousseau v. The United States,[*] particularly, the whole matter was carefully examined, and the court held, that while "the appellate powers of this court are not given by the judicial act, but are given by the Constitution," they are, nevertheless, "limited and regulated by that act, and by such other acts as have been passed on the subject." The court said, further, that the judicial act was an exercise of the power given by the Constitution to Congress "of making exceptions to the appellate jurisdiction of the Supreme Court." "They have described affirmatively," said the court, "its jurisdiction, and this affirmative description has been understood to imply a negation of the exercise of such appellate power as is not comprehended within it."

The principle that the affirmation of appellate jurisdiction implies the negation of all such jurisdiction not affirmed having been thus established, it was an almost necessary consequence that acts of Congress, providing for the exercise of jurisdiction, should come to be spoken of as acts granting jurisdiction, and not as acts making exceptions to the constitutional grant of it.

The exception to appellate jurisdiction in the case before us, however, is not an inference from the affirmation of other appellate jurisdiction. It is made in terms. The provision of the act of 1867, affirming the appellate jurisdiction of this court in cases of *habeas corpus* is expressly repealed. It is hardly possible to imagine a plainer instance of positive exception.

We are not at liberty to inquire into the motives of the legislature. We can only examine into its power under the Constitution; and the power to make exceptions to the appellate jurisdiction of this court is given by express words.

What, then, is the effect of the repealing act upon the case before us? We cannot doubt as to this. Without jurisdiction the court cannot proceed at all in any cause. Jurisdiction is power to declare the law, and when it ceases to exist, the only function remaining to the court is that of announcing the fact and dismissing the cause. And this is not less clear upon authority than upon principle.

Several cases were cited by the counsel for the petitioner in support of the position that jurisdiction of this case is not affected by the repealing act. But none of them, in our judgment, afford any support to it. They are all cases of the exercise of judicial power by the legislature,

[*] 6 Cranch, 312; Wiscart v. D'Auchy, 3 Dallas, 321.

or of legislative interference with courts in the exercising of continuing jurisdiction.

On the other hand, the general rule, supported by the best elementary writers is, that "when an act of the legislature is repealed, it must be considered, except as to transactions past and closed, as if it never existed." And the effect of repealing acts upon suits under acts repealed, has been determined by the adjudications of this court. The subject was fully considered in Norris v. Crocker, and more recently in Insurance Company v. Ritchie. In both of these cases it was held that no judgment could be rendered in a suit after the repeal of the act under which it was brought and prosecuted.

It is quite clear, therefore, that this court cannot proceed to pronounce judgment in this case, for it has no longer jurisdiction of the appeal; and judicial duty is not less fitly performed by declining ungranted jurisdiction than in exercising firmly that which the Constitution and the laws confer.

Counsel seem to have supposed, if effect be given to the repealing act in question, that the whole appellate power of the court, in cases of *habeas corpus*, is denied. But this is an error. The act of 1868 does not except from that jurisdiction any cases but appeals from Circuit Courts under the act of 1867. It does not affect the jurisdiction which was previously exercised.

The appeal of the petitioner in this case must be dismissed for want of jurisdiction.

EX PARTE YERGER, 75 U.S. (8 Wall.) 85 (1868). Petitioner, a private citizen and a civilian, had been arrested in Mississippi on a charge of murder. He was to be tried by a military commission, pursuant to the Act of March 2, 1867, establishing Reconstruction. He sought a writ of habeas corpus in federal court, alleging that his constitutional rights had been denied. The lower court found petitioner's detention to be lawful, and he sought a writ of certiorari to obtain review in the Supreme Court. The Supreme Court's jurisdiction was challenged on the grounds that the act of 1868 (involved in *McCardle*) eliminating Supreme Court appellate review of habeas corpus decisions provided for in 1867 precluded Supreme Court review. The Court responded that the 1868 act had repealed only the form of habeas corpus review provided for in the 1867 act, and had no effect whatsoever on the alternative method of obtaining habeas corpus review provided for in the Judiciary Act of 1789:

> "Our conclusion is, that none of the acts prior to 1867, authorizing this court to exercise appellate jurisdiction by means of the writ of *habeas corpus*, were repealed by the act of that year, and that the repealing section of the act of 1868 is limited in terms, and must

be limited in effect to the appellate jurisdiction authorized by the act of 1867.

"We could come to no other conclusion without holding that the whole appellate jurisdiction of this court, in cases of *habeas corpus*, conferred by the Constitution, recognized by law, and exercised from the foundation of the government hitherto, has been taken away, without the expression of such intent, and by mere implication, through the operation of the acts of 1867 and 1868." Id. at 106.

Notes

1. *McCardle* was the vortex of a complex and bitter political struggle over the validity of Congress' Reconstruction program. In the words of Professor Fairman, *McCardle* "was the case whereby Congressional Reconstruction was really being brought to book." C. Fairman, VI History of the Supreme Court of the United States: Reconstruction and Reunion 1864–88, part one 451 (1971). If the Court were to have invalidated the use of military trials, Congress would have been required to try the resisters before local juries. "Even if limited to that point, such a decision would have impaired the protective aspect of the Congressional program; moreover, Southern resisters and Democrats generally would have been emboldened when they could boast that 'the Reconstruction Act is unconstitutional.' The Republicans in Congress appreciated the seriousness of any adverse decision." Id. at 449. See also Kutler, Ex Parte McCardle: *Judicial Impotency? The Supreme Court and Reconstruction Reconsidered*, 72 Am.His.Rev. 835 (1967). Much more was involved, then, than whether a particular individual could obtain habeas corpus review in the Supreme Court.

2. Should *McCardle* be read "for all it might be worth"? Hart, The "Dialogue," supra, 66 Harv.L.Rev. at 1364. In other words, should the decision be taken to stand as precedent for the proposition that Congress has unlimited authority under the Exceptions Clause to limit the Supreme Court's appellate jurisdiction? Of what relevance to your answer is Ex Parte Yerger? Note that the Court reaffirmed *Yerger* in Felker v. Turpin, 518 U.S. 651 (1996) (holding that limits on the Supreme Court's appellate review of habeas corpus petitions do not preclude original jurisdiction on habeas). In *Felker*, however, the Court avoided, by means of statutory construction, the issue of the outer reach of congressional power to regulate the Supreme Court's appellate jurisdiction. See also Immigration and Naturalization Service v. St. Cyr, 533 U.S. 289 (2001) ("a serious suspension clause issue would be presented if we were to accept the INS's submission that the 1996 statutes have withdrawn that power from federal judges and provided no adequate substitute for its exercise.* * * The necessity of resolving such a serious and difficult constitutional issue—and the desirability of avoiding that necessity—simply reinforce the reasons for requiring a clear and unambiguous statement of constitutional intent."); Hamdan v. Rumsfeld, 548 U.S. ___, 126 S.Ct. 2749 (2006) (using "[o]rdinary principles of statutory construction" to conclude that Congress had not deprived the Court of appellate jurisdiction in a habeas case). But see Reno v. American–Arab Anti–Discrimination Committee, 525 U.S. 471, 488 (1999), refusing to invoke the doctrine of "constitutional doubt" where federal statutes made habeas relief unavail-

able to targeted aliens, because "an alien unlawfully in this country has no constitutional right to assert selective enforcement as a defense against his deportation."

3. Had Congress clearly intended in the 1868 act to repeal *all* avenues of habeas corpus review in the Supreme Court, would any constitutional provision have been violated? How about Article I, section 9, which guarantees the right of habeas corpus? The Supreme Court has held that due process does not guarantee a right of appellate review. See e.g., Lindsey v. Normet, 405 U.S. 56, 77 (1972); Griffin v. Illinois, 351 U.S. 12, 18 (1956). In light of this, how persuasive is the argument that denying Supreme Court review effectively denies the constitutional right of habeas corpus?

Nevertheless, Professor William Van Alstyne has argued that the Constitution may impose limits on Congress' power to restrict the Supreme Court's appellate jurisdiction:

> Without doubt, the Bill of Rights applies as do the several limitations flowing from article I, section 9. To exclude from review the claims of a readily identifiable group determined by the Court to have been disfavored by Congress as a device of legislative punishment, for instance, might be held to offend the ban on bills of attainder. An "exception" precluding redetermination in the Supreme Court of an alleged "fact" of obscenity when the Court regards the matter as one of "constitutional" fact might be held not to state an instance of excepting a case from appellate jurisdiction, but of impermissibly foreshortening the decisional process in a manner the Court would feel obliged to disregard in light of the first amendment. An exception to the scope of review applicable only in cases where the defendant availed himself of his right to trial by jury, but not when he agreed to a bench trial, moreover, might be held to offend the sixth or fourteenth amendments' protections of the right to trial by jury. Perhaps the simplest illustration would be an "exception" of cases based upon the appellant's race: an exception certain to be held offensive to the fifth amendment's dimension of equal protection. Expanding upon this example, one may plausibly argue that *whatever* basis of classification for excepting certain cases from the Court's appellate jurisdiction Congress may have used, it is necessarily subject to review to determine whether the class thus described is "arbitrary" or "invidious" in the sense condemned by whatever standards of equal protection appropriately applies to the subject matter.

> Where the class of excluded cases involves the exercise of "fundamental rights," the appropriate standard of judicial review is the more taxing one which denies any presumption of constitutionality and requires that the government justify the exceptional treatment of the class by demonstrating an imperative connection between the basis for singling out that class and a highly compelling, as well as licit, governmental interest. Arguably, this standard of fifth amendment equal protection review would be applicable to cases "excepted" from the appellate jurisdiction involving criminal convictions under anti-obscenity statutes punishing varieties of speech or expression claimed to be protected by

the first amendment—as simply one illustration of a class of cases involving "fundamental" rights.

Accordingly, the class of cases thus "excepted" by Congress should be sustained if (but only if) the government can articulate an imperative connection between that class of cases and a reason for excepting that class which is both licit and compelling. Plainly, considerations of alleged "judicial economy" or similar makeweights ought not be enough in respect to such cases, and the question must inevitably arise whether the most obvious reason would be deemed either licit or compelling by the Court: that Congress excepted that particular class of cases *precisely because it was dissatisfied with the manner in which the Supreme Court had been deciding them in the exercise of its power of substantive constitutional review.* Exactly at this juncture, the Court might again find itself involved in an additional investigation of the functions of the exceptions clause itself, but this time in a different way in order to resolve the fifth amendment objection to the manner in which Congress exercised its power.

If the exceptions clause meant to permit Congress to "check" the Court *specifically in the exercise of substantive constitutional review*, then the categorical exception of any group of cases made by Congress for that very reason cannot possibly be deemed offensive to the fifth amendment's equal protection concern: the exceptions clause *itself* would provide the source for the government's argument that that reason is both licit and compelling enough. If the clause is not seen as approving such a use of the exceptions power, on the other hand, it is difficult to imagine any other basis sufficient for the purpose. At this point, therefore, one's interest in the original understanding of the functions of the exceptions clause takes on a very different importance: not to determine what kinds of "exceptions" Congress may make under the clause *without reference to the fifth amendment*, but what kinds of exceptions Congress may make *given* the subsequent ratification of the fifth amendment *and its requirement of equal protection*? Correspondingly, there is no embarrassment if the answer that now emerges may be a different answer than the Court provided in Ex parte McCardle, which was decided long before judicial doctrine had evolved in this aspect of the fifth amendment. Specifically, the fact that consideration of the "exceptions" clause was apparently very casual, and that the examples of its appropriate use never involved any suggestion that it meant to provide a check against felt excesses of the Court in the exercise of substantive constitutional review, and the absence of expressed concern that Congress needed a means of curbing that review (except as to findings of fact), all may be useful to show that such a use is not made a licit and compelling reason by the clause itself. Thus, the use by Congress of the exceptions power to single out a class of cases involving fundamental rights, withdrawn from the Supreme Court's appellate jurisdiction only from dissatisfaction with the Court's exercise of its power of substantive constitutional review in respect to such cases, may, ironically, today be subject to fifth amendment challenge. On the other hand, a bill adopted from motives of retaliation against the Supreme Court would not necessarily betray that purpose on its face and might enable the government to argue that consistent with the face of the bill, it may have been the purpose of Congress simply to leave finality of decision with state courts—a purpose that does find some substantial measure of support in the origins of the exceptions clause and the Judiciary Act of 1789.

Nothing in the plenitude of the exceptions clause itself, moreover, nor in combination with any other provision in article III, implies that Congress could fashion a law enabling the government to deprive any person of life, liberty or property without due process; that is, without a fair opportunity to test any nonfrivolous objection to the government's action in an adversary adjudicative forum, including any substantive constitutional objections. Every case sustaining the power of Congress to forbid the adjudication of a federal question by the state judiciary has been at pains to note that in such circumstances another forum had been provided which the Court deemed sufficient in respect to procedural due process. Similarly, while plenary congressional authority over the jurisdiction of inferior federal courts, when combined with plenary congressional power to make exception to the appellate jurisdiction of the Supreme Court, may provide a possible means to oust certain cases entirely from the federal judiciary, the residual constitutional obligation of state judges "to support this Constitution" would then be drawn into play, exactly as Henry Hart quite properly observed.

But the point is not to exhaust the myriad ways in which the Bill of Rights or other parts of the Constitution function as a set of affirmative restrictions upon the exceptions power or upon any other power of Congress. Nor is it to suggest a sense of complacency that such safeguards are necessarily sufficient as a substitute for additional restrictions that some might prefer to add by amending the exceptions clause itself. To the contrary, it is only to indicate again that indeed they lie outside the clause.

Van Alstyne, *A Critical Guide to* Ex Parte McCardle, 15 Ariz.L.Rev. 229, 263–66 (1973).

How persuasive is the argument that selective curbing of Supreme Court review of one constitutional right violates equal protection? Might a greater equal protection problem be presented by limitation on Supreme Court power to hear cases challenging racial segregation in violation of the Fourteenth Amendment, than on the power to hear cases involving other constitutional rights, such as the free exercise of religion or free speech? See Redish, *Congressional Power to Limit Supreme Court Appellate Jurisdiction Under the Exceptions Clause: An Internal and External Examination*, 27 Vill.L.Rev. 900 (1982).

4. Are there any limits inherent in the exceptions clause itself on Congress' power to limit Supreme Court appellate jurisdiction?

Several commentators have argued that, despite the clause's seemingly unlimited language, Congress may not interfere with performance of the Supreme Court's "essential role." See Hart, supra, 66 Harv.L.Rev. at 1365; Ratner, *Congressional Power Over the Appellate Jurisdiction of the Supreme Court*, 109 U.Pa.L.Rev. 157 (1960). Professor Ratner describes these "essential functions" as: "(1) to provide a tribunal for the ultimate resolution of inconsistent or conflicting interpretations of federal law by state and federal courts, and (2) to provide a tribunal for maintaining the supremacy of federal law when it conflicts with state law or is challenged by state authority." 109 U.Pa.L.Rev. at 161. Where do you suppose these commentators find the "essential functions" thesis in the body of the Constitution? *Must* the theory be embodied in a specific constitutional provision before it can serve as a check on Congress?

Other commentators have found no basis for such a theory. According to Professor Van Alstyne, "[t]he power to make exceptions to Supreme Court appellate jurisdiction is a plenary power. It is given in express terms and without limitation, regardless of the more modest uses that might have been anticipated and, hopefully, generally to be respected by Congress as a matter of enlightened policy once the power was granted, as it was, to the fullest extent. In short, the clause is complete exactly as it stands * * *." Van Alstyne, supra, 15 Ariz.L.Rev. at 260. "In no opinion by the Supreme Court touching upon the subject, however," he writes, "is there any express or implied suggestion that the power to 'except' is limited to making 'inessential' exceptions." Id. at 257. See also Wechsler, *The Courts and the Constitution*, 65 Colum.L.Rev. 1001, 1005–06 (1965).

Other arguments for limiting the reach of the exceptions clause turn on historical factors. It is contended by some that the clause was inserted by the framers solely because of their concern over potential Supreme Court review of factual findings. See Van Alstyne, supra at 261; R. Berger, Congress v. The Supreme Court 286–87 (1969). Review the language of the Exceptions Clause carefully. Does its language lend itself to such a construction?

5. Berger makes the following argument in support of his contention that the exceptions clause deserves a narrow reading:

> The records * * * disclose that the Founders were deeply concerned with, and in no little part designed judicial review as a restraint on, *Congressional* excesses. If the Court was intended to curb Congressional excesses in appropriately presented "cases or controversies," and if an attempt to exercise that power might in turn be blocked by Congress as a judicial "excess," then the Convention was aimlessly going in circles. R. Berger, supra at 286 (emphasis in original).

Is Berger improperly equating *judicial* review with *Supreme Court* review? — *probably*

6. Consider the following argument: Legislative use of Congress' power under the exceptions clause is a more limited alternative to the amendment process. Thus, for example, if Congress were displeased with the Supreme Court's decision in Roe v. Wade, 410 U.S. 113 (1973), finding a constitutional right to abortion, it would cause less of a disruption if Congress were simply to remove legislatively Supreme Court jurisdiction to hear abortion cases than to enact a constitutional amendment banning abortion. Cf. Rice, *Congress and the Supreme Court's Jurisdiction*, 27 Vill.L.Rev. 959 (1982).

Do you agree? Is the practical effect of a limitation on Supreme Court jurisdiction the same as that of a constitutional amendment? — *No. Will get inconsistent lower decision*

7. Over the years, numerous bills have been introduced in Congress to limit the Supreme Court's appellate jurisdiction in one area or another. One example was the bill introduced by Senator Jenner, S. 2646, 85th Cong., 2d

Sess. (1958), which provided that "the Supreme Court shall have no jurisdiction to review, either by appeal, writ of certiorari, or otherwise, any case where there is drawn into question the validity of

"(1) any function or practice of, or the jurisdiction of, any committee or subcommittee of the United States Congress, or any action or proceeding against a witness charged with contempt of Congress;

"(2) any action, function, or practice of, or the jurisdiction of, any officer or agency of the executive branch of the Federal Government in the administration of any program established pursuant to an Act of Congress or otherwise for the elimination from service as employees in the executive branch of individuals whose retention may impair the security of the United States Government;

"(3) any statute or executive regulation of any State the general purpose of which is to control subversive activities within such State;

"(4) any rule, bylaw, or regulation adopted by a school board, board of education, board of trustees, or similar body, concerning subversive activities in its teaching body; and

"(5) any law, rule, or regulation of State, or of any board of bar examiners, or similar body, or of any action or proceeding taken pursuant to any such law, rule, or regulation pertaining to the admission of persons to the practice of law within such State."

In 1981, approximately twenty bills were introduced in Congress to limit Supreme Court or lower federal jurisdiction. Several of these were proposed constitutional amendments, while others were attempts to utilize the power under the Exceptions Clause. H.R. 761, 97th Cong., 1st Sess. introduced January 6, 1981 by Representative McDonald, for example, proposed elimination of federal court jurisdiction to issue any order having the effect of requiring an individual to attend any particular school. Do you think this law is constitutional, even under a broad reading of the exceptions clause? If you believe it does create potential constitutional problems, could you redraft it to accomplish fundamentally the same result but without many of those difficulties? See generally Constitutional Restraints Upon the Judiciary: Hearings Before the Subcommittee on the Constitution of the Committee on the Judiciary, United States Senate, 97th Cong., 1st Sess. (1981).

8. Professor James Pfander has suggested an alternative basis for limiting congressional power to regulate the Supreme Court's appellate jurisdiction. He argues that "the constitutional requirement of a supreme-inferior relationship between the Supreme Court and inferior federal courts may impose an important textual and structural limitation on what might otherwise appear to be the broad power of Congress to fashion exceptions to the Court's appellate jurisdiction." Pfander, *Jurisdiction-Stripping and the Supreme Court's Power to Supervise Inferior Tribunals*, 78 Tex.L.Rev. 1433, 1436 (2000). He argues that "[j]urisdiction strips that seek to prevent the Court from playing a supervisory role would represent a grave threat to the Court's role as the supreme federal court and its ability to confine inferior courts to the lawful exercise of their jurisdiction." Id. at 1511–1512. See also Caminker, *Why Must Inferior Courts Obey Superior Court Precedents?*, 46 Stan.L.Rev. 817 (1994).

9. Consider the following theory: The nation is considerably better off without a definitive Supreme Court interpretation of the exceptions clause than it would be with one. Do you agree? Why?

10. The literature on the subject of the Exceptions Clause is extensive. In addition to the sources already referred to, see J. Goebel, I History of the Supreme Court of the United States: Antecedents and Beginnings to 1801, 204–50, 430–49 (1971); Hardman, *The Doctrine of Political Accountability and Supreme Court Jurisdiction: Applying a New External Constraint to Congress's Exceptions Clause Power,* 106 Yale L.J. 197 (1996); Strong, *RX for a Nagging Constitutional Headache,* 8 San Diego L.Rev. 246 (1971); Forkosch, *The Exceptions and Regulations Clause of Article III and a Person's Constitutional Rights: Can the Latter be Limited by Congressional Power Under the Former?,* 72 W.Va.L.Rev. 238 (1970); Merry, *Scope of the Supreme Court's Appellate Jurisdiction: Historical Basis,* 47 Minn.L.Rev. 53 (1962).

11. A variation of the issue in *McCardle* was presented in United States v. Klein, 80 U.S. (13 Wall.) 128 (1871). The case is described in the following excerpt from M. Redish, Federal Jurisdiction: Tensions in the Allocation of Judicial Power 48–49 (2d ed.1990):

> Congress had provided that persons whose property had been seized during the Civil War could recover the property (or the proceeds from its sale) upon proof that they had not given aid or comfort to the enemy during the War. The Supreme Court had held that a presidential pardon for activities during the War constituted proof that the person had not given aid or comfort to the enemy. The Court's theory apparently was that the constitutional effect of a pardon, unless it is specifically limited by the President, is that the pardoned person is treated as if he had not committed the pardoned acts.
>
> Klein, representing a pardoned decedent, sued in the Court of Claims to recover the proceeds of seized property. Following the Supreme Court's precedent, the Court of Claims awarded relief. The government appealed, and while the case was pending in the Supreme Court, Congress passed legislation providing that federal courts should treat a pardon as proof that a person had been disloyal, and that the lower courts and the Supreme Court should dismiss the case seeking return of the property for want of jurisdiction.
>
> The Supreme Court held this limitation on its jurisdiction and the direction to treat pardons as proof of disloyalty unconstitutional. The Court made clear that it did not view the limitation on its jurisdiction as part of Congress' power to make exceptions and regulations to its appellate jurisdiction: "[t]he language of the proviso shows plainly that it does not intend to withhold appellate jurisdiction except as a means to an end * * *. It is evident from this statement that the denial of jurisdiction to this court, as well as to the Court of Claims, is founded solely on the application of a rule of decision ... prescribed by Congress." Using language which would seem to cast doubt on *Ex parte McCardle,* the Court suggested that there were constitutional problems because Congress had attempted to change the result in a case already pending before the Supreme Court and because the government was

attempting to alter the outcome of a case in which it was a party. But given the well established doctrine that courts are to apply the law as it exists at the time of the final judicial decision, neither of these factors can be considered the basis of the Court's decision. Absent fifth amendment due process retroactivity or taking of "vested" property right problems, Congress is generally free to alter rules of decision while a case is pending, even if the suit is one in which the government is a party.

The more plausible reading is that the rule of decision which the courts were in effect being directed to apply was unconstitutional because it denied the presidential pardon–which the President was constitutionally authorized to issue–the effect that the Court had ruled it had. Congress might have been free to rescind the statute providing for recovery of seized property, but so long as it allowed for recovery upon proof of loyalty, it had to consider pardoned persons loyal. *Klein* clearly affirms that there are limitations on Congress' power over jurisdiction. But whether *Klein* can be understood as establishing an independent separation-of-powers restraint which limits Congress' power is uncertain.

In United States v. Sioux Nation of Indians, 448 U.S. 371 (1980), the Court described the *Klein* case's rationale in the following manner: "[T]he [congressionally enacted] proviso was unconstitutional in two respects: First, it prescribed a rule of decision in a case pending before the courts, and did so in a manner that required the courts to decide a controversy in the Government's favor." Under this broader reading of *Klein,* the rule prescribed by Congress apparently need not itself be unconstitutional for the prescription to be invalid. Which of the two conceivable readings of the *Klein* holding better strikes an appropriate balance between congressional and judicial authority?

Consider the following argument: "The key theoretical insight that may be gleaned from *Klein* is that the judiciary—the one governmental branch insulated from the electorate—provides the only effective means of assuring that the democratic process operates in the manner necessary to the attainment of the normative goals that underlie the nation's chosen form of representative government. It does so by policing the legislative process to eliminate both micro and macro legislative deception." Redish & Pudelski, *Legislative Deception, Separation of Powers, and the Democratic Process: Harnessing the Political Theory of* United States v. Klein, 100 Nw.U.L.Rev. 437, 440 (2006). In what way might the legislation struck down in *Klein* be deemed a form of "legislative deception"? Consider the following suggested definition of the concept: "When a legislature engages in *micro* deception, it leaves the generalized substantive law intact, but legislatively directs that a particular litigation (or group of litigations) arising under that law be resolved in a manner inconsistent with the dictates of that preexisting generalized law. In the case of *macro* deception, in contrast, the legislature leaves substantive law unchanged on its face, but alters it in a generally applicable manner by enacting procedural or evidentiary modifications that have the effect of transforming the essence—or what can appropriately be described as the 'DNA'—of that law." Id. at 439.

§ 3. CONGRESSIONAL POWER TO CONTROL JUDICIAL DECISIONS

PLAUT v. SPENDTHRIFT FARM, INC.

Supreme Court of the United States, 1995.
514 U.S. 211.

JUSTICE SCALIA delivered the opinion of the Court.

The question presented in this case is whether § 27A(b) of the Securities Exchange Act of 1934, to the extent that it requires federal courts to reopen final judgments in private civil actions under § 10(b) of the Act, contravenes the Constitution's separation of powers or the Due Process Clause of the Fifth Amendment.

I

In 1987, petitioners brought a civil action against respondents in the United States District Court for the Eastern District of Kentucky. The complaint alleged that in 1983 and 1984 respondents had committed fraud and deceit in the sale of stock in violation of § 10(b) of the Securities Exchange Act of 1934 and Rule 10b–5 of the Securities and Exchange Commission. The case was mired in pretrial proceedings in the District Court until June 20, 1991, when we decided *Lampf, Pleva, Lipkind, Prupis & Petigrow v. Gilbertson*, 501 U.S. 350 (1991). *Lampf* held that "[l]itigation instituted pursuant to § 10(b) and Rule 10b–5 ... must be commenced within one year after the discovery of the facts constituting the violation and within three years after such violation." *Id.*, at 364. We applied that holding to the plaintiff-respondents in *Lampf* itself, found their suit untimely, and reinstated a summary judgment previously entered in favor of the defendant-petitioners. On the same day we decided *James B. Beam Distilling Co. v. Georgia*, 501 U.S. 529 (1991), in which a majority of the Court held, albeit in different opinions, that a new rule of federal law that is applied to the parties in the case announcing the rule must be applied as well to all cases pending on direct review. The joint effect of *Lampf* and *Beam* was to mandate application of the 1–year/3–year limitations period to petitioners' suit. The District Court, finding that petitioners' claims were untimely under the *Lampf* rule, dismissed their action with prejudice on August 13, 1991. Petitioners filed no appeal; the judgment accordingly became final 30 days later.

On December 19, 1991, the President signed the Federal Deposit Insurance Corporation Improvement Act of 1991, 105 Stat. 2236. Section 476 of the Act—a section that had nothing to do with FDIC improvements—became § 27A of the Securities Exchange Act of 1934, and was later codified as 15 U.S.C. § 78aa–1 (1988 ed., Supp. V). It provides:

"(a) Effect on pending causes of action

"The limitation period for any private civil action implied under section 78j(b) of this title [§ 10(b) of the Securities Exchange Act of

1934] that was commenced on or before June 19, 1991, shall be the limitation period provided by the laws applicable in the jurisdiction, including principles of retroactivity, as such laws existed on June 19, 1991.

"(b) Effect on dismissed causes of action

"Any private civil action implied under section 78j(b) of this title that was commenced on or before June 19, 1991—

"(1) which was dismissed as time barred subsequent to June 19, 1991, and

"(2) which would have been timely filed under the limitation period provided by the laws applicable in the jurisdiction, including principles of retroactivity, as such laws existed on June 19, 1991,

shall be reinstated on motion by the plaintiff not later than 60 days after December 19, 1991."

On February 11, 1992, petitioners returned to the District Court and filed a motion to reinstate the action previously dismissed with prejudice. The District Court found that the conditions set out in §§ 27A(b)(1) and (2) were met, so that petitioners' motion was required to be granted by the terms of the statute. It nonetheless denied the motion, agreeing with respondents that § 27A(b) is unconstitutional. The United States Court of Appeals for the Sixth Circuit affirmed. We granted certiorari.

II

[The Court began by rejecting several interpretations of § 27A(b) urged by respondents, which would allow the Court to affirm the courts below without reaching the constitutional question.] In short, there is no reasonable construction on which § 27A(b) does not require federal courts to reopen final judgments in suits dismissed with prejudice by virtue of *Lampf*.

III

Respondents submit that § 27A(b) violates both the separation of powers and the Due Process Clause of the Fifth Amendment. Because the latter submission, if correct, might dictate a similar result in a challenge to state legislation under the Fourteenth Amendment, the former is the narrower ground for adjudication of the constitutional questions in the case, and we therefore consider it first. *Ashwander v. TVA*, 297 U.S. 288, 347 (1936)(Brandeis, J., concurring). We conclude that in § 27A(b) Congress has exceeded its authority by requiring the federal courts to exercise "the judicial Power of the United States," U.S. Const., Art. III, § 1, in a manner repugnant to the text, structure and traditions of Article III.

Our decisions to date have identified two types of legislation that require federal courts to exercise the judicial power in a manner that Article III forbids. The first appears in *United States v. Klein*, 13 Wall.

128 (1872), where we refused to give effect to a statute that was said "[t]o prescribe rules of decision to the Judicial Department of the government in cases pending before it." *Id.*, 13 Wall., at 146. Whatever the precise scope of *Klein*, however, later decisions have made clear that its prohibition does not take hold when Congress "amend[s] applicable law." *Robertson v. Seattle Audubon Society*, 503 U.S. 429, 441 (1992). Section 27A(b) indisputably does set out substantive legal standards for the Judiciary to apply, and in that sense changes the law (even if solely retroactively). The second type of unconstitutional restriction upon the exercise of judicial power identified by past cases is exemplified by *Hayburn's Case*, 2 Dall. 409 (1792), which stands for the principle that Congress cannot vest review of the decisions of Article III courts in officials of the Executive Branch. Yet under any application of § 27A(b) only courts are involved; no officials of other departments sit in direct review of their decisions. Section 27A(b) therefore offends neither of these previously established prohibitions.

We think, however, that § 27A(b) offends a postulate of Article III just as deeply rooted in our law as those we have mentioned. Article III establishes a "judicial department" with the "province and duty . . . to say what the law is" in particular cases and controversies. *Marbury v. Madison*, 1 Cranch 137, 177 (1803). The record of history shows that the Framers crafted this charter of the judicial department with an expressed understanding that it gives the Federal Judiciary the power, not merely to rule on cases, but to *decide* them, subject to review only by superior courts in the Article III hierarchy—with an understanding, in short, that "a judgment conclusively resolves the case" because "a 'judicial Power' is one to render dispositive judgments." Easterbrook, Presidential Review, 40 Case W.Res.L.Rev. 905, 926 (1990). By retroactively commanding the federal courts to reopen final judgments, Congress has violated this fundamental principle.

A

[The Court canvassed the history of legislative and judicial powers up to the time of the framing, and then concluded:]

If the need for separation of legislative from judicial power was plain, the principal effect to be accomplished by that separation was even plainer. As Hamilton wrote in his exegesis of Article III, § 1, in Federalist No. 81:

> "It is not true . . . that the parliament of Great Britain, or the legislatures of the particular states, can rectify the exceptionable decisions of their respective courts, in any other sense than might be done by a future legislature of the United States. The theory neither of the British, nor the state constitutions, authorises the revisal of a judicial sentence, by a legislative act. . . . A legislature without exceeding its province cannot reverse a determination once made, in a particular case; though it may prescribe a new rule for future cases." The Federalist No. 81, p. 545 (J. Cooke ed. 1961).

The essential balance created by this allocation of authority was a simple one. The Legislature would be possessed of power to "prescrib[e] the rules by which the duties and rights of every citizen are to be regulated," but the power of "[t]he interpretation of the laws" would be "the proper and peculiar province of the courts." The Federalist No. 78, pp. 523, 525 (J. Cooke ed. 1961). See also Corwin, The Doctrine of Judicial Review, at 42. The Judiciary would be, "from the nature of its functions, ... the [department] least dangerous to the political rights of the constitution," not because its acts were subject to legislative correction, but because the binding effect of its acts was limited to particular cases and controversies. Thus, "though individual oppression may now and then proceed from the courts of justice, the general liberty of the people can never be endangered from that quarter: ... so long as the judiciary remains truly distinct from both the legislative and executive." The Federalist No. 78, pp. 522, 523 (J. Cooke ed. 1961).

Judicial decisions in the period immediately after ratification of the Constitution confirm the understanding that it forbade interference with the final judgments of courts. In *Calder v. Bull*, 3 Dall. 386 (1798), the Legislature of Connecticut had enacted a statute that set aside the final judgment of a state court in a civil case. Although the issue before this Court was the construction of the *Ex Post Facto* Clause, Art. I, § 10, Justice Iredell (a leading Federalist who had guided the Constitution to ratification in North Carolina) noted that

> "the Legislature of [Connecticut] has been in the uniform, uninterrupted, habit of exercising a general superintending power over its courts of law, by granting new trials. It may, indeed, appear strange to some of us, that in any form, there should exist a power to grant, with respect to suits depending or adjudged, new rights of trial, new privileges of proceeding, not previously recognized and regulated by positive institutions.... The power ... is judicial in its nature; and whenever it is exercised, as in the present instance, it is an exercise of judicial, not of legislative, authority." *Id.*, 3 Dall., at 398.

The state courts of the era showed a similar understanding of the separation of powers, in decisions that drew little distinction between the federal and state constitutions. To choose one representative example from a multitude: in *Bates v. Kimball*, 2 Chipman 77 (Vt.1824), a special Act of the Vermont Legislature authorized a party to appeal from the judgment of a court even though, under the general law, the time for appeal had expired. The court, noting that the unappealed judgment had become final, set itself the question "Have the Legislature power to vacate or annul an existing judgment between party and party?" *Id.*, at 83. The answer was emphatic: "The necessity of a distinct and separate existence of the three great departments of government ... had been proclaimed and enforced by ... Blackstone, Jefferson and Madison," and had been "sanctioned by the people of the United States, by being adopted in terms more or less explicit, into all their written constitutions." *Id.*, at 84. The power to annul a final judgment, the court held (citing *Hayburn's Case*, 2 Dall., at 410), was "an assumption of Judicial power," and therefore forbidden. *Bates v. Kimball, supra*, at 90.

* * *

B

Section 27A(b) effects a clear violation of the separation-of-powers principle we have just discussed. It is, of course, retroactive legislation, that is, legislation that prescribes what the law *was* at an earlier time, when the act whose effect is controlled by the legislation occurred—in this case, the filing of the initial Rule 10b–5 action in the District Court. When retroactive legislation requires its own application in a case already finally adjudicated, it does no more and no less than "reverse a determination once made, in a particular case." The Federalist No. 81, p. 545 (J. Cooke ed. 1961). Our decisions stemming from *Hayburn's Case*—although their precise holdings are not strictly applicable here—have uniformly provided fair warning that such an act exceeds the powers of Congress. * * *

It is true, as petitioners contend, that Congress can always revise the judgments of Article III courts in one sense: When a new law makes clear that it is retroactive, an appellate court must apply that law in reviewing judgments still on appeal that were rendered before the law was enacted, and must alter the outcome accordingly. See *United States v. Schooner Peggy*, 1 Cranch 103 (1801); *Landgraf v. USI Film Products*, 511 U.S. 244, 273–280 (1994). Since that is so, petitioners argue, federal courts must apply the "new" law created by § 27A(b) in finally adjudicated cases as well; for the line that separates lower court judgments that are pending on appeal (or may still be appealed), from lower-court judgments that are final, is determined by statute, see, *e.g.*, 28 U.S.C. § 2107(a)(30–day time limit for appeal to federal court of appeals), and so cannot possibly be a *constitutional* line. But a distinction between judgments from which all appeals have been forgone or completed, and judgments that remain on appeal (or subject to being appealed), is implicit in what Article III creates: not a batch of unconnected courts, but a judicial *department* composed of "inferior Courts" and "one supreme Court." Within that hierarchy, the decision of an inferior court is not (unless the time for appeal has expired) the final word of the department as a whole. It is the obligation of the last court in the hierarchy that rules on the case to give effect to Congress's latest enactment, even when that has the effect of overturning the judgment of an inferior court, since each court, at every level, must "decide according to existing laws." *Schooner Peggy, supra*, 1 Cranch, at 109. Having achieved finality, however, a judicial decision becomes the last word of the judicial department with regard to a particular case or controversy, and Congress may not declare by retroactive legislation that the law applicable *to that very case* was something other than what the courts said it was. Finality of a legal judgment is determined by statute, just as entitlement to a government benefit is a statutory creation; but that no more deprives the former of its constitutional significance for separation-of-powers analysis than it deprives the latter of its significance for due process purposes.

* * *

The central theme of the dissent is a variant on these arguments. The dissent maintains that *Lampf* "announced" a new statute of limitations in an act of "judicial ... lawmaking," that "changed the law." That statement, even if relevant, would be wrong. The point decided in *Lampf* had never before been addressed by this Court, and was therefore an open question, no matter what the lower courts had held at the time. But the more important point is that *Lampf* as such is irrelevant to this case. The dissent itself perceives that "[w]e would have the same issue to decide had Congress enacted the *Lampf* rule," and that the *Lampf* rule's genesis in judicial lawmaking rather than, shall we say, legislative lawmaking, "should not affect the separation-of-powers analysis." Just so. The issue here is not the validity or even the source of the legal rule that produced the Article III judgments, but rather the immunity from legislative abrogation of those judgments themselves. The separation-of-powers question before us has nothing to do with *Lampf*, and the dissent's attack on *Lampf* has nothing to do with the question before us.

C

Apart from the statute we review today, we know of no instance in which Congress has attempted to set aside the final judgment of an Article III court by retroactive legislation. That prolonged reticence would be amazing if such interference were not understood to be constitutionally proscribed. The closest analogue that the Government has been able to put forward is the statute at issue in *United States v. Sioux Nation*, 448 U.S. 371 (1980). That law required the Court of Claims "[n]otwithstanding any other provision of law . . . [to] review on the merits, without regard to the defense of res judicata or collateral estoppel," a Sioux claim for just compensation from the United States—even though the Court of Claims had previously heard and rejected that very claim. We considered and rejected separation-of-powers objections to the statute based upon *Hayburn's Case* and *United States v. Klein*. The basis for our rejection was a line of precedent (starting with *Cherokee Nation v. United States*, 270 U.S. 476 (1926)) that stood, we said, for the proposition that "Congress has the power to waive the res judicata effect of a prior judgment entered in the Government's favor on a claim against the United States." *Sioux Nation*, 448 U.S., at 397. And our holding was as narrow as the precedent on which we had relied: "In sum, ... Congress' mere waiver of the res judicata effect of a prior judicial decision rejecting the validity of a legal claim against the United States does not violate the doctrine of separation of powers." *Id.*, at 407.

The Solicitor General suggests that even if *Sioux Nation* is read in accord with its holding, it nonetheless establishes that Congress may require Article III courts to reopen their final judgments, since "if *res judicata* were compelled by Article III to safeguard the structural independence of the courts, the doctrine would not be subject to waiver by any party litigant." Brief for United States 27 (citing *Commodity Futures Trading Comm'n v. Schor*, 478 U.S. 833, 850–851 (1986)). But the proposition that legal defenses based upon doctrines central to the courts' structural independence can never be waived simply does not accord with our cases. Certainly one such doctrine consists of the "judicial Power" to disregard an unconstitutional statute, see *Marbury*, 1 Cranch, at 177; yet none would suggest that a litigant may never waive the defense that a statute is unconstitutional. What may follow from our holding that the judicial power unalterably includes the power to render final judgments, is not that waivers of res judicata are always impermissible, but rather that, as many federal Courts of Appeals have held, waivers of res judicata need not always be accepted—that trial courts may in appropriate cases raise the res judicata bar on their own motion. Waiver subject to the control of the courts themselves would obviously raise no issue of separation of powers, and would be precisely in accord with the language of the decision that the Solicitor General relies upon. We held in *Schor* that, although a litigant had consented to bring a state-law counterclaim before an Article I tribunal, we would nonetheless choose to consider his Article III challenge, because "where these Article III limitations are at issue, notions of consent and waiver cannot be *dispositive*."

* * *

Finally, petitioners liken § 27A(b) to Federal Rule of Civil Procedure 60(b), which authorizes courts to relieve parties from a final judgment for grounds such as excusable neglect, newly discovered evidence, fraud, or "any other reason justifying relief...." We see little resemblance. Rule 60(b), which authorizes discretionary judicial revision of judgments in the listed situations and in other "extraordinary circumstances," *Liljeberg v. Health Services Acquisition Corp.*, 486 U.S. 847, 864 (1988), does not impose any legislative mandate-to-reopen upon the courts, but merely reflects and confirms the courts' own inherent and discretionary power, "firmly established in English practice long before the foundation of our Republic," to set aside a judgment whose enforcement would work inequity. *Hazel-Atlas Glass Co. v. Hartford–Empire Co.*, 322 U.S. 238, 244 (1944). Thus, Rule 60(b), and the tradition that it embodies, would be relevant refutation of a claim that reopening a final judgment is always a denial of property without due process; but they are irrelevant to the claim that legislative instruction to reopen impinges upon the independent constitutional authority of the courts.

The dissent promises to provide "[a] few contemporary examples" of statutes retroactively requiring final judgments to be reopened, "to demonstrate that [such statutes] are ordinary products of the exercise of legislative power." That promise is not kept. The relevant retroactivity, of course, consists not of the requirement that there be set aside a judgment that has been rendered *prior to its being set aside*—for example, a statute passed today which says that all default judgments rendered in the future may be reopened within 90 days after their entry. In that sense, *all* requirements to reopen are "retroactive," and the designation is superfluous. Nothing we say today precludes a law such as that. The finality that a court can pronounce is no more than what the law in existence at the time of judgment will permit it to pronounce. If the law then applicable says that the judgment may be reopened for certain reasons, that limitation is built into the judgment itself, and its finality is so conditioned. The present case, however, involves a judgment that Congress subjected to a reopening requirement which did not exist when the judgment was pronounced. The dissent provides not a single clear prior instance of such congressional action.

* * *

We know of no previous instance in which Congress has enacted retroactive legislation requiring an Article III court to set aside a final judgment, and for good reason. The Constitution's separation of legislative and judicial powers denies it the authority to do so. Section 27A(b) is unconstitutional to the extent that it requires federal courts to reopen final judgments entered before its enactment. The judgment of the Court of Appeals is affirmed.

JUSTICE STEVENS, with whom JUSTICE GINSBURG joins, dissenting.

* * *

III.

The lack of precedent for the Court's holding is not, of course, a sufficient reason to reject it. Correct application of separation-of-powers principles, however, confirms that the Court has reached the wrong result. As our most recent major pronouncement on the separation of powers noted, "we have never held that the Constitution requires that the three branches of Government 'operate with absolute independence.'" *Morrison v. Olson*, 487 U.S. 654, 693–694 (1988)(quoting *United States v. Nixon*, 418 U.S. 683 (1974)). Rather, our jurisprudence reflects "Madison's flexible approach to separation of powers." *Mistretta v. United States*, 488 U.S. 361, 380 (1989). In accepting Madison's conception rather than any "hermetic division among the Branches," *id.*, at 381, "we have upheld statutory provisions that to some degree commingle the functions of the Branches, but that pose no danger of either aggrandizement or encroachment." *Id.*, at 382. Today's holding does not comport with these ideals.

Section 27A shares several important characteristics with the remedial statutes discussed above. It does not decide the merits of any issue in any litigation but merely removes an impediment to judicial decision on the merits. The impediment it removes would have produced inequity because the statute's beneficiaries did not cause the impediment. It requires a party invoking its benefits to file a motion within a specified time and to convince a court that the statute entitles the party to relief.

Most important, § 27A(b) specifies both a substantive rule to govern the reopening of a class of judgments—the pre-*Lampf* limitations rule—and a procedure for the courts to apply in determining whether a particular motion to reopen should be granted. These characteristics are quintessentially legislative. They reflect Congress' fealty to the separation of powers and its intention to avoid the sort of ad hoc excesses the Court rightly criticizes in colonial legislative practice. In my judgment, all of these elements distinguish § 27A from "judicial" action and confirm its constitutionality. A sensible analysis would at least consider them in the balance.

Instead, the Court myopically disposes of § 27A(b) by holding that Congress has no power to "requir[e] an Article III court to set aside a final judgment." That holding must mean one of two things. It could mean that Congress may not impose a mandatory duty on a court to set aside a judgment even if the court makes a particular finding, such as a finding of fraud or mistake, that Congress has not made. Such a rule, however, could not be correct. Although Rule 60(b), for example, merely authorizes federal courts to set aside judgments after making appropriate findings, Acts of Congress characteristically set standards that judges are obligated to enforce. Accordingly, Congress surely could add to Rule 60(b) certain instances in which courts *must* grant relief from final judgments if they make particular findings—for example, a finding that a member of the jury accepted a bribe from the prevailing party. The Court, therefore, must mean to hold that Congress may not *unconditionally* require an Article III court to set aside a final judgment. That rule is both unwise and beside the point of this case.

A simple hypothetical example will illustrate the practical failings of the Court's new rule. Suppose Congress, instead of endorsing the new limitations rule fashioned by the Court in *Lampf*, had decided to return to the pre-*Lampf* regime (or perhaps to enact a longer uniform statute). Subsection (a) of § 27 would simply have provided that the law in effect prior to June 19, 1991, would govern the timeliness of all 10b–5 actions. In that event, subsection (b) would still have been necessary to remedy the injustice caused by this Court's failure to exempt pending cases from its new rule. In my judgment, the statutory correction of the inequitable flaw in *Lampf* would be appropriate remedial legislation whether or not Congress had endorsed that decision's substantive limitations rule. The Court, unfortunately, appears equally consistent: Even though the class of dismissed 10b–5 plaintiffs in my hypothetical would have been subject to the same substantive rule as all other 10b–5 plaintiffs, the Court's reasoning would still reject subsection (b) as an impermissible exercise of "judicial" power.

The majority's rigid holding unnecessarily hinders the Government from addressing difficult issues that inevitably arise in a complex society. This Court, for example, lacks power to enlarge the time for filing petitions for certiorari in a civil case after 90 days from the entry of final judgment, no matter how strong the equities. See 28 U.S.C. § 2101(c). If an Act of God, such as a flood or an earthquake, sufficiently disrupted communications in a particular area to preclude filing for several days, the majority's reasoning would appear to bar Congress from addressing the resulting inequity. If Congress passed remedial legislation that retroactively granted movants from the disaster area extra time to file petitions or motions for extensions of time to file, today's holding presumably would compel us to strike down the legislation as an attack on the finality of judgments. Such a ruling, like today's holding, would gravely undermine federal courts' traditional power "to set aside a judgment whose enforcement would work inequity."

Notes

1. What, if anything, does *Plaut* tell us about the meaning of *Klein*?

2. Consider the possible relevance to *Plaut* of the Supreme Court's decision in Hayburn's Case, 2 U.S. (2 Dall. 409) 408 (1792). There the Court invalidated, on separation-of-powers grounds, a congressional directive that the federal courts accept or reject applications by Revolutionary War veterans for disability pensions. *Hayburn* "rightly establishes that Congress may not authorize an executive officer to review and reverse specific, individual federal court decisions." Redish, *Federal Judicial Independence: Constitutional and Political Perspectives*, 46 Mercer L.Rev. 697, 723 (1995). Is that the situation in *Plaut*?

3. The enactment of section 27A(b) tells us that Congress intended § 10(b) actions to have a longer statute of limitations period than that specified by the Court in *Lampf*. After *Plaut*, is there any way for Congress to correct the Supreme Court's mistaken interpretation of a federal statute of limitations? Should separation-of-powers principles—or anything else in Article III—preclude Congress from implementing its own determination of the appropriate statute of limitations for federal statutory claims?

4. Was the problem in *Plaut* that Congress acted too slowly or in the wrong manner, or was it that the Plauts did not foresee congressional action and thus did not appeal the district court's dismissal of their case? How should you advise your clients in the future, should a district court dismiss their claims on the basis of a recent Supreme Court decision? Is your answer consistent with good legal practice, in general?

5. Are you persuaded by the dissent's analogy to extending deadlines missed because of an Act of God? Should such extensions be granted by Congress or by the courts?

6. The 1995 Extradition Act, 18 U.S.C. § 3184, permits the Secretary of State to review judicial decisions of extraditability and to decline to extradite even where a judge has ordered extradition. Is the statute constitutional after *Plaut*? Compare Lobue v. Christopher, 893 F.Supp. 65 (D.D.C. 1995) (unconstitutional) with Cherry v. Warden, 1995 WL 598986 (S.D.N.Y. 1995) (constitutional). Is the case closer to *Sioux Nation* or to *Hayburn's Case*?

7. Consider the relevance of *Plaut* to Miller v. French, 530 U.S. 327 (2000), upholding the automatic stay provision of the Prison Litigation

Reform Act of 1995 (PLRA), 18 U.S.C. § 3626, which provides that any motion to terminate prospective relief under a "prison conditions" consent decree shall, after a specific period of time, unless the court within that time period reissues the prospective relief under the revised statutory standards, operate as an automatic stay of the decree. *Plaut* was inapplicable, the Court found, because that case had involved "legislation that attempted to reopen the dismissal of a suit seeking money damages." The Court reasoned that the PLRA affected only prospective relief, and in such a situation Congress may alter the law governing the situation controlled by that prospective relief, thereby requiring a change in that relief. The controlling law had been modified by Congress, the Court said, when the PLRA altered the substantive standards for the issuance of equitable relief—a congressional power originally held valid in Pennsylvania v. Wheeling & Belmont Bridge Co., 59 U.S. (18 How.) 421 (1855). Under the principle of *Wheeling Bridge*, the automatic stay "does not 'suspend' or reopen a judgment of an Article III court.* * * Instead, [the automatic stay provision] merely reflects the change implemented by [a separate provision], which does the 'heavy lifting' in the statutory scheme by establishing new standards for prospective relief."

In Pennsylvania v. Wheeling & Belmont Bridge Co., 54 U.S. (13 How.) 518 (1851) *(Wheeling Bridge* I), the Court held that a bridge across the Ohio River unlawfully obstructed the river's navigation and ordered that the bridge be permanently removed. Shortly thereafter, Congress enacted a law declaring the bridge to be a "lawful structur[e]," and that it could be maintained at its current site and elevation. After the bridge was destroyed in a storm, Pennsylvania sued to enjoin the bridge's reconstruction, arguing that the statute legalizing the bridge was unconstitutional because it effectively annulled the Court's earlier decision. In *Wheeling Bridge* II, relied on in *Miller*, the Court rejected this argument, even though the Court had, in the first case, enjoined the defendants from any continuance or reconstruction of the obstruction. The Court reasoned that because the decree entered in *Wheeling Bridge* I provided for prospective relief, the ongoing validity of that relief depended on whether or not the bridge continued to interfere with the right of navigation. When Congress altered the law so that the bridge was no longer an unlawful obstruction, the injunction needed to be modified to reflect that change. However, the result would have been different, the Court indicated, had the decision in the first case been an award of money damages.

Do you agree with the Court that *Wheeling Bridge* supports the PLRA's automatic stay provision? Are there no differences between the two situations? Contrast the different manner in which the congressional alteration of the underlying law is to be implemented in the two situations.

Justice Souter, dissenting in part in *Miller*, suggested that "applying the automatic stay may raise the due process issue, of whether a plaintiff has a fair chance to preserve an existing judgment that was valid when entered."

§ 4. CONGRESSIONAL POWER TO VEST ARTICLE III COURTS WITH NON–ARTICLE III POWER

NATIONAL MUTUAL INSURANCE CO. v. TIDEWATER TRANSFER CO., INC.

Supreme Court of the United States, 1949.
337 U.S. 582.

MR. JUSTICE JACKSON announced the judgment of the Court and an opinion in which MR. JUSTICE BLACK and MR. JUSTICE BURTON join.

This case calls up for review a holding that it is unconstitutional for Congress to open federal courts in the several states to action by a citizen of the District of Columbia against a citizen of one of the states. The petitioner, as plaintiff, commenced in the United States District Court for Maryland an action for a money judgment on a claim arising out of an insurance contract. No cause of action under the laws or Constitution of the United States was pleaded, jurisdiction being predicated only upon an allegation of diverse citizenship. The diversity set forth was that plaintiff is a corporation created by District of Columbia law, while the defendant is a corporation chartered by Virginia, amenable to suit in Maryland by virtue of a license to do business there. The learned District Judge concluded that, while this diversity met jurisdictional requirements under the Act of Congress,[1] it did not comply with diversity requirements of the Constitution as to federal jurisdiction, and so dismissed. The Court of Appeals, by a divided court, affirmed. Of twelve district courts that had considered the question up to the time review in this Court was sought, all except three had held the enabling Act unconstitutional, and the two Courts of Appeals which had spoken on the subject agreed with that conclusion. The controversy obviously was an appropriate one for review here and writ of certiorari issued in the case.

The history of the controversy begins with that of the Republic. In defining the cases and controversies to which the judicial power of the United States could extend, the Constitution included those "between Citizens of different States." In the Judiciary Act of 1789, Congress created a system of federal courts of first instance and gave them jurisdiction of suits "between a citizen of the State where the suit is brought, and a citizen of another State." In 1804, the Supreme Court, through Chief Justice Marshall, held that a citizen of the District of Columbia was not a citizen of a State within the meaning and intendment of this Act.[9] This decision closed federal courts in the states to citizens of the District of Columbia in diversity cases, and for 136 years they remained closed. In 1940 Congress enacted the statute challenged here. It confers on such courts jurisdiction if the action "Is between citizens of different States, or citizens of the District of Columbia, the

---

1. Act of April 20, 1940, c. 117, 54 Stat. 143. For terms of the statute see note 10.

9. Hepburn & Dundas v. Ellzey, 2 Cranch 445.

Territory of Hawaii, or Alaska, and any State or Territory."[10] The issue here depends upon the validity of this Act, which, in substance, was reenacted by a later Congress as part of the Judicial Code.

Before concentrating on detail, it may be well to place the general issue in a larger perspective. This constitutional issue affects only the mechanics of administering justice in our federation. It does not involve an extension or a denial of any fundamental right or immunity which goes to make up our freedoms. Those rights and freedoms do not include immunity from suit by a citizen of the District of Columbia or exemption from process of the federal courts. Defendant concedes that it can presently be sued in some court of law, if not this one, and it grants that Congress may make it suable at plaintiff's complaint in some, if not this, federal court. Defendant's contention only amounts to this: that it cannot be made to answer this plaintiff in the particular court which Congress has decided is the just and convenient forum.

D Contends

The considerations which bid us strictly to apply the Constitution to congressional enactments which invade fundamental freedoms or which reach for powers that would substantially disturb the balance between the Union and its component states, are not present here. In mere mechanics of government and administration we should, so far as the language of the great Charter fairly will permit, give Congress freedom to adapt its machinery to the needs of changing times. * * *

mere mechanics not substantive rights

(1) Our first inquiry is whether, under the third, or Judiciary, Article of the Constitution, extending the judicial power of the United States to cases or controversies "between Citizens of different States," a citizen of the District of Columbia has the standing of a citizen of one of the states of the Union. This is the question which the opinion of Chief Justice Marshall answered in the negative, by way of dicta if not of actual decision. Hepburn and Dundas v. Ellzey, 2 Cranch 445. To be sure, nothing was before that Court except interpretation of a statute which conferred jurisdiction substantially in the words of the Constitution with nothing in the text or context to show that Congress intended to regard the District as a state. But Marshall resolved the statutory question by invoking the analogy of the constitutional provisions of the same tenor and reasoned that the District was not a state for purposes of the Constitution and, hence, was not for purposes of the Act. * * *

No explicit congressional directive in earlier precedent

* * *

To now overrule this early decision of the Court on this point and hold that the District of Columbia is a state would, as that opinion pointed out, give to the word "state" a meaning in the Article which sets up the judicial establishment quite different from that which it carries in

---

10. The effect of the Act was to amend 28 U.S.C. (1946 ed.) § 41(1) so that it read in pertinent part: "The district courts shall have original jurisdiction as follows: ... Of all suits of a civil nature, at common law or in equity ... where the matter in contro- versy exceeds, exclusive of interest and costs, the sum or value of $3,000, and ... (b) Is between citizens of different States, or citizens of the District of Columbia, the Territory of Hawaii, or Alaska, and any State or Territory...."

those Articles which set up the political departments and in other Articles of the instrument. While the word is one which can contain many meanings, such inconsistency in a single instrument is to be implied only where the context clearly requires it. * * *

* * *

We therefore decline to overrule the opinion of Chief Justice Marshall, and we hold that the District of Columbia is not a state within Article III of the Constitution. In other words, cases between citizens of the District and those of the states were not included in the catalogue of controversies over which the Congress could give jurisdiction to the federal courts by virtue of Art. III.

This conclusion does not, however, determine that Congress lacks power under other provisions of the Constitution to enact this legislation. Congress, by the Act in question, sought not to challenge or disagree with the decision of Chief Justice Marshall that the District of Columbia is not a state for such purposes. It was careful to avoid conflict with that decision by basing the new legislation on powers that had not been relied upon by the First Congress in passing the Act of 1789.

The Judiciary Committee of the House of Representatives recommended the Act of April 20, 1940, as "a reasonable exercise of the constitutional power of Congress to legislate for the District of Columbia and for the Territories." This power the Constitution confers in broad terms. By Art. I, Congress is empowered "to exercise exclusive Legislation in all Cases whatsoever, over such District." And of course it was also authorized "To make all Laws which shall be necessary and proper for carrying into Execution" such powers. These provisions were not relevant in Chief Justice Marshall's interpretation of the Act of 1789 because it did not refer in terms to the District but only to states. * * *

It is elementary that the exclusive responsibility of Congress for the welfare of the District includes both power and duty to provide its inhabitants and citizens with courts adequate to adjudge not only controversies among themselves but also their claims against, as well as suits brought by, citizens of the various states. It long has been held that Congress may clothe District of Columbia courts not only with the jurisdiction and powers of federal courts in the several states but with such authority as a state may confer on her courts. Kendall v. United States, 12 Pet. 524, 619; Capital Traction Co. v. Hof, 174 U.S. 1; O'Donoghue v. United States, 289 U.S. 516. The defendant here does not challenge the power of Congress to assure justice to the citizens of the District by means of federal instrumentalities, or to empower a federal court within the District to run its process to summon defendants here from any part of the country. And no reason has been advanced why a special statutory court for cases of District citizens could not be authorized to proceed elsewhere in the United States to sit, where necessary or proper, to discharge the duties of Congress toward District citizens.

[handwritten margin note: Can't Combine Art I + III funcs]

However, it is contended that Congress may not combine this function, under Art. I, with those under Art. III, in district courts of the United States. Two objections are urged to this. One is that no jurisdiction other than specified in Art. III can be imposed on courts that exercise the judicial power of the United States thereunder. The other is that Art. I powers over the District of Columbia must be exercised solely within that geographic area.

Of course there are limits to the nature of duties which Congress may impose on the constitutional courts vested with the federal judicial power. The doctrine of separation of powers is fundamental in our system. It arises, however, not from Art. III nor any other single provision of the Constitution, but because "behind the words of the constitutional provisions are postulates which limit and control." Chief Justice Hughes in Monaco v. Mississippi, 292 U.S. 313, 323. The permeative nature of this doctrine was early recognized during the Constitutional Convention. Objection that the present provision giving federal courts jurisdiction of cases arising "under this Constitution" would permit usurpation of nonjudicial functions by the federal courts was overruled as unwarranted since it was "generally supposed that the jurisdiction given was constructively limited to cases of a Judiciary nature." 2 Farrand, Records of the Federal Convention, 430. And this statute reflects that doctrine. It does not authorize or require either the district courts or this Court to participate in any legislative, administrative, political or other nonjudicial function or to render any advisory opinion. The jurisdiction conferred is limited to controversies of a justiciable nature, the sole feature distinguishing them from countless other controversies handled by the same courts being the fact that one party is a District citizen. Nor has the Congress by this statute attempted to usurp any judicial power. It has deliberately chosen the district courts as the appropriate instrumentality through which to exercise part of the judicial functions incidental to exertion of sovereignty over the District and its citizens.

Unless we are to deny to Congress the same choice of means through which to govern the District of Columbia that we have held it to have in exercising other legislative powers enumerated in the same Article, we cannot hold that Congress lacked the power it sought to exercise in the Act before us.

It is too late to hold that judicial functions incidental to Art. I powers of Congress cannot be conferred on courts existing under Art. III, for it has been done with this Court's approval. O'Donoghue v. United States, 289 U.S. 516. *[handwritten margin note: ← Precedent]* In that case it was held that, although District of Columbia courts are Art. III courts, they can also exercise judicial power conferred by Congress pursuant to Art. I. The fact that District of Columbia courts, as local courts, can also be given administrative or legislative functions which other Art. III courts cannot exercise, does but emphasize the fact that, although the latter are limited to the exercise of judicial power, it may constitutionally be received from either Art. III or

Art. I, and that congressional power over the District, flowing from Art. I, is plenary in every respect.

* * *

Congress is given power by Art. I to pay debts of the United States. That involves as an incident the determination of disputed claims. We have held unanimously that congressional authority under Art. I, not the Art. III jurisdiction over suits to which the United States is a party, is the sole source of power to establish the Court of Claims and of the judicial power which that court exercises. Williams v. United States, 289 U.S. 553. In that decision we also noted that it is this same Art. I power that is conferred on district courts by the Tucker Act which authorizes them to hear and determine such claims in limited amounts. Since a legislative court such as the Court of Claims is "incapable of receiving" Art. III judicial power, American Insurance Co. v. Canter, 1 Pet. 511, 546, it is clear that the power thus exercised by that court and concurrently by the district courts flows from Art. I, not Art. III. Indeed, more recently and again unanimously, this Court has said that by the Tucker Act the Congress authorized the district courts to sit as a court of claims exercising the same but no more judicial power. * * * Congress has * * * recently conferred on the district courts exclusive jurisdiction of tort claims cognizable under the Federal Tort Claims Act, 60 Stat. 842, 843, also enacted pursuant to Art. I powers.

Congress also is given power in Art. I to make uniform laws on the subject of bankruptcies. That this, and not the judicial power under Art. III, is the source of our system of reorganizations and bankruptcy is obvious, Continental Illinois Nat. Bank & Trust Co. v. Chicago, Rock Island & Pacific R. Co., 294 U.S. 648. Not only may the district courts be required to handle these proceedings, but Congress may add to their jurisdiction cases between the trustee and others that, but for the bankruptcy powers, would be beyond their jurisdiction because of lack of diversity required under Art. III. Schumacher v. Beeler, 293 U.S. 367. In that case, Chief Justice Hughes for a unanimous court wrote that, by virtue of its Art. I authority over bankruptcies, the Congress could confer on the regular district courts jurisdiction of "all controversies at law and in equity, as distinguished from proceedings in bankruptcy, between trustees as such and adverse claimants" to the extent specified in § 23b of the Bankruptcy Act as amended. Such jurisdiction was there upheld in a plenary suit, in a district court, by which the trustee sought equitable relief relying on allegations raising only questions of Ohio law concerning the validity under that law of a sheriff's levy and execution. Possession by the trustee not being shown, and there being no diversity, jurisdiction in the district court could flow only from the statute. Chief Justice Hughes noted that the distinction between proceedings in bankruptcy and suits at law and in equity was recognized by the terms of the statute itself, but held that "Congress, by virtue of its constitutional authority over bankruptcies, could confer or withhold jurisdiction to entertain such suits and could prescribe the conditions upon which the federal courts should have jurisdiction.... Exercising that power, the Congress prescribed in § 23b the condition of consent on the part of the defendant sued by the trustee. Section 23b was thus in effect a grant of jurisdiction subject to that condition." 293 U.S. 367, 374. He concluded that the statute granted jurisdiction to the district court "although the bankrupt could not have brought suit there if proceedings in bankruptcy had not been instituted.... " 293 U.S. 367, 377. And he stated the correct view to be that § 23 conferred substantive jurisdiction, 293 U.S. 367, 371, disapproving statements in an earlier case that Congress lacked power to confer such jurisdiction. Id. 293 U.S. at page 377. Thus, the Court held that Congress had power to authorize an Art. III court to entertain a non-Art. III suit because such judicial power was conferred under Art. I. Indeed, the present Court has assumed, without even discussion, that Congress has such power. In Williams v. Austrian, 331 U.S. 642, 657, the Chief Justice, speaking for the Court, said that " ... Congress intended by the elimination of § 23 [from Chapter X of the Bankruptcy Act] to establish the jurisdiction of federal courts to hear plenary suits brought by a reorganization trustee, *even though diversity or other usual ground for federal jurisdiction is lacking.*" (Emphasis supplied.) * * *

This assumption by the Court in the *Beeler* and *Austrian* cases, that the Congress had power to confer on the district courts jurisdiction of nondiversity suits involving only state law questions, made unnecessary any discussion of the source of the assumed power. In view of Congress' plenary control over bankruptcies, the Court may have grounded such assumption on Art. I. Or it might have considered that the jurisdiction was based on Art. III, and statutes enacted pursuant to it, giving the district courts jurisdiction over suits arising under the Constitution and laws of the United States. Had the Court held such a view, this latter might have commended itself as the most obvious answer. Consequently, silence in this respect, in the decision of each case, seems significant, particularly in contrast with repeated reference to Art. I power in the *Beeler* case, and sweeping language in the *Austrian* case that such jurisdiction existed despite lack of diversity "or other usual ground for federal jurisdiction." Nevertheless, it is now asserted, in retrospect, that those cases did arise under the laws of the United States. No justification is offered for that conclusion and there is no effort to say just why or how the cases did so arise. This would indeed be difficult if we still adhere to the doctrine of Mr. Justice Holmes that "a suit arises under the law that creates the cause of action," American Well Works Co. v. Layne & Bowler Co., 241 U.S. 257, 260, for the cause of action in each case rested solely on state law.

* * *

Consequently, we can deny validity to this present Act of Congress, only by saying that the power over the District given by Art. I is somehow less ample than that over bankruptcy given by the same Article. If Congress could require this district court to decide this very case if it were brought by a trustee, it is hard to see why it may not require its decision for a solvent claimant when done in pursuance of other Art. I powers.

We conclude that where Congress in the exercise of its powers under Art. I finds it necessary to provide those on whom its power is exerted with access to some kind of court or tribunal for determination of controversies that are within the traditional concept of the justiciable, it may open the regular federal courts to them regardless of lack of diversity of citizenship. The basis of the holdings we have discussed is that, when Congress deems that for such purposes it owes a forum to claimants and trustees, it may execute its power in this manner. The Congress, with equal justification, apparently considers that it also owes such a forum to the residents of the District of Columbia in execution of its power and duty under the same Article. We do not see how the one could be sustained and the other denied.

We therefore hold that Congress may exert its power to govern the District of Columbia by imposing the judicial function of adjudicating justiciable controversies on the regular federal courts which under the Constitution it has the power to ordain and establish and which it may invest with jurisdiction and from which it may withhold jurisdiction "in the exact degrees and character which to Congress may seem proper for the public good." Lockerty v. Phillips, 319 U.S. 182, 187.

* * *

MR. JUSTICE RUTLEDGE, with whom MR. JUSTICE MURPHY agrees, concurring.

I join in the Court's judgment. But I strongly dissent from the reasons assigned to support it in the opinion of Mr. Justice Jackson.

While giving lip service to the venerable decision in Hepburn & Dundas v. Ellzey, 2 Cranch 445, and purporting to distinguish it, that opinion ignores nearly a century and a half of subsequent consistent construction. In all practical consequence, it would overrule that decision with its later reaffirmations. * * *

* * *

The opinion of Mr. Justice Jackson in words "reaffirms" [Chief Justice Marshall's] view of the diversity clause. Nevertheless, faced with an explicit congressional command to extend jurisdiction in nonfederal cases to the citizens of the District of Columbia, it finds that Congress has power to add to the Article III jurisdiction of federal district courts such further jurisdiction as Congress may think "necessary and proper," Const., Art. I, § 8, cl. 18, to implement its power of "exclusive Legislation," Const., Art. I, § 8, cl. 17, over the District of Columbia; and thereby to escape from the limitations of Article III.

From this reasoning I dissent. For I think that the Article III courts in the several states cannot be vested, by virtue of other provisions of the Constitution, with powers specifically denied them by the terms of

Article III. If we accept the elementary doctrine that the words of Article III are not self-exercising grants of jurisdiction to the inferior federal courts, then I think those words must mark the limits of the power Congress may confer on the district courts in the several states. And I do not think we or Congress can override those limits through invocation of Article I without making the Constitution a self-contradicting instrument. * * *

* * *

If Article III were no longer to serve as the criterion of district court jurisdiction, I should be at a loss to understand what tasks, within the constitutional competence of Congress, might not be assigned to district courts. At all events, intimations that district courts could only undertake the determination of "justiciable" controversies seem inappropriate, since the very clause of Article I today relied on has long been regarded as the source of the "legislative," Keller v. Potomac Electric Power Co., 261 U.S. 428, and "administrative," Postum Cereal Co. v. California Fig Nut Co., 272 U.S. 693, powers of the courts of the District of Columbia. * * *

[Justice Rutledge concurred, because he believed—unlike Justice Jackson—that Chief Justice Marshall's refusal to characterize the District of Columbia as a "State" for purposes of Article III should be overruled.]

* * *

MR. CHIEF JUSTICE VINSON, with whom MR. JUSTICE DOUGLAS joins, dissenting.

* * * I agree with the views expressed by Mr. Justice Frankfurter and Mr. Justice Rutledge which relate to the power of Congress under Art. I of the Constitution to vest federal district courts with jurisdiction over suits between citizens of States and the District of Columbia, and with the views of Mr. Justice Frankfurter and Mr. Justice Jackson as to the proper interpretation of the word "States" in the diversity clause of Art. III * * *.

* * *

MR. JUSTICE FRANKFURTER, with whom MR. JUSTICE REED concurs, dissenting.

No provisions of the Constitution, barring only those that draw on arithmetic, as in prescribing the qualifying age for a President and members of a Congress or the length of their tenure of office, are more explicit and specific than those pertaining to courts established under Article III. "The judicial power" which is "vested" in these tribunals and the safeguards under which their judges function are enumerated with particularity. Their tenure and compensation, the controversies which may be brought before them, and the distribution of original and appellate jurisdiction among these tribunals are defined and circumscribed, not left at large by vague and elastic phrasing. The precision which characterizes these portions of Article III is in striking contrast to the imprecision of so many other provisions of the Constitution dealing with other very vital aspects of government. This was not due to chance or ineptitude on the part of the Framers. The differences in subject-matter account for the drastic differences in treatment. Great concepts like "Commerce ... among the several States," "due process of law," "liberty," "property" were purposely left to gather meaning from experience. For they relate to the whole domain of social and economic fact, and the statesmen who founded this Nation knew too well that only a stagnant society remains unchanged. But when the Constitution in turn gives strict definition of power or specific limitations upon it we cannot extend the definition or remove the translation. Precisely because "it is *a constitution* we are expounding," M'Culloch v. Maryland, 4 Wheat. 316, 407, we ought not to take liberties with it.

There was deep distrust of a federal judicial system, as against the State judiciaries, in the Constitutional Convention. This distrust was reflected in the evolution of Article III. Moreover, when they dealt with the distribution of judicial power as between the courts of the States and the courts of the United States, the Framers were dealing with a technical subject in a professional way. More than that, since the judges of the courts for which Article III made provision not only had the last word (apart from amending the Constitution) but also enjoyed life tenure, it was an essential safeguard against control by the judiciary of its own jurisdiction, to define the jurisdiction of those courts with particularity. The Framers guarded against the self-will of the courts as well as against the will of Congress by marking with exactitude the outer limits of federal judicial power.

According to Article III, only "judicial power" can be "vested" in the courts established under it. At least this limitation, which has been the law of the land since 1792, Hayburn's Case, 2 Dall. 409, is not yet called into question. And so the President could not today elicit this Court's views on ticklish problems of international law any more than Washington was able to do in 1793.

But if courts established under Article III can exercise wider jurisdiction than that defined and confined by Article III, and if they are available to effectuate the various substantive powers of Congress, such as the power to legislate for the District of Columbia, what justification is there for interpreting Article III as imposing one restriction in the exercise of those other powers of the Congress—the restriction to the exercise of "judicial power"—yet not interpreting it as imposing the restrictions that are most explicit, namely, the particularization of the "cases" to which "the judicial Power shall extend"?

It is conceded that the claim for which access is sought in the District Court for Maryland, one of the courts established under Article III, is not included among the "cases" to which the judicial power can be made to extend. But if the precise enumeration of cases as to which Article III authorized Congress to grant jurisdiction to the United States

District Courts does not preclude Congress from vesting these courts with authority which Article III disallows, by what rule of reason is Congress to be precluded from bringing to its aid the advisory opinions of this Court or of the Courts of Appeals? In the exercise of its constitutional power to regulate commerce, to establish uniform rules of naturalization, to raise and support armies, or to execute any of the other powers of Congress that are no less vital than its power to legislate for the District of Columbia, the Congress may be greatly in need of informed and disinterested legal advice. If Congress may grant to the United States District Courts authority to act in situations in which Article III denies it, why may not this Court respond to calls upon it by Congress if confronted with the conscientious belief of Congress that such a call is made under the Necessary-and-Proper Clause in order to deal wisely and effectively with some substantive constitutional power of Congress? * * *

* * *

The diversity jurisdiction of the federal courts was probably the most tenuously founded and most unwillingly granted of all the heads of federal jurisdiction which Congress was empowered by Article III to confer. It is a matter of common knowledge that the jurisdiction of the federal courts based merely on diversity of citizenship has been more continuously under fire than any other. Inertia largely accounts for its retention. By withdrawing the meretricious advantages which diversity jurisdiction afforded one of the parties in some types of litigation, Erie R. Co. v. Tompkins, 304 U.S. 64, has happily eliminated some practical but indefensible reasons for its retention. An Act for the elimination of diversity jurisdiction could fairly be called an Act for the relief of the federal courts. Concededly, no great public interest or libertarian principle is at stake in the desire of a corporation which happens to have been chartered in the District of Columbia, to pursue its claim against a citizen of Maryland in the federal court in Maryland on the theory that the right of this artificial citizen of the District of Columbia cannot be vindicated in the State courts of Maryland.

But in any event, the dislocation of the Constitutional scheme for the establishment of the federal judiciary and the distribution of jurisdiction among its tribunals so carefully formulated in Article III is too heavy a price to pay for whatever advantage there may be to a citizen of the District, natural or artificial, to go to a federal court in a particular State instead of to the State court in suing a citizen of that State. Nor is it merely a dislocation for the purpose of accomplishing a result of trivial importance in the practical affairs of life. The process of reasoning by which this result is reached invites a use of the federal courts which breaks with the whole history of the federal judiciary and disregards the wise policy behind that history. It was because Article III defines and confines the limits of jurisdiction of the courts which are established under Article III that the first Court of Claims Act fell, Gordon v. United States, 2 Wall. 561. And it was in observance of these Constitutional limits that this Court had to decline appellate powers sought to be conferred by the Congress in an exercise of its legislative power over the District. Keller v. Potomac Electric Power Co., 261 U.S. 428.

To find a source for "the judicial Power," therefore, which may be exercised by courts established under Article III of the Constitution outside that Article would be to disregard the distribution of powers made by the Constitution.[3] The other alternative—to expand "the judicial Power" of Article III to include a controversy between a citizen of the District of Columbia and a citizen of one of the States by virtue of the provision extending "the judicial Power" to controversies "between Citizens of different States"—would disregard an explicit limitation of Article III. For a hundred and fifty years "States" as there used meant "States"—the political organizations that form the Union and alone have power to amend the Constitution. The word did not cover the district which was to become "the Seat of the Government of the United States," nor the "Territory" belonging to the United States, both of which the Constitution dealt with in differentiation from the States. A decent respect for unbroken history since the country's foundation, for contemporaneous interpretation by those best qualified to make it, for the capacity of the distinguished lawyers among the Framers to express themselves with precision when dealing with technical matters, unite to admonish against disregarding the explicit language of Article III extending the diversity jurisdiction of the federal courts "to Controversies . . . between Citizens of different States," not to controversies between "Citizens of different States, including the District and the Territory of the United States."

* * *

A substantial majority of the Court agrees that each of the two grounds urged in support of the attempt by Congress to extend diversity jurisdiction to cases involving citizens of the District of Columbia must be rejected—but not the same majority. And so, conflicting minorities in combination bring to pass a result—paradoxical as it may appear—which differing majorities of the Court find insupportable.

---

3. Reliance on Williams v. Austrian, 331 U.S. 642, 657, seems singularly inapposite. When a petition for bankruptcy is filed, there may be outstanding claims by the bankrupt against debtors and by creditors against the bankrupt. Of course Congress has power to determine whether all such claims—those for, and those against, the bankrupt estate—should be enforced through the federal courts. That a particular claim dissociated from the fact of bankruptcy would have to be brought in a State court for want of any ground of federal jurisdiction is irrelevant. This is so because in the exercise of its power to "pass uniform laws on the subject of bankruptcies" Congress may deem it desirable that the federal courts be utilized for all the claims that pertain to the bankrupt estate whether in the federal court in which the bankruptcy proceeding is pending or in a more convenient federal court. The congeries of controversies thus brought into being by reason of bankruptcy may be lodged in the federal courts because they arise under "the Laws of the United States," to wit, laws concerning the "subject of bankruptcies." It is a matter of congressional policy whether there must be a concourse of all claims affecting the bankrupt's estate in the federal court in which the bankruptcy proceeding is pending or whether auxiliary suits be pursued in other federal courts.

Notes

1. Note that although Justice Jackson's opinion announced the judgment of the Court, it spoke for only three Justices. The other members of the Court were all in agreement that an Article III federal court could not be required by Congress to hear matters falling outside the "judicial power" as defined in Article III, section 2. Why do you suppose the other Justices were so concerned about such a result? Consider closely the reasoning of Justice Frankfurter in his dissent.

2. How, if at all, does Justice Jackson's opinion respond to the points made by Justice Frankfurter? They seem to differ over whether a distinction can be drawn between Congress' giving *cases* to Article III courts that cover subject matter beyond Article III (which Jackson thinks should be allowed) and Congress' giving *tasks* to Article III courts that fall outside the "case or controversy" requirement of Article III (which both agree is improper). Do you think such a distinction can be drawn? Why is Justice Jackson more afraid of the latter than of the former?

Consider the debate between Justices Jackson and Frankfurter in light of the Court's decisions in Morrison v. Olson, 487 U.S. 654 (1988), and Mistretta v. United States, 488 U.S. 361 (1989).

Morrison involved a challenge to the Ethics in Government Act of 1978. Title VI of the Act creates a "Special Division", made up of Article III judges, to appoint independent counsel to investigate wrongdoing by government officials. The special division is also assigned various duties in connection with investigations—the power to grant extensions for preliminary investigations conducted by the Attorney General, the power to receive the Attorney General's report and the Independent Counsel's report on expenses, the power to terminate the Independent Counsel relationship, and related activities. Upholding the constitutionality of the scheme, the majority concluded that the duties prescribed under the Act are "directly analogous to functions that federal judges perform in other contexts." The powers "do not pose a sufficient threat of judicial intrusion into matters that are more properly within the Executive's authority to require that the Act be invalidated as inconsistent with Article III." 487 U.S. at 678–685.

In *Mistretta* the Court ruled that the statutorily required inclusion of three Article III judges on the United States Sentencing Commission does not violate separation-of-powers standards. The Commission was established by Congress with a charge to put an end to perceived inequities and disparities in federal criminal sentencing. To that end, the Commission was given power to promulgate binding sentencing guidelines on the basis of specified criteria. Again applying a functional analysis, the Court ruled that the scheme did not "accrete to a single Branch powers more appropriately diffused among separate Branches or * * * undermine the authority and independence of one or another coordinate Branch." 488 U.S. at 382. Moreover, "[i]t was the everyday business of judges, taken collectively, to evaluate and weigh the various aims of sentencing and to apply those aims to the individual cases that come before them." Id. at 395.

See M. Redish, Federal Jurisdiction: Tensions in the Allocation of Judicial Power, 18–19 (2d ed. 1990): "Could anyone imagine a law directing the federal judiciary to promulgate binding regulations enforcing the First Amendment's right of free speech could survive examination under the case-or-controversy requirement, on the grounds that the judiciary has traditionally developed the substance of first amendment law in the context of live cases?"

3.   Justice Jackson relied in part on O'Donoghue v. United States, 289 U.S. 516 (1933). There the Supreme Court held that federal courts in the District of Columbia were Article III courts, even though they had for many years performed certain administrative functions which fell outside the Supreme Court's definition of a "case." The Supreme Court has not approved use of this "dual status" outside of the District of Columbia, however, and the decision is no longer relevant even to the District, since Congress set up a dual system of courts there. District of Columbia Court Reorganization Act of 1970, Pub.L. No. 91–358, 84 Stat. 473 (1970). See Palmore v. United States, 411 U.S. 389 (1973); Chapter Three.

4.   For a thorough examination of *Tidewater,* see Cross, *Congressional Power to Extend Federal Jurisdiction to Disputes Outside Article III: A Critical Analysis from the Perspective of Bankruptcy,* 87 Nw.U.L.Rev. 1188 (1993).

Chapter 3

LEGISLATIVE COURTS

§ 1. THE BACKGROUND TO LEGISLATIVE COURTS: REVIEW OF "CONSTITUTIONAL FACTS"

CROWELL v. BENSON

Supreme Court of the United States, 1932.
285 U.S. 22.

Mr. Chief Justice Hughes delivered the opinion of the Court.

This suit was brought in the District Court to enjoin the enforcement of an award made by petitioner Crowell, as deputy commissioner of the United States Employees' Compensation Commission, in favor of the petitioner Knudsen and against the respondent Benson. The award was made under the Longshoremen's and Harbor Workers' Compensation Act * * * and rested upon the finding of the deputy commissioner that Knudsen was injured while in the employ of Benson and performing service upon the navigable waters of the United States. The complainant alleged that the award was contrary to law for the reason that Knudsen was not at the time of his injury an employee of the complainant and his claim was not "within the jurisdiction" of the deputy commissioner. An amended complaint charged that the Act was unconstitutional upon the grounds that it violated the due process clause of the Fifth Amendment, the provision of the Seventh Amendment as to trial by jury, that of the Fourth Amendment as to unreasonable search and seizure, and the provisions of Article III with respect to the judicial power of the United States. The District Judge denied motions to dismiss and granted a hearing *de novo* upon the facts and the law, expressing the opinion that the Act would be invalid if not construed to permit such a hearing. The case was transferred to the admiralty docket, answers were filed presenting the issue as to the fact of employment, and the evidence of both parties having been heard, the District Court decided that Knudsen was not in the employ of the petitioner and restrained the enforcement of the award. * * * The decree was affirmed by the Circuit Court of Appeals, * * * and this Court granted writs of certiorari. * * *

The question of the validity of the Act may be considered in relation to (1) its provisions defining substantive rights and (2) its procedural requirements.

First. The Act has two limitations that are fundamental. It deals exclusively with compensation in respect of disability or death resulting "from an injury occurring upon the navigable waters of the United States" if recovery "through workmen's compensation proceedings may not validly be provided by State law," and it applies only when the relation of master and servant exists. § 3. "Injury," within the statute, "means accidental injury or death arising out of and in the course of employment," and the term "employer" means one "any of whose employees are employed in maritime employment, in whole or in part," upon such navigable waters. § 2(2)(4). Employers are made liable for the payment to their employees of prescribed compensation "irrespective of fault as a cause for the injury." § 4. The liability is exclusive, unless the employer fails to secure payment of the compensation. § 5. The employer is required to furnish appropriate medical and other treatment. § 7. The compensation for temporary or permanent disability, total or partial, according to the statutory classification, and in case of the death of the employee, is fixed, being based upon prescribed percentages of average weekly wages, and the persons to whom payments are to be made are designated. §§ 6, 8, 9, 10. Employers must secure the payment of compensation by procuring insurance or by becoming self-insurers in the manner stipulated. § 32. Failure to provide such security is a misdemeanor. § 38.

As the Act relates solely to injuries occurring upon the navigable waters of the United States, it deals with the maritime law, applicable to matters that fall within the admiralty and maritime jurisdiction (Const. Art. III, § 2 * * *); and the general authority of the Congress to alter or revise the maritime law which shall prevail throughout the country is beyond dispute. * * *

Second. The objections to the procedural requirements of the Act relate to the extent of the administrative authority which it confers. The administration of the Act—"except as otherwise specifically provided"— was given to the United States Employees' Compensation Commission, which was authorized to establish compensation districts, appoint deputy commissioners, and make regulations. * * *

* * *

(1) The contention under the due process clause of the Fifth Amendment relates to the determination of questions of fact. Rulings of the deputy commissioner upon questions of law are without finality. So far as the latter are concerned, full opportunity is afforded for their determination by the Federal courts through proceedings to suspend or to set aside a compensation order, § 21(b), by the requirement that judgment is to be entered on a supplementary order declaring default only in case the order follows the law (§ 18), and by the provision that the issue of injunction or other process in a proceeding by a beneficiary

to compel obedience to a compensation order is dependent upon a determination by the court that the order was lawfully made and served. § 21(c). Moreover, the statute contains no express limitation attempting to preclude the court, in proceedings to set aside an order as not in accordance with law, from making its own examination and determination of facts whenever that is deemed to be necessary to enforce a constitutional right properly asserted. See Ohio Valley Water Co. v. Ben Avon Borough, 253 U.S. 287, 289; Ng Fung Ho v. White, 259 U.S. 276, 284, 285; Prendergast v. New York Telephone Co., 262 U.S. 43, 50; Tagg Bros. & Moorhead v. United States, 280 U.S. 420, 443, 444; Phillips v. Commissioner, 283 U. S. 589, 600. As the statute is to be construed so as to support rather than to defeat it, no such limitation is to be implied. Panama Railroad Co. v. Johnson, 264 U.S. 375, 390.

Apart from cases involving constitutional rights to be appropriately enforced by proceedings in court, there can be no doubt that the Act contemplates that, as to questions of fact arising with respect to injuries to employees within the purview of the Act, the findings of the deputy commissioner, supported by evidence and within the scope of his authority, shall be final. To hold otherwise would be to defeat the obvious purpose of the legislation to furnish a prompt, continuous, expert and inexpensive method for dealing with a class of questions of fact which are peculiarly suited to examination and determination by an administrative agency specially assigned to that task. * * *

* * *

(2) The contention based upon the judicial power of the United States, as extended "to all cases of admiralty and maritime jurisdiction" (Const. art. 3), presents a distinct question. In Murray's Lessee v. Hoboken Land and Improvement Company, 18 How. 272, 284, this Court, speaking through Mr. Justice Curtis, said: "To avoid misconstruction upon so grave a subject, we think it proper to state that we do not consider congress can either withdraw from judicial cognizance any matter which, from its nature, is the subject of a suit at the common law, or in equity, or admiralty; nor, on the other hand, can it bring under the judicial power a matter which, from its nature, is not a subject for judicial determination."

The question in the instant case, in this aspect, can be deemed to relate only to determinations of fact. The reservation of legal questions is to the same court that has jurisdiction in admiralty, and the mere fact that the court is not described as such is unimportant. Nor is the provision for injunction proceedings, § 21(b), open to objection. The Congress was at liberty to draw upon another system of procedure to equip the court with suitable and adequate means for enforcing the standards of the maritime law as defined by the Act. The Genesee Chief, 12 How. 443, 459, 460. Compare Panama R. Co. v. Johnson, supra, at page 388 of 264 U.S. By statute and rules, courts of admiralty may be empowered to grant injunctions, as in the case of limitation of liability proceedings. Hartford Accident & Indemnity Co. v. Southern Pacific Co.,

273 U.S. 207, 218. See, also, Marine Transit Corporation v. Dreyfus, 284 U.S. 263, decided January 4, 1932. The Congress did not attempt to define questions of law, and the generality of the description leaves no doubt of the intention to reserve to the Federal court full authority to pass upon all matters which this Court had held to fall within that category. There is thus no attempt to interfere with, but rather provision is made to facilitate, the exercise by the court of its jurisdiction to deny effect to any administrative finding which is without evidence, or "contrary to the indisputable character of the evidence," or where the hearing is "inadequate," or "unfair," or arbitrary in any respect. * * *

As to determinations of fact, the distinction is at once apparent between cases of private right and those which arise between the Government and persons subject to its authority in connection with the performance of the constitutional functions of the executive or legislative departments. The Court referred to this distinction in Murray's Lessee v. Hoboken Land and Improvement Co., *supra*, pointing out that "there are matters, involving public rights, which may be presented in such form that the judicial power is capable of acting on them, and which are susceptible of judicial determination, but which Congress may or may not bring within the cognizance of the courts of the United States, as it may deem proper." Thus the Congress, in exercising the powers confided to it, may establish "legislative" courts (as distinguished from "constitutional courts in which the judicial power conferred by the Constitution can be deposited") which are to form part of the government of territories or of the District of Columbia, or to serve as special tribunals "to examine and determine various matters, arising between the government and others, which from their nature do not require judicial determination and yet are susceptible of it." But "the mode of determining matters of this class is completely within congressional control. Congress may reserve to itself the power to decide, may delegate that power to executive officers, or may commit it to judicial tribunals." Ex parte Bakelite Corporation, 279 U.S. 438, 451. Familiar illustrations of administrative agencies created for the determination of such matters are found in connection with the exercise of the congressional power as to interstate and foreign commerce, taxation, immigration, the public lands, public health, the facilities of the post office, pensions and payments to veterans.

The present case does not fall within the categories just described but is one of private right, that is, of the liability of one individual to another under the law as defined. But in cases of that sort, there is no requirement that, in order to maintain the essential attributes of the judicial power, all determinations of fact in constitutional courts shall be made by judges. On the common law side of the Federal courts, the aid of juries is not only deemed appropriate but is required by the Constitution itself. In cases of equity and admiralty it is historic practice to call to the assistance of the courts, without the consent of the parties, masters and commissioners or assessors, to pass upon certain classes of questions, as, for example, to take and state an account or to find the amount of damages. While the reports of masters and commissioners in such cases are essentially of an advisory nature, it has not been the practice to disturb their findings when they are properly based upon evidence, in the absence of errors of law, and the parties have no right to demand that the court shall redetermine the facts thus found. * * *

* * *

In deciding whether the Congress, in enacting the statute under review, has exceeded the limits of its authority to prescribe procedure in cases of injury upon navigable waters, regard must be had, as in other cases where constitutional limits are invoked, not to mere matters of form but to the substance of what is required. The statute has a limited application, being confined to the relation of master and servant, and the method of determining the questions of fact, which arise in the routine of making compensation awards to employees under the Act, is necessary to its effective enforcement. The Act itself, where it applies, establishes the measure of the employer's liability, thus leaving open for determination the questions of fact as to the circumstances, nature, extent and consequences of the injuries sustained by the employee for which compensation is to be made in accordance with the prescribed standards. Findings of fact by the deputy commissioner upon such questions are closely analogous to the findings of the amount of damages that are made, according to familiar practice, by commissioners or assessors; and the reservation of full authority to the court to deal with matters of law provides for the appropriate exercise of the judicial function in this class of cases. For the purposes stated, we are unable to find any constitutional obstacle to the action of the Congress in availing itself of a method shown by experience to be essential in order to apply its standards to the thousands of cases involved, thus relieving the courts of a most serious burden while preserving their complete authority to insure the proper application of the law.

(3) What has been said thus far relates to the determination of claims of employees within the purview of the Act. A different question is presented where the determinations of fact are fundamental or "jurisdictional,"[17] in the sense that their existence is a condition precedent to the operation of the statutory scheme. These fundamental requirements are that the injury occur upon the navigable waters of the United States and that the relation of master and servant exist. These conditions are indispensable to the application of the statute, not only because the Congress has so provided explicitly (§ 3), but also because the power of the Congress to enact the legislation turns upon the existence of these conditions.

---

17. The term "jurisdictional," although frequently used, suggests analogies which are not complete when the reference is to administrative officials or bodies. See Interstate Commerce Commission v. Humboldt Steamship Co., 224 U.S. 474, 484. In relation to administrative agencies, the question in a given case is whether it falls within the scope of the authority validly conferred.

In amending and revising the maritime law, the Congress cannot reach beyond the constitutional limits which are inherent in the admiralty and maritime jurisdiction. Unless the injuries to which the Act relates occur upon the navigable waters of the United States, they fall outside that jurisdiction. Not only is navigability itself a question of fact, as waters that are navigable in fact are navigable in law, but, where navigability is not in dispute, the locality of the injury, that is, whether it has occurred upon the navigable waters of the United States, determines the existence of the congressional power to create the liability prescribed by the statute. Again, it cannot be maintained that the Congress has any general authority to amend the maritime law so as to establish liability without fault in maritime cases regardless of particular circumstances or relations. It is unnecessary to consider what circumstances or relations might permit the imposition of such a liability by amendment of the maritime law, but it is manifest that some suitable selection would be required. In the present instance, the Congress has imposed liability without fault only where the relation of master and servant exists in maritime employment and, while we hold that the Congress could do this, the fact of that relation is the pivot of the statute and, in the absence of any other justification, underlies the constitutionality of this enactment. If the person injured was not an employee of the person sought to be held, or if the injury did not occur upon the navigable waters of the United States, there is no ground for an assertion that the person against whom the proceeding was directed could constitutionally be subjected, in the absence of fault upon his part, to the liability which the statute creates.

In relation to these basic facts, the question is not the ordinary one as to the propriety of provision for administrative determinations. Nor have we simply the question of due process in relation to notice and hearing. It is rather a question of the appropriate maintenance of the Federal judicial power in requiring the observance of constitutional restrictions. It is the question whether the Congress may substitute for constitutional courts, in which the judicial power of the United States is vested, an administrative agency—in this instance a single deputy commissioner—for the final determination of the existence of the facts upon which the enforcement of the constitutional rights of the citizen depend. The recognition of the utility and convenience of administrative agencies for the investigation and finding of facts within their proper province, and the support of their authorized action, does not require the conclusion that there is no limitation of their use, and that the Congress could completely oust the courts of all determinations of fact by vesting the authority to make them with finality in its own instrumentalities or in the Executive Department. That would be to sap the judicial power as it exists under the Federal Constitution, and to establish a government of a bureaucratic character alien to our system, wherever fundamental rights depend, as not infrequently they do depend, upon the facts, and finality as to facts becomes in effect finality in law.

In this aspect of the question, the irrelevancy of State statutes and citations from State courts as to the distribution of State powers is apparent. A State may distribute its powers as it sees fit, provided only that it acts consistently with the essential demands of due process and does not transgress those restrictions of the Federal Constitution which are applicable to State authority. In relation to the Federal government, we have already noted the inappositeness to the present inquiry of decisions with respect to determinations of fact, upon evidence and within the authority conferred, made by administrative agencies which have been created to aid in the performance of governmental functions and where the mode of determination is within the control of the Congress * * *.

* * *

In cases brought to enforce constitutional rights, the judicial power of the United States necessarily extends to the independent determination of all questions, both of fact and law, necessary to the performance of that supreme function. The case of confiscation is illustrative, the ultimate conclusion almost invariably depending upon the decisions of questions of fact. This court has held the owner to be entitled to "a fair opportunity for submitting that issue to a judicial tribunal for determination upon its own independent judgment as to both law and facts." Ohio Valley Water Co. v. Ben Avon Borough, supra. * * * Jurisdiction in the Executive to order deportation exists only if the person arrested is an alien, and while, if there were jurisdiction, the findings of fact of the Executive Department would be conclusive, the claim of citizenship "is thus a denial of an essential jurisdictional fact" both in the statutory and the constitutional sense, and a writ of *habeas corpus* will issue "to determine the status." Persons claiming to be citizens of the United States "are entitled to a judicial determination of their claims," said this Court in Ng Fung Ho v. White, supra, at page 285 of 259 U.S., and in that case the cause was remanded to the Federal District Court "for trial in that court of the question of citizenship."

In the present instance, the argument that the Congress has constituted the deputy commissioner a fact-finding tribunal is unavailing, as the contention makes the untenable assumption that the constitutional courts may be deprived in all cases of the determination of facts upon evidence even though a constitutional right may be involved. Reference is also made to the power of the Congress to change the procedure in courts of admiralty, a power to which we have alluded in dealing with the function of the deputy commissioner in passing upon the compensation claims of employees. But when fundamental rights are in question, this Court has repeatedly emphasized "the difference in security of judicial over administrative action." Ng Fung Ho v. White, supra. Even where issues of fact are tried by juries in the Federal courts, such trials are under the constant superintendence of the trial judge. * * *

When the validity of an act of the Congress is drawn in question, and even if a serious doubt of constitutionality is raised, it is a cardinal principle that this Court will first ascertain whether a construction of the statute is fairly possible by which the question may be avoided. We are of the opinion that such a construction is permissible and should be adopted in the instant case. The Congress has not expressly provided that the determinations by the deputy commissioner of the fundamental or jurisdictional facts as to the locality of the injury and the existence of the relation of master and servant shall be final. The finality of such determinations of the deputy commissioner is predicated primarily upon the provision, § 19(a), that he "shall have full power and authority to hear and determine all questions in respect to such claim." But "such claim" is the claim for compensation under the Act and by its explicit provisions is that of an "employee," as defined in the Act, against his "employer." The fact of employment is an essential condition precedent to the right to make the claim. The other provision upon which the argument rests is that which authorizes the Federal court to set aside a compensation order if it is "not in accordance with law." § 21(b). In the absence of any provision as to the finality of the determination by the deputy commissioner of the jurisdictional fact of employment, the statute is open to the construction that the court in determining whether a compensation order is in accordance with law may determine the fact of employment which underlies the operation of the statute. And, to remove the question as to validity, we think that the statute should be so construed. * * *

Assuming that the Federal court may determine for itself the existence of these fundamental or jurisdictional facts, we come to the question,—Upon what record is the determination to be made? There is no provision of the statute which seeks to confine the court in such a case to the record before the deputy commissioner or to the evidence which he has taken. The remedy which the statute makes available is not by an appeal or by a writ of certiorari for a review of his determination upon the record before him. The remedy is "through injunction proceedings, mandatory or otherwise." § 21(b). The question in the instant case is not whether the deputy commissioner has acted improperly or arbitrarily as shown by the record of his proceedings in the course of administration in cases contemplated by the statute, but whether he has acted in a case to which the statute is inapplicable. By providing for injunction proceedings, the Congress evidently contemplated a suit as in equity, and in such a suit the complainant would have full opportunity to plead and prove either that the injury did not occur upon the navigable waters of the United States or that the relation of master and servant did not exist, and hence that the case lay outside the purview of the statute. As the question is one of the constitutional authority of the deputy commissioner as an administrative agency, the court is under no obligation to give weight to his proceedings pending the determination of that question. If the court finds that the facts existed which gave the deputy commissioner jurisdiction to pass upon the claim for compensation, the injunction will be denied in so far as these fundamental questions are concerned; if, on the contrary, the court is satisfied that

[handwritten margin note: De Novo Review]

the deputy commissioner had no jurisdiction of the proceedings before him, that determination will deprive them of their effectiveness for any purpose. We think that the essential independence of the exercise of the judicial power of the United States in the enforcement of constitutional rights requires that the Federal court should determine such an issue upon its own record and the facts elicited before it.

[handwritten margin note: Fed Ct should Determine the issue based upon its own finding]

* * *

Mr. Justice Brandeis, dissenting.

* * *

Fourth. Trial *de novo* of the issue of the existence of the employer-employee relation is not required by the due process clause. That clause ordinarily does not even require that parties shall be permitted to have a judicial tribunal pass upon the weight of the evidence introduced before the administrative body. * * * The findings of fact of the deputy commissioner, the Court now decides, are conclusive as to most issues, if supported by evidence. Yet as to the issue of employment the Court holds not only that such findings may not be declared final, but that it would create a serious constitutional doubt to construe the Act as committing to the deputy commissioner the simple function of collecting the evidence upon which the court will ultimately decide the issue.

[handwritten margin note: employment]

It is suggested that this exception is required as to issues of fact involving claims of constitutional right. For reasons which I shall later discuss, I cannot believe that the issue of employment is one of constitutional right. But even assuming it to be so, the conclusion does not follow that the trial of the issue must therefore be upon a record made in the district court. That the function of collecting evidence may be committed to an administrative tribunal is settled by a host of cases, and supported by persuasive analogies, none of which justify a distinction between issues of constitutional right and any others. * * *

* * *

Sixth. Even if the constitutional power of Congress to provide compensation is limited to cases in which the employer-employee relation exists, I see no basis for a contention that the denial of the right to a trial *de novo* upon the issue of employment is in any manner subversive of the independence of the federal judicial power. Nothing in the Constitution, or in any prior decision of this Court to which attention has been called, lends support to the doctrine that a judicial finding of any fact involved in any civil proceeding to enforce a pecuniary liability may not be made upon evidence introduced before a properly constituted administrative tribunal, or that a determination so made may not be deemed an independent judicial determination. Congress has repeatedly exercised authority to confer upon the tribunals which it creates, be they administrative bodies or courts of limited jurisdiction, the power to receive evidence concerning the facts upon which the exercise of federal power must be predicated, and to determine whether those facts exist. The power of Congress to provide by legislation for liability under certain circumstances subsumes the power to provide for the determination of the existence of those circumstances. It does not depend upon the absolute existence in reality of any fact.

* * *

The "judicial power" of Article III of the Constitution is the power of the federal government, and not of any inferior tribunal. There is in that Article nothing which requires any controversy to be determined as of first instance in the federal district courts. The jurisdiction of those courts is subject to the control of Congress. Matters which may be placed within their jurisdiction may instead be committed to the state courts. If there be any controversy to which the judicial power extends that may not be subjected to the conclusive determination of administrative bodies or federal legislative courts, it is not because of any prohibition against the diminution of the jurisdiction of the federal district courts as such, but because, under certain circumstances, the constitutional requirement of due process is a requirement of judicial process. An accumulation of precedents, already referred to, has established that in civil proceedings involving property rights determination of facts may constitutionally be made otherwise than judicially; and necessarily that evidence as to such facts may be taken outside of a court. I do not conceive that Article III has properly any bearing upon the question presented in this case.

* * *

Notes

1. Which factual issues did the Supreme Court hold had to be determined *de novo* by a court? What, if anything, is unique about these issues? See L. Jaffe, Judicial Control of Administrative Action 640, 641 (Student Ed. 1965).

2. What was the constitutional basis of Chief Justice Hughes' decision? Can you articulate his reasoning? See L. Jaffe, supra, at 639–40, 642.

3. *Crowell* is the most famous in a line of Supreme Court decisions dealing with similar issues. The first was Ohio Valley Water Co. v. Ben Avon Borough, 253 U.S. 287 (1920). The case concerned a rate set by a state regulatory commission alleged to be so low as to be confiscatory. The complaint sought the "independent judgment" of a state court on the question and the U.S. Supreme Court agreed, reasoning: "[I]f the owner claims confiscation of his property will result, the State must provide a fair opportunity for submitting that issue to a judicial tribunal for determination upon its own independent judgment as to both law and facts * * *." Id. at 289. Given what you have been told about the case, can you guess what the constitutional basis of the Court's decision was? Keep in mind that the federal separation-of-powers requirements of Article III have never been held applicable to the states.

Two years later, the Court decided Ng Fung Ho v. White, 259 U.S. 276 (1922). The Department of Labor had ordered deported two individuals who claimed they were United States citizens. The Court, in an opinion by Justice Brandeis, held that the deportees were entitled to a judicial determination of their claims of citizenship.

Crowell, ten years later, was the third case in the progression. It was followed by St. Joseph Stock Yards Co. v. United States, 298 U.S. 38 (1936). The case presented the issue of whether a federally-set rate order was confiscatory. While the Court continued to hold that the question of whether the rate actually was confiscatory was ultimately a judicial question, a *de novo* factual hearing in court was no longer held to be constitutionally required.

4. What is the basis of Justice Brandeis' dissent? Can you reconcile his dissent in *Crowell* with the fact that he wrote the opinion for the Court in *Ng Fung Ho*?

5. Serious question has been raised by commentators as to the continued vitality of *Crowell*. According to Professor Kenneth Culp Davis, for example, *Crowell* "probably is no longer law." K. Davis, 4 Administrative Law Treatise § 29.08, at 156 (1958). Cf. Schwartz, *Does the Ghost of* Crowell v. Benson *Still Walk?*, 98 U.Pa.L.Rev. 163 (1949). See also the opinion of Justice Frankfurter in Estep v. United States, 327 U.S. 114, 142 (1946) suggesting that "one had supposed that the doctrine had earned a deserved repose." In Associated Indemnity Corp. v. Shea, 455 F.2d 913 (5th Cir.1972) (per curiam), the court stated: "Whether any vestige of validity remains of the extensively criticized *Crowell* doctrine is extremely doubtful." Id. at 914 n.2. But at least in regard to issues of personal liberty, rather than property rights, it appears that the "constitutional fact" doctrine still has force. See, e.g., Jacobellis v. Ohio, 378 U.S. 184, 190 n. 6 (1964). In recent years, several lower court opinions have cited at least the broad implications of *Crowell* favorably. See, e.g., Feinberg v. Federal Deposit Insurance Corp., 522 F.2d 1335 (D.C.Cir.1975); Cross v. United States, 512 F.2d 1212 (4th Cir.1975) (en banc). Whatever else can be said about *Crowell*, the case has at least never been explicitly overruled by the Supreme Court. For a contemporaneous discussion of *Crowell*, see Dickinson, Crowell v. Benson: *Judicial Review of Administrative Determinations of Questions of "Constitutional Fact"*, 80 U.Pa.L.Rev. 1055 (1932). For more recent commentary, see Schwartz, *Nonacquiescence,* Crowell v. Benson, *and Administrative Adjudication,* 77 Geo. L.J. 1815 (1989).

6. Professor Henry Hart has argued that *Crowell* is in some senses like United States v. Klein [supra pp. 169–70]. He suggests that *Crowell* involved a statute the enforcement of which Congress had authorized in federal court. Though *Crowell* itself was not an "enforcement" case like *Klein* or *Yakus*, it was effectively a pre-enforcement case: "Under the Act the award was enforceable only by judicial process. Congress chose to give the employer a chance to challenge an award in advance of enforcement proceedings. The Court was certainly entitled to assume in those circumstances, wasn't it, that whatever would invalidate an award in enforcement proceedings would invalidate it also in an advance challenge?" Hart, *The Power of Congress to*

Limit the Jurisdiction of Federal Courts: An Exercise in Dialectic, 66 Harv.L.Rev. 1362, 1373 (1953).

Does Professor Hart accurately characterize the Court's analysis in *Crowell*? Was there anything in the opinion limiting the holding to these so-called "pre-enforcement" cases?

§ 2. LEGISLATIVE COURTS AND ARTICLE III

M. REDISH, FEDERAL JURISDICTION: TENSIONS IN THE ALLOCATION OF JUDICIAL POWER 53–64 (2d ed. 1990): The essential characteristic of the Article III courts * * * is the independence their judges possess with respect to the executive and legislative branches of the federal government. * * * However, Congress' power to create at least certain types of courts not subject to these protections has long been recognized. Congressional authority to establish such non-Article III courts does not derive from any explicit constitutional power. Rather, such power derives from the conclusion that Congress may create certain non-Article III courts pursuant to its enumerated powers in Article I, in combination with the "necessary and proper" clause. For example, Congress has employed its Article I power "to make Rules for the Government and Regulation of the land and naval Forces" to establish military tribunals whose judges do not have Article III protections. Similarly, Congress has utilized its power to govern territories provided by Article IV of the Constitution to establish territorial courts, and its Article I power to lay and collect taxes to establish the Tax Court. Courts established in this manner have been referred to as "Article I" or "legislative" courts. While it has not always been clear whether certain courts are of the Article I or Article III variety, the distinction has significant consequences. One distinguishing factor is the vast difference in the degree of independence possessed by the judges of the two types of courts. The business of the judiciary is often to review the constitutional legitimacy of the actions of the legislative or executive branches. To the extent that these branches retain power to retaliate against judges who displease them, it is at least conceivable that courts will be unable to review the activities of those branches with proper neutrality. It was for this very reason that the framers inserted the independence requirements in Article III. * * *

Another important consequence that flows from the distinction between Article I and Article III courts is that the former may be made to perform non-judicial functions which the latter, on the whole, may not.

Though Congress' power to establish Article I courts in certain areas is well established, the parameters, if any, of this power remain shrouded in uncertainty. The primary question concerns the extent to which Congress may invest Article I courts with the "judicial power" of the United States. In other words, to what extent may it delegate to Article I courts the categories of cases described in Article III, section 2 of the Constitution? If it were to be held that Article I bodies (which, in addition to legislative courts, include administrative agencies) could hear no case falling within the "judicial power," Congress' ability to make use of these institutions would be severely limited, if only because virtually all the controversies given for determination to these bodies could be deemed cases arising under the laws of the United States, a central segment of the "judicial power" described in Article III, section 2. On the other hand, if the authority of Article I courts to adjudicate controversies within the judicial power was unlimited, Congress could easily circumvent the independence protections of Article III, by simply vesting all judicial power in Article I courts. Any attempt to deal with these issues, however, must be preceded by an examination of the historical development of the concept of legislative courts.

The first decision recognizing the existence of legislative courts was *American Insurance Co. v. Canter* [26 U.S. (1 Pet.) 511 (1828)], in which Chief Justice Marshall stated that the judges of the territorial courts created by Congress for the territory of Florida did not have the protections of Article III, since those courts were not created pursuant to its provisions. The power they exercised, Marshall concluded, was not the "judicial power" described in Article III, section 2. Indeed, "[t]hey are incapable of receiving it." Marshall continued:

> They are legislative Courts, created in virtue of the general right of sovereignty which exists in the government, or in virtue of that clause which enables Congress to make all needful rules and regulations, respecting the territory belonging to the United States. The jurisdiction with which they are invested, is not a part of that judicial power which is defined in the 3d article of the Constitution, but is conferred by Congress, in the execution of those general powers which that body possesses over the territories of the United States.

Since the *Canter* decision, it has been well established that territorial courts are legislative courts. It has, therefore, been held that the salary of a territorial judge may be reduced and that he may be appointed for a limited term or removed from office.

The reasons for considering territorial courts to be Article I bodies are pragmatic in nature. Judges in the territories performed functions traditionally within the purview of both state and federal courts within states. If and when a territory became a state, a significant portion of the duties performed by its courts was to be assumed by a newly established state judiciary. If the judges of the territorial courts had the life tenure protections of Article III, Congress would have been hard pressed to know what to do with many of them.

* * *

Following two major Supreme Court decisions, both the Court of Claims and the Court of Customs Appeals * * * were also considered to be legislative courts. These conclusions were expressly rejected by the Supreme Court in its 1962 decision in Glidden Co. v. Zdanok. It is now accepted that these are Article III courts, and that as a result their judges have both tenure and salary protections. But while the conclusions in the two cases, Ex parte Bakelite Corp. [279 U.S. 438 (1929)] and Williams v. United States, [289 U.S. 553 (1933)], are clearly no longer the law, both decisions present contrasting and significant approaches to the questions of how much overlap of jurisdiction could exist between Article I and Article III courts—in other words, to the issue of how much of the "judicial power" as defined in Article III, section 2 can be exercised by an Article I court.

Bakelite concerned the power of the Court of Customs Appeals to entertain an appeal from a finding of the Tariff Commission that improper methods in the importation of articles in competition with Bakelite's products had been employed. Bakelite argued that since the Court of Customs Appeals was an Article III court, it lacked the authority to review the Commission's findings because there existed no "case or controversy." The Supreme Court held that the Court of Customs Appeals was an Article I court, rendering irrelevant the question of whether its jurisdiction included matter which an Article III court could not hear.

The Supreme Court decided *Williams* four years later. The case considered whether the salaries of judges sitting on the Court of Claims could be constitutionally reduced. If that court were an Article III court, the answer would be no; if it were an Article I court, the answer would be yes. The Supreme Court, consistent with its *Bakelite* dictum about the status of the Court of Claims, held that court to be of the Article I variety.

Thus, both decisions found that the courts involved were Article I bodies. But, as Professor Currie has correctly pointed out, "[i]n approaching the basic problem . . . *Bakelite* and *Williams* were at opposite poles." In *Bakelite*, the Court assumed an extensive overlap between the jurisdiction of Article I and Article III courts:

> Legislative courts . . . may be created as special tribunals to examine and determine various matters, arising between the government and others, which from their nature do not require judicial determination and yet are susceptible of it. The mode of determining matters of this class is completely within congressional control.

Since the matters heard by the Court of Customs Appeals "include nothing which inherently or necessarily requires judicial determination," that court could have been an Article I court, even though the cases before it fell within "judicial power" as defined in Article III, section 2. In other words, the court's jurisdiction included only those cases falling within Article III, section 2 which could be heard by courts of either the Article I or Article III variety.

Four years later in *Williams,* however, the Court's initial assumption, ultimately leading to the conclusion that the Court of Claims was an Article I court, was that no Article I court could adjudicate *any* matter falling within Article III, section 2. The Court relied on dictum from *Bakelite* in concluding that the function performed by the Court of

Claims is one which Congress has discretion either to exercise directly or to delegate to executive agencies. The Court also cited Chief Justice Marshall's decision in *Canter* for the proposition that "[t]he jurisdiction with which [legislative courts] are invested, is not a part of that judicial power which is defined in the 3d article of the Constitution * * *." Given these assumptions, the Court's decision seemed logically inescapable:

> And since Congress, whenever it thinks proper, undoubtedly may, without infringing the Constitution, confer upon an executive officer or administrative board, or an existing or specially constituted court, or retain for itself, the power to hear and determine controversies respecting claims against the United States, it follows indubitably that such power, in whatever guise or by whatever agency exercised, is no part of the judicial power vested in the constitutional courts by the third article.

Because the Court of Claims heard nothing but suits against the United States, and because suits against the United States were not part of the "judicial power" defined by Article III, the *Williams* Court concluded that the Court of Claims was a legislative court.

The Court faced certain difficulties, however, in reaching the conclusion that suits against the United States were not part of the "judicial power" defined in Article III, section 2. By its terms, that provision refers to "controversies to which the United States shall be a party," which would seem to include all cases heard by the Court of Claims. But the Court rejected the argument that suits against the United States fell within this category. Rather, the Court argued, the clause referred only to suits in which the United States was a plaintiff.

The Court's reasoning to support its conclusion could most charitably be described as strained. First, the Court noted that, unlike most of the other categories of cases referred to in Article III, this clause did not explicitly apply to "all" cases to which the United States was a party. The Court then concluded that since at the time of the framing of Article III, suits against the United States were barred by the doctrine of sovereign immunity, the framers could not have contemplated that the reference in Article III to suits involving the United States would include suits *against* the United States.

An easy answer to the Court's argument is that the provision in Article III could just as well have implied that *if and when* the United States waived sovereign immunity by consenting to suit, Article III would extend to such cases. Furthermore, whether or not suits against the United States could properly be classified as "controversies to which the United States is a party," there can be little question that suits brought pursuant to the Tucker Act or the Federal Tort Claims Act, which constitute the cases heard by the Court of Claims, "arise under" the laws of the United States, a central category of Article III jurisdiction.

After the *Bakelite* and *Williams* decisions, Congress enacted resolutions declaring that both courts were to be deemed "established under article III of the Constitution of the United States." It was not until the Supreme Court's 1962 decision in Glidden Co. v. Zdanok, [370 U.S. 530 (1962)], however, that the status of the Court of Claims and the Court of Customs and Patent Appeals as Article III courts was firmly established.*

In *Glidden,* the Supreme Court considered whether judges of these courts could properly sit by designation on Article III courts. The Court decided that since both courts were created pursuant to Article III, no constitutional violation resulted from the assignment of their judges to other Article III courts.

Justice Harlan delivered the plurality opinion, in which Justices Brennan and Stewart concurred. Justice Clark concurred separately in an opinion in which Chief Justice Warren joined. Justices Douglas and Black dissented. Justice Harlan emphasized that "we may not disregard Congress' declaration that [these courts] were created under Article III." He noted that "[a]t the time when *Bakelite* and *Williams* were decided, the Court did not have the benefit of this congressional understanding." Harlan went well beyond this limited basis for rejecting the *Bakelite* and *Williams* decisions, however. Both decisions, he stated, "have long been considered of questionable soundness." He found that "the crucial *non sequitur* of the *Bakelite* and *Williams* opinions" is that they assumed that because Congress *may* employ Article I tribunals, it *must* have employed them. His statement implicitly recognizes that, at least in certain instances, matters which may be heard by Article III courts may also be adjudicated by Article I bodies. Harlan thus accepted the reasoning—if not the actual holding—of *Bakelite*, that much of the Article III power could be vested in either Article I *or* Article III courts. His opinion is significant because it expressly rejected the assumption of the Court in *Williams* that because an Article I body could adjudicate suits against the United States, such suits could not be simultaneously considered Article III cases.

In two ways, then, *Glidden* did much to remove uncertainty in the law of legislative courts. First, it made clear beyond question that the two courts involved were Article III, rather than Article I courts. Second, on a more theoretical level, the Court once and for all erased any doubt that Article I courts can adjudicate at least some cases falling within Article III, section 2. But the vital issue left unanswered by the *Glidden* Court was the nature and extent of any limit on the authority of Article I courts to hear matters described in Article III, section 2. Thus, while it was clear after *Glidden* that a substantial body of cases existed which

---

* [Ed. Note: In the Federal Courts Improvement Act of 1982, 1982 Pub.L. 97–164, 96 Stat. 25, Congress merged the Court of Claims and the Court of Customs and Patent Appeals into a single Court of Appeals for the Federal Circuit, with expanded appellate jurisdiction for patent, government contract, trademark and international trade cases. The Act also provided for establishment of a new Claims Court to assume the prior Court of Claims trial jurisdiction.]

could be heard by either Article III courts or Article I courts, it was uncertain whether there existed *any* cases which could be heard by Article III courts but not by Article I courts. As noted previously, the answer to this question could have a dramatic effect on the independence of the federal judiciary. For if there were no limit on the overlap between the jurisdiction of Article I and Article III courts, Congress could easily circumvent the independence guarantees of Article III, simply by vesting all authority to adjudicate cases falling within the "judicial power" in Article I courts.

In *Bakelite,* it will be recalled, the Court implied that an Article I court could not hear cases which are "inherently judicial." This provides a basis for believing that there do exist cases which must be heard by Article III courts, at least if they are to be heard by the federal judiciary at all: those which can be classified as "inherently judicial." But the Court did not attempt to define this phrase, and the words are certainly not self-explanatory. The Court in *Glidden* compounded the confusion by explicitly leaving open the question of whether matters deemed "inherently judicial" could not be given to Article I courts. Thus, it remains uncertain both how we are to determine whether a case is to be considered "inherently judicial," and whether anything is to turn on that determination.

The uncertainty surrounding these questions was not diminished in the Supreme Court's decision in *Palmore v. United States* [411 U.S. 389 (1973)]. The issue was "whether a defendant charged with a felony under the District of Columbia Code may be tried by a judge who does not have protection with respect to tenure and salary under Article III of the Constitution." In the District of Columbia Court Reform and Criminal Procedure Act of 1970, Congress vested all authority to adjudicate local District of Columbia cases in a newly-created Superior Court. Judges of the Superior Court were to serve 15–year terms, and were subject to removal or suspension by a judicial commission. In establishing the Superior Courts, Congress expressly stated that they were Article I courts.

Palmore, who had been convicted in the Superior Court, argued that since his prosecution was a case "arising under the laws of the United States," a category of cases included in the "judicial power" described in Article III, he had the right to be judged by an individual who had the independence guarantees of that Article. Such a broadly phrased argument was doomed to fail, since it effectively reasserted the discredited theory that an Article I court could hear no matter falling within Article III, section 2. Even the narrower argument asserting only that no Article I court could deprive an individual of his personal liberty, however, would have been equally unsuccessful. For in response to Palmore, the Court cited three situations in which Congress had been allowed to invest judges lacking the independence protections of Article III with power to deprive individuals of personal liberty. Two of these * * * [are] the territorial and military courts. It is questionable, however, whether these traditional exceptions to the requirements of Article III support the *Palmore* decision. Rightly or wrongly, it has long been thought that citizens of the territories do not receive the benefit of all constitutional protections; no such conclusion has been reached for citizens of the District of Columbia. Similarly, it is doubtful that the exception from Article III for the military courts—premised on a supposed understanding of the framers' intent and the alleged unique exigencies of military discipline—should be found relevant to courts dealing with civilians living in the District of Columbia. The Court's third category included the state courts. The Court noted that Congress, if it so chooses, may vest power in the state courts to adjudicate federal criminal cases, yet state judges lack the guarantees of independence provided by Article III. Once again, the Court's analogy is dubious. While it is true that Congress may circumvent the lower federal judiciary by vesting federal judicial power in the state courts, and that state judges may lack the protections of salary and tenure afforded Article III judges, Congress lacks power to control either the salary or tenure of state judges. Although state judges may not be independent of their own legislature, they are independent of Congress and the President. It is, then, one thing to say that state courts may adjudicate federal criminal cases; it is quite another to hold that individuals directly subject to the control of the federal government may do so.

Perhaps the strongest argument in support of the *Palmore* decision—and the most limiting—is that in establishing courts to handle the local affairs of the District of Columbia, Congress acts in a manner analogous to a state legislature. The argument is that while Congress may be bound to vest jurisdiction over criminal cases of a traditional federal nature in Article III courts (or in state courts equally independent of the federal government), when acting in the capacity of a state legislature Congress is no more bound to adhere to the independence requirements of Article III than is a state legislature. The Court in *Palmore* relied, at least in part, on this rationale, and subsequent statements of both the Supreme Court and lower federal courts have underscored the importance of the state court analogy as a basis for the non-Article III status of District of Columbia judges. As noted previously, such an argument might be employed to justify the exception of territorial courts from the requirements of Article III, and to this extent, the Court's reliance on the territorial court precedents may be valid. Once again, however, it is necessary to point out the fallacy of this argument: while Article III does not limit state legislatures, it does limit Congress in all of its actions.

While congressional regulation of the District of Columbia judiciary has always been viewed as *sui generis,* certain language in the Court's opinion arguably extends its holding well beyond this limited factual situation. As partial justification for its conclusion that Congress may vest criminal jurisdiction in the District of Columbia Superior Courts, the Court stated:

From its own studies, Congress had concluded that there was a crisis in the judicial system of the District of Columbia, that case loads had become unmanageable, and that neither those matters of national concern nor those of strictly local cognizance were being promptly tried and disposed of by the existing court system.

The Court also noted that:

> Congress made a deliberate choice to create judgeships with terms of 15 years * * * and to subject judges in those positions to removal or suspension by a judicial commission under certain established circumstances. * * * It was thought that such a system would be more workable and efficient in administering and discharging the work of a multifaceted metropolitan court system.

Such reasoning would seem to justify Congress' circumvention of the requirements of Article III any time it is determined that such requirements would be unduly burdensome. It is true that such an argument could be—and has been—used to justify the Article I status of both territorial and military courts. But acceptance of inconvenience as a general rationale for the use of legislative courts to adjudicate fundamental constitutional rights could extend this practice well beyond the narrowly defined instances where it has been accepted to date, perhaps threatening the continued vitality of the Article III protections.

Notes

1. Why shouldn't Article III be given an absolute construction—i.e. construed to mean that no "judicial" power, as described in Article III, section 2, can be exercised by any governmental body other than an Article III court? Can it linguistically receive any *other* construction? Compare Redish, *Legislative Courts, Administrative Agencies and the* Northern Pipeline *Decision,* 1983 Duke L.J. 197, with Fallon, *Of Legislative Courts, Administrative Agencies, and Article III,* 101 Harv.L.Rev. 915 (1988). Professor Fallon suggests that "article III literalism [is] untenable" for three reasons: uncertain historical foundations, policy concerns, and "entrenched practice". However, he adds: "Insofar as article III literalism is unacceptable because of its incompatibility with entrenched practice and precedent, the very doctrines and institutions that demonstrate the theory's unworkability may pose threats to article III values. Those threats, although insufficient to establish the desirability of article III literalism, not only contribute to its allure, but also help to define the challenge that a better doctrine must meet." He adds, "although article III literalism is not sustainable, it is easy to understand the anxieties of those who resist relinquishing it." Can one logically both reject and rely upon the "literal" model of Article III? If Professor Fallon is correct in his perception of threats to Article III values from current practice, does it make sense to rely upon "entrenched practice" as a basis for rejecting a particular constitutional construction? How might such logic have worked in the case of "separate-but-equal" in 1954? See also Case, *Article I Courts, Substantive Rights, and Remedies for Government Misconduct,* 26 N.Ill.L.Rev. 101, 105 (2005): "A literal interpretation of Article III, demanding that all judicial decisions be made by judges with life tenure, has been soundly rejected by the Supreme Court's decision following Crowell [v. Benson]."

Professor Fallon ultimately suggests that "the best approach to the question of the permissible role of non-article III federal tribunals lies in an appellate review theory. The core claim of this theory is that sufficiently searching review of a legislative court's or administrative agency's decisions by a constitutional court will always satisfy the requirements of article III." For a similar view, see Redish, supra, 1983 Duke L.J. at 226–29. Do you agree? For an expression of doubt over the proposition "that [the] absolutist conception of article III is constitutionally required," see Saphire & Solomine, *Shoring up Article III: Legislative Court Doctrine in the Post*–FTC v. Schor *Era,* 68 B.U.L.Rev. 85, 152 (1988).

Professor Pfander has focused upon the congressional power to establish "tribunals" inferior to the Supreme Court, granted in Art. I, § 8, cl. 9. Distinguishing between "courts" referred to in Article III and "tribunals" mentioned in Article I, Pfander suggests that Article III can "be read to vest the judicial power in inferior federal 'courts' but not in some inferior 'tribunals' created under Article I. This interpretation suggests that Congress enjoys a degree of flexibility in creating Article I tribunals. On such a reading, the Inferior Tribunals Clause may empower Congress to create inferior 'tribunals' with judges who lack Article III protections. While these tribunals must remain inferior to the Supreme Court and the judicial department, Article I does not require that they employ life-tenured judges and Article III does not formally invest these tribunals with the judicial power of the United States." Pfander, *Article I Tribunals, Article III Courts, and the Judicial Power of the United States*, 118 Harv.L.Rev. 643, 650–51 (2004).

2. **Military Court Jurisdiction.** In Dynes v. Hoover, 61 U.S. (20 How.) 65, 79 (1857), the Supreme Court stated in dictum: "Congress has the power to provide for the trial and punishment of military and naval offenses in the manner then and now practiced by civilized nations * * *. [T]he power to do so is given without any connection between it and the 3d article of the Constitution * * *." See also United States ex rel. Toth v. Quarles, 350 U.S. 11, 17 (1955). Thus, it has long been established that military courts, even though they have broad power to impose criminal penalties, are not staffed by judges who have the independence protections of Article III. Can you think of a reason why such a lack of independence may be *especially* troubling in the military context?

What do you think of the following possible rationales for exempting military courts from the protections of Article III:

a. "There is a problem * * * of reconciling the constitutional policy favoring independent judges with other policies relating to expediency, as in * * * military cases in the field of battle, where it just is not convenient to call in the federal judge from Washington to hear a small disciplinary matter." D. Currie, Federal Jurisdiction in a Nutshell 40 (1976).

How compelling is an argument that disposes of constitutional guarantees on grounds of "expediency" or "convenience"? In any event, how valid is the "convenience" argument in the military context? What about the many times military courts operate in non-battle settings? Even during wartime, is the only alternative to non-independent military judges, as Professor Currie says, "the federal judge from Washington"?

    b.   Article I, section 8 of the Constitution gives Congress plenary power "[to] make Rules for the Government and Regulation of the land and naval Forces." Therefore Congress may exercise that power freely, without limitation by Article III.

    c.   In the Fifth Amendment the framers explicitly exempted from the requirement of a grand jury indictment those cases "arising in the land or naval forces, or in the Militia, when in actual service in time of War or public danger." This shows that the framers recognized the unique requirements of military justice. Therefore it is doubtful that the framers would have intended the limitations of Article III to apply to the military.

Because of the independence issue surrounding military courts, the Supreme Court has strictly confined the scope of military jurisdiction, generally excluding civilians from its reach. See, e.g., United States ex rel. Toth v. Quarles, supra. For an argument in favor of expanding military court jurisdiction over civilians, see Gibson, *Lack of Extraterritorial Jurisdiction Over Civilians: A New Look at an Old Problem*, 148 Mil.L.Rev. 114 (1995). On the general subject of the scope of military court jurisdiction, see Baldrate, *The Supreme Court's Role in Defining the Jurisdiction of Military Tribunals: A Study, Critique, & Proposal for* Hamdan v. Rumsfeld, 186 Mil.L.Rev. 1 (2005); Burris, *Time for Congressional Action: The Necessity of Delineating the Jurisdictional Responsibilities of Federal District Courts, Courts–Martial and Military Commissions to Try Violations of the Laws of War*, 2005 Fed.Cts.L.Rev. 4.

    3.   On the history of territorial courts, see Burnett, *Untied States: American Expansion and Territorial Deannexation*, 72 U.Chi.L.Rev. 797 (2005). There it is argued that Article III's exclusion from the territories has not altered the widespread assumption that otherwise the Constitution applies "in full" in the incorporated territories. Id at 824.

NORTHERN PIPELINE CONSTRUCTION CO. v. MARATHON PIPE LINE COMPANY

Supreme Court of the United States, 1982.
458 U.S. 50.

Justice Brennan announced the judgment of the Court and delivered an opinion in which Justice Marshall, Justice Blackmun, and Justice Stevens joined.

The question presented is whether the assignment by Congress to bankruptcy judges of the jurisdiction granted in § 241(a) of the Bankruptcy Act of 1978, 28 U.S.C. § 1471 (1976 ed., Supp. IV), violates Art. III of the Constitution.

I

A

In 1978, after almost ten years of study and investigation, Congress enacted a comprehensive revision of the bankruptcy laws. The Bankruptcy Act of 1978 (Act) made significant changes in both the substantive and procedural law of bankruptcy. It is the changes in the latter that are at issue in this case.

Before the Act, federal district courts served as bankruptcy courts and employed a "referee" system. Bankruptcy proceedings were generally conducted before referees, except in those instances in which the district court elected to withdraw a case from a referee. The referee's final order was appealable to the district court. The bankruptcy courts were vested with "summary jurisdiction"—that is, with jurisdiction over controversies involving property in the actual or constructive possession of the court. And, with consent, the bankruptcy court also had jurisdiction over some "plenary" matters—such as disputes involving property in the possession of a third person.

The Act eliminates the referee system and establishes "in each judicial district, as an adjunct to the district court for such district, a bankruptcy court which shall be a court of record known as the United States Bankruptcy Court for the district." 28 U.S.C. § 151(a) (1976 ed., Supp. IV). The judges of these courts are appointed to office for 14–year terms by the President, with the advice and consent of the Senate. §§ 152, 153(a). They are subject to removal by the "judicial council of the circuit" on account of "incompetence, misconduct, neglect of duty or physical or mental disability." § 153(b). In addition, the salaries of the bankruptcy judges are set by statute and are subject to adjustment under the Federal Salary Act, 2 U.S.C. §§ 351–361. 28 U.S.C. § 154 (1976 ed., Supp. IV).

The jurisdiction of the bankruptcy courts created by the Act is much broader than that exercised under the former referee system. This jurisdictional grant empowers bankruptcy courts to entertain a wide variety of cases involving claims that may affect the property of the estate once a petition has been filed under title 11 of the Act. Included within the bankruptcy courts' jurisdiction are suits to recover accounts, controversies involving exempt property, actions to avoid transfers and payments as preferences or fraudulent conveyances, and causes of action owned by the debtor at the time of the petition for bankruptcy. The bankruptcy courts can hear claims based on state law as well as those based on federal law.

The judges of the bankruptcy courts are vested with all of the "powers of a court of equity, law and admiralty," except that they "may not enjoin another court or punish a criminal contempt not committed in the presence of the judge of the court or warranting a punishment of imprisonment." 28 U.S.C. § 1481 (1976 ed., Supp. IV). In addition to this broad grant of power, Congress has allowed bankruptcy judges the power to hold jury trials, § 1480; to issue declaratory judgments, § 2201; to issue writs of habeas corpus under certain circumstances, § 2256; to issue all writs necessary in aid of the bankruptcy court's expanded jurisdiction, § 451; see 28 U.S.C. § 1651 (1976 ed.); and to issue any order, process or judgment that is necessary or appropriate to carry out the provisions of title 11, 11 U.S.C. § 105(a) (1976 ed., Supp. IV).

The Act also establishes a special procedure for appeals from orders of bankruptcy courts. The circuit council is empowered to direct the Chief Judge of the circuit to designate panels of three bankruptcy judges to hear appeals. 28 U.S.C. § 160 (1976 ed., Supp. IV). These panels have jurisdiction of all appeals from final judgments, orders, and decrees of bankruptcy courts, and, with leave of the panel, of interlocutory appeals. § 1482. If no such appeals panel is designated the district court is empowered to exercise appellate jurisdiction. § 1334. The court of appeals is given jurisdiction over appeals from the appellate panels or from the district court. § 1293. If the parties agree, a direct appeal to the court of appeals may be taken from a final judgment of a bankruptcy court. § 1293(b).

* * *

B

This case arises out of proceedings initiated in the United States Bankruptcy Court for the District of Minnesota after appellant Northern Pipeline Construction Co. (Northern) filed a petition for reorganization in January 1980. In March 1980 Northern, pursuant to the Act, filed in that court a suit against appellee Marathon Pipeline Co. (Marathon). Appellant sought damages for alleged breaches of contract and warranty, as well as for alleged misrepresentation, coercion, and duress. Marathon sought dismissal of the suit, on the ground that the Act unconstitutionally conferred Art. III judicial power upon judges who lacked life tenure and protection against salary diminution. The United States intervened to defend the validity of the statute.

The bankruptcy judge denied the motion to dismiss. * * * But on appeal the District Court entered an order granting the motion, on the ground that "the delegation of authority in 28 U.S.C. § 1471 to the Bankruptcy Judges to try cases otherwise relegated under the Constitution to Article III judges" was unconstitutional. Both the United States and Northern filed notices of appeal in this Court. * * *

II

A

Basic to the constitutional structure established by the Framers was their recognition that "The accumulation of all powers, legislative, executive, and judiciary, in the same hands, whether of one, a few, or many, and whether hereditary, self-appointed, or elective, may justly be pronounced the very definition of tyranny." The Federalist No. 47 (J. Madison), p. 300 (H. Lodge ed. 1888). To ensure against such tyranny, the Framers provided that the Federal Government would consist of three distinct Branches each to exercise one of the governmental powers recognized by the Framers as inherently distinct. "The Framers regarded the checks and balances that they had built into the tripartite Federal

Government as a self-executing safeguard against the encroachment or aggrandizement of one branch at the expense of the other." Buckley v. Valeo, 424 U.S. 1, 122 (1976) (*per curiam*).

The Federal Judiciary was therefore designed by the Framers to stand independent of the Executive and Legislature—to maintain the checks and balances of the constitutional structure, and also to guarantee that the process of adjudication itself remained impartial. Hamilton explained the importance of an independent Judiciary:

> "Periodical appointments, however regulated, or by whomsoever made, would, in some way or other, be fatal to [the courts'] necessary independence. If the power of making them was committed either to the Executive or legislature, there would be danger of an improper complaisance to the branch which possessed it; if to both, there would be an unwillingness to hazard the displeasure of either; if to the people, or to persons chosen by them for the special purpose, there would be too great a disposition to consult popularity, to justify a reliance that nothing would be consulted but the Constitution and the laws." The Federalist No. 78, p. 489 (H. Lodge ed. 1888).

The Court has only recently reaffirmed the significance of this feature of the Framers' design: "A Judiciary free from control by the Executive and Legislature is essential if there is a right to have claims decided by judges who are free from potential domination by other branches of government." United States v. Will, 449 U.S. 200, 217–218 (1980).

As an inseparable element of the constitutional system of checks and balances, and as a guarantee of judicial impartiality, Art. III both defines the power and protects the independence of the Judicial Branch. It provides that "The Judicial Power of the United States, shall be vested in one supreme Court, and in such inferior Courts as the Congress may from time to time ordain and establish." Art. III, § 1. The inexorable command of this provision is clear and definite: The judicial power of the United States must be exercised by courts having the attributes prescribed in Art. III. Those attributes are also clearly set forth:

> "The Judges, both of the supreme and inferior Courts, shall hold their Offices during good Behaviour, and shall, at stated Times, receive for their Services, a Compensation, which shall not be diminished during their Continuance in Office." Art. III, § 1.

The "good Behaviour" Clause guarantees that Art. III judges shall enjoy life tenure, subject only to removal by impeachment. Toth v. Quarles, 350 U.S. 11, 16 (1955). The Compensation Clause guarantees Art. III judges a fixed and irreducible compensation for their services. United States v. Will, supra, 449 U.S., at 218–221. Both of these provisions were incorporated into the Constitution to ensure the independence of the judiciary from the control of the executive and legislative branches of government.[10] As we have only recently emphasized,

---

10. These provisions serve other institutional values as well. The independence from political forces that they guarantee helps to promote public confidence in judi-

"The Compensation Clause has its roots in the longstanding Anglo–American tradition of an independent Judiciary," id., at 217, while the principle of life tenure can be traced back at least as far as the Act of Settlement in 1701, id., at 218. To be sure, both principles were eroded during the late colonial period, but that departure did not escape notice and indignant rejection by the Revolutionary generation. Indeed, the guarantees eventually included in Art. III were clearly foreshadowed in the Declaration of Independence, "which, among the injuries and usurpations recited against the King of Great Britain, declared that he had 'made judges dependent on his will alone, for the tenure of their offices, and the amount and payment of their salaries.' " O'Donoghue v. United States, 289 U.S. 516, 531 (1933). The Framers thus recognized that

> "Next to permanency in office, nothing can contribute more to the independence of the judges than a fixed provision for their support.... In the general course of human nature, *a power over a man's subsistence amounts to a power over his will*." The Federalist No. 79 (A. Hamilton), p. 491 (H. Lodge ed. 1888) (emphasis in original).[11]

In sum, our Constitution unambiguously enunciates a fundamental principle—that the "judicial Power of the United States" must be reposed in an independent Judiciary. It commands that the independence of the Judiciary be jealously guarded, and it provides clear institutional protections for that independence.

B

It is undisputed that the bankruptcy judges whose offices were created by the Bankruptcy Act of 1978 do not enjoy the protections constitutionally afforded to Art. III judges. The bankruptcy judges do not serve for life subject to their continued "good Behaviour." Rather, they are appointed for 14–year terms, and can be removed by the judicial council of the circuit in which they serve on grounds of "incompetence, misconduct, neglect of duty or physical or mental disability." Second, the salaries of the bankruptcy judges are not immune from diminution by Congress. * * * In short, there is no doubt that the bankruptcy judges created by the Act are not Art. III judges.

* * *

Appellants suggest two grounds for upholding the Act's conferral of broad adjudicative powers upon judges unprotected by Art. III. First, it is urged that "pursuant to its enumerated Article I powers, Congress may

---

cial determinations. See The Federalist No. 78 (A. Hamilton). The security that they provide to members of the Judicial Branch helps to attract well qualified persons to the federal bench. Ibid. The guarantee of life tenure insulates the individual judge from improper influences not only by other branches but by colleagues as well, and thus promotes judicial individualism. * * *

11. Further evidence of the Framers' concern for assuring the independence of the judicial branch may be found in the fact that the Constitutional Convention soundly defeated a proposal to allow the removal of judges by the executive and legislative branches. * * *

establish legislative courts that have jurisdiction to decide cases to which the Article III judicial power of the United States extends." Referring to our precedents upholding the validity of "legislative courts," appellants suggest that "the plenary grants of power in Article I permit Congress to establish non-Article III tribunals in 'specialized areas having particularized needs and warranting distinctive treatment,'·" such as the area of bankruptcy law. Second, appellants contend that even if the Constitution does require that this bankruptcy-related action be adjudicated in an Art. III court, the Act in fact satisfies that requirement. "Bankruptcy jurisdiction was vested in the district court" of the judicial district in which the bankruptcy court is located, "and the exercise of that jurisdiction by the adjunct bankruptcy court was made subject to appeal as of right to an Art. III court." Analogizing the role of the bankruptcy court to that of a special master, appellants urge us to conclude that this "adjunct" system established by Congress satisfies the requirements of Art. III. We consider these arguments in turn.

III

Congress did not constitute the bankruptcy courts as legislative courts.[13] Appellants contend, however, that the bankruptcy courts could have been so constituted, and that as a result the "adjunct" system in fact chosen by Congress does not impermissibly encroach upon the judicial power. In advancing this argument, appellants rely upon cases in which we have identified certain matters that "congress may or may not bring within the cognizance of [Art. III] courts, as it may deem proper." Murray's Lessee v. Hoboken Land and Improvement Co., 18 How. 272, 284 (1855).[14] But when properly understood, these precedents represent no broad departure from the constitutional command that the judicial power of the United States must be vested in Art. III courts.[15] Rather, they reduce to three narrow situations not subject to that command,

---

13. The Act designates the bankruptcy court in each district as an "adjunct" to the district court. 28 U.S.C. § 151(a) (1976 ed., Supp. IV). Neither House of Congress concluded that the bankruptcy courts should be established as independent legislative courts.

14. At one time, this Court suggested a rigid distinction between those subjects that could be considered only in Art. III courts and those that could be considered only in legislative courts. See Williams v. United States, 289 U.S. 553 (1933). But this suggested dichotomy has not withstood analysis. Our more recent cases clearly recognize that legislative courts may be granted jurisdiction over some cases and controversies to which the Art. III judicial power might also be extended. E.g., Palmore v. United States, 411 U.S. 389 (1973). See Glidden v. Zdanok, 370 U.S. 530, 549–551 (1962) (Opinion of Harlan, J.).

15. Justice White's dissent finds particular significance in the fact that Congress could have assigned all bankruptcy matters to the state courts. But, of course, virtually all matters that might be heard in Art. III courts could also be left by Congress to state courts. This fact is simply irrelevant to the question before us. Congress has no control over state court judges; accordingly the principle of separation of powers is not threatened by leaving the adjudication of federal disputes to such judges. The Framers chose to leave to Congress the precise role to be played by the lower federal courts to the administration of justice. See Hart and Wechsler's The Federal Courts and the Federal System, supra, at 11. But the Framers did not leave it to Congress to define the character of those courts—they were to be independent of the political branches and presided over by judges with guaranteed salary and life tenure.

each recognizing a circumstance in which the grant of power to the Legislative and Executive Branches was historically and constitutionally so exceptional that the congressional assertion of a power to create legislative courts was consistent with, rather than threatening to, the constitutional mandate of separation of powers. These precedents simply acknowledge that the literal command of Art. III, assigning the judicial power of the United States to courts insulated from Legislative or Executive interference, must be interpreted in light of the historical context in which the Constitution was written, and of the structural imperatives of the Constitution as a whole.

Appellants first rely upon a series of cases in which this Court has upheld the creation by Congress of non-Art. III "territorial courts." This exception from the general prescription of Art. III dates from the earliest days of the Republic, when it was perceived that the Framers intended that as to certain geographical areas, in which no State operated as sovereign, Congress was to exercise the general powers of government. For example, in American Ins. Co. v. Canter, 1 Pet. 511 (1828), the Court observed that Art. IV bestowed upon Congress alone a complete power of government over territories not within the States that comprised the United States. The Court then acknowledged Congress' authority to create courts for those territories that were not in conformity with Art. III. Such courts were

> "created in virtue of the general right of sovereignty which exists in the government, or in virtue of that clause which enables Congress to make all needful rules and regulations, respecting the territory belonging to the United States. The jurisdiction with which they are invested ... is conferred by Congress, in the execution of those general powers which that body possesses over the territories of the United States." * * * In legislating for them, Congress exercises the combined powers of the general, and of a state government." 1 Pet., at 546.

The Court followed the same reasoning when it reviewed Congress' creation of non-Art. III courts in the District of Columbia. It noted that there was in the District

> "no division of powers between the general and state governments. Congress has the entire control over the district for every purpose of government; and it is reasonable to suppose, that in organizing a judicial department here, all judicial power necessary for the purposes of government would be vested in the courts of justice." Kendall v. United States, 12 Pet. 524, 619 (1838).[16]

Appellants next advert to a second class of cases—those in which this Court has sustained the exercise by Congress and the Executive of the power to establish and administer courts martial. The situation in

---

16. We recently reaffirmed the principle, expressed in these early cases, that Art. I, § 8, cl. 17, provides that Congress shall have power "[t]o exercise exclusive legislation in all cases whatsoever, over" the District of Columbia. Palmore v. United States, 411 U.S. 389, 397 (1973).

these cases strongly resembles the situation with respect to territorial courts: It too involves a constitutional grant of power that has been historically understood as giving the political branches of Government extraordinary control over the precise subject matter at issue. Art. I, § 8, cls. 13, 14, confer upon Congress the power "to provide and maintain a Navy," and "to make Rules for the Government and Regulation of the land and naval Forces." The Fifth Amendment, which requires a presentment or indictment of a grand jury before a person may be held to answer for a capital or otherwise infamous crime, contains an express exception for "cases arising in the land or naval forces." And Art. II, § 2, cl. 1, provides that "The President shall be Commander in Chief of the Army and Navy of the United States, and of the Militia of the several States, when called into the actual Service of the United States." Noting these constitutional directives, the Court in Dynes v. Hoover, 20 How. 65 (1858), explained:

> "These provisions show that Congress has the power to provide for the trial and punishment of military and naval offences in the manner then and now practiced by civilized nations; and that the power to do so is given without any connection between it and the 3d article of the Constitution defining the judicial power of the United States; indeed, that the two powers are entirely independent of each other." Id., at 79.[17]

Finally, appellants rely on a third group of cases, in which this Court has upheld the constitutionality of legislative courts and administrative agencies created by Congress to adjudicate cases involving "public rights." The "public rights" doctrine was first set forth in Murray's Lessee v. Hoboken Land & Improvement Co., 18 How. 272 (1855):

> "[W]e do not consider congress can either withdraw from judicial cognizance any matter which, from its nature, is the subject of a suit at the common law, or in equity, or admiralty; nor, on the other hand, can it bring under the judicial power a matter which, from its nature, is not a subject for judicial determination. At the same time there are matters, *involving public rights*, which may be presented in such form that the judicial power is capable of acting on them, and which are susceptible of judicial determination, but which congress may or may not bring within the cognizance of the courts of the United States, as it may deem proper." Id., at 284 (emphasis added).

This doctrine may be explained in part by reference to the traditional principle of sovereign immunity, which recognizes that the Government may attach conditions to its consent to be sued. But the public-rights doctrine also draws upon the principle of separation of powers, and an historical understanding that certain prerogatives were reserved

---

17. See also Burns v. Wilson, 346 U.S. 137, 139–140 (1953). But this Court has been alert to ensure that Congress does not exceed the constitutional bounds and bring within the jurisdiction of the military courts matters beyond that jurisdiction, and property within the realm of "judicial power." See, e.g., Reid v. Covert; Toth v. Quarles, 350 U.S. 11 (1955).

to the political branches of government. The doctrine extends only to matters arising "between the Government and persons subject to its authority in connection with the performance of the constitutional functions of the executive or legislative departments," Crowell v. Benson, 285 U.S. 22, 50 (1932), and only to matters that historically could have been determined exclusively by those departments. The understanding of these cases is that the Framers expected that Congress would be free to commit such matters completely to non-judicial executive determination, and that as a result there can be no constitutional objection to Congress' employing the less drastic expedient of committing their determination to a legislative court or an administrative agency. Crowell v. Benson, supra, 285 U.S. at 50.

The public-rights doctrine is grounded in a historically recognized distinction between matters that could be conclusively determined by the Executive and Legislative Branches and matters that are "inherently . . . judicial." Ex parte Bakelite Corp., 279 U.S., at 458. See Murray's Lessee v. Hoboken Land & Improvement Co., supra, at 480–82. For example, the Court in *Murray's Lessee* looked to the law of England and the States at the time the Constitution was adopted, in order to determine whether the issue presented was customarily cognizable in the courts. Concluding that the matter had not traditionally been one for judicial determination, the Court perceived no bar to Congress' establishment of summary procedures, outside of Art. III courts, to collect a debt due to the Government from one of its customs agents.[20] On the same premise, the Court in Ex parte Bakelite Corp., supra, held that the Court of Customs Appeals had been properly constituted by Congress as a legislative court:

> "The *full* province of the court under the act creating it is that of determining matters arising between the Government and others in the executive administration and application of the customs laws. . . . The appeals include nothing which inherently or necessarily requires judicial determination, but only matters the determination of *which may be, and at times has been, committed exclusively to executive officers*." 279 U.S., at 458 (emphasis added).

The distinction between public rights and private rights has not been definitively explained in our precedents. Nor is it necessary to do so in the present case, for it suffices to observe that a matter of public rights must at a minimum arise "between the government and others." Ex Parte Bakelite Corp., supra, at 451.[23] In contrast, "the liability of one

20. Doubtless it could be argued that the need for independent judicial determination is greatest in cases arising between the government and an individual. But the rationale for the public-rights line of cases lies not in political theory, but rather in Congress' and this Court's understanding of what power was reserved to the Judiciary by the Constitution as a matter of historical fact.

23. Congress cannot "withdraw from [Art. III] judicial cognizance *any* matter which, *from its nature*, is the subject of a suit at common law, or in equity or admiralty." Murray's Lessee v. Hoboken Land & Improvement Co., 18 How., at 284 (emphasis added). It is thus clear that the presence of the United States as a proper party to the proceeding is a necessary but not sufficient means of distinguishing "private

individual to another under the law as defined," Crowell v. Benson, 285 U.S., at 51, is a matter of private rights. Our precedents clearly establish that *only* controversies in the former category may be removed from Art. III courts and delegated to legislative courts or administrative agencies for their determination. See Atlas Roofing Co. v. Occupational Safety Comm'n, 430 U.S., at 450, n. 7; Crowell v. Benson, supra, at 50–51. See also Katz, Federal Legislative Courts, 43 Harv.L.Rev. 894, 917–918 (1930).[24] Private-rights disputes, on the other hand, lie at the core of the historically recognized judicial power.

In sum, this Court has identified three situations in which Art. III does not bar the creation of legislative courts. In each of these situations, the Court has recognized certain exceptional powers bestowed upon Congress by the Constitution or by historical consensus. Only in the face of such an exceptional grant of power has the Court declined to hold the authority of Congress subject to the general prescriptions of Art. III.[25]

We discern no such exceptional grant of power applicable in the case before us. The courts created by the Bankruptcy Act of 1978 do not lie exclusively outside the States of the Federal Union, like those in the District of Columbia and the territories. Nor do the bankruptcy courts bear any resemblance to courts martial, which are founded upon the Constitution's grant of plenary authority over the Nation's military forces to the Legislative and Executive Branches. Finally, the substantive legal rights at issue in the present action cannot be deemed "public

rights" from "public rights." And it is also clear that even with respect to matters that arguably fall within the scope of the "public rights" doctrine, the presumption is in favor of Art. III courts. See Glidden v. Zdanok, 370 U.S. 530, 548–549, and n. 21 (1962) (opinion of Harlan, J.). Moreover, when Congress assigns these matters to administrative agencies, or to legislative courts, it has generally provided, and we have suggested that it may be required to provide, for Art. III judicial review. See Atlas Roofing Co. v. Occupational Safety Comm'n, 430 U.S. 442, 455, n. 13 (1977).

24. Of course, the public-rights doctrine does not extend to any criminal matters, although the government is a proper party. See, e.g., Toth v. Quarles, 350 U.S. 11 (1955).

25. The "unifying principle" that Justice White's dissent finds lacking in all of these cases * * * is to be found in the exceptional constitutional grants of power to Congress with respect to certain matters. Although the dissent is correct that these grants are not explicit in the language of the Constitution, they are nonetheless firmly established in our historical understanding of the constitutional structure. When these three exceptional grants are properly constrained, they do not threaten the Framers' vision of an independent federal judi-

ciary. What clearly remains subject to Art. III are all private adjudications in federal courts within the States—matters from their nature subject to "a suit at common law or in equity or admiralty"—and all criminal matters, with the narrow exception of military crimes. There is no doubt that when the Framers assigned the "judicial Power" to an independent Art. III branch, these matters lay at what they perceived to be the protected core of that power.

Although the dissent recognizes that the Framers had something important in mind when they assigned the judicial power of the United States to Art. III courts, it concludes that our cases and subsequent practice have eroded this conception. Unable to find a satisfactory theme in our precedents for analyzing this case, the dissent rejects all of them, as well as the historical understanding upon which they were based, in favor of an ad hoc balancing approach in which Congress can essentially determine for itself whether Art. III courts are required. * * *. But even the dissent recognizes that the notion that Congress rather than the Constitution should determine whether there is a need for independent federal courts cannot be what the Framers had in mind. * * *

rights." Appellants argue that a discharge in bankruptcy is indeed a "public right," similar to such congressionally created benefits as "radio station licenses, pilot licenses, and certificates for common carriers" granted by administrative agencies. * * * But the restructuring of debtor-creditor relations, which is at the core of the federal bankruptcy power, must be distinguished from the adjudication of state-created private rights, such as the right to recover contract damages that is at issue in this case. The former may well be a "public right," but the latter obviously is not. Appellant Northern's right to recover contract damages to augment its estate is "one of private right, that is, of the liability of one individual to another under the law as defined." Crowell v. Benson, 285 U.S., at 51.

Recognizing that the present case may not fall within the scope of any of any of our prior cases permitting the establishment of legislative courts, appellants argue that we should recognize an additional situation beyond the command of Art. III, sufficiently broad to sustain the Act. Appellants contend that Congress' constitutional authority to establish "uniform Laws on the subject of Bankruptcies throughout the United States," Art. I, § 8, cl. 4, carries with it an inherent power to establish legislative courts capable of adjudicating "bankruptcy related controversies." * * * In support of this argument, appellants rely primarily upon a quotation from the opinion in Palmore v. United States, 411 U.S. 389 (1973), in which we stated that

> "both Congress and this Court have recognized that ... the requirements of Art. III, which are applicable where laws of national applicability and affairs of national concern are at stake, must in proper circumstances give way to accommodate plenary grants of power to Congress to legislate with respect to specialized areas having particularized needs and warranting distinctive treatment." Id., 407–408.

Appellants cite this language to support their proposition that a bankruptcy court created by Congress under its Art. I powers is constitutional, because the law of bankruptcy is a "specialized area," and Congress has found a "particularized need" that warrants "distinctive treatment."

Appellants' contention, in essence, is that pursuant to any of its Art. I powers, Congress may create courts free of Art. III's requirements whenever it finds that course expedient. * * *

The flaw in appellants' analysis is that it provides no limiting principle. It thus threatens to supplant completely our system of adjudication in independent Art. III tribunals and replace it with a system of "specialized" legislative courts. True, appellants argue that under their analysis Congress could create legislative courts pursuant only to some "specific" Art. I power, and "only when there is a particularized need for distinctive treatment." They therefore assert, that their analysis would not permit Congress to replace the independent Art. III judiciary through a "wholesale assignment of federal judicial business to legislative courts." But these "limitations" are wholly illusory. For example, Art. I, § 8, empowers Congress to enact laws, *inter alia*, regulating interstate commerce and punishing certain crimes. Art. I, § 8, cls. 3, 6. On appellants' reasoning Congress could provide for the adjudication of these and "related" matters by judges and courts within Congress' exclusive control. The potential for encroachment upon powers reserved to the Judicial Branch through the device of "specialized" legislative courts is dramatically evidenced in the jurisdiction granted to the courts created by the Act before us. The broad range of questions that can be brought into a bankruptcy court because they are "related to cases under title 11," 28 U.S.C. § 1471(b), see supra, at 3, is the clearest proof that even when Congress acts through a "specialized" court, and pursuant to only one of its many Art. I powers, appellants' analysis fails to provide any real protection against the erosion of Art. III jurisdiction by the unilateral action of the political branches. In short, to accept appellants' reasoning, would require that we replace the principles delineated in our precedents, rooted in history and the Constitution, with a rule of broad legislative discretion that could effectively eviscerate the constitutional guarantee of an independent Judicial Branch of the Federal Government.[28]

Appellants' reliance upon *Palmore* for such broad legislative discretion is misplaced. In the context of the issue decided in that case, the language quoted from the *Palmore* opinion offers no substantial support for appellants' argument. *Palmore* was concerned with the courts of the District of Columbia, a unique federal enclave over which "Congress has ... entire control ... for every purpose of government." Kendall v. United States, 12 Pet. 524, 619 (1838). The "plenary authority" under the District of Columbia clause, Art. I, § 8 cl. 17, was the subject of the quoted passage and the powers granted under that clause are obviously different in kind from the other broad powers conferred on Congress: Congress' power over the District of Columbia encompasses the *full* authority of government, and thus, necessarily, the executive and judi-

---

28. Justice White's suggested "limitations" on Congress' power to create Art. I courts are even more transparent. Justice White's dissent suggest that Art. III "should be read as expressing one value that must be balanced against competing constitutional concerns and legislative responsibilities," and that the Court retains the final word on how the balance is to be struck. The dissent would find the Art. III "value" accommodated where appellate review to Art. III courts is provided and where the Art. I courts are "designed to deal with issues likely to be of little interest to the political branches." But the dissent's view that appellate review is sufficient to satisfy either the command or the purpose of Art. III is incorrect. And the suggestion that we should consider whether the Art. I courts are designed to deal with issues like-

ly to be of interest to the political branches would undermine the validity of the adjudications performed by most of the administrative agencies, on which validity the dissent so heavily relies.

In applying its ad hoc balancing approach to the facts of this case, the dissent rests on the justification that these courts differ from standard Art. III courts because of their "extreme specialization." As noted above, "extreme specialization" is hardly an accurate description of bankruptcy courts designed to adjudicate the entire range of federal and state controversies. Moreover, the special nature of bankruptcy adjudications is in no sense incompatible with performance of such functions in a tribunal afforded the protection of Art. III. * * *

cial powers as well as the legislative. This is a power that is clearly possessed by Congress only in limited geographic areas. *Palmore* itself makes this limitation clear. The quoted passage distinguishes the congressional powers at issue in *Palmore* from those in which the Art. III command of an independent Judiciary must be honored: where "laws of national applicability and affairs of national concern are at stake." 411 U.S., at 408. Laws respecting bankruptcy, like most laws enacted pursuant to the national powers catalogued in Art. I, § 8, are clearly laws of national applicability and affairs of national concern. Thus our reference in *Palmore* to "specialized areas having particularized needs" referred only to *geographic* areas, such as the District of Columbia or territories outside the States of the Federal Union. In light of the clear commands of Art. III, nothing held or said in *Palmore* can be taken to mean that in every area in which Congress may legislate, it may also create non-Art. III courts with Art. III powers.

In sum, Art. III bars Congress from establishing legislative courts to exercise jurisdiction over all matters related to those arising under the bankruptcy laws. The establishment of such courts does not fall within any of the historically recognized situations in which the general principle of independent adjudication commanded by Art. III does not apply. Nor can we discern any persuasive reason, in logic, history, or the Constitution, why the bankruptcy courts here established lie beyond the reach of Art. III.

IV

Appellants advance a second argument for upholding the constitutionality of the Act: that "viewed within the entire judicial framework set up by Congress," the bankruptcy court is merely an "adjunct" to the district court, and that the delegation of certain adjudicative functions to the bankruptcy court is accordingly consistent with the principle that the judicial power of the United States must be vested in Art. III courts. The question to which we turn, therefore, is whether the Act has retained "the essential attributes of the judicial power," Crowell v. Benson, supra, 285 U.S., at 51, in Art. III tribunals.[29]

The essential premise underlying appellants' argument is that even where the Constitution denies Congress the power to establish legislative courts, Congress possesses the authority to assign certain factfinding functions to adjunct tribunals. It is, of course, true that while the the power to adjudicate "private rights" must be vested in an Art. III court, see Part III, supra,

---

29. Justice White's dissent fails to distinguish between Congress' power to create adjuncts to Art. III courts, and Congress' power to create Art. I courts in limited circumstances. Congress' power to create adjuncts and assign them limited adjudicatory functions is in no sense an "exception" to Art. III. Rather, such an assignment is consistent with Art. III, so long as "the essential attributes of judicial power" are retained in the Art. III court. Crowell v. Benson, 285 U.S., at 51, and so long as Congress' adjustment of the traditional manner of adjudication can be sufficiently linked to its legislative power to define substantive rights * * *.

"this Court has accepted factfinding by an administrative agency, ... as an adjunct to the Art. III court, analogizing the agency to a jury or a special master and permitting it in admiralty cases to perform the function of a special master. Crowell v. Benson, 285 U.S. 22, 51–65 (1932)." Atlas Roofing Co. v. Occupational Safety Comm'n, 430 U.S. 442, 450, n. 7, (1977).

The use of administrative agencies as adjuncts was first upheld in Crowell v. Benson, supra. * * *

Crowell involved the adjudication of congressionally created rights. But this Court has sustained the use of adjunct fact-finders even in the adjudication of constitutional rights—so long as those adjuncts were subject to sufficient control by an Art. III district court. In United States v. Raddatz, supra, the Court upheld the 1978 Federal Magistrates Act, which permitted district court judges to refer certain pretrial motions, including suppression motions based on alleged violations of constitutional rights, to a magistrate for initial determination. The Court observed that the magistrate's proposed findings and recommendations were subject to *de novo* review by the district court, which was free to rehear the evidence or to call for additional evidence. Moreover, it was noted that the magistrate considered motions only upon reference from the district court, and that the magistrates were appointed, and subject to removal, by the district court. Id., at 685 (Blackmun, J., concurring). In short, the ultimate decision making authority respecting all pretrial motions clearly remained with the district court. Id., at 682. Under these circumstances, the Court held that the Act did not violate the constraints of Art. III.

Together these cases establish two principles that aid us in determining the extent to which Congress may constitutionally vest traditionally judicial functions in non-Art. III officers. First, it is clear that when Congress creates a substantive federal right, it possesses substantial discretion to prescribe the manner in which that right may be adjudicated—including the assignment to an adjunct of some functions historically performed by judges.[32] Thus *Crowell* recognized that Art. III does not require "all determinations of fact [to] be made by judges," with respect to congressionally created rights, some factual determinations may be made by a specialized factfinding tribunal designed by Congress, without constitutional bar. Second, the functions of the adjunct must be limited in such a way that "the essential attributes" of judicial power are retained in the Art. III court. Thus in upholding the adjunct scheme challenged in *Crowell*, the Court emphasized that "the reservation of full authority to the court to deal with matters of law provides for the appropriate exercise of the judicial function in this class of cases." Ibid.

32. Contrary to Justice White's suggestion, we do not concede that "Congress may provide for initial adjudications by Article I courts or administrative judges of all rights and duties arising under otherwise valid federal laws." Rather we simply reaffirm the holding of *Crowell*—that Congress may assign to non-Art. III bodies some adjudicatory functions. *Crowell* itself spoke of "specialized" functions. This case does not require us to specify further any limitations that may exist with respect to Congress' power to create adjuncts to assist in the adjudication of federal statutory rights.

And in refusing to invalidate the Magistrates Act at issue in *Raddatz*, the Court stressed that under the congressional scheme " '[t]he authority—and the responsibility—to make an informed, final determination ... remains with the judge,' " 447 U.S., at 682, quoting Mathews v. Weber, 423 U.S. 261, 271 (1976); the statute's delegation of power was therefore permissible, since "the ultimate decision is made by the district court," 447 U.S., at 683.

These two principles assist us in evaluating the "adjunct" scheme presented in this case. Appellants assume that Congress' power to create "adjuncts" to consider all cases related to those arising under title 11 is as great as it was in the circumstances of *Crowell*. But while *Crowell* certainly endorsed the proposition that Congress possesses broad discretion to assign factfinding functions to an adjunct created to aid in the adjudication of congressionally created statutory rights, *Crowell* does not support the further proposition necessary to appellants' argument—that Congress possesses the same degree of discretion in assigning traditionally judicial power to adjuncts engaged in the adjudication of rights *not* created by Congress. Indeed, the validity of this proposition was expressly denied in *Crowell* * * *.

* * * [A] distinction [between rights created by Congress and other rights] seems to us to be necessary in light of the delicate accommodations required by the principle of separation of powers reflected in Art. III. The constitutional system of checks and balances is designed to guard against "encroachment or aggrandizement" by Congress at the expense of the other branches of Government. But when Congress creates a statutory right, it clearly has the discretion, in defining that right to create presumptions, or assign burdens of proof, or prescribe remedies; it may also provide that persons seeking to vindicate that right must do so before particularized tribunals created to perform the specialized adjudicative tasks related to that right.[35] Such provisions do, in a sense, affect the exercise of judicial power, but they are also incidental to Congress' power to define the right that it has created. No comparable justification exists, however, when the right being adjudicated is not of congressional creation. In such a situation, substantial inroads into functions that have traditionally been performed by the judiciary cannot be characterized merely as incidental extensions of Congress' power to define rights that it has created. Rather, such inroads suggest unwarranted encroachments upon the judicial power of the United States, which our Constitution reserves for Art. III courts.

35. Drawing the line between permissible extensions of legislative power and impermissible incursions into judicial power is a delicate undertaking, for the powers of the Judicial and Legislative Branches are often overlapping. As Justice Frankfurter noted in a similar context, "To be sure, the content of the three authorities of government is not to be derived from an abstract analysis. The areas are partly interacting, not wholly disjointed." Youngstown Co. v. Sawyer, 343 U.S. 579, 610 (1952) (concurring opinion). The interaction between the Legislative and Judicial Branches is at its height where courts are adjudicating rights wholly of Congress' creation. Thus where Congress creates a substantive right, pursuant to one of its broad powers to make laws, Congress may have something to say about the proper manner of adjudicating that right.

We hold that the Bankruptcy Act of 1978 carries the possibility of such an unwarranted encroachment. Many of the rights subject to adjudication by the Act's bankruptcy courts * * * are not of Congress' creation. Indeed, the case before us, which centers upon appellant Northern's claim for damages for breach of contract and misrepresentation, involves a right created by *state* law, a right independent of and antecedent to the reorganization petition that conferred jurisdiction upon the bankruptcy court. Accordingly, Congress' authority to control the manner in which that right is adjudicated, through assignment of historically judicial functions to a non-Art. III "adjunct," plainly must be deemed at a minimum. Yet it is equally plain that Congress has vested the "adjunct" bankruptcy judges with powers over appellant's state-created right that far exceed the powers that it has vested in administrative agencies that adjudicate only rights of Congress' own creation.

Unlike the administrative scheme that we reviewed in *Crowell*, the Act vests all "essential attributes" of the judicial power of the United States in the "adjunct" bankruptcy court. First, the agency in *Crowell* made only specialized, narrowly confined factual determinations regarding a particularized area of law. In contrast, the subject matter jurisdiction of the bankruptcy courts encompasses not only traditional matters of bankruptcy, but also "all civil proceedings arising under title 11 or arising in or *related to* cases arising under title 11." 28 U.S.C. § 1471(b) (1976 ed., Supp. IV) (emphasis added). Second, while the agency in *Crowell* engaged in statutorily channeled factfinding functions, the bankruptcy courts exercise "*all* of the jurisdiction" conferred by the Act on the district courts, § 1471(b) (emphasis added). Third, the agency in *Crowell* possessed only a limited power to issue compensation orders pursuant to specialized procedures, and its orders could be enforced only by order of the district court. By contrast, the bankruptcy courts exercise all ordinary powers of district courts, including the power to preside over jury trials, the power to issue declaratory judgments, § 2201, the power to issue writs of habeas corpus, § 2256, and the power to issue any order, process or judgment appropriate for the enforcement of the provisions of title 11, 11 U.S.C. § 105(a) (1976 ed., Supp. IV). Fourth, while orders issued by the agency in *Crowell* were to be set aside if "not supported by the evidence," the judgments of the bankruptcy courts are apparently subject to review only under the more deferential "clearly erroneous" standard. Finally, the agency in *Crowell* was required by law to seek enforcement of its compensation orders in the district court. In contrast, the bankruptcy courts issue final judgments, which are binding and enforceable even in the absence of an appeal. In short, the "adjunct" bankruptcy courts created by the Act exercise jurisdiction behind the facade of a grant to the district courts* * *.

We conclude that 28 U.S.C. § 1471 (1976 ed., Supp. IV), as added by § 241(a) of the Bankruptcy Act of 1978, has impermissibly removed most, if not all, of "the essential attributes of the judicial power" from the Art. III district court, and has vested those attributes in a non-Art.

III adjunct. Such a grant of jurisdiction cannot be sustained as an exercise of Congress' power to create adjuncts to Art. III courts.

V

Having concluded that the broad grant of jurisdiction to the bankruptcy courts contained in § 241(a) is unconstitutional, we must now determine whether our holding should be applied retroactively to the effective date of the Act.[40] * * * It is plain that Congress' broad grant of judicial power to non-Art. III bankruptcy judges presents an unprecedented question of interpretation of Art. III. It is equally plain that retroactive application would not further the operation of our holding, and would surely visit substantial injustice and hardship upon those litigants who relied upon the Act's vesting of jurisdiction in the bankruptcy courts. We hold, therefore, that our decision today shall apply only prospectively.

* * *

JUSTICE REHNQUIST, with whom JUSTICE O'CONNOR joins, concurring in the judgment.

Were I to agree with the plurality that the question presented by this case is "whether the assignment by Congress to bankruptcy judges of the jurisdiction granted in * * * § 241(a) of the Bankruptcy Act of 1978 violates Art. III of the Constitution," * * * I would with considerable reluctance embark on the duty of deciding this broad question. But appellee Marathon Pipe Line Co. has not been subjected to the full range of authority granted Bankruptcy Courts by § 241(a). It was named as a defendant in a suit brought by appellant in a United States Bankruptcy Court. The suit sought damages for, *inter alia*, breaches of contract and warranty. Marathon moved to dismiss the action on the grounds that the Bankruptcy Act of 1978, which authorized the suit, violated Art. III of the Constitution insofar as it established Bankruptcy Judges whose tenure and salary protection do not conform to the requirements of Art. III.

---

40. It is clear that, at the least, the new bankruptcy judges cannot constitutionally be vested with jurisdiction to decide this state-law contract claim against Marathon. As part of a comprehensive restructuring of the bankruptcy laws, Congress has vested jurisdiction over this and all matters related to cases under title 11 in a single non-Art. III court, and has done so pursuant to a single statutory grant of jurisdiction. In these circumstances we cannot conclude that if Congress were aware that the grant of jurisdiction could not constitutionally encompass this and similar claims, it would simply remove the jurisdiction of the bankruptcy court over these matters, leaving the jurisdictional provision and adjudicatory structure intact with respect to other types of claims, and thus subject to Art. III constitutional challenge on a claim-by-claim basis. Indeed, we note that one of the express purposes of the Act was to ensure adjudication of all claims in a single forum and to avoid the delay and expense of jurisdictional disputes. See H.R.Rep.No.95–595, supra, p. 43–48; S.Rep. No.95–989, p. 17 (1978). Nor can we assume, as The Chief Justice suggests * * * that Congress' choice would be to have this case "routed to the United States district court of which the bankruptcy court is an adjunct." We think that it is for Congress to determine the proper manner of restructuring the Bankruptcy Act of 1978 to conform to the requirements of Art. III, in the way that will best effectuate the legislative purpose.

With the case in this posture, Marathon has simply been named defendant in a lawsuit about a contract, a lawsuit initiated by appellant Northern after having previously filed a petition for reorganization under the Bankruptcy Act. Marathon may object to proceeding further with this lawsuit on the grounds that if it is to be resolved by an agency of the United States, it may be resolved only by an agency which exercises "the judicial power of the United States" described by Art. III of the Constitution. But resolution of any objections it may make on this ground to the exercise of a different authority conferred on Bankruptcy Courts by the 1978 Act * * * should await the exercise of such authority.

> "This Court, as is the case with all federal courts, 'has no jurisdiction to pronounce any statute, either of a State or of the United States, void, because irreconcilable with the Constitution, except as it is called upon to adjudge the legal rights of litigants in actual controversies. In the exercise of that jurisdiction, it is bound by two rules, to which it has rigidly adhered, one, never to anticipate a question of constitutional law in advance of the necessity of deciding it; the other never to formulate a rule of constitutional law broader than is required by the precise facts to which it is to be applied.' Liverpool, New York & Philadelphia S. S. Co. v. Commissioners of Emigration, 113 U.S. 33, 39." United States v. Raines, 362 U.S. 17, 21 (1960).

Particularly in an area of constitutional law such as that of "Art. III Courts," with its frequently arcane distinctions and confusing precedents, rigorous adherence to the principle that this Court should decide no more of a constitutional question than is absolutely accords with both our decided cases and with sound judicial policy.

From the record before us, the lawsuit in which Marathon was named defendant seeks damages for breach of contract, misrepresentation, and other counts which are the stuff of the traditional actions at common law tried by the courts at Westminster in 1789. There is apparently no federal rule of decision provided for any of the issues in the lawsuit; the claims of Northern arise entirely under state law. * * *

The cases dealing with the authority of Congress to create courts other than by use of its power under Art. III do not admit of easy synthesis. * * * None of the cases has gone so far as to sanction the type of adjudication to which Marathon will be subjected against its will under the provisions of the 1978 Act. To whatever extent different powers granted under that Act might be sustained under the "public rights" doctrine of Murray's Lessee v. Hoboken Land & Improvement Co., 18 How. 272 (1855), and succeeding cases, I am satisfied that the adjudication of Northern's lawsuit cannot be so sustained.

I am likewise of the opinion that the extent of review by Art. III courts provided on appeal from a decision of the bankruptcy court in a case such as Northern's does not save the grant of authority to the latter under the rule espoused in Crowell v. Benson. All matters of fact and law in whatever domains of the law to which the parties' dispute may lead are to be resolved by the bankruptcy court in the first instance, with only traditional appellate review apparently contemplated by Art. III courts. Acting in this manner the bankruptcy court is not an "adjunct" of either the district court or the court of appeals.

I would, therefore, hold so much of the Bankruptcy Act of 1978 as enables a bankruptcy court to entertain and decide Northern's lawsuit over Marathon's objection to be violative of Art. III of the United States Constitution. Because I agree with the plurality that this grant of authority is not readily severable from the remaining grant of authority to bankruptcy courts under § 241(a), I concur in the judgment. * * *

CHIEF JUSTICE BURGER, dissenting.

I join JUSTICE WHITE's dissenting opinion, but I write separately to emphasize that, notwithstanding the plurality opinion, the Court does *not* hold today that Congress' broad grant of jurisdiction to the new bankruptcy courts is generally inconsistent with Art. III of the Constitution. Rather, the Court's holding is limited to the proposition stated by JUSTICE REHNQUIST in his concurrence in the judgment—that a "traditional" state common-law action, not made subject to a federal rule of decision, and related only peripherally to an adjudication of bankruptcy under federal law, must, absent the consent of the litigants, be heard by an "Art. III court" if it is to be heard by any court or agency of the United States. This limited holding, of course, does not suggest that there is something inherently unconstitutional about the new bankruptcy courts; nor does it preclude such courts from adjudicating all but a relatively narrow category of claims "arising under" or "arising in or related to cases under" the Bankruptcy Act.

* * *

JUSTICE WHITE, with whom THE CHIEF JUSTICE and JUSTICE POWELL join, dissenting.

Article III, § 1 of the Constitution is straight forward and uncomplicated on its face * * *. Any reader could easily take this provision to mean that although Congress was free to establish such lower courts as it saw fit, any court that it did establish would be an "inferior" court exercising "judicial power of the United States" and so must be manned by judges possessing both life-tenure and a guaranteed minimal income. This would be an eminently sensible reading and one that, as the plurality shows, is well-founded in both the documentary sources and the political doctrine of separation of powers that stands behind much of our constitutional structure.

If this simple reading were correct and we were free to disregard 150 years of history, this would be an easy case and the plurality opinion could end with its observation that "[i]t is undisputed that the bankruptcy judges whose offices were created by the Bankruptcy Reform Act of 1978 do not enjoy the protections constitutionally afforded to Art. III judges." The fact that the plurality must go on to deal with what has been characterized as one of the most confusing and controversial areas of constitutional law itself indicates the gross oversimplification implicit in the plurality's claim that "our Constitution unambiguously enunciates a fundamental principle—that the 'judicial Power of the United States' must be reposed in an independent Judiciary [and] provides clear institutional protections for that independence." While this is fine rhetoric, analytically it serves only to put a distracting and superficial gloss on a difficult question.

That question is what limits Art. III places on Congress' ability to create adjudicative institutions designed to carry out federal policy established pursuant to the substantive authority given Congress elsewhere in the Constitution. Whether fortunate or unfortunate, at this point in the history of constitutional law that question can no longer be answered by looking only to the constitutional text. This Court's cases construing that text must also be considered. In its attempt to pigeonhole these cases, the plurality does violence to their meaning and creates an artificial structure that itself lacks coherence.

I

* * *

* * * The plurality concedes that Congress may provide for initial adjudications by Art. I courts or administrative judges of all rights and duties arising under otherwise valid federal laws. There is no apparent reason why this principle should not extend to matters arising in federal bankruptcy proceedings. The Court attempts to escape the reach of prior decisions by contending that the bankrupt's claim against Marathon arose under state law. Non–Article III judges, in its view, cannot be vested with authority to adjudicate such issues. It then proceeds to strike down [§ 241(a)] on this ground. For several reasons, the Court's judgment is unsupportable.

* * *

The plurality concedes that in adjudications and discharges in bankruptcy, "the restructuring of debtor-creditor relations, which lies at the core of the federal bankruptcy power," and "the manner in which the rights of debtors and creditors are adjusted," are matters of federal law. Under the plurality's own interpretation of the cases, therefore, these matters could be heard and decided by Art. I judges. But because the bankruptcy judge is also given authority to hear a case like that of petitioner against Marathon, which the Court says is founded on state law, the Court holds that the section must be stricken down on its face. This is a grossly unwarranted emasculation of the scheme Congress has adopted. Even if the Court is correct that such a state law claim cannot be heard by a bankruptcy judge, there is no basis for doing more than declaring the section unconstitutional as applied to the claim against Marathon, leaving the section otherwise intact. In that event, cases such as this one would have to be heard by Art. III judges or by state courts— unless the defendant consents to suit before the bankruptcy judge—just as they were before the 1978 Act was adopted. But this would remove from the jurisdiction of the bankruptcy judges only a tiny fraction of the cases he is now empowered to adjudicate and would not otherwise limit his jurisdiction.[3]

* * *

The new aspect of the Bankruptcy Act of 1978 * * * is not the extension of federal jurisdiction to state law claims, but its extension to particular kinds of state law claims, such as contract cases against third parties or disputes involving property in the possession of a third person. Prior to 1978, a claim of a bankrupt against a third party, such as the claim against Marathon in this case, was not within the jurisdiction of the bankruptcy judge. * * *

* * *

III

A

The plurality contends that the precedents upholding Art. I courts can be reduced to three categories. First, there are territorial courts, which need not satisfy Art. III constraints because "the Framers intended that as to certain geographical areas ... Congress was to exercise the general powers of government." Second, there are courts-martial, which are exempt from Art. III limits because of a constitutional grant of power that has been "historically understood as giving the political branches of Government extraordinary control over the precise subject matter at issue." Finally, there are those legislative courts and administrative agencies that adjudicate cases involving public rights—controversies between the government and private parties—which are not covered by Art. III because the controversy could have been resolved by the executive alone without judicial review. Despite the plurality's attempt to cabin the domain of Art. I courts, it is quite unrealistic to consider these to be only three "narrow" limitations on or exceptions to the reach of Art. III. In fact, the plurality itself breaks the mold in its discussion of "adjuncts" in Part IV, when it announces that "when Congress creates a substantive federal right, it possesses substantial discretion to prescribe the manner in which that right may be adjudicated." Adjudications of federal rights may, according to the plurality, be committed to administrative agencies, as long as provision is made for judicial review.

* * *

3. The plurality attempts to justify its sweeping invalidation of [§ 241(a)], because of its inclusion of state-law claims, by suggesting that this statutory provision is non-severable. * * * The basis for the conclusion of nonseverability, however, is nothing more than a presumption: "Congress has vested jurisdiction over this and all matters related to cases under title 11 in a single non-Art. III court, and has done so pursuant to a single statutory grant of jurisdiction. In these circumstances, we cannot conclude that if Congress were aware that the grant of jurisdiction could not constitutionally encompass this and similar claims, it would simply remove the jurisdiction of the bankruptcy court over these matters." * * *

Instead of telling us what it is Art. I courts can and cannot do, the plurality presents us with a list of Art. I courts. When we try to distinguish those courts from their Art. III counterparts, we find—apart from the obvious lack of Art. III judges—a series of non-distinctions. By the plurality's own admission, Art. I courts can operate throughout the country, they can adjudicate both private and public rights, and they can adjudicate matters arising from congressional actions in those areas in which congressional control is "extraordinary." I cannot distinguish this last category from the general "arising under" jurisdiction of Art. III courts.

The plurality opinion has the appearance of limiting Art. I courts only because it fails to add together the sum of its parts. Rather than limiting each other, the principles relied upon complement each other; together they cover virtually the whole domain of possible areas of adjudication. Without a unifying principle, the plurality's argument reduces to the proposition that because bankruptcy courts are not sufficiently like any of these three exceptions, they may not be either Art. I courts or adjuncts to Art. III courts. But we need to know why bankruptcy courts can not qualify as Art. I courts in their own right.

* * *

IV

The complicated and contradictory history of the issue before us leads me to conclude that * * * [t]here is no difference in principle between the work that Congress may assign to an Art. I court and that which the Constitution assigns to Art. III courts. Unless we want to overrule a large number of our precedents upholding a variety of Art. I courts—not to speak of those Art. I courts that go by the contemporary name of "administrative agencies"—this conclusion is inevitable. It is too late to go back that far; too late to return to the simplicity of the principle pronounced in Art. III and defended so vigorously and persuasively by Hamilton in The Federalist Nos. 78–82.

To say that the Court has failed to articulate a principle by which we can test the constitutionality of a putative Art. I court, or that there is no such abstract principle, is not to say that this Court, must always defer to the legislative decision to create Art. I, rather than Art. III, courts. Art. III is not to be read out of the Constitution; rather, it should be read as expressing one value that must be balanced against competing constitutional values and legislative responsibilities. This Court retains the final word on how that balance is to be struck.

* * *

This was precisely the approach taken to this problem in Palmore v. United States, which, contrary to the suggestion of the majority, did not rest on any theory of territorial or geographical control. Rather, it rested on an evaluation of the strength of the legislative interest in pursuing in this manner one of its constitutionally assigned responsibilities—a responsibility not different in kind from numerous other legislative responsibilities. Thus, *Palmore* referred to the wide variety of Art. I courts, not just territorial courts. It is in this light that the critical statement of the case must be understood:

> "[T]he requirements of Art. III, which are applicable where laws of national applicability and affairs of national concern are at stake, must in proper circumstances give way to accommodate plenary grants of power to Congress to legislate with respect to specialized areas having particularized needs and warranting distinctive treatment."

I do not suggest that the Court should simply look to the strength of the legislative interest and ask itself if that interest is more compelling than the values furthered by Art. III. The inquiry should, rather, focus equally on those Art. III values and ask whether and to what extent the legislative scheme accommodates them or, conversely, substantially undermines them. The burden on Art. III values should then be measured against the values Congress hopes to serve through the use of Art. I courts.

To be more concrete: *Crowell,* supra, suggests that the presence of appellate review by an Art. III court will go a long way toward insuring a proper separation of powers. Appellate review of the decisions of legislative courts, like appellate review of state court decisions, provides a firm check on the ability of the political institutions of government to ignore or transgress constitutional limits on their own authority. Obviously, therefore, a scheme of Art. I courts that provides for appellate review by Art. III courts should be substantially less controversial than a legislative attempt entirely to avoid judicial review in a constitutional court.

Similarly, as long as the proposed Art. I courts are designed to deal with issues likely to be of little interest to the political branches, there is less reason to fear that such courts represent a dangerous accumulation of power in one of the political branches of government. Chief Justice Vinson suggested as much when he stated that the Court should guard against any congressional attempt "to transfer jurisdiction ... for the purpose of emasculating" constitutional courts. National Insurance Co. v. Tidewater Co., 337 U.S., at 644.

V

I believe that the new bankruptcy courts established by the Bankruptcy Act of 1978 * * * satisfy this standard.

First, ample provision is made for appellate review by Art. III courts. Appeals may in some circumstances be brought directly to the district courts. 28 U.S.C. § 1334. Decisions of the district courts are further appealable to the court of appeals. In other circumstances, appeals go first to a panel of bankruptcy judges, § 1482, and then to the court of appeals. In still other circumstances—when the parties agree—appeals may go directly to the court of appeals. In sum, there is in every instance a right of appeal to at least one Art. III court. Had Congress decided to assign all bankruptcy matters to the state courts, a power it clearly possesses, no greater review in an Art. III court would exist. Although I do not suggest that this analogy means that Congress may establish an Art. I court wherever it could have chosen to rely upon the state courts, it does suggest that the critical function of judicial review is being met in a manner that the Constitution suggests is sufficient.

Second, no one seriously argues that the Bankruptcy Act of 1978 represents an attempt by the political branches of government to aggrandize themselves at the expense of the third branch or an attempt to undermine the authority of constitutional courts in general. * * * Bankruptcy matters are, for the most part, private adjudications of little political significance. Although some bankruptcies may indeed present politically controversial circumstances or issues, Congress has far more direct ways to involve itself in such matters than through some sort of subtle, or not so subtle, influence on bankruptcy judges. Furthermore, were such circumstances to arise, the Due Process Clause might very well require that the matter be considered by an Art. III judge: Bankruptcy proceedings remain, after all, subject to all of the strictures of that constitutional provision.

Finally, I have no doubt that the ends that Congress sought to accomplish by creating a system of non-Art. III bankruptcy courts were at least as compelling as the ends found to be satisfactory in *Palmore,* supra, or the ends that have traditionally justified the creation of legislative courts. The stresses placed upon the old bankruptcy system by the tremendous increase in bankruptcy cases were well documented and were clearly a matter to which Congress could respond. I don't believe it is possible to challenge Congress' further determination that it was to create a specialized court to deal with bankruptcy matters. This was the nearly uniform conclusion of all those that testified before Congress on the question of reform of the bankruptcy system, as well as the conclusion of the Commission on Bankruptcy Laws established by Congress in 1970 to explore possible improvements in the system.

* * * Congress may legitimately consider the effect on the federal judiciary of the addition of several hundred specialized judges: We are, on the whole, a body of generalists. The addition of several hundred specialists may substantially change, whether for good or bad, the character of the federal bench. Moreover, Congress may have desired to maintain some flexibility in its possible future responses to the general problem of bankruptcy. There is no question that the existence of several hundred bankruptcy judges with life-tenure would have severely limited Congress' future options. Furthermore, the number of bankruptcies may fluctuate producing a substantially reduced need for bankruptcy judges. Congress may have thought that, in that event, a bankruptcy specialist should not as a general matter serve as a judge in the countless nonspecialized cases that come before the federal district courts. It would then face the prospect of large numbers of idle federal judges. Finally, Congress may have believed that the change from bankruptcy referees to Article I judges was far less dramatic, and so less disruptive of the

existing bankruptcy and constitutional court systems, than would be a change to Art. III judges.

[handwritten: D.C. as a state]

Notes

[handwritten: Bankrupcy]

1. In light of *Palmore,* the Court's most recent statement on the legislative court issue prior to *Northern Pipeline,* are you surprised by this decision? Is it consistent with the spirit and/or letter of *Palmore?* Could an argument be fashioned that in certain senses, *Northern Pipeline* is an easier case for upholding the use of a non-Article III court?

2. How successfully does Justice Brennan distinguish the work of administrative agencies from the work of the Bankruptcy Court for purposes of Article III? Do you understand Justice Brennan's suggested distinction between legislative courts on the one hand and federal court "adjuncts" on the other? Is it a valid distinction? How about Justice Brennan's distinction between cases involving "private" rights and those concerning so-called "public" rights? Are the latter any less a part of Article III's "judicial power" than the former? Is the need for an independent judiciary any less in cases involving the latter than in those involving the former?

3. How satisfactorily does Justice Brennan distinguish the situations in which the use of legislative courts had previously been approved? Does Justice Brennan develop a guiding principle on which to base future determinations about the constitutionality of legislative courts? Does Justice White? Which of the two principles do you find more persuasive? Do you find *either* of them to be persuasive? For a discussion of the constitutionality of courts-martial and territorial courts, see Stern, *What's a Constitution Among Friends?—Unbalancing Article III*, 146 U.Pa.L.Rev. 1043 (1998).

4. **Magistrate Judges and Article III.** In the Federal Magistrates Act of 1968, codified at 28 U.S.C. §§ 631–639, Congress provided magistrates (now referred to as "magistrate judges") an important role in the conduct of the business of the federal courts. Congress further expanded their role in both 1976 and 1979. Act of Oct. 21, 1976, Pub.L. No. 94–577, 90 Stat. 2729 (1976); Federal Magistrates Act of 1979, Pub.L. No. 96–82, 93 Stat. 643–45 (1979). Magistrate judges are appointed for an eight-year term [28 U.S.C. § 631(e)], and a magistrate may be removed from office during his term because of "incompetency, misconduct, neglect of duty, or physical or mental disability". The Act further provides that "a magistrate's office shall be terminated if the conference determines that the services performed by his office are no longer needed." Section 636(i). They thus are explicitly denied the salary and life tenure protection given to Article III judges.

[handwritten: No safeguards of Art III]

Because the Act vested broad power in non-Article III officials, concern was expressed, both prior to and after passage of the original act in 1968, concerning its constitutionality. See Mathews v. Weber, 423 U.S. 261, 269 (1976); TPO, Inc. v. McMillen, 460 F.2d 348, 352–354 (7th Cir.1972).

[handwritten: Raddatz]

In United States v. Raddatz, 447 U.S. 667 (1980), relied on in *Northern Pipeline,* the Supreme Court upheld the use of section 636(b) of the Federal Magistrates Act of 1979, 28 U.S.C. § 636(b), to authorize a magistrate to make factual findings at a suppression hearing in a criminal case, where the district judge exercises ultimate review and control. The Court believed that it "need not decide whether * * * Congress could constitutionally have delegated the task of rendering a final decision on a suppression motion to a non-Art. III officer." Id. at 681. Justice Blackmun, concurring, reasoned that "[w]e do not face a procedure under which 'Congress [has] delegate[d] to a non-Art. III judge the authority to make final determinations on issues of fact.' * * * Rather, we confront a procedure under which Congress has vested in Art. III judges the discretionary power to delegate certain functions to competent and impartial assistants, while ensuring that the judges retain complete supervisory control over the assistants' activities." Id. at 686. However, Justice Marshall, dissenting, argued that "[i]f the motion to suppress turns on issues of credibility that cannot be resolved on the basis of the record, and if the district judge does not hear the witnesses, the magistrate's report is no mere 'recommendation.' Unless the district judge ventures a blind guess, that report is effectively the final determination of the facts underlying the suppression motion." Id. at 703.

A provision of the Federal Magistrates Act of 1979, 28 U.S.C. § 636(c), allows magistrates to conduct civil trials with the consent of all the parties. Exactly how does this provision differ from the structure established in section 636(b), upheld in *Raddatz*? Do those differences make it more or less vulnerable to constitutional attack than section 636(b)? The provision was upheld in the post-*Northern Pipeline* lower court decision, Pacemaker Diagnostic Clinic of America, Inc. v. Instromedix, Inc., 725 F.2d 537 (9th Cir.1984), cert. denied, 469 U.S. 824 (1984) (en banc). The opinion, by then-Judge Kennedy, relied heavily on the presence of the consent requirement: "The Supreme Court has allowed criminal defendants to waive even fundamental rights. * * * We refuse to reach the anomalous result of forbidding waiver in a civil case of the personal right to an Article III judge." While he acknowledged that "[t]he purported waiver of the right to an Article III trial would not be an acceptable ground for avoiding the constitutional question if the alternative to the waiver were the imposition of serious burdens and costs on the litigant," he concluded that "[n]o such burdens or hardships have been demonstrated here." Id. at 543.

In Gomez v. United States, 490 U.S. 858 (1989), the Supreme Court held that section 636(b)(3) of the Federal Magistrates Act, which grants district courts authority to assign magistrates "such additional duties as are not inconsistent with the Constitution and laws of the United States", does not encompass the selection of a jury in a felony trial without the defendant's consent. In Peretz v. United States, 501 U.S. 923 (1991), the Court held that where a defendant does consent, magistrates may be assigned this duty: "Our decision that the procedure followed in *Raddatz* comported with Article III * * * requires the same conclusion respecting the procedure followed in this case." Id. at 939. Does this reasoning make sense, in light of the Court's previous holding in *Gomez* that absent such consent Article III would, in fact, be violated? Could the same be said of the procedure challenged in *Raddatz*? In dissent, Justice Marshall, speaking for three members of the Court, argued that "[o]ur reasoning in *Gomez* makes clear that the absence or presence of consent is entirely relevant to the * * * Act's prohibition upon magistrate jury selection in a felony trial." Id. at 940. For an argument in support of the expanded consensual use of magistrate judges in criminal proceedings see Note, *Consensual Sentencing in the Magistrate Court*, 75 Tex.L.Rev. 1161 (1997).

On the general issue, see Note, *Federal Magistrates and the Principles of Article III*, 97 Harv.L.Rev. 1947 (1984). In recent years, lower courts have upheld the use of magistrate judges in criminal or related proceedings, as long as the parties have consented. Lee Norris v. Schotten, 146 F.3d 314 (6th Cir.), *cert. denied*, 525 U.S. 935 (1998); United States v. Dees, 125 F.3d 261 (5th Cir.1997), *cert. denied*, 522 U.S. 1152 (1998).

5. The *Northern Pipeline* decision is criticized in Redish, *Legislative Courts Administrative Agencies, and the* Northern Pipeline *Decision,* 1983 Duke L.J. 197. There it is argued:

> [W]hat makes the [Court's] approval of the exercise of article I court authority over [public rights] cases so bizarre is the contrast to the type of case that the [public-private right] dichotomy dictates must be heard in article III courts: suits between private individuals involving state-created common law rights. Such cases barely fall within the categories of cases to which the judicial power is extended in article III, section 2. * * * Thus, the cases that, according to Justice Brennan, make up the 'core' of the federal judicial power, and therefore comprise the category of cases that may not be given for final resolution to an article I body, are those that barely fall within the judicial power in the first place.

[handwritten margin note: Art. I cases barely fall w/in Art III to begin with]

> * * *

> The public-private right dichotomy effectively frustrates the purposes served by the constitutional protections of judicial independence. The danger of both potential federal governmental domination of the federal judiciary and potential governmental displeasure with judicial decisions is at a minimum in suits between private individuals involving state-created common law rights. In contrast, the types of cases in which the dangers are greatest, those involving a dispute between private individuals and the federal government, are the very cases that Justice Brennan permits article I bodies to adjudicate. 1983 Duke L.J. at 208–10.

Another commentator has suggested that "*Northern Pipeline* was a curious, even ironic case to elicit concern that non-article III adjudicative bodies might undermine the vital role of article III courts in the constitutional scheme. * * * The case presented a state law contract dispute involving no diversity of citizenship—surely not the kind of case in which article III courts ever were expected to play a central role." Fallon, *Of Legislative Courts, Administrative Agencies, and Article III,* 101 Harv.L.Rev. 915, 927 (1988).

6. In 1984, Congress responded to *Northern Pipeline* with enactment of Pub.L. 98–353 (98th Cong.2d Sess.1984), the Bankruptcy Amendments and Federal Judgeship Act of 1984. The enactment came well after the Supreme Court's final stay of the effect of its decision. In effect, the amendments make bankruptcy courts "adjuncts" to the federal district courts. 28 U.S.C. § 151 now provides that bankruptcy judges shall constitute a unit of the district court. Another section provides that bankruptcy judges, appointed for a fourteen-year term "serve as officers of the United States district court established under Article III of the Constitution." 28 U.S.C. § 152(b). The

amendments authorize district judges to refer all proceedings arising under or related to a case under title II to the bankruptcy judges for the district. 28 U.S.C. § 157(a).

For cases not involving a "core proceeding" (a term defined to include such things as the administration of estates, allowance or disallowance of claims against an estate, estate property exemptions, and debt discharges), the bankruptcy judge submits his or her findings of fact and conclusions of law to the district judge, who proceeds to make the decision. The parties may request *de novo* review on any matter. 28 U.S.C. § 157(a)(1).

For discussions of the Article III implications of the current Bankruptcy Court structure, see Kar, *What Can Bankruptcy Law Tell Us About Article III and Vice Versa?*, 60 Mont.L.Rev. 415 (1999); Chemerinsky, *Decision-Makers: In Defense of Courts*, 71 Am.Bankr.L.J. 109 (1999); Crabb, *In Defense of Direct Appeals: A Further Reply to Professor Chemerinsky*, 71 Am.Bankr.L.J. 137 (1997).

THOMAS v. UNION CARBIDE AGRICULTURAL PRODUCTS CO., 473 U.S. 568 (1985): Pesticide Chemical manufacturers brought an action challenging the constitutionality of the binding arbitration provisions of the 1978 amendments to the Federal Insecticide, Fungicide, and Rodenticide Act [FIFRA], 61 Stat. 163, as amended, 7 U.S.C. § 136 et seq. Justice O'Connor delivered the opinion of the Court:

In this case we address whether Article III of the Constitution prohibits Congress from selecting binding arbitration with only limited judicial review as the mechanism for resolving disputes among participants in FIFRA's pesticide registration scheme. We conclude it does not and reverse the judgment below.

As a precondition for registration of a pesticide, manufacturers must submit research data to the Environmental Protection Agency (EPA), concerning the product's health, safety, and environmental effects. The 1972 Act established data sharing provisions intended to streamline pesticide registration procedures, increase competition, and avoid unnecessary duplication of data generation costs. Some evidence suggests that before 1972 data submitted by one registrant had 'as a matter of practice but without statutory authority, been considered by the Administrator to support the registration of the same or a similar product by another registrant.' * * * Such registrations were colloquially known as 'me too' or 'follow-on' registrations. Section 3(c)(1)(D) of the 1972 Act provided statutory authority for the use of previously submitted data as well as a scheme for sharing the costs of data generation. * * *

Congress enacted the original compensation provision in 1972 because it believed recognizing a limited proprietary interest in data submitted to support pesticide registrations would provide an added incentive beyond statutory patent protection for research and development of new pesticides. The data submitters, however, contended that basic health, safety, and environmental data essential to registration of a competing pesticide qualified for protection as a trade secret. With the EPA bogged down in cataloging data and the pesticide industry embroiled in litigation over what types of data could legitimately be designated 'trade secrets,' new pesticide registrations 'ground to a virtual halt.'

The 1978 amendments were a response to the 'logjam of litigation that resulted from controversies over data compensation and trade secret protection.' Congress viewed data-sharing as essential to the registration scheme, but concluded EPA must be relieved of the task of valuation because disputes regarding the compensation scheme had 'for all practical purposes, tied up their registration process' and '[EPA] lacked the expertise to establish the proper amount of compensation.' * * *

Against this background, Congress in 1978 amended § 3(c)(1)(D) and § 10(b) to clarify that the trade secret exemption from the data-consideration provision did not extend to health, safety, and environmental data. In addition, the 1978 amendments granted data submitters a 10–year period of exclusive use for data submitted after September 30, 1978, during which time the data may not be cited without original submitter's permission. § 3(c)(1)(D)(i).

Regarding compensation for use of data not protected by the 10–year exclusive use provision, the amendment substituted for the EPA Administrator's determination of the appropriate compensation a system of negotiation and binding arbitration to resolve compensation disputes among registrants. * * * The arbitrator's decision is subject to judicial review for only fraud, misrepresentation or other misconduct. The statute contains its own sanctions. Should an applicant or data submitter fail to comply with the scheme, the Administrator is required to cancel the new registration or to consider the data without compensation to the original submitter. The Administrator may also issue orders regarding sale or use of existing pesticide stocks.

* * *

Appellees contend that Article III bars Congress from requiring arbitration of disputes among registrants concerning compensation under FIFRA without also affording substantial review by tenured judges of the arbitrator's decision. Article III, § 1, establishes a broad policy that federal judicial power shall be vested in courts whose judges enjoy life tenure and fixed compensation. These requirements protect the role of the independent judiciary within the constitutional scheme of tripartite government and assure impartial adjudication in federal courts.

An absolute construction of Article III is not possible in this area of frequently arcane distinctions and confusing precedents. Northern Pipeline Co. v. Marathon Pipe Line Co., 458 U.S., at 90 (opinion concurring in judgment). * * *

* * *

Appellees contend that their claims to compensation under FIFRA are a matter of state law, and thus are encompassed by the holding of *Northern Pipeline.* We disagree. Any right to compensation from follow-on registrants under § 3(c)(1)(D)(ii) for EPA's use of data results from FIFRA and does not depend on or replace a right to such compensation under state law. * * * As a matter of state law, property rights in a trade secret are extinguished when a company discloses its trade secret to persons not obligated to protect the confidentiality of the information. * * * Therefore registrants who submit data with notice of the scheme established by the 1978 amendments, and its qualified protection of trade secrets as defined in § 10, can claim no property interest under state law in data subject to § 3(c)(1)(D)(ii). * * *

Alternatively, appellees contend that FIFRA confers a 'private right' to compensation, requiring either Article III adjudication or review by an Article III court sufficient to retain 'the essential attributes of the judicial power.' Northern Pipeline Co., 458 U.S., at 77, 85–86 (plurality opinion). This 'private right' argument rests on the distinction between public and private rights drawn by the plurality in *Northern Pipeline.* The *Northern Pipeline* plurality construed the Court's prior opinions to permit only three clearly defined exceptions to the rule of Article III adjudication: military tribunals, territorial courts, and decisions involving 'public' as opposed to 'private' rights. Drawing upon language in Crowell v. Benson, * * * the plurality defined 'public rights' authority in connection with the performance of the constitutional functions of the executive or legislative departments." * * * It identified 'private rights' as 'the liability of one individual to another under the law as defined.'

This theory that the public rights/private rights dichotomy provides a bright line test for determining the requirements of Article III did not command a majority of the Court in *Northern Pipeline.* Insofar as appellees interpret that case and *Crowell* as establishing that the right to an Article III forum is absolute unless the federal government is a party of record, we cannot agree. Cf. *Northern Pipeline Co.,* supra, at 71 (plurality) (noting that discharge in bankruptcy, which adjusts liabilities between individuals, is arguably a public right). Nor did a majority of the Court endorse the implication of the private right/public right dichotomy that Article III has no force simply because a dispute is between the Government and an individual.

* * *

Looking beyond form to the substance of what FIFRA accomplishes, we note several aspects of FIFRA that persuade us the arbitration scheme adopted by Congress does not contravene Article III. First, the right created by FIFRA is not a purely 'private' right, but bears many of the characteristics of a public right. Use of a registrant's data to support a follow-on registration serves a public purpose as an integral part of a program safeguarding the public health. Congress has the power, under Article I, to authorize an agency administering a complex regulatory scheme to allocate costs and benefits among voluntary participants in the program without providing an Article III adjudication. It also has the power to condition issuance of registrations or licenses on compliance with agency procedures. Article III is not so inflexible that it bars Congress from shifting the task of data valuation from the agency to the interested parties.

The 1978 amendments represent a pragmatic solution to the difficult problem of spreading the costs of generating adequate information regarding the safety, health, and environmental impact of a potentially dangerous product. * * *

The near disaster of the FIFRA 1972 amendments and the danger to public health of further delay in pesticide registration led Congress to select arbitration as the appropriate method of dispute resolution. Given the nature of the right at issue and the concerns motivating the legislature, we do not think this system threatens the independent role of the judiciary in our constitutional scheme. * * *

We note as well that the FIFRA arbitration scheme incorporates its own system of internal sanctions and relies only tangentially, if at all, on the Judicial Branch for enforcement. The danger of Congress or the Executive encroaching on the Article III judicial powers is at a minimum when no unwilling defendant is subjected to judicial enforcement power as a result of the agency 'adjudication.'

* * *

Finally, we note that FIFRA limits but does not preclude review of the arbitration proceeding by an Article III court. We conclude that, in the circumstances, the review afforded preserves the 'appropriate exercise of the judicial function.' FIFRA at a minimum allows private parties to secure Article III review of the arbitrator's 'findings and determination' for fraud, misconduct, or misrepresentation. This provision protects against arbitrators who abuse or exceed their powers or willfully misconstrue their mandate under the governing law. Moreover, review of constitutional error is preserved, and FIFRA, therefore, does not obstruct whatever judicial review might be required by due process. Cf. Crowell v. Benson, 285 U.S., at 46 (Brandeis, J., dissenting). * * *

* * *

Our holding is limited to the proposition that Congress, acting for a valid legislative purpose pursuant to its constitutional powers under Article I, may create a seemingly 'private' right that is so closely integrated into a public regulatory scheme as to be a matter appropriate for agency resolution with limited involvement by the Article III judiciary. To hold otherwise would be to erect a rigid and formalistic restraint on the ability of Congress to adopt innovative measures such as negotiation and arbitration with respect to rights created by a regulatory scheme.''

Justice Brennan, joined by Justices Marshall and Blackmun, concurred separately:

Analysis of the present case properly begins with the recognition that it differs substantially from the issue in *Northern Pipeline*. * * *

I agree with the Court that the determinative factor with respect to the proper characterization of the nature of the dispute in this case should not be the presence or absence of the government as a party. Despite the Court's contrary suggestions, the plurality opinion in *Northern Pipeline* suggests neither that the right to an Article III forum is absolute unless the federal government is a party of record nor that Article III has no force simply because a dispute is between the Government and an individual. * * * Properly understood, the analysis elaborated by the plurality in *Northern Pipeline* does not place the federal government in an Article III straightjacket whenever a dispute technically is one between private parties. We recognized that a bankruptcy adjudication, though technically a dispute among private parties, may well be properly characterized as a matter of public rights. * * *

Nor does the approach of the *Northern Pipeline* plurality opinion permit Congress to sap the judiciary of all its checking power whenever the Government is a party. The opinion made clear that 'the presence of the United States as a proper party to the proceeding is ... not [a] sufficient means of distinguishing' private rights 'from' public rights.'' 458 U.S., at 69, n.23. At a minimum, Art. III must bar Congress from assigning to an Art. I decisionmaker the ultimate disposition of challenges to the constitutionality of government action, either legislative or executive. Also, the plurality opinion was careful to leave open the question whether and to what extent even the resolution of public rights disputes might require some eventual review in an Art. III court in the exercise of its responsibility to check an impermissible accumulation of power in other branches of Government. * * *

Though the issue before us in this case is not free of doubt, in my judgment the FIFRA compensation scheme challenged in this case should be viewed as involving a matter of public rights as that term is understood in the line of cases culminating in *Northern Pipeline*. In one sense the question of proper compensation for a follow-on registrant's use of test data is, under the FIFRA scheme, a dispute about the liability of one individual to another under the law as defined, Crowell v. Benson, 285 U.S. 22, 51 (1932) (defining matters of private right). But the dispute arises in the context of a federal regulatory scheme that virtually occupies the field. * * * This case, in other words, involves not only the congressional prescription of a federal rule of decision to govern a private dispute but also the active participation of a federal regulatory agency in resolving the dispute. Although a compensation dispute under FI-FRA ultimately involves a determination of the duty owed one private party by another, at its heart the dispute involves the exercise of authority by a federal government arbitrator in the course of administration of FIFRA's comprehensive regulatory scheme. As such it partakes of the characteristics of a standard agency adjudication. * * *

Given that this dispute is properly understood as one involving a matter in which Congress has substantial latitude to make use of Art. I decisionmakers, the question remains whether the Constitution nevertheless imposes some requirement of Art. III supervision of the arbitrator's decisions under this scheme. In this case Congress has provided for review of arbitrators' decisions to ensure against 'fraud, misrepresentation, or misconduct.' The Court therefore need not reach the difficult question of whether Congress is always free to cut off all judicial review of decisions respecting such exercises of Art. I authority.

The review prescribed under FIFRA encompasses the authority to invalidate an arbitrator's decision when that decision exceeds the arbitrator's authority or exhibits a manifest disregard for the governing law. Such review preserves the judicial authority over questions of law in the present context."

Justice Stevens also concurred separately.

Notes

1. On what basis does the Court conclude that "this system [does not] threaten[ ] the independent role of the judiciary in our constitutional scheme"? Is the analysis persuasive? Under Article III, is it appropriate for the Court to make this analysis on a case-by-case basis? Is it arguable that this is the very practice Article III was attempting to prevent?

2. Is the Court effectively employing Justice White's *Northern Pipeline* balancing test? If so, in conducting this balancing process is it giving sufficient weight to the need for independence?

3. The Court emphasizes that the FIFRA arbitration scheme "relies only tangentially, if at all, on the Judicial Branch for enforcement." Why is that important?

4. Consider the scheme of judicial review of the arbitrator's decision discussed in the opinion. Could a persuasive argument be fashioned that such a scheme is more constitutionally suspect than one providing for no judicial review at all? In responding, reconsider your answer to question 3.

5. What is left of the public-private right dichotomy after this case? If it remains in effect, has it been altered? If so, do you think that it has been altered for the better?

6. Both the opinion of the Court and the concurring opinion of Justice Brennan emphasize that no state law claim is being adjudicated by an Article I court. Why does the Court believe this fact is important? *Is* it important?

COMMODITY FUTURES TRADING
COMMISSION v. SCHOR

Supreme Court of the United States, 1986.
478 U.S. 833.

JUSTICE O'CONNOR delivered the opinion of the Court.

State Law Counterclaims

The question presented is whether the Commodity Exchange Act (CEA or Act), 7 U.S.C. § 1 et seq., empowers the Commodity Futures Trading Commission (CFTC or Commission) to entertain state law counterclaims in reparation proceedings and, if so, whether that grant of authority violates Article III of the Constitution. *(Issue)*

I

The CEA broadly prohibits fraudulent and manipulative conduct in connection with commodity futures transactions. In 1974, Congress "overhaul[ed]" the Act in order to institute a more "comprehensive regulatory structure to oversee the volatile and esoteric futures trading complex." H.R.Rep. No. 93–975, p. 1 (1974). Congress also determined that the broad regulatory powers of the CEA were most appropriately vested in an agency which would be relatively *immune from the* "political winds that sweep Washington." It therefore created an independent agency, the CFTC, and entrusted to it sweeping authority to implement the CEA.

Among the duties assigned to the CFTC was the administration of a reparations procedure through which disgruntled customers of professional commodity brokers could seek redress for the brokers' violations of the Act or CFTC regulations. Thus, § 14 of the CEA provides that any person injured by such violations may apply to the Commission for an order directing the offender to pay reparations to the complainant and may enforce that order in federal district court. Congress intended this administrative procedure to be an "inexpensive and expeditious" alternative to existing fora available to aggrieved customers, namely, the courts and arbitration.

efficient alternative

In conformance with the congressional goal of promoting efficient dispute resolution, the CFTC promulgated a regulation in 1976 which allows it to adjudicate counterclaims "aris[ing] out of the transaction or occurrence or series of transactions or occurrences set forth in the complaint." This permissive counterclaim rule leaves the respondent in a reparations proceeding free to seek relief against the reparations complainant in other fora.

permissive counterclaim

The instant dispute arose in February 1980, when respondents Schor and Mortgage Services of America invoked the CFTC's reparations jurisdiction by filing complaints against petitioner ContiCommodity Services, Inc. (Conti), a commodity futures broker, and Richard L. Sandor, a Conti employee. Schor had an account with Conti which contained a debit balance because Schor's net futures trading losses and expenses, such as commissions, exceeded the funds deposited in the account. Schor alleged that this debit balance was the result of Conti's numerous violations of the CEA.

Before receiving notice that Schor had commenced the reparations proceeding, Conti had filed a diversity action in Federal District Court to recover the debit balance. Schor counterclaimed in this action, reiterating his charges that the debit balance was due to Conti's violations of the CEA. Schor also moved on two separate occasions to dismiss or stay the district court action * * *.

Although the District Court declined to stay or dismiss the suit, Conti voluntarily dismissed the federal court action and presented its debit balance claim by way of a counterclaim in the CFTC reparations proceeding. Conti denied violating the CEA and instead insisted that the debit balance resulted from Schor's trading, and was therefore a simple debt owed by Schor.

After discovery, briefing and a hearing, the Administrative Law Judge (ALJ) in Schor's reparations proceeding ruled in Conti's favor on both Schor's claims and Conti's counterclaims. After this ruling, Schor for the first time challenged the CFTC's statutory authority to adjudicate Conti's counterclaim. The ALJ rejected Schor's challenge, stating himself "bound by agency regulations and published agency policies." The Commission declined to review the decision and allowed it to become final, at which point Schor filed a petition for review with the Court of Appeals for the District of Columbia Circuit. Prior to oral argument, the Court of Appeals, *sua sponte,* raised the question of whether CFTC could constitutionally adjudicate Conti's counterclaims in light of *Northern Pipeline Construction Co. v. Marathon Pipe Line Co.,* in which this Court held that "Congress may not vest in a non-Article III court the power to adjudicate, render final judgment, and issue binding orders in a traditional contract action arising under state law, without consent of the litigants, and subject only to ordinary appellate review."

After briefing and argument, the Court of Appeals upheld the CFTC's decision on Schor's claim in most respects, but ordered the dismissal of Conti's counterclaims on the ground that "the CFTC lacks authority (subject matter competence) to adjudicate" common law counterclaims. In support of this latter ruling, the Court of Appeals reasoned that the CFTC's exercise of jurisdiction over Conti's common law counterclaim gave rise to "[s]erious constitutional problems" under *Northern Pipeline.* The Court of Appeals therefore concluded that, under well-established principles of statutory construction, the relevant inquiry was whether the CEA was " 'fairly susceptible' of [an alternative] construction," such that Article III objections, and thus un constitutional adjudication, could be avoided.

After examining the CEA and its legislative history, the court concluded that Congress had no "clearly expressed" or "explicit" intention to give the CFTC constitutionally questionable jurisdiction over state common law counterclaims. The Court of Appeals therefore "adopt[ed] the construction of the Act that avoids significant constitutional questions," reading the CEA to authorize the CFTC to adjudicate only those counterclaims alleging violations of the Act or CFTC regulations. Because Conti's counterclaims did not allege such violations, the Court of Appeals held that the CFTC exceeded its authority in adjudicating those claims, and ordered that the ALJ's decision on the claims be reversed and the claims dismissed for lack of jurisdiction.

     * * * This Court granted the CFTC's petition for certiorari, vacated the court of appeals' judgment, and remanded the case for further consideration in light of *Thomas* [*v. Union Carbide Agricultural Products Co.*]. * * *

     On remand, the Court of Appeals reinstated its prior judgment. * * *

* * *

II

     The Court of Appeals was correct in its understanding that "[f]ederal statutes are to be so construed as to avoid serious doubt of their constitutionality." Machinists v. Street, 367 U.S. 740, 749 (1961). * * * It is equally true, however, that this canon of construction does not give a court the prerogative to ignore the legislative will in order to avoid constitutional adjudication. * * *

     Assuming that the Court of Appeals correctly discerned a "serious" constitutional problem in the CFTC's adjudication of Conti's counterclaim, we nevertheless believe that the court was mistaken in finding that the CEA could fairly be read to preclude the CFTC's exercise of jurisdiction over that counterclaim. Our examination of the CEA and its legislative history and purpose reveals that Congress plainly intended the CFTC to decide counterclaims asserted by respondents in reparations proceedings, and just as plainly delegated to the CFTC the authority to fashion its counterclaim jurisdiction in the manner the CFTC determined to further the purposes of the reparations program.

* * *

     Reference to the instant controversy illustrates the crippling effect that the Court of Appeals' restrictive reading of the CFTC's counterclaim jurisdiction would have on the efficacy of the reparations remedy. The dispute between Schor and Conti is typical of the disputes adjudicated in reparations proceedings: a customer and a professional commodities broker agree that there is a debit balance in the customer's account, but the customer attributes the deficit to the broker's alleged CEA violations and the broker attributes it to the customer's lack of success in the market. The customer brings a reparations claim; the broker counterclaims for the amount of the debit balance. In the usual case, then, the counterclaim "arises out of precisely the same course of events" as the principal claim and requires resolution of many of the same disputed factual issues.

Under the Court of Appeals' approach, the entire dispute may not be resolved in the administrative forum. Consequently, the entire dispute will typically end up in court, for when the broker files suit to recover the debit balance, the customer will normally be compelled either by compulsory counterclaim rules or by the expense and inconvenience of litigating the same issues in two fora to forgo his reparations remedy and to litigate his claim in court. * * * In sum, as Schor himself aptly summarized, to require a bifurcated examination of the single dispute "would be to emasculate if not destroy the purposes of the Commodity Exchange Act to provide an efficient and relatively inexpensive forum for the resolution of disputes in futures trading."

* * *

In view of the abundant evidence that Congress both contemplated and authorized the CFTC's assertion of jurisdiction over Conti's common law counterclaim, we conclude that the Court of Appeals' analysis is untenable. The canon of construction that requires courts to avoid unconstitutional adjudication did not empower the Court of Appeals to manufacture a restriction on the CFTC's jurisdiction that was nowhere contemplated by Congress and to reject plain evidence of congressional intent because that intent was not specifically embodied in a statutory mandate. We therefore are squarely faced with the question of whether the CFTC's assumption of jurisdiction over common law counterclaims violates Article III of the Constitution.

III

Article III, § 1 directs that the "judicial Power of the United States shall be vested in one supreme Court and in such inferior Courts as the Congress may from time to time ordain and establish," and provides that these federal courts shall be staffed by judges who hold office during good behavior, and whose compensation shall not be diminished during tenure in office. Schor claims that these provisions prohibit Congress from authorizing the initial adjudication of common law counterclaims by the CFTC, an administrative agency whose adjudicatory officers do not enjoy the tenure and salary protections embodied in Article III.

Although our precedents in this area do not admit of easy synthesis, they do establish that the resolution of claims such as Schor's cannot turn on conclusory reference to the language of Article III. Rather, the constitutionality of a given congressional delegation of adjudicative functions to a non-Article III body must be assessed by reference to the purposes underlying the requirements of Article III. This inquiry, in turn, is guided by the principle that "practical attention to substance rather than doctrinaire reliance on formal categories should inform application of Article III." *Thomas.*

A

Article III, § 1 serves both to protect "the role of the independent judiciary within the constitutional scheme of tripartite government,"

Thomas, and to safeguard litigants' "right to have claims decided before judges who are free from potential domination by other branches of government." United States v. Will, 449 U.S. 200, 218 (1980). Although our cases have provided us with little occasion to discuss the nature or significance of this latter safeguard, our prior discussions of Article III, § 1's guarantee of an independent and impartial adjudication by the federal judiciary of matters within the judicial power of the United States intimated that this guarantee serves to protect primarily personal, rather than structural, interests.

Our precedents also demonstrate, however, that Article III does not confer on litigants an absolute right to the plenary consideration of every nature of claim by an Article III court. Moreover, as a personal right, Article III's guarantee of an impartial and independent federal adjudication is subject to waiver, just as are other personal constitutional rights that dictate the procedures by which civil and criminal matters must be tried. Indeed, the relevance of concepts of waiver to Article III challenges is demonstrated by our decision in *Northern Pipeline,* in which the absence of consent to an initial adjudication before a non-Article III tribunal was relied on as a significant factor in determining that Article III forbade such adjudication.

In the instant case, Schor indisputably waived any right he may have possessed to the full trial of Conti's counterclaim before an Article III court. Schor expressly demanded that Conti proceed on its counterclaim in the reparations proceeding rather than before the District Court, and was content to have the entire dispute settled in the forum he had selected until the ALJ ruled against him on all counts; it was only after the ALJ rendered a decision to which he objected that Schor raised any challenge to the CFTC's consideration of Conti's counterclaim.

Even were there no evidence of an express waiver here, Schor's election to forgo his right to proceed in state or federal court on his claim and his decision to seek relief instead in a CFTC reparations proceeding constituted an effective waiver. * * *

B

* * * Article III, § 1 safeguards the role of the Judicial Branch in our tripartite system by barring congressional attempts "to transfer jurisdiction [to non-Article III tribunals] for the purpose of emasculating" constitutional courts, National Insurance Co. v. Tidewater Co., 337 U.S. 582, 644 (1949) (Vinson, C.J., dissenting), and thereby preventing "the encroachment or aggrandizement of one branch at the expense of the other." Buckley v. Valeo, 424 U.S. 1, 122 (1976) (per curiam) *Northern Pipeline,* 458 U.S., at 57–58, 73–74, 83, 86; id., at 98, 115–116 (WHITE, J., dissenting). To the extent that this structural principle is implicated in a given case, the parties cannot by consent cure the constitutional difficulty for the same reason that the parties by consent cannot confer on federal courts subject matter jurisdiction beyond the limitations imposed by Article III, § 2. When these Article III limitations

are at issue, notions of consent and waiver cannot be dispositive because the limitations serve institutional interests that the parties cannot be expected to protect.

In determining the extent to which a given congressional decision to authorize the adjudication of Article III business in a non-Article III tribunal impermissibly threatens the institutional integrity of the Judicial Branch, the Court has declined to adopt formalistic and unbending rules. Although such rules might lend a greater degree of coherence to this area of the law, they might also unduly constrict Congress' ability to take needed and innovative action pursuant to its Article I powers. Thus, in reviewing Article III challenges, we have weighed a number of factors, none of which has been deemed determinative, with an eye to the practical effect that the congressional action will have on the constitutionally assigned role of the federal judiciary. Among the factors upon which we have focused are the extent to which the "essential attributes of judicial power" are reserved to Article III courts, and, conversely, the extent to which the non-Article III forum exercises the range of jurisdiction and powers normally vested only in Article III courts, the origins and importance of the right to be adjudicated, and the concerns that drove Congress to depart from the requirements of Article III.

An examination of the relative allocation of powers between the CFTC and Article III courts in light of the considerations given prominence in our precedents demonstrates that the congressional scheme does not impermissibly intrude on the province of the judiciary. The CFTC's adjudicatory powers depart from the traditional agency model in just one respect: the CFTC's jurisdiction over common law counterclaims. While wholesale importation of concepts of pendent or ancillary jurisdiction into the agency context may create greater constitutional difficulties, we decline to endorse an absolute prohibition on such jurisdiction out of fear of where some hypothetical "slippery slope" may deposit us. * * *

In the instant case, we are * * * persuaded that there is little practical reason to find that this single deviation from the agency model is fatal to the congressional scheme. Aside from its authorization of counterclaim jurisdiction, the CEA leaves far more of the "essential attributes of judicial power" to Article III courts than did that portion of the Bankruptcy Act found unconstitutional in *Northern Pipeline*. The CEA scheme in fact hews closely to the agency model approved by the Court in Crowell v. Benson, 285 U.S. 22 (1932).

The CFTC, like the agency in *Crowell*, deals only with a "particularized area of law," whereas the jurisdiction of the bankruptcy courts found unconstitutional in *Northern Pipeline* extended to broadly "all civil proceedings arising under title 11 or arising in or *related to* cases under title 11." CFTC orders, like those of the agency in *Crowell*, but unlike those of the bankruptcy courts under the 1978 Act, are enforceable only by order of the District Court. CFTC orders are also reviewed under the same "weight of the evidence" standard sustained in *Crowell*, rather than the more deferential standard found lacking in *Northern Pipeline*. The legal rulings of the CFTC, like the legal determinations of the agency in *Crowell*, are subject to *de novo* review. Finally, the CFTC, unlike the bankruptcy courts under the 1978 Act, does not exercise "all ordinary powers of district courts," and thus may not, for instance, preside over jury trials or issue writs of habeas corpus.

Of course, the nature of the claim has significance in our Article III analysis quite apart from the method prescribed for its adjudication. The counterclaim asserted in this case is a "private" right for which state law provides the rule of decision. It is therefore a claim of the kind assumed to be at the "core" of matters normally reserved to Article III courts. Yet this conclusion does not end our inquiry; just as this Court has rejected any attempt to make determinative for Article III purposes the distinction between public rights and private rights, *Thomas*, there is no reason inherent in separation of powers principles to accord the state law character of a claim talismanic power in Article III inquiries. See, e.g., *Northern Pipeline*, 458 U.S., at 68, n. 20, (WHITE, J., dissenting).

We have explained that "the public rights doctrine reflects simply a pragmatic understanding that when Congress selects a quasi-judicial method of resolving matters that 'could be conclusively determined by the Executive and Legislative Branches,' the danger of encroaching on the judicial powers" is less than when private rights, which are normally within the purview of the judiciary, are relegated as an initial matter to administrative adjudication. Similarly, the state law character of a claim is significant for purposes of determining the effect that an initial adjudication of those claims by a non-Article III tribunal will have on the separation of powers for the simple reason that private, common law rights were historically the types of matters subject to resolution by Article III courts. The risk that Congress may improperly have encroached on the federal judiciary is obviously magnified when Congress "withdraw[s] from judicial cognizance any matter which, from its nature, is the subject of a suit at the common law, or in equity, or admiralty" and which therefore has traditionally been tried in Article III courts, and allocates the decision of those matters to a non-Article III forum of its own creation. Accordingly, where private, common law rights are at stake, our examination of the congressional attempt to control the manner in which those rights are adjudicated has been searching. In this case, however, "[l]ooking beyond form to the substance of what" Congress has done, we are persuaded that the congressional authorization of limited CFTC jurisdiction over a narrow class of common law claims as an incident to the CFTC's primary, and unchallenged, adjudicative function does not create a substantial threat to the separation of powers.

It is clear that Congress has not attempted to "withdraw from judicial cognizance" the determination of Conti's right to the sum represented by the debit balance in Schor's account. Congress gave the CFTC the authority to adjudicate such matters, but the decision to invoke this forum is left entirely to the parties and the power of the federal judiciary to take jurisdiction of these matters is unaffected. In such circumstances, separation of powers concerns are diminished, for it seems self-evident that just as Congress may encourage parties to settle a dispute out of court or resort to arbitration without impermissible incursions on the separation of powers, Congress may make available a quasi-judicial mechanism through which willing parties may, at their option, elect to resolve their differences. This is not to say, of course, that if Congress created a phalanx of non-Article III tribunals equipped to handle the entire business of the Article III courts without any Article III supervision or control and without evidence of valid and specific legislative necessities, the fact that the parties had the election to proceed in their forum of choice would necessarily save the scheme from constitutional attack. But this case obviously bears no resemblance to such a scenario, given the degree of judicial control saved to the federal courts, as well as the congressional purpose behind the jurisdictional delegation, the demonstrated need for the delegation, and the limited nature of the delegation.

When Congress authorized the CFTC to adjudicate counterclaims, its primary focus was on making effective a specific and limited federal regulatory scheme, not on allocating jurisdiction among federal tribunals. Congress intended to create an inexpensive and expeditious alternative forum through which customers could enforce the provisions of the CEA against professional brokers. Its decision to endow the CFTC with jurisdiction over such reparations claims is readily understandable given the perception that the CFTC was relatively immune from political pressures, see H.R.Rep. No. 93–975, pp. 44, 70, and the obvious expertise that the Commission possesses in applying the CEA and its own regulations. This reparations scheme itself is of unquestioned constitutional validity. It was only to ensure the effectiveness of this scheme that Congress authorized the CFTC to assert jurisdiction over common law counterclaims. Indeed, as was explained above, absent the CFTC's exercise of that authority, the purposes of the reparations procedure would have been confounded.

It also bears emphasis that the CFTC's assertion of counterclaim jurisdiction is limited to that which is to make the reparations procedure workable. The CFTC adjudication of common law counterclaims is incidental to, and completely dependent upon, adjudication of reparations claims created by federal law, and in actual fact is limited to claims arising out of the same transaction or occurrence as the reparations claim.

In such circumstances, the magnitude of any intrusion on the Judicial Branch can only be termed *de minimis*. Conversely, were we to hold that the Legislative Branch may not permit such limited cognizance of common law counterclaims at the election of the parties, it is clear that we would "defeat the obvious purpose of the legislation to furnish a prompt, continuous, expert and inexpensive method for dealing with a class of questions of fact which are peculiarly suited to examination and determination by an administrative agency specially assigned to that task." Crowell v. Benson, 285 U.S., at 46. We do not think Article III compels this degree of prophylaxis.

* * * [W]e have * * * looked to a number of factors in evaluating the extent to which the congressional scheme endangers separation of powers principles under the circumstances presented, but have found no genuine threat to those principles to be present in this litigation.

In so doing, we have also been faithful to our Article III precedents, which counsel that bright line rules cannot effectively be employed to yield broad principles applicable in all Article III inquiries. Rather, due regard must be given in each case to the unique aspects of the congressional plan at issue and its practical consequences in light of the larger concerns that underlie Article III. We conclude that the limited jurisdiction that the CFTC asserts over state law claims as a incident to the adjudication of federal claims willingly submitted by the parties for initial agency adjudication does not contravene separation of powers principles or Article III.

c Federalism

Schor asserts that Article III, § 1, constrains Congress for reasons of federalism, as well as for reasons of separation of powers. He argues that the state law character of Conti's counterclaim transforms the central question in this case from whether Congress has trespassed upon the judicial powers of the Federal Government into whether Congress has invaded the prerogatives of state governments.

At the outset, we note that our prior precedents in this area have dealt only with separation of powers concerns, and have not intimated that principles of federalism impose limits on Congress' ability to delegate adjudicative functions to non-Article III tribunals. This absence of discussion regarding federalism is particularly telling in *Northern Pipeline*, where the Court based its analysis solely on the separation of powers principles inherent in Article III despite the fact that the claim sought to be adjudicated in the bankruptcy court was created by state law.

Even assuming that principles of federalism are relevant to Article III analysis, however, we are unpersuaded that those principles require the invalidation of the CFTC's counterclaim jurisdiction. The sole fact that Conti's counterclaim is resolved by a *federal* rather than a *state* tribunal could not be said to unduly impair state interests, for it is established that a federal court could, without constitutional hazard, decide a counterclaim such as the one asserted here under its ancillary jurisdiction, even if an independent jurisdictional basis for it were lacking. Given that the federal courts can and do exercise ancillary jurisdiction over counterclaims such as the one at issue here, the question becomes whether the fact that a federal agency rather than a federal Article III court initially hears the state law claim gives rise to a cognizably greater impairment of principles of federalism.

Schor argues that those framers opposed to diversity jurisdiction in the federal courts acquiesced in its inclusion in Article III only because they were assured that the federal judiciary would be protected by the tenure and salary provisions of Article III. He concludes, in essence, that to protect this constitutional compact, Article III should be read to absolutely preclude any adjudication of state law claims by federal decisionmakers that do not enjoy the Article III salary and tenure protections. We are unpersuaded by Schor's novel theory, which suffers from a number of flaws, the most important of which is that Schor identifies no historical support for the critical link he posits between the provisions of Article III that protect the independence of the federal judiciary and those provisions that define the extent of the judiciary's jurisdiction over state law claims.

The judgment of the Court of Appeals for the District of Columbia Circuit is reversed and the case remanded for further proceedings consistent with this opinion.

* * *

JUSTICE BRENNAN, with whom JUSTICE MARSHALL joins, dissenting.

* * *

On its face, Article III, § 1, seems to prohibit the vesting of *any* judicial functions in either the Legislative or the Executive Branches. The Court has, however, recognized three narrow exceptions to the otherwise absolute mandate of Article III: territorial courts, courts martial, and courts that adjudicate certain disputes concerning public rights. Unlike the Court, I would limit the judicial authority of non-Article III federal tribunals to these few, long-established exceptions and would countenance no further erosion of Article III's mandate.

I

The Framers knew that "[t]he accumulation of all powers, legislative, executive, and judiciary, in the same hands, whether of one, a few, or many, and whether hereditary, self-appointed, or elective, may justly be pronounced the very definition of tyranny." The Federalist No. 46, p. 334 (H. Dawson ed. 1876) (J. Madison). In order to prevent such tyranny, the Framers devised a governmental structure composed of three distinct branches—"a vigorous legislative branch," "a separate and wholly independent executive branch," and "a judicial branch equally independent." * * * The federal judicial power, then, must be exercised by judges who are independent of the executive and the legislature in order to maintain the checks and balances that are crucial to our constitutional structure.

The Framers also understood that a principal benefit of the separation of the judicial power from the legislative and executive powers would be the protection of individual litigants from decisionmakers susceptible to majoritarian pressures. Article III's salary and tenure provisions promote impartial adjudication by placing the judicial power of the United States "in a body of judges insulated from majoritarian pressures and thus able to enforce [federal law] without fear of reprisal or public rebuke." United States v. Raddatz, 447 U.S. 667, 704 (1980) (MARSHALL, J., dissenting). As Alexander Hamilton observed, "[t]hat inflexible and uniform adherence to the rights of the constitution and of individuals, which we perceive to be indispensable in the courts of justice can certainly not be expected from judges who hold their offices by a temporary commission." The Federalist No. 78, p. 546. This is so because

> "[i]f the power of making [periodic appointments] was committed either to the Executive or Legislature, there would be danger of an improper complaisance to the branch which possessed it; if to both, there would be an unwillingness to hazard the displeasure of either; if to the People, or to persons chosen by them for the special purpose, there would be too great a disposition to consult popularity, to justify a reliance that nothing would be consulted but the Constitution and the laws." Ibid.

"Next to permanency in office," Hamilton added, "nothing can contribute more to the independence of the Judges than a fixed provision for their support" because "*a power over a man's subsistence amounts to a power over his will.*" Id., at 548 (emphasis in original). * * *

These important functions of Article III are too central to our constitutional scheme to risk their incremental erosion. The exceptions we have recognized for territorial courts, courts martial, and administrative courts were each based on "certain exceptional powers bestowed upon Congress by the Constitution or by historical consensus." *Northern Pipeline*, supra, 458 U.S., at 70 (opinion of BRENNAN, J.). Here, however, there is no equally forceful reason to extend further these exceptions to situations that are distinguishable from existing precedents. Cf. Currie, Bankruptcy Judges and the Independent Judiciary, 16 Creighton L.Rev. 441, 445 (1983). The Court, however, engages in just such an extension. By sanctioning the adjudication of state-law counterclaims by a federal administrative agency, the Court far exceeds the analytic framework of our precedents.

More than a century ago, we recognized that Congress may not "withdraw from [Article III] judicial cognizance any matter *which, from its nature, is the subject of a suit at the common law, or in equity, or admiralty.*" *Murray's Lessee*, 18 How., at 284 (emphasis added). More recently, in *Northern Pipeline*, supra, the view of a majority of the Court that the breach-of-contract and misrepresentation claims at issue in that case lay "at the core of the historically recognized judicial power," and were "the stuff of the traditional actions at common law tried by the courts at Westminster in 1789," contributed significantly to the Court's conclusion that the bankruptcy courts could not constitutionally adjudicate Northern Pipeline's common-law claims. In the instant case, the Court lightly discards both history and our precedents. The Court attempts to support the substantial alteration it works today in our

Article III jurisprudence by pointing, *inter alia*, to legislative convenience; to the fact that Congress does not altogether eliminate federal court jurisdiction over ancillary state-law counterclaims; and to Schor's "consent" to CFTC adjudication of ContiCommodity's counterclaims.* In my view, the Court's effort fails.

II

The Court states that in reviewing Article III challenges, one of several factors we have taken into account is "the concerns that drove Congress to depart from the requirements of Article III." The Court identifies the desire of Congress "to create an inexpensive and expeditious alternative forum through which customers could enforce the provisions of the CEA against professional brokers" as the motivating congressional concern here. The Court further states that "[i]t was only to ensure the effectiveness of this scheme that Congress authorized the CFTC to assert jurisdiction over common-law counterclaims[;] ... absent the CFTC's exercise of that authority, the purposes of the reparations procedure would have been confounded." Were we to hold that the CFTC's authority to decide common-law counterclaims offends Article III, the Court declares, "it is clear that we would 'defeat the obvious purpose of the legislation.'" Article III, the Court concludes, does not "compe[l] this degree of prophylaxis."

I disagree—Article III's prophylactic protections were intended to prevent just this sort of abdication to claims of legislative convenience. The Court requires that the legislative interest in convenience and efficiency be weighed against the competing interest in judicial independence. In doing so, the Court pits an interest the benefits of which are immediate, concrete, and easily understood against one, the benefits of which are almost entirely prophylactic, and thus often seem remote and not worth the cost in any single case. Thus, while this balancing creates the illusion of objectivity and ineluctability, in fact the result was foreordained, because the balance is weighted against judicial independence. See Redish, Legislative Courts, Administrative Agencies, and the Northern Pipeline Decision, 1983 Duke L.J. 197, 221–222. The danger of the Court's balancing approach is, of course, that as individual cases accumulate in which the Court finds that the short-term benefits of efficiency outweigh the long-term benefits of judicial independence, the protections of Article III will be eviscerated.

Perhaps the resolution of reparations claims such as respondent's may be accomplished more conveniently under the Court's decision than

* The Court also rests its holding on the fact that Congress has not assigned the same sweeping judicial powers to the CFTC that it had assigned to the bankruptcy courts under the Bankruptcy Act of 1978 and that we held violated Article III in Northern Pipeline Co. v. Marathon Pipe Line Co., 458 U.S. 50 (1982). While I agree with the Court that the grant of judicial authority to the CFTC is significantly narrower in scope than the grant to the bankruptcy courts under the 1978 Act, in my view, that difference does not suffice to cure the constitutional defects raised by the grant of authority over state-law counterclaims to the CFTC.

under my approach, but the Framers foreswore this sort of convenience in order to preserve freedom. * * *

* * *

III

According to the Court, the intrusion into the province of the federal judiciary caused by the CFTC's authority to adjudicate state-law counterclaims is insignificant, both because the CFTC *shares* in, rather than displaces, federal district court jurisdiction over these claims and because only a very narrow class of state-law issues are involved. The "sharing" justification fails under the reasoning used by the Court to support the CFTC's authority. If the administrative reparations proceeding is so much more convenient and efficient than litigation in federal district court that abrogation of Article III's commands is warranted, it seems to me that complainants would rarely, if ever, choose to go to district court in the first instance. Thus, any "sharing" of jurisdiction is more illusory than real.

More importantly, the Court, in emphasizing that *this case* will permit solely a narrow class of state-law claims to be decided by a non-Article III court, ignores the fact that it establishes a broad principle. The decision today may authorize the administrative adjudication only of state-law claims that stem from the same transaction or set of facts that allow the customer of a professional commodity broker to initiate reparations proceedings before the CFTC, but the *reasoning* of this decision strongly suggests that, given "legislative necessity" and party consent, any federal agency may decide state-law issues that are ancillary to federal issues within the agency's jurisdiction. Thus, while in this case "the magnitude of intrusion on the judicial branch" may conceivably be characterized as *"de minimis,"* the potential impact of the Court's decision on federal court jurisdiction is substantial. The Court dismisses warnings about the dangers of its approach, asserting simply that it does not fear the slippery slope, and that this case does not involve the creation by Congress of a "phalanx of non-Article III tribunals equipped to handle the entire business of the Article III courts." A healthy respect for the precipice on which we stand is warranted, however, for this reason: Congress can seriously impair Article III's structural and individual protections without assigning away "the *entire* business of the Article III courts." It can do so by *diluting* the judicial power of the federal courts. And, contrary to the Court's intimations, dilution of judicial power operates to impair the protections of Article III regardless of whether Congress acted with the "good intention" of providing a more efficient dispute resolution system or with the "bad intention" of strengthening the Legislative Branch at the expense of the judiciary.

IV

The Court's reliance on Schor's "consent" to a non-Article III tribunal is also misplaced. The Court erroneously suggests that there is a clear division between the separation of powers and the impartial adjudication functions of Article III. The Court identifies Article III's structural, or separation of powers, function as preservation of the judiciary's domain from encroachment by another branch. The Court identifies the impartial adjudication function as the protection afforded by Article III to individual litigants against judges who may be dominated by other branches of government.

In my view, the structural and individual interests served by Article III are inseparable. The potential exists for individual litigants to be deprived of impartial decisionmakers only where federal officials who exercise judicial power are susceptible to congressional and executive pressure. That is, individual litigants may be harmed by the assignment of judicial power to non-Article III federal tribunals only where the Legislative or Executive Branches have encroached upon judicial authority and have thus threatened the separation of powers. The Court correctly recognizes that to the extent that Article III's structural concerns are implicated by a grant of judicial power to a non-Article III tribunal, "the parties cannot by consent cure the constitutional difficulty for the same reason that the parties by consent cannot confer on federal courts subject-matter jurisdiction beyond the limitations imposed by Article III, § 2." Because the individual and structural interests served by Article III are coextensive, I do not believe that a litigant may ever waive his right to an Article III tribunal where one is constitutionally required. In other words, consent is irrelevant to Article III analysis.

V

Our Constitution unambiguously enunciates a fundamental principle—that the "judicial power of the United States" be reposed in an independent judiciary. It is our obligation zealously to guard that independence so that our tripartite system of government remains strong and that individuals continue to be protected against decisionmakers subject to majoritarian pressures. Unfortunately, today the Court forsakes that obligation for expediency. I dissent.

Notes

1. What is left of Justice Brennan's *Northern Pipeline* analysis after this decision? Would it be reasonable to conclude that Justice White's balancing test is now the governing standard? See J. Pfander, Principles of Federal Jurisdiction 312 (2006): "With its retreat from the categorical rigidity of *Northern Pipeline*, *CFTC v. Schor* signals the advent of a balancing methodology that may tend to validate new Article I tribunals. A variety of factors will be included in the balance, including the individual's interest in an Article III forum and the threat posed to the judiciary's institutional role. So long as Congress acted for understandable reasons and did not act to undermine judicial independence, new legislation should raise few red flags." Should it matter that Congress's goal was not to undermine judicial independence?

2. What are Justice Brennan's criticisms of Justice White's balancing test? Are they persuasive?

3. Recall that in *Northern Pipeline,* Justice Brennan concluded that administrative agencies could adjudicate matters falling within Article III, because they served as "adjuncts" to the Article III courts. Could that reasoning have been used to justify the practice challenged in *Schor*? Why do you think Justice Brennan does not recognize the theory's applicability here?

4. What is Justice O'Connor's position on waiver of the Article III protection? Is it persuasive?

5. Exactly what is the "federalism" argument employed to justify the required use of Article III courts here? Is the argument persuasive? What is Justice O'Connor's response to this argument?

6. In Freytag v. Commissioner of Internal Revenue, 501 U.S. 868 (1991), the Supreme Court held that the Tax Court, though not an Article III court, constituted a "Court":

> The text of the Clause does not limit "the Courts of Law" to those courts established under Article III of the Constitution. * * * Congress' consistent interpretation of the Appointments Clause evinces a clear congressional understanding that Article I courts could be given the power to appoint.

Id. at 888, 890. The Court noted that "[o]ur cases involving non-Article III tribunals have held that these courts exercise the judicial power of the United States." Id. at 889.

In a separate opinion concurring in the judgment, Justice Scalia rejected the Court's view that the Tax Court is a "Court[] of Law" for purposes of the appointment clause. He believed that this reference in the appointments clause must have been intended to be confined to Article III courts, because "[t]he Framers contemplated no other national judicial tribunals." Moreover, he argued, this limitation "faithfully implement[ed] a considered political theory for the appointment of officers." "Even if legislators could not appoint themselves, they would be inclined to appoint their friends and supporters." To avoid the threat of "[i]nvasion by the legislature," the appointment power was given to members of the other branches, insulated from congressional pressure in ways that legislative courts are not. Justice Scalia ultimately concluded, however, that the Chief Judge of the Tax Court could be given the power of appointment, because he is one of "the Heads of Departments." Does this conclusion in any way undermine his reasoning in refusing to include the Tax Court as a Court of Law?

7. In Granfinanciera, S.A. v. Nordberg, 492 U.S. 33 (1989), the Court held that one who is sued by a trustee in bankruptcy for the fraudulent transfer of money, who has not submitted a claim against the bankrupt estate, possesses a constitutional right to jury trial. The trustee's cause of action involves a "private right" and is legal, not equitable. Justice Brennan, writing for the majority, offered this explanation of the "public rights" concept:

> In our most recent discussion of the "public rights" doctrine * * * we rejected the view that "a matter of public rights must at a minimum arise between the government and others." *Northern Pipeline Construc-*

tion Co. We held instead, that the federal government need not be a party for a case to revolve around "public rights". The crucial question, in cases not involving the federal government, is whether "Congress, acting for a valid legislative purpose * * *, [has] create[d] a seemingly 'private' right that is so closely integrated into a public regulatory scheme as to be a matter appropriate for agency resolution with limited involvement by the Article III judiciary." If a statutory right is not closely intertwined with a federal regulatory program Congress has power to enact, and if that right neither belongs to nor exists against the federal government, then it must be adjudicated by an Article III court. 492 U.S. at 54–55.

Granfinanciera is the aberration rather than the rule: the Court has generally upheld congressional denials of jury trials in cases heard by Article I courts. For a critique of this line of cases, see Redish & LaFave, *Seventh Amendment Right to Jury Trial in Non–Article III Proceedings: A Study in Dysfunctional Constitutional Theory*, 4 Wm. & Mary Bill of Rights J. 407 (1995). On the same issue, see Sward, *Legislative Courts, Article III and the Seventh Amendment*, 77 N.C.L.Rev. 1037 (1999).

8. A modern controversy implicating *Schor* involves the legislatively prescribed method of adjudication of certain disputes under the North American Free Trade Agreement (NAFTA). See Boyer, *Article III, The Foreign Relations Power, and the Binational Panel System of NAFTA*, 13 Int'l Tax & Bus.Law 101 (1996). The agreement creates a binational panel review system. according to Boyer, "[t]he principal purpose of the binational panel system is to replace domestic judicial review of antidumping and countervailing duty claims in cases involving NAFTA Parties." When invoked, the panels have full authority under NAFTA to review final determinations of antidumping claims by the competent investigating authority. United States law prohibits any judicial review on any question of law or fact where panel review has been requested. NAFTA Implementation Act, Pub. L. No. 103–182, 107 Stat. 2057, § 411(4)(c) (1993), amending 19 U.S.C.A. § 1516a(g)(2). Panelists are private individuals with a general familiarity with international trade law. Quite obviously, the panelists lack the independence protections of Article III. Do such panels violate Article III, pursuant to *Schor*? For the view that the panels survive *Schor*'s balancing test, see Boyer, 13 Int'l Tax & Bus.Law 101, supra. See also Metropoulos, *Constitutional Dimensions of the North American Free Trade Agreement*, 27 Cornell Int'l L.J. 141 (1994).

Chapter 4

RECURRING THEMES IN JUDICIAL FEDERALISM

EMPLOYERS ASS'N INC. v. UNITED STEELWORKERS OF AMERICA

United States District Court, District of Minnesota, 1992.
803 F.Supp. 1558.

ROSENBAUM, District Judge.

Minnesota's Striker Replacement Law, Minn.Stat. § 179.12(9) ("Striker Replacement Law" or "Act"), makes it an unfair labor practice, and an unlawful act, for an employer to hire, or threaten to hire, permanent replacement workers in the event of a lockout by an employer or during a strike by employees. The plaintiff claims that the Act is preempted by federal labor law, and therefore contravenes the Supremacy Clause of the United States Constitution, U.S. Const. art. VI, cl. 2.

Before the Court are plaintiff's motion for summary judgment and defendant's cross motion for dismissal. The plaintiff seeks a declaratory judgment finding Minnesota's Striker Replacement Law unconstitutional. The defendant contends that there is no justiciable case or controversy between the parties and, as a result, this Court lacks jurisdiction.

Briefs were submitted, and oral argument was heard on June 25, 1992. For the reasons set forth below, the Court finds that this case presents a justiciable controversy. The Court further holds that Minnesota's Striker Replacement Law is preempted by federal labor law. As a result, the Court finds the Act unconstitutional under the Supremacy Clause.

BACKGROUND

Plaintiff Employers Association, Inc. ("the Association"), is a Minnesota-incorporated membership organization consisting of more than 1,250 Minnesota employers. The Association provides labor relations specialists who assist over 200 of its members in the collective bargaining process throughout Minnesota. The Association and its member employers are "employers" as defined by the National Labor Relations Act (NLRA), 29 U.S.C. § 152(2), and the Minnesota Labor Relations Act (MLRA), Minn.Stat. § 179.01(3).

Defendant United Steelworkers of America ("USWA" or "Union") is a labor organization, as defined by the NLRA, 29 U.S.C. § 152(5), and the MLRA, Minn.Stat. § 179.01(6). The USWA is the exclusive bargaining representative of, and has bargained for, a number of plaintiff's members' employees. Notwithstanding the USWA's protestations to the contrary, there is no question that these parties will negotiate in the future.

The State of Minnesota ("the State") has intervened in this action to defend the constitutionality of the Striker Replacement Law, pursuant to Rule 24(a), Federal Rules of Civil Procedure.

ANALYSIS

A. The Striker Replacement Law

The striker replacement bill was passed by the 1991 Minnesota State legislature as an amendment to the Minnesota Labor Relations Act, Minn.Stat. §§ 179.01–179.17. The Striker Replacement Law provides:

> It is an unfair labor practice for an employer . . .
>
> (9) To grant or offer to grant the status of permanent replacement employee to a person for performing bargaining unit work for an employer during a lockout of employees in a labor organization or during a strike of employees in a labor organization authorized by a representative of employees. . . .

Minn.Stat. § 179.12(9) (1991).

Under the terms of the Act, if an employer hires or threatens to hire permanent replacement workers, a union may seek a temporary or permanent injunction in state court to enjoin the unfair labor practice. Id. § 179.14. An employer who violates the Striker Replacement Law is then precluded from exercising its own remedies which would otherwise be available under the MLRA. These remedies include the right to bring an injunction action in state court with respect to matters arising out of a labor dispute. Id. § 179.15.[6]

B. Justiciability

Plaintiff seeks a declaratory judgment that the Striker Replacement Law is preempted by federal labor law, as defined by the Supreme Court in Lodge 76, Int'l Ass'n of Machinists & Aerospace Workers, AFL–CIO v. Wisconsin Employment Relations Comm'n, 427 U.S. 132, 146 (1976)

---

6. The Act also declares that a violation of the Striker Replacement Law is an "unlawful act" under the MLRA. Id. § 179.12(10). * * * The violation of the Striker Replacement Law could well result in a misdemeanor prosecution * * *.

("*Machinists*"), and San Diego Building Trades Council v. Garmon, 359 U.S. 236 (1959) ("*Garmon*").

* * *

It is settled that one of the economic weapons available to an employer is the right to hire permanent replacement workers in the event of an economic strike. Belknap, Inc. v. Hale, 463 U.S. 491, 500 (1983); NLRB v. Mackay Radio & Telegraph Co., 304 U.S. 333, 347 (1938). "The presence of economic weapons *in reserve* and their actual exercise on occasion by the parties, is part and parcel of the system that the Wagner and Taft Hartley Acts have recognized." NLRB v. Insurance Agents' Int'l Union, AFL–CIO, 361 U.S. 477, 489 (1960) (emphasis added). The enactment of the Striker Replacement Law has removed this weapon from the plaintiff's bargaining arsenal, affecting the subtle balance established by Congress. This subtle but substantial shift in bargaining positions is neither hypothetical nor abstract. This material alteration of the collective bargaining relationship obviates any need to await a strike and actual invocation of the law.

* * *

D.   Preemption

The Supreme Court has enunciated two distinct preemption principles which define the "broadly pre-emptive scope of the NLRA...." Int'l Longshoremen's Ass'n, AFL–CIO v. Davis, 476 U.S. 380, 389 (1986). Under the first of these preemption principles, states are prohibited from regulating any "activity that the NLRA protects, prohibits or arguably protects or prohibits." *Garmon*, 359 U.S. at 236.[8] Under this so-called *Garmon* preemption principle, state law regulating conduct which is arguably protected or prohibited by the NLRA "must yield to the exclusive primary competence of the [National Labor Relations] Board" (NLRB). Id. at 245. "The *Garmon* rule is intended to preclude state interference with the NLRB's interpretation and active enforcement of the integrated scheme of regulation established by the NLRA." Golden State Transit Corp. v. City of Los Angeles, 475 U.S. 608, 613 (1986).

The *Garmon* court also articulated two limited exceptions to the broadly preemptive power of the NLRA. Under these exceptions, states may regulate activity which is only a "peripheral concern" of the NLRA, or they may regulate activity which "touch[es] interests ... deeply rooted in local feeling and responsibility." *Garmon*, 359 U.S. at 243–244.

In contrast to the *Garmon* rule, which prevents diminution of the NLRB's authority, the second preemption principle, the so-called *Machinists* rule, concerns those areas which Congress intended to leave "unrestricted by *any* governmental power to regulate." *Machinists*, 427

---

8. Clearly, where state law regulates conduct which is actually protected or prohibited by federal labor law, such direct conflict will result in preemption of the state law. Brown v. Hotel & Restaurant Employees & Bartenders, 468 U.S. 491, 503 (1984).

U.S. at 140 (emphasis in original). When it enacted the NLRA, Congress necessarily chose to regulate some aspects of labor activities and to leave others "to be controlled by the free play of economic forces." NLRB v. Nash–Finch Co., 404 U.S. 138, 144 (1971). Under this preemption principle, states are prohibited from regulating the self-help, economic weapons which fall into the "area of labor combat." *Machinists*, 427 U.S. at 146. "Congress meant that these activities, whether of employer or employees, were not to be regulable by States any more than by the NLRB...." Id. 427 U.S. at 149. "[B]oth [the NLRB and the States] are without authority to attempt to 'introduce some standard of properly balanced bargaining power' ... or to define 'what economic sanctions might be permitted negotiating parties in an' 'ideal' or 'balanced state of collective bargaining.' " *Machinists,* 427 U.S. at 150.

Congress's prohibition of specific economic weapons, and concomitant unwillingness to regulate others, was interpreted by the *Machinists* court as an intentional balancing of the conflicting interests of the union, the employees, the employer, and the community. The *Machinists* court concluded that "the exercise of plenary state authority to curtail or entirely prohibit self-help would frustrate effective implementation of the Act's processes." Id. at 148.

Plaintiff contends that the Striker Replacement Law raises preemption issues under both *Machinists* and *Garmon*. Plaintiff then argues that the Act cannot be upheld under *Garmon*'s "local interest" exception. In response, the defendant argues that neither *Garmon* nor *Machinists* is applicable. Rather, the defendant urges the Court to apply a few recent Supreme Court holdings which, in its view, disclose a strong presumption against federal preemption.

The State then advances the novel argument that the Act falls within *Garmon*'s "local interest" exception because it actually regulates the legal relationship between the permanent replacement workers and their employers. * * * Finally, the USWA argues that the Act falls within the "local interest exception" because the law was primarily intended to abate picket line violence. The USWA cites portions of the Act's legislative history to support the contention that the law was passed to address Minnesota's concern with strike-related misconduct and violence.

* * *

E. The Constitutionality of the Act

The Court finds that Minnesota's Striker Replacement Law, is unconstitutional under the *Machinists* preemption doctrine.

It is well-established federal labor law that an employer may hire permanent replacement workers during an economic strike by employees. Trans World Airlines, Inc. v. Independent Federation of Flight Attendants, 489 U.S. 426, 432–33 (1989); *Belknap,* 463 U.S. at 500; NLRB v. Erie Resistor Corp., 373 U.S. 221, 232 (1963); *Mackay Radio,*

304 U.S. at 333.[9] Minnesota's Striker Replacement Law flatly prohibits the employer's exercise of this well-established right by making the actual hiring of permanent replacements, or even the threat of doing so, an unfair labor practice under the MLRA.

The Act, then, forbids actions which federal labor law clearly permit. Therefore, the Court finds that the Striker Replacement Law is contrary to federal labor law and is preempted. The Act seeks to deny to an employer its protected right to "resort to economic weapons should more peaceful measures not avail." *Machinists*, 427 U.S. at 147. Because the Striker Replacement Law "add[s] to an employer's federal legal obligations in collective bargaining," the law is unconstitutional under the *Machinists* preemption doctrine. *Machinists*, 427 U.S. at 147.

* * *

Finally, the Court rejects the two arguments advanced by the State and the USWA that the Striker Replacement Law falls into the "local interest" exception. The State argues, first, that, since *Machinists*, the Court has carved out an area between individual employees and the employer where a state may engage in labor regulation. See Malone v. White Motor Corp., 435 U.S. 497 (1978); Metropolitan Life Ins. Co. v. Massachusetts, 471 U.S. 724 (1985); Fort Halifax Packing Co. v. Coyne, 482 U.S. 1 (1987); *Belknap*, 463 U.S. at 491. Secondly, the USWA contends that the "local interest" exception established in *Garmon* directly applies because Minnesota has a compelling state interest in preventing strike-related misconduct and violence. In its view, this compelling state interest arises when strikers face the loss of their jobs to permanent replacement workers. The Court addresses each argument in turn.

First, the Court cannot find that the Striker Replacement Law was intended to regulate the relationship between the individual employees and the employer. The present case is clearly distinguishable from those cited by the State. In *Malone*, the Court held that Minnesota's Private Pension Benefit Protection Act was not preempted by the NLRA. 435 U.S. at 512,. The Court found that Congress did not intend to remove bargained-for pension plans from substantive state or federal regulation. Id. In *Metropolitan Life*, the Court found no preemption of a Massachusetts statute which required that minimum mental health benefits be provided under certain health insurance policies. 471 U.S. at 758. In *Fort Halifax*, the Court held that the NLRA did not preempt a Maine statute which required employers to provide their employees with a one-time severance payment in the event of a plant closing. 482 U.S. at 23. In all three cases, the Court reasoned that Congress did not intend to exclude unionized workers from receiving the substantive benefits of a state's

---

9. The State has advanced the thesis that the underlying rationale of NLRB v. Mackay Radio & Telegraph Co., 304 U.S. 333 (1938), the first case to permit the hiring of permanent replacement workers, is in error. The State then suggests that this error has compounded itself over 50 years of Supreme Court precedent. Notwithstanding the academic theory suggesting "this error," this Court will follow Mackay Radio and its unvarying progeny.

minimum labor standards. This Court, granting a full and fair reading to
Minnesota's Striker Replacement Law, cannot find that this law is
designed to address minimum labor standards and state-regulated benefits.

The Court further finds that the precepts underlying *Belknap* are
inapplicable. In *Belknap,* the Court held that the NLRA did not preempt
a state court action brought by permanent strike replacements for
misrepresentation and breach of contract. The permanent replacements
sued when they were displaced to accommodate returning strikers. The
Court reasoned that permitting the state court action would not interfere with the carefully balanced relationship between the union and the
employer but, rather, would serve to protect the rights of innocent third
parties. Id. at 501. This Court has already rejected the State's argument
that the Minnesota Striker Replacement Law is directed toward the
relationship between permanent replacements and the employer. The
Act directly regulates the relationship between union members and the
employer. This case, therefore, is clearly distinguishable from *Belknap,*
which concerned the employer's relationship to third parties. In sum, the
Court cannot construe the Striker Replacement Law so that it falls into
those narrowly defined areas of state regulation which lie beyond the
Machinists doctrine.

Similarly, the Court rejects the USWA's argument that the law falls
within the *Garmon* "local interest" exception. The USWA contends that
the State has a legitimate interest in preventing picket-line violence and
promoting peaceful strike settlements. The legislative history makes
clear that the Act was motivated, at least in part, by precisely this
interest. The Court, of course, does not oppose such a goal.

The Court, however, cannot uphold the means by which the State
has attempted to achieve this laudable purpose. The Striker Replacement Law does not selectively address the right of an employee, an
employer, or the State to redress picket line violence. Instead, the State's
blanket prohibition of hiring permanent striker replacements directly
interferes with an employer's federally protected right to do so. The
State's attempt to avoid picket line violence by a blunderbuss prohibition
of a practice which has been protected by over fifty years of Supreme
Court precedent cannot stand. This is not a State adjustment of a locally
sensitive relationship. It is instead a reweaving of a critical thread in the
fabric of labor-management relations. Under the broadly preemptive
power of the NLRA, the State is simply without authority to introduce
its own standard of "properly balanced bargaining power." *Machinists,*
427 U.S. at 149–150. While Minnesota is certainly entitled to be concerned over picket line safety, this concern is too generalized to permit
the State to unilaterally redefine federal labor law.

* * *

Plaintiff's motion for summary judgment, seeking a declaratory
judgment finding Minnesota's Striker Replacement Law unconstitutional, is granted.

State SC overturned statute as preempted

MIDWEST MOTOR EXPRESS, INC. v. INTERNATIONAL BROTHERHOOD OF TEAMSTERS

Minnesota District Court, Second Judicial District, Ramsey County, 1992.
139 L.R.R.M. 2563.

COHEN, JUDGE.

FACTS

Plaintiff is a common carrier with facilities located at 2778 Cleveland Avenue North, Roseville, Minnesota. Defendant is the exclusive collective bargaining representative of certain employees of the plaintiff. Plaintiff and Defendant were parties to a collective bargaining agreement covering the bargaining unit employees at Roseville. On August 12, 1991, Defendant authorized and commenced a strike at the Roseville Facility. The strike was caused by failure of the parties to agree on a new collective bargaining agreement.

1991 Minn.Laws ch. 239, § 1, codified at Minn.Stat. § 179.12(9) makes it an unfair labor practice for an employer:

> [t]o grant or offer to grant the status of permanent replacement employee to a person for performing bargaining unit work for an employer during a lockout of employees in a labor organization or during a strike of employees in a labor organization authorized by a representative of employees.

Plaintiff has indicated an intention to hire permanent replacement workers at its Minnesota facilities if warranted by economic conditions. Plaintiff states that it has not yet hired any permanent replacements. Plaintiff's collective bargaining strategy has been adversely affected because of § 179.12(9). Plaintiff states that if it hires permanent replacements, it would subject itself to the loss of injunctive relief.

* * *

PREEMPTION

Does Fed law preempt state law?

Is the Minnesota Striker Replacement Legislation, Minn.Stat. § 179.12(9) which makes it unlawful for an employer to hire permanent strike replacements, preempted by the Federal National Labor Relations Act (NLRA), which permits but does not protect this practice; therefore making the statute unconstitutional?

HELD

Based upon a review of pertinent decisions of federal and state law this court concludes that the state statute is not preempted.

DISCUSSION

In San Diego Bldg. Trades Council v. Garmon, 359 U.S. 236, 244 (1959), the U.S. Supreme Court recognized federal preemption of state and local regulation that is actually or arguably either protected or prohibited by the NLRA. The exceptions to preemption are:

    1.   A State may regulate where the arguably protected or prohibited activity is merely a peripheral concern of the NLRA, or,

    2.   A State may regulate in this area if the conduct is so deeply rooted in local feeling and responsibility that it cannot be assumed that Congress intended to preempt the application of State law. Id. at 244.

Exception [margin note]

The second preemption doctrine is set forth in Lodge 76, Int'l. Assoc. of Machinists & Aerospace Workers v. Wisconsin Emp. Comm., 427 U.S. 132. The Court held that state and local governments are prohibited from regulating activities which congress intended to be left unrestricted by any governmental power. Id. at 140.

Garmon does not require preemption in the instant case. The hiring of permanent replacements is not prohibited in the NLRA. The NLRA does not confer to the employer a protectable right to hire permanent replacements but merely permits the practice. In *Garmon* the Minnesota statute is sustained under the compelling local interest exception.

Not Prohibited [margin note]

COMPELLING LOCAL INTEREST EXCEPTION

The Minnesota Legislature had strong reasons for the passage of Minn.Stat. § 179.12(9). In remarks before the Senate Employment Committee on March 25, 1991, Senator Chmielewski, sponsor of the bill, explained among other things, "What we're trying to do is restore the balance in the collective bargaining system, and that's what this is all about."

Restore Balance [margin note]

In addition, however, Senator Chmielewski stated, * * * "What this bill deals with is promoting some peaceful resolve to these issues, because what happened at the Hormel, for example, in Austin, and the Greyhound bus strike. A lot of violence happens because the workers are informed they have been permanently replaced, and that's a very big issue ... * * * the violence that occurs—actually shooting and slashing tires, all that kind of violence—you deal with it if you pass this kind of bill. This will not happen again, because strikers know that, in fact, their strike is temporary and they're not going to lose their benefits. They're not going to lose their jobs. When it's over with, they have to restore them back to where they came from."

Peaceful Resolution Prevent Violence [margin note]

Representative Anderson, the chief author of the bill, in testimony before the House Labor Management Relations Committee on February 25, 1991 stated, * * * [The right to hire permanent replacements] "gives the employer an unfair advantage. And so, I see the bill as a bill that will bring stability, more tranquility, more peacefulness to labor turmoil. I think that it will bring about more equity in cases of labor/management strife by giving employees somewhat of an equal opportunity to bring their point of view forth. I also think that it is a safety measure because in many instances when employees go on strike and they are, the

Unfair Advantage [margin note]

employer advertises that their replacements are permanent replacements, it great turmoil on the strike line."

* * *

Based upon legislative history, public safety appears to be a substantial part of the intent of the 1991 Minnesota Legislature in the passage
of § 179.12(9).

* * *

Plaintiff states, at page 16 of the Memorandum, " * * * Indeed, all
during committee hearings on this bill, the topic of safety was scarcely
mentioned. * * *." Plaintiff, again, in its Reply Memorandum at page 7
states, " * * * The comments of the bills' sponsors, Senator Chmielewski and Representative Anderson, leave no room for doubt that the
Minnesota Legislature was consciously seeking to redress what it perceived to be inequities in federal labor policy."

* * *

Plaintiff is dead wrong! The facts are contrary to its position. The
subject of violence on the picket line and in a strike situation was
advanced before legislative committees in strong words. There was
nothing wishy-washy about the language used by Senator Chmielewski.
Representative Anderson was likewise clear that he considered this as a
safety matter.

Minn.Stat. § 179.12(9) is not preempted because the State of Minnesota has a legitimate interest in regulating this area to prevent violence
and to promote the peaceful settlement and negotiating in strike situations.

Accordingly, Minnesota's interest in controlling certain conduct is
balanced against both the interference with the NLRB's ability to
adjudicate controversies committed to it by the NLRA and the risk that
the state will sanction conduct that the NLRA protects. See Belknap,
Inc. v. Hale, 463 U.S. 491 (1983).

Minnesota's regulation no more interferes with the NLRB's jurisdiction or impacts upon federal labor policy than that allowed in *Belknap.*

In *Belknap,* the Supreme Court permitted permanent strike replacements to use state law against the employer for breach of contract and
misrepresentation. Allowing this state court action, profoundly affected
the balance of power and the ability of the employer to hire permanent
strike replacements. The Supreme Court did not find preemption! The
Minnesota Statute in the instant case goes no further. In Minnesota the
public policy issue is prevention of violence on the picket line and during
a strike situation. Its concern is one of public safety.

Thus, *Belknap* supports the proposition that the State has a legitimate interest in legislating in this precise area and that this state
interest is not preempted under the rationale of either *Garmon* or
Machinists.

The *Machinist* doctrine does not compel preemption because the National Labor Relations Act does not, in unmistakably clear language declare that Congress intended this area to be free of state regulation. There is no indication that Congress intended that this conduct of prohibiting the hiring of permanent replacements be preempted and left to the free play of economic forces. The Statute does not deprive the employer of an economic weapon of self-help during a strike. Under Minnesota law the employer is able to hire replacement workers during a strike but simply not able to promise or grant those employees permanent status to the detriment of a striking bargaining unit employee.

[margin note: No indication Congress wanted to b. preconstat regulation]

Notes

1. Note that these two cases, raising exactly the same question, were decided within a few months of each other but reached opposite results. Does the federal trial court or the state trial court do a better job of analyzing United States Supreme Court precedent? Of protecting the supremacy of federal law? Of protecting state interests? Are you surprised by the results?

2. This pair of cases implicates the long-running debate about whether state trial courts are adequate for adjudicating federal questions, often characterized as an issue of whether there is parity between state and federal courts. Both the Supreme Court and scholarly commentators have frequently addressed the issue of parity. You will encounter the Court's views on the subject as you go through this section of the casebook. This chapter is meant as an introduction to this and other recurring issues.

[margin note: ISSUE]

Professor Burt Neuborne first raised the parity question in a 1977 article, *The Myth of Parity*. Commenting on Justice Powell's conclusion, in Stone v. Powell, 428 U.S. 465 (1976) [infra p. 658], that state and federal courts are functionally interchangeable when it comes to protecting constitutional rights, Professor Neuborne wrote:

> Unfortunately, I fear that the parity which Justice Powell celebrated in *Stone* exists only in his understandable wish that it were so. I suggest that the assumption of parity is, at best, a dangerous myth, fostering forum allocation decisions which channel constitutional adjudication under the illusion that state courts will vindicate federally secured constitutional rights as forcefully as would the lower federal courts. At worst, it provides a pretext for funneling federal constitutional decision-making into state court precisely because they are less likely to be receptive to vigorous enforcement of federal constitutional doctrine.

Neuborne, *The Myth of Parity*, 90 Harv.L.Rev. 1105, 1105–06 (1977).

Note that no participants in the parity debate question the good faith of state judges. Instead, Professor Neuborne and others who agree with his conclusions have focused on a number of "institutional" factors which contribute to the state courts' diminished capacity for enforcing federal rights. Other commentators have raised questions about these factors.

Technical Competence. Professor Neuborne suggested that federal trial judges tend to be more technically competent, because the federal bench is both smaller and better paid. "As in any bureaucracy, it is far easier to maintain a high level of quality when appointing a relatively small number of officials than when staffing a huge department." 90 Harv.L.Rev. at 1121. Moreover, Neuborne argued, the constitutionally-mandated appointment process for federal judges helps ensure high quality. An additional argument is that federal judges are more technically competent because their constant exposure to federal questions has led them to develop "a vast expertise in dealing with the intricacies of federal law." M. Redish, Federal Jurisdiction: Tensions in the Allocation of Judicial Power 2 (2d ed. 1989). Are these arguments persuasive? Does greater technical proficiency necessarily yield increased protection for constitutional rights? Erwin Chemerinsky points out that "[j]urists such as Justice Antonin Scalia and Ninth Circuit Judge Alex Kozinski are respected for their brilliance, but they hardly instill confidence that federal courts will protect individual rights more often than their state counterparts." Chemerinsky, *Ending the Parity Debate*, 71 B.U.L.Rev. 593, 599 (1991). Federal judges are often appointed from the ranks of state court judges—do they automatically become more competent when they ascend to the federal bench?

What about the relative caseloads and resources of state and federal judges? See R. Posner, The Federal Courts: Challenge and Reform 37–39 (rev.ed. 1996) (describing different "conditions of employment" of state and federal judges). If federal judges have lower caseloads and greater resources—as they generally do—are they more likely to produce a "better" product? Compare the two striker replacement cases: do you see evidence of more time (and perhaps better law clerks) in Judge Rosenbaum's opinion than in Judge Cohen's?

Psychological Set. Professor Neuborne also suggested that federal judges "often display an enhanced sense of bureaucratic receptivity to the pronouncements of the Supreme Court." Thus, he reasoned, federal judges "appear to recognize an affirmative obligation to carry out and even anticipate the direction of the Supreme Court," while state judges "appear to acknowledge only an obligation not to disobey clearly established law." Neuborne, supra, 90 Harv.L.Rev. at 1124–25. Do the two cases at the beginning of this chapter illustrate these tendencies? Do you agree with Professor Neuborne that the tendencies are likely to be widespread? Federal judges are also, according to Professor Neuborne, "an elite, prestigious, body, drawn primarily from a successful homogeneous socioeducational class—a class strongly imbued with the philosophical values of Locke and Mill (which the Bill of Rights in large measure tracks)." Id. at 1126. Do you see any problems with that argument?

Majoritarian Pressures. The most important factor relied on by those who believe that there is a serious gap between state and federal courts is that many state judges are subject to election or re-election. By virtue of the federal constitutional guarantee of lifetime tenure, however, federal judges are insulated from majoritarian pressures in a way that many of their state counterparts cannot be. "This insulation factor," wrote Neuborne, "explains the historical preference for federal enforcement of controversial constitutional norms." 90 Harv.L.Rev. at 1128. One state tried to reduce the majoritarian pressure on its judges through its code of judicial conduct, which prohibited candidates for judicial offices (including incumbent judges) from announcing their "views on disputed legal or political issues." The

Supreme Court invalidated the prohibition as a violation of candidates' First Amendment rights. Republican Party of Minnesota v. White, 536 U.S. 765 (2002).

Another article describes more bluntly the dangers of allowing state court judges to adjudicate constitutional challenges to state laws: "Imagine, for a moment, that the Chicago Cubs announced that from this point forward, they would hire umpires, unilaterally determine their salaries, and retain unreviewable discretion to fire them at any time. Can anyone imagine that we could trust a call at second base?" Redish, *Judicial Parity, Litigant Choice, and Democratic Theory: A Comment on Federal Jurisdiction and Constitutional Rights*, 36 UCLA L.Rev. 329, 333 (1988). See also Boutrous et al., State Judiciaries and Impartiality: Judging the Judges (1996) (detailing electoral and other pressures on state judges).

In light of the baseball analogy, consider the case of Cincinnati Reds player and manager Pete Rose. In 1989, while he was managing the Reds, Rose was accused of betting on baseball—a charge which, if proven, would likely lead to his permanent banishment from baseball. Baseball Commissioner Bartlett Giamatti—formerly president of Yale University—scheduled a hearing on the charges. Rose obtained a temporary injunction against the hearing from an Ohio state court in Cincinnati. The Ohio judge who issued the injunction was up for re-election the following year. Giamatti immediately removed the case to federal court on diversity grounds. In a hearing before the federal court to determine whether to remand to the state court, counsel for Giamatti argued that federal jurisdiction was necessary:

> In the State Court in Cincinnati, I need not describe Mr. Rose's standing. He is a local hero, perhaps the first citizen of Cincinnati. And Commissioner Giamatti is viewed suspiciously as a foreigner from New York, trapped in an ivory tower, accused of bias by Mr. Rose. Your Honor, this is a textbook example of why diversity jurisdiction was created in the Federal Courts and why it exists to this very day.

Rose v. Giamatti, 721 F.Supp. 906, 910 n. 2 (S.D.Ohio 1989). The federal court refused to remand, but before it could reach the merits of the dispute, "Rose, perhaps recognizing that he stood little chance of prevailing without a hometown advantage, terminated his counterattack and accepted a lifetime ban from baseball." Note, *"Root, Root, Root for the Home Team": Pete Rose, Nominal Parties, and Diversity Jurisdiction*, 66 N.Y.U.L.Rev. 148, 151 (1991). If a state court judge is unable to stand up to a local baseball hero, how likely is he or she to rule against state legislators? To stand up for the rights of unpopular speakers, religious groups, or political activists?

On the majoritarian-pressures argument, does empirical evidence—such as data on state and federal court decisions on constitutional issues—matter? The only empirical studies have reached conflicting results, and in any case may rely on questionable methodologies. See Solimine & Walker, *Constitutional Litigation in Federal and State Courts: An Empirical Analysis of Judicial Parity*, 10 Hastings Constit.L.Q. 213 (1983); Marvell, *The Rationales For Federal Question Jurisdiction: An Empirical Examination of Student Rights Litigation*, 1984 Wisc.L.Rev. 1315; Hellman, *Courting Disaster*, 39 Stan.L.Rev. 297, 313–14 (1986); Chemerinsky, *Parity Reconsidered: Defining A Role for the Federal Judiciary*, 36 UCLA L.Rev. 233, 262–69

(1988); Herman, *Why Parity Matters*, 71 B.U.L.Rev. 651, 658–59 n.29 (1991); Clermont & Eisenberg, *Do Case Outcomes Really Reveal Anything About the Legal System: Win Rates and Removal Jurisdiction*, 83 Cornell L.Rev. 581 (1998); Hanssen, *The Effect of Judicial Institutions on Uncertainty and the Rate of Litigation: The Election versus Appointment of State Judges*, 28 J.Legal Stud. 205 (1999); Gerry, *Parity Revisited: An Empirical Comparison of State and Lower Federal Court Interpretations of* Nollan v. California Coastal Commission, 23 Harv. J.L. & Pub.Pol'y 233 (1999); Solimine, *The Future of Parity*, 46 Wm. & Mary L.Rev. 1457 (2005); see also Pinello, *Linking Party to Judicial Ideology in American Courts: A Meta–Analysis*, 20 Justice Syst. J. 219 (1999) (finding stronger link between party affiliation and judicial ideology among federal judges than among state judges).

Indeed, is the parity debate really an empirical one at all? Doesn't one's view on the question of state court parity depend on *which* constitutional rights are seen as important? Consider the following argument:

> We are told that federal judges will be more receptive to constitutional values than state judges. What is really meant, however, is that federal judges will be more receptive to *some* constitutional values than state judges. And the hidden assumption of the argument is that the Constitution contains only one or two *sorts* of values: typically, those which protect the individual from the power of the state, and those which assure the superiority of federal to state law.

> But the Constitution contains other sorts of values as well. It gives the federal government powers, but also enacts limitations on those powers. *The limitations, too, count as setting forth constitutional values.* Will the federal judge be more sensitive than the state judge in insuring that these limitations are complied with? Whose institutional "set" is likely to make one more sensitive to the values underlying the tenth amendment?

Bator, *The State Courts and Federal Constitutional Litigation*, 22 Wm. & Mary L Rev. 605, 631–32 (1981). Is this a sufficient response to the argument that state court judges, unlike federal judges, are electorally accountable? Why do you think the framers of the Constitution provided for lifetime tenure for federal judges? Does the answer tell you anything about the validity of Professor Bator's arguments?

Professor Ann Althouse offers a different sort of response to the complaint that state court judges are electorally accountable:

> Federal court primatists * * * impugn the state courts for their responsiveness to political pressures. This reaction to state courts is understandable: State courts could not have desegregated the schools or reapportioned state legislatures in the 1960s. But this close connection to local political culture also represents a strength: When that culture includes a respect for rights, rights will have more staying power. The greater security for rights will come not from shoehorning more claims into federal courts but from effectively enlisting the state courts in rights enforcement.

Althouse, *Federal Jurisdiction and the Enforcement of Federal Rights: Can Congress Bring Back the Warren Era?*, 20 Law & Soc.Inquiry 1067, 1087–88

(1995). Does this recognition solve the parity problem? Is Professor Althouse simply offering a Hobson's choice: suffer with the problems of imposing federally-declared rights on hostile states, or take jurisdiction away from the federal courts and let state courts choose to protect no rights at all?

Some commentators have argued that the parity question has changed since Professor Neuborne's 1977 article. These commentators suggest that many years of conservative Republican appointments have made it "unrealistic to assume that federal courts are more likely than state courts to protect constitutional liberties." Chemerinsky, supra, 71 B.U.L.Rev. at 594. Professor William B. Rubenstein concludes as an empirical matter that "gay litigants seeking to establish and vindicate civil rights have generally fared better in state courts than they have in federal courts." Rubenstein, *The Myth of Superiority*, 16 Const. Commentary 599 (1999). See also Althouse, supra, 20 Law & Soc.Inquiry at 1070–71. One can respond that the point is "not so much whether the court will find in favor of the constitutional right, but whether, whatever the decision the court reaches, we can be assured that the decision was reached on the basis of a fair and neutral assessment of law, policy, and facts." Redish, supra, 36 UCLA L.Rev. at 337–38. Do the cases at the beginning of this chapter illustrate this last point? Even leaving aside recent appointments, is the relative competence of state and federal judges likely to be stable over time?

Professor Michael Wells adopts yet another approach to the parity debate. He argues that what is really at stake is not a high constitutional or moral question, but simply both sides competing for an edge in litigation: "The constitutional claimant seeks a forum that not only is constitutionally adequate but also accords her the benefit of the doubt on close questions. The state * * * seeks the benefits that accompany trying the case in the state system." Wells, *Behind the Parity Debate: The Decline of the Legal Process Tradition in the Federal Courts*, 71 B.U.L.Rev. 609, 617 (1991); see also Wells, *Naked Politics, Federal Courts Law, and the Canon of Acceptable Arguments*, 47 Emory L.J. 89 (1998). He condemns most of the debate over parity as mere rhetoric; he suggests that most scholarly arguments are attempts to disguise the fact that both sides are simply seeking a litigation advantage. Does Professor Wells' argument depend on an assumption that state courts are *adequate* to protect federal rights? Isn't that the very question at issue in the parity debate?

3.　Judge Rosenbaum's decision in *Steelworkers* was affirmed by the Eighth Circuit, 32 F.3d 1297 (8th Cir.1994), and Judge Cohen's decision in *Midwest Motor* was affirmed by the Minnesota Court of Appeals (the intermediate appellate court). 494 N.W.2d 895 (Minn.Ct.App.1993). But the Minnesota Supreme Court ultimately reversed the trial court, invalidating the striker-replacement statute as pre-empted. Midwest Motor Express, Inc. v. International Brotherhood of Teamsters, 512 N.W.2d 881 (Minn.1994). Does that fact influence your views on the parity debate? Which state courts should be compared to federal trial courts—state trial courts or state appellate courts? See Neuborne, supra, 90 Harv.L.Rev. at 1118–19 (because of fragility of some rights, and the importance of factfinding processes, state appellate review is not an adequate remedy for state trial court mistakes).

4. Why isn't United States Supreme Court review sufficient to remedy any disparity between state and federal courts? See Redish, supra, 36 UCLA L.Rev. at 336; Sager, *Constitutional Limitations on Congress' Authority to Regulate the Jurisdiction of the Federal Courts*, 95 Harv.L.Rev. 17 (1981); Eisenberg, *Congressional Authority to Restrict Lower Federal Court Jurisdiction*, 83 Yale L.J. 498 (1974).

5. What about the role of juries? Where factual questions are at issue, are there significant differences between state and federal juries? See Lowenfeld, Conflict of Laws: Documentary Materials 565 (1986). To what extent is judicial control of juries relevant? See Woolhandler & Collins, *The Article III Jury*, 87 Va.L.Rev. 587 (2001).

6. The parity question asks whether state courts are adequate fora for resolving federal questions. Another recurring question in judicial federalism—the flip side of the parity dispute—involves the extent to which federal courts should exercise restraint in order to avoid unnecessary interference with state legislative and judicial processes.

Justice Frankfurter was perhaps the primary architect of this aspect of judicial federalism, and his opinions remain among the most eloquent defenses of federal court deference to state processes. Justice Frankfurter—even before he ascended to the bench—believed that the federal courts should, if possible, avoid cases that were likely to "stir political friction inevitable to a conflict between state and national forces." Frankfurter & Landis, *The Business of the Supreme Court at October Term, 1929*, 44 Harv.L.Rev. 1, 59 (1930). For a review of Justice Frankfurter's views on judicial federalism, and his extensive influence on the development of the law, see McManamon, *Felix Frankfurter: The Architect of "Our Federalism,"* 27 Ga.L.Rev. 697 (1993).

Commentators have built on this idea of avoiding friction between state and federal courts. Consider the arguments of Professor Paul Bator:

> The problem of federalism * * * should not be seen in terms of the possible irritation of state judges at being reversed by federal district judges. The crucial issue is the possible damage done to the inner sense of responsibility, to the pride and conscientiousness, of a state judge in doing what is, after all, under the constitutional scheme a part of *his* business: the decision of federal questions properly raised in state litigation.

Bator, *Finality in Criminal Law and Federal Habeas Corpus for State Prisoners*, 76 Harv.L.Rev. 441, 505–06 (1963).

Too much interference not only causes friction, it also may ultimately reduce the power of the federal courts to protect rights: "The increased federalization of claims threatens to cheapen the special nature of federal court jurisdiction by making every state court matter a 'federal case.'" Friedman, *A Revisionist Theory of Abstention*, 88 Mich.L.Rev. 530, 549 (1989). See also A. Bickel, The Least Dangerous Branch (1962); Bator, supra, 76 Harv.L.Rev. at 506 (limits on federal jurisdiction help in "husbanding the intellectual and moral energies and intensities of our judges").

Isn't the key question the extent to which these negative effects of expansive federal jurisdiction are *necessary* to protect constitutional values? Does that question ultimately take us back to the parity debate?

7. Might all these questions be context-dependent? Professor Richard Fallon, in a wide-ranging critique of federal courts jurisprudence, characterizes the field's scholarship and decisionmaking as dominated by two conflicting ideological models: (1) The "Federalist" model, under which "states emerge as sovereign entities against which federal courts should exercise only limited powers"; and (2) the "Nationalist" model, which "minimizes the significance of state sovereignty in comparison to national interests and that posits a constitutional and statutory preference for federal over state courts as the guarantors of federal rights." Fallon argues that neither model should dominate federal jurisdictional analysis—answers should be derived from examinations of particular contexts rather than general assumptions about the relationship between state and federal courts. See Fallon, *The Ideologies of Federal Courts Law,* 74 Va.L.Rev. 1141, 1143–44 (1988). Professor Wells, on the other hand, responds that a " 'crudely political' view of judicial motivation yields a more plausible and more powerful account of most judges' behavior than does Fallon's thesis." Wells, *Rhetoric and Reality in the Law of Federal Courts: Professor Fallon's Faulty Premise,* 6 Const. Comm. 367, 368 (1989). See also Wells, supra, 71 B.U.L.Rev. at 644 ("One cannot fully and accurately explain the contemporary law of federal courts, or argue persuasively about what the rules should be and why, without acknowledging the systematic disparity between federal and state judges and the importance of substantive considerations in the resolution of jurisdictional issues.").

In this context, consider also the arguments of Professor Barry Friedman: "[N]ot every case falling within congressionally granted jurisdiction presents the concerns that motivated Congress to grant or expand federal jurisdiction." Friedman, supra, 88 Mich.L.Rev. at 547. He goes on to argue that in cases in which "legitimate state interests are present * * * and the case can be resolved in state court without threatening federal interests— either because no important federal interest is at stake or because direct review by the Supreme Court is adequate to the task," there is no need for unflagging insistence on federal jurisdiction. Id. at 550. How should we decide which cases "can be resolved in state court without threatening federal interests"? Into which category do the striker-replacement cases at the beginning of this chapter fall? Does your answer depend on having read the cases—or could you allocate the pre-emption question to state or federal court before knowing how each court decided?

8. Professors Robert Cover and Alexander Aleinikoff offer an alternative view on the recurring question of the appropriate division of jurisdiction between state and federal courts. They argue in favor of "dialectical federalism," a sort of ongoing dialogue between state and federal courts about constitutional rights. Cover & Aleinikoff, *Dialectical Federalism: Habeas Corpus and The Court,* 86 Yale L.J. 1035 (1977). See also Schapiro, *Interjurisdictional Enforcement of Rights in a Post-*Erie* World,* 46 Wm. & Mary L.Rev. 1399 (2005); Resnik, *History, Jurisdiction, and the Federal Courts: Changing Contexts, Selective Memories, and Limited Imagination,* 98 W.Va. L.Rev. 171 (1995).

In this dialogue, "state and federal courts [are] required both to speak and listen as equals." Cover & Aleinikoff, supra, 86 Yale L.J. at 1036. Professors Cover and Aleinikoff suggest that their model of dialogue "obtains whenever jurisdictional rules link state and federal tribunals and create areas of overlap in which neither system can claim total sovereignty." Id. at 1048. Do you think that any of the other participants in the parity debate disagree with the idea of dialogue? See M. Redish, Federal Jurisdiction: Tensions in the Allocation of Judicial Power 2 n.8 (1989) ("even a system premised on the primary role of federal courts as expositors of federal law will not totally remove state court opportunity to adjudicate issues of federal law, particularly in defense to state prosecutions"); Bator, supra, 22 Wm. & Mary L.Rev. at 624 ("no matter where we draw the line, it is virtually inevitable that the state courts will in fact continue to be asked to play a substantial role in the formulation and application of federal constitutional principles"). Isn't the devil in the details?

9. Keep all these debates in mind as you read through the cases in Chapters Five through Twelve: the cases will raise and reraise—and resolve in different ways—the questions about parity and judicial federalism.

For further general discussion of these recurring issues of judicial federalism, in addition to the articles cited in this chapter, see Schapiro, *Polyphonic Federalism: State Constitutions in the Federal Courts*, 87 Cal. L.Rev. 1409 (1999); Lee, *On the Received Wisdom in Federal Courts*, 147 U.Pa.L.Rev. 1111 (1999); Resnik, *Afterword: Federalism's Options*, 14 Yale L. & Pol'y Rev. 465 (1996); Rehnquist, *Taking Comity Seriously: How to Neutralize the Abstention Doctrine*, 46 Stan.L.Rev. 1049 (1994); Redish, *Reassessing the Allocation of Judicial Business Between State and Federal Courts: Federal Jurisdiction and "The Martian Chronicles,"* 78 Va.L.Rev. 1769 (1992); Solimine & Walker, *State Court Protection of Federal Constitutional Rights*, 12 Harv.J.L. & Pub.Pol'y 127 (1989); Collins, *Foreword: The Once "New Judicial Federalism" & Its Critics*, 64 Wash.L.Rev. 5 (1989); Wells, *Is Disparity A Problem?*, 22 Ga.L.Rev. 283 (1988); Resnik, *The Mythic Meaning of Article III Courts*, 56 U.Colo.L.Rev. 581 (1985); Zeigler, *Federal Court Reform of State Criminal Justice Systems: A Reassessment of the Younger Doctrine from a Modern Perspective*, 19 U.C.Davis L.Rev. 31 (1985); O'Connor, *Trends in the Relationship Between the Federal and State Courts From the Perspective of a State Court Judge*, 22 Wm. & Mary L. Rev. 801 (1981); Weinberg, *The New Judicial Federalism*, 29 Stan.L.Rev. 1192 (1977). For an interesting discussion of the relationship between these questions and questions regarding the jurisdiction and authority of international courts, see Young, *Institutional Settlement in a Globalizing Judicial System*, 54 Duke L.J. 1143 (2005).

Chapter 5

STATE COURTS AND FEDERAL POWER

§ 1. STATE COURT POWER TO ENFORCE FEDERAL LAW

CHARLES DOWD BOX CO., INC. v. COURTNEY, 368 U.S. 502 (1962): The question before the Court was whether jurisdiction to enforce section 301(a) of the Labor Management Relations Act of 1947 is exclusively federal. That provision states:

> (a) Suits for violation of contracts between an employer and a labor organization representing commerce * * * or between any such labor organization, may be brought in any district court of the United States having jurisdiction of the parties, without respect to the amount in controversy or without regard to the citizenship of the parties.

In Textile Workers Union of America v. Lincoln Mills of Alabama, 353 U.S. 448 (1957) [infra p. 723], the Court had held that this provision authorized the enforcing court to develop a federal common law of labor contracts. In *Charles Dowd* the Court, in an opinion by Justice Stewart, held that federal jurisdiction under section 301(a) was not exclusive:

> It has not been argued, nor could it be, that § 301(a) speaks in terms of exclusivity of federal court jurisdiction over controversies within the statute's purview. * * *

> * * *

> It is argued that the rationale of *Lincoln Mills* would be frustrated if state courts were allowed to exercise concurrent jurisdiction over suits within the purview of § 301(a). The task of formulating federal common law in this area of labor management relations must be entrusted exclusively to the federal courts, it is said, because participation by the state courts would lead to a disharmony incompatible with the *Lincoln Mills* concept of an all-embracing body of federal law. Only the federal judiciary, the argument goes, possesses both the familiarity with federal labor legislation and the monolithic judicial system necessary for the

281

proper achievement of the creative task envisioned by *Lincoln Mills.*
* * *

Whatever the merits of this argument as a matter of policy, we find nothing to indicate that Congress adopted such a policy in enacting § 301. The legislative history of the enactment nowhere suggests [such a policy] * * *.

We start with the premise that nothing in the concept of our federal system prevents state courts from enforcing rights created by federal law. Concurrent jurisdiction has been a common phenomenon in our judicial history, and exclusive federal court jurisdiction over cases arising under federal law has been the exception rather than the rule. This Court's approach to the question of whether Congress has ousted state courts of jurisdiction was enumerated * * * in Claflin v. Houseman, 93 U.S. 130, and has remained unmodified through the years. "The general question, whether State courts can exercise concurrent jurisdiction with the Federal courts in cases arising under the Constitution, laws, and treaties of the United States, has been elaborately discussed * * * [and] the result of these discussions has, in our judgment, been * * * to affirm the jurisdiction, where it is not excluded by express provision, or by incompatibility in its exercise arising from the nature of the particular case." To hold that § 301(a) operates to deprive the state courts of a substantial segment of their established jurisdiction over contract actions would thus be to disregard this consistent history of hospitable acceptance of concurrent jurisdiction. 368 U.S. at 506–08.

GULF OFFSHORE CO. v. MOBIL OIL CORP.

Supreme Court of the United States, 1981.
453 U.S. 473.

JUSTICE POWELL delivered the opinion of the Court.

This case requires us to determine whether federal courts have exclusive jurisdiction over personal injury and indemnity cases arising under the Outer Continental Shelf Lands Act, 67 Stat. 462, as amended, 43 U.S.C. § 1331 *et seq.* (1976 ed. and Supp. III). * * *

Respondent, Mobil Oil Corp., contracted with petitioner, Gulf Offshore Co., for the latter to perform certain completion operations on oil drilling platforms offshore of Louisiana. As part of the agreement, petitioner promised to indemnify Mobil for all claims resulting directly or indirectly from the work. While the work was in progress in September 1975, the advent of Hurricane Eloise required that workers be evacuated from oil platforms in the Gulf of Mexico.

Steven Gaedecke was an employee of petitioner working on an oil drilling platform above the seabed of the Outer Continental Shelf. As the storm approached, a boat chartered by Mobil took him safely aboard. Shortly thereafter, while assisting crewmen attempting to evacuate other workers from the platforms in turbulent sea, he was washed across the deck of the vessel by a wave. He suffered injuries primarily to his back.

Gaedecke brought this suit for damages in the District Court of Harris County, a Texas state court, alleging negligence by Mobil and the boatowner. Mobil filed a third-party complaint for indemnification against petitioner. In its third-party answer, petitioner denied that the state court had subject-matter jurisdiction over the third-party complaint. Petitioner argued that Mobil's cause of action arose under the Outer Continental Shelf Lands Act (OCSLA), and that OCSLA vested exclusive subject-matter jurisdiction in a United States district court. The Texas trial court rejected this contention, and the case went to trial before a jury.

In submitting the case to the jury, the trial court denied a request by petitioner to instruct them that personal injury damages awards are not subject to federal income taxation and that they should not increase or decrease an award in contemplation of tax consequences. The jury found Mobil negligent and awarded Gaedecke $900,000 for his injuries. The jury also found, however, that Gaedecke sustained his injuries while performing work subject to the contract of indemnification. Based on the two verdicts, the trial judge entered judgment against petitioner in the amount of $900,000.

The Texas Court of Civil Appeals affirmed. It held that the Texas state courts had subject-matter jurisdiction over the causes of action. It acknowledged that OCSLA governed the case, but found no explicit command in the Act that federal-court jurisdiction be exclusive. The court also observed that exclusive federal-court jurisdiction was unnecessary because the Act incorporates as federal law in personal injury actions the laws of the State adjacent to the scene of the events, when not inconsistent with other federal laws. 43 U.S.C. § 1333(a)(2). Thus, the court reasoned, "[t]he end result would be an application of the same laws no matter where the forum was located, whether state or federal." The court also held that the trial court did not err in refusing to instruct the jury that damages awards are not subject to federal income taxation. The Texas Supreme Court denied review.

* * *

The general principle of state-court jurisdiction over cases arising under federal laws is straightforward: state courts may assume subject-matter jurisdiction over a federal cause of action absent provision by Congress to the contrary or disabling incompatibility between the federal claim and state-court adjudication. Charles Dowd Box Co. v. Courtney, 368 U.S. 502, 507–508 (1962); Claflin v. Houseman, 93 U.S. 130, 136 (1876). This rule is premised on the relation between the States and the National Government within our federal system. See The Federalist No. 82 (Hamilton). The two exercise concurrent sovereignty, although the Constitution limits the powers of each and requires the States to recognize federal law as paramount. Federal law confers rights binding on state courts, the subject-matter jurisdiction of which is governed in the first instance by state laws.[4]

In considering the propriety of state-court jurisdiction over any particular federal claim, the Court begins with the presumption that state courts enjoy concurrent jurisdiction. See California v. Arizona, 440 U.S. 59, 66–67 (1979); Charles Dowd Box Co. v. Courtney, 368 U.S., at 507–508. Congress, however, may confine jurisdiction to the federal courts either explicitly or implicitly. Thus, the presumption of concurrent jurisdiction can be rebutted by an explicit statutory directive, by unmistakable implication from legislative history, or by a clear incompatibility between state-court jurisdiction and federal interests. * * *

No one argues that Congress explicitly granted federal courts exclusive jurisdiction over cases arising under OCSLA. Congress did grant United States district courts "original jurisdiction of cases and controversies arising out of or in connection with any operations conducted on the outer Continental Shelf...." 43 U.S.C. § 1333(b). It is black letter law, however, that the mere grant of jurisdiction to a federal court does not operate to oust a state court from concurrent jurisdiction over the cause of action.

OCSLA declares the Outer Continental Shelf to be an area of "exclusive federal jurisdiction." 43 U.S.C. § 1333(a)(1). Chevron Oil Co. v. Huson, 404 U.S. 97, 100 (1971).[7] Petitioner does contend that the assertion of exclusive political jurisdiction over the Shelf evinces a congressional intent that federal courts exercise exclusive jurisdiction over controversies arising from operations on the Shelf. This argument is premised on a perceived incompatibility between exclusive federal sovereignty over the Outer Continental Shelf and state-court jurisdiction over controversies relating to the Shelf. We think petitioner mistakes the

---

4. Permitting state courts to entertain federal causes of action facilitates the enforcement of federal rights. If Congress does not confer jurisdiction on federal courts to hear a particular federal claim, the state courts stand ready to vindicate the federal right, subject always to review, of course, in this Court. See Martin v. Hunter's Lessee, 1 Wheat. 304, 346–348 (1816). This practical concern was more important before the statutory creation in 1875 of general federal-question jurisdiction.

7. The legislative history confirms that the purpose of OCSLA was "to assert the exclusive jurisdiction and control of the Federal Government of the United States over the seabed and subsoil of the outer Continental Shelf, and to provide for the development of its vast mineral resources." S.Rep. No. 411, 83d Cong., 1st Sess., 2 (1953) (hereinafter 1953 S.Rep.). Congress enacted OCSLA in the wake of decisions by this Court that the Federal Government enjoyed sovereignty and ownership of the

seabed and subsoil of the Outer Continental Shelf to the exclusion of adjacent States. Congress chose to retain exclusive federal control of the administration of the Shelf because it underlay the high seas and the assertion of sovereignty there implicated the foreign policies of the Nation. Much of OCSLA provides a federal framework for the granting of leases for exploration and extraction of minerals from the submerged lands of the Shelf. See 43 U.S.C. §§ 1334–1343.

Congress was not unaware, however, of the close, longstanding relationship between the Shelf and the adjacent States. This concern manifested itself primarily in the incorporation of the law of adjacent States to fill gaps in federal law. It should be emphasized that this case only involves state-court jurisdiction over actions based on incorporated state law. We express no opinion on whether state courts enjoy concurrent jurisdiction over actions based on the substantive provisions of OCSLA.

purpose of OCSLA and the policies necessitating exclusive federal-court jurisdiction.

OCSLA extends the "Constitution and laws and civil and political jurisdiction of the United States" to the subsoil and seabed of the Outer Continental Shelf and to "artificial islands and fixed structures" built for discovery, extraction, and transportation of minerals. 43 U.S.C. § 1333(a)(1). All law applicable to the Outer Continental Shelf is federal law, but to fill the substantial "gaps" in the coverage of federal law, OCSLA borrows the "applicable and not inconsistent" laws of the adjacent States as surrogate federal law. Thus, a personal injury action involving events occurring on the Shelf is governed by federal law, the content of which is borrowed from the law of the adjacent State, here Louisiana. * * *

The OCSLA plan is not inimical to state-court jurisdiction over personal injury actions. Nothing inherent in exclusive federal sovereignty over a territory precludes a state court from entertaining a personal injury suit concerning events occurring in the territory and governed by federal law. * * * "The judiciary power of every government looks beyond its own local or municipal laws, and in civil cases lays hold of all subjects of litigation between parties within its jurisdiction, though the causes of dispute are relative to the laws of the most distant part of the globe." The Federalist No. 82, p. 514 (H. Lodge ed. 1908) (Hamilton), quoted in Claflin v. Houseman, 93 U.S., at 138. State courts routinely exercise subject-matter jurisdiction over civil cases arising from events in other States and governed by the other States' laws. That the location of the event giving rise to the suit is an area of exclusive federal jurisdiction rather than another State, does not introduce any new limitation on the forum State's subject-matter jurisdiction.

Section 1333(a)(3) provides that "adoption of State law as the law of the United States shall never be interpreted as a basis for claiming any interest in or jurisdiction on behalf of any State for any purpose over the seabed and subsoil of the outer Continental Shelf, or the property and natural resources thereof or the revenues therefrom." Petitioner argues that state-court jurisdiction over this personal injury case would contravene this provision. This argument again confuses the political jurisdiction of a State with its judicial jurisdiction. Section 1333(a)(3) speaks to the geographic boundaries of state sovereignty, because Congress primarily was concerned in enacting OCSLA to assure federal control over the Shelf and its resources. The language of the provision refers to "any interest in or jurisdiction over" real property, minerals, and revenues, not over causes of action. * * *

We do not think the legislative history of OCSLA can be read to rebut the presumption of concurrent state-court jurisdiction, given Congress' silence on the subject in the statute itself. Petitioner relies principally on criticisms by the two Senators from Louisiana, Ellender and Long, who opposed the bill that eventually became OCSLA. Yet "[t]he fears and doubts of the opposition are no authoritative guide to the construction of legislation." Schwegmann Bros. v. Calvert Distillers Corp., 341 U.S. 384, 394 (1951). Moreover, the amendments offered by the Senators sought to confer political control over the Shelf and its mineral wealth on the States, not jurisdiction on the state courts over OCSLA cases.

The operation of OCSLA will not be frustrated by state-court jurisdiction over personal injury actions. The factors generally recommending exclusive federal-court jurisdiction over an area of federal law include[12] the desirability of uniform interpretation, the expertise of federal judges in federal law, and the assumed greater hospitality of federal courts to peculiarly federal claims.[13] These factors cannot support exclusive federal jurisdiction over claims whose governing rules are borrowed from state law. There is no need for uniform interpretation of laws that vary from State to State. State judges have greater expertise in applying these laws and certainly cannot be thought unsympathetic to a claim only because it is labeled federal rather than state law.

Allowing personal injury and contract actions in state courts will advance interests identified by Congress in enacting OCSLA. A recurring consideration in the deliberations leading to enactment was "the special relationship between the men working on these [platforms] and the adjacent shore to which they commute to visit their families." Rodrigue v. Aetna Casualty Co., 395 U.S., [352], at 365. Allowing state-court jurisdiction over these cases will allow these workers, and their lawyers, to pursue individual claims in familiar, convenient, and possibly less expensive fora. * * *

In summary, nothing in the language, structure, legislative history, or underlying policies of OCSLA suggests that Congress intended federal courts to exercise exclusive jurisdiction over personal injury actions arising under OCSLA. The Texas courts had jurisdiction over this case.

Notes

1. Note that the Court in *Dowd* and *Gulf Offshore* relies heavily on the presumption of concurrent jurisdiction, enunciated in the 1876 decision of Claflin v. Houseman. While, as the *Dowd* Court states, the *Claflin* rule is considered good law, it has had a somewhat spotty history. See Redish & Muench, *Adjudication of Federal Causes of Action in State Court,* 75 Mich. L.Rev. 311, 316–25 (1976). In American National Red Cross v. S.G., A.E., 505 U.S. 247, 259 (1992), the Supreme Court, citing both *Claflin* and *Dowd,*

---

12. Exclusive federal-court jurisdiction over a cause of action generally is unnecessary to protect the parties. The plaintiff may choose the available forum he prefers, and the defendant may remove the case if it could have been brought originally in a federal court. 28 U.S.C. § 1441(b). Also, exclusive federal jurisdiction will not prevent a state court from deciding a federal question collaterally even if it would not

have subject-matter jurisdiction over a case raising the question directly. See Note, Exclusive Jurisdiction of Federal Courts in Private Civil Actions, 70 Harv.L.Rev. 509, 510 (1957).

13. See Redish & Muench, Adjudication of Federal Causes of Action in State Court, 75 Mich.L.Rev. 311, 329–335 (1976); Note, 70 Harv.L.Rev., supra n. 12, at 511–15.

noted that "[t]here is every reason to expect Congress to take great care in its use of explicit language when it wishes to confer exclusive jurisdiction, given our longstanding requirement to that effect."

2. How consistent is the *Claflin* rule with our traditions of judicial federalism? Should its presumption of concurrent jurisdiction be continued today?

3. Given the implicit assumptions about the important role of state courts as adjudicators of federal law contained in the *Claflin* presumption of concurrent jurisdiction, why do you suppose the *Claflin* Court included a doctrine of *impliedly* exclusive federal jurisdiction (i.e., its assertion that jurisdiction was concurrent "where it has not been excluded by express provision, *or by incompatibility in its exercise arising from the nature of the particular case*")? Classic examples of implied exclusive federal jurisdiction are the Sherman and Clayton antitrust laws. Can you fashion an argument to support a finding of implied exclusivity in the antitrust context? Are you persuaded?

4. Think about the factors identified in *Gulf Offshore* as relevant to the determination of exclusive federal jurisdiction, and consider *Tafflin v. Levitt*, 493 U.S. 455 (1990). In *Tafflin*, the Court held that state courts possess concurrent jurisdiction over civil claims arising under the Racketeer Influenced and Corrupt Organizations Act [RICO], 18 U.S.C. §§ 1961–68. Enacted as part of the Organized Crime Control Act of 1970, RICO is designed to prevent and punish "racketeering activity". The statute prohibits, among other things, the conduct of such activity to acquire an interest in or to establish or operate an enterprise engaged in or affecting interstate commerce. "Racketeering activity" is defined as any act in violation of several classes of state criminal law or of several specified federal criminal provisions. In addition to a criminal enforcement scheme, the statute establishes a system for civil enforcement, including a private cause of action.

On its face, the statute is silent on the issue of state court jurisdiction. Justice O'Connor, speaking for the Court, applied the *Gulf Offshore* test, and concluded that neither legislative history nor pragmatic considerations justified a finding of jurisdictional exclusivity:

> Our review of the legislative history * * * reveals no evidence that Congress even considered the question of concurrent state court jurisdiction over RICO claims, much less any suggestion that Congress affirmatively intended to confer exclusive jurisdiction over such claims on the federal courts. * * *

> * * *

> We perceive no "clear incompatibility" between state court jurisdiction over civil RICO actions and federal interests. * * *

> * * * [O]ur decision today creates no significant danger of inconsistent application of federal criminal law. Although petitioners' concern with the need for uniformity and consistency of federal criminal law is well-taken, federal courts * * * would retain full authority and responsibility for the interpretation and application of federal criminal laws, for they would not be bound by state court interpretations of the federal offenses constituting RICO's predicate acts. State courts adjudicating

civil RICO claims will, in addition, be guided by federal court interpretations of the relevant federal criminal statutes, just as federal courts sitting in diversity are guided by state court interpretations of state law. * * *

Moreover, * * * we have full faith in the ability of state courts to handle the complexities of civil RICO actions, particularly since many RICO cases involve asserted violations of state law * * *. 493 U.S. at 461–465.

In a separate concurring opinion, Justice Scalia, joined by Justice Kennedy, argued that "State courts have jurisdiction over federal causes of action not because it is 'conferred' upon them by the Congress * * *. It * * * takes an affirmative act of power under the Supremacy Clause to oust the States of jurisdiction * * *." He conceded, however, that perhaps "implied preclusion can be established by the fact that a statute expressly mentions only federal courts, plus the fact that state-court jurisdiction would plainly disrupt the statutory scheme." But "[i]f the phrase is interpreted more broadly than that * * * it has absolutely no foundation in our precedent." Id. at 469–472.

See also Yellow Freight System, Inc. v. Donnelly, 494 U.S. 820 (1990), where the Court held that federal courts do not have exclusive jurisdiction over Title VII actions. Writing for a unanimous Court, Justice Stevens determined that "without disagreeing with [the] persuasive showing that most legislators, judges, and administrators who have been involved in the enactment, amendment, enforcement, and interpretation of Title VII expected that such litigation would be processed exclusively in federal courts, we conclude that such anticipation does not overcome the presumption of concurrent jurisdiction that lies at the core of our federal system." Id. at 826.

See generally Solimine, *Rethinking Exclusive Federal Jurisdiction,* 52 U.Pitt.L.Rev. 383 (1991).

6. Why should Congress ever make federal jurisdiction exclusive? As long as Congress has made a federal forum available, any harm flowing from a plaintiff's choice of a state forum will be purely self-imposed. In thinking about this question, you might want to know that one example of a statute in which Congress has made federal jurisdiction explicitly exclusive is the patent and copyright jurisdictional statute. 28 U.S.C. § 1338(a). Why do you suppose Congress chose cases in these areas to be heard exclusively in federal court?

7. Consider the following argument: Even if it is appropriate on occasion for Congress to render federal jurisdiction exclusive, it is never appropriate for the courts to infer exclusive jurisdiction in the face of congressional silence. To do so is blatant substitution of the judiciary's will for that of Congress. For a contrary argument that at least in some contexts, the Constitution itself might require exclusive federal jurisdiction, see Collins, *The Federal Courts, the First Congress, and the Non–Settlement of 1789,* 91 Va.L.Rev. 1515 (2005).

10. What if an issue that has been exclusively vested by Congress in the federal courts is raised as a defense in the course of an adjudication in

state court of a state cause of action? For example, plaintiff patent-holder sues in state court for breach of a royalty agreement by a licensee. The licensee defends on the ground that plaintiff's patent is invalid under the federal patent law and therefore he is not liable to the plaintiff for production or sale of the patented item. Should the state court be allowed to decide the issue of patent validity, even though jurisdiction to adjudicate patent validity in a suit for patent infringement would be exclusively federal under 28 U.S.C. § 1338(a)?

In Lear, Inc. v. Adkins, 395 U.S. 653 (1969), the Supreme Court held that the state court had authority to consider patent validity in a suit for breach of the royalty agreement. What are the competing considerations? Cf. Chisum, *The Allocation of Jurisdiction Between State and Federal Courts in Patent Litigation,* 46 Wash.L.Rev. 633 (1971). If a state court is allowed to adjudicate the otherwise-"exclusive" federal issue as a defense, should the state court's finding have full collateral estoppel effect? Cf. Lyons v. Westinghouse Electric Corp., 222 F.2d 184 (2d Cir.), cert. denied, 350 U.S. 825 (1955). Again, what are the competing considerations?

11. The Court recently held that the presumption of concurrent jurisdiction does not apply to tribal courts, which have jurisdiction over federal questions only if a statute specifically provides for such jurisdiction. Nevada v. Hicks, 533 U.S. 353 (2001).

§ 2. STATE COURT OBLIGATION TO ENFORCE FEDERAL LAW

TESTA v. KATT

Supreme Court of the United States, 1947.
330 U.S. 386.

Mr. Justice Black delivered the opinion of the Court.

Section 205(e)[1] of the Emergency Price Control Act provides that a buyer of goods at above the prescribed ceiling price may sue the seller "in any court of competent jurisdiction" for not more than three times the amount of the overcharge plus costs and a reasonable attorney's fee. Section 205(c)[2] provides that federal district courts shall have jurisdic-

1. "(e) If any person selling a commodity violates a regulation, order, or price schedule prescribing a maximum price or maximum prices, the person who buys such commodity for use or consumption other than in the course of trade or business may, within one year from the date of the occurrence of the violation, except as hereinafter provided, bring an action against the seller on account of the overcharge. In such action, the seller shall be liable for reasonable attorney's fees and costs as determined by the court, plus whichever of the following sums is the greater: (1) Such amount not more than three times the amount of the overcharge, or the overcharges, upon which the action is based as the court in its discre-

tion may determine, or (2) an amount not less than $25 nor more than $50, as the court in its discretion may determine: * * *. Any action under this subsection by either the buyer or the Administrator, as the case may be, may be brought in any court of competent jurisdiction. * * * " 56 Stat. 34 as amended, 58 Stat. 632, 640, 50 U.S.C. App., Supp. V, § 925(e).

2. "The district courts shall have jurisdiction of criminal proceedings * * * and, concurrently with State and Territorial courts, of all other proceedings under section 205 of this Act. * * * " 56 Stat. 32, as amended, 58 Stat. 632, 640, 50 U.S.C. App., Supp. V, § 925(c).

tion of such suits "concurrently with State and Territorial courts." Such a suit under § 205(e) must be brought "in the district or county in which the defendant resides or has a place of business * * *."

The respondent was in the automobile business in Providence, Providence County, Rhode Island. In 1944 he sold an automobile to petitioner Testa, who also resides in Providence, for $1100, $210 above the ceiling price. The petitioner later filed this suit against respondent in the State District Court in Providence. Recovery was sought under § 205(e). The court awarded a judgment of treble damages and costs to petitioner. On appeal to the State Superior Court, where the trial was *de novo,* the petitioner was again awarded judgment, but only for the amount of the overcharge plus attorney's fees. Pending appeal from this judgment, the Price Administrator was allowed to intervene. On appeal, the State Supreme Court reversed. It interpreted § 205(e) to be "a penal statute in the international sense." It held that an action for violation of § 205(e) could not be maintained in the courts of that State. The State Supreme Court rested its holding on its earlier decision in Robinson v. Norato, 1945, 71 R.I. 256, in which it had reasoned that: A state need not enforce the penal laws of a government which is foreign in the international sense; § 205(e) is treated by Rhode Island as penal in that sense; the United States is "foreign" to the State in the "private international" as distinguished from the "public international" sense; hence Rhode Island courts, though their jurisdiction is adequate to enforce similar Rhode Island "penal" statutes, need not enforce § 205(e). Whether state courts may decline to enforce federal laws on these grounds is a question of great importance. For this reason, and because the Rhode Island Supreme Court's holding was alleged to conflict with this Court's previous holding in Mondou v. New York, N.H. & H.R. Co., 223 U.S. 1, we granted certiorari. 329 U.S. 703.

For the purposes of this case, we assume, without deciding, that § 205(e) is a penal statute in the "public international," "private international," or any other sense. So far as the question of whether the Rhode Island courts properly declined to try this action, it makes no difference into which of these categories the Rhode Island court chose to place the statute which Congress has passed. For we cannot accept the basic premise on which the Rhode Island Supreme Court held that it has no more obligation to enforce a valid penal law of the United States than it has to enforce a penal law of another state or a foreign country. Such a broad assumption flies in the face of the fact that the States of the Union constitute a nation. It disregards the purpose and effect of Article VI of the Constitution which provides: "This Constitution, and the Laws of the United States which shall be made in Pursuance thereof; and all Treaties made, or which shall be made, under the Authority of the United States, shall be the supreme Law of the Land; and the Judges in every State shall be bound thereby, any Thing in the Constitution or Laws of any State to the Contrary notwithstanding."

It cannot be assumed, the supremacy clause considered, that the responsibilities of a state to enforce the laws of a sister state are identical with its responsibilities to enforce federal laws. Such an assumption represents an erroneous evaluation of the statutes of Congress and the prior decisions of this Court in their historic setting. Those decisions establish that state courts do not bear the same relation to the United States that they do to foreign countries. The first Congress that convened after the Constitution was adopted conferred jurisdiction upon the state courts to enforce important federal civil laws, and succeeding Congresses conferred on the states jurisdiction over federal crimes and actions for penalties and forfeitures.

Enforcement of federal laws by state courts did not go unchallenged. Violent public controversies existed throughout the first part of the Nineteenth Century until the 1860's concerning the extent of the constitutional supremacy of the Federal Government. During that period there were instances in which this Court and state courts broadly questioned the power and duty of state courts to exercise their jurisdiction to enforce United States civil and penal statutes or the power of the Federal Government to require them to do so. But after the fundamental issues over the extent of federal supremacy had been resolved by war, this Court took occasion in 1876 to review the phase of the controversy concerning the relationship of state courts to the Federal Government. Claflin v. Houseman, 93 U.S. 130. The opinion of a unanimous court in that case was strongly buttressed by historic references and persuasive reasoning. It repudiated the assumption that federal laws can be considered by the states as though they were laws emanating from a foreign sovereign. Its teaching is that the Constitution and the laws passed pursuant to it are the supreme laws of the land, binding alike upon states, courts, and the people, "any thing in the Constitution or Laws of any State to the Contrary notwithstanding."[7] It asserted that the obligation of states to enforce these federal laws is not lessened by reason of the form in which they are cast or the remedy which they provide. And the Court stated that "If an act of Congress gives a penalty to a party aggrieved, without specifying a remedy for its enforcement, there is no reason why it should not be enforced, if not provided otherwise by some act of Congress, by a proper action in a state court." Id. 93 U.S. at page 137. And see United States v. Bank of New York & Trust Co., 296 U.S. 463, 479.

The *Claflin* opinion thus answered most of the arguments theretofore advanced against the power and duty of state courts to enforce federal penal laws. And since that decision, the remaining areas of doubt have been steadily narrowed. There have been statements in cases concerned with the obligation of states to give full faith and credit to the proceedings of sister states which suggested a theory contrary to that pronounced in the *Claflin* opinion. But when in Mondou v. New York, N.H. & H.R. Co., supra, this Court was presented with a case testing the power and duty of states to enforce federal laws, it found the solution in the broad principles announced in the *Claflin* opinion.

7. U.S. Const. Art. VI. See also Ex parte Siebold, 100 U.S. 371, 392–394.

The precise question in the *Mondou* case was whether rights arising under the Federal Employers' Liability Act, 36 Stat. 291, could "be enforced, as of right, in the courts of the States when their jurisdiction, as fixed by local laws, is adequate to the occasion * * *" Id. 223 U.S. at page 46. The Supreme Court of Connecticut had decided that they could not. Except for the penalty feature, the factors it considered and its reasoning were strikingly similar to that on which the Rhode Island Supreme Court declined to enforce the federal law here involved. But this Court held that the Connecticut court could not decline to entertain the action. The contention that enforcement of the congressionally created right was contrary to Connecticut policy was answered as follows:

> "The suggestion that the act of Congress is not in harmony with the policy of the State, and therefore that the courts of the State are free to decline jurisdiction, is quite inadmissible, because it presupposes what in legal contemplation does not exist. When Congress, in the exertion of the power confided to it by the Constitution, adopted that act, it spoke for all the people and all the States, and thereby established a policy for all. That policy is as much the policy of Connecticut as if the act had emanated from its own legislature, and should be respected accordingly in the courts of the State." Mondou v. New York, N.H. & H.R. Co., supra, 223 U.S. at page 57.

So here, the fact that Rhode Island has an established policy against enforcement by its courts of statutes of other states and the United States which it deems penal, cannot be accepted as a "valid excuse." Cf. Douglas v. New York, N.H. & H.R. Co., 279 U.S. 377, 388. For the policy of the federal Act is the prevailing policy in every state. Thus, in a case which chiefly relied upon the *Claflin* and *Mondou* precedents, this Court stated that a state court cannot "refuse to enforce the right arising from the law of the United States because of conceptions of impolicy or want of wisdom on the part of Congress in having called into play its lawful powers." Minneapolis & St. L.R. Co. v. Bombolis, 241 U.S. 211, 222.

* * *

It is conceded that this same type of claim arising under Rhode Island law would be enforced by that State's courts. Its courts have enforced claims for double damages growing out of the Fair Labor Standards Act. Thus the Rhode Island courts have jurisdiction adequate and appropriate under established local law to adjudicate this action. Under these circumstances the State courts are not free to refuse enforcement of petitioners' claim. See McKnett v. St. Louis & S.F.R. Co., 292 U.S. 230; and compare Herb v. Pitcairn, 324 U.S. 117; Id., 325 U.S. 77. The case is reversed and the cause is remanded for proceedings not inconsistent with this opinion.

Notes

1.   Compare *Testa* to Tarble's Case [supra p. 148]. In both cases, the Court appeared to emphasize post-Civil War federal supremacy. Yet in *Testa,* applying this supremacy, the Court held state courts *must* adjudicate federal rights; in *Tarble,* the Court held that state courts *could not* adjudicate federal rights. Are the two decisions inconsistent?

2.   From where does Congress derive constitutional power to compel state courts to adjudicate federal claims? Examine the text of the supremacy clause, Art. VI, cl. 2. Does that provision establish an independent congressional power to compel state courts to adjudicate federal claims? If not the supremacy clause, is the constitutional source of Congress's authority the enumeration of congressional powers in Art. I, section 8, combined with the necessary and proper clause?

In Printz v. United States, 521 U.S. 898 (1997), the Supreme Court held that the Constitution prohibited Congress from "commandeering" state executive officers to enforce and implement federal programs. In New York v. United States, 505 U.S. 144 (1992), the Court had reached a similar conclusion concerning congressional power to dictate that state legislatures enact specific legislation. Both decisions, however, distinguished *Testa,* primarily on the grounds of the supremacy clause's express reference to the obligation of state judges to obey federal law. Is this a persuasive distinction? A number of scholars have argued that the distinction between judicial and non-judicial state actors does not serve the values of federalism. See, e.g., Caminker, Printz, *State Sovereignty, and the Limits of Formalism,* 1997 Sup.Ct. Rev. 199; Adler & Kreimer, *The New Etiquette of Federalism:* New York, Printz, *and* Yeskey, 1998 Sup.Ct.Rev. 71. Does the supremacy clause's express reference to state judges imply that state executive officers are *not* obligated to obey federal law? Professor Caminker suggests that *Testa* rests on the general language of the supremacy clause, rather than on the specific reference to judges. Caminker, supra, 1997 Sup.Ct.Rev. at 213–15. See also Redish & Sklaver, *Federal Power to Commandeer State Courts: Implications for the Theory of Judicial Federalism,* 32 Ind.L.Rev. 71 (1998) (arguing that Congress's Article I authority to commandeer state courts necessarily extends to state executive officials as well).

Other articles discussing the relationship between *Testa* and *Printz* include Katz, *State Judges, State Officers, and Federal Commands After Seminole Tribe and* Printz, 1998 Wis.L.Rev. 1465; Hills, *The Political Economy of Cooperative Federalism: Why State Autonomy Makes Sense and "Dual Sovereignty" Doesn't,* 96 Mich.L.Rev. 813 (1998); Smith, *The Anticommandeering Principle and Congress's Power to Direct State Judicial Action: Congress's Power to Compel State Courts to Answer Certified Questions of State Law,* 31 Conn.L.Rev. 649 (1999).

3.   There is some dispute about whether the framers intended to allow Congress to coerce state courts to hear federal questions. Saikrishna Prakash, for example, argues that *Testa*'s rule is supported by historical evidence suggesting that the Framers not only assumed that Congress could compel state courts to hear federal questions, they also assumed that

Congress "could constitute state courts as inferior federal courts." Prakash, *Field Office Federalism*, 79 Va.L.Rev. 1957, 2007 (1993). Michael Collins, however, offers a historical refutation of these arguments and concludes that "there was almost no suggestion before this century that" Congress could compel state courts to accept federal jurisdiction. Collins, *Article III Cases, State Court Duties, and the Madisonian Compromise*, 1995 Wisc.L.Rev. 39, 135; see also Collins, *The Federal Courts, the First Congress, and the Non–Settlement of 1789*, 91 Va.L.Rev. 1515 (2005). Should the answer, in the context of both state courts and state executives, depend on balancing congressional need against the burden on state officials? See Jackson, *Federalism and the Uses and Limits of Law: Printz and Principle?* 111 Harv.L.Rev. 2180 (1998). For a thorough historical analysis, see Bellia, *Congressional Power and State Court Jurisdiction*, 94 Geo.L.J. 949 (2006).

4.   In holding that the state court must adjudicate the federal case, Justice Black emphasized that "this same type of claim arising under Rhode Island law would be enforced by that State's courts." Why should this fact be relevant?

5.   The Court held that Rhode Island's argument against hearing the case "cannot be accepted as a 'valid excuse.'" What *should* be accepted as a "valid excuse"? Consider Herb v. Pitcairn, 324 U.S. 117 (1945). The plaintiff had brought an action in a city court of Illinois under the Federal Employers' Liability Act. Under the Illinois Constitution, a city court did not have jurisdiction to hear cases based upon a cause of action (whether state or federal) that arose outside the city. The United States Supreme Court held that the city court was not compelled to hear the federal suit, because the case was not within the court's jurisdiction under state law.

Should the doctrine of *forum non conveniens* be accepted as a "valid excuse"? See Missouri ex rel. Southern Railway Co. v. Mayfield, 340 U.S. 1 (1950). Cf. Douglas v. New York, New Haven & Hartford Railroad Co., 279 U.S. 377 (1929). How about that the state does not enforce an "analogous right"? Professor Hart has described as an open question whether state courts can constitutionally be compelled to hear cases that do not involve analogous rights. Hart, *The Relations Between State and Federal Law*, 54 Colum.L.Rev. 489, 507–508 (1954). What do you think the term, "analogous right" means? If the term is given its most obvious interpretation, it seems to mean, simply, a substantive right that is similar or parallel to a right authorized under federal law. If this is in fact the term's meaning, do the policy considerations underlying the valid excuse doctrine support recognition of an excuse when the state does not itself provide a right similar to the federal one sought to be enforced in state court? See Sandalow, Henry v. Mississippi *and the Adequate State Ground: Proposals for a Revised Doctrine*, 1965 Sup.Ct.Rev. 187, 205; Note, *State Enforcement of Federally Created Rights*, 73 Harv.L.Rev. 1551, 1554–1555 (1960); Redish & Muench, *Adjudication of Federal Causes of Action in State Court*, 75 Mich.L.Rev. 311, 350–59 (1976). Does *Testa* arguably provide any support for the existence of such an excuse? See also Martinez v. California, 444 U.S. 277, 283–84 n. 7 (1980): "We note that where the same type of claim, if arising under state law, would be enforced in the state courts, the state courts are generally not free to refuse enforcement of the federal claim [citing *Testa*]." Does this statement provide support for the analogous right doctrine?

6. FERC v. Mississippi, 456 U.S. 742 (1982): The Public Utility Regulatory Policies Act of 1978 (PURPA), as part of a legislative package designed to combat the energy crisis, directed state utility regulatory commissions to develop and enforce certain types of standards against regulated utilities. The Court, in an opinion by Justice Blackmun, rejected a tenth amendment argument against the burdens on state agencies imposed by the Act:

> In essence, * * * the statute and the implementing regulations simply require the Mississippi authorities to adjudicate disputes arising under the statute. Dispute resolution of this kind is the very type of activity customarily engaged in by the Mississippi Public Service Commission.

> *Testa v. Katt* is instructive and controlling on this point. * * *

> * * * The Mississippi Commission has jurisdiction to entertain claims analogous to those granted by PURPA, and it can satisfy [the Act's] requirements simply by opening its doors to claimants. That the Commission has administrative as well as judicial duties is of no significance. Any other conclusion would allow the States to disregard both the preeminent position held by federal law throughout the Nation, and the congressional determination that the federal rights granted by PURPA can appropriately be enforced through state adjudicatory machinery. 456 U.S. at 760–61.

Consider the Court's reference to "analogous" claims. Is this an example of the "analogous rights" doctrine, or is it simply a reassertion of the "court-of-limited-jurisdiction" exception of Herb v. Pitcairn?

7. In Howlett v. Rose, 496 U.S. 356 (1990), the Court faced the question whether a state law defense of sovereign immunity is available to a school board in a section 1983 action brought in state court even though the defense would not be available if the action had been brought in a federal forum.

Howlett was a section 1983 action brought by a student in a Florida state court against a county school board and several school officials alleging Fourth and Fourteenth Amendment violations. The Florida courts dismissed the case, concluding that the defendants were protected by sovereign immunity: "When a section 1983 action is brought in state court, the sole question to be decided on the basis of state law is whether the state has waived its common law sovereign immunity * * *."

In reversing the Florida decision, Justice Stevens, writing for a unanimous Court, emphasized that the state court had extended absolute immunity to defendants "who would otherwise be subject to suit under sec. 1983 in federal court." If the Florida court meant to "hold that governmental entities subject to § 1983 liability enjoy an immunity over and above those already provided in § 1983, that holding directly violates federal law." If, on the other hand, the state court refused to take cognizance of a federal cause of action, that decision "violates the Supremacy Clause":

> Three corollaries follow from the proposition that "federal" law is part of the Law of the Land in the State: 1. A state court may not deny a federal right, when the parties and controversy are properly before it, in absence of a "valid excuse." * * * 2. An excuse that is inconsistent with or violates federal law is not a valid excuse: the Supremacy Clause

forbids state courts to disassociate themselves from federal law because of disagreement with its content or a refusal to recognize the superior authority of its source. * * * 3. When a state court refuses jurisdiction because of a neutral state rule regarding the administration of its courts, we must act with caution before deciding that it is obligated to entertain the claim. Id. at 369–72.

Emphasizing that the "State of Florida has constituted the Circuit Court for Pinellas County as a court of general jurisdiction", id. at 378, the Supreme Court found no neutral excuse to justify the refusal to entertain the federal claim.

8. Consider the following argument: "In the absence of a declaration by Congress that state courts must enforce rights that Congress has created, there appears to be no substantial reason why the Supreme Court should impose such an obligation." Sandalow, supra, 1965 Sup.Ct.Rev. at 207.

DICE v. AKRON, CANTON & YOUNGSTOWN RAILROAD CO.

Supreme Court of the United States, 1952.
342 U.S. 359.

Opinion of the Court by Mr. Justice Black, announced by Mr. Justice Douglas.

Petitioner, a railroad fireman, was seriously injured when an engine in which he was riding jumped the track. Alleging that his injuries were due to respondent's negligence, he brought this action for damages under the Federal Employers' Liability Act, 35 Stat. 65, 45 U.S.C. § 51 *et seq.*, in an Ohio court of common pleas. Respondent's defenses were (1) a denial of negligence and (2) a written document signed by petitioner purporting to release respondent in full for $924.63. Petitioner admitted that he had signed several receipts for payments made him in connection with his injuries but denied that he had made a full and complete settlement of all his claims. He alleged that the purported release was void because he had signed it relying on respondent's deliberately false statement that the document was nothing more than a mere receipt for back wages.

After both parties had introduced considerable evidence the jury found in favor of petitioner and awarded him a $25,000 verdict. The trial judge later entered judgment notwithstanding the verdict. In doing so he reappraised the evidence as to fraud, found that petitioner had been "guilty of supine negligence" in failing to read the release, and accordingly held that the facts did not "sustain either in law or equity the allegations of fraud by clear, unequivocal and convincing evidence." This judgment notwithstanding the verdict was reversed by the Court of Appeals of Summit County, Ohio, on the ground that under federal law, which controlled, the jury's verdict must stand because there was ample evidence to support its finding of fraud. The Ohio Supreme Court, one judge dissenting, reversed the Court of Appeals' judgment and sustained the trial court's action, holding that: ① Ohio, not federal, law governed;

②under that law petitioner, a man of ordinary intelligence who could read, was bound by the release even though he had been induced to sign it by the deliberately false statement that it was only a receipt for back wages; and ③ under controlling Ohio law factual issues as to fraud in the execution of this release were properly decided by the judge rather than by the jury. 155 Ohio St. 185. We granted certiorari because the decision of the Supreme Court of Ohio appeared to deviate from previous decisions of this Court that federal law governs cases arising under the Federal Employers' Liability Act.

First. We agree with the Court of Appeals of Summit County, Ohio, and the dissenting judge in the Ohio Supreme Court and hold that validity of releases under the Federal Employers' Liability Act raises a federal question to be determined by federal rather than state law. Congress in § 1 of the Act granted petitioner a right to recover against his employer for damages negligently inflicted. State laws are not controlling in determining what the incidents of this federal right shall be. Chesapeake & Ohio R. Co. v. Kuhn, 284 U.S. 44; Ricketts v. Pennsylvania R. Co., 2 Cir., 153 F.2d 757, 759. Manifestly the federal rights affording relief to injured railroad employees under a federally declared standard could be defeated if states were permitted to have the final say as to what defenses could and could not be properly interposed to suits under the Act. Moreover, only if federal law controls can the federal Act be given that uniform application throughout the country essential to effectuate its purposes. See Garrett v. Moore–McCormack Co., 317 U.S. 239, 244, and cases there cited. Releases and other devices designed to liquidate or defeat injured employees' claims play an important part in the federal Act's administration. Compare Duncan v. Thompson, 315 U.S. 1, 62 S.Ct. 422. Their validity is but one of the many interrelated questions that must constantly be determined in these cases according to a uniform federal law.

Second. In effect the Supreme Court of Ohio held that an employee trusts his employer at his peril, and that the negligence of an innocent worker is sufficient to enable his employer to benefit by its deliberate fraud. Application of so harsh a rule to defeat a railroad employee's claim is wholly incongruous with the general policy of the Act to give railroad employees a right to recover just compensation for injuries negligently inflicted by their employers. And this Ohio rule is out of harmony with modern judicial and legislative practice to relieve injured persons from the effect of releases fraudulently obtained. * * * We hold that the correct federal rule is that announced by the Court of Appeals of Summit County, Ohio, and the dissenting judge in the Ohio Supreme Court—a release of rights under the Act is void when the employee is induced to sign it by the deliberately false and material statements of the railroad's authorized representatives made to deceive the employee as to the contents of the release. The trial court's charge to the jury correctly stated this rule of law.

Third. Ohio provides and has here accorded petitioner the usual jury trial of factual issues relating to negligence. But Ohio treats factual questions of fraudulent releases differently. It permits the judge trying a negligence case to resolve all factual questions of fraud "other than fraud in the factum." The factual issue of fraud is thus split into fragments, some to be determined by the judge, others by the jury.

It is contended that since a state may consistently with the Federal Constitution provide for trial of cases under the Act by a nonunanimous verdict, Minneapolis & St. Louis R. Co. v. Bombolis, 241 U.S. 211, Ohio may lawfully eliminate trial by jury as to one phase of fraud while allowing jury trial as to all other issues raised. The *Bombolis* case might be more in point had Ohio abolished trial by jury in all negligence cases including those arising under the federal Act. But Ohio has not done this. It has provided jury trials for cases arising under the federal Act but seeks to single out one phase of the question of fraudulent releases for determination by a judge rather than by a jury. Compare Testa v. Katt, 330 U.S. 386.

We have previously held that "The right to trial by jury is 'a basic and fundamental feature of our system of federal jurisprudence'" and that it is "part and parcel of the remedy afforded railroad workers under the Employers Liability Act." Bailey v. Central Vermont Ry., 319 U.S. 350, 354. We also recognized in that case that to deprive railroad workers of the benefit of a jury trial where there is evidence to support negligence "is to take away a goodly portion of the relief which Congress has afforded them." It follows that the right to trial by jury is too substantial a part of the rights accorded by the Act to permit it to be classified as a mere "local rule of procedure" for denial in the manner that Ohio has here used.

The trial judge and the Ohio Supreme Court erred in holding that petitioner's rights were to be determined by Ohio law and in taking away petitioner's verdict when the issues of fraud had been submitted to the jury on conflicting evidence and determined in petitioner's favor. The judgment of the Court of Appeals of Summit County, Ohio, was correct and should not have been reversed by the Supreme Court of Ohio. The cause is reversed and remanded to the Supreme Court of Ohio for further action not inconsistent with this opinion.

MR. JUSTICE FRANKFURTER, whom MR. JUSTICE REED, MR. JUSTICE JACKSON and MR. JUSTICE BURTON join, concurring for reversal but dissenting from the Court's opinion.

Ohio, as do many other States, maintains the old division between law and equity as to the mode of trying issues, even though the same judge administers both. The Ohio Supreme Court has told us what, on one issue, is the division of functions in all negligence actions brought in the Ohio courts: "Where it is claimed that a release was induced by fraud (other than fraud in the factum) or by mistake, it is * * * necessary, before seeking to enforce a cause of action which such release purports to bar, that equitable relief from the release be secured." Thus, in all cases in Ohio, the judge is the trier of fact on this issue of fraud, rather than the jury. It is contended that the Federal Employers'

Liability Act requires that Ohio courts send the fraud issue to a jury in the cases founded on that Act. To require Ohio to try a particular issue before a different fact-finder in negligence actions brought under the Employers' Liability Act from the fact-finder on the identical issue in every other negligence case disregards the settled distribution of judicial power between Federal and State courts where Congress authorizes concurrent enforcement of federally-created rights.

It has been settled ever since the Second Employers' Liability Cases, 223 U.S. 1, that no State which gives its courts jurisdiction over common law actions for negligence may deny access to its courts for a negligence action founded on the Federal Employers' Liability Act. Nor may a State discriminate disadvantageously against actions for negligence under the Federal Act as compared with local causes of action in negligence. McKnett v. St. Louis & S.F.R. Co., 292 U.S. 230, 234; Missouri ex rel. Southern Ry. Co. v. Mayfield, 340 U.S. 1, 4. Conversely, however, simply because there is concurrent jurisdiction in Federal and State courts over actions under the Employers' Liability Act, a State is under no duty to treat actions arising under that Act differently from the way it adjudicates local actions for negligence, so far as the mechanics of litigation, the forms in which law is administered, are concerned. This surely covers the distribution of functions as between judge and jury in the determination of the issues in a negligence case.

In 1916 the Court decided without dissent that States in entertaining actions under the Federal Employers' Liability Act need not provide a jury system other than that established for local negligence actions. States are not compelled to provide the jury required of Federal courts by the Seventh Amendment. Minneapolis & St. L.R. Co. v. Bombolis, 241 U.S. 211. In the thirty-six years since this early decision after the enactment of the Federal Employers' Liability Act, 35 Stat. 65 (1908), the *Bombolis* case has often been cited by this Court but never questioned. Until today its significance has been to leave to States the choice of the fact-finding tribunal in all negligence actions, including those arising under the Federal Act. * * *

* * *

Although a State must entertain negligence suits brought under the Federal Employers' Liability Act if it entertains ordinary actions for negligence, it need conduct them only in the way in which it conducts the run of negligence litigation. The *Bombolis* case directly establishes that the Employers' Liability Act does not impose the jury requirements of the Seventh Amendment on the States *pro tanto* for Employers' Liability litigation. If its reasoning means anything, the *Bombolis* decision means that, if a State chooses not to have a jury at all, but to leave questions of fact in all negligence actions to a court, certainly the Employers' Liability Act does not require a State to have juries for negligence actions brought under the Federal Act in its courts. Or, if a State chooses to retain the old double system of courts, common law and equity—as did a good many States until the other day, and as four States still do—surely there is nothing in the Employers' Liability Act that requires traditional distribution of authority for disposing of legal issues as between common law and chancery courts to go by the board. And, if States are free to make a distribution of functions between equity and common law courts, it surely makes no rational difference whether a State chooses to provide that the same judge preside on both the common law and the chancery sides in a single litigation, instead of in separate rooms in the same building. So long as all negligence suits in a State are treated in the same way, by the same mode of disposing equitable, non-jury, and common law, jury issues, the State does not discriminate against Employer's Liability suits nor does it make any inroad upon substance.

* * * The State judges and local lawyers who must administer the Federal Employers' Liability Act in State courts are trained in the ways of local practice; it multiplies the difficulties and confuses the administration of justice to require, on purely theoretical grounds, a hybrid of State and Federal practice in the State courts as to a single class of cases. Nothing in the Employers' Liability Act or in the judicial enforcement of the Act for over forty years forces such judicial hybridization upon the States. * * *

Even though the method of trying the equitable issue of fraud which the State applies in all other negligence cases governs Employers' Liability cases, two questions remain for decision: Should the validity of the release be tested by a Federal or a State standard? And if by a Federal one, did the Ohio courts in the present case correctly administer the standard? If the States afford courts for enforcing the Federal Act, they must enforce the substance of the rights given by Congress. They cannot depreciate the legislative currency issued by Congress—either expressly or by local methods of enforcement that accomplish the same result. * * *

* * *

Notes

1. Why is *Dice* often referred to as a "converse-*Erie*" case?

2. What did the Court mean when it stated: "The *Bombolis* case might be more in point had Ohio abolished trial by jury in all negligence cases including those arising under the federal Act"? —Then could't force Ohio to hear cases

3. Is there any *constitutional* limitation on what procedures Congress may require state courts to follow in adjudicating federal suits? Could Congress constitutionally require state judges to stand on one leg while adjudicating federal cases? For discussions of mandating federal procedural rules in state courts, see Redish & Sklaver, *Federal Power to Commandeer State Courts: Implications for the Theory of Judicial Federalism*, 32 Ind. L.Rev. 71 (1998); Jackson, Printz *and* Testa: *The Infrastructure of Federal Supremacy*, 32 Ind.L.Rev. 111 (1998); Parmet, *Stealth Preemption: The Proposed Federalization of State Court Procedures*, 44 Vill.L.Rev. 1 (1999);

Bellia, *Federal Regulation of State Court Procedures*, 110 Yale L.J. 947 (2001).

4. What is Justice Frankfurter's reasoning to support his conclusion that the state court need not employ federal procedures? Is his reasoning persuasive?

5. Under Georgia state practice, great factual detail was required in a complaint. This was in contrast to federal procedure where, under Rule 8(a) of the Federal Rules of Civil Procedure, a considerably more liberal "notice pleading" system is applied. Georgia state courts dismissed a complaint brought under the Federal Employers' Liability Act because it failed to meet the requirements of Georgia pleading practice. Plaintiff, in the United States Supreme Court, argued that in adjudicating this federal cause of action, the Georgia courts should be required to follow federal pleading practice. What result? See Brown v. Western Railway of Alabama, 338 U.S. 294 (1949).

6. In Felder v. Casey, 487 U.S. 131 (1988), the Supreme Court held invalid the Wisconsin Supreme Court's reliance on the state's notice-of-claim statute to bar a suit brought under the federal civil rights laws, 42 U.S.C. § 1983. The state statute provided that before suit may be brought in state court against a state or local governmental entity or officer, the plaintiff must notify the defendant of the circumstances and amount of the claim within 120 days of the injury. Justice Brennan, writing for the Court, reasoned:

> The decision to subject state subdivisions to liability for violations of federal rights * * * was a choice that Congress, not the Wisconsin legislature, made, and it is a decision that the State has no authority to override. Thus, however understandable or laudable the State's interest in controlling liability expenses might otherwise be, it is patently incompatible with the compensatory goals of the federal legislation, as are the means the State has chosen to effectuate it.

* * *

> This burdening of a federal right, moreover, is not the natural or permissible consequence of an otherwise neutral, uniformly applicable state rule. Although it is true that the notice-of-claim statute does not discriminate between state and federal causes of action against local governments, the fact remains that the law's protection extends only to governmental defendants and this conditions the right to bring suit against the very persons and entities Congress intended to subject to liability. We therefore cannot accept the suggestion that this requirement is simply part of "the vast body of procedural rules, rooted in policies unrelated to the definition of any particular substantive cause of action, that forms no essential part of 'the cause of action' as applied to any given plaintiff." * * * [The] defendant-specific focus of the notice requirement serves to distinguish it, rather starkly, from rules uniformly applicable to all suits, much as rules governing service of process or substitution of parties * * *. That state courts will hear the entire § 1983 cause of action once a plaintiff complies with the notice-of-claim statute, therefore, in no way alters the fact that the statute discrimi-

nates against the precise type of claim Congress has created. Id. at 143–45.

Justice O'Connor, joined by the Chief Justice, dissented.

How do you think the Court would have held had the state's notice-of-claim statute applied to every suit brought in state court? How *should* the Court have held? Assume a state judicial system provides for little or no discovery. Should the Supreme Court hold that in a section 1983 suit the state court must make available all of the discovery devices provided for in the Federal Rules of Civil Procedure? What are the competing considerations?

7.   *Dice* was distinguished in Johnson v. Fankell, 520 U.S. 911 (1997). There the Supreme Court held that the exception to the final judgment rule of appealability that it had recognized in the federal courts for appeals of orders denying qualified officer immunity on section 1983 claims did not bind the state courts adjudicating similar qualified immunity defenses. In *Dice*, the Court said, "we made clear that Congress had provided in FELA that the jury trial procedure was to be part of claims brought under the Act. In this case, by contrast, Congress has mentioned nothing about interlocutory appeals in section 1983; rather, the right to an immediate appeal in the federal court system is found in section 1291 [the final judgment rule], which obviously has no application to state courts." Id. at 921 n.12. The Court therefore concluded that the right of interlocutory review "is a federal procedural right that simply does not apply in a nonfederal forum." Id. at 921. However, neither the text nor the history of 28 U.S.C.A. § 1291, embodying the final judgment rule, in any way provides the basis for an exception for appeal of claims of qualified immunity. Rather, it was the substantive policy which the Court had recognized underlying the qualified immunity defense in section 1983 actions which had originally led the Court to recognize the exception to the final judgment rule from orders denying that defense. Did the Court correctly apply *Dice*?

8.   On the converse *Erie* issue, see generally Note, *State Enforcement of Federally Created Rights,* 73 Harv.L.Rev. 1551 (1961).

Chapter 6

REMEDIES AGAINST STATE AND LOCAL ACTION: 42 U.S.C.A. § 1983

§ 1. UNDER COLOR OF LAW

MONROE v. PAPE

Supreme Court of the United States, 1961.
365 U.S. 167.

MR. JUSTICE DOUGLAS delivered the opinion of the Court.

This case presents important questions concerning the construction of R.S. § 1979, 42 U.S.C. § 1983, which reads as follows:

> "Every person who, under color of any statute, ordinance, regulation, custom, or usage, of any State or Territory, subjects, or causes to be subjected, any citizen of the United States or other person within the jurisdiction thereof to the deprivation of any rights, privileges, or immunities secured by the Constitution and laws, shall be liable to the party injured in an action at law, suit in equity, or other proper proceeding for redress."

The complaint alleges that 13 Chicago police officers broke into petitioners' home in the early morning, routed them from bed, made them stand naked in the living room, and ransacked every room, emptying drawers and ripping mattress covers. It further alleges that Mr. Monroe was then taken to the police station and detained on "open" charges for 10 hours, while he was interrogated about a two-day-old murder, that he was not taken before a magistrate, though one was accessible, that he was not permitted to call his family or attorney, that he was subsequently released without criminal charges being preferred against him. It is alleged that the officers had no search warrant and no arrest warrant and that they acted "under color of the statutes, ordinances, regulations, customs and usages" of Illinois and of the City of

Chicago. Federal jurisdiction was asserted under R.S. § 1979, which we have set out above, and 28 U.S.C. § 1343,[1] and 28 U.S.C. § 1331.

The City of Chicago moved to dismiss the complaint on the ground that it is not liable under the Civil Rights Acts nor for acts committed in performance of its governmental functions. All defendants moved to dismiss, alleging that the complaint alleged no cause of action under those Acts or under the Federal Constitution. The District Court dismissed the complaint. The Court of Appeals affirmed, 272 F.2d 365, relying on its earlier decision, Stift v. Lynch, 7 Cir., 267 F.2d 237. The case is here on a writ of certiorari which we granted because of a seeming conflict of that ruling with our prior cases.

I.

Petitioners claim that the invasion of their home and the subsequent search without a warrant and the arrest and detention of Mr. Monroe without a warrant and without arraignment constituted a deprivation of their "rights, privileges, or immunities secured by the Constitution" within the meaning of R.S. § 1979. It has been said that when 18 U.S.C. § 241, made criminal a conspiracy "to injure, oppress, threaten, or intimidate any citizen in the free exercise or enjoyment of any right or privilege secured to him by the Constitution," it embraced only rights that an individual has by reason of his relation to the central government, not to state governments. But the history of the section of the Civil Rights Act presently involved does not permit such a narrow interpretation.

Section 1979 came onto the books as § 1 of the Ku Klux Act of April 20, 1871. 17 Stat. 13. It was one of the means whereby Congress exercised the power vested in it by § 5 of the Fourteenth Amendment to enforce the provisions of that Amendment. Senator Edmunds, Chairman of the Senate Committee on the Judiciary, said concerning this section:

> "The first section is one that I believe nobody objects to, as defining the rights secured by the Constitution of the United States when they are assailed by any State law or under color of any State law, and it is merely carrying out the principles of the civil rights bill, which has since become a part of the Constitution," viz., the Fourteenth Amendment.

Its purpose is plain from the title of the legislation, "An Act to enforce the Provisions of the Fourteenth Amendment to the Constitution of the United States, and for other Purposes." 17 Stat. 13. Allegation of facts constituting a deprivation under color of state authority of a right guaranteed by the Fourteenth Amendment satisfies to that extent the

1. This section provides in material part:

"The district courts shall have original jurisdiction of any civil action authorized by law to be commenced by any person:

. . .

"(3) To redress the deprivation, under color of any State law, statute, ordinance, regulation, custom or usage, of any right, privilege or immunity secured by the Constitution of the United States or by any Act of Congress providing for equal rights of citizens or of all persons within the jurisdiction of the United States."

requirement of R.S. § 1979. See Douglas v. City of Jeannette, 319 U.S. 157, 161–162. So far petitioners are on solid ground. For the guarantee against unreasonable searches and seizures contained in the Fourth Amendment has been made applicable to the States by reason of the Due Process Clause of the Fourteenth Amendment. Wolf v. People of State of Colorado, 338 U.S. 25; Elkins v. United States, 364 U.S. 206, 213.

II.

There can be no doubt at least since Ex parte Virginia, 100 U.S. 339, 346–347, that Congress has the power to enforce provisions of the Fourteenth Amendment against those who carry a badge of authority of a State and represent it in some capacity, whether they act in accordance with their authority or misuse it. See Home Tel. & Tel. Co. v. City of Los Angeles, 227 U.S. 278, 287–296. The question with which we now deal is the narrower one of whether Congress, in enacting § 1979, meant to give a remedy to parties deprived of constitutional rights, privileges and immunities by an official's abuse of his position. We conclude that it did so intend.

It is argued that "under color of" enumerated state authority excludes acts of an official or policeman who can show no authority under state law, state custom, or state usage to do what he did. In this case it is said that these policemen, in breaking into petitioners' apartment, violated the Constitution and laws of Illinois. It is pointed out that under Illinois law a simple remedy is offered for that violation and that, so far as it appears, the courts of Illinois are available to give petitioners that full redress which the common law affords for violence done to a person; and it is earnestly argued that no "statute, ordinance, regulation, custom or usage" of Illinois bars that redress.

* * *

The legislation—in particular the section with which we are now concerned—had several purposes. There are threads of many thoughts running through the debates. One who reads them in their entirety sees that the present section had three main aims.

First, it might, of course, override certain kinds of state laws. Mr. Sloss of Alabama, in opposition, spoke of that object and emphasized that it was irrelevant because there were no such laws:

"The first section of this bill prohibits any invidious legislation by States against the rights or privileges of citizens of the United States. The object of this section is not very clear, as it is not pretended by its advocates on this floor that any State has passed any laws endangering the rights or privileges of the colored people."

Second, it provided a remedy where state law was inadequate. That aspect of the legislation was summed up as follows by Senator Sherman of Ohio:

" . . . it is said the reason is that any offense may be committed upon a negro by a white man, and a negro cannot testify in any case against a white man, so that the only way by which any conviction can be had in Kentucky in those cases is in the United States courts, because the United States courts enforce the United States laws by which negroes may testify.''

But the purposes were much broader. The *third* aim was to provide a federal remedy where the state remedy, though adequate in theory, was not available in practice. The opposition to the measure complained that "It overrides the reserved powers of the States," just as they argued that the second section of the bill "absorb[ed] the entire jurisdiction of the States over their local and domestic affairs."

This Act of April 20, 1871, sometimes called "the third 'force bill,' " was passed by a Congress that had the Klan "particularly in mind." The debates are replete with references to the lawless conditions existing in the South in 1871. There was available to the Congress during these debates a report, nearly 600 pages in length, dealing with the activities of the Klan and the inability of the state governments to cope with it. This report was drawn on by many of the speakers. It was not the unavailability of state remedies but the failure of certain States to enforce the laws with an equal hand that furnished the powerful momentum behind this "force bill."

* * *

Senator Pratt of Indiana spoke of the discrimination against Union sympathizers and Negroes in the actual enforcement of the laws:

"Plausibly and sophistically it is said the laws of North Carolina do not discriminate against them; that the provisions in favor of rights and liberties are general; that the courts are open to all; that juries, grand and petit, are commanded to hear and redress without distinction as to color, race, or political sentiment.

"But it is a fact, asserted in the report, that of the hundreds of outrages committed upon loyal people through the agency of this Ku Klux organization not one has been punished. This defect in the administration of the laws does not extend to other cases. Vigorously enough are the laws enforced against Union people. They only fail in efficiency when a man of known Union sentiments, white or black, invokes their aid. Then Justice closes the door of her temples."

* * *

The debates were long and extensive. It is abundantly clear that one reason the legislation was passed was to afford a federal right in federal courts because, by reason of prejudice, passion, neglect, intolerance or otherwise, state laws might not be enforced and the claims of citizens to the enjoyment of rights, privileges, and immunities guaranteed by the Fourteenth Amendment might be denied by the state agencies.

* * *

Although the legislation was enacted because of the conditions that existed in the South at that time, it is cast in general language and is as applicable to Illinois as it is to the States whose names were mentioned over and again in the debates. It is no answer that the State has a law which if enforced would give relief. The federal remedy is supplementary to the state remedy, and the latter need not be first sought and refused before the federal one is invoked. Hence the fact that Illinois by its constitution and laws outlaws unreasonable searches and seizures is no barrier to the present suit in the federal court.

State relief not enough to overcome fed protections

We had before us in United States v. Classic, supra, § 20 of the Criminal Code, 18 U.S.C. § 242, which provides a criminal punishment for anyone who "under color of any law, statute, ordinance, regulation, or custom" subjects any inhabitant of a State to the deprivation of "any rights, privileges, or immunities secured or protected by the Constitution or laws of the United States." * * * The right involved in the Classic case was the right of voters in a primary to have their votes counted. The laws of Louisiana required the defendants "to count the ballots, to record the result of the count, and to certify the result of the election." But according to the indictment they did not perform their duty. In an opinion written by Mr. Justice (later Chief Justice) Stone, in which Mr. Justice Roberts, Mr. Justice Reed, and Mr. Justice Frankfurter joined, the Court ruled, "Misuse of power, possessed by virtue of state law and made possible only because the wrongdoer is clothed with the authority of state law, is action taken 'under color of' state law." There was a dissenting opinion; but the ruling as to the meaning of "under color of" state law was not questioned.

Classic

Misuse of p[ower] granted under state law

That view of the meaning of the words "under color of" state law, 18 U.S.C. § 242, was reaffirmed in Screws v. United States, supra, 325 U.S. 108–113. * * * It was argued there, as it is here, that "under color of" state law included only action taken by officials pursuant to state law. We rejected that view.

Rejected

* * *

Mr. Shellabarger, reporting out the bill which became the Ku Klux Act, said of the provision with which we now deal:

> "The model for it will be found in the second section of the act of April 9, 1866, known as the 'civil rights act.' ... This section of this bill, on the same state of facts, not only provides a civil remedy for persons whose former condition may have been that of slaves, but also to all people where, under color of State law, they or any of them may be deprived of rights...."

Thus, it is beyond doubt that this phrase should be accorded the same construction in both statutes—in § 1979 and in 18 U.S.C. § 242.

* * *

We conclude that the meaning given "under color of" law in the *Classic* case and in the *Screws* and *Williams* cases was the correct one; and we adhere to it.

In the *Screws* case we dealt with a statute that imposed criminal penalties for acts "wilfully" done. We construed that word in its setting to mean the doing of an act with "a specific intent to deprive a person of a federal right." 325 U.S. at page 103. We do not think that gloss should be placed on § 1979 which we have here. The word "wilfully" does not appear in § 1979. Moreover, § 1979 provides a civil remedy, while in the *Screws* case we dealt with a criminal law challenged on the ground of vagueness. Section 1979 should be read against the background of tort liability that makes a man responsible for the natural consequences of his actions.

So far, then, the complaint states a cause of action. There remains to consider only a defense peculiar to the City of Chicago.

III.

The City of Chicago asserts that it is not liable under § 1979. We do not stop to explore the whole range of questions tendered us on this issue at oral argument and in the briefs. For we are of the opinion that Congress did not undertake to bring municipal corporations within the ambit of § 1979.

* * *

The response of the Congress to the proposal to make municipalities liable for certain actions being brought within federal purview by the Act of April 20, 1871, was so antagonistic that we cannot believe that the word "person" was used in this particular Act to include them. Accordingly we hold that the motion to dismiss the complaint against the City of Chicago was properly granted. But since the complaint should not have been dismissed against the officials the judgment must be and is reversed.

Reversed.

MR. JUSTICE HARLAN, whom MR. JUSTICE STEWART joins, concurring.

Were this case here as one of first impression, I would find the "under color of any statute" issue very close indeed. However, in *Classic* and *Screws* this Court considered a substantially identical statutory phrase to have a meaning which, unless we now retreat from it, requires that issue to go for the petitioners here.

From my point of view, the policy of *stare decisis,* as it should be applied in matters of statutory construction and, to a lesser extent, the indications of congressional acceptance of this Court's earlier interpretation, require that it appear beyond doubt from the legislative history of the 1871 statute that *Classic* and *Screws* misapprehended the meaning of the controlling provision, before a departure from what was decided in those cases would be justified. Since I can find no such justifying indication in that legislative history, I join the opinion of the Court.

Mr. Justice Frankfurter, dissenting except insofar as the Court holds that this action cannot be maintained against the City of Chicago.

* * *

This case squarely presents the question whether the intrusion of a city policeman for which that policeman can show no such authority at state law as could be successfully interposed in defense to a state-law action against him, is nonetheless to be regarded as "under color" of state authority within the meaning of R.S. § 1979. Respondents, in breaking into the Monroe apartment, violated the laws of the State of Illinois. Illinois law appears to offer a civil remedy for unlawful searches; petitioners do not claim that none is available. Rather they assert that they have been deprived of due process of law and of equal protection of the laws under color of state law, although from all that appears the courts of Illinois are available to give them the fullest redress which the common law affords for the violence done them, nor does any "statute, ordinance, regulation, custom, or usage" of the State of Illinois bar that redress. Did the enactment by Congress of § 1 of the Ku Klux Act of 1871 encompass such a situation?

That section, it has been noted, was patterned on the similar criminal provision of § 2, Act of April 9, 1866. The earlier Act had as its primary object the effective nullification of the Black Codes, those statutes of the Southern legislatures which had so burdened and disqualified the Negro as to make his emancipation appear illusory. The Act had been vetoed by President Johnson, whose veto message describes contemporary understanding of its second section; the section, he wrote,

> "seems to be designed to apply to some existing or future law of a State or Territory which may conflict with the provisions of the bill. . . . It provides for counteracting such forbidden legislation by imposing fine and imprisonment upon the legislators who may pass such conflicting laws, or upon the officers or agents who shall put, or attempt to put, them into execution. It means an official offense, not a common crime committed against law upon the persons or property of the black race. Such an act may deprive the black man of his property, but not of the right to hold property. It means a deprivation of the right itself, either by the State judiciary or the State Legislature."

And Senator Trumbull, then Chairman of the Senate Judiciary Committee, in his remarks urging its passage over the veto, expressed the intendment of the second section as those who voted for it read it:

> "If an offense is committed against a colored person simply because he is colored, in a State where the law affords him the same protection as if he were white, this act neither has nor was intended to have anything to do with his case, because he has adequate remedies in the State courts; but if he is discriminated against under

color of State laws because he is colored, then it becomes necessary to interfere for his protection."

* * *

The original text of the present § 1979 contained words, left out in the Revised Statutes, which clarified the objective to which the provision was addressed:

"That any person who, under color of any law, statute, ordinance, regulation, custom, or usage of any State, shall subject, or cause to be subjected, any person within the jurisdiction of the United States to the deprivation of any rights, privileges, or immunities secured by the Constitution of the United States, shall, *any such law, statute, ordinance, regulation, custom, or usage of the State to the contrary notwithstanding,* be liable to the party injured. . . ."

* * *

The Court now says, however, that "It was not the unavailability of state remedies but the failure of certain States to enforce the laws with an equal hand that furnished the powerful momentum behind this 'force bill.' "Of course, if the notion of "unavailability" of remedy is limited to mean an absence of statutory, paper right, this is in large part true. Insofar as the Court undertakes to demonstrate—as the bulk of its opinion seems to do—that § 1979 was meant to reach some instances of action not specifically authorized by the avowed, apparent, written law inscribed in the statute books of the States, the argument knocks at an open door. No one would or could, deny this, for by its express terms the statute comprehends deprivations of federal rights under color of any "statute, ordinance, regulation, *custom, or usage*" of a State. (Emphasis added.) The question is, *what* class of cases other than those involving state statute law were meant to be reached. And, with respect to this question, the Court's conclusion is undermined by the very portions of the legislative debates which it cites. For surely the misconduct of individual municipal police officers, subject to the effective oversight of appropriate state administrative and judicial authorities, presents a situation which differs *toto coelo* from one in which "Immunity is given to crime, and the records of the public tribunals are searched in vain for any evidence of effective redress," or in which murder rages while a State makes "no successful effort to bring the guilty to punishment or afford protection or redress," or in which the "State courts . . . [are] unable to enforce the criminal laws . . . or to suppress the disorders existing," or in which, in a State's "judicial tribunals one class is unable to secure that enforcement of their rights and punishment for their infraction which is accorded to another," or "of . . . hundreds of outrages . . . not one [is] punished," or "the courts of the . . . States fail and refuse to do their duty in the punishment of offenders against the law," or in which a "class of officers charged under the laws with their administration permanently and as a rule refuse to extend [their] protection." These statements indicate that Congress—made keenly aware by the post-bellum conditions in the South that States through their authorities could sanction offenses against the individual by settled practice which established state law as truly as written codes—designed § 1979 to reach, as well, official conduct which, because engaged in "permanently and as a rule," or "systematically," came through acceptance by law-administering officers to constitute "custom, or usage" having the cast of law. They do not indicate an attempt to reach, nor does the statute by its terms include, instances of acts in defiance of state law and which no settled state practice, no systematic pattern of official action or inaction, no "custom, or usage, of any State," insulates from effective and adequate reparation by the State's authorities.

Rather, all the evidence converges to the conclusion that Congress by § 1979 created a civil liability enforceable in the federal courts only in instances of injury for which redress was barred in the state courts because some "statute, ordinance, regulation, custom, or usage" sanctioned the grievance complained of. This purpose, manifested even by the so-called "Radical" Reconstruction Congress in 1871, accords with the presuppositions of our federal system. The jurisdiction which Article III of the Constitution conferred on the national judiciary reflected the assumption that the state courts, not the federal courts, would remain the primary guardians of that fundamental security of person and property which the long evolution of the common law had secured to one individual as against other individuals. The Fourteenth Amendment did not alter this basic aspect of our federalism.

* * *

The present case comes here from a judgment sustaining a motion to dismiss petitioners' complaint. That complaint, insofar as it describes the police intrusion, makes no allegation that that intrusion was authorized by state law other than the conclusory and unspecific claim that "During all times herein mentioned the individual defendants and each of them were acting under color of the statutes, ordinances, regulations, customs and usages of the State of Illinois, of the County of Cook and of the defendant City of Chicago." In the face of Illinois decisions holding such intrusions unlawful and in the absence of more precise factual averments to support its conclusion, such a complaint fails to state a claim under § 1979.

However, the complaint does allege, as to the ten-hour detention of Mr. Monroe, that "it was, and it is now, the custom or usage of the Police Department of the City of Chicago to arrest and confine individuals in the police stations and jail cells of the said department for long periods of time on 'open' charges." * * * Such averments do present facts which, admitted as true for purposes of a motion to dismiss, seem to sustain petitioners' claim that Mr. Monroe's detention—as contrasted with the night-time intrusion into the Monroe apartment—was "under color" of state authority.

Notes

1.   Bivens v. Six Unknown Named Agents of Federal Bureau of Narcotics, 403 U.S. 388 (1971), and its progeny [infra pp. 917–38], explore whether various constitutional provisions create implied causes of action against federal government officials. The *Bivens* inquiry is generally made unnecessary when constitutional claims "in * * * law [or] * * * in equity" are brought against state and local government actors under section 1983. The Civil Rights Attorney's Fees Awards Act of 1976 also allows the recovery of attorney fees in section 1983 cases. 42 U.S.C. § 1988; Pub.L. No. 94–559. As *Monroe* indicates, section 1983 is accompanied by a specific jurisdictional statute, 28 U.S.C. § 1343(3). Federal jurisdiction over section 1983 claims is not, however, exclusive. Therefore, section 1983 actions may be brought in state courts. See Steinglass, *The Emerging State Court § 1983 Action: A Procedural Review,* 38 U.Miami L.Rev. 381 (1984). In fact, as a general matter, competent state courts may not refuse to entertain section 1983 claims. Howlett v. Rose, 496 U.S. 356 (1990).

2.   Justice Douglas's opinion in *Monroe* turns extensively on the legislative history of section 1983. The Civil Rights Act of 1871, or the Ku Klux Act as it was referred to, was intended, in the Court's view, to "afford a federal right in federal courts because, by reason of prejudice, passion, neglect, intolerance or otherwise, state laws might not be enforced and * * * rights * * * guaranteed by the Fourteenth Amendment might be denied." 365 U.S. at 180. This history has been explored extensively in the literature. See Blackmun, *Section 1983 and Federal Protection of Individual Rights—Will the Statute Remain Alive or Fade Away?,* 60 N.Y.U.L.Rev. 1 (1985); Nichol, *Federalism, State Courts and Section 1983,* 73 Va.L.Rev. 959 (1987); Zagrans, *"Under Color of" What Law: A Reconstructed Model of Section 1983 Liability,* 71 Va.L.Rev. 499, 559 (1985) (section 1983 clearly meant to "create liability only for acts done with state authority."); Winter, *The Meaning of "Under Color of" Law,* 91 Mich.L.Rev. 323, 325 (1992) (referring to Zagrans–Frankfurter position: "Nothing could be further from the truth.").

Justice Frankfurter, of course, would have given section 1983 a far more restrictive interpretation. If the central concern of the framers of section 1983 was that state actors (including the judiciary) were dominated by the Klan and, therefore, applied local laws in dramatically biased ways, would Justice Frankfurter's interpretation of section 1983 thwart its primary purpose? On the other hand, does Justice Douglas conclude that action is "under color of" state law even if it is contrary to state law?

3.   Before the decision in *Monroe,* section 1983 actions were, relatively speaking, rarely filed. As recently as 1960, only 287 suits were filed in the entire country. By the late 1980s, however, over 40,000 section 1983 cases a year were brought in the federal courts. See generally, Eisenberg & Schwab, *The Reality of Constitutional Tort Litigation,* 72 Corn.L.Rev. 641 (1987). The great bulk of modern constitutional litigation now occurs through the conduit of section 1983. Many of the federal courts principles which follow in this casebook—abstention, the Anti–Injunction Act, "Our Federalism" and res judicata, for example—are strongly affected by the interpretation of section 1983. See generally Gressman, *The Unhappy History of Civil Rights*

Legislation, 50 Mich.L.Rev. 1323 (1952); Weinberg, *The* Monroe *Mystery Solved: Beyond the "Unhappy History" Theory of Civil Rights Litigation,* 1991 B.Y.U.L.Rev. 737; Beermann, *The Unhappy History of Civil Rights Legislation, Fifty Years Later*, 34 Conn.L.Rev. 981 (2002). The explosion of litigation and the far-reaching effects of section 1983 have led two commentators to call section 1983 a "super-statute." Eskridge & Ferejohn, *Super-Statutes*, 50 Duke L.J. 1215 (2001).

4. *Monroe* significantly expanded the meaning of "under color of law". In Lugar v. Edmondson Oil Co., 457 U.S. 922, 929 (1982), the Court indicated "it is clear that in a § 1983 action brought against a state official, the statutory requirement of action 'under color of state law' and the 'state action' requirement of the Fourteenth Amendment are identical." Cf. Polk County v. Dodson, 454 U.S. 312 (1981) (actions of public defender not under color of state law).

5. Section 1983 grants a cause of action against the deprivation of rights "secured by the Constitution and laws" of the United States. In Maine v. Thiboutot, 448 U.S. 1 (1980), the Supreme Court ruled that the statute means what it says and, therefore, provides a cause of action for violations of federal statutes as well as the Constitution. Wright v. Roanoke Redevelopment and Housing Authority, 479 U.S. 418, 423 (1987), in turn, ruled that a plaintiff alleging a violation of a federal statute will be permitted to sue under section 1983 unless (1) "the statute [does] not create enforceable rights * * * within the meaning of sec. 1983," or (2) "Congress has foreclosed such enforcement of the statute in the enactment itself." This is, the Court has held, "a different inquiry than that involved in determining whether a private right of action can be implied from a particular statute." Wilder v. Virginia Hospital Association, 496 U.S. 498, 508 (1990). "Because § 1983 provides an 'alternative source of express congressional authorization of private suits,'" the Court indicated in *Wilder,* "separation of powers concerns are not present in a § 1983 case. Id. at 509. Consistent with this view, we recognize an exception to the general rule that sec. 1983 provides a remedy for violation of federal statutory rights only when Congress has affirmatively withdrawn the remedy." See generally Jacques & Beermann, *Section 1983's "And Laws" Clause Run Amok: Civil Rights Attorney's Fees in Cellular Facilities Siting Disputes*, 81 B.U.L.Rev. 735 (2001); Monaghan, *Federal Statutory Review Under Section 1983 and the APA,* 91 Colum.L.Rev. 233 (1991).

6. *Monroe* establishes that a plaintiff may bring a section 1983 action without first exhausting state judicial remedies—the "federal remedy is supplementary to the state remedy, and the latter need not be first sought and refused before the federal one is invoked." 365 U.S. at 183. The same result holds for state administrative remedies. McNeese v. Board of Education, 373 U.S. 668 (1963); Patsy v. Board of Regents, 457 U.S. 496 (1982).

§ 2. LIABILITY

MONELL v. DEPARTMENT OF SOCIAL SERVICES

Supreme Court of the United States, 1978.
436 U.S. 658.

Justice Brennan delivered the opinion of the Court.

Petitioners, a class of female employees of the Department of Social Services and of the Board of Education of the city of New York, commenced this action under 42 U.S.C. § 1983 in July 1971. The gravamen of the complaint was that the Board and the Department had as a matter of official policy compelled pregnant employees to take unpaid leaves of absence before such leaves were required for medical reasons. Cf. Cleveland Board of Education v. LaFleur, 414 U.S. 632 (1974) [holding such leaves unconstitutional]. The suit sought injunctive relief and backpay for periods of unlawful forced leave. Named as defendants in the action were the Department and its Commissioner, the Board and its Chancellor, and the city of New York and its Mayor. In each case, the individual defendants were sued solely in their official capacities.

On cross-motions for summary judgment, the District Court for the Southern District of New York held moot petitioners' claims for injunctive and declaratory relief since the City of New York and the Board, after the filing of the complaint, had changed their policies relating to maternity leaves so that no pregnant employee would have to take leave unless she was medically unable to continue to perform her job. No one now challenges this conclusion. The court did conclude, however, that the acts complained of were unconstitutional under LaFleur, supra. Nonetheless plaintiffs' prayers for backpay were denied because any such damages would come ultimately from the City of New York and, therefore, to hold otherwise would be to "circumven[t]" the immunity conferred on municipalities by Monroe v. Pape, 365 U.S. 167 (1961).

On appeal, petitioners renewed their arguments that the Board of Education[1] was not a "municipality" within the meaning of Monroe v. Pape, supra, and that, in any event, the District Court had erred in barring a damages award against the individual defendants. The Court of Appeals for the Second Circuit rejected both contentions. The court first held that the Board of Education was not a "person" under § 1983 because "it performs a vital governmental function ... , and, significantly, while it has the right to determine how the funds appropriated to it shall be spent ... , it has no final say in deciding what its appropriations shall be." The individual defendants, however, were "persons" under § 1983, even when sued solely in their official capacities. Yet, because a damages award would "have to be paid by a city that was held not to be

4. Petitioners conceded that the Department of Social Services enjoys the same   status as New York City for Monroe purposes.

amenable to such an action in *Monroe v. Pape*," a damages action
against officials sued in their official capacities could not proceed.

We granted certiorari in this case to consider

"Whether local governmental officials and/or local independent
school boards are 'persons' within the meaning of 42 U.S.C. § 1983
when equitable relief in the nature of back pay is sought against
them in their official capacities?"

ISSUE

Although, after plenary consideration, we have decided the merits of
over a score of cases brought under § 1983 in which the principal
defendant was a school board—and, indeed, in some of which § 1983 and
its jurisdictional counterpart, 28 U.S.C. § 1343, provided the only basis
for jurisdiction—we indicated in Mt. Healthy City Board of Education v.
Doyle, 429 U.S. 274, 279 (1977), last Term that the question presented
here was open and would be decided "another day." That other day has
come and we now overrule Monroe v. Pape, supra, insofar as it holds
that local governments are wholly immune from suit under § 1983.[7]

I

In Monroe v. Pape, we held that "Congress did not undertake to
bring municipal corporations within the ambit of [§ 1983]." 365 U.S., at
187. The sole basis for this conclusion was an inference drawn from
Congress' rejection of the "Sherman amendment" to the bill which
became the Civil Rights Act of 1871, the precursor of § 1983. The
amendment would have held a municipal corporation liable for damage
done to the person or property of its inhabitants by *private* persons
"riotously and tumultuously assembled." Cong. Globe, 42d Cong., 1st
Sess., 749 (1871) (hereinafter Globe). Although the Sherman amendment
did not seek to amend § 1 of the Act, which is now § 1983, and although
the nature of the obligation created by that amendment was vastly
different from that created by § 1, the Court nonetheless concluded in
Monroe that Congress must have meant to exclude municipal corporations from the coverage of § 1 because " 'the House [in voting against
the Sherman amendment] had solemnly decided that in their judgment
Congress had no constitutional power to impose any *obligation* upon
county and town organizations, the mere instrumentality for the administration of state law.' " 365 U.S., at 190 (emphasis added), quoting
Globe 804 (Rep. Poland). This statement, we thought, showed that
Congress doubted its "constitutional power . . . to impose *civil liability*
on municipalities," 365 U.S., at 190 (emphasis added), and that such
doubt would have extended to any type of civil liability.

mere instrum
in adming
state law

A fresh analysis of the debate on the Civil Rights Act of 1871, and
particularly of the case law which each side mustered in its support,

7. However, we do uphold Monroe v.
Pape, insofar as it holds that the doctrine of
respondeat superior is not a basis for rendering municipalities liable under § 1983
for the constitutional torts of their employees. See Part II, infra.

shows, however, that *Monroe* incorrectly equated the "obligation" of which Representative Poland spoke with "civil liability."

* * *

[In Part I of the opinion, the Court analyzed the legislative history of § 1983 and the Sherman amendment, concluding that the 1871 Congress did intend to impose liability on municipalities.]

II

Our analysis of the legislative history of the Civil Rights Act of 1871 compels the conclusion that Congress *did* intend municipalities and other local government units to be included among those persons to whom § 1983 applies. Local governing bodies,[55] therefore, can be sued directly under § 1983 for monetary, declaratory, or injunctive relief where, as here, the action that is alleged to be unconstitutional implements or executes a policy statement, ordinance, regulation, or decision officially adopted and promulgated by that body's officers. Moreover, although the touchstone of the § 1983 action against a government body is an allegation that official policy is responsible for a deprivation of rights protected by the Constitution, local governments, like every other § 1983 "person," by the very terms of the statute, may be sued for constitutional deprivations visited pursuant to governmental "custom" even though such a custom has not received formal approval through the body's official decisionmaking channels. As Mr. Justice Harlan, writing for the Court, said in Adickes v. S. H. Kress & Co., 398 U.S. 144, 167–168 (1970): "Congress included customs and usages [in § 1983] because of the persistent and widespread discriminatory practices of state officials. . . . Although not authorized by written law, such practices of state officials could well be so permanent and well settled as to constitute a 'custom or usage' with the force of law."

On the other hand, the language of § 1983, read against the background of the same legislative history, compels the conclusion that Congress did not intend municipalities to be held liable unless action pursuant to official municipal policy of some nature caused a constitutional tort. In particular, we conclude that a municipality cannot be held liable *solely* because it employs a tortfeasor—or, in other words, a municipality cannot be held liable under § 1983 on a *respondeat superior* theory.

We begin with the language of § 1983 as originally passed:

> "*[A]ny person who,* under color of any law, statute, ordinance, regulation, custom, or usage of any State, *shall subject, or cause to be subjected,* any person . . . to the deprivation of any rights,

55. Since official-capacity suits generally represent only another way of pleading an action against an entity of which an officer is an agent—at least where Eleventh Amendment considerations do not control analysis—our holding today that local governments can be sued under § 1983 necessarily decides that local government officials sued in their official capacities are "persons" under § 1983 in those cases in which, as here, a local government would be suable in its own name.

privileges, or immunities secured by the Constitution of the United States, shall, any such law, statute, ordinance, regulation, custom, or usage of the State to the contrary notwithstanding, be liable to the party injured in any action at law, suit in equity, or other proper proceeding for redress...." 17 Stat. 13 (emphasis added).

The italicized language plainly imposes liability on a government that, under color of some official policy, "causes" an employee to violate another's constitutional rights. At the same time, that language cannot be easily read to impose liability vicariously on governing bodies solely on the basis of the existence of an employer-employee relationship with a tortfeasor. Indeed, the fact that Congress did specifically provide that A's tort became B's liability if B "caused" A to subject another to a tort suggests that Congress did not intend § 1983 liability to attach where such causation was absent.

Only if Causation

Equally important, creation of a federal law of *respondeat superior* would have raised all the constitutional problems associated with the obligation to keep the peace, an obligation Congress chose not to impose because it thought imposition of such an obligation unconstitutional. To this day, there is disagreement about the basis for imposing liability on an employer for the torts of an employee when the sole nexus between the employer and the tort is the fact of the employer-employee relationship. See W. Prosser, Law of Torts § 69, p. 459 (4th ed. 1971). Nonetheless, two justifications tend to stand out. First is the common-sense notion that no matter how blameless an employer appears to be in an individual case, accidents might nonetheless be reduced if employers had to bear the cost of accidents. See, e.g., ibid.; 2 F. Harper & F. James, Law of Torts, § 26.3, pp. 1368–1369 (1956). Second is the argument that the cost of accidents should be spread to the community as a whole on an insurance theory. See, e.g., id., § 26.5; Prosser, supra, at 459.

The first justification is of the same sort that was offered for statutes like the Sherman amendment: "The obligation to make compensation for injury resulting from riot is, by arbitrary enactment of statutes, affirmatory law, and the reason of passing the statute is to secure a more perfect police regulation." Globe 777 (Sen. Frelinghuysen). This justification was obviously insufficient to sustain the amendment against perceived constitutional difficulties and there is no reason to suppose that a more general liability imposed for a similar reason would have been thought less constitutionally objectionable. The second justification was similarly put forward as a justification for the Sherman amendment: "we do not look upon [the Sherman amendment] as a punishment.... It is a mutual insurance." Id., at 792 (Rep. Butler). Again, this justification was insufficient to sustain the amendment.

We conclude, therefore, that a local government may not be sued under § 1983 for an injury inflicted solely by its employees or agents. Instead, it is when execution of a government's policy or custom, whether made by its lawmakers or by those whose edicts or acts may fairly be said to represent official policy, inflicts the injury that the

not liable for injury inflicted solely by employee/agent

government as an entity is responsible under § 1983. Since this case unquestionably involves official policy as the moving force of the constitutional violation found by the District Court, we must reverse the judgment below. In so doing, we have no occasion to address, and do not address, what the full contours of municipal liability under § 1983 may be. We have attempted only to sketch so much of the § 1983 cause of action against a local government as is apparent from the history of the 1871 Act and our prior cases, and we expressly leave further development of this action to another day.

* * *

[The concurring opinions of JUSTICE POWELL and JUSTICE STEVENS, and the dissenting opinion of JUSTICE REHNQUIST, joined by the CHIEF JUSTICE, are omitted.]

Notes

1. Justice Rehnquist, dissenting in *Monell*, pointed out that Congress was in the process of considering a bill that would have amended section 1983 by removing the municipal immunity recognized in *Monroe*. Should that fact be relevant?

2. The Court held in Will v. Michigan Department of State Police, 491 U.S. 58 (1989), that a state and instrumentalities of a state are not "persons" subject to suit under section 1983 in either state or federal court. The *Will* decision is criticized in Burnham & Fayz, *The State as a "Non-Person" Under Section 1983: Some Comments on Will and Suggestions for the Future,* 70 Ore.L.Rev. 1 (1991).

3. The Court in *Monell* explained that *stare decisis* did not mandate retaining the *Monroe* rule, because municipalities could not claim a reliance interest in *Monroe's* immunity: "[I]t scarcely need be mentioned that nothing in *Monroe* encourages municipalities to violate constitutional rights or even suggests that such violations are anything other than completely wrong." 436 U.S. at 700. Does this statement prove too much? Does it undermine the Court's holding that municipalities cannot be held liable under a theory of *respondeat superior*?

4. The distinction between liability based on a municipal policy or custom and liability based on *respondeat superior* has caused the Court quite a bit of difficulty. Beyond the simple case of a declared policy issued by the municipality—as was the situation in *Monell*—when can wrongdoing by a city employee be attributed to the city?

In City of Oklahoma City v. Tuttle, 471 U.S. 808 (1985), plaintiff's husband was shot and killed by an Oklahoma City police officer. Plaintiff sued the city for damages under section 1983, alleging that its "policy" of inadequate training caused the police officer to use excessive force, violating the decedent's constitutional rights. The jury awarded the plaintiff $1,500,000. The Supreme Court ultimately reversed the jury's verdict on the ground that the single incident of police misbehavior—however egregious—could not by itself support a finding that a municipal policy caused the incident. The plurality opinion expressed concern that if a jury inferred a policy of inadequate training from a single incident, the jury might be imposing liability "simply because the municipality hired one 'bad apple.' " Id. at 821. See also id. at 831 (Brennan, J., concurring in judgment) ("To infer the existence of a city policy from the isolated misconduct of a single, low-level officer, and then to hold the city liable on the basis of that policy, would amount to permitting precisely the theory of strict *respondeat superior* liability rejected in *Monell*.") The Court reserved judgment on the extent to which inadequate training could *ever* constitute a municipal policy, and on the level of proof necessary to show that inadequate training caused the constitutional violations.

In Pembaur v. City of Cincinnati, 475 U.S. 469 (1986), the Court confronted the question of whether, after *Tuttle*, a single decision by a policy-making official could constitute city policy. In *Pembaur*, county police trying to serve a subpoena on Pembaur encountered resistance. They called the county prosecutor, who ordered them to serve the subpoena, the police then entered Pembaur's place of business by force. The question before the Supreme Court was whether that entry—held to be illegal—could subject the county to liability under *Monell*. The Court held that the county was liable, because the prosecutor had final authority to establish county policy with respect to the illegal entry. The Court rejected an argument that *Tuttle* prohibited imposing liability on the basis of a single action, holding that "municipal liability may be imposed for a single decision by municipal policymakers under appropriate circumstances." Id. at 480. Beyond that holding, the Court could not agree on much of the reasoning. Justice Brennan's plurality opinion would impose liability for a single decision as long as "the decisionmaker possesses final authority to establish municipal policy with respect to the action ordered." Id. 481. Justice Stevens, concurring in the judgment, would impose liability for *any* illegal action by an employee, under a theory of *respondeat superior*. (Justice Stevens did not join Part II of the Court's opinion in *Monell*, and he dissented in *Tuttle*, arguing that section 1983 established *respondeat superior* liability.) Justice O'Connor also concurred in the judgment in *Pembaur*, agreeing that in the particular circumstances the county prosecutor's decision constituted county policy. She refused to join much of the plurality opinion, however, because she was afraid that "the standard the majority articulates may be misread to expose municipalities to liability beyond that envisioned by the Court in *Monell*." Id. at 491.

5. The question of who constitutes a policymaking official, which divided the Court in *Pembaur*, has been particularly troublesome. Consider the following case:

CITY OF ST. LOUIS v. PRAPROTNIK
Supreme Court of the United States, 1988.
485 U.S. 112.

JUSTICE O'CONNOR announced the judgment of the Court and delivered an opinion, in which THE CHIEF JUSTICE, JUSTICE WHITE, and JUSTICE SCALIA join.

This case calls upon us to define the proper legal standard for determining when isolated decisions by municipal officials or employees may expose the municipality itself to liability under 42 U.S.C. § 1983.

The principal facts are not in dispute. Respondent James H. Praprotnik is an architect who began working for petitioner city of St. Louis in 1968. For several years, respondent consistently received favorable evaluations of his job performance, uncommonly quick promotions, and significant increases in salary. By 1980, he was serving in a management-level city planning position at petitioner's Community Development Agency (CDA).

The Director of CDA, Donald Spaid, had instituted a requirement that the agency's professional employees, including architects, obtain advance approval before taking on private clients. Respondent and other CDA employees objected to the requirement. In April 1980, respondent was suspended for 15 days by CDA's Director of Urban Design, Charles Kindleberger, for having accepted outside employment without prior approval. Respondent appealed to the city's Civil Service Commission, a body charged with reviewing employee grievances. Finding the penalty too harsh, the Commission reversed the suspension, awarded respondent backpay, and directed that he be reprimanded for having failed to secure a clear understanding of the rule.

The Commission's decision was not well received by respondent's supervisors at CDA. Kindleberger later testified that he believed respondent had lied to the Commission, and that Spaid was angry with respondent.

Respondent's next two annual job performance evaluations were markedly less favorable than those in previous years. In discussing one of these evaluations with respondent, Kindleberger apparently mentioned his displeasure with respondent's 1980 appeal to the Civil Service Commission. Respondent appealed both evaluations to the Department of Personnel. In each case, the Department ordered partial relief and was upheld by the city's Director of Personnel or the Civil Service Commission.

In April 1981, a new Mayor came into office, and Donald Spaid was replaced as Director of CDA by Frank Hamsher. As a result of budget cuts, a number of layoffs and transfers significantly reduced the size of CDA and of the planning section in which respondent worked. Respondent, however, was retained.

In the spring of 1982, a second round of layoffs and transfers occurred at CDA. At that time, the city's Heritage and Urban Design Commission (Heritage) was seeking approval to hire someone who was qualified in architecture and urban planning. Hamsher arranged with the Director of Heritage, Henry Jackson, for certain functions to be transferred from CDA to Heritage. This arrangement, which made it possible for Heritage to employ a relatively high-level "city planning manager," was approved by Jackson's supervisor, Thomas Nash. Hamsher then transferred respondent to Heritage to fill this position. [Praprotnik was eventually laid off from the Heritage position.]

Respondent objected to the transfer, and appealed to the Civil Service Commission. The Commission declined to hear the appeal because respondent had not suffered a reduction in his pay or grade. Respondent then filed suit in Federal District Court, alleging that the transfer was unconstitutional. The city was named as a defendant, along with Kindleberger, Hamsher, Jackson (whom respondent deleted from the list before trial), and Deborah Patterson, who had succeeded Hamsher at CDA.

* * *

The case went to trial on [the theory] that respondent's First Amendment rights had been violated through retaliatory actions taken in response to his appeal of his 1980 suspension * * *. The jury returned special verdicts exonerating each of the three individual defendants, but finding the city liable * * *. * * * [T]he city appealed.

* * * With one judge dissenting, * * * the panel affirmed the verdict holding the city liable for violating respondent's First Amendment rights. * * *

* * *

Turning to the question whether a rational jury could have concluded that respondent had been injured by an unconstitutional policy, the Court of Appeals found that respondent's transfer from CDA to Heritage had been "orchestrated" by Hamsher, that the transfer had amounted to a "constructive discharge," and that the injury had reached fruition when respondent was eventually laid off [from Heritage]. The court held that the jury's verdict exonerating Hamsher and the other individual defendants could be reconciled with a finding of liability against the city because "the named defendants were not the supervisors directly causing the lay off, when the actual damages arose."

The dissenting judge relied on our decision in Pembaur v. Cincinnati, 475 U.S. 469 (1986). He found that the power to set employment policy for petitioner city of St. Louis lay with the Mayor and Aldermen, who were authorized to enact ordinances, and with the Civil Service Commission, whose function was to hear appeals from city employees who believed that their rights under the city's Charter, or under applicable rules and ordinances, had not been properly respected. The dissent concluded that respondent had submitted no evidence proving that the Mayor and Aldermen, or the Commission, had established a policy of retaliating against employees for appealing from adverse personnel decisions. The dissenting judge also concluded that, even if there were such a policy, the record evidence would not support a finding that respondent was in fact transferred or laid off in retaliation for the 1980 appeal from his suspension.

We granted certiorari, and we now reverse.

* * *

III

A

* * *

Ten years ago, this Court held that municipalities and other bodies of local government are "persons" within the meaning of [§ 1983]. Such a body may therefore be sued directly if it is alleged to have caused a constitutional tort through "a policy statement, ordinance, regulation, or decision officially adopted and promulgated by that body's officers." Monell v. New York City Dept. of Social Services, 436 U.S. 658, 690 (1978). The Court pointed out that § 1983 also authorizes suit "for constitutional deprivations visited pursuant to governmental 'custom' even though such a custom has not received formal approval through the body's official decisionmaking channels." Id., at 690–691. At the same time, the Court rejected the use of the doctrine of *respondeat superior* and concluded that municipalities could be held liable only when an injury was inflicted by a government's "lawmakers or by those whose edicts or acts may fairly be said to represent official policy." Id., at 694.

Monell's rejection of *respondeat superior*, and its insistence that local governments could be held liable only for the results of unconstitutional governmental "policies," arose from the language and history of § 1983. For our purposes here, the crucial terms of the statute are those that provide for liability when a government "subjects [a person], or causes [that person] to be subjected," to a deprivation of constitutional rights. Aware that governmental bodies can act only through natural persons, the Court concluded that these governments should be held responsible when, and only when, their official policies cause their employees to violate another person's constitutional rights. Reading the statute's language in the light of its legislative history, the Court found that vicarious liability would be incompatible with the causation requirement set out on the face of § 1983. See id., at 691. That conclusion, like decisions that have widened the scope of § 1983 by recognizing constitutional rights that were unheard of in 1871, has been repeatedly reaffirmed. * * *

In *Monell* itself, it was undisputed that there had been an official policy requiring city employees to take actions that were unconstitutional under this Court's decisions. Without attempting to draw the line between actions taken pursuant to official policy and the independent actions of employees and agents, the *Monell* Court left the "full contours" of municipal liability under § 1983 to be developed further on "another day." 436 U.S., at 695.

In the years since *Monell* was decided, the Court has considered several cases involving isolated acts by government officials and employees. We have assumed that an unconstitutional governmental policy could be inferred from a single decision taken by the highest officials responsible for setting policy in that area of the government's business. See, e.g., Owen v. City of Independence, supra; Newport v. Fact Concerts, Inc., 453 U.S. 247 (1981). Cf. *Pembaur*, supra, 475 U.S., at 480. At the other end of the spectrum, we have held that an unjustified shooting by a police officer cannot, without more, be thought to result from official policy. [Oklahoma City v.] Tuttle, 471 U.S. [808], at 821 (plurality opinion); id., at 830–831, and n. 5 (Brennan, J., concurring in part and concurring in judgment).

Two Terms ago, in *Pembaur*, supra, we undertook to define more precisely when a decision on a single occasion may be enough to establish an unconstitutional municipal policy. Although the Court was unable to settle on a general formulation, Justice Brennan's opinion articulated several guiding principles. First, a majority of the Court agreed that municipalities may be held liable under § 1983 only for acts for which the municipality itself is actually responsible, "that is, acts which the municipality has officially sanctioned or ordered." Id., 475 U.S., at 480. Second, only those municipal officials who have "final policymaking authority" may by their actions subject the government to § 1983 liability. Id., at 483 (plurality opinion). Third, whether a particular official has "final policymaking authority" is a question of *state law*. Ibid. (plurality opinion). Fourth, the challenged action must have been taken pursuant to a policy adopted by the official or officials responsible under state law for making policy in that area of the city's business. Id., at 482–483, and n. 12 (plurality opinion).

* * * Today, we set out again to clarify the issue that we last addressed in *Pembaur*.

B

We begin by reiterating that the identification of policymaking officials is a question of state law. "Authority to make municipal policy may be granted directly by a legislative enactment or may be delegated by an official who possesses such authority, and of course, whether an official had final policymaking authority is a question of state law." Pembaur v. Cincinnati, supra, 475 U.S., at 483 (plurality opinion).[1] Thus the identification of policymaking officials is not a question of federal law, and it is not a question of fact in the usual sense. The States have extremely wide latitude in determining the form that local government takes, and local preferences have led to a profusion of distinct forms. Among the many kinds of municipal corporations, political subdivisions, and special districts of all sorts, one may expect to find a rich variety of ways in which the power of government is distributed among a host of

---

1. Unlike Justice Brennan, we would not replace this standard with a new approach in which state law becomes merely an "appropriate starting point" for an "assessment of a municipality's actual power structure." Municipalities cannot be expected to predict how courts or juries will assess their "actual power structures," and this uncertainty could easily lead to results that would be hard in practice to distinguish from the results of a regime governed by the doctrine of respondeat superior. It is one thing to charge a municipality with responsibility for the decisions of officials invested by law, or by a "custom or usage" having the force of law, with policymaking authority. It would be something else, and something inevitably more capricious, to hold a municipality responsible for every decision that is perceived as "final" through the lens of a particular factfinder's evaluation of the city's "actual power structure."

different officials and official bodies. Without attempting to canvass the numberless factual scenarios that may come to light in litigation, we can be confident that state law (which may include valid local ordinances and regulations) will always direct a court to some official or body that has the responsibility for making law or setting policy in any given area of a local government's business.

We are not, of course, predicting that state law will always speak with perfect clarity. We have no reason to suppose, however, that federal courts will face greater difficulties here than those that they routinely address in other contexts. We are also aware that there will be cases in which policymaking responsibility is shared among more than one official or body. In the case before us, for example, it appears that the Mayor and Aldermen are authorized to adopt such ordinances relating to personnel administration as are compatible with the City Charter. The Civil Service Commission, for its part, is required to "prescribe ... rules for the administration and enforcement of the provisions of this article, and of any ordinance adopted in pursuance thereof, and not inconsistent therewith." Assuming that applicable law does not make the decisions of the Commission reviewable by the Mayor and Aldermen, or vice versa, one would have to conclude that policy decisions made either by the Mayor and Aldermen or by the Commission would be attributable to the city itself. In any event, however, a federal court would not be justified in assuming that municipal policymaking authority lies somewhere other than where the applicable law purports to put it. And certainly there can be no justification for giving a jury the discretion to determine which officials are high enough in the government that their actions can be said to represent a decision of the government itself.

As the plurality in *Pembaur* recognized, special difficulties can arise when it is contended that a municipal policymaker has delegated his policymaking authority to another official. 475 U.S., at 482–483, and n. 12. If the mere exercise of discretion by an employee could give rise to a constitutional violation, the result would be indistinguishable from *respondeat superior* liability. If, however, a city's lawful policymakers could insulate the government from liability simply by delegating their policymaking authority to others, § 1983 could not serve its intended purpose. It may not be possible to draw an elegant line that will resolve this conundrum, but certain principles should provide useful guidance.

First, whatever analysis is used to identify municipal policymakers, egregious attempts by local governments to insulate themselves from liability for unconstitutional policies are precluded by a separate doctrine. Relying on the language of § 1983, the Court has long recognized that a plaintiff may be able to prove the existence of a widespread practice that, although not authorized by written law or express municipal policy, is "so permanent and well settled as to constitute a 'custom or usage' with the force of law." Adickes v. S.H. Kress & Co., 398 U.S. 144, 167–168 (1970). That principle, which has not been affected by *Monell* or subsequent cases, ensures that most deliberate municipal evasions of the Constitution will be sharply limited.

Second, as the *Pembaur* plurality recognized, the authority to make municipal policy is necessarily the authority to make *final* policy. 475 U.S., at 481–484. When an official's discretionary decisions are constrained by policies not of that official's making, those policies, rather than the subordinate's departures from them, are the act of the municipality. Similarly, when a subordinate's decision is subject to review by the municipality's authorized policymakers, they have retained the authority to measure the official's conduct for conformance with *their* policies. If the authorized policymakers approve a subordinate's decision and the basis for it, their ratification would be chargeable to the municipality because their decision is final.

C

Whatever refinements of these principles may be suggested in the future, we have little difficulty concluding that the Court of Appeals applied an incorrect legal standard in this case. In reaching this conclusion, we do not decide whether the First Amendment forbade the city to retaliate against respondent for having taken advantage of the grievance mechanism in 1980. Nor do we decide whether there was evidence in this record from which a rational jury could conclude either that such retaliation actually occurred or that respondent suffered any compensable injury from whatever retaliatory action may have been taken. Finally, we do not address petitioner's contention that the jury verdict exonerating the individual defendants cannot be reconciled with the verdict against the city. Even assuming that all these issues were properly resolved in respondent's favor, we would not be able to affirm the decision of the Court of Appeals.

The city cannot be held liable under § 1983 unless respondent proved the existence of an unconstitutional municipal policy. Respondent does not contend that anyone in city government ever promulgated, or even articulated, such a policy. Nor did he attempt to prove that such retaliation was ever directed against anyone other than himself. Respondent contends that the record can be read to establish that his supervisors were angered by his 1980 appeal to the Civil Service Commission; that new supervisors in a new administration chose, for reasons passed on through some informal means, to retaliate against respondent two years later by transferring him to another agency; and that this transfer was part of a scheme that led, another year and a half later, to his layoff. Even if one assumes that all this was true, it says nothing about the actions of those whom the law established as the makers of municipal policy in matters of personnel administration. The Mayor and Aldermen enacted no ordinance designed to retaliate against respondent or against similarly situated employees. On the contrary, the city established an independent Civil Service Commission and empowered it to review and correct improper personnel actions. Respondent does not deny that his repeated appeals from adverse personnel decisions repeatedly brought him at least partial relief, and the Civil Service Commission never so much as hinted that retaliatory transfers or layoffs were permissible.

Respondent points to no evidence indicating that the Commission delegated to anyone its final authority to interpret and enforce the following policy set out in Article XVIII of the city's Charter, § 2(a):

> "Merit and fitness. All appointments and promotions to positions in the service of the city and all measures for the control and regulation of employment in such positions, and separation therefrom, shall be on the sole basis of merit and fitness...."

The Court of Appeals concluded that "appointing authorities," like Hamsher and Killen, who had the authority to initiate transfers and layoffs, were municipal "policymakers." The court based this conclusion on its findings (1) that the decisions of these employees were not individually reviewed for "substantive propriety" by higher supervisory officials; and (2) that the Civil Service Commission decided appeals from such decisions, if at all, in a circumscribed manner that gave substantial deference to the original decisionmaker. We find these propositions insufficient to support the conclusion that Hamsher and Killen were authorized to establish employment policy for the city with respect to transfers and layoffs. To the contrary, the City Charter expressly states that the Civil Service Commission has the power and the duty:

> "To consider and determine any matter involved in the administration and enforcement of this [Civil Service] article and the rules and ordinances adopted in accordance therewith that may be referred to it for decision by the director [of personnel], or on appeal by any appointing authority, employee, or taxpayer of the city, from any act of the director or of any appointing authority. The decision of the commission in all such matters shall be final, subject, however, to any right of action under any law of the state or of the United States." St. Louis City Charter, Art. XVIII, § 7(d).

This case therefore resembles the hypothetical example in *Pembaur:* "[I]f [city] employment policy was set by the [Mayor and Aldermen and by the Civil Service Commission], only [those] bod[ies'] decisions would provide a basis for [city] liability. This would be true even if the [Mayor and Aldermen and the Commission] left the [appointing authorities] discretion to hire and fire employees and [they] exercised that discretion in an unconstitutional manner...." 475 U.S., at 483, n. 12. A majority of the Court of Appeals panel determined that the Civil Service Commission's review of individual employment actions gave too much deference to the decisions of appointing authorities like Hamsher and Killen. Simply going along with discretionary decisions made by one's subordinates, however, is not a delegation to them of the authority to make policy. It is equally consistent with a presumption that the subordinates are faithfully attempting to comply with the policies that are supposed to guide them. It would be a different matter if a particular decision by a subordinate was cast in the form of a policy statement and expressly approved by the supervising policymaker. It would also be a different matter if a series of decisions by a subordinate official manifested a "custom or usage" of which the supervisor must have been aware. In both those cases, the supervisor could realistically be deemed to have adopted a policy that happened to have been formulated or initiated by a lower ranking official. But the mere failure to investigate the basis of a subordinate's discretionary decisions does not amount to a delegation of policymaking authority, especially where (as here) the wrongfulness of the subordinate's decision arises from a retaliatory motive or other unstated rationale. In such circumstances, the purposes of § 1983 would not be served by treating a subordinate employee's decision as if it were a reflection of municipal policy.

Justice Brennan's opinion, concurring in the judgment, finds implications in our discussion that we do not think necessary or correct. We nowhere say or imply, for example, that "a municipal charter's precatory admonition against discrimination or any other employment practice not based on merit and fitness effectively insulates the municipality from any liability based on acts inconsistent with that policy." Rather, we would respect the decisions, embodied in state and local law, that allocate policymaking authority among particular individuals and bodies. Refusals to carry out stated policies could obviously help to show that a municipality's actual policies were different from the ones that had been announced. If such a showing were made, we would be confronted with a different case than the one we decide today.

Nor do we believe that we have left a "gaping hole" in § 1983 that needs to be filled with the vague concept of "*de facto* final policymaking authority." Except perhaps as a step towards overruling *Monell* and adopting the doctrine of *respondeat superior*, ad hoc searches for officials possessing such "*de facto*" authority would serve primarily to foster needless unpredictability in the application of § 1983.

IV

We cannot accept either the Court of Appeals' broad definition of municipal policymakers or respondent's suggestion that a jury should be entitled to define for itself which officials' decisions should expose a municipality to liability. Respondent has suggested that the record will support an inference that policymaking authority was in fact delegated to individuals who took retaliatory action against him and who were not exonerated by the jury. Respondent's arguments appear to depend on a legal standard similar to the one suggested in Justice Stevens' dissenting opinion, which we do not accept. Our examination of the record and state law, however, suggests that further review of this case may be warranted in light of the principles we have discussed. That task is best left to the Court of Appeals, which will be free to invite additional briefing and argument if necessary. Accordingly, the decision of the Court of Appeals is reversed, and the case is remanded for further proceedings consistent with this opinion.

It is so ordered.

JUSTICE KENNEDY took no part in the consideration or decision of this case.

JUSTICE BRENNAN, with whom JUSTICE MARSHALL and JUSTICE BLACKMUN join, concurring in the judgment.

Despite its somewhat confusing procedural background, this case at bottom presents a relatively straightforward question: whether respondent's supervisor at the Community Development Agency, Frank Hamsher, possessed the authority to establish final employment policy for the city of St. Louis such that the city can be held liable under 42 U.S.C. § 1983 for Hamsher's allegedly unlawful decision to transfer respondent to a dead-end job. Applying the test set out two Terms ago by the plurality in Pembaur v. Cincinnati, 475 U.S. 469 (1986), I conclude that Hamsher did not possess such authority and I therefore concur in the Court's judgment reversing the decision below. I write separately, however, because I believe that the commendable desire of today's plurality to "define more precisely when a decision on a single occasion may be enough" to subject a municipality to § 1983 liability, has led it to embrace a theory of municipal liability that is both unduly narrow and unrealistic, and one that ultimately would permit municipalities to insulate themselves from liability for the acts of all but a small minority of actual city policymakers.

* * *

II

In light of the jury instructions below, the central question before us is whether the city delegated to CDA Director Frank Hamsher the authority to establish final employment policy for the city respecting transfers. For if it did not, then his allegedly unlawful decision to move respondent to an unfulfilling, dead-end position is simply not an act for which the city can be held responsible under § 1983. I am constrained to conclude that Hamsher possessed no such policymaking power here, and that, on the contrary, his allegedly retaliatory act simply constituted an abuse of the discretionary authority the city had entrusted to him.

The scope of Hamsher's authority with respect to transfers derives its significance from our determination in Monell v. New York City Dept. of Social Services, 436 U.S. 658 (1978), that a municipality is not liable under § 1983 for each and every wrong committed by its employees. In rejecting the concept of vicarious municipal liability, we emphasized that "the touchstone of the § 1983 action against a government body is an allegation that official policy is responsible for the deprivation of rights protected by the Constitution." Id., at 690. More recently we have explained that the touchstone of "official policy" is designed "to distinguish acts of the *municipality* from acts of *employees* of the municipality, and thereby make clear that municipal liability is limited to action for which the municipality is actually responsible." Pembaur v. Cincinnati, 475 U.S., at 479–480 (emphasis in original).

Municipalities, of course, conduct much of the business of governing through human agents. Where those agents act in accordance with formal policies, or pursuant to informal practices "so permanent and well settled as to constitute a 'custom or usage' with the force of law," Adickes v. S.H. Kress & Co., 398 U.S. 144, 167–168 (1970), we naturally ascribe their acts to the municipalities themselves and hold the latter responsible for any resulting constitutional deprivations. *Monell*, which involved a challenge to a citywide policy requiring all pregnant employees to take unpaid leave after their fifth month of pregnancy, was just such a case. Nor have we ever doubted that a single decision of a city's properly constituted legislative body is a municipal act capable of subjecting the city to liability. See, e.g., Newport v. Fact Concerts, Inc., 453 U.S. 247 (1981) (City Council canceled concert permit for content-based reasons); Owen v. City of Independence, 445 U.S. 622 (1980) (City Council passed resolution firing Police Chief without any pretermination hearing). In these cases we neither required nor, as the plurality suggests, assumed that these decisions reflected generally applicable "policies" as that term is commonly understood, because it was perfectly obvious that the actions of the municipalities' policymaking organs, whether isolated or not, were properly charged to the municipalities themselves.[3] And, in *Pembaur* we recognized that "the power to establish policy is no more the exclusive province of the legislature at the local level than at the state or national level," 475 U.S., at 480, and that the isolated decision of an executive municipal policymaker, therefore, could likewise give rise to municipal liability under § 1983.

In concluding that Frank Hamsher was a policymaker, the Court of Appeals relied on the fact that the city had delegated to him "the authority, either directly or indirectly, to act on [its] behalf," and that his decisions within the scope of this delegated authority were effectively final. In *Pembaur*, however, we made clear that a municipality is not liable merely because the official who inflicted the constitutional injury had the final authority to *act* on its behalf; rather, as four of us explained, the official in question must possess "final authority to establish municipal policy with respect to the [challenged] action." 475 U.S., at 481. Thus, we noted, "[t]he fact that a particular official—even a policymaking official—has discretion in the exercise of particular functions does not, without more, give rise to municipal liability based on an exercise of that discretion." Id., at 481–482. By way of illustration, we explained that if, in a given county, the Board of County Commissioners established county employment policy and delegated to the County

---

3. The plurality's suggestion that in *Owen* and *Fact Concerts* we "*assumed*" that an unconstitutional governmental policy could be *inferred* from a single decision," elevates the identification of municipal policy from touchstone to talisman. Section 1983 imposes liability where a municipality "subjects [a person], or causes [a person] to be subjected ... to the deprivation of any rights, privileges, or immunities secured by the Constitution and laws...." Our decision in *Monell*, interpreting the statute to require a showing that such deprivations arise from municipal policy, did not employ the policy requirement as an end in itself, but rather as a means of determining which acts by municipal employees are properly attributed to the municipality. Congress, we held, did not intend to subject cities to liability simply because they employ tortfeasors. But where a municipality's governing legislative body inflicts the constitutional injury, the municipal policy inquiry is essentially superfluous: the city is liable under the statute whether its decision reflects a considered policy judgment or nothing more than the bare desire to inflict harm.

Sheriff alone the discretion to hire and fire employees, the county itself would not be liable if the Sheriff exercised this authority in an unconstitutional manner, because "the decision to act unlawfully would not be a decision of the Board." Id., at 483, n. 12. We pointed out, however, that in that same county the Sheriff could be the final policymaker in other areas, such as law enforcement practices, and that if so, his or her decisions in such matters *could* give rise to municipal liability. Ibid. In short, just as in *Owen* and *Fact Concerts* we deemed it fair to hold municipalities liable for the isolated, unconstitutional acts of their legislative bodies, regardless of whether those acts were meant to establish generally applicable "policies," so too in *Pembaur* four of us concluded that it is equally appropriate to hold municipalities accountable for the isolated constitutional injury inflicted by an executive final municipal policymaker, even though the decision giving rise to the injury is not intended to govern future situations. In either case, as long as the contested decision is made in an area over which the official or legislative body *could* establish a final policy capable of governing future municipal conduct, it is both fair and consistent with the purposes of § 1983 to treat the decision as that of the municipality itself, and to hold it liable for the resulting constitutional deprivation.

In my view, *Pembaur* controls this case. As an "appointing authority," Hamsher was empowered under the City Charter to initiate lateral transfers such as the one challenged here, subject to the approval of both the Director of Personnel and the appointing authority of the transferee agency. The Charter, however, nowhere confers upon agency heads any authority to establish city policy, final or otherwise, with respect to such transfers. Thus, for example, Hamsher was not authorized to promulgate binding guidelines or criteria governing how or when lateral transfers were to be accomplished. Nor does the record reveal that he in fact sought to exercise any such authority in these matters. There is no indication, for example, that Hamsher ever purported to institute or announce a practice of general applicability concerning transfers. Instead, the evidence discloses but one transfer decision—the one involving respondent—which Hamsher ostensibly undertook pursuant to a city-wide program of fiscal restraint and budgetary reductions. At most, then, the record demonstrates that Hamsher had the authority to determine how best to *effectuate* a policy announced by his superiors, rather than the power to *establish* that policy. Like the hypothetical Sheriff in *Pembaur*'s n. 12, Hamsher had discretionary authority to transfer CDA employees laterally; that he may have used this authority to punish respondent for the exercise of his First Amendment rights does not, without more, render the city liable for respondent's resulting constitutional injury. The court below did not suggest that either Killen or Nash, who together orchestrated respondent's ultimate layoff, shared Hamsher's constitutionally impermissible animus. Because the court identified only one unlawfully motivated municipal employee involved in respondent's transfer and layoff, and because that employee did not possess final policymaking authority with respect to the contested decision, the city may not be held accountable for any constitutional wrong respondent may have suffered.

III

These determinations, it seems to me, are sufficient to dispose of this case, and I therefore think it unnecessary to decide, as the plurality does, who the actual policymakers in St. Louis are. I question more than the mere necessity of these determinations, however, for I believe that in the course of passing on issues not before us, the plurality announces legal principles that are inconsistent with our earlier cases and unduly restrict the reach of § 1983 in cases involving municipalities.

The plurality begins its assessment of St. Louis' power structure by asserting that the identification of policymaking officials is a question of state law, by which it means that the question is neither one of federal law nor of fact, at least "not ... in the usual sense." Instead, the plurality explains, courts are to identify municipal policymakers by referring exclusively to applicable state statutory law. Not surprisingly, the plurality cites no authority for this startling proposition, nor could it, for we have never suggested that municipal liability should be determined in so formulaic and unrealistic a fashion. In any case in which the policymaking authority of a municipal tortfeasor is in doubt, state law will naturally be the appropriate starting point, but ultimately the factfinder must determine where such policymaking authority actually resides, and not simply "where the applicable law purports to put it." As the plurality itself acknowledges, local governing bodies may take myriad forms. We in no way slight the dignity of municipalities by recognizing that in not a few of them real and apparent authority may diverge, and that in still others state statutory law will simply fail to disclose where such authority ultimately rests. Indeed, in upholding the Court of Appeals' determination in *Pembaur* that the County Prosecutor was a policymaking official with respect to county law enforcement practices, a majority of this Court relied on testimony which revealed that the County Sheriff's office routinely forwarded certain matters to the Prosecutor and followed his instructions in those areas. See 475 U.S., at 485; ibid. (White, J., concurring); id., at 491 (O'Connor, J., concurring). While the majority splintered into three separate camps on the ultimate theory of municipal liability, and the case generated five opinions in all, not a single Member of the Court suggested that reliance on such extrastatutory evidence of the county's actual allocation of policymaking authority was in any way improper. Thus, although I agree with the plurality that juries should not be given open-ended "*discretion* to determine which officials are high enough in the government that their actions can be said to represent a decision of the government itself," juries can and must find the predicate facts necessary to a determination whether a given official possesses final policymaking authority. While the jury instructions in this case were regrettably vague, the plurality's solution tosses the baby out with the bath water. The identification of municipal policymakers is an essentially factual determination "in the usual sense," and is therefore rightly entrusted to a properly instructed jury.

Nor does the "custom or usage" doctrine adequately compensate for the inherent inflexibility of a rule that leaves the identification of policymakers exclusively to state statutory law. That doctrine, under which municipalities and States can be held liable for unconstitutional practices so well settled and permanent that they have the force of law, see Adickes v. S.H. Kress & Co., 398 U.S., at 167, has little if any bearing on the question whether a city has delegated *de facto* final policymaking authority to a given official. A city practice of delegating final policymaking authority to a subordinate or mid-level official would not be unconstitutional in and of itself, and an isolated unconstitutional act by an official entrusted with such authority would obviously not amount to a municipal "custom or usage." Under *Pembaur*, of course, such an isolated act *should* give rise to municipal liability. Yet a case such as this would fall through the gaping hole the plurality's construction leaves in § 1983, because state statutory law would not identify the municipal actor as a policymaking official, and a single constitutional deprivation, by definition, is not a well-settled and permanent municipal practice carrying the force of law.

For these same reasons, I cannot subscribe to the plurality's narrow and overly rigid view of when a municipal official's policymaking authority is "final." Attempting to place a gloss on *Pembaur*'s finality requirement, the plurality suggests that whenever the decisions of an official are subject to some form of review—however limited—that official's decisions are nonfinal. Under the plurality's theory, therefore, even where an official wields policymaking authority with respect to a challenged decision, the city would not be liable for that official's policy decision unless *reviewing* officials affirmatively approved both the "decision and the basis for it." Reviewing officials, however, may as a matter of practice never invoke their plenary oversight authority, or their review powers may be highly circumscribed. Under such circumstances, the subordinate's decision is in effect the final municipal pronouncement on the subject. Certainly a § 1983 plaintiff is entitled to place such considerations before the jury, for the law is concerned not with the niceties of legislative draftsmanship but with the realities of municipal decisionmaking, and any assessment of a municipality's actual power structure is necessarily a factual and practical one.[7]

7. The plurality also asserts that "[w]hen an official's discretionary decisions are constrained by policies not of that official's making, those policies, rather than the subordinate's departures from them, are the act of the municipality." While I have no quarrel with such a proposition in the abstract, I cannot accept the plurality's apparent view that a municipal charter's precatory admonition against discrimination or any other employment practice not based on merit and fitness effectively insu-

lates the municipality from any liability based on acts inconsistent with that policy. Again, the relevant inquiry is whether the policy in question is actually and effectively enforced through the city's review mechanisms. Thus in this case, a policy prohibiting lateral transfers for unconstitutional or discriminatory reasons would not shield the city from liability if an official possessing final policymaking authority over such transfers acted in violation of the prohibition, because the CSC would lack jurisdic-

Accordingly, I cannot endorse the plurality's determination, based on nothing more than its own review of the City Charter, that the Mayor, the Aldermen, and the CSC are the only policymakers for the city of St. Louis. While these officials may well have policymaking authority, that hardly ends the matter; the question before us is whether the officials responsible for respondent's allegedly unlawful transfer were final policymakers. As I have previously indicated, I do not believe that CDA Director Frank Hamsher possessed any policymaking authority with respect to lateral transfers and thus I do not believe that his allegedly improper decision to transfer respondent could, without more, give rise to municipal liability. Although the plurality reaches the same result, it does so by reasoning that because others could have reviewed the decisions of Hamsher and Killen, the latter officials simply could not have been final policymakers.

* * * Under the plurality's analysis, * * * even the hollowest promise of review is sufficient to divest all city officials save the mayor and governing legislative body of final policymaking authority. While clarity and ease of application may commend such a rule, we have remained steadfast in our conviction that Congress intended to hold municipalities accountable for those constitutional injuries inflicted not only by their lawmakers, but also "by those whose edicts or acts may fairly be said to represent official policy." *Monell*, 436 U.S., at 694. Because the plurality's mechanical "finality" test is fundamentally at odds with the pragmatic and factual inquiry contemplated by *Monell*, I cannot join what I perceive to be its unwarranted abandonment of the traditional factfinding process in § 1983 actions involving municipalities.

Finally, I think it necessary to emphasize that despite certain language in the plurality opinion suggesting otherwise, the Court today need not and therefore does not decide that a city can only be held liable under § 1983 where the plaintiff "prove[s] the existence of an unconstitutional municipal policy." Just last Term, we left open for the second time the question whether a city can be subjected to liability for a policy that, while not unconstitutional in and of itself, may give rise to constitutional deprivations. See Springfield v. Kibbe, 480 U.S. 257 (1987); see also Oklahoma City v. Tuttle, 471 U.S. 808 (1985). That question is certainly not presented by this case, and nothing we say today forecloses its future consideration.

IV

For the reasons stated above, I concur in the judgment of the Court reversing the decision below and remanding the case so that the Court of Appeals may determine whether respondent's layoff resulted from the actions of any improperly motivated final policymakers.

[The dissenting opinion of JUSTICE STEVENS is omitted.]

tion to review the decision and thus could not enforce the city policy. Where as here, however, the official merely possesses discretionary authority over transfers, the city policy is irrelevant, because the official's actions cannot subject the city to liability in any event.

Notes

1. On remand, the Court of Appeals found that the individuals responsible for Praprotnik's transfer (and ultimate lay-off) were not policy-making officials for purposes of personnel decisions, and thus that the city could not be held liable. Praprotnik v. City of St. Louis, 879 F.2d 1573 (8th Cir.1989).

2. In *Praprotnik*, as in *Pembaur* and *Tuttle*, there was no majority opinion. Those cases thus did not really resolve the difficult questions raised by *Monell*'s distinction between liability for municipal policies and mere *respondeat superior* liability. In City of Canton v. Harris, 489 U.S. 378 (1989), the Court finally reached agreement on some points. Plaintiff Harris was arrested by the Canton police, who then failed to give her necessary medical attention. She sued under section 1983, claiming that the lapse arose from the city's failure to train its police personnel. The Court, in a majority opinion by Justice White, held that "the inadequacy of police training may serve as the basis for § 1983 liability only where the failure to train amounts to deliberate indifference to the rights of persons with whom the police come into contact." Id. at 388. The Court explained that a failure to act can constitute an affirmative policy where, "in light of the duties assigned to specific officers or employees the need for more or different training is so obvious, and the inadequacy so likely to result in the violation of constitutional rights, that the policymakers of the city can reasonably be said to have been deliberately indifferent to the need." Id. at 390. The plaintiff must also "prove that the deficiency in training actually caused the police officers' unconstitutional conduct." Id. at 391.

The agreement in *Canton* was short-lived. In Board of County Commissioners of Bryan County v. Brown, 520 U.S. 397 (1997), a divided Court applied *Canton* and *Pembaur* to deny county liability on a claim that a county sheriff's failure to check a candidate's background before hiring him as a police officer led to plaintiff's injury at the hands of the officer. All members of the Court agreed that the sheriff was the policy-making official for the county on police hiring matters. But five Justices held that his single act of negligent hiring did not constitute the "deliberate indifference" necessary to trigger municipal liability. Justice O'Connor, writing for the majority, explained why a court must carefully scrutinize claims of inadequate screening:

> Where a plaintiff presents a § 1983 claim premised upon the inadequacy of an official's review of a prospective applicant's record, however, there is a particular danger that a municipality will be held liable for an injury not directly caused by a deliberate action attributable to the municipality itself. Every injury suffered at the hands of a municipal employee can be traced to a hiring decision in a "but-for" sense: But for the municipality's decision to hire the employee, the plaintiff would not have suffered the injury. To prevent municipal liability for a hiring decision from collapsing into *respondeat superior* liability, a court must carefully test the link between the policymaker's inadequate decision and the particular injury alleged. Id. at 410.

The Court went on to specify the necessary link between the inadequate screening and the plaintiff's injury: "Only where adequate scrutiny of an applicant's background would lead a reasonable policymaker to conclude that the plainly obvious consequence of the decision to hire the applicant would be the deprivation of a third party's federally protected right can the official's failure to adequately scrutinize the applicant's background constitution 'deliberate indifference.'" Id. at 411. Justices Souter, Stevens, Breyer, and Ginsburg dissented, arguing that the failure to screen satisfied the "deliberate indifference" standard.

3. Think about all the distinctions drawn in *Tuttle*, *Pembaur*, *Praprotnik*, *Canton*, and *Bryan County*. See also McMillian v. Monroe County, 520 U.S. 781 (1997) (Alabama county sheriffs are state, not county, policymakers when enforcing state law). Are these arcane distinctions necessary if the Court is to avoid imposing *respondeat superior* liability on municipalities? If so, does that suggest that perhaps *Monell*'s limitation on municipal liability should be overruled, allowing municipalities to be held liable for the acts of their employees? Consider Justice Breyer's dissent in *Bryan County*, joined by Justices Stevens and Ginsburg:

> Finally, relevant legal and factual circumstances may have changed in a way that affects likely reliance upon *Monell*'s liability limitation. The legal complexity * * * makes it difficult for municipalities to predict just when they will be held liable based upon "policy or custom." Moreover, their potential liability is, in a sense, greater than that of individuals, for they cannot assert the "qualified immunity" defenses that individuals may raise. Owen v. City of Independence, 445 U.S. 622 (1980). Further, many States have statutes that appear to, in effect, mimic *respondeat superior* by authorizing indemnification of employees found liable under § 1983 for actions within the scope of their employment. These statutes— valuable to government employees as well as to civil rights victims— can provide for payments from the government that are similar to those that would take place in the absence of *Monell*'s limitations. To the extent that they do so, municipal reliance upon the continuation of *Monell*'s "policy" limitation loses much of its significance. 520 U.S. at 436.

Should the *respondeat superior* part of *Monell* be overruled? Would it be fair to hold municipalities liable for the acts of their employees? Would it be consistent with section 1983 and its history? See Beerman, *Municipal Responsibility for Constitutional Torts*, 48 DePaul L.Rev. 627 (1999). One scholar examines the historical background of section 1983 and concludes that the *Monell* Court's historical analysis was "fatally flawed." Achtenberg, *Taking History Seriously: Municipal Liability Under 42 U.S.C. § 1983 and the Debate over Respondeat Superior*, 73 Fordham L.Rev. 2183 (2005). Going beyond *Monell*'s historical analysis, Professor Achtenberg concludes that although there are valid historical arguments on both sides, the best reading of the historical debate is that Congress intended to allow respondeat superior liability.

4. For scholarly discussion of *Monell* and its progeny, see generally Symposium, *Section 1983 Municipal Liability in Civil Rights Litigation*, 48

DePaul L.Rev. 619 (1999); Gilles, *Breaking the Code of Silence: Rediscovering "Custom" in Section 1983 Municipal Liability*, 80 B.U.L.Rev. 17 (2000); Kinports, *The Buck Does Not Stop Here: Supervisory Liability in Section 1983 Cases*, 1997 U.Ill.L.Rev. 147; Kritchevsky, *A Return to Owen: Depersonalizing Section 1983 Municipal Liability Litigation*, 41 Vill.L.Rev. 1381 (1996); Brown & Kerrigan, *42 U.S.C.A. § 1983: The Vehicle for Protecting Public Employees' Rights*, 47 Baylor L.Rev. 619 (1995); Cushman, *Municipal Liability Under § 1983: Toward a New Definition of Municipal Policymaker*, 34 B.C. L. Rev. 693 (1993); Lewis & Blumoff, *Reshaping Section 1983's Asymmetry*, 140 U.Pa.L.Rev. 755 (1992); Gerhardt, *The Monell Legacy: Balancing Federalism Concerns and Municipal Accountability Under Section 1983*, 62 S.Cal.L.Rev. 539 (1989); Schuck, *Municipal Liability Under Section 1983: Some Lessons from Tort Law and Organizational Theory*, 77 Geo. L.Rev. 1753 (1989); Welch & Hofmeister, Praprotnik, *Municipal Policy and Policymakers: the Supreme Court's Constriction of Municipal Liability*, 13 S.Ill.U.L.J. 857 (1989); Burke & Burton, *Defining the Contours of Municipal Liability Under 42 U.S.C.A. § 1983:* Monell *Through* City of Canton v. Harris, 18 Stetson L.Rev. 511 (1989); Kramer & Sykes, *Municipal Liability Under Section 1983: A Legal and Economic Analysis*, 1987 S.Ct.Rev. 249; Snyder, *The Final Authority Analysis: A Unified Approach to Municipal Liability Under Section 1983*, 1986 Wis.L.Rev. 633; Bandes, Monell, Parratt, Daniels, *and* Davidson: *Distinguishing a Custom or Policy from a Random, Unauthorized Act*, 72 Iowa L.Rev. 101 (1986); Whitman, *Government Responsibility for Constitutional Torts*, 85 Mich.L.Rev. 225 (1986).

§ 3. IMMUNITIES

HARLOW v. FITZGERALD

Supreme Court of the United States, 1982.
457 U.S. 800.

JUSTICE POWELL delivered the opinion of the Court.

The issue in this case is the scope of the immunity available to the senior aides and advisers of the President of the United States in a suit for damages based upon their official acts.

I

In this suit for civil damages petitioners Bryce Harlow and Alexander Butterfield are alleged to have participated in a conspiracy to violate the constitutional and statutory rights of the respondent A. Ernest Fitzgerald. Respondent avers that petitioners entered the conspiracy in their capacities as senior White House aides to former President Richard M. Nixon. [Fitzgerald alleged that the conspirators dismissed him from his position as an analyst for the Air Force in retaliation for his testimony before Congress regarding military cost overruns.]

* * *

II

As we reiterated today in Nixon v. Fitzgerald, 457 U.S. 731, our decisions consistently have held that government officials are entitled to some form of immunity from suits for damages. As recognized at common law, public officers require this protection to shield them from undue interference with their duties and from potentially disabling threats of liability.

Our decisions have recognized immunity defenses of two kinds. For officials whose special functions or constitutional status requires complete protection from suit, we have recognized the defense of "absolute immunity." The absolute immunity of legislators, in their legislative functions, see, e.g., Eastland v. United States Servicemen's Fund, 421 U.S. 491 (1975), and of judges, in their judicial functions, see, e.g., Stump v. Sparkman, 435 U.S. 349 (1978), now is well settled. Our decisions also have extended absolute immunity to certain officials of the Executive Branch. These include prosecutors and similar officials, see Butz v. Economou, 438 U.S. 478, 508–512(1978), executive officers engaged in adjudicative functions, id., at 513–517, and the President of the United States, see Nixon v. Fitzgerald, 457 U.S. 731.

For executive officials in general, however, our cases make plain that qualified immunity represents the norm. In Scheuer v. Rhodes, 416 U.S. 232 (1974), we acknowledged that high officials require greater protection than those with less complex discretionary responsibilities. Nonetheless, we held that a governor and his aides could receive the requisite protection from qualified or good-faith immunity. Id., at 247–248. In Butz v. Economou, supra, we extended the approach of Scheuer to high federal officials of the Executive Branch. Discussing in detail the considerations that also had underlain our decision in Scheuer, we explained that the recognition of a qualified immunity defense for high executives reflected an attempt to balance competing values: not only the importance of a damages remedy to protect the rights of citizens, 438 U.S., at 504–505, but also "the need to protect officials who are required to exercise their discretion and the related public interest in encouraging the vigorous exercise of official authority." Id., at 506. Without discounting the adverse consequences of denying high officials an absolute immunity from private lawsuits alleging constitutional violations—consequences found sufficient in Spalding v. Vilas, 161 U.S. 483 (1896), and Barr v. Matteo, 360 U.S. 564 (1959), to warrant extension to such officials of absolute immunity from suits at common law—we emphasized our expectation that insubstantial suits need not proceed to trial:

> "Insubstantial lawsuits can be quickly terminated by federal courts alert to the possibilities of artful pleading. Unless the complaint states a compensable claim for relief ... , it should not survive a motion to dismiss. Moreover, the Court recognized in Scheuer that damages suits concerning constitutional violations need not proceed to trial, but can be terminated on a properly supported motion for summary judgment based on the defense of immunity.... In responding to such a motion, plaintiffs may not play dog in the manger; and firm application of the Federal Rules of Civil Procedure will ensure that federal officials are not harassed by frivolous lawsuits." 438 U.S., at 507–508 (citations omitted).

Butz continued to acknowledge that the special functions of some officials might require absolute immunity. But the Court held that "federal officials who seek absolute exemption from personal liability for unconstitutional conduct must bear the burden of showing that public policy requires an exemption of that scope." Id., at 506. This we reaffirmed today in Nixon v. Fitzgerald, 457 U.S., at 747.

III

A

Petitioners argue that they are entitled to a blanket protection of absolute immunity as an incident of their offices as Presidential aides. In deciding this claim we do not write on an empty page. In Butz v. Economou, supra, the Secretary of Agriculture—a Cabinet official directly accountable to the President—asserted a defense of absolute official immunity from suit for civil damages. We rejected his claim. In so doing we did not question the power or the importance of the Secretary's office. Nor did we doubt the importance to the President of loyal and efficient subordinates in executing his duties of office. Yet we found these factors, alone, to be insufficient to justify absolute immunity. "[T]he greater power of [high] officials," we reasoned, "affords a greater potential for a regime of lawless conduct." 438 U.S., at 506. Damages actions against high officials were therefore "an important means of vindicating constitutional guarantees." Ibid. Moreover, we concluded that it would be "untenable to draw a distinction for purposes of immunity law between suits brought against state officials under [42 U.S.C.] § 1983 and suits brought directly under the Constitution against federal officials." Id., at 504.

Having decided in *Butz* that Members of the Cabinet ordinarily enjoy only qualified immunity from suit, we conclude today that it would be equally untenable to hold absolute immunity an incident of the office of every Presidential subordinate based in the White House. Members of the Cabinet are direct subordinates of the President, frequently with greater responsibilities, both to the President and to the Nation, than White House staff. The considerations that supported our decision in *Butz* apply with equal force to this case. It is no disparagement of the offices held by petitioners to hold that Presidential aides, like Members of the Cabinet, generally are entitled only to a qualified immunity.

* * *

IV

Even if they cannot establish that their official functions require absolute immunity, petitioners assert that public policy at least mandates an application of the qualified immunity standard that would permit the defeat of insubstantial claims without resort to trial. We agree.

A

The resolution of immunity questions inherently requires a balance between the evils inevitable in any available alternative. In situations of abuse of office, an action for damages may offer the only realistic avenue for vindication of constitutional guarantees. Butz v. Economou, supra, at 506; see Bivens v. Six Unknown Fed. Narcotics Agents, 403 U.S., at 410 ("For people in Bivens' shoes, it is damages or nothing"). It is this recognition that has required the denial of absolute immunity to most public officers. At the same time, however, it cannot be disputed seriously that claims frequently run against the innocent as well as the guilty— at a cost not only to the defendant officials, but to society as a whole. These social costs include the expenses of litigation, the diversion of official energy from pressing public issues, and the deterrence of able citizens from acceptance of public office. Finally, there is the danger that fear of being sued will "dampen the ardor of all but the most resolute, or the most irresponsible [public officials], in the unflinching discharge of their duties." Gregoire v. Biddle, 177 F.2d 579, 581 (C.A.2 1949), cert. denied, 339 U.S. 949 (1950).

In identifying qualified immunity as the best attainable accommodation of competing values, in *Butz*, supra, 438 U.S., at 507–508, as in *Scheuer*, 416 U.S., at 245–248, we relied on the assumption that this standard would permit "[i]nsubstantial lawsuits [to] be quickly terminated." 438 U.S., at 507–508. Yet petitioners advance persuasive arguments that the dismissal of insubstantial lawsuits without trial—a factor presupposed in the balance of competing interests struck by our prior cases—requires an adjustment of the "good faith" standard established by our decisions.

B

Qualified or "good faith" immunity is an affirmative defense that must be pleaded by a defendant official. Decisions of this Court have established that the "good faith" defense has both an ("objective") and a "subjective" aspect. The objective element involves a presumptive knowledge of and respect for "basic, unquestioned constitutional rights." Wood v. Strickland, 420 U.S. 308, 322 (1975). The subjective component refers to "permissible intentions." Ibid. Characteristically the Court has defined these elements by identifying the circumstances in which qualified immunity would *not* be available. Referring both to the objective and subjective elements, we have held that qualified immunity would be defeated if an official *"knew or reasonably should have known* that the action he took within his sphere of official responsibility would violate the constitutional rights of the [plaintiff], *or* if he took the action *with the malicious intention* to cause a deprivation of constitutional rights or other injury...." Ibid. (emphasis added).

The subjective element of the good-faith defense frequently has proved incompatible with our admonition in *Butz* that insubstantial claims should not proceed to trial. Rule 56 of the Federal Rules of Civil

Procedure provides that disputed questions of fact ordinarily may not be decided on motions for summary judgment. And an official's subjective good faith has been considered to be a question of fact that some courts have regarded as inherently requiring resolution by a jury.

In the context of *Butz'* attempted balancing of competing values, it now is clear that substantial costs attend the litigation of the subjective good faith of government officials. Not only are there the general costs of subjecting officials to the risks of trial—distraction of officials from their governmental duties, inhibition of discretionary action, and deterrence of able people from public service. There are special costs to "subjective" inquiries of this kind. Immunity generally is available only to officials performing discretionary functions. In contrast with the thought processes accompanying "ministerial" tasks, the judgments surrounding discretionary action almost inevitably are influenced by the decisionmaker's experiences, values, and emotions. These variables explain in part why questions of subjective intent so rarely can be decided by summary judgment. Yet they also frame a background in which there often is no clear end to the relevant evidence. Judicial inquiry into subjective motivation therefore may entail broad-ranging discovery and the deposing of numerous persons, including an official's professional colleagues. Inquiries of this kind can be peculiarly disruptive of effective government.

Consistently with the balance at which we aimed in *Butz*, we conclude today that bare allegations of malice should not suffice to subject government officials either to the costs of trial or to the burdens of broad-reaching discovery. We therefore hold that government officials performing discretionary functions, generally are shielded from liability for civil damages insofar as their conduct does not violate clearly established statutory or constitutional rights of which a reasonable person would have known.[30]

Reliance on the objective reasonableness of an official's conduct, as measured by reference to clearly established law, should avoid excessive disruption of government and permit the resolution of many insubstantial claims on summary judgment. On summary judgment, the judge appropriately may determine, not only the currently applicable law, but whether that law was clearly established at the time an action occurred. If the law at that time was not clearly established, an official could not reasonably be expected to anticipate subsequent legal developments, nor could he fairly be said to "know" that the law forbade conduct not previously identified as unlawful. Until this threshold immunity question is resolved, discovery should not be allowed. If the law was clearly

30. This case involves no issue concerning the elements of the immunity available to state officials sued for constitutional violations under 42 U.S.C. § 1983. We have found previously, however, that it would be "untenable to draw a distinction for purposes of immunity law between suits brought against state officials under § 1983 and suits brought directly under the Constitution against federal officials." Butz v. Economou, 438 U.S., at 504.

Our decision in no way diminishes the absolute immunity currently available to officials whose functions have been held to require a protection of this scope.

established, the immunity defense ordinarily should fail, since a reasonably competent public official should know the law governing his conduct. Nevertheless, if the official pleading the defense claims extraordinary circumstances and can prove that he neither knew nor should have known of the relevant legal standard, the defense should be sustained. But again, the defense would turn primarily on objective factors.

By defining the limits of qualified immunity essentially in objective terms, we provide no license to lawless conduct. The public interest in deterrence of unlawful conduct and in compensation of victims remains protected by a test that focuses on the objective legal reasonableness of an official's acts. Where an official could be expected to know that certain conduct would violate statutory or constitutional rights, he should be made to hesitate; and a person who suffers injury caused by such conduct may have a cause of action. But where an official's duties legitimately require action in which clearly established rights are not implicated, the public interest may be better served by action taken "with independence and without fear of consequences." Pierson v. Ray, 386 U.S. 547, 554 (1967).[34]

* * *

[The concurring opinions of JUSTICE BRENNAN and JUSTICE REHNQUIST, and the dissenting opinion of the CHIEF JUSTICE, are omitted.]

Notes

1. Note that *Harlow* was a suit against federal officials, brought directly under the Constitution, rather than a section 1983 suit against state officials. See Bivens v. Six Unknown Named Agents of Federal Bureau of Narcotics, 403 U.S. 388 (1971) [infra p. 917]. But as the Court made clear in note 30, the same immunities apply to both types of suits.

2. Does the *Harlow* standard provide enough protection for plaintiffs whose constitutional rights have been violated? Should an official who maliciously takes what turns out to be an unconstitutional action against an individual plaintiff be protected simply because the courts had not yet declared such an action unconstitutional?

What if a particularly perspicacious official takes action that he knows or suspects violates a constitutional right, but the right has not yet been clearly established? Consider the comments of Justice Brennan, concurring in *Harlow*: "[The standard adopted by the Court] would not allow the official who *actually knows* that he was violating the law to escape liability for his actions, even if he could not 'reasonably have been expected' to know what he actually did know." 457 U.S. at 821. Do you agree with Justice Brennan's reading of the majority opinion? If actual knowledge is sufficient to overcome qualified immunity, does the *Harlow* test really eliminate the subjective inquiry that the Court claims impedes quick dismissals?

34. We emphasize that our decision applies only to suits for civil *damages* arising from actions within the scope of an official's duties and in "objective" good faith. We express no view as to the conditions in which injunctive or declaratory relief might be available.

3.   How should a court determine whether official actions violate clearly established law? The Court has confronted the question in a variety of settings. In Wilson v. Layne, 526 U.S. 603 (1999), the Court unanimously held that police officers violated the fourth amendment when they brought members of the news media into a home while executing an arrest warrant. Nevertheless, the Court also held (Justice Stevens dissenting) that the officers were entitled to qualified immunity because the violation was not clearly established at the time of the officers' conduct. The Court noted that few cases on "ride-alongs" existed at the time, and characterized the state of the law as "undeveloped." It further noted that subsequent to the events that triggered the suit, a split in the circuits developed: "If judges thus disagree on a constitutional question, it is unfair to subject police to money damages for picking the losing side of the controversy." Id. at 618. In Saucier v. Katz, 533 U.S. 194 (2001), the Court stressed that the question of whether a right was clearly established "must be undertaken in light of the specific context of the case, not as a broad general proposition." Id. at 201. In *Saucier*, the plaintiff alleged the use of excessive force, and the Court held that qualified immunity was available because although the use of excessive force is clearly prohibited, it was not clearly established that the particular use of force was excessive. In Hope v. Pelzer, 536 U.S. 730 (2002), the Court found no immunity from an Eighth Amendment suit brought against Alabama prison guards. The Court concluded that the guards ought to have known that handcuffing prisoners to a "hitching post" for several hours, which forced them to stand almost motionless in the hot sun and exposed their skin to burns from the sun-heated metal handcuffs, constituted cruel and unusual punishment. Two years later, the Court held that police officers who execute a facially defective search warrant are not entitled to qualified immunity. Groh v. Ramirez, 540 U.S. 551 (2004). Most recently, the Court found that an officer who shot a fleeing felon in the back was entitled to qualified immunity because it was not clearly established that her conduct violated the Constitution in the "particularized" context of a fleeing felon whose flight put innocent third parties at risk. Brosseau v. Haugen, 543 U.S. 194 (2004). See generally Mitchell v. Forsyth, 472 U.S. 511 (1985); Saphire, *Qualified Immunity in Section 1983 Cases and the Role of State Decisional Law*, 35 Ariz.L.Rev. 621 (1993); Mandery, *Qualified Immunity or Absolute Impunity? The Moral Hazards of Extending Qualified Immunity to Lower–Level Public Officials*, 17 Harv.J.L. & Pub.Pol'y 479, 500–02 (1994).

4.   Section 1983 cases typically name individual officers of state or local government entities as defendants. When damages are sought, an official is often sued in his or her "personal" or "individual" capacity, rather than "official" capacity. In an official capacity suit, the plaintiff seeks compensation from the "government entity itself," thus potentially implicating the eleventh amendment. See Kentucky v. Graham, 473 U.S. 159, 166 (1985). In individual capacity suits, however, any judgment awarded to the plaintiff must be secured from the defendant's personal funds.

5.   As the *Harlow* opinion indicates, in an extensive series of decisions, the United States Supreme Court has recognized immunities from section 1983 damages claims for various government officials. Absolute immunities from suit have been afforded for legislative, judicial and prosecutorial actions. Executive and other governmental activities have typically received

qualified or good faith immunity. How does the Court square the granting of governmental immunities with the extremely broad "Every person" language of section 1983? With Marshall's eloquent declaration in *Marbury* that for every violation of right there must be a remedy? Is the immunity of government officials a statutory interpretation of section 1983, or a constitutional requirement? See Vazquez, *Eleventh Amendment Schizophrenia*, 75 Notre Dame L.Rev. 859, 900–08 (2000).

Besides removing the threat of litigation against conscientious but mistaken officials, does granting immunity have any other benefits? Professor John Jeffries argues that it "facilitates constitutional change by reducing the costs of innovation." Jeffries, *The Right–Remedy Gap in Constitutional Law*, 109 Yale L.J. 87, 90 (1999); see also Jeffries, *In Praise of the Eleventh Amendment and Section 1983*, 84 Va.L.Rev. 47, 78–81 (1998). Are you persuaded? Does Jeffries' argument focus too much on the *courts* as instruments of constitutional change?

6. **Prosecutorial Immunity.** Imbler v. Pachtman, 424 U.S. 409 (1976), recognized an absolute prosecutorial immunity—for matters "intimately associated with the judicial phase of the criminal process"—in section 1983 cases. Id. at 430. Since absolute immunity cannot be defeated even by claims of malice or improper motivation, it essentially eliminates the burden of defense, typically allowing dismissal on a Rule 12(b)(6) motion. Prosecutors enjoy only qualified or good faith immunity in their roles as investigator and administrator. See Burns v. Reed, 500 U.S. 478 (1991); Buckley v. Fitzsimmons, 509 U.S. 259 (1993); Kalina v. Fletcher, 522 U.S. 118 (1997). Isn't it likely that the specter of possible section 1983 damages claims will chill the exercise of independent judgment by prosecutors and other government officials in capacities beyond those "intimately associated with the judicial phase of the criminal process"? Does the distinction suggest that judges may employ a different standard for those state officials directly involved with the judicial process? Would it be possible to provide prosecutors sufficient protection through the use of good faith immunities combined with strict pleading and summary judgment rules? For an argument that prosecutors should not be afforded absolute immunity from section 1983 suits, see Johns, *Reconsidering Absolute Prosecutorial Immunity*, 2005 B.Y.U.L.Rev. 53.

7. **Judicial and Legislative Immunity.** In order to assure independent decisionmaking and to protect against repeated retaliation, the Court has long recognized an absolute judicial immunity in section 1983 cases as well. The immunity exists "however erroneous the act may have been, and however injurious in its consequences it may have proved to the plaintiff." Bradley v. Fisher, 80 U.S. (13 Wall.) 335, 347 (1871). In Stump v. Sparkman, 435 U.S. 349 (1978), for example, the Supreme Court dismissed a section 1983 damages claim against a state judge filed by a woman who had been sterilized without her knowledge at the age of 15. *Stump* presented an extremely harsh set of facts. The judge had approved an ex parte request for the sterilization by the woman's parents in an action which was not docketed or filed with the court clerk, and in which no hearing was held. The girl was told that her appendix was being removed and only learned of the action years later when she was unable to have children. And although the judge sat in a court of general jurisdiction, he apparently had no statutory

authority to issue the order in question. Nonetheless, the Court ruled that the suit challenged a "judicial act" normally "performed by judges" and was, therefore, not subject to suit. See also Dennis v. Sparks, 449 U.S. 24 (1980) and Mireles v. Waco, 502 U.S. 9 (1991) (absolute immunity granted where state judge allegedly ordered tardy public defender to be seized "with excessive force" and brought before court.) Judges, however, enjoy only good faith immunity for their administrative or executive actions. See Forrester v. White, 484 U.S. 219 (1988) (judge may be sued for sex discrimination in firing probation officer).

In Tenney v. Brandhove, 341 U.S. 367 (1951) the Court recognized an absolute immunity from section 1983 claims to protect the state legislative function. There a suit seeking damages from legislators and their aides who held state subversive activity hearings was dismissed because the challenged actions were "in a field where legislators traditionally have power to act." 341 U.S. at 379. The immunity extends, however, only to actions that are an "integral part of the deliberative and communicative process * * * with respect to the consideration and passage or rejection of proposed legislation or with respect to other matters * * * within the jurisdiction of either house." Gravel v. United States, 408 U.S. 606, 625 (1972) (scope of analogous federal legislative privilege.) The Supreme Court extended absolute immunity to local legislators engaged in legislative activities in Bogan v. Scott–Harris, 523 U.S. 44 (1998).

8. **Private Persons and Municipalities.** Private individuals who are amenable to suit under section 1983 have no immunities. See Wyatt v. Cole, 504 U.S. 158 (1992) (no immunity for private individuals who invoke state replevin, garnishment, or attachment statutes); Richardson v. McKnight, 521 U.S. 399 (1997) (no immunity for private prison guards). In Owen v. City of Independence, 445 U.S. 622 (1980), the Court ruled that local governments are liable under section 1983 for constitutional violations even if the actions are undertaken in good faith. *Owen* emphasized that municipalities enjoyed no good faith immunity in 1871. Moreover, allowing cities to claim qualified immunity would thwart the goals of deterrence and risk allocation. See generally, Nahmod, *Section 1983 Discourse: The Move From Constitution to Tort,* 77 Geo.L.Rev. 1719 (1989).

9. The President of the United States is absolutely immune from damage claims for acts committed in his official capacity. Nixon v. Fitzgerald, 457 U.S. 731 (1982). However, that immunity does not extend to suits for acts committed prior to the presidency, even if the suit is commenced during the presidency. Clinton v. Jones, 520 U.S. 681 (1997).

10. The issue of good faith immunity is a legal question to be decided by the court rather than the jury. Hunter v. Bryant, 502 U.S. 224 (1991). As a legal question, the crux of qualified immunity—whether a right was clearly established—is subject to de novo review on appeal. Elder v. Holloway, 510 U.S. 510 (1994). The denial of qualified immunity is immediately appealable in federal court, although state courts are not required to authorize immediate appeals. See Mitchell v. Forsyth, 472 U.S. 511 (1985) (federal court); Johnson v. Fankell, 520 U.S. 911 (1997) (state court).

11. For scholarly discussion of immunities, in addition to the articles mentioned in these notes, see generally P. Schuck, Suing Government:

Citizen Remedies for Official Wrongs (1983); Saiman, *Interpreting Immunity*, 7 U.Pa.J.Constit.L. 1155 (2005); Goldsmith, *Reforming the Civil Rights Act of 1871: The Problem of Police Perjury*, 80 Notre Dame L.Rev. 1259 (2005); Nahmod, *From the Courtroom to the Street: Court Orders and Section 1983*, 29 Hastings Constit.L.Q. 613 (2002); Hassel, *Living a Lie: The Cost of Qualified Immunity*, 64 Mo.L.Rev. 123 (1999); Armacost, *Qualified Immunity: Ignorance Excused*, 51 Vand.L.Rev. 583 (1998); Wright, *Qualified and Civic Immunity in Section 1983 Actions: What Do Justice and Efficiency Require?*, 49 Syracuse L.Rev. 1 (1998); Chen, *The Burdens of Qualified Immunity: Summary Judgment and the Role of Facts in Constitutional Tort Law*, 47 Am.U.L.Rev. 1 (1997); McNamara, Buckley, Imbler, *and* Stare Decisis: *The Present Predicament of Prosecutorial Immunity and an End to Its Absolute Means*, 59 Alb.L.Rev. 1135 (1996); Kinports, *Qualified Immunity in Section 1983 Cases: The Unanswered Questions*, 23 Ga.L.Rev. 597 (1989); Matasar, *Personal Immunities Under Section 1983: The Limits of the Court's Historical Analysis,* 40 Ark.L.Rev. 741 (1987); Cass, *Damage Suits Against Public Officers,* 129 U.Pa.L.Rev. 1110 (1981).

Chapter 7

STATE SOVEREIGN IMMUNITY

§ 1. FOUNDATIONS

The notion that the sovereign may not be sued without its consent is an ancient one, derived from English law. The doctrine still retains significant vitality as applied to the federal government, which even today may not be sued without its consent. But the question becomes more complicated in a federal system with dual sovereigns: what rule should apply when a citizen sues one sovereign in the courts of the other? The problems raised by suits against states in federal court have bedeviled American jurists since before the Constitution was adopted.

No explicit mention of state sovereign immunity was made in the body of the unamended Constitution. Indeed, Article III, section 2 extended the federal judicial power to suits between a state and a citizen of another state. That clause provoked controversy in the debates over the ratification of the Constitution. Consider the following excerpts from those debates, and try to determine what the founding generation thought about states' amenability to suit in federal court.

DEBATES IN THE VIRGINIA CONVENTION
June 19–20, 1788.
3 Elliot's Debates 526–27, 533, 543, 555.*

George Mason: "To controversies between a state and the citizens of another state."—How will their jurisdiction in this case do? Let gentlemen look at the westward. Claims respecting those lands, every liquidated account, or other claim against this state, will be tried before the federal court. Is not this disgraceful? Is this state to be brought to the bar of justice like a delinquent individual? Is the sovereignty of the state to be arraigned like a culprit, or private offender? Will the states undergo this mortification? I think this power perfectly unnecessary.

* * *

---

* Jonathan Elliot, The Debates in the State Conventions on the Adoption of the Federal Constitution (1866 ed.). With minor changes in punctuation and grammar, Elliot's version accords with that in X The Documentary History of the Ratification of the Constitution 1406, 1414, 1422–23, 1433 (1993).

James Madison: Its jurisdiction in controversies between a State and citizens of another state is much objected to, and perhaps without reason. It is not in the power of individuals to call any state into court. The only operation it can have, is that, if a state should wish to bring suit against a citizen, it must be brought before the federal court. * * * It appears to me that this can have no operation but this—to give a citizen a right to be heard in the federal courts; and if a state should condescend to be a party, this court may take cognizance of it.

* * *

Patrick Henry: As to controversies between a state and the citizens of another state, his [Madison's] construction of it is to me perfectly incomprehensible. He says it will seldom happen that a state has such demands on individuals. There is nothing to warrant such an assertion. But he says that the state may be plaintiff only. If gentlemen pervert the most clear expressions, and the usual meaning of the language of the people, there is an end of all argument. What says the paper? That it shall have cognizance of controversies between a state, and citizens of another state, without discriminating between plaintiff and defendant. What says the honorable gentleman? The contrary—that the the state can only be plaintiff.

* * *

John Marshall: With respect to disputes between *a state and the citizens of another state*, its jurisdiction has been decried with unusual vehemence. I hope that no gentleman will think that a state will be called at the bar of the federal court. * * * It is not rational to suppose that the sovereign power shall be dragged before a court. The intent is, to enable states to recover claims of individuals residing in other states. I contend this construction is warranted by the words.

FEDERALIST NO. 81

Alexander Hamilton.

I shall take occasion to mention here a supposition which has excited some alarm upon very mistaken grounds. It has been suggested that an assignment of the public securities of one State to the citizens of another would enable them to prosecute that State in the federal courts for the amount of the securities; a suggestion which the following considerations prove to be without foundation.

It is inherent in the nature of sovereignty not to be amenable to the suit of an individual *without its consent*. This is the general sense and the general practice of mankind; and the exemption, as one of the attributes of sovereignty, is now enjoyed by the government of every State in the Union. Unless, therefore, there is a surrender of this immunity in the plan of the convention, it will remain with the States and the danger intimated must be merely ideal. * * * A recurrence to the principles [earlier] established will satisfy us that there is no color to pretend that the State governments would, by the adoption of that plan, be divested of the privilege of paying their own debts in their own way, free from every constraint but that which flows from the obligations of good faith. The contracts between a nation and individuals are only binding on the conscience of the sovereign, and have no pretensions to a compulsive force. They confer no right of action independent of the sovereign will. To what purpose would it be to authorize suits against States for the debts they owe? How could recoveries be enforced? It is evident that it could not be done without waging war against the contracting State; and to ascribe to the federal courts, by mere implication, and in destruction of a pre-existing right of the State governments, a power which would involve such a consequence, would be altogether forced and unwarrantable.

Despite the fears of men like Patrick Henry and George Mason, the Constitution was successfully ratified. A mere five years later, however, their apprehensions were vindicated when the Supreme Court decided the following case:

CHISHOLM v. GEORGIA

Supreme Court of the United States, 1793.
2 U.S. (2 Dall.) 419.

[Chisholm, a citizen of South Carolina, sued the state of Georgia in the Supreme Court to recover debts on bonds issued by that state. Georgia objected on the ground that as a sovereign, it could not be sued in federal court without its consent.]

BLAIR, JUSTICE:*

In considering this important case, * * * [t]he Constitution of the United States is the only fountain from which I shall draw; the only authority to which I shall appeal. * * * What then do we find there requiring the submission of individual States to the judicial authority of the United States? This is expressly extended, among other things, to controversies between a State and citizens of another State. Is then the case before us one of that description? Undoubtedly it is, unless it may be a sufficient denial to say, that it is a controversy between a citizen of one State and another State. Can this change of order be an essential

---

* In 1794, the Justices announced their opinions seriatim, in reverse order of seniority. There was no opinion for the Court. This practice, patterned after English custom, was the usual one in the new United States until the tenure of Chief Justice John Marshall. Marshall introduced the idea of a common opinion for the Court. In *Chisholm*, Justice Iredell's opinion was in fact read first (and is printed that way in the U.S. Reports); since his was ultimately a dissenting opinion, however, it is reprinted here as the last opinion, in keeping with the more modern organization. We have also deviated in another way from the usual practice of reprinting cases exactly as they are reported: we have chosen not to retain the original italicization in this case, as it is frequent, archaic, and distracting.

change in the thing intended? And is this alone a sufficient ground from which to conclude, that the jurisdiction of this Court reaches the case where a State is Plaintiff, but not where it is Defendant? In this latter case, should any man be asked, whether it was not a controversy between a State and citizen of another State, must not the answer be in the affirmative? A dispute between A. and B. is surely a dispute between B. and A. Both cases, I have no doubt, were intended; and probably the State was first named, in respect to the dignity of a State. But that very dignity seems to have been thought a sufficient reason for confining the sense to the case where a State is plaintiff. It is, however, a sufficient answer to say, that our Constitution most certainly contemplates, in another branch of the cases enumerated, the maintaining [of] jurisdiction against a State, as Defendant; this is unequivocally asserted when the judicial power of the United States is extended to controversies between two or more States; for there, a State must, of necessity, be a Defendant. * * * It seems to me, that if this Court should refuse to hold jurisdiction of a case where a State is Defendant, it would renounce part of the authority conferred, and, consequently, part of the duty imposed on it by the Constitution; because it would be a refusal to take cognizance of a case where a State is a party. * * *

* * *

WILSON, JUSTICE:

This is a case of uncommon magnitude. One of the parties to it is a State; certainly respectable, claiming to be sovereign. The question to be determined is, whether this State, so respectable, and whose claim soars so high, is amenable to the jurisdiction of the Supreme Court of the United States? * * *

* * *

To the Constitution of the United States the term SOVEREIGN, is totally unknown. There is but one place where it could have been used with propriety. But, even in that place it would not, perhaps, have comported with the delicacy of those, who ordained and established that Constitution. They might have announced themselves "SOVEREIGN" people of the United States: But serenely conscious of the fact, they avoided the ostentatious declaration.

* * *

* * * As a Judge of this Court, I know, and can decide upon the knowledge, that the citizens of Georgia, when they acted upon the large scale of the Union, as a part of the "People of the United States," did not surrender the Supreme or sovereign Power to that State; but, as to the purposes of the Union, retained it to themselves. As to the purposes of the Union, therefore, Georgia is NOT a sovereign State. If the Judicial decision of this case forms one of those purposes; the allegation, that Georgia is a sovereign State, is unsupported by the fact. Whether the judicial decision of this cause is, or is not, one of those purposes, is a

question which will be examined particularly in a subsequent part of my argument.

* * *

The question now opens fairly to our view, could the people of those States, among whom were those of Georgia, bind those States, and Georgia among the others, by the Legislative, Executive, and Judicial power so vested? If the principles, on which I have founded myself, are just and true; this question must unavoidably receive an affirmative answer. If those States were the work of those people; those people, and, that I may apply the case closely, the people of Georgia, in particular, could alter, as they pleased, their former work: To any given degree, they could diminish as well as enlarge it. Any or all of the former State-powers, they could extinguish or transfer. The inference, which necessarily results, is, that the Constitution ordained and established by those people; and, still closely to apply the case, in particular by the people of Georgia, could vest jurisdiction or judicial power over those States and over the State of Georgia in particular.

* * *

Whoever considers, in a combined and comprehensive view, the general texture of the Constitution, will be satisfied, that the people of the United States intended to form themselves into a nation for national purposes. They instituted, for such purposes, a national Government, complete in all its parts, with powers Legislative, Executive and Judiciary; and, in all those powers, extending over the whole nation. Is it congruous, that, with regard to such purposes, any man or body of men, any person natural or artificial, should be permitted to claim successfully an entire exemption from the jurisdiction of the national Government? Would not such claims, crowned with success, be repugnant to our very existence as a nation? When so many trains of deduction, coming from different quarters, converge and unite, at last, in the same point; we may safely conclude, as the legitimate result of this Constitution, that the State of Georgia is amenable to the jurisdiction of this Court.

* * *

JAY, CHIEF JUSTICE:

The question we are now to decide has been accurately stated, viz. Is a State suable by individual citizens of another State?

* * *

* * * It is agreed, that one free citizen may sue another; the obvious dictates of justice, and the purposes of society demanding it. It is agreed, that one free citizen may sue any number on whom process can be conveniently executed; nay, in certain cases one citizen may sue forty thousand; for where a corporation is sued, all the members of it are Mactually sued, though not personally, sued. In this city there are forty odd thousand free citizens, all of whom may be collectively sued by any

individual citizen. In the State of Delaware, there are fifty odd thousand free citizens, and what reason can be assigned why a free citizen who has demands against them should not prosecute them? Can the difference between forty odd thousand, and fifty odd thousand make any distinction as to right? Is it not as easy, and as convenient to the public and parties, to serve a summons on the Governor and Attorney General of Delaware, as on the Mayor or other Officers of the Corporation of Philadelphia? Will it be said, that the fifty odd thousand citizens in Delaware being associated under a State Government, stand in a rank so superior to the forty odd thousand of Philadelphia, associated under their charter, that although it may become the latter to meet an individual on an equal footing in a Court of Justice, yet that such a procedure would not comport with the dignity of the former? In this land of equal liberty, shall forty odd thousand in one place be compellable to do justice, and yet fifty odd thousand in another place be privileged to do justice only as they may think proper? Such objections would not correspond with the equal rights we claim; with the equality we profess to admire and maintain, and with that popular sovereignty in which every citizen partakes. Grant that the Governor of Delaware holds an office of superior rank to the Mayor of Philadelphia, they are both nevertheless the officers of the people; and however more exalted the one may be than the other, yet in the opinion of those who dislike aristocracy, that circumstance cannot be a good reason for impeding the course of justice.

* * *

Let us now turn to the Constitution. The people therein declare, that their design in establishing it, comprehended six objects. 1st. To form a more perfect union. 2nd. To establish justice. 3rd. To ensure domestic tranquillity. 4th. To provide for the common defence. 5th. To promote the general welfare. 6th. To secure the blessings of liberty to themselves and their posterity. * * *

* * *

The exception contended for, would contradict and do violence to the great and leading principles of a free and equal national government, one of the great objects of which is, to ensure justice to all: To the few against the many, as well as to the many against the few. It would be strange, indeed, that the joint and equal sovereigns of this country, should, in the very Constitution by which they professed to establish justice, so far deviate from the plain path of equality and impartiality, as to give to the collective citizens of one State, a right of suing individual citizens of another State, and yet deny to those citizens a right of suing them. * * *

* * *

As this opinion, though deliberately formed, has been hastily reduced to writing between the intervals of the daily adjournments, and while my mind was occupied and wearied by the business of the day, I fear it is less concise and connected than it might otherwise have been. * * * Georgia has in strong language advocated the cause of republican equality: and there is reason to hope that the people of that State will yet perceive that it would not have been consistent with that equality, to have exempted the body of her citizens from that suability, which they are at this moment exercising against citizens of another State.

* * *

IREDELL, JUSTICE [dissenting]:

* * *

The question, as I before observed, is,—will an action of *assumpsit* lie against a State? If it will, it must be in virtue of the Constitution of the United States, and of some law of Congress conformable thereto. * * *

* * *

* * * I conceive, that all the Courts of the United States must receive, not merely their organization as to the number of Judges of which they are to consist; but all their authority, as to the manner of their proceeding, from the Legislature only. This appears to me to be one of those cases, with many others, in which an article of the Constitution cannot be effectuated without the intervention of the Legislative authority. * * * The Constitution intended this article so far at least to be the subject of a Legislative act. Having a right thus to establish the Court, and it being capable of being established in no other manner, I conceive it necessarily follows, that they are also to direct the manner of its proceedings. Upon this authority, there is, that I know, but one limit; that is, "that they shall not exceed their authority." If they do, I have no hesitation to say, that any act to that effect would be utterly void, because it would be inconsistent with the Constitution, which is a fundamental law paramount to all others, which we are not only bound to consult, but sworn to observe; and, therefore, where there is an interference, being superior in obligation to the other, we must unquestionably obey that in preference. Subject to this restriction, the whole business of organizing the Courts, and directing the methods of their proceeding where necessary, I conceive to be in the discretion of Congress. If it shall be found on this occasion, or on any other, that the remedies now in being are defective, for any purpose it is their duty to provide for, they no doubt will provide others. It is their duty to legislate so far as is necessary to carry the Constitution into effect. It is ours only to judge. We have no reason, nor any more right to distrust their doing their duty, than they have to distrust that we all do ours. * * *

* * *

* * * [W]e must receive our directions from the Legislature in this particular, and have no right to constitute ourselves an *ossicina brevium*, or take any other short method of doing what the Constitution has

chosen (and, in my opinion, with the most perfect propriety) should be done in another manner.

But the act of Congress has not been altogether silent upon this subject. The 14th sect. of the judicial act, provides in the following words: "All the before mentioned Courts of the United States, shall have power to issue writs of *feire facias*, *habeas corpus*, and all other writs not specially provided for by statute, which may be necessary for the exercise of their respective jurisdictions, and agreeable to the principles and usages of law." These words refer as well to the Supreme Court as to the other Courts of the United States. Whatever writs we issue, that are necessary for the exercise of our jurisdiction, must be agreeable to the principles and usages of law. This is a direction, I apprehend, we cannot supercede, because it may appear to us not sufficiently extensive. If it be not, we must wait till other remedies are provided by the same authority. From this it is plain that the Legislature did not chuse to leave to our own discretion the path to justice, but has prescribed one of its own. In doing so, it has, I think, wisely, referred us to principles and usages of law already well known, and by their precision calculated to guard against that innovating spirit of Courts of Justice, which the Attorney–General in another case reprobated with so much warmth, and with whose sentiments in that particular, I most cordially join. * * *

* * * I believe there is no doubt that neither in the State now in question, nor in any other in the Union, any particular Legislative mode, authorizing a compulsory suit for the recovery of money against a State, was in being either when the Constitution was adopted, or at the time the judicial act was passed.

The only principles of law, then, that can be regarded, are those common to all the States. I know of none such, which can affect this case, but those that are derived from what is properly termed "the common law," a law which I presume is the ground-work of the laws in every State in the Union, and which I consider, so far as it is applicable to the peculiar circumstances of the country, and where no special act of Legislation controls it, to be in force in each State, as it existed in England, (unaltered by any statute) at the time of the first settlement of the country. * * * But it is certain that in regard to any common law principle which can influence the question before us no alteration has been made by any statute, which could occasion the least material difference, or have any partial effect. * * *

* * * It follows, therefore, unquestionably, I think, that looking at the act of Congress, which I consider is on this occasion the limit of our authority (whatever further might be constitutionally, enacted) we can exercise no authority in the present instance consistently with the clear intention of the act, but such as a proper State Court would have been at least competent to exercise at the time the act was passed.

If therefore, no new remedy be provided (as plainly is the case), and consequently we have no other rule to govern us but the principles of the pre-existent laws, which must remain in force till superceded by others, then it is incumbent upon us to enquire, whether previous to the adoption of the Constitution (which period, or the period of passing the law, in respect to the object of this enquiry, is perfectly equal) an action of the nature like this before the Court could have been maintained against one of the States in the Union upon the principles of the common law, which I have shown to be alone applicable. If it could, I think it is now maintainable here; If it could not, I think, as the law stands at present, it is not maintainable; whatever opinion may be entertained; upon the construction of the Constitution, as to the power of Congress to authorize such a one. * * *

* * *

[After examining English precedents and their effect on American law, Justice Iredell concluded:] I have now, I think, established the following particulars. 1st. That the Constitution, so far as it respects the judicial authority, can only be carried into effect by acts of the Legislature appointing Courts, and prescribing their methods of proceeding. 2nd. That Congress has provided no new law in regard to this case, but expressly referred us to the old. 3rd. That there are no principles of the old law, to which, we must have recourse, that in any manner authorise the present suit, either by precedent or by analogy. The consequence of which, in my opinion, clearly is, that the suit in question cannot be maintained, nor, of course, the motion made upon it be complied with.

* * * My opinion being, that even if the Constitution would admit of the exercise of such a power, a new law is necessary for the purpose, since no part of the existing law applies, this alone is sufficient to justify my determination in the present case. So much, however, has been said on the Constitution, that it may not be improper to intimate that my present opinion is strongly against any construction of it, which will admit, under any circumstances, a compulsive suit against a State for the recovery of money. I think every word in the Constitution may have its full effect without involving this consequence, and that nothing but express words, or an insurmountable implication (neither of which I consider, can be found in this case) would authorise the deduction of so high a power. This opinion I hold, however, with all the reserve proper for one, which, according to my sentiments in this case, may be deemed in some measure extra-judicial. * * *

———

Largely in response to the decision in *Chisholm*, the eleventh amendment was adopted in 1795. That amendment provides: "The Judicial power of the United States shall not be construed to extend to any suit in law or equity, commenced or prosecuted against one of the United States by Citizens of another State, or by Citizens or Subjects of any Foreign State." For analysis of the amendment's historical background, see C. Warren, The Supreme Court in United States History (Vol. 1, 2d Ed. 1926); C. Jacobs, The Eleventh Amendment and Sovereign Immunity (1972); J. Orth, the Judicial Power of the United States: The Eleventh Amendment in American History (1987).

Notes

1. The eleventh amendment is widely thought to have adopted Justice Iredell's dissent in *Chisholm*. If that is true, what principles does the eleventh amendment reflect? In particular, did Justice Iredell think that the Constitution itself barred all suits against states? Did Marshall, Madison, or Hamilton think so? If Congress had, by the time Chisholm brought suit, enacted a statute that explicitly created federal court jurisdiction over diversity suits brought against states by citizens of another state, would Iredell have ruled differently? Can Congress respond to the eleventh amendment by passing such a statute? See Orth, *The Truth About Justice Iredell's Dissent in* Chisholm v. Georgia, 73 N.C.L.Rev. 255 (1994). For further information about *Chisholm* and other eighteenth century Supreme Court cases involving suits against states, as well as the history of the adoption of the eleventh amendment, see The Documentary History of the Supreme Court of the United States, 1789–1800, Volume 5: Suits Against States (M. Marcus, ed., 1994). For a brief history of English sovereign immunity, thought to have influenced the founding generation's understanding, see Seidman, *The Origins of Accountability: Everything I Know About the Sovereign's Immunity, I Learned from King Henry III*, 49 St. Louis U.L.J. 393 (2005).

2. Note that the language of the eleventh amendment mirrors the language of Article III, section 2, providing for jurisdiction in diversity suits involving a state. The amendment's protection appears to be limited to suits in law or equity—thus excluding suits in admiralty—and to suits brought against a state by citizens of *another* state. In Cohens v. Virginia, 19 U.S. (6 Wheat.) 264 (1821), the Court interpreted this language to permit a citizen to appeal his conviction, in the courts of his own state, to the Supreme Court. Chief Justice Marshall's opinion for the Court ruled that an appeal was not a suit, and that in any case the eleventh amendment prohibited only suits brought by citizens of other states (or of foreign states). He also suggested that the purpose of the amendment could not have been "to maintain the sovereignty of a State from the degradation supposed to attend a compulsory appearance before the tribunal of the nation," since some suits against states remained permissible despite the amendment. Id. at 406. Instead, Marshall intimated, it was probably designed to protect states from their creditors. In Osborn v. Bank of the United States, 22 U.S. (9 Wheat.) 738 (1824), Marshall further narrowed the reach of the eleventh amendment by allowing suits against state officers challenging acts performed in the course of their official duties: "The 11th amendment, which restrains the jurisdiction granted by the constitution over suits against States, is, of necessity, limited to those suits in which a State is a party on the record." Id. at 857.

3. Does the language of the eleventh amendment make sense? Why would the drafters have failed to protect states from suits in admiralty or suits by citizens of their own state? Was it mere oversight, brought about by a focus on *Chisholm*? Think about exactly what Mason and Henry were

worried about, how to interpret the responses by Madison and the others, and how the eleventh amendment might have assuaged Antifederalist fears. Are there reasons why the framers (of the Constitution or of the eleventh amendment) might have been more concerned about diversity suits against states than about federal question or admiralty suits? Compare your answers to these questions with those of the Court in the next case.

HANS v. LOUISIANA

Supreme Court of the United States, 1890.
134 U.S. 1.

[Hans, a citizen of Louisiana, sued in federal court to recover interest on bonds issued by that state. The state had amended its constitution to repudiate the bond debt, and Hans alleged that the state constitutional provisions violated the federal Constitution's contract clause.]

JUSTICE BRADLEY delivered the opinion of the Court:

The question is presented, whether a State can be sued in a Circuit Court of the United States by one of its own citizens upon a suggestion that the case is one that arises under the Constitution or laws of the United States.

* * *

That a State cannot be sued by a citizen of another State, or of a foreign state, on the mere ground that the case is one arising under the Constitution or laws of the United States, is clearly established by the decisions of this court in several recent cases. Louisiana v. Jumel, 107 U. S. 711; Hagood v. Southern, 117 U. S. 52; In re Ayers, 123 U. S. 443. Those were cases arising under the Constitution of the United States, upon laws complained of as impairing the obligation of contracts, one of which was the constitutional amendment of Louisiana complained of in the present case. Relief was sought against state officers who professed to act in obedience to those laws. This court held that the suits were virtually against the States themselves, and were consequently violative of the Eleventh Amendment of the Constitution, and could not be maintained. It was not denied that they presented cases arising under the Constitution; but, notwithstanding that, they were held to be prohibited by the [eleventh] amendment * * *.

In the present case the plaintiff in error contends that he, being a citizen of Louisiana, is not embarrassed by the obstacle of the Eleventh Amendment, inasmuch as that amendment only prohibits suits against a State which are brought by the citizens of another State, or by citizens or subjects of a foreign State. It is true, the amendment does so read; and if there were no other reason or ground for abating his suit, it might be maintainable; and then we should have this anomalous result, that in cases arising under the Constitution or laws of the United States, a State may be sued in the federal courts by its own citizens, though it cannot be sued for a like cause of action by the citizens of other States, or of a foreign state; and may be thus sued in the federal courts, although not allowing itself to be sued in its own courts. If this is the necessary consequence of the language of the constitution and the law, the result is no less startling and unexpected than was the original decision of this court, that, under the language of the Constitution and of the judiciary act of 1789, a State was liable to be sued by a citizen of another State or of a foreign country. That decision was made in the case of Chisholm v. Georgia and created such a shock of surprise throughout the country that, at the first meeting of Congress thereafter, the Eleventh Amendment to the Constitution was almost unanimously proposed, and was in due course adopted by the legislatures of the States. This amendment, expressing the will of the ultimate sovereignty of the whole country, superior to all legislatures and all courts, actually reversed the decision of the Supreme Court. It did not in terms prohibit suits by individuals against the States, but declared that the Constitution should not be construed to import any power to authorize the bringing of such suits. The language of the amendment is that "the judicial power of the United States *shall not be construed to extend* to any suit in law or equity, commenced or prosecuted against one of the United States by citizens of another State, or by citizens or subjects of any foreign state." The Supreme Court had construed the judicial power as extending to such a suit, and its decision was thus overruled. * * *

This view of the force and meaning of the amendment is important. It shows that, on this question of the suability of the States by individuals, the highest authority of this country was in accord rather with the minority than with the majority of the court in the decision of the case of Chisholm v. Georgia; and this fact lends additional interest to the able opinion of Mr. Justice Iredell on that occasion. * * * Justice Iredell * * * contended that it was not the intention to create new and unheard of remedies, by subjecting sovereign States to actions at the suit of individuals, (which he conclusively showed was never done before,) but only, by proper legislation, to invest the federal courts with jurisdiction to hear and determine controversies and cases, between the parties designated, that were properly susceptible of litigation in courts.

Looking back from our present stand-point at the decision in Chisholm v. Georgia, we do not greatly wonder at the effect which it had upon the country. Any such power as that of authorizing the federal judiciary to entertain suits by individuals against the States had been expressly disclaimed, and even resented, by the great defenders of the Constitution while it was on its trial before the American people. As some of their utterances are directly pertinent to the question now under consideration, we deem it proper to quote them.

[The Court then quoted the portion of Federalist No. 81 reproduced supra pp. 347–48, and the remarks of Madison and Marshall reproduced supra p. 347]

* * *

It seems to us that these views of those great advocates and defenders of the constitution were most sensible and just; and they apply equally to the present case as to that then under discussion. The letter is appealed to now, as it was then, as a ground for sustaining a suit brought by an individual against a State. The reason against it is as strong in this case as it was in that. It is an attempt to strain the Constitution and the law to a construction never imagined or dreamed of. Can we suppose that, when the Eleventh Amendment was adopted, it was understood to be left open for citizens of a State to sue their own state in the federal courts, whilst the idea of suits by citizens of other states, or of foreign states, was indignantly repelled? Suppose that Congress, when proposing the Eleventh Amendment, had appended to it a proviso that nothing therein contained should prevent a State from being sued by its own citizens in cases arising under the Constitution or laws of the United States: can we imagine that it would have been adopted by the States? The supposition that it would is almost an absurdity on its face.

The truth is that the cognizance of suits and actions unknown to the law, and forbidden by the law, was not contemplated by the Constitution when establishing the judicial power of the United States. * * *

* * *

But besides the presumption that no anomalous and unheard-of proceedings or suits were intended to be raised up by the Constitution— anomalous and unheard of when the Constitution was adopted,—an additional reason why the jurisdiction claimed for the Circuit Court does not exist is the language of the act of Congress by which its jurisdiction is conferred. The words are these: "The circuit courts of the United States shall have original cognizance, concurrent with the courts of the several States, of all suits of a civil nature, at common law or in equity, . . . arising under the Constitution or laws of the United States, or treaties," etc. "Concurrent with the courts of the several States." Does not this qualification show that Congress, in legislating to carry the Constitution into effect, did not intend to invest its courts with any new and strange jurisdictions? The state courts have no power to entertain suits by individuals against a State without its consent. Then how does the Circuit Court, having only concurrent jurisdiction, acquire any such power? It is true that the same qualification existed in the judiciary act of 1789, which was before the court in Chisholm v. Georgia, and the majority of the court did not think that it was sufficient to limit the jurisdiction of the Circuit Court. Justice Iredell thought differently. In view of the manner in which that decision was received by the country, the adoption of the Eleventh Amendment, the light of history and the reason of the thing, we think we are at liberty to prefer Justice Iredell's views in this regard.

Some reliance is placed by the plaintiff upon the observations of Chief Justice Marshall in Cohens v. Virginia, 6 Wheat. 264, 410. The Chief Justice was there considering the power of review exercisable by this court over the judgments of a state court, wherein it might be necessary to make the State itself a defendant in error. * * *

After * * * showing by incontestable argument that a writ of error to a judgment recovered by a State, in which the State is necessarily the defendant in error, is not a suit commenced or prosecuted against a State in the sense of the amendment, [Chief Justice Marshall] added that, if the court were mistaken in this, its error did not affect that case, because the writ of error therein was not prosecuted by "a citizen of another state" or "of any foreign state," and so was not affected by the amendment; but was governed by the general grant of judicial power, as extending "to all cases arising under the Constitution or laws of the United States, without respect to parties." *w/o respect to the parties*

It must be conceded that the last observation of the Chief Justice does favor the argument of the plaintiff. But the observation was unnecessary to the decision, and in that sense *extra judicial,* and, though made by one who seldom used words without due reflection, ought not to *important* outweigh the important considerations referred to which lead to a *considerations* different conclusion. With regard to the question then before the court, it may be observed that writs of error to judgments in favor of the crown, or of the State, had been known to the law from time immemorial, and had never been considered as exceptions to the rule, that an action does not lie against the sovereign.

* * *

The judgment of the Circuit Court is affirmed.

Notes

1. Does the reasoning of the Court in Hans v. Louisiana make any sense? Does the decision represent constitutional construction, or merely the application of a common law principle of sovereign immunity? What practical difference does it make? Cf. Employees v. Department of Public Health and Welfare of Missouri, 411 U.S. 279 (1973) (Brennan, J., dissenting): "*Hans* was a 'sovereign immunity' case pure and simple; no alleged bar in either Art. III or the Eleventh Amendment played any role whatever in that decision. Therefore * * * [there is] no support in *Hans* for bringing this suit by a State's own citizens within that prohibition. Stated simply, the holding of *Hans* is that ancient principles of sovereign immunity limit exercise of the federal power to suits against consenting States." Id. at 320–21. Is this an accurate characterization of the *Hans* holding? For a thorough scholarly account of sovereign immunity as a common law, rather than a constitutional, doctrine, see Field, *The Eleventh Amendment and Other Sovereign Immunity Doctrines: Part One*, 126 U.Pa.L.Rev. 515 (1978).

If, on the other hand, *Hans* was in fact a matter of constitutional construction, what provision of the Constitution is it invoking? Is it the eleventh amendment? If so, does the decision represent a legitimate linguistic construction of that provision? One commentator, in referring to both *Hans* and the decision in Ex parte New York, 256 U.S. 490 (1921), extending the eleventh amendment's bar to suits in admiralty, writes:

> The problem, of course, is that the results in *Hans* and *Ex parte New York* contradict the unambiguous limitations of the Eleventh Amend-

ment's text—a contradiction that suggests the clear error of the Supreme Court's first interpretive premise that the Amendment is in fact concerned with sovereign immunity. If coherence of general sovereign immunity doctrine is achieved only by mangling the Amendment's text, the obvious lesson should be that the Amendment was not designed to embody any such doctrine.

Worse yet, *Hans* and *Ex parte New York* succeed in patching holes in the Court's sovereign immunity theory only by tearing constitutional fabric in other spots. Even in some areas where Congress may constitutionally regulate state behavior, the Supreme Court denies it the power to provide full enforcement of its regulations in federal court. By reading the Eleventh Amendment's "state sovereign immunity" restrictions on federal *judicial* power to go far beyond the Tenth's "residuary state sovereignty" restrictions on federal *legislative* power, the Court has created a curious category of cases in which Congress may pass laws operating directly on states that can be enforced (if at all) only in state courts. The result is an inexplicable throwback to the jurisdictional regime of the Articles of Confederation. Amar, *Of Sovereignty and Federalism,* 96 Yale L.J. 1425, 1476–77 (1987).

For a thorough analysis of the eleventh amendment's history, from pre-*Chisholm* to post-*Hans,* see Gibbons, *The Eleventh Amendment and State Sovereign Immunity: A Reinterpretation,* 83 Colum.L.Rev. 1889 (1983). Judge Gibbons concludes that "[t]he history of the eleventh amendment is in large measure an unflinchingly political one. At the two major points in its history, the amendment's contours were shaped not by doctrinal reasoning but by the political exigencies of the times." 83 Colum.L.Rev. at 2003–04. In referring to *Hans,* he writes: "Regardless of the decision's political wisdom in 1890, its reasoning makes for very bad constitutional theory today." Id. at 2004. Another scholar, examining the history of *Hans*, is even more blunt about its political origins: "*Hans* should carry no generative authority in American constitutional law because it was the product of unprincipled expedience, a vicious and long-since repudiated racism, and a refusal to accept the constitutional principles embodied in the Fourteenth Amendment." Purcell, *The Particularly Dubious Case of* Hans v. Louisiana*: An Essay on Law, Race, History, and "Federal Courts,"* 81 N.Car.L.Rev. 1927, 1934 (2003).

In another thorough historical analysis, Professor (now Ninth Circuit Judge) William Fletcher concludes that "the adopters of the eleventh amendment did not specifically intend to forbid the exercise of federal question or admiralty jurisdiction over private suits against the states." Fletcher, *A Historical Interpretation of the Eleventh Amendment: A Narrow Construction of an Affirmative Grant of Jurisdiction Rather than a Prohibition Against Jurisdiction,* 35 Stan.L.Rev. 1033, 1036 (1983). His analysis, he contends, "will permit a natural and unforced reading of the amendment." Id. at 1037. Fletcher suggests that "[t]he eleventh amendment's failure to mention in-state citizens suggests that its drafters did not intend to reach federal question suits, for if they intended the amendment to forbid them, their drafting was extraordinarily inept." Id. at 1060.

His ultimate conclusion is "that the amendment was designed merely to *Limit* require a limiting construction of the state-citizen diversity clause." Id. at *Diversity* 1062. From this he infers the following: "If the eleventh amendment simply *Clause* required that the state-citizen diversity clause be construed to confer party-based jurisdiction only when the state is a plaintiff, the amendment itself did nothing to forbid private citizens' suits against the states in federal court." Id. at 1063. See also Gibbons, supra, 83 Colum.L.Rev. at 2004: "It is time for the Supreme Court to acknowledge that the eleventh amendment applies only to cases in which the jurisdiction of the federal court depends solely upon party status." Id. He refers to this view as "a strict construction of the eleventh amendment." Id.

Professor Fletcher's "diversity explanation" is further developed in Fletcher, *The Diversity Explanation of the Eleventh Amendment: A Reply to Critics,* 56 U.Chi.L.Rev. 1261 (1989). Justice Brennan advocated the diversity theory in his dissenting opinion in Welch v. Texas Dept. of Highways and Public Transp., 483 U.S. 468 (1987). The eleventh amendment, he suggested, "uses language identical to that in Article III to bar the extension of the judicial power to a suit 'against one of the United States by Citizens of another state, or by Citizens or subjects of any Foreign State.' The congruence of the language suggests that the Amendment specifically limits only the jurisdiction conferred by the above-referenced part of Article III. Thus, the Amendment bars only federal actions brought against a State by citizens of another state or by foreign aliens." 483 U.S. at 504. See also Jackson, *The Supreme Court, the Eleventh Amendment and State Sovereign Immunity,* 98 Yale L.J. 1, 6 (1988) (the "amendment was intended to repeal part of the diversity-based jurisdiction that had been construed to permit federal adjudication of state law claims"); Hovenkamp, *Judicial Restraint and Constitutional Federalism: The Supreme Court's* Lopez *and* Seminole Tribe *Decisions,* 96 Colum.L.Rev. 2213, 2240 (1996) ("In sum, its language indicates that the Eleventh Amendment was designed by its framers to place a limit on diversity actions by preserving traditional state sovereign immunity, a common law doctrine.")

The *Hans* Court relied in part on the statements of Madison, Hamilton, and Marshall for its conclusion that the framers of both the original Constitution and the eleventh amendment could not have meant to subject states to suit in federal court. But the scholars who favor the diversity explanation have a response: "Yet it is quite clear that the context of Hamilton's discussion in Federalist No. 81 was common law suits against states for reneging on debts.... Hamilton was not even discussing federal question lawsuits." Hovenkamp, supra, 96 Colum.L.Rev. at 2243. The same can be said of Marshall's and Madison's remarks.

Still, other scholars have lodged powerful attacks on the diversity theory. Professor William Marshall argues that the historical claims supporting the diversity theory are "ambiguous" or "inaccurate". Given the language of the eleventh amendment, which bars "any suit in law or equity," and almost a century of acceptance of *Hans,* "the diversity theorists have not adequately supported their contention that a proper historical understanding establishes that states should not be immune from federal question suits for monetary relief in federal court." W. Marshall, *The Diversity Theory of the Eleventh Amendment: A Critical Evaluation,* 102 Harv.L.Rev. 1372,

1375 (1989). Professor Lawrence Marshall asserts, more broadly, that "like *Hans,* both the diversity and congressional abrogation theories are thoroughly unfaithful to the essentially unambiguous dictates of the amendment's language." L. Marshall, *Fighting the Words of the Eleventh Amendment,* 102 Harv.L.Rev. 1342, 1343 (1989). See also, Massey, *State Sovereignty and the Tenth and Eleventh Amendments,* 56 U.Chi.L.Rev. 61 (1989) (diversity theorists are "revisionists"; the amendment sought to "create a party-based denial of jurisdiction to the federal courts that sweeps across all jurisdictional heads of Article III.") Professors Massey, Fletcher, and both Marshalls continue the debate in *Exchange on the Eleventh Amendment,* 57 U.Chi. L.Rev. 118–140 (1990).

The original proposal to protect states from federal court jurisdiction, made in the House of Representatives shortly after *Chisholm,* provides further inconclusive evidence:

> That no state shall be liable to be made a party defendant, in any of the judicial courts established, or which shall be established under the authority of the United States, at the suit of any person or persons whether a citizen or citizens, or a foreigner or foreigners, of any body politic or corporate, whether within or without the United States.

Congress never voted on this proposal, but the next day another proposal was introduced in the Senate with language almost identical to the amendment eventually adopted. What conclusion should we draw from the differences between the two versions? Professor William Casto suggests that Representative Theodore Sedgwick, who introduced the first proposal, and Senator Caleb Strong, both Massachusetts Federalists, shared politics and goals, and that the two versions should therefore be read as similar in scope and meaning. W. Casto, The Supreme Court in the Early Republic: The Chief Justiceships of John Jay and Oliver Ellsworth 197–208 (1995). An alternative interpretation is that Congress, having considered the broader Sedgwick proposal, deliberately chose to confine the reach of the eleventh amendment by using the language of diversity jurisdiction.

Professor Casto also notes an unsuccessful attempt to amend the language of the proposed eleventh amendment. Senator Albert Gallatin of Pennsylvania moved to exclude from the jurisdictional ban "cases arising under treaties made under the authority of the United States." Id. at 200. Professor Casto argues that the overwhelming defeat of this motion suggests both that Congress intended to prohibit more than party-based (i.e. diversity) suits. Adherents of the "diversity explanation" respond that Gallatin's motion was intended only to preserve jurisdiction in party-based suits involving treaty violations.

Moving in a different direction, scholars have also made the "rare" and "surprising" suggestion that in interpreting the eleventh amendment the Court should "simply follow the unambiguous dictates of the text"—rejecting both *Hans* and the diversity theory. See M. Redish, Federal Jurisdiction: Tensions in the Allocation of Judicial Power, 192 (2d ed. 1990) (arguing that "[w]hat may at first appear to be a puzzling dichotomy drawn by the drafters of the amendment"—that is, the amendment's protection from nonresident, but not resident, suits—"may well represent the most coherent outgrowth of the delicate balancing process inherent in * * * constitutional ratification." Id. at 193). Similarly, Professor Lawrence Marshall asserts that the "fallacy of the current eleventh amendment theories lies in their relentless demand for a single theoretical principle that can coherently explain the amendment, and even better, also explain how the amendment is consistent with the principles that give rise to the Constitution. This may be a fascinating exercise, but it surely fails to reflect the realities of the political process." L. Marshall, supra, 102 Harv.L.Rev. at 1353. Professor John Manning agrees, suggesting that both statutory and constitutional language—including the eleventh amendment—are the product of compromise and thus that courts should simply enforce the text of the amendment. Manning, *The Eleventh Amendment and the Reading of Precise Constitutional Texts*, 113 Yale L.J. 1663 (2004).

For further discussion of the diversity explanation and its critics, see Shreve, *Letting Go of the Eleventh Amendment,* 64 Ind.L.J. 601 (1989); Sherry, *The Eleventh Amendment and Stare Decisis: Overruling* Hans v. Louisiana, 57 U.Chi.L.Rev. 1260 (1990); Burnham, *Taming the Eleventh Amendment Without Overruling* Hans v. Louisiana, 40 Case W.Res.L.Rev. 931 (1991); Jackson, *One Hundred Years of Folly: The Eleventh Amendment and the 1988 Term,* 64 So.Cal.L.Rev. 51 (1990); Monaghan, *The Sovereign Immunity "Exception,"* 110 Harv.L.Rev. 102 (1996); Meltzer, *The* Seminole *Decision and State Sovereign Immunity,* 1996 Sup.Ct.Rev. 1; Vazquez, *What is Eleventh Amendment Immunity?* 106 Yale L.J. 1683 (1997); Bederman, *Admiralty and the Eleventh Amendment,* 72 Notre Dame L.Rev. 935 (1997); Pfander, *History and State Suability: An "Explanatory" Account of the Eleventh Amendment,* 83 Cornell L.Rev. 1269 (1998); Lee, *Making Sense of the Eleventh Amendment: International Law and State Sovereignty,* 96 Nw.U.L.Rev. 1027 (2002).

2. In McKesson Corp. v. Division of Alcoholic Beverages and Tobacco, 496 U.S. 18 (1990), a unanimous Court ruled that the eleventh amendment does not preclude the Supreme Court's exercise of appellate jurisdiction over cases brought against States that arise from state courts:

> Whereas the Eleventh Amendment has been construed so that a State retains immunity from original suit in federal court * * *, it is "inherent in the constitutional plan," that when a state court takes cognizance of a case, the State assents to appellate review by this Court of the federal issues raised in the case "whoever may be the parties to the original suit, whether private persons, or the state itself." We recognize what has long been implicit in our consistent practice and uniformly endorsed in our cases: the Eleventh Amendment does not constrain the appellate jurisdiction of the Supreme Court over cases arising from state courts.

See also South Central Bell Telephone Co. v. Alabama, 526 U.S. 160 (1999).

3. The Court has refused to apply the eleventh amendment in a number of other circumstances. The amendment, for example, does not bar a federal court action against a state filed by the United States. See United States v. Mississippi, 380 U.S. 128, 140–141 (1965). Nor does it prohibit suits by one state against another. See Colorado v. New Mexico, 459 U.S. 176, 182 n. 9 (1982).

The Court has also long held that the eleventh amendment does not bar suits against municipalities or political subdivisions of a state. See Mt. Healthy City School District Bd. of Education v. Doyle, 429 U.S. 274 (1977); Lincoln County v. Luning, 133 U.S. 529 (1890); Northern Ins. Co. of New York v. Chatham County, 547 U.S. ___, 126 S.Ct. 1689 (2006). Whether a particular defendant is a political subdivision amenable to suit or an agency of the state protected by the amendment can raise difficult issues, especially in the case of state universities. Although most state universities are protected by the eleventh amendment, some are not. Compare, e.g., Treleven v. University of Minnesota, 73 F.3d 816 (8th Cir.1996) (defendant is an arm of the state); Lassiter v. Alabama A & M University, 3 F.3d 1482 (11th Cir.1993), reversed on other grounds, 28 F.3d 1146 (11th Cir.1994) (en banc) (same); with Sherman v. Curators of the University of Missouri, 16 F.3d 860 (8th Cir.1994) (remanding for consideration of whether defendant is an arm of the state); Kovats v. Rutgers, the State University, 822 F.2d 1303 (3d Cir.1987) (defendant is not an arm of the state); Soni v. Board of Trustees of University of Tennessee, 513 F.2d 347 (6th Cir.1975) (court unsure whether defendant is an arm of the state). Cf. Regents of the University of California v. Doe, 519 U.S. 425 (1997) (mentioning but not resolving the issue).

4. States may waive their immunity, although mere participation in a federal program does not constitute consent to suit. See Edelman v. Jordan, 415 U.S. 651 (1974). Nor is giving consent to be sued in its own courts sufficient to waive a state's immunity from suit in federal court. See, e.g., Florida Dept. of Health and Rehabilitative Svcs. v. Florida Nursing Home Assn., 450 U.S. 147 (1981). The Court also recently reaffirmed that states cannot "constructively" waive their immunity merely by knowingly engaging in commercial activity that would subject private actors to suit. To be effective, a state's waiver must be clear and unequivocal. College Savings Bank v. Florida Prepaid Postsecondary Education Expense Board, 527 U.S. 666 (1999). Statutes giving consent to suit will be narrowly construed; the Court requires an express indication of consent to suit in federal court. See, e.g., Port Authority Trans–Hudson Corp. v. Feeney, 495 U.S. 299 (1990). The state may consent to suit through legislation or through judicial interpretation; whether attorneys for the state may waive sovereign immunity in any case is a matter of state law, and many states restrict attorneys' ability to do so. See, e.g., Dagnall v. Gegenheimer, 645 F.2d 2 (5th Cir.1981); Mazur v. Hymas, 678 F.Supp. 1473 (D.Idaho 1988).

Moreover, the waiver must be voluntary rather than coerced: although Congress may threaten to withhold "a gift or gratuity" if states refuse to waive immunity, Congress may not threaten states with a "sanction" for such a refusal. College Savings Bank at 687. Are there any circumstances under which the withholding of federal funds might constitute a sanction? See Jim C. v. Arkansas Department of Education, 235 F.3d 1079 (8th Cir.2000) (en banc) (majority holds that a state's "politically painful" choice between waiving sovereign immunity and forgoing $250 million dollars—12% of the state's annual education budget—in federal education funds is not coerced; dissent disagrees). See also discussion of Congress's options under South Dakota v. Dole, 483 U.S. 203 (1987), infra p. 420.

Finally, in Lapides v. Board of Regents of University System of Georgia, 535 U.S. 613 (2002), the Court unanimously held that if a state consents to suit in state court and then removes the case to federal court, it has waived immunity because it has "voluntarily invoked the federal court's jurisdiction." What if the state removes to federal court in a case in which it *would* be immune in state court? See Stewart v. North Carolina, 393 F.3d 484 (4th Cir.2005) (distinguishing *Lapides* and finding no waiver). For discussions of the Court's waiver doctrines, see Siegel, *Waivers of State Sovereign Immunity and the Ideology of the Eleventh Amendment*, 52 Duke L.J. 1167 (2003); Bohannon, *Beyond Abrogation of Sovereign Immunity: State Waivers, Private Contracts, and Federal Incentives*, 77 N.Y.U.L.Rev. 273 (2002); Seinfeld, *Waiver-in-Litigation: Eleventh Amendment Immunity and the Voluntariness Question*, 63 Ohio St.L.J. 871 (2002).

5.   Should the eleventh amendment protect states from individual complaints brought before federal administrative agencies? In Federal Maritime Commission v. South Carolina State Ports Authority, 535 U.S. 743 (2002), a divided Supreme Court held that it does. Justice Thomas's majority opinion concluded that requiring states to defend themselves against privately initiated complaints constitutes the same affront to state dignitary interests whether the complaint is brought before an Article III court or before a federal agency. The majority was careful to note that claims brought *by* a federal agency are outside the scope of the eleventh amendment, because they are suits by the United States. In light of this exception for suits by an agency, should it matter that Federal Maritime Commission orders are not self-executing, but must instead be enforced by a federal court at the behest of the Commission itself? The Court held the lack of enforcement power irrelevant: it reasoned that a state is "coerced" to defend itself before the Commission in order to avoid forfeiting some otherwise available defenses should the Commission seek enforcement in an Article III court.

§ 2.   INTERPRETATIONS

EX PARTE YOUNG

Supreme Court of the United States, 1908.
209 U.S. 123.

[This decision arose out of a habeas corpus proceeding brought by the Attorney General of Minnesota. He had been held in contempt for failing to comply with a federal court order not to institute state court proceedings against railroads to penalize them for violation of a state statute reducing their rates. The federal court injunction had been issued because the court had found that the rates set by the state law were so low as to be confiscatory and therefore constituted the taking of property without due process of law, in violation of the Fourteenth Amendment. Young argued that the federal proceeding in which he had been enjoined effectively constituted a suit against the state, in violation of the eleventh amendment.]

JUSTICE PECKHAM delivered the opinion of the court.

* * *

We have * * * upon this record the case of an unconstitutional act of the state legislature and an intention by the Attorney General of the

State to endeavor to enforce its provisions, to the injury of the company, in compelling it, at great expense, to defend legal proceedings of a complicated and unusual character, and involving questions of vast importance to all employés and officers of the company, as well as to the company itself. The question that arises is whether there is a remedy that the parties interested may resort to, by going into a Federal court of equity, in a case involving a violation of the Federal Constitution, and obtaining a judicial investigation of the problem, and pending its solution obtain freedom from suits, civil or criminal, by a temporary injunction, and if the question be finally decided favorably to the contention of the company, a permanent injunction restraining all such actions or proceedings.

This inquiry necessitates an examination of the most material and important objection made to the jurisdiction of the Circuit Court, the objection being that the suit is, in effect, one against the State of Minnesota, and that the injunction issued against the Attorney General illegally prohibits state action, either criminal or civil, to enforce obedience to the statutes of the State. This objection is to be considered with reference to the Eleventh and Fourteenth Amendments to the Federal Constitution. The Eleventh Amendment prohibits the commencement or prosecution of any suit against one of the United States by citizens of another State or citizens or subjects of any foreign State. The Fourteenth Amendment provides that no State shall deprive any person of life, liberty or property without due process of law, nor shall it deny to any person within its jurisdiction the equal protection of the laws.

The case before the Circuit Court proceeded upon the theory that the orders and acts heretofore mentioned would, if enforced, violate rights of the complainants protected by the latter Amendment. We think that whatever the rights of complainants may be, they are largely founded upon that Amendment, but a decision of this case does not require an examination or decision of the question whether its adoption in any way altered or limited the effect of the earlier Amendment. We may assume that each exists in full force, and that we must give to the Eleventh Amendment all the effect it naturally would have, without cutting it down or rendering its meaning any more narrow than the language, fairly interpreted, would warrant. It applies to a suit brought against a State by one of its own citizens as well as to a suit brought by a citizen of another State. Hans v. Louisiana, 134 U.S. 1. It was adopted after the decision of this court in Chisholm v. Georgia (1792), 2 Dall. 419, where it was held that a State might be sued by a citizen of another State. Since that time there have been many cases decided in this court involving the Eleventh Amendment, among them being Osborn v. United States Bank (1824), 9 Wheat. 738, 846, 857, which held that the Amendment applied only to those suits in which the State was a party on the record. In the subsequent case of Governor of Georgia v. Madrazo (1828), 1 Pet. 110, 122, 123, that holding was somewhat enlarged, and Chief Justice Marshall, delivering the opinion of the court, while citing Osborn v. United States Bank, supra, said that where the claim was made, as in the case then before the court, against the Governor of Georgia as governor, and the demand was made upon him, not personally, but officially (for moneys in the treasury of the State and for slaves in possession of the state government), the State might be considered as the party on the record and therefore the suit could not be maintained.

* * *

[After a detailed examination of precedent, the Court concluded:] The various authorities we have referred to furnish ample justification for the assertion that individuals, who, as officers of the State, are clothed with some duty in regard to the enforcement of the laws of the State, and who threaten and are about to commence proceedings, either of a civil or criminal nature, to enforce against parties affected an unconstitutional act, violating the Federal Constitution, may be enjoined by a Federal court of equity from such action.

* * *

* * * The act to be enforced is alleged to be unconstitutional, and if it be so, the use of the name of the State to enforce an unconstitutional act to the injury of complainants is a proceeding without the authority of and one which does not affect the State in its sovereign or governmental capacity. It is simply an illegal act upon the part of a state official in attempting by the use of the name of the State to enforce a legislative enactment which is void because unconstitutional. If the act which the state Attorney General seeks to enforce be a violation of the Federal Constitution, the officer in proceeding under such enactment comes into conflict with the superior authority of that Constitution, and he is in that case stripped of his official or representative character and is subjected in his person to the consequences of his individual conduct. The State has no power to impart to him any immunity from responsibility to the supreme authority of the United States. See In re Ayers * * *. It would be an injury to complainant to harass it with a multiplicity of suits or litigation generally in an endeavor to enforce penalties under an unconstitutional enactment, and to prevent it ought to be within the jurisdiction of a court of equity. If the question of unconstitutionality with reference, at least, to the Federal Constitution be first raised in a Federal court that court, as we think is shown by the authorities cited hereafter, has the right to decide it to the exclusion of all other courts.

* * *

And, again, it must be remembered that jurisdiction of this general character has, in fact, been exercised by Federal courts from the time of Osborn v. United States Bank up to the present; the only difference in regard to the case of Osborn and the case in hand being that in this case the injury complained of is the threatened commencement of suits, civil or criminal, to enforce the act, instead of, as in the *Osborn* case, an actual and direct trespass upon or interference with tangible property. A bill filed to prevent the commencement of suits to enforce an unconstitutional act, under the circumstances already mentioned, is no new invention, as we have already seen. The difference between an actual and direct interference with tangible property and the enjoining of state officers from enforcing an unconstitutional act, is not of a radical nature, and does not extend, in truth, the jurisdiction of the courts over the subject matter. In the case of the interference with property the person enjoined is assuming to act in his capacity as an official of the State, and justification for his interference is claimed by reason of his position as a state official. Such official cannot so justify when acting under an unconstitutional enactment of the legislature. So, where the state official, instead of directly interfering with tangible property, is about to commence suits, which have for their object the enforcement of an act which violates the Federal Constitution, to the great and irreparable injury of the complainants, he is seeking the same justification from the authority of the State as in other cases. The sovereignty of the State is, in reality, no more involved in one case than in the other. The State cannot in either case impart to the official immunity from responsibility to the supreme authority of the United States. See In re Ayers, 123 U.S. 507.

* * *

MR. JUSTICE HARLAN, dissenting.

* * *

Let it be observed that the suit instituted * * * in the Circuit Court of the United States was, as to the defendant Young, one against him *as, and only because he was*, Attorney General of Minnesota. No relief was sought against him individually but only in his capacity *as* Attorney General. And the manifest, indeed the avowed and admitted, object of seeking such relief was *to tie the hands* of the *State* so that it could not in any manner or by any mode of proceeding, *in its own courts*, test the validity of the statutes and orders in question. It would therefore seem clear that within the true meaning of the Eleventh Amendment the suit brought in the Federal court was one, in legal effect, against the State— as much so as if the State had been formally named on the record as a party—and therefore it was a suit to which, under the Amendment, so far as the State or its Attorney General was concerned, the judicial power of the United States did not and could not extend. If this proposition be sound it will follow—indeed, it is conceded that if, so far as relief is sought against the Attorney General of Minnesota, this be a suit against the State—then the order of the Federal court enjoining that officer from taking any action, suit, step or proceeding to compel the railway company to obey the Minnesota statute was beyond the jurisdiction of that court and wholly void; in which case, that officer was at liberty to proceed in the discharge of his official duties as defined by the laws of the State, and the order adjudging him to be in contempt for bringing the mandamus proceeding in the state court was a nullity.

* * * [T]he intangible thing, called a State, however extensive its powers, can never appear or be represented or known in any court in a

litigated case, except by and through its officers. When, therefore, the Federal court forbade the defendant Young, as Attorney General of Minnesota, from taking any action, suit, step or proceeding whatever looking to the enforcement of the statutes in question, it said in effect to the State of Minnesota: "It is true that the powers not delegated to the United States by the Constitution, nor prohibited by it to the States, are reserved to the States respectively or to its people, and it is true that under the Constitution the judicial power of the United States does not extend to any suit brought against a State by a citizen of another State or by a citizen or subject of a foreign State, yet the Federal court adjudges that you, the State, although a sovereign for many important governmental purposes, shall not appear in your own courts, by your law officer, with the view of enforcing, or even for determining the validity of the state enactments which the Federal court has, upon a preliminary hearing, declared to be in violation of the Constitution of the United States."

This principle, if firmly established, would work a radical change in our governmental system. It would inaugurate a new era in the American judicial system and in the relations of the National and state governments. It would enable the subordinate Federal courts to supervise and control the official action of the States as if they were "dependencies" or provinces. It would place the States of the Union in a condition of inferiority never dreamed of when the Constitution was adopted or when the Eleventh Amendment was made a part of the Supreme Law of the Land. I cannot suppose that the great men who framed the Constitution ever thought the time would come when a subordinate Federal court, having no power to compel a State, in its corporate capacity, to appear before it as a litigant, would yet assume to deprive a State of the right to be represented in its own courts by its regular law officer. That is what the court below did, as to Minnesota, when it adjudged that the appearance of the defendant Young *in the state court*, as the Attorney General of Minnesota, representing his State as its chief law officer, was a contempt of the authority of the Federal court, punishable by fine and imprisonment. Too little consequence has been attached to the fact that the courts of the States are under an obligation equally strong with that resting upon the courts of the Union to respect and enforce the provisions of the Federal Constitution as the Supreme Law of the Land, and to guard rights secured or guaranteed by that instrument. We must assume—a decent respect for the States requires us to assume—that the state courts will enforce every right secured by the Constitution. If they fail to do so, the party complaining has a clear remedy for the protection of his rights; for, he can come by writ of error, in an orderly, judicial way, from the highest court of the State to this tribunal for redress in respect of every right granted or secured by that instrument and denied by the state court. The state courts, it should be remembered, have jurisdiction concurrent with the courts of the United States of all suits of a civil nature, at common law or equity involving a prescribed amount, arising under the Constitution or laws of the United States. * * *

Notes

1. How realistic is the doctrine of Ex parte Young? Do you see any awkwardness in the doctrine, in light of the fact that the only reason Attorney General Young's conduct could be thought to violate the fourteenth amendment was that he was exercising state authority, which is required by the "state action" prerequisite of that amendment?

2. What would have been the legal and practical result if the Court had rejected the doctrine it ultimately adopted? Could the Court have achieved the same practical result accomplished by its doctrine through any alternative theory or theories? See Leonard, *Ubi Remedium Ibi Jus, Or, Where There's a Remedy, There's a Right: A Skeptic's Critique of* Ex parte Young, 54 Syracuse L.Rev. 215 (2004).

3. While the doctrine discussed in *Young* is today generally associated with that decision, its origins long precede *Young*. Recall that Chief Justice Marshall limited the reach of the eleventh amendment to cases in which a state was a named party. Osborn v. Bank of the United States, 22 U.S. (9 Wheat.) 738 (1824) [noted supra p. 355]. See also Allen v. Baltimore & Ohio Railroad Co., 114 U.S. 311 (1885), where the Supreme Court authorized a taxpayer's suit to enjoin a tax collector from seizing property for nonpayment of allegedly unconstitutional taxes. However, in applying the doctrine, the Court imposed an important limiting principle, as described in In re Ayers, 123 U.S. 443, 500–501 (1887):

> The vital principle in all such cases is that the defendants, though professing to act as officers of the State, are threatening a violation of the personal or property rights of the complainant, for which they are personally and individually liable * * *. The legislation under which the defendant justified being declared to be null and void as contrary to the Constitution of the United States, therefore left him defenseless, subject to answer to the consequences of his personal act in the seizure and detention of the plaintiff's property, and responsible for the damages occasioned thereby.

In *Ayers*, the Virginia legislature had authorized state officials to bring suit against anyone attempting to use certain bond coupons as payment of taxes, an action which holders of the coupons and the bonds sought an injunction to restrain state officers from suing under the law, contending that to do so would violate their constitutional rights. The Court held that the suit against the state officers could not be maintained, because "[t]he acts alleged * * * are violations of the assumed contract between the State of Virginia and the complainants, only as they are considered to be the acts of the State of Virginia. The defendants, as individuals, not being parties to that contract, are not capable in law of committing a breach of it." 123 U.S. at 503.

Can you articulate the logic behind the type of limitation fashioned in *Ayers*? Does it make sense?

4.   To what extent does the *Ayers* limitation survive Ex parte Young? How would the *Ayers* doctrine have applied to the facts in *Young*? In Georgia Railroad & Banking Co. v. Redwine, 342 U.S. 299 (1952), the Supreme Court, when presented with a defense by the state under *Ayers*, distinguished that case on the grounds that in *Ayers* there had been no allegation of deprivation of constitutional rights. This was a clear misstatement of the *Ayers* facts. In light of *Young*, need the Court in *Redwine* have attempted to distinguish *Ayers* on its facts?

5.   *Young* carries with it the power to enforce judgments, including consent decrees. In Frew v. Hawkins, 540 U.S. 431 (2004), plaintiffs sued state officials for allegedly violating federal Medicaid laws, requesting only prospective injunctive relief. The parties eventually entered into a consent decree, which was approved by the court. Plaintiffs later returned to federal court, alleging that the state officials had not fully complied with the terms of the consent decree. The defendants argued, and the Fifth Circuit agreed, that the eleventh amendment rendered the decree unenforceable unless the non-compliance with the decree also amounted to a violation of the underlying federal law. The Supreme Court unanimously reversed, holding that *Young* authorized the enforcement suit: "Federal courts are not reduced to approving consent decrees and hoping for compliance. Once entered, a consent decree may be enforced." Id. at 440.

6.   In Seminole Tribe of Florida v. Florida, 517 U.S. 44 (1996), the Supreme Court may have imposed some limits on Ex parte Young. The Seminole Tribe had sought an injunction ordering the state of Florida to negotiate over Indian gaming, as required by the federal Indian Gaming Regulation Act (IGRA). IGRA established a complicated set of procedures for enforcing the state's duty to negotiate, including not only a federal court suit but also appeals to mediators and ultimately to the Secretary of the Interior. The Court found Congress's direct attempt to subject states to suit unconstitutional [see infra p. 390], and then turned to whether the tribe could bring suit under the doctrine of Ex parte Young. In a puzzling few paragraphs, the Court concluded that it could not:

> Where Congress has created a remedial scheme for the enforcement of a particular federal right, we have, in suits against federal officers, refused to supplement that scheme with one created by the judiciary. Schweiker v. Chilicky, 487 U.S. 412 at 423 (1988) ("When the design of a Government program suggests that Congress has provided what it considers adequate remedial mechanisms for constitutional violations that may occur in the course of its administration, we have not created additional . . . remedies"). Here, of course, the question is not whether a remedy should be created, but instead is whether the Eleventh Amendment bar should be lifted, as it was in Ex parte Young, in order to allow a suit against a state officer. Nevertheless, we think that the same general principle applies: Therefore, where Congress has prescribed a detailed remedial scheme for the enforcement against a State of a statutorily created right, a court should hesitate before casting aside those limitations and permitting an action against a state officer based upon Ex parte Young.

Here, Congress intended § 2710(d)(3) to be enforced against the State in an action brought under § 2710(d)(7); the intricate procedures set forth in that provision show that Congress intended therein not only to define, but also significantly to limit, the duty imposed by § 2710(d)(3). For example, where the court finds that the State has failed to negotiate in good faith, the only remedy prescribed is an order directing the State and the Indian tribe to conclude a compact within 60 days. And if the parties disregard the court's order and fail to conclude a compact within the 60–day period, the only sanction is that each party then must submit a proposed compact to a mediator who selects the one which best embodies the terms of the Act. Finally, if the State fails to accept the compact selected by the mediator, the only sanction against it is that the mediator shall notify the Secretary of the Interior who then must prescribe regulations governing Class III gaming on the tribal lands at issue. By contrast with this quite modest set of sanctions, an action brought against a state official under Ex parte Young would expose that official to the full remedial powers of a federal court, including, presumably, contempt sanctions. If § 2710(d)(3) could be enforced in a suit under Ex parte Young, § 2710(d)(7) would have been superfluous; it is difficult to see why an Indian tribe would suffer through the intricate scheme of § 2710(d)(7) when more complete and more immediate relief would be available under Ex parte Young.

Here, of course, we have found that Congress does not have authority under the Constitution to make the State suable in federal court under § 2710(d)(7). Nevertheless, the fact that Congress chose to impose upon the State a liability which is significantly more limited than would be the liability imposed upon the state officer under Ex parte Young strongly indicates that Congress had no wish to create the latter under § 2710(d)(3). Nor are we free to rewrite the statutory scheme in order to approximate what we think Congress might have wanted had it known that § 2710(d)(7) was beyond its authority. If that effort is to be made, it should be made by Congress, and not by the federal courts. We hold that Ex parte Young is inapplicable to petitioner's suit against the Governor of Florida, and therefore that suit is barred by the Eleventh Amendment and must be dismissed for a lack of jurisdiction. Id. at 74–76.

Justice Souter's dissent took the majority to task for both its approach and its conclusion in rejecting the *Young* suit. He argued that the Court should not find a Congressional intent to bar an Ex parte Young suit absent a clear statement to that effect, and that in any case it was implausible that Congress in IGRA, having attempted unsuccessfully to subject states to suit directly, would have wanted to limit the availability of an Ex parte Young suit as an alternative. Souter also suggested that the majority confused the meaning of *Young*:

Young did not establish a new cause of action and it does not impose any particular procedural regime in the suits it permits. It stands, instead, for a jurisdictional rule by which paramount federal law may be enforced in a federal court by substituting a non-immune party (the state officer) for an immune one (the State itself). *Young* does no more and furnishes no authority for the Court's assumption that it somehow preempts procedural rules devised by Congress for particular kinds of cases that may depend on *Young* for federal jurisdiction. Id. at 177–78.

Do you understand the Court's interpretation of *Young?* In reading *Young*, did you think that congressional intent was relevant to the question of eleventh amendment immunity? Consider the following possible interpretations of *Seminole Tribe*:

(1) Congress did not intend to create any private cause of action under IGRA, and therefore Ex parte Young is irrelevant. See *Chilicky* [infra p. 936].

(2) Congress intended, in enacting IGRA, to restrict Ex parte Young in order to protect state sovereign immunity.

(3) Congress chose not to create an Ex parte Young cause of action under IGRA, and therefore no such cause of action exists in this case.

Which of these is the best interpretation of *Seminole Tribe?* Of *Young?* Professor Vicki Jackson has suggested that the Court in *Seminole Tribe* conflated two aspects of *Young*: one aspect implies a cause of action in the absence of a statutory mandate, and the other aspect simply holds that for purposes of the eleventh amendment, state officials are not identical to the state itself. Jackson, Seminole Tribe, *The Eleventh Amendment, and the Potential Evisceration of* Ex parte Young, 72 N.Y.U.L.Rev. 495 (1997). Which of these aspects of *Young* is relevant to *Seminole Tribe?* Which did the Court seem to focus on?

Note that one scholar has suggested that this portion of *Seminole Tribe* is merely "symbolic," and that "the rule of *Ex parte Young* remains in full force." Monaghan, *The Sovereign Immunity "Exception,"* 110 Harv.L.Rev. 102, 103 (1996). See also Meltzer, *The* Seminole *Decision and State Sovereign Immunity*, 1996 Sup.Ct.Rev. 1, 42 ("I do not view *Seminole* as a significant step in a general assault on private enforcement of federal law against state officials"); Currie, Ex Parte Young *After* Seminole Tribe, 72 N.Y.U.L.Rev. 547 (1997) ("Not to worry; *Ex parte Young* is alive and well and living in the Supreme Court"). Do you agree?

In Idaho v. Coeur d'Alene Tribe of Idaho, 521 U.S. 261 (1997), a majority of the Supreme Court appeared to back away from this part of *Seminole Tribe*, but continued to place limits on *Young* suits. A five to four majority held that the tribe could not bring a *Young* suit for declaratory and injunctive relief against Idaho officials, because the suit sought to "divest the State of all regulatory power" over certain disputed lands. Id. at 296. The suit thus encroached too closely on matters of state sovereignty, and, as Justice O'Connor's concurring opinion put it, "it simply cannot be said that the suit is not a suit against the State." Id. Is this different from any other suit under Ex parte Young?

Nevertheless, the Court made clear in *Coeur d'Alene* that *Young* still retained most of its vitality. Justice Kennedy, writing only for himself and Chief Justice Rehnquist, would have recast *Young* as a balancing test, in which the importance of the federal right, the availability of a state forum, and the need to accommodate state interests should all play a role. Justice O'Connor, joined by Justices Scalia and Thomas, would have no part of this: "[Justice Kennedy's] approach unnecessarily recharacterizes and narrows much of our *Young* jurisprudence. The parties have not briefed whether such a shift in the *Young* doctrine is warranted. In my view, it is not." Id. at 291. Justice O'Connor's opinion also rejected Justice Kennedy's attempt to use *Seminole Tribe's* citation of *Chilicky* to import into *Young* the analysis used in Bivens v. Six Unknown Named Federal Narcotics Agents, 403 U.S. 388 (1971) [infra p. 917]. Four Justices dissented from the Court's holding, but praised Justice O'Connor's opinion for "wisely reject[ing] [Justice Kennedy's] call for federal jurisdiction contingent on a case-by-case balancing * * *." 521 U.S. at 297. The Court reaffirmed the broad availability of *Ex parte Young* suits in Verizon Maryland, Inc. v. Public Service Comm'n of Maryland, 535 U.S. 635 (2002). For a discussion of *Coeur d'Alene*, see LaVelle, *Sanctioning a Tyranny: The Diminishment of* Ex Parte Young, *Expansion of* Hans *Immunity, and Denial of Indian Rights in* Coeur d'Alene Tribe, 31 Ariz.St.L.J. 787 (1999).

7. Was Ex parte Young an inevitable development after *Hans*? One scholar argues that "when *Hans* gave an expansive reading to the Eleventh Amendment in 1890, the *Lochner*-era substantive due process Court felt compelled to create the exception of *Ex parte Young*." Hovenkamp, *Judicial Restraint and Constitutional Federalism: The Supreme Court's* Lopez *and* Seminole Tribe *Decisions*, 96 Colum.L.Rev. 2213, 2246 (1996). During the expansion of civil rights under the Warren Court, *Young* similarly allowed the Court to police state violations of individual rights. One scholar suggests that as a result of *Young*, "[t]he Eleventh Amendment almost never matters." Jeffries, *In Praise of the Eleventh Amendment and Section 1983*, 84 Va.L.Rev. 47, 49 (1998); but see Brown, *The Failure of Fault Under § 1983: Municipal Liability For State Law Enforcement*, 84 Cornell L.Rev. 1503 (1999). Do you agree? Consider the next case in answering that question.

EDELMAN v. JORDAN

Supreme Court of the United States, 1974.
415 U.S. 651.

MR. JUSTICE REHNQUIST delivered the opinion of the Court.

Respondent John Jordan filed a complaint in the United States District Court for the Northern District of Illinois, individually and as a representative of a class, seeking declaratory and injunctive relief against two former directors of the Illinois Department of Public Aid, the director of the Cook County Department of Public Aid, and the comptroller of Cook County. Respondent alleged that these state officials were administering the federal-state programs of Aid to the Aged, Blind, or Disabled (AABD) in a manner inconsistent with various federal regulations and with the Fourteenth Amendment to the Constitution.[2]

2. In his complaint in the District Court, respondent claimed that the Illinois Department of Public Aid was not complying with federal regulations in its processing of public aid applications, and also that its refusal to process and allow respondent's claim for a period of four months, while processing and allowing the claims of those similarly situated, violated the Equal Protection Clause of the Fourteenth Amendment. Respondent asserted that the District Court could exercise jurisdiction over the cause by virtue of 28 U.S.C. §§ 1331 and 1343(3) and (4). Though not briefed by the parties before this Court, we think that under our decision in Hagans v. Lavine, 415

AABD is one of the categorical aid programs administered by the Illinois Department of Public Aid pursuant to the Illinois Public Aid Code, Ill.Rev.Stat., c. 23, §§ 3–1 through 3–12 (1973). Under the Social Security Act, the program is funded by the State and the Federal Governments. 42 U.S.C. §§ 1381–1385.[3] The Department of Health, Education, and Welfare (HEW), which administers these payments for the Federal Government issued regulations prescribing maximum permissible time standards within which States participating in the program had to process AABD applications. Those regulations originally issued in 1968 required at the time of the institution of this suit that eligibility determinations must be made by the States within 30 days of receipt of applications for aid to the aged and blind and within 45 days of receipt of applications for aid to the disabled. For those persons found eligible the assistance check was required to be received by them within the applicable time period. 45 CFR § 206.10(a)(3).

During the period in which the federal regulations went into effect, Illinois public aid officials were administering the benefits pursuant to their own regulations as provided in the Categorical Assistance Manual of the Illinois Department of Public Aid. Respondent's complaint charged that the Illinois defendants, operating under those regulations, were improperly authorizing grants to commence only with the month in which an application was approved and not including prior eligibility months for which an applicant was entitled to aid under federal law. The complaint also alleged that the Illinois defendants were not processing the applications within the applicable time requirements of the federal regulations; specifically, respondent alleged that his own application for disability benefits was not acted on by the Illinois Department of Public Aid for almost four months. Such actions of the Illinois officials were alleged to violate federal law and deny the equal protection of the laws. Respondent's prayer requested declaratory and injunctive relief, and specifically requested "a permanent injunction enjoining the defendants to award to the entire class of plaintiffs all AABD benefits wrongfully withheld."

In its judgment of March 15, 1972, the District Court declared § 4004 of the Illinois Manual to be invalid insofar as it was inconsistent with the federal regulations found in 45 CFR § 206.10(a)(3), and granted a permanent injunction requiring compliance with the federal time limits for processing and paying AABD applicants. The District Court, in paragraph 5 of its judgment, also ordered the state officials to "release and remit AABD benefits wrongfully withheld to all applicants for AABD in the State of Illinois who applied between July 1, 1968 [the date of the federal regulations] and April 16, 197[1] [the date of the preliminary

U.S. 528, the equal protection claim cannot be said to be "wholly insubstantial," and that therefore the District Court was correct in exercising pendent jurisdiction over the statutory claim.

3. Effective January 1, 1974, this AABD program was replaced by a similar program. See 42 U.S.C. §§ 801–805 (1970 ed., Supp. II).

injunction issued by the District Court] and were determined eligible. . . ."

On appeal to the United States Court of Appeals for the Seventh Circuit, the Illinois officials contended, *inter alia*, that the Eleventh Amendment barred the award of retroactive benefits, that the judgment of inconsistency between the federal regulations and the provisions of the Illinois Categorical Assistance Manual could be given prospective effect only and that the federal regulations in question were inconsistent with the Social Security Act itself. The Court of Appeals rejected these contentions and affirmed the judgment of the District Court. Jordan v. Weaver, 472 F.2d 985 (1973). * * * The petition for certiorari raised the same contentions urged by the petitioner in the Court of Appeals. Because we believe the Court of Appeals erred in its disposition of the Eleventh Amendment claim, we reverse that portion of the Court of Appeals decision which affirmed the District Court's order that retroactive benefits be paid by the Illinois state officials.

The historical basis of the Eleventh Amendment has been oft stated, and it represents one of the more dramatic examples of this Court's effort to derive meaning from the document given to the Nation by the Framers nearly 200 years ago. * * *

* * *

While the Amendment by its terms does not bar suits against a State by its own citizens, this Court has consistently held that an unconsenting State is immune from suits brought in federal courts by her own citizens as well as by citizens of another State. Hans v. Louisiana, 134 U.S. 1 (1890); * * * It is also well established that even though a State is not named a party to the action, the suit may nonetheless be barred by the Eleventh Amendment. In Ford Motor Co. v. Department of Treasury, 323 U.S. 459 (1945), the Court said:

> "[W]hen the action is in essence one for the recovery of money from the state, the state is the real, substantial party in interest and is entitled to invoke its sovereign immunity from suit even though individual officials are nominal defendants." Id., at 464.

Thus the rule has evolved that a suit by private parties seeking to impose a liability which must be paid from public funds in the state treasury is barred by the Eleventh Amendment. * * *

The Court of Appeals in this case, while recognizing that the *Hans* line of cases permitted the State to raise the Eleventh Amendment as a defense to suit by its own citizens, nevertheless concluded that the Amendment did not bar the award of retroactive payments of the statutory benefits found to have been wrongfully withheld. The Court of Appeals held that the above-cited cases, when read in light of this Court's landmark decision in Ex parte Young, 209 U.S. 123 (1908), do not preclude the grant of such a monetary award in the nature of equitable restitution.

Petitioner concedes that Ex parte Young is no bar to that part of the District Court's judgment that prospectively enjoined petitioner's predecessors from failing to process applications within the time limits established by the federal regulations. Petitioner argues, however, that Ex parte Young does not extend so far as to permit a suit which seeks the award of an accrued monetary liability which must be met from the general revenues of a State, absent consent or waiver by the State of its Eleventh Amendment immunity, and that therefore the award of retroactive benefits by the District Court was improper.

Ex parte Young was a watershed case in which this Court held that the Eleventh Amendment did not bar an action in the federal courts seeking to enjoin the Attorney General of Minnesota from enforcing a statute claimed to violate the Fourteenth Amendment of the United States Constitution. This holding has permitted the Civil War Amendments to the Constitution to serve as a sword, rather than merely as a shield, for those whom they were designed to protect. But the relief awarded in Ex parte Young was prospective only; the Attorney General of Minnesota was enjoined to conform his future conduct of that office to the requirement of the Fourteenth Amendment. Such relief is analogous to that awarded by the District Court in the prospective portion of is order under review in this case.

But the retroactive portion of the District Court's order here, which requires the payment of a very substantial amount of money which that court held should have been paid, but was not, stands on quite a different footing. These funds will obviously not be paid out of the pocket of petitioner Edelman. Addressing himself to a similar situation in Rothstein v. Wyman, 467 F.2d 226 (C.A.2 1972), cert. denied, 411 U.S. 921 (1973), Judge McGowan observed for the court:

> "It is not pretended that these payments are to come from the personal resources of these appellants. Appellees expressly contemplate that they will, rather, involve substantial expenditures from the public funds of the state. . . .

> "It is one thing to tell the Commissioner of Social Services that he must comply with the federal standards for the future if the state is to have the benefit of federal funds in the programs he administers. It is quite another thing to order the Commissioner to use state funds to make reparation for the past. The latter would appear to us to fall afoul of the Eleventh Amendment if that basic constitutional provision is to be conceived of as having any present force." 467 F.2d at 236–237 (footnotes omitted).

We agree with Judge McGowan's observations. The funds to satisfy the award in this case must inevitably come from the general revenues of the State of Illinois, and thus the award resembles far more closely the monetary award against the State itself, Ford Motor Co. v. Department of Treasury, supra, than it does the prospective injunctive relief awarded in Ex parte Young.

The Court of Appeals, in upholding the award in this case, held that it was permissible because it was in the form of "equitable restitution" instead of damages, and therefore capable of being tailored in such a way as to minimize disruptions of the state program of categorical assistance. But we must judge the award actually made in this case, and not one which might have been differently tailored in a different case, and we must judge it in the context of the important constitutional principle embodied in the eleventh amendment.[11]

We do not read Ex parte Young or subsequent holdings of this Court to indicate that any form of relief may be awarded against a state officer no matter how closely it may in practice resemble a money judgment payable out of the state treasury, so long as the relief may be labeled "equitable" in nature. The Court's opinion in Ex parte Young hewed to no such line. Its citation of Hagood v. Southern, 117 U.S. 52 (1886), and In re Ayers, 123 U.S. 443 (1887), which were both actions against state officers for specific performance of a contract to which the State was a party demonstrate that equitable relief may be barred by the Eleventh Amendment.

As in most areas of the law, the difference between the type of relief barred by the Eleventh Amendment and that permitted under Ex parte Young will not in many instances be that between day and night. The injunction issued in Ex parte Young was not totally without effect on the State's revenues, since the state law which the Attorney General was enjoined from enforcing provided substantial monetary penalties against railroads which did not conform to its provisions. Later cases from this Court have authorized equitable relief which has probably had greater impact on state treasuries than did that awarded in Ex parte Young. In Graham v. Richardson, 403 U.S. 365 (1971), Arizona and Pennsylvania welfare officials were prohibited from denying welfare benefits to otherwise qualified recipients who were aliens. In Goldberg v. Kelly, 397 U.S.

---

11. It may be true, as stated by our Brother Douglas in dissent, that "[m]ost welfare decisions by federal courts have a financial impact on the States." * * * But we cannot agree that such a financial impact is the same where a federal court applies Ex parte Young to grant prospective declaratory and injunctive relief, as opposed to an order of retroactive payments as was made in the instant case. It is not necessarily true that "[w]hether the decree is prospective only or requires payments for the weeks or months wrongfully skipped over by the state officials, the nature of the impact on the state treasury is precisely the same." * * * This argument neglects the fact that where the State has a definable allocation to be used in the payment of public aid benefits, and pursues a certain course of action such as the processing of applications within certain time periods as did Illinois here, the subsequent ordering by a federal court of retroactive payments

to correct delays in such processing will invariably mean there is less money available for payments for the continuing obligations of the public aid system.

As stated by Judge McGowan in Rothstein v. Wyman, 467 F.2d 226, 235 (C.A.2 1972):

"The second federal policy which might arguably be furthered by retroactive payments is the fundamental goal of congressional welfare legislation—the satisfaction of the ascertained needs of impoverished persons. Federal standards are designed to ensure that those needs are equitably met; and there may perhaps be cases in which the *prompt* payment of funds wrongfully withheld will serve that end. As time goes by, however, retroactive payments become compensatory rather than remedial; the coincidence between previously ascertained and existing needs becomes less clear."

254 (1970). New York City welfare officials were enjoined from following New York State procedures which authorized the termination of benefits paid to welfare recipients without prior hearing.[12] But the fiscal consequences to state treasuries in these cases were the necessary result of compliance with decrees which by their terms were prospective in nature. State officials, in order to shape their official conduct to the mandate of the Court's decrees, would more likely have to spend money from the state treasury than if they had been left free to pursue their previous course of conduct. Such an ancillary effect on the state treasury is a permissible and often an inevitable consequence of the principle announced in Ex parte Young, supra.

But that portion of the District Court's decree which petitioner challenges on Eleventh Amendment grounds goes much further than any of the cases cited. It requires payment of state funds, not as a necessary consequence of compliance in the future with a substantive federal-question determination, but as a form of compensation to those whose applications were processed on the slower time schedule at a time when petitioner was under no court-imposed obligation to conform to a different standard. While the Court of Appeals described this retroactive award of monetary relief as a form of "equitable restitution," it is in practical effect indistinguishable in many aspects from an award of damages against the State. It will to a virtual certainty be paid from state funds, and not from the pockets of the individual state officials who were the defendants in the action. It is measured in terms of a monetary loss resulting from a past breach of a legal duty on the part of the defendant state officials.

Were we to uphold this portion of the District Court's decree, we would be obligated to overrule the Court's holding in Ford Motor Co. v. Department of Treasury, supra. There a taxpayer, who had, under protest, paid taxes to the State of Indiana, sought a refund of those taxes from the Indiana state officials who were charged with their collection. The taxpayer claimed that the tax had been imposed in violation of the United States Constitution. The term "equitable restitution" would seem even more applicable to the relief sought in that case, since the taxpayer had at one time had the money, and paid it over to the State pursuant to an allegedly unconstitutional tax exaction. Yet this Court had no hesitation in holding that the taxpayer's action was a suit against the State, and barred by the Eleventh Amendment. We reach a similar

---

12. The Court of Appeals considered the Court's decision in Griffin v. School Board, 377 U.S. 218 (1964), to be of like import. But as may be seen from *Griffin's* citation of Lincoln County v. Luning, 133 U.S. 529 (1890), a county does not occupy the same position as a State for purposes of the Eleventh Amendment. See also Moor v. County of Alameda, 411 U.S. 693 (1973). The fact that the county policies executed by the county officials in *Griffin* were subject to the commands of the Fourteenth Amendment, but the county was not able to invoke the protection of the Eleventh Amendment, is no more than a recognition of the long-established rule that while county action is generally state action for purposes of the Fourteenth Amendment, a county defendant is not necessarily a state defendant for purposes of the Eleventh Amendment.

conclusion with respect to the retroactive portion of the relief awarded by the District Court in this case.

* * *

Three fairly recent District Court judgments requiring state directors of public aid to make the type of retroactive payment involved here have been summarily affirmed by this Court notwithstanding Eleventh Amendment contentions made by state officers who were appealing from the District Court judgment. Shapiro v. Thompson, 394 U.S. 618 (1969), is the only instance in which the Eleventh Amendment objection to such retroactive relief was actually presented to this Court in a case which was orally argued. The three-judge District Court in that case had ordered the retroactive payment of welfare benefits found by that court to have been unlawfully withheld because of residence requirements held violative of equal protection. This Court, while affirming the judgment, did not in its opinion refer to or substantively treat the Eleventh Amendment argument. Nor, of course, did the summary dispositions of the three District Court cases contain any substantive discussion of this or any other issues raised by the parties.

This case, therefore, is the first opportunity the Court has taken to fully explore and treat the Eleventh Amendment aspects of such relief in a written opinion. Shapiro v. Thompson and these three summary affirmances obviously are of precedential value in support of the contention that the Eleventh Amendment does not bar the relief awarded by the District Court in this case. Equally obviously, they are not of the same precedential value as would be an opinion of this Court treating the question on the merits. Since we deal with a constitutional question, we are less constrained by the principle of *stare decisis* than we are in other areas of the law. Having now had an opportunity to more fully consider the Eleventh Amendment issue after briefing and argument, we disapprove the Eleventh Amendment holdings of those cases to the extent that they are inconsistent with our holding today.

* * *

[The dissenting opinions of JUSTICES DOUGLAS, BRENNAN, and MARSHALL, with whom Justice BLACKMUN joined, are omitted.]

Notes

1. On what basis does Justice Rehnquist purport to distinguish Ex Parte Young? How persuasive is the distinction?

2. In Hutto v. Finney, 437 U.S. 678 (1978), the Supreme Court affirmed an award of attorney's fees, which were to be paid by the state, because of bad faith on the part of the state in failing to comply with a prior judicial order. Justice Stevens, speaking for the Court, distinguished *Edelman*:

[T]he Court emphasized in *Edelman* that the distinction [between prospective and retroactive relief] did not immunize the States from the obligation to obey costly federal-court orders. The cost of compliance is "ancillary" to the prospective order enforcing federal law * * *. The line between retroactive and prospective relief cannot be so rigid that it defeats the effective enforcement of prospective relief. Id. at 690.

In Missouri v. Jenkins, 491 U.S. 274, 279 (1989), the Court reaffirmed *Hutto.* ("[T]he holding of *Hutto* * * * was not just that Congress had spoken sufficiently clear to overcome Eleventh Amendment immunity in enacting section 1988, but rather that the Eleventh Amendment did not apply to an award of attorney's fees ancillary to a grant of prospective relief.")

3. Is the prospective-retrospective distinction drawn in *Edelman* defensible? By its terms, the eleventh amendment prohibits all suits against a state. If the Court concludes that the eleventh amendment is applicable, then, does it have authority to decide that certain types of relief against the state are permitted while others are barred? If, on the other hand, the Court concludes that the amendment is inapplicable or may be applicable but has been superceded by an exercise of congressional power, does the Court possess constitutional authority to limit the form of relief Congress chooses to make available? Furthermore, if the state is in fact immune as a sovereign, how can it be subject to any suits without its consent? See Gey, *The Myth of State Sovereignty*, 63 Ohio St.L.J. 1601 (2002). For a defense of the prospective-retrospective distinction on pragmatic grounds, see Hills, *The Eleventh Amendment as Curb on Bureaucratic Power*, 53 Stan.L.Rev. 1225 (2001).

4. Assuming that one accepts the theoretical validity of the prospective-retrospective dichotomy, how workable is the distinction in practice? In Milliken v. Bradley, 433 U.S. 267 (1977), for example, the Supreme Court upheld a desegregation decree requiring the expenditure of state funds to establish several remedial and compensatory educational programs. Despite the program's remedial nature, the Court determined that the remedy ordered was prospective:

> The decree to share future costs of educational components in this case fits squarely within the prospective-compliance exception reaffirmed by Edelman. * * * The educational components, which the District Court ordered into effect *prospectively*, are plainly designed to wipe out continuing conditions of inequality produced by the inherently unequal dual school system. * * *

> That the programs are also "compensatory" in nature does not change the fact that they are of a plan that operates *prospectively* to bring about the delayed benefits of a unitary school system. We therefore hold that * * * relief is not barred by the Eleventh Amendment. Id. at 289–90.

After Milliken was decided, Professor David Currie wrote that "Milliken was no more 'prospective' than * * * Edelman itself. In both cases the money was to be paid in the future in order to right a past wrong. If that is enough to make the order 'prospective', there is no such thing as a retrospective order; nobody is ever ordered to have paid yesterday." Currie, *Sovereign Immunity and Suits Against Government Officers*, 1984 Sup.Ct.Rev. 149, 162.

Consider also the Court's decision in Papasan v. Allain, 478 U.S. 265 (1986). The case concerned "the claims of school officials and [Chickasaw Indian] schoolchildren in 23 Northern Mississippi counties that they are being unlawfully denied the economic benefits of public school lands granted by the United States to the State of Mississippi * * *." One of the major issues was whether the suit was barred by the eleventh amendment.

The plaintiffs presented two substantive claims: (1) that "the state's sale of the Chickasaw Cession school lands and unwise investment of the proceeds in the 1850's had abrogated the State's trust obligation [under the trust granted by the United States] to hold [the] lands [in question] for the benefit of Chickasaw Cession schoolchildren in perpetuity", 478 U.S. at 274, and (2) that, because of the resulting, "dual treatment" of the Chickasaw schoolchildren and the "disparity in the level of school funds * * * that are available to the Chickasaw Cession schools as compared to the schools in the remainder of the State" the state had violated the fourteenth amendment's equal protection clause. Id. at 273. Plaintiff sought "the establishment of a fund in a suitable amount to be held in perpetual trust for the benefit of plaintiffs" or in the alternative the making available of lands of the same value as the original ones sold by the state. Id. at 275.

The Court, in an opinion by Justice White, found the claims under the trust barred by the eleventh amendment, but held that the equal protection claims were not similarly barred. In reaching these conclusions, the Court relied on the retroactive-prospective distinction:

> The petitioners claim that the federal grants of school lands to the State of Mississippi created a perpetual trust, with the State as trustee, for the benefit of the public schools. * * *
>
> * * * But * * * [t]he distinction between a continuing obligation on the part of the trustee and an ongoing liability for past breach of trust is essentially a formal distinction of the sort we rejected in Edelman. * * *
>
> The characterization in that case of the legal wrong as the continuing withholding of accrued benefits is very similar to the [plaintiffs'] characterization of the legal wrong here as the breach of a continuing obligation to meet trust responsibilities asserted by the [plaintiffs]. In both cases, the trustee is required, because of the past loss of the trust corpus, to use its own resources to take the place of the corpus or the lost income from the corpus. * * * That is, continuing payment of the income from the lost corpus is essentially equivalent in economic terms to a one-time restoration of the lost corpus itself * * *. Id. at 279–81.

As to the fourteenth amendment claim, however, the Court held:

> This alleged ongoing constitutional violation—the unequal distribution by the State of the benefits of the State's school lands—is precisely the type of continuing violation for which a remedy may permissibly be fashioned under Young. It may be that the current disparity results directly from the same actions in the past that are the subject of the [plaintiffs'] trust claims, but the essence of the equal protection allegation is the present disparity in the distribution of the benefits of state-held assets and not the past actions of the State. A remedy to eliminate this current disparity, even a remedy that might require the expenditure

of state funds, would ensure " 'compliance *in the future* with a substantive federal-question determination' " rather than bestow an award for accrued monetary liability. Id. at 282.

Justices Brennan, Marshall, Blackmun and Stevens dissented on the eleventh amendment issue, concluding, for various reasons, that the amendment was inapplicable.

Does the Court's *rejection* of plaintiffs' requested relief under the trust, but *acceptance* of much the same relief under the equal protection claim, make sense? How can one be deemed retroactive while the other is considered prospective? Is one in reality any less a suit against the state than the other? Does one undermine state interests more than the other? In any event, under the eleventh amendment, is it legitimate for the Court to ask the last question?

5. *Edelman* prohibits damage suits against the state itself. May plaintiffs seek compensation from a state official instead? What if the state is obligated, under state law, to indemnify the official? Compare Luder v. Endicott, 253 F.3d 1020 (7th Cir.2001) (eleventh amendment bars suit) with Cornforth v. University of Oklahoma, 263 F.3d 1129 (10th Cir.2001) (eleventh amendment does not bar suit).

THE ELEVENTH AMENDMENT AND STATE LAW

In PENNHURST STATE SCHOOL AND HOSPITAL v. HALDERMAN, 465 U.S. 89 (1984) (Pennhurst II), the Court considered the interplay between the *Young* and *Edelman* rules and state causes of action. Plaintiffs in that class action case had challenged conditions in a Pennsylvania institution for the care of the mentally retarded. They brought suit in federal district court against various state officials, alleging violation of several federal constitutional and statutory provisions and seeking only injunctive relief in the form of an order to improve conditions to meet the statutory and constitutional requirements. They also added a claim, under what is now called supplemental jurisdiction [Chapter Fifteen], alleging that conditions violated the Pennsylvania Mental Health and Mental Retardation Act of 1966 (MH/MR Act). Here, too, they sought only injunctive relief.

After a lengthy trial, the district court found violations of several federal constitutional provisions and the Pennsylvania statute, and ordered various improvements. The Court of Appeals affirmed most of the district court's decision, but solely on the ground that conditions at Pennhurst violated the federal Developmentally Disabled Assistance and Bill of Rights Act, 42 U.S.C. § 6010.

The Supreme Court reversed on the ground that section 6010 did not create any judicially enforceable substantive rights. It remanded the case to the Court of Appeals, inviting it to consider whether its remedial order could be supported on the basis on any other federal or state law. Pennhurst State School and Hospital v. Halderman, 451 U.S. 1 (1981) (Pennhurst I). On remand, the Court of Appeals reaffirmed its earlier judgment, this time basing its decision on the Pennsylvania MH/MR Act.

In *Pennhurst II*, the Supreme Court again reversed, this time finding the action under the Pennsylvania statute barred by the eleventh amendment. Recognizing that the plaintiffs' suit met the requirements of *Young* and *Edelman*, the Court nevertheless held that complying with *Young* and *Edelman* could not a save state cause of action from the strictures of the eleventh amendment. Justice Powell wrote for the five to four majority:

> We first address the contention that respondents' state-law claim is not barred by the Eleventh Amendment because it seeks only prospective relief as defined in Edelman v. Jordan. The Court of Appeals held that if the judgment below rested on federal law, it could be entered against petitioner state officials under the doctrine established in *Edelman* and *Young* even though the prospective financial burden was substantial and ongoing.[13] The court assumed, and respondents assert, that this reasoning applies as well when the official acts in violation of state law. This argument misconstrues the basis of the doctrine established in *Young* and *Edelman*.
>
> As discussed above, the injunction in *Young* was justified, notwithstanding the obvious impact on the State itself, on the view that sovereign immunity does not apply because an official who acts unconstitutionally is "stripped of his official or representative character," *Young*, 209 U.S., at 160. This rationale, of course, created the "well-recognized irony" that an official's unconstitutional conduct constitutes state action under the Fourteenth Amendment but not the Eleventh Amendment. Florida Department of State v. Treasure Salvors, Inc., 458 U.S. 670, 685 (1982) (opinion of Stevens, J.). Nonetheless, the *Young* doctrine has been accepted as necessary to permit the federal courts to vindicate federal rights and hold state officials responsible to "the supreme authority of the United States." As Justice Brennan has observed, "Ex parte Young was the culmination of efforts by this Court to harmonize the principles of the Eleventh Amendment with the effective supremacy of rights and powers secured elsewhere in the Constitution." Perez v. Ledesma, 401 U.S. 82, 106 (1971) (Brennan, J., concurring in part and dissenting in part). Our decisions repeatedly have emphasized that the *Young* doctrine rests on the need to promote the vindication of federal rights. See, e.g., Quern v. Jordan, 440 U.S. 332, 337 (1979)
>
> The Court also has recognized, however, that the need to promote the supremacy of federal law must be accommodated to the constitutional immunity of the States. This is the significance of Edelman v. Jordan. We recognized that the prospective relief au-

---

13. We do not decide whether the District Court would have jurisdiction under this reasoning to grant prospective relief on the basis of federal law, but we note that the scope of any such relief would be constrained by principles of comity and federalism. "Where, as here, the exercise of authority by state officials is attacked, federal courts must be constantly mindful of the 'special delicacy of the adjustment to be preserved between federal equitable power and State administration of its own law.'" Rizzo v. Goode, 423 U.S. 362, 378 (1976) (quoting Stefanelli v. Minard, 342 U.S. 117, 120 (1951)). [Footnote by the Court.]

thorized by *Young* "has permitted the Civil War Amendments to the Constitution to serve as a sword, rather than merely a shield, for those whom they were designed to protect." But we declined to extend the fiction of *Young* to encompass retroactive relief, for to do so would effectively eliminate the constitutional immunity of the States. Accordingly, we concluded that although the difference between permissible and impermissible relief "will not in many instances be that between day and night," an award of retroactive relief necessarily " 'fall[s] afoul of the Eleventh Amendment if that basic constitutional provision is to be conceived of as having any present force.' " Id. In sum, *Edelman*'s distinction between prospective and retroactive relief fulfills the underlying purpose of Ex parte Young while at the same time preserving to an important degree the constitutional immunity of the States.

This need to reconcile competing interests is wholly absent, however, when a plaintiff alleges that a state official has violated *state* law. In such a case the entire basis for the doctrine of *Young* and *Edelman* disappears. A federal court's grant of relief against state officials on the basis of state law, whether prospective or retroactive, does not vindicate the supreme authority of federal law. On the contrary, it is difficult to think of a greater intrusion on state sovereignty than when a federal court instructs state officials on how to conform their conduct to state law. Such a result conflicts directly with the principles of federalism that underlie the Eleventh Amendment. We conclude that *Young* and *Edelman* are inapplicable in a suit against state officials on the basis of state law. 465 U.S. at 104–06.

In a sharply worded dissent, Justice Stevens, writing for himself and Justices Brennan, Marshall, and Blackmun, accused the majority of overruling at least 28 Supreme Court cases. Justice Stevens argued that the majority failed to recognize that the "pivotal consideration in *Young* was that it was not the conduct of the sovereign that was at issue," and that it was therefore irrelevant whether the claim arose under state or federal law. Id. at 146. Moreover, he wrote, the Court's holding was detrimental to principles of federalism: "The majority's approach, which requires federal courts to ignore questions of state law and to rest their decisions on federal bases, will create more rather than less friction between the States and the federal judiciary." Id. at 151.

Justice Stevens began his opinion in *Pennhurst II* with the words: "This case has illuminated the character of an institution," referring to conditions at the Pennhurst institution. Id. at 126. He concluded his opinion, after arguing that the Court's holding ignored well-settled doctrine in various areas, "[a]s I said at the outset, this case has illuminated the character of an institution." Id. at 167. The next year, in Atascadero State Hospital v. Scanlon, 473 U.S. 234 (1985), Justice Stevens became the fourth member of the Court to urge the overruling of Hans v. Louisiana as an incorrect interpretation of the eleventh amendment. Having concluded in 1981 that *stare decisis* mandated the retention of Edelman v. Jordan despite its incorrectness, he noted in *Atascadero* that "a word of explanation is in order." 473 U.S. at 304. Since 1981, he wrote, "the Court has not felt constrained by *stare decisis* in its expansion of the protective mantle of sovereign immunity, having repudiated at least 28 cases in its decision in [*Pennhurst II*]." Id. He was therefore willing to overrule both *Edelman* and *Hans* itself.

Notes

1. Though the immediate result of the *Pennhurst* decision was a denial of federal court jurisdiction, might the Court's attempt to distinguish Ex parte Young ultimately lead to an *expansion* of federal court jurisdiction over state defendants? See Shapiro, *Wrong Turns: The Eleventh Amendment and the* Pennhurst *Case,* 98 Harv.L.Rev. 61, 83–84 (1984):

> Although I have considerable difficulty with the majority's casual dismissal of the authority-stripping rationale [of Ex parte Young] as a fiction, I see promise in the Court's emphasis on the subordination of immunity doctrine to federal interests. * * * A frank recognition that state sovereign immunity must consistently yield to the effective enforcement of federal law could have several beneficial effects.

> First, this recognition could lead to the abandonment of the requirement in some instances that when federal law permits a suit challenging state action, the suit must nevertheless be brought not against the state or one of its departments but against an individual officer. There may be a few occasions in which suit against the officer is truly appropriate; in others, the requirement is only a trap for the unwary.

> Second, it could lead to open acknowledgment that when Congress acts in pursuance of a valid federal interest, it may impose amenability to federal court suit on the state and its officers.

Might *Pennhurst's* "frank recognition" have just the opposite effect in the case of federal statutory claims against states and their officials? Perhaps the Court will eventually conclude that the importance of enforcing federal *statutory* federal rights lies somewhere in between enforcing federal *constitutional* rights and enforcing state law rights. If so, perhaps the *Young* fiction will become expendable for federal statutory claims as well. Might this explain the treatment of *Young* in *Seminole Tribe* [supra p. 371]?

Should the Court's exposure of the fictional nature of *Young* have any effect on the prospective-retroactive distinction drawn in *Edelman*? See Shapiro, supra, 98 Harv.L.Rev. at 84. What, if anything, does the Court say about this in *Pennhurst*?

2. Note that Professor Shapiro has "considerable difficulty with the majority's casual dismissal of the authority-stripping rationale as a fiction. * * *" Do you agree? See 98 Harv.L.Rev. at 84–85. See also Rudenstine, Pennhurst *and the Scope of Federal Judicial Power to Reform Social Institutions,* 6 Cardozo L.Rev. 71, 89 (1984):

> Powell took an extreme position when he dismissed the distinction in *Young* as a mere fiction. A state can act only through its agents. Yet it is untenable, at least in defining a state's constitutional immunity, to

claim that *every* act of *every* state employee is an act of the state. Even Powell retreated from this consequence, although it logically followed from his theoretical position. Obviously, Powell could have developed a theoretical model that defined the scope of a state's constitutional immunity and conformed with his conclusion in *Pennhurst*. But such a model would have implied approval of the *Young* distinction as a theoretical matter and focused discussion on its application. This step was counterproductive if his aim was to undermine all applications of *Young*.

Do you find this response to the criticism of the *Young* distinction as a fiction to be persuasive? Must one logically accept "that *every* act of *every* state employee is an act of the state" if one rejects *Young* as a fiction?

3. It has been suggested that *Pennhurst* "restricts access to federal courts by multiple-claim plaintiffs by biasing the choice of forum in favor of state courts." Brown, *Beyond* Pennhurst—*Protective Jurisdiction, the Eleventh Amendment, and the Power of Congress to Enlarge Federal Jurisdiction in Response to the Burger Court,* 71 Va.L.Rev. 343, 351 (1985). What do you think this means? Is it a correct assessment of *Pennhurst*'s impact?

Compare to Professor Brown's criticism of the use of the eleventh amendment as a bar to pendent jurisdiction, the defense of such a result by Professor Althouse:

> When the basis for suit is state law * * * there is not only an absence of * * * [a] federal interest, but also a risk of misinterpretation of state law. If *Young* applied in * * * cases [like *Pennhurst*], the state's statute would be isolated from the state courts, its interpretation and application severed from the gravitational pull of political accountability and transferred to federal court, a forum known and probably chosen for its political independence. The statute may be translated into remedies that the legislature did not contemplate, and, in a case like *Pennhurst*, remedies that the legislature—given its failure to fund the institution adequately—probably would have rejected. Of course, federal courts apply state law and we tolerate differences in result that ensue. But the eleventh amendment counsels hesitation. When the state has created a right running against itself, but has failed to take the additional step of consenting to suit in federal court, the federal court should find that jurisdiction properly belongs to the state courts. Althouse, *How to Build A Separate Sphere: Federal Courts and State Power,* 100 Harv.L.Rev. 1485, 1522–23 (1987).

4. Justice Powell also suggests that a federal court directive to state officials premised on state law involves a major "intrusion on state sovereignty." Do you agree? See Brown, supra, 71 Va.L.Rev. at 360.

5. **Pennhurst and "Institutional" Litigation.** To what extent do you think the Court's conclusion on the eleventh amendment was influenced by its broader concern about the role of the federal judiciary in overhauling state institutions, thereby unduly invading state autonomy? See Brown, supra, 71 Va.L.Rev. at 365–66; Rudenstine, supra, 6 Cardozo L.Rev. at 72 ("a careful reading of Powell's majority opinion in *Pennhurst* signals that five Justices want to limit the federal courts' power to vindicate *federal* rights in cases involving social institutions.") See also id. at 94. Do you agree

with Professor Rudenstine's assessment of Justice Powell's opinion? If so, do you think it is appropriate for the Court to employ the eleventh amendment for such a purpose?

6. Might a persuasive argument be fashioned that the doctrine of Ex parte Young should not be construed to authorize federal court suits seeking injunctions in such "institutional" litigations? Consider Rudenstine, supra, 6 Cardozo L.Rev. at 100–01:

> Though a state loses some autonomy every time a federal judge grants a prohibitory injunction, as Minnesota did in *Young,* the loss of state autonomy can be as great or greater when a federal judge grants an injunction that restructures a social institution such as a school or prison.
>
> Injunctions restructuring social institutions differ substantially in another respect from the prohibitory injunction approved by the Supreme Court in *Young.* The former can compromise the state's autonomy as much as, if not more than, an award of money damages, which the Court has decided is prohibited by the eleventh amendment. It is certainly arguable, therefore, that the current relief rule fashioned by the Supreme Court under the eleventh amendment should be changed so that federal courts are prohibited from granting all relief, or reversed so that federal courts have jurisdiction to grant damage awards and injunctions.

Do you think that the impact upon the state is likely to be qualitatively different in the event of an award of an injunction in an "institutional" litigation than in *Young* itself? Recall that Justice Rehnquist in *Edelman* acknowledged that "[t]he injunction issued in Ex parte Young was not totally without effect on the State's revenues, since the state law which the Attorney General was enjoined from enforcing provided substantial monetary penalties against railroads which did not conform to its provisions." 415 U.S. at 667. It is conceivable, of course, that the impact on state interests in the so-called "institutional" litigations will be more substantial than in a case like *Young.* However, does it necessarily follow that this *quantitative* difference justifies the drawing of a distinction for eleventh amendment purposes?

7. Green v. Mansour, 474 U.S. 64 (1985): Recipients of benefits under the federal Aid to Families With Dependent Children program filed class actions in federal court against the director of the Michigan Department of Social Services, arguing that her policies of prohibiting child care cost deduction and requiring inclusion of stepparents' income for purposes of determining eligibility violated relevant federal law. They sought an injunction, declaratory judgment, and notice relief. However, while the actions were pending, Congress amended the relevant federal statute expressly to require states to deduct child care expenses and to include stepparents' income.

The district court held that these changes rendered moot the claims for prospective injunctive relief, and that the remaining claims for declaratory and notice relief were barred by the eleventh amendment, because they amounted to retrospective relief barred by *Edelman.* The court of appeals affirmed, and so did the Supreme Court.

Justice Rehnquist, speaking for the majority, initially attempted to justify the continued use of *Edelman*'s prospective-retroactive distinction, in light of the Court's express recognition in *Pennhurst* of the fictitious nature of the *Young* doctrine:

> Both prospective and retrospective relief implicate Eleventh Amendment concerns, but the availability of prospective relief of the sort awarded in *Ex Parte Young* gives life to the Supremacy Clause. Remedies designed to end a continuing violation of federal law are necessary to vindicate the federal interest in assuring the supremacy of that law. * * * But compensatory or deterrence interests are insufficient to overcome the dictates of the Eleventh Amendment. 474 U.S. at 68.

Do you understand Justice Rehnquist's asserted justification for the *Edelman* dichotomy? Is it the same justification he relied on in *Edelman* itself?

Consider the following critique of the dichotomy's rationale adopted in *Green:* Once the Court acknowledges (as it did in *Pennhurst*) that a suit for *prospective* relief is in reality a suit "against the state", even though the state officer is named as the defendant, Justice Rehnquist's logic amounts to swimming half way across a river: By its terms, the eleventh amendment (and the general concept of sovereign immunity) prohibit *all* suits against the state. If the Court concludes the eleventh amendment is applicable, then, it has no authority to decide that *certain* types of relief against the state are permitted while others are not: the amendment prohibits *all* forms of relief against the state. If, on the other hand, the Court concludes that the amendment is inapplicable or may be and has been superseded by the exercise of congressional power, then the Court lacks constitutional authority to limit the form of relief Congress chooses to make available.

Do you agree with Justice Rehnquist that it is only *prospective* relief that "gives life to the Supremacy Clause"? Could not the deterrence effect of a damage award have much the same impact? Are the goals of compensating victims on the one hand and vindicating federal interests on the other mutually exclusive? Cf. Justice Brennan's dissent in Atascadero State Hospital v. Scanlon, 473 U.S. 234, 256–57 (1985): "A damages award may often be the only practical remedy available to the plaintiff, and the threat of a damages award may be the only effective deterrent to a defendant's willful violation of federal law." Indeed, in providing for *both* injunctive *and* damage relief in section 1983 civil rights suits, has not Congress concluded that federal interests can be vindicated either way? Is it proper for the Court to supercede Congress' judgment on this point, at least once the Court has conceded that either form of relief in reality constitutes a suit against the state?

In light of its continued adherence to the *Edelman* distinction, the Court in *Green* concluded that neither declaratory nor notice relief was permissible:

> [A] request for a limited notice order will escape the Eleventh Amendment bar if the notice is ancillary to the grant of some other appropriate relief that can be "noticed." Because there is no continuing violation of federal law to enjoin in this case, an injunction is not available.

* * *

We think that the award of a declaratory judgment in this situation would be useful in resolving the dispute over the past lawfulness of the respondent's action only if it might be offered in state court proceedings as res judicata on the issue of liability, leaving to the state courts only a form of accounting proceedings whereby damages or restitution would be computed. But the issuance of a declaratory judgment would have much the same effect as a full-fledged award of damages or restitution by the federal court, the latter kinds of relief being of course prohibited by the Eleventh Amendment. 474 U.S. at 71, 73.

Justice Marshall, joined by Justices Brennan and Stevens, dissented:

The notice relief at issue here imposes no significant cost to the State, creates no direct liabilities against the State, and respects the institutions of state government. * * * Indeed, notice of the availability of possible relief through existing state administrative remedies, where the state agency and state courts would be the sole arbiters of what relief would be granted, assists in the vindication of state law * * *. In the Eleventh Amendment balance set up by the majority opinion, it is thus hard to see what weight, if any, exists on the state's side of the scale, and why that weight should overcome the interests in vindicating federal law. Id. at 80.

Do you agree that the majority set up an eleventh amendment "balance"? If so, does this constitute a legitimate construction of the eleventh amendment? Justice Blackmun also dissented.

§ 3.   ABROGATION

SEMINOLE TRIBE OF FLORIDA v. FLORIDA

Supreme Court of the United States, 1996.
517 U.S. 44.

CHIEF JUSTICE REHNQUIST delivered the opinion of the Court.

The Indian Gaming Regulatory Act provides that an Indian tribe may conduct certain gaming activities only in conformance with a valid compact between the tribe and the State in which the gaming activities are located. 25 U.S.C. § 2710(d)(1)(C). The Act, passed by Congress under the Indian Commerce Clause, U.S. Const., Art. I, § 8, cl. 3, imposes upon the States a duty to negotiate in good faith with an Indian tribe toward the formation of a compact, § 2710(d)(3)(A), and authorizes a tribe to bring suit in federal court against a State in order to compel performance of that duty, § 2710(d)(7). We hold that notwithstanding Congress' clear intent to abrogate the States' sovereign immunity, the Indian Commerce Clause does not grant Congress that power, and therefore § 2710(d)(7) cannot grant jurisdiction over a State that does not consent to be sued. * * *

I

Congress passed the Indian Gaming Regulatory Act in 1988 in order to provide a statutory basis for the operation and regulation of gaming by Indian tribes. * * * [The Act provides that certain types of Indian gaming are lawful where they are:] "conducted in conformance with a Tribal–State compact entered into by the Indian tribe and the State under paragraph (3) that is in effect." § 2710(d)(1).

The "paragraph (3)" to which the last prerequisite of § 2710(d)(1) refers is § 2710(d)(3), which * * * describes the process by which a State and an Indian tribe begin negotiations toward a Tribal–State compact:

"(A) Any Indian tribe having jurisdiction over the Indian lands upon which a class III gaming activity is being conducted, or is to be conducted, shall request the State in which such lands are located to enter into negotiations for the purpose of entering into a Tribal–State compact governing the conduct of gaming activities. Upon receiving such a request, the State shall negotiate with the Indian tribe in good faith to enter into such a compact."

The State's obligation to "negotiate with the Indian tribe in good faith," is made judicially enforceable by §§ 2710(d)(7)(A)(i) and (B)(i):

"(A) The United States district courts shall have jurisdiction over—

"(i) any cause of action initiated by an Indian tribe arising from the failure of a State to enter into negotiations with the Indian tribe for the purpose of entering into a Tribal–State compact under paragraph (3) or to conduct such negotiations in good faith. . . .

"(B)(i) An Indian tribe may initiate a cause of action described in subparagraph (A)(i) only after the close of the 180–day period beginning on the date on which the Indian tribe requested the State to enter into negotiations under paragraph (3)(A)."

Sections 2710(d)(7)(B)(ii)-(vii) describe an elaborate remedial scheme designed to ensure the formation of a Tribal–State compact. * * *

In September 1991, the Seminole Tribe of Indians, petitioner, sued the State of Florida and its Governor, Lawton Chiles, respondents. Invoking jurisdiction under 25 U.S.C. § 2710(d)(7)(A), as well as 28 U.S.C. §§ 1331 and 1362, petitioner alleged that respondents had "refused to enter into any negotiation for inclusion of [certain gaming activities] in a tribal-state compact," thereby violating the "requirement of good faith negotiation" contained in § 2710(d)(3). Respondents moved to dismiss the complaint, arguing that the suit violated the State's sovereign immunity from suit in federal court. The District Court denied respondents' motion. * * *

The Court of Appeals for the Eleventh Circuit reversed the decision of the District Court, holding that the Eleventh Amendment barred petitioner's suit against respondents. * * *

Petitioner sought our review of the Eleventh Circuit's decision, and we granted certiorari in order to consider two questions: (1) Does the Eleventh Amendment prevent Congress from authorizing suits by Indian tribes against States for prospective injunctive relief to enforce legislation enacted pursuant to the Indian Commerce Clause?; and (2) Does the doctrine of Ex parte Young permit suits against a State's governor for prospective injunctive relief to enforce the good faith bargaining requirement of the Act? We answer the first question in the affirmative, the second in the negative, and we therefore affirm the Eleventh Circuit's dismissal of petitioner's suit.

The Eleventh Amendment provides:

"The Judicial power of the United States shall not be construed to extend to any suit in law or equity, commenced or prosecuted against one of the United States by Citizens of another State, or by Citizens or Subjects of any Foreign State."

Although the text of the Amendment would appear to restrict only the Article III diversity jurisdiction of the federal courts, "we have understood the Eleventh Amendment to stand not so much for what it says, but for the presupposition ... which it confirms." Blatchford v. Native Village of Noatak, 501 U.S. 775, 779 (1991). That presupposition, first observed over a century ago in Hans v. Louisiana, 134 U.S. 1 (1890), has two parts: first, that each State is a sovereign entity in our federal system; and second, that " '[i]t is inherent in the nature of sovereignty not to be amenable to the suit of an individual without its consent.' " Id., at 13 (emphasis deleted), quoting The Federalist No. 81, p.487 (C. Rossiter ed. 1961)(A. Hamilton). For over a century we have reaffirmed that federal jurisdiction over suits against unconsenting States "was not contemplated by the Constitution when establishing the judicial power of the United States." Hans.

Here, petitioner has sued the State of Florida and it is undisputed that Florida has not consented to the suit. See Blatchford (States by entering into the Constitution did not consent to suit by Indian tribes). Petitioner nevertheless contends that its suit is not barred by state sovereign immunity. First, it argues that Congress through the Act abrogated the States' sovereign immunity. Alternatively, petitioner maintains that its suit against the Governor may go forward under Ex parte Young. We consider each of those arguments in turn.

II

Petitioner argues that Congress through the Act abrogated the States' immunity from suit. In order to determine whether Congress has abrogated the States' sovereign immunity, we ask two questions: first, whether Congress has "unequivocally expresse[d] its intent to abrogate the immunity," Green v. Mansour, 474 U.S. 64, 68 (1985); and second, whether Congress has acted "pursuant to a valid exercise of power." Ibid.

A

Congress' intent to abrogate the States' immunity from suit must be obvious from "a clear legislative statement." Blatchford, 501 U.S., at 786. * * *

Here, we agree with the parties, with the Eleventh Circuit in the decision below, and with virtually every other court that has confronted the question that Congress has in § 2710(d)(7) provided an "unmistakably clear" statement of its intent to abrogate. * * *

B

Having concluded that Congress clearly intended to abrogate the States' sovereign immunity through § 2710(d)(7), we turn now to consider whether the Act was passed "pursuant to a valid exercise of power." *Green v. Mansour,* 474 U.S., at 68. * * *

* * *

Thus our inquiry into whether Congress has the power to abrogate unilaterally the States' immunity from suit is narrowly focused on one question: Was the Act in question passed pursuant to a constitutional provision granting Congress the power to abrogate? See, e.g., *Fitzpatrick v. Bitzer,* 427 U.S. 445, 452–456 (1976). Previously, in conducting that inquiry, we have found authority to abrogate under only two provisions of the Constitution. In *Fitzpatrick,* we recognized that the Fourteenth Amendment, by expanding federal power at the expense of state autonomy, had fundamentally altered the balance of state and federal power struck by the Constitution. *Id.,* at 455. We noted that § 1 of the Fourteenth Amendment contained prohibitions expressly directed at the States and that § 5 of the Amendment expressly provided that "The Congress shall have the power to enforce, by appropriate legislation, the provisions of this article." See id., at 453. We held that through the Fourteenth Amendment, federal power extended to intrude upon the province of the Eleventh Amendment and therefore that § 5 of the Fourteenth Amendment allowed Congress to abrogate the immunity from suit guaranteed by that Amendment.

In only one other case has congressional abrogation of the States' Eleventh Amendment immunity been upheld. In *Pennsylvania v. Union Gas Co.,* 491 U.S. 1 (1989), a plurality of the Court found that the Interstate Commerce Clause, Art. I, § 8, cl. 3, granted Congress the power to abrogate state sovereign immunity, stating that the power to regulate interstate commerce would be "incomplete without the authority to render States liable in damages." *Union Gas,* 491 U.S., at 19–20. Justice White added the fifth vote necessary to the result in that case, but wrote separately in order to express that he "[did] not agree with much of [the plurality's] reasoning." Id., at 57 (White, J., concurring in judgment in part and dissenting in part).

* * *

Both parties make their arguments from the plurality decision in *Union Gas,* and we, too, begin there. We think it clear that Justice Brennan's opinion finds Congress' power to abrogate under the Interstate Commerce Clause from the States' cession of their sovereignty when they gave Congress plenary power to regulate interstate commerce.

See *Union Gas*, 491 U.S., at 17 ("The important point ... is that the provision both expands federal power and contracts state power"). * * *

Following the rationale of the *Union Gas* plurality, our inquiry is limited to determining whether the Indian Commerce Clause, like the Interstate Commerce Clause, is a grant of authority to the Federal Government at the expense of the States. The answer to that question is obvious. If anything, the Indian Commerce Clause accomplishes a greater transfer of power from the States to the Federal Government than does the Interstate Commerce Clause. This is clear enough from the fact that the States still exercise some authority over interstate trade but have been divested of virtually all authority over Indian commerce and Indian tribes. Under the rationale of *Union Gas*, if the States' partial cession of authority over a particular area includes cession of the immunity from suit, then their virtually total cession of authority over a different area must also include cession of the immunity from suit. We agree with the petitioner that the plurality opinion in *Union Gas* allows no principled distinction in favor of the States to be drawn between the Indian Commerce Clause and the Interstate Commerce Clause.

Respondents argue, however, that we need not conclude that the Indian Commerce Clause grants the power to abrogate the States' sovereign immunity. Instead, they contend that if we find the rationale of the *Union Gas* plurality to extend to the Indian Commerce Clause, then "*Union Gas* should be reconsidered and overruled." Generally, the principle of *stare decisis*, and the interests that it serves, viz., "the evenhanded, predictable, and consistent development of legal principles, ... reliance on judicial decisions, and ... the actual and perceived integrity of the judicial process," counsel strongly against reconsideration of our precedent. Nevertheless, we always have treated *stare decisis* as a "principle of policy," and not as an "inexorable command." "[W]hen governing decisions are unworkable or are badly reasoned, 'this Court has never felt constrained to follow precedent.'" Our willingness to reconsider our earlier decisions has been "particularly true in constitutional cases, because in such cases 'correction through legislative action is practically impossible.'"

The Court in *Union Gas* reached a result without an expressed rationale agreed upon by a majority of the Court. We have already seen that Justice Brennan's opinion received the support of only three other Justices. Of the other five, Justice White, who provided the fifth vote for the result, wrote separately in order to indicate his disagreement with the majority's rationale, and four Justices joined together in a dissent that rejected the plurality's rationale. * * *

The plurality's rationale also deviated sharply from our established federalism jurisprudence and essentially eviscerated our decision in *Hans*. See *Union Gas, supra*, at 36 ("If *Hans* means only that federal-question suits for money damages against the States cannot be brought in federal court unless Congress clearly says so, it means nothing at all") (SCALIA, J., dissenting). It was well established in 1989 when *Union Gas* was decided that the Eleventh Amendment stood for the constitutional principle that state sovereign immunity limited the federal courts' jurisdiction under Article III. * * * As the dissent in *Union Gas* recognized, the plurality's conclusion—that Congress could under Article I expand the scope of the federal courts' jurisdiction under Article III—"contradict[ed] our unvarying approach to Article III as setting forth the exclusive catalog of permissible federal court jurisdiction." *Union Gas,* 491 U.S., at 39.

Never before the decision in *Union Gas* had we suggested that the bounds of Article III could be expanded by Congress operating pursuant to any constitutional provision other than the Fourteenth Amendment. Indeed, it had seemed fundamental that Congress could not expand the jurisdiction of the federal courts beyond the bounds of Article III. Marbury v. Madison, 1 Cranch 137 (1803). The plurality's citation of prior decisions for support was based upon what we believe to be a misreading of precedent. * * *

The plurality's extended reliance upon our decision in Fitzpatrick v. Bitzer, 427 U.S. 445 (1976), that Congress could under the Fourteenth Amendment abrogate the States' sovereign immunity was also, we believe, misplaced. *Fitzpatrick* was based upon a rationale wholly inapplicable to the Interstate Commerce Clause, viz., that the Fourteenth Amendment, adopted well after the adoption of the Eleventh Amendment and the ratification of the Constitution, operated to alter the preexisting balance between state and federal power achieved by Article III and the Eleventh Amendment. Id., at 454. As the dissent in *Union Gas* made clear, *Fitzpatrick* cannot be read to justify "limitation of the principle embodied in the Eleventh Amendment through appeal to antecedent provisions of the Constitution." *Union Gas,* 491 U.S., at 42 (SCALIA, J., dissenting).

In the five years since it was decided, *Union Gas* has proven to be a solitary departure from established law. * * * Reconsidering the decision in *Union Gas,* we conclude that none of the policies underlying *stare decisis* require our continuing adherence to its holding. The decision has, since its issuance, been of questionable precedential value, largely because a majority of the Court expressly disagreed with the rationale of the plurality. The case involved the interpretation of the Constitution and therefore may be altered only by constitutional amendment or revision by this Court. Finally, both the result in *Union Gas* and the plurality's rationale depart from our established understanding of the Eleventh Amendment and undermine the accepted function of Article III. We feel bound to conclude that *Union Gas* was wrongly decided and that it should be, and now is, overruled.

The dissent makes no effort to defend the decision in *Union Gas,* but nonetheless would find congressional power to abrogate in this case. Contending that our decision is a novel extension of the Eleventh Amendment, the dissent chides us for "attend[ing]" to dicta. We adhere in this case, however, not to mere *obiter dicta,* but rather to the well-established rationale upon which the Court based the results of its earlier decisions. When an opinion issues for the Court, it is not only the result but also those portions of the opinion necessary to that result by which we are bound. For over a century, we have grounded our decisions in the oft-repeated understanding of state sovereign immunity as an essential part of the Eleventh Amendment. In *Principality of Monaco v. Mississippi*, 292 U.S. 313 (1934), the Court held that the Eleventh Amendment barred a suit brought against a State by a foreign state. Chief Justice Hughes wrote for a unanimous Court:

> "[N]either the literal sweep of the words of Clause one of § 2 of Article III, nor the absence of restriction in the letter of the Eleventh Amendment, permits the conclusion that in all controversies of the sort described in Clause one, and omitted from the words of the Eleventh Amendment, a State may be sued without her consent. Thus Clause one specifically provides that the judicial power shall extend 'to all Cases, in Law and Equity, arising under this Constitution, the Laws of the United States, and Treaties made, or which shall be made, under their Authority.' But, although a case may arise under the Constitution and laws of the United States, the judicial power does not extend to it if the suit is sought to be prosecuted against a State, without her consent, by one of her own citizens. . . ."

> "Manifestly, we cannot rest with a mere literal application of the words of § 2 of Article III, or assume that the letter of the Eleventh Amendment exhausts the restrictions upon suits against non-consenting States. Behind the words of the constitutional provisions are postulates which limit and control. There is the essential postulate that the controversies, as contemplated, shall be found to be of a justiciable character. There is also the postulate that States of the Union, still possessing attributes of sovereignty, shall be immune from suits, without their consent, save where there has been a 'surrender of this immunity in the plan of the convention.' " Id., at 321–323 (citations and footnote omitted).

See *id.* at 329–330; see also *Pennhurst*, 465 U.S., at 98 ("In short, the principle of sovereign immunity is a constitutional limitation on the federal judicial power established in Art. III"). It is true that we have not had occasion previously to apply established Eleventh Amendment principles to the question whether Congress has the power to abrogate state sovereign immunity (save in *Union Gas*). But consideration of that question must proceed with fidelity to this century-old doctrine.

The dissent, to the contrary, disregards our case law in favor of a theory cobbled together from law review articles and its own version of historical events. The dissent cites not a single decision since *Hans* (other than *Union Gas*) that supports its view of state sovereign immunity, instead relying upon the now-discredited decision in Chisholm v. Georgia, 2 Dall. 419 (1793). Its undocumented and highly speculative extralegal explanation of the decision in *Hans* is a disservice to the Court's traditional method of adjudication.

* * *

Hans—with a much closer vantage point than the dissent—recognized that the decision in *Chisholm* was contrary to the well-understood meaning of the Constitution. The dissent's conclusion that the decision in *Chisholm* was "reasonable," certainly would have struck the Framers of the Eleventh Amendment as quite odd: that decision created "such a shock of surprise that the Eleventh Amendment was at once proposed and adopted." *Monaco*, supra, at 325. The dissent's lengthy analysis of the text of the Eleventh Amendment is directed at a straw man—we long have recognized that blind reliance upon the text of the Eleventh Amendment is " 'to strain the Constitution and the law to a construction never imagined or dreamed of.' " *Monaco*, 292 U.S., at 326, quoting *Hans*, 134 U.S., at 15. The text dealt in terms only with the problem presented by the decision in *Chisholm*; in light of the fact that the federal courts did not have federal question jurisdiction at the time the Amendment was passed (and would not have it until 1875), it seems unlikely that much thought was given to the prospect of federal question jurisdiction over the States.

That same consideration causes the dissent's criticism of the views of Marshall, Madison, and Hamilton to ring hollow. The dissent cites statements made by those three influential Framers, the most natural reading of which would preclude all federal jurisdiction over an unconsenting State.[12] Struggling against this reading, however, the dissent finds significant the absence of any contention that sovereign immunity would affect the new federal-question jurisdiction. But the lack of any statute vesting general federal question jurisdiction in the federal courts until much later makes the dissent's demand for greater specificity about a then-dormant jurisdiction overly exacting.[13]

12. We note here also that the dissent quotes selectively from the Framers' statements that it references. The dissent cites the following, for instance, as a statement made by Madison: "the Constitution 'give[s] a citizen a right to be heard in the federal courts; and if a state should condescend to be a party, this court may take cognizance of it.' " * * * But that statement, perhaps ambiguous when read in isolation, was preceded by the following: "[J]urisdiction in controversies between a state and citizens of another state is much objected to, and perhaps without reason. It is not in the power of individuals to call any state into court. The only operation it can have, is that, if a state should wish to bring a suit against a citizen, it must be brought before the federal courts. It appears to me that this can have no operation but this[.]" See 3 J. Elliot, Debates on the Federal Constitution 67 (1866).

13. Although the absence of any discussion dealing with federal question jurisdiction is therefore unremarkable, what is notably lacking in the Framers' statements is any mention of Congress' power to abrogate the States' immunity. The absence of any discussion of that power is particularly striking in light of the fact that the Framers virtually always were very specific about the exception to state sovereign immunity arising from a State's consent to suit. See, e.g., The Federalist No. 81, pp. 487–488 (C. Rossiter ed. 1961)(A.Hamilton)("It is inherent in the nature of sovereignty not to be amenable to the suit of an individual *without its consent*.... Unless, therefore, there is a surrender of this immunity in the plan of the convention, it will remain with the States and the danger intimated must be merely ideal.")(emphasis in the original); Madison in 3 Elliot, supra n. [12] ("It is not in the power of individuals to call any state

In putting forward a new theory of state sovereign immunity, the dissent develops its own vision of the political system created by the Framers, concluding with the statement that "[t]he Framer's principal objectives in rejecting English theories of unitary sovereignty ... would have been impeded if a new concept of sovereign immunity had taken its place in federal question cases, and would have been substantially thwarted if that new immunity had been held untouchable by any congressional effort to abrogate it."[14] This sweeping statement ignores the fact that the Nation survived for nearly two centuries without the question of the existence of such power ever being presented to this Court. And Congress itself waited nearly a century before even conferring federal question jurisdiction on the lower federal courts.[15]

In overruling *Union Gas* today, we reconfirm that the background principle of state sovereign immunity embodied in the Eleventh Amendment is not so ephemeral as to dissipate when the subject of the suit is an area, like the regulation of Indian commerce, that is under the exclusive control of the Federal Government. Even when the Constitution vests in Congress complete law-making authority over a particular area, the Eleventh Amendment prevents congressional authorization of suits by private parties against unconsenting States.[16] The Eleventh

into court.... [The Constitution] can have no operation but this: ... if a state should condescend to be a party, this court may take cognizance of it").

14. This argument wholly disregards other methods of ensuring the States' compliance with federal law: the Federal Government can bring suit in federal court against a State, see, e.g., United States v. Texas, 143 U.S. 621, 644–645 (1892)(finding such power necessary to the "permanence of the Union"); an individual can bring suit against a state officer in order to ensure that the officer's conduct is in compliance with federal law, see, e.g., Ex parte Young, 209 U.S. 123 (1908); and this Court is empowered to review a question of federal law arising from a state court decision where a State has consented to suit, see, e.g., Cohens v. Virginia, 6 Wheat. 264 (1821).

15. Justice Stevens, in his dissenting opinion, makes two points that merit separate response. First, he contends that no distinction may be drawn between state sovereign immunity and the immunity enjoyed by state and federal officials. But even assuming that the latter has no constitutional foundation, the distinction is clear: the Constitution specifically recognizes the States as sovereign entities, while government officials enjoy no such constitutional recognition. Second, Justice Stevens criticizes our prior decisions applying the "clear statement rule," suggesting that they were based upon an understanding that Article I allowed Congress to abrogate state sover-

eign immunity. His criticism, however, ignores the fact that many of those cases arose in the context of a statute passed under the Fourteenth Amendment, where Congress' authority to abrogate is undisputed. * * *

16. Justice Stevens understands our opinion to prohibit federal jurisdiction over suits to enforce the bankruptcy, copyright, and antitrust laws against the States. He notes that federal jurisdiction over those statutory schemes is exclusive, and therefore concludes that there is "no remedy" for state violations of those federal statutes.

That conclusion is exaggerated both in its substance and in its significance. First, Justice Stevens' statement is misleadingly overbroad. We have already seen that several avenues remain open for ensuring state compliance with federal law. Most notably, an individual may obtain injunctive relief under Ex parte Young in order to remedy a state officer's ongoing violation of federal law. See supra, at n. 14. Second, contrary to the implication of Justice Stevens' conclusion, it has not been widely thought that the federal antitrust, bankruptcy, or copyright statutes abrogated the States' sovereign immunity. * * * Although the copyright and bankruptcy laws have existed practically since our nation's inception, and the antitrust laws have been in force for over a century, there is no established tradition in the lower federal courts of allowing enforcement of those federal statutes against the States. * * *

Amendment restricts the judicial power under Article III, and Article I cannot be used to circumvent the constitutional limitations placed upon federal jurisdiction. Petitioner's suit against the State of Florida must be dismissed for a lack of jurisdiction.

* * *

JUSTICE STEVENS, dissenting.

This case is about power—the power of the Congress of the United States to create a private federal cause of action against a State, or its Governor, for the violation of a federal right. In Chisholm v. Georgia, 2 Dall. 419 (1793), the entire Court—including Justice Iredell whose dissent provided the blueprint for the Eleventh Amendment—assumed that Congress had such power. In Hans v. Louisiana, 134 U.S. 1 (1890)—a case the Court purports to follow today—the Court again assumed that Congress had such power. In Fitzpatrick v. Bitzer, 427 U.S. 445 (1976), and Pennsylvania v. Union Gas Co., 491 U.S. 1, 24 (1989)(Stevens, J., concurring), the Court squarely held that Congress has such power. In a series of cases beginning with Atascadero State Hospital v. Scanlon, 473 U.S. 234, 238–239 (1985), the Court formulated a special "clear statement rule" to determine whether specific Acts of Congress contained an effective exercise of that power. Nevertheless, in a sharp break with the past, today the Court holds that with the narrow and illogical exception of statutes enacted pursuant to the Enforcement Clause of the Fourteenth Amendment, Congress has no such power.

* * *

I

For the purpose of deciding this case, I can readily assume that Justice Iredell's dissent in Chisholm v. Georgia, 2 Dall., at 429–450, and the Court's opinion in Hans v. Louisiana, 134 U.S. 1 (1890), correctly stated the law that should govern our decision today. As I shall explain, both of those opinions relied on an interpretation of an Act of Congress rather than a want of congressional power to authorize a suit against the State.

In concluding that the federal courts could not entertain Chisholm's action against the State of Georgia, Justice Iredell relied on the text of the Judiciary Act of 1789, not the State's assertion that Article III did not extend the judicial power to suits against unconsenting States. Justice Iredell argued that, under Article III, federal courts possessed only such jurisdiction as Congress had provided, and that the Judiciary Act expressly limited federal-court jurisdiction to that which could be exercised in accordance with " 'the principles and usages of law.' " Chisholm v. Georgia, 2 Dall., at 434 (quoting § 14 of the Judiciary Act of 1789.) He reasoned that the inclusion of this phrase constituted a command to the federal courts to construe their jurisdiction in light of the prevailing common law, a background legal regime which he believed incorporated the doctrine of sovereign immunity. Chisholm v. Georgia, 2 Dall., at 434–436 (Iredell, J., dissenting).

Because Justice Iredell believed that the expansive text of Article III did not prevent Congress from imposing this common-law limitation on federal-court jurisdiction, he concluded that judges had no authority to entertain a suit against an unconsenting State. At the same time, although he acknowledged that the Constitution might allow Congress to extend federal-court jurisdiction to such an action, he concluded that the terms of the Judiciary Act of 1789 plainly had not done so.

> "[Congress'] direction, I apprehend, we cannot supersede because it may appear to us not sufficiently extensive. *If it be not, we must wait till other remedies are provided by the same authority.* From this it is plain that the Legislature did not chuse to leave to our own discretion the path to justice, but has prescribed one of its own. In doing so, it has, I think, wisely, referred us to principles and usages of law already well known. * * * " *Id.*, at 434 (emphasis added).

For Justice Iredell then, it was enough to assume that Article III *permitted* Congress to impose sovereign immunity as a jurisdictional limitation; he did not proceed to resolve the further question whether the Constitution went so far as to *prevent* Congress from withdrawing a State's immunity. Thus, it would be ironic to construe the *Chisholm* dissent as precedent for the conclusion that Article III limits Congress' power to determine the scope of a State's sovereign immunity in federal court.

The precise holding in *Chisholm* is difficult to state because each of the Justices in the majority wrote his own opinion. They seem to have held, however, not that the Judiciary Act of 1789 precluded the defense of sovereign immunity, but that Article III of the Constitution itself required the Supreme Court to entertain original actions against unconsenting States. I agree with Justice Iredell that such a construction of Article III is incorrect; that Article should not then have been construed, and should not now be construed, to prevent Congress from granting States a sovereign immunity defense in such cases. That reading of Article III, however, explains why the majority's holding in *Chisholm* could not have been reversed by a simple statutory amendment adopting Justice Iredell's interpretation of the Judiciary Act of 1789. There is a special irony in the fact that the error committed by the *Chisholm* majority was its decision that this Court, rather than Congress, should define the scope of the sovereign immunity defense. That, of course, is precisely the same error the Court commits today.

In light of the nature of the disagreement between Justice Iredell and his colleagues, *Chisholm*'s holding could have been overturned by simply amending the Constitution to restore to Congress the authority to recognize the doctrine. As it was, the plain text of the Eleventh Amendment would seem to go further and to limit the judicial power itself in a certain class of cases. In doing so, however, the Amendment's quite explicit text establishes only a partial bar to a federal court's power to entertain a suit against a State.

Justice Brennan has persuasively explained that the Eleventh Amendment's jurisdictional restriction is best understood to apply only to suits premised on diversity jurisdiction, see Atascadero State Hospital v. Scanlon, 473 U.S. 234, 247 (1985)(dissenting opinion), and Justice Scalia has agreed that the plain text of the Amendment cannot be read to apply to federal-question cases. See Pennsylvania v. Union Gas, 491 U.S., at 31 (dissenting opinion).[8] Whatever the precise dimensions of the Amendment, its express terms plainly do *not* apply to all suits brought against unconsenting States. The question thus becomes whether the relatively modest jurisdictional bar that the Eleventh Amendment imposes should be understood to reveal that a more general jurisdictional bar implicitly inheres in Article III.

The language of Article III certainly gives no indication that such an implicit bar exists. That provision's text specifically provides for federal-court jurisdiction over *all* cases arising under federal law. Moreover, as I have explained, Justice Iredell's dissent argued that it was the Judiciary Act of 1789, not Article III, that prevented the federal courts from entertaining Chisholm's diversity action against Georgia. Therefore, Justice Iredell's analysis at least suggests that it was by no means a fixed view at the time of the founding that Article III prevented Congress from rendering States suable in federal court by their own citizens. In sum, little more than speculation justifies the conclusion that the Eleventh Amendment's express but partial limitation on the scope of Article III reveals that an implicit but more general one was already in place.

II

The majority appears to acknowledge that one cannot deduce from either the text of Article III or the plain terms of the Eleventh Amendment that the judicial power does not extend to a congressionally created cause of action against a State brought by one of that State's citizens. Nevertheless, the majority asserts that precedent compels that same conclusion. I disagree. The majority relies first on our decision in Hans v. Louisiana, 134 U.S. 1 (1890), which involved a suit by a citizen of Louisiana against that State for a claimed violation of the Contracts Clause. The majority suggests that by dismissing the suit, *Hans* effectively held that federal courts have no power to hear federal question suits brought by same-state plaintiffs.

Hans does not hold, however, that the Eleventh Amendment, or any other constitutional provision, precludes federal courts from entertaining

---

8. Of course, even if the Eleventh Amendment applies to federal-question cases brought by a citizen of another State, its express terms pose no bar to a federal court assuming jurisdiction in a federal-question case brought by an in-state plaintiff pursuant to Congress' express authorization. As that is precisely the posture of the suit before us, and as it was also precisely the posture of the suit at issue in Pennsylvania v. Union Gas, there is no need to decide here whether Congress would be barred from authorizing out-of-state plaintiffs to enforce federal rights against States in federal court. * * *

*n does not bear
it where Act of Congress
limits it*

actions brought by citizens against their own States in the face of contrary congressional direction. * * * *Hans* instead reflects, at the most, this Court's conclusion that, as a matter of federal common law, federal courts should decline to entertain suits against unconsenting States. Because *Hans* did not announce a constitutionally mandated jurisdictional bar, one need not overrule *Hans*, or even question its reasoning, in order to conclude that Congress may direct the federal courts to reject sovereign immunity in those suits not mentioned by the Eleventh Amendment. Instead, one need only follow it.

Justice Bradley's somewhat cryptic opinion for the Court in *Hans* relied expressly on the reasoning of Justice Iredell's dissent in *Chisholm*, which, of course, was premised on the view that the doctrine of state sovereign immunity was a common-law rule that Congress had directed federal courts to respect, not a constitutional immunity that Congress was powerless to displace. For that reason, Justice Bradley explained that the State's immunity from suit by one of its own citizens was based not on a constitutional rule but rather on the fact that Congress had not, by legislation, attempted to overcome the common-law presumption of sovereign immunity. His analysis so clearly supports the position rejected by the majority today that it is worth quoting at length.

*ngress did
to overcome
mmon law
SI*

> "But besides the presumption that no anomalous and unheard of proceedings or suits were intended to be raised up by the Constitution—anomalous and unheard of when the Constitution was adopted—an additional reason why the jurisdiction claimed for the Circuit Court does not exist, is the language of an act of Congress by which its jurisdiction is conferred. The words are these: 'The circuit courts of the United States shall have original cognizance, concurrent with the courts of the several States, of all suits of a civil nature at common law or in equity, … arising under the Constitution or laws of the United States, or treaties,' etc.—'Concurrent with the Courts of the several States.' Does not this qualification show that Congress, in legislating to carry the Constitution into effect, did not intend to invest its courts with any new and strange jurisdictions? The state courts have no power to entertain suits by individuals against a State without its consent. Then how does the Circuit Court, having only concurrent jurisdiction, acquire any such power? It is true that the same qualification existed in the judiciary act of 1789, which was before the court in Chisholm v. Georgia, and the majority of the court did not think that it was sufficient to limit the jurisdiction of the Circuit Court. Justice Iredell thought differently. In view of the manner in which that decision was received by the country, the adoption of the Eleventh Amendment, the light of history and the reason of the thing, we think we are at liberty to prefer Justice Iredell's view in this regard." Hans v. Louisiana, 134 U.S., at 18–19.

As this passage demonstrates, *Hans* itself looked to see whether Congress had displaced the presumption that sovereign immunity obtains. Although the opinion did go to great lengths to establish the quite uncontroversial historical proposition that unconsenting States generally were not subject to suit, that entire discussion preceded the opinion's statutory analysis. See Hans v. Louisiana, 134 U.S. at 10–18. Thus, the opinion's thorough historical investigation served only to establish a presumption against jurisdiction that Congress must overcome, not an inviolable jurisdictional restriction that inheres in the Constitution itself.

Indeed, the very fact that the Court characterized the doctrine of sovereign immunity as a "presumption" confirms its assumption that it could be displaced. The *Hans* Court's inquiry into congressional intent would have been wholly inappropriate if it had believed that the doctrine of sovereign immunity was a constitutionally inviolable jurisdictional limitation. Thus, *Hans* provides no basis for the majority's conclusion that Congress is powerless to make States suable in cases not mentioned by the text of the Eleventh Amendment. Instead, *Hans* provides affirmative support for the view that Congress may create federal-court jurisdiction over private causes of action against unconsenting States brought by their own citizens.

* * *

Some of our precedents do state that the sovereign immunity doctrine rests on fundamental constitutional "postulates" and partakes of jurisdictional aspects rooted in Article III. Most notably, that reasoning underlies this Court's holding in Principality of Monaco v. Mississippi, 292 U.S. 313 (1934).

Monaco is a most inapt precedent for the majority's holding today. That case barred a foreign sovereign from suing a State in an equitable state law action to recover payments due on State bonds. It did not, however, involve a claim based on federal law. Instead, the case concerned a purely state law question to which the State had interposed a federal defense. Principality of Monaco v. Mississippi, 292 U.S. 313, 317 (1934). Thus, *Monaco* reveals little about the power of Congress to create a private federal cause of action to remedy a State's violation of federal law.

Moreover, although *Monaco* attributes a quasi-constitutional status to sovereign immunity, even in cases not covered by the Eleventh Amendment's plain text, that characterization does not constitute precedent for the proposition that Congress is powerless to displace a State's immunity. Our abstention doctrines have roots in both the Tenth Amendment and Article III, and thus may be said to rest on constitutional "postulates" or to partake of jurisdictional aspects. Yet it has not been thought that the Constitution would prohibit Congress from barring federal courts from abstaining. The majority offers no reason for making the federal common-law rule of sovereign immunity less susceptible to congressional displacement than any other quasi-jurisdictional common-law rule.

In this regard, I note that *Monaco* itself analogized sovereign immunity to the prudential doctrine that "controversies" identified in Article

III must be "justiciable" in order to be heard by federal courts. Id., at 329. The justiciability doctrine is a prudential rather than a jurisdictional one, and thus Congress' clearly expressed intention to create federal jurisdiction over a particular Article III controversy necessarily strips federal courts of the authority to decline jurisdiction on justiciability grounds. See Allen v. Wright, 468 U.S. 737, 791 (1984) (Stevens, J., dissenting); Flast v. Cohen, 392 U.S. 83, 100–101 (1968). For that reason, *Monaco*, by its own terms, fails to resolve the question before us.[11]

More generally, it is quite startling to learn that the *reasoning* of *Hans* and *Monaco* (even assuming that it did not undermine the majority's view) should have a *stare decisis* effect on the question whether Congress possesses the authority to provide a federal forum for the vindication of a federal right by a citizen against its own State. In light of the Court's development of a "clear-statement" line of jurisprudence, I would have thought that *Hans* and *Monaco* had at least left open the question whether Congress could permit the suit we consider here. Our clear-statement cases would have been all but unintelligible if *Hans* and *Monaco* had already established that Congress lacked the constitutional power to make States suable in federal court by individuals no matter how clear its intention to do so.

* * *

III

* * *

The fundamental error that continues to lead the Court astray is its failure to acknowledge that its modern embodiment of the ancient doctrine of sovereign immunity "has absolutely nothing to do with the limit on judicial power contained in the Eleventh Amendment." Id., at 25 (Stevens, J., concurring). It rests rather on concerns of federalism and comity that merit respect but are nevertheless, in cases such as the one before us, subordinate to the plenary power of Congress.

* * *

JUSTICE SOUTER, with whom JUSTICE GINSBURG and JUSTICE BREYER join, dissenting.

In holding the State of Florida immune to suit under the Indian Gaming Regulatory Act, the Court today holds for the first time since the founding of the Republic that Congress has no authority to subject a State to the jurisdiction of a federal court at the behest of an individual asserting a federal right. Although the Court invokes the Eleventh

---

11. Indeed, to the extent the reasoning of *Monaco* was premised on the ground that a contrary ruling might permit foreign governments and States indirectly to frustrate Congress' treaty power, Principality of Monaco v. Mississippi, 292 U.S. 313, 331 (1934), the opinion suggests that its outcome would have been quite different had Congress expressly authorized suits by foreign governments against individual States as part of its administration of foreign policy.

Amendment as authority for this proposition, the only sense in which that amendment might be claimed as pertinent here was tolerantly phrased by Justice Stevens in his concurring opinion in Pennsylvania v. Union Gas, 491 U.S. 1, 23 (1989)(Stevens, J., concurring). There, he explained how it has come about that we have two Eleventh Amendments, the one ratified in 1795, the other (so-called) invented by the Court nearly a century later in Hans v. Louisiana, 134 U.S. 1 (1890). Justice Stevens saw in that second Eleventh Amendment no bar to the exercise of congressional authority under the Commerce Clause in providing for suits on a federal question by individuals against a State, and I can only say that after my own canvass of the matter I believe he was entirely correct in that view, for reasons given below. His position, of course, was also the holding in *Union Gas*, which the Court now overrules and repudiates.

The fault I find with the majority today is not in its decision to reexamine *Union Gas*, for the Court in that case produced no majority for a single rationale supporting congressional authority. Instead, I part company from the Court because I am convinced that its decision is fundamentally mistaken, and for that reason I respectfully dissent.

I

It is useful to separate three questions: (1) whether the States enjoyed sovereign immunity if sued in their own courts in the period prior to ratification of the National Constitution; (2) if so, whether after ratification the States were entitled to claim some such immunity when sued in a federal court exercising jurisdiction either because the suit was between a State and a non-state litigant who was not its citizen, or because the issue in the case raised a federal question; and (3) whether any state sovereign immunity recognized in federal court may be abrogated by Congress.

The answer to the first question is not clear, although some of the Framers assumed that States did enjoy immunity in their own courts. The second question was not debated at the time of ratification, except as to citizen-state diversity jurisdiction; there was no unanimity, but in due course the Court in Chisholm v. Georgia, 2 Dall. 419 (1793), answered that a state defendant enjoyed no such immunity. As to federal question jurisdiction, state sovereign immunity seems not to have been debated prior to ratification, the silence probably showing a general understanding at the time that the States would have no immunity in such cases.

The adoption of the Eleventh Amendment soon changed the result in *Chisholm*, not by mentioning sovereign immunity, but by eliminating citizen-state diversity jurisdiction over cases with state defendants. I will explain why the Eleventh Amendment did not affect federal question jurisdiction, a notion that needs to be understood for the light it casts on the soundness of *Hans*'s holding that States did enjoy sovereign immunity in federal question suits. The *Hans* Court erroneously assumed that a

State could plead sovereign immunity against a noncitizen suing under federal question jurisdiction, and for that reason held that a State must enjoy the same protection in a suit by one of its citizens. The error of *Hans*'s reasoning is underscored by its clear inconsistency with the Founders' hostility to the implicit reception of common-law doctrine as federal law, and with the Founders' conception of sovereign power as divided between the States and the National Government for the sake of very practical objectives.

The Court's answer today to the third question is likewise at odds with the Founders' view that common law, when it was received into the new American legal systems, was always subject to legislative amendment. In ignoring the reasons for this pervasive understanding at the time of the ratification, and in holding that a nontextual common-law rule limits a clear grant of congressional power under Article I, the Court follows a course that has brought it to grief before in our history, and promises to do so again.

* * *

A

* * *

Whatever the scope of sovereign immunity might have been in the Colonies, however, or during the period of Confederation, the proposal to establish a National Government under the Constitution drafted in 1787 presented a prospect unknown to the common law prior to the American experience: the States would become parts of a system in which sovereignty over even domestic matters would be divided or parcelled out between the States and the Nation, the latter to be invested with its own judicial power and the right to prevail against the States whenever their respective substantive laws might be in conflict. With this prospect in mind, the 1787 Constitution might have addressed state sovereign immunity by eliminating whatever sovereign immunity the States previously had, as to any matter subject to federal law or jurisdiction; by recognizing an analogue to the old immunity in the new context of federal jurisdiction, but subject to abrogation as to any matter within that jurisdiction; or by enshrining a doctrine of inviolable state sovereign immunity in the text, thereby giving it constitutional protection in the new federal jurisdiction. See Field, The Eleventh Amendment and Other Sovereign Immunity Doctrines: Part One, 126 U. Pa. L. Rev. 515, 536–538 (1977).

* * *

* * * [T]here was no consensus on the issue [of state sovereign immunity among the Framers]. There was, on the contrary, a clear disagreement, which was left to fester during the ratification period, to be resolved only thereafter. One other point, however, was also clear: the debate addressed only the question whether ratification of the Constitution would, in diversity cases and without more, abrogate the state sovereign immunity or allow it to have some application. We have no record that anyone argued for the third option mentioned above, that the Constitution would affirmatively guarantee state sovereign immunity against any congressional action to the contrary. Nor would there have been any apparent justification for any such argument, since no clause in the proposed (and ratified) Constitution even so much as suggested such a position. It may have been reasonable to contend (as we will see that Madison, Marshall, and Hamilton did) that Article III would not alter States' pre-existing common-law immunity despite its unqualified grant of jurisdiction over diversity suits against States. But then, as now, there was no textual support for contending that Article III or any other provision would "constitutionalize" state sovereign immunity, and no one uttered any such contention.

B

The argument among the Framers and their friends about sovereign immunity in federal citizen-state diversity cases, in any event, was short lived and ended when this Court, in Chisholm v. Georgia, 2 Dall. 419 (1793), chose between the constitutional alternatives of abrogation and recognition of the immunity enjoyed at common law. The 4–to–1 majority adopted the reasonable (although not compelled) interpretation that the first of the two Citizen–State Diversity Clauses abrogated for purposes of federal jurisdiction any immunity the States might have enjoyed in their own courts, and Georgia was accordingly held subject to the judicial power in a common-law assumpsit action by a South Carolina citizen suing to collect a debt.[5] The case also settled, by implication, any question there could possibly have been about recognizing state sovereign immunity in actions depending on the federal question (or "arising under") head of jurisdiction as well. The constitutional text on federal question jurisdiction, after all, was just as devoid of immunity language as it was on citizen-state diversity, and at the time of *Chisholm* any influence that general common-law immunity might have had as an interpretive force in construing constitutional language would presumably have been no greater when addressing the federal question language

---

5. This lengthy discussion of the history of the Constitution's ratification, the Court's opinion in Chisholm v. Georgia, 2 Dall. 419 (1793) and the adoption of the Eleventh Amendment is necessary to explain why, in my view, the contentions in some of our earlier opinions that *Chisholm* created a great "shock of surprise" misread the history. See Principality of Monaco v. Mississippi, 292 U.S. 313 (1934). The Court's response to this historical analysis is simply to recite yet again *Monaco*'s erroneous assertion that *Chisholm* created a "such a shock of surprise that the Eleventh Amendment was at once proposed and adopted," 292 U.S., at 325. This response is, with respect, no response at all.

Monaco's *ipse dixit* that *Chisholm* created a "shock of surprise" does not make it so. * * *

Moreover, in this case, there is ample evidence contradicting the "shock of surprise" thesis. Contrary to *Monaco*'s suggestion, the Eleventh Amendment was not "at once proposed and adopted." Congress was in session when *Chisholm* was decided, and a constitutional amendment in response was proposed two days later, but Congress never acted on it, and in fact it was not until two years after *Chisholm* was handed down that an amendment was ratified. See Gibbons, The Eleventh Amendment and State Sovereign Immunity: A Reinterpretation, 83 Colum. L. Rev. 1889, 1926–1927 (1983).

of Article III than its Diversity Clauses. See Sherry, The Eleventh Amendment and Stare Decisis: Overruling Hans v. Louisiana, 57 U. Chi. L. Rev. 1260, 1270 (1990).

Although Justice Iredell's dissent in *Chisholm* seems at times to reserve judgment on what I have called the third question, whether Congress could authorize suits against the States, *Chisholm, supra,* at 434–435 (Iredell, J., dissenting), his argument is largely devoted to stating the position taken by several federalists that state sovereign immunity was cognizable under the Citizen–State Diversity Clauses, not that state immunity was somehow invisibly codified as an independent constitutional defense. * * *

C

The Eleventh Amendment, of course, repudiated *Chisholm* and clearly divested federal courts of some jurisdiction as to cases against state parties:

> "The Judicial power of the United States shall not be construed to extend to any suit in law or equity, commenced or prosecuted against one of the United States by Citizens of another State, or by Citizens or Subjects of any Foreign State."

There are two plausible readings of this provision's text. Under the first, it simply repeals the Citizen–State Diversity Clauses of Article III for all cases in which the State appears as a defendant. Under the second, it strips the federal courts of jurisdiction in any case in which a state defendant is sued by a citizen not its own, even if jurisdiction might otherwise rest on the existence of a federal question in the suit. Neither reading of the Amendment, of course, furnishes authority for the Court's view in today's case, but we need to choose between the competing readings for the light that will be shed on the *Hans* doctrine and the legitimacy of inflating that doctrine to the point of constitutional immutability as the Court has chosen to do.

The history and structure of the Eleventh Amendment convincingly show that it reaches only to suits subject to federal jurisdiction exclusively under the Citizen–State Diversity Clauses.[8] [Justice Souter here

---

8. The great weight of scholarly commentary agrees. See, e.g., Jackson, The Supreme Court, the Eleventh Amendment, and State Sovereign Immunity, 98 Yale L.J. 1 (1988); Amar, Of Sovereignty and Federalism, 96 Yale L.J. 1425 (1987); Fletcher, A Historical Interpretation of the Eleventh Amendment: A Narrow Construction of an Affirmative Grant of Jurisdiction Rather than a Prohibition Against Jurisdiction, 35 Stan. L. Rev. 1033 (1983); Gibbons, The Eleventh Amendment and State Sovereign Immunity: A Reinterpretation, 83 Colum. L. Rev. 1889 (1983); Field, The Eleventh Amendment and Other Sovereign Immunity Doctrines: Congressional Imposition of Suit Upon the States, 126 U. Pa. L. Rev. 1203 (1978). While a minority has adopted the second view set out above, see, e.g., Marshall, Fighting the Words of the Eleventh Amendment, 102 Harv. L. Rev. 1342 (1989); Massey, State Sovereignty and the Tenth and Eleventh Amendments, 56 U. Chi. L. Rev. 61 (1989), and others have criticized the diversity theory, see, e.g., Marshall, The Diversity Theory of the Eleventh Amendment: A Critical Evaluation, 102 Harv. L. Rev. 1372 (1989), I have discovered no commentator affirmatively advocating the position taken by the Court today. As one scholar has observed, the literature is "remarkably consistent in its

canvasses the historical evidence for the "diversity explanation," described in Note 1, supra pp. 359–63.] * * *

* * *

It should accordingly come as no surprise that the weightiest commentary following the amendment's adoption described it simply as constricting the scope of the Citizen–State Diversity Clauses. In Cohens v. Virginia, 6 Wheat. 264 (1821), for instance, Chief Justice Marshall, writing for the Court, emphasized that the amendment had no effect on federal courts' jurisdiction grounded on the "arising under" provision of Article III and concluded that "a case arising under the constitution or laws of the United States, is cognizable in the Courts of the Union, whoever may be the parties to that case." Id., at 383. The point of the Eleventh Amendment, according to *Cohens*, was to bar jurisdiction in suits at common law by Revolutionary War debt creditors, not "to strip the government of the means of protecting, by the instrumentality of its Courts, the constitution and laws from active violation." Id., at 407.

* * *

The good sense of this early construction of the Amendment as affecting the diversity jurisdiction and no more has the further virtue of making sense of this Court's repeated exercise of appellate jurisdiction in federal question suits brought against states in their own courts by out-of-staters. Exercising appellate jurisdiction in these cases would have been patent error if the Eleventh Amendment limited federal question jurisdiction, for the Amendment's unconditional language ("shall not be construed") makes no distinction between trial and appellate jurisdiction.[10] And yet, again and again we have entertained such appellate cases, even when brought against the State in its own name by a private plaintiff for money damages. The best explanation for our practice belongs to Chief Justice Marshall: the Eleventh Amendment bars only those suits in which the sole basis for federal jurisdiction is diversity of citizenship.

In sum, reading the Eleventh Amendment solely as a limit on citizen-state diversity jurisdiction has the virtue of coherence with this Court's practice, with the views of John Marshall, with the history of the Amendment's drafting, and with its allusive language. Today's majority does not appear to disagree, at least insofar as the constitutional text is

---

evaluation of the historical evidence and text of the amendment as not supporting a broad rule of constitutional immunity for states." Jackson, supra, at 44, n. 179.

10. We have generally rejected Eleventh Amendment challenges to our appellate jurisdiction on the specious ground that an appeal is not a "suit" for purposes of the Amendment. See, e.g., McKesson Corp. v. Division of Alcoholic Beverages and Tobacco, Dept. of Business Regulation, 496 U.S. 18, 27 (1990). Although *Cohens v. Virginia*, 6 Wheat. 264, 412 (1821), is cited for this

proposition, that case involved a State as plaintiff. See generally Jackson, "The Supreme Court, the Eleventh Amendment, and State Sovereign Immunity," 98 Yale L.J. 1, 32–35 (1988)(rejecting the appeal/suit distinction). The appeal/suit distinction, in any case, makes no sense. Whether or not an appeal is a "suit" in its own right, it is certainly a means by which an appellate court exercises jurisdiction over a "suit" that began in the courts below.

concerned; the Court concedes, after all, that "the text of the Amendment would appear to restrict only the Article III diversity jurisdiction of the federal courts."

Thus, regardless of which of the two plausible readings one adopts, the further point to note here is that there is no possible argument that the Eleventh Amendment, by its terms, deprives federal courts of jurisdiction over all citizen lawsuits against the States. Not even the Court advances that proposition, and there would be no textual basis for doing so.[12] Because the plaintiffs in today's case are citizens of the State that they are suing, the Eleventh Amendment simply does not apply to them. We must therefore look elsewhere for the source of that immunity by which the Court says their suit is barred from a federal court.[13]

II

The obvious place to look elsewhere, of course, is Hans v. Louisiana, and *Hans* was indeed a leap in the direction of today's holding, even though it does not take the Court all the way. The parties in *Hans* raised, and the Court in that case answered, only what I have called the second question, that is, whether the Constitution, without more, permits a State to plead sovereign immunity to bar the exercise of federal question jurisdiction. See id., at 9. Although the Court invoked a principle of sovereign immunity to cure what it took to be the Eleventh Amendment's anomaly of barring only those state suits brought by noncitizen plaintiffs, the *Hans* Court had no occasion to consider wheth-

12. The Court does suggest that the drafters of the Eleventh Amendment may not have had federal question jurisdiction in mind, in the apparent belief that this somehow supports its reading. The possibility, however, that those who drafted the Eleventh Amendment intended to deal "only with the problem presented by the decision in *Chisholm*" would demonstrate, if any demonstration beyond the clear language of the Eleventh Amendment were necessary, that the Eleventh Amendment was not intended to address the broader issue of federal question suits brought by citizens.

Moreover, the Court's point is built on a faulty foundation. The Court is simply incorrect in asserting that "the federal courts did not have federal question jurisdiction at the time the Amendment was passed." Article III, of course, provided for such jurisdiction, and early Congresses exercised their authority pursuant to Article III to confer jurisdiction on the federal courts to resolve various matters of federal law. In fact, only six years after the passage of the Eleventh Amendment, Congress enacted a statute providing for general federal question jurisdiction. It is, of course, true that this statute proved short-lived (it was repealed by the Act of Mar. 8, 1802, 2 Stat. 132), and that Congress did not pass another statute

conferring general federal jurisdiction until 1875, but the drafters of the Eleventh Amendment obviously could not have predicted such things. The real significance of the 1801 act is that it demonstrates the awareness among the Members of the early Congresses of the potential scope of Article III. This, in combination with the pre-Eleventh Amendment statutes that conferred federal question jurisdiction on the federal courts, cast considerable doubt on the Court's suggestion that the issue of federal question jurisdiction never occurred to the drafters of the Eleventh Amendment; on the contrary, just because these early statutes underscore the early Congresses' recognition of the availability of federal question jurisdiction, the silence of the Eleventh Amendment is all the more deafening.

13. The majority chides me that the "lengthy analysis of the text of the Eleventh Amendment is directed at a straw man." But plain text is the Man of Steel in a confrontation with "background principle[s]" and " 'postulates which limit and control.' " * * * That the Court thinks otherwise is an indication of just how far it has strayed beyond the boundaries of traditional constitutional analysis.

er Congress could abrogate that background immunity by statute. Indeed (except in the special circumstance of Congress's power to enforce the Civil War Amendments), this question never came before our Court until *Union Gas*, and any intimations of an answer in prior cases were mere dicta. In *Union Gas* the Court held that the immunity recognized in *Hans* had no constitutional status and was subject to congressional abrogation. Today the Court overrules *Union Gas* and holds just the opposite. In deciding how to choose between these two positions, the place to begin is with *Hans*'s holding that a principle of sovereign immunity derived from the common law insulates a state from federal question jurisdiction at the suit of its own citizen. A critical examination of that case will show that it was wrongly decided, as virtually every recent commentator has concluded. It follows that the Court's further step today of constitutionalizing *Hans*'s rule against abrogation by Congress compounds and immensely magnifies the century-old mistake of *Hans* itself and takes its place with other historic examples of textually untethered elevations of judicially derived rules to the status of inviolable constitutional law.

A

* * *

Taking *Hans* only as far as its holding, its vulnerability is apparent. The Court rested its opinion on avoiding the supposed anomaly of recognizing jurisdiction to entertain a citizen's federal question suit, but not one brought by a noncitizen. See *Hans*, supra, at 10–11. There was, however, no such anomaly at all. As already explained, federal question cases are not touched by the Eleventh Amendment, which leaves a State open to federal question suits by citizens and noncitizens alike. If Hans had been from Massachusetts the Eleventh Amendment would not have barred his action against Louisiana.

Although there was thus no anomaly to be cured by *Hans*, the case certainly created its own anomaly in leaving federal courts entirely without jurisdiction to enforce paramount federal law at the behest of a citizen against a State that broke it. It destroyed the congruence of the judicial power under Article III with the substantive guarantees of the Constitution, and with the provisions of statutes passed by Congress in the exercise of its power under Article I: when a State injured an individual in violation of federal law no federal forum could provide direct relief. Absent an alternative process to vindicate federal law John Marshall saw just what the consequences of this anomaly would be in the early Republic, and he took that consequence as good evidence that the Framers could never have intended such a scheme.

"Different States may entertain different opinions on the true construction of the constitutional powers of Congress. * * * In many States the judges are dependent for office and for salary on the will of the legislature. The constitution of the United States furnishes no security against the universal adoption of this principle. When we observe the importance which that constitution attaches to the independence of judges, we are less inclined to suppose that it can have intended to leave these constitutional questions to tribunals where this independence may not exist." Cohens v. Virginia, 6 Wheat., at 386–387.

And yet that is just what *Hans* threatened to do.

How such a result could have been threatened on the basis of a principle not so much as mentioned in the Constitution is difficult to understand. But history provides the explanation. * * * *Hans* was one episode in a long story of debt repudiation by the States of the former Confederacy after the end of Reconstruction. The turning point in the States' favor came with the Compromise of 1877, when the Republican party agreed effectively to end Reconstruction and to withdraw federal troops from the South in return for Southern acquiescence in the decision of the Electoral Commission that awarded the disputed 1876 presidential election to Rutherford B. Hayes. See J. Orth, Judicial Power of the United States: The Eleventh Amendment in American History 53–57 (1987); Gibbons, 83 Colum. L. Rev., at 1978–1982; see generally Foner, Reconstruction, at 575–587 (describing the events of 1877 and their aftermath). * * *

So it is that history explains, but does not honor, *Hans*. The ultimate demerit of the case centers, however, not on its politics but on the legal errors on which it rested. Before considering those errors, it is necessary to address the Court's contention that subsequent cases have read into *Hans* what was not there to begin with, that is, a background principle of sovereign immunity that is constitutional in stature and therefore unalterable by Congress.

* * *

III

Three critical errors in *Hans* weigh against constitutionalizing its holding as the majority does today. The first we have already seen: the *Hans* Court misread the Eleventh Amendment. It also misunderstood the conditions under which common-law doctrines were received or rejected at the time of the Founding, and it fundamentally mistook the very nature of sovereignty in the young Republic that was supposed to entail a State's immunity to federal question jurisdiction in a federal court. While I would not, as a matter of *stare decisis*, overrule *Hans* today, an understanding of its failings on these points will show how the Court today simply compounds already serious error in taking *Hans* the further step of investing its rule with constitutional inviolability against the considered judgment of Congress to abrogate it.

A

There is and could be no dispute that the doctrine of sovereign immunity that *Hans* purported to apply had its origins in the "familiar doctrine of the common law," "derived from the laws and practices of our English ancestors." Although statutes came to affect its importance in the succeeding centuries, the doctrine was never reduced to codification, and Americans took their understanding of immunity doctrine from Blackstone, see 3 W. Blackstone, Commentaries on the Laws of England ch. 17 (1768). Here, as in the mother country, it remained a common-law rule.

This fact of the doctrine's common-law status in the period covering the Founding and the later adoption of the Eleventh Amendment should have raised a warning flag to the *Hans* Court and it should do the same for the Court today. [Justice Souter here canvassed the historical record to show that the Framers did not incorporate the common law wholesale.]

* * *

C

The considerations expressed so far, based on text, *Chisholm*, caution in common-law reception, and sovereignty theory, have pointed both to the mistakes inherent in *Hans* and, even more strongly, to the error of today's holding. Although for reasons of *stare decisis* I would not today disturb the century-old precedent, I surely would not extend its error by placing the common-law immunity it mistakenly recognized beyond the power of Congress to abrogate. In doing just that, however, today's decision declaring state sovereign immunity itself immune from abrogation in federal question cases is open to a further set of objections peculiar to itself. For today's decision stands condemned alike by the Framers' abhorrence of any notion that such common-law rules as might be received into the new legal systems would be beyond the legislative power to alter or repeal, and by its resonance with this Court's previous essays in constitutionalizing common-law rules at the expense of legislative authority.

1

I have already pointed out how the views of the Framers reflected the caution of state constitutionalists and legislators over reception of common-law rules, a caution that the Framers exalted to the point of vigorous resistance to any idea that English common-law rules might be imported wholesale through the new Constitution. The state politicians also took pains to guarantee that once a common-law rule had been received, it would always be subject to legislative alteration, and again the state experience was reflected in the Framers' thought. Indeed, the Framers' very insistence that no common-law doctrine would be received by virtue of ratification was focused in their fear that elements of the common law might thereby have been placed beyond the power of Congress to alter by legislation.

* * *

*mmon law can
changed by
statute*

Virtually every state reception provision, be it constitutional or statutory, explicitly provided that the common law was subject to alteration by statute. * * * Just as the early state governments did not leave reception of the common law to implication, then, neither did they receive it as law immune to legislative alteration.

* * *

2

History confirms the wisdom of Madison's abhorrence of constitutionalizing common-law rules to place them beyond the reach of congressional amendment. The Framers feared judicial power over substantive policy and the ossification of law that would result from transforming common law into constitutional law, and their fears have been borne out every time the Court has ignored Madison's counsel on subjects that we generally group under economic and social policy. It is, in fact, remarkable that as we near the end of this century the Court should choose to open a new constitutional chapter in confining legislative judgments on these matters by resort to textually unwarranted common-law rules, for it was just this practice in the century's early decades that brought this Court to the nadir of competence that we identify with Lochner v. New York, 198 U.S. 45 (1905).

It was the defining characteristic of the *Lochner* era, and its characteristic vice, that the Court treated the common-law background (in those days, common-law property rights and contractual autonomy) as paramount, while regarding congressional legislation to abrogate the common law on these economic matters as constitutionally suspect. And yet the superseding lesson that seemed clear after West Coast Hotel Co. v. Parrish, 300 U.S. 379 (1937), that action within the legislative power is not subject to greater scrutiny merely because it trenches upon the case law's ordering of economic and social relationships, seems to have been lost on the Court.

The majority today, indeed, seems to be going *Lochner* one better. When the Court has previously constrained the express Article I powers by resort to common-law or background principles, it has done so at least in an ostensible effort to give content to some other written provision of the Constitution, like the Due Process Clause, the very object of which is to limit the exercise of governmental power. Some textual argument, at least, could be made that the Court was doing no more than defining one provision that happened to be at odds with another. Today, however, the Court is not struggling to fulfill a responsibility to reconcile two arguably conflicting and Delphic constitutional provisions, nor is it struggling with any Delphic text at all. For even the Court concedes that the Constitution's grant to Congress of plenary power over relations with Indian tribes at the expense of any state claim to the contrary is unmistakably clear, and this case does not even arguably implicate a textual trump to the grant of federal question jurisdiction.

* * *

V

* * *

There is an even more fundamental "clear statement" principle, however, that the Court abandons today. John Marshall recognized it over a century and a half ago in the very context of state sovereign immunity in federal question cases:

"The jurisdiction of the Court, then, being extended by the letter of the constitution to all cases arising under it, or under the laws of the United States, it follows that those who would withdraw any case of this description from that jurisdiction, must sustain the exemption they claim on the spirit and true meaning of the constitution, which spirit and true meaning must be so apparent as to overrule the words which its framers have employed." Cohens v. Virginia, 6 Wheat., at 379–380.

Because neither text, precedent, nor history supports the majority's abdication of our responsibility to exercise the jurisdiction entrusted to us in Article III, I would reverse the judgment of the Court of Appeals.

Notes

1. In light of the historical materials in section 1 of this chapter, do you think the majority or the dissent has the better argument? For purposes of determining Congress's authority to confer jurisdiction under the Indian Gaming Regulatory Act, does it matter whether the "diversity explanation" [supra pp. 359–63] is valid? For excellent discussions of *Seminole Tribe*, see Meltzer, *The* Seminole *Decision and State Sovereign Immunity*, 1996 Sup.Ct. Rev. 1; Monaghan, *The Sovereign Immunity "Exception,"* 110 Harv.L.Rev. 102 (1996); Vazquez, *What is Eleventh Amendment Immunity?* 106 Yale L.J. 1683 (1997); Symposium: Fear and Federalism, 23 Ohio N.U.L.Rev. 1179 (1997); Pfander, *An Intermediate Solution to State Sovereign Immunity: Federal Appellate Court Review of State–Court Judgments After* Seminole Tribe, 46 UCLA L.Rev. 161 (1998); Fitzgerald, *Beyond* Marbury: *Jurisdictional Self–Dealing in* Seminole Tribe, 52 Vand.L.Rev. 407 (1999). For additional historical analysis, see Rich, *Lessons of Charleston Harbor: The Rise, Fall, and Revival of Pro–Slavery Federalism*, 36 McGeorge L.Rev. 569 (2005).

2. Justice Souter believes that *Hans* is wrongly decided, but would not overrule it. One might make an argument that he is trying to show that two wrongs make a right: since the wrongly-decided *Hans* remains good law, Congress should have the unusual power of altering the eleventh amendment by statute, in order to ameliorate the harsh result of *Hans*. What is Justice Souter's response to such an argument? How many eleventh amendments do *you* think there are? Professor Caleb Nelson suggests that there are two strands of state sovereign immunity, one governed by the text and the other by notions of personal jurisdiction. Nelson, *Sovereign Immunity as a Doctrine of Personal Jurisdiction*, 115 Harv.L.Rev. 1559 (2002). Congress might be able to abrogate the latter, but not the former. Does Professor Nelson's scheme explain Justice Souter's dissent?

3. The majority quotes Principality of Monaco v. Mississippi, 292 U.S. 313 (1934) (which itself quotes Alexander Hamilton in Federalist No. 81), to hold that states are constitutionally immune from suit unless there has been a "surrender of this immunity in the plan of the convention." Ratification of the commerce clause, according to *Seminole Tribe*, was not such a surrender. Was ratification of any other part of Article I? In Central Virginia Community College v. Katz, 546 U.S. ___, 126 S.Ct. 990 (2006), a divided Court held that the bankruptcy clause (which follows the commerce clause in Article I, § 8) represents such a surrender. The majority concluded that the bankruptcy clause was designed to give Congress the power to ensure uniformity and to prevent "the rampant injustice resulting from States' refusal to respect one another's discharge orders." Is this purpose significantly different from the purpose of the commerce clause, which does not represent a surrender of immunity? Does the need for nationwide and uniform bankruptcy laws necessarily require states to surrender their immunity, or only their authority to pass individual and inconsistent bankruptcy schemes? The dissent in *Central Virginia Community College* concluded that "Nothing in the text, structure, or history of the Constitution indicates that the Bankruptcy Clause, in contrast to all of the other provisions of Article I, manifests the States' consent to be sued by private citizens." For a general critique of the "surrender in the plan of the convention" argument, see Pfander, *Waiver of Sovereign Immunity in the "Plan of the Convention,"* 1 Geo.J.L. & Pub. Pol'y 13 (2002).

4. In Fitzpatrick v. Bitzer, 427 U.S. 445 (1976), discussed in *Seminole Tribe*, the Court held that Congress may, pursuant to its power under section 5 of the fourteenth amendment to enforce that amendment's provisions, revoke state sovereign immunity. In reaching this conclusion, the Court, in an opinion by Justice Rehnquist, cited post-Civil War decisions "sanction[ing] intrusions by Congress, acting under the Civil War Amendments, into the judicial, executive, and legislative spheres of autonomy previously reserved to the States. The legislation considered in each case was grounded on the expansion of Congress' powers—with the corresponding diminution of state sovereignty—found to be intended by the Framers and made part of the Constitution upon the States' ratification of those Amendments * * *." 427 U.S. at 455–56. While the Court acknowledged that "none of these previous cases presented the question of the relationship between the Eleventh Amendment and the enforcement power granted to Congress under § 5 of the Fourteenth Amendment," it concluded "that the Eleventh Amendment, and the principle of state sovereignty which it embodies, are necessarily limited by the enforcement provisions of § 5 of the Fourteenth Amendment. * * * When Congress acts pursuant to § 5, not only is it exercising legislative authority that is plenary within the terms of the constitutional grant, it is exercising that authority under one section of a constitutional Amendment whose other sections by their own terms embody limitations on state authority." Id. at 456, 96 S.Ct. at 2671. See also Hutto v. Finney, 437 U.S. 678 (1978), where the Court, relying on *Fitzpatrick*, upheld application of the Civil Rights Attorney's Fees Awards Act of 1976, 42 U.S.C.A. § 1988, to cases in which state funds would be used to pay attorney's fees.

Do you understand why the majority in *Seminole Tribe* thinks that *Fitzpatrick* does not control? Does it make sense? Consider the following arguments:

> The temporal argument—that the Fourteenth Amendment postdates the Eleventh—fails on its own terms: on the one hand, * * * proponents of sovereign immunity view the principle underlying it as predating the Commerce Clause; on the other hand, the Reconstruction Amendments cannot have had the purpose of overruling the sovereign immunity recognized by the Eleventh Amendment, as that recognition was given only in subsequent decisions. Moreover, there is a deeper objection to the temporal argument: our practice when construing a positive enactment that has been amended—whether a Constitution or a statute—is not ordinarily to treat the later-added provision as trumping any predecessor. * * * Rather, we seek to make sense of the amended enactment as a whole. Suppose that Congress, fearing jury nullification, enacted a law providing that all federal court suits seeking damages for racial discrimination by state or local officials should be tried to a judge rather than a jury. If a defendant objected that the law denied the right to jury trial guaranteed by the Seventh Amendment, the response that the Fourteenth Amendment postdated the Seventh surely would not be adequate. Daniel J. Meltzer, *The* Seminole *Decision and State Sovereign Immunity*, 1996 Sup.Ct.Rev. 1, 21–22.

Are you persuaded? Are there other differences between the fourteenth amendment and the commerce clause that might justify a distinction?

5.) *Seminole Tribe* means that the question of abrogation of immunity depends on the scope of Congress's powers under section 5 of the Fourteenth Amendment. The Court's recent substantive pronouncements on section 5 have indicated a possible contraction of congressional power. In City of Boerne v. Flores, 521 U.S. 507 (1997), the Court construed Congress's section 5 powers very narrowly, striking down the Religious Freedom Restoration Act because Congress had attempted to protect free exercise "rights" beyond those protected by the Supreme Court's first amendment jurisprudence. See also United States v. Morrison, 529 U.S. 598 (2000) (construing section 5 powers narrowly).

The Court has applied *Seminole Tribe* and *City of Boerne* to strike down numerous congressional attempts to abrogate state sovereign immunity. It first clarified the standard in Florida Prepaid Postsecondary Education Expense Board v. College Savings Bank, 527 U.S. 627 (1999). To invoke its section 5 powers, Congress must both "identify conduct transgressing the Fourteenth Amendment's substantive provisions," and "tailor its legislative scheme to remedying or preventing such conduct." In *Florida Prepaid*, the Court held that Congress's attempt to subject states to suits for patent infringement failed this test, because Congress had not identified any "pattern of patent infringement by the states, let alone a pattern of constitutional violations." In Kimel v. Florida Board of Regents, 528 U.S. 62 (2000), the Court similarly held that states could not be subject to suit for violations of the federal Age Discrimination in Employment Act (ADEA). Prior precedent established that age discrimination violates the Fourteenth Amendment only when it is irrational, and, according to Justice O'Connor's majority opinion in *Kimel*, "Congress had virtually no reason to believe that state and local governments" were irrationally discriminating against employees on the basis of age. Thus Congress had no power to abrogate the states' sovereign immunity and subject them to suit under the ADEA. See also College Savings Bank v. Florida Prepaid Postsecondary Education Expense Board, 527 U.S. 666 (1999) (Lanham Act protections against false or misleading advertising not within section 5 powers).

More recently, the Supreme Court struck down Congress's attempt to abrogate state immunity from suit under Title I of the Americans with Disabilities Act (ADA). Board of Trustees of the University of Alabama v. Garrett, 531 U.S. 356 (2001). Title I of the ADA applies to employers, and both prohibits intentional discrimination against the disabled and requires employers to accommodate disabled workers unless doing so would create an undue hardship. Earlier precedent had established that there is no constitutional duty to accommodate disabilities, and that even intentional discrimination against the disabled is constitutional unless it is irrational. In a five-to-four ruling, the Court held that "[t]he legislative record of the ADA * * * simply fails to show that Congress did in fact identify a pattern of irrational state discrimination in employment against the disabled." In addition, according to the majority, even if a pattern of unconstitutional behavior had been identified, "the rights and remedies created by the ADA against the States would raise the same sort of concerns as to congruence and proportionality as were found in *City of Boerne*," because of the accommodation requirement.

What, if anything, is wrong with the line of cases culminating in *Garrett*? Is it that the Court too narrowly defined Congress's section 5 powers in *City of Boerne*? How *should* Congress's power to "enforce" the Fourteenth Amendment be defined, if not by reference to the judicial interpretation of that Amendment? See Caminker, *"Appropriate" Means–Ends Constraints on Section 5 Powers*, 53 Stan.L.Rev. 1127 (2001). Is the problem with *Garrett* instead that the Court is insufficiently deferential to Congress's judgment that states are violating the Constitution? Consider that both age discrimination and disability discrimination are constitutional unless irrational: is it likely that Congress could *ever* compile a credible record of a pattern of irrational discrimination? Note that one of the purported instances of irrational discrimination against the disabled, cited in Justice Breyer's dissent in *Garrett*, was that a blind person was denied a driver's license (Appendix C, item 01231). While this item is unusual, most of the other examples cited by Justice Breyer involve state refusals to spend money on accommodations. Do those examples provide evidence of unconstitutional state discrimination against the disabled (in other words, are they instances of irrational behavior)? Perhaps the real problem is that the Constitution does not prohibit all objectionable discriminatory behavior. If so, what should the solution be? What approach do we usually take when the Constitution does not go far enough? Why won't that solution work here?

Note that in most of the post-*Seminole Tribe* cases, the state defendant was acting as a market participant rather than a sovereign. Should that make a difference? See Fletcher, *The Eleventh Amendment: Unfinished Business*, 75 Notre Dame L.Rev. 843 (2000).

6. The Court has backed away from *Kimel* and *Garrett* in its two most recent cases. The federal Family and Medical Leave Act (FMLA) requires employers—including states—to allow eligible employees up to 12 weeks of unpaid leave to care for a new child or for a seriously ill family member. Although most Courts of Appeals concluded that the precedent required invalidation of the FMLA's attempted abrogation of state sovereign immunity, the Supreme Court upheld it in Nevada Department of Human Resources v. Hibbs, 538 U.S. 721 (2003). Chief Justice Rehnquist's opinion for a six-Justice majority found that Congress enacted the FMLA to combat gender discrimination. The Court held that it was a congruent and proportional remedy for the failure of some states to provide paternity leave, and a prophylactic measure to prevent states from denying family-care leave, because "two-thirds of the nonprofessional caregivers for older, chronically ill, or disabled persons are women," so that a no-leave policy "would exclude far more women than men in the workplace." Justice Kennedy argued in dissent that the evidence did not show a pattern of unconstitutional gender discrimination by state employers, and Justice Scalia's dissent suggested that, like the Voting Rights Act, the FMLA should have targeted only those states found to have engaged in unconstitutional acts.

Is the argument that a no-leave policy would exclude more women than men sufficient to justify the statute under *City of Boerne* and its progeny? Recall that under Washington v. Davis, 426 U.S. 229 (1976), and Personnel Administrator of Massachusetts v. Feeney, 442 U.S. 256 (1979), neutral practices with a disparate impact on a protected group do not violate the equal protection clause. Note that the Court in *Hibbs* distinguished *Kimel* and *Garrett* in part because gender discrimination, unlike discrimination based on age or disability, is subject to heightened scrutiny. Does that distinction support the Court's holding? Two federal appellate courts have subsequently distinguished *Hibbs* in cases involving denial of leave to care for *oneself* (also covered by the FMLA but not at issue in *Hibbs*), holding that the personal leave provision, unlike the family leave provision, does not address gender discrimination and is therefore an invalid abrogation. Touvell v. Ohio Dept. of Mental Retardation & Developmental Disabilities, 422 F.3d 392 (6th Cir.2005); Brockman v. Wyoming Department of Family Services, 342 F.3d 1159 (10th Cir.2003).

The Court also recently upheld the abrogation of immunity in Title II of the ADA, which prohibits discrimination (and requires accommodation) by public entities. Tennessee v. Lane, 541 U.S. 509 (2004), involved a wheelchair-bound plaintiff who alleged that the state's failure to accommodate his disability denied him access to state courts. A closely divided Supreme Court, relying on *Hibbs* and distinguishing *Garrett*, found the abrogation of immunity valid, allowing the plaintiff to sue for damages as well as injunctive relief. The majority relied on the history of discrimination against the disabled, although similar evidence had been held insufficient to justify the use of Congress's § 5 powers in *Garrett*. Ultimately, *Lane* may presage a case-by-case examination of the particular violation alleged. After noting that Title II sought to remedy not simply discrimination but the discriminatory infringement of fundamental constitutional rights such as access to courts, Justice O'Connor's majority opinion concluded:

Whatever might be said about Title II's other applications, the question validly presented in this case is not whether Congress can validly subject the States to private suits for money damages for failing to provide reasonable access to hockey rinks, or even to voting booths [both of which are covered by Title II], but whether Congress had the power under § 5 to enforce the constitutional right of access to the courts. Id. at 530–31.

Chief Justice Rehnquist's dissent, joined by Justices Kennedy and Thomas, found an insufficient pattern of constitutional violations by the states to justify the use of § 5: "[T]here is *nothing* in the legislative record or statutory findings to indicate that disabled persons were systematically denied the right to be present at criminal trials, denied the meaningful opportunity to be heard in civil cases, unconstitutionally excluded from jury service, or denied the right to attend criminal trials." Id. at 543. Justice Scalia also dissented, proposing to abandon the *City of Boerne* test: "The 'congruence and proportionality' standard, like all such flabby tests, is a standing invitation to judicial arbitrariness and policy-driven decisionmaking." Id. at 557–58.

Does the apparent inconsistency between *Kimel* and *Garrett* on the one hand, and *Hibbs* and *Lane* on the other, suggest that the Court is using an ad hoc balancing test rather than the test of *City of Boerne* and its progeny? For an argument to that effect, see Sherry, *The Unmaking of a Precedent*, 2003 Sup.Ct.Rev. 231.

7. For some of the voluminous literature on these post-*Seminole Tribe* cases, see J. Noonan, Narrowing the Nation's Power: The Supreme Court Sides With the States (2002); Symposium: State Sovereign Immunity and the Eleventh Amendment, 75 Notre Dame L.Rev. 817 (2000); Meltzer, *Overcoming Immunity: The Case of Federal Regulation of Intellectual Property*, 53 Stan.L.Rev. 1331 (2001); Volokh, *Sovereign Immunity and Intellectual Property*, 73 S.Cal.L.Rev. 1161 (2000); Althouse, *The* Alden *Trilogy: Still Searching for a Way to Enforce Federalism*, 31 Rutgers L.J. 631 (2000); Symposium on New Directions in Federalism, 33 Loyola L.A. L.Rev. 1275 (2000); Rich, *Privileges or Immunities: The Missing Link in Establishing Congressional Power to Abrogate State Eleventh Amendment Immunity*, 28 Hastings Const. L.Q. 235 (2001); Thomas, *Congress' Section 5 Power and Remedial Rights*, 34 U.C. Davis L.Rev. 673 (2001); Eastman, *A Seminole* Dissent? 1 Geo J.L. & Pub. Pol'y 29 (2002); Randall, *Sovereign Immunity and the Uses of History*, 81 Neb.L.Rev. 1 (2002); McCormick, *Federalism Re–Constructed: The Eleventh Amendment's Illogical Impact on Congress' Power*, 37 Ind.L.Rev. 345 (2004).

8. What are Congress's options for ensuring federal court enforcement of federal statutes after *Seminole Tribe* and its progeny? See generally Choper & Yoo, *Who's Afraid of the Eleventh Amendment? The Limited Impact of the Court's Sovereign Immunity Rulings*, 106 Colum.L.Rev. 213 (2006). Congress has conditioned the receipt of various types of federal funds on state waiver of sovereign immunity. Are these statutes constitutionally permissible? Do the funds have to be related in some way to the suits for which waiver is demanded? See South Dakota v. Dole, 483 U.S. 203 (1987) (there must be a nexus between the purpose of federal spending and any conditions placed upon it); compare Garcia v. S.U.N.Y. Health Sciences Ctr.,

280 F.3d 98 (2d Cir.2001) (rejecting waiver tied to funding) with Pace v. Bogalusa City School Board, 403 F.3d 272 (5th Cir.2005) (en banc) (upholding waiver tied to funding); A.W. v. Jersey City Public Schools, 341 F.3d 234 (3d Cir. 2003) (same); Jim C. v. Arkansas Dept. of Education, 235 F.3d 1079 (8th Cir.2000) (same); Litman v. George Mason Univ., 186 F.3d 544 (4th Cir.1999) (same); Innes v. Kansas State Univ., 184 F.3d 1275 (10th Cir.1999) (same). Is conditioning federal funds on state waivers of immunity consistent with the spirit of *Seminole Tribe* and the other cases? Is the resulting waiver voluntary? See supra p. 364; see also Kinports, *Implied Waiver after* Seminole Tribe, 82 Minn.L.Rev. 793 (1998); Baker, *Conditional Federal Spending and States' Rights*, 574 Annals (AAPSS) 104 (2001); Berman et al., *State Accountability for Violations of Intellectual Property Rights: How to "Fix"* Florida Prepaid *(And How* Not *To)*, 79 Tex.L.Rev. 1037 (2001); Zietlow, *Federalism's Paradox: The Spending Power and Waiver of Sovereign Immunity*, 37 Wake Forest L.Rev. 141 (2002).

9. Besides the approach taken in the *Seminole Tribe* dissents, scholars have suggested another interpretation of the eleventh amendment that conflicts with the holding of *Seminole Tribe*. Professors John Nowak and Laurence Tribe, in separate articles, both concluded that the eleventh amendment was designed to limit only the power of the federal *judicial* branch to abrogate state immunity; the purpose was not, however, to limit *Congress's* power to abrogate that immunity. John Nowak, *The Scope of Congressional Power to Create Causes of Action Against State Governments and the History of the Eleventh and Fourteenth Amendments*, 75 Colum.L.Rev. 1413 (1975); Laurence Tribe, *Intergovernmental Immunities in Litigation, Taxation, and Regulation: Separation of Powers Issues in Controversies About Federalism*, 89 Harv.L.Rev. 682 (1976). Professor Tribe relies in part on the language of the eleventh amendment to support his construction, since it "literally limits only the judicial power." Id. at 694.

Professor Nowak relies on historical considerations to support the position that the eleventh amendment limits only the federal judiciary. He argues that Article III's drafters were concerned over the potential power of the federal judiciary to revoke state sovereign immunity, and therefore concludes that "a convincing argument can be made that the drafters of the eleventh amendment were only responding to the judicial assumption of jurisdiction in suits brought by Tories against states." 75 Colum.L.Rev. at 1440. Others, however, have questioned the force of his historical evidence. See Baker, *Federalism and the Eleventh Amendment*, 48 U.Colo.L.Rev. 139, 182 (1977); Field, *The Eleventh Amendment and Other Sovereign Immunity Doctrines: Congressional Imposition of Suit Upon the States*, 126 U.Pa.L.Rev. 1203, 1260 (1978).

Both Nowak and Tribe also rely on considerations of social policy to support their theories. In Nowak's words, "the pragmatic problems of federalism posed by the eleventh amendment should be resolved by Congress, not by the judiciary. Congress is the only governmental entity which shares a dual responsibility to the state and federal systems and is accountable at both levels." Nowack, supra, 75 Colum.L.Rev. at 1441. Do you agree that wise social policy supports a dichotomy between judicial and congressional power to abrogate state sovereign immunity? Can a response to Nowak and Tribe be fashioned that, in interpreting the eleventh amendment, social policy considerations can play at most a limited role? To what extent is the result of this interpretation similar to the result of the diversity theory?

10. In *Seminole Tribe,* Justice Rehnquist reiterated—and the dissent did not dispute—the longstanding requirement that "Congress' intent to abrogate the States' immunity from suit must be obvious from a 'clear legislative statement.' " 517 U.S. at 55.

The Court gave a stringent reading to the clear statement rule in Dellmuth v. Muth, 491 U.S. 223 (1989). Refusing to allow suit against the state of Pennsylvania under the Education of the Handicapped Act of 1975, Justice Kennedy wrote for the Court that a "permissible inference" of state liability is not "the unequivocal declaration which * * * is necessary before we will determine that Congress intended to exercise its powers of abrogation." Id. at 232. A 1986 amendment to the Act provided that a reduction in attorney fees in certain cases is not applicable "if the court finds that the State or local education agency unreasonably protracted the final resolution of the action * * *." Id. at 228.

Similarly, the Court held in Quern v. Jordan, 440 U.S. 332 (1979), that 42 U.S.C. § 1983 does not abrogate state sovereign immunity. In light of the purposes of section 1983, discussed in the materials in Chapter Six, do you think Congress intended to abrogate state sovereign immunity when it enacted section 1983?

The clear statement rule is criticized in both Chemerinsky, *Congress, The Supreme Court, and the Eleventh Amendment: A Comment on the Decisions During the 1988–89 Term,* 39 DePaul L.Rev. 321 (1990) and W. Marshall, *The Eleventh Amendment, Process Federalism and the Clear Statement Rule,* 39 DePaul L.Rev. 345 (1990). Professor Chemerinsky argues that the requirement of unequivocal textual support for congressional intent is justified by neither the sovereign immunity nor the diversity jurisdiction theories of the eleventh amendment. Professor Marshall, on the other hand, suggests that the clear statement rule allows the Court to frustrate congressional intent when it considers state liability unattractive.

One defense of the clear statement rule is found in Cloherty, *Exclusive Jurisdiction and the Eleventh Amendment: Recognizing the Assumption of State Court Availability in the Clear Statement Compromise,* 82 Calif.L.Rev. 1287 (1994). Mr. Cloherty argues that the rule is a *"subconstitutional judicial compromise"* between adherents and critics of *Hans.* Id. at 1307. He also suggests that the rule should not apply in cases of exclusive federal jurisdiction, where no state court is available if the eleventh amendment precludes federal court adjudication. Does the "subconstitutional judicial compromise" theory hold up after *Seminole Tribe?*

11. After *Seminole Tribe,* what is the status of such doctrines as justiciability (discussed in Chapter One) and abstention (discussed in Chapters Eight and Ten)? Can Congress alter them by statute? If so, how is the *Hans* doctrine distinguishable?

STATE IMMUNITY FROM SUIT IN STATE COURT

What about federal claims against a state in *state* court? Although the eleventh amendment does not apply, state law doctrines of sovereign immunity might. Can Congress abrogate that immunity?

The Supreme Court decided a handful of cases arising in state courts prior to *Seminole Tribe*. In Howlett v. Rose, 496 U.S. 356 (1990), the Court held that state sovereign immunity doctrines, which protected *county* officials, could not bar a section 1983 suit brought against them in state court. The Court held that immunity from section 1983 liability could be no broader in state court than it would be in federal court.

In Reich v. Collins, 513 U.S. 106 (1994), the Court held that in some cases even states themselves may be sued without their consent in state court, despite the fact that federal suits would be barred by the eleventh amendment. The Court held that denying a state forum for a suit demanding the recovery of allegedly unconstitutional state taxes itself violates the due process clause, "the sovereign immunity States traditionally enjoy in their own courts notwithstanding." The Court then noted that the eleventh amendment would bar such a suit in federal court. One scholar has interpreted *Reich* to mean that "[i]n large measure, the Eleventh Amendment operates only as a forum selection clause": "state courts must provide adequate relief ... when state officials deprive persons of their property in violation of federal law." Monaghan, *The Sovereign Immunity "Exception,"* 110 Harv.L.Rev. 102, 125 (1996). See also Vazquez, *What is Eleventh Amendment Immunity?* 106 Yale L.J. 1683 (1997). Do you agree? Would it help to know that in 1794, Congress considered and overwhelmingly rejected limiting the proposed eleventh amendment to cases in which the defendant state "shall have previously made provision in their own Courts, whereby such suit may be prosecuted to effect"? See 4 Annals of Congress 30–31 (1794).

For other thoughtful discussions of some of these issues, see Pfander, *Rethinking the Supreme Court's Original Jurisdiction in State-Party Cases*, 82 Calif.L.Rev. 555 (1994); Gordon & Gross, *Justiciability of Federal Claims in State Court*, 59 Notre Dame L.Rev. 1145 (1984); Wolcher, *Sovereign Immunity and the Supremacy Clause: Damages Against States in Their Own Courts for Constitutional Violations*, 69 Calif.L.Rev. 189 (1981).

Think about *Howlett, Reich*, and *Seminole Tribe* as you read the following case:

ALDEN v. MAINE

Supreme Court of the United States, 1999.
527 U.S. 706.

JUSTICE KENNEDY delivered the opinion of the Court.

In 1992, petitioners, a group of probation officers, filed suit against their employer, the State of Maine, in the United States District Court for the District of Maine. The officers alleged the State had violated the overtime provisions of the Fair Labor Standards Act of 1938 (FLSA), and sought compensation and liquidated damages. While the suit was pending, this Court decided Seminole Tribe of Fla. v. Florida, 517 U.S. 44 (1996), which made it clear that Congress lacks power under Article I to abrogate the States' sovereign immunity from suits commenced or prosecuted in the federal courts. Upon consideration of *Seminole Tribe*, the District Court dismissed petitioners' action, and the Court of Appeals affirmed. Petitioners then filed the same action in state court. The state trial court dismissed the suit on the basis of sovereign immunity, and the Maine Supreme Judicial Court affirmed.

The Maine Supreme Judicial Court's decision conflicts with the decision of the Supreme Court of Arkansas, and calls into question the constitutionality of the provisions of the FLSA purporting to authorize private actions against States in their own courts without regard for consent. In light of the importance of the question presented and the conflict between the courts, we granted certiorari. The United States intervened as a petitioner to defend the statute.

We hold that the powers delegated to Congress under Article I of the United States Constitution do not include the power to subject nonconsenting States to private suits for damages in state courts. We decide as well that the State of Maine has not consented to suits for overtime pay and liquidated damages under the FLSA. On these premises we affirm the judgment sustaining dismissal of the suit.

I

The Eleventh Amendment makes explicit reference to the States' immunity from suits "commenced or prosecuted against one of the United States by Citizens of another State, or by Citizens or Subjects of any Foreign State." We have, as a result, sometimes referred to the States' immunity from suit as "Eleventh Amendment immunity." The phrase is convenient shorthand but something of a misnomer, for the sovereign immunity of the States neither derives from nor is limited by the terms of the Eleventh Amendment. Rather, as the Constitution's structure, and its history, and the authoritative interpretations by this Court make clear, the States' immunity from suit is a fundamental aspect of the sovereignty which the States enjoyed before the ratification of the Constitution, and which they retain today (either literally or by virtue of their admission into the Union upon an equal footing with the other States) except as altered by the plan of the Convention or certain constitutional Amendments.

* * *

B

The generation that designed and adopted our federal system considered immunity from private suits central to sovereign dignity. When the Constitution was ratified, it was well established in English law that the Crown could not be sued without consent in its own courts. * * *

* * *

[The Court here repeats the quotations from Hamilton, Madison, Marshall and others cited in *Hans* and *Seminole Tribe* and reproduced supra pp. 346–48.]

* * *

Despite the persuasive assurances of the Constitution's leading advocates and the expressed understanding of the only state conventions to address the issue in explicit terms, this Court held, just five years after the Constitution was adopted, that Article III authorized a private citizen of another State to sue the State of Georgia without its consent. Chisholm v. Georgia, 2 Dall. 419 (1793). * * *

* * *

The Court's decision "fell upon the country with a profound shock." 1 C. Warren, The Supreme Court in United States History 96 (rev. ed. 1926); accord, *Hans, supra,* at 11; Principality of Monaco v. Mississippi, 292 U.S. 313, 325 (1934); *Seminole Tribe,* 517 U.S., at 69. "Newspapers representing a rainbow of opinion protested what they viewed as an unexpected blow to state sovereignty. Others spoke more concretely of prospective raids on state treasuries." D. Currie, The Constitution in Congress: The Federalist Period 1789–1801, p. 196 (1997).

The States, in particular, responded with outrage to the decision. The Massachusetts Legislature, for example, denounced the decision as "repugnant to the first principles of a federal government," and called upon the State's Senators and Representatives to take all necessary steps to "remove any clause or article of the Constitution, which can be construed to imply or justify a decision, that, a State is compellable to answer in any suit by an individual or individuals in any Court of the United States." 15 Papers of Alexander Hamilton 314 (H. Syrett & J. Cooke eds. 1969). Georgia's response was more intemperate: Its House of Representatives passed a bill providing that anyone attempting to enforce the *Chisholm* decision would be " 'guilty of felony and shall suffer death, without benefit of clergy, by being hanged.' " Currie, *supra,* at 196.

* * *

It might be argued that the *Chisholm* decision was a correct interpretation of the constitutional design and that the Eleventh Amendment represented a deviation from the original understanding. This, however, seems unsupportable. First, despite the opinion of Justice Iredell, the majority failed to address either the practice or the understanding that prevailed in the States at the time the Constitution was adopted. Second, even a casual reading of the opinions suggests the majority suspected the decision would be unpopular and surprising. See, e.g., 2 Dall., at 454–455 (Wilson, J.) (condemning the prevailing conception of sovereignty); *id.*, at 468 (Cushing, J.) ("If the Constitution is found inconvenient in practice in this or any other particular, it is well that a regular mode is pointed out for amendment"); *id.*, at 478–479 (Jay, C.J.) ("[T]here is reason to hope that the people of [Georgia] will yet perceive that [sovereign immunity] would not have been consistent with [republican] equality"); cf. *id.*, at 419–420 (attorney for Chisholm) ("I did not want the remonstrance of Georgia, to satisfy me, that the motion, which I have made is unpopular. Before that remonstrance was read, I had learnt from the acts of another State, whose will must be always dear to me, that she too condemned it"). Finally, two Members of the majority acknowledged that the United States might well remain immune from suit despite Article III's grant of jurisdiction over "Controversies to which the United States shall be a Party," see *id.*, at 469 (Cushing, J.); *id.*, at 478 (Jay, C.J.), and, invoking the example of actions to collect debts incurred before the Constitution was adopted, one raised the possibility of "exceptions," suggesting the rule of the case might not "extend to all the demands, and to every kind of action," see *id.*, at 479 (Jay, C.J.). These concessions undercut the crucial premise that either the Constitution's literal text or the principal of popular sovereignty necessarily overrode widespread practice and opinion.

The text and history of the Eleventh Amendment also suggest that Congress acted not to change but to restore the original constitutional design. Although earlier drafts of the Amendment had been phrased as express limits on the judicial power granted in Article III, see, e.g., 3 Annals of Congress 651–652 (1793) ("The Judicial Power of the United States shall not extend to any suits in law or equity, commenced or prosecuted against one of the United States ..."), the adopted text addressed the proper interpretation of that provision of the original Constitution, see U.S. Const., Amdt. 11 ("The Judicial Power of the United States shall not be construed to extend to any suit in law or equity, commenced or prosecuted against one of the United States ..."). By its terms, then, the Eleventh Amendment did not redefine the federal judicial power but instead overruled the Court:

> "This amendment, expressing the will of the ultimate sovereignty of the whole country, superior to all legislatures and all courts, actually reversed the decision of the Supreme Court. It did not in terms prohibit suits by individuals against the States, but declared that the Constitution should not be construed to import any power to authorize the bringing of such suits.... The supreme court had construed

the judicial power as extending to such a suit, and its decision was thus overruled." *Hans*, 134 U.S., at 11.

* * *

Finally, the swiftness and near unanimity with which the Eleventh Amendment was adopted suggest "either that the Court had not captured the original understanding, or that the country had changed its collective mind most rapidly." D. Currie, The Constitution in the Supreme Court: The First Century 18, n. 101 (1985). The more reasonable interpretation, of course, is that regardless of the views of four Justices in *Chisholm*, the country as a whole—which had adopted the Constitution just five years earlier—had not understood the document to strip the States of their immunity from private suits. Cf. Currie, The Constitution in Congress, at 196 ("It is plain that just about everybody in Congress agreed the Supreme Court had misread the Constitution").

Although the dissent attempts to rewrite history to reflect a different original understanding, its evidence is unpersuasive. * * *

* * *

In short, the scanty and equivocal evidence offered by the dissent establishes no more than what is evident from the decision in *Chisholm*—that some members of the founding generation disagreed with Hamilton, Madison, Marshall, Iredell, and the only state conventions formally to address the matter. The events leading to the adoption of the Eleventh Amendment, however, make clear that the individuals who believed the Constitution stripped the States of their immunity from suit were at most a small minority.

Not only do the ratification debates and the events leading to the adoption of the Eleventh Amendment reveal the original understanding of the States' constitutional immunity from suit, they also underscore the importance of sovereign immunity to the founding generation. Simply put, "The Constitution never would have been ratified if the States and their courts were to be stripped of their sovereign authority except as expressly provided by the Constitution itself." Atascadero State Hospital v. Scanlon, 473 U.S. 234, 239, n. 2 (1985).

C

* * * In accordance with this understanding, we have recognized a "presumption that no anomalous and unheard-of proceedings or suits were intended to be raised up by the Constitution—anomalous and unheard of when the constitution was adopted." *Hans*, 134 U.S., at 18. As a consequence, we have looked to "history and experience, and the established order of things" *id.*, at 14, rather than "[a]dhering to the mere letter" of the Eleventh Amendment, *id.*, at 13, in determining the scope of the States' constitutional immunity from suit.

Following this approach, the Court has upheld States' assertions of sovereign immunity in various contexts falling outside the literal text of the Eleventh Amendment. In Hans v. Louisiana, the Court held that sovereign immunity barred a citizen from suing his own State under the federal-question head of jurisdiction. * * * Later decisions rejected similar requests to conform the principle of sovereign immunity to the strict language of the Eleventh Amendment in holding that nonconsenting States are immune from suits brought by federal corporations, Smith v. Reeves, 178 U.S. 436 (1900), foreign nations, *Principality of Monaco*, *supra*, or Indian tribes, Blatchford v. Native Village of Noatak, 501 U.S. 775 (1991), and in concluding that sovereign immunity is a defense to suits in admiralty, though the text of the Eleventh Amendment addresses only suits "in law or equity," Ex parte New York, 256 U.S. 490 (1921).

These holdings reflect a settled doctrinal understanding, consistent with the views of the leading advocates of the Constitution's ratification, that sovereign immunity derives not from the Eleventh Amendment but from the structure of the original Constitution itself. The Eleventh Amendment confirmed rather than established sovereign immunity as a constitutional principle; it follows that the scope of the States' immunity from suit is demarcated not by the text of the Amendment alone but by fundamental postulates implicit in the constitutional design. * * *

* * *

II

In this case we must determine whether Congress has the power, under Article I, to subject nonconsenting States to private suits in their own courts. As the foregoing discussion makes clear, the fact that the Eleventh Amendment by its terms limits only "[t]he Judicial power of the United States" does not resolve the question. To rest on the words of the Amendment alone would be to engage in the type of a historical literalism we have rejected in interpreting the scope of the States' sovereign immunity since the discredited decision in *Chisholm*.

While the constitutional principle of sovereign immunity does pose a bar to federal jurisdiction over suits against nonconsenting States, this is not the only structural basis of sovereign immunity implicit in the constitutional design. Rather, "[t]here is also the postulate that States of the Union, still possessing attributes of sovereignty, shall be immune from suits, without their consent, save where there has been 'a surrender of this immunity in the plan of the convention.' " [*Principality of Monaco*] (quoting The Federalist No. 81, at 487); accord, *Blatchford*, *supra*, at 781; *Seminole Tribe*, *supra*, at 68. This separate and distinct structural principle is not directly related to the scope of the judicial power established by Article III, but inheres in the system of federalism established by the Constitution. In exercising its Article I powers Congress may subject the States to private suits in their own courts only if there is "compelling evidence" that the States were required to surrender this power to Congress pursuant to the constitutional design.

A

* * *

1

* * *

The cases we have cited [culminating in *Seminole Tribe*], of course, came at last to the conclusion that neither the Supremacy Clause nor the enumerated powers of Congress confer authority to abrogate the States' immunity from suit in federal court. The logic of the decisions, however, does not turn on the forum in which the suits were prosecuted but extends to state-court suits as well.

* * *

Although the sovereign immunity of the States derives at least in part from the common-law tradition, the structure and history of the Constitution make clear that the immunity exists today by constitutional design. The dissent has provided no persuasive evidence that the founding generation regarded the States' sovereign immunity as defeasible by federal statute. * * *

* * *

2

There are isolated statements in some of our cases suggesting that the Eleventh Amendment is inapplicable in state courts. See Hilton v. South Carolina Public Railways Comm'n, 502 U.S. 197, 204–205 (1991); Will v. Michigan Dept. of State Police, 491 U.S. 58, 63 (1989); Atascadero State Hospital v. Scanlon, 473 U.S., at 239–240, n. 2; Maine v. Thiboutot, 448 U.S. 1, 9, n. 7 (1980); Nevada v. Hall, 440 U.S., at 418–421. This, of course, is a truism as to the literal terms of the Eleventh Amendment. As we have explained, however, the bare text of the Amendment is not an exhaustive description of the States' constitutional immunity from suit. The cases, furthermore, do not decide the question presented here—whether the States retain immunity from private suits in their own courts notwithstanding an attempted abrogation by the Congress.

Two of the cases discussing state-court immunity may be dismissed out of hand. The footnote digressions in *Atascadero State Hospital* and *Thiboutot* were irrelevant to either opinion's holding or rationale. The discussion in *Will* was also unnecessary to the decision; our holding that 42 U.S.C. § 1983 did not create a cause of action against the States rendered it unnecessary to determine the scope of the States' constitutional immunity from suit in their own courts. Our opinions in *Hilton* and *Hall*, however, require closer attention, for in those cases we sustained suits against States in state courts.

In *Hilton* we held that an injured employee of a state-owned railroad could sue his employer (an arm of the State) in state court under the Federal Employers' Liability Act (FELA). Our decision was "controlled and informed" by *stare decisis*. A generation earlier we had held that because the FELA made clear that all who operated railroads would be subject to suit by injured workers, States that chose to enter the railroad business after the statute's enactment impliedly waived their sovereign immunity from such suits. See *Parden, supra*. Some States had excluded railroad workers from the coverage of their workers' compensation statutes on the assumption that FELA provided adequate protection for those workers. *Hilton, supra*, at 202. Closing the courts to FELA suits against state employers would have dislodged settled expectations and required an extensive legislative response. *Ibid*.

There is language in *Hilton* which gives some support to the position of petitioners here but our decision did not squarely address, much less resolve, the question of Congress' power to abrogate States' immunity from suit in their own courts. The respondent in *Hilton*, the South Carolina Public Railways Commission, neither contested Congress' constitutional authority to subject it to suits for money damages nor raised sovereign immunity as an affirmative defense. Nor was the State's litigation strategy surprising. *Hilton* was litigated and decided in the wake of *Union Gas*, and before this Court's decisions in *New York*, *Printz*, and *Seminole Tribe*. At that time it may have appeared to the State that Congress' power to abrogate its immunity from suit in any court was not limited by the Constitution at all, so long as Congress made its intent sufficiently clear.

Furthermore, our decision in *Parden* was based on concepts of waiver and consent. Although later decisions have undermined the basis of *Parden*'s reasoning, we have not questioned the general proposition that a State may waive its sovereign immunity and consent to suit.

Hilton, then, must be read in light of the doctrinal basis of *Parden*, the issues presented and argued by the parties, and the substantial reliance interests drawn into question by the litigation. When so read, we believe the decision is best understood not as recognizing a congressional power to subject nonconsenting States to private suits in their own courts, nor even as endorsing the constructive waiver theory of *Parden*, but as simply adhering, as a matter of *stare decisis* and presumed historical fact, to the narrow proposition that certain States had consented to be sued by injured workers covered by the FELA, at least in their own courts.

[The Court distinguished *Hall* on the ground that it dealt only with Nevada's amenability to suit in the courts of another state, not in its own courts.]

Petitioners seek support in two additional decisions. In Reich v. Collins, 513 U.S. 106 (1994), we held that, despite its immunity from suit in federal court, a State which holds out what plainly appears to be "a clear and certain" postdeprivation remedy for taxes collected in violation of federal law may not declare, after disputed taxes have been paid in reliance on this remedy, that the remedy does not in fact exist. This case arose in the context of tax-refund litigation, where a State may deprive a taxpayer of all other means of challenging the validity of its tax laws by holding out what appears to be a "clear and certain" postdeprivation remedy. In this context, due process requires the State to provide the remedy it has promised. The obligation arises from the Constitution itself; *Reich* does not speak to the power of Congress to subject States to suits in their own courts.

In Howlett v. Rose, 496 U.S. 356 (1990), we held that a state court could not refuse to hear a § 1983 suit against a school board on the basis of sovereign immunity. The school board was not an arm of the State, however, so it could not assert any constitutional defense of sovereign immunity to which the State would have been entitled. In *Howlett*, then, the only question was "whether a state-law defense of 'sovereign immunity' is available to a school board otherwise subject to suit in a Florida court even though such a defense would not be available if the action had been brought in a federal forum." 496 U.S., at 358–359. The decision did not address the question of Congress' power to compel a state court to entertain an action against a nonconsenting State.

B

Whether Congress has authority under Article I to abrogate a State's immunity from suit in its own courts is, then, a question of first impression. In determining whether there is "compelling evidence" that this derogation of the States' sovereignty is "inherent in the constitutional compact," we continue our discussion of history, practice, precedent, and the structure of the Constitution.

1

We look first to evidence of the original understanding of the Constitution. Petitioners contend that because the ratification debates and the events surrounding the adoption of the Eleventh Amendment focused on the States' immunity from suit in federal courts, the historical record gives no instruction as to the founding generation's intent to preserve the States' immunity from suit in their own courts.

We believe, however, that the founders' silence is best explained by the simple fact that no one, not even the Constitution's most ardent opponents, suggested the document might strip the States of the immunity. In light of the overriding concern regarding the States' war-time debts, together with the well known creativity, foresight, and vivid imagination of the Constitution's opponents, the silence is most instructive. It suggests the sovereign's right to assert immunity from suit in its own courts was a principle so well established that no one conceived it would be altered by the new Constitution.

* * *

The response the Constitution's advocates gave to the argument is also telling. Relying on custom and practice—and, in particular, on the States' immunity from suit in their own courts, see 3 Elliot's Debates, at 555 (Marshall)—they contended that no individual could sue a sovereign without its consent. It is true the point was directed toward the power of the Federal Judiciary, for that was the only question at issue. The logic of the argument, however, applies with even greater force in the context of a suit prosecuted against a sovereign in its own courts, for in this setting, more than any other, sovereign immunity was long established and unquestioned. See *Hall, supra*, at 414.

Similarly, while the Eleventh Amendment by its terms addresses only "the Judicial power of the United States" "nothing in *Chisholm*, the catalyst for the Amendment, suggested the States were not immune from suits in their own courts. The only Justice to address the issue, in fact, was explicit in distinguishing between sovereign immunity in federal court and in a State's own courts." See 2 Dall., at 452 (Blair, J.) ("When sovereigns are sued in their own Courts, such a method [a petition of right] may have been established as the most respectful form of demand; but we are not now in a State–Court; and if sovereignty be an exemption from suit in any other than the sovereign's own Courts, it follows that when a State, by adopting the Constitution, has agreed to be amenable to the judicial power of the United States, she has, in that respect, given up her right of sovereignty").

The language of the Eleventh Amendment, furthermore, was directed toward the only provisions of the constitutional text believed to call the States' immunity from private suits into question. Although Article III expressly contemplated jurisdiction over suits between States and individuals, nothing in the Article or in any other part of the Constitution suggested the States could not assert immunity from private suit in their own courts or that Congress had the power to abrogate sovereign immunity there.

Finally, the Congress which endorsed the Eleventh Amendment rejected language limiting the Amendment's scope to cases where the States had made available a remedy in their own courts. Implicit in the proposal, it is evident, was the premise that the States retained their immunity and the concomitant authority to decide whether to allow private suits against the sovereign in their own courts.

In light of the language of the Constitution and the historical context, it is quite apparent why neither the ratification debates nor the language of the Eleventh Amendment addressed the States' immunity from suit in their own courts. The concerns voiced at the ratifying conventions, the furor raised by *Chisholm*, and the speed and unanimity with which the Amendment was adopted, moreover, underscore the jealous care with which the founding generation sought to preserve the sovereign immunity of the States. To read this history as permitting the inference that the Constitution stripped the States of immunity in their own courts and allowed Congress to subject them to suit there would turn on its head the concern of the founding generation—that Article III might be used to circumvent state-court immunity. In light of the historical record it is difficult to conceive that the Constitution would have been adopted if it had been understood to strip the States of immunity from suit in their own courts and cede to the Federal Government a power to subject nonconsenting States to private suits in these fora.

* * *

4

Our final consideration is whether a congressional power to subject nonconsenting States to private suits in their own courts is consistent with the structure of the Constitution. We look both to the essential principles of federalism and to the special role of the state courts in the constitutional design.

Although the Constitution grants broad powers to Congress, our federalism requires that Congress treat the States in a manner consistent with their status as residuary sovereigns and joint participants in the governance of the Nation. See, e.g., United States v. Lopez, 514 U.S., at 583 (concurring opinion); *Printz*, 521 U.S., at 935; *New York*, 505 U.S., at 188. The founding generation thought it "neither becoming nor convenient that the several States of the Union, invested with that large residuum of sovereignty which had not been delegated to the United States, should be summoned as defendants to answer the complaints of private persons." In re Ayers, 123 U.S., at 505. The principle of sovereign immunity preserved by constitutional design "thus accords the States the respect owed them as members of the federation." *Puerto Rico Aqueduct and Sewer Authority*, 506 U.S., at 146.

Petitioners contend that immunity from suit in federal court suffices to preserve the dignity of the States. Private suits against nonconsenting States, however, present "the indignity of subjecting a State to the coercive process of judicial tribunals at the instance of private parties," In re Ayers, *supra*, at 505; accord, *Seminole Tribe*, 517 U.S., at 58, regardless of the forum. Not only must a State defend or default but also it must face the prospect of being thrust, by federal fiat and against its will, into the disfavored status of a debtor, subject to the power of private citizens to levy on its treasury or perhaps even government buildings or property which the State administers on the public's behalf.

In some ways, of course, a congressional power to authorize private suits against nonconsenting States in their own courts would be even more offensive to state sovereignty than a power to authorize the suits in a federal forum. Although the immunity of one sovereign in the courts of another has often depended in part on comity or agreement, the immunity of a sovereign in its own courts has always been understood to be within the sole control of the sovereign itself. A power to press a State's own courts into federal service to coerce the other branches of the State, furthermore, is the power first to turn the State against itself and ultimately to commandeer the entire political machinery of the State against its will and at the behest of individuals. Such plenary federal control of state governmental processes denigrates the separate sovereignty of the States.

It is unquestioned that the Federal Government retains its own immunity from suit not only in state tribunals but also in its own courts. In light of our constitutional system recognizing the essential sovereignty of the States, we are reluctant to conclude that the States are not entitled to a reciprocal privilege.

Underlying constitutional form are considerations of great substance. Private suits against nonconsenting States—especially suits for money damages—may threaten the financial integrity of the States. It is indisputable that, at the time of the founding, many of the States could have been forced into insolvency but for their immunity from private suits for money damages. Even today, an unlimited congressional power to authorize suits in state court to levy upon the treasuries of the States for compensatory damages, attorney's fees, and even punitive damages could create staggering burdens, giving Congress a power and a leverage over the States that is not contemplated by our constitutional design. The potential national power would pose a severe and notorious danger to the States and their resources.

* * *

Congress cannot abrogate the States' sovereign immunity in federal court; were the rule to be different here, the National Government would wield greater power in the state courts than in its own judicial instrumentalities.

The resulting anomaly cannot be explained by reference to the special role of the state courts in the constitutional design. Although Congress may not require the legislative or executive branches of the States to enact or administer federal regulatory programs, see *Printz, supra*, at 935; *New York*, 505 U.S., at 188, it may require state courts of "adequate and appropriate" jurisdiction, *Testa*, 330 U.S., at 394, "to enforce federal prescriptions, insofar as those prescriptions relat[e] to matters appropriate for the judicial power," *Printz, supra*, at 907. It would be an unprecedented step, however, to infer from the fact that Congress may declare federal law binding and enforceable in state courts the further principle that Congress' authority to pursue federal objectives through the state judiciaries exceeds not only its power to press other branches of the State into its service but even its control over the federal courts themselves. The conclusion would imply that Congress may in some cases act only through instrumentalities of the States. * * *

* * *

We have recognized that Congress may require state courts to hear only "matters appropriate for the judicial power," *Printz*, 521 U.S., at 907. Our sovereign immunity precedents establish that suits against nonconsenting States are not "properly susceptible of litigation in courts," *Hans*, 134 U.S., at 12, and, as a result, that "[t]he 'entire judicial power granted by the Constitution' does not embrace authority to entertain such suits in the absence of the State's consent." *Principali-*

ty of Monaco, 292 U.S., at 329 (quoting *Ex parte New York*, 256 U.S., at 497). We are aware of no constitutional precept that would admit of a congressional power to require state courts to entertain federal suits which are not within the judicial power of the United States and could not be heard in federal courts. * * *

In light of history, practice, precedent, and the structure of the Constitution, we hold that the States retain immunity from private suit in their own courts, an immunity beyond the congressional power to abrogate by Article I legislation.

* * *

JUSTICE SOUTER, with whom JUSTICE STEVENS, JUSTICE GINSBURG, and JUSTICE BREYER join, dissenting.

* * *

Today's issue arises naturally in the aftermath of the decision in *Seminole Tribe*. The Court holds that the Constitution bars an individual suit against a State to enforce a federal statutory right under the Fair Labor Standards Act of 1938 (FLSA), when brought in the State's courts over its objection. In thus complementing its earlier decision, the Court of course confronts the fact that the state forum renders the Eleventh Amendment beside the point, and it has responded by discerning a simpler and more straightforward theory of state sovereign immunity than it found in *Seminole Tribe*: a State's sovereign immunity from all individual suits is a "fundamental aspect" of state sovereignty "confirm[ed]" by the Tenth Amendment. As a consequence, *Seminole Tribe*'s contorted reliance on the Eleventh Amendment and its background was presumably unnecessary; the Tenth would have done the work with an economy that the majority in *Seminole Tribe* would have welcomed. Indeed, if the Court's current reasoning is correct, the Eleventh Amendment itself was unnecessary. Whatever Article III may originally have said about the federal judicial power, the embarrassment to the State of Georgia occasioned by attempts in federal court to enforce the State's war debt could easily have been avoided if only the Court that decided *Chisholm v. Georgia*, 2 Dall. 419 (1793), had understood a State's inherent, Tenth Amendment right to be free of any judicial power, whether the court be state or federal, and whether the cause of action arise under state or federal law.

The sequence of the Court's positions prompts a suspicion of error, *No evidenc[e]* and skepticism is confirmed by scrutiny of the Court's efforts to justify its holding. There is no evidence that the Tenth Amendment constitutionalized a concept of sovereign immunity as inherent in the notion of statehood, and no evidence that any concept of inherent sovereign immunity was understood historically to apply when the sovereign sued was not the font of the law. Nor does the Court fare any better with its subsidiary lines of reasoning, that the state-court action is barred by the scheme of American federalism, a result supposedly confirmed by a history largely devoid of precursors to the action considered here. The

Court's federalism ignores the accepted authority of Congress to bind States under the FLSA and to provide for enforcement of federal rights in state court. The Court's history simply disparages the capacity of the Constitution to order relationships in a Republic that has changed since the founding.

On each point the Court has raised it is mistaken, and I respectfully dissent from its judgment.

I

* * *

* * * The Court's principal rationale for today's result * * * turns on history: was the * * * conception of sovereign immunity as inherent in any notion of an independent State widely held in the United States in the period preceding the ratification of 1788 (or the adoption of the Tenth Amendment in 1791)?

The answer is certainly no. There is almost no evidence that the generation of the Framers thought sovereign immunity was fundamental in the sense of being unalterable. Whether one looks at the period before the framing, to the ratification controversies, or to the early republican era, the evidence is the same. Some Framers thought sovereign immunity was an obsolete royal prerogative inapplicable in a republic; some thought sovereign immunity was a common-law power defeasible, like other common-law rights, by statute; and perhaps a few thought * * * that immunity was inherent in a sovereign because the body that made a law could not logically be bound by it. [That] thinking on the part of a doubtful few will not, however, support the Court's position.

* * *

If the * * * conception of sovereign immunity as an inherent characteristic of sovereignty enjoyed by the States had been broadly accepted at the time of the founding, one would expect to find it reflected somewhere in the five opinions delivered by the Court in Chisholm v. Georgia, 2 Dall. 419 (1793). Yet that view did not appear in any of them. * * *

* * *

* * * Not a single Justice suggested that sovereign immunity was an inherent and indefeasible right of statehood, and neither counsel for Georgia before the Circuit Court, nor Justice Iredell seems even to have conceived the possibility that the new Tenth Amendment produced the equivalent of such a doctrine. This dearth of support makes it very implausible for today's Court to argue that a substantial (let alone a dominant) body of thought at the time of the framing understood sovereign immunity to be an inherent right of statehood, adopted or confirmed by the Tenth Amendment.

The Court's discomfort is evident in its obvious recognition that its * * * Tenth Amendment conception of state sovereign immunity is insupportable if *Chisholm* stands. Hence the Court's attempt to discount the *Chisholm* opinions, an enterprise in which I believe it fails.

The Court, citing Hans v. Louisiana, 134 U.S. 1 (1890), says that the Eleventh Amendment "overruled" *Chisholm*, but the animadversion is beside the point. The significance of *Chisholm* is its indication that in 1788 and 1791 it was not generally assumed (indeed, hardly assumed at all) that a State's sovereign immunity from suit in its own courts was an inherent, and not merely a common-law, advantage. On the contrary, the testimony of five eminent legal minds of the day confirmed that virtually everyone who understood immunity to be legitimate saw it as a common-law prerogative (from which it follows that it was subject to abrogation by Congress as to a matter within Congress's Article I authority).

The Court does no better with its trio of arguments to undercut *Chisholm*'s legitimacy: that the *Chisholm* majority "failed to address either the practice or the understanding that prevailed in the States at the time the Constitution was adopted,"; that "the majority suspected the decision would be unpopular and surprising,"; and that "two Members of the majority acknowledged that the United States might well remain immune from suit despite" Article III. These three claims do not, of course, go to the question whether state sovereign immunity was understood to be "fundamental" or "inherent," but in any case, none of them is convincing.

With respect to the first, Justice Blair in fact did expressly refer to the practice of state sovereign immunity in state court, and acknowledged the petition of right as an appropriate and normal practice. This aside, the Court would have a legitimate point if it could show that the *Chisholm* majority took insufficient account of a body of practice that somehow indicated a widely held absolutist conception of state sovereign immunity untouchable and untouched by the Constitution. But of course it cannot.

As for the second point, it is a remarkable doctrine that would hold anticipation of unpopularity the benchmark of constitutional error. In any event, * * * [the] items [cited by the majority] boil down to the proposition that the Justices knew (as who could not, with such a case before him) that at the ratifying conventions the significance of sovereign immunity had been, as it still was, a matter of dispute. This reality does not detract from, but confirms, the view that the Framers showed no intent to recognize sovereign immunity as an immutably inherent power of the States.

As to the third objection, that two Justices noted that the United States might possess sovereign immunity notwithstanding Article III, * * * Chief Justice Jay thought this possibility was purely practical, not at all legal, and without any implication for state immunity vis-à-vis federal claims. Justice Cushing was so little troubled by the possibility he raised that he wrote, "If this be a necessary consequence, it must be so,"

Chisholm, supra, at 469, and simply suggested a textual reading that might have led to a different consequence.

Nor can the Court make good on its claim that the enactment of the Eleventh Amendment retrospectively reestablished the view that had already been established at the time of the framing (though eluding the perception of all but one Member of the Supreme Court), and hence "acted ... to restore the original constitutional design."[28] There was nothing "established" about the position espoused by Georgia in the effort to repudiate its debts, and the Court's implausible suggestion to the contrary merely echoes the brio of its remark in *Seminole Tribe* that *Chisholm* was "contrary to the well-understood meaning of the Constitution." 517 U.S., at 69 (citing Principality of Monaco v. Mississippi, 292 U.S. 313, 325 (1934)). The fact that *Chisholm* was no conceptual aberration is apparent from the ratification debates and the several state requests to rewrite Article III. There was no received view either of the role this sovereign immunity would play in the circumstances of the case or of a conceptual foundation for immunity doctrine at odds with *Chisholm*'s reading of Article III. As an author on whom the Court relies has it, "there was no unanimity among the Framers that immunity would exist," D. Currie, The Constitution in the Supreme Court: The First Century 19 (1985).

It should not be surprising, then, to realize that although much post-*Chisholm* discussion was disapproving (as the States saw their escape from debt cut off), the decision had champions "every bit as vigorous in defending their interpretation of the Constitution as were those partisans on the other side of the issue." Marcus & Wexler, Suits Against States: Diversity of Opinion In The 1790s, 1993 J. Sup. Ct. Hist. 73, 83; see, e.g., 5 Documentary History of the Supreme Court, *supra,* at 251–52, 252–53, 262–64, 268–69 (newspaper articles supporting holding in *Chisholm*); 5 Documentary History, *supra* n. 17, at 616 (statement of a Committee of Delaware Senate in support of holding in *Chisholm*). The federal citizen-state diversity jurisdiction was settled by the Eleventh Amendment; Article III was not "restored."

* * *

II

The Court's rationale for today's holding based on a conception of sovereign immunity as somehow fundamental to sovereignty or inherent in statehood fails for the lack of any substantial support for such a

---

28. It is interesting to note a case argued in the Supreme Court of Pennsylvania in 1798, in which counsel for the Commonwealth urged a version of the point that the Court makes here, and said that "[t]he language of the amendment, indeed, does not import an alteration of the Constitution, but an authoritative declaration of its true construction." Respublica v. Cobbett, 3 Dall. 467, 472 (Pa.1798). The Court expressly repudiated the historical component of this claim in an opinion by its Chief Justice: "When the judicial law [i.e., the Judiciary Act of 1789] was passed, the opinion prevailed that States might be sued, which by this amendment is settled otherwise." *Id.,* at 475 (M'Kean, C. J.).

conception in the thinking of the founding era. The Court cannot be counted out yet, however, for it has a second line of argument looking * * * to a structural basis in the Constitution's creation of a federal system. Immunity, the Court says, "inheres in the system of federalism established by the Constitution," its "contours [being] determined by the founders' understanding, not by the principles or limitations derived from natural law." Again, "[w]e look both to the essential principles of federalism and to the special role of the state courts in the constitutional design." That is, the Court believes that the federal constitutional structure itself necessitates recognition of some degree of state autonomy broad enough to include sovereign immunity from suit in a State's own courts, regardless of the federal source of the claim asserted against the State. If one were to read the Court's federal structure rationale in isolation from the preceding portions of the opinion, it would appear that the Court's position on state sovereign immunity might have been rested entirely on federalism alone. If it had been, however, I would still be in dissent, for the Court's argument that state court sovereign immunity on federal questions is inherent in the very concept of federal structure is demonstrably mistaken.

A

The National Constitution formally and finally repudiated the received political wisdom that a system of multiple sovereignties constituted the "great solecism of an imperium in imperio," cf. Bailyn, The Ideological Origins of the American Revolution, at 223. Once "the atom of sovereignty" had been split, U.S. Term Limits, Inc. v. Thornton, 514 U.S. 779, 838 (1995) (Kennedy, J., concurring), the general scheme of delegated sovereignty as between the two component governments of the federal system was clear, and was succinctly stated by Chief Justice Marshall: "In America, the powers of sovereignty are divided between the government of the Union, and those of the States. They are each sovereign, with respect to the objects committed to it, and neither sovereign with respect to the objects committed to the other." McCulloch v. Maryland, 4 Wheat. 316, 410 (1819).

Hence the flaw in the Court's appeal to federalism. The State of Maine is not sovereign with respect to the national objective of the FLSA.[33] It is not the authority that promulgated the FLSA, on which the right of action in this case depends. That authority is the United States acting through the Congress, whose legislative power under Article I of the Constitution to extend FLSA coverage to state employees has already

---

33. It is therefore sheer circularity for the Court to talk of the "anomaly," that would arise if a State could be sued on federal law in its own courts, when it may not be sued under federal law in federal court, Seminole Tribe, supra. The short and sufficient answer is that the anomaly is the Court's own creation: the Eleventh Amendment was never intended to bar federal-question suits against the States in federal court. The anomaly is that Seminole Tribe, an opinion purportedly grounded in the Eleventh Amendment, should now be used as a lever to argue for state sovereign immunity in state courts, to which the Eleventh Amendment by its terms does not apply.

been decided, see Garcia v. San Antonio Metropolitan Transit Authority, 469 U.S. 528 (1985), and is not contested here.

Nor can it be argued that because the State of Maine creates its own court system, it has authority to decide what sorts of claims may be entertained there, and thus in effect to control the right of action in this case. Maine has created state courts of general jurisdiction; once it has done so, the Supremacy Clause of the Constitution, Art. VI, cl. 2, which requires state courts to enforce federal law and state-court judges to be bound by it, requires the Maine courts to entertain this federal cause of action. Maine has advanced no " 'valid excuse,' " Howlett v. Rose, 496 U.S. 356, 369 (1990) (quoting Douglas v. New York, N. H. & H. R. Co., 279 U.S. 377, 387–88 (1929)), for its courts' refusal to hear federal-law claims in which Maine is a defendant, and sovereign immunity cannot be that excuse, simply because the State is not sovereign with respect to the subject of the claim against it. The Court's insistence that the federal structure bars Congress from making States susceptible to suit in their own courts is, then, plain mistake.

B

It is symptomatic of the weakness of the structural notion proffered by the Court that it seeks to buttress the argument by relying on "the dignity and respect afforded a State, which the immunity is designed to protect" and by invoking the many demands on a State's fisc. Apparently beguiled by Gilded Era language describing private suits against States as " 'neither becoming nor convenient,' " the Court calls "immunity from private suits central to sovereign dignity," and assumes that this "dignity" is a quality easily translated from the person of the King to the participatory abstraction of a republican State. The thoroughly anomalous character of this appeal to dignity is obvious from a reading of Blackstone's description of royal dignity, which he sets out as a premise of his discussion of sovereignty:

> "First, then, of the royal dignity. Under every monarchical establishment, it is necessary to distinguish the prince from his subjects.... The law therefore ascribes to the king ... certain attributes of a great and transcendent nature; by which the people are led to consider him in the light of a superior being, and to pay him that awful respect, which may enable him with greater ease to carry on the business of government. This is what I understand by the royal dignity, the several branches of which we will now proceed to examine." 1 Blackstone *241.

It would be hard to imagine anything more inimical to the republican conception, which rests on the understanding of its citizens precisely that the government is not above them, but of them, its actions being governed by law just like their own. Whatever justification there may be for an American government's immunity from private suit, it is not dignity.

* * *

III

If neither theory nor structure can supply the basis for the Court's conceptions of sovereign immunity and federalism, then perhaps history might. The Court apparently believes that because state courts have not historically entertained Commerce Clause-based federal-law claims against the States, such an innovation carries a presumption of unconstitutionality. At the outset, it has to be noted that this approach assumes a more cohesive record than history affords. In Hilton v. South Carolina Public Railways Comm'n, 502 U.S. 197 (1991) (Kennedy, J.), a case the Court labors mightily to distinguish, we held that a state-owned railroad could be sued in state court under the Federal Employers' Liability Act, notwithstanding the lack of an express congressional statement, because " 'the Eleventh Amendment does not apply in state courts.' " *Hilton*, *supra*, at 205 (quoting Will v. Michigan Dept. of State Police, 491 U.S. 58, 63–64 (1989)). But even if the record were less unkempt, the problem with arguing from historical practice in this case is that past practice, even if unbroken, provides no basis for demanding preservation when the conditions on which the practice depended have changed in a constitutionally relevant way.

It was at one time, though perhaps not from the framing, believed that "Congress' authority to regulate the States under the Commerce Clause" was limited by "certain underlying elements of political sovereignty ... deemed essential to the States' 'separate and independent existence.' " See *Garcia*, 469 U.S., at 547–548 (quoting Lane County v. Oregon, 7 Wall. 71, 76 (1869)). On this belief, the preordained balance between state and federal sovereignty was understood to trump the terms of Article I and preclude Congress from subjecting States to federal law on certain subjects. (From time to time, wage and hour regulation has been counted among those subjects.) As a consequence it was rare, if not unknown, for state courts to confront the situation in which federal law enacted under the Commerce Clause provided the authority for a private right of action against a State in state court. The question of state immunity from a Commerce Clause-based federal-law suit in state court thus tended not to arise for the simple reason that acts of Congress authorizing such suits did not exist.

Today, however, in light of *Garcia*, *supra* (overruling National League of Cities v. Usery, 426 U.S. 833 (1976)), the law is settled that federal legislation enacted under the Commerce Clause may bind the States without having to satisfy a test of undue incursion into state sovereignty. * * * Because the commerce power is no longer thought to be circumscribed, the dearth of prior private federal claims entertained against the States in state courts does not tell us anything, and reflects nothing but an earlier and less expansive application of the commerce power.

Least of all is it to the point for the Court to suggest that because the Framers would be surprised to find States subjected to a federal-law suit in their own courts under the commerce power, the suit must be prohibited by the Constitution. The Framers' intentions and expectations count so far as they point to the meaning of the Constitution's text or the fair implications of its structure, but they do not hover over the instrument to veto any application of its principles to a world that the Framers could not have anticipated.

If the Framers would be surprised to see States subjected to suit in their own courts under the commerce power, they would be astonished by the reach of Congress under the Commerce Clause generally. The proliferation of Government, State and Federal, would amaze the Framers, and the administrative state with its reams of regulations would leave them rubbing their eyes. But the Framers' surprise at, say, the FLSA, or the Federal Communications Commission, or the Federal Reserve Board is no threat to the constitutionality of any one of them, for a very fundamental reason:

> "[W]hen we are dealing with words that also are a constituent act, like the Constitution of the United States, we must realize that they have called into life a being the development of which could not have been foreseen completely by the most gifted of its begetters. It was enough for them to realize or to hope that they had created an organism; it has taken a century and has cost their successors much sweat and blood to prove that they created a nation. The case before us must be considered in the light of our whole experience and not merely in that of what was said a hundred years ago." Missouri v. Holland, 252 U.S. 416, 433 (1920) (Holmes, J.).

* * *

IV

* * *

B

The Court might respond to the charge that in practice it has vitiated *Garcia* by insisting, as counsel for Maine argued, that the United States may bring suit in federal court against a State for damages under the FLSA, on the authority of United States v. Texas, 143 U.S. 621, 644–645 (1892). It is true, of course, that the FLSA does authorize the Secretary of Labor to file suit seeking damages, but unless Congress plans a significant expansion of the National Government's litigating forces to provide a lawyer whenever private litigation is barred by today's decision and *Seminole Tribe*, the allusion to enforcement of private rights by the National Government is probably not much more than whimsy. Facing reality, Congress specifically found, as long ago as 1974, "that the enforcement capability of the Secretary of Labor is not alone sufficient to provide redress in all or even a substantial portion of the situations where compliance is not forthcoming voluntarily." S. Rep. No. 93–690, p. 27 (1974). One hopes that such voluntary compliance will prove more popular than it has in Maine, for there is no reason today to suspect that enforcement by the Secretary of Labor alone would likely prove adequate to assure compliance with this federal law in the multifarious circumstances of some 4.7 million employees of the 50 States of the Union.

The point is not that the difficulties of enforcement should drive the Court's decision, but simply that where Congress has created a private right to damages, it is implausible to claim that enforcement by a public authority without any incentive beyond its general enforcement power will ever afford the private right a traditionally adequate remedy. No one would think the remedy adequate if private tort claims against a State could only be brought by the National Government: the tradition of private enforcement, as old as the common law itself, is the benchmark. But wage claims have a lineage of private enforcement just as ancient, and a claim under the FLSA is a claim for wages due on work performed. Denying private enforcement of an FLSA claim is thus on par with closing the courthouse door to state tort victims unaccompanied by a lawyer from Washington.

So there is much irony in the Court's profession that it grounds its opinion on a deeply rooted historical tradition of sovereign immunity, when the Court abandons a principle nearly as inveterate, and much closer to the hearts of the Framers: that where there is a right, there must be a remedy. * * * The generation of the Framers thought the principle so crucial that several States put it into their constitutions. And when Chief Justice Marshall asked about Marbury, "If he has a right, and that right has been violated, do the laws of his country afford him a remedy?," Marbury v. Madison, 1 Cranch 137, 162 (1803), the question was rhetorical, and the answer clear:

> "The very essence of civil liberty certainly consists in the right of every individual to claim the protection of the laws, whenever he receives an injury. One of the first duties of government is to afford that protection. In Great Britain the king himself is sued in the respectful form of a petition, and he never fails to comply with the judgment of his court." *Id.*, at 163.

Yet today the Court has no qualms about saying frankly that the federal right to damages afforded by Congress under the FLSA cannot create a concomitant private remedy. * * *

V

* * * The resemblance of today's state sovereign immunity to the *Lochner* era's industrial due process is striking. The Court began this century by imputing immutable constitutional status to a conception of economic self-reliance that was never true to industrial life and grew insistently fictional with the years, and the Court has chosen to close the century by conferring like status on a conception of state sovereign immunity that is true neither to history nor to the structure of the Constitution. I expect the Court's late essay into immunity doctrine will prove the equal of its earlier experiment in laissez-faire, the one being as unrealistic as the other, as indefensible, and probably as fleeting.

Notes

1. Is the Court in *Alden* interpreting the tenth amendment, the eleventh amendment, or some other part of the Constitution? Is the majority's approach to constitutional interpretation in this case consistent with the usual approach of Justices Scalia and Thomas (both of whom joined the majority opinion)? See Young, Alden v. Maine *and the Jurisprudence of Structure*, 41 Wm. & Mary L.Rev. 1601 (2000).

2. How does the question raised in *Alden* differ from the one raised in *Seminole Tribe*? Is the result in *Alden* required by the holding in *Seminole Tribe*? Think about how much of the majority's argument depends on the reasoning that whatever limits apply to congressional power to abrogate immunity in the federal courts must necessarily also limit congressional power with regard to state courts. Is that the only argument in favor of *Alden*, or might *Alden* be defensible even if *Seminole Tribe* had gone the other way? Construct an argument that *Alden* would be *more* defensible if *Seminole Tribe* had gone the other way.

3. Notice the use of similar historical evidence and arguments in both *Seminole Tribe* and *Alden*. In which case does the historical evidence seem more directly relevant? Which case do you find more persuasive? Do you find the historical evidence or the federalism arguments more important in each case? For a further argument that sovereign immunity is not a *constitutional* doctrine, and that both *Seminole Tribe* and *Alden* were incorrectly decided, see Chemerinsky, *Against Sovereign Immunity*, 53 Stan.L.Rev. 1201 (2001).

4. Does the majority adequately distinguish earlier precedent, such as *Reich*, *Howlett*, and *Hilton*? Construct an argument that the Court considers the enforcement of federal statutory rights less important than the enforcement of federal constitutional rights. (Hint: You might want to think about the *Ex parte Young* portion of *Seminole Tribe*, about the difference between *Reich* and *Alden*, and about the Court's language in *Pennhurst*.)

5. The majority analogizes this suit to the one in *Chisholm*. Is the payment of money damages for violation of a federal law analogous to the payment of a debt owed by reason of a contract?

6. Is the majority correct that this decision will not encourage states to violate federal law? How would you advise a state that wishes to save money and is thinking about doing so by paying its employees less than the minimum wage? What if an underpaid state employee comes to you and asks whether there is any way to force the state to pay minimum wage, or to recover past underpayments? How would you advise Congress if it wishes to ensure that states will obey federal laws?

7. Consider the sovereign immunity decisions from *Seminole Tribe* to *Garrett*. How are state interests protected by these cases? Might Congress, frustrated in its attempt to subject states to suits, find other ways to intrude on state sovereignty, including direct regulation and conditional spending? See Young, *State Sovereign Immunity and the Future of Federalism*, 1999 Sup.Ct.Rev. 1. If plaintiffs are forced to resort to seeking injunctive relief (under *Ex parte Young*) rather than damages, might that actually be *more* intrusive on state sovereignty? See Karlan, *The Irony of Immunity: The*

Eleventh Amendment, Irreparable Injury, and Section 1983, 53 Stan.L.Rev. 1311 (2001).

8. For some of the extensive scholarship on *Alden*, see Siegel, *Congress's Power to Authorize Suits Against States*, 68 Geo.Wash.L.Rev. 44 (1999); Hartley, *The* Alden *Trilogy: Praise and Protest*, 23 Harv.J.Law & Pub.Pol'y 323 (1999); Symposium: State Sovereign Immunity and the Eleventh Amendment, 75 Notre Dame L.Rev. 817 (2000); Symposium: Federalism After *Alden*, 31 Rutgers L.J. 631 (2000); Vazquez, *Sovereign Immunity, Due Process, and the* Alden *Trilogy*, 109 Yale L.J. 1927 (2000); Brown, *Weathering Constitutional Change*, 2000 Ill.L.Rev. 1091; Hill, *In Defense of Our Law of Sovereign Immunity*, 42 B.C.L.Rev. 485 (2001); Caminker, *Judicial Solicitude for State Dignity*, 574 Annals (AAPSS) 81 (2001); Strasser, Chisholm, *The Eleventh Amendment, and Sovereign Immunity: On* Alden's *Return to Confederation Principles*, 28 Fla.St.U.L.Rev. 605 (2001); Weingberg, *Of Sovereignty and Union: The Legends of* Alden, 76 Notre Dame L.Rev. 1113 (2001); Gibson, *Congressional Authority to Induce Waivers of Sovereign Immunity: The Conditional Spending Power (and Beyond)*, 29 Hastings Constit.L.Q. 439 (2002). For a general critique of the notion of sovereign immunity as inconsistent with the rule of law, see D. Doernberg, Sovereign Immunity or the Rule of Law: The New Federalism's Choice (2005).

Chapter 8

ABSTENTION

even though the court has jurisdiction it should not exercise it

§ 1. THE VARIOUS ABSTENTION DOCTRINES

RAILROAD COMMISSION OF TEXAS v. PULLMAN CO.
Supreme Court of the United States, 1941.
312 U.S. 496.

Mr. Justice Frankfurter delivered the opinion of the Court.

In those sections of Texas where the local passenger traffic is slight, trains carry but one sleeping car. These trains, unlike trains having two or more sleepers, are without a Pullman conductor; the sleeper is in charge of a porter who is subject to the train conductor's control. As is well known, porters on Pullmans are colored and conductors are white. Addressing itself to this situation, the Texas Railroad Commission after due hearing ordered that "no sleeping car shall be operated on any line of railroad in the State of Texas . . . unless such cars are continuously in the charge of an employee . . . having the rank and position of Pullman conductor." Thereupon, the Pullman Company and the railroads affected brought this action in a federal district court to enjoin the Commission's order. Pullman porters were permitted to intervene as complainants, and Pullman conductors entered the litigation in support of the order. Three judges having been convened, the court enjoined enforcement of the order. From this decree, the case came here directly.

The Pullman Company and the railroads assailed the order as unauthorized by Texas law as well as violative of the Equal Protection, the Due Process and the Commerce Clauses of the Constitution. The intervening porters adopted these objections but mainly objected to the order as a discrimination against Negroes in violation of the Fourteenth Amendment.

The complaint of the Pullman porters undoubtedly tendered a substantial constitutional issue. It is more than substantial. It touches a sensitive area of social policy upon which the federal courts ought not to enter unless no alternative to its adjudication is open. Such constitution-

446

al adjudication plainly can be avoided if a definitive ruling on the state issue would terminate the controversy. It is therefore our duty to turn to a consideration of questions under Texas law.

The Commission found justification for its order in a Texas statute which we quote in the margin.[1] It is common ground that if the order is within the Commission's authority its subject matter must be included in the Commission's power to prevent "unjust discrimination . . . and to prevent any and all other abuses" in the conduct of railroads. Whether arrangements pertaining to the staffs of Pullman cars are covered by the Texas concept of "discrimination" is far from clear. What practices of the railroads may be deemed to be "abuses" subject to the Commission's correction is equally doubtful. Reading the Texas statutes and the Texas decisions as outsiders without special competence in Texas law, we would have little confidence in our independent judgment regarding the application of that law to the present situation. The lower court did deny that the Texas statutes sustained the Commission's assertion of power. And this represents the view of an able and experienced circuit judge of the circuit which includes Texas and of two capable district judges trained in Texas law. Had we or they no choice in the matter but to decide what is the law of the state, we should hesitate long before rejecting their forecast of Texas law. But no matter how seasoned the judgment of the district court may be, it cannot escape being a forecast rather than a determination. The last word on the meaning of Article 6445 of the Texas Civil Statutes, and therefore the last word on the statutory authority of the Railroad Commission in this case, belongs neither to us nor to the district court but to the supreme court of Texas. In this situation a federal court of equity is asked to decide an issue by making a tentative answer which may be displaced tomorrow by a state adjudication. The reign of law is hardly promoted if an unnecessary ruling of a federal court is thus supplanted by a controlling decision of a state court. The resources of equity are equal to an adjustment that will avoid the waste of a tentative decision as well as the friction of a premature constitutional adjudication.

An appeal to the chancellor, as we had occasion to recall only the other day, is an appeal to the "exercise of the sound discretion, which

---

1. Vernon's Anno. Texas Civil Statutes, Article 6445:

"Power and authority are hereby conferred upon the Railroad Commission of Texas over all railroads, and suburban, belt and terminal railroads, and over all public wharves, docks, piers, elevators, warehouses, sheds, tracks and other property used in connection therewith in this State, and over all persons, associations and corporations, private or municipal, owning or operating such railroad, wharf, dock, pier, elevator, warehouse, shed, track or other property to fix, and it is hereby made the duty of the said Commission to adopt all necessary rates, charges and regulations, to govern and regulate such railroads, persons, associations and corporations, and to correct abuses and prevent unjust discrimination in the rates, charges and tolls of such railroads, persons, associations and corporations, and to fix division of rates, charges and regulations between railroads and other utilities and common carriers where a division is proper and correct, and to prevent any and all other abuses in the conduct of their business and to do and perform such other duties and details in connection therewith as may be provided by law."

guides the determination of courts of equity." The history of equity jurisdiction is the history of regard for public consequences in employing the extraordinary remedy of the injunction. * * * Few public interests have a higher claim upon the discretion of a federal chancellor than the avoidance of needless friction with state policies, whether the policy relates to the enforcement of the criminal law, Fenner v. Boykin, 271 U.S. 240; Spielman Motor Co. v. Dodge, 295 U.S. 89; or the administration of a specialized scheme for liquidating embarrassed business enterprises, Pennsylvania v. Williams, 294 U.S. 176; or the final authority of a state court to interpret doubtful regulatory laws of the state, Gilchrist v. Interborough Co., 279 U.S. 159; cf. Hawks v. Hamill, 288 U.S. 52, 61. These cases reflect a doctrine of abstention appropriate to our federal system whereby the federal courts, "exercising a wise discretion," restrain their authority because of "scrupulous regard for the rightful independence of the state governments" and for the smooth working of the federal judiciary. See Cavanaugh v. Looney, 248 U.S. 453, 457; Di Giovanni v. Camden Ins. Assn., 296 U.S. 64, 73. This use of equitable powers is a contribution of the courts in furthering the harmonious relation between state and federal authority without the need of rigorous congressional restriction of those powers. * * *

Regard for these important considerations of policy in the administration of federal equity jurisdiction is decisive here. If there was no warrant in state law for the Commission's assumption of authority there is an end of the litigation; the constitutional issue does not arise. The law of Texas appears to furnish easy and ample means for determining the Commission's authority. Article 6453 of the Texas Civil Statutes gives a review of such an order in the state courts. Or, if there are difficulties in the way of this procedure of which we have not been apprised, the issue of state law may be settled by appropriate action on the part of the State to enforce obedience to the order. In the absence of any showing that these obvious methods for securing a definitive ruling in the state courts cannot be pursued with full protection of the constitutional claim, the district court should exercise its wise discretion by staying its hands.

We therefore remand the cause to the district court, with directions to retain the bill pending a determination of proceedings, to be brought with reasonable promptness, in the state court in conformity with this opinion. Compare Atlas Ins. Co. v. W. I. Southern, Inc., 306 U.S. 563, 573, and cases cited.

MR. JUSTICE ROBERTS took no part in the consideration or decision of this case.

Notes

1. **Abstention and Separation of Powers.** To what extent should the form of judge-made abstention recognized in *Pullman*—or any other form of judge-made abstention—be deemed an improper judicial usurpation of legislative authority, in violation of the principle of separation of powers?

Consider the argument made in Redish, *Abstention, Separation of Powers, and the Limits of the Judicial Function*, 94 Yale L.J. 71, 72–75 (1984):

> Presumably no one would deny that a federal court cannot legitimately invalidate a federal statute solely because of its unwise policies, or because it would make judges work harder than they believe they should, or because the judges themselves would not have enacted such legislation. Such behavior by the judiciary would amount to a blatant—and indefensible—usurpation of legislative authority. At most, the judiciary possesses authority to overturn federal legislation because it is unconstitutional, not because the judiciary considers it unwise. Yet, in a sense, the abstention doctrines amount to such usurpation.

> * * *

> The burden of production in the abstention debate has been improperly reversed. * * * Those who argue for * * * the continuation or expansion of existing "partial" abstention raise various arguments founded in either social policy, federalism, or judicial efficiency. They usually develop their arguments as if we were attempting to establish, on a totally clean slate, the wisest system of judicial federalism, in total disregard of the detailed and carefully balanced existing statutory network. * * *

> The central difficulty with the argument for abstention is the forum to which it has been directed. Nothing, of course, prevents those who believe in the fungibility of state and federal courts as protectors of federal rights from convincing Congress to repeal or substantially modify the broad jurisdiction it has vested in the federal courts. Generally, however, the arguments have been directed not to the legislative arena, but instead to the judicial forum, which is somehow believed to possess authority to alter or overrule the legislative directives.

> * * *

> One could persuasively argue that whatever social harms may flow from federal judicial enforcement of federal rights against state entities cannot—short of a finding of unconstitutionality—justify judicial abandonment of federal legislation.

> * * *

> [T]he interests of federalism would be sufficiently protected by existing statutorily dictated abstention, by long established equitable limitations, and by the contours and limits of the substantive federal right being enforced.

What responses can be made to the separation-of-powers critique of judge-made abstention? Consider the merits of the following possibilities:

a. Congress' failure to overrule judge-made abstention constitutes an implied legislative approval of the practice. For a response, see Redish, 94 Yale L.J. at 80–84.

b. At least in the case of *Pullman* abstention, legislative authority is not thwarted, because the practice results only in a *delay* of federal adjudication, rather than a complete abdication of federal judicial authority. See 94 Yale L.J. at 90.

c.   The practice of judge-made abstention is justified by the reasonable desire—one with which Congress would presumably concur if it had given the question any thought—to avoid so drastically negative an impact on federalism and state institutions that would result from the doctrines' abandonment. For a response, see 94 Yale L.J. at 90–98.

d.   Federal judicial abstention in section 1983 cases does not undermine the congressional will as embodied in that statute, because the state courts remain available to adjudicate and enforce those federal rights.

Consider also the argument made in Wells, *Why Professor Redish is Wrong About Abstention*, 19 Ga.L.Rev. 1097, 1097 (1985):

> A * * * basic flaw in the institutional argument against abstention is its reliance on a faulty premise: that Congress is responsible for the modern federal cause of action under 42 U.S.C.A. § 1983 against state actors to redress constitutional violations. Once this premise is accepted, it is easy to show that the abstention rules violate Congress' intent. The problem with the institutional argument is that the statute was never intended to create such a broad cause of action [as it has been construed to do]. * * * Abstention is more accurately viewed as a judge-made forum rule for a judge-made cause of action and thus can withstand the separation-of-powers attack mounted against it. * * *

There exists some debate about whether Professor Wells' criticisms of the judicial construction of section 1983 are valid. See Monroe v. Pape, 365 U.S. 167 (1961). Of course, if Professor Wells is incorrect in his critique, then his response to the separation-of-powers attack on abstention fails. However, assuming that his critique of section 1983's interpretation is accurate, does it logically follow that, once the Court establishes substantive law purporting to represent an interpretation of a federal statute, it has the authority to decline to enforce the statute, as interpreted? Could Professor Wells be accused of arguing that two wrongs make a right?

Professor David Shapiro has argued that "suggestions of an overriding obligation, subject only and at most to a few narrowly drawn exceptions, are far too grudging in their recognition of judicial discretion in matters of jurisdiction." Shapiro, *Jurisdiction and Discretion*, 60 N.Y.U.L.Rev. 543, 545 (1985). In support, he argues "that the existence of this discretion is much more pervasive than is generally realized, and that it has ancient and honorable roots at common law as well as in equity. Thus, far from amounting to judicial usurpation, open acknowledgment of reasoned discretion is wholly consistent with the Anglo–American legal tradition."

Is this argument persuasive? Does the fact that a practice has proceeded over a long period of time necessarily establish that that practice is consistent with the nation's democratic structure?

Keeping in mind the language of 28 U.S.C. § 1331, compare these analyses to the argument that "issues not controlled by the Constitution * * * are to be resolved on the basis of judicial policy assessment only to the extent the representative branches have not already made that policy choice through legislative action." Redish, *Federal Common Law, Political Legiti-*

macy, and the Interpretive Process: An "Institutionalist" Perspective, 83 Nw.U.L.Rev. 761, 768 (1989).

2. Can you articulate the rationale for *Pullman* abstention? Is the concern simply that federal courts are not as equipped as state courts to interpret state law? If so, is this principle in conflict with the accepted practice of having federal courts interpret and apply state law in diversity actions? Cf. Meredith v. City of Winter Haven, 320 U.S. 228 (1943). Could the purpose of *Pullman* abstention simply be concern about possible federal court disruption of state programs and policies? For *Pullman* abstention to apply, must a federal constitutional issue be present? Why?

3. Can you foresee any difficulties that are likely to arise in the use of *Pullman* abstention? Cf. Field, *The Abstention Doctrine Today,* 125 U.Pa. L.Rev. 590, 591 (1977) ("From the outset * * * *Pullman* abstention has proved far from ideal in practice.").

4. Consider that Erie R.R. v. Tompkins, 304 U.S. 64 (1938)(holding that federal courts should apply state law in diversity cases) was decided only three years before *Pullman.* Has *Erie's* maturation changed anything? See Rehnquist, *Taking Comity Seriously: How to Neutralize the Abstention Doctrine,* 46 Stan.L.Rev. 1049, 1096–98 (1994).

5. *Pullman* abstention is said to apply when the relevant state law is uncertain. What if the state law is challenged on the very ground that it is unconstitutionally vague? Under the logic of *Pullman,* should a federal court automatically abstain when such a challenge is made? See Baggett v. Bullitt, 377 U.S. 360, 375–376 (1964); Procunier v. Martinez, 416 U.S. 396, 401 (1974). What if, though the law on its face is unambiguous, the state courts have not yet construed it? See City of Houston v. Hill, 482 U.S. 451 (1987): "[W]hen a statute is not ambiguous, there is no need to abstain even if state courts have never interpreted the statute."

6. To what extent should use of *Pullman* abstention depend upon the availability of a viable opportunity to raise the relevant issues in state court? What if state law requires the plaintiff to raise the claim solely in an administrative proceeding? Cf. Lister v. Lucey, 575 F.2d 1325 (7th Cir.1978); Vickers v. Trainor, 546 F.2d 739 (7th Cir.1976); Committee for Public Education & Religious Liberty v. Rockefeller, 322 F.Supp. 678 (S.D.N.Y. 1971).

7. What if, in the course of a federal constitutional challenge to a state statute, the meaning of the state statute in question is not uncertain, but there exists a provision of the state constitution which might be construed to invalidate the challenged state law? Is your answer influenced by the fact that most, if not all state constitutions contain a clause roughly equivalent or identical to the due process clause of the fourteenth amendment? Consider the dissenting opinion of Chief Justice Burger in Wisconsin v. Constantineau, 400 U.S. 433, 439 (1971). A Wisconsin statute authorizing local police chiefs, without notice or hearing, to post notices in all retail liquor stores announcing that a particular individual was not allowed to purchase or receive liquor for one year was challenged on constitutional grounds in federal court. Because the state statute was not ambiguous, the majority rejected a plea for abstention. The Chief Justice, while acknowledging that the law was probably unconstitutional, suggested that it was "a very odd

business to strike down a state statute, on the books for almost 40 years, without any opportunity for the state courts to dispose of the problem either under the Wisconsin Constitution or the U.S. Constitution." Note that he did not limit his suggested role for the state court to interpretation of the *state* Constitution. Is the Chief Justice's analysis compelled by the *Pullman* doctrine? What role would the lower federal courts play under such an arrangement?

8.   Compare Chief Justice Burger's dissent in *Constantineau* with Reetz v. Bozanich, 397 U.S. 82 (1970). A challenge was made to fishing laws and regulations in Alaska under both the fourteenth amendment and a provision of the Alaska Constitution dealing specifically with fishing. The Court ordered abstention in part because the state constitutional provision might prove to be "the nub of the whole controversy." Chief Justice Burger could see no difference between *Constantineau* and *Reetz*. Can you? Cf. Fornaris v. Ridge Tool Co., 400 U.S. 41 (1970) (per curiam).

9.   With *Reetz* compare Harris County Commissioners Court v. Moore, 420 U.S. 77 (1975), which concerned an equal protection challenge to a redistricting plan for the County's justice of the peace precincts. Speaking for the Court, Justice Marshall chose to abstain because of the uncertain applicability of provisions of the state constitution regulating the manner of selection and removal of justices of the peace. In so doing he distinguished *Constantineau*:

> In Wisconsin v. Constantineau * * * we declined to order abstention where the federal due process claim was not complicated by an unresolved state-law question, even though plaintiffs might have sought relief under a similar provision of the state constitution. But where the challenged statute is part of an integrated scheme of related constitutional provisions, statutes, and regulations, and where the scheme as a whole calls for clarifying interpretation by the state courts, we have regularly required the district courts to abstain. 420 U.S. at 84–85 n. 8.

Justice Marshall argued that the same considerations relevant to *Pullman* abstention were applicable. Do you agree?

HAWAII HOUSING AUTHORITY v. MIDKIFF

Supreme Court of the United States, 1984.
467 U.S. 229.

JUSTICE O'CONNOR delivered the opinion of the Court.

The Fifth Amendment of the United States Constitution provides, in pertinent part, that "private property [shall not] be taken for public use, without just compensation." These cases present the question whether the Public Use Clause of that Amendment, made applicable to the States through the Fourteenth Amendment, prohibits the State of Hawaii from taking, with just compensation, title in real property from lessors and transferring it to lessees in order to reduce the concentration of ownership of fees simple in the State. We conclude that it does not.

I

A

The Hawaiian Islands were originally settled by Polynesian immigrants from the eastern Pacific. These settlers developed an economy around a feudal land tenure system in which one island high chief, the ali'i nui, controlled the land and assigned it for development to certain subchiefs. The subchiefs would then reassign the land to other lower ranking chiefs, who would administer the land and govern the farmers and other tenants working it. All land was held at the will of the ali'i nui and eventually had to be returned to his trust. There was no private ownership of land.

Beginning in the early 1800's, Hawaiian leaders and American settlers repeatedly attempted to divide the lands of the kingdom among the crown, the chiefs, and the common people. These efforts proved largely unsuccessful, however, and the land remained in the hands of a few. In the mid–1960's, after extensive hearings, the Hawaii Legislature discovered that, while the State and Federal Governments owned almost 49% of the State's land, another 47% was in the hands of only 72 private landowners. The legislature further found that 18 landholders, with tracts of 21,000 acres or more, owned more than 40% of this land and that, on Oahu, the most urbanized of the islands, 22 landowners owned 72.5% of the fee simple titles. The legislature concluded that concentrated land ownership was responsible for skewing the State's residential fee simple market, inflating land prices, and injuring the public tranquility and welfare.

To redress these problems, the legislature decided to compel the large landowners to break up their estates. The legislature considered requiring large landowners to sell lands which they were leasing to homeowners. However, the landowners strongly resisted this scheme, pointing out the significant federal tax liabilities they would incur. Indeed, the landowners claimed that the federal tax laws were the primary reason they previously had chosen to lease, and not sell, their lands. Therefore, to accommodate the needs of both lessors and lessees, the Hawaii Legislature enacted the Land Reform Act of 1967 (Act), Haw.Rev.Stat., ch. 516, which created a mechanism for condemning residential tracts and for transferring ownership of the condemned fees simple to existing lessees. By condemning the land in question, the Hawaii Legislature intended to make the land sales involuntary, thereby making the federal tax consequences less severe while still facilitating the redistribution of fees simple.

Under the Act's condemnation scheme, tenants living on single-family residential lots within developmental tracts at least five acres in size are entitled to ask the Hawaii Housing Authority (HHA) to condemn the property on which they live. When 25 eligible tenants, or tenants on half the lots in the tract, whichever is less, file appropriate applications, the Act authorizes HHA to hold a public hearing to determine whether acquisition by the State of all or part of the tract will "effectuate the public purposes" of the Act. If HHA finds that these public purposes will be served, it is authorized to designate some or all of the lots in the tract for acquisition. It then acquires, at prices set either by condemnation trial or by negotiation between lessors and lessees, the former fee owners' full "right, title, and interest" in the land.

After compensation has been set, HHA may sell the land titles to tenants who have applied for fee simple ownership. HHA is authorized to lend these tenants up to 90% of the purchase price, and it may condition final transfer on a right of first refusal for the first 10 years following sale. If HHA does not sell the lot to the tenant residing there, it may lease the lot or sell it to someone else, provided that public notice has been given. However, HHA may not sell to any one purchaser, or lease to any one tenant, more than one lot, and it may not operate for profit. In practice, funds to satisfy the condemnation awards have been supplied entirely by lessees. While the Act authorizes HHA to issue bonds and appropriate funds for acquisition, no bonds have issued and HHA has not supplied any funds for condemned lots.

B

In April 1977, HHA held a public hearing concerning the proposed acquisition of some of appellees' lands. HHA made the statutorily required finding that acquisition of appellees' lands would effectuate the public purposes of the Act. Then, in October 1978, it directed appellees to negotiate with certain lessees concerning the sale of the designated properties. Those negotiations failed, and HHA subsequently ordered appellees to submit to compulsory arbitration.

Rather than comply with the compulsory arbitration order, appellees filed suit, in February 1979, in United States District Court, asking that the Act be declared unconstitutional and that its enforcement be enjoined. The District Court temporarily restrained the State from proceeding against appellees' estates. Three months later, while declaring the compulsory arbitration and compensation formulae provisions of the Act unconstitutional, the District Court refused preliminarily to enjoin appellants from conducting the statutory designation and condemnation proceedings. Finally, in December 1979, it granted partial summary judgment to appellants, holding the remaining portion of the Act constitutional under the Public Use Clause. The District Court found that the Act's goals were within the bounds of the State's police powers and that the means the legislature had chosen to serve those goals were not arbitrary, capricious, or selected in bad faith.

The Court of Appeals for the Ninth Circuit reversed. First, the Court of Appeals decided that the District Court had permissibly chosen not to abstain from the exercise of its jurisdiction. Then, the Court of Appeals determined that the Hawaii Land Reform Act could not pass the requisite judicial scrutiny of the Public Use Clause. It found that the transfers contemplated by the Act were unlike those of takings previously held to constitute "public uses" by this Court. The court further determined that the public purposes offered by the Hawaii Legislature were not deserving of judicial deference. The court concluded that the Act was simply "a naked attempt on the part of the state of Hawaii to take the private property of A and transfer it to B solely for B's private use and benefit." One judge dissented.

* * * We now reverse.

II

We begin with the question whether the District Court abused its discretion in not abstaining from the exercise of its jurisdiction. The appellants have suggested as one alternative that perhaps abstention was required under the standards announced in Railroad Comm'n v. Pullman Co., 312 U.S. 496 (1941), and Younger v. Harris, 401 U.S. 37 (1971). We do not believe that abstention was required.

A

In Railroad Comm'n v. Pullman Co., supra, this Court held that federal courts should abstain from decision when difficult and unsettled questions of state law must be resolved before a substantial federal constitutional question can be decided. By abstaining in such cases, federal courts will avoid both unnecessary adjudication of federal questions and "needless friction with state policies. . . ." Id., 312 U.S., at 500. However, federal courts need not abstain on *Pullman* grounds when a state statute is not "fairly subject to an interpretation which will render unnecessary" the federal constitutional question. See Harman v. Forssenius, 380 U.S. 528, 535 (1965). *Pullman* abstention is limited to uncertain questions of state law because "[a]bstention from the exercise of federal jurisdiction is the exception, not the rule." Colorado River Water Conservation Dist. v. United States, 424 U.S. 800, 813 (1976).

In this case, there is no uncertain question of state law. The Hawaii Land Reform Act unambiguously provides that "[t]he use of the power . . . to condemn . . . is for a public use and purpose." Haw.Rev.Stat. § 516–83(a)(12) (1977); see also §§ 516–83(a)(10), (11), (13). There is no other provision of the Act—or, for that matter, of Hawaii law—which would suggest that § 516–83(a)(12) does not mean exactly what it says. Since "the naked question, uncomplicated by [ambiguous language], is whether the Act on its face is unconstitutional," Wisconsin v. Constantineau, 400 U.S. 433, 439 (1971), abstention from federal jurisdiction is not required.

The dissenting judge in the Court of Appeals suggested that, perhaps, the state courts could make resolution of the federal constitutional questions unnecessary by their construction of the Act. In the abstract, of course, such possibilities always exist. But the relevant inquiry is not whether there is a bare, though unlikely, possibility that state courts *might* render adjudication of the federal question unnecessary. Rather, "[w]e have frequently emphasized that abstention is not to be ordered unless the statute is of an uncertain nature, and is obviously susceptible of a limiting construction." Zwickler v. Koota, 389 U.S. 241, 251, and n. 14 (1967). These statutes are not of an uncertain nature and have no reasonable limiting construction. Therefore, *Pullman* abstention is unnecessary.

[Justice MARSHALL took no part in the consideration or decision of this case.]

Notes

1. How does the formulation of the abstention doctrine in *Midkiff* differ from the formulation in *Pullman*? Under the *Midkiff* formulation, should the Court have abstained in *Pullman* itself?

2. In Brockett v. Spokane Arcades, Inc., 472 U.S. 491 (1985), the Supreme Court's majority held that use of the word "lust" in a state's obscenity statute in its definition of "prurient interest" was not constitutionally overbroad. In a separate concurring opinion, Justice O'Connor, joined by Justice Rehnquist and Chief Justice Burger, argued that the Court should not have reached the constitutional merits, but instead should have invoked *Pullman* abstention. She relied in part on *Midkiff:* "Attention to the policies underlying abstention makes clear that in the circumstances of this case, a federal court should await a definitive construction by a state court rather than precipitously indulging a facial challenge to the constitutional validity of a state statute. There can be no doubt that a state obscenity statute concerns important state interests. * * * The nature of the overbreadth claim advanced by appellees suggest that abstention was required because the Washington statute is 'fairly subject to an interpretation which will render unnecessary or substantially modify the federal constitutional question.' Harman v. Forssenius, 380 U.S. 528, 535 (1965)." She rejected the lower Court's view that *Pullman* abstention should "almost never" apply when a state statute is challenged on First Amendment grounds. "This Court has never endorsed such a proposition," she asserted.

OTHER TYPES OF ABSTENTION

In addition to *Pullman*, the Court has authorized abstention in a variety of other circumstances. One form of abstention derives from the Court's decision in Louisiana Power & Light Co. v. City of Thibodaux, 360 U.S. 25 (1959). The city had filed a petition for expropriation in Louisiana state court, seeking to obtain the company's property. The company, a Florida corporation, removed the case to federal district court on the basis of diversity of citizenship. The district court stayed the proceedings so that the state statute on which the city's expropriation order was based could be construed by the Louisiana Supreme Court. The Supreme Court affirmed the district court's decision to abstain, noting that the "statute has never been interpreted, in respect to a situation like that before the [district court], by the Louisiana courts," and recognizing that "[i]nformed local courts may find meaning not discernible to the outsider." Id. at 30.

The basis for abstention in *Thibodaux* is unclear. The Court was not attempting to avoid or moot a delicate constitutional question, since none was involved. It is not likely that the mere presence of an uncertain issue of state law was sufficient for the Court to authorize abstention; such a rationale would have substantially undermined long established Supreme Court doctrine, and the *Thibodaux* Court did not suggest that it was doing any such thing.

Justice Frankfurter's opinion for the Court does suggest that certain unique factors existed which might be thought to limit the abstention authorized in the case. The most significant fact is that the case involved eminent domain, a proceeding that, according to Justice Frankfurter, "is of a special and peculiar nature," and "intimately involved with sovereign prerogative" Id. at 28. He therefore concluded:

> The special nature of eminent domain justifies a district judge, when his familiarity with the problem of local law so counsels him, to ascertain the meaning of a disputed state statute from the only tribunal empowered to speak definitively—the courts of the state under whose statute eminent domain is sought to be exercised— rather than himself make a dubious and tentative forecast. Id. at 29.

In another decision handed down the same day, however, the Court made clear that *both* an unclear state law and a connection to state sovereign prerogative were necessary to justify abstention. In County of Allegheny v. Frank Mashuda Co., 360 U.S. 185 (1959), the Board of County Commissioners had employed the state's eminent domain statutes to appropriate certain property owned by the company for the claimed purpose of improving and enlarging the Pittsburgh Airport. After condemnation, it became known that the County had leased the property for use by a private business. Under the law of Pennsylvania, it was clearly established that eminent domain could not be employed for private use. Suit was filed in federal court on the basis of diversity of citizenship, seeking the ouster of both the County and the lessees, and damages or injunctive relief. The district court dismissed the case in order to avoid interference with a state condemnation proceeding.

Although in *Thibodaux* the Court had emphasized the discretion of the district judge to choose to abstain, the Court in *Mashuda* reversed the district court's decision to dismiss. Justice Brennan, speaking for the Court, concluded that "adjudication of the issues in this case by the District Court would present no hazard of disrupting federal-state relations," id. at 189–90, because "[t]he only question for decision is [a] purely factual [one]." Id. at 190. The clearest explanation of the distinction between *Mashuda* and *Thibodaux* is found in Justice Stewart's concurring opinion in *Thibodaux*:

> This case is totally unlike *County of Allegheny v. Mashuda Co.* except for the coincidence that both cases involve eminent domain proceedings. * * * The Court ... holds in [*Mashuda*] that, since the controlling state law is clear and only factual issues need be re-

solved, there is no occasion in the interest of justice to refrain from prompt adjudication. 360 U.S. at 31.

Perhaps the most appropriate synthesis of the two decisions, then, is that eminent domain will be a sufficient basis for abstention, but only if there exists a significant, unclear question of state law. Unfortunately, subsequent Supreme Court statements on the scope of *Thibodaux* abstention have done little to reduce the confusion. In *Harris County Commissioners Court v. Moore*, 420 U.S. 77 (1975), for example, the Court appeared to expand *Thibodaux* well beyond its eminent domain context by noting that abstention had been employed in cases such as *Thibodaux* "when the state-law questions have concerned matters peculiarly within the province of the local courts," id. at 83–84, a characterization which can most charitably be called unhelpful. In a recent restatement of the abstention doctrine in *Colorado River Water Conservation District v. United States*, 424 U.S. 800 (1976), the Court stated that the scope of the eminent domain power of municipalities in controversy in *Thibodaux* was a "difficult questio[n] of state law bearing on policy problems of substantial public import whose importance transcends the result in the case then at bar." Id. at 814. Again, the Court's statement leaves considerable room for debate over the outer limits of this category of abstention.

The Court has most recently described the difference between *Thibodaux* and *Mashuda* in different terms:

> Unlike in *Thibodaux*, however, the District Court in [*Mashuda*] had not merely stayed adjudication of the federal action pending the resolution of an issue in state court, but rather had dismissed the federal action altogether. Based in large measure on this distinction, we reversed the District Court's order. Quackenbush v. Allstate Insurance Co., 517 U.S. 706, 721 (1996).

Is this a persuasive distinction?

What interest lies behind *Thibodaux* abstention? Is it state sovereignty? If so, how broadly should that interest be defined? If it goes beyond eminent domain, will it undermine diversity jurisdiction? Even if there are no satisfactory answers to these questions, *Thibodaux* abstention may be less problematic than some other types of abstention, as long as it is limited to cases within diversity jurisdiction. Consider the questions of parity and judicial federalism raised in Chapter Four: might they have more force with regard to federal question jurisdiction than diversity jurisdiction? On the other hand, consider that *Thibodaux* itself involved a dispute between a Louisiana city and a Florida corporation; did the corporation rightly distrust the Louisiana courts? In any case, does the Court's narrowing of the contours of federal jurisdiction in diversity cases undermine the congressional determination to grant diversity jurisdiction?

Another form of abstention is associated with the Supreme Court's 1943 decision in Burford v. Sun Oil Co., 319 U.S. 315 (1943). The case concerned a challenge to a Texas Railroad Commission order granting

Burford a permit to drill oil wells. Though jurisdiction was premised partially on the basis of diversity of citizenship, Sun Oil also contested the Commission's order on due process grounds. The Court, in an opinion by Justice Black, concluded that abstention on the part of the federal court was appropriate. In reaching this conclusion, the Court described in detail the administrative and judicial network established by the Texas legislature for regulating the production of oil and gas, emphasizing both the importance of the subject of regulation to the state's domestic interests and the delicate relation between the Commission and the state courts which reviewed its orders. Federal court review of the Commission's work, said Justice Black, had resulted in "[t]he very 'confusion' which the Texas legislature and Supreme Court feared might result from review by many state courts of the Railroad Commission's orders * * *." Id. at 327.

Commentators have on occasion referred to *Burford* as an example of "administrative" abstention, and at least one subsequent Supreme Court opinion supports this characterization. See, e.g., Field, *Abstention in Constitutional Cases: The Scope of the* Pullman *Abstention Doctrine*, 122 U.Pa.L.Rev.1071, 1154 (1974); *Mashuda*, 360 U.S. at 189; England v. Louisiana State Board of Medical Examiners, 375 U.S. 411, 415 n. 5 (1964) [infra p. 473]. But another commentator has stated that "*Burford* may be said to be simply an example of the broad equitable principle of comity—leaving to a state the determination of its own policies." Liebenthal, *A Dialogue on* England: *The* England *Case, Its Effect on the Abstention Doctrine, and Some Suggested Solutions*, 18 W. Res. L. Rev. 157, 161 (1966). See also Woolhandler & Collins, *The Article III Jury*, 87 Va.L.Rev. 587, 680–84 (2001) (suggesting that Justice Black used abstention as a method of reducing federal judicial control over states). The Court itself has more recently characterized *Burford* as a case in which "exercise of federal review of the question in a case and in similar cases would be disruptive of state efforts to establish a coherent policy with respect to a matter of substantial public concern." Colorado River Water Conservation District v. United States, 424 U.S. 800, 814 (1976) [infra p. 461].

In a more recent decision where *Burford* abstention was considered, the Court decided that the doctrine was inapplicable. In Zablocki v. Redhail, 434 U.S. 374 (1978), the Court held that a Wisconsin statute providing that a Wisconsin resident under a legal obligation to support children not in his or her custody may not marry without first obtaining court permission violated the fourteenth amendment's equal protection clause. Appellant argued that, in light of *Burford*, the district court should have abstained out of "regard for the independence of state governments in carrying out their domestic policy." 434 U.S. at 380 n. 5. The Court responded that "[u]nlike *Burford* ... this case does not involve complex issues of state law, resolution of which would be 'disruptive of state efforts to establish a coherent policy with respect to a matter of substantial public concern.'" Id. The Court added that "there is, of course, no doctrine requiring abstention merely because resolution

of a federal question may result in the overturning of a state policy." Id.
Most recently, the Court has held that even in the rare cases in which
Burford abstention is appropriate, the federal court should stay, rather
than dismiss, the action. Quackenbush v. Allstate Insurance Co., 517
U.S. 706 (1996). For an unusual recent example of *Burford* abstention,
see Chiropractic America v. Lavecchia, 180 F.3d 99 (3d Cir.1999).

en where applied stay other than dismiss

There is some question about the nature and degree of uncertainty
which must be found in the state law before *Burford* abstention will
apply. Justice Black's opinion contains several references to the difficulty
in interpreting the applicable state law and the tentative nature of any
federal interpretation of it. However, in contrast to the situation in
Thibodaux, the Court's concern was not as much with the uncertainty of
the specific state law issue presented in that particular case as with the
broad state law quagmire in which the federal courts would find themselves if they ventured into the general area.

Note also that *Burford*, unlike *Thibodaux*, involved a federal constitutional question. Does this make *Burford* abstention more problematic?
Consider the following argument:

> *Burford* presented a constitutional question. Though the Court has
> let nothing turn on this factor in developing the two forms of
> abstention, the issue arguably should have received closer scrutiny.
> While ideally it might be more appropriate to have state courts wade
> through complex state administrative schemes because of their
> presumed expertise in and sympathy towards state policies, the
> opposite could be said to be true of the interest in having the federal
> judiciary adjudicate issues of federal law. Federal courts might be
> well advised to take into account a state's legitimate interest in
> resolving its own problems, but it does not automatically follow that
> they should willingly abdicate their responsibility to interpret feder-
> al law and protect federal rights. M. Redish, Federal Jurisdiction:
> Tensions in the Allocation of Judicial Power 294 (2d ed. 1990).

importance of having fed const'l question?

See also Colorado River Water Conservation District v. United States,
424 U.S. 800, 814 n. 21 (1976) ("the presence of a federal basis for
jurisdiction may raise the level of justification needed for abstention").
Might this fact also explain why Justice Frankfurter, who wrote the
opinions in both *Pullman* and *Thibodaux*, dissented in *Burford*? For
further discussion of *Burford* abstention, see Woolhandler & Collins,
Judicial Federalism and the Administrative States, 87 Calif.L.Rev. 613
(1999); Young, *Federal Court Abstention and State Administrative Law
from* Burford *to* Ankendbrandt: *Fifty Years of Judicial Federalism Under*
Burford v. Sun Oil Co. *and Kindred Doctrines*, 42 DePaul L.Rev. 859
(1993).

The Court has also required federal courts to abstain in another
situation. In Scott v. Germano, 381 U.S. 407 (1965), the Court vacated a
lower court decision invalidating an Illinois statute apportioning the
Illinois legislature. The lower court had held that the state apportionment scheme violated the "one person, one vote" rule of Reynolds v.

Sims, 377 U.S. 533 (1964). After the order was issued, the Illinois supreme court also invalidated the apportionment statute, and ordered the state legislature to enact a constitutionally valid scheme. The Supreme Court held in *Germano* that the federal district court should have stayed any further proceedings, pending the efforts of the Illinois legislature to enact such legislation. The Court has more recently described this type of abstention as a requirement that "federal judges * * * defer consideration of disputes involving redistricting where the State, through its legislative or judicial branch, has begun to address that highly political task itself." Growe v. Emison, 507 U.S. 25, 33 (1993). See also Lawyer v. Department of Justice, 521 U.S. 567 (1997). A federal court is not required to abstain if it becomes clear that the state will be unable to successfully reapportion in time for an upcoming election. Branch v. Smith, 538 U.S. 254 (2003). Is reapportionment abstention more or less appropriate than *Burford* or *Thibodaux* abstention?

Finally, one other type of abstention deserves a brief mention. When a federal court is asked to rule on whether a tribal court has jurisdiction, the Supreme Court has said that "considerations of comity" require the federal court to abstain until after the tribal court "has had a full opportunity to determine its own jurisdiction." National Farmers Union Ins. Cos. v. Crow Tribe, 471 U.S. 845 (1985); see also Iowa Mut. Ins. Co. v. LaPlante, 480 U.S. 9 (1987). In El Paso Natural Gas Co. v. Neztsosie, 526 U.S. 473 (1999), the Court held that this abstention doctrine does not apply to suits covered by the Price–Anderson Act, in which "Congress expressed an unmistakable preference for a federal forum."

§ 2. PARALLEL STATE AND FEDERAL PROCEEDINGS

COLORADO RIVER WATER CONSERVATION DISTRICT v. UNITED STATES

Supreme Court of the United States, 1976.
424 U.S. 800.

MR. JUSTICE BRENNAN delivered the opinion of the Court.

The McCarran Amendment, 66 Stat. 560, 43 U.S.C. § 666, provides that "consent is hereby given to join the United States as a defendant in any suit (1) for the adjudication of rights to the use of water of a river system or other source, or (2) for the administration of such rights, where it appears that the United States is the owner of or is in the process of acquiring water rights by appropriation under State law, by purchase, by exchange, or otherwise, and the United States is a necessary party to such suit." The questions presented by this case concern the effect of the McCarran Amendment upon the jurisdiction of the federal district courts under 28 U.S.C. § 1345 over suits for determination of water rights brought by the United States as trustee for certain Indian tribes and as owner of various non-Indian Government claims.[1]

1. The McCarran Amendment (also known as the McCarran Water Rights Suit Act), 43 U.S.C. § 666, as codified, provides in full text:

I

It is probable that no problem of the Southwest section of the Nation is more critical than that of scarcity of water. As southwestern populations have grown, conflicting claims to this scarce resource have increased. To meet these claims, several Southwestern States have established elaborate procedures for allocation of water and adjudication of conflicting claims to that resource. In 1969, Colorado enacted its Water Rights Determination and Administration Act in an effort to revamp its legal procedures for determining claims to water within the State.

Under the Colorado Act, the State is divided into seven Water Divisions, each Division encompassing one or more entire drainage basins for the larger rivers in Colorado. Adjudication of water claims within each Division occurs on a continuous basis. Each month, Water Referees in each Division rule on applications for water rights filed within the preceding five months or refer those applications to the Water Judge of their Division. Every six months, the Water Judge passes on referred applications and contested decisions by Referees. A State Engineer and engineers for each Division are responsible for the administration and distribution of the waters of the State according to the determinations in each Division.

Colorado applies the doctrine of prior appropriation in establishing rights to the use of water. Under that doctrine, one acquires a right to water by diverting it from its natural source and applying it to some beneficial use. Continued beneficial use of the water is required in order to maintain the right. In periods of shortage, priority among confirmed rights is determined according to the date of initial diversion.

The reserved rights of the United States extend to Indian reservations, Winters v. United States, 207 U.S. 564 (1908), and other federal

"(a) Consent is hereby given to join the United States as a defendant in any suit (1) for the adjudication of rights to the use of water of a river system or other source, or (2) for the administration of such rights, where it appears that the United States is the owner of or is in the process of acquiring water rights by appropriation under State law, by purchase, by exchange, or otherwise, and the United States is a necessary party to such suit. The United States, when a party to any such suit, shall (1) be deemed to have waived any right to plead that the State laws are inapplicable or that the United States is not amenable thereto by reason of its sovereignty, and (2) shall be subject to the judgments, orders, and decrees of the court having jurisdiction, and may obtain review thereof, in the same manner and to the same extent as a private individual under like circumstances: *Provided*, That no judgment for costs shall

be entered against the United States in any such suit.

"(b) Summons or other process in any such suit shall be served upon the Attorney General or his designated representative.

"(c) Nothing in this Act shall be construed as authorizing the joinder of the United States in any suit or controversy in the Supreme Court of the United States involving the right of States to the use of the water of any interstate stream."

Title 28 U.S.C. § 1345 provides:

"Except as otherwise provided by Act of Congress, the district courts shall have original jurisdiction of all civil actions, suits or proceedings commenced by the United States, or by any agency or officer thereof expressly authorized to sue by Act of Congress."

lands, such as national parks and forests, Arizona v. California, 373 U.S. 546 (1963). The reserved rights claimed by the United States in this case affect waters within Colorado Water Division No. 7. On November 14, 1972, the Government instituted this suit in the United States District Court for the District of Colorado, invoking the court's jurisdiction under 28 U.S.C. § 1345. The District Court is located in Denver, some 300 miles from Division 7. The suit, against some 1,000 water users, sought declaration of the Government's rights to waters in certain rivers and their tributaries located in Division 7. In the suit, the Government asserted reserved rights on its own behalf and on behalf of certain Indian tribes, as well as rights based on state law. It sought appointment of a water master to administer any waters decreed to the United States. Prior to institution of this suit, the Government had pursued adjudication of non-Indian reserved rights and other water claims based on state law in Water Divisions 4, 5, and 6, and the Government continues to participate fully in those Divisions.

Shortly after the federal suit was commenced, one of the defendants in that suit filed an application in the state court for Division 7, seeking an order directing service of process on the United States in order to make it a party to proceedings in Division 7 for the purpose of adjudicating all of the Government's claims, both state and federal. On January 3, 1973, the United States was served pursuant to authority of the McCarran Amendment. Several defendants and intervenors in the federal proceeding then filed a motion in the District Court to dismiss on the ground that under the Amendment, the court was without jurisdiction to determine federal water rights. Without deciding the jurisdictional question, the District Court, on June 21, 1973, granted the motion in an unreported oral opinion stating that the doctrine of abstention required deference to the proceedings in Division 7. On appeal, the Court of Appeals for the Tenth Circuit reversed, United States v. Akin, 504 F.2d 115 (1974), holding that the suit of the United States was within district-court jurisdiction under 28 U.S.C. § 1345, and that abstention was inappropriate. We granted certiorari to consider the important questions of whether the McCarran Amendment terminated jurisdiction of federal courts to adjudicate federal water rights and whether, if that jurisdiction was not terminated, the District Court's dismissal in this case was nevertheless appropriate. 421 U.S. 946. We reverse.

* * *

III

We turn * * * to the question whether this suit * * * was properly dismissed in view of the concurrent state proceedings in Division 7.

A

First, we consider whether the McCarran Amendment provided consent to determine federal reserved rights held on behalf of Indians in state court. * * *

* * *

Not only the Amendment's language, but also its underlying policy, dictates a construction including Indian rights in its provisions. * * *

* * *

B

Next, we consider whether the District Court's dismissal was appropriate under the doctrine of abstention. We hold that the dismissal cannot be supported under that doctrine in any of its forms.

Abstention from the exercise of federal jurisdiction is the exception, not the rule. "The doctrine of abstention, under which a District Court may decline to exercise or postpone the exercise of its jurisdiction, is an extraordinary and narrow exception to the duty of a District Court to adjudicate a controversy properly before it. Abdication of the obligation to decide cases can be justified under this doctrine only in the exceptional circumstances where the order to the parties to repair to the State court would clearly serve an important countervailing interest." County of Allegheny v. Frank Mashuda Co., 360 U.S. 185, 188–189 (1959). "[I]t was never a doctrine of equity that a federal court should exercise its judicial discretion to dismiss a suit merely because a State court could entertain it." Alabama Pub. Serv. Comm'n v. Southern R. Co., 341 U.S. 341, 361 (1951) (Frankfurter, J., concurring in result). Our decisions have confined the circumstances appropriate for abstention to three general categories.

(a) Abstention is appropriate "in cases presenting a federal constitutional issue which might be mooted or presented in a different posture by a state court determination of pertinent state law." County of Allegheny v. Frank Mashuda Co., supra, at 189. See, e.g., Lake Carriers' Assn. v. MacMullan, 406 U.S. 498 (1972); United Gas Pipe Line Co. v. Ideal Cement Co., 369 U.S. 134 (1962); Railroad Comm'n of Texas v. Pullman Co., 312 U.S. 496 (1941). This case, however, presents no federal constitutional issue for decision.

(b) Abstention is also appropriate where there have been presented difficult questions of state law bearing on policy problems of substantial public import whose importance transcends the result in the case then at bar. Louisiana Power & Light Co. v. City of Thibodaux, 360 U.S. 25 (1959), for example, involved such a question. In particular, the concern there was with the scope of the eminent domain power of municipalities under state law. See also Kaiser Steel Corp. v. W. S. Ranch Co., 391 U.S. 593 (1968); Hawks v. Hamill, 288 U.S. 52 (1933). In some cases, however, the state question itself need not be determinative of state policy. It is enough that exercise of federal review of the question in a case and in similar cases would be disruptive of state efforts to establish a coherent policy with respect to a matter of substantial public concern. In Burford v. Sun Oil Co., 319 U.S. 315 (1943); for example, the Court held that a suit seeking review of the reasonableness under Texas state law of a state commission's permit to drill oil wells should have been dismissed by the District Court. The reasonableness of the permit in that case was not of transcendent importance, but review of reasonableness by the federal courts in that and future cases, where the State had established its own elaborate review system for dealing with the geological complexities of oil and gas fields, would have had an impermissibly disruptive effect on state policy for the management of those fields. See also Alabama Pub. Serv. Comm'n v. Southern R. Co., supra.[21]

The present case clearly does not fall within this second category of abstention. While state claims are involved in the case, the state law to be applied appears to be settled. No questions bearing on state policy are presented for decision. Nor will decision of the state claims impair efforts to implement state policy as in *Burford*. To be sure, the federal claims that are involved in the case go to the establishment of water rights which may conflict with similar rights based on state law. But the mere potential for conflict in the results of adjudications, does not, without more, warrant staying exercise of federal jurisdiction. See Meredith v. Winter Haven, 320 U.S. 228(1943); Kline v. Burke Constr. Co., 260 U.S. 226 (1922); McClellan v. Carland, 217 U.S. 268 (1910). The potential conflict here, involving state claims and federal claims, would not be such as to impair impermissibly the State's effort to effect its policy respecting the allocation of state waters. Nor would exercise of federal jurisdiction here interrupt any such efforts by restraining the exercise of authority vested in state officers. See Pennsylvania v. Williams, 294 U.S. 176 (1935); Hawks v. Hamill, supra.

(c) Finally, abstention is appropriate where, absent bad faith, harassment, or a patently invalid state statute, federal jurisdiction has been invoked for the purpose of restraining state criminal proceedings, Younger v. Harris, 401 U.S. 37 (1971); Douglas v. City of Jeannette, 319 U.S. 157 (1943); state nuisance proceedings antecedent to a criminal prosecution, which are directed at obtaining the closure of places exhibiting obscene films, Huffman v. Pursue, Ltd., 420 U.S. 592 (1975); or collection of state taxes, Great Lakes Dredge & Dock Co. v. Huffman, 319 U.S. 293 (1943). Like the previous two categories, this category also does not include this case. We deal here neither with a criminal proceeding, nor such a nuisance proceeding, nor a tax collection. We also do not

---

21. We note that Burford v. Sun Oil Co., and Alabama Pub. Serv. Comm'n v. Southern R. Co., differ from Louisiana Power & Light Co. v. City of Thibodaux, and County of Allegheny v. Frank Mashuda Co., in that the former two cases, unlike the latter two, raised colorable constitutional claims and were therefore brought under federal-question, as well as diversity, jurisdiction. While abstention in *Burford* and *Alabama Pub. Serv.* had the effect of avoiding a federal constitutional issue, the opinions indicate that this was not an additional ground for abstention in those cases. See Alabama Pub. Serv. Comm'n v. Southern R. Co., 341 U.S., at 344; Burford v. Sun Oil Co., 319 U.S., at 334; H. Hart & H. Wechsler, The Federal Courts and the Federal System 1005 (2d ed. 1973) ("The two groups of cases share at least one common characteristic: the Pullman purpose of avoiding the necessity for federal constitutional adjudication is not relevant"). We have held, of course, that the opportunity to avoid decision of a constitutional question does not alone justify abstention by a federal court. See Harman v. Forssenius, 380 U.S. 528 (1965); Baggett v. Bullitt, 377 U.S. 360 (1964). Indeed, the presence of a federal basis for jurisdiction may raise the level of justification needed for abstention. See Burford v. Sun Oil Co., supra, 319 U.S., at 318 n. 5; Hawks v. Hamill, 288 U.S., at 61, 53 S.Ct., at 243.

deal with an attempt to restrain such actions or to seek a declaratory judgment as to the validity of a state criminal law under which criminal proceedings are pending in a state court.

C

Although this case falls within none of the abstention categories, there are principles unrelated to considerations of proper constitutional adjudication and regard for federal-state relations which govern in situations involving the contemporaneous exercise of concurrent jurisdictions, either by federal courts or by state and federal courts. These principles rest on considerations of "[w]ise judicial administration, giving regard to conservation of judicial resources and comprehensive disposition of litigation." Kerotest Mfg. Co. v. C–O–Two Fire Equipment Co., 342 U.S. 180, 183 (1952). Generally, as between state and federal courts, the rule is that "the pendency of an action in the state court is no bar to proceedings concerning the same matter in the Federal court having jurisdiction. . . ." McClellan v. Carland, supra, 217 U.S. at 282. See Donovan v. City of Dallas, 377 U.S. 408 (1964). As between federal district courts, however, though no precise rule has evolved, the general principle is to avoid duplicative litigation. See Kerotest Mfg. Co. v. C–O–Two Fire Equipment Co., supra; Steelman v. All Continent Corp., 301 U.S. 278 (1937); Landis v. North American Co., 299 U.S. 248, 254 (1936). This difference in general approach between state-federal concurrent jurisdiction and wholly federal concurrent jurisdiction stems from the virtually unflagging obligation of the federal courts to exercise the jurisdiction given them. Given this obligation, and the absence of weightier considerations of constitutional adjudication and state-federal relations, the circumstances permitting the dismissal of a federal suit due to the presence of a concurrent state proceeding for reasons of wise judicial administration are considerably more limited than the circumstances appropriate for abstention. The former circumstances, though exceptional, do nevertheless exist.

It has been held, for example, that the court first assuming jurisdiction over property may exercise that jurisdiction to the exclusion of other courts. * * * In assessing the appropriateness of dismissal in the event of an exercise of concurrent jurisdiction, a federal court may also consider such factors as the inconvenience of the federal forum, cf. Gulf Oil Corp. v. Gilbert, 330 U.S. 501 (1947); the desirability of avoiding piecemeal litigation, cf. Brillhart v. Excess Ins. Co., 316 U.S. 491, 495 (1942); and the order in which jurisdiction was obtained by the concurrent forums, Pacific Live Stock Co. v. Oregon Water Bd., 241 U.S. 440, 447 (1916). No one factor is necessarily determinative; a carefully considered judgment taking into account both the obligation to exercise jurisdiction and the combination of factors counselling against that exercise is required. Only the clearest of justifications will warrant dismissal.

Turning to the present case, a number of factors clearly counsel against concurrent federal proceedings. The most important of these is the McCarran Amendment itself. The clear federal policy evinced by that legislation is the avoidance of piecemeal adjudication of water rights in a river system. This policy is akin to that underlying the rule requiring that jurisdiction be yielded to the court first acquiring control of property, for the concern in such instances is with avoiding the generation of additional litigation through permitting inconsistent dispositions of property. This concern is heightened with respect to water rights, the relationships among which are highly interdependent. Indeed, we have recognized that actions seeking the allocation of water essentially involve the disposition of property and are best conducted in unified proceedings. The consent to jurisdiction given by the McCarran Amendment bespeaks a policy that recognizes the availability of comprehensive state systems for adjudication of water rights as the means for achieving these goals.

As has already been observed, the Colorado Water Rights Determination and Administration Act established such a system for the adjudication and management of rights to the use of the State's waters. * * *

Beyond the congressional policy expressed by the McCarran Amendment and consistent with furtherance of that policy, we also find significant (a) the apparent absence of any proceedings in the District Court, other than the filing of the complaint, prior to the motion to dismiss, (b) the extensive involvement of state water rights occasioned by this suit naming 1,000 defendants, (c) the 300–mile distance between the District Court in Denver and the court in Division 7, and (d) the existing participation by the Government in Division 4, 5, and 6 proceedings. We emphasize, however, that we do not overlook the heavy obligation to exercise jurisdiction. We need not decide, for example, whether, despite the McCarran Amendment, dismissal would be warranted if more extensive proceedings had occurred in the District Court prior to dismissal, if the involvement of state water rights were less extensive than it is here, or if the state proceeding were in some respect inadequate to resolve the federal claims. But the opposing factors here, particularly the policy underlying the McCarran Amendment, justify the District Court's dismissal in this particular case.

The judgment of the Court of Appeals is reversed and the judgment of the District Court dismissing the complaint is affirmed for the reasons here stated.

MR. JUSTICE STEWART, with whom MR. JUSTICE BLACKMUN and MR. JUSTICE STEVENS concur, dissenting.

The Court says that the United States District Court for the District of Colorado clearly had jurisdiction over this lawsuit. I agree. The Court further says that the McCarran Amendment "in no way diminished" the District Court's jurisdiction. I agree. The Court also says that federal courts have a "virtually unflagging obligation . . . to exercise the jurisdiction given them." I agree. And finally, the Court says that nothing in the abstention doctrine "in any of its forms" justified the District Court's dismissal of the Government's complaint. I agree. These views would seem to lead ineluctably to the conclusion that the District Court was wrong in dismissing the complaint. Yet the Court holds that the order of dismissal was "appropriate." With that conclusion I must respectfully disagree.

In holding that the United States shall not be allowed to proceed with its lawsuit, the Court relies principally on cases reflecting the rule that where "control of the property which is the subject of the suit [is necessary] in order to proceed with the cause and to grant the relief sought, the jurisdiction of one court must of necessity yield to that of the other." Penn General Casualty Co. v. Pennsylvania ex rel. Schnader, 294 U.S. 189, 195. See also Donovan v. City of Dallas, 377 U.S. 408; Princess Lida v. Thompson, 305 U.S. 456; United States v. Bank of New York Co., 296 U.S. 463. But, as those cases make clear, this rule applies only when exclusive control over the subject matter is necessary to effectuate a court's judgment. 1A J. Moore, Federal Practice ¶ 0.214 (1974). Here the federal court did not need to obtain *in rem* or *quasi in rem* jurisdiction in order to decide the issues before it. The court was asked simply to determine as a matter of federal law whether federal reservations of water rights had occurred, and, if so, the date and scope of the reservations. The District Court could make such a determination without having control of the river.

The rule invoked by the Court thus does not support the conclusion that it reaches. * * *

* * *

The Court's principal reason for deciding to close the doors of the federal courthouse to the United States in this case seems to stem from the view that its decision will avoid piecemeal adjudication of water rights. To the extent that this view is based on the special considerations governing *in rem* proceedings, it is without precedential basis, as the decisions discussed above demonstrate. To the extent that the Court's view is based on the realistic practicalities of this case, it is simply wrong, because the relegation of the Government to the state courts will not avoid piecemeal litigation.

The Colorado courts are currently engaged in two types of proceedings under the State's water-rights law. First, they are processing new claims to water based on recent appropriations. Second, they are integrating these new awards of water rights with all past decisions awarding such rights into one all-inclusive tabulation for each water source. The claims of the United States that are involved in this case have not been adjudicated in the past. Yet they do not involve recent appropriations of water. In fact, these claims are wholly dissimilar to normal state water claims, because they are not based on actual beneficial use of water but rather on an intention formed at the time the federal land use was established to reserve a certain amount of water to support the federal reservations. The state court will, therefore, have to conduct separate proceedings to determine these claims. * * *

As the Court says, it is the virtual "unflagging obligation" of a federal court to exercise the jurisdiction that has been conferred upon it. Obedience to that obligation is particularly "appropriate" in this case, for at least two reasons.

First, the issues involved are issues of federal law. A federal court is more likely than a state court to be familiar with federal water law and to have had experience in interpreting the relevant federal statutes, regulations, and Indian treaties. Moreover, if tried in a federal court, these issues of federal law will be reviewable in a federal appellate court, whereas federal judicial review of the state courts' resolution of issues of federal law will be possible only on review by this Court in the exercise of its certiorari jurisdiction.

Second, some of the federal claims in this lawsuit relate to water reserved for Indian reservations. It is not necessary to determine that there is no state-court jurisdiction of these claims to support the proposition that a federal court is a more appropriate forum than a state court for determination of questions of life-and-death importance to Indians. This Court has long recognized that " '[t]he policy of leaving Indians free from state jurisdiction and control is deeply rooted in the Nation's history.' " McClanahan v. Arizona State Tax Comm'n, 411 U.S. 164, 168, quoting Rice v. Olson, 324 U.S. 786, 789.

The Court says that "[o]nly the clearest of justifications will warrant dismissal" of a lawsuit within the jurisdiction of a federal court. In my opinion there was no justification at all for the District Court's order of dismissal in this case.

I would affirm the judgment of the Court of Appeals.

[The dissenting opinion of JUSTICE STEVENS is omitted.]

Notes

1. How should *Colorado River* be applied in cases where the federal litigant seeks a declaratory judgment? Consider Wilton v. Seven Falls Co., 515 U.S. 277 (1995). The Court in *Wilton* held unanimously that a district court's decision to stay a declaratory judgment action during the pendency of parallel state court proceedings is not controlled by the "exceptional circumstances" test of *Colorado River*, but rather by the broader discretionary standards set forth in Brillhart v. Excess Ins. Co., 316 U.S. 491 (1942)(and applied by the plurality in *Will*). Justice O'Connor's opinion for the Court interpreted the Declaratory Judgment Act "to confer on federal courts unique and substantial discretion in deciding whether to declare the rights of litigants." 515 U.S. at 286. That Act, she contended, "created an opportunity, rather than a duty, to grant a new form of relief to qualifying litigants." Id. at 288. As to petitioners' claim that *Colorado River* and its progeny had undermined *Brillhart*, the Court held: "We disagree. * * * No subsequent case, in our view, has called into question the application of the *Brillhart* standard to the *Brillhart* facts." Id. at 286.

Are you persuaded that there is a sufficient difference between suits seeking a declaratory judgment and suits seeking other relief to justify the different standards for abstention? Is the underlying assumption of *Colorado River*, that a federal court has an obligation to exercise jurisdiction absent "exceptional circumstances," any more valid in non-declaratory judgment suits than it is in declaratory judgment suits? See Rehnquist, *Taking Comity Seriously: How to Neutralize the Abstention Doctrine*, 46 Stan.L.Rev. 1049, 1102–08 (1994). Where do interpleader suits fit in? See NYLife Distributors, Inc. v. Adherence Group, Inc., 72 F.3d 371 (3d Cir.1995).

Lower courts are still struggling with the application of *Wilton* and *Colorado River*. In Youell v. Exxon Corp., 48 F.3d 105 (2d Cir.1995), the Second Circuit applied the *Colorado River* "exceptional circumstances" test to reverse a district court's decision to abstain in the *Exxon Valdez* case. After the Supreme Court vacated the judgment and remanded for reconsideration in light of *Wilton*, the Second Circuit applied *Brillhart* and nevertheless reaffirmed its earlier holding. It found the district court's dismissal to be an abuse of discretion because the case raised "a novel issue of federal admiralty law." Youell v. Exxon Corp., 74 F.3d 373 (2d Cir.1996). *Wilton* is discussed in Giesel, *The Expanded Discretion of Lower Courts to Regulate Access to the Federal Courts After* Wilton v. Seven Falls Co.: *Declaratory Judgment Actions and Implications Far Beyond*, 33 Hous.L.Rev. 393 (1996).

2. *Colorado River* abstention is criticized in Mullenix, *A Branch Too Far: Pruning the Abstention Doctrine,* 75 Geo.L.J. 99 (1986). Professor Mullenix refers to this form of abstention as "an invidious encroachment on the constitutional and statutory rights of federal litigants. If the courts desire to reduce their dockets, they should persuade Congress to abolish diversity jurisdiction or enact other palliative measures. The Supreme Court is not empowered to sanction the fabrication of an artificial abstention doctrine as a means of docket clearing." Id. at 101. She refers to *Colorado River* as "merely a doctrine of judicial convenience that has no place in American jurisprudence * * *." She distinguishes the other forms of abstention, because they were "based in large part on the 'desire to preserve harmonious federal-state relations.'" Id. at 105. Is it possible to rationalize *Colorado River* on grounds of federalism, as well as judicial convenience?

3. Do you think that Justice Brennan established a strong basis in *Colorado River* for concluding that the "exceptional circumstances" requirement, justifying federal court dismissal in favor of a parallel state court proceeding, was met in that case? How do each of the criteria mentioned by Justice Brennan for determining exceptional circumstances apply to the facts of *Colorado River*?

4. Consider the effect on *Colorado River* abstention of Moses H. Cone Memorial Hospital v. Mercury Construction Corp., 460 U.S. 1 (1983). The federal case was a petition for an order to compel arbitration of a contract dispute between a contractor and a hospital pursuant to section 4 of the United States Arbitration Act, 9 U.S.C.A. § 4. The case was filed by the contractor. Prior to the filing of the federal action, the hospital had filed a state action seeking a declaration that it was not liable to the contractor and that there was no right to arbitration. In addition, it sought a stay of arbitration. On the hospital's motion, the federal district court stayed the federal action pending resolution of the state court suit, because the two suits involved the identical issue of the arbitrability of the contractor's

claims. The court of appeals reversed the stay and remanded for entry of an order compelling arbitration. The Supreme Court, in an opinion by Justice Brennan, affirmed the court of appeals' decision. In discussing *Colorado River,* the Court stated:

> [T]he decision whether to dismiss a federal action because of parallel state-court litigation does not rest on a mechanical checklist, but on a careful balancing of the important factors as they apply in a given case, with the balance heavily weighted in favor of the exercise of jurisdiction. The weight to be given to any one factor may vary greatly from case to case, depending on the particular setting of the case. *Colorado River* itself illustrates this principle in operation.

* * *

Applying the *Colorado River* factors to this case, it is clear that there was no showing of the requisite exceptional circumstances to justify the District Court's stay.

* * * There was no assumption by either court of jurisdiction over any res or property, nor is there any contention that the federal forum was any less convenient to the parties than the state forum. The remaining factors—avoidance of piecemeal litigation and the order in which jurisdiction was obtained by the concurrent forums—far from supporting the stay, actually counsel against it.

There is no force here to the consideration that was paramount in *Colorado River* itself—the danger of piecemeal litigation.

The Hospital points out that it has two substantive disputes here—one with Mercury, concerning Mercury's claim for delay and impact costs, and the other with the Architect, concerning the Hospital's claim for indemnity for any liability it may have to Mercury. The latter dispute cannot be sent to arbitration without the Architect's consent. It is true, therefore, that if Mercury obtains an arbitration order for its dispute, the Hospital will be forced to resolve those related disputes in different forums. That misfortune, however, is not the result of any choice between the federal and state courts, it occurs because the relevant federal law *requires* piecemeal resolution when necessary to give effect to an arbitration agreement.

* * *

* * * The Hospital argues that the stay was proper because the state-court suit was filed some 19 days before the federal suit. * * *

* * * [T]he Hospital's priority argument gives too mechanical a reading to the "priority" element of the *Colorado River* balance. This factor, as with the other *Colorado River* factors, is to be applied in a pragmatic, flexible manner with a view to the realities of the case at hand. Thus, priority should not be measured exclusively by which complaint was filed first, but rather in terms of how much progress has been made in the two actions. * * * In realistic terms, the federal suit was running well ahead of the state suit at the very time that the District Court decided to refuse to adjudicate the case.

This refusal to precede was plainly erroneous in view of Congress's clear intent, in the Arbitration Act, to move the parties to an arbitrable dispute out of the court and into arbitration as quickly and easily as possible. * * *

* * *

Finally, in this case an important reason against allowing a stay is the probable inadequacy of the state-court proceeding to protect Mercury's rights. * * * [T]here was, at a minimum, substantial room for doubt that Mercury could obtain from the state court an order compelling the Hospital to arbitrate. Id. at 16–27.

Are *Colorado River* and *Moses H. Cone* distinguishable? If not, which is likely to prove to be the exception, and which the rule?

Note that in *Moses H. Cone,* the Court emphasized "the fact that federal law provides the rule of decision on the merits." Id. at 23. It also noted: "Although in some rare circumstances the presence of state-law issues may weigh in favor of * * * surrender, the presence of federal-law issues must always be a major consideration weighing against surrender." Id. at 26. Is this a proper factor to examine? Consider the criticism presented by Professor Mullenix:

> [T]he Supreme Court has reversed the normal ordering of procedural concerns. Usually, proper jurisdiction is established first, and the choice of law follows. * * * The choice of law factor, however, requires a fortiori that the choice of law precede determination of jurisdiction. The * * * standard thus has the choice of law tail wagging the jurisdictional dog. If a court discerns state law issues, the choice of law factor, counsels surrender of federal jurisdiction, but if a court finds federal law issues, surrender of jurisdiction is discouraged. This is a novel proposition. Choice of law considerations have nothing to do with proper jurisdiction and certainly should not affect surrender of proper jurisdiction. Mullenix, *A Branch Too Far: Pruning the Abstention Doctrine,* 75 Geo.L.J. 99, 126 (1986).

Is this a valid criticism? Does the abstention test really reverse the proper order of analyzing choice of law and jurisdictional questions?

5. Consider the following argument: After *Moses H. Cone,* courts will rarely abstain in cases raising a federal issue. At the same time, however, Supreme Court interpretation of the Anti–Injunction Act [discussed in Chapter Nine] means that federal courts will rarely be able to enjoin parallel state cases. Thus in most instances, parallel state and federal cases will *both* continue, creating duplicative proceedings that waste judicial resources and are potentially harassing. See Redish, *Intersystemic Redundancy and Federal Court Power: Proposing a Zero Tolerance Solution to the Duplicative Litigation Problem,* 75 Notre Dame L.Rev. 1347 (2000). This article argues that we should adopt a "zero tolerance" posture toward such duplicative proceedings: in every case, the federal court should *either* abstain or enjoin the state court, but remains agnostic on the choice between the two alternatives. Isn't the choice between the alternatives the key question, however? How would you structure the choice between staying the federal action and enjoining the state action? Does the approach in this article require us, in the name of

efficiency, to choose between respect for state courts on the one hand and providing a federal forum for federal questions on the other? Do we always have to make that choice in the types of cases discussed throughout this book?

§ 3.   PROCEDURAL ASPECTS

ENGLAND v. LOUISIANA STATE BOARD OF MEDICAL EXAMINERS

Supreme Court of the United States, 1964.
375 U.S. 411.

MR. JUSTICE BRENNAN delivered the opinion of the Court.

Appellants are graduates of schools of chiropractic who seek to practice in Louisiana without complying with the educational requirements of the Louisiana Medical Practice Act, Title 37, La.Rev.Stat. §§ 1261–1290. They brought this action against respondent Louisiana State Board of Medical Examiners in the Federal District Court for the Eastern District of Louisiana, seeking an injunction and a declaration that, as applied to them, the Act violated the Fourteenth Amendment. A statutory three-judge court invoked, *sua sponte,* the doctrine of abstention, on the ground that "The state court might effectively end this controversy by a determination that chiropractors are not governed by the statute," and entered an order "staying further proceedings in this Court until the courts of the State of Louisiana shall have been afforded an opportunity to determine the issues here presented, and retaining jurisdiction to take such steps as may be necessary for the just disposition of the litigation should anything prevent a prompt state court determination."

Appellants thereupon brought proceedings in the Louisiana courts. They did not restrict those proceedings to the question whether the Medical Practice Act applied to chiropractors. They unreservedly submitted for decision, and briefed and argued, their contention that the Act, if applicable to chiropractors, violated the Fourteenth Amendment. The state proceedings terminated with a decision by the Louisiana Supreme Court declining to review an intermediate appellate court's holding both that the Medical Practice Act applied to chiropractors and that, as so applied, it did not violate the Fourteenth Amendment. La.App., 126 So.2d 51.

Appellants then returned to the District Court, where they were met with a motion by appellees to dismiss the federal action. This motion was granted, on the ground that "since the courts of Louisiana have passed on all issues raised, including the claims of deprivation under the Federal Constitution, this court, having no power to review those proceedings, must dismiss the complaint. The proper remedy was by appeal to the Supreme Court of the United States." The court saw the case as illustrating "the dilemma of a litigant who has invoked the jurisdiction of a federal court to assert a claimed constitutional right and finds himself remitted to the state tribunals." The dilemma, said the court, was that "On the one hand, in view of Government & Civic Employees Organizing Committee v. Windsor, 353 U.S. 364, he dare not restrict his state court case to local law issues. On the other, if, as required by Windsor, he raises the federal questions there, well established principles will bar a relitigation of those issues in the United States District Court. . . . Since, in the usual case, no question not already passed on by the state courts will remain, he is thereby effectively deprived of a federal forum for the adjudication of his federal claims." 194 F.Supp. 521, 522. Appellants appealed directly to this Court under 28 U.S.C. § 1253, and we noted probable jurisdiction. We reverse and remand to the District Court for decision on the merits of appellants' Fourteenth Amendment claims.

There are fundamental objections to any conclusion that a litigant who has properly invoked the jurisdiction of a Federal District Court to consider federal constitutional claims can be compelled, without his consent and through no fault of his own, to accept instead a state court's determination of those claims.[5] Such a result would be at war with the unqualified terms in which Congress, pursuant to constitutional authorization, has conferred specific categories of jurisdiction upon the federal courts, and with the principle that "When a Federal court is properly appealed to in a case over which it has by law jurisdiction, it is its duty to take such jurisdiction. . . The right of a party plaintiff to choose a Federal court where there is a choice cannot be properly denied." Willcox v. Consolidated Gas Co., 212 U.S. 19, 40. Nor does anything in the abstention doctrine require or support such a result. Abstention is a judge-fashioned vehicle for according appropriate deference to the "respective competence of the state and federal court systems." Louisiana P. & L. Co. v. Thibodaux, 360 U.S. 25, 29. Its recognition of the role of state courts as the final expositors of state law implies no disregard for the primacy of the federal judiciary in deciding questions of federal law. Accordingly, we have on several occasions explicitly recognized that abstention "does not, of course, involve the abdication of federal jurisdiction, but only the postponement of its exercise." Harrison v. NAACP, 360 U.S. 167, 177; accord, Louisiana P. & L. Co. v. Thibodaux, supra, 360 U.S., at 29.[7]

---

5. At least this is true in a case, like the instant one, not involving the possibility of unwarranted disruption of a state administrative process. Compare Burford v. Sun Oil Co., 319 U.S. 315; Alabama Public Service Comm'n v. Southern R. Co., 341 U.S. 341.

7. The doctrine contemplates only "that controversies involving unsettled questions of state law [may] be decided in the state tribunals preliminary to a federal court's consideration of the underlying federal constitutional questions," City of Meridian v. Southern Bell Tel. & Tel. Co., 358 U.S. 639, 640; "that decision of the federal question

be deferred until the potentially controlling state-law issue is authoritatively put to rest," United Gas Pipe Line Co. v. Ideal Cement Co., 369 U.S. 134, 135–136; "that federal courts do not decide questions of constitutionality on the basis of preliminary guesses regarding local law," Spector Motor Service, Inc. v. McLaughlin, 323 U.S. 101, 105; "that these enactments should be exposed to state construction or limiting interpretation before the federal courts are asked to decide upon their constitutionality," Harrison v. NAACP, 360 U.S. 167, 178.

It is true that, after a post-abstention determination and rejection of his federal claims by the state courts, a litigant could seek direct review in this Court. NAACP v. Button, 371 U.S. 415; Lassiter v. Northampton County Board of Elections, 360 U.S. 45. But such review, even when available by appeal rather than only by discretionary writ of certiorari, is an inadequate substitute for the initial District Court determination * * * to which the litigant is entitled in the federal courts. This is true as to issues of law; it is especially true as to issues of fact. Limiting the litigant to review here would deny him the benefit of a federal trial court's role in constructing a record and making fact findings. How the facts are found will often dictate the decision of federal claims. "It is the typical, not the rare, case in which constitutional claims turn upon the resolution of contested factual issues." Townsend v. Sain, 372 U.S. 293, 312. "There is always in litigation a margin of error, representing error in factfinding. . . ." Speiser v. Randall, 357 U.S. 513, 525. Thus in cases where, but for the application of the abstention doctrine, the primary fact determination would have been by the District Court, a litigant may not be unwillingly deprived of that determination. The possibility of appellate review by this Court of a state court determination may not be substituted, against a party's wishes, for his right to litigate his federal claims fully in the federal courts. We made this clear only last Term in NAACP v. Button, supra, 371 U.S., at 427, when we said that "a party has the right to return to the District Court, after obtaining the authoritative state court construction for which the court abstained, for a final determination of his claim."

We also made clear in *Button*, however, that a party may elect to forgo that right. Our holding in that case was that a judgment of the Virginia Supreme Court of Appeals upon federal issues submitted to the state tribunals by parties remitted there under the abstention doctrine was "final" for purposes of our review under 28 U.S.C. § 1257. In so determining, we held that the petitioner had elected "to seek a complete and final adjudication of [its] rights in the state courts" and thus not to return to the District Court, and that it had manifested this election "by seeking from the Richmond Circuit Court 'a binding adjudication' of all its claims and a permanent injunction as well as declaratory relief, by making no reservation to the disposition of the entire case by the state courts, and by coming here directly on certiorari." 371 U.S., at 427–428. We fashioned the rule recognizing such an election because we saw no inconsistency with the abstention doctrine in allowing a litigant to decide, once the federal court has abstained and compelled him to proceed in the state courts in any event, to abandon his original choice of a federal forum and submit his entire case to the state courts, relying on the opportunity to come here directly if the state decision on his federal claims should go against him. Such a choice by a litigant serves to avoid much of the delay and expense to which application of the abstention doctrine inevitably gives rise; when the choice is voluntarily made, we see no reason why it should not be given effect.

In *Button*, we had no need to determine what steps, if any, short of those taken by the petitioner there would suffice to manifest the election. The instant case, where appellants did not attempt to come directly to this Court but sought to return to the District Court, requires such a determination. The line drawn should be bright and clear, so that litigants shunted from federal to state courts by application of the abstention doctrine will not be exposed, not only to unusual expense and delay, but also to procedural traps operating to deprive them of their right to a District Court determination of their federal claims. It might be argued that nothing short of what was done in *Button* should suffice—that a litigant should retain the right to return to the District Court unless he not only litigates his federal claims in the state tribunals but seeks review of the state decision in this Court. But we see no reason why a party, after unreservedly litigating his federal claims in the state courts although not required to do so, should be allowed to ignore the adverse state decision and start all over again in the District Court. Such a rule would not only countenance an unnecessary increase in the length and cost of the litigation; it would also be a potential source of friction between the state and federal judiciaries. We implicitly rejected such a rule in *Button*, when we stated that a party elects to forgo his right to return to the District Court by a decision "to seek a complete and final adjudication of his rights in the state courts." We now explicitly hold that if a party freely and without reservation submits his federal claims for decision by the state courts, litigates them there, and has them decided there, then—whether or not he seeks direct review of the state decision in this Court—he has elected to forgo his right to return to the District Court.

This rule requires clarification of our decision in Government & Civic Employees Organizing Committee, C.I.O. v. Windsor, 353 U.S. 364, the case referred to by the District Court. The plaintiffs in *Windsor* had submitted to the state courts only the question whether the state statute they challenged applied to them, and had not "advanced" or "presented" to those courts their contentions against the statute's constitutionality. We held that "the bare adjudication by the Alabama Supreme Court that the [appellant] union is subject to this Act does not suffice, since that court was not asked to interpret the statute in light of the constitutional objections presented to the District Court. If appellants' freedom-of-expression and equal-protection arguments had been presented to the state court, it might have construed the statute in a different manner." 353 U.S., at 366. On oral argument in the instant case, we were advised that appellants' submission of their federal claims to the state courts had been motivated primarily by a belief that *Windsor* required this. The District Court likewise thought that under *Windsor* a party is required to litigate his federal question in the state courts and "dare not restrict his state court case to local law issues." 194 F.Supp., at 522. Others have read *Windsor* the same way. It should not be so read. The case does not mean that a party must litigate his federal claims in the state courts, but only that he must inform those courts what his federal claims are, so that the state statute may be construed "in light of" those claims. Thus mere compliance with *Windsor* will not support a conclusion, much less create a presumption, that a litigant has freely and without reservation litigated his federal claims in the state courts and so elected not to return to the District Court.

We recognize that in the heat of litigation a party may find it difficult to avoid doing more than is required by *Windsor*. This would be particularly true in the typical case, such as the instant one, where the state courts are asked to construe a state statute against the backdrop of a federal constitutional challenge. The litigant denying the statute's applicability may be led not merely to state his federal constitutional claim but to argue it, for if he can persuade the state court that application of the statute to him would offend the Federal Constitution, he will ordinarily have persuaded it that the statute should not be construed as applicable to him. In addition, the parties cannot prevent the state court from rendering a decision on the federal question if it chooses to do so; and even if such a decision is not explicit, a holding that the statute is applicable may arguably imply, in view of the constitutional objections to such a construction, that the court considers the constitutional challenge to be without merit.

Despite these uncertainties arising from application of *Windsor*—which decision, we repeat, does not require that federal claims be actually litigated in the state courts—a party may readily forestall any conclusion that he has elected not to return to the District Court. He may accomplish this by making on the state record the "reservation to the disposition of the entire case by the state courts" that we referred to in *Button*. That is, he may inform the state courts that he is exposing his federal claims there only for the purpose of complying with *Windsor*, and that he intends, should the state courts hold against him on the question of state law, to return to the District Court for disposition of his federal contentions. Such an explicit reservation is not indispensable; the litigant is in no event to be denied his right to return to the District Court unless it clearly appears that he voluntarily did more than *Windsor* required and fully litigated his federal claims in the state courts. When the reservation has been made, however, his right to return will in all events be preserved.[13]

On the record in the instant case, the rule we announce today would call for affirmance of the District Court's judgment. But we are unwilling

---

13. The reservation may be made by any party to the litigation. Usually the plaintiff will have made the original choice to litigate in the federal court, but the defendant also, by virtue of the removal jurisdiction, 28 U.S.C. § 1441(b), has a right to litigate the federal question there. Once issue has been joined in the federal court, no party is entitled to insist, over another's objection, upon a binding state court determination of the federal question. Thus, while a plaintiff who unreservedly litigates his federal claims in the state courts may thereby elect to forgo his own right to return to the District Court, he cannot impair the corresponding right of the defendant. The latter may protect his right by either declining to oppose the plaintiff's federal claim in the state court or opposing it with the appropriate reservation. It may well be, of course, that a refusal to litigate or a reservation by any party will deter the state court from deciding the federal question.

to apply the rule against these appellants. As we have noted, their primary reason for litigating their federal claims in the state courts was assertedly a view that *Windsor* required them to do so. That view was mistaken, and will not avail other litigants who rely upon it after today's decision. But we cannot say, in the face of the support given the view by respectable authorities, including the court below, that appellants were unreasonable in holding it or acting upon it. We therefore hold that the District Court should not have dismissed their action. The judgment is reversed, and the case is remanded for further proceedings consistent with this opinion.

* * *

[The concurring opinion of JUSTICE DOUGLAS and the opinion of JUSTICE BLACK, concurring in part and dissenting in part, are omitted.]

Notes

1.   To which of the various abstention doctrines, if any, should the procedure adopted in *England* not apply? Should it apply outside the context of abstention, to cases in which a plaintiff is involuntarily forced into state court by other doctrines such as the *Pennhurst* doctrine [supra p. 383]? See Friedman, *Under the Law of Federal Jurisdiction: Allocating Cases Between Federal and State Courts*, 104 Colum.L.Rev. 1211 (2004). Reconsider this question when you study the preclusion doctrines addressed in Chapter Eleven.

2.   The *England* procedure has been subjected to significant attack. The American Law Institute, for example, has stated that "[t]o shuttle the cases back and forth from state to federal court * * * 'operates to require piecemeal adjudication in many courts * * * thereby delaying ultimate adjudication on the merits for an undue length of time.' " American Law Institute, Study of the Division of Jurisdiction Between State and Federal Courts 285 (1969) (quoting Baggett v. Bullitt, 377 U.S. 360, 378–379 (1964)). The ALI has suggested that the *England* procedure be replaced by a procedure that prevents return of the case to federal court, as long as available state procedures are adequate. See also Kurland, *Toward a Co-Operative Judicial Federalism: The Federal Court Abstention Doctrine*, 24 F.R.D. 481, 489 (1959), suggesting that in cases of *Pullman* abstention it would be appropriate for the state courts to decide the entire case, subject to possible review in the United States Supreme Court. Are these proposals preferable to the *England* procedure? What are their advantages and disadvantages? Note that the Supreme Court adheres to the *England* procedure. American Trial Lawyers Association v. New Jersey Supreme Court, 409 U.S. 467, 469 (1973) (per curiam).

3.   One of the most significant problems inherent in the *England* procedure is determining whether the federal plaintiff has waived his right to return to federal court. The problem is compounded by the Court's requirement that the federal issues be presented to the state court, whether or not the state court will be chosen by the parties to adjudicate those federal issues. Why do you suppose the Court added this requirement? Do its

benefits outweigh the possible increase in confusion on the waiver issue that results? What do you think is the best way for a federal court plaintiff, while in state court because of abstention, to avoid a finding of waiver of his right to return to federal court?

A plaintiff who makes an *England reservation in state court* must be careful not to "broaden the scope of the state court's review beyond the decision of the antecedent state-law issue." San Remo Hotel v. City and County of San Francisco, 545 U.S. 323 (2005). In *San Remo Hotel*, the Court found the *England* reservation ineffective—thus depriving the plaintiffs of the opportunity to relitigate in federal court—because by presenting broad claims to the state court, the plaintiffs "effectively asked the state court to resolve the same federal issues they asked it to reserve."

4. What should happen if, after a federal court has abstained on *Pullman* grounds, the state court decides the case against the plaintiff on state law procedural grounds, without ever reaching the interpretation of the challenged law? Cf. Ratcliff v. County of Buncombe, 759 F.2d 1183 (4th Cir.1985).

5. Under certain circumstances, the Supreme Court will authorize what it describes as outright "dismissal" of the federal action because of *Pullman* abstention. In Harris County Commissioners Court v. Moore, 420 U.S. 77 (1975), the Court directed dismissal in an abstention case, "[i]n order to remove any possible obstacles to state-court jurisdiction * * *." Id. at 88. The problem arose because the Texas Supreme Court had held that it lacked authority to issue declaratory relief while the federal court retained jurisdiction. However, the United States Supreme Court's "dismissal" was "without prejudice so that any remaining federal claim may be raised in a federal forum after the Texas courts have been given the opportunity to address the state-law questions in this case." Id. at 88–89.

6. A possible alternative to the abstention procedure is certification, which allows a federal court—when authorized to do so by state statute or state court rule—to refer unsettled issues of state law directly to the state's highest court for decision. Under this procedure, the case itself remains in federal court. The time and expense of the abstention procedure are thereby avoided. The value of the certification procedure has been generally recognized. See, e.g., Field, *The Abstention Doctrine Today*, 125 U.Pa.L.Rev. 590, 605 (1977); Note, *Inter-Jurisdictional Certification: Beyond Abstention Toward Cooperative Judicial Federalism*, 111 U.Pa.L.Rev. 344 (1963).

[margin note: Certificatic]

In Bellotti v. Baird, 428 U.S. 132 (1976), the Supreme Court emphasized the availability of certification under Massachusetts law in concluding that abstention was appropriate, despite the need for a speedy resolution.

[margin note: Bellotti]

In Virginia v. American Booksellers Association, Inc., 484 U.S. 383 (1988), the Court declined to review the constitutionality of a state statute making it unlawful "to knowingly display for commercial purpose in a manner whereby juveniles may examine and peruse 'visual or written material' that 'depicts sexually explicit nudity, sexual conduct, or sadomasochistic abuse and which is harmful to juveniles.'" Instead, the Court chose to take advantage of Virginia's certification procedure in order to obtain "the Virginia Supreme Court's interpretation of key provisions of the statute." The Court reasoned that

[u]nder these unusual circumstances, where it appears the State will decline to defend a statute if it is read one way and where the nature and substance of plaintiffs' constitutional challenge is drastically altered if the statute is read another way, it is essential that we have the benefit of the law's authoritative construction from the Virginia Supreme Court. Certification, in contrast to the more cumbersome and (in this context) problematic abstention doctrine, is a method by which we may expeditiously obtain that construction. * * * Consequently, we shall resort to its certification Rule * * * to ask the Virginia Supreme Court whether any of the books introduced by plaintiffs as exhibits below fall within the scope of the amended statute, and how such decisions should take into account juveniles' differing ages and levels of maturity. Id. at 395–96.

See also Vickers v. Trainor, 546 F.2d 739 (7th Cir.1976), where the court noted the absence of the availability of certification as one factor leading it to decline to abstain. It should be noted, however, that the Supreme Court in *Bellotti* expressly rejected the principle that the absence of a state certification procedure in itself is a sufficient basis for precluding abstention. Many states have not adopted a certification procedure. Should the principle rejected in *Bellotti* be accepted?

On the other hand, should the existence of a certification procedure *automatically* dictate resort to that procedure, rather than retention of the case in federal court? See City of Houston v. Hill, 482 U.S. 451 (1987), where the Court, after holding that a challenged state law was unambiguous, even though it had not yet been construed by the state appellate courts, stated: "It would be manifestly inappropriate to certify a question in a case where, as here, there is no uncertain question of state law whose resolution might affect the pending federal claim. * * * A federal court may not properly ask a state court if it would care in effect to rewrite a statute."

In Arizonans for Official English v. Arizona, 520 U.S. 43 (1997), the Supreme Court further muddied the waters on abstention and certification. In that case, two lower federal courts had held unconstitutional an Arizona ballot initiative making English the state's official language. The Supreme Court indicated that such a ruling was premature, because the initiative was unclear and uninterpreted by the state courts. Justice Ginsburg's opinion for a unanimous Court suggested that the district court should have certified the "novel or unsettled questions of state law" to the Arizona Supreme Court. Id. at 77.

Although that ruling is consistent with earlier cases, some of the language in the opinion suggests that certification might be governed by different rules than abstention. Justice Ginsburg suggested that "[c]ertification today covers territory once dominated by a deferral device called '*Pullman* abstention.'" Id. She also stated:

> Blending abstention with certification, the Ninth Circuit found "no unique circumstances in this case militating in favor of certification." Novel, unsettled questions of state law, however, not "unique circumstances," are necessary before federal courts may avail themselves of state certification procedures. Those procedures do not entail the delays,

expense, and procedural complexity that generally attend abstention decisions. Id. at 79.

This passage might be interpreted as simply reaffirming the holding of *Midkiff* [supra p. 452] that *Pullman* abstention or its substitute, certification, are appropriate where a federal court cannot resolve a federal question without first resolving unsettled issues of state law. Might this passage also be interpreted as drawing a distinction between "abstention," which requires "unique circumstances" because of its cumbersome character, and "certification," which does not? Should such a distinction be drawn?

The use of certification in diversity cases is somewhat controversial. Can you see why some commentators would reject the procedure's use in such cases? What impact might widespread use of certification by the federal courts in diversity cases have on the frequency of use of the diversity jurisdiction? Would this impact be good or bad? In Lehman Brothers v. Schein, 416 U.S. 386 (1974), a diversity case, the Supreme Court expressed great enthusiasm for the procedure, noting that it "does, of course, in the long run save time, energy, and resources and helps build a cooperative judicial federalism." 416 U.S. at 391. On the general issue of certification, see Mattis, *Certification of Question of State Law: An Impractical Tool in the Hands of the Federal Courts*, 23 U.Miami L.Rev. 717 (1969); Lillich & Mundy, *Federal Court Certification of Doubtful State Law Questions*, 18 U.C.L.A.L.Rev. 888 (1971); Selya, *Certified Madness: Ask A Silly Question*, 29 Suffolk U.L.Rev. 677 (1995). For an analysis of certification from a jurisprudential perspective, see Le Bel, *Legal Positivism and Federalism: The Certification Experience*, 19 Ga.L.Rev. 999 (1985); Cochran, *Federal Court Certification of Questions of State Law to State Courts: A Theoretical and Empirical Study*, 29 J.Legis. 157 (2003); Calabresi, *Federal and State Courts: Restoring a Workable Balance*, 78 N.Y.U.L.Rev. 1293 (2003).

7. On the general issue of the *England* procedure, see Liebenthal, *A Dialogue on* England: *The* England *Case, Its Effect on the Abstention Doctrine, and Some Suggested Solutions*, 18 W.Res.L.Rev. 157 (1966).

Chapter 9

ANTI–INJUNCTION ACT

§ 1. HISTORICAL BACKGROUND

TOUCEY v. NEW YORK LIFE INSURANCE CO.

Supreme Court of the United States, 1941.
314 U.S. 118.

MR. JUSTICE FRANKFURTER delivered the opinion of the Court.

These cases were argued in succession and are dealt with in a single opinion because the controlling question in both is the same: Does a federal court have power to stay a proceeding in a state court simply because the claim in controversy has previously been adjudicated in the federal court?

In 1935, Toucey brought suit against the New York Life Insurance Company in a Missouri state court. He alleged that in 1924 the company issued him a life insurance policy providing for monthly disability benefits and for the waiver of premiums during disability; that he became disabled in April, 1933, and that the defendant fraudulently concealed the disability provisions from him; that the defendant unlawfully cancelled the policy for nonpayment of premiums; that in September, 1935, he discovered the existence of the disability provisions; that he then applied to the company for reinstatement of the policy and for the payment of disability benefits, and that the company refused.

The suit was removed to the federal District Court for the Western District of Missouri, the plaintiff being a citizen of Missouri, the defendant a New York corporation, and the amount in controversy exceeding $3,000. All of the material allegations of the bill were denied. The district court dismissed the bill, finding that there was no fraud on the defendant's part and that the plaintiff was not disabled within the meaning of the policy. No appeal was taken.

In 1937, an action at law was brought against the insurance company in the Missouri state court by one Shay, a resident of the District of Columbia. He alleged that he was Toucey's assignee and that Toucey's disability entitled him to judgment. It does not appear that the insurance

482

company filed an answer or any other pleading. Instead, a "supplemental bill" was filed in the Western District of Missouri, setting forth the history of the litigation between the parties, alleging that the assignment to Shay was made in order to avoid federal jurisdiction, and praying that Toucey be enjoined from bringing any suit for the purpose of readjudicating the issues settled by the federal decree and from further prosecuting the Shay suit.

A preliminary injunction was granted, and affirmed by the Circuit Court of Appeals for the Eighth Circuit. The court held that Toucey's claim in the prior suit rested upon proof of his disability, and that this issue, necessarily involved in the Shay proceeding, had been conclusively determined in the insurance company's favor. Section 265 of the Judicial Code, 36 Stat. 1162, 28 U.S.C. § 379, [the Anti–Injunction Statute] was construed not to deprive a federal court of the power to enjoin state court proceedings where an injunction is "necessary to preserve to litigants the fruits of, or to effectuate the lawful decrees of the federal courts." Certiorari was denied, 307 U.S. 638, and the injunction was made permanent. Toucey appealed and the Circuit Court of Appeals again affirmed, 112 F.2d 927. In view of the importance of the questions presented, we granted certiorari. The decision below was affirmed by an equally divided Court, and the case is now before us on rehearing.

* * *

The courts below have thus decided that the previous federal judgments are *res judicata* in the state proceedings, and that therefore, notwithstanding the prohibitory provisions of § 265, the federal courts may use their injunctive powers to save the defendants in the state proceedings the inconvenience of pleading and proving *res judicata*.

First. Section 265—"a limitation of the power of the federal courts dating almost from the beginning of our history and expressing an important Congressional policy—to prevent needless friction between state and federal courts," Oklahoma Packing Co. v. Oklahoma Gas & Electric Co., 309 U.S. 4, 8, 9—is derived from § 5 of the Act of March 2, 1793, 1 Stat. 335: " . . . nor shall a writ of injunction be granted [by any court of the United States] to stay proceedings in any court of a state * * *" In its present form, 36 Stat. 1162, 28 U.S.C. § 379, the provision reads as follows: "The writ of injunction shall not be granted by any court of the United States to stay proceedings in any court of a State, except in cases where such injunction may be authorized by any law relating to proceedings in bankruptcy."[2]

The history of this provision in the Judiciary Act of 1793 is not fully known. * * *

* * *

2. Formulated as a contraction of the federal courts' equity jurisdiction, the Act of 1793 "limits their general equity powers in respect to the granting of a particular form of equitable relief; that is, it prevents them from granting relief by way of injunction in the cases included within its inhibitions." Smith v. Apple, 264 U.S. 274, 279. See Treinies v. Sunshine Mining Co., 308 U.S. 66, 74.

There is no record of any debates over the statute. See 3 Annals of Congress (1791–93). It has been suggested that the provision reflected the then strong feeling against the unwarranted intrusion of federal courts upon state sovereignty. Chisholm v. Georgia, 2 Dall. 419, was decided on February 18, 1793, less than two weeks before the provision was enacted into law. The significance of this proximity is doubtful. Compare Warren, *Federal and State Court Interference*, 43 Harv.L.Rev. 345, 347–48, with Gunter v. Atlantic Coast Line, 200 U.S. 273, 291, 292. Much more probable is the suggestion that the provision reflected the prevailing prejudices against equity jurisdiction. * * *

Regardless of the various influences which shaped the enactment of § 5 of the Act of March 2, 1793, the purpose and direction underlying the provision are manifest from its terms: proceedings in the state courts should be free from interference by federal injunction. The provision expresses on its face the duty of "hands off" by the federal courts in the use of the injunction to stay litigation in a state court.

Second. The language of the Act of 1793 was unqualified: " ... nor shall a writ of injunction be granted to stay proceedings in any court of a state ..." 1 Stat. 335. In the course of one hundred and fifty years, Congress has made few withdrawals from this sweeping prohibition:

(1) *Bankruptcy proceedings*. This is the only legislative exception which has been incorporated directly into § 265: " * * * except in cases where such injunction may be authorized by any law relating to proceedings in bankruptcy." 36 Stat. 1162. This provision, based upon § 21 of the Bankruptcy Act of 1867, 14 Stat. 526, was inserted in the Act of 1793 by the Revisers. R.S. § 720; see Proposed Draft of Revision of U.S. Statutes (1872), vol. 1, p. 418.

(2) *Removal of actions*. The Removal Acts, ever since the Act of September 24, 1789, 1 Stat. 73, 79, have provided that whenever any party entitled to remove a suit shall file with the state court a proper petition for removal and a bond with good and sufficient surety, it shall then be the duty of the state court to accept such petition and bond "and proceed no further in the cause." Section 265 has always been deemed inapplicable to removal proceedings. Dietzsch v. Huidekoper, 103 U.S. 494; Madisonville Traction Co. v. St. Bernard Mining Co., 196 U.S. 239. The true rationale of these decisions is that the Removal Acts qualify *pro tanto* the Act of 1793. Subsequent decisions have clarified the loose ground advanced in French v. Hay, 22 Wall. 250, 253, note. See Kline v. Burke Construction Co., 260 U.S. 226; Taylor and Willis, *The Power of Federal Courts to Enjoin Proceedings in State Courts*, 42 Yale L.J. 1169, 1174–75; compare Bryant v. Atlantic Coast Line R. Co., 92 F.2d 569, 571.

(3) *Limitation of shipowners' liability*. The Act of 1851 limiting the liability of shipowners provides that after a shipowner transfers his interest in the vessel to a trustee for the benefit of the claimants, "all claims and proceedings against the owner or owners shall cease." 9 Stat. 635, 636. Being a "subsequent statute" to the Act of 1793, this provision

operates as an implied legislative amendment to it. Providence & N. Y. S. S. Co. v. Hill Mfg. Co., 109 U.S. 578, 599; see Admiralty Rule 51.

(4) *Interpleader*. The Interpleader Act of 1926, 44 Stat. 416, amended the 1917 Interpleader Act, 39 Stat. 929, to provide as follows: "Notwithstanding any provision of the Judicial Code to the contrary, said [district] court shall have power to issue its process for all such claimants and to issue an order of injunction against each of them, enjoining them from instituting or prosecuting any suit or proceeding in any State court or in any other Federal court ..." See Dugas v. American Surety Co., 300 U.S. 414, 428; Treinies v. Sunshine Mining Co., 308 U.S. 66, 74.

(5) *Frazier-Lemke Act*. The filing of a petition for relief under this Act subjects the farmer and his property, wherever located, to the "exclusive jurisdiction" of the federal court. And except with the consent of the court, specified proceedings against the farmer or his property "shall not be instituted, or if instituted at any time prior to the filing of a petition under this section, shall not be maintained, in any court ..." 47 Stat. 1473. See Kalb v. Feuerstein, 308 U.S. 433.

Third. This brings us to applications of § 265 apart from these statutory qualifications. The early decisions of this Court applied the Act of 1793 as a matter of course. However, a line of cases beginning with Hagan v. Lucas, 10 Pet. 400, holds that the court, whether federal or state, which first takes possession of a *res* withdraws the property from the reach of the other. Taylor v. Carryl, 20 How. 583, 597; Freeman v. Howe, 24 How. 450. See Kline v. Burke Construction Co., 260 U.S. 226, 235: "The rank and authority of the [federal and state] courts are equal but both courts cannot possess or control the same thing at the same time, and any attempt to do so would result in unseemly conflict. The rule, therefore, that the court first acquiring jurisdiction shall proceed without interference from a court of the other jurisdiction is a rule of right and of law based upon necessity, and where the necessity, actual or potential, does not exist, the rule does not apply. Since that necessity does exist in actions *in rem* and does not exist in actions *in personam*, involving a question of personal liability only, the rule applies in the former but does not apply in the latter."

The Act of 1793 expresses the desire of Congress to avoid friction between the federal government and the states resulting from the intrusion of federal authority into the orderly functioning of a state's judicial process. The reciprocal doctrine of the *res* cases is but an application of the reason underlying the Act. Contest between the representatives of two distinct judicial systems over the same physical property would give rise to actual physical friction. The rule has become well settled, therefore, that § 265 does not preclude the use of the injunction by a federal court to restrain state proceedings seeking to interfere with property in the custody of the court.[6] Farmers' Loan &

---

6. The extent to which a federal court's exclusive control over the *res* may require use of the injunction to effectuate its decrees *in rem* is illustrated by Riverdale Cot-

Trust Co. v. Lake Street R. Co., 177 U.S. 51, 61; Kline v. Burke Construction Co., 260 U.S. 226, 229, 235; Lion Bonding & Surety Co. v. Karatz, 262 U.S. 77, 88, 89; see Warren, *Federal and State Court Interference*, 43 Harv.L.Rev. 345, 359–66. And where a state court first acquires control of the *res*, the federal courts are disabled from exercising any power over it, by injunction or otherwise. Palmer v. Texas, 212 U.S. 118.

Another group of cases is said to constitute an exception to § 265, namely, where federal courts have enjoined litigants from enforcing judgments fraudulently obtained in the state courts. Marshall v. Holmes, 141 U.S. 589; Simon v. Southern Railway Co., 236 U.S. 115; Essanay Film Co. v. Kane, 258 U.S. 358; Atchison, T. & S. F. R. Co. v. Wells, 265 U.S. 101; Wells Fargo & Co. v. Taylor, 254 U.S. 175. In the *Simon* case, Mr. Justice Lamar undertook to rationalize this class of cases by regarding a state court "proceeding" as completed once judgment is secured, with the result that an injunction against levying execution does not stay a judicial "proceeding." 236 U.S. at 124. But this construction of § 265 was rejected in Hill v. Martin, 296 U.S. 393, 403: * * * However, the opinion cites the *Wells Fargo and Essanay Film* cases in a footnote dealing with "the recognized exceptions to § 265." 296 U.S. 403, note 19. The foundation of these cases is thus very doubtful. However, we need not undertake to reexamine them here since, in any event, they do not govern the cases at bar.

Fourth. We come then to the so-called "relitigation" cases * * * [cases which the Court attempted to distinguish].

Fifth. We find, therefore, that apart from Congressional authorization, only one "exception" has been imbedded in § 265 by judicial construction, to wit, the *res* cases. The fact that one exception has found its way into § 265 is no justification for making another. Furthermore, the *res* exception, having its roots in the same policy from which sprang § 265, has had an uninterrupted and firmly established acceptance in the decisions. The rule of the *res* cases was unequivocally on the books when Congress reenacted the original § 5 of the Act of 1793, first by the Revised Statutes of 1874 and later by the Judicial Code in 1911.

In striking contrast are the "relitigation cases." Loose language and a sporadic, ill-considered decision cannot be held to have imbedded in our law a doctrine which so patently violates the expressed prohibition of Congress. We are not dealing here with a settled course of decisions, erroneous in original but around which substantial interests have clustered. Only a few recent and episodic utterances furnish a tenuous basis for the exception which we are now asked explicitly to sanction. Whatever justification there may be for turning past error into law when reasonable expectations would thereby be defeated, no such justification

ton Mills v. Alabama & G. Manufacturing Co., 198 U.S. 188; Julian v. Central Trust Co., 193 U.S. 93; and Local Loan Co. v.   Hunt, 292 U.S. 234, 241. Cf. Ex parte Baldwin, 291 U.S. 610, 615, 54 S.Ct. 551, 553.

can be urged on behalf of a procedural doctrine in the distribution of judicial power between federal and state courts. It denies reality to suggest that litigants have shaped their conduct in reliance upon some loose talk in past decisions in the application of § 265 * * *.

It is indulging in the merest fiction to suggest that the doctrine which for the first time we are asked to pronounce with our eyes open and in the light of full consideration, was so obviously and firmly part of the texture of our law that Congress in effect enacted it through its silence. There is no occasion here to regard the silence of Congress as more commanding than its own plainly and unmistakably spoken words. * * *

* * *

* * * We must be scrupulous in our regard for the limits within which Congress has confined the authority of the courts of its own creation.

Reversed.

* * *

Mr. Justice Reed, dissenting:

The controlling issue in * * * *Toucey* * * * is the power of a federal court to protect those who have obtained its decrees against an effort to force relitigation of the same causes of action in the state courts. Questions of *res judicata* seem inapposite for the conclusion. We are not concerned in either case with the effect of the decrees if and when they might be pleaded in the state actions. Since federal jurisdiction in each case depended upon diversity, their effect as a pleaded bar to recovery in the state suits would depend upon the faith and credit by law or usage given like judgments of courts of the state containing the federal district. But when the preliminary question is the meaning and application of the federal decree as a basis for a conclusion as to whether or not the decree shall be enforced by further steps, it is entirely a federal question. It is immaterial from that point of view whether the federal jurisdiction was bottomed originally on diversity, or the Constitution or laws of the United States. The power to give effect to the judgments of federal courts rests with Congress. * * *

* * *

* * * Granted that § 265 is not a sentence or section of a legislative scheme whose meaning is to be sought in the purpose of the entire enactment or series of enactments, we are nevertheless led by the judicial history intervening since its passage to look beyond the literal language and give weight to those decisions which had added to its content before the reenactment in the Judicial Code. In the Senate Report of the Special Joint Committee on Revision and Codification no change in language was suggested. Yet the Committee, as indicative of the then state of the law, cited numerous cases which are relitigation cases and are analyzed or referred to later in this opinion. We are all the

more persuaded to believe that the Code of 1911 intended to accept this early legislation with its judicial gloss because of the alternative offered. This alternative is that a federal judgment entered perhaps after years of expense in money and energy and after the production of thousands of pages of evidence comes to nothing that is final. It is to be only the basis for a plea of *res judicata* which is to be examined by another court, unfamiliar with the record already made, to determine whether the issues were or were not settled by the former adjudication. We, too, desire that the difficulties innate in the federal system of government may be smoothed away without a clash of sovereignties, but we find no cause for alarm in affirming a court which forbids parties bound by its decree to fight the battle over on another day and field. We should not, in reaching for theoretical symmetry, hamper the efficiency and needlessly break the continuity of our judicial methodology. A decree forbidding a defeated party from setting up any right, anywhere, based upon claims adjudged, is the usual form where injunctions are appropriate for determining controversies.

* * *

The Chief Justice and Mr. Justice Roberts concur in this dissent.

Notes

1.   Primarily in response to *Toucey*, Congress adopted the 1948 revision of the Anti–Injunction Act, presently codified in 28 U.S.C. § 2283, which provides: "A court of the United States may not grant an injunction to stay proceedings in a State Court except as expressly authorized by Act of Congress, or where necessary in aid of its jurisdiction, or to protect or effectuate its judgments." The Reviser's Note states in full:

> An exception as to Acts of Congress relating to bankruptcy was omitted and the general exception substituted to cover all exceptions.

> The phrase "in aid of its jurisdiction" was added to conform to section 1651 of this title and to make clear the recognized power of the Federal courts to stay proceedings in State cases removed to the district courts.

> The exceptions specifically include the words "to protect or effectuate its judgments," for lack of which the Supreme Court held that the Federal courts are without power to enjoin relitigation of cases and controversies fully adjudicated by such courts. (See Toucey v. New York Life Insurance Co.,) 314 U.S. 118. A vigorous dissenting opinion (62 S.Ct. 148) notes that at the time of the 1911 revision of the Judicial Code, the power of the courts of the United States to protect their judgments was unquestioned and that the revisers of that code noted no change and Congress intended no change).

> Therefore the revised section restores the basic law as generally understood and interpreted prior to the *Toucey* decision.

Changes were made in phraseology. 28 U.S.C. § 2283.

2. As the following sections will demonstrate, the revised Anti–Injunction Act has had a rocky history in the courts. In the words of one commentator, "the courts have * * * treat[ed] the statutory language somewhat like silly putty, stretching it and squashing it * * *." Wood, *Fine-Tuning Judicial Federalism: A Proposal for Reform of the Anti–Injunction Act,* 1990 B.Y.U.L.Rev. 289, 289–90. The same commentator suggests that "[i]n the end, the goal of a bright-line anti-injunction standard may be doomed never to succeed, because it attempts to incorporate two mutually inconsistent imperatives: first, respecting the autonomy of the state courts as adjudicators of equal dignity to the federal courts; and second, protecting superior federal interests, both substantive and procedural." Id. at 290.

3. For analysis of the history of the Anti–Injunction Act prior to its 1948 revision, see Durfee & Sloss, *Federal Injunction Against Proceedings in State Courts: The Life History of a Statute,* 30 Mich.L.Rev. 1145 (1932); Taylor & Willis, *The Power of Federal Courts to Enjoin Proceedings in State Courts,* 42 Yale L.J. 1169 (1933); Warren, *Federal and State Court Interference,* 43 Harv.L.Rev. 345 (1930).

4. Note that "[t]he Anti–Injunction Act applies although the injunction would be directed at a litigant * * * instead of the state court proceeding itself. * * * The Anti–Injunction Act also applies to declaratory judgments if those judgments have the same effect as an injunction." California v. Randtron, 268 F.3d 891, 896 (9th Cir.2001).

5. The Supreme Court has not resolved the question whether the Anti–Injunction Act's bar applies only to attempts to enjoin judicial proceedings, and not administrative proceedings. Gibson v. Berryhill, 411 U.S. 564, 573 n. 12 (1973). However, "every circuit to have addressed the question has held that it does not [apply to attempts to enjoin administrative proceedings]." Entergy, Arkansas, Inc. v. Nebraska, 210 F.3d 887, 900 (8th Cir.2000).

§ 2. THE "RELITIGATION" EXCEPTION

PARSONS STEEL, INC. v. FIRST ALABAMA BANK

Supreme Court of the United States, 1986.
474 U.S. 518.

JUSTICE REHNQUIST delivered the opinion of the Court.

The Full Faith and Credit Act, 28 U.S.C. § 1738, requires federal courts as well as state courts to give state judicial proceedings "the same full faith and credit ... as they have by law or usage in the courts of such State ... from which they are taken." The Anti–Injunction Act, 28 U.S.C. § 2283, generally prohibits a federal court from granting an injunction to stay proceedings in a state court, but excepts from that prohibition the issuance of an injunction by a federal court "where necessary ... to protect or effectuate its judgments." In the present case the Court of Appeals for the Eleventh Circuit held that the quoted exception to the latter Act worked a *pro tanto* amendment to the former, so that a federal court might issue an injunction against state-court proceedings even though the prevailing party in the federal suit had litigated in the state court and lost on the res judicata effect of the federal judgment. We granted certiorari to consider this question, and now reverse the judgment of the Court of Appeals.

Petitioners Parsons Steel, Inc., and Jim and Melba Parsons sued respondents First Alabama Bank of Montgomery and Edward Herbert, a bank officer, in Alabama state court in February 1979, essentially alleging that the bank had fraudulently induced the Parsons to permit a third person to take control of a subsidiary of Parsons Steel and eventually to obtain complete ownership of the subsidiary. The subsidiary was adjudicated an involuntary bankrupt in April 1979, and the trustee in bankruptcy was added as a party plaintiff in the state action. In May 1979 Parsons Steel and the Parsons sued the bank in the United States District Court for the District of Alabama, alleging that the same conduct on the part of the bank that was the subject of the state-court suit also violated the Bank Holding Company Act (BHCA) amendments, 12 U.S.C. §§ 1971–1978. The trustee in bankruptcy chose not to participate in the federal action.

The parties conducted joint discovery in the federal and state actions. The federal action proceeded to trial on the issue of liability before the state action went to trial. A jury returned a verdict in favor of petitioners, but the District Court granted judgment n.o.v. to the bank. That judgment was affirmed on appeal. Parsons Steel, Inc. v. First Alabama Bank of Montgomery, 679 F.2d 242 (C.A.11 1982). After the federal judgment was entered, respondents pleaded in the state action the defenses of res judicata and collateral estoppel based on that judgment. The Alabama court, however, ruled that res judicata did not bar the state action. Almost a year after the federal judgment was entered, the state complaint was amended to include a Uniform Commercial Code (UCC) claim that the bank's foreclosure sale of the subsidiary's assets was commercially unreasonable. A jury returned a general verdict in favor of petitioners, awarding a total of four million and one dollars in damages.

Having lost in state court, respondents returned to the District Court that had previously entered judgment in the bank's favor and filed the present injunctive action against petitioners, the plaintiffs in the state action.[1] The District Court found that the federal BHCA suit and the state action were based on the same factual allegations and claimed substantially the same damages. The court held that the state claims should have been raised in the federal action as pendent to the BHCA claim and accordingly that the BHCA judgment barred the state claims under res judicata. Determining that the Alabama judgment in effect nullified the earlier federal-court judgment in favor of the bank, the District Court enjoined petitioners from further prosecuting the state action.

---

1. Although the opinion of the Court of Appeals does not mention it, respondents apparently also filed in state court a timely post-trial motion for new trial or judgment n.o.v.

A divided panel of the Court of Appeals affirmed in relevant part, holding that the issuance of the injunction was not "an abuse of discretion" by the District Court. The majority first agreed with the District Court that the fraud and UCC claims presented issues of fact and law that could have been and should have been raised in the same action as the BHCA claim. Thus the parties to the BHCA action and their privies, including the trustee in bankruptcy, were barred by res judicata from raising these claims in state court after the entry of the federal judgment.

The majority then held that the injunction was proper under the so-called "relitigation exception" to the Anti–Injunction Act, 28 U.S.C. § 2283, which provides:

> "A court of the United States may not grant an injunction to stay proceedings in a State court except as expressly authorized by Act of Congress, or where necessary in aid of its jurisdiction, or *to protect or effectuate its judgments*" (emphasis added).

In reaching this holding, the majority explicitly declined to consider the possible preclusive effect, pursuant to the Full Faith and Credit Act, 28 U.S.C. § 1738,[2] of the state court's determination after full litigation by the parties that the earlier federal-court judgment did not bar the state action. According to the majority, "while a federal court is generally bound by other state court determinations, the relitigation exception empowers a federal court to be the final adjudicator as to the res judicata effects of its prior judgments on a subsequent state action."

Finally, the majority ruled that respondents had not waived their right to an injunction by waiting until after the trial in the state action was completed. The majority concluded that the state-court pleadings were so vague that it was not clear until after trial that essentially the same cause of action was involved as the BHCA claim and that the earlier federal judgment was in danger of being nullified. According to the majority, the Anti–Injunction Act does not limit the power of a federal court to protect its judgment "to specific points in time in state court trials or appellate procedure."

* * *

In our view, the majority of the Court of Appeals gave unwarrantedly short shrift to the important values of federalism and comity embodied in the Full Faith and Credit Act. * * * "It has long been established that § 1738 does not allow federal courts to employ their own rules of res judicata in determining the effect of state judgments. Rather, it goes beyond the common law and commands a federal court to accept the rules chosen by the State from which the judgment is taken." Kremer v. Chemical Construction Corp., 456 U.S. 461, 481–482 (1982). * * *

2. The Full Faith and Credit Act provides, in pertinent part, that state judicial proceedings "shall have the same full faith and credit in every court within the United States ... as they have by law or usage in the courts of such State ... from which they are taken."

In the instant case, however, the Court of Appeals did not consider the possible preclusive effect under Alabama law of the state-court judgment, and particularly of the state court's ·resolution of the res judicata issue, concluding instead that the relitigation exception to the Anti–Injunction Act limits the Full Faith and Credit Act. We do not agree. "[A]n exception to § 1738 will not be recognized unless a later statute contains an express or implied partial repeal." *Kremer,* supra, at 468; Allen v. McCurry, 449 U.S. 90, 99 (1980). Here, as in *Kremer,* there is no claim of an express repeal; rather, the Court of Appeals found an implied repeal. " 'It is, of course, a cardinal principle of statutory construction that repeals by implication are not favored,' Radzanower v. Touche Ross & Co., 426 U.S. 148, 154 (1976); United States v. United Continental Tuna Corp., 425 U.S. 164, 168 (1976), and whenever possible, statutes should be read consistently." 456 U.S., at 468. We believe that the Anti–Injunction Act and the Full Faith and Credit Act can be construed consistently, simply by limiting the relitigation exception of the Anti–Injunction Act to those situations in which the state court has not yet ruled on the merits of the res judicata issue. Once the state court has finally rejected a claim of res judicata, then the Full Faith and Credit Act becomes applicable and federal courts must turn to state law to determine the preclusive effect of the state court's decision.

The contrary holding of the Court of Appeals apparently was based on the fact that Congress in 1948 amended the Anti–Injunction Act to overrule this Court's decision in Toucey v. New York Life Insurance Co., 314 U.S. 118 (1941), in favor of the understanding of prior law expressed in Justice Reed's dissenting opinion. See Revisor's Note to 1948 Revision of Anti–Injunction Act, 28 U.S.C., p. 377. But the instant case is a far cry from *Toucey,* and one may fully accept the logic of Justice Reed's dissent without concluding that it sanctions the result reached by the Court of Appeals here. In each of the several cases involved in *Toucey,* the prevailing party in the federal action sought an injunction against relitigation in state court as soon as the opposing party commenced the state action, and before there was any resolution of the res judicata issue by the state court. In the instant case, on the other hand, respondents chose to fight out the res judicata issue in state court first, and only after losing there did they return to federal court for another try.

The Court of Appeals also felt that the District Court's injunction would discourage inefficient simultaneous litigation in state and federal courts on the same issue—that is, the res judicata effect of the prior federal judgment. But this is one of the costs of our dual court system:

> "In short, the state and federal courts had concurrent jurisdiction in this case, and neither court was free to prevent either party from simultaneously pursuing claims in both courts." Atlantic Coast Line R. Co. v. Locomotive Engineers, 398 U.S. 281, 295 (1970).

Indeed, this case is similar to *Atlantic Coast Line* in which we held that the various exceptions to the Anti–Injunction Act did not permit a federal court to enjoin state proceedings in circumstances more threatening to federal jurisdiction than the circumstances of this case. There we stated that the phrase "to protect or effectuate its judgments" authorized a federal injunction of state proceedings only "to prevent a state court from so interfering with a federal court's consideration or disposition of a case as to seriously impair the federal court's flexibility and authority to decide that case."

We hold, therefore, that the Court of Appeals erred by refusing to consider the possible preclusive effect, under Alabama law, of the state-court judgment. Even if the state court mistakenly rejected respondents' claim of res judicata, this does not justify the highly intrusive remedy of a federal-court injunction against the enforcement of the state-court judgment. Rather, the Full Faith and Credit Act requires that federal courts give the state court judgment, and particularly the state court's resolution of the res judicata issue, the same preclusive effect it would have had in another court of the same State. Challenges to the correctness of a state court's determination as to the conclusive effect of a federal judgment must be pursued by way of appeal through the state-court system and certiorari from this Court.

We think the District Court is best situated to determine and apply Alabama preclusion law in the first instance. Should the District Court conclude that the state-court judgment is not entitled to preclusive effect under Alabama law and the Full Faith and Credit Act, it would then be in the best position to decide the propriety of a federal-court injunction under the general principles of equity, comity, and federalism discussed in Mitchum v. Foster, 407 U.S. 225, 243 (1972).

Notes

1. How, if at all, does the practice under the relitigation exception differ from the traditional operation of the *res judicata* doctrine? Why could the sanctity of the federal judgment not be preserved simply by the pleading of *res judicata* in the subsequent state proceeding?

2. What is the rationale for the relitigation exception? See Justice Reed's dissent in *Toucey*. Is there any reason this logic should be limited to situations where the prior judgment is federal and the subsequent litigation is in state court?

3. To what extent should a federal court be permitted to enjoin a state court action in order to protect a judgment issued by another federal district court? See Smith v. Woosley, 399 F.3d 428 (2d Cir.2005), where the court upheld a Connecticut district court's injunction of a state court action to protect the prior judgment of a Pennsylvania district court. While the court acknowledged that this was a strained reading of the text of the relitigation exception, "the equities overwhelmingly favor" the injunction, in order to protect the interests of the successful litigant in the Pennsylvania action. For the contrary position, see Alton Box Board Co. v. Esprit de Corp., 682 F.2d 1267 (9th Cir.1982).

4. Prior to *Parsons Steel*, it was not entirely clear whether a federal court, before issuing an injunction under the relitigation exception, had to

allow the state court to rule on the claim of res judicata deriving from the earlier federal judgment. The American Law Institute had argued that "[t]he requirements of irreparable harm and lack of any other adequate remedy apply implicitly under the [anti-injunction] statute * * *." ALI, Study of the Division of Jurisdiction Between State and Federal Courts 306 (1969). The study therefore concluded that the relitigation exception would not generally be employed, since the federal court would defer to the state court to apply res judicata principles. Id. How does this approach differ from the holding in Parsons Steel? _ must occur b/f state Ct judgment

5. After *Parsons Steel*, under what circumstances will a federal court be authorized to employ the relitigation exception? Can it *ever* be used? Presumably, if the litigant seeking to protect the federal judgment eschews state court and instead goes in the first instance to the federal court that issued the judgment, then the bar of *Parsons* would not apply. However, even when that litigant goes first to state court and there seeks, unsuccessfully, to raise the defense of res judicata, federal courts have, on occasion, permitted him to go to federal court for relief. This has occurred when the state court's rejection of the res judicata defense would itself not receive collateral estoppel effect under state law because of its lack of finality. See, e.g., Vines v. University of Louisiana at Monroe, 398 F.3d 700 (5th Cir. 2005),cert. denied, ___ U.S. ___, 126 S.Ct. 1019 (2006). However, even when the state court's rejection of the res judicata defense need not be adhered to in the federal court as a matter of collateral estoppel because of its lack of finality, the federal court may nevertheless exercise its inherent equitable discretion not to enjoin the state action, due to federalism and comity concerns. See, e.g., Ramsden v. Agribank, FCB 214 F.3d 865 (7th Cir.), 531 U.S. 1036 (2000).

6. The Court in *Parsons Steel* believed that the approach used by the court of appeals "gave unwarrantedly short shrift to the important values of federalism and comity embodied in the Full Faith and Credit Act." Consider the following argument: The approach adopted by the Court is considerably *less* deferential to the interests of the state courts than is the approach adopted by the court of appeals.

7. In the *Atlantic Coast Line* case discussed by the Court in *Parsons Steel* (another aspect of which is examined infra p. 511), an employer sought an injunction in federal court against a union's picketing. The court denied the request, and the employer then obtained an injunction in Florida state court. After a subsequent Supreme Court decision recognizing a federal right to picket, the union attempted unsuccessfully to have the state court vacate its injunction. It then successfully sought to have the federal court enjoin the employer from enforcing the state court order. The union argued that the injunction fell within two of the exceptions to the Anti–Injunction Act, including the relitigation exception. The argument was that when the federal court originally denied the requested injunction, it had implicitly held that the union had a federally protected right to picket.

The Court held in Chick Kam Choo v. Exxon Corporation, 486 U.S. 140 (1988), that "an essential prerequisite for applying the relitigation exception is that the claims or issues which the federal injunction insulates from litigation in state proceedings actually have been decided by the federal court."

8. The lower courts generally apply a four-part test to determine the applicability of the relitigation exception: (1) "the parties in a later action must be identical to (or at least in privity with) the parties in a prior action"; (2) "the judgment in the prior action must have been rendered by a court of competent jurisdiction"; (3) "the prior action must have concluded with a final judgment on the merits"; and (4) "the same claim or cause of action must be involved in both suits." New York Life Ins. Co. v. Gillispie, 203 F.3d 384, 387 (5th Cir.2000). Note that "[i]t is insufficient that a claim or issue could have been raised in the prior action: The relitigation exception requires that the claims or issues that the federal injunction is to insulate from litigation in state proceedings 'actually have been decided by the federal court.'" Regions Bank of Louisiana v. Rivet, 224 F.3d 483, 488 (5th Cir.2000), quoting Chick Kam Choo v. Exxon Corp., 486 U.S. 140, 148 (1988).

9. *The Relitigation Exception and Class Actions.* On occasion, federal courts have relied on the relitigation exception to enjoin class actions in state court where the state and federal certification standards are the same and the federal court has previously found the class uncertifiable. See, e.g., In re Bridgestone/Firestone, Inc., Tires Products Liability Litigation, 333 F.3d 763 (7th Cir.), cert. denied, 537 U.S. 1105 (2003). But see Canady v. Allstate Ins. Co., 282 F.3d 1005 (8th Cir.2002) (holding that denial of class certification does not constitute a final judgment on the merits sufficient to satisfy the requirements of res judicata). On the subject, see generally Moorcroft, Note, *The Path to Preclusion: Federal Injunctive Relief Against Nationwide Classes in State Court,* 54 Duke L.J. 221 (2004); Wasserman, *Dueling Class Actions,* 80 B.U.L.Rev. 461 (2000).

10. Consider the following argument: The relitigation exception is premised on a fear that state courts, which are generally unfamiliar with the nuances of federal law, will be unable to grasp the full ramifications of the prior federal court judgment. If accepted, would this argument perhaps prove too much? See Redish, *The Anti–Injunction Statute Reconsidered,* 44 U.Chi.L.Rev. 717, 722–26 (1977).

§ 3.   THE "EXPRESSLY AUTHORIZED" EXCEPTION

MITCHUM v. FOSTER

Supreme Court of the United States, 1972.
407 U.S. 225.

MR. JUSTICE STEWART delivered the opinion of the Court.

The federal anti-injunction statute provides that a federal court "may not grant an injunction to stay proceedings in a State court except as expressly authorized by Act of Congress, or where necessary in aid of its jurisdiction, or to protect or effectuate its judgments."[1] An Act of Congress, 42 U.S.C. § 1983, expressly authorizes a "suit in equity" to

---

1.   28 U.S.C. § 2283.

redress "the deprivation," under the color of state law, "of any rights, privileges, or immunities secured by the Constitution. . . . ."[2] The question before us is whether this "Act of Congress" comes within the "expressly authorized" exception of the anti-injunction statute so as to permit a federal court in a § 1983 suit to grant an injunction to stay a proceeding pending in a state court. This question, which has divided the federal courts,[3] has lurked in the background of many of our recent cases, but we have not until today explicitly decided it.[4]

I

The prosecuting attorney of Bay County, Florida, brought a proceeding in a Florida court to close down the appellant's bookstore as a public nuisance under the claimed authority of Florida law. The state court entered a preliminary order prohibiting continued operation of the bookstore. After further inconclusive proceedings in the state courts, the appellant filed a complaint in the United States District Court for the Northern District of Florida, alleging that the actions of the state judicial and law enforcement officials were depriving him of rights protected by the First and Fourteenth Amendments. Relying upon 42 U.S.C. § 1983,[5] he asked for injunctive and declaratory relief against the state court proceedings, on the ground that Florida laws were being unconstitutionally applied by the state court so as to cause him great and irreparable harm. A single federal district judge issued temporary restraining orders, and a three-judge court was convened pursuant to 28 U.S.C. §§ 2281 and 2284. After a hearing, the three-judge court dissolved the temporary restraining orders and refused to enjoin the state court proceeding, holding that the "injunctive relief sought here as to the proceedings pending in the Florida courts does not come under any of the exceptions

2. The statute provides in full: "Every person who, under color of any statute, ordinance, regulation, custom, or usage, of any State or Territory, subjects, or causes to be subjected, any citizen of the United States or other person within the jurisdiction thereof to the deprivation of any rights, privileges, or immunities secured by the Constitution and laws, shall be liable to the party injured in an action at law, suit in equity, or other proper proceeding for redress."

3. Compare Cooper v. Hutchinson, 184 F.2d 119 (C.A.3) (§ 1983 is an "expressly authorized" exception), with Baines v. City of Danville, 337 F.2d 579 (C.A.4) (§ 1983 is not an "expressly authorized" exception).

4. See Dombrowski v. Pfister, 380 U.S. 479, 484 n. 2; Cameron v. Johnson, 390 U.S. 611, 613 n. 3; Younger v. Harris, 401 U.S. 37, 54. See also Lynch v. Household Finance Corp., 405 U.S. 538, 556; Roudebush v. Hartke, 405 U.S. 15.

In *Younger,* supra, Mr. Justice Douglas was the only member of the Court who took

a position on the question now before us. He expressed the view that § 1983 is included in the "expressly authorized exception to § 2283. . . ." 401 U.S., at 62. Cf. id., at 54 (Stewart, J., joined by Harlan, J., concurring); Perez v. Ledesma, 401 U.S. 82, 120 n. 14 (separate opinion of Brennan, J., joined by White and Marshall, JJ.).

5. Federal jurisdiction was based upon 28 U.S.C. § 1343(3). The statute states in relevant part:

"The district courts shall have original jurisdiction of any civil action authorized by law to be commenced by any person:

. . .

"(3) To redress the deprivation, under color of any State law, statute, ordinance, regulation, custom or usage, of any right, privilege or immunity secured by the Constitution of the United States or by any Act of Congress providing for equal rights of citizens or of all persons within the jurisdiction of the United States."

set forth in Section 2283. It is not expressly authorized by Act of Congress, it is not necessary in the aid of this court's jurisdiction, and it is not sought in order to protect or effectuate any judgment of this court." 315 F.Supp. 1387, 1389. An appeal was brought directly here under 28 U.S.C. § 1253, and we noted probable jurisdiction.

II

In denying injunctive relief, the District Court relied on this Court's decision in Atlantic Coast Line R. Co. v. Brotherhood of Locomotive Engineers, 398 U.S. 281. The *Atlantic Coast Line* case did not deal with the "expressly authorized" exception of the anti-injunction statute,[7] but the Court's opinion in that case does bring into sharp focus the critical importance of the question now before us. For in that case we expressly rejected the view that the anti-injunction statute merely states a flexible doctrine of comity, and made clear that the statute imposes an absolute ban upon the issuance of a federal injunction against a pending state court proceeding in the absence of one of the recognized exceptions * * *.

It follows, in the present context, that if 42 U.S.C. § 1983 is not within the "expressly authorized" exception of the anti-injunction statute, then a federal equity court is wholly without power to grant any relief in a § 1983 suit seeking to stay a state court proceeding. In short, if a § 1983 action is not an "expressly authorized" statutory exception, the anti-injunction law absolutely prohibits in such an action all federal equitable intervention in a pending state court proceeding, whether civil or criminal, and regardless of how extraordinary the particular circumstances may be.

Last Term, in Younger v. Harris, 401 U.S. 37, and its companion cases,[9] the Court dealt at length with the subject of federal judicial intervention in pending state criminal prosecutions. In *Younger* a three-judge federal district court in a § 1983 action had enjoined a criminal prosecution pending in a California court. In asking us to reverse that judgment, the appellant argued that the injunction was in violation of the federal anti-injunction statute. But the Court carefully eschewed any reliance on the statute in reversing the judgment, basing its decision instead upon what the Court called "Our Federalism"—upon "the national policy forbidding federal courts to stay or enjoin pending state court proceedings except under special circumstances."

In *Younger*, this Court emphatically reaffirmed "the fundamental policy against federal interference with state criminal prosecutions." It made clear that even "the possible unconstitutionality of a statute 'on its face' does not in itself justify an injunction against good-faith attempts

---

7. At issue were the other two exceptions of the anti-injunction statute: "where necessary in aid of its jurisdiction, or to protect or effectuate its judgments." Atlantic Coast Line R. Co. v. Brotherhood of Locomotive Engineers, 398 U.S. 281, 288.

9. Samuels v. Mackell, 401 U.S. 66; Boyle v. Landry, 401 U. S. 77; Perez v. Ledesma, 401 U.S. 82; Dyson v. Stein, 401 U.S. 200; Byrne v. Karalexis, 401 U.S. 216.

to enforce it.'' At the same time, however, the Court clearly left room for federal injunctive intervention in a pending state court prosecution in certain exceptional circumstances—where irreparable injury is ''both great and immediate,'' where the state law is '' 'flagrantly and patently violative of express constitutional prohibitions,' '' or where there is a showing of ''bad faith, harassment, or . . . other unusual circumstances that would call for equitable relief.'' In the companion case of Perez v. Ledesma, 401 U.S. 82, the Court said that ''[o]nly in cases of proven harassment or prosecutions undertaken by state officials in bad faith without hope of obtaining a valid conviction and perhaps in other extraordinary circumstances where irreparable injury can be shown is federal injunctive relief against pending state prosecutions appropriate.'' See also Dyson v. Stein, 401 U.S. 200, 203.

While the Court in *Younger* and its companion cases expressly disavowed deciding the question now before us—whether § 1983 comes within the ''expressly authorized'' exception of the anti-injunction statute—it is evident that our decisions in those cases cannot be disregarded in deciding this question. In the first place, if § 1983 is not within the statutory exception, then the anti-injunction statute would have absolutely barred the injunction issued in *Younger*, as the appellant in that case argued, and there would have been no occasion whatever for the Court to decide that case upon the ''policy'' ground of ''Our Federalism.'' Secondly, if § 1983 is not within the ''expressly authorized'' exception of the anti-injunction statute, then we must overrule *Younger* and its companion cases insofar as they recognized the permissibility of injunctive relief against pending criminal prosecutions in certain limited and exceptional circumstances. For, under the doctrine of *Atlantic Coast Line*, the anti-injunction statute would, in a § 1983 case, then be an ''absolute prohibition'' against federal equity intervention in a pending state criminal *or* civil proceeding—under any circumstances whatever.

The *Atlantic Coast Line* and *Younger* cases thus serve to delineate both the importance and the finality of the question now before us. And it is in the shadow of those cases that the question must be decided.

III

* * *

Despite the seemingly uncompromising language of the anti-injunction statute prior to 1948, the Court soon recognized that exceptions must be made to its blanket prohibition if the import and purpose of other Acts of Congress were to be given their intended scope. So it was that, in addition to the bankruptcy law exception that Congress explicitly recognized in 1874, the Court through the years found that federal courts were empowered to enjoin state court proceedings, despite the anti-injunction statute, in carrying out the will of Congress under at least six other federal laws. These covered a broad spectrum of congressional action: (1) legislation providing for removal of litigation from state to federal courts,[12] (2) legislation limiting the liability of shipowners,[13] (3) legislation providing for federal interpleader actions,[14] (4) legislation conferring federal jurisdiction over farm mortgages,[15] (5) legislation governing federal habeas corpus proceedings,[16] and (6) legislation providing for control of prices.[17]

In addition to the exceptions to the anti-injunction statute found to be embodied in these various Acts of Congress, the Court recognized other "implied" exceptions to the blanket prohibition of the anti-injunction statute. One was an "in rem" exception allowing a federal court to enjoin a state court proceeding in order to protect its jurisdiction of a *res* over which it had first acquired jurisdiction.[18] Another was a "relitigation" exception, permitting a federal court to enjoin relitigation in a state court of issues already decided in federal litigation.[19] Still a third exception, more recently developed, permits a federal injunction of state court proceedings when the plaintiff in the federal court is the United States itself, or a federal agency asserting "superior federal interests."[20]

In *Toucey v. New York Life Ins.* Co., 314 U.S. 118, the Court in 1941 issued an opinion casting considerable doubt upon the approach to the anti-injunction statute reflected in its previous decisions. The Court's

---

12. See French v. Hay, 22 Wall. 250; Kline v. Burke Construction Co., 260 U.S. 226. The federal removal provisions, both civil and criminal, 28 U.S.C. §§ 1441–1450, provide that once a copy of the removal petition is filed with the clerk of the state court, the "State court shall proceed no further unless and until the case is remanded." 28 U.S.C. § 1446(e).

13. See Providence & N.Y.S.S. Co. v. Hill Mfg. Co., 109 U.S. 578. The Act of 1851, 9 Stat. 635, as amended, provides that once a shipowner has deposited with the court an amount equal to the value of his interest in the ship, "all claims and proceedings against the owner with respect to the matter in question shall cease." 46 U.S.C. § 185.

14. See Treinies v. Sunshine Mining Co., 308 U.S. 66. The Interpleader Act of 1926, 44 Stat. 416, as currently written provides that in "any civil action of interpleader ... a district court may ... enter its order restraining [all claimants] ... from instituting or prosecuting any proceeding in any State or United States court affecting the property, instrument or obligation involved in the interpleader action." 28 U.S.C. § 2361.

15. See Kalb v. Feuerstein, 308 U.S. 433. The Frazier–Lemke Farm–Mortgage Act, as amended in 1935, 49 Stat. 944, provides that in situations to which it is applicable a federal court shall "stay all judicial or official proceedings in any court." 11 U.S.C. § 203(s)(2) (1940 ed.).

16. See Ex parte Royall, 117 U.S. 241, 248–249. The Federal Habeas Corpus Act provides that a federal court before which a habeas corpus proceeding is pending may "stay any proceeding against the person detained in any State Court ... for any matter involved in the habeas corpus proceeding." 28 U.S.C. § 2251.

17. Section 205(a) of the Emergency Price Control Act of 1942, 56 Stat. 33, provided that the Price Administrator could request a federal district court to enjoin acts that violated or threatened to violate the Act. In Porter v. Dicken, 328 U.S. 252, we held that this authority was broad enough to justify an injunction to restrain state court proceedings. Id., at 255. The Emergency Price Control Act was thus considered a congressionally authorized exception to the anti-injunction statute. Ibid.; see also Bowles v. Willingham, 321 U.S. 503. Section 205(a) expired in 1947. Act of July 25, 1946, 60 Stat. 664.

18. See, e.g., Toucey v. New York Life Ins. Co., 314 U.S., at 135–136; Freeman v. Howe, 24 How. 450; Kline v. Burke Construction Co., 260 U.S. 226.

19. See, e.g., Toucey, supra, at 137–141; Dial v. Reynolds, 96 U.S. 340; Supreme Tribe of Ben-Hur v. Cauble, 255 U.S. 356. See generally 1A J. Moore, Federal Practice 2302–2311 (1965).

20. Leiter Minerals Inc. v. United States, 352 U.S. 220; NLRB v. Nash–Finch Co., 404 U.S. 138.

opinion expressly disavowed the "relitigation" exception to the statute, and emphasized generally the importance of recognizing the statute's basic directive "of 'hands off' by the federal courts in the use of the injunction to stay litigation in a state court." 314 U.S., at 132. The congressional response to *Toucey* was the enactment in 1948 of the anti-injunction statute in its present form in 28 U.S.C. § 2283, which, as the Reviser's Note makes evident, served not only to overrule the specific holding of *Toucey*,[21] but to restore "the basic law as generally understood and interpreted prior to the *Toucey* decision."[22]

We proceed, then, upon the understanding that in determining whether § 1983 comes within the "expressly authorized" exception of the anti-injunction statute, the criteria to be applied are those reflected in the Court's decisions prior to *Toucey*.[23] A review of those decisions makes reasonably clear what the relevant criteria are. In the first place, it is evident that, in order to qualify under the "expressly authorized" exception of the anti-injunction statute, a federal law need not contain an express reference to that statute. As the Court has said, "no prescribed formula is required; an authorization need not expressly refer to § 2283." Amalgamated Clothing Workers of America v. Richman Bros. Co., 348 U.S. 511, 516. Indeed, none of the previously recognized statutory exceptions contains any such reference.[24] Secondly, a federal law need not expressly authorize an injunction of a state court proceeding in order to qualify as an exception. Three of the six previously recognized statutory exceptions contain no such authorization.[25] Thirdly, it is clear that, in order to qualify as an "expressly authorized" exception to the anti-injunction statute, an Act of Congress must have created a specific and uniquely federal right or remedy, enforceable in a federal court of equity, that could be frustrated if the federal court were not empowered to enjoin a state court proceeding. This is not to say that in order to come within the exception an Act of Congress must, on its face and in every one of its provisions, be totally incompatible with the

---

21. The Reviser's Note states in part: "The exceptions specifically include the words 'to protect or effectuate its judgments,' for lack of which the Supreme Court held that the Federal courts are without power to enjoin relitigation of cases and controversies fully adjudicated by such courts. (See Toucey v. New York Life Insurance Co., 314 U.S. 118. A vigorous dissenting opinion [314 U.S. 141] notes that at the time of the 1911 revision of the Judicial Code, the power of the courts ... of the United States to protect their judgments was unquestioned and that the revisers of that code noted no change and Congress intended no change." H.R.Rep. No. 308, 80th Cong., 1st Sess., A181–182 (1947).

22. Ibid.

23. Cf. Amalgamated Clothing Workers v. Richman Bros. Co., 348 U.S. 511, 521 (dissenting opinion).

24. See nn. 12, 13, 14, 15, 16, and 17, supra.

25. See nn. 12, 13, and 17, supra. The federal courts have found that other Acts of Congress that do not refer to § 2283 or to injunctions against state court proceedings nonetheless come within the "expressly authorized" language of the anti-injunction statute. See, e.g., Walling v. Black Diamond Coal Mining Co., 59 F.Supp. 348, 351 (W.D.Ky.) (the Fair Labor Standards Act); Okin v. SEC, 161 F.2d 978, 980 (C.A.2) (the Public Utility Holding Company Act); Dilworth v. Riner, 343 F.2d 226, 230 (C.A.5) (the 1964 Civil Rights Act); Studebaker Corp. v. Gittlin, 360 F.2d 692 (C.A.2) (the Securities and Exchange Act).

prohibition of the anti-injunction statute.[26] The test, rather, is whether an Act of Congress, clearly creating a federal right or remedy enforceable in a federal court of equity, could be given its intended scope only by the stay of a state court proceeding. See *Toucey, supra,* at 132–134; *Kline v. Burke Construction Co.,* 260 U.S. 226; *Providence & N. Y. S. S. Co. v. Hill Mfg. Co.,* 109 U.S. 578, 599; *Treinies v. Sunshine Mining Co.,* 308 U.S. 66, 78; *Kalb v. Feuerstein,* 308 U.S. 433; *Bowles v. Willingham,* 321 U.S. 503.

With these criteria in view, we turn to consideration of 42 U.S.C. § 1983.

IV

Section 1983 was originally § 1 of the Civil Rights Act of 1871. 17 Stat. 13. It was "modeled" on § 2 of the Civil Rights Act of 1866, 14 Stat. 27,[27] and was enacted for the express purpose of "enforc[ing] the Provisions of the Fourteenth Amendment." 17 Stat. 13. The predecessor of § 1983 was thus an important part of the basic alteration in our federal system wrought in the Reconstruction era through federal legislation and constitutional amendment.[28] As a result of the new structure of law that emerged in the post-Civil War era—and especially of the Fourteenth Amendment, which was its centerpiece—the role of the Federal Government as a guarantor of basic federal rights against state power was clearly established. *Monroe v. Pape,* 365 U.S. 167; *McNeese v. Board of Education,* 373 U.S. 668; *Shelley v. Kraemer,* 334 U.S. 1; *Zwickler v. Koota,* 389 U.S. 241, 245–249; H. Flack, The Adoption of the Fourteenth Amendment (1908); J. tenBroek, The Anti–Slavery Origins of the Fourteenth Amendment (1951). Section 1983 opened the federal courts to private citizens offering a uniquely federal remedy against incursions under the claimed authority of state law upon rights secured by the Constitution and laws of the Nation.

It is clear from the legislative debates surrounding passage of § 1983's predecessor that the Act was intended to enforce the provisions of the Fourteenth Amendment "against State action, ... whether that action be executive, legislative, or *judicial.*" *Ex parte Virginia,* 100 U.S. 339, 346 (emphasis supplied). Proponents of the legislation noted that state courts were being used to harass and injure individuals, either because the state courts were powerless to stop deprivations or were in

26. Cf. *Baines v. City of Danville,* 337 F.2d 579 (C.A.4).

27. See remarks of Representative Shellabarger, chairman of the House Select Committee which drafted the Civil Rights Act of 1871, Cong. Globe, 42d Cong., 1st Sess., App. 68 (1871), and *Lynch v. Household Finance Corp.,* 405 U.S. 538, 545 n. 9.

28. In addition to proposing the Thirteenth, Fourteenth, and Fifteenth Amendments, Congress, from 1866 to 1875, enacted the following civil rights legislation: Act of April 9, 1866, 14 Stat. 27; Act of May 31, 1870, 16 Stat. 140; Act of April 20, 1871, 17 Stat. 13; and Act of March 1, 1875, 18 Stat. 335. In 1875, Congress also passed the general federal-question provision, giving federal courts the power to hear suits arising under Art. III, § 2, of the Constitution. Act of March 3, 1875, 18 Stat. 470. This is the predecessor of 28 U.S.C. § 1331.

league with those who were bent upon abrogation of federally protected rights.

* * *

Those who opposed the Act of 1871 clearly recognized that the proponents were extending federal power in an attempt to remedy the state courts' failure to secure federal rights. The debate was not about whether the predecessor of § 1983 extended to actions of state courts, but whether this innovation was necessary or desirable.

This legislative history makes evident that Congress clearly conceived that it was altering the relationship between the States and the Nation with respect to the protection of federally created rights; it was concerned that state instrumentalities could not protect those rights; it realized that state officers might, in fact, be antipathetic to the vindication of those rights; and it believed that these failings extended to the state courts.

V

Section 1983 was thus a product of a vast transformation from the concepts of federalism that had prevailed in the late 18th century when the anti-injunction statute was enacted. The very purpose of § 1983 was to interpose the federal courts between the States and the people, as guardians of the people's federal rights—to protect the people from unconstitutional action under color of state law, "whether that action be executive, legislative, or judicial." Ex parte Virginia, 100 U.S., at 346. In carrying out that purpose, Congress plainly authorized the federal courts to issue injunctions in § 1983 actions, by expressly authorizing a "suit in equity" as one of the means of redress. And this Court long ago recognized that federal injunctive relief against a state court proceeding can in some circumstances be essential to prevent great, immediate, and irreparable loss of a person's constitutional rights. Ex parte Young, 209 U.S. 123; cf. Truax v. Raich, 239 U.S. 33; Dombrowski v. Pfister, 380 U.S. 479. For these reasons we conclude that, under the criteria established in our previous decisions construing the anti-injunction statute, § 1983 is an Act of Congress that falls within the "expressly authorized" exception of that law.

In so concluding, we do not question or qualify in any way the principles of equity, comity, and federalism that must restrain a federal court when asked to enjoin a state court proceeding. These principles, in the context of state criminal prosecutions, were canvassed at length last Term in Younger v. Harris, 401 U.S. 37; and its companion cases. They are principles that have been emphasized by this Court many times in the past. Fenner v. Boykin, 271 U.S. 240; Spielman Motor Sales Co. v. Dodge, 295 U.S. 89; Beal v. Missouri Pac. R. Corp., 312 U.S. 45; Watson v. Buck, 313 U.S. 387; Williams v. Miller, 317 U.S. 599; Douglas v. City of Jeannette, 319 U.S. 157; Stefanelli v. Minard, 342 U.S. 117; Cameron v. Johnson, 390 U.S. 611. Today we decide only that the District Court in this case was in error in holding that, because of the anti-injunction statute, it was absolutely without power in this § 1983 action to enjoin a proceeding pending in a state court under any circumstances whatsoever.

The judgment is reversed and the case is remanded to the District Court for further proceedings consistent with this opinion.

[The concurring opinion of CHIEF JUSTICE BURGER is omitted.]

Notes

1. Does section 1983 "expressly" authorize an injunction of state proceedings, as you commonly understand that term?

2. The Court, relying on the Reviser's Note, concluded that "the criteria to be applied are those reflected in the Court's decisions prior to *Toucey*." The Court therefore believed it could rely on pre-*Toucey* precedents in interpreting the "expressly authorized" exception. Look again at the Reviser's Note, supra p. 488. Does it support the Court's conclusion that "pre-*Toucey*" cases are relevant to interpretation of the "expressly authorized" exception?

3. In finding that section 1983 could be viewed as an "expressly" authorized exception, the Court stated that "a federal law need not expressly authorize an injunction of a state court proceeding in order to qualify as an exception." Look carefully at the precedents the Court cites to support this conclusion. Assuming "pre-*Toucey*" precedents are relevant, do those cases help the Court in the context of section 1983?

4. In *Younger v. Harris*, 401 U.S. 37 (1971) [infra p. 523], the Supreme Court decided—one year before *Mitchum*—that, purely as a matter of judge-made federalism and comity, federal courts could not enjoin ongoing state criminal proceedings to protect rights under section 1983. It did so in part because to allow such injunctions would insult state courts by questioning their ability to enforce and protect federal rights. Is there an arguable inconsistency between the logic of *Mitchum* and that of *Younger*? If so, can the two be reconciled?

5. Although the Reviser's Note is not of much help on the question, why do you suppose Congress would require that a legislative exception to the Anti–Injunction Act be "express"? What safeguards does that requirement impose? Does the *Mitchum* test preserve those safeguards? See Redish, *The Anti–Injunction Statute Reconsidered*, 44 U.Chi.L.Rev. 717, 733–39 (1977).

6. Consider the following commentary on *Mitchum*: "However poorly grounded in statutory text, the decision has enormous practical significance for public law litigation. It means that parties (like the freedom riders) may pursue federal injunctive relief against a pending state court criminal prosecution on the ground that the prosecution violates federal constitutional rights." J. Pfander, Principles of Federal Jurisdiction 262 (2006). Professor Pfander further notes, however, that "the authority recognized in *Mitchum v. Foster* is not unlimited; the federal plaintiff must still make a case for injunctive relief," and "the federal plaintiff must also thread the

increasingly elaborate procedural needles created by the doctrine of equitable restraint [established in *Younger*]." Id.

    7. How easy to apply is the test developed in *Mitchum* for use of the "expressly authorized" exception? In answering, consider the following case.

    VENDO CO. v. LEKTRO–VEND CORP., 433 U.S. 623 (1977). The issue in the case was whether "§ 16 of the Clayton Act, which authorizes a private action to redress violations of the anti-trust laws, comes within the 'expressly authorized' exception to § 2283". Id. at 630. The petitioner had sued the respondents in Illinois state court for breach of noncompetition covenants. The respondents proceeded to file suit against the petitioner in federal court, arguing that the covenant forming the basis for the state court action constituted an unreasonable restraint of trade in violation of sections 1 and 2 of the Sherman Act. The federal court action remained dormant while the state action proceeded. However, after the Illinois Supreme Court affirmed an award for violation of the agreement, the respondents obtained a preliminary injunction from the federal court against collection of the state court judgment. The district court found that its injunction fell within both the "expressly authorized" and "necessary-in-aid-of-jurisdiction" exceptions to section 2283. The Seventh Circuit affirmed, but a divided Supreme Court reversed.

    Three opinions were written. The opinion announcing the Court's judgment was written by Justice Rehnquist and concurred in by Justices Stewart and Powell. Justice Blackmun, joined by Chief Justice Burger, concurred separately, and Justice Stevens, joined by Justice Brennan, Marshall and White, dissented.

    Section 16 provides in relevant part:

> [A]ny person * * * shall be entitled to sue for and have injunctive relief, in any court of the United States having jurisdiction over the parties, against threatened loss or damage by violation of the anti-trust laws * * * when and under the same conditions and principles as injunctive relief against threatened conduct that will cause loss or damage is granted by courts of equity, under the rules governing such proceedings * * *.

    Justice Rehnquist first noted that "[o]n its face, the language merely authorizes private injunctive relief for antitrust violations." He then rejected the lower courts' reliance on *Mitchum* as a basis on which to find section 16 an "expressly authorized" exception:

> The private action for damages conferred by the Clayton Act is a 'uniquely federal right or remedy,' in that actions based upon it may be brought only in the federal courts * * *. It thus meets the first part of the test laid down in the language quoted from *Mitchum*.

failspart

But that authorization for private action does not meet the second part of the *Mitchum* test; it is not an 'Act of Congress ... [which] could be given its intended scope only by the stay of a state court proceeding' Crucial to our determination in *Mitchum* that 42 U.S.C. § 1983 fulfilled this requirement–but wholly lacking here– was our recognition that one of the clear congressional concerns underlying the enactment of § 1983 was the possibility that state courts, as well as other branches of state government, might be used as instruments to deny citizens their rights under the Federal Constitution * * *.

* * *

Thus, in *Mitchum*, absence of express language authorization for enjoining state-court proceedings in § 1983 actions was cured by the presence of relevant legislative history. In this case, however, neither the respondents nor the courts below have called to our attention any similar legislative history in connection with the enactment of § 16 of the Clayton Act. Id. at 632–34.

Justice Blackmun, concurring, expressed the view that "application of the *Mitchum* test for deciding whether a statute is an 'expressly authorized' exception * * * shows that § 16 is such an exception under narrowly limited circumstances." However, he concluded that "no injunction may issue against currently pending state-court proceedings unless those proceedings are themselves part of a 'pattern of baseless, repetitive claims' that are being used as an anticompetitive device, all the traditional prerequisites for equitable relief are satisfied, and the only way to give the antitrust laws their intended scope is by staying the state proceedings." Id. at 643–44. He drew support from the antitrust decision, California Motor Transport Co. v. Trucking Unlimited, 404 U.S. 508 (1972), which, according to Blackmun, required institution of more than a single judicial proceeding to constitute a violation of the antitrust laws. In a footnote, he added: "Since I believe that federal courts should be hesitant indeed to enjoin ongoing state-court proceedings, I am of the opinion that a pattern of baseless, repetitive claims or some equivalent showing of grave abuse of the state courts must exist before an injunction would be proper." Id. at 644. Since no such finding had been made by the district court in the instant case, the injunction had to be denied.

Currently pending

Justice Stevens, dissenting, argued, first: "Since § 16 of the Clayton Act is an Act of Congress which expressly authorizes an injunction against a state-court proceeding which violates the antitrust laws, the plain language of the anti-injunction statute excepts this kind of injunction from its coverage." Id. at 654. He also relied on *Mitchum*: "Section 16 of the Clayton Act created a federal remedy which can only be given its intended scope if it includes the power to stay state-court proceedings in appropriate cases." Id. at 656–657. He relied on legislative history indicating that the antitrust laws were to be supported by "all remedial

Plain lang

process or writs proper and necessary to enforce its provisions." Id. at 657.

Stevens also rejected Justice Blackmun's interpretation of *California Motor Transport* as requiring a multiplicity of suits, rather than a single suit, for an antitrust violation to exist.

Notes

1.   After this decision, could you confidently advise a client whether section 16 of the Clayton Act is ever to be viewed as an "expressly authorized" exception to the Anti–Injunction Act? In answering, note that Justice Blackmun's concurring opinion, speaking for two justices, was necessary to make up a five-person majority, since Justice Stevens, dissenting, spoke for three justices.

2.   Exactly what do you understand Justice Blackmun to be saying? Do you find his footnote confusing in any way? Is it clear whether his conclusion is based on an interpretation of the substantive reach of the antitrust laws, of the Anti–Injunction Statute, or of both?

3.   How persuasive is Justice Stevens' suggested interpretation of the "expressly authorized" exception?

4.   What effect, if any, should *Vendo* have on the *Mitchum* test? See In re BankAmerica Corp. Securities Litigation, 263 F.3d 795, 801, n. 3 (8th Cir.2001), cert. denied, 535 U.S. 970 (2002).

5.   An application of the *Mitchum* test came in Casa Marie, Inc. v. Superior Court of Puerto Rico, 988 F.2d 252 (1st Cir.1993). The District Court had held that Title VIII of the Fair Housing Act, 42 U.S.C.A. § 3604, which prohibits discrimination in housing against people with a handicap, met *Mitchum*'s requirements for an "expressly authorized" exception. Section 3613(a) gives private litigants the right to challenge discriminatory practices. The District Court had concluded that "[a]pplying the *Mitchum* test, we find that the Fair Housing Act is an Act of Congress that has created uniquely federal rights, enforceable in a court of equity by private parties." 752 F.Supp. 1152, 1170 (D.Puerto Rico 1990). That court relied heavily on the fact that the legislative history of the 1988 amendments to the Act intended "that courts be able to award all remedies provided under" its provisions. It noted that "[i]t is obvious that state courts could be used to apply facially-neutral zoning laws, building codes, restrictive covenants, and other state statutory law related to the regulating [of] housing." Id. at 1171.

The Court of Appeals reversed, expressing an inability "to discern any statutory language or legislative history which indicates that Congress expressly excepted Title VIII claims from the operation of the Anti–Injunction Act." 988 F.2d at 261. The court noted that "Congress contemplated concurrent state-federal court jurisdiction over Title VIII claims" and reasoned that "the vesting of concurrent jurisdiction would seem to imply a vote of confidence in the integrity and competence of state courts to adjudicate Title VIII claims." Id. at 262. How persuasive is this argument, given that jurisdiction over section 1983 claims is also concurrent? In responding to the argument "that Congress implicitly demonstrated mistrust of state and local *government in general* by enabling private litigants to sue for federal injunctive relief against municipalities which enact or enforce zoning ordinances in a discriminatory fashion," the court stated that such reasoning "distends the [Anti–Injunction] Act's restrictive language (*expressly* authorized by Act of Congress) to absurd limits. If *Mitchum*'s second prong were to be considered satisfied whenever Congress enacted a statute authorizing injunctive relief, or by the mere fact that a local government *might* be made a defendant in a particular case, the rule requiring narrow construction of the Act's exceptions would be rendered largely meaningless, and with it the general presumption that state *courts* are competent to protect federal rights." 988 F.2d at 262. Is the court's analysis a criticism of the lower court's misuse of *Mitchum,* or of *Mitchum* itself?

6. On occasion, federal courts have found other statutes to satisfy *Mitchum*'s version of the "expressly authorized" exception. See, e.g., Martin v. Constance, 843 F.Supp. 1321 (E.D.Mo.1994) (Fair Housing Act); AT & T Management Pension Plan v. Tucker, 902 F.Supp. 1168 (C.D.Cal.1995) (Employee Retirement Income Security Act). See also United States v. Lewis, 411 F.3d 838, 845 (7th Cir.2005) (18 U.S.C. § 1514, protecting victims and witnesses of federal crimes from "harassment," is an expressly authorized exception under *Mitchum*, because "[d]espite the language of the statute, the 'expressly authorized' exceptions need not be spelled out"). But see Denny's Inc. v. Cake, 364 F.3d 521, 524 (4th Cir.), cert. denied, 543 U.S. 940 (2004) (finding that § 1132(a) of Employment Retirement Income Security Act (ERISA), which provides that a participant's beneficiary or fiduciary may bring an ERISA enforcement action in federal court "to enjoin any act or practice which violates any provision of this subchapter," constitutes an expressly authorized exception to the Anti–Injunction Act is "unpersuasive").

§ 4. THE "IN AID OF JURISDICTION" EXCEPTION

KLINE v. BURKE CONSTR. CO.

Supreme Court of the United States, 1922.
260 U.S. 226.

MR. JUSTICE SUTHERLAND delivered the opinion of the Court.

The Burke Construction Company, a corporation organized under the laws of the State of Missouri, brought an action at law against petitioners in the United States District Court for the Western District of Arkansas on February 16, 1920. The jurisdiction of that court was invoked upon the ground of diversity of citizenship, the petitioners being citizens of the State of Arkansas. The action was for breach of a contract between the parties, whereby the Construction Company had engaged to pave certain streets in the town of Texarkana. A trial was had before the court and a jury which resulted in a disagreement.

Subsequent to the commencement of the action by the Construction Company, viz., on March 19, 1920, petitioners instituted a suit in equity against that Company in a state chancery court of the State of Arkansas, upon the same contract, joining as defendants the sureties on the bond which had been given for the faithful performance of the contract. The bill in the latter suit alleged that the Construction Company had abandoned its contract and judgment was sought against the sureties as well as against the company. The bill asked an accounting with reference to the work which had been done and which remained to be done under the contract, and prayed judgment in the sum of $88,000.

In the action brought by the Construction Company the petitioners filed an answer and cross complaint, setting up, in substance, the same matters which were set forth in their bill in the state court. In the equity suit the Construction Company filed an answer and cross complaint, setting up the matters charged in its complaint in the action at law. Thus the two cases presented substantially the same issues, the only differences being those resulting from the addition of the sureties as parties defendant in the equity suit. Both actions were *in personam*, the ultimate relief sought in each case being for a money judgment only.

The equity suit was removed to the United States District Court upon the petition of the Construction Company upon the ground that the Company and the petitioners were citizens of different States and that the controversy between them was a separable controversy, and upon the further ground that a federal question was involved. Petitioners moved to remand. The District Court sustained the motion and the equity suit was thereupon remanded to the State Chancery Court, where it is still pending.

After the mistrial of the action at law in the United States District Court, the Construction Company filed a bill of complaint as a dependent bill to its action at law, by which it sought to enjoin the petitioners from further prosecuting the suit in equity in the State Chancery Court. The United States District Court denied the injunction and an appeal was taken to the Circuit Court of Appeals for the Eighth Circuit. That court reversed the decision of the District Court and remanded the case with instructions to issue an injunction against the prosecution of the suit in equity in the State Chancery Court. From that decree the case comes here upon writ of certiorari.

Section 265 of the Judicial Code provides: "The writ of injunction shall not be granted by any court of the United States to stay proceedings in any court of a State, except in cases where such injunction may be authorized by any law relating to proceedings in bankruptcy." But this section is to be construed in connection with § 262, which authorizes the United States courts "to issue all writs not specifically provided for by statute, which may be necessary for the exercise of their respective jurisdictions, and agreeable to the usages and principles of law." See Julian v. Central Trust Co., 193 U.S. 93, 112; Lanning v. Osborne, (C.C.) 79 Fed. 657, 662. It is settled that where a federal court has first acquired jurisdiction of the subject-matter of a cause, it may enjoin the parties from proceeding in a state court of concurrent jurisdiction where the effect of the action would be to defeat or impair the jurisdiction of the federal court. Where the action is *in rem* the effect is to draw to the federal court the possession or control, actual or potential, of the *res*, and the exercise by the state court of jurisdiction over the same *res* necessarily impairs, and may defeat, the jurisdiction of the federal court already attached. The converse of the rule is equally true, that where the jurisdiction of the state court has first attached, the federal court is precluded from exercising its jurisdiction over the same *res* to defeat or impair the state court's jurisdiction.

constitutional

* * *

But a controversy is not a thing, and a controversy over a mere question of personal liability does not involve the possession or control of a thing, and an action brought to enforce such a liability does not tend to impair or defeat the jurisdiction of the court in which a prior action for the same cause is pending. Each court is free to proceed in its own way and in its own time, without reference to the proceedings in the other court. Whenever a judgment is rendered in one of the courts and pleaded in the other, the effect of that judgment is to be determined by the application of the principles of *res adjudicata* by the court in which the action is still pending in the orderly exercise of its jurisdiction, as it would determine any other question of fact or law arising in the progress of the case. The rule, therefore, has become generally established that where the action first brought is *in personam* and seeks only a personal judgment, another action for the same cause in another jurisdiction is not precluded. * * *

res judicata

Rule

* * *

It is said * * * that if the second suit may be prosecuted so as to secure an adjudication in a state court before the action of the federal court can be adjudicated, then the federal court's adjudication would be made futile because before it is rendered the controversy will have become *res adjudicata* by the adjudication of the state court. Such a result, it is urged, cannot be allowed because the Construction Company brought its action in the federal court in pursuance "of a grant of this right in the Constitution and the acts of Congress" and it may not be deprived of that constitutional right by a subsequent suit in a state court.

Constitutional Right

* * *

The right of a litigant to maintain an action in a federal court on the ground that there is a controversy between citizens of different States is not one derived from the Constitution of the United States, unless in a very indirect sense. Certainly it is not a right *granted* by the Constitution. The applicable provisions, so far as necessary to be quoted here, are contained in Article III. Section 1 of that Article provides, "The judicial power of the United States shall be vested in one Supreme Court, and in such inferior courts as the Congress may from time to time ordain and establish." By § 2 of the same Article it is provided that the judicial power shall extend to certain designated cases and controversies and, among them, "to controversies ... between citizens of different

States...." The effect of these provisions is not to vest jurisdiction in the inferior courts over the designated cases and controversies but to delimit those in respect of which Congress may confer jurisdiction upon such courts as it creates. Only the jurisdiction of the Supreme Court is derived directly from the Constitution. Every other court created by the general government derives its jurisdiction wholly from the authority of Congress. That body may give, withhold or restrict such jurisdiction at its discretion, provided it be not extended beyond the boundaries fixed by the Constitution. Turner v. Bank of North America, 4 Dall. 8, 10; United States v. Hudson & Goodwin, 7 Cranch, 32; Sheldon v. Sill, 8 How. 441, 448; Stevenson v. Fain, 195 U.S. 165. The Constitution simply gives to the inferior courts the capacity to take jurisdiction in the enumerated cases, but it requires an act of Congress to confer it. The Mayor v. Cooper, 6 Wall. 247, 252. And the jurisdiction having been conferred may, at the will of Congress, be taken away in whole or in part; and if withdrawn without a saving clause all pending cases though cognizable when commenced must fall. The Assessors v. Osbornes, 9 Wall. 567, 575. A right which thus comes into existence only by virtue of an act of Congress, and which may be withdrawn by an act of Congress after its exercise has begun, cannot well be described as a constitutional right. The Construction Company, however, had the undoubted right under the statute to invoke the jurisdiction of the federal court and that court was bound to take the case and proceed to judgment. It could not abdicate its authority or duty in favor of the state jurisdiction. Chicot County v. Sherwood, 148 U.S. 529, 533; McClellan v. Carland, 217 U.S. 268, 282. But, while this is true, it is likewise true that the state court had jurisdiction of the suit instituted by petitioners. Indeed, since the case presented by that suit was such as to preclude its removal to the federal jurisdiction, the state jurisdiction in that particular suit was exclusive. It was, therefore, equally the duty of the state court to take the case and proceed to judgment. There can be no question of judicial supremacy, or of superiority of individual right. The well established rule, to which we have referred, that where the action is one *in rem* that court—whether state or federal—which first acquires jurisdiction draws to itself the exclusive authority to control and dispose of the *res*, involves the conclusion that the rights of the litigants to invoke the jurisdiction of the respective courts are of equal rank. See Heidritter v. Elizabeth Oil–Cloth Co., 112 U.S. 294, 305. The rank and authority of the courts are equal but both courts cannot possess or control the same thing at the same time, and any attempt to do so would result in unseemly conflict. The rule, therefore, that the court first acquiring jurisdiction shall proceed without interference from a court of the other jurisdiction is a rule of right and of law based upon necessity, and where the necessity, actual or potential, does not exist, the rule does not apply. Since that necessity does exist in actions *in rem* and does not exist in actions *in personam*, involving a question of personal liability only, the rule applies in the former but does not apply in the latter.

ATLANTIC COAST LINE R. R. v. BROTHERHOOD OF LOCOMO-
TIVE ENGINEERS, 398 U.S. 281 (1970).

In 1967 BLE [Brotherhood of Locomotive Engineers] began picketing the Moncrief Yard, a switching yard located near Jacksonville,
Florida, and wholly owned and operated by ACL [Atlantic Coast
Line]. As soon as this picketing began ACL went into federal court
seeking an injunction. When the federal judge denied the request,
ACL immediately went into state court and there succeeded in
obtaining an injunction. No further legal action was taken in this
dispute until two years later in 1969, after this Court's decision in
Brotherhood of Railroad Trainmen v. Jacksonville Terminal Co., 394
U.S. 369 (1969). In that case the Court considered the validity of a
state injunction against picketing by the BLE and other unions at
the Jacksonville Terminal, located immediately next to Moncrief
Yard. The Court reviewed the factual situation surrounding the
Jacksonville Terminal picketing and concluded that the unions had
a federally protected right to picket under the Railway Labor Act, 44
Stat. 577, as amended 45 U.S.C.A. § 151 et seq., and that that right
could not be interfered with by state court injunctions. * * * [T]he
respondent BLE filed a motion in state court to dissolve the Moncrief Yard injunction, arguing that under the *Jacksonville Terminal*
decision the injunction was improper. The state judge refused to
dissolve the injunction, holding that this Court's *Jacksonville Terminal* decision was not controlling. The union did not elect to appeal
that decision directly, but instead went back into the federal court
and requested an injunction against the enforcement of the state
court injunction. The District Judge granted the injunction and
upon application, a stay of that injunction, pending the filing and
disposition of a petition for certiorari, was granted. 396 U.S. 1201
(1969). The Court of Appeals summarily affirmed on the parties'
stipulation, and we granted a petition for certiorari to consider the
validity of the federal court's injunction against the state court. 398
U.S. at 283–84.

After disposing of the union's contention that the injunction was
proper as a means of "protect[ing] or effectuat[ing]" the district court's
earlier denial of an injunction, the Court, per Justice Black, concluded
that the injunction was not authorized by the "in aid of jurisdiction"
exception. Justice Black reasoned that "a federal court does not have
inherent power to ignore the limitations of § 2283 and to enjoin state
court proceedings merely because those proceedings interfere with a
protected federal right or invade an area preempted by federal law, even
when the interference is unmistakably clear." Id. at 294. The "in aid of
jurisdiction" exception, he said, "implies something similar to the concept of injunctions to 'protect or effectuate' judgments. Both exceptions
to the general prohibition of § 2283 imply that some federal injunctive

relief may be necessary to prevent a state court from so interfering with a federal court's consideration or disposition of a case as to seriously impair the federal court's flexibility and authority to decide that case." Id. at 295. In the present case, Black said, "the state and federal courts had concurrent jurisdiction * * *, and neither court was free to prevent either party from simultaneously pursuing claims in both courts. Kline v. Burke Constr. Co., 260 U.S. 226 (1922). * * * [L]ower federal courts possess no power whatever to sit in direct review of state court decisions. If the union was adversely affected by the state court's decision, it was free to seek vindication of its federal right in the Florida appellate courts and ultimately, if necessary, in this Court." Id. at 295–96.

Notes

1.   Is it true that, as *Kline* assumes, a state court action will impair the exercise of a federal court's jurisdiction when the two concurrent proceedings are in rem, but not when they are in personam? Assume concurrent state and federal in personam proceedings; if the state action is completed first, what is likely to be the effect of that decision in the federal proceeding? Do you believe such an effect constitutes an "impairment" of the federal court's jurisdiction? If so, would not an injunction of the state proceeding logically seem to be "in aid of" the federal court's jurisdiction?

2.   After *Atlantic Coast Line*, is the *Kline* rule still good law? Is there some basis for confusion on the point, in light of the language employed in *Atlantic Coast Line*? Cf. In re Glenn W. Turner Enterprises Litigation, 521 F.2d 775, 780 (3d Cir.1975). Many courts continue to follow the *Kline* rule. See, e.g., In re BankAmerica Corp., 263 F.3d 795, 801 (8th Cir.2001), cert. denied, 535 U.S. 970 (2002) ("Because both the state-court and federal-court actions are in personam proceedings, the * * * injunction does not fit within the Anti–Injunction Act's exceptions for injunctions in aid of the district court's jurisdiction." (citing *Kline*)). But see Winkler v. Eli Lilly & Co., 101 F.3d 1196, 1202 (7th Cir.1996): "We agree that the 'necessary in aid of jurisdiction' exception should be construed 'to empower the federal court to enjoin a concurrent state proceeding that might render the exercise of the federal court's jurisdiction nugatory.'" On occasion courts have carved exceptions to the *Kline* rule for multidistrict or complex litigation (see note 5), and for school desegregation cases. Garcia v. Bauza–Salas, 862 F.2d 905, 909 (1st Cir.1988).

3.   If the judicial history of *Kline* were put aside, what would be the most rational interpretation of the language of the "in aid of jurisdiction" exception? Consider the argument made in M. Redish, Federal Jurisdiction: Tensions in the Allocation of Judicial Power 326–27 (2d ed. 1990):

> Neither the *Kline* opinion nor the cases following *Kline* explain why the impairment of a federal court's "jurisdiction" is greater where the concurrent actions are in rem. If the federal court is hearing an in personam action, the conclusion of a concurrent state proceeding in the same matter will greatly restrict the freedom of the federal court, since the federal court will be found by the doctrines of res judicata and

collateral estoppel to apply most, if not all, of the factual findings and legal conclusions of the state court.

4. County of Imperial v. Munoz, 449 U.S. 54 (1980): The county obtained an injunction in California state court prohibiting the owner of a tract of land from selling water from a well on the premises for use outside the county, in violation of a conditional use permit required by a county zoning ordinance. The California Supreme Court affirmed, and the United States Supreme Court dismissed the appeal. Shortly after the California Supreme Court had disposed of the case, merchants who had arranged for the sale of the water brought an action in federal district court seeking declaratory and injunctive relief to prevent the county from enforcing the terms of the conditional permit, arguing that the terms violated the Commerce Clause of the Constitution. The federal court then issued a preliminary injunction, and the court of appeals affirmed. The United States Supreme Court, however, vacated the injunction, rejecting the lower courts' conclusion that the Anti–Injunction Act was inapplicable to the case. The court of appeals had reasoned that the state trial proceedings had terminated and therefore the injunction did not violate the rule that the Anti–Injunction Act cannot be evaded by addressing a federal injunction to the parties rather than to the state court. But the Supreme Court concluded:

> In our view the threshold reasoning of the Court of Appeals disregarded the teaching of this Court's opinion in Atlantic Coast Line R. Co. v. Locomotive Engineers * * *. In that case, the railroad had secured a state-court injunction prohibiting the union from picketing a railroad facility. Two years later, the union tried but failed to convince the state court to dissolve the injunction in light of an intervening decision of this Court. The union did not appeal that decision, but instead persuaded a federal court to enjoin the railroad "from giving effect to or availing [itself] of the benefits of" the state-court injunction. * * * This Court held that "although this federal injunction is in terms directed only at the railroad it is an injunction 'to stay proceedings in a State court.'"
> * * * The view of the Court of Appeals in the present case that after a state court has entered an injunction, its proceedings are concluded for the purposes of the Anti–Injunction Act was thus contrary to the square holding of the *Atlantic Coast Line* case.

Id. at 58–59.

The Court noted further that "[n]either the District Court nor the Court of Appeals addressed the question whether respondents in this case [i.e., the merchants who brought the federal action] were 'strangers to the state court proceeding' who were not bound 'as though [they were parties] to the litigation in the state court.' [citing Hale v. Bimco Trading, Inc., 306 U.S. 375, 378 (1939)]". Unless respondents were such "strangers", the injunction they sought was barred by the Act. Id. at 59–60. Should the applicability of the Anti–Injunction Act be held to turn on whether the party seeking the federal injunction is a party to the state action being enjoined?

Finally, the Court rejected the argument that because the federal court needed to preserve the effectiveness of its jurisdiction over Commerce Clause cases the federal injunction fell within the "in aid of jurisdiction" exception to the Act: "This argument proves too much, since by its reasoning the exception, and not the rule, would always apply." Id. at 60, n. 4. How persuasive is this argument as a basis for rejecting a broader interpretation of the "in aid of jurisdiction" exception?

5. *The Anti–Injunction Act and Complex Litigation*. The *Kline* rule potentially causes significant problems for a federal court adjudicating mass tort claims or other complex litigation when parallel state proceedings are taking place. See Note, *Procedural Impediments to the Resolution of Mass Tort Cases: The Anti–Injunction Act and the Due Process Clause*, 12 Ohio St.J.Disp.Resol. 485 (1997). Under the reasoning of *Kline*, the federal court may not enjoin a parallel in personam state proceeding on the basis of the in-aid-of-jurisdiction exception. See In re Federal Skywalk Cases, 680 F.2d 1175 (8th Cir.), cert. denied, 459 U.S. 988 (1982) (court rejects argument that a corporation's assets should be treated as a res for purposes of in-aid-of-jurisdiction exception). Yet if federal courts may not enjoin such parallel state litigation—which is a relatively common occurrence in the event of mass tort litigation—it risks imposing significant litigation burdens on the parties.

Because of such concerns, a number of federal courts have concluded that, at least under limited circumstances, such parallel state litigation does, in fact, fall within the in-aid-of-jurisdiction exception, despite the absence of either Supreme Court guidance or authorization. For example, in In re Joint Eastern and Southern District Asbestos Litigation, 134 F.R.D. 32 (E.D.N.Y. 1990), Judge Jack Weinstein issued an injunction against state proceedings which he deemed to interfere with the settlement of a no-opt-out class action in federal court. He noted that the defendant would likely go bankrupt if parallel proceedings were allowed.

In Doctor's Associates, Inc. v. Distajo, 944 F.Supp. 1007 (D.Conn.1996), the district court held that the Anti–Injunction Act did not forbid it from enjoining franchisees' state court proceedings concerning contractual disputes with the franchisor, because such action fell within the in-aid-of-jurisdiction exception. The court noted that it was "on the verge of resolving this matter" and that "[o]nly two issues remanded by the Court of Appeals remain to be decided." It added that "[t]he parties, lawyers, and witnesses could be spared great time and expense" if the issues were litigated in a single forum. In so holding, the district court was following the lead of the Second Circuit, which had held in In re Baldwin–United Corporation, 770 F.2d 328 (2d Cir.1985), that a district court could enjoin parallel state litigation that threatened a settlement that that court was about to approve. See also In re Prudential Ins. Co., 261 F.3d 355 (3d Cir.2001) (upholding injunction of state action threatening to litigate issues barred by the settlement reached in a complex multidistrict litigation); In re Diet Drugs, 369 F.3d 293, 306 (3d Cir.2004) (citation omitted): "One instance where we have determined that a federal court may enjoin state court proceedings to protect its jurisdiction is when a federal court is 'entertaining complex litigation, especially when it involves a substantial class of persons from multiple states, or represents a consolidation of cases from multiple districts.' "

Can these decisions be reconciled with *Kline*? If not, which of the two approaches makes more sense as a construction of the in-aid-of-jurisdiction exception? What are the risks of both approaches?

In contrast to its decision in *Baldwin-United*, the Second Circuit in Retirement Systems of Alabama v. J.P. Morgan Chase & Co., 386 F.3d 419 (2d Cir.2004), held that an injunction of parallel state court litigation by a federal district court hearing a multidistrict federal securities action violated the Anti–Injunction Act. "Clearly," the court reasoned, "our decision in *Baldwin-United* did not create a blanket rule or presumption that a federal court in any multidistrict action may enjoin parallel state proceedings. We held that an injunction of related state court proceedings could be warranted even in an *in personam* action, but it was crucial to our analysis that most of the defendants had already settled * * *." Id. at 427–28. Moreover, "[e]ven if defendants had demonstrated that, as in *Baldwin-United*, a prompt settlement in the Securities Litigation was likely, they have failed to explain how the District Court's injunction was necessary to protect that prospective settlement." Id. at 428.

The American Law Institute has proposed a statute providing that when actions are transferred and consolidated, "the transferee court may enjoin transactionally related proceedings, or portions thereof, pending is any state or federal court whenever it determines that continuation of those actions substantially impairs or interferes with the consolidated actions and that an injunction would promote the just, efficient, and fair resolution of the actions before it." American Law Institute, Complex Litigation: Statutory Recommendations and Analysis § 5.04(a)(1994). The accompanying comments note that "[t]he injunction should be as narrow as possible to meet its objective of protecting the transferee court from undue intrusion." Comment a, at 264. The power is intended to be discretionary, with the court considering such factors as how far the individual actions have progressed, the degree of duplication, the presence of federal, law issues, and the interests of nonparties. On the subject, see generally Sherman, *Antisuit Injunction and Notice of Intervention and Preclusion: Complementary Devices to Prevent Duplicative Litigation*, 1995 B.Y.U.L.Rev. 925; Comment, *Antisuit Injunctions Under the Complex Litigation Proposal: Harmonizing The Sirens' Song of Efficiency and Fairness With the Hymn of Judicial Federalism and Comity*, 1995 B.Y.U.L.Rev. 1041; Schillinger, *Preventing Duplicative Mass Tort Litigation Through the Limited Resources Doctrine*, 14 Rev.Litig. 465 (1995); Note, *Procedural Impediments to the Resolution of Mass Tort Cases: The Anti–Injunction Act and the Due Process Clause*, 12 Ohio St. J.Disp.Resol. 485 (1997).

6. One area in which the case law historically appears to deviate from the *Kline* principle is the insurance field. The insurance company seeks a declaratory judgment in federal court that a particular policy is invalid, generally because of fraud. The insured or the beneficiary then proceeds to file an action in state court, seeking to recover under the policy. Generally, such policies contain what is known as an "uncontestability clause," which states that after a specified period the insured is barred from contesting the policy's validity. Therefore if the state court action is filed after that period has run, the insurer is defenseless on the fraud issue. Even if the insurer's federal declaratory judgment action is filed prior to the running of the contestability period, if the state action is filed after that period has run, conclusion of the state action would likely render useless any relief obtained by the insurer in the federal action. However, if the insurer sought to have

the federal court enjoin the state action, the federal court would be required to deal with the Anti–Injunction Statute. Yet federal courts traditionally felt free to enjoin the state action. See e.g., Hesselberg v. Aetna Life Insurance Co., 102 F.2d 23, 27 (8th Cir.1939); Jamerson v. Alliance Insurance Co. of Philadelphia, 87 F.2d 253, 256 (7th Cir.), cert. denied, 300 U.S. 683 (1937); Provident Mutual Life Insurance Co. of Philadelphia v. Parsons, 70 F.2d 863, 868 (4th Cir.), cert. denied 293 U.S. 582 (1934). Do you see why these cases might be thought to constitute departures from *Kline*?

7.   In Leiter Minerals, Inc. v. United States, 352 U.S. 220, 225–226 (1957), the Supreme Court held section 2283 inapplicable to injunctions sought by the United States. Justice Frankfurter, speaking for the Court, reasoned: "The statute is designed to prevent conflict between federal and state courts. This policy is much more compelling when it is the litigation of private parties which threatens to draw the two judicial systems into conflict than when it is the United States which seeks a stay to prevent threatened irreparable injury to a national interest. The frustration of superior federal interests that would ensue from precluding the Federal Government from obtaining a stay of state court proceedings except under the severe restrictions of 28 U.S.C. § 2283 would be so great that we cannot reasonably impute such a purpose to Congress from the general language of 28 U.S.C. § 2283 alone."

In *Atlantic Coast Line*, however, the Court explicitly held "that any injunction against state court proceedings otherwise proper under general equitable principles must be based on one of the specific statutory exceptions to § 2283 if it is to be upheld." Atlantic Coast Line Railroad Co. v. BLE, 398 U.S. 281, 287 (1970). One might reasonably think that such a statement would have implicitly overruled *Leiter Minerals*, since that decision had recognized an exception not mentioned in the statute itself. But in NLRB v. Nash–Finch Co., 404 U.S. 138, 144–147 (1971), the Court made clear that not only was *Leiter Minerals* still good law, but that the exception recognized there was actually extended to injunctions sought by federal agencies. Thus today, the result in *Capital Service* could be justified on the basis of *Nash-Finch*.

8.   The American Law Institute proposed a revision of the Anti–Injunction Act. Its proposed section 1372 reads as follows:

A court of the United States shall not grant an injunction to stay proceedings in a State court, including the enforcement of a judgment of a State court, unless such an injunction is otherwise warranted, and: (1) an Act of Congress authorizes such relief or provides that other proceedings shall cease; or (2) the injunction is requested by the United States, or an officer or agency thereof; or (3) the injunction is necessary to protect the jurisdiction of the court over property in its custody or subject to its control; or (4) the injunction is in aid of a claim for interpleader; or (5) the injunction is necessary to protect or effectuate an existing judgment of the court; or (6) the injunction is sought to preserve temporarily the status quo pending determination of whether this section permits grant of a permanent injunction; or (7) the injunction is to restrain a criminal prosecution that should not be permitted to continue either because the statute or other law that is the basis of the prosecution plainly cannot constitutionally be applied to the party seeking the injunction or because the prosecution is so plainly discriminatory as to amount to a denial of the equal protection of the laws.

American Law Institute, Study of Division of Jurisdiction Between State and Federal Courts 51–52 (1969).

Does this proposal resolve many or all of the problems with the present statute?

9. **Injunction of Federal Judicial Proceedings.** Although no statute explicitly prohibits state courts from enjoining federal judicial proceedings, it was held in Donovan v. City of Dallas, 377 U.S. 408 (1964), that a state court could not enjoin an overlapping in personam federal proceeding. Does this holding make sense? Is it consistent with the traditions of American judicial federalism? The Court recognized an exception to its bar for cases in which the state court initially obtained custody of the "res", or property, in dispute and where jurisdiction is in rem, rather than in personam. The distinction drawn by the Court thus parallels the *Kline* dichotomy in regard to federal court power to enjoin state judicial proceedings. *See generally* Arnold, *State Power to Enjoin Federal Court Proceedings*, 51 Va.L.Rev. 59 (1965); Note, *State Injunction of Proceedings in Federal Courts*, 75 Yale L.J. 150 (1965).

What if one federal court is asked to enjoin another federal court? In Kerotest Manufacturing Co. v. C–O–Two Fire Equipment Co., 342 U.S. 180 (1952), C–O–Two, a Delaware corporation with offices in New Jersey, commenced an action in the District Court for the Northern District of Illinois against the Acme Equipment Company for "making and causing to be made and selling and using" devices which were allegedly infringing C–O–Two's patents. A month-and-a-half later, Kerotest, a Pennsylvania Corporation, filed an action against C–O–Two in the District Court of Delaware for a declaration that the patents sued on in the Illinois action are invalid and that the devices which Kerotest manufactures and supplies to Acme do not infringe C–O–Two's patents. C–O–Two then joined Kerotest, who was subject to service of process in Illinois, as a defendant in the Illinois action. C–O–Two then sought to stay the Delaware action while Kerotest sought to have the Delaware federal court enjoin C–O–Two from prosecuting the Illinois action. The district court refused to enjoin the Illinois proceeding and instead stayed its own proceeding for 90 days to get more information about the Illinois suit, and its decision was affirmed by the Third Circuit. During the 90–day period, the Illinois court added Kerotest as a defendant and denied Acme's motion to stay its proceeding. After the 90 days, both parties renewed their motions in the Delaware proceeding, and the district court (a different judge sitting) enjoined C–O–Two from proceeding in the Illinois suit against Kerotest and denied the stay of its own action. The Third Circuit reversed, reasoning that " 'the whole of the war and all the parties to it are in the Chicago theatre and there only can it be fought to a finish as the litigations are now cast. On the other hand if the battle is waged in the Delaware arena there is a strong probability that the Chicago suit nonetheless would have to be proceeded with for Acme is not and cannot be made a party to the Delaware litigation. The Chicago suit when adjudicated will bind all the parties in both cases. Why, under the circumstances, should there be two litigations where one will suffice? We can find no adequate reason. We assume, of course, that there will be prompt action in the Chicago theatre.' " 342 U.S. at 183.

The Supreme Court, in an opinion by Justice Frankfurter, affirmed: "The factors relevant to wise administration here are equitable in nature. Necessarily, an ample degree of discretion, appropriate for disciplined and experienced judges, must be left to the lower courts. The conclusion which we are asked to upset derives from an extended and careful study of the circumstances of this litigation. Such an estimate here led the Court of Appeals twice to conclude that all interests will be best served by prosecution of the single suit in Illinois. Even if we had more doubts than we do about the analysis made by the Court of Appeals, we would not feel justified in displacing its judgment with ours." Id. at 183–84.

Why should the Supreme Court "not feel justified" in replacing the Court of Appeals' decision with its own? Are there any factors that establish the issue in *Kerotest* as one especially suited for the exercise of lower court discretion? What do you suppose the Supreme Court would have done had the Third Circuit affirmed the injunction of the Illinois proceeding, and the Illinois federal court had enjoined the parties from pursuing the Delaware proceeding?

§ 5. OTHER STATUTORY RESTRICTIONS ON FEDERAL IN-JUNCTIONS AGAINST STATE ACTIVITIES

In addition to the Anti–Injunction Act, 28 U.S.C. § 2283, there are two other major statutory restrictions on federal court authority to enjoin state activities. One is the Tax Injunction Act of 1937, now 28 U.S.C. § 1341, which provides that "[t]he district courts shall not enjoin, suspend or restrain the assessment, levy or collection of any tax under State law where a plain, speedy and efficient remedy may be had in the courts of such State. The Act, adopted in 1937, 'reflects a congressional concern to confine federal intervention in state government * * *.'" Arkansas v. Farm Credit Services of Central Arkansas, 520 U.S. 821, 826–27 (1997). "The States' interest in the integrity of their own processes," the Supreme Court has stated, "is of particular moment respecting questions of state taxation," because "[t]he power to tax is basic to the power of the State to exist." Id. at 826. The other is the Johnson Act of 1934, now 28 U.S.C. § 1342, which provides:

> The district courts shall not enjoin, suspend or restrain the opera-tion of, or compliance with, any order affecting rates chargeable by a public utility and made by a State administrative agency or a rate-making body of a State political subdivision, where:
>
> (1) Jurisdiction is based solely on diversity of citizenship or repugnance of the order to the Federal Constitution; and,
>
> (2) The order does not interfere with interstate commerce; and,
>
> (3) The order has been made after reasonable notice and hear-ing; and,

(4) A plain, speedy and efficient remedy may be had in the courts of such State.

Why do you suppose Congress selected the areas of state taxation and administrative decisionmaking to be generally excluded from federal judicial review?

Note that an important issue in application of both statutes will be whether the state courts provide "a plain, speedy and efficient remedy". The Supreme Court has found such a remedy to be present, where the individual's only remedy is as a defense to a suit to collect the tax (Kohn v. Central Distributing Co., 306 U.S. 531 (1939)), and where the individual must pay the tax before he can challenge it in a suit for a refund (Matthews v. Rodgers, 284 U.S. 521 (1932)). However, where state procedure requires a multiplicity of suits, federal jurisdiction has been allowed. Georgia Railroad & Banking Co. v. Redwine, 342 U.S. 299 (1952).

In Rosewell v. LaSalle National Bank, 450 U.S. 503 (1981), the Supreme Court held that an Illinois statute met the "plain, speedy and efficient" requirement, even though it required real property owners who challenge their property rights first to exhaust their administrative remedy before they could challenge their taxes (after paying them) in a state court action, with a customary delay of two years between initial protest and payment of refund, with no interest. The Court, in an opinion by Justice Brennan, interpreted the statutory phrase to require the meeting of only *procedural* criteria, and then concluded that "[t]here is no doubt that the Illinois state-court refund procedure provides the taxpayer with a 'full hearing and judicial determination' at which she may raise any and all constitutional objections to the tax." Id. at 514. Pointing to the long delays in both state and federal court dockets, the Court decided that "[c]ast in this light, [the taxpayer's] 2–year wait, regrettably, is not unusual", and therefore did not violate the requirement that the state court remedy be "speedy". Id. at 520. As to the failure of the state to provide interest, the Court noted that if she indeed had a federal right to interest, "she could assert this right in the state court proceeding." Id. at 515. The Court reasoned that

> this legislation was first and foremost a vehicle to limit drastically federal district court jurisdiction to interfere with so important a local concern as the collection of taxes. * * *
>
> When it passed the Act, Congress knew that state tax systems commonly provided for payment of taxes under protest with subsequent refund as their exclusive remedy. * * *
>
> It is only common sense to presume that Congress was also aware that some of these same States did not pay interest on their refunds to taxpayers, following the then familiar rule that interest in refund actions was recoverable only when expressly allowed by statute * * *. It would be wholly unreasonable, therefore, to construe a statute passed to limit federal court interference in state tax matters to mean that Congress nevertheless wanted taxpayers from

States not paying interest on refunds to have unimpaired access to the federal courts. If Congress had meant to carve out such an expansive exception, one would expect to find some mention of it. The statute's broad prophylactic language is incompatible with such an interpretation. Id. at 522–24.

Are you persuaded by the Court's reliance on the statutory language?

In addition to the bar of the Tax Injunction Act, the Court has recognized non-statutory limits of comity on the power of the federal courts to interfere with state taxing systems. In Fair Assessment in Real Estate Association, Inc. v. McNary, 454 U.S. 100 (1981), the Court held that comity bars taxpayers' damage actions brought in federal court pursuant to the federal civil rights statute, 42 U.S.C. § 1983, to redress allegedly unconstitutional administration of a state tax system:

> [P]etitioners contend that damages actions are inherently less disruptive of state tax systems than injunctions or declaratory judgments, and therefore should not be barred * * *. Petitioners emphasize that their § 1983 claim seeks recovery from individual state officers, not from state coffers, and that the doctrine of qualified immunity will protect such officers' good faith actions and will thus avoid chilling their administration of the [state] tax scheme.
>
> We disagree. Petitioners will not recover damages under § 1983 unless a district court first determines that respondents' administration of the County tax system violated petitioners' constitutional rights. * * * We are convinced that such a determination would be fully as intrusive as the equitable actions that are barred by principles of comity. Id. at 113.

Justice Brennan, speaking for four Justices, dissented:

> The jurisdiction of the federal courts over cases such as the present one reflects a considered Congressional judgment. * * * Where Congress has granted the federal courts jurisdiction, we are not free to repudiate that authority. Id. at 123–24.

Could it be persuasively argued that Congress' failure expressly to ban the award of damages in the Tax Injunction Act implies that Congress was not concerned about the possible dangers of awarding such relief? Alternatively, could it be argued that the Court's decision proves too much, in that its logic would apply to *every* section 1983 suit challenging state or local governmental practice, thereby effectively removing a federal forum for the adjudication of suits brought under section 1983? If so, would that be a bad thing? Would it be inconsistent with the logic of *Mitchum*? Consider particularly Justice Brennan's position when reading the following chapter.

Note that the Tax Injunction Act prohibits a federal court from "enjoin[ing]" the assessment, levy or collection of a state tax. Should the Act be construed to bar declaratory judgments? In California v. Grace Brethren Church, 457 U.S. 393 (1982), the Court held that "the Act also prohibits a district court from issuing a declaratory judgment holding state tax laws unconstitutional." A federal district court had held that payments under California's unemployment compensation tax scheme, which is federally approved under the Federal Unemployment Tax Act, to employees of nonchurch-affiliated religious schools would violate the first amendment. In holding that both federal court injunctive and declaratory relief were barred by the Tax Injunction Act, the Supreme Court avoided the substantive constitutional challenge to the tax scheme. The Court emphasized that the Tax Injunction Act's prohibitions were not limited to the issuance of injunctions, but include in their bar the power of a federal court to "suspend" or "restrain": "Because the declaratory judgment 'procedure may in every practical sense operate to suspend collection of the state taxes until the litigation is ended,' Great Lakes Dredge & Dock Co. v. Huffman, 319 U.S. 293, 299 (1943), the very language of the Act suggests that a federal court is prohibited from issuing declaratory relief in state tax cases." The Court concluded that "because Congress' intent in enacting the Tax Injunction Act was to prevent federal court interference with the assessment and collection of state taxes, we hold that the Act prohibits declaratory as well as injunctive relief."

Justice Stevens, joined by Justice Blackmun, dissented:

The preclusion of federal injunctive relief [in the Tax Injunction Act] was a response to a specific problem that concerned Congress in 1937. In the States in which taxpayers were required to challenge a tax assessment in a refund suit, only taxpayers that could sue state taxing authorities in federal court could obtain injunctive relief. The privileged taxpayers were primarily the foreign corporations that could invoke federal diversity jurisdiction. These federal suits were objectionable not only because of this discrimination but also because state treasuries often were deprived of tax revenues while the federal suits were adjudicated and because the federal suits involved only state-law questions that were more appropriate for state-court resolution. * * *

A literal reading of the Tax Injunction Act manifestly does not preclude the declaratory judgment entered in this case. Nor do the concerns that gave rise to its enactment require such a bar. Appellee's challenge is based on the Federal Constitution and is directed at a federal-state program administered according to federal requirements. Only federal questions are involved. Id. at 420–21.

Are you persuaded by Justice Stevens' reasoning? If the only concern of the drafters of the Tax Injunction Act were the one described by Justice Stevens, could that concern not have been satisfied by less restrictive legislation? Consider also his argument that "[o]nly federal questions are involved." Is there anything in the language of the Tax Injunction Act (or of the Anti–Injunction Act, for that matter) which recognizes an exception for cases in which only federal questions are involved? *Should* such an exception exist?

In Hibbs v. Winn, 542 U.S. 88 (2004), the Supreme Court held that the Tax Injuction Act did not apply to bar an action in which taxpayers challenged an Arizona statute permitting tax credits for contributions to non-profit organizations supporting parochial schools as violative of the Establishment Clause. The Court's ruling was predicated on the fact that the taxpayers sought injunctive relief prohibiting the tax credits, a declaration that the statute violated the Establishment Clause, and an order that in the future all such contributions be paid into a state general tax fund, rather than avoidance of payment of taxes or to otherwise interfere with state tax collection.

In reaching this result, Justice Ginsburg, speaking for the Court, relied on an interpretation of the word "assessment" as found in 28 U.S.C. § 1341 and concluded that the word is "closely tied to the collection of a tax" and does not signify "the entire plan or scheme fixed upon for charging or taxing." She expressed the view that "Congress trained its attention on taxpayers who sought to avoid paying their tax bill by pursuing a challenge route other than the one specified by the taxing authority. Nowhere does the legislative history announce a sweeping congressional direction to prevent 'federal-court interference with all aspects of state tax administration.' " Id. at 105.

In a vigorous dissent, Justice Kennedy, joined by Chief Justice Rehnquist and Justices Scalia and Thomas, argued that the majority opinion "shows great skepticism for the state courts' ability to vindicate constitutional wrongs." And further that, "[d]ismissive treatment of state courts is particularly unjustified since the TIA, by express terms, provides a federal safeguard: The Act lifts its bar on federal court intervention when state courts fail to provide 'a plain, speedy, and efficient remedy.' " Id. at 113.

According to one commentator, "[b]y refusing to interpret the Act as requiring a complete bar to federal jurisdiction over challenges to state tax systems, the Court has signaled a limit to the gradual expansion of the Act's scope and has brought it back in line with the more limited purpose that Congress intended for it." Note, *The Supreme Court, Leading Cases 2003 Term*, 118 Harv.L.Rev. 248, 486 (2004).

How would *Hibbs* apply to the following situation: The American Civil Liberties Union sues in federal court to challenge a specialty license program which makes available a license plate bearing the words "Choose Life" and subsequently pays a percentage of the license fees to pro-life groups. Compare Henderson v. Stalder, 407 F.3d 351 (5th Cir. 2005), cert. denied sub nom. Keeler v. Stalder, 2006 WL 1725640 (2006) (suit barred by Tax Injunction Act) with ACLU of Tennessee v. Bredesen, 441 F.3d 370 (6th Cir.), cert. denied, ___ U.S. ___, 126 S.Ct. 2972 (2006) (suit not barred by Tax Injunction Act).

Chapter 10

"OUR FEDERALISM"

YOUNGER v. HARRIS

Supreme Court of the United States, 1971.
401 U.S. 37.

MR. JUSTICE BLACK delivered the opinion of the Court.

Appellee, John Harris, Jr., was indicted in a California state court, charged with violation of the California Penal Code §§ 11400 and 11401, known as the California Criminal Syndicalism Act * * *. He then filed a complaint in the Federal District Court, asking that court to enjoin the appellant, Younger, the District Attorney of Los Angeles County, from prosecuting him, and alleging that the prosecution and even the presence of the Act inhibited him in the exercise of his rights of free speech and press, rights guaranteed him by the First and Fourteenth Amendments. Appellees Jim Dan and Diane Hirsch intervened as plaintiffs in the suit, claiming that the prosecution of Harris would inhibit them as members of the Progressive Labor Party from peacefully advocating the program of their party, which was to replace capitalism with socialism and to abolish the profit system of production in this country. Appellee Farrell Broslawsky, an instructor in history at Los Angeles Valley College, also intervened claiming that the prosecution of Harris made him uncertain as to whether he could teach about the doctrines of Karl Marx or read from the Communist Manifesto as part of his classwork. All claimed that unless the United States court restrained the state prosecution of Harris each would suffer immediate and irreparable injury. A three-judge Federal District Court, convened pursuant to 28 U.S.C. § 2284, held that it had jurisdiction and power to restrain the District Attorney from prosecuting, held that the State's Criminal Syndicalism Act was void for vagueness and overbreadth in violation of the First and Fourteenth Amendments, and accordingly restrained the District Attorney from "further prosecution of the currently pending action against plaintiff Harris for alleged violation of the Act."

The case is before us on appeal by the State's District Attorney Younger, pursuant to 28 U.S.C. § 1253. In his notice of appeal and his jurisdictional statement appellant presented two questions: (1) whether the decision of this Court in Whitney v. California, 274 U.S. 357, holding California's law constitutional in 1927 was binding on the District Court and (2) whether the State's law is constitutional on its face. In this Court the brief for the State of California, filed at our request, also argues that only Harris, who was indicted, has standing to challenge the State's law, and that issuance of the injunction was a violation of a longstanding judicial policy and of 28 U.S.C. § 2283, which provides:

> "A court of the United States may not grant an injunction to stay proceedings in a State court except as expressly authorized by Act of Congress, or where necessary in aid of its jurisdiction, or to protect or effectuate its judgments."

See, e.g., Atlantic Coast Line R. Co. v. Engineers, 398 U.S. 281, 285–286 (1970). Without regard to the questions raised about Whitney v. California, supra, since overruled by Brandenburg v. Ohio, 395 U.S. 444 (1969), or the constitutionality of the state law, we have concluded that the judgment of the District Court, enjoining appellant Younger from prosecuting under these California statutes, must be reversed as a violation of the national policy forbidding federal courts to stay or enjoin pending state court proceedings except under special circumstances. We express no view about the circumstances under which federal courts may act when there is no prosecution pending in state courts at the time the federal proceeding is begun.

HELD

I

Appellee Harris has been indicted, and was actually being prosecuted by California for a violation of its Criminal Syndicalism Act at the time this suit was filed. He thus has an acute, live controversy with the State and its prosecutor. But none of the other parties plaintiff in the District Court, Dan, Hirsch, or Broslawsky, has such a controversy. None has been indicted, arrested, or even threatened by the prosecutor. * * *

Whatever right Harris, who is being prosecuted under the state syndicalism law may have, Dan, Hirsch, and Broslawsky cannot share it with him. If these three had alleged that they would be prosecuted for the conduct they planned to engage in, and if the District Court had found this allegation to be true—either on the admission of the State's district attorney or on any other evidence—then a genuine controversy might be said to exist. But here appellees Dan, Hirsch, and Broslawsky do not claim that they have ever been threatened with prosecution, that a prosecution is likely, or even that a prosecution is remotely possible. They claim the right to bring this suit solely because, in the language of their complaint, they "feel inhibited." We do not think this allegation, even if true, is sufficient to bring the equitable jurisdiction of the federal courts into play to enjoin a pending state prosecution. A federal lawsuit to stop a prosecution in a state court is a serious matter. And persons having no fears of state prosecution except those that are imaginary or speculative, are not to be accepted as appropriate plaintiffs in such cases. See Golden v. Zwickler, 394 U.S. 103 (1969). Since Harris is actually

Hart is is the only appropria party!

being prosecuted under the challenged laws, however, we proceed with him as a proper party.

II

Since the beginning of this country's history Congress has, subject to few exceptions, manifested a desire to permit state courts to try state cases free from interference by federal courts. In 1793 an Act unconditionally provided: "[Nor shall a writ of injunction be granted to stay proceedings in any court of a state...." 1 Stat. 335, c. 22, § 5.] A comparison of the 1793 Act with 28 U.S.C. § 2283, its present-day successor, graphically illustrates how few and minor have been the exceptions granted from the flat, prohibitory language of the old Act. During all this lapse of years from 1793 to 1970 the statutory exceptions to the 1793 congressional enactment have been only three: (1) "except as expressly authorized by Act of Congress';" (2) "where necessary in aid of its jurisdiction"; and (3) "to protect or effectuate its judgments." In addition, a judicial exception to the longstanding policy evidenced by the statute has been made where a person about to be prosecuted in a state court can show that he will, if the proceeding in the state court is not enjoined, suffer irreparable damages. See Ex parte Young, 209 U.S. 123 (1908).

3 exception

irreparable damages

The precise reasons for this longstanding public policy against federal court interference with state court proceedings have never been specifically identified but the primary sources of the policy are plain. One is the basic doctrine of equity jurisprudence that courts of equity should not act, and particularly should not act to restrain a criminal prosecution, when the moving party has an adequate remedy at law and will not suffer irreparable injury if denied equitable relief. The doctrine may originally have grown out of circumstances peculiar to the English judicial system and not applicable in this country, but its fundamental purpose of restraining equity jurisdiction within narrow limits is equally important under our Constitution, in order to prevent erosion of the role of the jury and avoid a duplication of legal proceedings and legal sanctions where a single suit would be adequate to protect the rights asserted. This underlying reason for restraining courts of equity from interfering with criminal prosecutions is reinforced by an even more vital consideration, the notion of "comity," that is, a proper respect for state functions, a recognition of the fact that the entire country is made up of a Union of separate state governments, and a continuance of the belief that the National Government will fare best if the States and their institutions are left free to perform their separate functions in their separate ways. This, perhaps for lack of a better and clearer way to describe it, is referred to by many as "Our Federalism" and one familiar with the profound debates that ushered our Federal Constitution into existence is bound to respect those who remain loyal to the ideals and dreams of "Our Federalism." The concept does not mean blind deference to "States' Rights" any more than it means centralization of control over every important issue in our National Government and its courts.

The Framers rejected both these courses. What the concept does represent is a system in which there is sensitivity to the legitimate interests of both State and National Governments, and in which the National Government, anxious though it may be to vindicate and protect federal rights and federal interests, always endeavors to do so in ways that will not unduly interfere with the legitimate activities of the States. It should never be forgotten that this slogan, "Our Federalism," born in the early struggling days of our Union of States, occupies a highly important place in our Nation's history and its future.

This brief discussion should be enough to suggest some of the reasons why it has been perfectly natural for our cases to repeat time and time again that the normal thing to do when federal courts are asked to enjoin pending proceedings in state courts is not to issue such injunctions. In Fenner v. Boykin, 271 U.S. 240 (1926), suit had been brought in the Federal District Court seeking to enjoin state prosecutions under a recently enacted state law that allegedly interfered with the free flow of interstate commerce. The Court, in a unanimous opinion made clear that such a suit, even with respect to state criminal proceedings not yet formally instituted, could be proper only under very special circumstances:

> "Ex parte Young, 209 U.S. 123, and following cases have established the doctrine that when absolutely necessary for protection of constitutional rights courts of the United States have power to enjoin state officers from instituting criminal actions. But this may not be done except under extraordinary circumstances where the danger of irreparable loss is both great and immediate. Ordinarily there should be no interference with such officers; primarily, they are charged with the duty of prosecuting offenders against the laws of the State and must decide when and how this is to be done. The accused should first set up and rely upon his defense in the state courts, even though this involves a challenge of the validity of some statute, unless it plainly appears that this course would not afford adequate protection." Id., at 243–44.

These principles, made clear in the *Fenner* case, have been repeatedly followed and reaffirmed in other cases involving threatened prosecutions. See, e.g., Spielman Motor Sales Co. v. Dodge, 295 U.S. 89 (1935); Beal v. Missouri Pac. R. Co., 312 U.S. 45 (1941); Watson v. Buck, 313 U.S. 387 (1941); Williams v. Miller, 317 U.S. 599 (1942); Douglas v. City of Jeannette, 319 U.S. 157 (1943).

In all of these cases the Court stressed the importance of showing irreparable injury, the traditional prerequisite to obtaining an injunction. In addition, however, the Court also made clear that in view of the fundamental policy against federal interference with state criminal prosecutions, even irreparable injury is insufficient unless it is "both great and immediate." *Fenner*, supra. Certain types of injury, in particular, the cost, anxiety, and inconvenience of having to defend against a single criminal prosecution, could not by themselves be considered "irreparable" in the special legal sense of that term. Instead, the threat to the plaintiff's federally protected rights must be one that cannot be eliminated by his defense against a single criminal prosecution. See, e.g., Ex parte Young, supra, at 145–147. Thus, in the *Buck* case, supra, at 400, we stressed:

> "Federal injunctions against state criminal statutes, either in their entirety or with respect to their separate and distinct prohibitions, are not to be granted as a matter of course, even if such statutes are unconstitutional. 'No citizen or member of the community is immune from prosecution, in good faith, for his alleged criminal acts. The imminence of such a prosecution even though alleged to be unauthorized and hence unlawful is not alone ground for relief in equity which exerts its extraordinary powers only to prevent irreparable injury to the plaintiff who seeks its aid.' Beal v. Missouri Pacific Railroad Corp., 312 U.S. 45, 49."

And similarly, in *Douglas*, supra, we made clear, after reaffirming this rule, that:

> "It does not appear from the record that petitioners have been threatened with any injury other than that incidental to every criminal proceeding brought lawfully and in good faith...." 319 U.S., at 164.

This is where the law stood when the Court decided Dombrowski v. Pfister, 380 U.S. 479 (1965), and held that an injunction against the enforcement of certain state criminal statutes could properly issue under the circumstances presented in that case. In *Dombrowski*, unlike many of the earlier cases denying injunctions, the complaint made substantial allegations that:

> "the threats to enforce the statutes against appellants are not made with any expectation of securing valid convictions, but rather are part of a plan to employ arrests, seizures, and threats of prosecution under color of the statutes to harass appellants and discourage them and their supporters from asserting and attempting to vindicate the constitutional rights of Negro citizens of Louisiana." 380 U.S., at 482.

The appellants in *Dombrowski* had offered to prove that their offices had been raided and all their files and records seized pursuant to search and arrest warrants that were later summarily vacated by a state judge for lack of probable cause. They also offered to prove that despite the state court order quashing the warrants and suppressing the evidence seized, the prosecutor was continuing to threaten to initiate new prosecutions of appellants under the same statutes, was holding public hearings at which photostatic copies of the illegally seized documents were being used, and was threatening to use other copies of the illegally seized documents to obtain grand jury indictments against the appellants on charges of violating the same statutes. These circumstances, as viewed by the Court sufficiently establish the kind of irreparable injury, above and beyond that associated with the defense of a single prosecution brought in good faith, that had always been considered sufficient to justify federal intervention. See, e.g., *Beal*, supra, at 50. Indeed, after quoting the Court's statement in *Douglas* concerning the very restricted circumstances under which an injunction could be justified, the Court in *Dombrowski* went on to say:

> "But the allegations in this complaint depict a situation in which defense of the State's criminal prosecution will not assure adequate vindication of constitutional rights. They suggest that a substantial loss of or impairment of freedoms of expression will occur if appellants must await the state court's disposition and ultimate review in this Court of any adverse determination. These allegations, if true, clearly show irreparable injury." 380 U.S., at 485–486.

And the Court made clear that even under these circumstances the District Court issuing the injunction would have continuing power to lift it at any time and remit the plaintiffs to the state courts if circumstances warranted. 380 U.S., at 491, 492. Similarly, in Cameron v. Johnson, 390 U.S. 611 (1968), a divided Court denied an injunction after finding that the record did not establish the necessary bad faith and harassment; the dissenting Justices themselves stressed the very limited role to be allowed for federal injunctions against state criminal prosecutions and differed with the Court only on the question whether the particular facts of that case were sufficient to show that the prosecution was brought in bad faith.

It is against the background of these principles that we must judge the propriety of an injunction under the circumstances of the present case. Here a proceeding was already pending in the state court, affording Harris an opportunity to raise his constitutional claims. There is no suggestion that this single prosecution against Harris is brought in bad faith or is only one of a series of repeated prosecutions to which he will be subjected. In other words, the injury that Harris faces is solely "that incidental to every criminal proceeding brought lawfully and in good faith," *Douglas*, supra, and therefore under the settled doctrine we have already described he is not entitled to equitable relief "even if such statutes are unconstitutional," *Buck*, supra.

The District Court, however, thought that the *Dombrowski* decision substantially broadened the availability of injunctions against state criminal prosecutions and that under that decision the federal courts may give equitable relief, without regard to any showing of bad faith or harassment, whenever a state statute is found "on its face" to be vague or overly broad, in violation of the First Amendment. We recognize that there are some statements in the *Dombrowski* opinion that would seem to support this argument. But, as we have already seen, such statements were unnecessary to the decision of that case, because the Court found that the plaintiffs had alleged a basis for equitable relief under the long-established standards. In addition, we do not regard the reasons adduced to support this position as sufficient to justify such a substantial departure from the established doctrines regarding the availability of injunctive relief. It is undoubtedly true, as the Court stated in *Dombrowski*, that "[a] criminal prosecution under a statute regulating expression usually involves imponderables and contingencies that themselves may inhibit the full exercise of First Amendment freedoms." 380 U.S., at 486. But this sort of "chilling effect," as the Court called it, should not by itself justify federal intervention. In the first place, the chilling effect cannot be satisfactorily eliminated by federal injunctive relief. In *Dombrowski* itself the Court stated that the injunction to be issued there could be lifted if the State obtained an "acceptable limiting construction" from the state courts. The Court then made clear that once this was done, prosecutions could then be brought for conduct occurring before the narrowing construction was made, and proper convictions could stand so long as the defendants were not deprived of fair warning. 380 U.S., at 491 n. 7. The kind of relief granted in *Dombrowski* thus does not effectively eliminate uncertainty as to the coverage of the state statute and leaves most citizens with virtually the same doubts as before regarding the danger that their conduct might eventually be subjected to criminal sanctions. The chilling effect can, of course, be eliminated by an injunction that would prohibit any prosecution whatever for conduct occurring prior to a satisfactory rewriting of the statute. But the States would then be stripped of all power to prosecute even the socially dangerous and constitutionally unprotected conduct that had been covered by the statute, until a new statute could be passed by the state legislature and approved by the federal courts in potentially lengthy trial and appellate proceedings. Thus, in *Dombrowski* itself the Court carefully reaffirmed the principle that even in the direct prosecution in the State's own courts, a valid narrowing construction can be applied to conduct occurring prior to the date when the narrowing construction was made, in the absence of fair warning problems.

Moreover, the existence of a "chilling effect," even in the area of First Amendment rights, has never been considered a sufficient basis, in and of itself, for prohibiting state action. Where a statute does not directly abridge free speech, but—while regulating a subject within the State's power—tends to have the incidental effect of inhibiting First Amendment rights, it is well settled that the statute can be upheld if the effect on speech is minor in relation to the need for control of the conduct and the lack of alternative means for doing so. * * *

Beyond all this is another, more basic consideration. Procedures for testing the constitutionality of a statute "on its face" in the manner apparently contemplated by *Dombrowski*, and for then enjoining all action to enforce the statute until the State can obtain court approval for a modified version, are fundamentally at odds with the function of the federal courts in our constitutional plan. The power and duty of the judiciary to declare laws unconstitutional is in the final analysis derived from its responsibility for resolving concrete disputes brought before the courts for decision; a statute apparently governing a dispute cannot be applied by judges, consistently with their obligations under the Supremacy Clause, when such an application of the statute would conflict with the Constitution. Marbury v. Madison, 5 U.S. (1 Cranch) 137 (1803). But this vital responsibility, broad as it is, does not amount to an unlimited power to survey the statute books and pass judgment on laws before the courts are called upon to enforce them. Ever since the Constitutional Convention rejected a proposal for having members of the Supreme Court render advice concerning pending legislation it has been clear that, even when suits of this kind involve a "case or controversy" sufficient to satisfy the requirements of Article III of the Constitution, the task of analyzing a proposed statute, pinpointing its deficiencies, and requiring correction of these deficiencies before the statute is put into effect, is rarely if ever an appropriate task for the judiciary. The combination of the relative remoteness of the controversy, the impact on the legislative process of the relief sought, and above all the speculative and amorphous nature of the required line-by-line analysis of detailed statutes ordinarily results in a kind of case that is wholly unsatisfactory for deciding constitutional questions, whichever way they might be decided. In light of this fundamental conception of the Framers as to the proper place of the federal courts in the governmental processes of passing and enforcing laws, it can seldom be appropriate for these courts to exercise any such power of prior approval or veto over the legislative process.

For these reasons, fundamental not only to our federal system but also to the basic functions of the Judicial Branch of the National Government under our Constitution, we hold that the *Dombrowski* decision should not be regarded as having upset the settled doctrines that have always confined very narrowly the availability of injunctive relief against state criminal prosecutions. We do not think that opinion stands for the proposition that a federal court can properly enjoin enforcement of a statute solely on the basis of a showing that the statute "on its face" abridges First Amendment rights. There may, of course, be extraordinary circumstances in which the necessary irreparable injury can be shown even in the absence of the usual prerequisites of bad faith and harassment. For example, as long ago as the *Buck* case, supra, we indicated:

> "It is of course conceivable that a statute might be flagrantly and patently violative of express constitutional prohibitions in every clause, sentence and paragraph, and in whatever manner and against whomever an effort might be made to apply it." 313 U.S., at 402.

Other unusual situations calling for federal intervention might also arise, but there is no point in our attempting now to specify what they might be. It is sufficient for purposes of the present case to hold, as we do, that the possible unconstitutionality of a statute "on its face" does not in itself justify an injunction against good-faith attempts to enforce it, and that appellee Harris has failed to make any showing of bad faith, harassment, or any other unusual circumstance that would call for equitable relief. Because our holding rests on the absence of the factors necessary under equitable principles to justify federal intervention, we have no occasion to consider whether 28 U.S.C. § 2283, which prohibits an injunction against state court proceedings "except as expressly authorized by Act of Congress" would in and of itself be controlling under the circumstances of this case.

* * *

MR. JUSTICE BRENNAN, with whom MR. JUSTICE WHITE and MR. JUSTICE MARSHALL join, concurring in the result.

I agree that the judgment of the District Court should be reversed. Appellee Harris had been indicted for violations of the California Criminal Syndicalism Act before he sued in federal court. He has not alleged that the prosecution was brought in bad faith to harass him. His constitutional contentions may be adequately adjudicated in the state criminal proceeding, and federal intervention at his instance was therefore improper.

* * *

MR. JUSTICE DOUGLAS, dissenting.

The fact that we are in a period of history when enormous extrajudicial sanctions are imposed on those who assert their First Amendment rights in unpopular causes emphasizes the wisdom of Dombrowski v. Pfister, 380 U.S. 479. There we recognized that in times of repression, when interests with powerful spokesmen generate symbolic pogroms against nonconformists, the federal judiciary, charged by Congress with special vigilance for protection of civil rights, has special responsibilities to prevent an erosion of the individual's constitutional rights.

Dombrowski represents an exception to the general rule that federal courts should not interfere with state criminal prosecutions. The exception does not arise merely because prosecutions are threatened to which the First Amendment will be the proffered defense. *Dombrowski* governs statutes which are a blunderbuss by themselves or when used *en masse*—those that have an "overbroad" sweep. "If the rule were otherwise, the contours of regulation would have to be hammered out case by case—and tested only by those hardy enough to risk criminal prosecution to determine the proper scope of regulation." Id., at 487. It was in the context of overbroad state statutes that we spoke of the "chilling effect upon the exercise of First Amendment rights" caused by state prosecutions. Ibid.

* * *

The special circumstances when federal intervention in a state criminal proceeding is permissible are not restricted to bad faith on the part of state officials or the threat of multiple prosecutions. They also exist where for any reason the state statute being enforced is unconstitutional on its face. * * *

Our *Dombrowski* decision was only another facet of the same problem.

In *Younger*, "criminal syndicalism" is defined so broadly as to jeopardize "teaching" that socialism is preferable to free enterprise.

Harris' "crime" was distributing leaflets advocating change in industrial ownership through political action. The statute under which he was indicted was the one involved in Whitney v. California, 274 U.S. 357, a decision we overruled in Brandenburg v. Ohio, 395 U.S. 444, 449.

If the "advocacy" which Harris used was an attempt at persuasion through the use of bullets, bombs, and arson, we would have a different case. But Harris is charged only with distributing leaflets advocating political action toward his objective. He tried unsuccessfully to have the state court dismiss the indictment on constitutional grounds. He resorted to the state appellate court for writs of prohibition to prevent the trial, but to no avail. He went to the federal court as a matter of last resort in an effort to keep this unconstitutional trial from being saddled on him.

* * *

[The concurring opinion of JUSTICE STEWART, joined by JUSTICE HARLAN, is omitted.]

Notes

1. **Pre-Younger History.** The traditional version of pre-*Younger* history is generally well described in the case itself. The problem of federal court interference with state criminal proceedings was first recognized in Ex parte Young, 209 U.S. 123 (1908). There the Supreme Court upheld the federal court's power to enjoin the filing of a prosecution in state court by a state official. In so holding, however, the Court noted that the federal court could not, "of course, interfere in a case where the proceedings were already pending in a state court." Id. at 162. In the decisions cited in *Younger*, including Fenner v. Boykin, 271 U.S. 240 (1926), Watson v. Buck, 313 U.S. 387 (1941); Beal v. Missouri Pac. R.R. Corp., 312 U.S. 45 (1941); and Spielman Motor Sales Co., Inc. v. Dodge, 295 U.S. 89 (1935), the Court expounded upon the principle first enunciated as dictum in *Young*. In Douglas v. City of Jeannette, 319 U.S. 157 (1943), also relied upon in *Younger*, Jehovah's Witnesses sought to restrain the city from enforcing an ordinance prohibiting the solicitation of merchandise orders without first obtaining a license and paying a license tax. The very same day on which *Douglas* was decided, the Court invalidated that ordinance in Murdock v. Pennsylvania, 319 U.S. 105 (1943). The *Douglas* Court held that "courts of equity in the exercise of their discretionary powers should * * * refus[e] to interfere with or embarrass threatened proceedings in state courts save in those exceptional cases which call for the interposition of a court of equity to prevent irreparable injury which is clear and imminent * * *." 319 U.S. at 163. No irreparable danger was imminent in *Douglas*, said the Court, because "the lawfulness or constitutionality of the statute or ordinance on

State court can decide constitutions

which the prosecution is based may be determined as readily [by the state court] in the criminal case as in a suit for an injunction." Id.

Several commentators have challenged this "traditional" interpretation of the pre-*Younger* case law. See Laycock, *Federal Interference with State Prosecutions: The Cases* Dombrowski *Forgot*, 46 U.Chi.L.Rev. 636 (1979); Soifer & Macgill, *The* Younger *Doctrine: Reconstructing Reconstruction*, 55 Tex.L.Rev. 1141 (1977); B. Wechsler, *Federal Courts, State Criminal Law and the First Amendment*, 49 N.Y.U.L.Rev. 740 (1974). According to Professor Burton Wechsler, for example, "beginning with the last decade of the nineteenth century federal trial courts have liberally exerted their power to invalidate state criminal law and enjoin its enforcement; and, with the exception of a brief period between 1941 and 1943, the Supreme Court has given massive support to this particular use of federal judicial power." 49 N.Y.U.L.Rev. at 743. Professor Laycock notes that "[e]ven in the early forties, the dominant line of cases freely granting injunctions did not die out." 46 U.Chi.L.Rev. at 645. He adds: "Following *Douglas*, the Court continued to give conflicting signals." Professor Laycock's analysis, however, emphasizes injunctions of prospective proceedings, an issue not specifically dealt with in *Younger*.

For two different views of the origins of the term "Our Federalism," see Collins, *Whose Federalism?*, 9 Const.Commentary 75 (1992); McManamon, *Felix Frankfurter: The Architect of "Our Federalism,"* 27 Ga.L.Rev. 697 (1993).

2. **The Dombrowski Case.** In Dombrowski v. Pfister, 380 U.S. 479 (1965), plaintiffs, members of a civil rights organization, had sought declaratory and injunctive relief in federal court to prevent Louisiana officials from prosecuting them for violations of the state's internal security law. They alleged "that the threats to enforce the statutes against [them] are not made with any expectation of securing valid convictions, but rather are part of a plan to employ arrests, seizures, and threats of prosecution under color of the statutes to harass [them] and discourage them and their supporters from asserting and attempting to vindicate the constitutional rights of Negro citizens of Louisiana." Id. at 482. Justice Brennan, speaking for the majority, ordered an injunction of the threatened prosecutions. He acknowledged that ordinarily, a defense to a criminal prosecution would provide an adequate remedy. The allegations, however, "depict a situation in which defense of the State's criminal prosecution will not assure adequate vindication of constitutional rights," Id. at 485. This was because "[a] criminal prosecution under a statute regulating expression usually involves imponderables and contingencies that themselves may inhibit the full exercise of First Amendment freedoms * * *. When the statutes also have an overbroad sweep, as is here alleged, the hazard of loss or substantial impairment of those precious rights may be critical * * *. The assumption that defense of a criminal prosecution will generally assure ample vindication of constitutional rights is unfounded in such cases." Id. at 486.

Justice Brennan characterized the case as one in which only future, rather than ongoing prosecutions were being enjoined. Professor Laycock has seriously questioned the historical accuracy of Justice Brennan's approach in *Dombrowski*. Laycock, supra, 46 U.Chi.L.Rev. 636 (1979). Brennan accepted the equitable framework set out in Douglas v. City of Jeannette, under which there existed a presumption of adequacy of the defense to the state criminal prosecution. However, Brennan carved out an exception for the special facts of *Dombrowski*. See generally Fiss, *Dombrowski*, 86 Yale L.J. 1103 (1977). According to Laycock, "*Dombrowski* is a dramatic example of judicial oversight. The Court announced a rule that had not been the law for at least two decades, if ever, that was inconsistent with the overwhelmingly dominant line of precedent for the previous sixty years, and that the majority apparently disagreed with as a matter of policy. Because the mistake went undetected, *Dombrowski* was greeted as an expansion of the right to prospective relief when in fact it was the opposite." 46 U.Chi.L.Rev. at 688. He is certainly correct in stating that the case was seen as an expansion of a federal right to relief. See, e.g., Sedler, *The* Dombrowski-*Type Suit as an Effective Weapon for Social Change: Reflections from Without and Within*, 18 U.Kan.L.Rev. 237, 244–45 (1970); Maraist, *Federal Injunctive Relief Against State Court Proceedings: The Significance of* Dombrowski, 48 Tex.L.Rev. 535 (1970); Boyer, *Federal Injunctive Relief: A Counterpoise Against the Use of State Criminal Prosecutions Designed to Deter the Exercise of Preferred Constitutional Rights*, 13 How.L.Rev. 51 (1967).

Consider how Justice Black in *Younger* disposed of the argued relevance of *Dombrowski*. Is it persuasive? You should be aware that in a certain sense, at least, the language in *Dombrowski* cited by Justice Black, emphasizing the alleged bad faith of the prosecution, was taken out of context. The language had been used by Justice Brennan solely in response to the contention that *Pullman*-abstention was appropriate, 380 U.S. at 489–90, though Justice Brennan himself confused the situation by recharacterizing his *Dombrowski* opinion three years later. Cameron v. Johnson, 390 U.S. 611 (1968). In any event, isn't there a very easy way to distinguish *Dombrowski* from *Younger*?

3. Of what relevance to Justice Black's analysis is the Anti–Injunction Act? Is his use of the Act legitimate?

4. To what state interests is Justice Black giving deference in *Younger*? State courts? State prosecutors? State legislatures? The state judicial process? All of the above? See generally Redish, *The Doctrine of Younger v. Harris: Deference in Search of a Rationale*, 63 Cornell L.Rev. 463 (1978). In his dissent in *Dombrowski*, Justice Harlan criticized the majority for making "the unarticulated assumption that state courts will not be as prone as federal courts to vindicate constitutional rights promptly and effectively." 380 U.S. at 499. Do you think that the awarding of federal injunctive relief against an ongoing state prosecution necessarily makes this assumption? If so, does this fact justify a prohibition on the awarding of such relief? Can you articulate an argument in support of the proposition that the limits imposed on the federal courts in *Younger* are justified by a need to defer to state legislative policies and/or prosecutorial and executive officer discretion? Are there any problems with the argument? What, if anything, is lost as a result of the *Younger* limit on federal court authority? On balance, do you think the doctrine is a wise one? For a critique of the conceivable state interests served by *Younger*, see L. Yackle, Reclaiming the Federal Courts 128–31 (1994).

One scholar has suggested that the best justification for *Younger* abstention is "avoiding the friction inherent in duplicative proceedings." Rehnquist, *Taking Comity Seriously: How to Neutralize the Abstention Doctrine*, 46 Stan.L.Rev. 1049, 1089 (1994). Do you agree? What sorts of rules would follow from such a justification? Would it matter whether the federal suit sought injunctive relief or merely damages? See id. at 1113–14.

Professor Ann Althouse argues that abstention fosters better constitutional interpretation by state courts: too much federal interference with state courts, she suggests, may diminish the capacity of state tribunals to enforce federal law—both through an effective declaration of mistrust and by depriving local courts of opportunities to gain experience in the enforcement of federal law. See Althouse, *The Misguided Search for State Interest in Abstention Cases: Observations on the Occasion of Pennzoil v. Texaco*, 63 N.Y.U.L.Rev. 1051 (1988). Even assuming that the empirical basis for these claims is sound, is she simply advocating sacrificing the interests of *present* constitutional litigants for the interests of *future* constitutional litigants? See Lee, *On the Received Wisdom in Federal Courts*, 147 U.Pa.L.Rev. 1111, 1115 (1999): "Providing the state courts with additional constitutional claims risks sacrificing individual liberty in some localities for the prospect of increasing individual liberties in other localities. The liberty of some is gambled with, in the hope of increasing the total amount of liberty of others in the system."

5. **Younger and Legislative Intent.** One scholar has argued "that the federal courts' refusal to use their equitable power to reform state justice systems directly contravenes the intent of the Reconstruction Congresses that adopted the fourteenth amendment and enacted section 1983." Zeigler, *A Reassessment of the* Younger *Doctrine In Light of the Legislative History of Reconstruction,* 1983 Duke L.J. 987, 988. Did not the Supreme Court itself reach a similar conclusion in *Mitchum v. Foster* [supra p. 495]? If so, how can the Court reconcile *Younger* with legislative intent? Does it even attempt to do so in *Younger*? Compare the broader discussion about abstention and separation of powers [supra pp. 448–50].

Consider the following defense of judge-made abstention in section 1983 actions from a separation-of-powers perspective:

[The *Younger* doctrine] is the correct enterprise not only because this is institutionally the "correct" or "best" solution, but also because it seems to me to be the proper interpretation of the governing authoritative statutes. * * * Statutes such as § 1983 * * * use language which, if woodenly and anachronistically read, can be interpreted to provide an "absolute" right of access to the federal courts. But these statutes were themselves passed against the background of a large body of standing law on matters of substance, remedy, and jurisdiction. * * * The fact that a given remedial doctrine is not explicitly mentioned therefore does not automatically mean that the new statute was intended wholly to supersede it. Thus, to give an example, it seems to me implausible to assume that the cause of action created by and the jurisdiction granted in the Civil Rights Act of 1871 [i.e., section 1983 and 28 U.S.C. § 1343] were meant wholly to supersede the preexisting equity doctrine that a good faith criminal prosecution will not ordinarily be enjoined simply because the plaintiff asserts that he has a valid defense to it.

Bator, *The State Courts and Federal Constitutional Litigation*, 22 Wm. & Mary L.Rev. 605, 622 (1981).

Do you find Professor Bator's argument persuasive? Is your answer affected by learning that, at the time of the original enactment of section 1983's predecessor, the equitable doctrine concerning a refusal to enjoin criminal prosecutions, to which Professor Bator refers, did not apply across jurisdictional lines? In other words, the principle, as understood, precluded federal equitable relief *only* against *federal* criminal prosecutions. See Whitten, *Federal Declaratory and Injunctive Interference with State Court Proceedings: The Supreme Court and the Limits of Judicial Discretion*, 53 N.C.L.Rev. 591, 637–38 (1975).

Do you agree with Professor Bator that it is only a "wooden" interpretation of the statutory language that could lead one to conclude that the *Younger* doctrine contravenes congressional intent? Reconsider the Court's explanation of the congressional rationale for enactment of the Civil Rights Act of 1871 described in *Mitchum*. See also Zeigler, 1983 Duke L.J. at 989–90: "The record shows that Congress's primary concern was the continuing violence and maladministration of justice in the South. Congress's main purpose in passing the fourteenth amendment and in enacting wave after wave of enforcement legislation was to accomplish a systemic reform of southern criminal and civil justice systems. The record further shows that the federal courts were to be the primary enforcers of this program through substantial intervention in the day-to-day workings of southern justice systems. Congress firmly and repeatedly rejected the notion that the federal courts should stay their hand in favor of theoretically available, but demonstrably ineffective, state court remedies." If this description of the legislative intent is historically accurate, is it conceivable that Congress would have contemplated an equitable limitation on the authority of federal courts to enjoin state criminal proceedings? Cf. Redish, *Abstention, Separation of Powers, and the Limits of the Judicial Function*, 94 Yale L.J. 71, 88 (1984): "[T]he combined effect—if not the motivation—of the Court's decisions in *Younger* and *Mitchum* is that the federal judiciary has arrogated to itself the authority to decide when to enjoin state court proceedings. It is difficult to imagine a starker illustration of judicial usurpation of legislative authority."

Interestingly, in a subsequent decision the Court rejected a judge-made limitation on section 1983 relief, even though such a limitation was not precluded on the face of the statute, because of its inconsistency with congressional intent. In Patsy v. Board of Regents, 457 U.S. 496 (1982), the Court rejected imposition of a requirement of exhaustion of state administrative remedies in section 1983 actions, in part because such a requirement was deemed inconsistent with congressional intent. In so holding, the Court noted that "legislative purpose * * * is of paramount importance in the exhaustion context because Congress is vested with the power to prescribe the basic procedural scheme under which claims may be heard in federal courts. * * * [T]he initial question whether exhaustion is required should be answered by reference to congressional intent; and a court should not defer the exercise of jurisdiction under a federal statute unless it is consistent with that intent." Id. at 501–02. Did the Court in *Younger* undertake such an examination of congressional intent? Should it have? Is the situation in *Patsy* distinguishable? See Zeigler, supra, 1983 Duke L.J. at 991, n. 19.

6. The fundamental assumption of the *Younger* doctrine, of course, is that an individual who believes an ongoing state prosecution threatens his constitutional rights has an adequate remedy available in the defense to his prosecution. How "adequate" a protector of constitutional rights is the ability to raise a defense to a criminal prosecution likely to be? In addition to the concerns about parity, addressed in Chapter Four, consider Laycock, *Federal Interference With State Prosecutions: The Need for Prospective Relief*, 1977 Sup.Ct.Rev. 193. Professor Laycock argues that "in many cases the criminal defense cannot provide an adequate remedy, because the criminal court cannot grant interlocutory, prospective, or class relief." Id. at 194. He notes that "*Younger* does not merely deny an injunction against the pending prosecution; it denies any relief that depends on resolution of the constitutional issue raised in the state case." Id. at 196. Does the situation described by Professor Laycock present a real problem? Do any of the exceptions described in *Younger* reach this issue? If not, could we devise a new exception that would deal with the problem? What would be left of the *Younger* doctrine if such an exception were devised? *Should* such an exception be devised? Consider particularly Laycock's argument concerning the possible need for class relief. Under what circumstances is such class relief likely to be necessary? Is there anything in the *Younger* opinion that speaks to the issue? Assuming class relief is needed, is it really necessary to create an exception to the *Younger* doctrine for such relief to be made available?

7. What exceptions does the Court recognize to the *Younger* doctrine? Are these exceptions consistent with the policies underlying the doctrine in the first place? In Gerstein v. Pugh, 420 U.S. 103 (1975), the Court upheld the issuance of a federal injunction requiring the holding of a probable cause hearing prior to trial, because "[t]he injunction was not directed at the state prosecutions as such, but only at the legality of pretrial detention without a judicial hearing, an issue that could not be raised in defense of the criminal prosecution." Id. at 108 n.9. Is this exception consistent with the underlying rationale of *Younger*? See also Gibson v. Berryhill, 411 U.S. 564 (1973), where the Court held *Younger* inapplicable because the state adjudicatory body, the State Board of Optometry, "was so biased by prejudgment and pecuniary interest that it could not constitutionally conduct hearings looking toward the revocation of appellees' license to practice optometry." Id. at 578. Is this exception consistent with the policies behind *Younger*?

For the view "that the exceptions to the noninterference rules [limiting federal court interference with state court proceedings] are consistent with the basic policies behind the noninterference rules themselves," see Collins, *The Right to Avoid Trial: Justifying Federal Court Intervention Into Ongoing State Court Proceedings*, 66 N.C.L.Rev. 49, 52 (1987). For a suggestion that the exceptions for bad faith prosecutions and patently unconstitutional statutes are inconsistent with *Younger*, see Rehnquist, *Taking Comity Seriously: How to Neutralize the Abstention Doctrine*, 46 Stan.L.Rev. 1049, 1113 (1994). See generally Wingate, *The Bad Faith–Harassment Exception to the* Younger *Doctrine: Exploring the Empty Universe*, 5 Rev. of Litig. 123 (1986).

8. *Our Federalism and Preemption.* On occasion courts have deemed to be an exception to *Younger* those cases in which the constitutional challenge to the state statute is premised on federal preemption. See, e.g., Baggett v. Dept. of Professional Regulation, Bd. of Pilot Commissioners, 717 F.2d 521 (11th Cir.1983). The reasoning for this exception is that the state has no interest in creating or enforcing laws where the federal government has preempted the particular area of law. Gartrell Constr. Inc. v. Aubry, 940 F.2d 437, 441 (9th Cir.1991). Does this reasoning adequately distinguish other applications of *Younger* abstention? If the challenged state law is unconstitutional because it violates the First Amendment, does the state possess any stronger interest in enforcing it? See Daniel Jordan Simon, Comment, *Abstention Preemption: How the Federal Courts Have Opened the Door to the Eradication of "Our Federalism,"* 99 Nw.U.L.Rev. 1355, 1386 (2005): "No justification exists under the current framework of the *Younger* abstention doctrine defined by the Supreme Court that supports treating preemption claims as special."

9. *United States as a party.* In United States v. Morros, 268 F.3d 695 (9th Cir.2001), the court held the *Younger* doctrine inapplicable in cases in which the United States is a party. The decision is criticized in Beck, Note, *The Ninth Circuit's Message to Nevada: You're Not Getting Any* Younger, 3 Nev.L.J. 592 (2003).

10. *Younger* has been the subject of extensive scholarly commentary. In addition to the articles already cited, see Althouse, *The Misguided Search for State Interest in Abstention Cases: Observations on the Occasion of* Pennzoil v. Texaco, 63 N.Y.U.L.Rev. 1051 (1988); Althouse, *Tapping the State Court Resource,* 44 Vand.L.Rev. 953 (1991); Brown, *Where Federalism and Separation of Powers Collide—Rethinking* Younger *Abstention,* 59 Geo.Wash.L.Rev. 114 (1990); Friedman, *A Revisionist Theory of Abstention,* 88 Mich.L.Rev. 530 (1989); Theis, *Younger v. Harris: Federalism in Context,* 33 Hast.L.J. 103 (1981); Weinberg, *The New Judicial Federalism: Where We Are Now,* 19 Ga.L.Rev. 1075 (1985) and *Developments in the Law: Section 1983 and Federalism,* 90 Harv. L.Rev. 1133 (1977).

SAMUELS v. MACKELL

Supreme Court of the United States, 1971.
401 U.S. 66.

Mr. Justice Black delivered the opinion of the Court.

The appellants in these two cases were all indicted in a New York state court on charges of criminal anarchy, in violation of §§ 160, 161, 163, and 580(1) of the New York Penal Law. They later filed these actions in federal district court, alleging (1) that the anarchy statute was void for vagueness in violation of due process, and an abridgment of free speech, press, and assembly, in violation of the First and Fourteenth Amendments; (2) that the anarchy statute had been pre-empted by federal law; and (3) that the New York laws under which the grand jury had been drawn violated the Due Process and Equal Protection Clauses of the Fourteenth Amendment because they disqualified from jury service any member of the community who did not own real or personal property of the value of at least $250, and because the laws furnished no definite standards for determining how jurors were to be selected. Appellants charged that trial of these indictments in state courts would harass them, and cause them to suffer irreparable damages, and they therefore prayed that the state courts should be enjoined from further proceedings. In the alternative, appellants asked the District Court to enter a declaratory judgment to the effect that the challenged state laws were unconstitutional and void on the same grounds. The three-judge court, convened pursuant to 28 U.S.C. § 2284, held that the New York criminal anarchy law was constitutional as it had been construed by the New York courts and held that the complaints should therefore be dismissed.

In Younger v. Harris, we today decided on facts very similar to the facts in these cases that a United States District Court could not issue an injunction to stay proceedings pending in a state criminal court at the time the federal suit was begun. This was because it did not appear from the record that the plaintiffs would suffer immediate irreparable injury in accord with the rule set out in Douglas v. City of Jeannette, 319 U.S. 157 (1943), and many other cases. Since in the present case there is likewise no sufficient showing in the record that the plaintiffs have suffered or would suffer irreparable injury, our decision in the *Younger* case is dispositive of the prayers for injunctions here. The plaintiffs in the present cases also included in their complaints an alternative prayer for a declaratory judgment, but for the reasons indicated below, we hold that this alternative prayer does not require a different result, and that under the circumstances of these cases, the plaintiffs were not entitled to federal relief, declaratory or injunctive. Accordingly we affirm the judgment of the District Court, although not for the reasons given in that court's opinion.

In our opinion in the *Younger* case, we set out in detail the historical and practical basis for the settled doctrine of equity that a federal court should not enjoin a state criminal prosecution begun prior to the institution of the federal suit except in very unusual situations, where necessary to prevent immediate irreparable injury. The question presented here is whether under ordinary circumstances the same considerations that require the withholding of injunctive relief will make declaratory relief equally inappropriate. The question is not, however, a novel one. It was presented and fully considered by this Court in Great Lakes Co. v. Huffman, 319 U.S. 293 (1943). We find the reasoning of this Court in the *Great Lakes* case fully persuasive and think that its holding is controlling here.

In the *Great Lakes* case several employers had brought suit against a Louisiana state official, seeking a declaratory judgment that the State's unemployment compensation law, which required the employers to make contributions to a state compensation fund, was unconstitutional. The lower courts had dismissed the complaint on the ground that the challenged law was constitutional. This Court affirmed the dismissal, "but solely on the ground that, in the appropriate exercise of the court's discretion, relief by way of a declaratory judgment should have been denied without consideration of the merits." Id., at 301–302. The Court, in a unanimous opinion written by Mr. Chief Justice Stone, noted first that under long-settled principles of equity, the federal courts could not have enjoined the Louisiana official from collecting the state tax at issue there unless, as was not true in that case, there was no adequate remedy available in the courts of the State. This judicial doctrine had been approved by Congress in the then-recent Tax Injunction Act of 1937, 50 Stat. 738, now 28 U.S.C. § 1341. Although the declaratory judgment sought by the plaintiffs was a statutory remedy rather than a traditional form of equitable relief, the Court made clear that a suit for declaratory judgment was nevertheless "essentially an equitable cause of action," and was "analogous to the equity jurisdiction in suits *quia timet* or for a decree quieting title." 319 U.S., at 300. In addition, the legislative history of the Federal Declaratory Judgment Act of 1934, 48 Stat. 955, as amended, 28 U.S.C. § 2201, showed that Congress had explicitly contemplated that the courts would decide to grant or withhold declaratory relief on the basis of traditional equitable principles. Accordingly, the Court held that in an action for a declaratory judgment, "the district court was as free as in any other suit in equity to grant or withhold the relief prayed, upon equitable grounds." * * *

The continuing validity of the Court's holding in the *Great Lakes* case has been repeatedly recognized and reaffirmed by this Court. * * * Although we have found no case in this Court dealing with the application of this doctrine to cases in which the relief sought affects state criminal prosecutions rather than state tax collections, we can perceive no relevant difference between the two situations with respect to the limited question whether, in cases where the criminal proceeding was begun prior to the federal civil suit, the propriety of declaratory and injunctive relief should be judged by essentially the same standards. In both situations deeply rooted and long-settled principles of equity have narrowly restricted the scope for federal intervention, and ordinarily a declaratory judgment will result in precisely the same interference with and disruption of state proceedings that the long-standing policy limiting injunctions was designed to avoid. This is true for at least two reasons. In the first place, the Declaratory Judgment Act provides that after a declaratory judgment is issued the district court may enforce it by granting "[f]urther necessary or proper relief," 28 U.S.C. § 2202, and therefore a declaratory judgment issued while state proceedings are pending might serve as the basis for a subsequent injunction against those proceedings to "protect or effectuate" the declaratory judgment, 28 U.S.C. § 2283, and thus result in a clearly improper interference with the state proceedings. Secondly, even if the declaratory judgment is not used as a basis for actually issuing an injunction, the declaratory relief alone has virtually the same practical impact as a formal injunction would. * * * We therefore hold that, in cases where the state criminal prosecution was begun prior to the federal suit, the same equitable principles relevant to the propriety of an injunction must be taken into consideration by federal district courts in determining whether to issue a declaratory judgment, and that where an injunction would be impermissible under these principles, declaratory relief should ordinarily be denied as well.

We do not mean to suggest that a declaratory judgment should never be issued in cases of this type if it has been concluded that injunctive relief would be improper. There may be unusual circumstances in which an injunction might be withheld because, despite a plaintiff's strong claim for relief under the established standards, the injunctive remedy seemed particularly intrusive or offensive; in such a situation, a declaratory judgment might be appropriate and might not be contrary to the basic equitable doctrines governing the availability of relief. Ordinarily, however, the practical effect of the two forms of relief will be virtually identical, and the basic policy against federal interference with pending state criminal prosecutions will be frustrated as much by a declaratory judgment as it would be by an injunction.

For the reasons we have stated, we hold that the court below erred in proceeding to a consideration of the merits of the New York criminal anarchy law. * * *

* * *

Mr. Justice Brennan, with whom Mr. Justice White and Mr. Justice Marshall join, concurring in the result.

I agree that the judgment of the District Court should be affirmed. All the appellants had been indicted for violation of the New York Criminal Anarchy Law before their suit in federal court was filed. They have not alleged facts amounting to bad-faith harassment. Therefore, neither a declaratory judgment nor an injunction would be proper.

[The concurring opinion of Justice Douglas is omitted.]

Notes

1. Does the decision in *Samuels* follow inescapably from the decision in *Younger*? Why or why not?

2. What exception or exceptions does the Court recognize to its ban on the issuance of declaratory judgments by federal courts against an ongoing state prosecution? Under what circumstances do you think the exceptions are likely to apply? Does the Court give any indication?

3. Keep *Samuels* closely in mind when you read the following case.

STEFFEL v. THOMPSON

Supreme Court of the United States, 1974.
415 U.S. 452.

Mr. Justice Brennan delivered the opinion of the Court.

When a state criminal proceeding under a disputed state criminal statute is pending against a federal plaintiff at the time his federal complaint is filed, Younger v. Harris, 401 U.S. 37, and Samuels v. Mackell, 401 U.S. 66 (1971), held, respectively, that, unless bad-faith enforcement or other special circumstances are demonstrated, principles of equity, comity, and federalism preclude issuance of a federal injunction restraining enforcement of the criminal statute and, in all but unusual circumstances, a declaratory judgment upon the constitutionality of the statute. This case presents the important question reserved in Samuels v. Mackell, id., at 73–74, whether declaratory relief is precluded when a state prosecution has been threatened, but is not pending, and a showing of bad-faith enforcement or other special circumstances has not been made.

Petitioner, and others, filed a complaint in the District Court for the Northern District of Georgia, invoking the Civil Rights Act of 1871, 42 U.S.C. § 1983, and its jurisdictional implementation, 28 U.S.C. § 1343. The complaint requested a declaratory judgment pursuant to 28 U.S.C. §§ 2201–2202, that Ga. Code Ann. § 26–1503 (1972) was being applied in violation of petitioner's First and Fourteenth Amendment rights, and an injunction restraining respondents—the solicitor of the Civil and Criminal Court of DeKalb County, the chief of the DeKalb County Police, the owner of the North DeKalb Shopping Center, and the manager of that shopping center—from enforcing the statute so as to interfere with petitioner's constitutionally protected activities.

The parties stipulated to the relevant facts: On October 8, 1970, while petitioner and other individuals were distributing handbills protesting American involvement in Vietnam on an exterior sidewalk of the North DeKalb Shopping Center, shopping center employees asked them to stop handbilling and leave. They declined to do so, and police officers were summoned. The officers told them that they would be arrested if they did not stop handbilling. The group then left to avoid arrest. Two days later petitioner and a companion returned to the shopping center and again began handbilling. The manager of the center called the police, and petitioner and his companion were once again told that failure to stop their handbilling would result in their arrests. Petitioner left to avoid arrest. His companion stayed, however, continued handbilling, and was arrested and subsequently arraigned on a charge of criminal trespass in violation of § 26–1503. Petitioner alleged in his complaint that, although he desired to return to the shopping center to distribute handbills, he had not done so because of his concern that he, too, would be arrested for violation of § 26–1503; the parties stipulated that, if petitioner returned and refused upon request to stop handbilling, a warrant would be sworn out and he might be arrested and charged with a violation of the Georgia statute.

After hearing, the District Court denied all relief and dismissed the action, finding that "no meaningful contention can be made that the state has [acted] or will in the future act in bad faith," and therefore "the rudiments of an active controversy between the parties ... [are] lacking." 334 F.Supp. 1386, 1389–1390 (1971). Petitioner appealed only from the denial of declaratory relief.[6] The Court of Appeals for the Fifth Circuit, one judge concurring in the result, affirmed the District Court's judgment refusing declaratory relief. Becker v. Thompson, 459 F.2d 919 (1972). The court recognized that the holdings of Younger v. Harris, 401 U.S. 37 (1971), and Samuels v. Mackell, 401 U.S. 66 (1971), were expressly limited to situations where state prosecutions were pending when the federal action commenced, but was of the view that Younger v. Harris "made it clear beyond peradventure that irreparable injury must be measured by bad faith harassment and such test must be applied to a request for injunctive relief against *threatened* state court criminal prosecution" as well as against a pending prosecution; and, furthermore, since the opinion in Samuels v. Mackell reasoned that declaratory relief would normally disrupt the state criminal justice system in the manner of injunctive relief, it followed that "the same test of bad faith harassment is prerequisite ... for declaratory relief in a threatened prosecution." * * *

We granted certiorari, and now reverse.

I

At the threshold we must consider whether petitioner presents an "actual controversy," a requirement imposed by Art. III of the Constitution and the express terms of the Federal Declaratory Judgment Act, 28 U.S.C. § 2201.

Unlike three of the appellees in Younger v. Harris, 401 U.S., at 41, petitioner has alleged threats of prosecution that cannot be characterized as "imaginary or speculative," id., at 42. He has been twice warned to stop handbilling that he claims is constitutionally protected and has been told by the police that if he again handbills at the shopping center and disobeys a warning to stop he will likely be prosecuted. The prosecution of petitioner's handbilling companion is ample demonstration that petitioner's concern with arrest has not been "chimerical," Poe v. Ullman, 367 U.S. 497, 508 (1961). In these circumstances, it is not necessary that petitioner first expose himself to actual arrest or prosecution to be entitled to challenge a statute that he claims deters the exercise of his constitutional rights. * * *

6. Petitioner's notice of appeal challenged the denial of both injunctive and declaratory relief. However, in his appellate brief, he abandoned his appeal from denial of injunctive relief. Becker v. Thompson, 459 F.2d 919, 921 (CA5 1972).

II

We now turn to the question of whether the District Court and the Court of Appeals correctly found petitioner's request for declaratory relief inappropriate.

Sensitive to principles of equity, comity, and federalism, we recognized in Younger v. Harris, supra, that federal courts should ordinarily refrain from enjoining ongoing state criminal prosecutions. We were cognizant that a pending state proceeding, in all but unusual cases, would provide the federal plaintiff with the necessary vehicle for vindicating his constitutional rights, and, in that circumstance, the restraining of an ongoing prosecution would entail an unseemly failure to give effect to the principle that state courts have the solemn responsibility, equally with the federal courts "to guard, enforce, and protect every right granted or secured by the Constitution of the United States. . . ." Robb v. Connolly, 111 U.S. 624, 637 (1884). In Samuels v. Mackell, supra, the Court also found that the same principles ordinarily would be flouted by issuance of a federal declaratory judgment when a state proceeding was pending, since the intrusive effect of declaratory relief "will result in precisely the same interference with and disruption of state proceedings that the long-standing policy limiting injunctions was designed to avoid." 401 U.S., at 72. * * *

Neither *Younger* nor *Samuels*, however, decided the question whether federal intervention might be permissible in the absence of a pending state prosecution. In *Younger*, the Court said:

"We express no view about the circumstances under which federal courts may act when there is no prosecution pending in state courts at the time the federal proceeding is begun." 401 U.S., at 41.

Similarly, in Samuels v. Mackell, the Court stated:

"We, of course, express no views on the propriety of declaratory relief when no state proceeding is pending at the time the federal suit is begun." 401 U.S., at 73–74.

These reservations anticipated the Court's recognition that the relevant principles of equity, comity, and federalism "have little force in the absence of a pending state proceeding." Lake Carriers' Assn. v. MacMullan, 406 U.S. 498, 509 (1972). When no state criminal proceeding is pending at the time the federal complaint is filed, federal intervention does not result in duplicative legal proceedings or disruption of the state criminal justice system; nor can federal intervention, in that circumstance, be interpreted as reflecting negatively upon the state court's ability to enforce constitutional principles. In addition, while a pending state prosecution provides the federal plaintiff with a concrete opportunity to vindicate his constitutional rights, a refusal on the part of the federal courts to intervene when no state proceeding is pending may place the hapless plaintiff between the Scylla of intentionally flouting state law and the Charybdis of forgoing what he believes to be constitutionally protected activity in order to avoid becoming enmeshed in a criminal proceeding. Cf. Dombrowski v. Pfister, 380 U.S. 479, 490 (1965).

When no state proceeding is pending and thus considerations of equity, comity, and federalism have little vitality, the propriety of granting federal declaratory relief may properly be considered independently of a request for injunctive relief. Here, the Court of Appeals held that, because injunctive relief would not be appropriate since petitioner failed to demonstrate irreparable injury—a traditional prerequisite to injunctive relief, e.g., Dombrowski v. Pfister, supra—it followed that declaratory relief was also inappropriate. Even if the Court of Appeals correctly viewed injunctive relief as inappropriate—a question we need not reach today since petitioner has abandoned his request for that remedy, see n. 6 supra—[12] the court erred in treating the requests for injunctive and declaratory relief as a single issue. "[W]hen no state prosecution is pending and the only question is whether declaratory relief is appropriate[,] ... the congressional scheme that makes the federal courts the primary guardians of constitutional rights, and the express congressional authorization of declaratory relief, afforded because it is a less harsh and abrasive remedy than the injunction, become the factors of primary significance." Perez v. Ledesma, 401 U.S. 82, 104 (1971) (separate opinion of Brennan, J.).

The subject matter jurisdiction of the lower federal courts was greatly expanded in the wake of the Civil War. A pervasive sense of nationalism led to enactment of the Civil Rights Act of 1871, 17 Stat. 13, empowering the lower federal courts to determine the constitutionality of actions, taken by persons under color of state law, allegedly depriving other individuals of rights guaranteed by the Constitution and federal law, see 42 U.S.C. § 1983, 28 U.S.C. § 1343(3).[13] Four years later, in the Judiciary Act of March 3, 1875, 18 Stat. 470, Congress conferred upon the lower federal courts, for but the second time in their nearly century-old history, general federal-question jurisdiction subject only to a jurisdictional-amount requirement, see 28 U.S.C. § 1331.[14] With this latter

---

12. We note that, in those cases where injunctive relief has been sought to restrain an imminent, but not yet pending, prosecution *for past conduct,* sufficient injury has not been found to warrant injunctive relief, see Beal v. Missouri Pacific R. Co., 312 U.S. 45 (1941); Spielman Motor Sales Co. v. Dodge, 295 U.S. 89 (1935); Fenner v. Boykin, 271 U.S. 240 (1926). There is some question, however, whether a showing of irreparable injury might be made in a case where, although no prosecution is pending or impending, an individual demonstrates that he will be required to *forgo* constitutionally protected activity in order to avoid arrest. Compare Dombrowski v. Pfister, 380 U.S. 479 (1965); Hygrade Provision Co. v. Sherman, 266 U.S. 497 (1925); and Terrace v. Thompson, 263 U.S. 197, 214, 216 (1923), with Douglas v. City of Jeannette, 319 U.S.

157 (1943); see generally Note, Implications of the Younger Cases for the Availability of Federal Equitable Relief When No State Prosecution is Pending, 72 Col.L.Rev. 874 (1972).

13. "Sensitiveness to 'states' rights', fear of rivalry with state courts and respect for state sentiment, were swept aside by the great impulse of national feeling born of the Civil War. Nationalism was triumphant; in national administration was sought its vindication. The new exertions of federal power were no longer trusted to the enforcement of state agencies." F. Frankfurter & J. Landis, The Business of the Supreme Court 64 (1928).

14. In the last days of the John Adams administration, general federal-question jurisdiction had been granted to the federal

enactment, the lower federal courts "ceased to be restricted tribunals of fair dealing between citizens of different states and became the *primary* and powerful reliances for vindicating every right given by the Constitution, the laws, and treaties of the United States." F. Frankfurter & J. Landis, The Business of the Supreme Court 65 (1928) (emphasis added). These two statutes, together with the Court's decision in Ex parte Young, 209 U.S. 123 (1908)—holding that state officials who threaten to enforce an unconstitutional state statute may be enjoined by a federal court of equity and that a federal court may, in appropriate circumstances, enjoin future state criminal prosecutions under the unconstitutional Act—have "established the modern framework for federal protection of constitutional rights from state interference." Perez v. Ledesma, supra, at 107 (separate opinion of Brennan, J.).

A "storm of controversy" raged in the wake of Ex parte Young, focusing principally on the power of a single federal judge to grant *ex parte* interlocutory injunctions against the enforcement of state statutes, H. Hart & H. Wechsler, The Federal Courts and the Federal System 967 (2d ed. 1973); see generally Goldstein v. Cox, 396 U.S. 471 (1970); Hutcheson, A Case for Three Judges, 47 Harv.L.Rev. 795, 804–805 (1934). * * * From a State's viewpoint the granting of injunctive relief—even by these courts of special dignity—"rather clumsily" crippled state enforcement of its statutes pending further review, see H. R. Rep. No. 288, 70th Cong., 1st Sess., 2 (1928); H. R. Rep. No. 94, 71st Cong., 2d Sess., 2 (1929); H. R. Rep. No. 627, 72d Cong., 1st Sess., 2 (1932). Furthermore, plaintiffs were dissatisfied with this method of testing the constitutionality of state statutes, since it placed upon them the burden of demonstrating the traditional prerequisites to equitable relief—most importantly, irreparable injury. See, e.g., Fenner v. Boykin, 271 U.S. 240, 243 (1926).

To dispel these difficulties, Congress in 1934 enacted the Declaratory Judgment Act, 28 U.S.C. §§ 2201–2202. That Congress plainly intended declaratory relief to act as an alternative to the strong medicine of the injunction and to be utilized to test the constitutionality of state criminal statutes in cases where injunctive relief would be unavailable is amply evidenced by the legislative history of the Act * * *.

* * *

It was this history that formed the backdrop to our decision in Zwickler v. Koota, 389 U.S. 241 (1967), where a state criminal statute was attacked on grounds of unconstitutional overbreadth and no state prosecution was pending against the federal plaintiff. There, we found error in a three-judge district court's considering, as a single question, the propriety of granting injunctive and declaratory relief. Although we noted that injunctive relief might well be unavailable under principles of equity jurisprudence canvassed in Douglas v. City of Jeannette, 319 U.S. 157 (1943), we held that "a federal district court has the duty to decide

courts by § 11 of the Midnight Judges Act, 2 Stat. 92 (1801). The Act was repealed only one year later by § 1 of the Act of Mar. 8, 1802, 2 Stat. 132.

the appropriateness and the merits of the declaratory request irrespective of its conclusion as to the propriety of the issuance of the injunction." 389 U.S., at 254. Only one year ago, we reaffirmed the Zwickler v. Koota holding in Roe v. Wade, 410 U.S. 113 (1973), and Doe v. Bolton, 410 U.S. 179 (1973). In those two cases, we declined to decide whether the District Courts had properly denied to the federal plaintiffs, against whom no prosecutions were pending, injunctive relief restraining enforcement of the Texas and Georgia criminal abortion statutes; instead, we affirmed the issuance of declaratory judgments of unconstitutionality, anticipating that these would be given effect by state authorities. We said:

> "The Court has recognized that *different considerations* enter into a federal court's decision as to declaratory relief, on the one hand, and injunctive relief, on the other. Zwickler v. Koota, 389 U.S. 241, 252–255, (1967); Dombrowski v. Pfister, 380 U.S. 479 (1965)." Roe v. Wade, supra, at 166 (emphasis added).

See Doe v. Bolton, supra, at 201.

The "different considerations" entering into a decision whether to grant declaratory relief have their origins in the preceding historical summary. First, as Congress recognized in 1934, a declaratory judgment will have a less intrusive effect on the administration of state criminal laws. As was observed in Perez v. Ledesma, 401 U.S., at 124–126 (separate opinion of Brennan, J.):

> "Of course, a favorable declaratory judgment may nevertheless be valuable to the plaintiff though it cannot make even an unconstitutional statute disappear. A state statute may be declared unconstitutional *in toto*—that is, incapable of having constitutional applications; or it may be declared unconstitutionally vague or overbroad— that is, incapable of being constitutionally applied to the full extent of its purport. In either case, a federal declaration of unconstitutionality reflects the opinion of the federal court that the statute cannot be fully enforced. If a declaration of total unconstitutionality is affirmed by this Court, it follows that this Court stands ready to reverse any conviction under the statute. If a declaration of partial unconstitutionality is affirmed by this Court, the implication is that this Court will overturn particular applications of the statute, but that if the statute is narrowly construed by the state courts it will not be incapable of constitutional applications. Accordingly, the declaration does not necessarily bar prosecutions under the statute, as a broad injunction would. Thus, where the highest court of a State has had an opportunity to give a statute regulating expression a narrowing or clarifying construction but has failed to do so, and later a federal court declares the statute unconstitutionally vague or overbroad, it may well be open to a state prosecutor, after the federal court decision, to bring a prosecution under the statute if he reasonably believes that the defendant's conduct is not constitutionally protected and that the state courts may give the statute a

construction so as to yield a constitutionally valid conviction. Even where a declaration of unconstitutionality is not reviewed by this Court, the declaration may still be able to cut down the deterrent effect of an unconstitutional state statute. The persuasive force of the court's opinion and judgment may lead state prosecutors, courts, and legislators to reconsider their respective responsibilities toward the statute. Enforcement policies or judicial construction may be changed, or the legislature may repeal the statute and start anew. Finally, the federal court judgment may have some *res judicata* effect, though this point is not free from difficulty and the governing rules remain to be developed with a view to the proper workings of a federal system. What is clear, however, is that even though a declaratory judgment has 'the force and effect of a final judgment,' 28 U.S.C. § 2201, it is a much milder form of relief than an injunction. Though it may be persuasive, it is not ultimately coercive; noncompliance with it may be inappropriate, but is not contempt." (Footnote omitted.)

Second, engrafting upon the Declaratory Judgment Act a requirement that all of the traditional equitable prerequisites to the issuance of an injunction be satisfied before the issuance of a declaratory judgment is considered would defy Congress' intent to make declaratory relief available in cases where an injunction would be inappropriate.

"Were the law to be that a plaintiff could not obtain a declaratory judgment that a local ordinance was unconstitutional when no state prosecution is pending unless he could allege and prove circumstances justifying a federal injunction of an existing state prosecution, the Federal Declaratory Judgment Act would have been *pro tanto* repealed." Wulp v. Corcoran, 454 F.2d 826, 832 (C.A.1 1972) (Coffin, J.).

See Perez v. Ledesma, 401 U.S., at 116 (separate opinion of Brennan, J.). Thus, the Court of Appeals was in error when it ruled that a failure to demonstrate irreparable injury—a traditional prerequisite to injunctive relief, having no equivalent in the law of declaratory judgments, see Aetna Life Ins. Co. v. Haworth, 300 U.S. 227, 241 (1937); Nashville, C. & St. L. R. Co. v. Wallace, 288 U.S. 249, 264 (1933)—precluded the granting of declaratory relief.

The only occasions where this Court has disregarded these "different considerations" and found that a preclusion of injunctive relief inevitably led to a denial of declaratory relief have been cases in which principles of federalism militated altogether against federal intervention in a class of adjudications. See Great Lakes Dredge & Dock Co. v. Huffman, 319 U.S. 293 (1943) (federal policy against interfering with the enforcement of state tax laws); Samuels v. Mackell, 401 U.S. 66 (1971). In the instant case, principles of federalism not only do not preclude federal intervention, they compel it. Requiring the federal courts totally to step aside when no state criminal prosecution is pending against the federal plaintiff would turn federalism on its head. When federal claims are premised on 42 U.S.C. § 1983 and 28 U.S.C. § 1343(3)—as they are *exhaustion of state judicial remedies not required* here—we have not required exhaustion of state judicial or administrative remedies, recognizing the paramount role Congress has assigned to the federal courts to protect constitutional rights. See, e.g., McNeese v. Board of Education, 373 U.S. 668 (1963); Monroe v. Pape, 365 U.S. 167 (1961). But exhaustion of state remedies is precisely what would be required if both federal injunctive and declaratory relief were unavailable in a case where no state prosecution had been commenced.

III

Respondents, however, relying principally upon our decision in Cameron v. Johnson, 390 U.S. 611 (1968), argue that, although it may be appropriate to issue a declaratory judgment when no state criminal proceeding is pending and the attack is upon the *facial validity* of a state criminal statute, such a step would be improper where, as here, the attack is merely upon the constitutionality of the statute as applied, since the State's interest in unencumbered enforcement of its laws outweighs the minimal federal interest in protecting the constitutional rights of only a single individual. We reject the argument.

* * *

Rule We therefore hold that, regardless of whether injunctive relief may be appropriate, federal declaratory relief is not precluded when no state prosecution is pending and a federal plaintiff demonstrates a genuine threat of enforcement of a disputed state criminal statute, whether an attack is made on the constitutionality of the statute on its face or as applied. The judgment of the Court of Appeals is reversed, and the case is remanded for further proceedings consistent with this opinion. *Constitutional as applied or its face or as applied*

It is so ordered.

MR. JUSTICE STEWART, with whom THE CHIEF JUSTICE joins, concurring.

While joining the opinion of the Court, I add a word by way of emphasis.

Our decision today must not be understood as authorizing the invocation of federal declaratory judgment jurisdiction by a person who thinks a state criminal law is unconstitutional, even if he genuinely feels "chilled" in his freedom of action by the law's existence, and even if he honestly entertains the subjective belief that he may now or in the future be prosecuted under it.

As the Court stated in Younger v. Harris, 401 U.S. 37, 52:

"The power and duty of the judiciary to declare laws unconstitutional is in the final analysis derived from its responsibility for resolving concrete disputes brought before the courts for decision. . . ." *Concrete Disputes*

See also Boyle v. Landry, 401 U.S. 77, 80–81.

The petitioner in this case has succeeded in objectively showing that the threat of imminent arrest, corroborated by the actual arrest of his companion, has created an actual concrete controversy between himself and the agents of the State. He has, therefore, demonstrated "a genuine threat of enforcement of a disputed state criminal statute. . . ." Cases where such a "genuine threat" can be demonstrated will, I think, be exceedingly rare.

MR. JUSTICE WHITE, concurring.

I offer the following few words in light of Mr. Justice Rehnquist's concurrence in which he discusses the impact on a pending federal action of a later filed criminal prosecution against the federal plaintiff, whether a federal court may enjoin a state criminal prosecution under a statute the federal court has earlier declared unconstitutional at the suit of the defendant now being prosecuted, and the question whether that declaratory judgment is res judicata in such a later filed state criminal action.

It should be noted, first, that his views on these issues are neither expressly nor impliedly embraced by the Court's opinion filed today. Second, my own tentative views on these questions are somewhat contrary to my Brother's.

At this writing at least, I would anticipate that a final declaratory judgment entered by a federal court holding particular conduct of the federal plaintiff to be immune on federal constitutional grounds from prosecution under state law should be accorded res judicata effect in any later prosecution of that very conduct. There would also, I think, be additional circumstances in which the federal judgment should be considered as more than a mere precedent bearing on the issue before the state court.

Neither can I at this stage agree that the federal court, having rendered a declaratory judgment in favor of the plaintiff, could not enjoin a later state prosecution for conduct that the federal court has declared immune. The Declaratory Judgment Act itself provides that a "declaration shall have the force and effect of a final judgment or decree," 28 U.S.C. § 2201; eminent authority anticipated that declaratory judgments would be res judicata, E. Borchard, Declaratory Judgments 10–11 (2d ed. 1941); and there is every reason for not reducing declaratory judgments to mere advisory opinions. Toucey v. New York Life Insurance Co., 314 U.S. 118 (1941), once expressed the view that 28 U.S.C. § 2283 forbade injunctions against relitigation in state courts of federally decided issues, but the section was then amended to overrule that case, the consequence being that "[i]t is clear that the Toucey rule is gone, and that to protect or effectuate its judgment a federal court may enjoin relitigation in the state court." C. Wright, Federal Courts 180 (2d ed. 1970). I see no more reason here to hold that the federal plaintiff must always rely solely on his plea of res judicata in the state courts. The statute provides for "[f]urther necessary or proper relief . . . against any adverse party whose rights have been determined by such judgment," 28 U.S.C. § 2202, and it would not seem improper to enjoin local prosecutors who refuse to observe adverse federal judgments.

* * *

Mr. Justice Rehnquist, with whom The Chief Justice joins, concurring.

I concur in the opinion of the Court. Although my reading of the legislative history of the Declaratory Judgment Act of 1934 suggests that its primary purpose was to enable persons to obtain a definition of their rights before an actual injury had occurred, rather than to palliate any controversy arising from Ex parte Young, 209 U.S. 123 (1908). Congress apparently was aware at the time it passed the Act that persons threatened with state criminal prosecutions might choose to forgo the offending conduct and instead seek a federal declaration of their rights. Use of the declaratory judgment procedure in the circumstances presented by this case seems consistent with that congressional expectation.

If this case were the Court's first opportunity to deal with this area of law, I would be content to let the matter rest there. But, as our cases abundantly illustrate, this area of law is in constant litigation, and it is an area through which our decisions have traced a path that may accurately be described as sinuous. Attempting to accommodate the principles of the new declaratory judgment procedure with other more established principles—in particular a proper regard for the relationship between the independent state and federal judiciary systems—this Court has acted both to advance and to limit the Act. Because the opinion today may possibly be read by resourceful counsel as commencing a new and less restrictive curve in this path of adjudication, I feel it is important to emphasize what the opinion does and does not say.

To begin with, it seems appropriate to restate the obvious: the Court's decision today deals only with declaratory relief and with threatened prosecutions. The case provides no authority for the granting of any injunctive relief nor does it provide authority for the granting of any relief at all when prosecutions are pending. The Court quite properly leaves for another day whether the granting of a declaratory judgment by a federal court will have any subsequent res judicata effect or will perhaps support the issuance of a later federal injunction. * * *

* * *

* * * I do not believe that today's decision can properly be raised to support the issuance of a federal injunction based upon a favorable declaratory judgment. The Court's description of declaratory relief as "'a milder alternative to the injunction remedy,'" having a "less intrusive effect on the administration of state criminal laws" than an injunction, indicates to me critical distinctions which make declaratory relief appropriate where injunctive relief would not be. It would all but totally obscure these important distinctions if a successful application for declaratory relief came to be regarded, not as the conclusion of a lawsuit, but as a giant step toward obtaining an injunction against a subsequent criminal prosecution. The availability of injunctive relief must be considered with an eye toward the important policies of federalism which this Court has often recognized.

If the rationale of cases such as *Younger* and *Samuels* turned in any way upon the relative ease with which a federal district court could reach a conclusion about the constitutionality of a challenged state statute, a preexisting judgment declaring the statute unconstitutional as applied to a particular plaintiff would, of course, be a factor favoring the issuance of an injunction as "further relief" under the Declaratory Judgment Act. But, except for statutes that are " 'flagrantly and patently violative of express constitutional prohibitions in every clause, sentence and paragraph ... ,' " *Younger v. Harris*, the rationale of those cases has no such basis. Their direction that federal courts not interfere with state prosecutions does not vary depending on the closeness of the constitutional issue or on the degree of confidence which the federal court possesses in the correctness of its conclusions on the constitutional point. Those decisions instead depend upon considerations relevant to the harmonious operation of separate federal and state court systems, with a special regard for the State's interest in enforcing its own criminal laws, considerations which are as relevant in guiding the action of a federal court which has previously issued a declaratory judgment as they are in guiding the action of one which has not. While the result may be that injunctive relief is not available as "further relief" under the Declaratory Judgment Act in this particular class of cases whereas it would be in similar cases not involving considerations of federalism, this would be no more a *pro tanto* repeal of that provision of the Declaratory Judgment Act than was *Younger* a *pro tanto* repeal of the All Writs Act, 28 U.S.C. § 1651.

A declaratory judgment is simply a statement of rights, not a binding order supplemented by continuing sanctions. State authorities may choose to be guided by the judgment of a lower federal court, but they are not compelled to follow the decision by threat of contempt or other penalties. If the federal plaintiff pursues the conduct for which he was previously threatened with arrest and is in fact arrested, he may not return the controversy to federal court, although he may, of course, raise the federal declaratory judgment in the state court for whatever value it may prove to have.[3] In any event, the defendant at that point is able to present his case for full consideration by a state court charged, as are the federal courts, to preserve the defendant's constitutional rights. Federal interference with this process would involve precisely the same concerns discussed in *Younger* and recited in the Court's opinion in this case.

Notes

1. On what grounds does the Court in *Steffel* distinguish future prosecutions from the ongoing prosecution involved in *Younger*? Is the asserted

---

3. The Court's opinion notes that the possible res judicata effect of a federal declaratory judgment in a subsequent state court prosecution is a question " 'not free from difficulty.' " I express no opinion on that issue here. However, I do note that the federal decision would not be accorded the *stare decisis* effect in state court that it would have in a subsequent proceeding within the same federal jurisdiction. Although the state court would not be compelled to follow the federal holding, the opinion might, of course, be viewed as highly persuasive.

basis for the distinction consistent with all of the rationales for the deference of the *Younger* doctrine? See Redish, *The Doctrine of* Younger v. Harris: *Deference in Search of a Rationale*, 63 Cornell L.Rev. 463, 473–77 (1978). Is it consistent with *any* of them? Consider Whitten, *Federal Declaratory and Injunctive Interference with State Court Proceedings: The Supreme Court and the Limits of Judicial Discretion*, 53 N.C.L.Rev. 591, 675–76 (1975):

> With regard to the distinction suggested between injunctive relief against future, as opposed to pending, state prosecutions, it is difficult to believe that any such distinction provides a viable means of preventing the sort of harm to state interests that the Court was concerned about in *Younger* * * *. [I]t is difficult to see why such considerations [of equity, comity and federalism] have "little vitality" in the absence of a pending proceeding * * *. [I]n many cases the disruption to state interests caused by preventing a future prosecution is just as great as if the prosecution is pending.

Is this persuasive? If so, to which conclusion does it lead you, rejection of *Steffel* or rejection of *Younger*?

2. Is *Steffel* limited to allowing federal *declaratory* relief against future state prosecutions? The Court did not expressly consider the propriety of either preliminary or permanent *injunctive* relief against a future prosecution. However, can you reason from the logic of the Court's opinion to determine whether injunctive relief should also be deemed available? How helpful are the opinions of Justices White and Rehnquist on this question? If declaratory relief against future prosecutions is allowed, can injunctive relief be rationally distinguished? Is *Samuels* relevant to your answer?

3. In part, the issue left unresolved in *Steffel* was answered in Doran v. Salem Inn, Inc., 422 U.S. 922 (1975). The district court had awarded a preliminary injunction, pending outcome of the federal action, against future state prosecutions of two parties against whom no prosecution had been filed. Justice Rehnquist, speaking for the Court, noted, the two parties "were assuredly entitled to declaratory relief, and since we have previously recognized that '[o]rdinarily ... the practical effect of [injunctive and declaratory] relief will be virtually identical,' *Samuels*, 401 U.S., at 73, we think that [the two parties] were entitled to have their claims for preliminary injunctive relief considered without regard to *Younger*'s restrictions." 422 U.S., at 930–931.

The opinion emphasized, however, that the Court was deciding only the issue of the availability of *preliminary* injunctive relief:

> At the conclusion of a successful federal challenge to a state statute or local ordinance, a district court can generally protect the interests of a federal plaintiff by entering a declaratory judgment, and therefore the stronger injunctive medicine will be unnecessary. But prior to final judgment there is no established declaratory remedy comparable to a preliminary injunction; unless preliminary relief is available upon a proper showing, plaintiffs in some situations may suffer unnecessary and substantial irreparable harm. Moreover, neither declaratory nor injunctive relief can directly interfere with enforcement of contested statutes or ordinances except with respect to the particular federal

plaintiffs, and the State is free to prosecute others who may violate the statute. Id. at 931.

Are the asserted bases on which to distinguish preliminary from permanent injunctive relief persuasive? Is Justice Rehnquist's reasoning in the above-quoted passage consistent with the rationale of *Samuels*? Cf. Fiss, *Dombrowski*, 86 Yale L.J. 1103, 1145 (1977) ("with *Steffel* and [*Doran*] on the books, the next step—bringing final statutory injunctions under the access rules for declaratory judgments—seemed small and almost predictable"). Is this a proper reading of *Doran*?

4. The permanent injunction issue may—or may not—have been resolved in Wooley v. Maynard, 430 U.S. 705 (1977). The federal court plaintiff had been prosecuted and convicted on several occasions for concealing the state slogan, "live free or die" on his New Hampshire license plates. Before another state prosecution was filed, he sought an injunction on the ground that requiring him to display the slogan violated the first amendment. The Court, in an opinion by Chief Justice Burger, authorized permanent injunctive relief against future prosecutions. In so holding, the Court reasoned in the following manner:

> In *Younger* the Court recognized that principles of judicial economy, as well as proper state-federal relations, preclude federal courts from exercising equitable jurisdiction to enjoin ongoing state prosecutions. However, when a genuine threat of prosecution exists, a litigant is entitled to resort to a federal forum to seek redress for an alleged deprivation of federal rights. See Steffel v. Thompson, 415 U.S. 452 (1974); Doran v. Salem Inn, Inc., 422 U.S. 922, 930–931 (1975). *Younger* principles aside, a litigant is entitled to resort to a federal forum in seeking redress under 42 U.S.C. § 1983 for an alleged deprivation of federal rights. Huffman v. Pursue, Ltd., 420 U.S. 592, 609–610, n. 21 (1975). Mr. Maynard now finds himself placed "between the Scylla of intentionally flouting state law and the Charybdis of forgoing what he believes to be constitutionally protected activity in order to avoid becoming enmeshed in [another] criminal proceeding." Steffel v. Thompson, supra, 415 U.S., at 462. Mrs. Maynard, as joint owner of the family automobiles, is no less likely than her husband to be subjected to state prosecution. Under these circumstances he cannot be denied consideration of a federal remedy.

> Appellants, however, point out that Maynard failed to seek review of his criminal convictions and cite Huffman v. Pursue, Ltd., supra, for the propositions that "a necessary concomitant of *Younger* is that a party in appellee's posture must exhaust his state appellate remedies before seeking relief in the District Court," 420 U.S., at 608, and that "*Younger* standards must be met to justify federal intervention in a state judicial proceeding as to which a losing litigant has not exhausted his state appellate remedies," id., at 609. *Huffman*, however, is inapposite. There the appellee was seeking to prevent, by means of federal intervention, enforcement of a state-court judgment declaring its theater a nuisance. We held that appellee's failure to exhaust its state appeals barred federal intervention under the principles of *Younger*: "Federal post-trial intervention, in a fashion designed to annul the results of a

state trial ... deprives the States of a function which quite legitimately is left to them, that of overseeing trial court dispositions of constitutional issues which arise in civil litigation over which they have jurisdiction." Ibid.

Here, however, the suit is in no way "designed to annul the results of a state trial" since the relief sought is wholly prospective, to preclude further prosecution under a statute alleged to violate appellees' constitutional rights. Maynard has already sustained convictions and has served a sentence of imprisonment for his prior offenses. He does not seek to have his record expunged, or to annul any collateral effects those convictions may have, e.g., upon his driving privileges. The Maynards seek only to be free from prosecutions for future violations of the same statutes. *Younger* does not bar federal jurisdiction.

In their complaint, the Maynards sought both declaratory and injunctive relief against the enforcement of the New Hampshire statutes. We have recognized that although " '[o]rdinarily ... the practical effect of [injunctive and declaratory] relief will be virtually identical,' " *Doran v. Salem Inn, supra,* 422 U.S., at 931, quoting *Samuels v. Mackell,* 401 U.S. 66, 73, (1971), a "district court can generally protect the interests of a federal plaintiff by entering a declaratory judgment, and therefore the stronger injunctive medicine will be unnecessary." *Doran, supra,* 422 U.S. at 931. It is correct that generally a court will not enjoin "the enforcement of a criminal statute even though unconstitutional," *Spielman Motor Co. v. Dodge,* 295 U.S. 89, 95 (1935), since "[s]uch a result seriously impairs the State's interest in enforcing its criminal laws, and implicates the concerns for federalism which lie at the heart of *Younger*," *Doran, supra,* 422 U.S., at 931. But this is not an absolute policy and in some circumstances injunctive relief may be appropriate. "To justify such interference there must be exceptional circumstances and a clear showing that an injunction is necessary in order to afford adequate protection of constitutional rights." *Spielman Motor Co., supra,* 295 U.S., at 95.

We have such a situation here for, as we have noted, three successive prosecutions were undertaken against Mr. Maynard in the span of five weeks. This is quite different from a claim for federal equitable relief when a prosecution is threatened for the first time. The threat of repeated prosecutions in the future against both him and his wife, and the effect of such a continuing threat on their ability to perform the ordinary tasks of daily life which require an automobile, is sufficient to justify injunctive relief. Cf. *Douglas v. City of Jeannette,* 319 U.S. 157 (1943). We are therefore unwilling to say that the District Court was limited to granting declaratory relief. *Wooley,* 430 U.S. at 710–12.

Several commentators have read *Wooley* to represent an extension of *Steffel* and *Doran* to permanent injunctive relief. See, e.g., Shreve, *Federal Jurisdiction: The Perils and Rewards of Pulling Things Together,* 80 Mich.L.Rev. 688, 692 n. 21 (1982). Do you agree? Can the Court's authorization of permanent injunctive relief be explained any other way?

In *Zablocki v. Redhail,* 434 U.S. 374 (1978), the Supreme Court affirmed a lower federal court's award of permanent injunctive relief, prohibiting county clerks from enforcing a Wisconsin statute providing that any resident having minor children not in his custody and which he is under an obligation to support by court order or judgment may not marry without court approval. The law had been found to violate the equal protection clause of the fourteenth amendment. In a footnote, the Supreme Court noted that "the District Court was correct in finding * * * *Younger* inapplicable, since there was no pending state-court proceeding* in which appellee could have challenged the statute", citing *Wooley*, 434 U.S., at 380 n. 5. While this statement appears to resolve the issue left unresolved in *Doran*, it should be noted that the injunctive relief was not against the conduct of a state criminal prosecution, the type of situation involved in *Younger*, *Steffel*, *Doran*, and *Wooley*.

More recently, in Morales v. TWA, Inc., 504 U.S. 374 (1992), the Supreme Court upheld, at least in part, the issuance of an injunction against a state attorney general prohibiting enforcement proceedings under state advertising laws which were deemed preempted by federal airline regulations. No enforcement actions were pending against the plaintiff airlines, but they had been served with notices of "intent to sue". The justices found the irreparable injury and inadequate remedy at law requirements met "when enforcement actions are imminent * * * when repetitive penalties attach to continuing or repeated violations and the moving party lacks the realistic option of violating the law once and raising its federal defenses." Id. at 381.

5. It has been suggested that a combination of *Steffel* and *Younger* creates a "kind of 'Catch 22' for plaintiffs." *Developments in the Law: Section 1983 and Federalism*, 90 Harv.L.Rev. 1133, 1278 (1977). What do you think this means?

6. Should the *Younger* doctrine apply to cases in which only monetary damages, rather than equitable relief, are sought in the federal action? Does the logic of *Younger* extend to such cases? The issue was expressly left unresolved in Deakins v. Monaghan, 484 U.S. 193, 202 (1988), because the district court had dismissed the federal suit and the Supreme Court concluded that "even if the *Younger* doctrine requires abstention here, the District Court has no discretion to dismiss rather than to stay claims for monetary relief that cannot be redressed in the state proceeding." Why is a stay more appropriate than a dismissal in such a case? Note that while a stay is employed in *Pullman* abstention [supra p. 446], in the *Younger* line of cases federal claims are traditionally dismissed.

Should *Younger* deference apply where, although no state prosecution has begun, the state grand jury is in the process of conducting an investigation at the time the federal action is filed? The Court in *Deakins* also avoided decision of this issue, on mootness grounds. In Morales v. TWA, Inc., 504 U.S. 374, 381 n. 1 (1992), the Court described the *Younger* doctrine as imposing "heightened requirements for an injunction to restrain an already-pending or an about-to-be-pending state criminal action." But during the same term, in Ankenbrandt v. Richards, 504 U.S. 689, 705 (1992), the Court indicated that it had "never applied the notions of comity so critical to *Younger*'s 'Our Federalism' when no state proceeding was pending."

Should the *Younger* doctrine apply to a federal suit which seeks to enjoin a state court's gag order, where federal plaintiffs, although affected by the gag order, are not parties to the state court suit and have not been permitted to intervene? See FOCUS v. Allegheny County Court of Common Pleas, 75 F.3d 834 (3d Cir.1996). Is the affront to the state judiciary any different in these circumstances? What alternatives do the plaintiffs have?

HICKS v. MIRANDA

Supreme Court of the United States, 1975.
422 U.S. 332.

MR. JUSTICE WHITE delivered the opinion of the Court.

* * *

I

On November 23 and 24, 1973, pursuant to four separate warrants issued seriatim, the police seized four copies of the film "Deep Throat," each of which had been shown at the Pussycat Theatre in Buena Park, Orange County, Cal. On November 26 an eight-count criminal misdemeanor charge was filed in the Orange County Municipal Court against two employees of the theater, each film seized being the subject matter of two counts in the complaint. Also on November 26, the Superior Court of Orange County ordered appellees to show cause why "Deep Throat" should not be declared obscene, an immediate hearing being available to appellees, who appeared that day, objected on state-law grounds to the court's jurisdiction to conduct such a proceeding, purported to "reserve" all federal questions, and refused further to participate. Thereupon, on November 27 the Superior Court held a hearing, viewed the film, took evidence, and then declared the movie to be obscene and ordered seized all copies of it that might be found at the theater. This judgment and order were not appealed by appellees.

Instead, on November 29, they filed this suit in the District Court against appellants—four police officers of Buena Park and the District Attorney and Assistant District Attorney of Orange County. The complaint recited the seizures and the proceedings in the Superior Court, stated that the action was for an injunction against the enforcement of the California obscenity statute, and prayed for judgment declaring the obscenity statute unconstitutional, and for an injunction ordering the return of all copies of the film, but permitting one of the films to be duplicated before its return.

A temporary restraining order was requested and denied, the District Judge finding the proof of irreparable injury to be lacking and an insufficient likelihood of prevailing on the merits to warrant an injunction. He requested the convening of a three-judge court, however, to consider the constitutionality of the statute. Such a court was then designated on January 8, 1974.

Service of the complaint was completed on January 14, 1974, and answers and motions to dismiss, as well as a motion for summary judgment, were filed by appellants. Appellees moved for a preliminary injunction. None of the motions was granted and no hearings held, all of the issues being ordered submitted on briefs and affidavits. The Attorney General of California also appeared * * *.

Meanwhile, on January 15, the criminal complaint pending in the Municipal Court had been amended by naming appellees as additional parties defendant and by adding four conspiracy counts, one relating to each of the seized films. Also, on motions of the defendants in that case, two of the films were ordered suppressed on the ground that the two search warrants for seizing "Deep Throat" last issued, one on November 23 and the other on November 24, did not sufficiently allege that the films to be seized under those warrants differed from each other and from the films previously seized, the final two seizures being said to be invalid multiple seizures. Immediately after this order, which was later appealed and reversed, the defense and the prosecution stipulated that for purposes of the trial, which was expected to be forthcoming, the four prints of the film would be considered identical and only one copy would have to be proved at trial.

On June 4, 1974, the three-judge court issued its judgment and opinion declaring the California obscenity statute to be unconstitutional for failure to satisfy the requirements of *Miller I* and ordering appellants to return to appellees all copies of "Deep Throat" which had been seized as well as to refrain from making any additional seizures. Appellants' claim that Younger v. Harris, 401 U.S. 37 (1971), and Samuels v. Mackell, 401 U.S. 66 (1971), required dismissal of the case was rejected, the court holding that no criminal charges were pending in the state court against appellees and that in any event the pattern of search warrants and seizures demonstrated bad faith and harassment on the part of the authorities, all of which relieved the court from the strictures of Younger v. Harris, supra, and its related cases.

Appellants filed various motions for rehearing, to amend the judgment, and for relief from judgment, also later calling the court's attention to two developments they considered important: First, the dismissal on July 25, 1974, "for want of a substantial federal question" of the appeal in Miller v. California, 418 U.S. 915 (*Miller II*), from a judgment of the Superior Court, Appellate Department, Orange County, California, sustaining the constitutionality of the very California obscenity statute which the District Court had declared unconstitutional; second, the reversal by the Superior Court, Appellate Department, of the suppression order which had been issued in the criminal case pending in the Municipal Court, the *per curiam* reversal citing Aday v. Superior Court, 55 Cal.2d 789, 13 Cal.Rptr. 415, 362 P.2d 47 (1961), and saying the "*requisite prompt adversary determination of obscenity under* Heller v. New York . . . has been held."

On September 30, the three-judge court denied appellants' motions, reaffirmed its June 4 Younger v. Harris ruling and, after concluding it was not bound by the dismissal of *Miller II*, adhered to its judgment that the California statute was invalid under the Federal Constitution. * * *

* * *

III

The District Court committed error in reaching the merits of this case despite the appellants' insistence that it be dismissed under Younger v. Harris, 401 U.S. 37 (1971), and Samuels v. Mackell, 401 U.S. 66 (1971). When they filed their federal complaint, no state criminal proceedings were pending against appellees by name; but two employees of the theater had been charged and four copies of "Deep Throat" belonging to appellees had been seized, were being held, and had been declared to be obscene and seizable by the Superior Court. Appellees had a substantial stake in the state proceedings, so much so that they sought federal relief, demanding that the state statute be declared void and their films be returned to them. Obviously, their interests and those of their employees were intertwined; and, as we have pointed out, the federal action sought to interfere with the pending state prosecution. Absent a clear showing that appellees, whose lawyers also represented their employees, could not seek the return of their property in the state proceedings and see to it that their federal claims were presented there, the requirements of Younger v. Harris could not be avoided on the ground that no criminal prosecution was pending against appellees on the date the federal complaint was filed. The rule in Younger v. Harris is designed to "permit state courts to try state cases free from interference by federal courts," 401 U.S., at 43, particularly where the party to the federal case may fully litigate his claim before the state court. Plainly, "[t]he same comity considerations apply," Allee v. Medrano, 416 U.S. 802, 831 (1974) (Burger, C. J., concurring), where the interference is sought by some, such as appellees, not parties to the state case.

What is more, on the day following the completion of service of the complaint, appellees were charged along with their employees in Municipal Court. Neither Steffel v. Thompson, 415 U.S. 452 (1974), nor any other case in this Court has held that for Younger v. Harris to apply, the state criminal proceedings must be pending on the day the federal case is filed. Indeed, the issue has been left open; and we now hold that where state criminal proceedings are begun against the federal plaintiffs after the federal complaint is filed but before any proceedings of substance on the merits have taken place in the federal court, the principles of Younger v. Harris should apply in full force. Here, appellees were charged on January 15, prior to answering the federal case and prior to any proceedings whatsoever before the three-judge court. Unless we are to trivialize the principles of Younger v. Harris, the federal complaint should have been dismissed on the appellants' motion absent satisfactory proof of those extraordinary circumstances calling into play one of the limited exceptions to the rule of Younger v. Harris and related cases.

vague + conclusory

The District Court concluded that extraordinary circumstances had been shown in the form of official harassment and bad faith, but this was also error. The relevant findings of the District Court were vague and conclusory. There were references to the "pattern of seizure" and to "the evidence brought to light by the petition for rehearing"; and the unexplicated conclusion was then drawn that "regardless of the nature of any judicial proceeding," the police were bent on banishing "Deep Throat" from Buena Park. Yet each step in the pattern of seizures condemned by the District Court was authorized by judicial warrant or order; and the District Court did not purport to invalidate any of the four warrants, in any way to question the propriety of the proceedings in the Superior Court, or even to mention the reversal of the suppression order in the Appellate Department of that court. Absent at least some effort by the District Court to impeach the entitlement of the prosecuting officials to rely on repeated judicial authorization for their conduct, we cannot agree that bad faith and harassment were made out. Indeed, such conclusion would not necessarily follow even if it were shown that the state courts were in error on some one or more issues of state or federal law.

* * *

MR. JUSTICE STEWART, with whom MR. JUSTICE DOUGLAS, MR. JUSTICE BRENNAN, and MR. JUSTICE MARSHALL join, dissenting.

* * *

In Steffel v. Thompson, 415 U.S. 452, the Court unanimously held that the principles of equity, comity, and federalism embodied in Younger v. Harris, 401 U.S. 37, and Samuels v. Mackell, 401 U.S. 66, do not preclude a federal district court from entertaining an action to declare unconstitutional a state criminal statute when a state criminal prosecution is threatened but not pending at the time the federal complaint is filed. Today the Court holds that the *Steffel* decision is inoperative if a state criminal charge is filed at any point after the commencement of the federal action "before any proceedings of substance on the merits have taken place in the federal court." Any other rule, says the Court, would "trivialize" the principles of Younger v. Harris. I think this ruling "trivializes" *Steffel,* decided just last Term, and is inconsistent with those same principles of equity, comity, and federalism.[1]

---

1. There is the additional difficulty that the precise meaning of the rule the Court today adopts is a good deal less than apparent. What are "proceedings of substance on the merits"? Presumably, the proceedings must be both "on the merits" and "of substance." Does this mean, then, that months of discovery activity would be insufficient if no question on the merits is presented to the court during that time? What proceedings "on the merits" are sufficient is also unclear. An application for a temporary restraining order or a preliminary injunction requires the court to make an assessment about the likelihood of success on the merits. Indeed, in this case, appellees filed an application for a temporary restraining order along with six supporting affidavits on November 29, 1973. Appellants responded on December 3, 1973, with six affidavits of their own as well as additional documents. On December 28, 1973, Judge Lydick denied the request for a temporary restraining order, in part because appellees "have failed totally to make that showing of . . .

There is, to be sure, something unseemly about having the applicability of the *Younger* doctrine turn solely on the outcome of a race to the courthouse. The rule the Court adopts today, however, does not eliminate that race; it merely permits the State to leave the mark later, run a shorter course, and arrive first at the finish line. This rule seems to me to result from a failure to evaluate the state and federal interests as of the time the state prosecution was commenced.

As of the time when its jurisdiction is invoked in a *Steffel* situation, a federal court is called upon to vindicate federal constitutional rights when no other remedy is available to the federal plaintiff. The Court has recognized that at this point in the proceedings no substantial state interests counsel the federal court to stay its hand. Thus, in Lake Carriers' Assn. v. MacMullan, 406 U.S. 498, we noted that "considerations of equity practice and comity in our federal system ... have little force in the absence of a pending state proceeding." Id., at 509. * * *

* * *

The duty of the federal courts to adjudicate and vindicate federal constitutional rights is, of course, shared with state courts, but there can be no doubt that the federal courts are "the primary and powerful reliances for vindicating every right given by the Constitution, the laws, and treaties of the United States." F. Frankfurter & J. Landis, The Business of the Supreme Court: A Study in the Federal Judicial System 65 (1927). The statute under which this action was brought, 42 U.S.C. § 1983, established in our law "the role of the Federal Government as a guarantor of basic federal rights against state power." Mitchum v. Foster, 407 U.S. 225, 239. Indeed, "[t]he very purpose of § 1983 was to interpose the federal courts between the States and the people." Id., at 242. See also Zwickler v. Koota, 389 U.S. 241, 245, 248; McNeese v. Board of Education, 373 U.S. 668; Monroe v. Pape, 365 U.S. 167. And this central interest of a federal court as guarantor of constitutional rights is fully implicated from the moment its jurisdiction is invoked. How, then, does the subsequent filing of a state criminal charge change the situation from one in which the federal court's dismissal of the action under *Younger* principles "would turn federalism on its head" to one in which *failure* to dismiss would "trivialize" those same principles?

A State has a vital interest in the enforcement of its criminal law, and this Court has said time and again that it will sanction little federal interference with that important state function. E.g., Kugler v. Helfant, 421 U.S. 117. But there is nothing in our decision in *Steffel* that requires a State to stay its hand during the pendency of the federal litigation. If, in the interest of efficiency, the State wishes to refrain from actively prosecuting the criminal charge pending the outcome of the federal

likelihood of prevailing on the merits needed to justify the issuance of a temporary restraining order." These proceedings, the Court says implicitly, were not sufficient to satisfy the test it announces. Why that should be, even in terms of the Court's holding, is a mystery.

declaratory judgment suit, it may, of course, do so. But no decision of this Court requires it to make that choice.

The Court today, however, goes much further than simply recognizing the right of the State to proceed with the orderly administration of its criminal law; it ousts the federal courts from their historic role as the "primary reliances" for vindicating constitutional freedoms. This is no less offensive to "Our Federalism" than the federal injunction restraining pending state criminal proceedings condemned in Younger v. Harris. The concept of federalism requires "sensitivity to the legitimate interests of *both* State and National governments." 401 U.S., at 44 (emphasis added). Younger v. Harris and its companion cases reflect the principles that the federal judiciary must refrain from interfering with the legitimate functioning of state courts. But surely the converse is a principle no less valid.

The Court's new rule creates a reality which few state prosecutors can be expected to ignore. It is an open invitation to state officials to institute state proceedings in order to defeat federal jurisdiction. One need not impugn the motives of state officials to suppose that they would rather prosecute a criminal suit in state court than defend a civil case in a federal forum. Today's opinion virtually instructs state officials to answer federal complaints with state indictments. Today, the State must file a criminal charge to secure dismissal of the federal litigation; perhaps tomorrow an action "akin to a criminal proceeding" will serve the purpose, see Huffman v. Pursue, Ltd., supra; and the day may not be far off when any state civil action will do.

The doctrine of Younger v. Harris reflects an accommodation of competing interests. The rule announced today distorts that balance beyond recognition.

[The concurring opinion of CHIEF JUSTICE BURGER is omitted.]

Notes

1. What is the Court's rationale in *Hicks*? Does the decision necessarily follow from *Younger*?

2. What does Justice Stewart mean when he suggests that the decision in *Hicks* "trivializes" *Steffel*? Is there any way for a would-be federal court plaintiff to circumvent this difficulty? In answering, recall *Doran* [supra p. 553]. Does that decision provide any aid to the federal court plaintiff?

3. What do you think the Court means by "proceedings of substance on the merits"? How persuasive are Justice Stewart's criticisms of the use of the phrase? Note that in *Hicks* itself, the Court found the *denial* of a temporary restraining order does not constitute proceedings of substance on the merits. Should the *issuance*, by the federal court, of a temporary restraining order be deemed to be such proceedings? Cf. Graham v. Breier, 418 F.Supp. 73, 77 (E.D.Wis.1976). See Hawaii Housing Authority v. Midkiff, 467 U.S. 229 (1984) ("Whether issuance of [a] * * * temporary restraining order was a substantial federal court action or not, issuance of the * * *

preliminary injunction certainly was * * *. A federal court action in which a preliminary injunction is granted has proceeded well beyond the 'embryonic state', and considerations of economy, equity, and federalism counsel against *Younger*-abstention at that point." Id. at 237.)

4. **Post-Trial Intervention.** *Younger* held that a federal court could not enjoin an ongoing state criminal proceeding. What if federal intervention is sought after the state proceeding is completed and the defendant has been convicted? In Huffman v. Pursue, Ltd., 420 U.S. 592 (1975), a state trial court had ordered an adult theater closed as a nuisance and all its property used in its operation seized. Instead of appealing the state court decision within the state court system, the theater owner brought a section 1983 action in federal court seeking to enjoin enforcement of the state court judgment. The Supreme Court rejected the attempt to obtain federal relief, reasoning that "a necessary concomitant of *Younger* is that a party * * * must exhaust his state appellate remedies before seeking relief in the District Court." Id. at 608. In elaborating, the Court stated:

> Virtually all of the evils at which *Younger* is directed would inhere in federal intervention prior to completion of state appellate proceedings, just as surely as they would if such intervention occurred at or before trial. Intervention at the later stage is if anything more highly duplicative, since an entire trial has already taken place, and it is also a direct aspersion on the capabilities and good faith of state appellate courts * * *.

> Federal post-trial intervention, in a fashion designed to annul the results of a state trial, also deprives the States of a function which quite legitimately is left to them, that of overseeing trial court dispositions of constitutional issues which arise in civil litigation over which they have jurisdiction. We think this consideration to be of some importance because it is typically a judicial system's appellate courts which are by their nature a litigant's most appropriate forum for the resolution of constitutional contentions. Especially is this true when, as here, the constitutional issue involves a statute which is capable of judicial narrowing. In short, we do not believe that a State's judicial system would be fairly accorded the opportunity to resolve federal issues arising in its courts if a federal district court were permitted to substitute itself for the State's appellate courts. Id. at 608–09.

Huffman was not a pure criminal proceeding, but the Court's reasoning in rejecting post-trial federal intervention would seem to apply with at least as much force in such cases. Is the Court's reasoning persuasive? To what extent is the Court's reasoning equally applicable to the affording of federal habeas corpus review of a state criminal conviction, after a state defendant has exhausted the available state review processes?

In City of Columbus v. Leonard, 443 U.S. 905 (1979), Justice Rehnquist, joined by Chief Justice Burger and Justice Blackmun, dissented from a denial of certiorari in a case which Justice Rehnquist deemed controlled by the above-quoted portions of *Huffman*. Respondents had been dismissed from the Columbus police department for deliberately removing the American Flag emblem from their uniforms during a public demonstration. After their dismissal, the respondents requested hearings before the police hearing board, a state-created body charged with reviewing challenged dismissals of officers. After their requests were granted, respondents filed a section 1983 action in federal court, alleging violations of the fourteenth amendment and of a Columbus ordinance. Their dismissals were subsequently upheld by the police board. Instead of seeking review of these decisions within the state court system, they then pursued their federal court action. Though the district court denied their requested relief on *Younger* grounds, the Court of Appeals for the Fifth Circuit reversed, holding that the district court should have reached the merits. 551 F.2d 974 (5th Cir.1977) (en banc).

Justice Rehnquist argued that while unlike *Huffman*, these proceedings had been initiated by the individuals, not the state, "this only strengthens the rationale for requiring respondents to exhaust their state appellate remedies. Respondents invoked the resources of the State to vindicate what they believed to have been illegal dismissals. Having lost the first round of this contest, they should not be allowed to abandon it and transfer the contest to another arena." 443 U.S., at 909. He distinguished Monroe v. Pape, 365 U.S. 167 (1961), which held that an individual need not exhaust state judicial remedies prior to obtaining federal judicial vindication of his section 1983 rights, because "[i]n *Monroe*, we merely held that a federal plaintiff need not *initiate* state proceedings before filing a § 1983 action." 443 U.S. at 910.

Do you agree that federal judicial restraint in *Leonard* is dictated by the reasoning and holding in *Huffman*? Are the two distinguishable? Exactly what state interests are undermined by allowing federal judicial intervention in *Leonard*? Would Justice Rehnquist's reasoning have led to the same conclusion if, after requesting the administrative hearings, the respondents had abandoned that course of action prior to the actual hearings? If the police board was required by state law automatically to review every dismissal? Is Justice Rehnquist correct in thinking that *Monroe* is distinguishable? Justice Rehnquist added that in any event, "the time may now be ripe for a reconsideration of the Court's conclusion in *Monroe* that the 'federal remedy is supplementary to the state remedy, and the latter need not be first sought and refused before the federal one is invoked.' * * * [T]he Court believed that this conclusion followed from the purpose of the Civil Rights Act 'to provide a federal remedy where the state remedy, though adequate in theory, *was not available in practice.*' * * * But this purpose need not bar exhaustion where the State can demonstrate that there is an available and adequate state remedy." Id. at 911. Do you agree with Justice Rehnquist's call for abandonment of *Monroe*'s no-judicial-exhaustion rule? How viable is an approach that requires the federal court, in each case, to determine whether there is an "available and adequate state remedy"? Might such an approach be thought to *increase* friction within the federal system? If such a standard were adopted, which party should have the burden of proof on this issue? What factors would be relevant in making the determination?

5. **Younger and State Administrative Remedies.** To what extent should the the *Younger* doctrine apply to noncriminal state administrative proceedings? Note that the Court applies *Younger* to some noncriminal judicial proceedings [see infra p. 566]. Consider the decision in Middlesex County Ethics Committee v. Garden State Bar Association, 457 U.S. 423 (1982). The case dealt with whether *Younger* bars federal injunctive relief

against a state attorney disciplinary proceeding, challenged on the grounds that the proceeding violated the attorney's first amendment rights. The Court, in an opinion by Chief Justice Burger, held that the federal relief was in fact barred by *Younger*:

> The policies underlying *Younger* are fully applicable to noncriminal judicial proceedings when important state interests are involved. The importance of the state interest may be demonstrated by the fact that the noncriminal proceedings bear a close relationship to proceedings criminal in nature, as in *Huffman*. Proceedings necessary for the vindication of important state policies or for the functioning of the state judicial system also evidence the state's substantial interest in the litigation [citing *Trainor*] * * *.
>
> * * *
>
> The State * * * has an extremely important interest in maintaining and assuring the professional conduct of the attorneys it licenses. States traditionally have exercised extensive control over the professional conduct of attorneys. Id. at 432–34.

Do you agree with the decision in *Middlesex*? Does it necessarily follow from *Younger*? Does the Chief Justice effectively impose a requirement of exhaustion of state administrative remedies prior to federal adjudication of section 1983 claims?

Compare to *Middlesex* the Court's decision in Patsy v. Board of Regents, 457 U.S. 496 (1982). There the Court, in an opinion by Justice Marshall, held that exhaustion of state administrative remedies is not a prerequisite to a civil rights action brought pursuant to section 1983. The Court reasoned that "in passing [section 1983], Congress assigned to the federal courts a paramount role in protecting constitutional rights," id. at 503, and that "the 1871 Congress would not have wanted to impose an exhaustion requirement." Id. at 505. The Court described Congress's motivation: "A major factor motivating the expansion of federal jurisdiction * * * was the belief of the 1871 Congress that the state authorities had been unable or unwilling to protect the constitutional rights of individuals or to punish those who violated these rights. * * * Of primary importance to the exhaustion question was the mistrust that the 1871 Congress held for the factfinding processes of state institutions." Id. at 505–06.

Is it possible to reconcile *Patsy* with *Middlesex*? Is it possible to reconcile *Patsy* with the entire line of *Younger* cases? Note that the Court in *Patsy* focused its inquiry heavily on legislative intent. Did the Court do the same in *Younger*? Should it have? If it had, might the same reasoning that led it to reject exhaustion of state administrative remedies as inconsistent with congressional intent have led it to reject *Younger* abstention, as well? For a more recent application of *Younger* to state administrative proceedings, see Ohio Civil Rights Commission v. Dayton Christian Schools, Inc., 477 U.S. 619 (1986). Judge Harry Edwards, of the United States Court of Appeals for the District of Columbia Circuit, notes that this line of cases arguably "suggests that the resolution of federal challenges to state action should be left to state courts, even in the absence of an ongoing state judicial proceeding, if the suit concerns important state activities." Edwards, *The Changing Notion of "Our Federalism"*, 33 Wayne L.Rev. 1015, 1029 (1987).

6. *Younger* abstention was ruled inappropriate in New Orleans Public Service, Inc. v. Council of New Orleans, 491 U.S. 350 (1989). There, an electric utility challenged the results of a City Council rate-making proceeding in federal court on preemption grounds. The utility also sought review of the City Council decision in state court. Writing for the Court, Justice Scalia reversed the federal court's decision to abstain:

> Although our concern for comity and federalism has led us to expand the protection of *Younger* beyond state criminal prosecutions, to civil enforcement proceedings, and even to civil proceedings involving certain orders that are uniquely in furtherance of the state courts' ability to perform their judicial functions, it has never been suggested that *Younger* requires abstention in deference to a state judicial proceeding reviewing legislative or executive action. Such a broad abstention requirement would make a mockery of the rule that only exceptional circumstances justify a federal court's refusal to decide a case in deference to the States. Id. at 367–68.

In response to the claim that the federal trial court should have abstained to the continuation of the Council proceeding, the Court replied that "[the] case for abstention still requires, however, that the *Council proceeding* be the sort of proceeding entitled to *Younger* treatment. We think that it is not. * * * [W]e have never extended [*Younger*] to proceedings that are not 'judicial in nature' ". Id. at 369–70.

7. Consider the relevance of *Middlesex* to the following suit: Foster children in physical custody of the state of Florida bring a civil rights action in federal court challenging the constitutionality of various aspects of Florida's foster care system. The state had filed dependency petitions in state court against each foster child named as plaintiff in the federal civil rights action. See 31 Foster Children v. Bush, 329 F.3d 1255 (11th Cir.2003) (finding abstention required under *Middlesex*). For criticism of this holding, see Meltzer, Note, *Dismissing the Foster Children: The Eleventh Circuit's Misapplication and Improper Expansion of the* Younger *Abstention Doctrine in* Bonnie L. v. Bush, 70 Brook.L.Rev. 635 (2004–05).

YOUNGER AND CIVIL CASES

The Supreme Court has extended *Younger* abstention to some civil cases, although has not always been clear *which* types of civil cases qualify. In Huffman v. Pursue, Ltd., 420 U.S. 592 (1975), state officials instituted a proceeding under a state statute which deemed the exhibition of obscene films to be a nuisance and provided for the seizure and sale of the offending materials. The defendant sought federal equitable relief on first amendment grounds. In holding the *Younger* doctrine applicable to this technically civil proceeding, the Supreme Court noted that "we deal here with a state proceeding which in most important respects is more akin to a criminal prosecution than are most civil cases." Id. at 604. Not only was the state a party, but the nuisance action was characterized as "in aid of and closely related to criminal statutes." Id. *Younger*'s "more vital consideration" of comity counselled restraint even in the absence of a criminal case.

Huffman's rationale was extended to state civil enforcement actions in Juidice v. Vail, 430 U.S. 327 (1977). There a judgment debtor had been held in contempt by a state court. He sought to have the statutory provisions authorizing enforcement through contempt declared unconstitutional in federal court. In reversing the injunction, the Supreme Court held that the *Younger* principles "apply to a case in which the State's contempt process is involved. The contempt power lies at the core of the administration of a State's judicial system." Id. at 335.

Trainor v. Hernandez, 431 U.S. 434 (1977), applied the *Younger* doctrine to a state civil suit filed to obtain the return of welfare funds allegedly wrongfully received. In the state civil action, the state attached funds of the defendants. In response, the defendants filed a federal suit challenging the constitutionality of the state attachment procedure. The Supreme Court held that the *Younger* doctrine applied. "[T]he State was a party to the suit in its role of administering public-assistance programs. Both the suit and the accompanying writ of attachment were brought to vindicate important state policies such as the fiscal integrity of those programs." Id. at 444. The majority indicated, however, that "we have no occasion to decide whether *Younger* principles apply to all civil litigation." Id. at 444.

After considering these three cases, can you identify any tests for determining whether *Younger* should apply to a civil case? Will it ever apply to a civil case between private parties, in which the state is not involved? Consider the next case.

PENNZOIL COMPANY v. TEXACO, INC.

Supreme Court of the United States, 1987.
481 U.S. 1.

Justice Powell delivered the opinion of the Court.

The principal issue in this case is whether a federal district court lawfully may enjoin a plaintiff who has prevailed in a trial in state court from executing the judgment in its favor pending appeal of that judgment to a state appellate court.

I

Getty Oil Co. and appellant Pennzoil Co. negotiated an agreement under which Pennzoil was to purchase about three-sevenths of Getty's outstanding shares for $110 a share. Appellee Texaco, Inc. eventually purchased the shares for $128 a share. On February 8, 1984, Pennzoil filed a complaint against Texaco in the Harris County District Court, a state court located in Houston, Texas, the site of Pennzoil's corporate headquarters. The complaint alleged that Texaco tortiously had induced Getty to breach a contract to sell its shares to Pennzoil; Pennzoil sought actual damages of $7.53 billion and punitive damages in the same amount. On November 19, 1985, a jury returned a verdict in favor of Pennzoil, finding actual damages of $7.53 billion and punitive damages of $3 billion. The parties anticipated that the judgment, including prejudgment interest, would exceed $11 billion.

Although the parties disagree about the details, it was clear that the expected judgment would give Pennzoil significant rights under Texas law. By recording an abstract of a judgment in the real property records of any of the 254 counties in Texas, a judgment creditor can secure a lien on all of a judgment debtor's real property located in that county. See Tex.Prop.Code Ann. §§ 52.001–.006 (1984). If a judgment creditor wishes to have the judgment enforced by state officials so that it can take possession of any of the debtor's assets, it may secure a writ of execution from the clerk of the court that issued the judgment. See Tex.Rule Civ.Proc. 627.[1] Rule 627 provides that such a writ usually can be obtained "after the expiration of thirty days from the time a final judgment is signed."[2] But the judgment debtor "may suspend the execution of the judgment by filing a good and sufficient bond to be approved by the clerk." Rule 364(a). See Rule 368.[3] For a money judgment, "the amount of the bond ... shall be at least the amount of the judgment, interest, and costs." Rule 364(b).[4]

* * * The amount of the bond required by Rule 364(b) would have been more than $13 billion. It is clear that Texaco would not have been able to post such a bond. Accordingly, "the business and financial community concluded that Pennzoil would be able, under the lien and bond provisions of Texas law, to commence enforcement of any judgment entered on the verdict before Texaco's appeals had been resolved." (District Court's Supplemental Finding of Fact 40, Jan. 10, 1986). The effects on Texaco were substantial: the price of its stock dropped markedly; it had difficulty obtaining credit; the rating of its bonds was lowered; and its trade creditors refused to sell it crude oil on customary terms.

---

1. A writ of execution is "[a]ddressed to any sheriff or constable in the State of Texas [and] enables the official to levy on a debtor's nonexempt real and personal property, within the official's county." 5 W. Dorsaneo, Texas Litigation Guide § 132.02[1], p. 132–7 (1986).

2. If the judgment debtor files a motion for new trial, the clerk cannot issue a writ of execution until the motion for new trial is denied or overruled by operation of law. Rule 627. If a trial judge does not act on a motion for new trial, it is deemed to be overruled by operation of law 75 days after the judgment originally was signed. Rule 329b(c).

3. Filing a supersedeas bond would not prevent Pennzoil from securing judgment liens against Texaco's real property. See

Tex.Prop.Code Ann. § 52.002 (1984) (directing clerk to issue an abstract of the judgment "[o]n application of a person in whose favor a judgment is rendered"; no exception for superseded judgments); Thulemeyer v. Jones, 37 Tex. 560, 571 (1872). The bond's only effect would be to prevent Pennzoil from executing the judgment and obtaining Texaco's property.

4. A judgment debtor also may suspend execution by filing "cash or other negotiable obligation of the government of the United States of America or any agency thereof, or with leave of court, ... a negotiable obligation of any bank ... in the amount fixed for the surety bond." Rule 14c.

Texaco did not argue to the trial court that the judgment, or execution of the judgment, conflicted with federal law. Rather, on December 10, 1985—before the Texas court entered judgment[5]—Texaco filed this action in the United States District Court for the Southern District of New York * * *. Texaco alleged that the Texas proceedings violated rights secured to Texaco by the Constitution and various federal statutes.[6] It asked the District Court to enjoin Pennzoil from taking any action to enforce the judgment. Pennzoil's response, and basic position, was that the District Court could not hear the case. First, it argued that the Anti–Injunction Act, 28 U.S.C. § 2283, barred issuance of an injunction. It further contended that the court should abstain under the doctrine of Younger v. Harris, 401 U.S. 37 (1971). * * *

The District Court rejected all of these arguments. * * * It found *Younger* abstention unwarranted because it did not believe issuance of an injunction would "interfere with a state official's pursuit of a fundamental state interest." * * *

The District Court justified its decision to grant injunctive relief by evaluating the prospects of Texaco's succeeding in its appeal in the Texas state courts. It considered the merits of the various challenges Texaco had made before the Texas Court of Appeals and concluded that these challenges "present generally fair grounds for litigation." * * * It concluded that application of the lien and bond provisions effectively would deny Texaco a right to appeal. It thought that the private interests and the State's interests favored protecting Texaco's right to appeal. Relying on its view of the merits of the state court appeal, the court found the risk of erroneous deprivation "quite severe." Finally, it viewed the administrative burden on the State as "slight." In light of these factors, the District Court concluded that Texaco's constitutional claims had "a very clear probability of success." Accordingly, the court issued a preliminary injunction.

On appeal, the Court of Appeals for the Second Circuit affirmed. * * *

* * *

[T]he court held that abstention was unnecessary. First, it addressed *Pullman* abstention, see Railroad Comm'n v. Pullman Co., 312 U.S. 496 (1941). It rejected that ground of abstention, holding that "the mere

---

5. * * *

So far as we know, Texaco has never presented to the Texas courts the challenges it makes in this case against the bond and lien provisions under federal law. Three days after it filed its federal lawsuit, Texaco did ask the Texas trial court informally for a hearing concerning possible modification of the judgment under Texas law. That request eventually was denied, because it failed to comply with Texas procedural rules.

6. Texaco claimed that the judgment itself conflicted with the Full Faith and Credit Clause, the Commerce Clause, the Williams Act, and the Securities Exchange Act of 1934. Texaco also argued that application of the Texas bond and lien provisions would violate the Due Process and Equal Protection Clauses of the Fourteenth Amendment to the Federal Constitution.

possibility that the Texas courts would find Rule 364 [concerning the supersedeas bond requirements] unconstitutional as applied does not call for *Pullman* abstention." Next, it rejected *Younger* abstention. It thought that "[t]he state interests at stake in this proceeding differ in both kind and degree from those present in the six cases in which the Supreme Court held that *Younger* applied." Moreover, it thought that Texas had failed to "provide adequate procedures for adjudication of Texaco's federal claims." Turning to the merits, it agreed with the District Court that Texaco had established a likelihood of success on its constitutional claims and that the balance of hardships favored Texaco. Accordingly, it affirmed the grant of injunctive relief.[8]

* * * We reverse.

II

The courts below should have abstained under the principles of federalism enunciated in Younger v. Harris, 401 U.S. 37 (1971). Both the District Court and the Court of Appeals failed to recognize the significant interests harmed by their unprecedented intrusion into the Texas judicial system. Similarly, neither of those courts applied the appropriate standard in determining whether adequate relief was available in the Texas courts.

A

The first ground for the *Younger* decision was "the basic doctrine of equity jurisprudence that courts of equity should not act, and particularly should not act to restrain a criminal prosecution, when the moving party has an adequate remedy at law." The Court also offered a second explanation for its decision:

> "This underlying reason ... is reinforced by an even more vital consideration, the notion of 'comity,' that is, a proper respect for state functions, a recognition of the fact that the entire country is made up of a Union of separate state governments, and a continuance of the belief that the National Government will fare best if the States and their institutions are left free to perform their separate functions in their separate ways.... The concept does not mean blind deference to 'States' Rights' any more than it means centralization of control over every important issue in our National Government and its courts. The Framers rejected both these courses. What the concept does represent is a system in which there is sensitivity to the legitimate interests of both State and National Governments, and in which the National Government, anxious though it may be to vindicate and protect federal rights and federal interests, always endeavors to do so in ways that will not unduly interfere with the legitimate activities of the States."

---

8. Although the District Court had entered only a preliminary injunction, the Court of Appeals concluded that the record was sufficiently undisputed to justify entering a permanent injunction. Thus, it did not remand the case to the District Court for further proceedings on the merits.

This concern mandates application of *Younger* abstention not only when the pending state proceedings are criminal, but also when certain civil proceedings are pending, if the State's interests in the proceeding are so important that exercise of the federal judicial power would disregard the comity between the States and the National Government. E.g., Huffman v. Pursue, Ltd., 420 U.S. 592, 603–605 (1975).

Another important reason for abstention is to avoid unwarranted determination of federal constitutional questions. When federal courts interpret state statutes in a way that raises federal constitutional questions, "a constitutional determination is predicated on a reading of the statute that is not binding on state courts and may be discredited at any time—thus essentially rendering the federal-court decision advisory and the litigation underlying it meaningless." Moore v. Sims, 442 U.S. 415, 428 (1979). See Trainor v. Hernandez, 431 U.S. 434, 445 (1977).[9] This concern has special significance in this case. Because Texaco chose not to present to the Texas courts the constitutional claims asserted in this case, it is impossible to be certain that the governing Texas statutes and procedural rules actually raise these claims. Moreover, the Texas Constitution contains an "open courts" provision, Art. I, § 13,[10] that appears to address Texaco's claims more specifically than the Due Process Clause of the Fourteenth Amendment. Thus, when this case was filed in Federal Court, it was entirely possible that the Texas courts would have resolved this case on state statutory or constitutional grounds, without reaching the federal constitutional questions Texaco raises in this case. As we have noted, *Younger* abstention in situations like this "offers the opportunity for narrowing constructions that might obviate the constitutional problem and intelligently mediate federal constitutional concerns and state interests." *Moore v. Sims,* supra, at 429–430.

Texaco's principal argument against *Younger* abstention is that exercise of the District Court's power did not implicate a "vital" or "important" state interest. This argument reflects a misreading of our precedents. This Court repeatedly has recognized that the States have important interests in administering certain aspects of their judicial systems. In Juidice v. Vail, 430 U.S. 327 (1977), we held that a federal court should have abstained from adjudicating a challenge to a State's

9. In some cases, the probability that any federal adjudication would be effectively advisory is so great that this concern alone is sufficient to justify abstention, even if there are no pending state proceedings in which the question could be raised. See Railroad Comm'n of Texas v. Pullman Co., 312 U.S. 496 (1941). Because appellant has not argued in this Court that *Pullman* abstention is proper, we decline to address Justice Blackmun's conclusion that *Pullman* abstention is the appropriate disposition of this case. We merely note that considerations similar to those that mandate *Pullman* abstention are relevant to a

court's decision whether to abstain under *Younger.* Cf. Moore v. Sims, 442 U.S. 415, 428 (1979). The various types of abstention are not rigid pigeonholes into which federal courts must try to fit cases. Rather, they reflect a complex of considerations designed to soften the tensions inherent in a system that contemplates parallel judicial processes.

10. Article I, § 13 provides: "All courts shall be open, and every person for an injury done him, in his lands, goods, person or reputation, shall have remedy by due course of law."

contempt process. The Court's reasoning in that case informs our decision today:

> "A State's interest in the contempt process, through which it vindicates the regular operation of its judicial system, so long as that system itself affords the opportunity to pursue federal claims within it, is surely an important interest. Perhaps it is not quite as important as is the State's interest in the enforcement of its criminal laws, *Younger,* supra, or even its interest in the maintenance of a quasi-criminal proceeding such as was involved in *Huffman,* supra. But we think it is of sufficiently great import to require application of the principles of those cases."

Our comments on why the contempt power was sufficiently important to justify abstention also are illuminating: "Contempt in these cases, serves, of course, to vindicate and preserve the private interests of competing litigants, ... but its purpose is by no means spent upon purely private concerns. It stands in aid of the authority of the judicial system, so that its orders and judgments are not rendered nugatory."

The reasoning of *Juidice* controls here. That case rests on the importance to the States of enforcing the orders and judgments of their courts. There is little difference between the State's interest in forcing persons to transfer property in response to a court's judgment and in forcing persons to respond to the court's process on pain of contempt. Both *Juidice* and this case involve challenges to the processes by which the State compels compliance with the judgments of its courts.[12] Not only would federal injunctions in such cases interfere with the execution of state judgments, but they would do so on grounds that challenge the very process by which those judgments were obtained. So long as those challenges relate to pending state proceedings, proper respect for the ability of state courts to resolve federal questions presented in state court litigation mandates that the federal court stay its hand.[13]

B

Texaco also argues that *Younger* abstention was inappropriate because no Texas court could have heard Texaco's constitutional claims within the limited time available to Texaco. But the burden on this point

---

12. Thus, contrary to Justice Stevens' suggestion, the State of Texas has an interest in this proceeding "that goes beyond its interest as adjudicator of wholly private disputes." Our opinion does not hold that *Younger* abstention is always appropriate whenever a civil proceeding is pending in a state court. Rather, as in *Juidice,* we rely on the State's interest in protecting "the authority of the judicial system, so that its orders and judgments are not rendered nugatory."

13. Texaco also suggests that abstention is unwarranted because of the absence of a state judicial proceeding with respect to which the Federal District Court should have abstained. Texaco argues that "the Texas judiciary plays no role" in execution of judgments. We reject this assertion. There is at least one pending judicial proceeding in the state courts; the lawsuit out of which Texaco's constitutional claims arose is now pending before a Texas Court of Appeals in Houston, Texas. As we explain infra, we are not convinced that Texaco could not have secured judicial relief in those proceedings.

rests on the federal plaintiff to show "that state procedural law barred presentation of [its] claims." Moore v. Sims, 442 U.S., at 432. * * *

Moreover, denigrations of the procedural protections afforded by Texas law hardly come from Texaco with good grace, as it apparently made no effort under Texas law to secure the relief sought in this case. Article VI of the United States Constitution declares that "the Judges in every State shall be bound" by the Federal Constitution, laws, and treaties. We cannot assume that state judges will interpret ambiguities in state procedural law to bar presentation of federal claims. Accordingly, when a litigant has not attempted to present his federal claims in related state court proceedings, a federal court should assume that state procedures will afford an adequate remedy, in the absence of unambiguous authority to the contrary.

The "open courts" provision of the Texas Constitution, Article I, § 13, has considerable relevance here. * * * "The common thread of [the Texas Supreme Court's] decisions construing the open courts provision is that the legislature has no power to make a remedy by due course of law contingent on an impossible condition." Nelson v. Krusen, 678 S.W.2d 918, 921 (Tex.1984). In light of this demonstrable and longstanding commitment of the Texas Supreme Court to provide access to the state courts, we are reluctant to conclude that Texas courts would have construed state procedural rules to deny Texaco an effective opportunity to raise its constitutional claims.

Against this background, Texaco's submission that the Texas courts were incapable of hearing its constitutional claims is plainly insufficient. Both of the courts below found that the Texas trial court had the power to consider constitutional challenges to the enforcement provisions. * * * Texaco has cited no statute or case clearly indicating that Texas courts lack such power.[15] Accordingly, Texaco has failed to meet its burden on this point.[16]

---

15. Texaco relies on the language of Texas Rule of Civil Procedure 364, that lists no exceptions to the requirement that an appellant file a bond to suspend execution of a money judgment pending appeal. Texaco also relies on cases noting that Rule 364 requires appellants to post bond in the full amount of the judgment. E.g., Kennesaw Life and Accident Insurance Co. v. Streetman, 644 S.W.2d 915, 916–917 (Tex.App.—Austin 1983, writ refused n.r.e.). But these cases do not involve claims that the requirements of Rule 364 violate other statutes or the Federal Constitution. Thus, they have "absolutely nothing to say with respect to" Texaco's claims that Rule 364 violates the Federal Constitution. See Huffman v. Pursue, Ltd., 420 U.S. 592, 610 (1975).

Also, the language of Rule 364 suggests that a trial court could suspend the bond requirement if it concluded that application of the bond requirement would violate the Federal Constitution. Rule 364(a) provides:

"*Unless otherwise provided by law* or these rules, an appellant may suspend the execution of the judgment by a good and sufficient bond." (emphasis added) Texaco has failed to demonstrate that Texas courts would not construe the phrase "otherwise provided by law" to encompass claims made under the Federal Constitution. We cannot assume that Texas courts would refuse to construe the Rule, or to apply their inherent powers, to provide a forum to adjudicate substantial federal constitutional claims.

16. We recognize that the trial court no longer has jurisdiction over the case. Thus, relief is no longer available to Texaco from the trial court. But Texaco cannot escape *Younger* abstention by failing to assert its state remedies in a timely manner. In any event, the Texas Supreme Court and the Texas Court of Appeals arguably have the authority to suspend the supersedeas requirement to protect their appellate jurisdiction.

In sum, the lower courts should have deferred on principles of comity to the pending state proceedings. They erred in accepting Texaco's assertions as to the inadequacies of Texas procedure to provide effective relief. It is true that this case presents an unusual fact situation, never before addressed by the Texas courts, and that Texaco urgently desired prompt relief. But we cannot say that those courts, when this suit was filed, would have been any less inclined than a federal court to address and decide the federal constitutional claims. Because Texaco apparently did not give the Texas courts an opportunity to adjudicate its constitutional claims, and because Texaco cannot demonstrate that the Texas courts were not then open to adjudicate its claims, there is no basis for concluding that the Texas law and procedures were so deficient that *Younger* abstention is inappropriate. Accordingly, we conclude that the District Court should have abstained.

III

In this opinion, we have addressed the situation that existed on the morning of December 10, 1985, when this case was filed in the United States District Court for the Southern District of New York. We recognize that much has transpired in the Texas courts since then. Later that day, the Texas trial court entered judgment. On February 12 of this year, the Texas Court of Appeals substantially affirmed the judgment. We are not unmindful of the unique importance to Texaco of having its challenges to that judgment authoritatively considered and resolved. We of course express no opinion on the merits of those challenges. Similarly, we express no opinion on the claims Texaco has raised in this case against the Texas bond and lien provisions, nor on the possibility that Texaco now could raise these claims in the Texas courts, see n. 16, supra. Today we decide only that it was inappropriate for the District Court to entertain these claims. If, and when, the Texas courts render a final decision on any federal issue presented by this litigation, review may be sought in this Court in the customary manner.

* * *

JUSTICE BRENNAN, with whom JUSTICE MARSHALL joins, concurring in the judgment.

Texaco's claim that the Texas bond and lien provisions violate the Fourteenth Amendment is without merit. While Texaco cannot, consistent with due process and equal protection, be arbitrarily denied the right to a meaningful opportunity to be heard on appeal, this right can be adequately vindicated even if Texaco were forced to file for bankruptcy.

I believe that the Court should have confronted the merits of this case. I wholeheartedly concur with Justice Stevens' conclusion that a creditor's invocation of a State's postjudgment collection procedures constitutes action under color of state law within the meaning of 42 U.S.C. § 1983.

I also agree with his conclusion that the District Court was not required to abstain under the principles enunciated in *Younger v. Harris*. I adhere to my view that *Younger* is, in general, inapplicable to civil proceedings, especially when a plaintiff brings a § 1983 action alleging violation of federal constitutional rights. See Huffman v. Pursue, Ltd., 420 U.S. 592, 613 (1975) (BRENNAN, J., dissenting) (*Younger* held "that federal courts should not interfere with pending state *criminal* proceedings, except under extraordinary circumstances") (emphasis in original); Juidice v. Vail, 430 U.S. 327, 342 (1977) (BRENNAN, J., dissenting) ("In congressional contemplation, the pendency of state civil proceedings was to be wholly irrelevant. 'The very purpose of § 1983 was to interpose the federal courts between the States and the people, as guardians of the people's federal rights' ") (quoting Mitchum v. Foster, 407 U.S. 225, 242 (1972)).

The State's interest in this case is negligible. The State of Texas— not a party in this appeal—expressly represented to the Court of Appeals that it "has no interest in the underlying action," except in its fair adjudication. The Court identifies the State's interest as enforcing "the authority of the judicial system, so that its orders and judgments are not rendered nugatory." Yet, the District Court found that "Pennzoil publicly admitted that Texaco's assets are sufficient to satisfy the Judgment even without liens or a bond." "Thus Pennzoil's interest in protecting the full amount of its judgment during the appellate process is reasonably secured by the substantial excess of Texaco's net worth over the amount of Pennzoil's judgment."

Indeed, the interest in enforcing the bond and lien requirement is privately held by Pennzoil, not by the State of Texas. The Court of Appeals correctly stated that this "is a suit between two private parties stemming from the defendant's alleged tortious interference with the plaintiff's contract with a third private party." Pennzoil was free to waive the bond and lien requirements under Texas law, without asking the State of Texas for permission. * * * The State's decision to grant private parties unilateral power to invoke, or not invoke, the State's bond and lien provisions demonstrates that the State has no independent interest in the enforcement of those provisions.

Texaco filed this § 1983 suit claiming only violations of *federal* statutory and constitutional law. * * * Today the Court holds that this § 1983 suit should be filed instead in Texas courts, offering to Texaco the unsolicited advice to bring its claims under the "open courts" provision of the Texas Constitution. This "blind deference to 'States' Rights' " hardly shows "sensitivity to the legitimate interests of *both* State *and National* Governments."[1]

* * *

1. Although the Court's opinion is based on a rather diffuse rationale, I read the opinion as narrowly limited by the unique factual circumstances of the case. The

While I agree with Justice Stevens that Texaco's claim is "plainly without merit," my reasons for so concluding are different. * * * While "a cost requirement, valid on its face, may offend due process because it operates to foreclose a particular party's opportunity to be heard," Boddie v. Connecticut, 401 U.S. 371, 380 (1971), in this case, Texaco clearly could exercise its right to appeal in order to protect its corporate interests even if it were forced to file for bankruptcy under Chapter Eleven. 11 U.S.C. § 362. Texaco, or its successor in interest, could go forward with the appeal, and if it did prevail on its appeal in Texas courts, the bankruptcy proceedings could be terminated. § 1112. Texaco simply fails to show how the initiation of corporate reorganization activities would prevent it from obtaining meaningful appellate review.

I reach this conclusion on the narrow facts before us. Thus, this case is different from the more troublesome situation where a particular corporate litigant has such special attributes as an organization that a trustee in bankruptcy, in its stead, could not effectively advance the organization's interests on an appeal. Moreover, the underlying issues in this case—arising out of a commercial contract dispute—do not involve fundamental constitutional rights. * * *

Given the particular facts of this case, I would reverse the judgment of the Court of Appeals, and remand the case with instructions to dismiss the complaint.

JUSTICE BLACKMUN, concurring in the judgment.

I, too, conclude, as do Justice Brennan and Justice Stevens, that a creditor's invocation of a State's post-judgment collection procedures constitutes action under color of state law within the reach of 42 U.S.C. § 1983. * * * I also agree with them that the District Court was correct in not abstaining under the principles enunciated in Younger v. Harris. In my view, to rule otherwise would expand the *Younger* doctrine to an unprecedented extent and would effectively allow the invocation of *Younger* abstention whenever any state proceeding is ongoing, no matter how attenuated the State's interests are in that proceeding and no matter what abuses the federal plaintiff might be sustaining.

* * *

Court is responding to "an unusual fact situation, never before addressed by the Texas courts," or by this Court. The Court bases its holding on several dependent considerations. First, the Court acknowledges that today's extension of the *Younger* doctrine applies only "when certain civil proceedings are pending, if the State's interests in the proceeding are so important that exercise of the federal judicial power would disregard the comity between the States and the National Government." Second, the Court emphasizes that in this instance "it is impossible to be certain that the govern-ing Texas statutes and procedural rules actually raise [Texaco's] claims," and that the Texas Constitution contains an "open courts" provision "that appears to address Texaco's claims more specifically" than the Federal Constitution. Third, the Court heavily relies on the State's particular interest in enforcing bond and lien requirements to prevent state court judgments, which have been already pronounced, from being rendered "nugatory." The unique and extraordinary circumstances of this case should limit its influence in determining the outer limits of the *Younger* doctrine.

I conclude instead that this case presents an example of the "narrowly limited 'special circumstances,'" Zwickler v. Koota, 389 U.S. 241, 248 (1967), quoting Propper v. Clark, 337 U.S. 472, 492 (1949), where the District Court should have abstained under the principles announced in Railroad Comm'n of Texas v. Pullman Co., 312 U.S. 496 (1941). Although the *Pullman* issue was not pressed before us it was considered by the Court of Appeals and rejected. In particular, the court determined that "there [was] nothing unclear or uncertain about the Texas lien and bond provisions" and that abstention was not demanded when there was only a "mere possibility" that the Texas courts would find such provisions unconstitutional. I disagree. If the extensive briefing by the parties on the numerous Texas statutes and constitutional provisions at issue here suggests anything, it is that on the unique facts of this case "unsettled questions of state law must be resolved before a substantial federal constitutional question can be decided," Hawaii Housing Authority v. Midkiff, 467 U.S. 229, 236 (1984), because "the state courts may interpret [the] challenged state statute[s] so as to eliminate, or at least to alter materially, the constitutional question presented." Ohio Bureau of Employment Services v. Hodory, 431 U.S. 471, 477 (1977). The possibility of such a state law resolution of this dispute seems to me still to exist.

JUSTICE STEVENS, with whom JUSTICE MARSHALL joins, concurring in the judgment.

In my opinion Texaco's claim that the Texas judgment lien and supersedeas bond provisions violate the Fourteenth Amendment is plainly without merit. The injunction against enforcement of those provisions must therefore be dissolved. I rest my analysis on this ground because I cannot agree with the grounds upon which the Court disposes of the case. In my view the District Court and the Court of Appeals were correct to hold that a creditor's invocation of a State's postjudgment collection procedures constitutes action "under color of" state law within the meaning of 42 U.S.C. § 1983, and that there is no basis for abstention in this case.[2]

* * *

[The concurring opinions of JUSTICE SCALIA, with whom JUSTICE O'CONNOR joins, and of JUSTICE MARSHALL are omitted.]

---

2. As the Court of Appeals explained: "The state interests at stake in this proceeding differ in both kind and in degree" from the cases in which the Court has held *Younger* abstention appropriate. As Justice Brennan's analysis points out, the issue of whether "proceedings implicate important state interests" is quite distinct from the question of whether there is an ongoing proceeding. See Middlesex Ethics Comm. v. Garden State Bar Assn., 457 U.S. 423, 432 (1982). Although we have often wrestled with deciding whether a particular exercise of state enforcement power implicates an "important state interest," we have invariably required that the State have a *substantive* interest in the ongoing proceeding, an interest that goes beyond its interest as adjudicator of wholly private disputes. By abandoning this critical limitation, the Court cuts the *Younger* doctrine adrift from its original doctrinal moorings which dealt with the States' interest in enforcing their criminal laws, and the federal courts' longstanding reluctance to interfere with such proceedings.

Skip to Chap 13
712

Notes

1. Does the application of *Younger* abstention in *Pennzoil* follow logically from its use in *Trainor* and *Juidice*? Do you agree with Justice Brennan's assertion that "[t]he State's interest in this case is negligible"? Is the state's interest any less here than in *Juidice*? Is it accurate to say that, after *Pennzoil*, the *Younger* doctrine has finally been extended to *all* civil cases?

2. Does Justice Powell's opinion effectively amount to adoption of an exhaustion-of-state-judicial remedies requirement? If so, is such a conclusion reconcilable with the reasoning of Patsy v. Board of Regents, 457 U.S. 496 (1982) [supra p. 536]? Justice Powell relies on the fact that "the Texas Constitution contains an 'open courts' provision that appears to address Texaco's claims more specifically than the Due Process Clause of the Fourteenth Amendment." Does this statement imply adoption of an exhaustion-of-state-*law* requirement? Is there anything in the logic of the *Younger* doctrine to support such a requirement?

3. Note that Justice Blackmun urges reliance on *Pullman* abstention, rather than *Younger* abstention. Do you agree? Does it make any practical difference which of the two forms of abstention is employed? Could a persuasive argument be fashioned that Justice Powell's opinion effectively, if not explicitly, relied more on the logic of *Pullman* than of *Younger?*

4. For other commentary on *Pennzoil*, see, e.g., Stravitz, *Younger Abstention Reaches A Civil Maturity,* 57 Ford.L.Rev. 997 (1989) ("After *Pennzoil* there is no principled basis to limit *Younger* abstention to criminal, quasi-criminal, and civil enforcement cases."); Vairo, *Making Younger Civil: The Consequences of Federal Court Deference to State Court Proceedings: A Response to Professor Stravitz,* 58 Ford.L.Rev. 173 (1989).

5. *Younger and Money Damages.* According to one commentator, while the Supreme Court has authorized "modest expansion" of the civil application of *Younger,* "[w]ithin the lower courts, the *Younger* doctrine's expansion has been far more sweeping. A plurality of circuit courts of appeals have held that *Younger* abstention applies not only to federal claims seeking equitable relief, but also to actions seeking money damages only." Estrada, *Pushing Doctrinal Limits: The Trend Toward Applying* Younger *Abstention to Claims for Monetary Damages and Raising* Younger *Abstention Sua Sponte on Appeal,* 81 N.Dak.L.Rev. 475 (2005). The Supreme Court has expressly reserved the issue. Deakins v. Monaghan, 484 U.S. 193, 202 (1988). Illustrative of the lower courts' view is Gilbertson v. Albright, 381 F.3d 965 (9th Cir.2004) (en banc), where the court reasoned: "[i]t would frustrate the state's interest in administering its judicial system, cast negative light on the state court's ability to enforce constitutional principles, and put the federal court in the position of prematurely or unnecessarily deciding a question of federal constitutional law, adjudication of a § 1983 claim for money damages would be just as intrusive as a declaratory judgment." Id. at 980.

Chapter 11

RES JUDICATA IN THE FEDERAL SYSTEM

ALLEN v. McCURRY

Supreme Court of the United States, 1980.
449 U.S. 90.

Justice Stewart delivered the opinion of the Court.

At a hearing before his criminal trial in a Missouri court, the respondent, Willie McCurry, invoked the Fourth and Fourteenth Amendments to suppress evidence that had been seized by the police. The trial court denied the suppression motion in part, and McCurry was subsequently convicted after a jury trial. The conviction was later affirmed on appeal. Because he did not assert that the state courts had denied him a "full and fair opportunity" to litigate his search and seizure claim, McCurry was barred by this Court's decision in Stone v. Powell, 428 U.S. 465, from seeking a writ of habeas corpus in a federal district court. Nevertheless, he sought federal-court redress for the alleged constitutional violation by bringing a damages suit under 42 U.S.C. § 1983 against the officers who had entered his home and seized the evidence in question. We granted certiorari to consider whether the unavailability of federal habeas corpus prevented the police officers from raising the state courts' partial rejection of McCurry's constitutional claim as a collateral estoppel defense to the § 1983 suit against them for damages.

I

In April 1977, several undercover police officers, following an informant's tip that McCurry was dealing in heroin, went to his house in St. Louis, Mo., to attempt a purchase. Two officers, petitioners Allen and Jacobsmeyer, knocked on the front door, while the other officers hid nearby. When McCurry opened the door, the two officers asked to buy some heroin "caps." McCurry went back into the house and returned soon thereafter, firing a pistol at and seriously wounding Allen and Jacobsmeyer. After a gun battle with the other officers and their reinforcements, McCurry retreated into the house; he emerged again when the police demanded that he surrender. Several officers then

579

entered the house without a warrant, purportedly to search for other persons inside. One of the officers seized drugs and other contraband that lay in plain view, as well as additional contraband he found in dresser drawers and in auto tires on the porch.

McCurry was charged with possession of heroin and assault with intent to kill. At the pretrial suppression hearing, the trial judge excluded the evidence seized from the dresser drawers and tires, but denied suppression of the evidence found in plain view. McCurry was convicted of both the heroin and assault offenses.

McCurry subsequently filed the present § 1983 action for $1 million in damages against petitioners Allen and Jacobsmeyer, other unnamed individual police officers, and the city of St. Louis and its police department. The complaint alleged a conspiracy to violate McCurry's Fourth Amendment rights, an unconstitutional search and seizure of his house, and an assault on him by unknown police officers after he had been arrested and handcuffed. The petitioners moved for summary judgment. The District Court apparently understood the gist of the complaint to be the allegedly unconstitutional search and seizure and granted summary judgment, holding that collateral estoppel prevented McCurry from relitigating the search-and-seizure question already decided against him in the state courts.

The Court of Appeals reversed the judgment and remanded the case for trial. * * *

II

The federal courts have traditionally adhered to the related doctrines of res judicata and collateral estoppel. Under res judicata, a final judgment on the merits of an action precludes the parties or their privies from relitigating issues that were or could have been raised in that action. Under collateral estoppel, once a court has decided an issue of fact or law necessary to its judgment, that decision may preclude relitigation of the issue in a suit on a different cause of action involving a party to the first case. * * * [5] As this Court and other courts have often recognized, res judicata and collateral estoppel relieve parties of the cost and vexation of multiple lawsuits, conserve judicial resources, and, by preventing inconsistent decisions, encourage reliance on adjudication.

In recent years, this Court has reaffirmed the benefits of collateral estoppel in particular, finding the policies underlying it to apply in contexts not formerly recognized at common law. * * * But one general limitation the Court has repeatedly recognized is that the concept of

---

5. The Restatement of Judgments now speaks of res judicata as "claim preclusion" and collateral estoppel as "issue preclusion." Restatement (Second) of Judgments § 74 (Tent. Draft No. 3, Apr. 15, 1976). Some courts and commentators use "res judicata" as generally meaning both forms of preclusion.

Contrary to a suggestion in the dissenting opinion, this case does not involve the question whether a § 1983 claimant can litigate in federal court an issue he might have raised but did not raise in previous litigation.

collateral estoppel cannot apply when the party against whom the earlier decision is asserted did not have a "full and fair opportunity" to litigate that issue in the earlier case.[7]

The federal courts generally have also consistently accorded preclusive effect to issues decided by state courts. Thus, res judicata and collateral estoppel not only reduce unnecessary litigation and foster reliance on adjudication, but also promote the comity between state and federal courts that has been recognized as a bulwark of the federal system. See Younger v. Harris, 401 U.S. 37, 43–45.

Indeed, though the federal courts may look to the common law or to the policies supporting res judicata and collateral estoppel in assessing the preclusive effect of decisions of other federal courts, Congress has specifically required all federal courts to give preclusive effect to state-court judgments whenever the courts of the State from which the judgments emerged would do so:

> "[J]udicial proceedings [of any court of any State] shall have the same full faith and credit in every court within the United States and its Territories and Possessions as they have by law or usage in the courts of such State * * *." 28 U.S.C. § 1738 (1976).[8]

It is against this background that we examine the relationship of § 1983 and collateral estoppel, and the decision of the Court of Appeals in this case.

III

This Court has never directly decided whether the rules of res judicata and collateral estoppel are generally applicable to § 1983 actions. But in Preiser v. Rodriguez, 411 U.S. 475, 497, the Court noted with implicit approval the view of other federal courts that res judicata principles fully apply to civil rights suits brought under that statute. * * *

Because the requirement of mutuality of estoppel was still alive in the federal courts until well into this century, the drafters of the 1871 Civil Rights Act, of which § 1983 is a part, may have had less reason to concern themselves with rules of preclusion than a modern Congress would. Nevertheless, in 1871 res judicata and collateral estoppel could

---

7. * * * Contrary to the suggestion of the dissent, our decision today does not "fashion" any new more stringent doctrine of collateral estoppel, nor does it hold that the collateral-estoppel effect of a state-court decision turns on the single factor of whether the State gave the federal claimant a full and fair opportunity to litigate a federal question. Our decision does not "fashion" any doctrine of collateral estoppel at all. Rather, it construes § 1983 to determine whether the conventional doctrine of collateral estoppel applies to the case at hand. It must be emphasized that the question whether any exceptions or qualifications within the bounds of that doctrine might ultimately defeat a collateral-estoppel defense in this case is not before us.

8. This statute has existed in essentially unchanged form since its enactment just after the ratification of the Constitution, Act of May 26, 1790, ch. 11, 1 Stat. 122, and its re-enactment soon thereafter, Act of Mar. 27, 1804, ch. 56, 2 Stat. 298–299. Congress has also provided means for authenticating the records of the state proceedings to which the federal courts are to give full faith and credit. 28 U.S.C. § 1738.

certainly have applied in federal suits following state-court litigation between the same parties or their privies, and nothing in the language of § 1983 remotely expresses any congressional intent to contravene the common-law rules of preclusion or to repeal the express statutory requirements of the predecessor of 28 U.S.C. § 1738. Section 1983 creates a new federal cause of action. It says nothing about the preclusive effect of state-court judgments.[12]

Moreover, the legislative history of § 1983 does not in any clear way suggest that Congress intended to repeal or restrict the traditional doctrines of preclusion. The main goal of the Act was to override the corrupting influence of the Ku Klux Klan and its sympathizers on the governments and law enforcement agencies of the Southern States, see Monroe v. Pape, 365 U.S. 167, 174, and of course the debates show that one strong motive behind its enactment was grave congressional concern that the state courts had been deficient in protecting federal rights, Mitchum v. Foster, 407 U.S. 225, 241–242; Monroe v. Pape, supra, at 180,. But in the context of the legislative history as a whole, this congressional concern lends only the most equivocal support to any argument that, in cases where the state courts have recognized the constitutional claims asserted and provided fair procedures for determining them, Congress intended to override § 1738 or the common-law rules of collateral estoppel and res judicata. Since repeals by implication are disfavored, much clearer support than this would be required to hold that § 1738 and the traditional rules of preclusion are not applicable to § 1983 suits.

As the Court has understood the history of the legislation, Congress realized that in enacting § 1983 it was altering the balance of judicial power between the state and federal courts. See Mitchum v. Foster, supra, at 241. But in doing so, Congress was adding to the jurisdiction of the federal courts, not subtracting from that of the state courts. See Monroe v. Pape, supra, at 183 ("The federal remedy is supplementary to the state remedy * * * ").[14] The debates contain several references to the concurrent jurisdiction of the state courts over federal questions, and numerous suggestions that the state courts would retain their estab-

---

12. By contrast, the roughly contemporaneous statute extending the federal writ of habeas corpus to state prisoners expressly rendered "null and void" any state-court proceeding inconsistent with the decision of a federal habeas court, Act of Feb. 5, 1867, ch. 28, § 1, 14 Stat. 385, 386 (current version at 28 U.S.C. § 2254), and the modern habeas statute also expressly adverts to the effect of state-court criminal judgments by requiring the applicant for the writ to exhaust his state-court remedies, 28 U.S.C. § 2254(b), and by presuming a state-court resolution of a factual issue to be correct except in eight specific circumstances, § 2254(d). In any event, the traditional exception to res judicata for habeas corpus review, see Preiser v. Rodriguez, 411 U.S.

475, 497, provides no analogy to § 1983 cases, since that exception finds its source in the unique purpose of habeas corpus—to release the applicant for the writ from unlawful confinement.

14. To the extent that Congress in the post-Civil War period did intend to deny full faith and credit to state-court decisions on constitutional issues, it expressly chose the very different means of postjudgment removal for state court defendants whose civil rights were threatened by biased state courts and who therefore "are denied or cannot enforce [their civil rights] in the courts or judicial tribunals of the State." Act of Apr. 9, 1866, ch. 31, § 3, 14 Stat. 27.

lished jurisdiction so that they could, when the then current political passions abated, demonstrate a new sensitivity to federal rights.

To the extent that it did intend to change the balance of power over federal questions between the state and federal courts, the 42d Congress was acting in a way thoroughly consistent with the doctrines of preclusion. In reviewing the legislative history of § 1983 in Monroe v. Pape, supra, the Court inferred that Congress had intended a federal remedy in three circumstances: where state substantive law was facially unconstitutional, where state procedural law was inadequate to allow full litigation of a constitutional claim, and where state procedural law, though adequate in theory, was inadequate in practice. In short, the federal courts could step in where the state courts were unable or unwilling to protect federal rights. This understanding of § 1983 might well support an exception to res judicata and collateral estoppel where state law did not provide fair procedures for the litigation of constitutional claims, or where a state court failed to even acknowledge the existence of the constitutional principle on which a litigant based his claim. Such an exception, however, would be essentially the same as the important general limit on rules of preclusion that already exists: Collateral estoppel does not apply where the party against whom an earlier court decision is asserted did not have a full and fair opportunity to litigate the claim or issue decided by the first court. But the Court's view of § 1983 in *Monroe* lends no strength to any argument that Congress intended to allow relitigation of federal issues decided after a full and fair hearing in a state court simply because the state court's decision may have been erroneous.

* * *

The actual basis of the Court of Appeals' holding appears to be a generally framed principle that every person asserting a federal right is entitled to one unencumbered opportunity to litigate that right in a federal district court, regardless of the legal posture in which the federal claim arises. But the authority for this principle is difficult to discern. It cannot lie in the Constitution, which makes no such guarantee, but leaves the scope of the jurisdiction of the federal district courts to the wisdom of Congress. And no such authority is to be found in § 1983 itself. For reasons already discussed at length, nothing in the language or legislative history of § 1983 proves any congressional intent to deny binding effect to a state-court judgment or decision when the state court, acting within its proper jurisdiction, has given the parties a full and fair opportunity to litigate federal claims, and thereby has shown itself willing and able to protect federal rights. And nothing in the legislative history of § 1983 reveals any purpose to afford less deference to judgments in state criminal proceedings than to those in state civil proceedings. There is, in short, no reason to believe that Congress intended to provide a person claiming a federal right an unrestricted opportunity to relitigate an issue already decided in state court simply because the issue arose in a state proceeding in which he would rather not have been engaged at all.

Through § 1983, the 42d Congress intended to afford an opportunity for legal and equitable relief in a federal court for certain types of injuries. It is difficult to believe that the drafters of that Act considered it a substitute for a federal writ of habeas corpus, the purpose of which is not to redress civil injury, but to release the applicant from unlawful physical confinement, Preiser v. Rodriguez, 411 U.S., at 484; Fay v. Noia, 372 U.S. 391, 399, n. 5,[24] particularly in light of the extremely narrow scope of federal habeas relief for state prisoners in 1871.

The only other conceivable basis for finding a universal right to litigate a federal claim in a federal district court is hardly a legal basis at all, but rather a general distrust of the capacity of the state courts to render correct decisions on constitutional issues. * * *

The Court of Appeals erred in holding that McCurry's inability to obtain federal habeas corpus relief upon his Fourth Amendment claim renders the doctrine of collateral estoppel inapplicable to his § 1983 suit. * * *

* * *

Justice Blackmun, with whom Justice Brennan and Justice Marshall join, dissenting.

* * *

The Court today holds that notions of collateral estoppel apply with full force to this suit brought under 42 U.S.C. § 1983. In my view, the Court, in so ruling, ignores the clear import of the legislative history of that statute and disregards the important federal policies that underlie its enforcement. It also shows itself insensitive both to the significant differences between the § 1983 remedy and the exclusionary rule, and to the pressures upon a criminal defendant that make a free choice of forum illusory. I do not doubt that principles of preclusion are to be given such effect as is appropriate in a § 1983 action. In many cases, the denial of res judicata or collateral estoppel effect would serve no purpose and would harm relations between federal and state tribunals. Nonetheless, the Court's analysis in this particular case is unacceptable to me. It works injustice on this § 1983 plaintiff, and it makes more difficult the consistent protection of constitutional rights, a consideration that was at the core of the enactors' intent. * * *

In deciding whether a common-law doctrine is to apply to § 1983 when the statute itself is silent, prior cases uniformly have accorded the intent of the legislators great weight. * * * This very proper inquiry must be made in order to ensure that § 1983 will continue to serve the

---

24. Under the modern statute, federal habeas corpus is bounded by a requirement of exhaustion of state remedies and by special procedural rules, 28 U.S.C. § 2254, which have no counterparts in § 1983, and which therefore demonstrate the continuing illogic of treating federal habeas and § 1983 suits as fungible remedies for constitutional violations.

important goals intended for it by the 42d Congress. In the present case, however, the Court minimizes the significance of the legislative history and discounts its own prior explicit interpretations of the statute. Its discussion is limited to articulating what it terms the single fundamental principle of res judicata and collateral estoppel.

Respondent's position merits a quite different analysis. Although the legislators of the 42d Congress did not expressly state whether the then existing common-law doctrine of preclusion would survive enactment of § 1983, they plainly anticipated more than the creation of a federal statutory remedy to be administered indifferently by either a state or a federal court. The legislative intent, as expressed by supporters and understood by opponents, was to restructure relations between the state and federal courts. Congress deliberately opened the federal courts to individual citizens in response to the States' failure to provide justice in their own courts. Contrary to the view presently expressed by the Court, the 42d Congress was not concerned solely with procedural regularity. Even where there was procedural regularity, which the Court today so stresses, Congress believed that substantive justice was unobtainable. The availability of the federal forum was not meant to turn on whether, in an individual case, the state procedures were adequate. Assessing the state of affairs as a whole, Congress specifically made a determination that federal oversight of constitutional determinations through the federal courts was necessary to ensure the effective enforcement of constitutional rights.

That the new federal jurisdiction was conceived of as concurrent with state jurisdiction does not alter the significance of Congress' opening the federal courts to these claims. Congress consciously acted in the broadest possible manner. The legislators perceived that justice was not being done in the States then dominated by the Klan, and it seems senseless to suppose that they would have intended the federal courts to give full preclusive effect to prior state adjudications. That supposition would contradict their obvious aim to right the wrongs perpetuated in those same courts.

I appreciate that the legislative history is capable of alternative interpretations. * * * I would have thought, however, that our prior decisions made very clear which reading is required. The Court repeatedly has recognized that § 1983 embodies a strong congressional policy in favor of federal courts' acting as the primary and final arbiters of constitutional rights. In Monroe v. Pape, the Court held that Congress passed the legislation in order to substitute a federal forum for the ineffective, although plainly available, state remedies:

> "It is abundantly clear that one reason the legislation was passed was to afford a federal right in federal courts because, by reason of prejudice, passion, neglect, intolerance or otherwise, state laws might not be enforced and the claims of citizens to the enjoyment of rights, privileges, and immunities guaranteed by the Fourteenth Amendment might be denied by the state agencies."

The Court appears to me to misconstrue the plain meaning of *Monroe*. It states that in that case, "the Court inferred that Congress had intended a federal remedy in three circumstances: where state substantive law was facially unconstitutional, where state procedural law was inadequate to allow full litigation of a constitutional claim, and where state procedural law, though adequate in theory, was inadequate in practice." It is true that the Court in *Monroe* described those three circumstances as the "three main aims" of the legislation. Yet in that case, the Court's recounting of the legislative history and its articulation of these three purposes were intended only as illustrative of *why* the 42d Congress chose to establish a federal remedy in federal court, not as a delineation of *when* the remedy would be available. The Court's conclusion was that this remedy was to be available no matter what the circumstances of state law:

> "It is no answer that the State has a law which if enforced would give relief. The federal remedy is supplementary to the state remedy, and the latter need not be first sought and refused before the federal one is invoked. Hence the fact that Illinois by its constitution and laws outlaws unreasonable searches and seizures is no barrier to the present suit in the federal court."

In Mitchum v. Foster, 407 U.S. 225 (1972), the Court reiterated its understanding of the effect of § 1983 upon state and federal relations:

> "Section 1983 was thus a product of a vast transformation from the concepts of federalism that had prevailed in the late 18th century.... The very purpose of § 1983 was to interpose the federal courts between the States and the people, as guardians of the people's federal rights—to protect the people from unconstitutional action under color of state law, 'whether that action be executive, legislative, or judicial.' Ex parte Virginia, 100 U.S. [339], at 346."[11]

At the very least, it is inconsistent now to narrow, if not repudiate, the meaning of *Monroe* and *Mitchum* and to alter our prior understanding of the distribution of power between the state and federal courts.

* * *

The Court now fashions a new doctrine of preclusion, applicable only to actions brought under § 1983, that is more strict and more confining than the federal rules of preclusion applied in other cases. In Montana v. United States, 440 U.S. 147 (1979), the Court pronounced three major factors to be considered in determining whether collateral estoppel serves as a barrier in the federal court:

11. The Court also stated:

"This legislative history makes evident that Congress clearly conceived that it was altering the relationship between the States and the Nation with respect to the protection of federally created rights; it was concerned that state instrumentalities could not protect those rights; it realized that state officers might, in fact, be antipathetic to the vindication of those rights; and it believed that these failings extended to the state courts."

"[W]hether the issues presented * * * are in substance the same * * *; whether controlling facts or legal principles have changed significantly since the state-court judgment; and finally, whether other special circumstances warrant an exception to the normal rules of preclusion." Id., at 155.

But now the Court states that the collateral-estoppel effect of prior state adjudication should turn on only one factor, namely, what it considers the "one general limitation" inherent in the doctrine of preclusion: "that the concept of collateral estoppel cannot apply when the party against whom the earlier decision is asserted did not have a 'full and fair opportunity' to litigate that issue in the earlier case." If that one factor is present, the Court asserts, the litigant properly should be barred from relitigating the issue in federal court.[12] One cannot deny that this factor is an important one. I do not believe, however, that the doctrine of preclusion requires the inquiry to be so narrow, and my understanding of the policies underlying § 1983 would lead me to consider all relevant factors in each case before concluding that preclusion was warranted.

In this case, the police officers seek to prevent a criminal defendant from relitigating the constitutionality of their conduct in searching his house, after the state trial court had found that conduct in part violative of the defendant's Fourth Amendment rights and in part justified by the circumstances. * * *

The following factors persuade me to conclude that this respondent should not be precluded from asserting his claim in federal court. First, at the time § 1983 was passed, a nonparty's ability, as a practical matter, to invoke collateral estoppel was nonexistent. One could not preclude an opponent from relitigating an issue in a new cause of action, though that issue had been determined conclusively in a prior proceeding, unless there was "mutuality." Additionally, the definitions of "cause of action" and "issue" were narrow. As a result, and obviously, no preclusive effect could arise out of a criminal proceeding that would affect subsequent *civil* litigation. Thus, the 42d Congress could not have anticipated or approved that a criminal defendant, tried and convicted in state court, would be precluded from raising against police officers a constitutional claim arising out of his arrest.

Also, the process of deciding in a state criminal trial whether to exclude or admit evidence is not at all the equivalent of a § 1983 proceeding. The remedy sought in the latter is utterly different. In bringing the civil suit the criminal defendant does not seek to challenge his conviction collaterally. At most, he wins damages. In contrast, the exclusion of evidence may prevent a criminal conviction. A trial court, faced with the decision whether to exclude relevant evidence, confronts institutional pressures that may cause it to give a different shape to the

12. This articulation of the preclusion doctrine of course would bar a § 1983 litigant from relitigating any issue he *might* have raised, as well as any issue he actually litigated in his criminal trial.

Fourth Amendment right from what would result in civil litigation of a damages claim. Also, the issue whether to exclude evidence is subsidiary to the purpose of a criminal trial, which is to determine the guilt or innocence of the defendant, and a trial court, at least subconsciously, must weigh the potential damage to the truth-seeking process caused by excluding relevant evidence.

A state criminal defendant cannot be held to have chosen "voluntarily" to litigate his Fourth Amendment claim in the state court. The risk of conviction puts pressure upon him to raise all possible defenses. He also faces uncertainty about the wisdom of forgoing litigation on *any* issue, for there is the possibility that he will be held to have waived his right to appeal on that issue. The "deliberate bypass" of state procedures, which the imposition of collateral estoppel under these circumstances encourages, surely is not a preferred goal. To hold that a criminal defendant who raises a Fourth Amendment claim at his criminal trial "freely and without reservation submits his federal claims for decision by the state courts," see England v. Medical Examiners, 375 U.S., at 419, is to deny reality. The criminal defendant is an involuntary litigant in the state tribunal, and against him all the forces of the State are arrayed. To force him to a choice between forgoing either a potential defense or a federal forum for hearing his constitutional civil claim is fundamentally unfair.

* * *

MIGRA v. WARREN CITY SCHOOL DISTRICT BOARD OF EDUCATION

Supreme Court of the United States, 1984.
465 U.S. 75.

JUSTICE BLACKMUN delivered the opinion of the Court.

This case raises issues concerning the claim preclusive effect[1] of a state-court judgment in the context of a subsequent suit, under 42 U.S.C. §§ 1983 and 1985 (1976 ed., Supp. V), in federal court.

1. The preclusive effects of former adjudication are discussed in varying and, at times, seemingly conflicting terminology, attributable to the evolution of preclusion concepts over the years. These effects are referred to collectively by most commentators as the doctrine of "res judicata." See Restatement (Second) of Judgments, Introductory Note before ch. 3 (1982); 18 C. Wright, A. Miller, & E. Cooper, Federal Practice and Procedure § 4402 (1981). Res judicata is often analyzed further to consist of two preclusion concepts: "issue preclusion" and "claim preclusion." Issue preclusion refers to the effect of a judgment in foreclosing relitigation of a matter that has been litigated and decided. See Restatement, supra, § 27. This effect also is re-

ferred to as direct or collateral estoppel. Claim preclusion refers to the effect of a judgment in foreclosing litigation of a matter that never has been litigated, because of a determination that it should have been advanced in an earlier suit. Claim preclusion therefore encompasses the law of merger and bar.

This Court on more than one occasion has used the term "res judicata" in a narrow sense, so as to exclude issue preclusion or collateral estoppel. See e.g., Allen v. McCurry, 449 U.S. 90, 94 (1980); Brown v. Felsen, 442 U.S. 127 (1979). When using that formulation, "res judicata" becomes virtually synonymous with "claim preclusion." In order to avoid confusion resulting

I

Petitioner, Dr. Ethel D. Migra, was employed by the Warren [Ohio] City School District Board of Education from August 1976 to June 1979. She served as supervisor of elementary education. Her employment was on an annual basis under written contracts for successive school years.

On April 17, 1979, at a regularly scheduled meeting, the Board, with all five of its members present, unanimously adopted a resolution renewing Dr. Migra's employment as supervisor for the 1979–1980 school year. Being advised of this, she accepted the renewed appointment by letter dated April 18 delivered to a member of the Board on April 23. Early the following morning her letter was passed on to the Superintendent of Schools and to the Board's President.

The Board, however, held a special meeting, called by its President, on the morning of April 24. Although there appear to have been some irregularities about the call, four of the five members of the Board were present. The President first read Dr. Migra's acceptance letter. Then, after disposing of other business, a motion was made and adopted, by a vote of three to one, not to renew petitioner's employment for the 1979–1980 school year. Dr. Migra was given written notice of this nonrenewal and never received a written contract of employment for that year. The Board's absent member, James Culver, learned of the special meeting and of Dr. Migra's termination after he returned from Florida on April 25 where he had attended a National School Boards Convention.

Petitioner brought suit in the Court of Common Pleas of Trumbull County, Ohio, against the Board and its three members who had voted not to renew her employment. The complaint, although in five counts, presented what the parties now accept as essentially two causes of action, namely, breach of contract by the Board, and wrongful interference by the individual members with petitioner's contract of employment. The state court, after a bench trial, "reserved and continued" the "issue of conspiracy" and did not reach the question of the individual members' liability. It ruled that under Ohio law petitioner had accepted the employment proffered for 1979–1980, that this created a binding contract between her and the Board, and that the Board's subsequent action purporting not to renew the employment relationship had no legal effect. The court awarded Dr. Migra reinstatement to her position and compensatory damages. Thereafter, petitioner moved the state trial court to dismiss without prejudice "the issue of the conspiracy and individual board member liability." That motion was granted. The Ohio Court of Appeals, Eleventh District, in an unreported opinion, affirmed the judgment of the Court of Common Pleas. Review was denied by the Supreme Court of Ohio.

from the two uses of "res judicata," this opinion utilizes the term "claim preclusion" to refer to the preclusive effect of a judgment in foreclosing relitigation of matters that should have been raised in an earlier suit. For a helpful explanation of preclusion vocabulary, see Wright, et al., supra, § 4402.

In July 1980, Dr. Migra filed the present action in the United States District Court for the Northern District of Ohio against the Board, its then individual members, and the Superintendent of Schools. App. 3. Her complaint alleged that Dr. Migra had become the director of a commission appointed by the Board to fashion a voluntary plan for the desegregation of the District's elementary schools; that she had prepared a social studies curriculum; that the individual defendants objected to and opposed the curriculum and resisted the desegregation plan; that hostility and ill will toward petitioner developed; and that, as a consequence, the individual defendants determined not to renew petitioner's contract of employment. Id., at 5–6. Many of the alleged facts had been proved in the earlier state-court litigation. Dr. Migra claimed that the Board's actions were intended to punish her for the exercise of her First Amendment rights. She also claimed that the actions deprived her of property without due process and denied her equal protection. Her federal claim thus arose under the First, Fifth and Fourteenth Amendments and 42 U.S.C. §§ 1983 and 1985. She requested injunctive relief and compensatory and punitive damages. Answers were filed in due course and shortly thereafter the defendants moved for summary judgment on the basis of res judicata and the bar of the statute of limitations.

The District Court granted summary judgment for the defendants and dismissed the complaint. The United States Court of Appeals for the Sixth Circuit, by a short unreported order, affirmed. * * *

II

The Constitution's Full Faith and Credit Clause[4] is implemented by the Federal Full Faith and Credit Statute, 28 U.S.C. § 1738. That statute reads in pertinent part:

> Such Acts, records and judicial proceedings or copies thereof, so authenticated, shall have the same full faith and credit in every court within the United States and its Territories and Possessions as they have by law or usage in the courts of such State, Territory or Possession from which they are taken.

It is now settled that a federal court must give to a state-court judgment the same preclusive effect as would be given that judgment under the law of the State in which the judgment was rendered. In Allen v. McCurry, 449 U.S. 90 (1980), this Court said:

> Indeed, though the federal courts may look to the common law or to the policies supporting res judicata and collateral estoppel in assessing the preclusive effect of decisions of other federal courts, Congress has specifically required all federal courts to give preclu-

---

4. "Full Faith and Credit shall be given in each State to the public Acts, Records, and judicial Proceedings of every other State. And the Congress may by general Laws prescribe the Manner in which such Acts, Records and Proceedings shall be proved, and the Effect thereof." U.S. Const., Art. IV, § 1.

sive effect to state-court judgments whenever the courts of the State from which the judgments emerged would do so.... Id., at 96.

This principle was restated in Kremer v. Chemical Construction Corp., 456 U.S. 461 (1982):

> Section 1738 requires federal courts to give the same preclusive effect to state court judgments that those judgments would be given in the courts of the State from which the judgments emerged. Id., at 466.

Accordingly, in the absence of federal law modifying the operation of § 1738, the preclusive effect in federal court of petitioner's state-court judgment is determined by Ohio law.

In *Allen,* the Court considered whether 42 U.S.C. § 1983 modified the operation of § 1738 so that a state-court judgment was to receive less than normal preclusive effect in a suit brought in federal court under § 1983. In that case, the respondent had been convicted in a state-court criminal proceeding. In that proceeding, the respondent sought to suppress certain evidence against him on the ground that it had been obtained in violation of the Fourth Amendment. The trial court denied the motion to suppress. The respondent then brought a § 1983 suit in federal court against the officers who had seized the evidence. The District Court held the suit barred by collateral estoppel (issue preclusion) because the issue of a Fourth Amendment violation had been resolved against the respondent by the denial of his suppression motion in the criminal trial. The Court of Appeals reversed. That court concluded that, because a § 1983 suit was the respondent's only route to a federal forum for his constitutional claim,[5] and because one of § 1983's underlying purposes was to provide a federal cause of action in situations where state courts were not adequately protecting individual rights, the respondent should be allowed to proceed to trial in federal court unencumbered by collateral estoppel. This Court, however, reversed the Court of Appeals, explaining:

> [N]othing in the language of § 1983 remotely expresses any congressional intent to contravene the common-law rules of preclusion or to repeal the express statutory requirements of the predecessor of 28 U.S.C. § 1738.... Section 1983 creates a new federal cause of action. It says nothing about the preclusive effect of state-court judgments.

> Moreover, the legislative history of § 1983 does not in any clear way suggest that Congress intended to repeal or restrict the traditional doctrines of preclusion. * * * [T]he legislative history as a whole * * * lends only the most equivocal support to any argument that, in cases where the state courts have recognized the constitutional claims asserted and provided fair procedures for determining

---

5.　The respondent had not asserted that the state courts had denied him a "full and fair opportunity" to litigate his search and seizure claim; he therefore was barred by Stone v. Powell, 428 U.S. 465 (1976), from seeking a writ of habeas corpus in federal district court.

them, Congress intended to override § 1738 or the common-law
rules of collateral estoppel and res judicata. Since repeals by implication are disfavored * * * much clearer support than this would be
required to hold that § 1738 and the traditional rules of preclusion
are not applicable to § 1983 suits.

Allen therefore made clear that issues actually litigated in a state-court
proceeding are entitled to the same preclusive effect in a subsequent
federal § 1983 suit as they enjoy in the courts of the State where the
judgment was rendered.

The Court in *Allen* left open the possibility, however, that the
preclusive effect of a state-court judgment might be different as to a
federal issue that a § 1983 litigant could have raised but did not raise in
the earlier state-court proceeding.[6] That is the central issue to be
resolved in the present case. Petitioner did not litigate her § 1983 claim
in state court, and she asserts that the state-court judgment should not
preclude her suit in federal court simply because her federal claim could
have been litigated in the state-court proceeding. Thus, petitioner urges
this Court to interpret the interplay of § 1738 and § 1983 in such a way
as to accord state-court judgments preclusive effect in § 1983 suits only
as to issues actually litigated in state court.

It is difficult to see how the policy concerns underlying § 1983
would justify a distinction between the issue preclusive and claim preclusive effects of state-court judgments. The argument that state-court
judgments should have less preclusive effect in § 1983 suits than in
other federal suits is based on Congress' expressed concern over the
adequacy of state courts as protectors of federal rights. See, e.g., Mitchum v. Foster, 407 U.S. 225, 241–242 (1972). *Allen* recognized that the
enactment of § 1983 was motivated partially out of such concern, but
Allen nevertheless held that § 1983 did not open the way to relitigation
of an issue that had been determined in a state criminal proceeding. Any
distrust of state courts that would justify a limitation on the preclusive
effect of state judgments in § 1983 suits would presumably apply equally
to issues that actually were decided in a state-court as well as to those
that could have been. If § 1983 created an exception to the general
preclusive effect accorded to state-court judgments, such an exception
would seem to require similar treatment of both issue preclusion and
claim preclusion. Having rejected in *Allen* the view that state-court
judgments have no issue preclusive effect in § 1983 suits, we must reject
the view that § 1983 prevents the judgment in petitioner's state-court
proceeding from creating a claim preclusion bar in this case.

Petitioner suggests that to give state-court judgments full issue
preclusive effect but not claim preclusive effect would enable litigants to
bring their state claims in state court and their federal claims in federal
court, thereby taking advantage of the relative expertise of both forums.

---

6. Most federal courts that have faced   sion is applicable to a § 1983 action. * * *
this question have ruled that claim preclu-

Although such a division may seem attractive from a plaintiff's perspective, it is not the system established by § 1738. That statute embodies the view that it is more important to give full faith and credit to state-court judgments than to ensure separate forums for federal and state claims. This reflects a variety of concerns, including notions of comity, the need to prevent vexatious litigation, and a desire to conserve judicial resources.

In the present litigation, petitioner does not claim that the state court would not have adjudicated her federal claims had she presented them in her original suit in state court. Alternatively, petitioner could have obtained a federal forum for her federal claim by litigating it first in a federal court.[7] Section 1983, however, does not override state preclusion law and guarantee petitioner a right to proceed to judgment in state court on her state claims and then turn to federal court for adjudication of her federal claims. We hold, therefore, that petitioner's state-court judgment in this litigation has the same claim preclusive effect in federal court that the judgment would have in the Ohio state courts.

III

It appears to us that preclusion law in Ohio has experienced a gradual evolution, and that Ohio courts recently have applied preclusion concepts more broadly than in the past. * * *

* * *

In reading the opinion of the District Court in the present litigation, we are unable to determine whether that court was applying what it thought was the Ohio law of preclusion. * * * Our holding today makes clear that Ohio state preclusion law is to be applied to this case. Prudence also dictates that it is the District Court, in the first instance, not this Court, that should interpret Ohio preclusion law and apply it.

The judgment of the Court of Appeals, accordingly, is vacated and the case is remanded to that court so that it may instruct the District Court to conduct such further proceedings as are required by, and are consistent with, this opinion.

It is so ordered.

---

7. The author of this opinion was in dissent in *Allen.* The rationale of that dissent, however, was based largely on the fact that the § 1983 plaintiff in that case first litigated his constitutional claim in state court in the posture of his being a *defendant* in a criminal proceeding. In this case, petitioner was in an offensive posture in her state court proceeding, and could have proceeded first in federal court had she wanted to litigate her federal claim in a federal forum.

In the event that a § 1983 plaintiff's federal and state law claims are sufficiently intertwined that the federal court abstains from passing on the federal claims without first allowing the state court to address the state law issues, the plaintiff can preserve his right to a federal forum for his federal claims by informing the state court of his intention to return to federal court on his federal claims following litigation of his state claims in state court. See, e.g., England v. Louisiana State Board of Medical Examiners, 375 U.S. 411 (1964).

JUSTICE WHITE, with whom THE CHIEF JUSTICE and JUSTICE POWELL join, concurring.

In Union & Planters' Bank v. Memphis, 189 U.S. 71, 75, this Court held that a federal court "can accord [a state judgment] no greater efficacy" than would the judgment-rendering state. That holding has been adhered to on at least three occasions since that time. Oklahoma Packing Co. v. Oklahoma Gas & Electric Co., 309 U.S. 4, 7–8 (1940); Wright v. Georgia R.R. & Banking Co., 216 U.S. 420, 429 (1910); City of Covington v. First National Bank, 198 U.S. 100, 107–109 (1905). The Court has also indicated that the states are bound by a similar rule under the full faith and credit clause. Public Works v. Columbia College, 17 Wall. 521, 529 (1873). The Court is thus justified in this case to rule that preclusion in this case must be determined under state law, even if there would be preclusion under federal standards.

This construction of § 1738 and its predecessors is unfortunate. In terms of the purpose of that section, which is to require federal courts to give effect to state-court judgments, there is no reason to hold that a federal court may not give preclusive effect to a state judgment simply because the judgment would not bar relitigation in the state courts. If the federal courts have developed rules of res judicata and collateral estoppel that prevent relitigation in circumstances that would not be preclusive in state courts, the federal courts should be free to apply them, the parties then being free to relitigate in the state courts. The contrary construction of § 1738 is nevertheless one of long standing, and Congress has not seen fit to disturb it, however justified such an action might have been.

Accordingly, I join the opinion of the Court.

Notes

1. Do you agree with the majority's conclusion in *McCurry* that a federal court is bound by collateral estoppel and section 1738 to enforce state court findings in a section 1983 civil rights action? What are the competing considerations? How persuasive on the collateral estoppel issue is Justice Stewart's argument that portions of section 1983's legislative history indicate a congressional desire to maintain the concurrent jurisdiction of state courts? Does this fact demonstrate anything more than that the state courts were not to be deprived of their jurisdiction to hear these issues in cases before them? Does this logically imply that the federal courts in subsequent cases are to be bound by state court findings?

2. Can *McCurry* and *Mitchum* [supra p. 495] be rationalized? Recall that in *Mitchum* the Court held that section 1983 was an "expressly authorized" exception to the Anti–Injunction Act, because the legislative history revealed a serious congressional concern about the competence of state courts to enforce federal rights. Cf. Nichol, *Federalism, State Courts, and Section 1983,* 73 Va.L.Rev. 959, 1008 (1987), commenting that "[the] conclusion [that section 1738 requires collateral estoppel in section 1983 actions] may be the correct one, though it seems a strange way to treat a

federal cause of action that was designed, at least in part, to operate against state tribunals." Justice Stewart wrote in *McCurry* that in enacting section 1983, "Congress was adding to the jurisdiction of the federal courts, not subtracting from that of the state courts." 449 U.S. at 99. If this were true, on what basis could the Court in *Mitchum* conclude that the enactment of section 1983 authorized a federal court to enjoin a state court proceeding?

3.   Does the decision in *McCurry* flow logically from the comity considerations invoked in Younger v. Harris [supra p. 523]? Consider the argument that "[i]f *Younger* completely bars injunctive oversight of pending claims * * * and principles of collateral estoppel prevent even subsequent equitable or declaratory review of state judicial process, the sweep is clean. A cause of action that was designed in no small measure to ensure state judicial accountability essentially has no applicability to state courts. If section 1738 does demand preclusion in section 1983 cases, therefore, the call for a meaningful exception to the *Younger* principle is heightened, rather than diminished." Nichol, supra, 73 Va.L.Rev. at 1008–09.

4.   Are you persuaded by Justice Blackmun's distinction between *McCurry* and *Migra* in footnote 7 of his majority opinion? Why should it make a difference whether the plaintiff in federal court had been a plaintiff, rather than a defendant, in the earlier state court proceeding? In *San Remo Hotel v. City and County of San Francisco*, 545 U.S. 323 (2005), the Court confirmed that it is irrelevant whether the plaintiff chose the state forum or was forced into it. In *San Remo Hotel*, the Court of Appeals found plaintiffs' takings claims unripe because plaintiffs had not tried to obtain compensation for the alleged taking through the state court system. Accordingly, the plaintiffs took their claim to state court. The state supreme court, analyzing the takings question under both state and federal law, held that there had been no unconstitutional taking. Returning to federal court, plaintiffs argued for an exception to § 1738 on the ground that the Supreme Court's own ripeness doctrines *required* them to litigate first in state court. The Court rejected the argument, holding that there is no "right to vindicate * * * federal claims in a federal forum," and noting that without congressional authorization, the Court has no power to create an exception to § 1738. Id. at 325.

5.   Recall that where a federal court abstains in order to allow a state court to interpret ambiguous state laws, the plaintiff (who initiated both the original suit in federal court and the later state suit) is permitted to return to federal court for resolution of any remaining federal questions, under England v. Louisiana State Board of Medical Examiners, 375 U.S. 411 (1964) [supra p. 473]. If the state court in this situation has also reached the federal questions, should its decision be given preclusive effect when the plaintiff returns to federal court? Is that situation distinguishable from *Migra* or *San Remo Hotel*? See Friedman, *Under the Law of Federal Jurisdiction: Allocating Cases Between Federal and State Courts*, 104 Colum.L.Rev. 1211 (2004).

6.   Is Justice White's suggestion in his concurrence in *Migra* consistent with section 1738? With the majority opinions in *Migra* and *McCurry*? In Marrese v. American Academy of Orthopaedic Surgeons, 470 U.S. 373 (1985), a majority of the Court explicitly rejected the scheme proposed by Justice White in *Migra*: section 1738, the Court said, does not allow "a

federal court to give a state court judgment greater preclusive effect than the state courts themselves would give to it." Id. at 383.

7.   In Kremer v. Chemical Construction Corp., 456 U.S. 461 (1982), the Supreme Court held that Title VII of the 1964 Civil Rights Act (prohibiting discrimination in employment) did not create an exception to section 1738. The Court reasoned that "[n]othing in the legislative history of the 1964 Act suggests that Congress considered it necessary or desirable to provide an absolute right to relitigate in federal court an issue resolved by a state court." Id. at 473. Thus a plaintiff who litigated his claim of employment discrimination in state court, under state law, was subsequently precluded from bringing a Title VII action in federal court.

8.   On the issue of the preclusive effect of state court judgments in section 1983 actions, see generally Lilly, *The Symmetry of Preclusion*, 54 Ohio St.L.J. 289 (1993); Moore, *Justice Blackmun and Preclusion in the State–Federal Context*, 97 Dickinson L.Rev. 465 (1993); *Symposium: Preclusion in a Federal System*, 70 Cornell L.Rev. 599 (1985); Note, *The Preclusive Effect of State Judgments on Subsequent 1983 Actions*, 78 Colum.L.Rev. 610 (1978); Averitt, *Federal Section 1983 Actions After State Court Judgment*, 44 U.Colo.L.Rev. 191 (1972). See also Degnan, *Federalized Res Judicata*, 85 Yale L.J. 741 (1976).

9.   **Preclusive Effect of Prior Federal Court Judgments**. The question of the preclusive effect of a prior *federal* court judgment also raises choice of law questions. It is settled that when the initial judgment was issued by a federal court sitting in federal question jurisdiction, federal common law governs any subsequent court's resolution of preclusion questions. See, e.g., Deposit Bank v. Frankfort, 191 U.S. 499 (1903). What law should govern preclusion questions if the federal court that issued the judgment was sitting in diversity jurisdiction? In Semtek International, Inc. v. Lockheed Martin Corp., 531 U.S. 497 (2001), the Court resolved a split among lower courts on this issue. After concluding that the case was not governed by any Federal Rule of Civil Procedure, the Court discussed Dupasseur v. Rochereau, 88 U.S. (21 Wall.) 130 (1874), in which the Court held that "the res judicata effect of a federal diversity judgment 'is such as would belong to judgments of the State courts rendered under similar circumstances:' "

> The reasoning of [the *Deposit Bank*] line of cases suggests, moreover, that even when States are allowed to give federal judgments (notably, judgments in diversity cases) no more than the effect accorded to state judgments, that disposition is by direction of *this* Court, which has the last word on the claim preclusive effect of *all* federal judgments. * * * In other words, in *Dupasseur* the State was allowed (indeed, required) to give a federal diversity judgment no more effect than it would accord one of its own judgments only because reference to state law was *the federal rule that this Court deemed appropriate*. In short, federal common law governs the claim-preclusive effect of a dismissal by a federal court sitting in diversity.
>
> It is left to us, then, to determine the appropriate federal rule. And despite the sea change that has occurred in the background law since *DuPasseur* was decided—not only repeal of the Conformity Act but also

the watershed decision of this Court in *Erie*—we think the result decreed by *DuPasseur* continues to be correct for diversity cases. * * * This is, it seems to us, a classic case for adopting, as the federally prescribed rule of decision, the law that would be applied by state courts in the State in which the federal diversity court sits. As we have alluded to above, any other rule would produce the sort of "forum-shopping . . . and . . . inequitable administration of the laws" that *Erie* seeks to avoid. * * *

This federal reference to state law will not obtain, of course, in situations in which the state law is incompatible with federal interests.

Is *Semtek* just an application of *Erie*, based on a conclusion that preclusion law must be treated as substantive rather than procedural? All previous cases in the *Erie* line, however, explicitly discussed the distinction between substance and procedure, and also defined the question as whether state law should *displace* federal common law. The *Semtek* Court seems instead to focus on determining the appropriate content of the governing federal common law rule. Moreover, *Semtek* governs both federal and state court consideration of the preclusive effect of a prior federal judgment, complicating the question (see Dice v. Akron, Canton & Youngstown Railroad Co., supra p. 296). But if *Semtek* is not based on *Erie*, why should the governing rule vary from state to state? What might the Court mean by incompatibility with federal interests? For a critique of *Semtek*, see Woolley, *The Sources of Federal Preclusion Law after* Semtek, 72 U.Cin.L.Rev. 527 (2003).

MATSUSHITA ELECTRIC INDUSTRIAL CO., LTD. v. EPSTEIN

Supreme Court of the United States, 1996.
516 U.S. 367.

JUSTICE THOMAS delivered the opinion of the Court.

This case presents the question whether a federal court may withhold full faith and credit from a state-court judgment approving a class-action settlement simply because the settlement releases claims within the exclusive jurisdiction of the federal courts. The answer is no. Absent a partial repeal of the Full Faith and Credit Act, 28 U.S.C. § 1738, by another federal statute, a federal court must give the judgment the same effect that it would have in the courts of the State in which it was rendered.

I

In 1990, petitioner Matsushita Electric Industrial Co. made a tender offer for the common stock of MCA, Inc., a Delaware corporation. The tender offer not only resulted in Matsushita's acquisition of MCA, but also precipitated two lawsuits on behalf of the holders of MCA's common stock. First, a class action was filed in the Delaware Court of Chancery against MCA and its directors for breach of fiduciary duty in failing to maximize shareholder value. The complaint was later amended to state additional claims against MCA's directors for, *inter alia*, waste of corporate assets by exposing MCA to liability under the federal securities laws. In addition, Matsushita was added as a defendant and was accused of conspiring with MCA's directors to violate Delaware law. The Delaware suit was based purely on state-law claims.

While the state class action was pending, the instant suit was filed in Federal District Court in California. The complaint named Matsushita as a defendant and alleged that Matsushita's tender offer violated Securities Exchange Commission (SEC) Rules 10b–3 and 14d–10. These Rules were created by the SEC pursuant to the 1968 Williams Act Amendments to the Securities Exchange Act of 1934 (Exchange Act), 48 Stat. 881, as amended, 15 U.S.C. § 78a *et seq.* Section 27 of the Exchange Act confers exclusive jurisdiction upon the federal courts for suits brought to enforce the Act or rules and regulations promulgated thereunder. See 15 U.S.C. § 78aa. The District Court declined to certify the class, entered summary judgment for Matsushita, and dismissed the case. The plaintiffs appealed to the Court of Appeals for the Ninth Circuit.

After the federal plaintiffs filed their notice of appeal but before the Ninth Circuit handed down a decision, the parties to the Delaware suit negotiated a settlement.[2] In exchange for a global release of all claims arising out of the Matsushita–MCA acquisition, the defendants would deposit $2 million into a settlement fund to be distributed *pro rata* to the members of the class. As required by Delaware Chancery Rule 23, which is modeled on Federal Rule of Civil Procedure 23, the Chancery Court certified the class for purposes of settlement and approved a notice of the proposed settlement. The notice informed the class members of their right to request exclusion from the settlement class and to appear and present argument at a scheduled hearing to determine the fairness of the settlement. In particular, the notice stated that "[b]y filing a valid Request for Exclusion, a member of the Settlement Class will not be precluded by the Settlement from individually seeking to pursue the claims alleged in the ... California Federal Actions, ... or any other claim relating to the events at issue in the Delaware Actions." Two such notices were mailed to the class members and the notice was also published in the national edition of the Wall Street Journal. The Chancery Court then held a hearing. After argument from several objectors, the Court found the class representation adequate and the settlement fair.

The order and final judgment of the Chancery Court incorporated the terms of the settlement agreement, providing:

> "All claims, rights and causes of action (state or federal, including but not limited to claims arising under the federal securities law, any rules or regulations promulgated thereunder, or otherwise), whether known or unknown that are, could have been or might in the future be asserted by any of the plaintiffs or any member of the

---

2. A previous settlement was rejected by the Court of Chancery as unfair to the class. See In re MCA, Inc. Shareholders Litigation, 598 A.2d 687 (1991).

Settlement Class *(other than those who have validly requested exclusion therefrom)*, ... in connection with or that arise now or hereafter out of the Merger Agreement, the Tender Offer, the Distribution Agreement, the Capital Contribution Agreement, the employee compensation arrangements, the Tender Agreements, the Initial Proposed Settlement, this Settlement ... *and including without limitation the claims asserted in the California Federal Actions* ... are hereby compromised, settled, released and discharged with prejudice by virtue of the proceedings herein and this Order and Final Judgment." (emphasis added).

The judgment also stated that the notice met all the requirements of due process. The Delaware Supreme Court affirmed.

Respondents were members of both the state and federal plaintiff classes. Following issuance of the notice of proposed settlement of the Delaware litigation, respondents neither opted out of the settlement class nor appeared at the hearing to contest the settlement or the representation of the class. On appeal in the Ninth Circuit, petitioner Matsushita invoked the Delaware judgment as a bar to further prosecution of that action under the Full Faith and Credit Act, 28 U.S.C. § 1738.

The Ninth Circuit rejected petitioner's argument, ruling that § 1738 did not apply. Instead, the Court of Appeals fashioned a test under which the preclusive force of a state court settlement judgment is limited to those claims that "could ... have been extinguished by the issue preclusive effect of an adjudication of the state claims." The lower courts have taken varying approaches to determining the preclusive effect of a state court judgment, entered in a class or derivative action, that provides for the release of exclusively federal claims. We granted certiorari to clarify this important area of federal law.

II

The Full Faith and Credit Act mandates that the "judicial proceedings" of any State "shall have the same full faith and credit in every court within the United States ... as they have by law or usage in the courts of such State ... from which they are taken." 28 U.S.C. § 1738. The Act thus directs all courts to treat a state court judgment with the same respect that it would receive in the courts of the rendering state. Federal courts may not "employ their own rules ... in determining the effect of state judgments," but must "accept the rules chosen by the State from which the judgment is taken." Kremer v. Chemical Constr. Corp., 456 U.S. 461, 481–482 (1982). Because the Court of Appeals failed to follow the dictates of the Act, we reverse.

A

The state court judgment in this case differs in two respects from the judgments that we have previously considered in our cases under the Full Faith and Credit Act. As respondents and the Court of Appeals stressed, the judgment was the product of a class action and incorporated a settlement agreement releasing claims within the exclusive jurisdiction of the federal courts. Though respondents urge "the irrelevance of section 1738 to this litigation," we do not think that either of these features exempts the judgment from the operation of § 1738.

That the judgment at issue is the result of a class action, rather than a suit brought by an individual, does not undermine the initial applicability of § 1738. The judgment of a state court in a class action is plainly the product of a "judicial proceeding" within the meaning of § 1738. Therefore, a judgment entered in a class action, like any other judgment entered in a state judicial proceeding, is presumptively entitled to full faith and credit under the express terms of the Act.

Further, § 1738 is not irrelevant simply because the judgment in question might work to bar the litigation of exclusively federal claims. Our decision in Marrese v. American Academy of Orthopaedic Surgeons, 470 U.S. 373 (1985), made clear that where § 1738 is raised as a defense in a subsequent suit, the fact that an allegedly precluded "claim is within the exclusive jurisdiction of the federal courts *does not necessarily make § 1738 inapplicable.*" Id., at 380 (emphasis added). In so holding, we relied primarily on Kremer v. Chemical Constr. Corp., supra, which held, without deciding whether Title VII claims are exclusively federal, that state court proceedings may be issue preclusive in Title VII suits in federal court. *Kremer,* we said, "implies that absent an exception to § 1738, state law determines at least the ... preclusive effect of a prior state judgment in a subsequent action involving a claim within the exclusive jurisdiction of the federal courts." *Marrese,* 470 U.S., at 381. Accordingly, we decided that "a state court judgment may in some circumstances have preclusive effect in a subsequent action within the exclusive jurisdiction of the federal courts." Id., at 380.

In *Marrese,* we discussed Nash County Board of Education v. Biltmore Co., 640 F.2d 484 (C.A.4), cert. denied, 454 U.S. 878 (1981), a case that concerned a state court settlement judgment. In *Nash,* the question was whether the judgment, which approved the settlement of state antitrust claims, prevented the litigation of exclusively federal antitrust claims. See 470 U.S., at 382, n. 2. We suggested that the approach outlined in *Marrese* would also apply in cases like *Nash* that involve judgments upon settlement: that is, § 1738 would control at the outset. See ibid. In accord with these precedents, we conclude that § 1738 is generally applicable in cases in which the state court judgment at issue incorporates a class action settlement releasing claims solely within the jurisdiction of the federal courts.

B

Marrese provides the analytical framework for deciding whether the Delaware court's judgment precludes this exclusively federal action. When faced with a state court judgment relating to an exclusively federal claim, a federal court must first look to the law of the rendering State to ascertain the effect of the judgment. See id., at 381–382. If state law indicates that the particular claim or issue would be barred from litigation in a court of that state, then the federal court must next decide whether, "as an exception to § 1738," it "should refuse to give preclusive effect to [the] state court judgment." Id., at 383. See also Migra v. Warren City School Dist. Bd. of Ed., 465 U.S. 75, 80 (1984)("[I]n the absence of federal law modifying the operation of § 1738, the preclusive effect in federal court of [a] state-court judgment is determined by [state] law").

1

We observed in *Marrese* that the inquiry into state law would not always yield a direct answer. Usually, "a state court will not have occasion to address the specific question whether a state judgment has issue or claim preclusive effect in a later action that can be brought only in federal court." 470 U.S., at 381–382. * * * Here, in addition to providing rules regarding the preclusive force of class-action settlement judgments in subsequent suits in state court, the Delaware courts have also spoken to the particular effect of such judgments in federal court.

Delaware has traditionally treated the impact of settlement judgments on subsequent litigation in state court as a question of claim preclusion. * * *

In Nottingham [Partners v. Dana, 564 A.2d 1089 (1989)], a class action, the Delaware Supreme Court approved a settlement that released claims then pending in federal court. In approving that settlement, the *Nottingham* Court appears to have eliminated the * * * requirement that the claims could have been raised in the suit that produced the settlement, at least with respect to class actions:

> " '[I]n order to achieve a comprehensive settlement that would prevent relitigation of settled questions at the core of a class action, a court may permit the release of a claim based on the identical factual predicate as that underlying the claims in the settled class action even though the claim was not presented and might not have been presentable in the class action.' " 564 A.2d, at 1106.

These cases indicate that even if, as here, a claim could not have been raised in the court that rendered the settlement judgment in a class action, a Delaware court would still find that the judgment bars subsequent pursuit of the claim.

The Delaware Supreme Court has further manifested its understanding that when the Court of Chancery approves a global release of claims, its settlement judgment should preclude on-going or future federal court litigation of any released claims. In *Nottingham*, the Court stated that "[t]he validity of executing a general release in conjunction with the termination of litigation has long been recognized by the Delaware courts. More specifically, the Court of Chancery has a history of approving settlements that have implicitly or explicitly included a general release, which would also release federal claims." 564 A.2d, at

1105 (citation omitted). Though the Delaware Supreme Court correctly recognized in *Nottingham* that it lacked actual authority to order the dismissal of any case pending in federal court, it asserted that state-court approval of the settlement would have the collateral effect of preventing class members from prosecuting their claims in federal court. Perhaps the clearest statement of the Delaware Chancery Court's view on this matter was articulated in the suit preceding this one: "When a state court settlement of a class action releases all claims which arise out of the challenged transaction and is determined to be fair and to have met all due process requirements, the class members are bound by the release or the doctrine of issue preclusion. Class members cannot subsequently relitigate the claims barred by the settlement in a federal court." In re MCA, Inc. Shareholders Litigation, 598 A.2d 687, 691 (1991).[4] We are aware of no Delaware case that suggests otherwise.

Given these statements of Delaware law, we think that a Delaware court would afford preclusive effect to the settlement judgment in this case, notwithstanding the fact that respondents could not have pressed their Exchange Act claims in the Court of Chancery. The claims are clearly within the scope of the release in the judgment, since the judgment specifically refers to this lawsuit. * * * Respondents do not deny that, as shareholders of MCA's common stock, they were part of the plaintiff class and that they never opted out; they are bound, then, by the judgment.

2

Because it appears that the settlement judgment would be res judicata under Delaware law, we proceed to the second step of the *Marrese* analysis and ask whether § 27 of the Exchange Act, which confers exclusive jurisdiction upon the federal courts for suits arising under the Act, partially repealed § 1738. Section 27 contains no express language regarding its relationship with § 1738 or the preclusive effect of related state court proceedings. Thus, any modification of § 1738 by § 27 must be implied. In deciding whether § 27 impliedly created an exception to § 1738, the "general question is whether the concerns underlying a particular grant of exclusive jurisdiction justify a finding of an implied partial repeal of § 1738." *Marrese*, 470 U.S., at 386. "Resolution of this question will depend on the particular federal statute as well as the nature of the claim or issue involved in the subsequent federal action.... [T]he primary consideration must be the intent of Congress." Ibid.

As a historical matter, we have seldom, if ever, held that a federal statute impliedly repealed § 1738. See Parsons Steel, Inc. v. First Ala-

---

4. In fact, the Chancery Court rejected the first settlement, which contained no opt-out provision, as unfair to the class precisely because it believed that the settlement would preclude the class from pursuing their exclusively federal claims in federal court. See In re MCA Inc. Shareholders Litigation, 598 A.2d 687, 692 (1991)("[I]f this Court provides for the release of all the claims arising out of the challenged transaction, the claims which the Objectors have asserted in the federal suit will likely be forever barred").

bama Bank, 474 U.S. 518, 523–524 (1986)(Anti–Injunction Act does not limit § 1738); Migra v. Warren City School Dist. Bd. of Ed., 465 U.S. 75, 83–85 (1984)(§ 1983 does not limit claim preclusion under § 1738); Kremer v. Chemical Constr. Corp., 456 U.S. 461, 468–476 (1982)(Title VII of the Civil Rights Act of 1964 does not limit § 1738); Allen v. McCurry, 449 U.S. 90, 96–105 (1980)(§ 1983 does not limit issue preclusion under § 1738). But cf. Brown v. Felsen, 442 U.S. 127, 138–139 (1979)(declining to give claim preclusive effect to prior state court debt collection proceeding in federal bankruptcy suit, without discussing § 1738, state law or implied repeals). The rarity with which we have discovered implied repeals is due to the relatively stringent standard for such findings, namely, that there be an " 'irreconcilable conflict' " between the two federal statutes at issue. Kremer v. Chemical Constr. Corp., *supra*, at 468 (quoting Radzanower v. Touche Ross & Co., 426 U.S. 148, 154 (1976)).

Section 27 provides that "[t]he district courts of the United States ... shall have exclusive jurisdiction ... of all suits in equity and actions at law brought to enforce any liability or duty created by this chapter or the rules and regulations thereunder." 15 U.S.C. § 78aa. There is no suggestion in § 27 that Congress meant for plaintiffs with Exchange Act claims to have more than one day in court to challenge the legality of a securities transaction. Though the statute plainly mandates that suits alleging violations of the Exchange Act may be maintained only in federal court, nothing in the language of § 27 "remotely expresses any congressional intent to contravene the common-law rules of preclusion or to repeal the express statutory requirements of ... 28 U.S.C. § 1738." Allen v. McCurry, supra, at 97–98.

Nor does § 27 evince any intent to prevent litigants in state court— whether suing as individuals or as part of a class—from voluntarily releasing Exchange Act claims in judicially approved settlements. While § 27 prohibits state courts from adjudicating claims arising under the Exchange Act, it does not prohibit state courts from approving the release of Exchange Act claims in the settlement of suits over which they have properly exercised jurisdiction, *i.e.*, suits arising under state law or under federal law for which there is concurrent jurisdiction. In this case, for example, the Delaware action was not "brought to enforce" any rights or obligations under the Act. The Delaware court asserted judicial power over a complaint asserting purely state law causes of action and, after the parties agreed to settle, certified the class and approved the settlement pursuant to the requirements of Delaware Rule of Chancery 23 and the Due Process Clause. Thus, the Delaware court never trespassed upon the exclusive territory of the federal courts, but merely approved the settlement of a common-law suit pursuant to state and nonexclusive federal law. While it is true that the state court assessed the general worth of the federal claims in determining the fairness of the settlement, such assessment does not amount to a judgment on the merits of the claims. The Delaware court never purported to resolve the merits of the Exchange Act claims in the course of appraising the settlement; indeed, it expressly disavowed that purpose.

The legislative history of the Exchange Act elucidates no specific purpose on the part of Congress in enacting § 27. We may presume, however, that Congress intended § 27 to serve at least the general purposes underlying most grants of exclusive jurisdiction: "to achieve greater uniformity of construction and more effective and expert application of that law." When a state court upholds a settlement that releases claims under the Exchange Act, it threatens neither of these policies. There is no danger that state court judges who are not fully expert in federal securities law will say definitively what the Exchange Act means and enforce legal liabilities and duties thereunder. And the uniform construction of the Act is unaffected by a state court's approval of a proposed settlement because the state court does not adjudicate the Exchange Act claims but only evaluates the overall fairness of the settlement, generally by applying its own business judgment to the facts of the case.

Furthermore, other provisions of the Exchange Act suggest that Congress did not intend to create an exception to § 1738 for suits alleging violations of the Act. Congress plainly contemplated the possibility of dual litigation in state and federal courts relating to securities transactions. See 15 U.S.C. § 78bb(a) (preserving "all other rights and remedies that may exist at law or in equity"). And all that Congress chose to say about the consequences of such litigation is that plaintiffs ought not obtain double recovery. See ibid. Congress said nothing to modify the background rule that where a state-court judgment precedes that of a federal court, the federal court must give full faith and credit to the state court judgment.

Finally, precedent supports the conclusion that the concerns underlying the grant of exclusive jurisdiction in § 27 are not undermined by state-court approval of settlements releasing Exchange Act claims. We have held that state court proceedings may, in various ways, subsequently affect the litigation of exclusively federal claims without running afoul of the federal jurisdictional grant in question. In Becher v. Contoure Laboratories, Inc., 279 U.S. 388 (1929)(cited in *Marrese*, 470 U.S., at 381), we held that state court findings of fact were issue preclusive in federal patent suits. We did so with full recognition that "the logical conclusion from the establishing of [the state law] claim is that Becher's patent is void." 279 U.S., at 391. *Becher* reasoned that although "decrees validating or invalidating patents belong to the Courts of the United States," that "does not give sacrosanctity to facts that may be conclusive upon the question in issue." Ibid. Similarly, while binding legal determinations of rights and liabilities under the Exchange Act are for federal courts only, there is nothing sacred about the approval of settlements of suits arising under state law, even where the parties agree to release exclusively federal claims. See also Brown v. Felsen, 442 U.S., at 139, n. 10 (noting that "[i]f, in the course of adjudicating a state-law question, a state court should determine factual issues using standards identical to those of § 17, then collateral estoppel, in the absence of countervailing statutory policy, would bar relitigation of those issues in the bankruptcy court"); Pratt v. Paris Gaslight & Coke Co., 168 U.S. 255, 258 (1897)(when a state court has jurisdiction of the parties and the subject matter of the complaint, the state court may decide the validity of a patent when that issue is raised as a defense).

We have also held that Exchange Act claims may be resolved by arbitration rather than litigation in federal court. In Shearson/American Express Inc. v. McMahon, 482 U.S. 220 (1987), we found that parties to an arbitration agreement could waive the right to have their Exchange Act claims tried in federal court and agree to arbitrate the claims. Id., at 227–228,. It follows that state court litigants ought also to be able to waive, or "release," the right to litigate Exchange Act claims in a federal forum as part of a settlement agreement. As *Shearson/American Express, Inc.* demonstrates, a statute conferring exclusive federal jurisdiction for a certain class of claims does not necessarily require resolution of those claims in a federal court.

Taken together, these cases stand for the general proposition that even when exclusively federal claims are at stake, there is no "universal right to litigate a federal claim in a federal district court." Allen v. McCurry, 449 U.S., at 105. If class action plaintiffs wish to preserve absolutely their right to litigate exclusively federal claims in federal court, they should either opt out of the settlement class or object to the release of any exclusively federal claims. In fact, some of the plaintiffs in the Delaware class action requested exclusion from the settlement class. They are now proceeding in federal court with their federal claims, unimpeded by the Delaware judgment.

In the end, §§ 27 and 1738 "do not pose an either-or proposition." Connecticut Nat. Bank v. Germain, 503 U.S. 249, 253 (1992). They can be reconciled by reading § 1738 to mandate full faith and credit of state court judgments incorporating global settlements, provided the rendering court had jurisdiction over the underlying suit itself, and by reading § 27 to prohibit state courts from exercising jurisdiction over suits arising under the Exchange Act. Congress' intent to provide an exclusive federal forum for adjudication of suits to enforce the Exchange Act is clear enough. But we can find no suggestion in § 27 that Congress meant to override the "principles of comity and repose embodied in § 1738," Kremer v. Chemical Constr. Corp., 456 U.S., at 463, by allowing plaintiffs with Exchange Act claims to release those claims in state court and then litigate them in federal court. We conclude that the Delaware courts would give the settlement judgment preclusive effect in a subsequent proceeding and, further, that § 27 did not effect a partial repeal of § 1738.

C

* * *

As explained above, the state court in this case clearly possessed jurisdiction over the subject matter of the underlying suit and over the defendants. Only if this were not so—for instance, if the complaint alleged violations of the Exchange Act and the Delaware court rendered a judgment on the merits of those claims—would the exception to § 1738

for lack of subject-matter jurisdiction apply. Where, as here, the rendering court in fact had subject-matter jurisdiction, the subject-matter jurisdiction exception to full faith and credit is simply inapposite. In such a case, the relevance of a federal statute that provides for exclusive federal jurisdiction is not to the state court's possession of jurisdiction *per se*, but to the existence of a partial repeal of § 1738.

* * *

JUSTICE GINSBURG, with whom JUSTICE STEVENS joins, and with whom JUSTICE SOUTER joins as to Part II–B, concurring in part and dissenting in part.

I join the Court's judgment to the extent that it remands the case to the Ninth Circuit. I agree that a remand is in order because the Court of Appeals did not attend to this Court's reading of 28 U.S.C. § 1738 in a controlling decision, *Kremer*. But I would not endeavor, as the Court does, to speak the first word on the content of Delaware preclusion law. Instead, I would follow our standard practice of remitting that issue for decision, in the first instance, by the lower federal courts. See, e.g., *Marrese*.

I write separately to emphasize a point key to the application of § 1738: A state-court judgment generally is not entitled to full faith and credit unless it satisfies the requirements of the Fourteenth Amendment's Due Process Clause. See *Kremer*, 456 U.S., at 482–483. In the class action setting, adequate representation is among the due process ingredients that must be supplied if the judgment is to bind absent class members.

* * *

II

A

Section 1738's full faith and credit instruction, as the Court indicates, requires the forum asked to recognize a judgment first to determine the preclusive effect the judgment would have in the rendering court. See *Kremer*, 456 U.S., at 466; *Marrese*, 470 U.S., at 381. Because the Ninth Circuit did not evaluate the preclusive effect of the Delaware judgment through the lens of that State's preclusion law, I would remand for that determination. See id., at 386–387; *Migra*, 465 U.S. at 87 ("Prudence ... dictates that it is the District Court, in the first instance, not this Court, that should interpret Ohio preclusion law and apply it.").[4]

---

4. In its endeavor to forecast Delaware preclusion law, the Court appears to have blended the "identical factual predicate" test applied by the Delaware Supreme

B

Every State's law on the preclusiveness of judgments is pervasively affected by the supreme law of the land. To be valid in the rendition forum, and entitled to recognition nationally, a state court's judgment must measure up to the requirements of the Fourteenth Amendment's Due Process Clause. *Kremer*, 456 U.S., at 482–483 "A State may not grant preclusive effect in its own courts to a constitutionally infirm judgment, and other state and federal courts are not required to accord full faith and credit to such a judgment." Id., at 482 (footnote omitted).

* * *

In Delaware, the constitutional due process requirement of adequate representation is embodied in Delaware Court of Chancery's Rule 23, a class action rule modeled on its federal counterpart. Delaware requires, as a prerequisite to class certification, that the named plaintiffs "fairly and adequately protect the interests of the class." Del.Ch. Rule 23(a)(4). In Prezant [v. De Angelis, 636 A.2d 915 (1994)] the Delaware Supreme Court considered whether adequate class representation was "a *sine qua non* for approval of a class action settlement," and concluded that it was. *Prezant*, 636 A.2d, at 920, 926. The state high court overturned a judgment and remanded a settlement because the Court of Chancery had failed to make an explicit finding of adequate representation. Id., at 926.

* * *

In the instant case, the Epstein plaintiffs challenge the preclusive effect of the Delaware settlement, arguing that the Vice Chancellor never in fact made the constitutionally required determination of adequate representation. They contend that the state court left unresolved key questions: notably, did the class representatives share substantial common interests with the absent class members, and did counsel in Delaware vigorously press the interests of the class in negotiating the settlement. * * *

Mindful that this is a court of final review and not first view, I do not address the merits of the Epstein plaintiffs' contentions, or Matsushita's counterargument that the issue of adequate representation was resolved by full and fair litigation in the Delaware Court of Chancery. These arguments remain open for airing on remand. I stress, however, the centrality of the procedural due process protection of adequate representation in class action lawsuits, emphatically including those resolved by settlement.

Notes

1. Does it make sense to employ *state* preclusion principles to determine whether a case falling within the exclusive jurisdiction of the federal

Court in Nottingham Partners v. Dana, 564 A.2d 1089, 1106–1107 (1989), with the broader "same transaction" test advanced by Matsushita.

courts is barred by res judicata? Does it make sense *ever* to allow a previous state judgment to bar a subsequent suit within the exclusive jurisdiction of the federal courts? What are the competing considerations? If your answer to either or both of these questions is that state law should not be relevant, what do you do about section 1738? See Burbank, *Afterwords: A Response to Professor Hazard and a Comment on* Marrese, 70 Cornell L.Rev. 659 (1985).

2.   In *Marrese* (discussed in *Matsushita*), the parties disagreed about whether Illinois law mandated preclusion. The Court remanded the case back to the lower courts, suggesting that the "dispute is best resolved in the first instance by the District Court." Marrese v. American Academy of Orthopaedic Surgeons, 470 U.S. 373, 387 (1985). Should the Court have followed the same approach in *Matsushita*? Why do you think it did not do so? For a suggestion that the Supreme Court got Delaware law wrong, see *Supreme Court 1995 Term: Leading Case*, 110 Harv.L.Rev. 295 (1996).

3.   Is there any difference between applying state preclusion law to a judgment after trial, as in *Marrese*, and applying state preclusion law to a judgment embodying a settlement, as in *Matsushita*? Do the plaintiffs' options differ? Consider that in the Seventh Circuit en banc opinion reversed by the Supreme Court in *Marrese*, Judge Posner, speaking for the majority, rejected the contention that res judicata did not bar the federal antitrust suit because the federal antitrust claim could not have been raised in state court: "The plaintiffs could, however, have joined with their other state claims a claim under the Illinois Antitrust Act, and if that Act is materially identical to the Sherman Act their failure to do so bars this suit." 726 F.2d 1150, 1153 (7th Cir.1984). How would such a test apply to the facts of *Matsushita*?

4.   What evidence might convince the Court that Congress intended to override section 1738? In *McCurry*, the Court concluded that Congress did not intend a partial repeal of section 1738 when it enacted section 1983, which creates a new substantive cause of action but does not limit jurisdiction to the federal courts. In *Matsushita*, the Court concluded that Congress did not intend a partial repeal of section 1738 when it enacted the Securities Exchange Act, which not only creates causes of action but also confers exclusive jurisdiction upon the federal courts. Did the Court use the same standards in determining Congressional intent in the two cases? Should it have?

5.   **Preclusive Effect of State Administrative Proceedings.** In University of Tennessee v. Elliott, 478 U.S. 788 (1986), the Court held that unreviewed state administrative proceedings had no preclusive effect on an employee's claims in federal court under Title VII of the Civil Rights Act of 1964, prohibiting employment discrimination. It also held, however, that the state administrative proceedings did have preclusive effect on the employee's claims under the Reconstruction civil rights statutes.

In an opinion by Justice White, the Court initially noted the inapplicability of section 1738: "Although § 1738 is a governing statute with regard to the judgments and records of state courts, because § 1738 antedates the development of administrative agencies it clearly does not represent a congressional determination that the decisions of state administrative agencies should not be given preclusive effect." 478 U.S. at 794. Though the

Court noted that "we have frequently fashioned federal common-law rules of preclusion in the absence of a governing statute," id., it concluded that "Congress did not intend unreviewed state administrative proceedings to have preclusive effect on Title VII claims." Id. at 796.

But while holding that its earlier decisions in *Allen* and *Migra* "are not controlling in this case, where § 1738 does not apply," it noted that "they support the view that Congress, in enacting the Reconstruction civil rights statutes, did not intend to create an exception to general rules of preclusion." Id. at 796–97. Does this conclusion represent a proper interpretation of those earlier decisions? The Court also reasoned "that giving preclusive effect to administrative factfinding serves the value underlying general principles of collateral estoppel: enforcing repose." It added that "[h]aving federal courts give preclusive effect to the factfinding of state administrative tribunals also serves the value of federalism," relying by analogy on the fact "that the Full Faith and Credit Clause compels the States to give preclusive effect to the factfinding of an administrative tribunal in a sister State." Id. at 798.

Justice Stevens, joined by Justices Brennan and Blackmun, dissented from the finding of preclusion for the claims under the Reconstruction civil rights acts:

> Preclusion of claims brought under the post-Civil War Acts does not advance the objectives typically associated with finality or federalism. In the employment setting which concerns us here, precluding civil rights claims based on the Reconstruction statutes fails to conserve the resources of either the litigants or the courts, because complainant's companion Title VII claim will still go to federal court under today's decision. Nor does preclusion show respect for state administrative determinations, because litigants apprised of this decision will presumably forego state administrative determinations for the same reason they currently forego state judicial review of those determinations—to protect their entitlement to a federal forum.

* * *

> * * * Due respect for the intent of the Congress that enacted the Civil Rights Act of 1871, as revealed in the voluminous legislative history of that Act, should preclude the Court from creating a judge-made rule that bars access to the express legislative remedy enacted by Congress. 478 U.S. at 800–02.

The Court relied on *Elliot* in Astoria Federal Savings & Loan Ass'n v. Solimino, 501 U.S. 104 (1991), holding that state administrative proceedings have no preclusive effect in federal suits brought under the Age Discrimination in Employment Act (ADEA), which was modelled on Title VII.

PRECLUSION BEYOND SECTION 1738: THE
ROOKER–FELDMAN DOCTRINE

EXXON MOBIL CORPORATION v. SAUDI BASIC INDUSTRIES CORPORATION

Supreme Court of the United States, 2005
544 U.S. 280

JUSTICE GINSBURG delivered the opinion of the Court.

This case concerns what has come to be known as the *Rooker-Feldman* doctrine, applied by this Court only twice, first in Rooker v. Fidelity Trust Co., 263 U.S. 413, 44 S.Ct. 149 (1923), then, 60 years later, in District of Columbia Court of Appeals v. Feldman, 460 U.S. 462 (1983). Variously interpreted in the lower courts, the doctrine has sometimes been construed to extend far beyond the contours of the *Rooker* and *Feldman* cases, overriding Congress' conferral of federal-court jurisdiction concurrent with jurisdiction exercised by state courts, and superseding the ordinary application of preclusion law pursuant to 28 U.S.C. § 1738. See, e.g., Moccio v. New York State Office of Court Admin., 95 F.3d 195, 199–200 (C.A.2 1996).

Rooker was a suit commenced in Federal District Court to have a judgment of a state court, adverse to the federal court plaintiffs, "declared null and void." 263 U.S., at 414. In *Feldman,* parties unsuccessful in the District of Columbia Court of Appeals (the District's highest court) commenced a federal-court action against the very court that had rejected their applications. Holding the federal suits impermissible, we emphasized that appellate jurisdiction to reverse or modify a state-court judgment is lodged, initially by § 25 of the Judiciary Act of 1789, 1 Stat. 85, and now by 28 U.S.C. § 1257, exclusively in this Court. Federal district courts, we noted, are empowered to exercise original, not appellate, jurisdiction. Plaintiffs in *Rooker* and *Feldman* had litigated and lost in state court. Their federal complaints, we observed, essentially invited federal courts of first instance to review and reverse unfavorable state-court judgments. We declared such suits out of bounds, *i.e.,* properly dismissed for want of subject-matter jurisdiction.

The *Rooker-Feldman* doctrine, we hold today, is confined to cases of the kind from which the doctrine acquired its name: cases brought by state-court losers complaining of injuries caused by state-court judgments rendered before the district court proceedings commenced and inviting district court review and rejection of those judgments. *Rooker-Feldman* does not otherwise override or supplant preclusion doctrine or augment the circumscribed doctrines that allow federal courts to stay or dismiss proceedings in deference to state-court actions.

In the case before us, the Court of Appeals for the Third Circuit misperceived the narrow ground occupied by *Rooker-Feldman*, and consequently erred in ordering the federal action dismissed for lack of subject-matter jurisdiction. We therefore reverse the Third Circuit's judgment.

I

In Rooker v. Fidelity Trust Co., 263 U.S. 413, the parties defeated in state court turned to a Federal District Court for relief. Alleging that the adverse state-court judgment was rendered in contravention of the Constitution, they asked the federal court to declare it "null and void." Id., at 414–415. This Court noted preliminarily that the state court had acted within its jurisdiction. Id., at 415. If the state-court decision was wrong, the Court explained, "that did not make the judgment void, but merely left it open to reversal or modification in an appropriate and timely appellate proceeding." Ibid. Federal district courts, the *Rooker* Court recognized, lacked the requisite appellate authority, for their jurisdiction was "strictly original." Id., at 416. Among federal courts, the *Rooker* Court clarified, Congress had empowered only this Court to exercise appellate authority "to reverse or modify" a state-court judgment. Ibid. Accordingly, the Court affirmed a decree dismissing the suit for lack of jurisdiction. Id., at 415, 417.

Sixty years later, the Court decided District of Columbia Court of Appeals v. Feldman, 460 U.S. 462. The two plaintiffs in that case, Hickey and Feldman, neither of whom had graduated from an accredited law school, petitioned the District of Columbia Court of Appeals to waive a court Rule that required D.C. bar applicants to have graduated from a law school approved by the American Bar Association. After the D.C. court denied their waiver requests, Hickey and Feldman filed suits in the United States District Court for the District of Columbia. Id., at 465–473. The District Court and the Court of Appeals for the District of Columbia Circuit disagreed on the question whether the federal suit could be maintained, and we granted certiorari. Id., at 474–475.

Recalling *Rooker,* this Court's opinion in *Feldman* observed first that the District Court lacked authority to review a final judicial determination of the D.C. high court. "Review of such determinations," the *Feldman* opinion reiterated, "can be obtained only in this Court." 460 U.S., at 476. The "crucial question," the Court next stated, was whether the proceedings in the D.C. court were "judicial in nature." Ibid. Addressing that question, the Court concluded that the D.C. court had acted both judicially and legislatively.

In applying the accreditation Rule to the Hickey and Feldman waiver petitions, this Court determined, the D.C. court had acted judicially. Id., at 479–482. As to that adjudication, *Feldman* held, this Court alone among federal courts had review authority. Hence, "to the extent that Hickey and Feldman sought review in the District Court of the District of Columbia Court of Appeals' denial of their petitions for waiver, the District Court lacked subject-matter jurisdiction over their complaints." Id., at 482. But that determination did not dispose of the entire case, for in promulgating the bar admission rule, this Court said, the D.C. court had acted legislatively, not judicially. Id., at 485–486. "Challenges to the constitutionality of state bar rules," the Court elaborated, "do not necessarily require a United States district court to review a final state-court judgment in a judicial proceeding." Id., at 486. Thus, the Court reasoned, 28 U.S.C. § 1257 did not bar District Court proceedings addressed to the validity of the accreditation Rule itself. *Feldman,* 460 U.S., at 486. The Rule could be contested in federal court, this Court held, so long as plaintiffs did not seek review of the Rule's application in a particular case. Ibid.

The Court endeavored to separate elements of the Hickey and Feldman complaints that failed the jurisdictional threshold from those that survived jurisdictional inspection. Plaintiffs had urged that the District of Columbia Court of Appeals acted arbitrarily in denying the waiver petitions of Hickey and Feldman, given that court's "former policy of granting waivers to graduates of unaccredited law schools." Ibid. That charge, the Court held, could not be pursued, for it was "inextricably intertwined with the District of Columbia Court of Appeals' decisions, in judicial proceedings, to deny [plaintiffs'] petitions." Id., at 486–487.

On the other hand, the Court said, plaintiffs could maintain "claims that the [bar admission] rule is unconstitutional because it creates an irrebuttable presumption that only graduates of accredited law schools are fit to practice law, discriminates against those who have obtained equivalent legal training by other means, and impermissibly delegates the District of Columbia Court of Appeals' power to regulate the bar to the American Bar Association," for those claims "do not require review of a judicial decision in a particular case." Id., at 487. * * *

Since *Feldman,* this Court has never applied *Rooker-Feldman* to dismiss an action for want of jurisdiction. The few decisions that have mentioned *Rooker* and *Feldman* have done so only in passing or to explain why those cases did not dictate dismissal. * * *

II

In 1980, two subsidiaries of petitioner Exxon Mobil Corporation (then the separate companies Exxon Corp. and Mobil Corp.) formed joint ventures with respondent Saudi Basic Industries Corp. (SABIC) to produce polyethylene in Saudi Arabia. Two decades later, the parties began to dispute royalties that SABIC had charged the joint ventures for sublicenses to a polyethylene manufacturing method.

SABIC preemptively sued the two ExxonMobil subsidiaries in Delaware Superior Court in July 2000 seeking a declaratory judgment that the royalty charges were proper under the joint venture agreements. About two weeks later, ExxonMobil and its subsidiaries countersued SABIC in the United States District Court for the District of New Jersey, alleging that SABIC overcharged the joint ventures for the sublicenses. ExxonMobil invoked subject-matter jurisdiction in the New Jersey action under 28 U.S.C. § 1330, which authorizes district courts to adjudicate actions against foreign states.

In January 2002, the ExxonMobil subsidiaries answered SABIC's state-court complaint, asserting as counterclaims the same claims ExxonMobil had made in the federal suit in New Jersey. The state suit went to trial in March 2003, and the jury returned a verdict of over $400 million in favor of the ExxonMobil subsidiaries. SABIC appealed the judgment entered on the verdict to the Delaware Supreme Court.

Before the state-court trial, SABIC moved to dismiss the federal suit, alleging, *inter alia,* immunity under the Foreign Sovereign Immunities Act of 1976, 28 U.S.C. § 1602 *et seq.* * * *. The Federal District Court denied SABIC's motion to dismiss. SABIC took an interlocutory appeal, and the Court of Appeals heard argument in December 2003, over eight months after the state-court jury verdict.

The Court of Appeals, on its own motion, raised the question whether "subject matter jurisdiction over this case fails under the *Rooker-Feldman* doctrine because ExxonMobil's claims have already been litigated in state court." The court did not question the District Court's possession of subject-matter jurisdiction at the outset of the suit, but held that federal jurisdiction terminated when the Delaware Superior Court entered judgment on the jury verdict. The court rejected ExxonMobil's argument that *Rooker-Feldman* could not apply because ExxonMobil filed its federal complaint well before the state-court judgment. The only relevant consideration, the court stated, "is whether the state judgment precedes a federal judgment on the same claims." If *Rooker-Feldman* did not apply to federal actions filed prior to a state-court judgment, the Court of Appeals worried, "we would be encouraging parties to maintain federal actions as 'insurance policies' while their state court claims were pending." Once ExxonMobil's claims had been litigated to a judgment in state court, the Court of Appeals held, *Rooker-Feldman* "preclude[d][the] federal district court from proceeding."

ExxonMobil, at that point prevailing in Delaware, was not seeking to overturn the state-court judgment. Nevertheless, the Court of Appeals hypothesized that, if SABIC won on appeal in Delaware, ExxonMobil would be endeavoring in the federal action to "invalidate" the state-court judgment, "the very situation," the court concluded, "contemplated by *Rooker-Feldman's* 'inextricably intertwined' bar."

We granted certiorari to resolve conflict among the Courts of Appeals over the scope of the *Rooker-Feldman* doctrine. We now reverse the judgment of the Court of Appeals for the Third Circuit.

III

Rooker and *Feldman* exhibit the limited circumstances in which this Court's appellate jurisdiction over state-court judgments, 28 U.S.C. § 1257, precludes a United States district court from exercising subject-matter jurisdiction in an action it would otherwise be empowered to adjudicate under a congressional grant of authority, e.g., § 1330 (suits against foreign states), § 1331 (federal question), and § 1332 (diversity). In both cases, the losing party in state court filed suit in federal court after the state proceedings ended, complaining of an injury caused by the state-court judgment and seeking review and rejection of that judgment. Plaintiffs in both cases, alleging federal-question jurisdiction, called upon the District Court to overturn an injurious state-court judgment. Because § 1257, as long interpreted, vests authority to review a state court's judgment solely in this Court, the District Courts in *Rooker* and *Feldman* lacked subject-matter jurisdiction.

When there is parallel state and federal litigation, *Rooker-Feldman* is not triggered simply by the entry of judgment in state court. This Court has repeatedly held that "the pendency of an action in the state court is no bar to proceedings concerning the same matter in the Federal court having jurisdiction." McClellan v. Carland, 217 U.S. 268, 282 (1910) * * *. Comity or abstention doctrines may, in various circumstances, permit or require the federal court to stay or dismiss the federal action in favor of the state-court litigation. See, e.g., Colorado River Water Conservation Dist. v. United States, 424 U.S. 800 (1976); Younger v. Harris, 401 U.S. 37 (1971); Burford v. Sun Oil Co., 319 U.S. 315 (1943); Railroad Comm'n of Tex. v. Pullman Co., 312 U.S. 496 (1941). But neither *Rooker* nor *Feldman* supports the notion that properly invoked concurrent jurisdiction vanishes if a state court reaches judgment on the same or related question while the case remains *sub judice* in a federal court.

Disposition of the federal action, once the state-court adjudication is complete, would be governed by preclusion law. The Full Faith and Credit Act, 28 U.S.C. § 1738, * * * requires the federal court to "give the same preclusive effect to a state-court judgment as another court of that State would give." Parsons Steel, Inc. v. First Alabama Bank, 474 U.S. 518, 523 (1986); accord Matsushita Elec. Industrial Co. v. Epstein, 516 U.S. 367, 373 (1996); Marrese v. American Academy of Orthopaedic Surgeons, 470 U.S. 373, 380–381 (1985). Preclusion, of course, is not a jurisdictional matter. In parallel litigation, a federal court may be bound to recognize the claim-and issue-preclusive effects of a state-court judgment, but federal jurisdiction over an action does not terminate automatically on the entry of judgment in the state court.

Nor does § 1257 stop a district court from exercising subject-matter jurisdiction simply because a party attempts to litigate in federal court a matter previously litigated in state court. If a federal plaintiff "present[s] some independent claim, albeit one that denies a legal conclusion that a state court has reached in a case to which he was a party . . ., then there is jurisdiction and state law determines whether the defendant prevails under principles of preclusion." GASH Assocs. v. Village of Rosemont, 995 F.2d 726, 728 (C.A.7 1993); accord Noel v. Hall, 341 F.3d 1148, 1163–1164 (C.A.9 2003).

This case surely is not the "paradigm situation in which *Rooker-Feldman* precludes a federal district court from proceeding." ExxonMobil plainly has not repaired to federal court to undo the Delaware judgment in its favor. Rather, it appears ExxonMobil filed suit in Federal District Court (only two weeks after SABIC filed in Delaware and well before any judgment in state court) to protect itself in the event it lost in state court on grounds (such as the state statute of limitations) that might not preclude relief in the federal venue. *Rooker-Feldman* did not prevent the District Court from exercising jurisdiction when ExxonMobil filed the federal action, and it did not emerge to vanquish jurisdiction after ExxonMobil prevailed in the Delaware courts.

* * *

For the reasons stated, the judgment of the Court of Appeals for the Third Circuit is reversed, and the case is remanded for further proceedings consistent with this opinion.

Notes

1. Consider the relationships among the *Rooker-Feldman* doctrine, res judicata, and the abstention doctrine of Younger v. Harris, 401 U.S. 37 (1971) [supra p. 523]. What does *Rooker-Feldman* add to the other doctrines? In other words, under what circumstances—if any—might *Rooker-Feldman alone* bar an exercise of federal review that would otherwise be permitted? You should note, incidentally, that *Rooker-Feldman* does not apply to writs of habeas corpus; the habeas statute explicitly permits lower federal court review of state court judgments. [See Chapter Twelve.]

2. *Exxon Mobil* was widely viewed as significantly narrowing the scope of the *Rooker-Feldman* doctrine as it had been developed by lower courts. See, e.g., Lance v. Dennis, 546 U.S. ___, 126 S.Ct. 1198 (2006) (Stevens, J., dissenting): "Last Term, in Justice Ginsburg's lucid opinion on *Exxon Mobil Corp. v. Saudi Basic Industries Corp.* * * *, the Court finally interred the so-called '*Rooker-Feldman* doctrine.'" Prior to *Exxon Mobil*, lower courts had expanded the doctrine well beyond suits that explicitly seek review of a state-court judgment. Most circuits described *Rooker-Feldman* as barring any suit in which the federal relief would nullify or modify the state judgment, or in which the federal court could not rule for the plaintiff without holding the state court judgment erroneous, or which raised claims "inextricably intertwined" with the state court judgment.

Is the *Rooker-Feldman* doctrine necessary in order to keep parties who are dissatisfied with state proceedings from "jumping ship" and going directly to federal district court rather than continuing in the state system and eventually appealing to the United States Supreme Court? Can *Rooker–Feldman* continue to serve that purpose after *Exxon Mobil*? Consider the following case: A cattle-yard and a landowner enter into an agreement under which the cattle-yard pays the landlord an annual fee in exchange for an easement allowing cattle to travel over a walkway on the landowner's property. The landowner subsequently removes the walkway. The cattle-yard sues in state court for breach of contract. The landowner defends on the ground that the cattle-yard failed to pay the contractual fees, and also counterclaims for the fees. The counterclaim is dismissed because the landowner had previously assigned that portion of the contract to an unrelated third party. After a jury trial, the cattle-yard prevails and is awarded damages. The landowner appeals, with no success. During the pendency of the appeal, the third party reassigns the contract for fees back to the landowner, who brings suit against the cattle-yard in federal court to collect the fees (the parties are diverse and the jurisdictional minimum is satisfied). Should the case be dismissed under § 1738? Under *Younger v. Harris*? Under *Rooker–Feldman* as interpreted by *Exxon Mobil*? If none of those doctrines bars the suit, is that an acceptable result? See Canal Capital Corp. v. Valley Pride Pack, Inc., 169 F.3d 508 (8th Cir.1999).

3.   The Court in *Exxon Mobil* limited *Rooker-Feldman* to cases in which "the losing party in state court filed suit in federal court after the state proceedings ended." Does that mean that there must be a final order? A judgment reviewable by the United States Supreme Court? See Federacion de Maestros de Puerto Rico v. Junta de Relaciones del Trabajo de Puerto Rico, 410 F.3d 17 (2005).

4.   For general scholarly discussion of *Rooker-Feldman* prior to *Exxon Mobil*, see Sherry, *Judicial Federalism in the Trenches: The* Rooker–Feldman *Doctrine in Action*, 74 Notre Dame L.Rev. 1085 (1999); Friedman & Gaylord, Rooker–Feldman, *From the Ground Up*, 74 Notre Dame L.Rev. 1129 (1999); Bandes, *The* Rooker–Feldman *Doctrine: Evaluating Its Jurisdictional Status*, 74 Notre Dame L.Rev. 1175 (1999); Beermann, *Comments on* Rooker–Feldman *or Let State Law Be Our Guide*, 74 Notre Dame L.Rev. 1209 (1999); Thompson, *The* Rooker–Feldman *Doctrine and the Subject Matter Jurisdiction of Federal District Courts*, 42 Rutgers L.Rev. 859 (1990); Beermann, *Government Official Torts and the Takings Clause: Federalism and State Sovereign Immunity*, 68 B.U.L.Rev. 277, 340–42 (1988); Chang, *Rediscovering the* Rooker *Doctrine: Section 1983, Res Judicata and the Federal Courts*, 31 Hastings L.J. 1337 (1980); Currie, *Res Judicata: The Neglected Defense*, 45 U.Chi.L.Rev. 317 (1978).

Chapter 12

HABEAS CORPUS

§ 1. INTRODUCTION

PURPOSES OF THE WRIT OF HABEAS CORPUS

Habeas corpus (Latin for "you have the body") was originally an ancient common law writ designed to test the legality of confinement. The writ is mentioned in both the Magna Carta and the Constitution (Article I, section 9). Today, federal habeas law is governed by a federal statute, 28 U.S.C. §§ 2241–2266 [reprinted in Appendix B], with a significant judicial gloss.

A federal petition for a writ of habeas corpus may be filed by a state or federal prisoner who alleges that he or she is imprisoned illegally. The Supreme Court described the breadth of the writ in Preiser v. Rodriguez, 411 U.S. 475 (1973):

> The original view of a habeas corpus attack upon detention under a judicial order was a limited one. The relevant inquiry was confined to determining simply whether or not the committing court had been possessed of jurisdiction. But, over the years, the writ of habeas corpus evolved as a remedy available to effect discharge from any confinement contrary to the Constitution or fundamental law, even though imposed pursuant to conviction by a court of competent jurisdiction. Thus, whether the petitioner's challenge to his custody is that the statute under which he stands convicted is unconstitutional, * * * that he has been imprisoned prior to trial on account of a defective judgment against him, * * * that he is unlawfully confined in the wrong institution, * * * that he was denied his constitutional rights at trial, * * * that the guilty plea was invalid, * * * that he is being unlawfully detained by the Executive or the military, * * * or that his parole was unlawfully revoked, causing him to be reincarcerated in prison * * *—in each case his grievance is that he is being unlawfully subjected to physical restraint, and in each case habeas corpus has been accepted as the specific instrument to obtain release from such confinement. 411 U.S. at 485–86.

617

Habeas corpus is the only circumstance in which state court judgments can be reviewed by *lower* federal courts. Moreover, in ruling on a habeas petition, the federal court does not give preclusive or res judicata effect to any previous state court judgments. Habeas thus appears to be an exception to the general rule, explored in previous chapters, that federal courts other than the United States Supreme Court are not entitled to pre-empt or second-guess state court rulings. The existence of habeas is therefore something of an anomaly.

Scholars have offered a number of alternative explanations for this apparent anomaly. The explanations fall into three main categories. The largest group of scholars argues that the availability of federal habeas to review state court convictions is a way of ensuring that federal rights can be litigated in federal court. Some of these scholars have suggested that habeas is a substitute for removal jurisdiction in civil cases, or for the increasingly rare discretionary Supreme Court review. See, e.g., L. Yackle, Reclaiming the Federal Courts (1994); Yackle, *The Habeas Hagioscope*, 66 S.Cal.L.Rev. 2331 (1993); Yackle, *Explaining Habeas Corpus*, 60 N.Y.U.L.Rev. 991 (1985); Friedman, Pas De Deux: *The Supreme Court and the Habeas Courts*, 66 S.Cal.L.Rev. 2467 (1993); Liebman, *Apocalypse Next Time? The Anachronistic Attack on Habeas Corpus/Direct Review Parity*, 92 Colum.L.Rev. 1997 (1992). See also Woolhandler, *Demodeling Habeas*, 45 Stan.L.Rev. 575 (1993). If these scholars are correct, can habeas be reconciled with the logic of the doctrine of Younger v. Harris [supra p. 523]?

Professor Paul Bator offered a second justification for the existence of habeas: as an oversight mechanism to ensure that state court proceedings are fair as a whole. Bator, *Finality in Criminal Law and Federal Habeas Corpus for State Prisoners*, 76 Harv.L.Rev. 441 (1963). Finally, Judge Henry Friendly suggested that the purpose of federal habeas is to free the innocent: the writ, Friendly argued, should only be used when the state court reached an incorrect result, not simply when its procedures were flawed. Friendly, *Is Innocence Irrelevant? Collateral Attack on Criminal Judgments*, 38 U.Chi.L.Rev. 142 (1970). Why is lower federal court review necessary to vindicate either of these goals? Wouldn't Supreme Court review suffice?

The debate over the purposes—and thus the appropriate scope—of habeas implicates the question of parity between state and federal courts, discussed in Chapter Four. Will federal court judges—who hold lifetime tenure—be more likely than state judges—who often must stand for re-election—to uphold the constitutional rights of criminal defendants? One commentator concludes that "[i]n criminal cases, enforcing the law may cost [state judges] their jobs. An elected judge who upholds a constitutional right of a person accused of child molestation, murder, or some other crime may be signing his or her own political death warrant." Bright, *Is Fairness Irrelevant? The Evisceration of Federal Habeas Corpus Review and Limits on the Ability of State Courts to Protect Fundamental Rights*, 54 Wash. & Lee L.Rev. 1 (1997); see also Tabak, *Capital Punishment: Is There Any Habeas Left in This Corpus?*,

27 Loy.Chi.L.J. 523 (1996). Various commentators catalogue successful political campaigns against the re-election of judges who have voted to uphold constitutional rights of criminal defendants. Professor Bright describes a campaign against Tennessee supreme court justice Penny White, in which her Republican opponents alleged that she "puts the rights of criminals before the rights of victims." A campaign brochure mailed to voters included the following: "Richard Odom was convicted of repeatedly raping and stabbing to death a 78 year old Memphis woman. However, Penny White felt the crime wasn't heinous enough for the death penalty—so she struck it down." Bright, supra, 54 Wash. & Lee L.Rev. at 11. A former North Carolina supreme court chief justice described his campaign for re-election:

> Some of the campaign debates got really grizzly. My opponents would bring up all the times I had dissented in cases involving the imposition of the death penalty, and I had to come back and demonstrate all the times I had concurred in cases sustaining the death penalty.

Exum, *Politics and the Death Penalty: Can Rational Discourse and Due Process Survive the Perceived Political Pressure?*, 21 Fordham Urb.L.J. 239, 271 (1994). One statistical study of Louisiana state supreme court justices showed that even among justices generally supportive of criminal defendants' rights, constituent preferences exerted an influence on the justices' votes in capital cases. Hall, *Constituent Influence in State Supreme Courts: Conceptual Notes and a Case Study*, 49 J.Pol. 1117 (1987). Is the parity problem more acute in criminal cases? Does that justify habeas review?

Keep all these debates in mind as you read through the cases in this chapter, and consider what doctrinal changes might follow from them. For an overview of these and other rationales for habeas, see Lee, *The Theories of Federal Habeas Corpus*, 72 Wash.U.L.Q. 151 (1994); McCord, *Visions of Habeas*, 1994 B.Y.U.L.Rev. 735; Hoffman & Stuntz, *Habeas After the Revolution*, 1993 Sup.Ct.Rev. 65. For discussions of the historical origins of the writ, see C. Federman, The Body and the State: Habeas Corpus and American Jurisprudence (2006); Forsythe, *The Historical Origins of Broad Federal Habeas Review Reconsidered*, 70 Notre Dame L.Rev. 1079 (1995).

You should also note that despite the controversy generated by the availability of federal habeas review of state convictions, federal courts in fact rarely overturn such convictions on collateral review. One recent study concludes that federal courts grant fewer than one percent of habeas petitions brought by state prisoners. Flango & McKenna, *Federal Habeas Corpus Review of State Court Convictions*, 31 Cal.W.L.Rev. 237, 259 (1995). Moreover, habeas jurisdiction is not a significant burden on the federal courts: only about five percent of the federal district court caseload consists of habeas petitions brought by state prisoners. Lay, *The Writ of Habeas Corpus: A Complex Procedure for a Simple Process*, 77 Minn.L.Rev. 1015, 1043–44 & n.162 (1993).

PROCEDURAL MATTERS

The Custody Requirement. 28 U.S.C. § 2441(c) limits the availability of habeas to petitioners alleging that they are in "custody" in violation of federal law. According to Professor Yackle, "[t]he modern 'custody' requirement has ancient roots, bearing a correlative relation to the function of the writ in the seventeenth century—to secure the release of persons who were wrongfully confined. * * * The 'custody' requirement is, then, no mere artificial prerequisite to a habeas action, designed to restrict access to those most in need of judicial attention. It is part and parcel of what habeas corpus is, what it means, or, at least, what it has been and meant traditionally." Yackle, *Explaining Habeas Corpus*, 60 N.Y.U.L.Rev. 991, 999 (1985). Does the "custody" requirement make sense from the perspective of modern judicial federalism? If we value the availability of a federal forum to adjudicate federal constitutional claims, should it matter whether the penalty imposed by the state court was a fine, rather than imprisonment? Note that in order to meet the "custody" requirement, actual physical incarceration is no longer essential. See Hensley v. Municipal Court, 411 U.S. 345, 349 (1973) (restraints flowing from bail or release on personal recognizance sufficient to constitute "custody"). Also, a prisoner who is serving consecutive sentences "remains 'in custody' under all of his sentences until all are served." Garlotte v. Fordice, 515 U.S. 39, 41 (1995).

The Court has recently addressed the related question of whether prisoners may challenge a sentence that was enhanced as a result of an earlier, allegedly unconstitutional, conviction. The Court held that where the earlier conviction is itself no longer subject to either direct or collateral review, neither state nor federal prisoners may attack the use of the earlier conviction in enhancing the current sentence (unless the earlier conviction was obtained in violation of the Sixth Amendment right to adequate counsel). Daniels v. United States, 532 U.S. 374 (2001) (federal prisoners); Lackawanna County District Attorney v. Coss, 532 U.S. 394 (2001) (state prisoners).

The Unlawfulness Requirement. Section 2241(c) also limits habeas to a few categories of prisoners, including prisoners held pursuant to federal convictions and state prisoners whose custody is "in violation of the Constitution or laws or treaties of the United States." The Supreme Court has interpreted both these provisions to limit statutory claims: neither state nor federal prisoners may raise non-constitutional claims on habeas unless the error alleged is "a fundamental defect which inherently results in a complete miscarriage of justice, [or] an omission inconsistent with the rudimentary demands of fair procedure." Hill v. United States, 368 U.S. 424, 428 (1962) (federal prisoners); Reed v. Farley, 512 U.S. 339 (1994) (applying *Hill* rule to federal habeas petitions brought by state prisoners).

The "unlawfulness" of the custody is also brought into question if an alleged constitutional error at trial might be considered harmless.

The standard for determining harmless error is in some doubt. In Brecht v. Abrahamson, 507 U.S. 619 (1993) the Court held that habeas petitioners must establish that the constitutional error " 'had substantial and injurious effect or influence in determining the jury's verdict.' " Id. at 619, 637 (quoting Kotteakos v. U.S., 328 U.S. 750, 776 (1946)). In so holding, the Court rejected petitioner's argument that claims on collateral review should be subject to the same standard as claims on direct review. The latter standard requires the government to prove that the error was "harmless beyond a reasonable state of doubt." Chapman v. California, 386 U.S. 18 (1967). The Court in *Brecht* justified the distinction between direct and collateral review on several grounds, including the need for finality and the notion that habeas is designed to remedy grievous wrongs. Justice White, joined by Justices Blackmun and Souter, dissented, suggesting that the majority's distinction meant that "the fate of one in state custody turns on * * * whether we choose to review his claims on certiorari." 507 U.S. at 644. Justice O'Connor also dissented, urging the Court to continue applying the *Chapman* standard on collateral review.

Two years later, in O'Neal v. McAninch, 513 U.S. 432 (1995), the Court confronted a claim of constitutional error at trial about which the federal habeas court "is in *grave doubt* about whether or not that error is harmless," that is, "in the judge's mind, the matter is so evenly balanced that he feels himself in virtual equipoise as to the harmlessness of the error." Id. at 435. The Court held that in such circumstances, the error must be deemed to meet the *Brecht* standard of harmfulness. Justice Breyer, who had not been on the Court in 1993, wrote the majority opinion. Rounding out the majority: Justices Souter and O'Connor, who had dissented in *Brecht*, Justice Stevens, who had filed a concurrence in *Brecht* stressing the similarity between the two standards, Justice Ginsburg, who had not been on the Court in 1993, and Justice Kennedy. Justice Thomas wrote a dissenting opinion, joined by Justice Scalia and the Chief Justice. Is *O'Neal* consistent with *Brecht*? For critiques of *Brecht*, see Liebman & Hertz, Brecht v. Abrahamson: *Harmful Error in Habeas Corpus Law*, 84 J.Crim.L. & Criminology 1109 (1994); Gershman, *The Gate is Open But the Door is Locked—Habeas Corpus and Harmless Error*, 51 Wash. & Lee L.Rev. 115 (1994).

Under either *O'Neal* or *Brecht*, how should a habeas court evaluate errors that may be harmless alone but might cumulatively deprive the defendant of a fair trial? See Van Cleave, *When Is an Error Not an "Error"? Habeas Corpus and Cumulative Error Analysis*, 46 Baylor L.Rev. 59 (1994).

Statute of Limitations. Originally, the federal habeas provisions contained no statute of limitations; prisoners were permitted to bring a petition for the writ at any time. In 1996, Congress enacted the Antiterrorism and Effective Death Penalty Act of 1996 (AEDPA), which, among other changes, placed a one-year statute of limitations for the filing of habeas petitions. 28 U.S.C. §§ 2244(d) (state prisoners) and 2255 (federal prisoners). The statute of limitations begins to run when the judgment of conviction becomes final through direct review or the expiration of time for seeking review, 28 U.S.C. § 2244(d)(2); it is tolled during the pendency of "a properly filed application for State post-conviction or other collateral review," 28 U.S.C. § 2244(d)(2).

The statute of limitations provision has created numerous questions, and the Supreme Court has decided a series of cases interpreting the provision. See Day v. McDonough, 547 U.S. ___, 126 S.Ct. 1675 (2006) (federal court has discretion to dismiss petition as untimely, *sua sponte*, even if state does not raise statute of limitations defense in its answer); Evans v. Chavis, 546 U.S. ___, 126 S.Ct. 846 (2006) (if state law would deem notice of appeal in state collateral review proceedings unreasonable and therefore untimely, state collateral review application was not "pending" during that delay); Mayle v. Felix, 545 U.S. 644 (2005); (amended petition does not relate back unless the new claims arise from a "common core of operative facts"; it is not sufficient that the new claims relate to the same conviction as the prior claims); Dodd v. United States, 545 U.S. 353 (2005) (statute of limitations begins to run on date Supreme Court declares a newly available constitutional right, not on date Supreme Court makes it retroactive to cases on collateral review); Pace v. DiGuglielmo, 544 U.S. 408 (2005) (untimely state collateral appeals are not "properly filed"; leaving open whether equitable tolling might apply); Johnson v. United States, 544 U.S. 295 (2005) (for challenge to sentenced enhanced by prior conviction, statute of limitations begins to run on date prisoner receives notice that prior conviction has been vacated, as long as prisoner acted with due diligence in attacking prior conviction); Carey v. Saffold, 536 U.S. 214 (2002) (state collateral review is still "pending" during interval between state lower court judgment and filing of state appeal); Duncan v. Walker, 533 U.S. 167 (2001) (federal habeas petition is not "other collateral review" and does not toll statute of limitations).

Note that AEDPA also made other changes to the habeas statutes. Cases decided before 1996, therefore, might be affected by some of these changes. For overviews of AEDPA, see Yackle, *A Primer on the New Habeas Corpus Statute*, 44 Buff.L.Rev. 381 (1996); Note, *Rewriting the Great Writ: Standards of Review for Habeas Corpus Under the New 28 U.S.C. § 2254*, 110 Harv.L.Rev. 1868 (1997); Blume, *AEDPA: The "Hype" and the "Bite,"* 91 Cornell L.Rev. 259 (2006).

Habeas Corpus and the War on Terrorism. The Supreme Court has decided several important cases interpreting the reach of the writ of habeas corpus to individuals incarcerated by the executive branch as part of the war on terrorism. In two cases, the petitioners—whom the government alleged were enemy combatants in the war on terrorism—were being held indefinitely, with no criminal charges and no opportunity to rebut the government's allegations against them. In the most recent case, the petitioners alleged that their impending trials in front of military commissions violated both federal and international law.

Rasul v. Bush, 542 U.S. 466 (2004), involved foreign nationals captured abroad during hostilities in Afghanistan. The military held them at Guantanamo Naval Base, an American naval base on the island of Cuba. The base is leased from the Cuban government. The lease provides that while "ultimate sovereignty" over the land remains with Cuba, "the United States shall exercise complete jurisdiction and control" over it. The lease will remain in effect permanently unless the United States agrees to abandon the base. The question in *Rasul* was whether, as a matter of statutory construction, the writ of habeas corpus was available to prisoners held on Guantanamo. Six Justices held that it was, analyzing the history of the writ from its common law origins to its modern statutory form to conclude that it reached at least territory within the peacetime control of the United States.

Hamdi v. Rumsfeld, 542 U.S. 507 (2004), involved an American citizen captured by American allies during military activities in Afghanistan. The allies turned him over to the United States military, who first detained him at Guantanamo and then, upon the discovery that he was an American citizen, transferred him to a naval brig in Virginia. The government, contending that he was an "enemy combatant," held him without access to counsel, without giving him any opportunity to rebut his status as an enemy combatant, and without charging him with a crime. Hamdi sought a writ of habeas corpus, demanding access to counsel, an evidentiary hearing, and release from "unlawful" custody. After the Court of Appeals for the Fourth Circuit upheld the detention and its terms, a divided Supreme Court reversed. Four Justices, in a plurality opinion written by Justice O'Connor, concluded that one important purpose of habeas is to test the legality of executive branch detentions. The plurality therefore balanced Hamdi's interest in liberty against the government's military and security needs. It concluded that Hamdi was entitled to counsel and to a hearing before an impartial judicial tribunal, but that the hearing need not comport with all of the ordinary requirements of the Due Process Clause. In particular, in remanding the case ultimately back to the district court, the plurality allowed the district court judge to rely on hearsay evidence by the government, and to adopt a rebuttable presumption that the government's factual assertions were correct, thus shifting the burden of proof to Hamdi. Justices Souter and Ginsburg concurred in the judgment only. These two Justices would have held the detention to be prohibited by federal statutory law, and would not have reached the question of the process that might be due to Hamdi. In order to "give practical effect" to the conclusions of eight Justices, however, they concurred in the decision to vacate and remand for a hearing. Justice Scalia, writing a dissenting opinion for himself and Justice Stevens, would have gone even further, holding the detention of an American citizen, without charging him with a crime, to be unconstitutional. Justice Thomas was the only Justice who voted to uphold the government's actions in their entirety and to affirm the Court of Appeals.

In Hamdan v. Rumsfeld, 548 U.S. ___, 126 S.Ct. 2749 (2006), the Court held that the jurisdictional sections of the Detainee Treatment Act of 2005, 28 U.S.C. § 2241(e) [reprinted in Appendix B], did not apply to cases pending at the time of its enactment. The Court declined to consider whether the Act might have unconstitutionally suspended the writ of habeas corpus.

For further discussion of this emerging area of habeas corpus law, see Chemerinsky, *Ignoring the Rule of Law: The Courts and the Guantanamo Detainees*, 25 T. Jefferson L.Rev. 303 (2003); Priester, *Return of the Great Writ: Judicial Review, Due Process, and the Detention of Alleged Terrorists as Enemy Combatants*, 37 Rutgers L.J. 39 (2005); Morrison, Hamdi's *Habeas Puzzle: Suspension as Authorization?* 91 Cornell L.Rev. 411 (2006); Pfander, *The Limits of Habeas Jurisdiction and the Global War on Terror*, 91 Cornell L.Rev. 497 (2006); Yoo, *Courts at War*, 91 Cornell L.Rev. 573 (2006).

§ 2.   THE EXHAUSTION REQUIREMENT

ROSE v. LUNDY

Supreme Court of the United States, 1982.
455 U.S. 509.

JUSTICE O'CONNOR delivered the opinion of the Court, except as to Part III–C.

In this case we consider whether the exhaustion rule in 28 U.S.C. §§ 2254(b), (c) requires a federal district court to dismiss a petition for a writ of habeas corpus containing any claims that have not been exhausted in the state courts. Because a rule requiring exhaustion of all claims furthers the purposes underlying the habeas statute, we hold that a district court must dismiss such "mixed petitions," leaving the prisoner with the choice of returning to state court to exhaust his claims or of amending or resubmitting the habeas petition to present only exhausted claims to the district court.

I

Following a jury trial, respondent Noah Lundy was convicted on charges of rape and crime against nature, and sentenced to the Tennessee State Penitentiary. After the Tennessee Court of Criminal Appeals affirmed the convictions and the Tennessee Supreme Court denied review, the respondent filed an unsuccessful petition for postconviction relief in the Knox County Criminal Court.

The respondent subsequently filed a petition in federal District Court for a writ of habeas corpus under 28 U.S.C. § 2254, alleging four grounds for relief: (1) that he had been denied the right to confrontation because the trial court limited the defense counsel's questioning of the victim; (2) that he had been denied the right to a fair trial because the prosecuting attorney stated that the respondent had a violent character; (3) that he had been denied the right to a fair trial because the prosecutor improperly remarked in his closing argument that the State's evidence was uncontradicted; and (4) that the trial judge improperly instructed the jury that every witness is presumed to swear the truth. After reviewing the state-court records, however, the District Court concluded that it could not consider claims three and four "in the constitutional framework" because the respondent had not exhausted his state remedies for those grounds. The court nevertheless stated that "in assessing the atmosphere of the cause taken as a whole these items may be referred to collaterally."

Apparently in an effort to assess the "atmosphere" of the trial, the District Court reviewed the state trial transcript and identified 10 instances of prosecutorial misconduct, only 5 of which the respondent had raised before the state courts. In addition, although purportedly not ruling on the respondent's fourth ground for relief—that the state trial judge improperly charged that "every witness is presumed to swear the truth"—the court nonetheless held that the jury instruction, coupled with both the restriction of counsel's cross-examination of the victim and the prosecutor's "personal testimony" on the weight of the State's evidence, violated the respondent's right to a fair trial. In conclusion, the District Court stated:

> "Also, subject to the question of exhaustion of state remedies, where there is added to the trial atmosphere the comment of the Attorney General that the only story presented to the jury was by the state's witnesses there is such mixture of violations that one cannot be separated from and considered independently of the others.
>
> . . .
>
> " . . . Under the charge as given, the limitation of cross examination of the victim, and the flagrant prosecutorial misconduct this court is compelled to find that petitioner did not receive a fair trial, his Sixth Amendment rights were violated and the jury poisoned by the prosecutorial misconduct."

In short, the District Court considered several instances of prosecutorial misconduct never challenged in the state trial or appellate courts, or even raised in the respondent's habeas petition.

The Sixth Circuit affirmed the judgment of the District Court * * *. The court specifically rejected the State's argument that the District Court should have dismissed the petition because it included both exhausted and unexhausted claims.

II

The petitioner urges this Court to apply a "total exhaustion" rule requiring district courts to dismiss every habeas corpus petition that contains both exhausted and unexhausted claims. The petitioner argues at length that such a rule furthers the policy of comity underlying the exhaustion doctrine because it gives the state courts the first opportunity to correct federal constitutional errors and minimizes federal interference and disruption of state judicial proceedings. The petitioner also believes that uniform adherence to a total exhaustion rule reduces the amount of piecemeal habeas litigation.

Under the petitioner's approach, a district court would dismiss a petition containing both exhausted and unexhausted claims, giving the prisoner the choice of returning to state court to litigate his unexhausted claims, or of proceeding with only his exhausted claims in federal court. The petitioner believes that a prisoner would be reluctant to choose the latter route since a district court could, in appropriate circumstances under Habeas Corpus Rule 9(b), dismiss subsequent federal habeas petitions as an abuse of the writ.[6] In other words, if the prisoner amended the petition to delete the unexhausted claims or immediately refiled in federal court a petition alleging only his exhausted claims, he could lose the opportunity to litigate his presently unexhausted claims in federal court. * * *

III

A

The exhaustion doctrine existed long before its codification by Congress in 1948. In Ex parte Royall, 117 U.S. 241, 251 (1886), this Court wrote that as a matter of comity, federal courts should not consider a claim in a habeas corpus petition until after the state courts have had an opportunity to act:

> "The injunction to hear the case summarily, and thereupon 'to dispose of the party as law and justice require' does not deprive the court of discretion as to the time and mode in which it will exert the powers conferred upon it. That discretion should be exercised in the light of the relations existing, under our system of government, between the judicial tribunals of the Union and of the States, and in recognition of the fact that the public good requires that those relations be not disturbed by unnecessary conflict between courts equally bound to guard and protect rights secured by the Constitution."

Subsequent cases refined the principle that state remedies must be exhausted except in unusual circumstances. * * * None of these cases, however, specifically applied the exhaustion doctrine to habeas petitions containing both exhausted and unexhausted claims.

In 1948, Congress codified the exhaustion doctrine in 28 U.S.C. § 2254 * * *. Section 2254,[9] however, does not directly address the

---

6. Rule 9(b) provides that

"[a] second or successive petition may be dismissed if the judge finds that it fails to allege new or different grounds for relief and the prior determination was on the merits or, if new and different grounds are alleged, the judge finds that the failure of the petitioner to assert

those grounds in a prior petition constituted an abuse of the writ."
* * *

9. Section 2254 in part provides:

"(b) An application for a writ of habeas corpus in behalf of a person in custody pursuant to the judgment of a State court shall not be granted unless it appears

problem of mixed petitions. To be sure, the provision states that a remedy is not exhausted if there exists a state procedure to raise "the question presented," but we believe this phrase to be too ambiguous to sustain the conclusion that Congress intended to either permit or prohibit review of mixed petitions. Because the legislative history of § 2254, as well as the pre–1948 cases, contains no reference to the problem of mixed petitions, in all likelihood Congress never thought of the problem. Consequently, we must analyze the policies underlying the statutory provision to determine its proper scope. * * *

B

The exhaustion doctrine is principally designed to protect the state courts' role in the enforcement of federal law and prevent disruption of state judicial proceedings. Under our federal system, the federal and state "courts [are] equally bound to guard and protect rights secured by the Constitution." Ex parte Royall, 117 U.S., at 251. Because "it would be unseemly in our dual system of government for a federal district court to upset a state court conviction without an opportunity to the state courts to correct a constitutional violation," federal courts apply the doctrine of comity, which "teaches that one court should defer action on causes properly within its jurisdiction until the courts of another sovereignty with concurrent powers, and already cognizant of the litigation, have had an opportunity to pass upon the matter." Darr v. Burford, 339 U.S. 200, 204 (1950). See Duckworth v. Serrano, 454 U.S. 1, 3 (1981) (per curiam) (noting that the exhaustion requirement "serves to minimize friction between our federal and state systems of justice by allowing the State an initial opportunity to pass upon and correct alleged violations of prisoners' federal rights").

A rigorously enforced total exhaustion rule will encourage state prisoners to seek full relief first from the state courts, thus giving those courts the first opportunity to review all claims of constitutional error. As the number of prisoners who exhaust all of their federal claims increases, state courts may become increasingly familiar with and hospitable toward federal constitutional issues. Equally as important, federal claims that have been fully exhausted in state courts will more often be accompanied by a complete factual record to aid the federal courts in their review. Cf. 28 U.S.C. § 2254(d) (requiring a federal court reviewing a habeas petition to presume as correct factual findings made by a state court).

The facts of the present case underscore the need for a rule encouraging exhaustion of all federal claims. In his opinion, the District Court Judge wrote that "there is such mixture of violations that one

---

that the applicant has exhausted the remedies available in the courts of the State, or that there is either an absence of available State corrective process or the existence of circumstances rendering such process ineffective to protect the rights of the prisoner.

"(c) An applicant shall not be deemed to have exhausted the remedies available in the courts of the State, within the meaning of this section, if he has the right under the law of the State to raise, by any available procedure, the question presented."

cannot be separated from and considered independently of the others." Because the two unexhausted claims for relief were intertwined with the exhausted ones, the judge apparently considered all of the claims in ruling on the petition. Requiring dismissal of petitions containing both exhausted and unexhausted claims will relieve the district courts of the difficult if not impossible task of deciding when claims are related, and will reduce the temptation to consider unexhausted claims.

In his dissent, Justice Stevens suggests that the District Court properly evaluated the respondent's two exhausted claims "in the context of the entire trial." Unquestionably, however, the District Court erred in considering unexhausted claims, for § 2254(b) expressly requires the prisoner to exhaust "the remedies available in the courts of the State." Moreover, to the extent that exhausted and unexhausted claims are interrelated, the general rule among the Courts of Appeals is to dismiss mixed habeas petitions for exhaustion of all such claims.

Rather than an "adventure in unnecessary lawmaking" our holdings today reflect our interpretation of a federal statute on the basis of its language and legislative history, and consistent with its underlying policies. There is no basis to believe that today's holdings will "complicate and delay" the resolution of habeas petitions (Stevens, J.,) or will serve to "trap the unwary pro se prisoner." (Blackmun, J.) On the contrary, our interpretation of §§ 2254(b), (c) provides a simple and clear instruction to potential litigants: before you bring any claims to federal court, be sure that you first have taken each one to state court. Just as pro se petitioners have managed to use the federal habeas machinery, so too should they be able to master this straightforward exhaustion requirement. Those prisoners who misunderstand this requirement and submit mixed petitions nevertheless are entitled to resubmit a petition with only exhausted claims or to exhaust the remainder of their claims.

Rather than increasing the burden on federal courts, strict enforcement of the exhaustion requirement will encourage habeas petitioners to exhaust all of their claims in state court and to present the federal court with a single habeas petition. To the extent that the exhaustion requirement reduces piecemeal litigation, both the courts and the prisoners should benefit, for as a result the district court will be more likely to review all of the prisoner's claims in a single proceeding, thus providing for a more focused and thorough review.

C

The prisoner's principal interest, of course, is in obtaining speedy federal relief on his claims. A total exhaustion rule will not impair that interest since he can always amend the petition to delete the unexhausted claims, rather than returning to state court to exhaust all of his claims. By invoking this procedure, however, the prisoner would risk forfeiting consideration of his unexhausted claims in federal court. Under 28 U.S.C. § 2254 Rule 9(b), a district court may dismiss subsequent petitions if it finds that "the failure of the petitioner to assert those [new] grounds in a prior petition constituted an abuse of the writ." The Advisory Committee to the Rules notes that Rule 9(b) incorporates the judge-made principle governing the abuse of the writ set forth in Sanders v. United States, 373 U.S. 1, 18 (1963), where this Court stated:

> "[I]f a prisoner deliberately withholds one of two grounds for federal collateral relief at the time of filing his first application, in the hope of being granted two hearings rather than one or for some other such reason, he may be deemed to have waived his right to a hearing on a second application presenting the withheld ground. The same may be true if, as in *Wong Doo*, the prisoner deliberately abandons one of his grounds at the first hearing. Nothing in the traditions of habeas corpus requires the federal courts to tolerate needless piecemeal litigation, or to entertain collateral proceedings whose only purpose is to vex, harass, or delay."

Thus a prisoner who decides to proceed only with his exhausted claims and deliberately sets aside his unexhausted claims risks dismissal of subsequent federal petitions.

IV

In sum, because a total exhaustion rule promotes comity and does not unreasonably impair the prisoner's right to relief, we hold that a district court must dismiss habeas petitions containing both unexhausted and exhausted claims.

JUSTICE BLACKMUN, concurring in the judgment.

* * *

The Court correctly observes, that neither the language nor the legislative history of the exhaustion provisions of sec. 2254(b) and (c) mandates dismissal of a habeas petition containing both exhausted and unexhausted claims. Nor does precedent dictate the result here. * * *

* * *

In some respects, the Court's ruling appears more destructive than solicitous of federal-state comity. Remitting a habeas petitioner to state court to exhaust a patently frivolous ground for relief hardly demonstrates respect for the state courts. The state judiciary's time and resources are then spent rejecting the obviously meritless unexhausted claim, which doubtless will receive little or no attention in the subsequent federal proceeding that focuses on the substantial exhausted claim. I can "conceive of no reason why the State would wish to burden its judicial calendar with a narrow issue the resolution of which is predetermined by established federal principals." * * *

* * *

The Court's interest in efficient administration of the federal courts * * * does not require dismissal of mixed habeas petitions. In fact, the concern militates against the approach taken by the Court today. In order to comply with the Court's ruling, a federal court will now have to review the record in a sec. 2254 proceeding at least summarily in order to determine whether all claims have been exhausted. In many cases a decision on the merits will involve only negligible additional effort. And in other cases the court may not realize that one of a number of claims is unexhausted until after substantial work has been done. If the district court must nevertheless dismiss the entire petition until all grounds have been exhausted, the prisoner will likely return to federal court eventually, thereby necessitating duplicative examination of the record and consideration of the exhausted claims—perhaps by another judge. Moreover, when the sec. 2254 petition does find its way back to federal court, the record on the exhausted grounds for relief may well be stale and resolution of the merits more difficult.

* * *

I therefore would remand the case, directing that the courts below dismiss respondent's unexhausted claims and examine those that have been properly presented to the state courts in order to determine whether they are interrelated with the unexhausted grounds and, if not, whether they warrant collateral relief.

* * *

JUSTICE BRENNAN, with whom JUSTICE MARSHALL joins, concurring in part and dissenting in part.

* * *

The plurality's conclusion simply distorts the meaning of [Sanders v. United States, 373 U.S. 1 (1963)]. Sanders was plainly concerned with "a prisoner *deliberately* withholding one of two grounds" for relief "in hope of being granted two hearings rather than one or for some other such reason." Sanders also notes that waiver might be inferred where "the prisoner *deliberately abandons* one of his grounds at the first hearing." Finally, Sanders states that dismissal is appropriate either when a court is faced with "*needless* piecemeal litigation" or with "collateral proceedings *whose only purpose is to vex, harass, or delay.*" Thus Sanders made it crystal clear that dismissal for "abuse of the writ" is *only* appropriate when a prisoner was free to include all of his claims in his first petition, but *knowingly* and *deliberately* chose not to do so in order to get more than "one bite at the apple." The plurality's opinion obviously would allow dismissal in a much broader class of cases than Sanders permits.

* * *

I conclude that when a prisoner's original, "mixed" habeas petition is dismissed without any examination of its claims on the merits, and when the prisoner later brings a second petition based on the previously unexhausted claims that had earlier been refused a hearing, then the remedy of dismissal for "abuse of the writ" cannot be employed against a second petition, absent unusual factual circumstances truly suggesting abuse. * * *

[The opinions of JUSTICE WHITE and JUSTICE STEVENS are omitted.]

Notes

1. What is the rationale for the judicial exhaustion requirement in habeas cases? Is it wise? To what extent does the rationale support the majority's decision in *Rose*? For general discussions of the exhaustion requirement, see Amsterdam, *Criminal Prosecutions Affecting Federally Guaranteed Civil Rights: Federal Removal and Habeas Corpus Jurisdiction to Abort State Court Trial*, 113 U.Pa.L.Rev. 793 (1965); *Developments in the Law—Federal Habeas Corpus*, 83 Harv.L.Rev. 1038, 1093 (1970); Henderson, *Thanks, but No Thanks: State Supreme Courts' Attempts to Remove Themselves from the Federal Habeas Exhaustion Requirement*, 51 Case W.Res. L.Rev. 201 (2000). For other cases construing the exhaustion requirement, see Duncan v. Henry, 513 U.S. 364 (1995); O'Sullivan v. Boerckel, 526 U.S. 838 (1999).

2. In AEDPA, Congress modified the exhaustion requirement to make it a one-way ratchet. 28 U.S.C. § 2254(b)(2) now reads: "An application for a writ of habeas corpus may be denied on the merits, notwithstanding the failure of the applicant to exhaust the remedies available in the courts of the State." Does that mean that a federal habeas court may look at the merits of an unexhausted claim? What if the court does so and concludes that the claim is meritorious? If a federal habeas court, presented with a mixed petition, denies the unexhausted claim on the merits under § 2254(b)(2), what should it do with the exhausted claim—is that claim now cognizable despite *Rose*, because it is no longer in a mixed petition?

3. As noted earlier [supra p. 621], AEDPA also imposed a one-year statute of limitations on habeas petitions. *Rose* requires the prisoner to bring both claims together, or risk losing the one subsequently brought. Read the statute of limitations provision, 28 U.S.C. § 2244(d) [reproduced in Appendix B]. While the prisoner is exhausting an unexhausted claim, does the statute of limitations keep running on the exhausted claim? If so, what options are available to a prisoner who has one exhausted and one unexhausted claim? In this regard, consider Rhines v. Weber, 544 U.S. 269, 275–78 (2005):

> As a result of the interplay between AEDPA's 1–year statute of limitations and *Lundy*'s dismissal requirement, petitioners who come to federal court with "mixed" petitions run the risk of forever losing their opportunity for any federal review of their unexhausted claims. * * *

> We recognize the gravity of this problem and the difficulty it has posed for petitioners and federal district courts alike. In an attempt to solve the problem, some district courts have adopted a version of the "stay-and-abeyance" procedure employed by the District Court below. Under this procedure, rather than dismiss the mixed petition pursuant to *Lundy*, a district court might stay the petition and hold it in abeyance while the petitioner returns to state court to exhaust his previously unexhausted claims. Once the petitioner exhausts his state remedies,

the district court will lift the stay and allow the petitioner to proceed in federal court.

District courts do ordinarily have authority to issue stays, where such a stay would be a proper exercise of discretion. AEDPA does not deprive district courts of that authority * * * but it does circumscribe their discretion. Any solution to this problem must therefore be compatible with AEDPA's purposes.

One of the statute's purposes is to "reduce delays in the execution of state and federal criminal sentences, particularly in capital cases." AEDPA's 1–year limitations period "quite plainly serves the well-recognized interest in the finality of state court judgments." * * *

* * * AEDPA [also] encourages petitioners to seek relief from state courts in the first instance by tolling the 1–year limitations period while a "properly filed application for State post-conviction or other collateral review" is pending. * * *

Stay and abeyance, if employed too frequently, has the potential to undermine these twin purposes. Staying a federal habeas petition frustrates AEDPA's objective of encouraging finality by allowing a petitioner to delay the resolution of the federal proceedings. It also undermines AEDPA's goal of streamlining federal habeas proceedings by decreasing a petitioner's incentive to exhaust all his claims in state court prior to filing his federal petition. * * *

For these reasons, stay and abeyance should be available only in limited circumstances. Because granting a stay effectively excuses a petitioner's failure to present his claims first to the state courts, stay and abeyance is only appropriate when the district court determines there was good cause for the petitioner's failure to exhaust his claims first in state court. Moreover, even if a petitioner had good cause for that failure, the district court would abuse its discretion if it were to grant him a stay when his unexhausted claims are plainly meritless. * * *

Even where stay and abeyance is appropriate, the district court's discretion in structuring the stay is limited by the timeliness concerns reflected in AEDPA. A mixed petition should not be stayed indefinitely. Though, generally, a prisoner's "principal interest . . . is in obtaining speedy federal relief on his claims," not all petitioners have an incentive to obtain federal relief as quickly as possible. In particular, capital petitioners might deliberately engage in dilatory tactics to prolong their incarceration and avoid execution of the sentence of death.* * * Thus, district courts should place reasonable time limits on a petitioner's trip to state court and back.

In light of the requirement that the petitioner show good cause for the failure to exhaust, how useful do you think the stay-and-abeyance procedure will prove? Note the Court's recognition that capital petitioners might have interests in delaying: Will the Court's insistence on time limits prevent dilatory tactics, or will it cut off potentially meritorious claims if state courts move slowly despite a petitioner's best efforts? Does the reasonableness of the Court's compromise in *Rhines* depend on what percentage of claims are likely meritorious?

4. In McCleskey v. Zant, 499 U.S. 467 (1991) the Supreme Court adopted a modified version of Justice O'Connor's suggestion, in Part III–C of *Rose*, dealing with subsequent petitions. The Court held in *McCleskey* that successive petitions should be examined under the rigorous "cause and prejudice" standard, developed in the procedural default cases. [See infra pp. 637–57.] The *McCleskey* standard itself was superseded by new provisions in the AEDPA. See 28 U.S.C. § 2244(b)(2) [discussed infra p. 655].

5. **Distinguishing Between Habeas Corpus and Section 1983.** Though an exhaustion requirement is imposed in habeas cases, civil rights suits under section 1983 have no such requirement, either for judicial or administrative remedies. However, it has not always been easy to distinguish the two situations. In Wilkinson v. Dotson, 544 U.S. 74 (2005), the Court surveyed the precedent and concluded that inmates challenging the procedures applied in parole hearings may bring suit under section 1983:

> Two state prisoners brought an action under 42 U.S.C. § 1983 claiming that Ohio's state parole procedures violate the Federal Constitution. The prisoners seek declaratory and injunctive relief. The question before us is whether they may bring such an action under [§ 1983], or whether they must instead seek relief exclusively under the federal habeas corpus statutes. We conclude that these actions may be brought under § 1983.

* * *

> This Court has held that a prisoner in state custody cannot use a § 1983 action to challenge "the fact or duration of his confinement." *Preiser v. Rodriguez,* 411 U.S. 475, 489 (1973); see also *Wolff v. McDonnell,* 418 U.S. 539, 554 (1974); *Heck v. Humphrey,* 512 U.S. 477, 481 (1994); *Edwards v. Balisok,* 520 U.S. 641, 648 (1997). He must seek federal habeas corpus relief (or appropriate state relief) instead.

> Ohio points out that the inmates in these cases attack their parole-eligibility proceedings (Dotson) and parole-suitability proceedings (Johnson) only because they believe that victory on their claims will lead to speedier release from prison. Consequently, Ohio argues, the prisoners' lawsuits, in effect, collaterally attack the *duration* of their confinement; hence, such a claim may only be brought through a habeas corpus action, not through § 1983.

> The problem with Ohio's argument lies in its jump from a true premise (that in all likelihood the prisoners hope these actions will help bring about earlier release) to a faulty conclusion (that habeas is their sole avenue for relief). A consideration of this Court's case law makes clear that the connection between the constitutionality of the prisoners' parole proceedings and release from confinement is too tenuous here to achieve Ohio's legal door-closing objective.

> The Court initially addressed the relationship between § 1983 and the federal habeas statutes in *Preiser v. Rodriguez, supra.* In that case, state prisoners brought civil rights actions attacking the constitutionality of prison disciplinary proceedings that had led to the deprivation of

their good-time credits.* * * The Court conceded that the language of § 1983 literally covers their claims. * * * But, the Court noted, the language of the federal habeas statutes applies as well. * * * Moreover, the Court observed, the language of the habeas statute is more specific, and the writ's history makes clear that it traditionally "has been accepted as the specific instrument to obtain release from [unlawful] confinement." *Preiser,* 411 U.S., at 486. Finally, habeas corpus actions require a petitioner fully to exhaust state remedies, which § 1983 does not. * * * These considerations of linguistic specificity, history, and comity led the Court to find an implicit exception from § 1983's otherwise broad scope for actions that lie "within the core of habeas corpus." *Preiser,* 411 U.S., at 487.

Defining the scope of that exception, the Court concluded that a § 1983 action will not lie when a state prisoner challenges "the fact or duration of his confinement," *id.,* at 489, and seeks either "immediate release from prison," or the "shortening" of his term of confinement, *id.,* at 482. Because an action for restoration of good-time credits in effect demands immediate release or a shorter period of detention, it attacks "the very duration of . . . physical confinement," *id.,* at 487–488, and thus lies at "the core of habeas corpus," *id.,* at 487. Therefore, the Court held, the *Preiser* prisoners could not pursue their claims under § 1983.

In *Wolff v. McDonnell, supra,* the Court elaborated the contours of this habeas corpus "core." As in *Preiser,* state prisoners brought a § 1983 action challenging prison officials' revocation of good-time credits by means of constitutionally deficient disciplinary proceedings. * * * The Court held that the prisoners could not use § 1983 to obtain restoration of the credits because *Preiser* had held that "an injunction restoring good time improperly taken is foreclosed." 418 U.S., at 555. But the inmates *could* use § 1983 to obtain a declaration ("as a predicate to" their requested damages award) that the disciplinary procedures were invalid. *Ibid.* They could also seek "by way of ancillary relief[,] an otherwise proper injunction enjoining the *prospective* enforcement of invalid prison regulations." *Ibid.* (emphasis added). In neither case would victory for the prisoners necessarily have meant immediate release or a shorter period of incarceration; the prisoners attacked only the "wrong procedures, not . . . the wrong result (*i.e.,* [the denial of] good-time credits)." *Heck, supra,* at 483 (discussing *Wolff*).

In *Heck,* the Court considered a different, but related, circumstance. A state prisoner brought a § 1983 action for damages, challenging the conduct of state officials who, the prisoner claimed, had unconstitutionally caused his conviction by improperly investigating his crime and destroying evidence. 512 U.S., at 479. The Court pointed to "the hoary principle that civil tort actions are not appropriate vehicles for challenging the validity of outstanding criminal judgments." *Id.,* at 486. And it held that where "establishing the basis for the damages claim necessarily demonstrates the invalidity of the conviction," *id.,* at 481–482, a § 1983 action will not lie "unless . . . the conviction or sentence has already been invalidated," *id.,* at 487. The Court then added that, where the § 1983 action, "even if successful, will *not* demonstrate the invalidity of any outstanding criminal judgment ..., the action should be allowed to proceed." *Ibid.*

Finally, in *Edwards v. Balisok, supra,* the Court returned to the prison disciplinary procedure context of the kind it had addressed previously in *Preiser* and *Wolff.* Balisok sought "a declaration that the procedures employed by state officials [to deprive him of good-time credits] violated due process, ... damages for use of the unconstitutional procedures, [and] an injunction to prevent future violations." 520 U.S., at 643. Applying *Heck,* the Court found that habeas was the sole vehicle for the inmate's constitutional challenge insofar as the prisoner sought declaratory relief and money damages, because the "principal procedural defect complained of," namely deceit and bias on the part of the decisionmaker, "would, if established, necessarily imply the invalidity of the deprivation of [Balisok's] good-time credits." 520 U.S., at 646. Hence, success on the prisoner's claim for money damages (and the accompanying claim for declaratory relief) would "necessarily imply the invalidity of the punishment imposed." *Id.,* at 648. Nonetheless, the prisoner's claim for an injunction barring *future* unconstitutional procedures did *not* fall within habeas' exclusive domain. That is because "[o]rdinarily, a prayer for such prospective relief will not 'necessarily imply' the invalidity of a previous loss of good-time credits." *Ibid.*

Throughout the legal journey from *Preiser* to *Balisok,* the Court has focused on the need to ensure that state prisoners use only habeas corpus (or similar state) remedies when they seek to invalidate the duration of their confinement–either *directly* through an injunction compelling speedier release or *indirectly* through a judicial determination that necessarily implies the unlawfulness of the State's custody. Thus, *Preiser* found an implied exception to § 1983's coverage where the claim seeks—not where it simply "relates to"—"core" habeas corpus relief, *i.e.,* where a state prisoner requests present or future release. * * * *Wolff* makes clear that § 1983 remains available for procedural challenges where success in the action *would not necessarily* spell immediate or speedier release for the prisoner. *Heck* specifies that a prisoner cannot use § 1983 to obtain damages where success *would necessarily* imply the unlawfulness of a (not previously invalidated) conviction or sentence. And *Balisok,* like *Wolff,* demonstrates that habeas remedies do not displace § 1983 actions where success in the civil rights suit would not necessarily vitiate the legality of (not previously invalidated) state confinement. These cases, taken together, indicate that a state prisoner's § 1983 action is barred (absent prior invalidation)—no matter the relief sought (damages or equitable relief), no matter the target of the prisoner's suit (state conduct leading to conviction or internal prison proceedings)—*if* success in that action would necessarily demonstrate the invalidity of confinement or its duration.

Applying these principles to the present case, we conclude that respondents' claims are cognizable under § 1983, *i.e.,* they do not fall within the implicit habeas exception. Dotson and Johnson seek relief that will render invalid the state procedures used to deny parole eligibility (Dotson) and parole suitability (Johnson). * * * Neither respondent seeks an injunction ordering his immediate or speedier release into the community. * * * And as in *Wolff,* a favorable judgment will not "necessarily imply the invalidity of [their] conviction[s] or sentence[s]." *Heck, supra,* at 487. Success for Dotson does not mean immediate release from confinement or a shorter stay in prison; it means at most new eligibility review, which at most will speed *consideration* of a new parole application. Success for Johnson means at most a new parole hearing at which Ohio parole authorities may, in their discretion, decline to shorten his prison term. * * * Because neither prisoner's claim would necessarily spell speedier release, neither lies at "the core of habeas corpus." *Preiser,* 411 U.S., at 489. * * * 544 U.S. at 76–82.

Justice Kennedy dissented, criticizing the majority's reliance on the fact that a new parole hearing would not necessarily result in granting parole to the petitioners:

The primary reason offered for the Court's holding is that an order entitling a prisoner to a new parole proceeding might not result in his early release. That reason, however, applies with equal logic and force to a sentencing proceeding. And since it is elementary that habeas is the appropriate remedy for challenging a sentence, something must be quite wrong with the Court's own first premise.

Everyone knows that when a prisoner succeeds in a habeas action and obtains a new sentencing hearing, the sentence may or may not be reduced. The sentence can end up being just the same, or perhaps longer. The prisoner's early release is by no means assured simply because the first sentence was found unlawful. Yet no one would say that an attack on judicial sentencing proceedings following conviction may be raised through an action under § 1983. The inconsistency in the Court's treatment of sentencing proceedings and parole proceedings is thus difficult to justify. Id. at 88.

Are there any reasons to treat differently a parole hearing and a sentencing hearing? One difference is that state *courts* conduct sentencing hearings and impose sentences, while parole decisions are usually made by *non-judicial* bodies. If that explains the distinction, however, shouldn't the majority rest its holding on the identity of the decision-maker whose decision is being challenged rather than on the consequences of upholding the challenge? Think about the extent to which notions of comity and federalism underlie the exhaustion requirement. Should the decisions of state prison wardens and parole boards be subject to the same deference as the decisions of state judges? If not, was *Preiser* itself incorrectly decided?

The Supreme Court has most recently applied the *Preiser* line of cases to hold that a challenge to a particular mix of drugs for lethal injection, as a violation of the eighth amendment's ban on cruel and unusual punishment, can be brought under section 1983. See Hill v. McDonough 547 U.S. ___, 126 S.Ct. 2096 (2006). For a discussion of challenges to lethal injection, see Dow et al., *The Extraordinary Execution of Billy Vickers, the Banality of Death, and the Demise of Post–Conviction Review*, 13 Wm. & Mary Bill of Rights J. 521 (2004).

§ 3. PROCEDURAL DEFAULT

WAINWRIGHT v. SYKES

Supreme Court of the United States 1977.
433 U.S. 72.

Mr. Justice Rehnquist delivered the opinion of the Court.

We granted certiorari to consider the availability of federal habeas corpus to review a state convict's claim that testimony was admitted at his trial in violation of his rights under Miranda v. Arizona, 384 U.S. 436 (1966), a claim which the Florida courts have previously refused to consider on the merits because of noncompliance with a state contemporaneous-objection rule. Petitioner Wainwright, on behalf of the State of Florida, here challenges a decision of the Court of Appeals for the Fifth Circuit ordering a hearing in state court on the merits of respondent's contention.

Respondent Sykes was convicted of third-degree murder after a jury trial in the Circuit Court of DeSoto County. He testified at trial that on the evening of January 8, 1972, he told his wife to summon the police because he had just shot Willie Gilbert. Other evidence indicated that when the police arrived at respondent's trailer home, they found Gilbert dead of a shotgun wound, lying a few feet from the front porch. Shortly after their arrival, respondent came from across the road and volunteered that he had shot Gilbert, and a few minutes later respondent's wife approached the police and told them the same thing. Sykes was immediately arrested and taken to the police station.

Once there, it is conceded that he was read his *Miranda* rights, and that he declined to seek the aid of counsel and indicated a desire to talk. He then made a statement, which was admitted into evidence at trial through the testimony of the two officers who heard it, to the effect that he had shot Gilbert from the front porch of his trailer home. There were several references during the trial to respondent's consumption of alcohol during the preceding day and to his apparent state of intoxication, facts which were acknowledged by the officers who arrived at the scene. At no time during the trial, however, was the admissibility of any of respondent's statements challenged by his counsel on the ground that respondent had not understood the *Miranda* warnings. Nor did the trial judge question their admissibility on his own motion or hold a factfinding hearing bearing on that issue.

Respondent appealed his conviction, but apparently did not challenge the admissibility of the inculpatory statements. He later filed in the trial court a motion to vacate the conviction and, in the State District Court of Appeals and Supreme Court, petitions for habeas corpus. These filings, apparently for the first time, challenged the statements made to police on grounds of involuntariness. In all of these efforts respondent was unsuccessful.

Having failed in the Florida courts, respondent initiated the present action under 28 U.S.C. § 2254, asserting the inadmissibility of his statements by reason of his lack of understanding of the *Miranda* warnings. The United States District Court for the Middle District of Florida ruled that Jackson v. Denno, 378 U.S. 368 (1964), requires a hearing in a state criminal trial prior to the admission of an inculpatory out-of-court statement by the defendant. It held further that respondent had not lost his right to assert such a claim by failing to object at trial or on direct appeal, since only "exceptional circumstances" of "strategic decisions at trial" can create such a bar to raising federal constitutional claims in a federal habeas action. The court stayed issuance of the writ to allow the state court to hold a hearing on the "voluntariness" of the statements.

Petitioner warden appealed this decision to the United States Court of Appeals for the Fifth Circuit. * * *

[The court of appeals affirmed the district court, holding that under Fay v. Noia, 372 U.S. 391 (1963),] the failure to comply with the rule requiring objection at the trial would only bar review of the suppression claim where the right to object was deliberately bypassed for reasons relating to trial tactics. * * *

The simple legal question before the Court calls for a construction of the language of 28 U.S.C. § 2254(a), which provides that the federal courts shall entertain an application for a writ of habeas corpus "in behalf of a person in custody pursuant to the judgment of a state court only on the ground that he is in custody in violation of the Constitution or laws or treaties of the United States." * * *

* * * Where the habeas petitioner challenges a final judgment of conviction rendered by a state court, this Court has been called upon to decide no fewer than four different questions, all to a degree interrelated with one another: (1) What types of federal claims may a federal habeas court properly consider? (2) Where a federal claim is cognizable by a federal habeas court, to what extent must that court defer to a resolution of the claim in prior state proceedings? (3) To what extent must the petitioner who seeks federal habeas exhaust state remedies before resorting to the federal court? (4) In what instances will an adequate and independent state ground bar consideration of otherwise cognizable federal issues on federal habeas review?

Each of these four issues has spawned its share of litigation. * * *

* * *

There is no need to consider here in greater detail these first three areas of controversy attendant to federal habeas review of state convictions. Only the fourth area—the adequacy of state grounds to bar federal habeas review—is presented in this case. * * *

As to the role of adequate and independent state grounds, it is a well-established principle of federalism that a state decision resting on an adequate foundation of state substantive law is immune from review in the federal courts. Fox Film Corp. v. Muller, 296 U.S. 207 (1935); Murdock v. Memphis, 20 Wall. 590 (1875). The application of this principle in the context of a federal habeas proceeding has therefore excluded from consideration any questions of state *substantive* law, and thus effectively barred federal habeas review where questions of that sort are either the only ones raised by a petitioner or are in themselves dispositive of his case. The area of controversy which has developed has concerned the reviewability of federal claims which the state court has declined to pass on because not presented in the manner prescribed by its *procedural* rules. The adequacy of such an independent state procedural ground to prevent federal habeas review of the underlying federal issue has been treated very differently than where the state-law ground is substantive. * * *

* * *

In Fay v. Noia, supra, respondent Noia sought federal habeas to review a claim that his state-court conviction had resulted from the introduction of a coerced confession in violation of the Fifth Amendment to the United States Constitution. While the convictions of his two codefendants were reversed on that ground in collateral proceedings following their appeals, Noia did not appeal and the New York courts ruled that his subsequent *coram nobis* action was barred on account of that failure. This Court held that petitioner was nonetheless entitled to raise the claim in federal habeas, and thereby overruled its decision 10 years earlier in Brown v. Allen, * * *:

> "[T]he doctrine under which state procedural defaults are held to constitute an adequate and independent state law ground barring direct Supreme Court review is not to be extended to limit the power granted the federal courts under the federal habeas statute." 372 U.S., at 399.

As a matter of comity but not of federal power, the Court acknowledged "a limited discretion in the federal judge to deny relief * * * to an applicant who had deliberately by-passed the orderly procedure of the state courts and in so doing has forfeited his state court remedies." Id., at 438. In so stating, the Court made clear that the waiver must be knowing and actual—" 'an intentional relinquishment or abandonment of a known right or privilege.' " Id., at 439, quoting Johnson v. Zerbst, 304 U.S., at 464. Noting petitioner's "grisly choice" between acceptance of his life sentence and pursuit of an appeal which might culminate in a sentence of death, the Court concluded that there had been no deliberate bypass of the right to have the federal issues reviewed through a state appeal.

A decade later we decided Davis v. United States, supra, in which a federal prisoner's application under 28 U.S.C. § 2255 sought for the first time to challenge the makeup of the grand jury which indicted him. The Government contended that he was barred by the requirement of Fed. Rule Crim.Proc. 12(b)(2) providing that such challenges must be raised "by motion before trial." The Rule further provides that failure to so object constitutes a waiver of the objection, but that "the court for cause shown may grant relief from the waiver." We noted that the Rule "promulgated by this Court and, pursuant to 18 U.S.C. § 3771, 'adopted' by Congress, governs by its terms the manner in which the claims of defects in the institution of criminal proceedings may be waived," and held that this standard contained in the Rule, rather than the Fay v. Noia concept of waiver, should pertain in federal habeas as on direct review. Referring to previous constructions of Rule 12(b)(2), we concluded that review of the claim should be barred on habeas, as on direct appeal, absent a showing of cause for the noncompliance and some showing of actual prejudice resulting from the alleged constitutional violation.

Last Term, in Francis v. Henderson, the rule of *Davis* was applied to the parallel case of a state procedural requirement that challenges to grand jury composition be raised before trial. The Court noted that there was power in the federal courts to entertain an application in such a case, but rested its holding on "considerations of comity and concerns for the orderly administration of criminal justice...." 425 U.S., at 538–539. While there was no counterpart provision of the state rule which allowed an exception upon some showing of cause, the Court concluded that the standard derived from the Federal Rule should nonetheless be applied in that context since " '[t]here is no reason to ... give greater preclusive effect to procedural defaults by federal defendants than to similar defaults by state defendants.' " Id., at 542, quoting Kaufman v. United States, 394 U.S. 217, 228 (1969). As applied to the federal petitions of state convicts, the *Davis* cause-and-prejudice standard was thus incorporated directly into the body of law governing the availability of federal habeas corpus review.

To the extent that the dicta of Fay v. Noia may be thought to have laid down an all-inclusive rule rendering state contemporaneous-objection rules ineffective to bar review of underlying federal claims in federal habeas proceedings—absent a "knowing waiver" or a "deliberate bypass" of the right to so object—its effect was limited by *Francis*, which applied a different rule and barred a habeas challenge to the makeup of a grand jury. Petitioner Wainwright in this case urges that we further confine its effect by applying the principle enunciated in *Francis* to a claimed error in the admission of a defendant's confession.

* * *

We * * * conclude that Florida procedure did, consistently with the United States Constitution, require that respondent's confession be challenged at trial or not at all, and thus his failure to timely object to its admission amounted to an independent and adequate state procedural ground which would have prevented direct review here. See Henry v. Mississippi, 379 U.S. 443 (1965). We thus come to the crux of this case. Shall the rule of Francis v. Henderson, * * * barring federal habeas review absent a showing of "cause" and "prejudice" attendant to a state procedural waiver, be applied to a waived objection to the admission of a confession at trial? We answer that question in the affirmative.

* * * We leave open for resolution in future decisions the precise definition of the "cause"-and-"prejudice" standard, and note here only that it is narrower than the standard set forth in dicta in Fay v. Noia, which would make federal habeas review generally available to state convicts absent a knowing and deliberate waiver of the federal constitutional contention. It is the sweeping language of Fay v. Noia, going far beyond the facts of the case eliciting it, which we today reject.[12]

The reasons for our rejection of it are several. The contemporaneous-objection rule itself is by no means peculiar to Florida, and deserves greater respect than Fay gives it, both for the fact that it is employed by a coordinate jurisdiction within the federal system and for the many interests which it serves in its own right. A contemporaneous objection enables the record to be made with respect to the constitutional claim when the recollections of witnesses are freshest, not years later in a federal habeas proceeding. It enables the judge who observed the demeanor of those witnesses to make the factual determinations necessary for properly deciding the federal constitutional question. While the 1966 amendment to § 2254 requires deference to be given to such determinations made by state courts, the determinations themselves are less apt to be made in the first instance if there is no contemporaneous objection to the admission of the evidence on federal constitutional grounds.

A contemporaneous-objection rule may lead to the exclusion of the evidence objected to, thereby making a major contribution to finality in criminal litigation. Without the evidence claimed to be vulnerable on federal constitutional grounds, the jury may acquit the defendant, and that will be the end of the case; or it may nonetheless convict the defendant, and he will have one less federal constitutional claim to assert in his federal habeas petition. If the state trial judge admits the evidence in question after a full hearing, the federal habeas court pursuant to the 1966 amendment to § 2254 will gain significant guidance from the state ruling in this regard. Subtler considerations as well militate in favor of honoring a state contemporaneous-objection rule. An objection on the spot may force the prosecution to take a hard look at its hole card, and even if the prosecutor thinks that the state trial judge will admit the evidence he must contemplate the possibility of reversal by the state

---

12. We have no occasion today to consider the *Fay* rule as applied to the facts there confronting the Court. Whether the *Francis* rule should preclude federal habeas review of claims not made in accordance with state procedure where the criminal defendant has surrendered, other than for reasons of tactical advantage, the right to have all of his claims of trial error considered by a state appellate court, we leave for another day.

The Court in *Fay* stated its knowing-and-deliberate-waiver rule in language which applied not only to the waiver of the right to appeal, but to failures to raise individual substantive objections in the state trial. Then, with a single sentence in a footnote, the Court swept aside all decisions of this Court "to the extent that [they] may be read to suggest a standard of discretion in federal habeas corpus proceedings different from what we lay down today...." 372 U.S., at 439 n. 44. We do not choose to paint with a similarly broad brush here.

appellate courts or the ultimate issuance of a federal writ of habeas corpus based on the impropriety of the state court's rejection of the federal constitutional claim.

We think that the rule of Fay v. Noia, broadly stated, may encourage "sandbagging" on the part of defense lawyers, who may take their chances on a verdict of not guilty in a state trial court with the intent to raise their constitutional claims in a federal habeas court if their initial gamble does not pay off. The refusal of federal habeas courts to honor contemporaneous-objection rules may also make state courts themselves less stringent in their enforcement. Under the rule of Fay v. Noia, state appellate courts know that a federal constitutional issue raised for the first time in the proceeding before them may well be decided in any event by a federal *habeas* tribunal. Thus, their choice is between addressing the issue notwithstanding the petitioner's failure to timely object, or else face the prospect that the federal habeas court will decide the question without the benefit of their views.

The failure of the federal habeas courts generally to require compliance with a contemporaneous-objection rule tends to detract from the perception of the trial of a criminal case in state court as a decisive and portentous event. A defendant has been accused of a serious crime, and this is the time and place set for him to be tried by a jury of his peers and found either guilty or not guilty by that jury. To the greatest extent possible all which bear on this charge should be determined in this proceeding: the accused is in the courtroom, the jury is in the box, the judge is on the bench, and the witnesses, having been subpoenaed and duly sworn, await their turn to testify. Society's resources have been concentrated at that time and place in order to decide, within the limits of human fallibility, the question of guilt or innocence of one of its citizens. Any procedural rule which encourages the result that those proceedings be as free of error as possible is thoroughly desirable, and the contemporaneous-objection rule surely falls within this classification.

We believe the adoption of the *Francis* rule in this situation will have the salutary effect of making the state trial on the merits the "main event," so to speak, rather than a "tryout on the road" for what will later be the determinative federal habeas hearing. There is nothing in the Constitution or in the language of § 2254 which requires that the state trial on the issue of guilt or innocence be devoted largely to the testimony of fact witnesses directed to the elements of the state crime, while only later will there occur in a federal habeas hearing a full airing of the federal constitutional claims which were not raised in the state proceedings. If a criminal defendant thinks that an action of the state trial court is about to deprive him of a federal constitutional right there is every reason for his following state procedure in making known his objection.

The "cause"-and-"prejudice" exception of the *Francis* rule will afford an adequate guarantee, we think, that the rule will not prevent a federal habeas court from adjudicating for the first time the federal constitutional claim of a defendant who in the absence of such an adjudication will be the victim of a miscarriage of justice. Whatever precise content may be given those terms by later cases, we feel confident in holding without further elaboration that they do not exist here. Respondent has advanced no explanation whatever for his failure to object at trial,[14] and, as the proceeding unfolded, the trial judge is certainly not to be faulted for failing to question the admission of the confession himself. The other evidence of guilt presented at trial, moreover, was substantial to a degree that would negate any possibility of actual prejudice resulting to the respondent from the admission of his inculpatory statement.

We accordingly conclude that the judgment of the Court of Appeals for the Fifth Circuit must be reversed, and the cause remanded to the United States District Court for the Middle District of Florida with instructions to dismiss respondent's petition for a writ of habeas corpus.

Mr. Justice Brennan, with whom Mr. Justice Marshall joins, dissenting.

[margin note: DISSENT]

Over the course of the last decade, the deliberate-bypass standard announced in Fay v. Noia has played a central role in efforts by the federal judiciary to accommodate the constitutional rights of the individual with the States' interests in the integrity of their judicial procedural regimes. The Court today decides that this standard should no longer apply with respect to procedural defaults occurring during the trial of a criminal defendant. In its place, the Court adopts the two-part "cause"-and-"prejudice" test originally developed in Davis v. United States and Francis v. Henderson. As was true with these earlier cases, however, today's decision makes no effort to provide concrete guidance as to the content of those terms. More particularly, left unanswered is the thorny question that must be recognized to be central to a realistic rationalization of this area of law: How should the federal habeas court treat a procedural default in a state court that is attributable purely and simply to the error or negligence of a defendant's trial counsel? Because this key issue remains unresolved, I shall attempt in this opinion a re-examination of the policies that should inform—and in *Fay* did inform—the selection of the standard governing the availability of federal habeas corpus jurisdiction in the face of an intervening procedural default in the state court.

[margin note: what about atty negligence]

I

I begin with the threshold question: What is the meaning and import of a procedural default? If it could be assumed that a procedural default more often than not is the product of a defendant's conscious refusal to abide by the duly constituted, legitimate processes of the state courts, then I might agree that a regime of collateral review weighted in

---

14. In Henry v. Mississippi, 379 U.S., at 451, the Court noted that decisions of counsel relating to trial strategy, even when made without the consultation of the defen- dant, would bar direct federal review of claims thereby forgone, except where "the circumstances are exceptional." * * *

favor of a State's procedural rules would be warranted. *Fay*, however, recognized that such rarely is the case; and therein lies *Fay*'s basic unwillingness to embrace a view of habeas jurisdiction that results in "an airtight system of [procedural] forfeitures."

This, of course, is not to deny that there are times when the failure to heed a state procedural requirement stems from an intentional decision to avoid the presentation of constitutional claims to the state forum. *Fay* was not insensitive to this possibility. Indeed, the very purpose of its bypass test is to detect and enforce such intentional procedural forfeitures of outstanding constitutionally based claims. *Fay* does so through application of the longstanding rule used to test whether action or inaction on the part of a criminal defendant should be construed as a decision to surrender the assertion of rights secured by the Constitution: To be an effective waiver, there must be "an intentional relinquishment or abandonment of a known right or privilege." Johnson v. Zerbst, 304 U.S. 458, 464 (1938). Incorporating this standard, *Fay* recognized that if one "understandingly and knowingly forewent the privilege of seeking to vindicate his federal claims in the state courts, whether for strategic, tactical or any other reasons that can fairly be described as the deliberate by-passing of state procedures, then it is open to the federal court on habeas to deny him all relief. . . ." For this reason, the Court's assertion that it "think[s]" that the *Fay* rule encourages intentional "sandbagging" on the part of the defense lawyers is without basis, * * * certainly the Court points to no cases or commentary arising during the past 15 years of actual use of the *Fay* test to support this criticism. Rather, a consistent reading of case law demonstrates that the bypass formula has provided a workable vehicle for protecting the integrity of state rules in those instances when such protection would be both meaningful and just.

But having created the bypass exception to the availability of collateral review, *Fay* recognized that intentional, tactical forfeitures are not the norm upon which to build a rational system of federal habeas jurisdiction. In the ordinary case, litigants simply have no incentive to slight the state tribunal, since constitutional adjudication on the state and federal levels are not mutually exclusive. * * * Under the regime of collateral review recognized since the days of Brown v. Allen, and enforced by the *Fay* bypass test, no rational lawyer would risk the "sandbagging" feared by the Court.[5] If a constitutional challenge is not

---

5. In brief, the defense lawyer would face two options: (1) He could elect to present his constitutional claims to the state courts in a proper fashion. If the state trial court is persuaded that a constitutional breach has occurred, the remedies dictated by the Constitution would be imposed, the defense would be bolstered, and the prosecution accordingly weakened, perhaps precluded altogether. If the state court rejects the properly tendered claims, the defense has lost nothing: Appellate review before the state courts and federal habeas consideration are preserved. (2) He could elect to "sandbag." This presumably means, first, that he would hold back the presentation of his constitutional claim to the trial court, thereby increasing the likelihood of a conviction since the prosecution would be able to present evidence that, while arguably constitutionally deficient, may be highly prejudicial to the defense. Second, he would thereby have forfeited all state review and remedies with respect to these claims (sub-

properly raised on the state level, the explanation generally will be found elsewhere than in an intentional tactical decision.

In brief then, any realistic system of federal habeas corpus jurisdiction must be premised on the reality that the ordinary procedural default is born of the inadvertence, negligence, inexperience, or incompetence of trial counsel. The case under consideration today is typical. The Court makes no effort to identify a tactical motive for the failure of Sykes' attorney to challenge the admissibility or reliability of a highly inculpatory statement. * * *

* * *

III

A regime of federal habeas corpus jurisdiction that permits the reopening of state procedural defaults does not invalidate any state procedural rule as such; Florida's courts remain entirely free to enforce their own rules as they choose, and to deny any and all state rights and remedies to a defendant who fails to comply with applicable state procedure. The relevant inquiry is whether more is required—specifically, whether the fulfillment of important interests of the State necessitates that federal courts be called upon to impose additional sanctions for inadvertent noncompliance with state procedural requirements such as the contemporaneous-objection rule involved here.

Florida, of course, can point to a variety of legitimate interests in seeking allegiance to its reasonable procedural requirements, the contemporaneous-objection rule included. As *Fay* recognized, a trial, like any organized activity, must conform to coherent process, and "there must be sanctions for the flouting of such procedure." The strict enforcement of procedural defaults, therefore, may be seen as a means of deterring any tendency on the part of the defense to slight the state forum, to deny state judges their due opportunity for playing a meaningful role in the evolving task of constitutional adjudication, or to mock the needed finality of criminal trials. All of these interests are referred to by the Court in various forms.

The question remains, however, whether any of these policies or interests are efficiently and fairly served by enforcing both intentional and inadvertent defaults pursuant to the identical stringent standard. I remain convinced that when one pierces the surface justifications for a harsher rule posited by the Court, no standard stricter than *Fay*'s deliberate-bypass test is realistically defensible.

ject to whatever "plain error" rule is available). Third, to carry out his scheme, he would now be compelled to deceive the federal habeas court and to convince the judge that he did not "deliberately bypass" the state procedures. If he loses on this gamble, all federal review would be barred, and his "sandbagging" would have resulted in nothing but the forfeiture of all judicial review of his client's claims. The Court, without substantiation, apparently believes that a meaningful number of lawyers are induced into option 2 by *Fay*. I do not. That belief simply offends common sense.

Punishing a lawyer's unintentional errors by closing the federal courthouse door to his client is both a senseless and misdirected method of deterring the slighting of state rules. It is senseless because unplanned and unintentional action of any kind generally is not subject to deterrence; and, to the extent that it is hoped that a threatened sanction addressed to the defense will induce greater care and caution on the part of trial lawyers, thereby forestalling negligent conduct or error, the potential loss of all valuable state remedies would be sufficient to this end. And it is a misdirected sanction because even if the penalization of incompetence or carelessness will encourage more thorough legal training and trial preparation, the habeas applicant, as opposed to his lawyer, hardly is the proper recipient of such a penalty. Especially with fundamental constitutional rights at stake, no fictional relationship of principal-agent or the like can justify holding the criminal defendant accountable for the naked errors of his attorney. This is especially true when so many indigent defendants are without any realistic choice in selecting who ultimately represents them at trial. Indeed, if responsibility for error must be apportioned between the parties, it is the State, through its attorney's admissions and certification policies, that is more fairly held to blame for the fact that practicing lawyers too often are ill-prepared or ill-equipped to act carefully and knowledgeably when faced with decisions governed by state procedural requirements.

* * *

IV

Perhaps the primary virtue of *Fay* is that the bypass test at least yields a coherent yardstick for federal district courts in rationalizing their power of collateral review. * * * In contrast, although some four years have passed since its introduction in Davis v. United States, the only thing clear about the Court's "cause"-and-"prejudice" standard is that it exhibits the notable tendency of keeping prisoners in jail without addressing their constitutional complaints. Hence, as of today, all we know of the "cause" standard is its requirement that habeas applicants bear an undefined burden of explanation for the failure to obey the state rule * * *. Left unresolved is whether a habeas petitioner like Sykes can adequately discharge this burden by offering the commonplace and truthful explanation for his default: attorney ignorance or error beyond the client's control. The "prejudice" inquiry, meanwhile, appears to bear a strong resemblance to harmless-error doctrine. * * * I disagree with the Court's appraisal of the harmlessness of the admission of respondent's confession, but if this is what is meant by prejudice, respondent's constitutional contentions could be as quickly and easily disposed of in this regard by permitting federal courts to reach the merits of his complaint. In the absence of a persuasive alternative formulation to the bypass test, I would simply affirm the judgment of the Court of Appeals and allow Sykes his day in court on the ground that the failure of timely objection in this instance was not a tactical or deliberate decision but stemmed from a lawyer's error that should not be permitted to bind his client.

* * *

[The concurring opinions of CHIEF JUSTICE BURGER, JUSTICE STEVENS and JUSTICE WHITE are omitted.]

Notes

1. The impact of Fay v. Noia, 372 U.S. 391 (1963), discussed extensively in *Sykes*, was described in Cover & Aleinikoff, *Dialectical Federalism: Habeas Corpus and the Court*, 86 Yale L.J. 1035, 1042–43 (1977):

> *Fay* guaranteed * * * broad independent review in three ways. First, it reaffirmed the doctrine of Brown v. Allen that state court adjudication could not estop federal court adjudication. Second, it held that defendants could not lose their opportunity to raise federal claims in federal court unless they had "deliberately by-passed" state procedures for adjudicating such claims. This high waiver standard was reinforced by a third principle: waiver depended upon "the considered choice" of the defendant; the acts of counsel would not automatically bind the client.
>
> *Fay* certainly increased the number of claims brought in federal court, but it did so in a way that avoided difficult questions concerning the relation of counsel to client and the standards for judicial behavior. Rather than determining whether counsel's behavior was such that it was fair to attribute his acts to his client, a federal court would rule on the underlying right at issue unless the defendant himself had bypassed state adjudication. Similarly, federal courts avoided potentially insulting inquiries into the reasons for the failure of the trial judge to raise and correct errors not called to his attention by the defense.

2. The Court in *Sykes* and subsequent cases is concerned with the possibility of "sandbagging:" a defendant might purposely refrain from making a claim at trial or on direct appeal in order to save the claim for federal habeas review. Is the cause-and-prejudice rule of *Sykes* necessary to prevent sandbagging, or would the rule of *Fay* adequately protect against such tactics? Recall that habeas petitions are not subject to ordinary res judicata rules. How likely is it that a defendant would deliberately withhold a claim from the state courts, only to raise it on federal collateral appeal? Do 28 U.S.C. §§ 2254(d) and 2254(e), [reproduced in Appendix B] newly enacted as part of the AEDPA, make sandbagging more likely?

3. The Court has revisited the question of "cause" on several occasions. The most common reason for failure to raise a claim in a timely manner is attorney inadvertence. In Murray v. Carrier, 477 U.S. 478 (1986), the Court held that attorney inadvertence does not constitute cause unless the attorney's mistakes rise to the level of a sixth amendment violation of the right to counsel. The Court reasoned that the costs associated with entertaining defaulted petitions—identified in *Sykes*—"do not disappear when the default stems from counsel's ignorance or inadvertence rather than from a deliberate decision, for whatever reason, to withhold a claim." Id. at 487. Indeed, the Court suggested, those costs would increase were

attorney inadvertence to constitute cause: "In order to determine whether there was cause for a procedural default, federal habeas courts would routinely be required to hold evidentiary hearings to determine what prompted counsel's failure to raise the claim in question." Id. Note that the procedural default rules apply all the way down: a prisoner cannot use a *defaulted* ineffective assistance of counsel claim to excuse a procedural default, unless he can show cause and prejudice with regard to the defaulted ineffective assistance claim. Edwards v. Carpenter, 529 U.S. 446 (2000). However, a claim of ineffective assistance of counsel is not defaulted just because it is not raised on direct review; it may be raised for the first time on state collateral review. Massaro v. United States, 538 U.S. 500 (2003).

4.   The Court in *Carrier* also listed some circumstances which *would* constitute cause. Justice O'Connor's majority opinion noted that "a showing that the factual or legal basis for a claim was not reasonably available to counsel, or that 'some interference by officials,' made compliance impracticable, would constitute cause under this standard." 477 U.S. at 488. See also Reed v. Ross, 468 U.S. 1, 16 (1984) (cause standard satisfied "where a constitutional claim is so novel that its legal basis is not reasonably available to counsel").

Although novel law or facts thus theoretically meet the cause standard, the Court has subsequently narrowed this means of satisfying *Sykes*. In Smith v. Murray, 477 U.S. 527 (1986), the Court held that a claim previously rejected in other cases by the state supreme court was not "unavailable." After petitioner's direct appeals were exhausted, the state supreme court changed its earlier rule, partly as a result of intervening United States Supreme Court decisions. Nevertheless, the Supreme Court in *Smith* held that the claim had always been "available": "the question is not whether subsequent legal developments have made counsel's task easier, but whether at the time of the default the claim was 'available' at all." Id. at 537. The Court found that Smith's claim was "available," because "various forms of the claim he now advances had been percolating in the lower courts for years at the time of his original appeal." Id.

The impact of novel legal doctrine was further elaborated in Teague v. Lane, 489 U.S. 288 (1989) [infra p. 679]. In *Teague*, the Court held that (with narrow exceptions), no "new rule" could be applied to cases on collateral appeal. The Court thus refused to reach the merits of any petition advancing a constitutional challenge not already well-established by precedent. After *Teague*, is there anything left of the idea of novel law as an excuse for procedural default?

In McCleskey v. Zant, 499 U.S. 467 (1991), the Supreme Court narrowed even more the scope of a novel or unavailable claim, this time in the context of a petition relying on previously unavailable *facts*. In that case, the petitioner had failed to raise a claim, under Massiah v. United States, 377 U.S. 201 (1964), that the state made a secret agreement with his cellmate, who then deliberately elicited incriminating statements from McCleskey. The cellmate's *advance* involvement with the police—which was necessary for a *Massiah* violation—did not come to light until after McCleskey had filed a federal habeas petition, although McCleskey did know that the cellmate had reported their conversations to the police. The Court found that McCleskey was nevertheless barred from raising the *Massiah* claim in a subsequent petition. Justice Kennedy's opinion for the majority reasoned:

> Abuse of the writ doctrine examines *petitioner's* conduct: the question is whether petitioner possessed, or by reasonable means could have obtained, a sufficient basis to allege a claim in the first petition and pursue the matter through the habeas process. The requirement of cause in the abuse-of-the-write context is based on the principle that petitioner must conduct a reasonable and diligent investigation aimed at including all relevant claims and grounds for relief in the first federal habeas petition. If what petitioner knows or could discover upon reasonable investigation supports a claim for relief in a federal habeas petition, what he does not know is irrelevant. Omission of the claim will not be excused merely because evidence discovered later might also have supported or strengthened the claim.

* * *

The 21–page document [detailing the state's agreement with the cellmate] unavailable to McCleskey at the time of the first petition does not establish that McCleskey had cause for failing to raise the *Massiah* claim at the outset. Based on testimony and questioning at trial, McCleskey knew that he had confessed the murder during jail-cell conversations with Evans [the cellmate], knew that Evans claimed to be a relative of [one of McCleskey's accomplices] during the conversations, and knew that Evans told the police about the conversations. Knowledge of these facts alone would have put McCleskey on notice to pursue the *Massiah* claim in his first federal habeas petition * * *. 499 U.S. at 498–99.

5. Amadeo v. Zant, 486 U.S. 214 (1988), was the apparently rare case which meets the "interference by state officials" standard. There the Court unanimously found cause for failure to raise a claim that the jury had been selected unconstitutionally. While the defendant's appeal was pending, discovery in an independent lawsuit revealed written evidence that the District Attorney had intentionally limited the number of blacks and women placed on master jury lists. The Court ruled that the deliberate concealment by local officials constituted cause. See also Banks v. Dretke, 540 U.S. 668 (2004) (prosecutorial misconduct in failing to produce exculpatory evidence constitutes cause).

6. Coleman v. Thompson, 501 U.S. 722 (1991), finally overruled Fay v. Noia. Like *Fay, Coleman* involved a state procedural default in the appellate process. The Court held that even the right to appeal could be forfeited by a procedural lapse.

7. In Harris v. Reed, 489 U.S. 255 (1989), the Court extended the "plain statement" rule of Michigan v. Long, 463 U.S. 1032 (1983) [infra p. 997], to habeas review. Writing for the majority, Justice Blackmun concluded that "habeas review * * * presents the same problem of ambiguity that this Court resolved in Michigan v. Long". Id. at 262. Thus, a procedural default precludes review only if the state court "clearly and expressly" relies on the waiver as a basis for rejecting the federal claim.

In Coleman v. Thompson, 501 U.S. 722 (1991), however, the Court ruled that *Harris*'s presumption applies only to cases in which "the decision of the last state court to which the petitioner presented his federal claims * * * fairly appear[s] to rest primarily on federal law or to be interwoven with federal law." 501 U.S. at 735. Accordingly, a conviction upheld by the Virginia Supreme Court merely by declaring "upon consideration [of the papers filed], the [state's] motion to dismiss is granted" did not run afoul of the rule of Michigan v. Long. Can this be squared with Harris v. Reed?

8. **Beyond cause and prejudice.** The Court applied the cause and prejudice standard to successive petitions (considered as an abuse of the writ) in McCleskey v. Zant, 499 U.S. 467 (1991). Although AEDPA may have altered the standard for successive petitions—a question considered infra p. 655—it did not do so for defaulted petitions. Thus the cause-and-prejudice cases before 1996, including those involving successive petitions, still govern procedurally defaulted petitions. The most important of those cases create and define a "safety valve" for the cause and prejudice standard, which allows a federal court to reach the merits of procedurally defaulted claims if failure to hear the claim would constitute a "miscarriage of justice." Kuhlmann v. Wilson, 477 U.S. 436, 452 (1986). In thinking about the possible reasons for and contours of such an exception, consider the following case:

SCHLUP v. DELO

Supreme Court of the United States, 1995.
513 U.S. 298.

JUSTICE STEVENS delivered the opinion of the Court.

Petitioner Lloyd E. Schlup, Jr., a Missouri prisoner currently under a sentence of death, filed a second federal habeas corpus petition alleging that constitutional error deprived the jury of critical evidence that would have established his innocence. The District Court, without conducting an evidentiary hearing, declined to reach the merits of the petition, holding that petitioner could not satisfy the threshold showing of "actual innocence" required by Sawyer v. Whitley, 505 U.S. 333 (1992). Under *Sawyer*, the petitioner must show "by clear and convincing evidence that but for a constitutional error, no reasonable juror would have found the petitioner" guilty. The Court of Appeals affirmed. We granted certiorari to consider whether the *Sawyer* standard provides adequate protection against the kind of miscarriage of justice that would result from the execution of a person who is actually innocent.

* * *

II

[After being convicted of the murder of another inmate, Schlup exhausted his state remedies and then filed a federal habeas corpus petition. After that petition was denied, he filed a second petition alleging new errors and also claiming actual innocence.]

On August 23, 1993, without holding a hearing, the District Court dismissed Schlup's second habeas petition and vacated the stay of execution that was then in effect. The District Court concluded that Schlup's various filings did not provide adequate cause for failing to raise his new claims more promptly. Moreover, the Court concluded that Schlup had failed to meet the *Sawyer* standard for showing that a refusal to entertain those claims would result in a fundamental miscarriage of justice. * * *

* * *

Petitioner then sought from the Court of Appeals a stay of execution pending the resolution of his appeal. Relying on Justice Powell's plurality opinion in Kuhlmann v. Wilson, 477 U.S. 436 (1986), Schlup argued that the District Court should have entertained his second habeas corpus petition, because he had supplemented his constitutional claim "with a colorable showing of factual innocence." Id., at 454.

On October 15, 1993, the Court of Appeals denied the stay application. * * * [T]he majority held that petitioner's claim of innocence was governed by the standard announced in *Sawyer*, and it concluded that under that standard, the evidence of Schlup's guilt that had been adduced at trial foreclosed consideration of petitioner's current constitutional claims.

* * *

On November 17, 1993, the Court of Appeals denied a suggestion for rehearing en banc. Dissenting from that denial, three judges joined an opinion describing the question whether the majority should have applied the standard announced in *Sawyer*, rather than the *Kuhlmann* standard as "a question of great importance in habeas corpus jurisprudence." We granted certiorari to consider that question.

III

As a preliminary matter, it is important to explain the difference between Schlup's claim of actual innocence and the claim of actual innocence asserted in Herrera v. Collins, 506 U.S. 390 (1993). In *Herrera*, the petitioner advanced his claim of innocence to support a novel substantive constitutional claim, namely that the execution of an innocent person would violate the Eighth Amendment. Under petitioner's theory in *Herrera*, even if the proceedings that had resulted in his conviction and sentence were entirely fair and error-free, his innocence would render his execution a "constitutionally intolerable event." Id., at 439 (O'Connor, J., concurring).

Schlup's claim of innocence, on the other hand, is procedural, rather than substantive. His constitutional claims are based not on his innocence, but rather on his contention that the ineffectiveness of his counsel, see Strickland v. Washington, 466 U.S. 668 (1984), and the withholding of evidence by the prosecution, see Brady v. Maryland, 373 U.S. 83 (1963), denied him the full panoply of protections afforded to criminal defendants by the Constitution. Schlup, however, faces procedural obstacles that he must overcome before a federal court may address the merits of those constitutional claims. Because Schlup has been unable to establish "cause and prejudice" sufficient to excuse his failure to present his evidence in support of his first federal petition, see McCleskey v. Zant, 499 U.S. 467, 493–494 (1991), Schlup may obtain review of his constitutional claims only if he falls within the "narrow class of cases ... implicating a fundamental miscarriage of justice." Id., at 494. Schlup's claim of innocence is offered only to bring him within this "narrow class of cases."

* * *

IV

* * *

To ensure that the fundamental miscarriage of justice exception would remain "rare" and would only be applied in the "extraordinary case," while at the same time ensuring that the exception would extend relief to those who were truly deserving, this Court explicitly tied the miscarriage of justice exception to the petitioner's innocence. In *Kuhlmann*, for example, Justice Powell concluded that a prisoner retains an overriding "interest in obtaining his release from custody if he is innocent of the charge for which he was incarcerated. That interest does not extend, however, to prisoners whose guilt is conceded or plain." 477 U.S., at 452. Similarly, Justice O'Connor wrote in *Carrier* that "in an extraordinary case, where a constitutional violation has probably resulted in the conviction of one who is actually innocent, a federal habeas court may grant the writ even in the absence of a showing of cause for the procedural default." 477 U.S., at 496; see also Smith v. Murray, 477 U.S., at 537, quoting *Carrier*, 477 U.S., at 496.

* * *

In the years following *Kuhlmann* and *Carrier*, we did not expound further on the actual innocence exception. In those few cases that mentioned the standard, the Court continued to rely on the formulations set forth in *Kuhlmann* and *Carrier*. In *McCleskey*, for example, while establishing that cause and prejudice would generally define the situations in which a federal court might entertain an abusive petition, the Court recognized an exception for cases in which the constitutional violation "probably has caused the conviction of one innocent of the crime." 499 U.S., at 494, citing *Carrier*, 477 U.S., at 485.

Then, in *Sawyer*, the Court examined the miscarriage of justice exception as applied to a petitioner who claimed he was "actually innocent of the death penalty." In that opinion, the Court struggled to define "actual innocence" in the context of a petitioner's claim that his death sentence was inappropriate. The Court concluded that such actual innocence "must focus on those elements which render a defendant eligible for the death penalty." 505 U.S., at 347. However, in addition to defining what it means to be "innocent" of the death penalty, the Court departed from *Carrier*'s use of "probably" and adopted a more exacting standard of proof to govern these claims: the Court held that a habeas petitioner "must show by *clear and convincing* evidence that but for a constitutional error, no reasonable juror would have found the petitioner eligible for the death penalty." 505 U.S., at 336 (emphasis added). No attempt was made in *Sawyer* to reconcile this stricter standard with *Carrier*'s use of "probably."

V

In evaluating Schlup's claim of innocence, the Court of Appeals applied Eighth Circuit precedent holding that *Sawyer*, rather than *Carrier*, supplied the proper legal standard. The Court then purported to apply the *Sawyer* standard. Schlup argues that *Sawyer* has no application to a petitioner who claims that he is actually innocent of the crime, and that the Court of Appeals misapplied *Sawyer* in any event. Respondent contends that the Court of Appeals was correct in both its selection and its application of the *Sawyer* standard. Though the Court of Appeals seems to have misapplied *Sawyer*, we do not rest our decision on that ground because we conclude that in a case such as this, the *Sawyer* standard does not apply.

As we have stated, the fundamental miscarriage of justice exception seeks to balance the societal interests in finality, comity, and conservation of scarce judicial resources with the individual interest in justice that arises in the extraordinary case. We conclude that *Carrier*, rather than *Sawyer*, properly strikes that balance when the claimed injustice is that constitutional error has resulted in the conviction of one who is actually innocent of the crime.

Claims of actual innocence pose less of a threat to scarce judicial resources and to principles of finality and comity than do claims that focus solely on the erroneous imposition of the death penalty. Though challenges to the propriety of imposing a sentence of death are routinely asserted in capital cases, experience has taught us that a substantial claim that constitutional error has caused the conviction of an innocent person is extremely rare. To be credible, such a claim requires petitioner to support his allegations of constitutional error with new reliable evidence—whether it be exculpatory scientific evidence, trustworthy eyewitness accounts, or critical physical evidence—that was not presented at trial. Because such evidence is obviously unavailable in the vast majority of cases, claims of actual innocence are rarely successful. Even under the pre-*Sawyer* regime, "in virtually every case, the allegation of actual innocence has been summarily rejected." The threat to judicial resources, finality, and comity posed by claims of actual innocence is thus significantly less than that posed by claims relating only to sentencing.

Of greater importance, the individual interest in avoiding injustice is most compelling in the context of actual innocence. The quintessential miscarriage of justice is the execution of a person who is entirely innocent. Indeed, concern about the injustice that results from the conviction of an innocent person has long been at the core of our criminal justice system. That concern is reflected, for example, in the "fundamental value determination of our society that it is far worse to convict an innocent man than to let a guilty man go free." In re Winship, 397 U.S. 358, 372 (1970)(Harlan, J., concurring).

The overriding importance of this greater individual interest merits protection by imposing a somewhat less exacting standard of proof on a habeas petitioner alleging a fundamental miscarriage of justice than on one alleging that his sentence is too severe. As this Court has noted, "a standard of proof represents an attempt to instruct the factfinder concerning the degree of confidence our society thinks he should have in the correctness of factual conclusions for a particular type of adjudication." In re Winship, 397 U.S., at 370 (Harlan, J., concurring). The standard of proof thus reflects "the relative importance attached to the ultimate decision." Though the *Sawyer* standard was fashioned to reflect the relative importance of a claim of an erroneous sentence, application of that standard to petitioners such as Schlup would give insufficient weight to the correspondingly greater injustice that is implicated by a claim of actual innocence. The paramount importance of avoiding the injustice of executing one who is actually innocent thus requires application of the *Carrier* standard.

* * *

Accordingly, we hold that the *Carrier* "probably resulted" standard rather than the more stringent *Sawyer* standard must govern the miscarriage of justice inquiry when a petitioner who has been sentenced to death raises a claim of actual innocence to avoid a procedural bar to the consideration of the merits of his constitutional claims.

VI

The *Carrier* standard requires the habeas petitioner to show that "a constitutional violation has probably resulted in the conviction of one who is actually innocent." 477 U.S., at 496. To establish the requisite probability, the petitioner must show that it is more likely than not that no reasonable juror would have convicted him in the light of the new evidence. The petitioner thus is required to make a stronger showing than that needed to establish prejudice. At the same time, the showing of "more likely than not" imposes a lower burden of proof than the "clear and convincing" standard required under *Sawyer*. The *Carrier* standard thus ensures that petitioner's case is truly "extraordinary," *McCleskey*, 499 U.S., at 494, while still providing petitioner a meaningful avenue by which to avoid a manifest injustice.

[The Court then remanded the case for a determination of whether petitioner had met the *Carrier* standard.]

[The concurring opinion of JUSTICE O'CONNOR, and the dissenting opinions of CHIEF JUSTICE REHNQUIST and JUSTICE SCALIA, are omitted.]

Notes

1. The Court in *Schlup* drew a distinction between those claiming to be innocent of the crime and those claiming to be "innocent of the death penalty." Is that distinction justified? If there is a distinction, in which case should the federal courts be more available for constitutional challenges?

2. Should the "actual innocence" exception to the cause and prejudice standard apply where a petitioner seeks to challenge a noncapital sentence, alleging not that he was innocent of the crime but that the sentence was imposed unconstitutionally? Should *Carrier* or *Sawyer* govern? See Sticha, *To Be or Not To Be? The Actual Innocence Exception in Noncapital Sentencing Cases*, 80 Minn.L.Rev. 1615 (1996). Note that the Supreme Court has held that "a federal court faced with allegations of actual innocence, whether of the sentence or of the crime charged, must first address all nondefaulted claims for comparable relief and other grounds for cause to excuse the procedural default." Dretke v. Haley, 541 U.S. 386, 393–94 (2004).

3. The Court found the "actual innocence" standard satisfied in House v. Bell, 547 U.S. ___, 126 S.Ct. 2064 (2006). The Court stressed that while *Schlup* "permits review only in the ' "extraordinary" ' case," it "does not require absolute certainty about the petitioner's guilt or innocence." In *House*, "the central forensic proof connecting House to the crime," had been "called into question" by subsequent DNA testing, and House had "put forward substantial evidence pointing to a different suspect." Thus, despite the fact that the new evidence did not provide "conclusive exoneration," it was sufficient to allow House to raise his defaulted claims despite the absence of cause and prejudice.

4. Does the cause and prejudice standard applied in *Schlup* still govern subsequent petitions, or is it now limited once again to defaulted claims? Consider 28 U.S.C. § 2244(b)(2), enacted as part of AEDPA in 1996:

> A claim presented in a second or successive habeas corpus application under section 2254 that was not presented in a prior application shall be dismissed unless—
>
> (A) the applicant shows that the claim relies on a new rule of constitutional law, made retroactive to cases on collateral review by the Supreme Court, that was previously unavailable; or
>
> (B)(i) the factual predicate for the claim could not have been discovered previously through the exercise of due diligence; and
>
> (ii) the facts underlying the claim, if proven and viewed in light of the evidence as a whole, would be sufficient to establish by clear and convincing evidence that, but for constitutional error, no reasonable factfinder would have found the applicant guilty of the underlying offense.

How does section 2244(b)(2) differ from the cause and prejudice standard applied in *Schlup*? From the standard applied in *Sawyer*? How would those cases have come out under the new statute? The Supreme Court has indicated in dicta that the miscarriage of justice standard is "somewhat more lenient than the standard of § 2244(b)(2)(B)." Calderon v. Thompson,

523 U.S. 538 (1998). The Court has also held that " 'actual innocence' means factual innocence, not mere legal insufficiency." Thus "the Government is not limited to the existing record to rebut any showing that petitioner might make," and "should be permitted to present any admissible evidence of petitioner's guilt." Bousley v. United States, 523 U.S. 614 (1998).

Notice that section 2244(b)(2) applies only to successive petitions, not to procedurally defaulted petitions. Should the same standard govern both circumstances? The Court first extended the cause and prejudice standard from defaulted to successive petitions in McCleskey v. Zant, 499 U.S. 467 (1991). Justice Kennedy's opinion for the majority in *McCleskey* catalogued the costs imposed by federal habeas review on finality, on state integrity, and on scarce federal judicial resources, and concluded:

> The federal writ of habeas corpus overrides all these considerations, essential as they are to the rule of law, when a petitioner raises meritorious constitutional claims in a proper manner in a habeas petition. Our procedural default jurisprudence and abuse-of-the-writ jurisprudence help define this dimension of procedural regularity. Both doctrines impose on petitioners a burden of reasonable compliance with procedures designed to discourage baseless claims and to keep the system open for valid ones; both recognize the law's interest in finality; and both invoke equitable principles to define the court's discretion to excuse pleading and procedural requirements for petitioners who could not comply with them in the exercise of reasonable care and diligence. * * * [T]he doctrines of procedural default and abuse of the writ are both designed to lessen the injury to a State that results through reexamination of a state conviction on the ground that the State did not have the opportunity to address at a prior, appropriate time; and both doctrines seek to vindicate the State's interest in the finality of its criminal judgments. 499 U.S. at 492–93.

Are you persuaded? In House v. Bell, 547 U.S. ___, 126 S.Ct. 2064 (2006), the Court held that § 2244(b)(2) applies only to successive petitions, and that defaulted petitions are still subject to the *Schlup* standard.

5.   Courts have had some difficulty in defining what constitutes a petition for habeas corpus for purposes of determining whether a pending application is a "successive petition." See Stewart v. Martinez–Villareal, 523 U.S. 637 (1998) (if earlier petition was dismissed on procedural grounds, subsequent petition is not "successive" for purposes of 2244(b)(1)); Slack v. McDaniel, 529 U.S. 473 (2000) (same with regard to 2244(b)(2)); Castro v. United States, 540 U.S. 375 (2003) (motion for a new trial can be considered a petition for habeas corpus, triggering ban on subsequent petitions); Gonzalez v. Crosby, 545 U.S. 524 (2005) (some motions for relief from final judgment under Fed.R.Civ.P. 60(b) are successive petitions).

6.   Consider the various exhaustion and procedural default rules together. Does the resulting complexity undermine the purposes of the writ, especially in light of the fact that a majority of habeas petitioners proceed *pro se*? You should know that in 1988, Congress passed legislation providing that "[i]n any postconviction proceeding under section 2254 or 2255 of Title 28, seeking to vacate or set aside a death sentence, any defendant who is or

becomes financially unable to obtain adequate representation * * * shall be entitled to the appointment of one or more attorneys." 21 U.S.C. § 848(q)(4)(B). The Supreme Court has held that this provision is triggered by the mere filing of a request for the appointment of counsel in a habeas proceeding; a formal habeas petition need not have been filed. McFarland v. Scott, 512 U.S. 849 (1994). The Court characterized the statute as reflecting a "recognition that federal habeas corpus has a particularly important role to play in promoting fundamental fairness in the imposition of the death penalty." Id. at 859. Is *McFarland* (and the statute it interprets) consistent with the different levels of proof required of petitioners in *Sawyer* and *Schlup*?

Even in capital cases, is providing appointed attorneys to habeas petitioners the best way to remedy defects in the criminal justice system? See McFarland v. Scott, 512 U.S. 1256, 1260–61 (1994)(denial of certiorari) (Blackmun, J., dissenting):

> Jesus Romero's attorney failed to present any evidence at the penalty phase and delivered a closing argument totalling 29 words. Although the attorney later was suspended on unrelated grounds, Romero's ineffective assistance claim was rejected by the Court of Appeals for the Fifth Circuit. * * * Romero was executed in 1992. Larry Heath was represented on direct appeal by counsel who filed a 6–page brief before the Alabama Court of Criminal Appeals. The attorney failed to appear for oral argument before the Alabama Supreme Court and filed a brief in that court containing a 1–page argument and citing a single case. * * * Heath was executed in Alabama in 1992.

> James Messer, a mentally impaired capital defendant, was represented by an attorney who at the trial's guilt phase presented *no* defense, made no objections, and emphasized the horror of the capital crime in his closing statement. At the penalty phase, the attorney presented no evidence of mental impairment, failed to introduce other substantial mitigating evidence, and again repeatedly suggested in closing that death was the appropriate punishment. The Eleventh Circuit refused to grant relief * * * and this Court denied certiorari. * * * Messer was executed in 1988.

For further examples of poor legal representation of capital defendants, see Bright, *Is Fairness Irrelevant?: The Evisceration of Federal Habeas Corpus Review and Limits on the Ability of State Courts to Protect Fundamental Rights*, 54 Wash. & Lee L.Rev. 1, 17–23 (1997). For other views on the role of habeas corpus in capital cases, see D. Dow, Executed on a Technicality: Lethal Injustice on America's Death Row (2005); Hammel, *Diabolical Federalism: A Functional Critique and Proposed Reconstruction of Death Penalty Federal Habeas*, 39 Am.Crim.L.Rev. 1 (2002); Liebman, *The Overproduction of Death*, 100 Colum.L.Rev. 2030 (2000); Kozinski, *Tinkering With Death*, 72 New Yorker 48 (No. 46, Feb. 10, 1997); Reinhardt, *The Anatomy of an Execution: Fairness vs. "Process,"* 74 N.Y.U.L.Rev. 313 (1999).

§ 4. SCOPE OF REVIEW

STONE v. POWELL

Supreme Court of the United States, 1976.
428 U.S. 465.

MR. JUSTICE POWELL delivered the opinion of the Court.

Respondents in these cases were convicted of criminal offenses in state courts, and their convictions were affirmed on appeal. The prosecution in each case relied upon evidence obtained by searches and seizures alleged by respondents to have been unlawful. Each respondent subsequently sought relief in a Federal District Court by filing a petition for a writ of federal habeas corpus under 28 U.S.C.A. § 2254. The question presented is whether a federal court should consider, in ruling on a petition for habeas corpus relief filed by a state prisoner, a claim that evidence obtained by an unconstitutional search or seizure was introduced at his trial, when he has previously been afforded an opportunity for full and fair litigation of his claim in the state courts. The issue is of considerable importance to the administration of criminal justice.

I

* * *

A

Respondent Lloyd Powell was convicted of murder in June 1968 after trial in a California state court. At about midnight on February 17, 1968, he and three companions entered the Bonanza Liquor Store in San Bernardino, Cal., where Powell became involved in an altercation with Gerald Parsons, the store manager, over the theft of a bottle of wine. In the scuffling that followed Powell shot and killed Parsons' wife. Ten hours later an officer of the Henderson, Nev., Police Department arrested Powell for violation of the Henderson vagrancy ordinance, and in the search incident to the arrest discovered a .38–caliber revolver with six expended cartridges in the cylinder.

Powell was extradited to California and convicted of second-degree murder in the Superior Court of San Bernardino County. Parsons and Powell's accomplices at the liquor store testified against him. A criminologist testified that the revolver found on Powell was the gun that killed Parsons' wife. The trial court rejected Powell's contention that testimony by the Henderson police officer as to the search and the discovery of the revolver should have been excluded because the vagrancy ordinance was unconstitutional. In October 1969, the conviction was affirmed by a California District Court of Appeal. Although the issue was duly presented, that court found it unnecessary to pass upon the legality of the arrest and search because it concluded that the error, if any, in admitting the testimony of the Henderson officer was harmless beyond a reasonable doubt under Chapman v. California, 386 U.S. 18 (1967). The Supreme Court of California denied Powell's petition for habeas corpus relief.

In August 1971 Powell filed an amended petition for a writ of federal habeas corpus under 28 U.S.C. § 2254 in the United States District Court for the Northern District of California, contending that the testimony concerning the .38–caliber revolver should have been excluded as the fruit of an illegal search. He argued that his arrest had been unlawful because the Henderson vagrancy ordinance was unconstitutionally vague, and that the arresting officer lacked probable cause to believe that he was violating it. The District Court concluded that the arresting officer had probable cause and held that even if the vagrancy ordinance was unconstitutional, the deterrent purpose of the exclusionary rule does not require that it be applied to bar admission of the fruits of a search incident to an otherwise valid arrest. In the alternative, that court agreed with the California District Court of Appeal that the admission of the evidence concerning Powell's arrest, if error, was harmless beyond a reasonable doubt.

In December 1974, the Court of Appeals for the Ninth Circuit reversed. 507 F.2d 93. The court concluded that the vagrancy ordinance was unconstitutionally vague, that Powell's arrest was therefore illegal, and that although exclusion of the evidence would serve no deterrent purpose with regard to police officers who were enforcing statutes in good faith, exclusion would serve the public interest by deterring legislators from enacting unconstitutional statutes. Id., at 98. After an independent review of the evidence the court concluded that the admission of the evidence was not harmless error since it supported the testimony of Parsons and Powell's accomplices. Id., at 99.

* * *

Petitioners Stone and Wolff, the wardens of the respective state prisons where Powell and Rice are incarcerated, petitioned for review of these decisions, raising questions concerning the scope of federal habeas corpus and the role of the exclusionary rule upon collateral review of cases involving Fourth Amendment claims. We granted their petitions for certiorari. 422 U.S. 1055 (1975). We now reverse.

II

The authority of federal courts to issue the writ of habeas corpus *ad subjiciendum* was included in the first grant of federal-court jurisdiction, made by the Judiciary Act of 1789, c. 20, § 14, 1 Stat. 81, with the limitation that the writ extend only to prisoners held in custody by the United States. The original statutory authorization did not define the substantive reach of writ. It merely stated that the courts of the United States "shall have power to issue writs of ... *habeas corpus* ... " Ibid. The courts defined the scope of the writ in accordance with the common law and limited it to an inquiry as to the jurisdiction of the sentencing tribunal. See, e.g., Ex parte Watkins, 3 Pet. 193 (1830) (Marshall, C. J.).

In 1867 the writ was extended to state petitioners. Act of Feb. 5, 1867, c. 28, § 1, 14 Stat. 385. Under the 1867 Act federal courts were authorized to give relief in "all cases where any person may be restrained of his or her liberty in violation of the constitution, or of any treaty or law of the United States...." But the limitation of federal habeas corpus jurisdiction to consideration of the jurisdiction of the sentencing court persisted. * * * And, although the concept of "jurisdiction" was subjected to considerable strain as the substantive scope of the writ was expanded, this expansion was limited to only a few classes of cases until Frank v. Mangum, 237 U.S. 309. * * *

In the landmark decision in Brown v. Allen, 344 U.S. 443, 482–487 (1953), the scope of the writ was expanded still further. In that case and its companion case, Daniels v. Allen, state prisoners applied for federal habeas corpus relief claiming that the trial courts had erred in failing to quash their indictments due to alleged discrimination in the selection of grand jurors and in ruling certain confessions admissible. In *Brown*, the highest court of the State had rejected these claims on direct appeal, State v. Brown, 233 N.C. 202, and this Court had denied certiorari, 341 U.S. 943 (1951). Despite the apparent adequacy of the state corrective process, the Court reviewed the denial of the writ of habeas corpus and held that Brown was entitled to a full reconsideration of these constitutional claims, including, if appropriate, a hearing in the Federal District Court. In *Daniels*, however, the State Supreme Court on direct review had refused to consider the appeal because the papers were filed out of time. This Court held that since the state-court judgment rested on a reasonable application of the State's legitimate procedural rules, a ground that would have barred direct review of his federal claims by this Court, the District Court lacked authority to grant habeas corpus relief. See 344 U.S., at 458, 486.

This final barrier to broad collateral re-examination of state criminal convictions in federal habeas corpus proceedings was removed in Fay v. Noia, 372 U.S. 391 (1963). Noia and two codefendants had been convicted of felony murder. The sole evidence against each defendant was a signed confession. Noia's codefendants, but not Noia himself, appealed their convictions. Although their appeals were unsuccessful, in subsequent state proceedings they were able to establish that their confessions had been coerced and their convictions therefore procured in violation of the Constitution. In a subsequent federal habeas corpus proceeding, it was stipulated that Noia's confession also had been coerced, but the District Court followed *Daniels* in holding that Noia's failure to appeal barred habeas corpus review. * * * The Court of Appeals reversed, ordering that Noia's conviction be set aside and that he be released from custody or that a new trial be granted. This Court affirmed the grant of the writ, narrowly restricting the circumstances in which a federal court may refuse to consider the merits of federal constitutional claims.

During the period in which the substantive scope of the writ was expanded, the Court did not consider whether exceptions to full review might exist with respect to particular categories of constitutional claims. Prior to the Court's decision in Kaufman v. United States, 394 U.S. 217 (1969), however, a substantial majority of the Federal Courts of Appeals had concluded that collateral review of search-and-seizure claims was inappropriate on motions filed by federal prisoners under 28 U.S.C. § 2255, the modern postconviction procedure available to federal prisoners in lieu of habeas corpus. The primary rationale advanced in support of those decisions was that Fourth Amendment violations are different in kind from denials of Fifth or Sixth Amendment rights in that claims of illegal search and seizure do not "impugn the integrity of the fact-finding process or challenge evidence as inherently unreliable; rather, the exclusion of illegally seized evidence is simply a prophylactic device intended generally to deter Fourth Amendment violations by law enforcement officers." 394 U.S., at 224. See Thornton v. United States, 368 F.2d 822 (1966).

Kaufman rejected this rationale and held that search-and-seizure claims are cognizable in § 2255 proceedings. The Court noted that "the federal habeas remedy extends to state prisoners alleging that unconstitutionally obtained evidence was admitted against them at trial," 394 U.S., at 225, citing, e.g., Mancusi v. DeForte, 392 U.S. 364 (1968); Carafas v. LaVallee, 391 U.S. 234 (1968), and concluded, as a matter of statutory construction, that there was no basis for restricting "access by federal prisoners with illegal search-and-seizure claims to federal collateral remedies, while placing no similar restriction on access by state prisoners," 394 U.S., at 226. Although in recent years the view has been expressed that the Court should re-examine the substantive scope of federal habeas jurisdiction and limit collateral review of search-and-seizure claims "solely to the question of whether the petitioner was provided a fair opportunity to raise and have adjudicated the question in state courts," Schneckloth v. Bustamonte, 412 U.S. 218 (1973) (Powell, J., concurring), the Court, without discussion or consideration of the issue, has continued to accept jurisdiction in cases raising such claims. * * *

* * * We hold * * * that where the State has provided an opportunity for full and fair litigation of a Fourth Amendment claim, the Constitution does not require that a state prisoner be granted federal habeas corpus relief on the ground that evidence obtained in an unconstitutional search or seizure was introduced at his trial.

* * *

IV

* * * The question is whether state prisoners—who have been afforded the opportunity for full and fair consideration of their reliance upon the exclusionary rule with respect to seized evidence by the state courts at trial and on direct review—may invoke their claim again on federal habeas corpus review. The answer is to be found by weighing the utility of the exclusionary rule against the costs of extending it to collateral review of Fourth Amendment claims.

The costs of applying the exclusionary rule even at trial and on direct review are well known: the focus of the trial, and the attention of the participants therein, are diverted from the ultimate question of guilt or innocence that should be the central concern in a criminal proceeding. Moreover, the physical evidence sought to be excluded is typically reliable and often the most probative information bearing on the guilt or innocence of the defendant. * * * Application of the rule thus deflects the truthfinding process and often frees the guilty. The disparity in particular cases between the error committed by the police officer and the windfall afforded a guilty defendant by application of the rule is contrary to the idea of proportionality that is essential to the concept of justice. * * * These long-recognized costs of the rule persist when a criminal conviction is sought to be overturned on collateral review on the ground that a search-and-seizure claim was erroneously rejected by two or more tiers of state courts.

Evidence obtained by police officers in violation of the Fourth Amendment is excluded at trial in the hope that the frequency of future violations will decrease. Despite the absence of supportive empirical evidence, we have assumed that the immediate effect of exclusion will be to discourage law enforcement officials from violating the Fourth Amendment by removing the incentive to disregard it. More importantly, over the long term, this demonstration that our society attaches serious consequences to violation of constitutional rights is thought to encourage those who formulate law enforcement policies, and the officers who implement them, to incorporate Fourth Amendment ideals into their value system.

We adhere to the view that these considerations support the implementation of the exclusionary rule at trial and its enforcement on direct appeal of state-court convictions. But the additional contribution, if any, of the consideration of search-and-seizure claims of state prisoners on collateral review is small in relation to the costs. To be sure, each case in which such claim is considered may add marginally to an awareness of the values protected by the Fourth Amendment. There is no reason to believe, however, that the overall educative effect of the exclusionary rule would be appreciably diminished if search-and-seizure claims could not be raised in federal habeas corpus review of state convictions. Nor is there reason to assume that any specific disincentive already created by the risk of exclusion of evidence at trial or the reversal of convictions on direct review would be enhanced if there were the further risk that a conviction obtained in state court and affirmed on direct review might be overturned, in collateral proceedings often occurring years after the incarceration of the defendant. The view that the deterrence of Fourth Amendment violations would be furthered rests on the dubious assumption that law enforcement authorities would fear that federal habeas review might reveal flaws in a search or seizure that went undetected at trial and on appeal. Even if one rationally could assume that some additional incremental deterrent effect would be present in isolated cases, the resulting advance of the legitimate goal of furthering Fourth Amendment rights would be outweighed by the acknowledged costs to other values vital to a rational system of criminal justice.

In sum, we conclude that where the State has provided an opportunity for full and fair litigation of a Fourth Amendment claim, a state prisoner may not be granted federal habeas corpus relief on the ground that evidence obtained in an unconstitutional search or seizure was introduced at his trial. In this context the contribution of the exclusionary rule, if any, to the effectuation of the Fourth Amendment is minimal and the substantial societal costs of application of the rule persist with special force.

* * *

Mr. Justice Brennan, with whom Mr. Justice Marshall concurs, dissenting.

* * *

The Court's opinion does not specify the particular basis on which it denies federal habeas jurisdiction over claims of Fourth Amendment violations brought by state prisoners. The Court insists that its holding is based on the Constitution, * * * but in light of the explicit language of 28 U.S.C. § 2254 (significantly not even mentioned by the Court), I can only presume that the Court intends to be understood to hold either that respondents are not, as a matter of statutory construction, "in custody in violation of the Constitution or laws ... of the United States," or that " 'considerations of comity and concerns for the orderly administration of criminal justice,' " * * * are sufficient to allow this Court to rewrite jurisdictional statutes enacted by Congress. Neither ground of decision is tenable; the former is simply illogical, and the latter is an arrogation of power committed solely to the Congress.

I

Much of the Court's analysis implies that respondents are not entitled to habeas relief because they are not being unconstitutionally detained. Although purportedly adhering to the principle that the Fourth and Fourteenth Amendments "require exclusion" of evidence seized in violation of their commands, * * * the Court informs us that there has merely been a "view" in our cases that "the effectuation of the Fourth Amendment ... requires the granting of habeas corpus relief when a prisoner has been convicted in state court on the basis of evidence obtained in an illegal search or seizure.... " * * * Applying a "balancing test," the Court then concludes that this "view" is unjustified and that the policies of the Fourth Amendment would not be implemented if claims to the benefits of the exclusionary rule were cognizable in collateral attacks on state-court convictions.

Understandably the Court must purport to cast its holding in constitutional terms, because that avoids a direct confrontation with the incontrovertible facts that the habeas statutes have heretofore always been construed to grant jurisdiction to entertain Fourth Amendment claims of both state and federal prisoners, that Fourth Amendment principles have been applied in decisions on the merits in numerous cases on collateral review of final convictions, and that Congress has legislatively accepted our interpretation of congressional intent as to the necessary scope and function of habeas relief. Indeed, the Court reaches its result without explicitly overruling any of our plethora of precedents inconsistent with that result or even discussing principles of *stare decisis*. Rather, the Court asserts, in essence, that the Justices joining those prior decisions or reaching the merits of Fourth Amendment claims simply overlooked the obvious constitutional dimension to the problem in adhering to the "view" that granting collateral relief when state courts erroneously decide Fourth Amendment issues would effectuate the principles underlying that Amendment. But, shorn of the rhetoric of "interest balancing" used to obscure what is at stake in this case, it is evident that today's attempt to rest the decision on the Constitution must fail so long as Mapp v. Ohio, 367 U.S. 643 (1961), remains undisturbed.

Under *Mapp*, as a matter of federal constitutional law, a state court *must* exclude evidence from the trial of an individual whose Fourth and Fourteenth Amendment rights were violated by a search or seizure that directly or indirectly resulted in the acquisition of that evidence. * * * When a state court admits such evidence, it has committed a *constitutional* error, and unless that error is harmless under federal standards, see, e.g., Chapman v. California, 386 U.S. 18 (1967), it follows ineluctably that the defendant has been placed "in custody in violation of the Constitution" within the comprehension of 28 U.S.C. § 2254. In short, it escapes me as to what logic can support the assertion that the defendant's unconstitutional confinement obtains during the process of direct review, no matter how long that process takes, but that the unconstitutionality then suddenly dissipates at the moment the claim is asserted in a collateral attack on the conviction.

The only conceivable rationale upon which the Court's "constitutional" thesis might rest is the statement that "the [exclusionary] rule is not a personal constitutional right.... Instead, 'the rule is a judicially created remedy designed to safeguard Fourth Amendment rights generally through its deterrent effect.' " * * * However the Court reinterprets *Mapp*, and whatever the rationale now attributed to *Mapp*'s holding or the purpose ascribed to the exclusionary rule, the prevailing constitutional *rule* is that unconstitutionally seized evidence *cannot be admitted* in the criminal trial of a person whose federal constitutional rights were violated by the search or seizure. The erroneous admission of such evidence is a violation of the Federal Constitution—*Mapp* inexorably means at least this much, or there would be no basis for applying the exclusionary rule in state criminal proceedings—and an accused against whom such evidence is admitted has been convicted in derogation of rights mandated by, and is "in custody in violation of," the Constitution of the United States. Indeed, since state courts violate the strictures of the Federal Constitution by admitting such evidence, then even if federal habeas review did not directly effectuate Fourth Amendment values, a proposition I deny, that review would nevertheless serve to effectuate what is concededly a constitutional principle concerning admissibility of evidence at trial.

* * * It is simply inconceivable that that constitutional deprivation suddenly vanishes after the appellate process has been exhausted. And as between this Court on certiorari, and federal districts courts on habeas, it is for *Congress* to decide what the most efficacious method is for enforcing *federal* constitutional rights and asserting the primacy of federal law. * * * The Court, however, simply ignores the settled principle that for purposes of adjudicating constitutional claims Congress, which has the power to do so under Art. III of the Constitution, has effectively cast the district courts sitting in habeas in the role of surrogate Supreme Courts.

* * *

* * * There is no foundation in the language or history of the habeas statutes for discriminating between types of constitutional transgressions, and efforts to relegate certain categories of claims to the status of "second-class rights" by excluding them from that jurisdiction have been repulsed. Today's opinion, however, marks the triumph of those who have sought to establish a hierarchy of constitutional rights, and to deny for all practical purposes a federal forum for review of those rights that this Court deems less worthy or important. Without even paying the slightest deference to principles of *stare decisis* or acknowledging Congress' failure for two decades to alter the habeas statutes in light of our interpretation of congressional intent to render all federal constitutional contentions cognizable on habeas, the Court today rewrites Congress' jurisdictional statutes as heretofore construed and bars access to federal courts by state prisoners with constitutional claims distasteful to a majority of my Brethren. * * *

[The concurring opinion of CHIEF JUSTICE BURGER is omitted.]

Notes

1. Exactly what issue or issues did the Court in *Stone* decide? Is it more accurate to characterize the decision as a habeas corpus decision, as a fourth amendment decision, or as a combination of the two? Cf. Cover & Aleinikoff, *Dialectical Federalism: Habeas Corpus and the Court,* 86 Yale L.J. 1035, 1087–88 (1977).

2. The Supreme Court has repeatedly refused to extend *Stone* beyond fourth amendment claims. In Rose v. Mitchell, 443 U.S. 545 (1979), the Court, in an opinion by Justice Blackmun, held "that a claim of discrimination in the selection of the grand jury differs so fundamentally from application on habeas of the Fourth Amendment exclusionary rule that the reasoning of *Stone v. Powell* should not be extended to foreclose habeas review of such claims in federal court." Id. at 560–61. The Court reasoned that "[i]n Fourth Amendment cases, courts are called upon to evaluate the actions of the police in seizing evidence, and this Court believed that state courts were as capable of performing this task as federal habeas courts. But

claims that the state judiciary itself has purposely violated the Equal Protection Clause are different. There is a need in such cases to ensure that an independent means of obtaining review by a federal court is available on a broader basis than review only by this Court will permit. A federal forum must be available if a full and fair hearing of such claims is to be had." Id. at 561.

In Kimmelman v. Morrison, 477 U.S. 365 (1986), the Court ruled that a sixth amendment claim of ineffective assistance of counsel was cognizable on habeas review, even though the principal allegation of inadequate representation rested on counsel's failure to file a timely motion to suppress evidence allegedly obtained in violation of the fourth amendment. Justice Brennan's majority opinion distinguished between fourth and sixth amendment rights:

Although it is frequently invoked in criminal trials, the Fourth Amendment is not a trial right; the protection it affords against governmental intrusion into one's home and affairs pertains to all citizens. * * *

The right to counsel is a fundamental right of criminal defendants; it assures the fairness, and thus the legitimacy, of our adversary process. * * *

* * *

* * * In determining [in *Stone*] that federal courts should withhold habeas review where the State has provided an opportunity for full and fair litigation of a Fourth Amendment claim, the Court found it crucial that the remedy for Fourth Amendment violations provided by the exclusionary rule "is not a personal constitutional right." The Court expressed the understanding that the rule "is not calculated to redress the injury to the privacy of the victim of the search and seizure"; instead, the Court explained, the exclusionary rule is predominantly a " 'judicially created' " structural remedy " 'designed to safeguard Fourth Amendment rights generally through its deterrent effect.' " * * *

* * *

In contrast to the habeas petition in *Stone*, who sought merely to avail himself of the exclusionary rule, Morrison seeks direct federal habeas protection of his personal right to effective assistance of counsel.

The right of an accused to counsel is beyond question a fundamental right. Without counsel, the right to a fair trial itself would be of little consequence, for it is through counsel that the accused secures his other rights. * * * [T]he right to counsel is the right to effective assistance of counsel.

Because collateral review will frequently be the only means through which an accused can effectuate the right to counsel, restricting the litigation of some Sixth Amendment claims to trial and direct review would seriously interfere with an accused's right to effective representation. 477 U.S. at 374–78.

Justice Powell, joined by Chief Justice Burger and Justice Rehnquist, concurred in the judgment, but wrote separately to question whether "the admission of illegally seized but reliable evidence can ever constitute 'prejudice' under [the ineffective assistance of counsel cases.]" 477 U.S. at 391.

After *Stone*, *Mitchell*, and *Kimmelman*, should *Miranda* violations (the admission of a confession elicited in the absence of warnings) be cognizable on habeas? Consider the following case.

WITHROW v. WILLIAMS

Supreme Court of the United States, 1993.
507 U.S. 680.

Justice SOUTER delivered the opinion of the Court.

In Stone v. Powell, 428 U.S. 465 (1976), we held that when a State has given a full and fair chance to litigate a Fourth Amendment claim, federal habeas review is not available to a state prisoner alleging that his conviction rests on evidence obtained through an unconstitutional search or seizure. Today we hold that *Stone*'s restriction on the exercise of federal habeas jurisdiction does not extend to a state prisoner's claim that his conviction rests on statements obtained in violation of the safeguards mandated by Miranda v. Arizona, 384 U.S. 436 (1966).

I

Police officers in Romulus, Michigan, learned that respondent, Robert Allen Williams, Jr., might have information about a double murder committed on April 6, 1985. On April 10, two officers called at Williams's house and asked him to the police station for questioning. Williams agreed to go. The officers searched Williams, but did not handcuff him, and they all drove to the station in an unmarked car. One officer, Sergeant David Early, later testified that Williams was not under arrest at this time, although a contemporaneous police report indicates that the officers arrested Williams at his residence.

At the station, the officers questioned Williams about his knowledge of the crime. Although he first denied any involvement, he soon began to implicate himself, and the officers continued their questioning, assuring Williams that their only concern was the identity of the "shooter." After consulting each other, the officers decided not to advise Williams of his rights under Miranda v. Arizona, supra. When Williams persisted in denying involvement, Sergeant Early reproved him:

> "You know everything that went down. You just don't want to talk about it. What it's gonna amount to is you can talk about it now and give us the truth and we're gonna check it out and see if it fits or else we're simply gonna charge you and lock you up and you can just tell it to a defense attorney and let him try and prove differently."

The reproof apparently worked, for Williams then admitted he had furnished the murder weapon to the killer, who had called Williams after the crime and told him where he had discarded the weapon and other incriminating items. Williams maintained that he had not been present at the crime scene.

Only at this point, some 40 minutes after they began questioning him, did the officers advise Williams of his *Miranda* rights. Williams waived those rights and during subsequent questioning made several more inculpatory statements. Despite his prior denial, Williams admitted that he had driven the murderer to and from the scene of the crime, had witnessed the murders, and had helped the murderer dispose of incriminating evidence. The officers interrogated Williams again on April 11 and April 12, and, on April 12, the State formally charged him with murder.

Before trial, Williams moved to suppress his responses to the interrogations, and the trial court suppressed the statements of April 11 and April 12 as the products of improper delay in arraignment under Michigan law. The court declined to suppress the statements of April 10, however, ruling that the police had given Williams a timely warning of his *Miranda* rights. * * *

[After Williams' conviction and appeal, he petitioned the federal district court for a writ of habeas corpus, alleging violation of his *Miranda* rights. The district court granted the writ, and the court of appeals affirmed. The state petitioned for certiorari, arguing that Williams' *Miranda* claim should not be cognizable on habeas.]

II

We have made it clear that *Stone*'s limitation on federal habeas relief was not jurisdictional in nature, but rested on prudential concerns counseling against the application of the Fourth Amendment exclusionary rule on collateral review. See *Stone,* supra, 428 U.S., at 494–495, n. 37. We simply concluded in *Stone* that the costs of applying the exclusionary rule on collateral review outweighed any potential advantage to be gained by applying it there. *Stone,* supra, 428 U.S., at 489–495.

We recognized that the exclusionary rule, held applicable to the States in Mapp v. Ohio, 367 U.S. 643, (1961), "is not a personal constitutional right"; it fails to redress "the injury to the privacy of the victim of the search or seizure" at issue, "for any '[r]eparation comes too late.' " *Stone,* supra, 428 U.S., at 486 (quoting Linkletter v. Walker, 381 U.S. 618, 637 (1965)). The rule serves instead to deter future Fourth Amendment violations, and we reasoned that its application on collateral review would only marginally advance this interest in deterrence. *Stone,* 428 U.S., at 493. On the other side of the ledger, the costs of applying the exclusionary rule on habeas were comparatively great. We reasoned that doing so would not only exclude reliable evidence and divert attention from the central question of guilt, but would also intrude upon the public interest in " '(i) the most effective utilization of limited judicial resources, (ii) the necessity of finality in criminal trials, (iii) the minimization of friction between our federal and state systems of justice, and (iv) the maintenance of the constitutional balance upon which the doctrine of federalism is founded.' " Id., at 491, n. 31 (quoting Schneckloth v. Bustamonte, 412 U.S. 218, 259 (1973) (Powell, J., concurring)).

Over the years, we have repeatedly declined to extend the rule in *Stone* beyond its original bounds. * * *

* * *

In this case, the argument for extending *Stone* again falls short. * * *

* * *

Petitioner, supported by the United States as *amicus curiae*, argues that *Miranda*'s safeguards are not constitutional in character, but merely "prophylactic," and that in consequence habeas review should not extend to a claim that a state conviction rests on statements obtained in the absence of those safeguards. We accept petitioner's premise for purposes of this case, but not her conclusion.

The *Miranda* Court did of course caution that the Constitution requires no "particular solution for the inherent compulsions of the interrogation process," and left it open to a State to meet its burden by adopting "other procedures ... at least as effective in apprising accused persons" of their rights. 384 U.S., at 467. The Court indeed acknowledged that, in barring introduction of a statement obtained without the required warnings, *Miranda* might exclude a confession that we would not condemn as "involuntary in traditional terms," id., at 457, and for this reason we have sometimes called the *Miranda* safeguards "prophylactic" in nature. Calling the *Miranda* safeguards "prophylactic," however, is a far cry from putting *Miranda* on all fours with *Mapp*, or from rendering *Miranda* subject to *Stone*.

As we explained in *Stone*, the *Mapp* rule "is not a personal constitutional right," but serves to deter future constitutional violations; although it mitigates the juridical consequences of invading the defendant's privacy, the exclusion of evidence at trial can do nothing to remedy the completed and wholly extrajudicial Fourth Amendment violation. *Stone*, 428 U.S., at 486. Nor can the *Mapp* rule be thought to enhance the soundness of the criminal process by improving the reliability of evidence introduced at trial. Quite the contrary, as we explained in *Stone*, the evidence excluded under *Mapp* "is typically reliable and often the most probative information bearing on the guilt or innocence of the defendant." 428 U.S., at 490.

Miranda differs from *Mapp* in both respects. "Prophylactic" though it may be, in protecting a defendant's Fifth Amendment privilege against self-incrimination, *Miranda* safeguards "a fundamental *trial* right." The privilege embodies "principles of humanity and civil liberty, which had been secured in the mother country only after years of struggle," and reflects

"many of our fundamental values and most noble aspirations: ... our preference for an accusatorial rather than an inquisitorial system of criminal justice; our fear that self-incriminating statements will be elicited by inhumane treatment and abuses; our sense of fair play which dictates 'a fair state-individual balance by requiring the government to leave the individual alone until good cause is shown for disturbing him and by requiring the government in its contest with the individual to shoulder the entire load;' our respect for the inviolability of the human personality and of the right of each individual 'to a private enclave where he may lead a private life;' our distrust of self-deprecatory statements; and our realization that the privilege, while sometimes 'a shelter to the guilty,' is often 'a protection to the innocent.' " Murphy v. Waterfront Comm'n of New York Harbor, 378 U.S. 52, 55 (1964) (citations omitted).

Nor does the Fifth Amendment "trial right" protected by *Miranda* serve some value necessarily divorced from the correct ascertainment of guilt. "[A] system of criminal law enforcement which comes to depend on the confession 'will, in the long run, be less reliable and more subject to abuses' than a system relying on independent investigation." Michigan v. Tucker, supra, 417 U.S., at 448, n. 23 (quoting Escobedo v. Illinois, 378 U.S. 478, 488–489 (1964)). By bracing against "the possibility of unreliable statements in every instance of in-custody interrogation," *Miranda* serves to guard against "the use of unreliable statements at trial." Johnson v. New Jersey, 384 U.S. 719, 730 (1966).

Finally, and most importantly, eliminating review of *Miranda* claims would not significantly benefit the federal courts in their exercise of habeas jurisdiction, or advance the cause of federalism in any substantial way. As one *amicus* concedes, eliminating habeas review of *Miranda* issues would not prevent a state prisoner from simply converting his barred *Miranda* claim into a due process claim that his conviction rested on an involuntary confession. Indeed, although counsel could provide us with no empirical basis for projecting the consequence of adopting petitioner's position, it seems reasonable to suppose that virtually all *Miranda* claims would simply be recast in this way.[5]

If that is so, the federal courts would certainly not have heard the last of *Miranda* on collateral review. Under the due process approach, as we have already seen, courts look to the totality of circumstances to determine whether a confession was voluntary. * * * We could lock the front door against *Miranda*, but not the back.

We thus fail to see how abdicating *Miranda*'s bright-line (or, at least, brighter-line) rules in favor of an exhaustive totality-of-circumstances approach on habeas would do much of anything to lighten the burdens placed on busy federal courts. We likewise fail to see how purporting to eliminate *Miranda* issues from federal habeas would go very far to relieve such tensions as *Miranda* may now raise between the two judicial systems. Relegation of habeas petitioners to straight involuntariness claims would not likely reduce the amount of litigation, and each such claim would in any event present a legal question requiring an

---

5. Justice O'Connor is confident that many such claims would be unjustified, but that is beside the point. Justifiability is not much of a gatekeeper on habeas.

"independent federal determination" on habeas. Miller v. Fenton, 474 U.S., at 112.

One might argue that tension results between the two judicial systems whenever a federal habeas court overturns a state conviction on finding that the state court let in a voluntary confession obtained by the police without the *Miranda* safeguards. And one would have to concede that this has occurred in the past, and doubtless will occur again. It is not reasonable, however, to expect such occurrences to be frequent enough to amount to a substantial cost of reviewing *Miranda* claims on habeas or to raise federal-state tensions to an appreciable degree. We must remember in this regard that *Miranda* came down some 27 years ago. In that time, law enforcement has grown in constitutional as well as technological sophistication, and there is little reason to believe that the police today are unable, or even generally unwilling, to satisfy *Miranda*'s requirements. And if, finally, one should question the need for federal collateral review of requirements that merit such respect, the answer simply is that the respect is sustained in no small part by the existence of such review. "It is the occasional abuse that the federal writ of habeas corpus stands ready to correct." *Jackson*, 443 U.S., at 322.

* * *

IV

The judgment of the Court of Appeals is affirmed in part and reversed in part, and the case is remanded for further proceedings consistent with this opinion.

It is so ordered.

Justice O'CONNOR, with whom THE CHIEF JUSTICE joins, concurring in part and dissenting in part.

Today the Court permits the federal courts to overturn on habeas the conviction of a double murderer, not on the basis of an inexorable constitutional or statutory command, but because it believes the result desirable from the standpoint of equity and judicial administration. Because the principles that inform our habeas jurisprudence—finality, federalism, and fairness—counsel decisively against the result the Court reaches, I respectfully dissent from this holding.

* * *

II

In *Stone*, the Court explained that the exclusionary rule of Mapp v. Ohio, 367 U.S. 643 (1961), was not an inevitable product of the Constitution but instead " 'a judicially created remedy.' " *Stone, supra*, 428 U.S., at 486 (quoting United States v. Calandra, 414 U.S. 338, 348 (1974)). By threatening to exclude highly probative and sometimes critical evidence, the exclusionary rule "is thought to encourage those who formulate law enforcement policies, and the officers who implement them, to incorporate Fourth Amendment ideals into their value system." *Stone*, 428 U.S., at 492. The deterrent effect is strong: Any transgression of the Fourth Amendment carries the risk that evidence will be excluded at trial. Nonetheless, this increased sensitivity to Fourth Amendment values carries a high cost. Exclusion not only deprives the jury of probative and sometimes dispositive evidence, but also "deflects the truthfinding process and often frees the guilty." Id., at 490. * * *

While that cost is considered acceptable when a case is on direct review, the balance shifts decisively once the case is on habeas. There is little marginal benefit to enforcing the exclusionary rule on habeas; the penalty of exclusion comes too late to produce a noticeable deterrent effect. Id., at 493. Moreover, the rule "divert[s attention] from the ultimate question of guilt," squanders scarce federal judicial resources, intrudes on the interest in finality, creates friction between the state and federal systems of justice, and upsets the "constitutional balance upon which the doctrine of federalism is founded." Id., at 490, 491, n. 31 (quoting Schneckloth v. Bustamonte, 412 U.S. 218, 259 (1973) (Powell, J., concurring)). Because application of the exclusionary rule on habeas "offend[s] important principles of federalism and finality in the criminal law which have long informed the federal courts' exercise of habeas jurisdiction," Duckworth, 492 U.S., at 208 (O'Connor, J., concurring), we held in Stone that such claims would no longer be cognizable on habeas so long as the State already had provided the defendant with a full and fair opportunity to litigate.

I continue to believe that these same considerations apply to Miranda claims with equal, if not greater, force. Like the suppression of the fruits of an illegal search or seizure, the exclusion of statements obtained in violation of Miranda is not constitutionally required. This Court repeatedly has held that Miranda's warning requirement is not a dictate of the Fifth Amendment itself, but a prophylactic rule. Because Miranda "sweeps more broadly than the Fifth Amendment itself," it excludes some confessions even though the Constitution would not. Oregon v. Elstad, 470 U.S. 298, 306 (1985). Indeed, "in the individual case, Miranda's preventive medicine [often] provides a remedy even to the defendant who has suffered no identifiable constitutional harm." Id., at 307.

Miranda's overbreadth, of course, is not without justification. The exclusion of unwarned statements provides a strong incentive for the police to adopt "procedural safeguards," Miranda, 384 U.S., at 444, against the exaction of compelled or involuntary statements. It also promotes institutional respect for constitutional values. But, like the exclusionary rule for illegally seized evidence, Miranda's prophylactic rule does so at a substantial cost. Unlike involuntary or compelled statements—which are of dubious reliability and are therefore inadmissible for any purpose—confessions obtained in violation of Miranda are not necessarily untrustworthy. In fact, because voluntary statements are "trustworthy" even when obtained without proper warnings, Johnson v. New Jersey, 384 U.S. 719, 731 (1966), their suppression actually impairs the pursuit of truth by concealing probative information from the trier of fact.

When the case is on direct review, that damage to the truth-seeking function is deemed an acceptable sacrifice for the deterrence and respect for constitutional values that the *Miranda* rule brings. But once a case is on collateral review, the balance between the costs and benefits shifts; the interests of federalism, finality, and fairness compel *Miranda's* exclusion from habeas. The benefit of enforcing *Miranda* through habeas is marginal at best. To the extent *Miranda* ensures the exclusion of involuntary statements, that task can be performed more accurately by adjudicating the voluntariness question directly. And, to the extent exclusion of voluntary but unwarned confessions serves a deterrent function, "[t]he awarding of habeas relief years after conviction will often strike like lightning, and it is absurd to think that this added possibility ... will have any appreciable effect on police training or behavior." *Duckworth, supra,* 492 U.S., at 211 (O'Connor, J., concurring). * * *

Despite its meager benefits, the relitigation of *Miranda* claims on habeas imposes substantial costs. Just like the application of the exclusionary rule, application of *Miranda's* prophylactic rule on habeas consumes scarce judicial resources on an issue unrelated to guilt or innocence. No less than the exclusionary rule, it undercuts finality. It creates tension between the state and federal courts. And it upsets the division of responsibilities that underlies our federal system. But most troubling of all, *Miranda's* application on habeas sometimes precludes the just application of law altogether. The order excluding the statement will often be issued "years after trial, when a new trial may be a practical impossibility." *Duckworth,* 492 U.S., at 211 (O'Connor, J., concurring). Whether the Court admits it or not, the grim result of applying *Miranda* on habeas will be, time and time again, "the release of an admittedly guilty individual who may pose a continuing threat to society." Ibid.

Any rule that so demonstrably renders truth and society "the loser," McNeil v. Wisconsin, 501 U.S., at 181, " 'bear[s] a heavy burden of justification, and must be carefully limited to the circumstances in which it will pay its way by deterring official lawlessness.' " United States v. Leon, 468 U.S. 897, 908, n. 6 (1984) (quoting Illinois v. Gates, 462 U.S. 213, 257–258 (1983) (White, J., concurring in judgment)). That burden is heavier still on collateral review. In light of the meager deterrent benefit it brings and the tremendous costs it imposes, in my view application of Miranda's prophylactic rule on habeas "falls short" of justification.

III

The Court identifies a number of differences that, in its view, distinguish this case from Stone v. Powell. I am sympathetic to the Court's concerns but find them misplaced nonetheless.

The first difference the Court identifies concerns the nature of the right protected. *Miranda,* the Court correctly points out, fosters Fifth

Amendment, rather than Fourth Amendment, values. The Court then offers a defense of the Fifth Amendment, reminding us that it is " 'a fundamental trial right' " that reflects " 'principles of humanity and civil liberty' "; that it was secured " 'after years of struggle' "; and that it does not serve "some value necessarily divorced from the correct ascertainment of guilt." The Court's spirited defense of the Fifth Amendment is, of course, entirely beside the point. The question is not whether *true* Fifth Amendment claims—the extraction and use of *compelled* testimony—should be cognizable on habeas. It is whether violations of *Miranda*'s prophylactic rule, which excludes from trial voluntary confessions obtained without the benefit of *Miranda*'s now-familiar warnings, should be. The questions are not the same; nor are their answers.

To say that the Fifth Amendment is a " 'fundamental *trial* right,' " is thus both correct and irrelevant. *Miranda*'s warning requirement may bear many labels, but "fundamental trial right" is not among them. Long before *Miranda* was decided, it was well established that the Fifth Amendment prohibited the introduction of compelled or involuntary confessions at trial. And long before *Miranda,* the courts enforced that prohibition by asking a simple and direct question: Was "the confession the product of an essentially free and unconstrained choice," or was the defendant's will "overborne"? Schneckloth v. Bustamonte, 412 U.S., at 225 (quoting Culombe v. Connecticut, 367 U.S. 568 (1961)). *Miranda*'s innovation was its introduction of the warning requirement: It commanded the police to issue warnings (or establish other procedural safeguards) before obtaining a statement through custodial interrogation. And it backed that prophylactic rule with a similarly prophylactic remedy—the requirement that unwarned custodial statements, even if wholly voluntary, be excluded at trial. Excluding violations of *Miranda*'s prophylactic suppression requirement from habeas would not leave true Fifth Amendment violations unredressed. Prisoners still would be able to seek relief by "invok[ing] a substantive test of voluntariness" or demonstrating prohibited coercion directly. The Court concedes as much.

Excluding *Miranda* claims from habeas, then, denies collateral relief only in those cases in which the prisoner's statement was neither compelled nor involuntary but merely obtained without the benefit of *Miranda*'s prophylactic warnings. The availability of a suppression remedy in such cases cannot be labeled a "fundamental trial right," for there is no constitutional right to the suppression of *voluntary* statements. Quite the opposite: The Fifth Amendment, by its terms, prohibits only *compelled* self-incrimination; it makes no mention of "unwarned" statements. On that much, our cases could not be clearer. As a result, the failure to issue warnings does "not abridge [the] constitutional privilege against compulsory self-incrimination, but depart[s] only from the prophylactic standards later laid down by this Court in *Miranda*." *Tucker,* supra, 417 U.S., at 446. If the principles of federalism, finality, and fairness ever counsel in favor of withholding relief on habeas, surely they do so where there is no constitutional harm to remedy.

Similarly unpersuasive is the Court's related argument that the Fifth Amendment trial right is not "necessarily divorced" from the interest of reliability. Whatever the Fifth Amendment's relationship to reliability, *Miranda*'s prophylactic rule is not merely "divorced" from the quest for truth but at war with it as well. The absence of *Miranda* warnings does not by some mysterious alchemy convert a voluntary and trustworthy statement into an involuntary and unreliable one. To suggest otherwise is both unrealistic and contrary to precedent. As I explained above, we have held over and over again that the exclusion of unwarned but voluntary statements not only fails to advance the cause of accuracy but impedes it by depriving the jury of trustworthy evidence. In fact, we have determined that the damage *Miranda* does to the truth-seeking mission of the criminal trial can become intolerable. We therefore have limited the extent of the suppression remedy, see Harris v. New York, 401 U.S. 222, 224–226 (1971) (unwarned but voluntary statement may be used for impeachment), and dispensed with it entirely elsewhere, see *Quarles,* supra (unwarned statement may be used for any purpose where statement was obtained under exigent circumstances bearing on public safety). * * *

The consideration the Court identifies as being "most importan[t]" of all is an entirely pragmatic one. Specifically, the Court "project[s]" that excluding *Miranda* questions from habeas will not significantly promote efficiency or federalism because some *Miranda* issues are relevant to a statement's voluntariness. It is true that barring *Miranda* claims from habeas poses no barrier to the adjudication of voluntariness questions. But that does not make it "reasonable to suppose that virtually all *Miranda* claims [will] simply be recast" and litigated as voluntariness claims. Involuntariness requires coercive state action, such as trickery, psychological pressure, or mistreatment. A *Miranda* claim, by contrast, requires no evidence of police overreaching whatsoever; it is enough that law enforcement officers commit a technical error. Even the forgetful failure to issue warnings to the most wary, knowledgeable, and seasoned of criminals will do. Given the Court's unqualified trust in the willingness of police officers to satisfy *Miranda*'s requirements, its suggestion that their every failure to do so involves coercion seems to me ironic. If the police have truly grown in "constitutional ... sophistication," then certainly it is reasonable to suppose that most technical errors in the administration of *Miranda*'s warnings are just that.

In any event, I see no need to resort to supposition. The published decisions of the lower federal courts show that what the Court assumes to be true demonstrably is not. In case after case, the courts are asked on habeas to decide purely technical *Miranda* questions that contain not even a hint of police overreaching. And in case after case, no voluntariness issue is raised, primarily because none exists. Whether the suspect was in "custody," whether or not there was "interrogation," whether warnings were given or were adequate, whether the defendant's equivocal statement constituted an invocation of rights, whether waiver was knowing and intelligent—this is the stuff that *Miranda* claims are made of. While these questions create litigable issues under *Miranda,* they generally do not indicate the existence of coercion—pressure tactics, deprivations, or exploitations of the defendant's weaknesses—sufficient to establish involuntariness.

Even assuming that many *Miranda* claims could "simply be recast" as voluntariness claims, it does not follow that barring *Miranda*'s prophylactic rule from habeas would unduly complicate their resolution. The Court labels *Miranda* a "bright-line (or, at least, brighter-line) rul[e]" and involuntariness an "exhaustive totality-of-circumstances approach," but surely those labels overstate the differences. *Miranda,* for all its alleged brightness, is not without its difficulties; and voluntariness is not without its strengths. Justice White so observed in his *Miranda* dissent, noting that the Court could not claim that

> "judicial time and effort ... will be conserved because of the ease of application of the [*Miranda*] rule. [*Miranda*] leaves open such questions as whether the accused was in custody, whether his statements were spontaneous or the product of interrogation, whether the accused has effectively waived his rights, ... all of which are certain to prove productive of uncertainty during investigation and litigation during prosecution." *Miranda,* supra, 384 U.S., at 544–545.

Experience has proved Justice White's prediction correct. *Miranda* creates as many close questions as it resolves. * * *

* * *

[The dissenting opinion of Justice Scalia is omitted.]

Notes

1. Are *Miranda* violations distinguishable from fourth amendment violations? Given *Stone* and *Kimmelman,* does the majority or the dissent present the more persuasive arguments?

2. In Herrera v. Collins, 506 U.S. 390 (1993), the Court refused to allow a habeas petitioner (who had been sentenced to death) to present a claim of actual innocence ten years after his conviction, when no independent constitutional violation was alleged. Writing for the Court, Chief Justice Rehnquist explained:

> Claims of actual innocence based on newly discovered evidence have never been held to state a ground for federal habeas relief absent an independent constitutional violation occurring in the underlying state criminal proceeding. * * * This rule is grounded in the principle that federal habeas courts sit to ensure that individuals are not imprisoned in violation of the Constitution—not to correct errors of fact. See, e.g., Moore v. Dempsey, 261 U.S. 86, 87–88 (1923) (Holmes, J.) ("[W]hat we have to deal with [on habeas review] is not the petitioners' innocence or guilt but solely the question whether their constitutional rights have been preserved"). * * *

More recent authority construing federal habeas statutes speaks in a similar vein. "Federal courts are not forums in which to litigate state trials." Barefoot v. Estelle, 463 U.S. 880, 887 (1983). "The guilt or innocence determination in state criminal trials is a decisive and portentous event." Wainwright v. Sykes, 433 U.S. 72, 90 (1977). "Society's resources have been concentrated at that time and place in order to decide, within the limits of human fallibility, the question of guilt or innocence of one of its citizens." Ibid. Few rulings would be more disruptive of our federal system than to provide for federal habeas review of free-standing claims of actual innocence. 506 U.S. at 400–01.

Justice O'Connor, joined by Justice Kennedy, wrote separately to emphasize that "the execution of a legally and factually innocent person would be a constitutionally intolerable event." Id. at 419. She joined the majority opinion, however, because she believed that Herrera was not innocent. Justice White concurred in the judgment only, and also "assume[d]" that it would be unconstitutional to execute an innocent person. Id. at 429. Justice Blackmun, joined by Justices Stevens and Souter, did more than assume the unconstitutionality of of such an event: "Nothing could be more contrary to contemporary standards of decency, or more shocking to the conscience, than to execute a person who is actually innocent." Id. at 430.

Professor Barry Friedman argues that despite the Justices' attempt "to conceal [the] holding," Herrera "actually held, by a vote of 9–0, that innocent people cannot be executed, and that if state channels to review a claim of actual innocence are not open then the federal habeas courts will hear the claim." Friedman, *Failed Enterprise: The Supreme Court's Habeas Reform*, 83 Cal.L.Rev. 485, 509 (1995). He suggests that the Court was virtually foreclosed from any other holding by the "cause-and-prejudice" line of cases. In House v. Bell, 547 U.S. ___, 126 S.Ct. 2064 (2006), the Court again refused to decide whether a claim of innocence is constitutionally cognizable, noting that "whatever burden a hypothetical freestanding innocence claim would require, this petitioner has not satisfied it." For a discussion of state methods of reviewing claims of actual innocence, see Anderson, *Responding to the Challenge of Actual Innocence Claims after Herrera v. Collins*, 71 Temple L.Rev. 489 (1998).

3. *Herrera* squarely raises an issue touched on in both *Stone* and *Withrow*: To what extent should the availability of habeas corpus turn on the innocence of the petitioner? Should a double standard of habeas review be established, with closer collateral federal scrutiny given to alleged constitutional defects that might result in an innocent man being convicted? Cf. Kaufman v. United States, 394 U.S. 217, 235 (1969) (Black, J., dissenting) ("the defendant's guilt or innocence is at least one of the vital considerations in determining whether collateral relief should be available to a convicted defendant.").

Consider Soloff, *Litigation and Relitigation: The Uncertain Status of Federal Habeas Corpus for State Prisoners*, 6 Hofstra L.Rev. 297, 310 (1978):

> The role which guilt or innocence might play in defining the scope of habeas corpus review for claims brought by state prisoners is limited at best. If the underlying premise of the scope of collateral review is that a mechanism should be continuously available to relitigate constitutional claims, then innocence is irrelevant. That is, if the right is enforceable in the first instance irrespective of its bearing on guilt or innocence, the

rationale of relitigation requires that it remain enforceable. Thus, in this context, to the extent that the guilt-innocence inquiry equates justice only with 'correct' results and pays no attention to the means used to secure those results, it is too narrow.

If, on the other hand, the underlying premise of the scope of collateral review is that there should be no relitigation of claims which have been fully and fairly litigated, even if only in the state courts, then the colorable claim of innocence acts as a kind of judicial safety valve. It allows relitigation even though the underlying process appears adequate because of some perception that the wrong result has been reached. In this context, the idea is expansive rather than restrictive.

Contrast with that view the position taken in Friendly, *Is Innocence Irrelevant? Collateral Attack on Criminal Judgments*, 38 U.Chi.L.Rev. 142 (1970). Judge Friendly finds that the needed finality of criminal convictions is significantly undermined by the availability of collateral review, and would therefore generally limit the availability of such review, but he would allow an exception to this principle "where a convicted defendant makes a colorable showing that an error, whether 'constitutional' or not, may be producing the continued punishment of an innocent man." Id. at 160. Under his standard, "the petitioner for collateral attack must show a fair probability that, in light of all the evidence, including that alleged to have been illegally admitted (but with due regard to any unreliability of it) and evidence tenably claimed to have been wrongly excluded or to have become available only after the trial, the trier of the facts would have entertained a reasonable doubt of his guilt." Id.

Think about the cases in this chapter that you have read so far. Do you think the Supreme Court views the purpose of habeas as primarily to protect the innocent, to ensure constitutionally adequate trials, or to deter state courts from constitutional violations? Do the cases give inconsistent answers? Professor Evan Tsen Lee suggests that choosing among these rationales is in fact misguided. Lee, *The Theories of Federal Habeas Corpus*, 72 Wash.U.L.Q. 151 (1994). Professor Lee advocates instead a "hybrid" theory of habeas, which would incorporate many rationales. Professors Joseph Hoffmann and William Stuntz take a somewhat different approach, suggesting that there ought to be two "tracks" for federal habeas petitions:

> On the first track, petitioners who can demonstrate a reasonable probability of innocence would receive de novo review of their federal claims, free of the restrictions currently imposed by the habeas doctrines of procedural default and retroactivity. On the second track, petitioners who cannot make a sufficient showing of innocence would have their federal claims * * * reviewed solely to determine if the state court acted reasonably in denying them.

Hoffmann & Stuntz, *Habeas After the Revolution*, 1993 Sup.Ct.Rev. 65, 69. For a critique of innocence-based reform suggestions, see Hammel, *Diabolical Federalism: A Functional Critique and Proposed Reconstruction of Death Penalty Federal Habeas*, 39 Am.Crim.L.Rev. 1, 36–41 (2002).

TEAGUE v. LANE

Supreme Court of the United States, 1989.
489 U.S. 288.

Justice O'Connor announced the judgment of the Court and delivered the opinion of the Court with respect to Parts I, II, and III, and an opinion with respect to Parts IV and V; in which The Chief Justice, Justice Scalia, and Justice Kennedy join.

In Taylor v. Louisiana, 419 U.S. 522 (1975), this Court held that the Sixth Amendment required that the jury venire be drawn from a fair cross section of the community. The Court stated, however, that "in holding that petit juries must be drawn from a source fairly representative of the community we impose no requirement that petit juries actually chosen must mirror the community and reflect the various distinctive groups in the population. Defendants are not entitled to a jury of any particular composition." The principal question presented in this case is whether the Sixth Amendment's fair cross section requirement should now be extended to the petit jury. Because we adopt Justice Harlan's approach to retroactivity for cases on collateral review, we leave the resolution of that question for another day.

I

Petitioner, a black man, was convicted by an all-white Illinois jury of three counts of attempted murder, two counts of armed robbery, and one count of aggravated battery. During jury selection for petitioner's trial, the prosecutor used all 10 of his peremptory challenges to exclude blacks. Petitioner's counsel used one of his 10 peremptory challenges to exclude a black woman who was married to a police officer. After the prosecutor had struck six blacks, petitioner's counsel moved for a mistrial. The trial court denied the motion. When the prosecutor struck four more blacks, petitioner's counsel again moved for a mistrial, arguing that petitioner was "entitled to a jury of his peers." The prosecutor defended the challenges by stating that he was trying to achieve a balance of men and women on the jury. The trial court denied the motion, reasoning that the jury "appear[ed] to be a fair [one]."

* * *

[After unsuccessful state court appeals,] [p]etitioner * * * filed a petition for a writ of habeas corpus in the United States District Court for the Northern District of Illinois. Petitioner repeated his fair cross section claim, and argued that the opinions of several Justices concurring in and dissenting from the denial of certiorari in McCray v. New York, 461 U.S. 961 (1983), had invited a reexamination of Swain v. Alabama, 380 U.S. 202 (1965), which prohibited States from purposefully and systematically denying blacks the opportunity to serve on juries. He also argued, for the first time, that under *Swain* a prosecutor could be questioned about his use of peremptory challenges once he volunteered an explanation. The District Court, though sympathetic to petitioner's arguments, held that it was bound by *Swain* and Circuit precedent.

On appeal, petitioner repeated his fair cross section claim and his *McCray* argument. A panel of the Court of Appeals agreed with petitioner that the Sixth Amendment's fair cross section requirement applied to the petit jury and held that petitioner had made out a prima facie case of discrimination. A majority of the judges on the Court of Appeals voted to rehear the case en banc, and the panel opinion was vacated. Rehearing was postponed until after our decision in Batson v. Kentucky, 476 U.S. 79 (1986), which overruled a portion of *Swain*. After *Batson* was decided, the Court of Appeals held that petitioner could not benefit from the rule in that case because Allen v. Hardy, 478 U.S. 255 (1986), had held that *Batson* would not be applied retroactively to cases on collateral review. The Court of Appeals rejected petitioner's fair cross section claim, holding that the fair cross section requirement was limited to the jury venire. * * *

II

Petitioner's first contention is that he should receive the benefit of our decision in *Batson* even though his conviction became final before *Batson* was decided. * * *

In *Batson,* the Court overruled that portion of *Swain* setting forth the evidentiary showing necessary to make out a prima facie case of racial discrimination under the Equal Protection Clause. The Court held that a defendant can establish a prima facie case by showing that he is a "member of a cognizable racial group," that the prosecutor exercised "peremptory challenges to remove from the venire members of the defendant's race," and that those "facts and any other relevant circumstances raise an inference that the prosecutor used that practice to exclude the veniremen from the petit jury on account of their race." * * *

In Allen v. Hardy, the Court held that *Batson* constituted an "explicit and substantial break with prior precedent" because it overruled a portion of *Swain*. Employing the retroactivity standard of Linkletter v. Walker, 381 U.S. 618, 636 (1965), the Court concluded that the rule announced in *Batson* should not be applied retroactively on collateral review of convictions that became final before *Batson* was announced. The Court defined final to mean a case " 'where the judgment of conviction was rendered, the availability of appeal exhausted, and the time for petition for certiorari had elapsed before our decision in' *Batson* [.]"

Petitioner's conviction became final two and a half years prior to *Batson,* thus depriving petitioner of any benefit from the rule announced in that case. * * *

* * * We find that *Allen v. Hardy* is dispositive, and that petitioner cannot benefit from the rule announced in *Batson*.

III

Petitioner's second contention is that he has established a violation of the Equal Protection Clause under *Swain.* * * *

* * *

* * * [W]e hold that petitioner's *Swain* claim is procedurally barred, and do not address its merits.

* * *

IV

Petitioner's third and final contention is that the Sixth Amendment's fair cross section requirement applies to the petit jury. As we noted at the outset, *Taylor* expressly stated that the fair cross section requirement does not apply to the petit jury. Petitioner nevertheless contends that the *ratio decidendi* of *Taylor* cannot be limited to the jury venire, and he urges adoption of a new rule. Because we hold that the rule urged by petitioner should not be applied retroactively to cases on collateral review, we decline to address petitioner's contention.

A

In the past, the Court has, without discussion, often applied a new constitutional rule of criminal procedure to the defendant in the case announcing the new rule, and has confronted the question of retroactivity later when a different defendant sought the benefit of that rule. In several cases, however, the Court has addressed the retroactivity question in the very case announcing the new rule. These two lines of cases do not have a unifying theme, and we think it is time to clarify how the question of retroactivity should be resolved for cases on collateral review.

* * *

In our view, the question "of whether a decision [announcing a new rule should] be given prospective or retroactive effect should be faced at the time of [that] decision." Mishkin, Foreword: the High Court, the Great Writ, and the Due Process of Time and Law, 79 Harv.L.Rev. 56, 64 (1965). Retroactivity is properly treated as a threshold question, for, once a new rule is applied to the defendant in the case announcing the rule, even-handed justice requires that it be applied retroactively to all who are similarly situated. Thus, before deciding whether the fair cross section requirement should be extended to the petit jury, we should ask whether such a rule would be applied retroactively to the case at issue. This retroactivity determination would normally entail application of the *Linkletter* standard, but we believe that our approach to retroactivity for cases on collateral review requires modification.

It is admittedly often difficult to determine when a case announces a new rule, and we do not attempt to define the spectrum of what may or may not constitute a new rule for retroactivity purposes. In general, however, a case announces a new rule when it breaks new ground or imposes a new obligation on the States or the Federal Government. See, e.g., Rock v. Arkansas, 483 U.S. 44, 62 (1987) (*per se* rule excluding all hypnotically refreshed testimony infringes impermissibly on a criminal defendant's right to testify on his behalf); Ford v. Wainwright, 477 U.S. 399, 410 (1986) (Eighth Amendment prohibits the execution of prisoners who are insane). To put it differently, a case announces a new rule if the result was not *dictated* by precedent existing at the time the defendant's conviction became final. Given the strong language in *Taylor* and our statement in Akins v. Texas, 325 U.S. 398 (1945), that "[f]airness in [jury] selection has never been held to require proportional representation of races upon a jury," application of the fair cross section requirement to the petit jury would be a new rule.

Not all new rules have been uniformly treated for retroactivity purposes. Nearly a quarter of a century ago, in *Linkletter,* the Court attempted to set some standards by which to determine the retroactivity of new rules. The question in *Linkletter* was whether Mapp v. Ohio, which made the exclusionary rule applicable to the States, should be applied retroactively to cases on collateral review. The Court determined that the retroactivity of *Mapp* should be determined by examining the purpose of the exclusionary rule, the reliance of the States on prior law, and the effect on the administration of justice of a retroactive application of the exclusionary rule. Using that standard, the Court held that *Mapp* would only apply to trials commencing after that case was decided.

The *Linkletter* retroactivity standard has not led to consistent results. Instead, it has been used to limit application of certain new rules to cases on direct review, other new rules only to the defendants in the cases announcing such rules, and still other new rules to cases in which trials have not yet commenced. Not surprisingly, commentators have "had a veritable field day" with the *Linkletter* standard, with much of the discussion being "more than mildly negative." Beytagh, Ten Years of Non–Retroactivity: A Critique and a Proposal, 61 Va.L.Rev. 1557, 1558, and n. 3 (1975).

Application of the *Linkletter* standard led to the disparate treatment of similarly situated defendants on direct review. For example, in Miranda v. Arizona, 384 U.S. 436, 467–473 (1966), the Court held that, absent other effective measures to protect the Fifth Amendment privilege against self-incrimination, a person in custody must be warned prior to interrogation that he has certain rights, including the right to remain silent. The Court applied that new rule to the defendants in *Miranda* and its companion cases, and held that their convictions could not stand because they had been interrogated without the proper warnings. In Johnson v. New Jersey, 384 U.S. 719, 733–735 (1966), the Court held under the *Linkletter* standard that *Miranda* would only be applied to trials commencing after that decision had been announced. Because the defendant in *Johnson,* like the defendants in *Miranda,* was on direct review of his conviction, the Court's refusal to give *Mapp* retroactive effect resulted in unequal treatment of those who were similarly situated. This inequity also generated vehement criticism.

Dissatisfied with the *Linkletter* standard, Justice Harlan advocated a different approach to retroactivity. He argued that new rules should always be applied retroactively to cases on direct review, but that generally they should not be applied retroactively to criminal cases on collateral review. See Mackey v. United States, 401 U.S. 667, 675 (1971) [separate opinion of Harlan, J.].

In Griffith v. Kentucky, 479 U.S. 314 (1987), we rejected as unprincipled and inequitable the *Linkletter* standard for cases pending on direct review at the time a new rule is announced, and adopted the first part of the retroactivity approach advocated by Justice Harlan. We agreed with Justice Harlan that "failure to apply a newly declared constitutional rule to criminal cases pending on direct review violates basic norms of constitutional adjudication." We gave two reasons for our decision. First, because we can only promulgate new rules in specific cases and cannot possibly decide all cases in which review is sought, "the integrity of judicial review" requires the application of the new rule to "all similar cases pending on direct review." We quoted approvingly from Justice Harlan's separate opinion in *Mackey:*

> " 'If we do not resolve all cases before us on direct review in light of our best understanding of governing constitutional principles, it is difficult to see why we should so adjudicate any case at all.... In truth, the Court's assertion of power to disregard current law in adjudicating cases before us that have not already run the full course of appellate review is quite simply an assertion that our constitutional function is not one of adjudication but in effect of legislation.' "

Second, because "selective application of new rules violates the principle of treating similarly situated defendants the same," we refused to continue to tolerate the inequity that resulted from not applying new rules retroactively to defendants whose cases had not yet become final. Although new rules that constituted clear breaks with the past generally were not given retroactive effect under the *Linkletter* standard, we held that "a new rule for the conduct of criminal prosecutions is to be applied retroactively to all cases, state or federal, pending on direct review or not yet final, with no exception for cases in which the new rule constitutes a 'clear break' with the past."

The *Linkletter* standard also led to unfortunate disparity in the treatment of similarly situated defendants on collateral review. An example will best illustrate the point. In Edwards v. Arizona, 451 U.S. 477, 484–487 (1981), the Court held that once a person invokes his right to have counsel present during custodial interrogation, a valid waiver of that right cannot be inferred from the fact that the person responded to police-initiated questioning. It was not until Solem v. Stumes, 465 U.S. 638 (1984), that the Court held, under the *Linkletter* standard, that *Edwards* was not to be applied retroactively to cases on collateral review. In the interim, several lower federal courts had come to the opposite conclusion and had applied *Edwards* to cases that had become final before that decision was announced. Thus, some defendants on collateral review whose *Edwards* claims were adjudicated prior to *Stumes* received the benefit of *Edwards*, while those whose *Edwards* claims had not been addressed prior to *Stumes* did not. This disparity in treatment was a product of two factors: our failure to treat retroactivity as a threshold question and the *Linkletter* standard's inability to account for the nature and function of collateral review. Having decided to rectify the first of those inadequacies, we now turn to the second.

B

Justice Harlan believed that new rules generally should not be applied retroactively to cases on collateral review. He argued that retroactivity for cases on collateral review could "be responsibly [determined] only by focusing, in the first instance, on the nature, function, and scope of the adjudicatory process in which such cases arise. The relevant frame of reference, in other words, is not the purpose of the new rule whose benefit the [defendant] seeks, but instead the purposes for which the writ of habeas corpus is made available." *Mackey,* 401 U.S., at 682 (separate opinion). With regard to the nature of habeas corpus, Justice Harlan wrote:

> "Habeas corpus always has been a *collateral* remedy, providing an avenue for upsetting judgments that have become otherwise final. It is not designed as a substitute for direct review. The interest in leaving concluded litigation in a state of repose, that is, reducing the controversy to a final judgment not subject to further judicial revision, may quite legitimately be found by those responsible for defining the scope of the writ to outweigh in some, many, or most instances the competing interest in readjudicating convictions according to all legal standards in effect when a habeas petition is filed."

Given the "broad scope of constitutional issues cognizable on habeas," Justice Harlan argued that it is "sounder, in adjudicating habeas petitions, generally to apply the law prevailing at the time a conviction became final than it is to seek to dispose of [habeas] cases on the basis of intervening changes in constitutional interpretation." As he had explained in *Desist,* "the threat of habeas serves as a necessary incentive for trial and appellate judges throughout the land to conduct their proceedings in a manner consistent with established constitutional principles. In order to perform this deterrence function, the habeas court need only apply the constitutional standards that prevailed at the time the original proceedings took place."

Justice Harlan identified only two exceptions to his general rule of nonretroactivity for cases on collateral review. First, a new rule should be applied retroactively if it places "certain kinds of primary, private individual conduct beyond the power of the criminal law-making authority to proscribe." Second, a new rule should be applied retroactively if it requires the observance of "those procedures that . . . are 'implicit in the concept of ordered liberty.' " Id., at 693 (quoting Palko v. Connecticut, 302 U.S. 319, 325 (1937) (Cardozo, J.)).

* * *

We agree with Justice Harlan's description of the function of habeas corpus. "[T]he Court never has defined the scope of the writ simply by reference to a perceived need to assure that an individual accused of crime is afforded a trial free of constitutional error." Kuhlmann v. Wilson, 477 U.S. 436, 447 (1986) (plurality opinion). Rather, we have recognized that interests of comity and finality must also be considered in determining the proper scope of habeas review. Thus, if a defendant fails to comply with state procedural rules and is barred from litigating a particular constitutional claim in state court, the claim can be considered on federal habeas only if the defendant shows cause for the default and actual prejudice resulting therefrom. We have declined to make the application of the procedural default rule dependent on the magnitude of the constitutional claim at issue, or on the State's interest in the enforcement of its procedural rule.

* * *

* * * Application of constitutional rules not in existence at the time a conviction became final seriously undermines the principle of finality which is essential to the operation of our criminal justice system. Without finality, the criminal law is deprived of much of its deterrent effect. The fact that life and liberty are at stake in criminal prosecutions "shows only that 'conventional notions of finality' should not have *as much* place in criminal as in civil litigation, not that they should have *none.*" Friendly, Is Innocence Irrelevant? Collateral Attacks on Criminal Judgments, 38 U.Chi.L.Rev. 142, 150 (1970). "[I]f a criminal judgment is ever to be final, the notion of legality must at some point include the assignment of final competence to determine legality." Bator, Finality in Criminal Law and Federal Habeas Corpus for State Prisoners, 76 Harv. L.Rev. 441, 450–451 (1963).

As explained by Professor Mishkin:

> "From this aspect, the *Linkletter* problem becomes not so much one of prospectivity or retroactivity of the rule but rather of the availability of collateral attack—in [that] case federal habeas corpus—to go behind the otherwise final judgment of conviction.... For the potential availability of collateral attack is what created the 'retroactivity' problem of *Linkletter* in the first place; there seems little doubt that without that possibility the Court would have given short shrift to any arguments for 'prospective limitation' of the *Mapp* rule." Mishkin, Foreword, 79 Harv.L.Rev., at 77–78 (footnote omitted).

The "costs imposed upon the State[s] by retroactive application of new rules of constitutional law on habeas corpus ... generally far outweigh the benefits of this application." In many ways the application of new rules to cases on collateral review may be more intrusive than the enjoining of criminal prosecutions, cf. Younger v. Harris, 401 U.S. 37, 43–54 (1971), for it *continually* forces the States to marshall resources in order to keep in prison defendants whose trials and appeals conformed to then-existing constitutional standards. Furthermore, as we recognized in Engle v. Isaac, "[s]tate courts are understandably frustrated when they faithfully apply existing constitutional law only to have a federal court discover, during a [habeas] proceeding, new constitutional commands."

We find these criticisms to be persuasive, and we now adopt Justice Harlan's view of retroactivity for cases on collateral review. Unless they fall within an exception to the general rule, new constitutional rules of criminal procedure will not be applicable to those cases which have become final before the new rules are announced.

V

Petitioner's conviction became final in 1983. As a result, the rule petitioner urges would not be applicable to this case, which is on collateral review, unless it would fall within an exception.

The first exception suggested by Justice Harlan—that a new rule should be applied retroactively if it places "certain kinds of primary, private individual conduct beyond the power of the criminal law-making authority to proscribe" is not relevant here. Application of the fair cross section requirement to the petit jury would not accord constitutional protection to any primary activity whatsoever.

The second exception suggested by Justice Harlan—that a new rule should be applied retroactively if it requires the observance of "those procedures that ... are 'implicit in the concept of ordered liberty,' "—we apply with a modification. The language used by Justice Harlan in *Mackey* leaves no doubt that he meant the second exception to be reserved for watershed rules of criminal procedure:

> "Typically, it should be the case that any conviction free from federal constitutional error at the time it became final, will be found, upon reflection, to have been fundamentally fair and conducted under those procedures essential to the substance of a full hearing. However, in some situations it might be that time and growth in social capacity, as well as judicial perceptions of what we can rightly demand of the adjudicatory process, will properly alter our understanding of the *bedrock procedural elements* that must be found to vitiate the fairness of a particular conviction. For example, such, in my view is the case with the right to counsel at trial now held a necessary condition precedent to any conviction for a serious crime."

In *Desist,* Justice Harlan had reasoned that one of the two principal functions of habeas corpus was "to assure that no man has been incarcerated under a procedure which creates an impermissibly large risk that the innocent will be convicted," and concluded "from this that all 'new' constitutional rules which significantly improve the pre-existing factfinding procedures are to be retroactively applied on habeas." 394

U.S., at 262. In *Mackey,* Justice Harlan gave three reasons for shifting to the less defined *Palko* approach. First, he observed that recent precedent led "ineluctably . . . to the conclusion that it is not a principal purpose of the writ to inquire whether a criminal convict did in fact commit the deed alleged." Second, he noted that cases such as Coleman v. Alabama, 399 U.S. 1 (1970) (invalidating lineup procedures in the absence of counsel), gave him reason to doubt the marginal effectiveness of claimed improvements in factfinding. Third, he found "inherently intractable the purported distinction between those new rules that are designed to improve the factfinding process and those designed principally to further other values."

We believe it desirable to combine the accuracy element of the *Desist* version of the second exception with the *Mackey* requirement that the procedure at issue must implicate the fundamental fairness of the trial. Were we to employ the *Palko* test without more, we would be doing little more than importing into a very different context the terms of the debate over incorporation. Reviving the *Palko* test now, in this area of law, would be unnecessarily anachronistic. Moreover, since *Mackey* was decided, our cases have moved in the direction of reaffirming the relevance of the likely accuracy of convictions in determining the available scope of habeas review. * * * Finally, we believe that Justice Harlan's concerns about the difficulty in identifying both the existence and the value of accuracy-enhancing procedural rules can be addressed by limiting the scope of the second exception to those new procedures without which the likelihood of an accurate conviction is seriously diminished.

Because we operate from the premise that such procedures would be so central to an accurate determination of innocence or guilt, we believe it unlikely that many such components of basic due process have yet to emerge. We are also of the view that such rules are "best illustrated by recalling the classic grounds for the issuance of a writ of habeas corpus— that the proceeding was dominated by mob violence; that the prosecutor knowingly made use of perjured testimony; or that the conviction was based on a confession extorted from the defendant by brutal methods." Rose v. Lundy, 455 U.S. 509, 544 (1982) (Stevens, J., dissenting).

An examination of our decision in *Taylor* applying the fair cross section requirement to the jury venire leads inexorably to the conclusion that adoption of the rule petitioner urges would be a far cry from the kind of absolute prerequisite to fundamental fairness that is "implicit in the concept of ordered liberty." The requirement that the jury venire be composed of a fair cross section of the community is based on the role of the jury in our system. Because the purpose of the jury is to guard against arbitrary abuses of power by interposing the common-sense judgment of the community between the State and the defendant, the jury venire cannot be composed only of special segments of the population. "Community participation in the administration of the criminal law . . . is not only consistent with our democratic heritage but is also critical to public confidence in the fairness of the criminal justice system."

Taylor, 419 U.S., at 530. But as we stated in Daniel v. Louisiana, 420 U.S. 31, 32 (1975), which held that *Taylor* was not to be given retroactive effect, the fair cross section requirement "[does] not rest on the premise that every criminal trial, or any particular trial, [is] necessarily unfair because it [is] not conducted in accordance with what we determined to be the requirements of the Sixth Amendment." Because the absence of a fair cross section on the jury venire does not undermine the fundamental fairness that must underlie a conviction or seriously diminish the likelihood of obtaining an accurate conviction, we conclude that a rule requiring that petit juries be composed of a fair cross section of the community would not be a "bedrock procedural element" that would be retroactively applied under the second exception we have articulated.

Were we to recognize the new rule urged by petitioner in this case, we would have to give petitioner the benefit of that new rule even though it would not be applied retroactively to others similarly situated. In the words of Justice Brennan, such an inequitable result would be "an unavoidable consequence of the necessity that constitutional adjudications not stand as mere dictum." Stovall v. Denno, 388 U.S. [293 (1967)]. But the harm caused by the failure to treat similarly situated defendants alike cannot be exaggerated: such inequitable treatment "hardly comports with the ideal of 'administration of justice with an even hand.' " Our refusal to allow such disparate treatment in the direct review context led us to adopt the first part of Justice Harlan's retroactivity approach in *Griffith.* "The fact that the new rule may constitute a clear break with the past has no bearing on the 'actual inequity that results' when only one of many similarly situated defendants receives the benefit of the new rule."

If there were no other way to avoid rendering advisory opinions, we might well agree that the inequitable treatment described above is "an insignificant cost for adherence to sound principles of decisionmaking." But there is a more principled way of dealing with the problem. We can simply refuse to announce a new rule in a given case unless the rule would be applied retroactively to the defendant in the case and to all others similarly situated. We think this approach is a sound one. Not only does it eliminate any problems of rendering advisory opinions, it also avoids the inequity resulting from the uneven application of new rules to similarly situated defendants. We therefore hold that, implicit in the retroactivity approach we adopt today, is the principle that habeas corpus cannot be used as a vehicle to create new constitutional rules of criminal procedure unless those rules would be applied retroactively to *all* defendants on collateral review through one of the two exceptions we have articulated. Because a decision extending the fair cross section requirement to the petit jury would not be applied retroactively to cases on collateral review under the approach we adopt today, we do not address petitioner's claim.

For the reasons set forth above, the judgment of the Court of Appeals is affirmed.

It is so ordered.

Justice White, concurring in part and concurring in the judgment.

I join Parts I, II, and III of Justice O'Connor's opinion. Otherwise, I concur only in the judgment.

Our opinion in Stovall v. Denno articulated a three-factor formula for determining the retroactivity of decisions changing the constitutional rules of criminal procedure. The formula, which applied whether a case was on direct review or arose in collateral proceedings, involved consideration of the purpose of the new rule, the extent of reliance on the old rule, and the effect on the administration of justice of retroactive application of the new rule. In a series of cases, however, the Court has departed from *Stovall* and has held that decisions changing the governing rules in criminal cases will be applied retroactively to all cases then pending on direct review, e.g., United States v. Johnson, 457 U.S. 537 (1982); Shea v. Louisiana, 470 U.S. 51 (1985); Griffith v. Kentucky, 479 U.S. 314 (1987). I dissented in those cases, believing that *Stovall* was the sounder approach. Other Justices, including The Chief Justice and Justice O'Connor, joined my dissents in those cases. The Chief Justice indicated in *Shea* and *Griffith,* and Justice O'Connor has now concluded, that the *Stovall* formula should also be abandoned in cases where convictions have become final and the issue of retroactivity arises in collateral proceedings.

I regret the course the Court has taken to this point, but cases like *Johnson, Shea,* and *Griffith* have been decided, and I have insufficient reason to continue to object to them. In light of those decisions, the result reached in Parts IV and V of Justice O'Connor's opinion is an acceptable application in collateral proceedings of the theories embraced by the Court in cases dealing with direct review, and I concur in that result. If we are wrong in construing the reach of the habeas corpus statutes, Congress can of course correct us; but because the Court's recent decisions dealing with direct review appear to have constitutional underpinnings, see e.g., Griffith v. Kentucky, correction of our error, if error there is, perhaps lies with us, not Congress.

Justice Blackmun, concurring in part and concurring in the judgment.

I join Part I of Justice Stevens' opinion, concurring in part and concurring in the judgment. So far as the petitioner's claim based upon Swain v. Alabama is concerned, I concur in the result.

Justice Stevens, with whom Justice Blackmun joins as to Part I, concurring in part and concurring in the judgment.

I

For the reasons stated in Part III of Justice Brennan's dissent, I am persuaded this petitioner has alleged a violation of the Sixth Amendment. I also believe the Court should decide that question in his favor. I do not agree with Justice O'Connor's assumption that a ruling in petitioner's favor on the merits of the Sixth Amendment issue would require that his conviction be set aside.

When a criminal defendant claims that a procedural error tainted his conviction, an appellate court often decides whether error occurred before deciding whether that error requires reversal or should be classified as harmless. I would follow a parallel approach in cases raising novel questions of constitutional law on collateral review, first determining whether the trial process violated any of the petitioner's constitutional rights and then deciding whether the petitioner is entitled to relief. If error occurred, factors relating to retroactivity—most importantly, the magnitude of unfairness—should be examined before granting the petitioner relief. Proceeding in reverse, a plurality of the Court today declares that a new rule should not apply retroactively without ever deciding whether there is such a rule.

In general, I share Justice Harlan's views about retroactivity. * * *

I do not agree, however, with the plurality's dicta proposing a "modification" of Justice Harlan's fundamental fairness exception. "[I]t has been the law, presumably for at least as long as anyone currently in jail has been incarcerated," Justice Harlan wrote, "that procedures utilized to convict them must have been fundamentally fair, that is, in accordance with the command of the Fourteenth Amendment that '[n]o State shall ... deprive any person of life, liberty, or property, without due process of law.'" *Mackey,* 401 U.S., at 689. * * * In embracing Justice Cardozo's notion that errors "violat[ing] those 'fundamental principles of liberty and justice which lie at the base of all our civil and political institutions,'" Palko v. Connecticut, must be rectified, Justice Harlan expressly rejected a previous statement linking the fundamental fairness exception to factual innocence. *Mackey,* supra, 401 U.S., at 694.

The plurality wrongly resuscitates Justice Harlan's early view, indicating that the only procedural errors deserving correction on collateral review are those that undermine "an accurate determination of innocence or guilt. . . . " I cannot agree that it is "unnecessarily anachronistic," to issue a writ of habeas corpus to a petitioner convicted in a manner that violates fundamental principles of liberty. Furthermore, a touchstone of factual innocence would provide little guidance in certain important types of cases, such as those challenging the constitutionality of capital sentencing hearings. Even when assessing errors at the guilt phase of a trial, factual innocence is too capricious a factor by which to determine if a procedural change is sufficiently "bedrock" or "watershed" to justify application of the fundamental fairness exception. In contrast, given our century-old proclamation that the Constitution does not allow exclusion of jurors because of race, Strauder v. West Virginia, 100 U.S. 303 (1880), a rule promoting selection of juries free from racial bias clearly implicates concerns of fundamental fairness.

As a matter of first impression, therefore, I would conclude that a guilty verdict delivered by a jury whose impartiality might have been eroded by racial prejudice is fundamentally unfair. Constraining that conclusion is the Court's holding in Allen v. Hardy, 478 U.S. 255 (1986)—an opinion I did not join—that Batson v. Kentucky cannot be applied retroactively to permit collateral review of convictions that became final before it was decided. It is true that the *Batson* decision rested on the Equal Protection Clause of the Fourteenth Amendment and that this case raises a Sixth Amendment issue. In both cases, however, petitioners pressed their objections to the jury selection on both grounds. Both cases concern the constitutionality of allowing the use of peremptories to yield a jury that may be biased against a defendant on account of race. Identical practical ramifications will ensue from our holdings in both cases. Thus if there is no fundamental unfairness in denying retroactive relief to a petitioner denied his Fourteenth Amendment right to a fairly chosen jury, as the Court held in *Allen,* there cannot be fundamental unfairness in denying this petitioner relief for the violation of his Sixth Amendment right to an impartial jury. I therefore agree that the judgment of the Court of Appeals must be affirmed.

* * *

JUSTICE BRENNAN, with whom JUSTICE MARSHALL joins, dissenting.

Today a plurality of this Court, without benefit of briefing and oral argument, adopts a novel threshold test for federal review of state criminal convictions on habeas corpus. It does so without regard for— indeed, without even mentioning—our contrary decisions over the past 35 years delineating the broad scope of habeas relief. The plurality further appears oblivious to the importance we have consistently accorded the principle of *stare decisis* in nonconstitutional cases. Out of an exaggerated concern for treating similarly situated habeas petitioners the same, the plurality would for the first time preclude the federal courts from considering on collateral review a vast range of important constitutional challenges; where those challenges have merit, it would bar the vindication of personal constitutional rights and deny society a check against further violations until the same claim is presented on direct review. In my view, the plurality's "blind adherence to the principle of treating like cases alike" amounts to "letting the tail wag the dog" when it stymies the resolution of substantial and unheralded constitutional questions. Griffith v. Kentucky, 479 U.S. 314, 332 (1987) (White, J., dissenting). Because I cannot acquiesce in this unprecedented curtailment of the reach of the Great Writ, particularly in the absence of any discussion of these momentous changes by the parties or the lower courts, I dissent.

Notes

1. The Court initially experienced some difficulty in applying *Teague.* In Penry v. Lynaugh, 492 U.S. 302 (1989), a majority (including Justice White) embraced the *Teague* standard and extended its use to habeas review of capital cases. The Justices also unanimously concluded that a claim that

the Eighth Amendment's prohibition of cruel and unusual punishments prohibits the execution of a mentally retarded person is cognizable on federal habeas. Although the requested rule was characterized as "new", the Court held that "a new rule placing a certain class of individuals beyond the State's power to punish by death is analogous to a new rule placing certain conduct beyond the State's power to punish at all." *Teague*'s first exception, therefore, was applicable. 492 U.S. at 330.

Penry also argued, however, that he had been sentenced to death in violation of the eighth amendment because the jury was not adequately instructed to take into consideration all of his mitigating evidence. On this issue, Justice O'Connor disagreed with the other members of the *Teague* plurality and wrote, for a bare majority, that the "relief Penry seeks does not 'impos[e] a new obligation' on the State of Texas." Id. at 315. Rather, the Court was "simply asked to [apply] a well-established constitutional principle to * * * a case which is closely analogous to those which have been previously considered in the prior case law." Id. at 314. Justice Scalia wrote, dissenting in part, that it "is rare that a principle of law as significant as that in *Teague* is adopted and gutted in the same Term." Id. at 353.

Justice Scalia's pessimism, however, was premature. The Supreme Court has since regularly found routine habeas claims to be barred under *Teague*. In many of the cases, the "new rule" contended for by petitioner had in fact been adopted by the Supreme Court in an unrelated case decided after petitioner's direct appeals had become final. Nonetheless, the Court barred the claim under *Teague*. In one of the most recent cases, the Court explained why this is so: A claim is barred under *Teague*, the Court said in Lambrix v. Singletary, 520 U.S. 518, 538 (1997), unless it "was *dictated* by precedent—i.e. *no other* interpretation was reasonable." The fact that the Court might have actually adopted the rule in another case, Justice Scalia's majority opinion noted, shows only that the rule is "a reasonable interpretation of prior law—perhaps even the most reasonable one." Id. Reasonableness, however, does not satisfy *Teague*'s strict requirement. For other cases holding new rules inapplicable to cases on collateral review, see Beard v. Banks, 542 U.S. 406 (2004); Schriro v. Summerlin, 542 U.S. 348 (2004); Bousley v. United States, 523 U.S. 614 (1998).

2.   Can *Teague*'s prohibition of the use of new rules in habeas cases benefit a petitioner? What if the petitioner relies on a constitutional rule that was in existence at the time of trial but subsequently overruled? In Lockhart v. Fretwell, 506 U.S. 364 (1993), the Court indicated that the *Teague* rule is designed to protect a state's interest in the finality of its judgments. Accordingly, the "State will benefit from our *Teague* decision in some federal habeas cases, while the habeas petitioner will not. * * * [This] is a perfectly logical limitation of *Teague* to the circumstances which gave rise to it." Id. at 373.

3.   Congress may have incorporated the *Teague* concept of retroactivity in the AEDPA. Section 2244(b)(2) allows successive petitions only if the petitioner can show either new facts or "a new rule of constitutional law, made retroactive to cases on collateral review by the Supreme Court." What if a new rule, announced by the Court in a case on direct review, *should* be made retroactive under the *Teague* standards, but the Supreme Court has

not yet decided the retroactivity question at the time the petitioner files a second or subsequent petition resting on the newly announced rule? Under *Teague*, can the Court decide the retroactivity question in the petitioner's case? Under § 2244(b)(2) can the Court decide the question in the petitioner's case? See Tyler v. Cain, 533 U.S. 656 (2001) (Court cannot decide retroactivity question because federal courts cannot even hear the petition unless the Supreme Court has *already* made the new rule retroactive in a case on direct appeal); see also Horn v. Banks, 536 U.S. 266 (2002) (Court of Appeals must decide properly raised retroactivity question before proceeding to § 2254(d) analysis).

4. The Court has made clear that *Teague* is not a jurisdictional rule, and can be waived by the State. See Godinez v. Moran, 509 U.S. 389 (1993). The consequences of this holding have been somewhat inconsistent. In Caspari v. Bohlen, 510 U.S. 383 (1994), the Court reached the *Teague* question despite the fact that it was not a question presented in the petition for certiorari (although the State did argue it in its petition and briefs), because it was a "necessary predicate to the resolution of the question presented in the petition." Id. at 390. In Schiro v. Farley, 510 U.S. 222 (1994), however, the Court declined to consider the State's *Teague* argument (made in its briefs on the merits) because it had not been argued in opposition to the petition for certiorari. If *Teague* is not jurisdictional, on what basis can the Supreme Court apply it?

5. Some scholars have argued that cases such as *Teague*, which cut back on the availability of federal habeas review, represent unwarranted judicial activism. Others argue that it is Brown v. Allen's expansion of habeas which constitutes the unwarranted activism, and that *Teague* is a necessary return to the *status quo ante*. Professor Jordan Steiker denies both these claims, emphasizing instead the equitable nature of the writ of habeas corpus:

> [T]he scope of federal habeas has always been fashioned as a matter of federal common-law and court-identified equitable principles. The Court has consistently ignored statutory language in determining the availability of a habeas forum. In addition, at each important moment in habeas law, the Court has rejected wholesale jurisdictional barriers to habeas. Instead, the Court has found broad jurisdictional power under the habeas statute but has exercised equitable discretion in barring particular petitioners.

Steiker, *Innocence and Federal Habeas*, 41 U.C.L.A.L.Rev. 303, 309 (1993). Is Professor Steiker offering a description or a justification of current habeas jurisprudence? Is the approach he identifies consistent with the Constitution?

For other scholarly comments on *Teague* and its progeny, see Hoffman, *Retroactivity and the Great Writ: How Congress Should Respond to Teague v. Lane,* 1990 B.Y.U.L.Rev. 183; Arkin, *The Prisoner's Dilemma: Life in the Lower Federal Courts After Teague v. Lane,* 69 N.C.L.Rev. 371 (1991); Kinports, *Habeas Corpus, Qualified Immunity and Crystal Balls: Predicting the Course of Constitutional Law,* 33 Ariz.L.Rev. 115 (1991); Fallon & Meltzer, *New Law, Non–Retroactivity and Constitutional Remedies,* 104 Harv.L.Rev. 1731 (1991); Yackle, *The Habeas Hagioscope,* 66 S.Cal.L.Rev.

2331 (1993); Bandes, *Taking Justice To Its Logical Extreme: A Comment on* Teague v. Lane, 66 S.Cal.L.Rev. 2453 (1993); Friedman, *Pas De Deux: The Supreme Court and The Habeas Courts*, 66 S.Cal.L.Rev. 2467 (1993); Meyer, *"Nothing We Say Matters": Teague and New Rules*, 61 U.Chi.L.Rev. 423 (1994); Bryant, *Retroactive Application of "New Rules" and the Antiterrorism and Effective Death Penalty Act*, 70 Geo.Wash.L.Rev. 1 (2002); Entzeroth, *Reflections on Fifteen Years of the* Teague v. Lane *Retroactivity Paradigm: A Study of the Persistence, the Pervasiveness, and the Perversity of the Court's Doctrine*, 35 N.Mex.L.Rev. 161 (2005).

§ 5. DEFERENCE TO STATE COURT DECISIONS

The exhaustion requirement and the rules governing procedural default ensure that federal habeas courts will almost always be considering claims that have already been adjudicated by state courts. How should the federal court treat a prior state adjudication?

Although federal courts considering habeas petitions have never been required to accord state decisions the full res judicata effect that would be required under section 1738 [discussed in Chapter Eleven], the question of the appropriate deference to state court determinations has been a source of continuing difficulty for both Congress and the Court. In 1966, Congress attempted to codify existing case law by specifying that a state court finding of fact "shall be presumed to be correct" unless any of 8 listed exceptions applied. The exceptions, taken mostly from Townsend v. Sain, 372 U.S. 293, (1963), were designed to identify circumstances under which state court findings of fact might be unreliable. The Supreme Court, applying the statutory provisions, gradually narrowed the scope of the exceptions and broadened the category of "findings of fact," but it consistently maintained that pure questions of law were to be decided *de novo* by the habeas court. See, e.g., Miller v. Fenton, 474 U.S. 104 (1985).

AEDPA, enacted in 1996, altered the statutory provisions governing the treatment of state court decisions. No longer limited to findings of fact, § 2254(d) now reads:

(d) An application for a writ of habeas corpus on behalf of a person in custody pursuant to the judgment of a State court shall not be granted with respect to any claim that was adjudicated on the merits in State court proceedings unless the adjudication of the claim—

(1) resulted in a decision that was contrary to, or involved an unreasonable application of, clearly established federal law, as determined by the Supreme Court of the United States; or

(2) resulted in a decision that was based on an unreasonable determination of the facts in light of the evidence presented in the State court proceeding.

The Supreme Court interpreted the new § 2254(d) in the following case:

WILLIAMS v. TAYLOR

Supreme Court of the United States, 2000.
529 U.S. 362.

JUSTICE STEVENS announced the judgement of the Court and delivered the opinion of the Court with respect to Parts, I, III, and IV, and an opinion with respect to Parts II and V.*

The questions presented are whether Terry Williams' constitutional right to the effective assistance of counsel as defined in Strickland v. Washington, 466 U.S. 668 (1984), was violated, and whether the judgment of the Virginia Supreme Court refusing to set aside his death sentence "was contrary to, or involved an unreasonable application of, clearly established Federal law, as determined by the Supreme Court of the United States," within the meaning of 28 U.S.C. § 2254(d)(1). We answer both questions affirmatively.

[handwritten margin notes: unreas app of fed law? (6th amend right to counsel)]

I

On November 3, 1985, Harris Stone was found dead in his residence on Henry Street in Danville, Virginia. * * * [O]n April 25, 1986, [the police] obtained several statements from [Williams]. In one Williams admitted that, after Stone refused to lend him "a couple of dollars," he had killed Stone with a mattock and took the money from his wallet. In September 1986, Williams was convicted of robbery and capital murder.

At Williams' sentencing hearing, the prosecution proved that Williams had been convicted of armed robbery in 1976 and burglary and grand larceny in 1982. The prosecution also introduced the written confessions that Williams had made in April. The prosecution described two auto thefts and two separate violent assaults on elderly victims perpetrated after the Stone murder. * * * Williams had also been convicted of arson for setting a fire in the jail while awaiting trial in this case. Two expert witnesses employed by the State testified that there was a "high probability" that Williams would pose a serious continuing threat to society.

The evidence offered by Williams' trial counsel at the sentencing hearing consisted of the testimony of Williams' mother, two neighbors, and a taped excerpt from a statement by a psychiatrist. One of the neighbors had not been previously interviewed by defense counsel, but was noticed by counsel in the audience during the proceedings and asked to testify on the spot. The three witnesses briefly described Williams as a "nice boy" and not a violent person. The recorded psychiatrist's testimony did little more than relate Williams' statement during an examination that in the course of one of his earlier robberies, he had removed the bullets from a gun so as not to injure anyone.

* Justice Souter, Justice Ginsburg, and Justice Breyer join this opinion in its en- tirety. Justice O'Connor and Justice Kennedy join Parts I, III, and IV of this opinion.

* * * The weight of defense counsel's closing * * * was devoted to explaining that it was difficult to find a reason why the jury should spare Williams' life.[2]

The jury found a probability of future dangerousness and unanimously fixed Williams' punishment at death. The trial judge concluded that such punishment was "proper" and "just" and imposed the death sentence. The Virginia Supreme Court affirmed the conviction and sentence. * * *

State Habeas Corpus Proceedings

In 1988 Williams filed for state collateral relief in the Danville Circuit Court. * * * [T]he Circuit Court (the same judge who had presided over Williams' trial and sentencing) held an evidentiary hearing on Williams' claim that trial counsel had been ineffective. Based on the evidence adduced after two days of hearings, Judge Ingram found that Williams' conviction was valid, but that his trial attorneys had been ineffective during sentencing. Among the evidence reviewed that had not been presented at trial were documents prepared in connection with Williams' commitment when he was 11 years old that dramatically described mistreatment, abuse, and neglect during his early childhood, as well as testimony that he was "borderline mentally retarded," had suffered repeated head injuries, and might have mental impairments organic in origin. The habeas hearing also revealed that the same experts who had testified on the State's behalf at trial believed that Williams, if kept in a "structured environment," would not pose a future danger to society.

* * * [Judge Ingram found that if Williams had had competent counsel] "there is a reasonable probability that the result of the sentencing phase would have been different." Judge Ingram therefore recommended that Williams be granted a rehearing on the sentencing phase of his trial.

The Virginia Supreme Court did not accept that recommendation. Although it assumed, without deciding, that trial counsel had been ineffective, it disagreed with the trial judge's conclusion that Williams had suffered sufficient prejudice to warrant relief. Treating the prejudice inquiry as a mixed question of law and fact, the Virginia Supreme Court accepted the factual determination that available evidence in mitigation had not been presented at the trial, but held that the trial judge had misapplied the law in two respects. First, relying on our decision in Lockhart v. Fretwell, 506 U.S. 364 (1993), the court held that it was wrong for the trial judge to rely "on mere outcome determination" when assessing prejudice. * * *

2. In defense counsel's words: "I will admit too that it is very difficult to ask you to show mercy to a man who maybe has not shown much mercy himself. I doubt very seriously that he thought much about mercy when he was in Mr. Stone's bedroom that night with him. I doubt very seriously that he had mercy very highly on his mind when he was walking along West Green and the incident with Alberta Stroud. I doubt very seriously that he had mercy on his mind when he took two cars that didn't belong to him. Admittedly it is very difficult to get up and ask that you give this man mercy when he has shown so little of it himself. But I would ask that you would."

The court then reviewed the prosecution evidence supporting the "future dangerousness" aggravating circumstance, reciting Williams' criminal history, including the several most recent offenses to which he had confessed. In comparison, it found that the excluded mitigating evidence—which it characterized as merely indicating "that numerous people, mostly relatives, thought that defendant was nonviolent and could cope very well in a structured environment,"—"barely would have altered the profile of this defendant that was presented to the jury." On this basis, the court concluded that there was no reasonable possibility that the omitted evidence would have affected the jury's sentencing recommendation, and that Williams had failed to demonstrate that his sentencing proceeding was fundamentally unfair.

Federal Habeas Corpus Proceedings

Having exhausted his state remedies, Williams sought a federal writ of habeas corpus pursuant to 28 U.S.C. § 2254. After reviewing the state habeas hearing transcript and the state courts' findings of fact and conclusions of law, the federal trial judge agreed with the Virginia trial judge: The death sentence was constitutionally infirm.

* * * He identified five categories of mitigating evidence that counsel had failed to introduce, and he rejected the argument that counsel's failure to conduct an adequate investigation had been a strategic decision to rely almost entirely on the fact that Williams had voluntarily confessed.

* * *

Turning to the prejudice issue, the judge determined that there was "a reasonable probability that, but for counsel's unprofessional errors, the result of the proceeding would have been different." He found that the Virginia Supreme Court had erroneously assumed that *Lockhart* had modified the *Strickland* standard for determining prejudice, and that it had made an important error of fact in discussing its finding of no prejudice. Having introduced his analysis of Williams' claim with the standard of review applicable on habeas appeals provided by 28 U.S.C. § 2254(d), the judge concluded that those errors established that the Virginia Supreme Court's decision "was contrary to, or involved an unreasonable application of, clearly established Federal law" within the meaning of § 2254(d)(1).

The Federal Court of Appeals reversed. It construed § 2254(d)(1) as prohibiting the grant of habeas corpus relief unless the state court "decided the question by interpreting or applying the relevant precedent in a manner that reasonable jurists would all agree is unreasonable." Applying that standard, it could not say that the Virginia Supreme Court's decision on the prejudice issue was an unreasonable application of the tests developed in either *Strickland* or *Lockhart*. It explained that the evidence that Williams presented a future danger to society was "simply overwhelming," it endorsed the Virginia Supreme Court's interpretation of *Lockhart*, and it characterized the state court's understanding of the facts in this case as "reasonable."

We granted certiorari and now reverse.

II

* * *

The warden here contends that federal habeas corpus relief is prohibited by the amendment to 28 U.S.C. § 2254, enacted as a part of the Antiterrorism and Effective Death Penalty Act of 1996 (AEDPA). The relevant portion of that amendment provides:

> "(d) An application for a writ of habeas corpus on behalf of a person in custody pursuant to the judgment of a State court shall not be granted with respect to any claim that was adjudicated on the merits in State court proceedings unless the adjudication of the claim—
>
> "(1) resulted in a decision that was contrary to, or involved an unreasonable application of, clearly established Federal law, as determined by the Supreme Court of the United States. . . ."

In this case, the Court of Appeals applied the construction of the amendment that it had adopted in its earlier opinion in Green v. French, 143 F.3d 865 (C.A.4 1998). It read the amendment as prohibiting federal courts from issuing the writ unless:

> "(a) the state court decision is in 'square conflict' with Supreme Court precedent that is controlling as to law and fact or (b) if no such controlling decision exists, 'the state court's resolution of a question of pure law rests upon an objectively unreasonable derivation of legal principles from the relevant [S]upreme [C]ourt precedents, or if its decision rests upon an objectively unreasonable application of established principles to new facts,' " 163 F.3d, at 865 (quoting *Green*, 143 F.3d, at 870).

Accordingly, it held that a federal court may issue habeas relief only if "the state courts have decided the question by interpreting or applying the relevant precedent in a manner that reasonable jurists would all agree is unreasonable."

We are convinced that that interpretation of the amendment is incorrect. It would impose a test for determining when a legal rule is clearly established that simply cannot be squared with the real practice of decisional law. It would apply a standard for determining the "reasonableness" of state-court decisions that is not contained in the statute itself, and that Congress surely did not intend. And it would wrongly require the federal courts, including this Court, to defer to state judges' interpretations of federal law.

As the Fourth Circuit would have it, a state-court judgment is "unreasonable" in the face of federal law only if all reasonable jurists would agree that the state court was unreasonable. Thus, in this case, for example, even if the Virginia Supreme Court misread our opinion in

Lockhart, we could not grant relief unless we believed that none of the judges who agreed with the state court's interpretation of that case was a "reasonable jurist." But the statute says nothing about "reasonable judges," presumably because all, or virtually all, such judges occasionally commit error; they make decisions that in retrospect may be characterized as "unreasonable." Indeed, it is most unlikely that Congress would deliberately impose such a requirement of unanimity on federal judges. As Congress is acutely aware, reasonable lawyers and lawgivers regularly disagree with one another. Congress surely did not intend that the views of one such judge who might think that relief is not warranted in a particular case should always have greater weight than the contrary, considered judgment of several other reasonable judges.

The inquiry mandated by the amendment relates to the way in which a federal habeas court exercises its duty to decide constitutional questions; the amendment does not alter the underlying grant of jurisdiction in § 2254(a). When federal judges exercise their federal-question jurisdiction under the "judicial Power" of Article III of the Constitution, it is "emphatically the province and duty" of those judges to "say what the law is." Marbury v. Madison, 1 Cranch 137, 177 (1803). At the core of this power is the federal courts' independent responsibility—independent from its coequal branches in the Federal Government, and independent from the separate authority of the several States—to interpret federal law. A construction of AEDPA that would require the federal courts to cede this authority to the courts of the States would be inconsistent with the practice that federal judges have traditionally followed in discharging their duties under Article III of the Constitution. If Congress had intended to require such an important change in the exercise of our jurisdiction, we believe it would have spoken with much greater clarity than is found in the text of AEDPA.

This basic premise informs our interpretation of both parts of § 2254(d)(1): first, the requirement that the determinations of state courts be tested only against "clearly established Federal law, as determined by the Supreme Court of the United States," and second, the prohibition on the issuance of the writ unless the state court's decision is "contrary to, or involved an unreasonable application of," that clearly established law. We address each part in turn.

The "clearly established law" requirement

In Teague v. Lane, 489 U.S. 288 (1989), we held that the petitioner was not entitled to federal habeas relief because he was relying on a rule of federal law that had not been announced until after his state conviction became final. The anti-retroactivity rule recognized in *Teague*, which prohibits reliance on "new rules," is the functional equivalent of a statutory provision commanding exclusive reliance on "clearly established law." * * * It is perfectly clear that AEDPA codifies *Teague* to the extent that *Teague* requires federal habeas courts to deny relief that is contingent upon a rule of law not clearly established at the time the state conviction became final.

* * *

To this, AEDPA has added, immediately following the "clearly established law" requirement, a clause limiting the area of relevant law to that "determined by the Supreme Court of the United States." If this Court has not broken sufficient legal ground to establish an asked-for constitutional principle, the lower federal courts cannot themselves establish such a principle with clarity sufficient to satisfy the AEDPA bar. In this respect, we agree with the Seventh Circuit that this clause "extends the principle of *Teague* by limiting the source of doctrine on which a federal court may rely in addressing the application for a writ." Lindh v. Murphy, 96 F.3d 856, 869 (C.A.7 1996). * * *

* * *

The "contrary to, or an unreasonable application of," requirement

The message that Congress intended to convey by using the phrases, "contrary to" and "unreasonable application of" is not entirely clear. * * *

* * *

The statutory text likewise does not obviously prescribe a specific, recognizable standard of review for dealing with either phrase. Significantly, it does not use any term, such as "*de novo*" or "plain error," that would easily identify a familiar standard of review. Rather, the text is fairly read simply as a command that a federal court not issue the habeas writ unless the state court was wrong as a matter of law or unreasonable in its application of law in a given case. The suggestion that a wrong state-court "decision"—a legal judgment rendered "after consideration of *facts, and ... law,*" Black's Law Dictionary 407 (6th ed.1990) (emphasis added)—may no longer be redressed through habeas (because it is unreachable under the "unreasonable application" phrase) is based on a mistaken insistence that the § 2254(d)(1) phrases have not only independent, but mutually exclusive, meanings. Whether or not a federal court can issue the writ "under [the] 'unreasonable application' clause," the statute is clear that habeas may issue under § 2254(d)(1) if a state court "decision" is "contrary to ... clearly established Federal law." We thus anticipate that there will be a variety of cases, like this one, in which both phrases may be implicated.

Even though we cannot conclude that the phrases establish "a body of rigid rules," they do express a "mood" that the federal judiciary must respect. In this respect, it seems clear that Congress intended federal judges to attend with the utmost care to state-court decisions, including all of the reasons supporting their decisions, before concluding that those proceedings were infected by constitutional error sufficiently serious to warrant the issuance of the writ. Likewise, the statute in a separate provision provides for the habeas remedy when a state-court decision "was based on an unreasonable determination of the facts *in light of the evidence presented in the State court proceeding.*" 28 U.S.C. § 2254(d)(2)(emphasis added). While this provision is not before us in this case, it provides relevant context for our interpretation of § 2254(d)(1); in this respect, it bolsters our conviction that federal habeas courts must make as the starting point of their analysis the state courts' determinations of fact, including that aspect of a "mixed question" that rests on a finding of fact. AEDPA plainly sought to ensure a level of "deference to the determinations of state courts," provided those determinations did not conflict with federal law or apply federal law in an unreasonable way. Congress wished to curb delays, to prevent "retrials" on federal habeas, and to give effect to state convictions to the extent possible under law. When federal courts are able to fulfill these goals within the bounds of the law, AEDPA instructs them to do so.

On the other hand, it is significant that the word "deference" does not appear in the text of the statute itself. Neither the legislative history, nor the statutory text, suggests any difference in the so-called "deference" depending on which of the two phrases is implicated. Whatever "deference" Congress had in mind with respect to both phrases, it surely is not a requirement that federal courts actually defer to a state-court application of the federal law that is, in the independent judgment of the federal court, in error. As Judge Easterbrook noted with respect to the phrase "contrary to":

> "Section 2254(d) requires us to give state courts' opinions a respectful reading, and to listen carefully to their conclusions, but when the state court addresses a legal question, it is the law 'as determined by the Supreme Court of the United States' that prevails.' " *Lindh*, 96 F.3d, at 869.

Our disagreement with Justice O'Connor about the precise meaning of the phrase "contrary to," and the word "unreasonable," is, of course, important, but should affect only a narrow category of cases. The simplest and first definition of "contrary to" as a phrase is "in conflict with." Webster's Ninth New Collegiate Dictionary 285 (1983). In this sense, we think the phrase surely capacious enough to include a finding that the state-court "decision" is simply "erroneous" or wrong. (We hasten to add that even "diametrically different" from, or "opposite" to, an established federal law would seem to include "decisions" that are wrong in light of that law.) And there is nothing in the phrase "contrary to"—as Justice O'Connor appears to agree—that implies anything less than independent review by the federal courts. Moreover, state-court decisions that do not "conflict" with federal law will rarely be "unreasonable" under either her reading of the statute or ours. We all agree that state-court judgments must be upheld unless, after the closest examination of the state-court judgment, a federal court is firmly convinced that a federal constitutional right has been violated. Our difference is as to the cases in which, at first-blush, a state-court judgment seems entirely reasonable, but thorough analysis by a federal court produces a firm conviction that that judgment is infected by constitutional error. In our view, such an erroneous judgment is "unreasonable" within the meaning of the act even though that conclusion was not immediately apparent.

In sum, the statute directs federal courts to attend to every state-court judgment with utmost care, but it does not require them to defer to the opinion of every reasonable state-court judge on the content of federal law. If, after carefully weighing all the reasons for accepting a state court's judgment, a federal court is convinced that a prisoner's custody—or, as in this case, his sentence of death—violates the Constitution, that independent judgment should prevail. Otherwise the federal "law as determined by the Supreme Court of the United States" might be applied by the federal courts one way in Virginia and another way in California. In light of the well-recognized interest in ensuring that federal courts interpret federal law in a uniform way, we are convinced that Congress did not intend the statute to produce such a result.

III

In this case, Williams contends that he was denied his constitutionally guaranteed right to the effective assistance of counsel when his trial lawyers failed to investigate and to present substantial mitigating evidence to the sentencing jury. The threshold question under AEDPA is whether Williams seeks to apply a rule of law that was clearly established at the time his state-court conviction became final. That question is easily answered because the merits of his claim are squarely governed by our holding in Strickland v. Washington, 466 U.S. 668 (1984).

* * *

* * * Williams is therefore entitled to relief if the Virginia Supreme Court's decision rejecting his ineffective-assistance claim was either "contrary to, or involved an unreasonable application of," that established law. It was both.

IV

The Virginia Supreme Court erred in holding that our decision in Lockhart v. Fretwell, 506 U.S. 364 (1993), modified or in some way supplanted the rule set down in *Strickland*. * * *

* * *

* * * The trial judge analyzed the ineffective-assistance claim under the correct standard; the Virginia Supreme Court did not.

We are likewise persuaded that the Virginia trial judge correctly applied both components of that standard to Williams' ineffectiveness claim. * * *

* * *

We are also persuaded, unlike the Virginia Supreme Court, that counsel's unprofessional service prejudiced Williams within the meaning of *Strickland*. After hearing the additional evidence developed in the postconviction proceedings, the very judge who presided at Williams' trial and who once determined that the death penalty was "just" and "appropriate," concluded that there existed "a reasonable probability that the result of the sentencing phase would have been different" if the jury had heard that evidence. * * *

The Virginia Supreme Court's own analysis of prejudice reaching the contrary conclusion was thus unreasonable in at least two respects. First, as we have already explained, the State Supreme Court mischaracterized at best the appropriate rule, made clear by this Court in *Strickland*, for determining whether counsel's assistance was effective within the meaning of the Constitution. While it may also have conducted an "outcome determinative" analysis of its own, it is evident to us that the court's decision turned on its erroneous view that a "mere" difference in outcome is not sufficient to establish constitutionally ineffective assistance of counsel. Its analysis in this respect was thus not only "contrary to," but also, inasmuch as the Virginia Supreme Court relied on the inapplicable exception recognized in *Lockhart*, an "unreasonable application of" the clear law as established by this Court.

Second, the State Supreme Court's prejudice determination was unreasonable insofar as it failed to evaluate the totality of the available mitigation evidence—both that adduced at trial, and the evidence adduced in the habeas proceeding—in reweighing it against the evidence in aggravation. * * *

V

In our judgment, the state trial judge was correct both in his recognition of the established legal standard for determining counsel's effectiveness, and in his conclusion that the entire postconviction record, viewed as a whole and cumulative of mitigation evidence presented originally, raised "a reasonable probability that the result of the sentencing proceeding would have been different" if competent counsel had presented and explained the significance of all the available evidence. It follows that the Virginia Supreme Court rendered a "decision that was contrary to, or involved an unreasonable application of, clearly established Federal law." Williams' constitutional right to the effective assistance of counsel as defined in Strickland v. Washington, 466 U.S. 668 (1984), was violated.

Accordingly, the judgment of the Court of Appeals is reversed, and the case is remanded for further proceedings consistent with this opinion.

JUSTICE O'CONNOR delivered the opinion of the Court with respect to Part II * * *, concurred in part, and concurred in the judgment.*

---

* Justice Kennedy joins this opinion in its entirety. The Chief Justice and Justice Thomas join this opinion with respect to Part II. Justice Scalia joins this opinion with respect to Part II * * *.

In 1996, Congress enacted the Antiterrorism and Effective Death Penalty Act (AEDPA). In that Act, Congress placed a new restriction on the power of federal courts to grant writs of habeas corpus to state prisoners. The relevant provision, 28 U.S.C. § 2254(d)(1), prohibits a federal court from granting an application for a writ of habeas corpus with respect to a claim adjudicated on the merits in state court unless that adjudication "resulted in a decision that was contrary to, or involved an unreasonable application of, clearly established Federal law, as determined by the Supreme Court of the United States." The Court holds today that the Virginia Supreme Court's adjudication of Terry Williams' application for state habeas corpus relief resulted in just such a decision. I agree with that determination and join Parts I, III, and IV of the Court's opinion. Because I disagree, however, with the interpretation of § 2254(d)(1) set forth in Part II of Justice STEVENS' opinion, I write separately to explain my views.

I

Before 1996, this Court held that a federal court entertaining a state prisoner's application for habeas relief must exercise its independent judgment when deciding both questions of constitutional law and mixed constitutional questions (i.e., application of constitutional law to fact). * * *

* * *

If today's case were governed by the federal habeas statute prior to Congress' enactment of AEDPA in 1996, I would agree with Justice STEVENS that Williams' petition for habeas relief must be granted if we, in our independent judgment, were to conclude that his Sixth Amendment right to effective assistance of counsel was violated.

II

A

Williams' case is *not* governed by the pre–1996 version of the habeas statute. Because he filed his petition in December 1997, Williams' case is governed by the statute as amended by AEDPA. * * *

Justice Stevens' opinion in Part II essentially contends that § 2254(d)(1) does not alter the previously settled rule of independent review. Indeed, the opinion concludes its statutory inquiry with the somewhat empty finding that § 2254(d)(1) does no more than express a " 'mood' that the federal judiciary must respect." For Justice Stevens, the congressionally enacted "mood" has two important qualities. First, "federal courts [must] attend to every state-court judgment with utmost care" by "carefully weighing all the reasons for accepting a state court's judgment." Second, if a federal court undertakes that careful review and yet remains convinced that a prisoner's custody violates the Constitution, "that independent judgment should prevail."

One need look no further than our decision in *Miller* to see that Justice Stevens' interpretation of § 2254(d)(1) gives the 1996 amendment no effect whatsoever. The command that federal courts should now use the "utmost care" by "carefully weighing" the reasons supporting a state court's judgment echoes our pre-AEDPA statement in *Miller* that federal habeas courts "should, of course, give great weight to the considered conclusions of a coequal state judiciary." 474 U.S., at 112. Similarly, the requirement that the independent judgment of a federal court must in the end prevail essentially repeats the conclusion we reached in the very next sentence in *Miller* with respect to the specific issue presented there: "But, as we now reaffirm, the ultimate question whether, under the totality of the circumstances, the challenged confession was obtained in a manner compatible with the requirements of the Constitution *is a matter for independent federal determination.*" *Ibid.* (emphasis added).

That Justice Stevens would find the new § 2254(d)(1) to have no effect on the prior law of habeas corpus is remarkable given his apparent acknowledgment that Congress wished to bring change to the field. ("Congress wished to curb delays, to prevent 'retrials' on federal habeas, and to give effect to state convictions to the extent possible under law"). That acknowledgment is correct and significant to this case. It cannot be disputed that Congress viewed § 2254(d)(1) as an important means by which its goals for habeas reform would be achieved.

Justice Stevens arrives at his erroneous interpretation by means of one critical misstep. He fails to give independent meaning to both the "contrary to" and "unreasonable application" clauses of the statute. ("We are not persuaded that the phrases define two mutually exclusive categories of questions"). By reading § 2254(d)(1) as one general restriction on the power of the federal habeas court, Justice Stevens manages to avoid confronting the specific meaning of the statute's "unreasonable application" clause and its ramifications for the independent-review rule. It is, however, a cardinal principle of statutory construction that we must "give effect, if possible, to every clause and word of a statute." Section 2254(d)(1) defines two categories of cases in which a state prisoner may obtain federal habeas relief with respect to a claim adjudicated on the merits in state court. Under the statute, a federal court may grant a writ of habeas corpus if the relevant state-court decision was either (1) "*contrary to* . . . clearly established Federal law, as determined by the Supreme Court of the United States," or (2) "*involved an unreasonable application of* . . . clearly established Federal law, as determined by the Supreme Court of the United States." (Emphases added.)

The Court of Appeals for the Fourth Circuit properly accorded both the "contrary to" and "unreasonable application" clauses independent meaning. The Fourth Circuit's interpretation of § 2254(d)(1) in Williams' case relied, in turn, on that court's previous decision in Green

v. French, 143 F.3d 865 (1998). With respect to the first of the two
statutory clauses, the Fourth Circuit held in *Green* that a state-court
decision can be "contrary to" this Court's clearly established precedent
in two ways. First, a state-court decision is contrary to this Court's
precedent if the state court arrives at a conclusion opposite to that
reached by this Court on a question of law. Second, a state-court decision
is also contrary to this Court's precedent if the state court confronts
facts that are materially indistinguishable from a relevant Supreme
Court precedent and arrives at a result opposite to ours.

The word "contrary" is commonly understood to mean "diametrically different," "opposite in character or nature," or "mutually opposed."
Webster's Third New International Dictionary 495 (1976). The text of
§ 2254(d)(1) therefore suggests that the state court's decision must be
substantially different from the relevant precedent of this Court. The
Fourth Circuit's interpretation of the "contrary to" clause accurately
reflects this textual meaning. A state-court decision will certainly be
contrary to our clearly established precedent if the state court applies a
rule that contradicts the governing law set forth in our cases. Take, for
example, our decision in Strickland v. Washington, 466 U.S. 668 (1984).
If a state court were to reject a prisoner's claim of ineffective assistance
of counsel on the grounds that the prisoner had not established by a
preponderance of the evidence that the result of his criminal proceeding
would have been different, that decision would be "diametrically different," "opposite in character or nature," and "mutually opposed" to our
clearly established precedent because we held in *Strickland* that the
prisoner need only demonstrate a "reasonable probability that ... the
result of the proceeding would have been different." Id., at 694. A state-
court decision will also be contrary to this Court's clearly established
precedent if the state court confronts a set of facts that are materially
indistinguishable from a decision of this Court and nevertheless arrives
at a result different from our precedent. Accordingly, in either of these
two scenarios, a federal court will be unconstrained by § 2254(d)(1)
because the state-court decision falls within that provision's "contrary
to" clause.

On the other hand, a run-of-the-mill state-court decision applying
the correct legal rule from our cases to the facts of a prisoner's case
would not fit comfortably within § 2254(d)(1)'s "contrary to" clause.
Assume, for example, that a state-court decision on a prisoner's ineffective-assistance claim correctly identifies *Strickland* as the controlling
legal authority and, applying that framework, rejects the prisoner's
claim. Quite clearly, the state-court decision would be in accord with our
decision in *Strickland* as to the legal prerequisites for establishing an
ineffective-assistance claim, even assuming the federal court considering
the prisoner's habeas application might reach a different result applying
the *Strickland* framework itself. It is difficult, however, to describe such
a run-of-the-mill state-court decision as "diametrically different" from,
"opposite in character or nature" from, or "mutually opposed" to
Strickland, our clearly established precedent. Although the state-court

decision may be contrary to the federal court's conception of how *Strickland* ought to be applied in that particular case, the decision is not "mutually opposed" to *Strickland* itself.

Justice Stevens would instead construe § 2254(d)(1)'s "contrary to" clause to encompass such a routine state-court decision. That construction, however, saps the "unreasonable application" clause of any meaning. If a federal habeas court can, under the "contrary to" clause, issue the writ whenever it concludes that the state court's application of clearly established federal law was incorrect, the "unreasonable application" clause becomes a nullity. We must, however, if possible, give meaning to every clause of the statute. Justice Stevens not only makes no attempt to do so, but also construes the "contrary to" clause in a manner that ensures that the "unreasonable application" clause will have no independent meaning. We reject that expansive interpretation of the statute. Reading § 2254(d)(1)'s "contrary to" clause to permit a federal court to grant relief in cases where a state court's error is limited to the manner in which it *applies* Supreme Court precedent is suspect given the logical and natural fit of the neighboring "unreasonable application" clause to such cases.

The Fourth Circuit's interpretation of the "unreasonable application" clause of § 2254(d)(1) is generally correct. That court held in *Green* that a state-court decision can involve an "unreasonable application" of this Court's clearly established precedent in two ways. First, a state-court decision involves an unreasonable application of this Court's precedent if the state court identifies the correct governing legal rule from this Court's cases but unreasonably applies it to the facts of the particular state prisoner's case. Second, a state-court decision also involves an unreasonable application of this Court's precedent if the state court either unreasonably extends a legal principle from our precedent to a new context where it should not apply or unreasonably refuses to extend that principle to a new context where it should apply.

A state-court decision that correctly identifies the governing legal rule but applies it unreasonably to the facts of a particular prisoner's case certainly would qualify as a decision "involv[ing] an unreasonable application of . . . clearly established Federal law." Indeed, we used the almost identical phrase "application of law" to describe a state court's application of law to fact in the certiorari question we posed to the parties in *Wright*.

The Fourth Circuit also held in *Green* that state-court decisions that unreasonably extend a legal principle from our precedent to a new context where it should not apply (or unreasonably refuse to extend a legal principle to a new context where it should apply) should be analyzed under § 2254(d)(1)'s "unreasonable application" clause. Although that holding may perhaps be correct, the classification does have some problems of precision. Just as it is sometimes difficult to distinguish a mixed question of law and fact from a question of fact, it will often be difficult to identify separately those state-court decisions that involve an unreasonable application of a legal principle (or an unreasonable failure to apply a legal principle) to a new context. Indeed, on the one hand, in some cases it will be hard to distinguish a decision involving an unreasonable extension of a legal principle from a decision involving an unreasonable application of law to facts. On the other hand, in many of the same cases it will also be difficult to distinguish a decision involving an unreasonable extension of a legal principle from a decision that "arrives at a conclusion opposite to that reached by this Court on a question of law." Today's case does not require us to decide how such "extension of legal principle" cases should be treated under § 2254(d)(1). For now it is sufficient to hold that when a state-court decision unreasonably applies the law of this Court to the facts of a prisoner's case, a federal court applying § 2254(d)(1) may conclude that the state-court decision falls within that provision's "unreasonable application" clause.

B

There remains the task of defining what exactly qualifies as an "unreasonable application" of law under § 2254(d)(1). The Fourth Circuit held in *Green* that a state-court decision involves an "unreasonable application of ... clearly established Federal law" only if the state court has applied federal law "in a manner that reasonable jurists would all agree is unreasonable." The placement of this additional overlay on the "unreasonable application" clause was erroneous. * * *

Defining an "unreasonable application" by reference to a "reasonable jurist," however, is of little assistance to the courts that must apply § 2254(d)(1) and, in fact, may be misleading. Stated simply, a federal habeas court making the "unreasonable application" inquiry should ask whether the state court's application of clearly established federal law was objectively unreasonable. The federal habeas court should not transform the inquiry into a subjective one by resting its determination instead on the simple fact that at least one of the Nation's jurists has applied the relevant federal law in the same manner the state court did in the habeas petitioner's case. The "all reasonable jurists" standard would tend to mislead federal habeas courts by focusing their attention on a subjective inquiry rather than on an objective one. * * * As I explained in *Wright* with respect to the "reasonable jurist" standard in the *Teague* context, "[e]ven though we have characterized the new rule inquiry as whether 'reasonable jurists' could disagree as to whether a result is dictated by precedent, the standard for determining when a case establishes a new rule is 'objective,' and the mere existence of conflicting authority does not necessarily mean a rule is new." 505 U.S., at 304 (citation omitted).

The term "unreasonable" is no doubt difficult to define. That said, it is a common term in the legal world and, accordingly, federal judges are familiar with its meaning. For purposes of today's opinion, the most important point is that an *unreasonable* application of federal law is different from an *incorrect* application of federal law. * * *

* * *

Throughout this discussion the meaning of the phrase "clearly established Federal law, as determined by the Supreme Court of the United States" has been put to the side. That statutory phrase refers to the holdings, as opposed to the dicta, of this Court's decisions as of the time of the relevant state-court decision. In this respect, the "clearly established Federal law" phrase bears only a slight connection to our *Teague* jurisprudence. With one caveat, whatever would qualify as an old rule under our *Teague* jurisprudence will constitute "clearly established Federal law, as determined by the Supreme Court of the United States" under § 2254(d)(1). The one caveat, as the statutory language makes clear, is that § 2254(d)(1) restricts the source of clearly established law to this Court's jurisprudence.

In sum, § 2254(d)(1) places a new constraint on the power of a federal habeas court to grant a state prisoner's application for a writ of habeas corpus with respect to claims adjudicated on the merits in state court. Under § 2254(d)(1), the writ may issue only if one of the following two conditions is satisfied—the state-court adjudication resulted in a decision that (1) "was contrary to . . . clearly established Federal law, as determined by the Supreme Court of the United States," or (2) "involved an unreasonable application of . . . clearly established Federal law, as determined by the Supreme Court of the United States." Under the "contrary to" clause, a federal habeas court may grant the writ if the state court arrives at a conclusion opposite to that reached by this Court on a question of law or if the state court decides a case differently than this Court has on a set of materially indistinguishable facts. Under the "unreasonable application" clause, a federal habeas court may grant the writ if the state court identifies the correct governing legal principle from this Court's decisions but unreasonably applies that principle to the facts of the prisoner's case.

III

Although I disagree with Justice Stevens concerning the standard we must apply under § 2254(d)(1) in evaluating Terry Williams' claims on habeas, I agree with the Court that the Virginia Supreme Court's adjudication of Williams' claim of ineffective assistance of counsel resulted in a decision that was both contrary to and involved an unreasonable application of this Court's clearly established precedent. Specifically, I believe that the Court's discussion in Parts III and IV is correct and that it demonstrates the reasons that the Virginia Supreme Court's decision in Williams' case, even under the interpretation of § 2254(d)(1) I have set forth above, was both contrary to and involved an unreasonable application of our precedent.

* * *

[The dissenting opinion of CHIEF JUSTICE REHNQUIST, with whom JUSTICE SCALIA and JUSTICE THOMAS join, is omitted.]

Notes

1. The dispute between Justice Stevens and Justice O'Connor centers on the meaning of the phrase "contrary to, or an unreasonable application of" federal law. Who gets the better of the argument? What was Congress trying to do in enacting § 2254(d)(1)?

2. Justice O'Connor suggests that not every "incorrect" application of federal law is an "unreasonable" application. What sorts of cases might fall into this category of "wrong, but not unreasonable" holdings? Is the existence of this category inconsistent with *Marbury*? See Liebman & Ryan, *"Some Effectual Power:" The Quantity and Quality of Decisionmaking Required of Article III Courts*, 98 Colum.L.Rev. 696, 868–73 (1998); Liebman, *An "Effective Death Penalty"? AEDPA and Error Detection in Capital Cases*, 67 Brook.L.Rev. 411 (2001). Is Justice O'Connor's position consistent with the purposes of habeas corpus? See Chen, *Shadow Law: Reasonable Unreasonableness, Habeas Theory, and the Nature of Legal Rules*, 2 Buff. Crim.L.Rev.535 (1999). For commentary on *Williams*, see Pettys, *Federal Habeas Relief and the New Tolerance for "Reasonably Erroneous" Applications of Federal Law*, 63 Ohio St.L.J. 731 (2002); Berry, *Seeking Clarity in the Federal Habeas Fog: Determining What Constitutes "Clearly Established" Law Under the Antiterrorism and Effective Death Penalty Act*, 54 Cath.U.L.Rev. 747 (2005).

3. In Simmons v. South Carolina, 512 U.S. 154 (1994), the Supreme Court held that a jury determining whether to impose a death sentence must be told if the defendant would be ineligible for parole if the jury imposed life imprisonment instead. Under a Virginia "three-strikes" law, a defendant who is convicted of a third specified crime of violence is ineligible for parole. However, Virginia law also provides that convictions are not final until the jury renders its verdict *and* the judge enters a final judgment of conviction. In Ramdass v. Angelone, 530 U.S. 156 (2000), a Virginia defendant was convicted of his third murder. At the time the jury considered his sentence, a final judgment had been entered on only one of his two prior convictions. The other judgment was entered shortly thereafter. The Virginia Supreme Court held that at the time of sentencing, Ramdass was *not* parole ineligible under the state's three-strikes law, and thus that *Simmons* did not apply. It affirmed Ramdass's death sentence despite the fact that the trial judge had refused Ramdass's request to inform the jury that he would be ineligible for parole should they impose life imprisonment. Is the Virginia court's ruling "contrary to, or an unreasonable application of" *Simmons*? Is this an example of what Justice O'Connor in *Williams* describes as an "unreasonabl[e] refus[al] to extend a legal principle to a new context where it should apply"?

4. The Court again found a state court application of Supreme Court precedent to be "unreasonable" in Penry v. Johnson, 532 U.S. 782 (2001). Despite the Court's finding of unreasonableness in *Williams* and *Penry*,

however, subsequent cases have shown that § 2254(d) imposes severe limitations on the federal courts' ability to grant the writ. Between 2002 and 2006, the Supreme Court reversed fourteen cases in which lower courts had found a state ruling to be contrary to, or an unreasonable application of, established precedent. See Rice v. Collins, 546 U.S. ___, 126 S.Ct. 969 (2006); Bradshaw v. Richey, 546 U.S. ___, 126 S.Ct. 602 (2005); Kane v. Garcia Espitia, 546 U.S. ___, 126 S.Ct. 407 (2005); Brown v. Payton, 544 U.S. 133 (2005); Bell v. Cone, 543 U.S. 447 (2005); Holland v. Jackson, 542 U.S. 649 (2004); Yarborough v. Alvarado, 541 U.S. 652 (2004); Middleton v. McNeil, 541 U.S. 433 (2004); Mitchell v. Esparza, 540 U.S. 12 (2003); Yarborough v. Gentry, 540 U.S. 1 (2003); Price v. Vincent, 538 U.S. 634 (2003); Lockyer v. Andrade, 538 U.S. 63 (2003); Woodford v. Visciotti, 537 U.S. 19 (2002); Early v. Packer, 537 U.S. 3 (2002). A divided Court did find the requisite unreasonableness, entitling the petitioner to habeas relief, in Miller–El v. Dretke, 545 U.S. 231 (2005), involving claims of race discrimination in jury selection.

5. How can part II of Justice O'Connor's opinion be the majority opinion? Notice that Chief Justice Rehnquist and Justices Scalia and Thomas dissent from the judgment—because they would affirm the Fourth Circuit—but nevertheless join part II of Justice O'Connor's opinion. Among the six Justices voting to reverse the Fourth Circuit, four Justices sign on to part II of the Stevens opinion and only two support part II of the O'Connor opinion. Thus, without the votes of the dissenters, Justice Stevens' part II would represent a plurality opinion. But the Court itself labelled Justice O'Connor's part II as a majority opinion, because of the votes of the three dissenters. Should dissenting Justices be able to cast the deciding votes in a dispute among the majority in this way?

6. In many of the recent cases limiting habeas review, the Court relies on goals of finality, federalism, and judicial economy. Professor Barry Friedman has recently suggested that viewed in light of these goals, the Supreme Court's habeas jurisdiction over the last two decades has been a failure. Friedman, *Failed Enterprise: The Supreme Court's Habeas Reform*, 83 Cal. L.Rev. 485 (1995). Instead, Professor Friedman suggests, the cases have created unwarranted doctrinal complexity which has led to increased litigation, burdening both state and federal courts with procedural matters far from the core substantive questions that habeas review is designed to resolve. See also Lay, *The Writ of Habeas Corpus: A Complex Procedure for a Simple Process*, 77 Minn.L.Rev. 1015, 1036–38 (1993); Yackle, *State Convicts and Federal Courts: Reopening the Habeas Corpus Debate*, 91 Cornell L.Rev. 541 (2006). Having read all the cases in this chapter, are you persuaded?

Chapter 13

FEDERAL QUESTION
JURISDICTION

§ 1.   THE CONSTITUTIONAL SCOPE

OSBORN v. BANK OF THE UNITED STATES

Supreme Court of the United States, 1824.
22 U.S. (9 Wheat.) 738.

Appeal from the Circuit Court of Ohio.

The bill filed in this cause, was exhibited in the Court below, at September term, 1819, in the name of the respondents, and signed by solicitors of the Court, praying an injunction to restrain Ralph Osborn, Auditor of the State of Ohio, from proceeding against the complainants, under an act of the Legislature of that State, passed February the 8th, 1819, entitled, "An act to levy and collect a tax from all banks, and individuals, and companies, and associations of individuals, that may transact banking business in this State, without being allowed to do so by the laws thereof." This act, after reciting that the Bank of the United States pursued its operations contrary to a law of the State, enacted, that if, after the 1st day of the following September, the said Bank, or any other, should continue to transact business in the State, it should be liable to an annual tax of 50,000 dollars on each office of discount and deposit. And that on the 15th day of September, the Auditor should charge such tax to the Bank, and should make out his warrant, under his seal of office, directed to any person, commanding him to collect the said tax, who should enter the banking house, and demand the same, and if payment should not be made, should levy the amount on the money or other goods of the Bank, the money to be retained, and the goods to be sold * * * If no effects should be found in the banking room, the person having the warrant was authorized to go into every room, vault, & c. and to open every chest, & c. in search of what might satisfy his warrant.

The bill, after reciting this act, stated, that Ralph Osborn is the Auditor, and gives out, & c. that he will execute the said act. It was exhibited in open Court, on the 14th of September, and, notice of the application having been given to the defendant, Osborn, an order was made, awarding the injunction on the execution of bonds and security in the sum of 100,000 dollars; after which, a subpoena was issued, on which the order that had been made for the injunction was endorsed by the solicitors for the plaintiffs; and a memorandum, that bond with security had been given by the plaintiffs, was endorsed by the clerk; and a power to James M'Dowell to serve the same, was endorsed by the Marshal. * * *

The amended bill charges, that, subsequent to the service of the subpoena and injunction, to wit, on the 17th of September, 1819, J. L. Harper, who was employed by Osborn to collect the tax, and well knew that an injunction had been allowed, proceeded by violence to the office of the Bank at Chilicothe, and took therefrom 100,000 dollars, in specie and bank notes, belonging to, or in deposit with, the plaintiffs. That this money was delivered to H. M. Curry, who was then Treasurer of the State, or to the defendant, Osborn, both of whom had notice of the illegal seizure, and paid no consideration for the amount, but received it to keep it on safe deposit. That Curry did keep the same until he delivered it over to one S. Sullivan, his successor as Treasurer. That neither Curry nor Sullivan held the said money in their character as Treasurer, but as individuals. The bill prays, that the said H. M. Curry, late Treasurer, S. Sullivan, the present Treasurer, and R. Osborn, in their official and private characters, and the said J. L. Harper, may be made defendants; that they may make discovery, and may be enjoined from using or paying away the coin or notes taken from the Bank, may be decreed to restore the same, and may be enjoined from proceeding further under the said act.

* * *

The cause came on to be heard * * * and upon the decrees *nisi*, against Osborn and Harper, and the Court pronounced a decree directing them to restore to the Bank the sum of 100,000 dollars, with interest on 19,830 dollars, the amount of specie in the hands of Sullivan. The cause was then brought, by appeal, to this Court.

* * *

MR. CHIEF JUSTICE MARSHALL delivered the opinion of the Court, and, after stating the case, proceeded as follows:

At the close of the argument, a point was suggested, of such vital importance, as to induce the Court to request that it might be particularly spoken to. That point is, the right of the Bank to sue in the Courts of the United States. It has been argued, and ought to be disposed of, before we proceed to the actual exercise of jurisdiction, by deciding on the rights of the parties.

The appellants contest the jurisdiction of the Court on two grounds:

1st. That the act of Congress has not given it.

2d. That, under the constitution, Congress cannot give it.

1.   The first part of the objection depends entirely on the language of the act. The words are, that the Bank shall be "made able and capable in law," "to sue and be sued, plead and be impleaded, answer and be answered, defend and be defended, in all State Courts having competent jurisdiction, and in any Circuit Court of the United States."

These words seem to the Court to admit of but one interpretation. They cannot be made plainer by explanation. They give, expressly, the right "to sue and be sued," "in every Circuit Court of the United States," and it would be difficult to substitute other terms which would be more direct and appropriate for the purpose. The argument of the appellants is founded on the opinion of this Court, in The Bank of the United States v. Deveaux, (5 Cranch, 85.) In that case it was decided, that the former Bank of the United States was not enabled, by the act which incorporated it, to sue in the federal Courts. The words of the 3d section of that act are, that the Bank may "sue and be sued," & c. "in Courts of record, or any other place whatsoever." The Court was of opinion, that these general words, which are usual in all acts of incorporation, gave only a general capacity to sue, not a particular privilege to sue in the Courts of the United States; and this opinion was strengthened by the circumstance that the 9th rule of the 7th section of the same act, subjects the directors, in case of excess in contracting debt, to be sued in their private capacity, "in any Court of record of the United States, or either of them." The express grant of jurisdiction to the federal Courts, in this case, was considered as having some influence on the construction of the general words of the 3d section, which does not mention those Courts. Whether this decision be right or wrong, it amounts only to a declaration, that a general capacity in the Bank to sue, without mentioning the Courts of the Union, may not give a right to sue in those Courts. To infer from this, that words expressly conferring a right to sue in those Courts, do not give the right, is surely a conclusion which the premises do not warrant.

The act of incorporation, then, confers jurisdiction on the Circuit Courts of the United States, if Congress can confer it.

2.   We will now consider the constitutionality of the clause in the act of incorporation, which authorizes the Bank to sue in the federal Courts.

In support of this clause, it is said, that the legislative, executive, and judicial powers, of every well constructed government, are co-extensive with each other; that is, they are potentially co-extensive. The executive department may constitutionally execute every law which the Legislature may constitutionally make, and the judicial department may receive from the Legislature the power of construing every such law. All governments which are not extremely defective in their organization, must possess, within themselves, the means of expounding, as well as enforcing, their own laws. If we examine the constitution of the United States, we find that its framers kept this great political principle in view. The 2d article vests the whole executive power in the President; and the

3d article declares, "that the judicial power shall extend to all cases in law and equity, arising under this constitution, the laws of the United States, and treaties made, or which shall be made, under their authority."

This clause enables the judicial department to receive jurisdiction to the full extent of the constitution, laws, and treaties of the United States, when any question respecting them shall assume such a form that the judicial power is capable of acting on it. That power is capable of acting only when the subject is submitted to it by a party who asserts his rights in the form prescribed by law. It then becomes a case, and the constitution declares, that the judicial power shall extend to all cases arising under the constitution, laws, and treaties of the United States.

The suit of The Bank of the United States v. Osborn and others, is a case, and the question is, whether it arises under a law of the United States?

The appellants contend, that it does not, because several questions may arise in it, which depend on the general principles of the law, not on any act of Congress.

If this were sufficient to withdraw a case from the jurisdiction of the federal Courts, almost every case, although involving the construction of a law, would be withdrawn; and a clause in the constitution, relating to a subject of vital importance to the government, and expressed in the most comprehensive terms, would be construed to mean almost nothing. There is scarcely any case, every part of which depends on the constitution, laws, or treaties of the United States. The questions, whether the fact alleged as the foundation of the action, be real or fictitious; whether the conduct of the plaintiff has been such as to entitle him to maintain his action; whether his right is barred; whether he has received satisfaction, or has in any manner released his claims, are questions, some or all of which may occur in almost every case; and if their existence be sufficient to arrest the jurisdiction of the Court, words which seem intended to be as extensive as the constitution, laws, and treaties of the Union, which seem designed to give the Courts of the government the construction of all its acts, so far as they affect the rights of individuals, would be reduced to almost nothing.

In those cases in which original jurisdiction is given to the Supreme Court, the judicial power of the United States cannot be exercised in its appellate form. In every other case, the power is to be exercised in its original or appellate form, or both, as the wisdom of Congress may direct. With the exception of these cases, in which original jurisdiction is given to this Court, there is none to which the judicial power extends, from which the original jurisdiction of the inferior Courts is excluded by the constitution. Original jurisdiction, so far as the constitution gives a rule, is co-extensive with the judicial power. We find, in the constitution, no prohibition to its exercise, in every case in which the judicial power can be exercised. It would be a very bold construction to say, that this power could be applied in its appellate form only, to the most important class of cases to which it is applicable.

The Constitution establishes the Supreme Court, and defines its jurisdiction. It enumerates cases in which its jurisdiction is original and exclusive; and then defines that which is appellate, but does not insinuate, that in any such case, the power cannot be exercised in its original form by Courts of original jurisdiction. It is not insinuated, that the judicial power, in cases depending on the character of the cause, cannot be exercised in the first instance, in the Courts of the Union, but must first be exercised in the tribunals of the State; tribunals over which the government of the Union has no adequate control, and which may be closed to any claim asserted under a law of the United States.

We perceive, then, no ground on which the proposition can be maintained, that Congress is incapable of giving the Circuit Courts original jurisdiction, in any case to which the appellate jurisdiction extends.

We ask, then, if it can be sufficient to exclude this jurisdiction, that the case involves questions depending on general principles? A cause may depend on several questions of fact and law. Some of these may depend on the construction of a law of the United States; others on principles unconnected with that law. If it be a sufficient foundation for jurisdiction, that the title or right set up by the party, may be defeated by one construction of the constitution or law of the United States, and sustained by the opposite construction, provided the facts necessary to support the action be made out, then all the other questions must be decided as incidental to this, which gives that jurisdiction. Those other questions cannot arrest the proceedings. Under this construction, the judicial power of the Union extends effectively and beneficially to that most important class of cases, which depend on the character of the cause. On the opposite construction, the judicial power never can be extended to a whole case, as expressed by the constitution, but to those parts of cases only which present the particular question involving the construction of the constitution or the law. We say it never can be extended to the whole case, because, if the circumstance that other points are involved in it, shall disable Congress from authorizing the Courts of the Union to take jurisdiction of the original cause, it equally disables Congress from authorizing those Courts to take jurisdiction of the whole cause, on an appeal, and thus will be restricted to a single question in that cause; and words obviously intended to secure to those who claim rights under the constitution, laws, or treaties of the United States, a trial in the federal Courts, will be restricted to the insecure remedy of an appeal upon an insulated point, after it has received that shape which may be given to it by another tribunal, into which he is forced against his will.

We think, then, that when a question to which the judicial power of the Union is extended by the constitution, forms an ingredient of the original cause, it is in the power of Congress to give the Circuit Courts jurisdiction of that cause, although other questions of fact or of law may be involved in it.

The case of the Bank is, we think, a very strong case of this description. The charter of incorporation not only creates it, but gives it every faculty which it possesses. The power to acquire rights of any description, to transact business of any description, to make contracts of any description, to sue on those contracts, is given and measured by its charter, and that charter is a law of the United States. This being can acquire no right, make no contract, bring no suit, which is not authorized by a law of the United States. It is not only itself the mere creature of a law, but all its actions and all its rights are dependant on the same law. Can a being, thus constituted, have a case which does not arise literally, as well as substantially, under the law?

Take the case of a contract, which is put as the strongest against the Bank.

When a Bank sues, the first question which presents itself, and which lies at the foundation of the cause, is, has this legal entity a right to sue? Has it a right to come, not into this Court particularly, but into any Court? This depends on a law of the United States. The next question is, has this being a right to make this particular contract? If this question be decided in the negative, the cause is determined against the plaintiff; and this question, too, depends entirely on a law of the United States. These are important questions, and they exist in every possible case. The right to sue, if decided once, is decided for ever; but the power of Congress was exercised antecedently to the first decision on that right, and if it was constitutional then, it cannot cease to be so, because the particular question is decided. It may be revived at the will of the party, and most probably would be renewed, were the tribunal to be changed. But the question respecting the right to make a particular contract, or to acquire a particular property, or to sue on account of a particular injury, belongs to every particular case, and may be renewed in every case. The question forms an original ingredient in every cause. Whether it be in fact relied on or not, in the defence, it is still a part of the cause, and may be relied on. The right of the plaintiff to sue, cannot depend on the defence which the defendant may choose to set up. His right to sue is anterior to that defence, and must depend on the state of things when the action is brought. The questions which the case involves, then, must determine its character, whether those questions be made in the cause or not.

The appellants say, that the case arises on the contract; but the validity of the contract depends on a law of the United States, and the plaintiff is compelled, in every case, to show its validity. The case arises emphatically under the law. The act of Congress is its foundation. The contract could never have been made, but under the authority of that act. The act itself is the first ingredient in the case, is its origin, is that from which every other part arises. That other questions may also arise, as the execution of the contract, or its performance, cannot change the case, or give it any other origin than the charter of incorporation. The action still originates in, and is sustained by, that charter.

* * *

naturalized citizen comparison

It is said, that a clear distinction exists between the party and the cause; that the party may originate under a law with which the cause has no connection; and that Congress may, with the same propriety, give a naturalized citizen, who is the mere creature of a law, a right to sue in the Courts of the United States, as give that right to the Bank.

This distinction is not denied; and, if the act of Congress was a simple act of incorporation, and contained nothing more, it might be entitled to great consideration. But the act does not stop with incorporating the Bank. It proceeds to bestow upon the being it has made, all the faculties and capacities which that being possesses. Every act of the Bank grows out of this law, and is tested by it. To use the language of the constitution, every act of the Bank arises out of this law.

A naturalized citizen is indeed made a citizen under an act of Congress, but the act does not proceed to give, to regulate, or to prescribe his capacities. He becomes a member of the society, possessing all the rights of a native citizen, and standing, in the view of the constitution, on the footing of a native. The constitution does not authorize Congress to enlarge or abridge those rights. The simple power of the national Legislature, is to prescribe a uniform rule of naturalization, and the exercise of this power exhausts it, so far as respects the individual. The constitution then takes him up, and, among other rights, extends to him the capacity of suing in the Courts of the United States, precisely under the same circumstances under which a native might sue. He is distinguishable in nothing from a native citizen, except so far as the constitution makes the distinction. The law makes none.

There is, then, no resemblance between the act incorporating the Bank, and the general naturalization law.

Upon the best consideration we have been able to bestow on this subject, we are of opinion, that the clause in the act of incorporation, enabling the Bank to sue in the Courts of the United States, is consistent with the constitution, and to be obeyed in all Courts.

* * *

MR. JUSTICE JOHNSON. The argument in this cause presents three questions: 1. Has Congress granted to the Bank of the United States, an unlimited right of suing in the Courts of the United States? 2. Could Congress constitutionally grant such a right? and 3. Has the power of the Court been legally and constitutionally exercised in this suit?

I have very little doubt that the public mind will be easily reconciled to the decision of the Court here rendered; for, whether necessary or unnecessary originally, a state of things has now grown up, in some of the States, which renders all the protection necessary, that the general government can give to this Bank. The policy of the decision is obvious, that is, if the Bank is to be sustained; and few will bestow upon its legal correctness, the reflection, that it is necessary to test it by the constitution and laws, under which it is rendered.

* * *

In the present instance, I cannot persuade myself, that the constitution sanctions the vesting of the right of action in this Bank, in cases in which the privilege is exclusively personal, or in any case, merely on the ground that a question might *possibly* be raised in it, involving the constitution, or constitutionality of a law, of the United States.

When laws were heretofore passed for raising a revenue by a duty on stamped paper, the tax was quietly acquiesced in, notwithstanding it entrenched so closely on the unquestionable power of the States over the law of contracts; but had the same law which declared void contracts not written upon stamped paper, declared, that every person holding such paper should be entitled to bring his action "in any Circuit Court" of the United States, it is confidently believed that there could have been but one opinion on the constitutionality of such a provision. The whole jurisdiction over contracts, might thus have been taken from the State Courts, and conferred upon those of the United States. Nor would the evil have rested there; by a similar exercise of power, imposing a stamp on deeds generally, jurisdiction over the territory of the State, whoever might be parties, even between citizens of the same State—jurisdiction of suits instituted for the recovery of legacies or distributive portions of intestates' estates—jurisdiction, in fact, over almost every possible case, might be transferred to the Courts of the United States. Wills may be required to be executed on stamped paper; taxes may be, and have been, imposed upon legacies and distributions; and, in all such cases, there is not only a possibility, but a probability, that a question may arise, involving the constitutionality, construction, & c. of a law of the United States. If the circumstance, that the questions which the case involves, are to determine its character, whether those questions be made in the case or not, then every case here alluded to, may as well be transferred to the jurisdiction of the United States, as those to which this Bank is a party. But still farther, as was justly insisted in argument, there is not a tract of land in the United States, acquired under laws of the United States, whatever be the number of mesne transfers that it may have undergone, over which the jurisdiction of the Courts of the United States might not be extended by Congress, upon the very principle on which the right of suit in this Bank is here maintained. Nor is the case of the alien, put in argument, at all inapplicable. The one acquires its character of individual property, as the other does his political existence, under a law of the United States; and there is not a suit which may be instituted to recover the one, nor an action of ejectment to be brought by the other, in which a right acquired under a law of the United States, does not lie as essentially at the basis of the right of action, as in the suits brought by this Bank. It is no answer to the argument, to say, that the law of the United States is but ancillary to the constitution, as to the alien; for the constitution could do nothing for him without the law: and, whether the question be upon law or constitution, still if the possibility of its arising be a sufficient circumstance to bring it within the jurisdiction of the United States Courts, that possibility exists with regard to every suit affected by alien disabilities; to real actions in time of peace—to all actions in time of war.

I cannot persuade myself, then, that, with these palpable consequences in view, Congress ever could have intended to vest in the Bank of the United States, the right of suit to the extent here claimed. * * *

* * *

I will dwell no longer on a point, which is in fact secondary and subordinate; for if Congress can vest this jurisdiction, and the people will it, the act may be amended, and the jurisdiction vested. I next proceed to consider, more distinctly, the constitutional question, on the right to vest the jurisdiction to the extent here contended for.

* * *

I have never understood any one to question the right of Congress to vest original jurisdiction in its inferior Courts, in cases coming properly within the description of "cases arising under the laws of the United States;" but surely it must first be ascertained, in some proper mode, that the cases are such as the constitution describes. By possibility, a constitutional question may be raised in any conceivable suit that may be instituted; but that would be a very insufficient ground for assuming universal jurisdiction; and yet, that a question has been made, as that, for instance, on the Bank charter, and may again be made, seems still worse, as a ground for extending jurisdiction. For, the folly of raising it again in every suit instituted by the Bank, is too great, to suppose it possible. Yet this supposition, and this alone, would seem to justify vesting the Bank with an unlimited right to sue in the federal Courts. Indeed, I cannot perceive how, with ordinary correctness, a question can be said to be involved in a cause, which only may possibly be made, but which, in fact, is the very last question that there is any probability will be made; or rather, how that can any longer be denominated a question, which has been put out of existence by a solemn decision. The constitution presumes, that the decisions of the supreme tribunal will be acquiesced in; and after disposing of the few questions which the constitution refers to it, all the minor questions belong properly to the State jurisdictions, and never were intended to be taken away in mass.

Efforts have been made to fix the precise sense of the constitution, when it vests jurisdiction in the general government, in "cases arising under the laws of the United States." To me, the question appears susceptible of a very simple solution; that all depends upon the identity of the case supposed; according to which idea, a case may be such in its very existence, or it may become such in its progress. An action may "live, move, and have its being," in a law of the United States; such as that given for the violation of a patent-right, and four or five different actions given by this act of incorporation; particularly that against the President and Directors for over-issuing; in all of which cases the plaintiff must count upon the law itself as the ground of his action. And of the other description, would have been an action of trespass, in this case, had remedy been sought for an actual levy of the tax imposed. * * * In this class of cases, the occurrence of a question makes the case, and transfers it, as provided for under the twenty-fifth section of the Judiciary Act, to the jurisdiction of the United States. And this appears to me to present the only sound and practical construction of the constitution on this subject; for no other cases does it regard as necessary to place under the control of the general government. It is only when the case exhibits one or the other of these characteristics, that it is acted upon by the constitution. Where no question is raised, there can be no contrariety of construction; and what else had the constitution to guard against? As to cases of the first description, *ex necessitate rei*, the Courts of the United States must be susceptible of original jurisdiction; and as to all other cases, I should hold them, also, susceptible of original jurisdiction, if it were practicable, in the nature of things, to make out the definition of the case, so as to bring it under the constitution judicially, upon an original suit. But until the plaintiff can control the defendant in his pleadings, I see no practical mode of determining when the case does occur, otherwise than by permitting the cause to advance until the case for which the constitution provides shall actually arise. If it never occurs, there can be nothing to complain of; and such are the provisions of the twenty-fifth section. The cause might be transferred to the Circuit Court before an adjudication takes place; but I can perceive no earlier stage at which it can possibly be predicated of such a case, that it is one within the constitution; nor any possible necessity for transferring it then, or until the Court has acted upon it to the prejudice of the claims of the United States. It is not, therefore, because Congress may not vest an *original* jurisdiction, where they can constitutionally vest in the Circuit Courts *appellate* jurisdiction, that I object to this general grant of the right to sue; but, because that the peculiar nature of this jurisdiction is such, as to render it impossible to exercise it in a strictly original form, and because the principle of a possible occurrence of a question as a ground of jurisdiction, is transcending the bounds of the constitution, and placing it on a ground which will admit of an *enormous accession*, if not an *unlimited assumption*, of jurisdiction.

Notes

1. Was there any doubt that the claim presented in *Osborn* "arose" under federal law? The hypothetical case Marshall described in *Osborn* was actually similar to a companion case, Bank of the United States v. Planters' Bank of Georgia, 22 U.S. (9 Wheat.) 904 (1824).

2. How would you describe the principle Marshall develops to determine whether a case "arises under" federal law for constitutional purposes? Do you believe this to be a valid reading of the constitutional language?

"Fed. Ingred"; "could be raised"

What practical value do you suppose such an interpretation might have? See Chadbourn & Levin, *Original Jurisdiction of Federal Questions*, 90 U.Pa. L.Rev. 639, 649 (1942). Can you see any possible difficulties with Marshall's approach? According to one commentator, the theory of "arising under" adopted by Marshall in *Osborn* represented "a distinctly unorthodox and novel view." Engdahl, *Federal Question Jurisdiction Under the 1789 Judiciary Act,* 14 Okla.City L.Rev. 521, 527 (1989). Another commentator has examined the historical context of *Osborn* and concluded that modern courts and commentators have read it too broadly: "an ingredient" of the cause of action meant something different under the nineteenth-century formal, remedies-based definition of a "cause of action" than it does under today's broader more transactional concept. Bellia, *Article III and the Cause of Action*, 89 Iowa L.Rev. 777 (2004). What should we make of such a historical argument? Does it prove too much?

3. Professor Paul Mishkin has argued that "the purpose of the *Osborn* decision was the protection of the Bank in all its legal relations, including those governed wholly by state law." Mishkin, *The Federal "Question" in the District Courts*, 53 Colum.L.Rev. 157, 187 (1953). Is Marshall's test for "arising under" jurisdiction so limited? Would it make sense to limit it in this manner?

4. What alternative interpretations of the constitutional language does dissenting Justice Johnson suggest? Is it preferable to Marshall's?

5. In American National Red Cross v. S.G., A.E., 505 U.S. 247 (1992), the Supreme Court adhered to *Osborn*'s interpretation of capacity-granting statutes. Writing for the majority, Justice Souter indicated that a congressional charter's "sue and be sued" provision may be read to confer federal jurisdiction if it specifically mentions the federal courts. However, a mere grant of general corporate capacity—such as "in courts of record"—is insufficient.

Justice Souter expressed the belief that "[o]ur holding leaves the jurisdiction of the federal courts well within Article III's limits," noting that "[a]s long ago as *Osborn,* this Court held that Article III's 'arising under' jurisdiction is broad enough to authorize Congress to confer federal court jurisdiction over federally chartered corporations" and that the Court had "consistently reaffirmed the breadth of this holding." Id. at 264.

Justice Scalia, writing for four dissenters, called the Court's opinion a "wonderland of linguistic confusion in which words are sometimes read to mean only what they say and other times read also to mean what they do not say * * *." Id. at 265.

6. The current status of the *Osborn* doctrine is not entirely settled. See Gully v. First National Bank in Meridian, 299 U.S. 109, 113 (1936); People of Puerto Rico v. Russell & Co., 288 U.S. 476, 485 (1933). In regard to this issue, consider the *Lincoln Mills* case, which follows.

TEXTILE WORKERS UNION OF AMERICA
v. LINCOLN MILLS OF ALABAMA

Supreme Court of the United States, 1957.
353 U.S. 448.

MR. JUSTICE DOUGLAS delivered the opinion of the Court.

Petitioner-union entered into a collective bargaining agreement in 1953 with respondent-employer, the agreement to run one year and from year to year thereafter, unless terminated on specified notices. The agreement provided that there would be no strikes or work stoppages and that grievances would be handled pursuant to a specified procedure. The last step in the grievance procedure—a step that could be taken by either party—was arbitration.

This controversy involves several grievances that concern work loads and work assignments. The grievances were processed through the various steps in the grievance procedure and were finally denied by the employer. The union requested arbitration, and the employer refused. Thereupon the union brought this suit in the District Court to compel arbitration.

The District Court concluded that it had jurisdiction and ordered the employer to comply with the grievance arbitration provisions of the collective bargaining agreement. The Court of Appeals reversed by a divided vote. 230 F.2d 81. It held that, although the District Court had jurisdiction to entertain the suit, the court had no authority founded either in federal or state law to grant the relief. The case is here on a petition for a writ of certiorari which we granted because of the importance of the problem and the contrariety of views in the courts. 352 U.S. 821.

The starting point of our inquiry is § 301 of the Labor Management Relations Act of 1947, 61 Stat. 156, 29 U.S.C. § 185, which provides:

(a) "Suits for violation of contracts between an employer and a labor organization representing employees in an industry affecting commerce as defined in this chapter, or between any such labor organizations, may be brought in any district court of the United States having jurisdiction of the parties, without respect to the amount in controversy or without regard to the citizenship of the parties."

(b) "Any labor organization which represents employees in an industry affecting commerce as defined in this chapter and any employer whose activities affect commerce as defined in this chapter shall be bound by the acts of its agents. Any such labor organization may sue or be sued as an entity and in behalf of the employees whom it represents in the courts of the United States. Any money judgment against a labor organization in a district court of the United States shall be enforceable only against the organization as an entity and against its assets, and shall not be enforceable against any individual member or his assets."

There has been considerable litigation involving § 301 and courts have construed it differently. There is one view that § 301(a) merely gives federal district courts jurisdiction in controversies that involve labor organizations in industries affecting commerce, without regard to diversity of citizenship or the amount in controversy. Under that view § 301(a) would not be the source of substantive law; it would neither supply federal law to resolve these controversies nor turn the federal judges to state law for answers to the questions. Other courts—the overwhelming number of them—hold that § 301(a) is more than jurisdictional—that it authorizes federal courts to fashion a body of federal law for the enforcement of these collective bargaining agreements and includes within that federal law specific performance of promises to arbitrate grievances under collective bargaining agreements. Perhaps the leading decision representing that point of view is the one rendered by Judge Wyzanski in Textile Workers Union of America (C.I.O.) v. American Thread Co., D.C., 113 F.Supp. 137. That is our construction of § 301(a), which means that the agreement to arbitrate grievance disputes, contained in this collective bargaining agreement, should be specifically enforced.

From the face of the Act it is apparent that § 301(a) and § 301(b) supplement one another. Section 301(b) makes it possible for a labor organization, representing employees in an industry affecting commerce, to sue and be sued as an entity in the federal courts. Section 301(b) in other words provides the procedural remedy lacking at common law. Section 301(a) certainly does something more than that. Plainly, it supplies the basis upon which the federal district courts may take jurisdiction and apply the procedural rule of § 301(b). The question is whether § 301(a) is more than jurisdictional.

* * *

It seems * * * clear to us that Congress adopted a policy which placed sanctions behind agreements to arbitrate grievance disputes, by implication rejecting the common-law rule, discussed in Red Cross Line v. Atlantic Fruit Co., 264 U.S. 109, against enforcement of executory agreements to arbitrate. We would undercut the Act and defeat its policy if we read § 301 narrowly as only conferring jurisdiction over labor organizations.

* * *

Mr. Justice Black took no part in the consideration or decision of this case.

Mr. Justice Burton, whom Mr. Justice Harlan joins, concurring in the result.

This suit was brought in a United States District Court under § 301 of the Labor Management Relations Act of 1947, 61 Stat. 156, 29 U.S.C.

§ 185, seeking specific enforcement of the arbitration provisions of a collective-bargaining contract. The District Court had jurisdiction over the action since it involved an obligation running to a union—a union controversy—and not uniquely personal rights of employees sought to be enforced by a union. Cf. Association of Westinghouse Employees v. Westinghouse Elec. Corp., 348 U.S. 437. Having jurisdiction over the suit, the court was not powerless to fashion an appropriate federal remedy. The power to decree specific performance of a collectively bargained agreement to arbitrate finds its source in § 301 itself, and in a Federal District Court's inherent equitable powers, nurtured by a congressional policy to encourage and enforce labor arbitration in industries affecting commerce.

I do not subscribe to the conclusion of the Court that the substantive law to be applied in a suit under § 301 is federal law. At the same time, I agree with Judge Magruder in International Brotherhood v. W. L. Mead, Inc., 1 Cir., 230 F.2d 576, that some federal rights may necessarily be involved in a § 301 case, and hence that the constitutionality of § 301 can be upheld as a congressional grant to Federal District Courts of what has been called "protective jurisdiction."

     MR. JUSTICE FRANKFURTER, dissenting.

The Court has avoided the difficult problems raised by § 301 of the Taft–Hartley Act, 61 Stat. 156, 29 U.S.C. § 185, by attributing to the section an occult content. This plainly procedural section is transmuted into a mandate to the federal courts to fashion a whole body of substantive federal law appropriate for the complicated and touchy problems raised by collective bargaining. I have set forth in my opinion in Employees v. Westinghouse Corp. the detailed reasons why I believe that § 301 cannot be so construed, even if constitutional questions cannot be avoided. 348 U.S. 437, 441–449, 452–459. But the Court has a "clear" and contrary conclusion emerge from the "somewhat," to say the least, "cloudy and confusing legislative history." This is more than can be fairly asked even from the alchemy of construction. * * *

* * *

The second ground of my dissent from the Court's action is more fundamental. Since I do not agree with the Court's conclusion that federal substantive law is to govern in actions under § 301, I am forced to consider the serious constitutional question that was adumbrated in the *Westinghouse* case, 348 U.S., at 449–452, the constitutionality of a grant of jurisdiction to federal courts over contracts that came into being entirely by virtue of state substantive law, a jurisdiction not based on diversity of citizenship, yet one in which a federal court would, as in diversity cases, act in effect merely as another court of the State in which it sits. The scope of allowable federal judicial power that this grant must satisfy is constitutionally described as "Cases, in Law and Equity, arising under this Constitution, the Laws of the United States, and Treaties made, or which shall be made, under their Authority." Art. III, § 2. While interpretive decisions are legion under general statutory grants of jurisdiction strikingly similar to this constitutional wording, it is generally recognized that the full constitutional power has not been exhausted by these statutes. See, e.g., Mishkin, The Federal "Question" in the District Courts, 53 Col.L.Rev. 157, 160; Shulman and Jaegerman, Some Jurisdictional Limitations on Federal Procedure, 45 Yale L.J. 393, 405, n. 47; Wechsler, Federal Jurisdiction and the Revision of the Judicial Code, 13 Law & Contemp.Prob., 216, 224–225.

Almost without exception, decisions under the general statutory grants have tested jurisdiction in terms of the presence, as an integral part of plaintiff's cause of action, of an issue calling for interpretation or application of federal law. E.g., Gully v. First National Bank, 299 U.S. 109. Although it has sometimes been suggested that the "cause of action" must derive from federal law, see American Well Works Co. v. Layne & Bowler Co., 241 U.S. 257, 260, it has been found sufficient that some aspect of federal law is essential to plaintiff's success. Smith v. Kansas City Title & Trust Co., 255 U.S. 180. The litigation-provoking problem has been the degree to which federal law must be in the forefront of the case and not collateral, peripheral or remote.

In a few exceptional cases, arising under special jurisdictional grants, the criteria by which the prominence of the federal question is measured against constitutional requirements have been found satisfied under circumstances suggesting a variant theory of the nature of these requirements. The first, and the leading case in the field, is Osborn v. Bank of the United States, 9 Wheat. 738. There, Chief Justice Marshall sustained federal jurisdiction in a situation—hypothetical in the case before him but presented by the companion case of Bank of the United States v. Planters' Bank, 9 Wheat. 904—involving suit by a federally incorporated bank upon a contract. Despite the assumption that the cause of action and the interpretation of the contract would be governed by state law, the case was found to "arise under the laws of the United States" because the propriety and scope of a federally granted authority to enter into contracts and to litigate might well be challenged. This reasoning was subsequently applied to sustain jurisdiction in actions against federally chartered railroad corporations. Pacific Railroad Removal Cases (Union Pac. Ry. Co. v. Myers), 115 U.S. 1. The traditional interpretation of this series of cases is that federal jurisdiction under the "arising" clause of the Constitution, though limited to cases involving potential federal questions, has such flexibility that Congress may confer it whenever there exists in the background some federal proposition that might be challenged, despite the remoteness of the likelihood of actual presentation of such a federal question.[4]

The views expressed in Osborn and the Pacific Railroad Removal Cases were severely restricted in construing general grants of jurisdiction. But the Court later sustained this jurisdictional section of the Bankruptcy Act of 1898:

4. Osborn might possibly be limited on the ground that a federal instrumentality, the Bank of the United States, was in- volved,* * * but such an explanation could not suffice to narrow the holding in the Pacific Railroad Removal Cases.

"The United States district courts shall have jurisdiction of all controversies at law and in equity, as distinguished from proceedings in bankruptcy, between trustees as such and adverse claimants concerning the property acquired or claimed by the trustees, in the same manner and to the same extent only as though bankruptcy proceedings had not been instituted and such controversies had been between the bankrupts and such adverse claimants." § 23(a), as amended, 44 Stat. 664, 11 U.S.C.A. § 46, sub. a.

Under this provision the trustee could pursue in a federal court a private cause of action arising under and wholly governed by state law. Schumacher v. Beeler,* 293 U.S. 367; Williams v. Austrian, 331 U.S. 642 (Chandler Act of 1938, 52 Stat. 840, 11 U.S.C.A. § 1 et seq.). To be sure, the cases did not discuss the basis of jurisdiction. It has been suggested that they merely represent an extension of the approach of the *Osborn* case; the trustee's right to sue might be challenged on obviously federal grounds—absence of bankruptcy or irregularity of the trustee's appointment or of the bankruptcy proceedings. National Mutual Ins. Co. of Dist. of Col. v. Tidewater Transfer Co., 337 U.S. 582, 611–613 (Rutledge, J., concurring). So viewed, this type of litigation implicates a potential federal question.

Apparently relying on the extent to which the bankruptcy cases involve only remotely a federal question, Mr. Justice Jackson concluded in National Mutual Insurance Co. of Dist. of Col. v. Tidewater Transfer Co., 337 U.S. 582, that Congress may confer jurisdiction on the District Courts as incidental to its powers under Article I. No attempt was made to reconcile this view with the restrictions of Article III; a majority of the Court recognized that Article III defined the bounds of valid jurisdictional legislation and rejected the notion that jurisdictional grants can go outside these limits.

With this background, many theories have been proposed to sustain the constitutional validity of § 301. In Textile Workers Union of America (C.I.O.) v. American Thread Co., D.C., 113 F.Supp. 137, 140, Judge Wyzanski suggested, among other possibilities, that § 301 might be read as containing a direction that controversies affecting interstate commerce should be governed by federal law incorporating state law by reference, and that such controversies would then arise under a valid federal law as required by Article III. Whatever may be said of the assumption regarding the validity of federal jurisdiction under an affirmative declaration by Congress that state law should be applied as federal law by federal courts to contract disputes affecting commerce, we cannot argumentatively legislate for Congress when Congress has failed to legislate. To do so disrespects legislative responsibility and disregards judicial limitations.

---

* [Note that contrary to Justice Frankfurter's interpretation, *Schumacher* actually upheld jurisdiction under § 23(b) rather than § 23(a). § 23(a) *denies* jurisdiction in the absence of a federal claim, while § 23(b) makes an exception to § 23(a)'s limit when the other party consented. However, the point made by Justice Frankfurter is unaffected by this error.]

Another theory, relying on *Osborn* and the bankruptcy cases, has been proposed which would achieve results similar to those attainable under Mr. Justice Jackson's view, but which purports to respect the "arising" clause of Article III. See Hart and Wechsler, The Federal Courts and the Federal System, pp. 744–747; Wechsler, Federal Jurisdiction and the Revision of the Judicial Code, 13 Law & Contemp.Prob. 216, 224–225; International Brotherhood of Teamsters, etc. v. W. L. Mead, Inc., 1 Cir., 230 F.2d 576. Called "protective jurisdiction," the suggestion is that in any case for which Congress has the constitutional power to prescribe federal rules of decision and thus confer "true" federal question jurisdiction, it may, without so doing, enact a jurisdictional statute, which will provide a federal forum for the application of state statute and decisional law. Analysis of the "protective jurisdiction" theory might also be attempted in terms of the language of Article III—construing "laws" to include jurisdictional statutes where Congress could have legislated substantively in a field. This is but another way of saying that because Congress could have legislated substantively and thereby could give rise to litigation under a statute of the United States, it can provide a federal forum for state-created rights although it chose not to adopt state law as federal law or to originate federal rights.

Surely the truly technical restrictions of Article III are not met or respected by a beguiling phrase that the greater power here must necessarily include the lesser. In the compromise of federal and state interests leading to distribution of jealously guarded judicial power in a federal system, see 13 Cornell L.Q. 499, it is obvious that very different considerations apply to cases involving questions of federal law and those turning solely on state law. It may be that the ambiguity of the phrase "arising under the laws of the United States" leaves room for more than traditional theory could accommodate. But, under the theory of "protective jurisdiction," the "arising under" jurisdiction of the federal courts would be vastly extended. For example, every contract or tort arising out of a contract affecting commerce might be a potential cause of action in the federal courts, even though only state law was involved in the decision of the case. At least in *Osborn* and the bankruptcy cases, a substantive federal law was present somewhere in the background. * * * But this theory rests on the supposition that Congress could enact substantive federal law to govern the particular case. It was not held in those cases, nor is it clear, that federal law could be held to govern the transactions of all persons who subsequently become bankrupt, or of all suits of a Bank of the United States. See Mishkin, The Federal "Question" in the District Courts, 53 Col.L.Rev. 157, 189.

"Protective jurisdiction," once the label is discarded, cannot be justified under any view of the allowable scope to be given to Article III. "Protective jurisdiction" is a misused label for the statute we are here considering. That rubric is properly descriptive of safeguarding some of the indisputable, staple business of the federal courts. It is a radiation of an existing jurisdiction. See Adams v. United States ex rel. McCann, 317 U.S. 269; 28 U.S.C. § 2283. "Protective jurisdiction" cannot generate an independent source for adjudication outside of the Article III sanctions and what Congress has defined. The theory must have as its sole justification a belief in the inadequacy of state tribunals in determining state law. The Constitution reflects such a belief in the specific situation within which the Diversity Clause was confined. The intention to remedy such supposed defects was exhausted in this provision of Article III.[5] That this "protective" theory was not adopted by Chief Justice Marshall at a time when conditions might have presented more substantial justification strongly suggests its lack of constitutional merit. Moreover, Congress in its consideration of § 301 nowhere suggested dissatisfaction with the ability of state courts to administer state law properly. Its concern was to provide access to the federal courts for easier enforcement of state-created rights.

Another theory also relies on *Osborn* and the bankruptcy cases as an implicit recognition of the propriety of the exercise of some sort of "protective jurisdiction" by the federal courts. Mishkin, *op. cit.* supra, 53 Col.L.Rev. 157, 184 *et seq.* Professor Mishkin tends to view the assertion of such a jurisdiction, in the absence of any exercise of substantive powers, as irreconcilable with the "arising" clause since the case would then arise only under the jurisdictional statute itself, and he is reluctant to find a constitutional basis for the grant of power outside Article III. Professor Mishkin also notes that the only purpose of such a statute would be to insure impartiality to some litigant, an objection inconsistent with Article III's recognition of "protective jurisdiction" only in the specified situation of diverse citizenship. But where Congress has "an articulated and active federal policy regulating a field, the 'arising under' clause of Article III apparently permits the conferring of jurisdiction on the national courts of all cases in the area—including those substantively governed by state law." Id., at 192. In such cases, the protection being offered is not to the suitor, as in diversity cases, but to the "congressional legislative program." Thus he supports § 301: "even though the rules governing collective bargaining agreements continue to be state-fashioned, nonetheless the mode of their application and enforcement may play a very substantial part in the labor-management relations of interstate industry and commerce—an area in which the national government has labored long and hard." Id., at 196.

Insofar as state law governs the case, Professor Mishkin's theory is quite similar to that advanced by Professors Hart and Wechsler and

---

5. To be sure, the Court upheld the removal statute for suits or prosecutions commenced in a state court against federal revenue officers on account of any act committed under color of office. Tennessee v. Davis, 100 U.S. 257. The Court, however, construed the action of Congress in defining the powers of revenue agents as giving them a substantive defense against prosecution under state law for commission of acts "warranted by the Federal authority they possess." Id., 100 U.S. at page 263. That put federal law in the forefront as a defense. In any event, the fact that officers of the Federal Government were parties may be considered sufficient to afford access to the federal forum. See In re Debs, 158 U.S. 564, 584–586; Mishkin, 53 Col.L.Rev., at 193: "Without doubt, a federal forum should be available for all suits involving the Government, its agents and instrumentalities, regardless of the source of the substantive rule."

followed by the Court of Appeals for the First Circuit: The substantive power of Congress, although not exercised to govern the particular "case," gives "arising under" jurisdiction to the federal courts despite governing state law. The second "protective jurisdiction" theory has the dubious advantage of limiting incursions on state judicial power to situations in which the State's feelings may have been tempered by early substantive federal invasions.

* * *

I believe that we should not extend the precedents of *Osborn* and the *Pacific Railroad Removal Cases* to this case, even though there be some elements of analytical similarity. *Osborn*, the foundation for the *Removal Cases*, appears to have been based on premises that today, viewed in the light of the jurisdictional philosophy of Gully v. First National Bank, are subject to criticism. The basic premise was that every case in which a federal question might arise must be capable of being commenced in the federal courts, and when so commenced it might, because jurisdiction must be judged at the outset, be concluded there despite the fact that the federal question was never raised. Marshall's holding was undoubtedly influenced by his fear that the bank might suffer hostile treatment in the state courts that could not be remedied by an appeal on an isolated federal question. There is nothing in Article III that affirmatively supports the view that original jurisdiction over cases involving federal questions must extend to every case in which there is the potentiality of appellate jurisdiction. We also have become familiar with removal procedures that could be adapted to alleviate any remaining fears by providing for removal to a federal court whenever a federal question was raised. In view of these developments, we would not be justified in perpetuating a principle that permits assertion of original federal jurisdiction on the remote possibility of presentation of a federal question. Indeed, Congress, by largely withdrawing the jurisdiction that the *Pacific Railroad Removal Cases* recognized, and this Court, by refusing to perpetuate it under general grants of jurisdiction, see Gully v. First National Bank, supra, have already done much to recognize the changed atmosphere.

Analysis of the bankruptcy power also reveals a superficial analogy to § 301. The trustee enforces a cause of action acquired under state law by the bankrupt. Federal law merely provides for the appointment of the trustee, vests the cause of action in him, and confers jurisdiction on the federal courts. Section 301 similarly takes the rights and liabilities which under state law are vested distributively in the individual members of a union and vests them in the union for purposes of actions in federal courts, wherein the unions are authorized to sue and be sued as an entity. While the authority of the trustee depends on the existence of a bankrupt and on the propriety of the proceedings leading to the trustee's appointment, both of which depend on federal law, there are similar federal propositions that may be essential to an action under § 301. Thus, the validity of the contract may in any case be challenged on the ground that the labor organization negotiating it was not the representative of the employees concerned, a question that has been held to be federal, La Crosse Telephone Corp. v. Wisconsin Employment Relations Board, 336 U.S. 18, or on the ground that subsequent change in the representative status of the union has affected the continued validity of the agreement. Perhaps also the qualifications imposed on a union's right to utilize the facilities of the National Labor Relations Board, dependent on the filing of non-Communist affidavits required by § 9(h) and the information and reports required by § 9(f) and (g), might be read as restrictions on the right of the union to sue under § 301, again providing a federal basis for challenge to the union's authority. Consequently, were the bankruptcy cases to be viewed as dependent solely on the background existence of federal questions, there would be little analytical basis for distinguishing actions under § 301. But the bankruptcy decisions may be justified by the scope of the bankruptcy power, which may be deemed to sweep within its scope interests analytically outside the "federal question" category, but sufficiently related to the main purpose of bankruptcy to call for comprehensive treatment. See National Mutual Ins. Co. of Dist. of Col. v. Tidewater Transfer Co., 337 U.S. 582, 652, Note 3 (concurring in part, dissenting in part). Also, although a particular suit may be brought by a trustee in a district other than the one in which the principal proceedings are pending, if all the suits by the trustee, even though in many federal courts, are regarded as one litigation for the collection and apportionment of the bankrupt's property, a particular suit by the trustee, under state law, to recover a specific piece of property might be analogized to the ancillary or pendent jurisdiction cases in which, in the disposition of a cause of action, federal courts may pass on state grounds for recovery that are joined to federal grounds. See Hurn v. Oursler, 289 U.S. 238; Siler v. Louisville & Nashville R. Co., 213 U.S. 175; but see Mishkin, 53 Col.L.Rev., at 194, n. 161.

If there is in the phrase "arising under the laws of the United States" leeway for expansion of our concepts of jurisdiction, the history of Article III suggests that the area is not great and that it will require the presence of some substantial federal interest, one of greater weight and dignity than questionable doubt concerning the effectiveness of state procedure. The bankruptcy cases might possibly be viewed as such an expansion. But even so, not merely convenient judicial administration but the whole purpose of the congressional legislative program—conservation and equitable distribution of the bankrupt's estate in carrying out the constitutional power over bankruptcy—required the availability of federal jurisdiction to avoid expense and delay. Nothing pertaining to § 301 suggests vesting the federal courts with sweeping power under the Commerce Clause comparable to that vested in the federal courts under the bankruptcy power.

Notes

1. Could the constitutionality of section 301(a), assuming it were to be construed as solely a jurisdictional statute, have been established by use of *Osborn*? *Yes — Fed. ? would possibly arise in §301 case – p. 730-31*

2. Consider the "protective jurisdiction" theories described in Justice Frankfurter's dissent. Note that the two versions, one developed by Professor Wechsler and the other by Professor Mishkin, are very different in both rationale and effect. Wechsler's theory turns on the logical premise that the "greater" includes the "lesser". Wechsler provides the following example:

> Where * * * Congress by the commerce power can declare as federal law that contracts of a given kind are valid and enforceable, it must be free to take the lesser step of drawing suits upon such contracts to the district courts without displacement of the states as sources of the operative, substantive law.

Wechsler, *Federal Jurisdiction and the Revision of the Judicial Code*, 13 Law & Contemp.Prob. 216, 224 (1948).

Mishkin's theory, on the other hand, is that "where there is an articulated and active federal policy regulating a field, the 'arising under' clause of Article III apparently permits the conferring of jurisdiction on the national courts of all cases in the area—including those substantively governed by state law." 53 Colum.L.Rev. at 192. For a critique of protective jurisdiction, see Pfander, *The* Tidewater *Problem: Article III and Constitutional Change*, 79 Notre Dame L.Rev. 1925 (2004).

3. Which of the two theories provides Congress broader authority to vest "arising under" jurisdiction in the federal courts? How, for example, would the two theories apply to the *Lincoln Mills* situation? Which of the two theories was Justice Burton referring to when he made reference to the principle of protective jurisdiction in his concurring opinion? *— Mishkin "policy"*

4. Do either or both theories of protective jurisdiction represent a proper construction of the "arising under" provision of Article III? Why? *No, Both go beyond.*

5. How does *Osborn* square with the two theories of protective jurisdiction? Does Wechsler's theory in any way go beyond Marshall's principle? Mishkin believes *Osborn* is an illustration of his theory. Do you agree? For another theory of protective jurisdiction, see Segall, *Article III as a Grant of Power: Protective Jurisdiction, Federalism, and the Federal Courts*, 54 Fla. L.Rev. 361 (2002) (arguing that a case "can 'arise under' federal law, for Article III purposes, when Congress uses federal jurisdiction to further legitimate Article I interests"). *"Arising under given very broad interp.*

6. Consider the bankruptcy cases described in Justice Frankfurter's dissent. Justice Frankfurter suggests that there exists only "a superficial analogy" between the bankruptcy decisions and section 301(a). Does he adequately distinguish the two? To what extent are the bankruptcy cases explainable in terms of either or both protective jurisdiction theories? In terms of *Osborn*? See generally Cross, *Congressional Power to Extend Federal Jurisdiction to Disputes Outside Article III: A Critical Analysis from the Perspective of Bankruptcy*, 87 Nw.U.L.Rev. 1188 (1993).

7. The Supreme Court's most recent detailed statement on the constitutional scope of the "arising under" clause came in the decision in Verlinden B.V. v. Central Bank of Nigeria, 461 U.S. 480 (1983). The issue, in the Court's words, was "whether the Foreign Sovereign Immunities Act of 1976, by authorizing a foreign plaintiff to sue a foreign state in a United States District Court on a non-federal cause of action, violates Article III of the Constitution." Section 2 of the Act extended federal jurisdiction to "civil action[s] against a foreign state * * * as to any claim for relief in personam with respect to which the foreign state is not entitled to immunity either under * * * this title or under any applicable international agreement." The Court found that it "need not now * * * decide the precise boundaries of Article III jurisdiction," because "the present case does not involve a mere speculative possibility that a federal question may arise at some point in the proceeding. Rather, a suit against a foreign state under this Act necessarily raises questions of substantive federal law at the very outset, and hence clearly 'arises under' federal law, as that term is used in Article III."

This was because

[t]he statute must be applied in the District Courts in every action against a foreign sovereign, since subject matter jurisdiction in any such action depends on the existence of one of the specified exceptions to foreign sovereign immunity. * * * At the threshold of every action in a District Court against a foreign state, therefore, the court must satisfy itself that one of the exceptions applies—and in doing so it must apply the detailed federal law standards set forth in the Act. Accordingly, an action against a foreign sovereign arises under federal law, for purposes of Article III jurisdiction.

461 U.S. at 493–94.

In a footnote, the Court concluded that "[i]n view of our conclusion that proper actions by foreign plaintiffs under the Foreign Sovereign Immunities Act are within Article III 'arising under' jurisdiction, we need not consider petitioner's alternative argument that the Act is constitutional as an aspect of so-called 'protective jurisdiction.'" Id. at 491 n.17.

In Mesa v. California, 489 U.S. 121 (1989), the Supreme Court construed the Federal Officer Removal Statute, 28 U.S.C.A. § 1442, to require the presence of a federal defense before removal could be invoked. In so holding, the Court suggested that an opposite construction would lead to serious "arising under" problems under Article III. The decision was openly negative towards the concept of protective jurisdiction:

We have, in the past, not found the need to adopt a theory of "protective jurisdiction" to support Art. III "arising under" jurisdiction * * * and we do not see any need for doing so here because we do not recognize any federal interests that are not protected by limiting removal to situations in which a federal defense is alleged.

Id. at 137.

In a separate concurring opinion, however, Justice Brennan pointed out that "[i]t is not at all inconceivable * * * that Congress' concern about local hostility to federal authority could come into play in some circumstances where the federal officer is unable to present any 'federal defense.' " Id. at 140.

Despite *Mesa*, at least one post-*Mesa* lower federal court has commented favorably on the theory of protective jurisdiction. Kolibash v. Committee on Legal Ethics, 872 F.2d 571, 575 (4th Cir.1989).

§ 2. THE STATUTORY FRAMEWORK

INTRODUCTION

The similarity between the language of the "arising under" provision of Article III and that of the general federal question statute, 28 U.S.C. § 1331, appearing in Appendix B, is striking. According to one commentator, the primary drafter of the Senate bill that eventually became the first version of the general grant in 1875 did in fact intend to vest full constitutional authority under the "arising under" provision in the lower federal courts. It is also claimed that whatever little contemporary legal commentary that existed concurred in this interpretation. Forrester, *The Nature of a "Federal Question"*, 16 Tul.L.Rev. 362, 374–75 (1942). However, as will be seen from the cases in this section, the statutory grant has never received the broad interpretation traditionally given to the constitutional language.

One simple and oft-cited interpretation of the statutory "arising under" language comes from Justice Holmes's majority opinion in American Well Works Co. v. Layne & Bowler Co., 241 U.S 257, 260 (1916): "A suit arises under the law that creates the cause of action." This formulation works well for cases in which the plaintiff alleges a federal cause of action, but it creates problems in other cases. Consider whether the following cases could be brought in federal court:

a.   A former patent holder sues his assignee to recover royalties which had been agreed upon. See Albright v. Teas, 106 U.S. 613 (1883).

b.   A patent holder sues to enjoin an alleged infringement; the defense is made that the defendant's actions were justified by a license contract. See White v. Rankin, 144 U.S. 628 (1892).

c.   Patent holder sues for the purchase price of a patented machine, and the defense is made that the plaintiff's patent is void. Cf. Pratt v. Paris Gas Light & Coke Co., 168 U.S. 255 (1897).

In each case, consider the purposes that are served by allocating "federal question" cases to federal court. In light of these purposes, might the *American Well Works* principle be deemed unduly narrow? In particular, think about about what issues are, as a practical matter, likely to dominate the litigation.

A recurring question about the application of *American Well Works* is how to treat cases in which a federal question is embedded in a state cause of action. The Court has struggled repeatedly with this dilemma, as the cases in this section demonstrate.

SMITH v. KANSAS CITY TITLE & TRUST CO.

Supreme Court of the United States, 1921.
255 U.S. 180.

imbedded Fed. Issue

Mr. Justice Day delivered the opinion of the court.

A bill was filed in the United States District Court for the Western Division of the Western District of Missouri by a shareholder in the Kansas City Title & Trust Company to enjoin the Company, its officers, agents and employees from investing the funds of the Company in farm loan bonds issued by Federal Land Banks or Joint Stock Land Banks under authority of the Federal Farm Loan Act of July 17, 1916, c. 245, 39 Stat. 360, as amended January 18, 1918, c. 9, 40 Stat. 431.

The relief was sought on the ground that these acts were beyond the constitutional power of Congress. The bill avers that the Board of Directors of the Company are about to invest its funds in the bonds to the amount of $10,000 in each of the classes described, and will do so unless enjoined by the court in this action. The bill avers the formation of twelve Federal Land Banks, and twenty-one Joint Stock Land Banks under the provisions of the act.

* * *

* * * The bill avers that the defendant Trust Company is authorized to buy, invest in and sell government, state and municipal and other bonds, but it cannot buy, invest in or sell any such bonds, papers, stocks or securities which are not authorized to be issued by a valid law or which are not investment securities, but that nevertheless it is about to invest in Farm Loan Bonds; that the Trust Company has been induced to direct its officers to make the investment by reason of its reliance upon the provisions of the Farm Loan Acts, especially §§ 21, 26 and 27, by which the Farm Loan Bonds are declared to be instrumentalities of the Government of the United States, and as such with the income derived therefrom, are declared to be exempt from federal, state, municipal and local taxation, and are further declared to be lawful investments for all fiduciary and trust funds. The bill further avers that the acts by which it is attempted to authorize the bonds are wholly illegal, void and unconstitutional and of no effect because unauthorized by the Constitution of the United States.

The bill prays that the acts of Congress authorizing the creation of the banks, especially §§ 21, 26 and 27 thereof, shall be adjudged and decreed to be unconstitutional, void and of no effect, and that the issuance of the Farm Loan Bonds, and the taxation exemption feature thereof, shall be adjudged and decreed to be invalid.

* * *

No objection is made to the federal jurisdiction, either original or appellate, by the parties to this suit, but that question will be first examined. The Company is authorized to invest its funds in legal securities only. The attack upon the proposed investment in the bonds described is because of the alleged unconstitutionality of the acts of Congress undertaking to organize the banks and authorize the issue of the bonds. No other reason is set forth in the bill as a ground of objection to the proposed investment by the Board of Directors acting in the Company's behalf. As diversity of citizenship is lacking, the jurisdiction of the District Court depends upon whether the cause of action set forth arises under the Constitution or laws of the United States. * * *

The general rule is that where it appears from the bill or statement of the plaintiff that the right to relief depends upon the construction or application of the Constitution or laws of the United States, and that such federal claim is not merely colorable, and rests upon a reasonable foundation, the District Court has jurisdiction under this provision.

At an early date, considering the grant of constitutional power to confer jurisdiction upon the federal courts, Chief Justice Marshall said: "A case in law or equity consists of the right of the one party, as well as of the other, and may truly be said to arise under the Constitution or a law of the United States, whenever its correct decision depends on the construction of either," Cohens v. Virginia, 6 Wheat. 264, 379; and again, when "the title or right set up by the party may be defeated by one construction of the Constitution or law of the United States, and sustained by the opposite construction." Osborn v. Bank of the United States, 9 Wheat. 738, 822. * * *

This characterization of a suit arising under the Constitution or laws of the United States has been followed in many decisions of this and other federal courts. * * *

* * *

The jurisdiction of this court is to be determined upon the principles laid down in the cases referred to. In the instant case the averments of the bill show that the directors were proceeding to make the investments in view of the act authorizing the bonds about to be purchased, maintaining that the act authorizing them was constitutional and the bonds valid and desirable investments. The objecting shareholder avers in the bill that the securities were issued under an unconstitutional law, and hence of no validity. It is, therefore, apparent that the controversy concerns the constitutional validity of an act of Congress which is directly drawn in question. The decision depends upon the determination of this issue.

* * * We are, therefore, of the opinion that the District Court had jurisdiction under the averments of the bill, and that a direct appeal to this court upon constitutional grounds is authorized.

* * *

[T]he decree of the District Court is affirmed.

MR. JUSTICE BRANDEIS took no part in the consideration or decision of this case.

MR. JUSTICE HOLMES dissenting.

No doubt it is desirable that the question raised in this case should be set at rest, but that can be done by the Courts of the United States only within the limits of the jurisdiction conferred upon them by the Constitution and the laws of the United States. As this suit was brought by a citizen of Missouri against a Missouri corporation the single ground upon which the jurisdiction of the District Court can be maintained is that the suit "arises under the Constitution or laws of the United States" within the meaning of § 24 of the Judicial Code. I am of opinion that this case does not arise in that way and therefore that the bill should have been dismissed.

It is evident that the cause of action arises not under any law of the United States but wholly under Missouri law. The defendant is a Missouri corporation and the right claimed is that of a stockholder to prevent the directors from doing an act, that is, making an investment, alleged to be contrary to their duty. But the scope of their duty depends upon the charter of their corporation and other laws of Missouri. If those laws had authorized the investment in terms the plaintiff would have had no case, and this seems to me to make manifest what I am unable to deem even debatable, that, as I have said, the cause of action arises wholly under Missouri law. If the Missouri law authorizes or forbids the investment according to the determination of this Court upon a point under the Constitution or acts of Congress, still that point is material only because the Missouri law saw fit to make it so. The whole foundation of the duty is Missouri law, which at its sole will incorporated the other law as it might incorporate a document. The other law or document depends for its relevance and effect not on its own force but upon the law that took it up, so I repeat once more the cause of action arises wholly from the law of the State.

But it seems to me that a suit cannot be said to arise under any other law than that which creates the cause of action. It may be enough that the law relied upon creates a part of the cause of action although not the whole, as held in Osborn v. Bank of the United States, 9 Wheat. 738, 819–823, which perhaps is all that is meant by the less guarded expressions in Cohens v. Virginia, 6 Wheat. 264, 379. I am content to assume this to be so, although the *Osborn Case* has been criticized and regretted. But the law must create at least a part of the cause of action by its own force, for it is the suit, not a question in the suit, that must arise under the law of the United States. The mere adoption by a state law of a United States law as a criterion or test, when the law of the United States has no force *proprio vigore*, does not cause a case under the state law to be also a case under the law of the United States, and so it has been decided by this Court again and again. Miller v. Swann, 150 U.S. 132, 136, 137; Louisville & Nashville R. R. Co. v. Western Union Telegraph Co., 237 U.S. 300, 303. See also Shoshone Mining Co. v. Rutter, 177 U.S. 505, 508, 509.

* * *

MR. JUSTICE McREYNOLDS concurs in this dissent. In view of our opinion that this Court has no jurisdiction we express no judgment on the merits.

Notes

1.   How would you describe the Court's method of determining whether a case "arises under" federal law? How, if at all, does this approach differ from the one used in *American Well Works*? Which of the two approaches do you find to be a more appropriate interpretation of the "federal question" statute?

2.   How would the *Smith* test apply to the following situation: A state legislature enacts a law which provides that any activity found to violate the federal Sherman Antitrust Act when conducted in interstate commerce will be deemed a violation of state law if conducted exclusively within the state. A non-diverse suit is brought in federal court, alleging that certain activity conducted exclusively within the state is a violation of the state statute, because if the exact same activity had taken place in interstate commerce it would have violated the Sherman Act. *Should* "federal question" jurisdiction be found in such a case? Once again, in answering consider the purposes served by allowing federal questions to be heard in federal court. If you believe that "federal question" jurisdiction should *not* be found in the hypothetical, can you distinguish *Smith* on the facts?

3.   Relevant to this discussion is Moore v. Chesapeake & Ohio Railway Co., 291 U.S. 205 (1934). There the Supreme Court held that "federal question" jurisdiction could not be found where a state has incorporated federal law by reference within its own law. The specific issue in the case was one of venue, which in turn was to be determined by whether the case rested "solely on diversity of citizenship", or instead could also be deemed to "arise under" federal law. Suit was brought under the Employers' Liability Act of Kentucky. That act provided that an employee could not be held guilty of contributory negligence or assumption of risk in any case "where the violation by such common carrier of any statute, state or federal, enacted for the safety of employees contributed to the injury or death of such employee." 291 U.S. at 213. The Federal Safety Appliance Act, which itself did not provide for a cause of action, dictated the use of certain equipment on all cars employed on any railroad used in interstate commerce. Apparently the railroad cars in question were in fact used in interstate commerce. The Supreme Court held that the state law had intended to include reference to the federal act. An important issue in the case, therefore, would be whether the defendant had violated the terms of the federal statute. However, the Supreme Court concluded that the case did not "arise under" the federal safety appliance act in the district court.

Professor Currie has suggested that *Smith* and *Moore* are irreconcilable. "In *Moore* as well as in *Smith*", he wrote, "the result turned upon the construction of federal law, but in both cases the federal law provided no remedy." D. Currie, Federal Jurisdiction in a Nutshell 109 (2d Ed. 1981). In support of Professor Currie's position, it is worthy of note that the Court in *Moore* acknowledged that "[q]uestions arising in actions in state courts to recover for injuries sustained by employees in intrastate commerce and relating to the scope or construction of the Federal Safety Appliance Acts are, of course, federal questions which may appropriately be reviewed in this Court." 291 U.S. at 214. The Court was thus making clear that a "federal question" did exist in the case for purposes of Supreme Court review, but not for the "arising under" jurisdiction of the federal district courts. Note that the two decisions might be distinguished on their facts. In *Moore*, the federal issue was made relevant only by means of a defense to the plaintiff's complaint. In *Smith*, on the other hand, the issue of federal law appeared in the complaint. Under the doctrine of Louisville & Nashville Railroad Co. v. Mottley, 211 U.S. 149 (1908) [infra p. 763], whether the federal issue appears on the face of the well-pleaded complaint is determinative of "federal question" jurisdiction. The Court in *Moore*, however, did not explicitly base its decision to reject "federal question" jurisdiction on this ground. On the issue of the possible inconsistency between these two decisions, see the *Merrell Dow* case [infra p. 741].

To the extent *Smith* and *Moore* are in fact inconsistent, it appeared clear, at least until *Merrell Dow* [infra p. 741], that the *Smith* doctrine prevailed in the lower federal courts. For example, Judge Friendly in T. B. Harms Co. v. Eliscu, 339 F.2d 823, 827 (2d Cir.1964), cert. denied, 381 U.S. 915 (1965), referred to *Smith* as a "path-breaking opinion * * *."

4.   Development of the *Smith* doctrine led Judge Friendly in *Harms* to suggest that "Holmes' formula [in *American Well Works*] is [today] more useful for inclusion than for the exclusion for which it was intended." 339 F.2d at 827. What does this mean?

5.   Consider Shoshone Mining Co. v. Rutter, 177 U.S. 505 (1900). In an attempt to provide a mechanism for settling conflicting claims to mines, Congress enacted a statute establishing a system allowing miners to file patents on their claims. If an adverse claim was filed, the adverse claimant could bring suit in a "court of competent jurisdiction" to determine ownership. The statute further provided that the right to possession was to be determined by "local customs or rules of miners in the several mining districts, so far as the same are applicable and not inconsistent with the laws of the United States." Id. at U.S. 508. In denying the existence of federal question jurisdiction in suits brought pursuant to the federal act, the Supreme Court reasoned:

> Inasmuch * * * as the "adverse suit" to determine the right of possession may not involve any question as to the construction or effect of the Constitution or laws of the United States, but may present simply a question of fact as to the time of the discovery of mineral, the location of the claim on the ground, or a determination of the meaning and effect of certain local rules and customs prescribed by the miners of the district, or the effect of state statutes, it would seem to follow that it is not one which necessarily arises under the Constitution and laws of the United States. Id. at 509.

In light of *Shoshone*, which remains good law today even though it preceded decisions in *American Well Works* and *Smith*, is Judge Friendly correct when he says that Holmes' principle in *American Well Works* is now used for purposes of inclusion, rather than the exclusion for which it was originally decided? How would use of the *American Well Works* principle have affected decision in *Shoshone*? Can the decision in *Shoshone* be reconciled with the interpretation of "arising under" developed in *Smith*?

Should the *Shoshone* decision be raised to the level of *constitutional* interpretation of "arising under"? In other words, if Congress had stated explicitly that it had intended the federal courts to have "federal question" jurisdiction in cases brought pursuant to the statute, could it have done so? Recall *Osborn* and the varying theories of protective jurisdiction discussed supra. How would those constitutional doctrines apply to such a situation?

Viewing *Shoshone* as merely an interpretation of the *statutory* "arising under" jurisdiction (which is actually all the case decided), was the decision a wise one? Consider Cohen, *The Broken Compass: The Requirement That a Case Arise "Directly" Under Federal Law*, 115 U.Pa.L.Rev. 890, 903 (1967):

> Even if all lawyers will agree that the plaintiff's cause of action in *Shoshone* is federal (state law merely being incorporated by reference), it does not follow that the Court reached the "wrong" result. The Court was properly concerned with the volume of litigation which a contrary decision would have loosed upon federal trial courts * * *. The Court, for pragmatic reasons, had refused to extend the jurisdiction to a large class of cases which would, in most instances, involve no clearly defined federal interest and no issue of federal law.

To a similar effect, see Mishkin, supra, 53 Colum.L.Rev. at 162.

Professor Currie, on the other hand, has criticized the decision in *Shoshone*. "[S]ince both the right and the remedy were created by federal law," he asserts, "the fact that certain matters were to be decided as state law would decide them does not seem to indicate a lack of federal interest in the case, any more than a state would be without concern as to the operation of its own courts merely because it had incorporated the federal rules." D. Currie, supra at 111.

Which of the two positions do you find more persuasive?

6. Gully v. First National Bank in Meridian, 299 U.S. 109 (1936). A Mississippi tax collector had sued in state court for taxes claimed to be due. These taxes were originally to have been paid by a bank that had become insolvent, and its assets and liabilities were assumed by the defendant bank pursuant to a contract. The claim was made that the defendant had failed to meet its contractual obligation to pay the taxes. Defendant removed the case to federal court, claiming that federal question jurisdiction was present because "the power to lay a tax upon the shares of national banks has its origin and measure in the provisions of a federal statute * * *." 299 U.S. at 112. In an opinion by Justice Cardozo, the Court denied federal jurisdiction. "The most one can say", said Cardozo, "is that a question of federal law is lurking in the background * * *. A dispute so doubtful and conjectural, so far removed from plain necessity, is unavailing to extinguish the jurisdiction of the states." Id. at 117. The goal in interpreting "arising under" jurisdiction, he said, is to formulate "the distinction between controversies that are basic and those that are collateral. * * * *" Id. at 118. His broader synthesis for measuring "arising under" jurisdiction was that

a right or immunity created by the Constitution or laws of the United States must be an element, and an essential one, of the plaintiff's cause of action * * *. The right or immunity must be such that it will be supported if the Constitution or laws of the United States are given one construction or effect, and defeated if they receive another.

Id. at 112.

How would *Smith* and *Shoshone* have been decided under the *Gully* test? How would *Gully* have been decided under the tests of each of those decisions, or under *American Well Works*? Under *Gully*, would there be "federal question" jurisdiction in a case brought pursuant to the federal antitrust laws alleging price-fixing where the only issue to be litigated was the factual one of whether the defendants had actually communicated with each other before setting their prices? For an analysis of *Gully*, as well as of the other decisions considered in this section, see Cohen, supra, 115 U.Pa. L.Rev. 890. Professor Cohen argues that in cases involving a mixture of state and federal law, "federal question" jurisdiction should be found only when the case "requires expertise in the construction of the federal law involved in the case, and a sympathetic forum for trial of factual issues related to the existence of a claimed federal right * * *." 115 U.Pa.L.Rev. at 906. Is this a workable standard? How would it have applied to *Smith*? *Shoshone*? *Gully*?

7. Professor Mishkin has suggested that "the criterion for original federal jurisdiction [is] a substantial claim founded 'directly' upon federal law * * *." 53 Colum.L.Rev. at 168. This language has been widely followed in the lower federal courts. See, e.g., Mescalero Apache Tribe v. Martinez, 519 F.2d 479, 481 (10th Cir.1975); Baker v. FCH Services, Inc., 376 F.Supp. 1365, 1367 (S.D.N.Y.1974); Davidson v. General Finance Corp., 295 F.Supp. 878, 881 (N.D.Ga.1968). Can you define the word, "directly", as it is used in the Mishkin standard? How would it apply to the facts of the major Supreme Court decisions discussed here?

8. On the issue of federal question jurisdiction, see generally M. Redish, Federal Jurisdiction: Tensions in the Allocation of Judicial Power 83–117 (2d ed. 1990); Hornstein, *Federalism, Judicial Power and the "Arising Under" Jurisdiction of the Federal Courts: A Hierarchical Analysis*, 56 Ind.L.J. 563 (1981).

MERRELL DOW PHARMACEUTICALS INC. v. THOMPSON

Supreme Court of the United States, 1986.
478 U.S. 804.

JUSTICE STEVENS delivered the opinion of the Court.

The question presented is whether the incorporation of a federal standard in a state-law private action, when Congress has intended that there not be a federal private action for violations of that federal standard, makes the action one "arising under the Constitution, laws, or treaties of the United States," 28 U.S.C. § 1331.

I

The Thompson respondents are residents of Canada and the Mac-Tavishes reside in Scotland. They filed virtually identical complaints against petitioner, a corporation, that manufactures and distributes the drug Bendectin. The complaints were filed in the Court of Common Pleas in Hamilton County, Ohio. Each complaint alleged that a child was born with multiple deformities as a result of the mother's ingestion of Bendectin during pregnancy. In five of the six counts, the recovery of substantial damages was requested on common-law theories of negligence, breach of warranty, strict liability, fraud, and gross negligence. In Count IV, respondents alleged that the drug Bendectin was "misbranded" in violation of the Federal Food, Drug, and Cosmetic Act (FDCA), 52 Stat. 1040, as amended, 21 U.S.C. § 301 et seq. (1982 ed., Supp. II), because its labeling did not provide adequate warning that its use was potentially dangerous. Paragraph 26 alleged that the violation of the FDCA "in the promotion" of Bendectin "constitutes a rebuttable presumption of negligence." Paragraph 27 alleged that the "violation of said federal statutes directly and proximately caused the injuries suffered" by the two infants.

Petitioner filed a timely petition for removal from the state court to the Federal District Court alleging that the action was "founded, in part, on an alleged claim arising under the laws of the United States." After removal, the two cases were consolidated. Respondents filed a motion to remand to the state forum on the ground that the federal court lacked subject-matter jurisdiction. Relying on our decision in Smith v. Kansas City Title & Trust Co., 255 U.S. 180 (1921), the District Court held that Count IV of the complaint alleged a cause of action arising under federal law and denied the motion to remand. It then granted petitioner's motion to dismiss on *forum non conveniens* grounds.

The Court of Appeals for the Sixth Circuit reversed. After quoting one sentence from the concluding paragraph in our recent opinion in Franchise Tax Board v. Construction Laborers Vacation Trust, 463 U.S. 1 (1983)[2], and noting "that the FDCA does not create or imply a private right of action for individuals injured as a result of violations of the Act," it explained:

> "Federal question jurisdiction would, thus, exist only if plaintiffs' right to relief *depended necessarily* on a substantial question of federal law. Plaintiffs' causes of action referred to the FDCA merely as one available criterion for determining whether Merrell Dow was negligent. Because the jury could find negligence on the part of Merrell Dow without finding a violation of the FDCA, the plaintiffs' causes of action did not depend necessarily upon a question of federal law. Consequently, the causes of action did not arise under federal law and, therefore, were improperly removed to federal court."

2. " 'Under our interpretations, Congress has given the lower courts jurisdiction to hear, originally or by removal from a state court, only those cases in which a well-pleaded complaint establishes either that federal law creates the cause of action or that the plaintiff's right to relief necessarily depends on resolution of a substantial question of federal law.' " 766 F.2d, at 1006 (quoting *Franchise Tax Board,* 463 U.S., at 28).

We granted certiorari, and we now affirm.

II

Article III of the Constitution gives the federal courts power to hear cases "arising under" federal statutes. That grant of power, however, is not self-executing, and it was not until the Judiciary Act of 1875 that Congress gave the federal courts general federal-question jurisdiction. Although the constitutional meaning of "arising under" may extend to all cases in which a federal question is "an ingredient" of the action, Osborn v. Bank of the United States, 9 Wheat. 738, 823 (1824), we have long construed the statutory grant of federal-question jurisdiction as conferring a more limited power.

Under our longstanding interpretation of the current statutory scheme, the question whether a claim "arises under" federal law must be determined by reference to the "well-pleaded complaint." A defense that raises a federal question is inadequate to confer federal jurisdiction. Louisville & Nashville R. Co. v. Mottley, 211 U.S. 149 (1908). Since a defendant may remove a case only if the claim could have been brought in federal court, 28 U.S.C. § 1441(b), moreover, the question for removal jurisdiction must also be determined by reference to the "well-pleaded complaint."

As was true in *Franchise Tax Board*, the propriety of the removal in this case thus turns on whether the case falls within the original "federal question" jurisdiction of the federal courts. There is no "single, precise definition" of that concept; rather, "the phrase 'arising under' masks a welter of issues regarding the interrelation of federal and state authority and the proper management of the federal judicial system."

This much, however, is clear. The "vast majority" of cases that come within this grant of jurisdiction are covered by Justice Holmes' statement that a " 'suit arises under the law that creates the cause of action.' " quoting American Well Works Co. v. Layne & Bowler Co., 241 U.S. 257, 260 (1916). Thus, the vast majority of cases brought under the general federal-question jurisdiction of the federal courts are those in which federal law creates the cause of action.

We have, however, also noted that a case may arise under federal law "where the vindication of a right under state law necessarily turned on some construction of federal law." Franchise Tax Board, 463 U.S., at 9.[5] * * *

5. The case most frequently cited for that proposition is Smith v. Kansas City Title & Trust Co., 255 U.S. 180 (1921). In that case the Court upheld federal jurisdiction of a shareholder's bill to enjoin the corporation from purchasing bonds issued by the federal land banks under the authority of the Federal Farm Loan Act on the ground that the federal statute that authorized the issuance of the bonds was unconstitutional. The Court stated:

"The general rule is that where it appears from the bill or statement of the plaintiff that the right to relief depends upon the construction or application of the Constitution or laws of the United States, and that such federal claim is not merely colorable, and rests upon a reasonable foundation, the District Court has jurisdiction under this provision."

This case does not pose a federal question of the first kind; respondents do not allege that federal law creates any of the causes of action that they have asserted.[6] This case thus poses what Justice Frankfurter called the "litigation-provoking problem," Textile Workers v. Lincoln Mills, 353 U.S. 448, 470 (1957) (dissenting opinion)—the presence of a federal issue in a state-created cause of action.

In undertaking this inquiry into whether jurisdiction may lie for the presence of a federal issue in a nonfederal cause of action, it is, of course, appropriate to begin by referring to our understanding of the statute conferring federal-question jurisdiction. We have consistently emphasized that, in exploring the outer reaches of § 1331, determinations about federal jurisdiction require sensitive judgments about congressional intent, judicial power, and the federal system. "If the history of the interpretation of judiciary legislation teaches us anything, it teaches the duty to reject treating such statutes as a wooden set of self-sufficient words.... The Act of 1875 is broadly phrased, but it has been continuously construed and limited in the light of the history that produced it, the demands of reason and coherence, and the dictates of sound judicial policy which have emerged from the Act's function as a provision in the mosaic of federal judiciary legislation." Romero v. International Terminal Operating Co., 358 U.S., at 379. * * *

In this case, both parties agree with the Court of Appeals' conclusion that there is no federal cause of action for FDCA violations. For purposes of our decision, we assume that this is a correct interpretation of the FDCA. Thus, as the case comes to us, it is appropriate to assume that, under the settled framework for evaluating whether a federal cause of action lies, some combination of the following factors is present: (1) the plaintiffs are not part of the class for whose special benefit the statute was passed; (2) the indicia of legislative intent reveal no congressional purpose to provide a private cause of action; (3) a federal cause of action would not further the underlying purposes of the legislative scheme; and (4) the respondents' cause of action is a subject traditionally relegated to state law.[7] In short, Congress did not intend a private federal remedy for violations of the statute that it enacted.

The effect of this view, expressed over Justice Holmes' vigorous dissent, on his *American Well Works* formulation has been often noted. See, e.g., Franchise Tax Board, 463 U.S., at 9 ("[I]t is well settled that Justice Holmes' test is more useful for describing the vast majority of cases that come within the district courts' original jurisdiction than it is for describing which cases are beyond district court jurisdiction"); T.B. Harms Co. v. Eliscu, 339 F.2d 823, 827 (C.A.2 1964) (Friendly, J.) ("It has come to be realized that Mr. Justice Holmes' formula is more useful for inclusion than for the exclusion for which it was intended").

6. Jurisdiction may not be sustained on a theory that the plaintiff has not advanced. See Healy v. Sea Gull Specialty Co., 237 U.S. 479, 480 (1915) ("[T]he plaintiff is absolute master of what jurisdiction he will appeal to"); The Fair v. Kohler Die and Specialty Co., 228 U.S. 22, 25 (1913) ("[T]he party who brings a suit is master to decide what law he will rely upon").

7. See California v. Sierra Club, 451 U.S. 287, 293 (1981); Cannon v. University of Chicago, 441 U.S. 677, 689–709 (1979); Cort v. Ash, 422 U.S. 66, 78 (1975).

This is the first case in which we have reviewed this type of jurisdictional claim in light of these factors. That this is so is not surprising. The development of our framework for determining whether a private cause of action exists has proceeded only in the last 11 years, and its inception represented a significant change in our approach to congressional silence on the provision of federal remedies.[8]

The recent character of that development does not, however, diminish its importance. Indeed, the very reasons for the development of the modern implied remedy doctrine—the "increased complexity of federal legislation and the increased volume of federal litigation," as well as "the desirability of a more careful scrutiny of legislative intent," Merrill Lynch, Pierce, Fenner & Smith v. Curran, 456 U.S. 353, 377 (1982) (footnote omitted)—are precisely the kind of considerations that should inform the concern for "practicality and necessity" that *Franchise Tax Board* advised for the construction of § 1331 when jurisdiction is asserted because of the presence of a federal issue in a state cause of action.

Purposes

The significance of the necessary assumption that there is no federal private cause of action thus cannot be overstated. For the ultimate import of such a conclusion, as we have repeatedly emphasized, is that it would flout congressional intent to provide a private federal remedy for the violation of the federal statute. We think it would similarly flout, or at least undermine, congressional intent to conclude that the federal courts might nevertheless exercise federal-question jurisdiction and provide remedies for violations of that federal statute solely because the violation of the federal statute is said to be a "rebuttable presumption" or a "proximate cause" under state law, rather than a federal action under federal law.[10]

III

Petitioner advances three arguments to support its position that, even in the face of this congressional preclusion of a federal cause of action for a violation of the federal statute, federal-question jurisdiction may lie for the violation of the federal statute as an element of a state cause of action.

3 argument

---

8. See Merrill Lynch, Pierce, Fenner & Smith v. Curran, 456 U.S. 353, 377 (1982) ("In 1975 the Court unanimously decided to modify its approach to the question whether a federal statute includes a private right of action"). Cf. Middlesex County Sewerage Authority v. National Sea Clammers Assn., 453 U.S. 1, 25 (1981) (STEVENS, J., concurring in judgment in part and dissenting in part) ("In 1975, in Cort v. Ash, 422 U.S. 66, the Court cut back on the simple common-law presumption by fashioning a four-factor formula that led to the denial of relief in that case").

10. When we conclude that Congress has decided not to provide a particular federal remedy, we are not free to "supplement" that decision in a way that makes it "meaningless." Cf. Mobil Oil Corp. v. Higginbotham, 436 U.S. 618, 625 (1978) (When Congress "does speak directly to a question, the courts are not free to 'supplement' Congress' answer so thoroughly that the Act becomes meaningless"). See also California v. Sierra Club, 451 U.S., at 297 ("The federal judiciary will not engraft a remedy on a statute, no matter how salutary, that Congress did not intend to provide").

First, petitioner contends that the case represents a straightforward application of the statement in *Franchise Tax Board* that federal-question jurisdiction is appropriate when "it appears that some substantial, disputed question of federal law is a necessary element of one of the well-pleaded state claims." *Franchise Tax Board,* however, did not purport to disturb the long-settled understanding that the mere presence of a federal issue in a state cause of action does not automatically confer federal-question jurisdiction. * * *

* * * Given the significance of the assumed congressional determination to preclude federal private remedies, the presence of the federal issue as an element of the state tort is not the kind of adjudication for which jurisdiction would serve congressional purposes and the federal system. This conclusion is fully consistent with the very sentence relied on so heavily by petitioner. We simply conclude that the congressional determination that there should be no federal remedy for the violation of this federal statute is tantamount to a congressional conclusion that the presence of a claimed violation of the statute as an element of a state cause of action is insufficiently "substantial" to confer federal-question jurisdiction.[12]

---

12. Several commentators have suggested that our § 1331 decisions can best be understood as an evaluation of the *nature* of the federal interest at stake. See, e.g., Shapiro, Jurisdiction and Discretion, 60 N.Y.U.L.Rev. 543, 568 (1985); C. Wright, Federal Courts 96 (4th ed. 1983); Cohen, The Broken Compass: The Requirement That A Case Arise 'Directly' Under Federal Law, 115 U.Pa.L.Rev. 890, 916 (1967). * * *

Focusing on the nature of the federal interest, moreover, suggests that the widely perceived "irreconcilable" conflict between the finding of federal jurisdiction in Smith v. Kansas City Title & Trust Co., 255 U.S. 180 (1921) and the finding of no jurisdiction in Moore v. Chesapeake & Ohio R. Co., 291 U.S. 205 (1934), see, e.g., M. Redish, Federal Jurisdiction: Tensions in the Allocation of Judicial Power 67 (1980), is far from clear. For the difference in results can be seen as manifestations of the differences in the nature of the federal issues at stake. In *Smith,* as the Court emphasized, the issue was the constitutionality of an important federal statute. See 255 U.S., at 201 ("It is ... apparent that the controversy concerns the constitutional validity of an act of Congress which is directly drawn in question. The decision depends upon the determination of this issue"). In *Moore,* in contrast, the Court emphasized that the violation of the federal standard as an element of state tort recovery did not fundamentally change the state tort nature of the action. See 291 U.S., at 216–217 (" 'The action fell within

the familiar category of cases involving the duty of a master to his servant. This duty is defined by the common law, except as it may be modified by legislation. The federal statute, in the present case, touched the duty of the master at a single point and, save as provided in the statute, the right of the plaintiff to recover was left to be determined by the law of the State' ") (quoting Minneapolis, St. P. & S.S.M.R. Co. v. Popplar, 237 U.S. 369, 372 (1915)).

The importance of the nature of the federal issue in federal question jurisdiction is highlighted by the fact that, despite the usual reliability of the Holmes test as an inclusionary principle, this Court has sometimes found that formally federal causes of action were not properly brought under federal-question jurisdiction because of the overwhelming predominance of state-law issues. See Shulthis v. McDougal, 225 U.S. 561, 569–570 (1912) ("A suit to enforce a right which takes its origin in the laws of the United States is not necessarily, or for that reason alone, one arising under those laws, for a suit does not so arise unless it really and substantially involves a dispute or controversy respecting the validity, construction or effect of such a law, upon the determination of which the result depends. This is especially so of a suit involving rights to land acquired under a law of the United States. If it were not, every suit to establish title to land in the central and western States would so arise, as all titles in those States are traceable back to those

Second, petitioner contends that there is a powerful federal interest in seeing that the federal statute is given uniform interpretations, and that federal review is the best way of insuring such uniformity. In addition to the significance of the congressional decision to preclude a federal remedy, we do not agree with petitioner's characterization of the federal interest and its implications for federal-question jurisdiction. To the extent that petitioner is arguing that state use and interpretation of the FDCA pose a threat to the order and stability of the FDCA regime, petitioner should be arguing, not that federal courts should be able to review and enforce state FDCA-based causes of action as an aspect of federal-question jurisdiction, but that the FDCA pre-empts state-court jurisdiction over the issue in dispute. Petitioner's concern about the uniformity of interpretation, moreover, is considerably mitigated by the fact that, even if there is no original district court jurisdiction for these kinds of action, this Court retains power to review the decision of a federal issue in a state cause of action.[14]

Role of Appellate review

Finally, petitioner argues that, whatever the general rule, there are special circumstances that justify federal-question jurisdiction in this case. Petitioner emphasizes that it is unclear whether the FDCA applies to sales in Canada and Scotland; there is, therefore, a special reason for having a federal court answer the novel federal question relating to the extraterritorial meaning of the Act. We reject this argument. We do not believe the question whether a particular claim arises under federal law depends on the novelty of the federal issue. Although it is true that federal jurisdiction cannot be based on a frivolous or insubstantial federal question, "the interrelation of federal and state authority and the proper management of the federal judicial system," *Franchise Tax Board,* 463 U.S., at 8, would be ill-served by a rule that made the existence of federal-question jurisdiction depend on the district court's case-by-case appraisal of the novelty of the federal question asserted as an element of the state tort. The novelty of an FDCA issue is not sufficient to give it status as a federal cause of action; nor should it be

laws"); Shoshone Mining Co. v. Rutter, 177 U.S. 505, 507 (1900) ("We pointed out in the former opinion that it was well settled that a suit to enforce a right which takes its origin in the laws of the United States is not necessarily one arising under the Constitution or laws of the United States, within the meaning of the jurisdiction clauses, for if it did every action to establish title to real estate (at least in the newer States) would be such a one, as all titles in those States come from the United States or by virtue of its laws").

14. See Moore v. Chesapeake & Ohio R. Co., 291 U.S. 205, 214–215 (1934) ("Questions arising in actions in state courts to recover for injuries sustained by employees in intrastate commerce and relating to the scope or construction of the Federal Safety Appliance Acts are, of course, federal questions which may appropriately be reviewed in this Court.... But it does not follow that a suit brought under the state statute which defines liability to employees who are injured while engaged in intrastate commerce, and brings within the purview of the statute a breach of the duty imposed by the federal statute, should be regarded as a suit arising under the laws of the United States and cognizable in the federal court in the absence of diversity of citizenship"). Cf. *Franchise Tax Board,* 463 U.S., at 12, n. 12 ("[T]he absence of original jurisdiction does not mean that there is no federal forum in which a preemption defense may be heard. If the state courts reject a claim of federal pre-emption, that decision may ultimately be reviewed on appeal by this Court").

sufficient to give a state-based FDCA claim status as a jurisdiction-triggering federal question.[15]

IV

We conclude that a complaint alleging a violation of a federal statute as an element of a state cause of action, when Congress has determined that there should be no private, federal cause of action for the violation, does not state a claim "arising under the Constitution, laws, or treaties of the United States." 28 U.S.C. § 1331.

The judgment of the Court of Appeals is affirmed.

JUSTICE BRENNAN, with whom JUSTICE WHITE, JUSTICE MARSHALL, and JUSTICE BLACKMUN join, dissenting.

* * *

* * * I believe that the limitation on federal jurisdiction recognized by the Court today is inconsistent with the purposes of § 1331. Therefore, I respectfully dissent.

I

While the majority of cases covered by § 1331 may well be described by Justice Holmes' adage that "a suit arises under the law that creates the cause of action," American Well Works Co. v. Layne & Bowler Co., 241 U.S. 257, 260 (1916), it is firmly settled that there may be federal question jurisdiction even though both the right asserted and the remedy sought by the plaintiff are state created. See C. Wright, Federal Courts § 17, pp. 95–96 (4th ed. 1983) (hereinafter Wright); M. Redish, Federal Jurisdiction: Tensions in the Allocation of Judicial Power 64–71 (1980) (hereinafter Redish). The rule as to such cases was stated in what Judge Friendly described as "[t]he path-breaking opinion" in Smith v. Kansas City Title & Trust Co., 255 U.S. 180 (1921). T.B. Harms Co. v. Eliscu, 339 F.2d 823, 827 (C.A.2 1964). In *Smith*, a shareholder of the defendant corporation brought suit in the federal court to enjoin the defendant from investing corporate funds in bonds issued under the authority of the Federal Farm Loan Act. The plaintiff alleged that Missouri law imposed a fiduciary duty on the corporation to invest only in bonds that were authorized by a valid law and argued that, because the Farm Loan Act was unconstitutional, the defendant could not purchase bonds issued under its authority. Although the cause of action was wholly state

15. Petitioner also contends that the Court of Appeals opinion rests on a view that federal question jurisdiction was inappropriate because, whatever the role of the federal issue in the FDCA-related count, the plaintiff could recover on other, strictly state law claims. See 766 F.2d, at 1006 (noting that "the jury could find negligence on the part of Merrell Dow without finding a violation of the FDCA"). To the extent that the opinion can be read to express such a view, we agree that it was erroneous. If the FDCA-related count presented a sufficient federal question, its relationship to the other, state-law claims would be determined by the ordinary principles of pendent jurisdiction described in Mine Workers v. Gibbs, 383 U.S. 715 (1966). For the reasons that we have stated, however, there is no federal-question jurisdiction even with that possible error corrected.

created, the Court held that there was original federal jurisdiction over the case:

> "The general rule is that where it appears from the bill or statement of the plaintiff that the right to relief depends upon the construction or application of the Constitution or laws of the United States, and that such federal claim is not merely colorable, and rests upon a reasonable foundation, the District Court has jurisdiction under [the statute granting federal question jurisdiction]." 255 U.S., at 199.

The continuing vitality of *Smith* is beyond challenge. We have cited it approvingly on numerous occasions, and reaffirmed its holding several times—most recently just three Terms ago by a unanimous Court in Franchise Tax Board v. Construction Laborers Vacation Trust, 463 U.S., at 9. Furthermore, the principle of the *Smith* case has been recognized and endorsed by most commentators as well. Redish 67, 69; American Law Institute, Study of the Division of Jurisdiction Between State and Federal Courts 178 (1969) (hereinafter ALI); Wright § 17, p. 96; P. Bator, P. Mishkin, D. Shapiro, & H. Wechsler, Hart & Wechsler's The Federal Courts and the Federal System 889 (2d ed. 1973); Mishkin, The Federal "Question" in the District Courts, 53 Colum.L.Rev. 157, 166 (1953); Wechsler, Federal Jurisdiction and the Revision of the Judicial Code, 13 Law & Contemp.Prob. 216, 225 (1948).[1]

---

1. Some commentators have argued that the result in *Smith* conflicts with our decision in Moore v. Chesapeake & Ohio Ry., 291 U.S. 205 (1934). See, e.g., Greene, Hybrid State Law in the Federal Courts, 83 Harv.L.Rev. 289, 323 (1969). In *Moore,* the plaintiff brought an action under Kentucky's Employer Liability Act, which provided that a plaintiff could not be held responsible for contributory negligence or assumption of risk where his injury resulted from the violation of any state or federal statute enacted for the safety of employees. The plaintiff in *Moore* alleged that his injury was due to the defendant's failure to comply with the Federal Safety Appliance Act; therefore, an important issue in the adjudication of the state cause of action was whether the terms of the federal law had been violated. The Court could have dismissed the complaint on the ground that the federal issue would arise only in response to a defense of contributory negligence or assumption of risk, and that therefore there was no jurisdiction under the well-pleaded complaint rule. Instead, the Court held that "a suit brought under the state statute which defines liability to employees who are injured while engaged in intrastate commerce, and brings within the purview of the statute a breach of the duty imposed by the federal statute, should [not] be regarded as a suit arising under the laws of the United States and cognizable in the federal court in the absence of diversity of citizenship." 291 U.S., at 214–215.

The Court suggests that *Smith* and *Moore* may be reconciled if one views the question whether there is jurisdiction under § 1331 as turning upon "an evaluation of the *nature* of the federal interest at stake." Thus, the Court explains, while in *Smith* the issue was the constitutionality of "an important federal statute," in *Moore* the federal interest was less significant in that "the violation of the federal standard as an element of state tort recovery did not fundamentally change the state tort nature of the action."

In one sense, the Court is correct in asserting that we can reconcile *Smith* and *Moore* on the ground that the "nature" of the federal interest was more significant in *Smith* than in *Moore*. Indeed, as the Court appears to believe, we could reconcile many of the seemingly inconsistent results that have been reached under § 1331 with such a test. But this is so only because a test based upon an ad hoc evaluation of the importance of the federal issue is infinitely malleable: at what point does a federal interest become strong enough to create jurisdiction? What principles guide the determination whether a statute is "important" or not? Why, for instance, was the statute in

There is, to my mind, no question that there is federal jurisdiction over the respondents' fourth cause of action under the rule set forth in *Smith* and reaffirmed in *Franchise Tax Board*. Respondents pleaded that petitioner's labeling of the drug Bendectin constituted "misbranding" in violation of §§ 201 and 502(f)(2), and (j) of the Federal Food, Drug, and Cosmetics Act (FDCA), 52 Stat. 1040, as amended, 21 U.S.C. § 301 et seq. (1982 ed. Supp. II), and that this violation "directly and proximately caused" their injuries. Respondents asserted in the complaint that this violation established petitioner's negligence *per se* and entitled them to recover damages without more. No other basis for finding petitioner negligent was asserted in connection with this claim. As pleaded, then, respondents' "right to relief depend[ed] upon the construction or application of the Constitution or laws of the United States." *Smith,* 255 U.S., at 199.[2] Furthermore, although petitioner disputes its liability under the FDCA, it concedes that respondents' claim that petitioner violated the FDCA is "colorable, and rests upon a reasonable foundation." *Smith,* supra, 255 U.S., at 199. Of course, since petitioner must make this concession to prevail in this Court, it need not be accepted at face value. However, independent examination of respondents' claim substantiates the conclusion that it is neither frivolous nor meritless. As stated in the complaint, a drug is "misbranded" under the FDCA if "the labeling or advertising fails to reveal facts material ... with respect to consequences which may result from the use of the article to which the

Smith so "important" that direct review of a state court decision (under our mandatory appellate jurisdiction) would have been inadequate? Would the result in *Moore* have been different if the federal issue had been a more important element of the tort claim? The point is that if one makes the test sufficiently vague and general, virtually any set of results can be "reconciled." However, the inevitable—and undesirable—result of a test such as that suggested in the Court's footnote 12 is that federal jurisdiction turns in every case on an appraisal of the federal issue, its importance and its relation to state law issues. Yet it is precisely because the Court believes that federal jurisdiction would be "ill-served" by such a case-by-case appraisal that it rejects petitioners' claim that the difficulty and importance of the statutory issue presented by their claim suffices to confer jurisdiction under § 1331. The Court cannot have it both ways.

My own view is in accord with those commentators who view the results in *Smith* and *Moore* as irreconcilable. See, e.g., Redish 67; Currie, Federal Jurisdiction in a Nutshell 109 (2d ed. 1981). That fact does not trouble me greatly, however, for I view *Moore* as having been a "sport" at the time it was decided and having long been in a state of innocuous desuetude. Unlike the jurisdictional holding in *Smith,* the jurisdic-

tional holding in *Moore* has never been relied upon or even cited by this Court. *Moore* has similarly borne little fruit in the lower courts, leading Professor Redish to conclude after comparing the vitality of *Smith* and *Moore* that "the principle enunciated in *Smith* is the one widely followed by modern lower federal courts." Redish 67. Finally, as noted in text, the commentators have also preferred *Smith*. *Moore* simply has not survived the test of time; it is presently moribund, and, to the extent that it is inconsistent with the well-established rule of the *Smith* case, it ought to be overruled.

2. As the Court correctly notes, the Court of Appeals erred in holding that respondents' right to relief did not depend upon the resolution of a federal question because respondents might prevail on one of their other, wholly state law claims. The fourth cause of action presents an independent and independently sufficient claim for relief. Whether it "arises under" federal law within the meaning of § 1331 must therefore be determined without reference to any other claims, as if only that claim was asserted. If, after such consideration, it is determined that there is jurisdiction, the plaintiff may join additional state law claims meeting the test for pendent jurisdiction set forth in Mine Workers v. Gibbs, 383 U.S. 715 (1966).

labeling or advertising relates.... " 21 U.S.C. § 321(n). Obviously, the possibility that a mother's ingestion of Bendectin during pregnancy could produce malformed children is material. Petitioner's principal defense is that the Act does not govern the branding of drugs that are sold in foreign countries. It is certainly not immediately obvious whether this argument is correct. Thus, the statutory question is one which "discloses a need for determining the meaning or application of [the FDCA]," T.B. Harms v. Eliscu, 339 F.2d, at 827, and the claim raised by the fourth cause of action is one "arising under" federal law within the meaning of § 1331.

II

The Court apparently does not disagree with any of this—except, of course, for the conclusion. According to the Court, if we assume that Congress did not intend for there to be a private federal cause of action under a particular federal law (and, presumably, *a fortiori* if Congress' decision not to create a private remedy is express), we must also assume that Congress did not intend for there to be federal jurisdiction over a state cause of action that is determined by that federal law. Therefore, assuming—only because the parties have made a similar assumption— that there is no private cause of action under the FDCA,[4] the Court holds that there is no federal jurisdiction over the plaintiff's claim:

> " * * * [T]he ultimate import of such a conclusion, as we have repeatedly emphasized, is that it would flout congressional intent to provide a private federal remedy for the violation of the federal statute. We think it would similarly flout, or at least undermine, congressional intent to conclude that the federal courts might nevertheless exercise federal-question jurisdiction and provide remedies for violations of that federal statute solely because the violation of the federal statute is said to be a 'rebuttable presumption' or a 'proximate cause' under state law, rather than a federal action under federal law."

The Court nowhere explains the basis for this conclusion. Yet it is hardly self-evident. Why should the fact that Congress chose not to create a private federal *remedy* mean that Congress would not want there to be federal *jurisdiction* to adjudicate a state claim that imposes liability for violating the federal law? Clearly, the decision not to provide a private federal remedy should not affect federal jurisdiction unless the reasons Congress withholds a federal remedy are also reasons for with-

[handwritten margin note: disagreement w/ reasoning]

---

4. It bears emphasizing that the Court does *not* hold that there is no private cause of action under the FDCA. Rather, it expressly states that "[f]or purposes of our decision, we assume that this is a correct interpretation of the FDCA." The Court simply holds petitioner to its concession that the FDCA provides no private remedy, and decides petitioner's claim on the basis of this concession. I shall do the same.

Under the Court's analysis, however, if a party persuaded a court that there is a private cause of action under the FDCA, there would be federal jurisdiction under *Smith* and *Franchise Tax Board* over a state cause of action making violations of the FDCA actionable. Such jurisdiction would apparently exist even if the plaintiff did not seek the federal remedy.

holding federal jurisdiction. Thus, it is necessary to examine the reasons for Congress' decisions to grant or withhold both federal jurisdiction and private remedies, something the Court has not done.

A

In the early days of our Republic, Congress was content to leave the task of interpreting and applying federal laws in the first instance to the state courts; with one shortlived exception, Congress did not grant the inferior federal courts original jurisdiction over cases arising under federal law until 1875. Judiciary Act of 1875, ch. 137, § 1, 18 Stat. 470. The reasons Congress found it necessary to add this jurisdiction to the district courts are well known. First, Congress recognized "the importance, and even necessity of *uniformity* of decisions throughout the whole United States, upon all subjects within the purview of the constitution." Martin v. Hunter's Lessee, 1 Wheat., at 347–348 (Story, J.) (emphasis in original). See also, Comment, Federal Preemption, Removal Jurisdiction, and the Well–Pleaded Complaint Rule, 51 U.Chi.L.Rev. 634, 636 (1984); D. Currie, Federal Courts 160 (3d ed. 1982). Concededly, because federal jurisdiction is not always exclusive and because federal courts may disagree with one another, absolute uniformity has not been obtained even under § 1331. However, while perfect uniformity may not have been achieved, experience indicates that the availability of a federal forum in federal question cases has done much to advance that goal. This, in fact, was the conclusion of the American Law Institute's Study of the Division of Jurisdiction Between State and Federal Courts. ALI 164–168.

In addition, § 1331 has provided for adjudication in a forum that specializes in federal law and that is therefore more likely to apply that law correctly. Because federal question cases constitute the basic grist for federal tribunals, "the federal courts have acquired a considerable expertise in the interpretation and application of federal law." ALI 164–165. By contrast, "it is apparent that federal question cases must form a very small part of the business of [state] courts." ALI 165. As a result, the federal courts are comparatively more skilled at interpreting and applying federal law, and are much more likely correctly to divine Congress' intent in enacting legislation.[6] See ibid.; Redish 71; Currie 160;

---

6. Another reason Congress conferred original federal question jurisdiction on the district courts was its belief that state courts are hostile to assertions of federal rights. See Hornstein 564–565; Comment 636; Redish 71. Although this concern may be less compelling today than it once was, the American Law Institute reported as recently as 1969 that "it is difficult to avoid concluding that federal courts are more likely to apply federal law sympathetically and understandingly than are state courts." ALI 166. In any event, this rationale is, like the rationale based on the expertise of the federal courts, simply an expression of Congress' belief that federal courts are more likely to interpret federal law correctly.

One might argue that this Court's appellate jurisdiction over state court judgments in cases arising under federal law can be depended upon to correct erroneous state court decisions and to insure that federal law is interpreted and applied uniformly. However, as any experienced observer of this Court can attest, "Supreme Court review of state courts, limited by docket pressures, narrow review of the facts, the debilitating possibilities of delay, and the necessity of deferring to adequate state

Comment 636; Hornstein, Federalism, Judicial Power and the "Arising Under" Jurisdiction of the Federal Courts: A Hierarchical Analysis, 56 Ind.L.J. 563, 564–565 (1981).

These reasons for having original federal question jurisdiction explain why cases like this one and *Smith*—i.e., cases where the cause of action is a creature of state law, but an essential element of the claim is federal—"arise under" federal law within the meaning of § 1331. Congress passes laws in order to shape behavior; a federal law expresses Congress' determination that there is a federal interest in having individuals or other entities conform their actions to a particular norm established by that law. Because all laws are imprecise to some degree, disputes inevitably arise over what specifically Congress intended to require or permit. It is the duty of courts to interpret these laws and apply them in such a way that the congressional purpose is realized. As noted above, Congress granted the district courts power to hear cases "arising under" federal law in order to enhance the likelihood that federal laws would be interpreted more correctly and applied more uniformly. In other words, Congress determined that the availability of a federal forum to adjudicate cases involving federal questions would make it more likely that federal laws would shape behavior in the way that Congress intended.

By making federal law an essential element of a state law claim, the State places the federal law into a context where it will operate to shape behavior: the threat of liability will force individuals to conform their conduct to interpretations of the federal law made by courts adjudicating the state law claim. It will not matter to an individual found liable whether the officer who arrives at his door to execute judgment is wearing a state or a federal uniform; all he cares about is the fact that a sanction is being imposed—and may be imposed again in the future—because he failed to comply with the federal law. Consequently, the possibility that the federal law will be incorrectly interpreted in the context of adjudicating the state law claim implicates the concerns that led Congress to grant the district courts power to adjudicate cases involving federal questions in precisely the same way as if it was federal law that "created" the cause of action. It therefore follows that there is federal jurisdiction under § 1331.

B

The only remaining question is whether the assumption that Congress decided not to create a private cause of action alters this analysis in a way that makes it inappropriate to exercise original federal jurisdiction. According to the Court, "the very reasons for the development of the modern implied remedy doctrine" support the conclusion that, where the legislative history of a particular law shows (whether expressly or by

grounds of decision, cannot do the whole job." Currie 160. Indeed, having served on this Court for 30 years, it is clear to me that, realistically, it cannot even come close to "doing the whole job" and that § 1331 is essential if federal rights are to be adequately protected.

inference) that Congress intended for there to be no private federal remedy, it must also mean that Congress would not want federal courts to exercise jurisdiction over a state law claim making violations of that federal law actionable. These reasons are " 'the increased complexity of federal legislation,' " " 'the increased volume of federal litigation,' " and " 'the desirability of a more careful scrutiny of legislative intent.' " (quoting Merrill Lynch, Pierce, Fenner & Smith v. Curran, 456 U.S. 353, 377 (1982)).

These reasons simply do not justify the Court's holding. Given the relative expertise of the federal courts in interpreting federal law, the increased complexity of federal legislation argues rather strongly in *favor* of recognizing federal jurisdiction. And, while the increased volume of litigation may appropriately be considered in connection with reasoned arguments that justify limiting the reach of § 1331, I do not believe that the day has yet arrived when this Court may trim a statute solely because it thinks that Congress made it too broad.

This leaves only the third reason: " 'the desirability of a more careful scrutiny of legislative intent.' " I certainly subscribe to the proposition that the Court should consider legislative intent in determining whether or not there is jurisdiction under § 1331. But the Court has not examined the purposes underlying either the FDCA or § 1331 in reaching its conclusion that Congress' presumed decision not to provide a private federal remedy under the FDCA must be taken to withdraw federal jurisdiction over a private state remedy that imposes liability for violating the FDCA. Moreover, such an examination demonstrates not only that it is consistent with legislative intent to find that there is federal jurisdiction over such a claim, but, indeed, that it is the Court's contrary conclusion that is inconsistent with congressional intent.

The enforcement scheme established by the FDCA is typical of other, similarly broad regulatory schemes. Primary responsibility for overseeing implementation of the Act has been conferred upon a specialized administrative agency, here the Food and Drug Administration (FDA).[8] Congress has provided the FDA with a wide-ranging arsenal of weapons to combat violations of the FDCA, including authority to obtain an ex parte court order for the seizure of goods subject to the Act, authority to initiate proceedings in a federal district court to enjoin continuing violations of the FDCA, and authority to request a United States Attorney to bring criminal proceedings against violators. Significantly, the FDA has no independent enforcement authority; final enforcement must come from the federal courts, which have exclusive jurisdiction over actions under the FDCA. Thus, while the initial interpretive function has been delegated to an expert administrative body whose interpretations are entitled to considerable deference, final re-

---

8. The Federal Trade Commission retains regulatory and enforcement authority over the advertising (as opposed to the labeling) of foods, drugs and cosmetics. See 15 U.S.C. §§ 52–55.

sponsibility for interpreting the statute in order to carry out the legislative mandate belongs to the federal courts. * * *

Given that Congress structured the FDCA so that all express remedies are provided by the federal courts, it seems rather strange to conclude that it either "flout[s]" or "undermine[s]" congressional intent for the federal courts to adjudicate a private state law remedy that is based upon violating the FDCA. * * *

It may be that a decision by Congress not to create a private remedy is intended to preclude all private enforcement. If that is so, then a state cause of action that makes relief available to private individuals for violations of the FDCA is pre-empted. But if Congress' decision not to provide a private federal remedy does *not* pre-empt such a state remedy, then, in light of the FDCA's clear policy of relying on the federal courts for enforcement, it also should not foreclose federal jurisdiction over that state remedy. Both § 1331 and the enforcement provisions of the FDCA reflect Congress' strong desire to utilize the federal courts to interpret and enforce the FDCA, and it is therefore at odds with both these statutes to recognize a private state law remedy for violating the FDCA but to hold that this remedy cannot be adjudicated in the federal courts.

The Court's contrary conclusion requires inferring from Congress' decision not to create a private federal remedy that, while some private enforcement is permissible in state courts, it is "bad" if that enforcement comes from the *federal* courts. But that is simply illogical. Congress' decision to withhold a private right of action and to rely instead on public enforcement reflects congressional concern with obtaining more accurate implementation and more coordinated enforcement of a regulatory scheme. These reasons are closely related to the Congress' reasons for giving federal courts original federal question jurisdiction. Thus, if anything, Congress' decision not to create a private remedy *strengthens* the argument in favor of finding federal jurisdiction over a state remedy that is not preempted.

Notes

1.   Examine how the Court relies for its conclusion that federal question jurisdiction does not extend to suits brought under state law involving the federal Food, Drug, and Cosmetic Act on the fact that no implied federal cause of action had been found under the Act. Is this a valid connection? Does it follow that because Congress did not intend there to exist a federal private damage remedy under the Act, *when and if* a state chooses to provide a cause of action for violations of the Act Congress would not want the federal courts to hear these state law suits? Is the nature of the federal interests the same in the two situations?

2.   Is the Court confusing the *substantive* issue of federal preemption with the *jurisdictional* issue of federal court authority to adjudicate?

3.   How does the Court respond to the argument that federal jurisdiction is necessary to preserve uniformity in interpretation of the federal Act? Is the Court's response persuasive?

4. Justice Brennan, in dissent, argues that "if anything, Congress' decision not to create a private remedy *strengthens* the argument in favor of finding federal jurisdiction over a state remedy that is not preempted." Do you understand the point he is making? Is he correct? *Are* there significant federal interest in the adjudication of suits such as *Merrell Dow*, justifying the extension of federal question jurisdiction?

5. Consider how the Court attempts to reconcile *Moore* and *Smith*. Is the Court's analysis persuasive? What is Justice Brennan's position on the issue?

6. What is left of *Smith* after *Merrell Dow*? Is it possible to predict, on the basis of the Court's opinion, under what circumstances federal question jurisdiction will extend to state causes of action involving an issue of federal law? See Redish, *Reassessing the Allocation of Judicial Business Between State and Federal Courts: Federal Jurisdiction and "The Martian Chronicles,"* 78 Va.L.Rev. 1769, 1794 (1992), suggesting that the majority's test "resembles more the free-standing, subjective, and individualized determination of Judge Wapner than a coherent, generalizable jurisdictional doctrine." In that regard, consider the following case:

GRABLE & SONS METAL PRODUCTS, INC. v. DARUE ENGINEERING & MANUFACTURING

Supreme Court of the United States, 2005.
545 U.S. 308.

JUSTICE SOUTER delivered the opinion of the Court.

The question is whether want of a federal cause of action to try claims of title to land obtained at a federal tax sale precludes removal to federal court of a state action with non-diverse parties raising a disputed issue of federal title law. We answer no, and hold that the national interest in providing a federal forum for federal tax litigation is sufficiently substantial to support the exercise of federal question jurisdiction over the disputed issue on removal, which would not distort any division of labor between the state and federal courts, provided or assumed by Congress.

I

In 1994, the Internal Revenue Service seized Michigan real property belonging to petitioner Grable & Sons Metal Products, Inc., to satisfy Grable's federal tax delinquency. Title 26 U.S.C. § 6335 required the IRS to give notice of the seizure, and there is no dispute that Grable received actual notice by certified mail before the IRS sold the property to respondent Darue Engineering & Manufacturing. Although Grable also received notice of the sale itself, it did not exercise its statutory right to redeem the property within 180 days of the sale, § 6337(b)(1), and after that period had passed, the Government gave Darue a quit-claim deed. § 6339.

Five years later, Grable brought a quiet title action in state court, claiming that Darue's record title was invalid because the IRS had failed to notify Grable of its seizure of the property in the exact manner required by § 6335(a), which provides that written notice must be "given by the Secretary to the owner of the property [or] left at his usual place of abode or business." Grable said that the statute required personal service, not service by certified mail.

Darue removed the case to Federal District Court as presenting a federal question, because the claim of title depended on the interpretation of the notice statute in the federal tax law. The District Court declined to remand the case at Grable's behest after finding that the "claim does pose a significant question of federal law," and ruling that Grable's lack of a federal right of action to enforce its claim against Darue did not bar the exercise of federal jurisdiction. On the merits, the court granted summary judgment to Darue, holding that although § 6335 by its terms required personal service, substantial compliance with the statute was enough.

The Court of Appeals for the Sixth Circuit affirmed. On the jurisdictional question, the panel thought it sufficed that the title claim raised an issue of federal law that had to be resolved, and implicated a substantial federal interest (in construing federal tax law). The court went on to affirm the District Court's judgment on the merits. We granted certiorari on the jurisdictional question alone, to resolve a split within the Courts of Appeals on whether Merrell Dow Pharmaceuticals Inc. v. Thompson, 478 U.S. 804 (1986), always requires a federal cause of action as a condition for exercising federal-question jurisdiction. We now affirm.

II

Darue was entitled to remove the quiet title action if Grable could have brought it in federal district court originally, 28 U.S.C. § 1441(a), as a civil action "arising under the Constitution, laws, or treaties of the United States," § 1331. This provision for federal-question jurisdiction is invoked by and large by plaintiffs pleading a cause of action created by federal law (e.g., claims under 42 U.S.C. § 1983). There is, however, another longstanding, if less frequently encountered, variety of federal "arising under" jurisdiction, this Court having recognized for nearly 100 years that in certain cases federal question jurisdiction will lie over state-law claims that implicate significant federal issues. E.g., Hopkins v. Walker, 244 U.S. 486, 490–491 (1917). The doctrine captures the commonsense notion that a federal court ought to be able to hear claims recognized under state law that nonetheless turn on substantial questions of federal law, and thus justify resort to the experience, solicitude, and hope of uniformity that a federal forum offers on federal issues.
* * *

The classic example is Smith v. Kansas City Title & Trust Co., 255 U.S. 180 (1921), a suit by a shareholder claiming that the defendant corporation could not lawfully buy certain bonds of the National Government because their issuance was unconstitutional. Although Missouri law provided the cause of action, the Court recognized federal-question jurisdiction because the principal issue in the case was the federal constitutionality of the bond issue. *Smith* thus held, in a somewhat generous statement of the scope of the doctrine, that a state-law claim could give rise to federal-question jurisdiction so long as it "appears from the [complaint] that the right to relief depends upon the construction or application of [federal law]." Id., at 199.

The *Smith* statement has been subject to some trimming to fit earlier and later cases recognizing the vitality of the basic doctrine, but shying away from the expansive view that mere need to apply federal law in a state-law claim will suffice to open the "arising under" door. As early as 1912, this Court had confined federal-question jurisdiction over state-law claims to those that "really and substantially involv[e] a dispute or controversy respecting the validity, construction or effect of [federal] law." Shulthis v. McDougal, 225 U.S. 561, 569 (1912). This limitation was the ancestor of Justice Cardozo's later explanation that a request to exercise federal-question jurisdiction over a state action calls for a "common-sense accommodation of judgment to [the] kaleidoscopic situations" that present a federal issue, in "a selective process which picks the substantial causes out of the web and lays the other ones aside." Gully v. First Nat. Bank in Meridian, 299 U.S. 109, 117–118 (1936). It has in fact become a constant refrain in such cases that federal jurisdiction demands not only a contested federal issue, but a substantial one, indicating a serious federal interest in claiming the advantages thought to be inherent in a federal forum. E.g., Chicago v. International College of Surgeons, 522 U.S. 156, 164 (1997); Merrell Dow, supra, at 814, n. 12; Franchise Tax Bd. of Cal. v. Construction Laborers Vacation Trust for Southern Cal., 463 U.S. 1, 28 (1983).

But even when the state action discloses a contested and substantial federal question, the exercise of federal jurisdiction is subject to a possible veto. For the federal issue will ultimately qualify for a federal forum only if federal jurisdiction is consistent with congressional judgment about the sound division of labor between state and federal courts governing the application of § 1331. Thus, *Franchise Tax Bd.* explained that the appropriateness of a federal forum to hear an embedded issue could be evaluated only after considering the "welter of issues regarding the interrelation of federal and state authority and the proper management of the federal judicial system." Id., at 8. Because arising-under jurisdiction to hear a state-law claim always raises the possibility of upsetting the state-federal line drawn (or at least assumed) by Congress, the presence of a disputed federal issue and the ostensible importance of a federal forum are never necessarily dispositive; there must always be an assessment of any disruptive portent in exercising federal jurisdiction. See also *Merrell Dow, supra,* at 810.

These considerations have kept us from stating a "single, precise, all-embracing" test for jurisdiction over federal issues embedded in state-law claims between nondiverse parties. We have not kept them out simply because they appeared in state raiment, as Justice Holmes would have done, see *Smith, supra,* at 214 (dissenting opinion), but neither have we treated "federal issue" as a password opening federal courts to any state action embracing a point of federal law. Instead, the question is, does a state-law claim necessarily raise a stated federal issue, actually disputed and substantial, which a federal forum may entertain without disturbing any congressionally approved balance of federal and state judicial responsibilities.

III

A

This case warrants federal jurisdiction. Grable's state complaint must specify "the facts establishing the superiority of [its] claim," and Grable has premised its superior title claim on a failure by the IRS to give it adequate notice, as defined by federal law. Whether Grable was given notice within the meaning of the federal statute is thus an essential element of its quiet title claim, and the meaning of the federal statute is actually in dispute; it appears to be the only legal or factual issue contested in the case. The meaning of the federal tax provision is an important issue of federal law that sensibly belongs in a federal court. The Government has a strong interest in the "prompt and certain collection of delinquent taxes," and the ability of the IRS to satisfy its claims from the property of delinquents requires clear terms of notice to allow buyers like Darue to satisfy themselves that the Service has touched the bases necessary for good title. The Government thus has a direct interest in the availability of a federal forum to vindicate its own administrative action, and buyers (as well as tax delinquents) may find it valuable to come before judges used to federal tax matters. Finally, because it will be the rare state title case that raises a contested matter of federal law, federal jurisdiction to resolve genuine disagreement over federal tax title provisions will portend only a microscopic effect on the federal-state division of labor.

This conclusion puts us in venerable company, quiet title actions having been the subject of some of the earliest exercises of federal-question jurisdiction over state-law claims. * * *

B

Merrell Dow Pharmaceuticals Inc. v. Thompson, 478 U.S. 804 (1986), on which Grable rests its position, is not to the contrary. *Merrell Dow* considered a state tort claim resting in part on the allegation that the defendant drug company had violated a federal misbranding prohibition, and was thus presumptively negligent under Ohio law. Id., at 806. The Court assumed that federal law would have to be applied to resolve the claim, but after closely examining the strength of the federal interest at stake and the implications of opening the federal forum, held federal jurisdiction unavailable. Congress had not provided a private federal cause of action for violation of the federal branding requirement, and the

Court found "it would ... flout, or at least undermine, congressional intent to conclude that federal courts might nevertheless exercise federal-question jurisdiction and provide remedies for violations of that federal statute solely because the violation ... is said to be a ... 'proximate cause' under state law." Id., at 812.

Because federal law provides for no quiet title action that could be brought against Darue, Grable argues that there can be no federal jurisdiction here, stressing some broad language in *Merrell Dow* (including the passage just quoted) that on its face supports Grable's position. But an opinion is to be read as a whole, and *Merrell Dow* cannot be read whole as overturning decades of precedent, as it would have done by effectively adopting the Holmes dissent in *Smith,* and converting a federal cause of action from a sufficient condition for federal-question jurisdiction into a necessary one.

In the first place, *Merrell Dow* disclaimed the adoption of any bright-line rule, as when the Court reiterated that "in exploring the outer reaches of § 1331, determinations about federal jurisdiction require sensitive judgments about congressional intent, judicial power, and the federal system." 478 U.S., at 810. The opinion included a lengthy footnote explaining that questions of jurisdiction over state-law claims require "careful judgments," id., at 814, about the "nature of the federal interest at stake," id., at 814, n. 12 (emphasis deleted). And as a final indication that it did not mean to make a federal right of action mandatory, it expressly approved the exercise of jurisdiction sustained in *Smith,* despite the want of any federal cause of action available to *Smith's* shareholder plaintiff. 478 U.S., at 814, n. 12. *Merrell Dow* then, did not toss out, but specifically retained the contextual enquiry that had been *Smith's* hallmark for over 60 years. At the end of *Merrell Dow,* Justice Holmes was still dissenting.

Accordingly, *Merrell Dow* should be read in its entirety as treating the absence of a federal private right of action as evidence relevant to, but not dispositive of, the "sensitive judgments about congressional intent" that § 1331 requires. The absence of any federal cause of action affected *Merrell Dow's* result two ways. The Court saw the fact as worth some consideration in the assessment of substantiality. But its primary importance emerged when the Court treated the combination of no federal cause of action and no preemption of state remedies for misbranding as an important clue to Congress's conception of the scope of jurisdiction to be exercised under § 1331. The Court saw the missing cause of action not as a missing federal door key, always required, but as a missing welcome mat, required in the circumstances, when exercising federal jurisdiction over a state misbranding action would have attracted a horde of original filings and removal cases raising other state claims with embedded federal issues. For if the federal labeling standard without a federal cause of action could get a state claim into federal court, so could any other federal standard without a federal cause of action. And that would have meant a tremendous number of cases.

* * * Expressing concern over the "increased volume of federal litigation," and noting the importance of adhering to "legislative intent," *Merrell Dow* thought it improbable that the Congress, having made no provision for a federal cause of action, would have meant to welcome any state-law tort case implicating federal law "solely because the violation of the federal statute is said to [create] a rebuttable presumption [of negligence] ... under state law." 478 U.S., at 811–812 (internal quotation marks omitted). In this situation, no welcome mat meant keep out. *Merrell Dow's* analysis thus fits within the framework of examining the importance of having a federal forum for the issue, and the consistency of such a forum with Congress's intended division of labor between state and federal courts.

As already indicated, however, a comparable analysis yields a different jurisdictional conclusion in this case. Although Congress also indicated ambivalence in this case by providing no private right of action to Grable, it is the rare state quiet title action that involves contested issues of federal law. Consequently, jurisdiction over actions like Grable's would not materially affect, or threaten to affect, the normal currents of litigation. Given the absence of threatening structural consequences and the clear interest the Government, its buyers, and its delinquents have in the availability of a federal forum, there is no good reason to shirk from federal jurisdiction over the dispositive and contested federal issue at the heart of the state-law title claim.

IV

The judgment of the Court of Appeals, upholding federal jurisdiction over Grable's quiet title action, is affirmed.

It is so ordered.

Justice Thomas, concurring.

The Court faithfully applies our precedents interpreting 28 U.S.C. § 1331 to authorize federal-court jurisdiction over some cases in which state law creates the cause of action but requires determination of an issue of federal law, e.g., Smith v. Kansas City Title & Trust Co., 255 U.S. 180 (1921); Merrell Dow Pharmaceuticals Inc. v. Thompson, 478 U.S. 804 (1986). In this case, no one has asked us to overrule those precedents and adopt the rule Justice Holmes set forth in American Well Works Co. v. Layne & Bowler Co., 241 U.S. 257 (1916), limiting § 1331 jurisdiction to cases in which federal law creates the cause of action pleaded on the face of the plaintiff's complaint. Id., at 260. In an appropriate case, and perhaps with the benefit of better evidence as to the original meaning of § 1331's text, I would be willing to consider that course.

Jurisdictional rules should be clear. Whatever the virtues of the *Smith* standard, it is anything but clear. * * *

Whatever the vices of the *American Well Works* rule, it is clear. Moreover, it accounts for the " 'vast majority' " of cases that come within § 1331 under our current case law, *Merrell Dow, supra,* at 808 (quoting Franchise Tax Bd. of Cal. v. Construction Laborers Vacation Trust for Southern Cal., 463 U.S. 1, 9 (1983))—further indication that trying to sort out which cases fall within the smaller *Smith* category may not be worth the effort it entails. Accordingly, I would be willing in appropriate circumstances to reconsider our interpretation of § 1331.

Notes

1. Would you have predicted the result in *Grable* based on your own reading of *Merrell Dow*? Did *Grable* apply *Merrell Dow* or modify it? Note that *Grable* does not cite *Moore* even once, although *Merrell Dow* purported to rely on it quite heavily.

2. Does *Grable* give more or less guidance to lower courts than *Merrell Dow* does? If you believe that neither case gives sufficient guidance, try to come up with a rule that is clear *and* takes into account federal interests, state interests, fairness to litigants, and deference to Congress. Does your rule look anything like Justice Thomas' proposal to return to *American Well Works*?

3. The Supreme Court distinguished *Grable* in Empire Healthchoice Assurance, Inc. v. McVeigh, 547 U.S. ___, 126 S.Ct. 2121 (2006). In *Empire,* an insurer who contracted with the federal government to cover federal employees sought to recover previously disbursed benefits, which it alleged had been recovered by the beneficiary in a state court tort suit. While a federal statute governed the relationship between the insurer and the government, and also pre-empted state law on coverage and benefits, the statute said nothing about subrogation and did not confer federal jurisdiction. Among other arguments, the insurer contended that the suit was within federal question jurisdiction under *Grable* because federal law was a "necessary element" of the insurer's claim for relief. The Court rejected that argument, concluding that the suit did "not fit within the special and small category" defined by *Grable*:

> This case is poles apart from *Grable*. The dispute there centered on the action of a federal agency (IRS) and its compatibility with a federal statute, the question qualified as "substantial," and its resolution was both dispositive of the case and would be controlling in numerous other cases. Here, the reimbursement claim was triggered, not by the action of any federal department, agency, or service, but by the settlement of a personal-injury action launched in state court, and the bottom-line practical issue is the share of that settlement properly payable to Empire.

> *Grable* presented a nearly "pure issue of law," one "that could be settled once and for all and thereafter would govern numerous tax sale cases." In contrast, Empire's reimbursement claim * * * is fact-bound and situation-specific.

Courts of Appeals had split on the question resolved by *Empire*. In light of *Grable,* are you surprised that some Courts of Appeals thought there was jurisdiction in this situation? Is the Supreme Court likely to have to decide many more cases clarifying *Grable*?

§ 3.   THE "WELL–PLEADED COMPLAINT" RULE

LOUISVILLE AND NASHVILLE RAILROAD CO. v. MOTTLEY

Supreme Court of the United States, 1908.
211 U.S. 149.

The appellees (husband and wife), being residents and citizens of Kentucky, brought this suit in equity in the Circuit Court of the United States for the Western District of Kentucky against the appellant, a railroad company and a citizen of the same State. The object of the suit was to compel the specific performance of the following contract:

"Louisville, Ky., Oct. 2nd, 1871.

"The Louisville & Nashville Railroad Company in consideration that E. L. Mottley and wife, Annie E. Mottley, have this day released Company from all damages or claims for damages for injuries received by them on the 7th of September, 1871, in consequence of a collision of trains on the railroad of said Company at Randolph's Station, Jefferson County, Ky., hereby agrees to issue free passes on said Railroad and branches now existing or to exist, to said E. L. & Annie E. Mottley for the remainder of the present year, and thereafter, to renew said passes annually during the lives of said Mottley and wife or either of them."

The bill alleged that in September, 1871, plaintiffs, while passengers upon the defendant railroad, were injured by the defendant's negligence, and released their respective claims for damages in consideration of the agreement for transportation during their lives, expressed in the contract. It is alleged that the contract was performed by the defendant up to January 1, 1907, when the defendant declined to renew the passes. The bill then alleges that the refusal to comply with the contract was based solely upon that part of the act of Congress of June 29, 1906, 34 Stat. 584, which forbids the giving of free passes or free transportation. The bill further alleges: First, that the act of Congress referred to does not prohibit the giving of passes under the circumstances of this case; and, second, that if the law is to be construed as prohibiting such passes, it is in conflict with the Fifth Amendment of the Constitution, because it deprives the plaintiffs of their property without due process of law. The defendant demurred to the bill. The judge of the Circuit Court overruled the demurrer, entered a decree for the relief prayed for, and the defendant appealed directly to this court.

MR. JUSTICE MOODY, after making the foregoing statement, delivered the opinion of the court.

Two questions of law were raised by the demurrer to the bill, were brought here by appeal, and have been argued before us. They are, first, whether that part of the act of Congress of June 29, 1906 (34 Stat. 584), which forbids the giving of free passes or the collection of any different compensation for transportation of passengers than that specified in the tariff filed, makes it unlawful to perform a contract for transportation of persons, who in good faith, before the passage of the act, had accepted such contract in satisfaction of a valid cause of action against the railroad; and, second, [whether the statute, if it should be construed to render such a contract unlawful, is in violation of the Fifth Amendment of the Constitution of the United States. We do not deem it necessary, however, to consider either of these questions, because, in our opinion, the court below was without jurisdiction of the cause. Neither party has questioned that jurisdiction, but it is the duty of this court to see to it that the jurisdiction of the Circuit Court, which is defined and limited by statute, is not exceeded. This duty we have frequently performed of our own motion. Mansfield, C. & L. M. R. Co. v. Swan, 111 U.S. 379, 382; King Iron Bridge & Mfg. Co. v. Otoe County, 120 U.S. 225; Blacklock v. Small, 127 U.S. 96, 105; Cameron v. Hodges, 127 U.S. 322, 326; Metcalf v. Watertown, 128 U.S. 586, 587; Continental Nat. Bank v. Buford, 191 U.S. 119.

There was no diversity of citizenship and it is not and cannot be suggested that there was any ground of jurisdiction, except that the case was a "suit ... arising under the Constitution and laws of the United States." Act of August 13, 1888, c. 866, 25 Stat. 433, 434. It is the settled interpretation of these words, as used in this statute, conferring jurisdiction, that a suit arises under the Constitution and laws of the United States only when the plaintiff's statement of his own cause of action shows that it is based upon those laws or that Constitution. It is not enough that the plaintiff alleges some anticipated defense to his cause of action and asserts that the defense is invalidated by some provision of the Constitution of the United States. Although such allegations show that very likely, in the course of the litigation, a question under the Constitution would arise, they do not show that the suit, that is, the plaintiff's original cause of action, arises under the Constitution. * * *

* * *

The interpretation of the act which we have stated was first announced in Metcalf v. Watertown, 128 U.S. 586, and has since been repeated and applied * * * The application of this rule to the case at bar is decisive against the jurisdiction of the Circuit Court.

* * *

Notes

1. Is the "well-pleaded complaint" rule described in *Mottley* an interpretation of the constitutional "arising under" provision or of the statutory "arising under" provision? What practical difference does it make?

2. What qualification, if any, does the phrase "well-pleaded" add to the rule? → No anticipation of defense

3. After this decision, the Mottleys brought their suit in state court. As expected, the defendant raised its federal defense and when the case ultimately reached the United States Supreme Court, the Court decided the

federal issue against the Mottleys. In light of this subsequent history, could it be persuasively argued that the Supreme Court should have saved everybody the time and trouble by simply deciding the federal issue when the original federal suit first reached it?

4. Consider the following arguments in support of the "well-pleaded complaint" rule:

> a. Until a federal issue appears in a case, a federal court lacks legal authority to demand a response from the defendant.

> b. Extending "federal question" jurisdiction to cases where the federal issue is presented only in defense would substantially increase the burdens on the lower federal courts.

> c. If "federal question" jurisdiction were permitted to attach simply on the basis of plaintiff's speculation that a defendant would respond by raising a defense based on federal law, the federal court could be forced to waste significant time and effort which will ultimately prove to be fruitless since the case will have to be dismissed.

If you find the argument fashioned in c. persuasive, to what extent is the difficulty met by allowing removal to federal court, by either plaintiff or defendant, of a state court action where a federal issue is raised initially as a defense? See, for example, the American Law Institute's proposed section 1312(a)(2), which would allow removal "by any defendant, or any plaintiff, by or against whom, subsequent to the initial pleading, a substantial defense arising under the Constitution, laws, or treaties of the United States is properly asserted that, if sustained, would be dispositive of the action or of all counterclaims therein * * *." American Law Institute, Study of the Division of Jurisdiction Between State and Federal Courts 25–27 (1969). Why should such a removal statute require that the federal claim be "dispositive" of one or more of the claims if sustained? The ALI urged continuation of the $10,000 jurisdictional amount requirement in these removal cases, though it recommended its abandonment in more traditional federal question cases (where the requirement has in fact been removed by Congress). Do you understand why this distinction should be drawn? In addition, the ALI suggested that its proposed removal statute not apply to such cases as those in which a constitutional defense of lack of jurisdiction over the person was asserted, or those brought by the state to enforce its laws (including, of course, criminal prosecutions). Do you understand why the ALI would choose to exclude such cases?

5. For a recent application of *Mottley*, see Holmes Group, Inc. v. Vornado Air Circulation Systems, Inc., 535 U.S. 826 (2002) (Court of Appeals for the Federal Circuit has no jurisdiction over cases which contain a patent-law counterclaim but no claim in the complaint arising under federal patent law); see also Cotropia, *Counterclaims, the Well–Pleaded Complaint, and Federal Jurisdiction*, 33 Hofstra L.Rev. 1 (2004).

SKELLY OIL CO. v. PHILLIPS PETROLEUM CO.

Supreme Court of the United States, 1950.
339 U.S. 667.

MR. JUSTICE FRANKFURTER delivered the opinion of the Court.

In 1945, Michigan–Wisconsin Pipe Line Company sought from the Federal Power Commission a certificate of public convenience and necessity, required by § 7(c) of the Natural Gas Act, 52 Stat. 825, as amended, 15 U.S.C. § 717f(c), 15 U.S.C.A. § 717f(c), for the construction and operation of a pipe line to carry natural gas from Texas to Michigan and Wisconsin. A prerequisite for such a certificate is adequate reserves of gas. To obtain these reserves Michigan–Wisconsin entered into an agreement with Phillips Petroleum Company on December 11, 1945, whereby the latter undertook to make available gas from the Hugoton Gas Field, sprawling over Kansas, Oklahoma and Texas, which it produced or purchased from others. Phillips had contracted with petitioners, Skelly Oil Company, Stanolind Oil and Gas Company, and Magnolia Petroleum Company, to purchase gas produced by them in the Hugoton Field for resale to Michigan–Wisconsin. Each contract provided that "in the event Michigan–Wisconsin Pipe Line Company shall fail to secure from the Federal Power Commission on or before [October 1, 1946] a certificate of public convenience and necessity for the construction and operation of its pipe line, Seller [a petitioner] shall have the right to terminate this contract by written notice to Buyer [Phillips] delivered to Buyer at any time after December 1, 1946, but before the issuance of such certificate." The legal significance of this provision is at the core of this litigation.

The Federal Power Commission, in response to the application of Michigan–Wisconsin, on November 30, 1946, ordered that "A certificate of public convenience and necessity be and it is hereby issued to applicant [Michigan–Wisconsin], upon the terms and conditions of this order," listing among the conditions that there be no transportation or sale of natural gas by means of the sanctioned facilities until all necessary authorizations were obtained from the State of Wisconsin and the communities proposed to be served, that Michigan–Wisconsin should have the approval of the Securities and Exchange Commission for its plan of financing, that the applicant should file for the approval of the Commission a schedule of reasonable rates, and that the sanctioned facilities should not be used for the transportation of gas to Detroit and Ann Arbor except with due regard for the rights and duties of Panhandle Eastern Pipe Line Company, which had intervened before the Federal Power Commission, in its established service for resale in these areas, such rights and duties to be set forth in a supplemental order. It was also provided that Michigan–Wisconsin should have fifteen days from the issue of the supplemental order to notify the Commission whether the certificate "as herein issued is acceptable to it." Finally, the Commission's order provided that for purposes of computing the time within which applications for rehearing could be filed, "the date of issuance of this order shall be deemed to be the date of issuance of the opinions, or of the supplemental order referred to herein, whichever may be the later." 5 F.P.C. 953, 954, 956.

News of the Commission's action was released on November 30, 1946, but the actual content of the order was not made public until December 2, 1946. Petitioners severally, on December 2, 1946, gave notice to Phillips of termination of their contracts on the ground that Michigan–Wisconsin had not received a certificate of public convenience and necessity. Thereupon Michigan–Wisconsin and Phillips brought suit against petitioners in the District Court for the Northern District of Oklahoma. Alleging that a certificate of public convenience and necessity, "within the meaning of said Natural Gas Act and said contracts" had been issued prior to petitioners' attempt at termination of the contracts, they invoked the Federal Declaratory Judgment Act for a declaration that the contracts were still "in effect and binding upon the parties thereto." Motions by petitioners to have Michigan–Wisconsin dropped as a party plaintiff were sustained, but motions to dismiss the complaint for want of jurisdiction were denied. The case then went to the merits, and the District Court decreed that the contracts between Phillips and petitioners had not been "effectively terminated and that each of such contracts remain [*sic*] in full force and effect." The Court of Appeals for the Tenth Circuit affirmed, 174 F.2d 89, and we brought the case here, 338 U.S. 846, because it raises in sharp form the question whether a suit like this "arises under the Constitution, laws or treaties of the United States," 28 U.S.C. § 1331, so as to enable District Courts to give declaratory relief under the Declaratory Judgment Act. 48 Stat. 955, as amended, now 28 U.S.C. § 2201.

"[T]he operation of the Declaratory Judgment Act is procedural only." Aetna Life Ins. Co. v. Haworth, 300 U.S. 227, 240. Congress enlarged the range of remedies available in the federal courts but did not extend their jurisdiction. When concerned as we are with the power of the inferior federal courts to entertain litigation within the restricted area to which the Constitution and Acts of Congress confine them, "jurisdiction" means the kinds of issues which give right of entrance to federal courts. Jurisdiction in this sense was not altered by the Declaratory Judgment Act. Prior to that Act, a federal court would entertain a suit on a contract only if the plaintiff asked for an immediately enforceable remedy like money damages or an injunction, but such relief could only be given if the requisites of jurisdiction, in the sense of a federal right or diversity, provided foundation for resort to the federal courts. The Declaratory Judgment Act allowed relief to be given by way of recognizing the plaintiff's right even though no immediate enforcement of it was asked. But the requirements of jurisdiction—the limited subject matters which alone Congress had authorized the District Courts to adjudicate—were not impliedly repealed or modified. See Great Lakes Dredge & Dock Co. v. Huffman, 319 U.S. 293, 300; Colegrove v. Green, 328 U.S. 549, 551–552.

If Phillips sought damages from petitioners or specific performance of their contracts, it could not bring suit in a United States District Court on the theory that it was asserting a federal right. And for the simple reason that such a suit would "arise" under the State law governing the contracts. Whatever federal claim Phillips may be able to urge would in any event be injected into the case only in anticipation of a defense to be asserted by petitioners. "Not every question of federal law emerging in a suit is proof that a federal law is the basis of the suit." Gully v. First National Bank, 299 U.S. 109, 115; compare 28 U.S.C. § 1257, with 28 U.S.C. § 1331. Ever since Metcalf v. Watertown, 128 U.S. 586, 589, it has been settled doctrine that where a suit is brought in the federal courts "upon the sole ground that the determination of the suit depends upon some question of a Federal nature, it must appear, at the outset, from the declaration or the bill of the party suing, that the suit is of that character." But "a suggestion of one party, that the other will or may set up a claim under the Constitution or laws of the United States, does not make the suit one arising under that Constitution or those laws." Tennessee v. Union & Planters' Bank, 152 U.S. 454, 464. The plaintiff's claim itself must present a federal question "unaided by anything alleged in anticipation of avoidance of defenses which it is thought the defendant may interpose." Taylor v. Anderson, 234 U.S. 74, 75–76; Louisville & Nashville R. Co. v. Mottley, 211 U.S. 149, 152.

These decisions reflect the current of jurisdictional legislation since the Act of March 3, 1875, 18 Stat. 470, first entrusted to the lower federal courts wide jurisdiction in cases "arising under this Constitution, the Laws of the United States, and Treaties." U.S.Const. Art. III, § 2. "The change is in accordance with the general policy of these acts, manifest upon their face, and often recognized by this court, to contract the jurisdiction of the Circuit Courts [which became the District Courts] of the United States." Tennessee v. Union & Planters' Bank, supra, 152 U.S. at page 462. See also Arkansas v. Kansas & Texas Coal Co., 183 U.S. 185, 188, and Gully v. First National Bank, supra, 299 U.S. at page 112–114. With exceptions not now relevant Congress has narrowed the opportunities for entrance into the federal courts, and this Court has been more careful than in earlier days in enforcing these jurisdictional limitations. See Gully v. First National Bank, supra, 299 U.S. at page 113.

To be observant of these restrictions is not to indulge in formalism or sterile technicality. It would turn into the federal courts a vast current of litigation indubitably arising under State law, in the sense that the right to be vindicated was State-created, if a suit for a declaration of rights could be brought into the federal courts merely because an anticipated defense derived from federal law. Not only would this unduly swell the volume of litigation in the District Courts but it would also embarrass those courts—and this Court on potential review—in that matters of local law may often be involved, and the District Courts may either have to decide doubtful questions of State law or hold cases pending disposition of such State issues by State courts. To sanction suits for declarative relief as within the jurisdiction of the District Courts merely because, as in this case, artful pleading anticipates a defense based on federal law would contravene the whole trend of jurisdictional legislation by Congress, disregard the effective functioning of the federal judicial system and distort the limited procedural purpose of the Declaratory Judgment Act. See *Developments in the Law—Declaratory Judgments—1941–1949*, 62 Harv.L.Rev. 787, 802–803 (1949). Since the matter in controversy as to which Phillips asked for a declaratory judgment is not one that "arises under the ... laws ... of the United States" and since as to Skelly and Stanolind jurisdiction cannot be sustained on the score of diversity of citizenship, the proceedings against them should have been dismissed.

As to Magnolia, a Texas corporation, a different situation is presented. Since Phillips was a Delaware corporation, there is diversity of citizenship. * * *

         * * *

* * * [W]e think that the proper disposition requires that we vacate the judgment as to Magnolia and remand the case in order that the Court of Appeals either itself or by sending the case back to the District Court can further explore, through ways that may be appropriate, the issues which have been laid bare. * * *

In respect to Magnolia, the judgment of the Court of Appeals is vacated and the cause remanded for further proceedings not inconsistent with this opinion. As to Skelly and Stanolind, we reverse the judgment with directions that the cause be dismissed.

MR. JUSTICE BLACK agrees with the Court of Appeals and would affirm its judgment.

MR. JUSTICE DOUGLAS took no part in the consideration or disposition of this case.

MR. CHIEF JUSTICE VINSON, with whom MR. JUSTICE BURTON joins, dissenting in part.

I concur in that part of the Court's judgment that directs dismissal of the cause as to Skelly and Stanolind. I have real doubts as to whether there is a federal question here at all, even though interpretation of the contract between private parties requires an interpretation of a federal statute and the action of a federal regulatory body. But the Court finds it unnecessary to reach that question because it holds that the federal question, if any, is not a part of the plaintiff's claim and that jurisdiction does not, therefore, attach. While this result is not a necessary one, I am not prepared to dissent from it at this time.

But I am forced to dissent from the vacation and remand of the cause in respect to Magnolia. I think that, as to this petitioner, the judgment of the Court of Appeals should be affirmed. * * *

Notes

1. Is the Court's decision in *Skelly* compelled by *Mottley*? Are there any grounds on which the two decisions may be distinguished?

2. Plaintiff in *Skelly* attempted to employ the declaratory judgment device as a means of gaining entrance to federal court. The declaratory judgment action was developed to remedy situations "where one of the parties to a dispute had no way to take the initiative to get it judicially settled and where he would be seriously prejudiced by the other party's delay in initiating proceedings for this purpose." F. James, Civil Procedure 26 (1965). An example of a classic declaratory judgment action is a suit brought by a party who wishes not to comply with the requirements of a contract on the grounds that the contract is void, but who does not wish to risk having to pay damages if he is wrong in believing the contract is void. The party, who is actually a prospective defendant in a suit for breach of contract, may prior to breaching seek a declaratory judgment that the contract is void. If he wins the suit, he will be freed from his obligation to perform; if he loses, he will not have breached his contract. Another example is a suit for a declaratory judgment by a prospective marcher who believes that the refusal of local officials to issue him a parade permit violates his first amendment rights. If he wins, he can march; if he loses, he will not have risked prosecution. Was the suit in *Skelly* an illustration of a classic declaratory judgment action? Are there any grounds on which to distinguish a classic declaratory judgment suit from the *Mottley* principle? Consider the rationales suggested previously to justify the *Mottley* rule. Are any or all of them inapplicable to a classic declaratory judgment action?

3. What did Chief Justice Vinson mean when he stated that he had "real doubts as to whether there is a federal question here at all * * * "?

4. Oneida Indian Nation v. County of Oneida, 414 U.S. 661 (1974): The Oneida Indians brought an action in federal court for the fair rental value for a specified period of certain land that they had ceded to New York State in 1795. They alleged that the cession violated federal treaties and a federal statute, and was therefore void. The lower courts dismissed the action, holding that it arose under state law. The court of appeals held that although decision would ultimately turn on whether the 1795 cession complied with a federal statute, that federal issue did not appear as part of the cause of action. Suit was therefore barred by the "well-pleaded complaint" rule.

The Supreme Court reversed, holding that the complaint in this case "asserts a present right to possession under federal law." 414 U.S. at 675. "Here, the right to possession itself is claimed to arise under federal law in the first instance." Id. at 676. "In the present case * * * the assertion of a federal controversy does not rest solely on the claim of a right to possession derived from a federal grant of title whose scope will be governed by state law. Rather, it rests on the not insubstantial claim that federal law now protects, and has continuously protected from the time of the formation of the United States, possessory right to tribal lands, wholly apart from the application of state law principles which normally and separately protect a valid right of possession." Id. at 677. Justice Rehnquist, in an opinion joined by Justice Powell, concurred separately: "The opinion for the Court today should give no comfort to persons with garden-variety ejectment claims who, for one reason or another, are covetously eyeing the door to the federal courthouse. The general standards for determining federal jurisdiction, and in particular the standards for evaluating compliance with the well-pleaded complaint rule, will retain their traditional vigor tomorrow as today." Id. at 684. Note that 28 U.S.C. § 1362 provides that "[t]he district courts shall have original jurisdiction of all civil actions brought by any Indian tribe or band with a governing body duly recognized by the Secretary of the Interior, wherein the matter in controversy arises under the Constitution, laws, or treaties of the United States." Both section 1331 and 1362 were relied upon as bases of jurisdiction. However, the Court did not explicitly limit its holding to an interpretation of the scope of section 1362's "arising under" requirement. On the general issue of federal question jurisdiction and the law of Native Americans, see Arrow, *Federal Question Doctrines and American Indian Law,* 14 Okla.City U.L.Rev. 263 (1989).

5. Phillips Petroleum Co. v. Texaco, Inc., 415 U.S. 125 (1974) (per curiam): Texaco sued in federal court, asserting that it had not been compensated for the helium constituent of natural gas sold by Texaco to Phillips and claiming that it was entitled to the reasonable value of the helium. There was no diversity of citizenship, and jurisdiction was premised solely on 28 U.S.C. § 1331(a). Texaco relied on an earlier Tenth Circuit decision in an interpleader action in which, Texaco argued, the court had read the National Gas Act and section 11 of the Helium Conservation Act together to imply a federal cause of action for the recovery of the reasonable value of the helium constituent in natural gas. However, the Supreme Court concluded that the earlier Tenth Circuit decision had "simply held that payment for natural gas at rates established or permitted by the [Federal Power] Commission under the authority of the Natural Gas Act will not be regarded as payment for the helium constituent and cannot be asserted as a defense to a suit for the recovery of the value of that helium. In short, the federal statutory provisions do not * * * create a federal right of recovery, but only preclude the interposition of a plea of payment to defeat a quasi-contractual suit for the value of the helium." 415 U.S. at 128.

6. Consider the relevance of *Skelly* and *Mottley* to the decision in Duke Power Co. v. Carolina Environmental Study Group, Inc., 438 U.S. 59 (1978). Plaintiffs challenged the constitutionality of the provision of the Price–Anderson Act, 42 U.S.C. § 2210, imposing a $560 million limitation on private liability for nuclear accidents resulting from the operation of federally licensed private nuclear power plants. The suit was brought in federal court against the United States Nuclear Regulatory Commission (which was responsible for issuing licenses) and the Duke Power Company, a public utility engaged in the construction of nuclear power plants. Plaintiffs sought a declaratory judgment that the Act violated the due process clause of the Fifth Amendment.

Though the jurisdictional issue had not been raised before, both the majority and dissenting opinions considered whether the case "arose" under federal law. The opinion of Chief Justice Burger, for the majority, held that the requirements of section 1331 were met because plaintiffs were "making two basic challenges to the Act—both of which find their moorings in the Fifth Amendment." Dissenting Justice Rehnquist, however, argued that the federal issues effectively arose in anticipation of a federal defense under the Price–Anderson Act.

Consider the following hypothetical reconstruction of the *Duke Power* facts: Assume a major nuclear power accident, resulting in damages of catastrophic proportions, well beyond the $560 million limit imposed by the Price–Anderson Act. The survivors have filed a class action suit against the operator of the nuclear power plant, seeking damages either under a theory of negligence or under a theory of strict tort liability. Under *Mottley* and *Skelly*, could such a suit be brought in federal court? Does it matter that much of the case will ultimately turn on the constitutionality of the limit imposed by the Price–Anderson Act? *Should* such a suit be able to be heard in federal court?

FRANCHISE TAX BOARD OF THE STATE OF CALIFORNIA v. CONSTRUCTION LABORERS VACATION TRUST FOR SOUTHERN CALIFORNIA

Supreme Court of the United States, 1983.
463 U.S. 1.

JUSTICE BRENNAN delivered the opinion of the Court.

The principal question in dispute between the parties is whether the Employment Retirement Income Security Act of 1974 (ERISA), 88 Stat. 829, codified at 29 U.S.C. §§ 1001 et seq., permits state tax authorities to collect unpaid state income taxes by levying on funds held in trust for the taxpayers under an ERISA-covered vacation benefit plan. The issue is an important one, which affects thousands of federally regulated trusts and all non-federal tax collection systems, and it must eventually receive a definitive, uniform resolution. Nevertheless, for reasons involving perhaps more history than logic, we hold that the lower federal courts had no jurisdiction to decide the question in the case before us, and we vacate the judgment and remand the case with instructions to remand it to the state court from which it was removed.

I

None of the relevant facts is in dispute. Appellee Construction Laborers Vacation Trust for Southern California (CLVT) is a trust established by an agreement between four associations of employers active in the construction industry in Southern California and the Southern California District Council of Laborers, an arm of the District Council and affiliated locals of the Laborers' International Union of North America. The purpose of the agreement and trust was to establish a mechanism for administering the provisions of a collective bargaining agreement that grants construction workers a yearly paid vacation. The trust agreement expressly proscribes any assignment, pledge, or encumbrance of funds held in trust by CLVT. The plan that CLVT administers is unquestionably an "employee welfare benefit plan" within the meaning of § 3 of ERISA, 29 U.S.C. § 1002(1), and CLVT and its individual trustees are thereby subject to extensive regulation under titles I and III of ERISA.

Appellant Franchise Tax Board is a California agency charged with enforcement of that State's personal income tax law. California law authorizes appellant to require any person in possession of "credits or other personal property belonging to a taxpayer" "to withhold ... the amount of any tax, interest, or penalties due from the taxpayer ... and to transmit the amount withheld to the Franchise Tax Board." Cal.Rev. & Tax Code Ann. § 18817 (West Supp.1982). Any person who, upon notice by the Franchise Tax Board, fails to comply with its request to withhold and to transmit funds becomes personally liable for the amounts identified in the notice. § 18818.

In June 1980, the Franchise Tax Board filed a complaint in state court against CLVT and its trustees. Under the heading "First Cause of Action," appellant alleged that CLVT had failed to comply with three levies issued under § 18817, concluding with the allegation that it had been "damaged in a sum * * * not to exceed $380.56 plus interest from June 1, 1980." Under the heading "Second Cause of Action," appellant incorporated its previous allegations and added:

> There was at the time of the levies alleged above and continues to be an actual controversy between the parties concerning their respective legal rights and duties. The Board [appellant] contends that defendants [CLVT] are obligated and required by law to pay over to the Board all amounts held ... in favor of the Board's delinquent taxpayers. On the other hand, defendants contend that section 514 of ERISA preempts state law and that the trustees lack the power to honor the levies made upon them by the State of California.

> * * * [D]efendants will continue to refuse to honor the Board's levies in this regard. Accordingly, a declaration by this court of the parties' respective rights is required to fully and finally resolve this controversy.

In a prayer for relief, appellant requested damages for defendants' failure to honor the levies and a declaration that defendants are "legally obligated to honor all future levies by the Board." Id., at 9.[5]

CLVT removed the case to the United States District Court for the Central District of California, and the court denied the Franchise Tax Board's motion for remand to the state court. On the merits, the District Court ruled that ERISA did not preempt the State's power to levy on funds held in trust by CLVT. CLVT appealed, and the Court of Appeals reversed. On petition for rehearing, the Franchise Tax Board renewed its argument that the District Court lacked jurisdiction over the complaint in this case. * * * We now hold that this case was not within the

---

5. The complaint does not identify statutory authority for the relief requested; in- deed, the only statute mentioned on the face of the complaint is ERISA. * * *

removal jurisdiction conferred by 28 U.S.C. § 1441, and therefore we do not reach the merits of the preemption question.

II

The jurisdictional structure at issue in this case has remained basically unchanged for the past century. With exceptions not relevant here, "any civil action brought in a State court of which the district courts of the United States have original jurisdiction, may be removed by the defendant or the defendants, to the district court of the United States for the district and division embracing the place where such action is pending." 28 U.S.C. § 1441. If it appears before final judgment that a case was not properly removed, because it was not within the original jurisdiction of the United States district courts, the district court must remand it to the state court from which it was removed. See § 1447(c). For this case—as for many cases where there is no diversity of citizenship between the parties—the propriety of removal turns on whether the case falls within the original "federal question" jurisdiction of the United States district courts: "The district courts shall have jurisdiction of all civil actions arising under the Constitution, laws, or treaties of the United States." 28 U.S.C. § 1331 (1976 ed., Supp. V).[7]

Since the first version of § 1331 was enacted, Act of Mar. 3, 1875, ch. 137, § 1, 18 Stat. 470, the statutory phrase "arising under the Constitution, laws, or treaties of the United States" has resisted all attempts to frame a single, precise definition for determining which cases fall within, and which cases fall outside, the original jurisdiction of the district courts. Especially when considered in light of § 1441's removal jurisdiction, the phrase "arising under" masks a welter of issues regarding the interrelation of federal and state authority and the proper management of the federal judicial system.[8]

The most familiar definition of the statutory "arising under" limitation is Justice Holmes' statement, "A suit arises under the law that creates the cause of action." American Well Works Co. v. Layne & Bowler Co., 241 U.S. 257, 260 (1916). However, it is well settled that Justice Holmes' test is more useful for describing the vast majority of cases that come within the district courts' original jurisdiction than it is for describing which cases are beyond district court jurisdiction. We have often held that a case "arose under" federal law where the vindication of

---

7. ERISA may also be an "Act of Congress regulating commerce" within the meaning of 28 U.S.C. § 1337, but we have not distinguished between the "arising under" standards of § 1337 and § 1331. See, e.g., Skelly Oil Co. v. Phillips Petroleum Co., 339 U.S. 667 (1950).

8. The statute's "arising under" language tracks similar language in art. III, § 2 of the Constitution, which has been construed as permitting Congress to extend Federal Jurisdiction to any case of which federal law potentially "forms an ingredi-

ent," see Osborn v. Bank of the United States, 9 Wheat. 738, 823 (1824), and its limited legislative history suggests that the 44th Congress may have meant to "confer the whole power which the Constitution conferred," 2 Cong.Rec. 4986 (1874) (remarks of Sen. Carpenter). Nevertheless, we have only recently reaffirmed what has long been recognized—that "Article III 'arising under' jurisdiction is broader than federal question jurisdiction under § 1331." Verlinden B.V. v. Central Bank of Nigeria, 461 U.S. 480, 495 (1983).

a right under state law necessarily turned on some construction of federal law, see, e.g. Smith v. Kansas City Title & Trust Co., 255 U.S. 180 (1921); Hopkins v. Walker, 244 U.S. 486 (1917), and even the most ardent proponent of the Holmes test has admitted that it has been rejected as an exclusionary principle, see Flournoy v. Wiener, 321 U.S. 253, 270–272 (1944) (Frankfurter, J., dissenting). See also T.B. Harms Co. v. Eliscu, 339 F.2d 823, 827 (C.A.2 1964) (Friendly, J.). Leading commentators have suggested that for purposes of § 1331 an action "arises under" federal law "if in order for the plaintiff to secure the relief sought he will be obliged to establish both the correctness and the applicability to his case of a proposition of federal law." P. Bator, P. Mishkin, D. Shapiro & H. Wechsler, Hart & Wechsler's The Federal Courts and the Federal System 889 (2d ed. 1973) (hereinafter Hart & Wechsler); cf. T.B. Harms Co., supra ("a case may 'arise under' a law of the United States if the complaint discloses a need for determining the meaning or application of such a law").

One powerful doctrine has emerged, however—the "well-pleaded complaint" rule—which as a practical matter severely limits the number of cases in which state law "creates the cause of action" that may be initiated in or removed to federal district court, thereby avoiding more-or-less automatically a number of potentially serious federal-state conflicts. Thus, a federal court does not have original jurisdiction over a case in which the complaint presents a state-law cause of action, but also asserts that federal law deprives the defendant of a defense he may raise, Taylor v. Anderson, supra; Louisville & Nashville R. Co. v. Mottley, 211 U.S. 149 (1908), or that a federal defense the defendant may raise is not sufficient to defeat the claim, Tennessee v. Union & Planters' Bank, 152 U.S. 454 (1894). * * * For better or worse, under the present statutory scheme as it has existed since 1887, a defendant may not remove a case to federal court unless the plaintiff's complaint establishes that the case "arises under" federal law.[9] "[A] right or immunity created by the Constitution or laws of the United States must be an element, and an

9. The well-pleaded complaint rule applies to the original jurisdiction of the district courts as well as to their removal jurisdiction. See Phillips Petroleum Co. v. Texaco, Inc., 415 U.S. 125, 127 (1974) (per curiam) (case brought originally in federal court); Pan American Petroleum Corp. v. Superior Court, 366 U.S. 656, 663 (1961) (attack on jurisdiction of state court).

It is possible to conceive of a rational jurisdictional system in which the answer as well as the complaint would be consulted before a determination was made whether the case "arose under" federal law, or in which original and removal jurisdiction were not co-extensive. Indeed, until the 1887 amendments to the 1875 Act, Act of Mar. 3, 1887, ch. 373, 24 Stat. 552, as amended by Act of Aug. 13, 1888, ch. 866, 25 Stat. 433, the well-pleaded complaint rule was not applied in full force to cases removed from state court; the defendant's petition for removal could furnish the necessary guarantee that the case necessarily presented a substantial question of federal law. See Railroad Co. v. Mississippi, 102 U.S. 135, 140 (1880); Gold–Washing & Water Co. v. Keyes, 96 U.S. 199, 203–204 (1877). Commentators have repeatedly proposed that some mechanism be established to permit removal of cases in which a federal defense may be dispositive. See, e.g., American Law Institute, Study of the Division of Jurisdiction Between State and Federal Courts § 1312, at 188–194 (1969) (ALI Study); Wechsler, Federal Jurisdiction and the Revision of the Judicial Code, 13 Law & Contemp.Prob. 216, 233–234 (1948). But those proposals have not been adopted.

essential one, of the plaintiff's cause of action." Gully v. First National Bank, 299 U.S. 109, 112 (1936).

For many cases in which federal law becomes relevant only insofar as it sets bounds for the operation of state authority, the well-pleaded complaint rule makes sense as a quick rule of thumb. * * *

The rule, however, may produce awkward results, especially in cases in which neither the obligation created by state law nor the defendant's factual failure to comply are in dispute, and both parties admit that the only question for decision is raised by a federal preemption defense. Nevertheless, it has been correctly understood to apply in such situations. As we said in Gully, "By unimpeachable authority, a suit brought upon a state statute does not arise under an act of Congress or the Constitution of the United States because prohibited thereby." 299 U.S., at 116.[12]

III

Simply to state these principles is not to apply them to the case at hand. Appellants' complaint sets forth two "causes of action," one of which expressly refers to ERISA; if either comes within the original jurisdiction of the federal courts, removal was proper as to the whole case. See 28 U.S.C. § 1441(c). Although appellant's complaint does not specifically assert any particular statutory entitlement for the relief it seeks, the language of the complaint suggests (and the parties do not dispute) that appellant's "first cause of action" states a claim under Cal.Rev. & Tax.Code § 18818, and its "second cause of action" states a claim under California's Declaratory Judgment Act, Cal.Civ.Proc.Code § 1060 (West 1980). As an initial proposition, then, the "law that creates the cause of action" is state law, and original federal jurisdiction is unavailable unless it appears that some substantial, disputed question of federal law is a necessary element of one of the well-pleaded state claims, or that one or the other claim is "really" one of federal law.

A

Even though state law creates appellant's causes of action, its case might still "arise under" the laws of the United States if a well-pleaded complaint established that its right to relief under state law requires resolution of a substantial question of federal law in dispute between the parties. For appellant's first cause of action—to enforce its levy, under § 18818—a straightforward application of the well-pleaded complaint rule precludes original federal court jurisdiction. California law establishes a set of conditions, without reference to federal law, under which a tax levy may be enforced; federal law becomes relevant only by way of a

---

12. Note, however, that a claim of federal preemption does not always arise as a defense to a coercive action. See infra, n. 20. And, of course, the absence of original jurisdiction does not mean that there is no federal forum in which a preemption defense may be heard. If the state courts reject a claim of federal preemption, that decision may ultimately be reviewed on appeal by this Court. See, e.g., Fidelity Federal Savings & Loan Assn. v. de la Cuesta, 458 U.S. 141 (1982). * * *.

defense to an obligation created entirely by state law, and then only if appellant has made out a valid claim for relief under state law. * * * The well-pleaded complaint rule was framed to deal with precisely such a situation. As we discuss above, since 1887 it has been settled law that a case may not be removed to federal court on the basis of a federal defense, including the defense of preemption, even if the defense is anticipated in the plaintiff's complaint, and even if both parties admit that the defense is the only question truly at issue in the case.

Appellant's declaratory judgment action poses a more difficult problem. Whereas the question of federal preemption is relevant to appellant's first cause of action only as a potential defense, it is a necessary element of the declaratory judgment claim. Under Cal.Civ.Proc.Code § 1060, a party with an interest in property may bring an action for a declaration of another party's legal rights and duties with respect to that property upon showing that there is an "actual controversy relating to the respective rights and duties" of the parties. The only questions in dispute between the parties in this case concern the rights and duties of CLVT and its trustees under ERISA. Not only does appellant's request for a declaratory judgment under California law clearly encompass questions governed by ERISA, but appellant's complaint identifies no other questions as a subject of controversy between the parties. Such questions must be raised in a well-pleaded complaint for a declaratory judgment. Therefore, it is clear on the face of its well-pleaded complaint that appellant may not obtain the relief it seeks in its second cause of action ("[t]hat the court declare defendants legally obligated to honor all future levies by the Board upon [CLVT],") without a construction of ERISA and/or an adjudication of its preemptive effect and constitutionality—all questions of federal law.

Appellant argues that original federal court jurisdiction over such a complaint is foreclosed by our decision in Skelly Oil Co. v. Phillips Petroleum Co., 339 U.S. 667 (1950). As we shall see, however, *Skelly Oil* is not directly controlling.

* * *

* * * *Skelly Oil* has come to stand for the proposition that "if, but for the availability of the declaratory judgment procedure, the federal claim would arise only as a defense to a state created action, jurisdiction is lacking." 10A C. Wright, A. Miller & M. Kane, Federal Practice and Procedure § 2767, at 744–745 (2d ed. 1983). Cf. Public Service Comm'n v. Wycoff, 344 U.S. 237, 248 (1952) (dictum).[14]

---

14. In *Wycoff,* a company that transported films between various points within the State of Utah sought a declaratory judgment that a state regulatory commission had no power to forbid it to transport over routes authorized by the Interstate Commerce Commission. However, "[i]t offered no evidence whatever of any past, pending or threatened action by the Utah Commis-

sion." 344 U.S., at 240. We held that there was no jurisdiction, essentially because the dispute had "not yet matured to a point where we can see what, if any, concrete controversy will develop." Id., at 245. We also added:

"Where the complaint in an action for declaratory judgment seeks in essence to assert a defense to an impending or threat-

1. As an initial matter, we must decide whether the doctrine of *Skelly Oil* limits original federal court jurisdiction under § 1331—and by extension removal jurisdiction under § 1441—when a question of federal law appears on the face of a well-pleaded complaint for a state law declaratory judgment. Apparently, it is a question of first impression. * * * *Skelly Oil* relied significantly on the precise contours of the federal Declaratory Judgment Act as well as of § 1331. Cf. 339 U.S., at 674 (stressing the need to respect "the limited procedural purpose of the Declaratory Judgment Act"). The Court's emphasis that the Declaratory Judgment Act was intended to affect only the remedies available in a federal district court, not the court's jurisdiction, was critical to the Court's reasoning. Our interpretation of the federal Declaratory Judgment Act in *Skelly Oil* does not apply of its own force to *state* declaratory judgment statutes, many of which antedate the federal statute, see Developments in the Law—Declaratory Judgments—1941–1949, 62 Harv.L.Rev. 787, 790–791 (1949). * * *

Yet while *Skelly Oil* itself is limited to the federal Declaratory Judgment Act, fidelity to its spirit leads us to extend it to state declaratory judgment actions as well. If federal district courts could take jurisdiction, either originally or by removal, of state declaratory judgment claims raising questions of federal law, without regard to the doctrine of *Skelly Oil*, the federal Declaratory Judgment Act—with the limitations *Skelly Oil* read into it—would become a dead letter. For any case in which a state declaratory judgment action was available, litigants could get into federal court for a declaratory judgment despite our interpretation of § 2201, simply by pleading an adequate state claim for a declaration of federal law. Having interpreted the Declaratory Judgment Act of 1934 to include certain limitations on the jurisdiction of federal district courts to entertain declaratory judgment suits, we should be extremely hesitant to interpret the Judiciary Act of 1875 and its 1887 amendments in a way that renders the limitations in the later statute nugatory. Therefore, we hold that under the jurisdictional statutes as they now stand[17] federal courts do not have original jurisdiction, nor do

ened state court action, it is the character of the threatened action, and not of the defense, which will determine whether there is federal-question jurisdiction in the District Court. If the cause of action, which the declaratory defendant threatens to assert, does not itself involve a claim under federal law, it is doubtful if a federal court may entertain an action for a declaratory judgment establishing a defense to that claim. This is dubious even though the declaratory complaint sets forth a claim of federal right, if that right is in reality in the nature of a defense to a threatened cause of action. Federal courts will not seize litigations from state courts merely because one, normally a defendant, goes to federal court to begin his federal-law defense before the state court begins the case under state law." Id., at 248.

17. It is not beyond the power of Congress to confer a right to a declaratory judgment in a case or controversy arising under federal law—within the meaning of the Constitution or of § 1331—without regard to *Skelly Oil's* particular application of the well-pleaded complaint rule. The 1969 ALI report strongly criticized the *Skelly Oil* doctrine: "If no other changes were to be made in federal question jurisdiction, it is arguable that such language, and the historical test it seems to embody, should be repudiated." ALI Study § 1311, at 170–171. Nevertheless, Congress has declined to make such a change.—At this point, any adjustment in the system that has evolved

they acquire jurisdiction on removal, when a federal question is presented by a complaint for a state declaratory judgment, but *Skelly Oil* would bar jurisdiction if the plaintiff had sought a federal declaratory judgment.

2. The question, then, is whether a federal district court could take jurisdiction of appellant's declaratory judgment claim had it been brought under 28 U.S.C. § 2201.[18] The application of *Skelly Oil* to such a suit is somewhat unclear. Federal courts have regularly taken original jurisdiction over declaratory judgment suits in which, if the declaratory judgment defendant brought a coercive action to enforce its rights, that suit would necessarily present a federal question.[19] Section 502(a)(3) of ERISA specifically grants trustees of ERISA-covered plans like CLVT a cause of action for injunctive relief when their rights and duties under ERISA are at issue, and that action is exclusively governed by federal law.[20] If CLVT could have sought an injunction under ERISA against application to it of state regulations that require acts inconsistent with ERISA,[21] does a declaratory judgment suit by the State "arise under" federal law?

under the *Skelly Oil* rule must come from Congress.

18. It may seem odd that, for purposes of determining whether removal was proper, we analyze a claim brought under state law, in state court, by a party who has continuously objected to district court jurisdiction over its case, as if that party had been trying to get original federal court jurisdiction all along. That irony, however, is a more-or-less constant feature of the removal statute, under which a case is removable if a federal district court could have taken jurisdiction had the same complaint been filed. See Wechsler, Federal Jurisdiction and the Revision of the Judicial Code, 13 Law & Contemp.Prob. 216, 234 (1948).

19. For instance, federal courts have consistently adjudicated suits by alleged patent infringers to declare a patent invalid, on the theory that an infringement suit by the declaratory judgment defendant would raise a federal question over which the federal courts have exclusive jurisdiction. See E. Edelmann & Co. v. Triple–A Specialty Co., 88 F.2d 852 (C.A.7 1937); Hart & Wechsler 896–897. Taking jurisdiction over this type of suit is consistent with the dictum in Public Service Comm'n of Utah v. Wycoff Co., 344 U.S. 237, 248 (1952), see supra, n. 14, in which we stated only that a declaratory judgment plaintiff could not get original federal jurisdiction if the anticipated lawsuit by the declaratory judgment defendant would *not* "arise under" federal law. It is also consistent with the nature of the declaratory remedy itself, which was designed to permit adjudication

of either party's claims of right. See E. Borchard, Declaratory Judgments 15–18, 23–25 (1934).

20. Section 502(a)(3) provides:

"[A civil action may be brought] by a participant, beneficiary, or fiduciary (A) to enjoin any act or practice which violates any provision of this subchapter or the terms of the plan, or (B) to obtain other appropriate equitable relief (i) to redress such violations or (ii) to enforce any provision of this subchapter.... " 29 U.S.C. § 1132(a)(3).

* * *

Even if ERISA did not expressly provide jurisdiction, CLVT might have been able to obtain federal jurisdiction under the doctrine applied in some cases that a person subject to a scheme of federal regulation may sue in federal court to enjoin application to him of conflicting state regulations, and a declaratory judgment action by the same person does not necessarily run afoul of the *Skelly Oil* doctrine. See, e.g., Lake Carriers' Assn. v. MacMullan, 406 U.S. 498, 506–508 (1972); Rath Packing Co. v. Becker, 530 F.2d 1295, 1303–1306 (C.A.9 1975), aff'd sub nom. Jones v. Rath Packing Co., 430 U.S. 519 (1977); First Federal Savings & Loan of Boston v. Greenwald, 591 F.2d, at 423, and n. 8.

21. We express no opinion, however, whether a party in CLVT's position could sue under ERISA to enjoin or to declare invalid a state tax levy, despite the Tax Injunction Act, 28 U.S.C. § 1341. See Cali-

We think not. We have always interpreted what *Skelly Oil* called "the current of jurisdictional legislation since the Act of March 3, 1875," 339 U.S., at 673, with an eye to practicality and necessity. "What is needed is something of that common-sense accommodation of judgment to kaleidoscopic situations which characterizes the law in its treatment of causation * * * a selective process which picks the substantial causes out of the web and lays the other ones aside." Gully v. First National Bank, 299 U.S., at 117–118. There are good reasons why the federal courts should not entertain suits by the States to declare the validity of their regulations despite possibly conflicting federal law. States are not significantly prejudiced by an inability to come to federal court for a declaratory judgment in advance of a possible injunctive suit by a person subject to federal regulation. They have a variety of means by which they can enforce their own laws in their own courts, and they do not suffer if the preemption questions such enforcement may raise are tested there.[22] The express grant of federal jurisdiction in ERISA is limited to suits brought by certain parties, * * * as to whom Congress presumably determined that a right to enter federal court was necessary to further the statute's purposes.[23] It did not go so far as to provide that any suit *against* such parties must also be brought in federal court when they themselves did not choose to sue. The situation presented by a State's suit for a declaration of the validity of state law is sufficiently removed from the spirit of necessity and careful limitation of district court jurisdiction that informed our statutory interpretation in *Skelly Oil* and *Gully* to convince us that, until Congress informs us otherwise, such a suit is not within the original jurisdiction of the United States district courts. Accordingly, the same suit brought originally in state court is not removable either.

* * *

IV

Our concern in this case is consistent application of a system of statutes conferring original federal court jurisdiction, as they have been

fornia v. Grace Brethren Church, 457 U.S. 393 (1982). To do so, it would have to show either that state law provided no "speedy and efficient remedy" or that Congress intended § 502 of ERISA to be an exception to the Tax Injunction Act.

22. Indeed, as appellant's strategy in this case shows, they may often be willing to go to great lengths to avoid federal-court resolution of a preemption question. Realistically, there is little prospect that States will flood the federal courts with declaratory judgment actions; most questions will arise, as in this case, because a State has sought a declaration in state court and the defendant has removed the case to federal court. Accordingly, it is perhaps appropriate to note that considerations of comity make us reluctant to snatch cases which a State

has brought from the courts of that State, unless some clear rule demands it.

23. Cf. nn. 19 and 20, supra. Alleged patent infringers, for example, have a clear interest in swift resolution of the federal issue of patent validity—they are liable for damages if it turns out they are infringing a patent, and they frequently have a delicate network of contractual arrangements with third parties that is dependent on their right to sell or license a product. Parties subject to conflicting state and federal regulatory schemes also have a clear interest in sorting out the scope of each government's authority, especially where they face a threat of liability if the application of federal law is not quickly made clear.

interpreted by this Court over many years. Under our interpretations, Congress has given the lower federal courts jurisdiction to hear, originally or by removal from a state court, only those cases in which a well-pleaded complaint establishes either that federal law creates the cause of action or that the plaintiff's right to relief necessarily depends on resolution of a substantial question of federal law. We hold that a suit by state tax authorities both to enforce its levies against funds held in trust pursuant to an ERISA-covered employee benefit plan, and to declare the validity of the levies notwithstanding ERISA, is neither a creature of ERISA itself nor a suit of which the federal courts will take jurisdiction because it turns on a question of federal law. Accordingly, we vacate the judgment of the Court of Appeals and remand so that this case may be remanded to the Superior Court of the State of California for the County of Los Angeles.

Notes

1.   The well-pleaded complaint rule has often been criticized for drawing an irrational distinction between federal issues raised in the plaintiff's complaint on the one hand and in the defendant's answer on the other. It has been suggested that a defendant who presents a federal defense should be allowed to remove the case to federal court. Judge Richard Posner, however, has suggested that "[t]he distinction is not quite so arbitrary as it sounds." R. Posner, The Federal Courts: Crisis and Reform 190 (1985):

> In many [such cases] the federal defense would have little merit—would, indeed, have been concocted purely to confer federal jurisdiction—yet this fact might be impossible to determine, with any confidence, without having a trial before the trial. Of course, frivolous federal claims are also a problem when only plaintiffs can use them to get into court, but a less serious problem. If the plaintiff gets thrown out of federal court because his claim is frivolous, and must start over in state court, he has lost time; and the loss may be fatal if meanwhile the statute of limitations has run. But the defendant may be delighted to see the plaintiff's case thrown out of federal court when the court discovers that the federal defense is frivolous.

Do you agree that the frivolousness of the federal defense could not likely be determined "without having a trial before the trial"? Is it clear that the danger to which Judge Posner refers is limited primarily to defendants? Might not a plaintiff, intent on harassing a defendant and/or increasing the defendant's expenses in order to encourage settlement of a sham claim (i.e., a "strike suit"), seek to file a frivolous federal claim? Might not a plaintiff—even one possessing a legitimate state claim—consider adding a "trumped up" federal issue to his complaint, in order to obtain the shorter dockets, more advanced discovery procedures, and possibly better qualified judges in federal court? In any event, does the danger to which Judge Posner refers outbalance the value of having adjudicated in federal court cases that will ultimately turn on an important and/or unsettled issue of federal law, albeit one raised exclusively as a defense? Does Posner's argument have relevance for the declaratory judgment issue in *Skelly* and *Franchise Tax Board*?

2.   Does the decision in *Franchise Tax Board* follow inescapably from *Skelly?* Do you agree with Justice Brennan that *Skelly* must be extended to state declaratory judgment actions because "[i]f federal district courts could take jurisdiction * * * of state declaratory judgment claims raising questions of federal law * * * the Federal Declaratory Judgment Act—with the limitations *Skelly Oil* read into it—would become a dead letter"? 463 U.S. at 18. If this were true, so what? As long as assumed congressional intent in the Federal Declaratory Judgment Act not to extend federal jurisdiction is not undermined, why should it make a difference that such an "extension" results from use of a *state* declaratory judgment action?

3.   How important to the Court's decision is the fact that the suit had originally been filed by a state agency? Is there a fallacy in the Court's logic that "[t]here are good reasons why the federal courts should not entertain suits by the States to declare the validity of their regulations despite possibly conflicting federal law"? Recall that the state agency originally filed its declaratory judgment action in *state* court, and that it was the *private defendant* who had sought a federal forum by attempting to remove the case to federal court.

4.   Consider the post-*Franchise Tax Board* decision in Metropolitan Life Ins. Co. v. Taylor, 481 U.S. 58 (1987). An employer and insurer defendants in a state proceeding brought by a former employee alleging various state causes of action, including breach of contract and wrongful termination of disability benefits, removed the case to federal district court, contending that the state claims were preempted by ERISA, a federal employee benefits statute. The court of appeals found the case non-removable on "well-pleaded complaint" grounds. The Supreme Court, in an opinion by Justice O'Connor, reversed. While describing the "well-pleaded complaint" rule as "the basic principle marking the boundaries of the federal question jurisdiction of the federal district courts," she nevertheless found the doctrine inapplicable:

> Federal pre-emption is ordinarily a federal defense to the plaintiff's suit. As a defense, it does not appear on the face of a well-pleaded complaint, and, therefore, does not authorize removal to federal court. One corollary of the well-pleaded complaint rule developed in the case law, however, is that Congress may so completely pre-empt a particular area, that any civil complaint raising this select group of claims is necessarily federal in character. For 20 years, this Court has singled out claims pre-empted by § 301 of the Labor Management Relations Act for such special treatment. Avco Corp. v. Machinists, 390 U.S. 557 (1968).

*   *   *

There is no dispute in this case that Taylor's complaint, although pre-empted by ERISA, purported to raise only state law causes of action. * * * In *Franchise Tax Board*, the Court held that ERISA pre-emption, without more, does not convert a state claim into an action arising under federal law. The Court suggested, however, that a state action that was not only pre-empted by ERISA, but also came "within" the scope of § 502(a) of ERISA [providing an exclusive federal cause of action for resolution of ERISA disputes] might fall within the *Avco* rule. The claim in this case, unlike the state tax collection suit in *Franchise*

Tax Board, is within the scope of § 502(a) and we therefore must face the question specifically reserved by *Franchise Tax Board.*

In the absence of explicit direction from Congress, this question would be a close one. * * * [W]e would be reluctant to find that extraordinary pre-emptive power, such as has been found with respect to § 301 of the LMRA, that converts an ordinary state common law complaint into one stating a federal claim for purposes of the well-pleaded complaint rule. But the language of the jurisdictional subsection of ERISA's civil enforcement provisions closely parallels that of § 301 of the LMRA. * * * The presumption that similar language in two labor law statutes has a similar meaning is fully confirmed by the legislative history of ERISA's civil enforcement provisions.

* * *

Accordingly, this suit, though it purports to raise only state law claims, is necessarily federal in character by virtue of the clearly manifested intent of Congress. Id. at 63–67.

Justice Brennan, joined by Justice Marshall, concurred separately:

While I join in the Court's opinion, I note that our decision should not be interpreted as adopting a broad rule that *any* defense premised on congressional intent to preempt state law is sufficient to establish removal jurisdiction. The Court holds only removal jurisdiction exists when, as here, "Congress has *clearly* manifested an intent to make causes of action * * * *removable to federal court.*" In future cases involving other statutes, the prudent course for a federal court that does not find a clear congressional intent to create removal jurisdiction will be to remand the case to state court. Id. at 67–68.

Metropolitan Life was followed in Board of Trustees, Local 25 v. The Madison Hotel, Inc., 97 F.3d 1479 (D.C.Cir.1996). There the court held that the issue of federal preemption under ERISA provided federal question jurisdiction over a collection action by the boards of trustees of three employee benefit funds against an employer, alleging breach of a settlement agreement. See also Balcorta v. Twentieth Century–Fox Film Corp., 208 F.3d 1102, 1107 (9th Cir.2000) (noting the existence of "a corollary to the well-pleaded complaint rule, known as the 'complete preemption' doctrine.").

For a general discussion of preemption jurisdiction, see Jordan, *The Complete Preemption Dilemma: A Legal Process Perspective*, 31 Wake Forest L.Rev. 927 (1996). Professor Jordan advocates an expanded version of the preemption-jurisdiction doctrine, arguing that removal should be allowed "when the federal law involved preempts the state law upon which the suit is barred—even in the absence of a superseding federal cause of action," since "[s]uch a suit may be characterized as 'federal in nature' because, if the state law has been displaced, the federal nature of the suit predominates." Id. at 998–99.

5. On the "well-pleaded complaint" issue, see generally Collins, *The Unhappy History of Federal Question Removal,* 71 Iowa L.Rev. 717 (1986); Segreti, *Vesting the Whole "Arising Under" Power of the District Courts in Federal Preemption Cases,* 37 Okla.L.Rev. 439 (1984).

6. For an application of the well-pleaded complaint rule, see Oklahoma Tax Commission v. Graham, 489 U.S. 838 (1989). The suit involved a state attempt to recover taxes from Native American tribes. The Court concluded that tribal "immunity may provide a federal defense to Oklahoma's claims. But it has long been settled that the existence of a federal immunity to the claims asserted does not convert a suit otherwise arising under state law into one which, in the statutory sense, arises under federal law."

7. Professors Doernberg and Mushlin argue, based on an extensive review of legislative history, that Congress did intend to expand federal jurisdiction through the Declaratory Judgment Act. See, Doernberg & Mushlin, *The Trojan Horse: How the Declaratory Judgment Act Created a Cause of Action and Expanded Federal Jurisdiction While The Supreme Court Wasn't Looking,* 36 U.C.L.A.L.Rev. 529 (1989).

Chapter 14

DIVERSITY JURISDICTION

§ 1. THE BASIC POLICIES

STRAWBRIDGE v. CURTISS

Supreme Court of the United States, 1806.
7 U.S. (3 Cranch) 267.

This was an appeal from a decree of the circuit court, for the district of Massachusetts, which dismissed the complainants' bill in chancery, for want of jurisdiction.

Some of the complainants were alleged to be citizens of the state of Massachusetts. The defendants were also stated to be citizens of the same state, excepting Curtiss, who was averred to be a citizen of the state of Vermont, and upon whom the subpoena was served in that state.

* * *

On a subsequent day, MARSHALL, CH. J. delivered the opinion of the court.

The court has considered this case, and is of opinion that the jurisdiction cannot be supported.

The words of the act of congress are, "where an alien is a party; or the suit is between a citizen of a state where the suit is brought, and a citizen of another state."

The court understands these expressions to mean, that each distinct interest should be represented by persons, all of whom are entitled to sue, or may be sued, in the federal courts. That is, that where the interest is joint, each of the persons concerned in that interest must be competent to sue, or liable to be sued, in those courts.

Complete diversity

But the court does not mean to give an opinion in the case where several parties represent several distinct interests, and some of those parties are, and others are not, competent to sue, or liable to be sued, in the courts of the United States.

Decree affirmed.

Notes

1. **History, Purposes and Current Viability of Diversity Jurisdiction.** The necessary statutory authorization for "diversity jurisdiction" appears in 28 U.S.C. § 1332, which states: "The district courts shall have jurisdiction of all civil actions where the matter in controversy exceeds the sum or value of $75,000, exclusive of interests and costs, and is between * * * citizens of different states." Section 1332(c)(2) now indicates as well that "an alien admitted to the United States for permanent residence shall be deemed to be a citizen of the state in which such alien is domiciled." See Appendix B. There is some debate over the reasons for the framers' original inclusion of diversity jurisdiction in Article III, section 2. It has often been thought that its purpose was to avoid potential prejudice against out-of-staters in state courts. See the opinion of Chief Justice Marshall in Bank of the United States v. Deveaux, 9 U.S. (5 Cranch) 61, 87 (1809). Cf. Frank, *Historical Bases of the Federal Judicial System*, 13 Law & Contemp.Prob. 1 (1948); Yntema & Jaffin, *Preliminary Analysis of Concurrent Jurisdiction*, 79 U.Pa.L.Rev. 869 (1931).

One respected commentator has concluded that "there was little cause to fear that the state tribunals would be hostile to litigants from other states." Friendly, *The Historic Basis of Diversity Jurisdiction*, 41 Harv. L.Rev. 483, 497 (1928). While Friendly notes the absence of substantial debate over the diversity issue among the drafters of Article III and only a lackluster defense of the jurisdiction against heavy attack in the states, he asserts that "the desire to protect creditors against legislation favorable to debtors was a principal reason for the grant of diversity jurisdiction, and * * * as a reason it was by no means without validity." Id. at 496–497. This was because "there was much reason to fear that the courts of a state having laws favorable to debtors would apply these laws in favor of their own residents even though the debt was payable in another state * * *." Id. at 496. He further cites the close ties that many state legislatures had with state judges. Id. at 497–498.

Whichever of these two conceivable grounds in support of diversity jurisdiction actually prompted the jurisdiction's adoption, how legitimate do you suppose these grounds are today? What other arguments, if any, may be made to support the continued use of the diversity jurisdiction? Consider Frank, *For Maintaining Diversity Jurisdiction*, 73 Yale L.J. 7 (1963). There three basic values of the diversity jurisdiction are noted: (a) litigants are generally satisfied with the justice obtained in federal court in diversity cases; (b) there exists an "educational value [in] having two systems in interaction", resulting in benefits to both state and federal systems (the "widespread emulation in the states" of the Federal Rules of Civil Procedure is cited); and (c) "there are elements of prejudice and competence deserving to be taken into account." Id. at 10–12. Additionally, Frank notes that "[t]he system works well. There is no good reason for changing it." See also Frank, *The Case for Diversity Jurisdiction*, 16 Harv.J.Legis. 403 (1979).

Contrast with Frank's position that taken in H. Friendly, Federal Jurisdiction: A General View 139–152 (1973). There it is argued that (a) diversity results in a "diversion of judge-power urgently needed for tasks which only federal courts can handle or which, because of their expertise, they can handle significantly better than the courts of a state"; (b) in diversity cases "federal courts cannot discharge the important objective of making law", because under the well-known rule in Erie R. Co. v. Tompkins, 304 U.S. 64 (1938), federal courts must apply state substantive law in such cases; and (c) "the very availability of litigation in a federal court postpones an authoritative decision by the state courts that otherwise would be inevitable." Friendly also notes, presumably speaking from personal experience, that "the dullest cases, at least in the truly civil field, are generally those arising from the diversity jurisdiction", said in response to the argument that the diversity jurisdiction might add intellectual breadth to federal judges.

How persuasive do you find the respective arguments of Frank and Friendly? In response to the argument about avoiding state court prejudice, Friendly notes that "the aid a federal court can give in avoiding prejudice against an out-of-stater at least in jury cases is exceedingly limited." What if you could be convinced that plaintiffs' attorneys virtually never choose the federal forum in a diversity case because of fear or prejudice against out-of-staters, but do so largely because of the generally higher quality of judges and procedures often thought to be available in the federal courts? Is this, standing alone, a sufficient basis for maintaining the diversity jurisdiction?

More recently, Professor Debra Bassett has argued that the "local bias" that is held to justify diversity jurisdiction stems from stereotypes about rural populations as provincial and unintelligent. Bassett, *The Hidden Bias in Diversity Jurisdiction*, 81 Wash.U.L.Q. 119 (2003). She argues that diversity jurisdiction itself perpetuates this bias against rural areas. Are you persuaded?

The debate over the future of diversity jurisdiction has continued to rage, fueled, at least in part, by the recommendations of the Federal Courts Study Committee. The proposals of the 15–month study, submitted to Congress in 1990, include a recommendation that diversity jurisdiction be significantly reduced. The report is reprinted in 22 Conn.L.Rev. 733 (1990). It indicates that diversity jurisdiction accounts for "almost one in every four cases in the district courts, about one of every two civil trials, about one of every ten appeals, and more than one in every ten dollars in the federal budget." Accordingly, the Committee recommended that "Congress * * * limit federal jurisdiction based on diversity of citizenship to complex multi-state litigation, interpleader, and suits involving aliens. At the least, [Congress] should effect changes to curtail the most obvious problems of the current jurisdiction." Professor Larry Kramer, who served as a reporter to the study committee, makes similar arguments in *Diversity Jurisdiction*, 1990 B.Y.U.L.Rev. 97. Echoing some of the positions of Judge Friendly, Judge Sloviter has argued that given *Erie*'s demand for the application of state law, the policies which support the federal abstention doctrines also suggest the abolition of diversity jurisdiction. See Sloviter, *A Federal Judge Views Diversity Jurisdiction Through the Lens of Federalism*, 78 Va.L.Rev. 1671 (1992).

For an analysis of some of the beneficial by-products of diversity's abolition, see Rowe, *Abolishing Diversity Jurisdiction: Positive Side Effects and Potential for Further Reforms*, 92 Harv.L.Rev. 963 (1979). Professor Rowe argues that "the considerable simplification in federal practice resulting from abolition would be an important benefit of the measure, rendering mostly superfluous the 'enormous infrastructure that has grown up to support and to define the diversity jurisdiction.' [Quoting the words of Professor Currie]. Many complex problems that are largely products of the diversity jurisdiction would virtually disappear. Beyond these benefits, abolition would facilitate several decisional developments and statutory and rule reforms that are now difficult or impossible because of problems that flow from diversity jurisdiction. Taking full advantage of these opportunities would lead to a federal judicial system different in important respects from the present one, but with characteristics that would be attractive to many—a system with authority to serve process nationwide and across national boundaries to the limits permitted by the Constitution, having uniform ancillary jurisdiction to dispose of matters not within its original competence but closely enough related to claims properly before it, and devoted primarily to the articulation and enforcement of our national law." Id. at 1101.

2. **Suggested Alternative Modifications of Diversity.** Some commentators, recognizing some degree of validity in both positions, have urged modifications of diversity, short of total abolition. One such proposal was made in Shapiro, *Federal Diversity Jurisdiction: A Survey and a Proposal*, 91 Harv.L.Rev. 317 (1977). On the basis of a questionnaire sent to all active federal district and appellate judges, Professor Shapiro concludes that "[t]here appears to be a good deal of evidence to support the view that diversity jurisdiction may be more warranted, and more useful, in some districts than in others." Id. at 339. This is because "[f]ederal districts vary widely in population, urban or rural character, types of cases filed in the federal courts, and docket congestion. Moreover, there seem to be different perceptions among judges in different districts about the quality of state justice, the extent to which an out-of-state litigant receives, or thinks he is receiving, a fair trial in a state court, and the extent to which state courts regard the contribution of their federal colleagues as useful." Id. Believing that "a simple choice between retention and abolition of diversity jurisdiction may be too inflexible", Shapiro suggests that "the best plan * * * may be to give each district a choice, to be exercised by a majority of that district's judges on regular active status after adequate notice and opportunity for comment, among (a) retention of the present scheme of diversity jurisdiction, (b) adoption of the ALI proposal, and (c) abolition of diversity jurisdiction within its borders." Id. at 340. The ALI proposal to which Shapiro refers is considered below. As a general matter, what do you think of a plan which allows each district to make its own decisions?

In 1969, the American Law Institute proposed a new section of the Judicial Code, providing that "[n]o person can invoke [the diversity] jurisdiction, either originally or on removal, in any district in a State of which he is a citizen." Proposed section 1302(a). Proposed section 1302(b) provides in part: "No corporation incorporated or having its principal place of business in the United States, and no partnership, unincorporated association, or sole proprietorship having its principal place of business in the United States, that has and for a period of more than two years has maintained a local establishment in a State, can invoke [the diversity] jurisdiction, either originally or on removal, in any district in that State in any action arising out of the activities of that establishment." The subsection proceeds to define the term, "local establishment". Subsection (c) applies the rule of subsection (b) to individuals. Subsection (d) provides: "No person can invoke [the diversity] jurisdiction, either originally or on removal, in any circumstances in which that person, or an individual whose interests or estate that person represents, would have been barred under subsections (b) or (c) of this section from doing so at the time the defendant's acts or omissions giving rise to the claim occurred." American Law Institute, Study of the Division of Jurisdiction Between State and Federal Courts 12–13 (1969).

In December 1995, the Judicial Conference of the United States approved a Long Range Plan for the Federal Courts, intended to guide congressional action. The Plan recommended reducing diversity jurisdiction by (1) eliminating it altogether in cases "in which the plaintiff is a citizen of the state in which the federal district court is located"; and (2) changing amount-in-controversy requirements to disregard punitive damages, raise the amount and index it to inflation, and require that "parties invoking diversity jurisdiction plead specific facts showing that the jurisdictional amount-in-controversy requirement has been satisfied." An earlier version of the Plan, prepared by a committee and subsequently revised by the Judicial Conference, had also included as an alternative recommendation that diversity jurisdiction be eliminated except in "actions involving aliens, interpleader actions, and cases in which the petitioner can clearly demonstrate the need for a federal forum."

Compare these proposals to the text of the present diversity statute, 28 U.S.C. § 1332 [in Appendix B]. Exactly what changes has the ALI proposed? What do you suppose are the rationales for these suggested changes? See generally ALI, supra, at 123–32. Do you think the changes go far enough? Too far? Aren't needed in the first place?

3. **The "Complete Diversity" Requirement.** Until 1967, it remained uncertain whether Chief Justice Marshall's requirement of complete diversity in *Strawbridge* represented an interpretation of the diversity provision of Article III, section 2, or of the statute creating diversity jurisdiction. What difference does it make? In that year, the Supreme Court decided State Farm Fire & Casualty Co. v. Tashire, 386 U.S. 523 (1967). There the Court interpreted the federal interpleader statute, 28 U.S.C. § 1335, to require only minimal diversity among claimants, and upheld the constitutionality of the statute as a proper exercise of the diversity jurisdiction. See also Caterpillar Inc. v. Lewis, 519 U.S. 61 (1996) (complete diversity requirement is "a matter of statutory construction").

What is the justification for the complete diversity requirement? Consider the following hypothetical: A, a resident of Illinois, and B, a resident of New York, sue C, a resident of Illinois, in state court in Illinois. If the justification for the diversity jurisdiction is the avoidance of potential prejudice against out-of-staters, is that justification rendered inapplicable here, because of the absence of complete diversity? Might it make a difference whether the claims of the two plaintiffs are joint? In other words, what if the court could conceivably find for one plaintiff, but not the other? Consider the following alternative hypothetical: A, a resident of Illinois, and B, a resident of New York, sue C, a resident of Illinois, in New York state court (having obtained proper personal jurisdiction over C). Is the avoidance of prejudice to out-of-staters also not applicable here, because of the absence of complete diversity? For a discussion of *Strawbridge* and the complete diversity requirement, see Currie, *The Federal Courts and the American Law Institute, Part I*, 36 U.Chi.L.Rev. 1, 18–21 (1968). Professor Currie suggests that "[i]f one is really concerned with providing a federal forum to protect a foreign litigant from possible bias, a reexamination of *Strawbridge* is in order * * *." Id. at 19. Consider the following argument: The valid justification for the complete diversity requirement is, simply, that it reduces the number of cases which properly fall within the diversity jurisdiction, thereby reducing the workload of the federal courts. The complete diversity requirement is criticized in Redish, *Reassessing the Allocation of Judicial Business Between State and Federal Courts: Federal Jurisdiction and "The Martian Chronicles"*, 78 Va.L.Rev. 1769 (1992).

Congress has recently enacted two different statutes conferring federal jurisdiction on the basis of minimal, rather than complete, diversity. The Multiparty, Multiforum Trial Jurisdiction Act of 2002, 28 U.S.C. § 1369, grants jurisdiction—with some exceptions—over "any civil action involving minimal diversity between adverse parties that arises from a single accident, where at least 75 natural persons have died in the accident at a discrete location." In the Class Action Fairness Act of 2003, Congress amended § 1332 to authorize federal jurisdiction over most class actions with minimal diversity and an amount in controversy above five million dollars. The legislative history of both statutes suggests a mistrust of state courts in multi-plaintiff tort suits against corporations. In light of the studies suggesting that the costs of diversity jurisdiction might outweigh its benefits, are these new extensions of diversity jurisdiction wise? As long as the complete diversity requirement still exists in most cases, should there be statutory exceptions for these kinds of cases? See generally Floyd, *The Limits of Minimal Diversity*, 55 Hastings L.J. 613 (2004).

4. The 1988 amendments to section 1332, quoted above, seem to extend diversity jurisdiction to an action by a resident alien domiciled in one state against a resident alien domiciled in another. Is that consistent with the diversity clauses of Article III of the United States Constitution?

§ 2. CORPORATIONS AND ASSOCIATIONS

PETERSON v. COOLEY

United States Court of Appeals, Fourth Circuit, 1998.
142 F.3d 181.

4th Cir.
1998

Before WILKINSON, Chief Judge, and WIDENER and NIEMEYER, Circuit Judges.

WILKINSON, Chief Judge.

Barrie and Nancy Peterson sued William Cooley, Mid–Pacific Funding Corporation, and C.F. Trust, Inc. for tortious interference with contractual relations and statutory conspiracy to injure their business, Va. Code Ann. § 18.2–499. The district court granted summary judgment in favor of the defendants on the grounds that no contract existed and that the defendants acted properly in pursuit of legitimate business purposes. The Petersons appeal, arguing both that the district court lacked diversity jurisdiction and that it erred in dismissing their claims on summary judgment. We hold that there is diversity of citizenship here, and that the defendants' motion for summary judgment was properly granted. Accordingly, we affirm the judgment of the district court. * * *

II.

We first consider the Petersons' claim that this case should be remanded to state court for lack of complete diversity between the parties. Specifically, they argue that C.F. Trust is a citizen of Virginia, the same state of which they are citizens. * * * As a corporation, C.F. Trust is considered "to be a citizen of any State by which it has been incorporated and of the State where it has its principal place of business." § 1332(c)(1). Because C.F. Trust is incorporated in Florida, the question of whether [jurisdiction is] appropriate turns on whether the corporation has its principal place of business in Virginia.

We have approved two tests for ascertaining a corporation's principal place of business for jurisdictional purposes, but have endorsed neither to the exclusion of the other. The first test, now commonly referred to as the nerve center test, "makes the 'home office,' or place where the corporation's officers direct, control, and coordinate its activities, determinative." The second test, normally termed the place of operations test, instead "looks to the place where the bulk of corporate activity takes place."

We believe that application of the nerve center test is more appropriate here. The place of operations test presumes the existence of physical operations by which a corporation's presence in different states can be measured. As a result, the test is applied when a company has multiple centers of manufacturing, purchasing, or sales. By contrast, a corporation engaged primarily in the ownership and management of investment assets such as debt or equities is not really geographically bound. Because such corporations can readily transfer and move their investment assets, a jurisdictional test focusing on the location of operations makes little sense.

C.F. Trust is essentially a passive investment vehicle. The corporation was set up solely to acquire and own the 1993 notes. Accordingly, C.F. Trust does not have any manufacturing plants, purchasing centers, or sales facilities—the normal indicia of a corporation's place of operations. C.F. Trust owns only the 1993 notes—investment assets—and not the Virginia property by which the notes are secured. Given these facts, we believe that application of the place of operations test would be inappropriate.

The Petersons concede that if the nerve center test is applied, C.F. Trust's principal place of business cannot be Virginia and complete diversity of citizenship exists. We agree. Courts normally find the nerve center "where the activities of the corporation are controlled and direct- ed," or "where its executive headquarters are located." C.F. Trust's president, corporate office, and corporate books and records are located in Coral Gables, Florida. The corporation's two vice presidents are also permanent residents of Florida. Clearly, the direction and management of the corporation radiates out from Florida. It is easy therefore to conclude that under the nerve center test C.F. Trust's principal place of business for purposes of 28 U.S.C. § 1332(c)(1) is Florida, and not Virginia.

Even were we to follow the Petersons' suggestion and apply the place of operations test, our conclusion would not change. Initially, C.F. Trust has no operations in Virginia. The corporation has no offices or personnel in Virginia, and none of C.F. Trust's directors, officers, or shareholders are residents or citizens of Virginia. Furthermore, any operations C.F. Trust does conduct are outside Virginia. When applying the place of operations test, courts must consider the nature of a corporation's activity: "whether it is active or passive and whether it is labor-intensive or management-demanding." As we have already noted, C.F. Trust's only connection to Virginia is as a passive investor in notes secured by real estate located in the Commonwealth. C.F. Trust's only operations are therefore managerial in nature and are controlled and directed from Florida. Like its nerve center then, C.F. Trust's place of operations is Florida.

The Petersons argue, however, that C.F. Trust's acquisition of a certificate of authority to transact business in Virginia proves the Commonwealth is its place of operations. We do not find this certificate to be determinative of our jurisdictional inquiry. The mere fact that C.F. Trust is permitted to transact business in Virginia is irrelevant because the corporation does not actually conduct any operations within the Commonwealth. Other courts have similarly declined to attach signifi- cance to a corporation's authority to transact business within a state when other factors tend to show the corporation's principal place of business is in a different state. * * *

Finally, other courts' decisions support the result we reach today. In Vareka Invs., N.V. v. American Inv. Properties, Inc., 724 F.2d 907, 910 (11th Cir.1984), the corporation in question "was formed as a passive investment vehicle in order to invest funds in United States real estate." The corporation was not involved in the day-to-day operation of the Florida commercial real estate; it had no employees in Florida; and its corporate books and records were in Ecuador. Applying a jurisdictional test that incorporated elements of both the nerve center and place of operations tests, the Eleventh Circuit found the corporation's principal place of business to be Ecuador, and not Florida. We agree with the reasoning of cases like *Vareka* and hold that C.F. Trust's principal place of business is Florida. Accordingly, the diversity of citizenship between the parties was complete and [federal jurisdiction] was proper.

Notes

1. **The General Matter of Corporate Citizenship for Purposes of Diversity Jurisdiction.** In Bank of the United States v. Deveaux, 9 U.S. (5 Cranch) 61 (1809), Chief Justice Marshall held that a corporation, as an "invisible, intangible, and artificial being," retained the citizenship of all of its stockholders. In Louisville, Cincinnati & Charleston Railroad Co. v. Letson, 43 U.S. (2 How.) 497 (1844), the Supreme Court overruled *Deveaux* by holding: "A corporation created by a state to perform its functions under the authority of that state and only suable there, though it may have members out of the state, seems to us to be a person, though an artificial one, inhabiting and belonging to that state, and therefore entitled, for the purpose of suing and being sued, to be deemed a citizen of that state." Id. at 555. However, in Marshall v. Baltimore & Ohio Railroad Co., 57 U.S. (16 How.) 314 (1853), the Court modified its rationale for this doctrine. Relying on the assumption in Bank of Augusta v. Earle, 38 U.S. (13 Pet.) 519 (1839), that "a corporation can have no legal existence out of the boundaries of the sovereignty by which it is created," id. at 588, the Court imposed an irrebuttable presumption that all of the stockholders were citizens of the state of incorporation. In so reasoning, the Court brought its rationale, if not its rule, closer to the *Deveaux* principle. To this very day, then, a corporation is deemed a citizen of the state of its incorporation. In light of this presumption, should diversity jurisdiction *never* extend to a shareholder's derivative action? See Doctor v. Harrington, 196 U.S. 579 (1905).

2. How different do you think the "nerve center" and "place of activities" tests are? Does the difficulty in determining which test to use suggest that section 1332(c) should be altered in any way? Should a corporation be found to be a citizen of more than merely its state of incorporation and "principal place of business"? If so, how would you phrase the extension? Recall that many deem the primary justification for the diversity jurisdiction to be the avoidance of prejudice to out-of-staters. Of what relevance, if any, is this fact to your answer?

3. In Tosco Corp. v. Communities For a Better Environment, 236 F.3d 495 (9th Cir.2001), defendant sought to dismiss a tort suit because of a lack of diversity. Defendant alleged that plaintiff's principal place of business was California (which would destroy diversity) because California was plaintiff's "place of operations." Plaintiff, on the other hand, argued that Connecticut was its principal place of business under the "nerve center" test. In finding for defendant, the court reasoned:

> Federal courts generally use one of two tests to determine a corporation's principal place of business. First, the "place of operations test" locates a corporation's principal place of business in the state which "contains a substantial predominance of corporate operations.* * *" Second, the "nerve center test" locates a corporations's principal place of business in the state where the majority of its executive and administrative functions are performed.* * * The "nerve center" test should be used only when no state contains a substantial predominance of the corporation's business activities. Thus, the Ninth Circuit applies the

place of operations test unless the plaintiff shows that its activities do not substantially predominate in any one state.

Id. at 500.

4. Proposed section 1302(b) of the ALI's revision of the Judicial Code provides that "no corporation incorporated or having its principal place of business in the United States * * * that has and for a period of more than two years has maintained a local establishment in a State, can invoke [the diversity] jurisdiction, either originally or on removal, in any district in that State in any action arising out of the activities of that establishment." The term "local establishment" is defined to mean "a fixed place of business where or in connection with which, as a regular part of such business: (1) services are rendered or accommodations furnished to persons within the State; (2) sales, delivery, or distribution of goods are made to persons within the State by one regularly maintaining a stock of goods or a showroom for the display of samples within the State; (3) sales of insurance, securities, or other intangibles, or of real property or interests therein, are made to persons within the State; (4) production or processing takes place. Dealings carried on through an independent commission agent, broker, or custodian do not give rise to a local establishment."

"The provisions of this subsection shall apply only to entities organized or operated primarily for the purpose of conducting a trade, investment, or other business enterprise." In what way would the ALI's proposal alter the current rule about corporations? Is its proposal preferable?

5. **The Problem of Multiple Incorporation.** Certain corporations have traditionally been allowed to incorporate in more than one state. According to Professor Currie, "[t]o indulge in understatement, the Supreme Court's attempts to fit these creatures into the diversity scheme left something to be desired." Currie, *The Federal Courts and the American Law Institute, Part I*, 36 U.Chi.L.Rev. 1, 39 (1968). He suggests that in the nineteenth century, the Court "announced three mutually inconsistent rules without disowning any of them * * *." Id. at 40. The first was that a corporation chartered in two states was to be deemed a citizen of both, thus destroying complete diversity in a suit involving a citizen of either state. Next, the Court held such corporations to be citizens of only the forum state, if that state was one of its places of incorporation. Finally, the Court seemed to hold that a multi-state corporation was diverse to everyone. See generally Weckstein, *Multi-State Corporations and Diversity of Citizenship: A Field Day for Fictions*, 31 Tenn.L.Rev. 195 (1964). According to Professor Weckstein, the dominant rule, at least prior to the 1958 amendment, was the so-called "forum rule", the second test described by Professor Currie, though Weckstein acknowledges that "its acceptance has not come easy." Id. at 198. See Seavey v. Boston & Maine Railroad, 197 F.2d 485 (1st Cir.1952); Jacobson v. New York, New Haven & Hartford Railroad Co., 206 F.2d 153 (1st Cir.1953), affirmed per curiam, 347 U.S. 909, 74 S.Ct. 474, 98 L.Ed. 1067. But cf. Currie, supra, 36 U.Chi.L.Rev. at 41. Weckstein argues that "the 1958 Amendment to § 1332 has eliminated the pre-existing 'forum' doctrine, and makes a corporation a citizen of every state in which it has been freely and actually incorporated (as well as of the state where it has its principal place of business)." 31 Tenn.L.Rev. at 216. Professor Currie,

however, suggests the statute is "opaque" on the issue. 36 U.Chi.L.Rev. at 42. Does adoption of the 1958 amendment necessarily do away with the "forum" rule in the event of multiple incorporation? Professor Currie suggests that the "forum" rule "is defensible in terms of diversity policy." Id. Do you agree?

<h2 style="text-align:center">UNITED STEELWORKERS OF AMERICA,
AFL–CIO v. R. H. BOULIGNY, INC.</h2>

Supreme Court of the United States, 1965.
382 U.S. 145.

MR. JUSTICE FORTAS delivered the opinion of the Court.

Respondent, a North Carolina corporation, brought this action in a North Carolina state court. It sought $200,000 in damages for defamation alleged to have occurred during the course of the United Steelworkers' campaign to unionize respondent's employees. The Steelworkers, an unincorporated labor union whose principal place of business purportedly is Pennsylvania, removed the case to a Federal District Court. The union asserted not only federal-question jurisdiction, but that for purposes of the diversity jurisdiction it was a citizen of Pennsylvania, although some of its members were North Carolinians.

The corporation sought to have the case remanded to the state courts, contending that its complaint raised no federal questions and relying upon the generally prevailing principle that an unincorporated association's citizenship is that of each of its members. But the District Court retained jurisdiction. The District Judge noted "a trend to treat unincorporated associations in the same manner as corporations and to treat them as citizens of the state wherein the principal office is located." Divining "no common sense reason for treating an unincorporated national labor union differently from a corporation," he declined to follow what he styled "the poorer reasoned but more firmly established rule" of Chapman v. Barney, 129 U.S. 677.

On interlocutory appeal the Court of Appeals for the Fourth Circuit reversed and directed that the case be remanded to the state courts. Certiorari was granted, so that we might decide whether an unincorporated labor union is to be treated as a citizen for purposes of federal diversity jurisdiction, without regard to the citizenship of its members. Because we believe this properly a matter for legislative consideration which cannot adequately or appropriately be dealt with by this Court, we affirm the decision of the Court of Appeals.

Article III, § 2, of the Constitution provides:

> "The judicial Power shall extend ... to Controversies ... between Citizens of different States...."

Congress lost no time in implementing the grant. In 1789 it provided for federal jurisdiction in suits "between a citizen of the State where the suit is brought, and a citizen of another State." There shortly arose the question as to whether a corporation—a creature of state law—is to be deemed a "citizen" for purposes of the statute. This Court, through Chief Justice Marshall, initially responded in the negative, holding that a corporation was not a "citizen" and that it might sue and be sued under the diversity statute only if none of its shareholders was a co-citizen of any opposing party. Bank of the United States v. Deveaux, 5 Cranch 61. In 1844 the Court reversed itself and ruled that a corporation was to be treated as a citizen of the State which created it. Louisville, C. & C. R. Co. v. Letson, 2 How. 497. Ten years later, the Court reached the same result by a different approach. In a compromise destined to endure for over a century, the Court indulged in the fiction that, although a corporation was not itself a citizen for diversity purposes, its shareholders would conclusively be presumed citizens of the incorporating State. Marshall v. Baltimore & O. R. Co., 16 How. 314.

Congress re-entered the lists in 1875, significantly expanding diversity jurisdiction by deleting the requirement imposed in 1789 that one of the parties must be a citizen of the forum State. The resulting increase in the quantity of diversity litigation, however, cooled enthusiasts of the jurisdiction, and in 1887 and 1888 Congress enacted sharp curbs. It quadrupled the jurisdictional amount, confined the right of removal to nonresident defendants, reinstituted protections against jurisdiction by collusive assignment, and narrowed venue.

It was in this climate that the Court in 1889 decided Chapman v. Barney, supra. On its own motion the Court observed that plaintiff was a joint stock company and not a corporation or natural person. It held that although plaintiff was endowed by New York with capacity to sue, it could not be considered a "citizen" for diversity purposes. 129 U.S., at 682.

In recent years courts and commentators have reflected dissatisfaction with the rule of Chapman v. Barney. The distinction between the "personality" and "citizenship" of corporations and that of labor unions and other unincorporated associations, it is increasingly argued, has become artificial and unreal. The mere fact that a corporation is endowed with a birth certificate is, they say, of no consequence. In truth and in fact, they point out, many voluntary associations and labor unions are indistinguishable from corporations in terms of the reality of function and structure, and to say that the latter are juridical persons and "citizens" and the former are not is to base a distinction upon an inadequate and irrelevant difference. They assert, with considerable merit, that it is not good judicial administration, nor is it fair, to remit a labor union or other unincorporated association to vagaries of jurisdiction determined by the citizenship of its members and to disregard the fact that unions and associations may exist and have an identity and a local habitation of their own.

The force of these arguments in relation to the diversity jurisdiction is particularized by petitioner's showing in this case. Petitioner argues that one of the purposes underlying the jurisdiction—protection of the nonresident litigant from local prejudice—is especially applicable to the modern labor union. According to the argument, when the nonresident defendant is a major union, local juries may be tempted to favor local interests at its expense. Juries may also be influenced by the fear that unionization would adversely affect the economy of the community and its customs and practices in the field of race relations. In support of these contentions, petitioner has exhibited material showing that during organizational campaigns like that involved in this case, localities have been saturated with propaganda concerning such economic and racial fears. Extending diversity jurisdiction to unions, says petitioner, would make available the advantages of federal procedure, Article III judges less exposed to local pressures than their state court counterparts, juries selected from wider geographical areas, review in appellate courts reflecting a multistate perspective, and more effective review by this Court.

juries might fear union

We are of the view that these arguments, however appealing, are addressed to an inappropriate forum, and that pleas for extension of the diversity jurisdiction to hitherto uncovered broad categories of litigants ought to be made to the Congress and not to the courts.

these pleas are appealing but should be made to Congr

Petitioner urges that in Puerto Rico v. Russell & Co., 288 U.S. 476, we have heretofore breached the doctrinal wall of Chapman v. Barney and, that step having been taken, there is now no necessity for enlisting the assistance of Congress. But *Russell* does not furnish the precedent which petitioner seeks. The problem which it presented was that of fitting an exotic creation of the civil law, the *sociedad en comandita*, into a federal scheme which knew it not. The Organic Act of Puerto Rico conferred jurisdiction upon the federal court if all the parties on either side of a controversy were citizens of a foreign state or "citizens of a State, Territory or District of the United States not domiciled in Puerto Rico." All of the *sociedad's* members were nonresidents of Puerto Rico, and jurisdiction lay in the federal court if they were the "parties" to the action. But this Court held that the *sociedad* itself, not its members, was the party, doing so on a basis that is of no help to petitioner. It did so because, as Justice Stone stated for the Court, in "[t]he tradition of the civil law, as expressed in the Code of Puerto Rico," "the *sociedad* is consistently regarded as a juridical person." 288 U.S., at 480–481. Accordingly, the Court held that the *sociedad*, Russell & Co., was a citizen domiciled in Puerto Rico, within the meaning of the Organic Act, and ordered the case remanded to the insular courts. It should be noted that the effect of *Russell* was to contract jurisdiction of the federal court in Puerto Rico.[10]

* * *

10. As the Court noted in *Russell*, 288 U.S., at 482, the effect of its decision was to prevent nonresidents from organizing *sociedads* to carry on business in Puerto Rico and then "remove from the Insular Courts controversies arising under local law." The Court of Appeals for the Second Circuit in *Mason*, 334 F.2d, at 397, n. 8, seems to assert that *Russell* had the effect of broad- ening the diversity jurisdiction. We do not agree. At the time *Russell* was decided, Puerto Rico was not considered a "State" for purposes of the federal diversity jurisdiction statute. Accordingly, a *sociedad*, although recognized as a citizen of Puerto Rico in *Russell*, could not avail itself of the general diversity statute.

Whether unincorporated labor unions ought to be assimilated to the status of corporations for diversity purposes, how such citizenship is to be determined, and what if any related rules ought to apply, are decisions which we believe suited to the legislative and not the judicial branch, regardless of our views as to the intrinsic merits of petitioner's argument—merits stoutly attested by widespread support for the recognition of labor unions as juridical personalities.

We affirm the decision below.

e agree but defer

Notes

1. Why are there likely to be a smaller number of diversity cases involving associations heard in federal court under the *Chapman* rule than under a rule that the citizenship of an association is determined by, for example, the location of its principal place of business? *members from many states*

2. Do you agree with the Court that the arguments here favoring a change in the diversity rule regarding associations "are addressed to an inappropriate forum"? Would it have violated congressional intent for the Court to have redefined the "citizenship" of associations? Would it have done so any more than do the decisions limiting the reach of diversity jurisdiction to matters involving probate or domestic relations [infra pp. 803–13]?

3. Does the Court adequately distinguish Puerto Rico v. Russell & Co.? Cf. Brocki v. American Express Co., 279 F.2d 785 (6th Cir.), certiorari denied 364 U.S. 871 (1960).

4. The Court suggests that it would be difficult for it to devise a general rule to determine the citizenship of associations. Do you agree?

5. Does the holding in *Bouligny* make sense as a policy matter? Cf. Consumers Savings Bank v. Touche Ross & Co., 613 F.Supp. 249, 252 (D.Mass.1985), commenting on application of the holding to multi-state partnerships:

> It may not be illogical to contend that, as a matter of policy, a large, multi-state general partnership should be treated like a corporation or an express trust for diversity purposes. Since 1789, diversity jurisdiction has existed to protect non-resident litigants from local prejudice and perceived professional inferiority of state courts. Corporations receive the benefit of access to the federal courts on the basis of diversity jurisdiction in all but one or two states. 28 U.S.C. § 1332(c). Yet the present rule concerning unincorporated associations may exclude a large, multi-state partnership * * * from receiving the benefit of diversity jurisdiction in virtually every state.

Can the Court's decision be properly justified on the simple grounds that the need for diversity jurisdiction is questionable and that while a repeal of diversity requires congressional action, the Court should do nothing that would in any way extend diversity's reach?

6. Rule 23.2 of the Federal Rules of Civil Procedure provides in part:

An action brought by or against the members of an unincorporated association as a class by naming certain members as representative parties may be maintained only if it appears that the representative parties will fairly and adequately protect the interests of the association and its members.

What impact, if any, should this Rule have on the *Chapman* rule? Note that even if suing in the association's name does not avoid the barrier of the *Chapman* rule, a class action under Rule 23, with one of the members of the association as the named plaintiff, might have that result. This is because of the ancillary jurisdiction doctrine of Supreme Tribe of Ben–Hur v. Cauble, 255 U.S. 356 (1921), which looks only to the citizenship of the representative party in determining whether diversity is present. See Chapter Fifteen. Nevertheless, it may not always be that easy to meet all of the requirements of Rule 23 to qualify as a class action.

7. Navarro Savings Association v. Lee, 446 U.S. 458 (1980): The Supreme Court held that individual trustees of a business trust may invoke the diversity jurisdiction on the basis of their own citizenship, without regard to the citizenship of the trust beneficiaries. The Court did not accept the argument that the "trust form masks an unincorporated association of individual[s] * * * ", even though it was contended "that certain features of the trust's operations also characterize the operations of an association: centralized management, continuity of enterprise, and unlimited duration." 446 U.S. at 461. "We need not reject the argument that [the trust] shares some attributes of an association. In certain respects, a business trust also resembles a corporation * * *. [T]he question is whether [the trust's] trustees are real parties to this controversy for purposes of a federal court's diversity jurisdiction." Id. at 462. The Court concluded that the trustees were real parties in interest, noting that "[t]here is no allegation of sham or collusion." Id. at 465.

Justice Blackmun dissented:

I am particularly troubled by the Court's intimation that business trusts are to be treated differently from other functionally analogous business associations—partnerships, limited partnerships, joint stock companies, and the like. I fear that, at bottom, the Court's distinction between business trusts and these other enterprises hinges on the laws of title to the trust assets, * * * a formalistic criterion having little to do with a realistic assessment of the respective degrees of control over the trust's activities that may be exercised by shareholders and trustees.

Id. at 475–476.

Justice Blackmun concluded that the citizenship of the trust should be determined according to the citizenship of the beneficiaries, because of "the pervasive measure of control that * * * shareholders possess over the trustees' actions taken in their behalf." Id. at 476.

8. In Carden v. Arkoma Associates, 494 U.S. 185 (1990) the Court held that the citizenship of all partners in a limited partnership, rather than only the citizenship of the general partners or the state where the partnership is created, governs the determination of citizenship for jurisdictional purposes. Writing for the Court, Justice Scalia explained:

[T]he course we take today does not so much disregard the policy of accommodating our diversity jurisdiction to the changing realities of commercial organization, as it honors the more important policy leaving that to the people's elected representatives. Such accommodation is not only performed more legitimately by Congress than by courts, but it is performed more intelligently by legislation than by interpretation of the statutory word "citizen."

Id. at 197.

§ 3. DETERMINATION OF DOMICILE

STINE v. MOORE

United States Court of Appeals, Fifth Circuit, 1954.
213 F.2d 446.

HOLMES, CIRCUIT JUDGE.

This is an action for damages for the alleged breach of a contract with reference to the rental of land. The amount involved exceeds three thousand dollars, exclusive of interest and costs, and federal jurisdiction is based solely upon diversity of citizenship between the parties. The complaint alleged that the plaintiff was a citizen of Louisiana, residing in the Lake Charles division of the Western District thereof, and that the defendant was a citizen and resident of Texas. The defendant, appearing in person and by attorney, moved to dismiss the action for lack of the requisite diversity of citizenship. Contrary to the allegations of plaintiff's complaint, the defendant alleged that he was a citizen of Louisiana and resided in the same parish in which the plaintiff had his domicile.

The issue as to the defendant's citizenship being joined and trial had thereon, the court below sustained the motion to dismiss and entered judgment accordingly, from which this appeal was taken. There was ample evidence to sustain the court's finding that the defendant was a citizen of Louisiana. In addition, the court wrote an opinion on the law of the case that needs no elaboration on our part. We fully concur both in its findings of fact and conclusions of law, which in substance were as follows:

> The burden of proving diversity jurisdiction, when challenged, is upon the plaintiff; but when it is shown, as in this case, that the appellant had a former domicile in Texas, the presumption is that it continues to exist, and the burden shifts to the defendant to prove that it has changed. It is not disputed that, until the year 1947, following his marriage in 1946, the defendant resided and had his domicile in Orange, Texas. Since then he has done many things which, on their face, tend to support the conclusion that he intended to retain his domicile in Texas, such as paying poll taxes and voting in that state, making returns and paying Louisiana income taxes as a non-resident, maintaining a residence and post-office box through which he received some of his mail at his former address in Orange, Texas, and making his federal income-tax returns from that address.

Nevertheless, he did move to Louisiana with the bona fide intention of remaining there permanently, which is the true test; and he has, beyond question, continued to live at Gum Cove plantation in Cameron Parish, Louisiana, since moving there in 1947. He and his wife both testified that they made this change on the advice of appellant's doctor, and expect to continue there "from now on out." The house in Orange, which he still owns, is occupied by his mother and sisters, though a room or accommodations therein are kept for his use when he returns to visit in that city.

If the appellant made the change of residence from Texas to Louisiana with the bona fide intention of making Louisiana his home and living there permanently, then his domicile and citizenship were changed from Texas to Louisiana. Bouvier defines domicile as that place where a man has his true, fixed, and permanent home and principal establishment, and to which he has the intention of returning whenever he is absent therefrom, citing numerous authorities including one from Texas and one from Louisiana. Bouv.Law Dict. Rawle's Third Revision, p. 915. Many people think that they can have their permanent home and live indefinitely in one state, yet retain their citizenship and right to vote in another; but this is a very questionable idea if put to the test in any particular case. Cf. Hall v. Godchaux, 149 La. 734, 90 So. 145, and authorities therein cited.

With respect to the diversity jurisdiction of the federal courts, citizenship has the same meaning as domicile. It imports permanent residence in a particular state with the intention of remaining, and is not dependent on birth. Residence alone is not the equivalent of citizenship, although the place of residence is prima facie the domicile; and citizenship is not necessarily lost by protracted absence from home, where the intention to return remains. Mere mental fixing of citizenship is not sufficient. What is in another man's mind must be determined by what he does as well as by what he says. 35 C.J.S., Federal Courts, § 56.

Residence in fact, and the intention of making the place of residence one's home, are essential elements of domicile. Words may be evidence of a man's intention to establish his domicile at a particular place of residence, but they cannot supply the fact of his domicile there. In such circumstances, the actual fact of residence and a real intention of remaining there, as disclosed by his entire course of conduct, are the controlling factors in ascertaining his domicile. As stated by Mr. Justice Stone: "When one intends the facts to which the law attaches consequences, he must abide the consequences whether intended or not." State of Texas v. Florida, 306 U.S. 398, 425.

Any person, *sui juris*, may make a bona fide change of domicile at any time, and we agree with the court below that the appellant had both the residence in fact and the purpose to make Louisiana his home in 1947, which constituted a change of his domicile from Texas to Louisiana. Accordingly, the judgment appealed from should be affirmed.

Affirmed.

Notes

1. If a litigant's domicile is in dispute, what sorts of objective criteria should be considered in making that determination? What arguably relevant criteria do you believe should not be considered? For other cases determining domicile in difficult contexts, see Sheehan v. Gustafson, 967 F.2d 1214 (8th Cir.1992); Lundquist v. Precision Valley Aviation, Inc., 946 F.2d 8 (1st Cir.1991). See generally Note, *Evidentiary Factors in the Determination of Domicile*, 61 Harv.L.Rev. 1232 (1948).

2. In a case that is removed to federal court where jurisdiction is based on diversity of citizenship, should the relevant point for measuring the litigants' domicile be the date the case was filed originally in state court, the date the case was removed to federal court, or both? See, e.g., Koenigsberger v. Richmond Silver Mining Co., 158 U.S. 41 (1895).

3. Should changes in domicile after the case is placed in federal court be deemed relevant? See Smith v. Sperling, 354 U.S. 91, 93 n. 1 (1957): "[J]urisdiction, once attached, is not impaired by a party's later change of domicile." Why do you think this is the rule? The Court recently reaffirmed the rule that a change of domicile that takes place after filing does not affect a court's jurisdiction. In Grupo Dataflux v. Atlas Global Group, L.P., 541 U.S. 567 (2004), a Texas partnership that included some Mexican partners sued a Mexican corporation in federal court on state law causes of action. No one noticed the jurisdictional difficulty, and the case proceeded towards trial. Before the trial began, the Mexican partners left the partnership (in a transaction unrelated to the ongoing lawsuit). After trial, but before entry of judgment, the defendant filed a motion to dismiss on the ground that there had not been complete diversity at the time of filing. Although the district court granted the motion, the Court of Appeals reversed, holding that under Caterpillar Inc. v. Lewis, 519 U.S. 61 (1996) [infra p. 876], a defect in jurisdiction that is unnoticed before judgment but remedied before the trial begins does not deprive the federal court of jurisdiction. The Supreme Court reversed the Court of Appeals, distinguishing *Caterpillar* on the ground that it had involved the *dismissal* of the diversity-destroying party, while *Grupo Dataflux* involved *change in domicile* of one of the parties. Should that make such a significant difference? See Simpson–Wood, *Has the Seductive Siren of Judicial Frugality Ceased to Sing?: Dataflux and its Family Tree*, 53 Drake L.Rev. 281 (2005).

4. In Newman–Green, Inc. v. Alfonzo–Larrain, 490 U.S. 826 (1989) the Supreme Court held that a United States citizen who is not domiciled in any state has no citizenship for purposes of section 1332.

5. Given the difficulties that may occur in determining domicile, why not simply accept the litigants' representations on the question, unless that representation is unquestionably contradicted by the facts?

§ 4. JUDICIALLY IMPOSED LIMITS ON THE EXERCISE OF DIVERSITY JURISDICTION

MARSHALL v. MARSHALL

Supreme Court of the United States, 2006.
547 U.S. ___, 126 S.Ct. 1735.

JUSTICE GINSBURG delivered the opinion of the Court.

In *Cohens v. Virginia,* Chief Justice Marshall famously cautioned: "It is most true that this Court will not take jurisdiction if it should not: but it is equally true, that it must take jurisdiction, if it should.... We have no more right to decline the exercise of jurisdiction which is given, than to usurp that which is not given." 6 Wheat. 264, 404 (1821). Among longstanding limitations on federal jurisdiction otherwise properly exercised are the so-called "domestic relations" and "probate" exceptions. Neither is compelled by the text of the Constitution or federal statute. Both are judicially created doctrines stemming in large measure from misty understandings of English legal history. See, *e.g.,* Atwood, Domestic Relations Cases in Federal Court: Toward a Principled Exercise of Jurisdiction, 35 Hastings L.J. 571, 584–588 (1984); *Spindel v. Spindel,* 283 F.Supp. 797, 802 (E.D.N.Y.1968) (collecting cases and commentary revealing vulnerability of historical explanation for domestic relations exception); Winkler, The Probate Jurisdiction of the Federal Courts, 14 Probate L.J. 77, 125–126, and n. 256 (1997) (describing historical explanation for probate exception as "an exercise in mythography"). In the years following Marshall's 1821 pronouncement, courts have sometimes lost sight of his admonition and have rendered decisions expansively interpreting the two exceptions. In *Ankenbrandt v. Richards,* 504 U.S. 689 (1992), this Court reined in the "domestic relations exception." Earlier, in *Markham v. Allen,* 326 U.S. 490 (1946), the Court endeavored similarly to curtail the "probate exception."

Nevertheless, the Ninth Circuit in the instant case read the probate exception broadly to exclude from the federal courts' adjudicatory authority "not only direct challenges to a will or trust, but also questions which would ordinarily be decided by a probate court in determining the validity of the decedent's estate planning instrument." 392 F.3d 1118, 1133 (C.A.9 2004). The Court of Appeals further held that a State's vesting of exclusive jurisdiction over probate matters in a special court strips federal courts of jurisdiction to entertain any "probate related matter," including claims respecting "tax liability, debt, gift, [or] tort." *Id.,* at 1136. We hold that the Ninth Circuit had no warrant from Congress, or from decisions of this Court, for its sweeping extension of the probate exception.

I

Petitioner, Vickie Lynn Marshall (Vickie), also known as Anna Nicole Smith, is the surviving widow of J. Howard Marshall II (J. Howard). Vickie and J. Howard met in October 1991. After a courtship lasting more than two years, they were married on June 27, 1994. J. Howard died on August 4, 1995. Although he lavished gifts and significant sums of money on Vickie during their courtship and marriage, J. Howard did not include anything for Vickie in his will. According to Vickie, J. Howard intended to provide for her financial security through a gift in the form of a "catch-all" trust.

Respondent, E. Pierce Marshall (Pierce), one of J. Howard's sons, was the ultimate beneficiary of J. Howard's estate plan, which consisted of a living trust and a "pourover" will. Under the terms of the will, all of J. Howard's assets not already included in the trust were to be transferred to the trust upon his death.

Competing claims regarding J. Howard's fortune ignited proceedings in both state and federal courts. In January 1996, while J. Howard's estate was subject to ongoing proceedings in Probate Court in Harris County, Texas, Vickie filed for bankruptcy under Chapter 11 of the Bankruptcy Code, 11 U.S.C. § 1101 *et seq.,* in the United States Bankruptcy Court for the Central District of California. * * * In June 1996, Pierce filed a proof of claim in the federal bankruptcy proceeding, * * * alleging that Vickie had defamed him when, shortly after J. Howard's death, lawyers representing Vickie told members of the press that Pierce had engaged in forgery, fraud, and overreaching to gain control of his father's assets. * * * Pierce sought a declaration that the debt he asserted in that claim was not dischargeable in bankruptcy. * * * Vickie answered, asserting truth as a defense. She also filed counterclaims, among them a claim that Pierce had tortiously interfered with a gift she expected. * * * Vickie alleged that Pierce prevented the transfer of his father's intended gift to her by, among other things: effectively imprisoning J. Howard against his wishes; surrounding him with hired guards for the purpose of preventing personal contact between him and Vickie; making misrepresentations to J. Howard; and transferring property against J. Howard's expressed wishes. * * *

Vickie's tortious interference counterclaim turned her objection to Pierce's claim into an adversary proceeding. * * * In that proceeding, the Bankruptcy Court granted summary judgment in favor of Vickie on Pierce's claim and, after a trial on the merits, entered judgment for Vickie on her tortious interference counterclaim. * * * The court awarded Vickie compensatory damages of more than $449 million–less whatever she recovered in the ongoing probate action in Texas–as well as $25 million in punitive damages. * * *

Pierce filed a post-trial motion to dismiss for lack of subject-matter jurisdiction, asserting that Vickie's tortious interference claim could be tried only in the Texas probate proceedings. * * * Relying on this Court's decision in *Markham,* the [bankruptcy] court observed that a federal court has jurisdiction to "adjudicate rights in probate property, so long as its final judgment does not undertake to interfere with the state court's possession of the property." * * *

* * *

Adopting and supplementing the Bankruptcy Court's findings, the District Court determined that Pierce had tortiously interfered with Vickie's expectancy. Specifically, the District Court found that J. Howard directed his lawyers to prepare an *inter vivos* trust for Vickie consisting of half the appreciation of his assets from the date of their marriage. * * * It further found that Pierce conspired to suppress or destroy the trust instrument and to strip J. Howard of his assets by backdating, altering, and otherwise falsifying documents, arranging for surveillance of J. Howard and Vickie, and presenting documents to J. Howard under false pretenses. * * * Based on these findings, the District Court awarded Vickie some $44.3 million in compensatory damages. * * * In addition, finding "overwhelming" evidence of Pierce's "willfulness, maliciousness, and fraud," the District Court awarded an equal amount in punitive damages. * * *

The Court of Appeals for the Ninth Circuit reversed. The appeals court recognized that Vickie's claim "does not involve the administration of an estate, the probate of a will, or any other purely probate matter." 392 F.3d, at 1133. Nevertheless, the court held that the probate exception bars federal jurisdiction in this case. In the Ninth Circuit's view, a claim falls within the probate exception if it raises "questions which would ordinarily be decided by a probate court in determining the validity of the decedent's estate planning instrument," whether those questions involve "fraud, undue influence [, or] tortious interference with the testator's intent." *Ibid.*

The Ninth Circuit was also of the view that state-court delineation of a probate court's exclusive adjudicatory authority could control federal subject-matter jurisdiction. In this regard, the Court of Appeals stated: "Where a state has relegated jurisdiction over probate matters to a special court and [the] state's trial courts of general jurisdiction do not have jurisdiction to hear probate matters, then federal courts also lack jurisdiction over probate matters." *Id.*, at 1136. Noting that "[t]he [P]robate [C]ourt ruled it had exclusive jurisdiction over all of Vickie['s] claims," the Ninth Circuit held that "ruling ... binding on the United States [D]istrict [C]ourt." *Ibid.* (citing *Durfee v. Duke,* 375 U.S. 106, 115–116 (1963)).

We granted certiorari * * * to resolve the apparent confusion among federal courts concerning the scope of the probate exception. Satisfied that the instant case does not fall within the ambit of the narrow exception recognized by our decisions, we reverse the Ninth Circuit's judgment.

II

In *Ankenbrandt v. Richards,* 504 U.S. 689 (1992), we addressed both the derivation and the limits of the "domestic relations exception" to the exercise of federal jurisdiction. Carol Ankenbrandt, a citizen of Missouri, brought suit in Federal District Court on behalf of her daughters, naming as defendants their father (Ankenbrandt's former husband) and his female companion, both citizens of Louisiana. *Id.*, at 691. Ankenbrandt's complaint sought damages for the defendants' alleged sexual and physical abuse of the children. *Ibid.* Federal jurisdiction was predicated on diversity of citizenship. *Ibid.* (citing 28 U.S.C. § 1332). The District Court dismissed the case for lack of subject-matter jurisdiction, holding that Ankenbrandt's suit fell within "the 'domestic relations' exception to diversity jurisdiction." 504 U.S., at 692. The Court of Appeals agreed and affirmed. *Ibid.* We reversed the Court of Appeals' judgment. *Id.*, at 706–707.

Holding that the District Court improperly refrained from exercising jurisdiction over Ankenbrandt's tort claim, *id.*, at 704, we traced explanation of the current domestic relations exception to *Barber v. Barber,* 21 How. 582 (1859). See *Ankenbrandt,* 504 U.S., at 693–695. In *Barber,* the Court upheld federal-court authority, in a diversity case, to enforce an alimony award decreed by a state court. In dicta, however, the *Barber* Court announced–without citation or discussion–that federal courts lack jurisdiction over suits for divorce or the allowance of alimony. 21 How., at 584–589; see *Ankenbrandt,* 504 U.S., at 693–695.

Finding no Article III impediment to federal-court jurisdiction in domestic relations cases, *id.*, at 695–697, the Court in *Ankenbrandt* anchored the exception in Congress' original provision for diversity jurisdiction, *id.*, at 698–701. Beginning at the beginning, the Court recalled:

> "The Judiciary Act of 1789 provided that 'the circuit courts shall have original cognizance, concurrent with the courts of the several States, of *all suits of a civil nature at common law or in equity, where the matter in dispute exceeds,* exclusive of costs, the sum or value of *five hundred dollars,* and ... an alien is a party, or the suit is *between a citizen of the State where the suit is brought, and a citizen of another State.*' " *Id.*, at 698 (quoting Act of Sept. 24, 1789, § 11, 1 Stat. 78; emphasis added in *Ankenbrandt*).

The defining phrase, "all suits of a civil nature at common law or in equity," the Court stressed, remained in successive statutory provisions for diversity jurisdiction until 1948, when Congress adopted the more economical phrase, "all civil actions." 504 U.S., at 698,; 1948 Judicial Code and Judiciary Act, 62 Stat. 930, 28 U.S.C. § 1332.

The *Barber* majority, we acknowledged in *Ankenbrandt,* did not expressly tie its announcement of a domestic relations exception to the text of the diversity statute. 504 U.S., at 698. But the dissenters in that case made the connection. They stated that English courts of chancery lacked authority to issue divorce and alimony decrees. Because "the jurisdiction of the courts of the United States in chancery is bounded by that of the chancery in England," *Barber,* 21 How., at 605 (opinion of Daniel, J.), the dissenters reasoned, our federal courts similarly lack authority to decree divorces or award alimony, *ibid.* Such relief, in other words, would not fall within the diversity statute's original grant of jurisdiction over "all suits of a civil nature at common law or in equity." We concluded in *Ankenbrandt* that "it may be inferred fairly that the jurisdictional limitation recognized by the *[Barber]* Court rested on th[e] statutory basis" indicated by the dissenters in that case. 504 U.S., at 699.

We were "content" in *Ankenbrandt* "to rest our conclusion that a domestic relations exception exists as a matter of statutory construction not on the accuracy of the historical justifications on which [the exception] was seemingly based." *Id.,* at 700. "[R]ather," we relied on "Congress' apparent acceptance of this construction of the diversity jurisdiction provisions in the years prior to 1948, when the statute limited jurisdiction to 'suits of a civil nature at common law or in equity.' " *Ibid.* * * * We further determined that Congress did not intend to terminate the exception in 1948 when it "replace[d] the law/equity distinction with the phrase 'all civil actions.' " 504 U.S., at 700. Absent contrary indications, we presumed that Congress meant to leave undisturbed "the Court's nearly century-long interpretation" of the diversity statute "to contain an exception for certain domestic relations matters." *Ibid.*

We nevertheless emphasized in *Ankenbrandt* that the exception covers only "a narrow range of domestic relations issues." *Id.,* at 701. The *Barber* Court itself, we reminded, "sanctioned the exercise of federal jurisdiction over the enforcement of an alimony decree that had been properly obtained in a state court of competent jurisdiction." 504 U.S., at 702. Noting that some lower federal courts had applied the domestic relations exception "well beyond the circumscribed situations posed by *Barber* and its progeny," *id.,* at 701, we clarified that only "divorce, alimony, and child custody decrees" remain outside federal jurisdictional bounds, *id.,* at 703, 704. While recognizing the "special proficiency developed by state tribunals ... in handling issues that arise in the granting of [divorce, alimony, and child custody] decrees," *id.,* at 704, we viewed federal courts as equally equipped to deal with complaints alleging the commission of torts, *ibid.*

III

Federal jurisdiction in this case is premised on 28 U.S.C. § 1334, the statute vesting in federal district courts jurisdiction in bankruptcy cases and related proceedings. Decisions of this Court have recognized a "probate exception," kin to the domestic relations exception, to otherwise proper federal jurisdiction. See *Markham v. Allen,* 326 U.S., at 494; see also *Sutton v. English,* 246 U.S. 199 (1918); *Waterman v. Canal–Louisiana Bank & Trust Co.,* 215 U.S. 33 (1909). Like the domestic relations exception, the probate exception has been linked to language contained in the Judiciary Act of 1789.

Markham, the Court's most recent and pathmarking pronouncement on the probate exception, stated that "the equity jurisdiction conferred by the Judiciary Act of 1789 ..., which is that of the English Court of Chancery in 1789, did not extend to probate matters." 326 U.S., at 494. See generally Nicolas, Fighting the Probate Mafia: A Dissection of the Probate Exception to Federal Jurisdiction, 74 S. Cal. L.Rev. 1479 (2001). As in *Ankenbrandt,* so in this case, "[w]e have no occasion . . . to join the historical debate" over the scope of English chancery jurisdiction in 1789, 504 U.S., at 699, for Vickie Marshall's claim falls far outside the bounds of the probate exception described in *Markham*. We therefore need not consider in this case whether there exists any uncodified probate exception to federal bankruptcy jurisdiction under § 1334.

In *Markham,* the plaintiff Alien Property Custodian[4] commenced suit in Federal District Court against an executor and resident heirs to determine the Custodian's asserted rights regarding a decedent's estate. 326 U.S., at 491–492. Jurisdiction was predicated on § 24(1) of the Judicial Code, now 28 U.S.C. § 1345, which provides for federal jurisdiction over suits brought by an officer of the United States. At the time the federal suit commenced, the estate was undergoing probate administration in a state court. The Custodian had issued an order vesting in himself all right, title, and interest of German legatees. He sought and gained in the District Court a judgment determining that the resident heirs had no interest in the estate, and that the Custodian, substituting himself for the German legatees, was entitled to the entire net estate, including specified real estate passing under the will.

Reversing the Ninth Circuit, which had ordered the case dismissed for want of federal subject-matter jurisdiction, this Court held that federal jurisdiction was properly invoked. The Court first stated:

> "It is true that a federal court has no jurisdiction to probate a will or administer an estate. . . . But it has been established by a long series of decisions of this Court that federal courts of equity have jurisdiction to entertain suits 'in favor of creditors, legatees and heirs' and other claimants against a decedent's estate 'to establish their claims' so long as the federal court does not interfere with the probate proceedings or assume general jurisdiction of the probate or control of the property in the custody of the state court." 326 U.S., at 494 (quoting *Waterman,* 215 U.S., at 43).

Next, the Court described a probate exception of distinctly limited scope:

> "[W]hile a federal court may not exercise its jurisdiction to disturb or affect the possession of property in the custody of a state court, . . . it may exercise its jurisdiction to adjudicate rights in such property where the final judgment does not undertake to interfere

---

4. Section 6 of the Trading with the Enemy Act, 40 Stat. 415, 50 U.S.C.App., authorizes the President to appoint an official known as the "alien property custodian," who is responsible for "receiv[ing,] . . . hold [ing], administer[ing], and account[ing] for" "all money and property in the United States due or belonging to an enemy, or ally of enemy. . . ." The Act was originally enacted during World War I "to permit, under careful safeguards and restrictions, certain kinds of business to be carried on" among warring nations, and to "provid[e] for the care and administration of the property and property rights of enemies and their allies in this country pending the war." *Markham v. Cabell,* 326 U.S. 404, 414, n. 1 (1945) (Burton, J., concurring) (quoting S.Rep. No. 113, 65th Cong., 1st Sess., p. 1 (1917)).

[handwritten margin note: Markham — fed Ct can make determinations so long as doa not disturb the]

with the state court's possession save to the extent that the state court is bound by the judgment to recognize the right adjudicated by the federal court." 326 U.S., at 494.

The first of the above-quoted passages from *Markham* is not a model of clear statement. The Court observed that federal courts have jurisdiction to entertain suits to determine the rights of creditors, legatees, heirs, and other claimants against a decedent's estate, "so long as the federal court does not *interfere with the probate proceedings.*" *Ibid.* (emphasis added). Lower federal courts have puzzled over the meaning of the words "interfere with the probate proceedings," and some have read those words to block federal jurisdiction over a range of matters well beyond probate of a will or administration of a decedent's estate. * * *

We read *Markham*'s enigmatic words, in sync with the second above-quoted passage, to proscribe "disturb[ing] or affect[ing] the possession of property in the custody of a state court." 326 U.S., at 494. True, that reading renders the first-quoted passage in part redundant, but redundancy in this context, we do not doubt, is preferable to incoherence. In short, we comprehend the "interference" language in *Markham* as essentially a reiteration of the general principle that, when one court is exercising *in rem* jurisdiction over a *res*, a second court will not assume *in rem* jurisdiction over the same *res*. * * * Thus, the probate exception reserves to state probate courts the probate or annulment of a will and the administration of a decedent's estate; it also precludes federal courts from endeavoring to dispose of property that is in the custody of a state probate court. But it does not bar federal courts from adjudicating matters outside those confines and otherwise within federal jurisdiction.

A

As the Court of Appeals correctly observed, Vickie's claim does not "involve the administration of an estate, the probate of a will, or any other purely probate matter." 392 F.3d, at 1133. Provoked by Pierce's claim in the bankruptcy proceedings, Vickie's claim, like Carol Ankenbrandt's, alleges a widely recognized tort. See *King v. Acker,* 725 S.W.2d 750, 754 (Tex.App.1987); Restatement (Second) of Torts § 774B (1979) ("One who by fraud, duress or other tortious means intentionally prevents another from receiving from a third person an inheritance or gift that [s]he would otherwise have received is subject to liability to the other for loss of the inheritance or gift."). Vickie seeks an *in personam* judgment against Pierce, not the probate or annulment of a will. Cf. *Sutton,* 246 U.S., at 208 (suit to annul a will found "supplemental to the proceedings for probate of the will" and therefore not cognizable in federal court). Nor does she seek to reach a *res* in the custody of a state court. See *Markham,* 326 U.S., at 494.

Furthermore, no "sound policy considerations" militate in favor of extending the probate exception to cover the case at hand. Cf. *Ankenbrandt,* 504 U.S., at 703. Trial courts, both federal and state, often address conduct of the kind Vickie alleges. State probate courts possess no "special proficiency ... in handling [such] issues." Cf. *id.*, at 704.

B

The Court of Appeals advanced an alternate basis for its conclusion that the federal courts lack jurisdiction over Vickie's claim. Noting that the Texas Probate Court "ruled it had exclusive jurisdiction over all of Vickie Lynn Marshall's claims against E. Pierce Marshall," the Ninth Circuit held that "ruling ... binding on the United States [D]istrict [C]ourt." 392 F.3d, at 1136. We reject that determination.

Texas courts have recognized a state-law tort action for interference with an expected inheritance or gift, modeled on the Restatement formulation. * * * [5] It is clear, under *Erie R. Co. v. Tompkins,* 304 U.S. 64 (1938), that Texas law governs the substantive elements of Vickie's tortious interference claim. It is also clear, however, that Texas may not reserve to its probate courts the exclusive right to adjudicate a transitory tort. We have long recognized that "a State cannot create a transitory cause of action and at the same time destroy the right to sue on that transitory cause of action in any court having jurisdiction." *Tennessee Coal, Iron & R. Co. v. George,* 233 U.S. 354 (1914). Jurisdiction is determined "by the law of the court's creation and cannot be defeated by the extraterritorial operation of a [state] statute ..., even though it created the right of action." *Ibid.* Directly on point, we have held that the jurisdiction of the federal courts, "having existed from the beginning of the Federal government, [can] not be impaired by subsequent state legislation creating courts of probate." *McClellan v. Carland,* 217 U.S. 268, 281 (1910) (upholding federal jurisdiction over action by heirs of decedent, who died intestate, to determine their rights in the estate (citing *Waterman,* 215 U.S. 33)).

Our decision in *Durfee v. Duke,* 375 U.S. 106 (1963), relied upon by the Ninth Circuit, 392 F.3d, at 1136, is not to the contrary. *Durfee* stands only for the proposition that a state court's final judgment determining *its own* jurisdiction ordinarily qualifies for full faith and credit, so long as the jurisdictional issue was fully and fairly litigated in the court that rendered the judgment. See 375 U.S., at 111. At issue here, however, is not the Texas Probate Court's jurisdiction, but the federal courts' jurisdiction to entertain Vickie's tortious interference claim. Under our federal system, Texas cannot render its probate courts exclusively competent to entertain a claim of that genre. We therefore hold that the District Court properly asserted jurisdiction over Vickie's counterclaim against Pierce.

5. Pierce maintains that * * * Texas decisions support his contention that preclusion principles bar Vickie's claim. * * * Vickie argues to the contrary. * * * The matter of preclusion remains open for consideration on remand.

* * *

For the reasons stated, the judgment of the Court of Appeals for the Ninth Circuit is reversed, and the case is remanded for further proceedings consistent with this opinion.

It is so ordered.

JUSTICE STEVENS, concurring in part and concurring in the judgment.

The administration of decedents' estates typically is governed by rules of state law and conducted by state probate courts. Occasionally, however, disputes between interested parties arise, either in the probate proceeding itself or elsewhere, that qualify as cases or controversies that federal courts have jurisdiction to decide. * * * In her opinion for the Court, Justice GINSBURG has cogently explained why this is such a case. I write separately to explain why I do not believe there is any "probate exception" that ousts a federal court of jurisdiction it otherwise possesses.

The familiar aphorism that hard cases make bad law should extend to easy cases as well. *Markham v. Allen,* 326 U.S. 490, (1946), like this case, was an easy case. In *Markham,* as here, it was unnecessary to question the historical or logical underpinnings of the probate exception to federal jurisdiction because, whatever the scope of the supposed exception, it did not extend to the case at hand. But *Markham's* obiter dicta–dicta that the Court now describes as redundant if not incoherent– generated both confusion and abdication of the obligation Chief Justice Marshall so famously articulated, see *Cohens v. Virginia,* 6 Wheat. 264, 404 (1821). While the Court today rightly abandons much of that dicta, I would go further.

The Court is content to adopt the approach it followed in *Ankenbrandt v. Richards,* 504 U.S. 689 (1992), and to accept as foundation for the probate exception *Markham's* bald assertion that the English High Court of Chancery's jurisdiction did not "extend to probate matters" in 1789. 326 U.S., at 495. I would not accept that premise. Not only had the theory *Markham* espoused been only sporadically and tentatively cited as justification for the exception,[1] but the most comprehensive article on the subject has persuasively demonstrated that *Markham's* assertion is "an exercise in mythography."[2]

Markham's theory apparently is the source of the Court's reformulated exception, which "reserves to state probate courts the probate or annulment of a will and the administration of a decedent's estate." * * * Although undoubtedly narrower in scope than *Markham's* ill-considered

---

1. Notably, Justice Joseph Bradley, a strong proponent of the theory that federal courts sitting in equity cannot exercise jurisdiction over probate matters because in England in 1789 such jurisdiction belonged to the ecclesiastical courts, see *Case of Broderick's Will,* 21 Wall. 503 (1875), *Gaines v. Fuentes,* 92 U.S. 10, 24–25 (1876) (dissenting opinion), urged that "even in matters savoring of [e]cclesiastical process, after an issue has been formed between definite parties," the controversy should be heard by a federal court. See *Rosenbaum v. Bauer,* 120 U.S. 450, 460–461 (1887) (dissenting opinion) (citing *Gaines,* 92 U.S., at 17, and *Hess v. Reynolds,* 113 U.S. 73 (1885)).

2. Winkler, The Probate Jurisdiction of the Federal Courts, 14 Probate L.J. 77, 126 (1997); * * * Winkler also observes, citing Charles Dickens' Bleak House (1853), that *Markham's* "suggestion that the High Court of Chancery had lacked jurisdiction to 'administer an estate' was preposterous." 14 Probate L. J., at 125, and n. 256.

description of the probate carve-out, this description also sweeps too broadly. For the Court has correctly upheld the exercise of federal jurisdiction over actions involving the annulment of wills and the administration of decedents' estates. In *Gaines v. Fuentes,* 92 U.S. 10 (1876), for example, the Court held that a defendant in an action to annul a will should be permitted to remove the case to federal court. In so doing, it explained:

> "[W]henever a controversy in a suit ... arises respecting the validity or construction of a will, or the enforcement of a decree admitting it to probate, there is no more reason why the Federal courts should not take jurisdiction of the case than there is that they should not take jurisdiction of any other controversy between the parties." *Id.,* at 22.

Likewise, in *Payne v. Hook,* 7 Wall. 425 (1869), the Court explained that it was "well settled that a court of chancery, as an incident to its power to enforce trusts, and make those holding a fiduciary relation account, has jurisdiction to compel executors and administrators to account and distribute the assets in their hands." *Id.,* 7 Wall., at 431. (In that same case, a federal court later appointed a Special Master to administer the estate. This Court upheld some of the Master's determinations and rejected others. See *Hook v. Payne,* 14 Wall. 252, 255 (1872).)

To be sure, there are cases that support limitations on federal courts' jurisdiction over the probate and annulment of wills and the administration of decedents' estates. But careful examination reveals that at least most of the limitations so recognized stem not from some *sui generis* exception, but rather from generally applicable jurisdictional rules. * * * Whatever the continuing viability of these individual rules, together they are more than adequate to the task of cabining federal courts' jurisdiction. They require no helping hand from the so-called probate exception.

Rather than preserving whatever vitality that the "exception" has retained as a result of the *Markham* dicta, I would provide the creature with a decent burial in a grave adjacent to the resting place of the *Rooker-Feldman* doctrine. See *Lance v. Dennis,* 546 U.S. ___, ___ (2006) (STEVENS, J., dissenting).

Notes

1. Although jurisdiction in *Marshall* stems from federal bankruptcy law rather than from § 1332, the probate exception more often arises in the context of diversity jurisdiction. Notice also that the Court relies heavily on *Ankenbrandt*, a diversity case that narrowed the domestic relations exception to federal jurisdiction. The decision in *Marshall* thus narrows the availability of the probate exception in diversity as well as federal question cases. But the Court does leave open the possibility that as a matter of statutory interpretation, the probate exception—even in its more limited form—does not apply at all in bankruptcy. Should the domestic relations and probate exceptions apply in cases that rest on a jurisdictional basis other than diversity?

2.　Is there anything unique about probate and domestic relations that justifies special, judicially-imposed limitations on federal jurisdiction? Consider the following arguments in support of the probate exception:

> One [practical reason for the probate exception] is the promotion of legal certainty. If an issue may end up being litigated in either a state or a federal court, its resolution is less certain, less predictable, than if it can be litigated in one or the other forum only, even if the same substantive law is applied. Certainty is desirable in every area of the law but has been thought especially so with regard to the transfer of property at death. There are obstacles enough to effectuating testamentary intentions, legal uncertainty ought not be one of them.

＊　＊　＊

> A more compelling reason for the probate exception is judicial economy. When a person dies, his will has to be admitted to probate somewhere, or if he dies intestate the control of his property has to be vested in some court initially, and it is hard to imagine in either case how the initial jurisdiction over the decedent's estate could be elsewhere than in a state court. ＊ ＊ ＊ If the probate proceeding thus must begin in state court, the interest in judicial economy argues for keeping it there until it is concluded.

Dragan v. Miller, 679 F.2d 712, 714 (7th Cir.)(Posner, J.), cert. denied, 459 U.S. 1017 (1982).

3.　Of what relevance is the historical evidence? In *Dragan*, Judge Posner noted that the probate exception had only "shoddy" historical underpinnings. 679 F.2d at 713. Justice Stevens—and perhaps the majority—seems to agree. If the historical evidence persuasively shows that English courts *did* have jurisdiction over probate and domestic relations cases, should the exceptions be abolished?

4.　As the Court notes, lower courts have tended to interpret both exceptions broadly. See, e.g., McLaughlin v. Cotner, 193 F.3d 410 (6th Cir.1999) (domestic relations exception was applicable to preclude jurisdiction over former wife's suit against former husband alleging breach of agreement for sale of real estate where alleged contract was part of separation agreement incorporated into a divorce decree). In this regard, consider the following proposition: The Court's attempt in *Marshall* and *Ankenbrandt* to limit the two exceptions is worse than *either* allowing broad exceptions *or* abolishing the exceptions altogether.

5.　Professor Naomi Cahn argues that the exclusion of family law cases from the federal courts is based not only on the fact that family law is "a traditional area of state regulation" but also on a perception that it is "out of place in the federal courts." Cahn, *Family Law, Federalism, and the Federal Courts*, 79 Iowa L.Rev. 1073, 1073–74 (1994). Professor Cahn suggests that this latter perception is the result of gender bias, and proposes opening the federal courts to at least some family law cases.

§ 5.   JURISDICTIONAL AMOUNT

NELSON v. KEEFER

United States Court of Appeals, Third Circuit, 1971.
451 F.2d 289.

ALDISERT, CIRCUIT JUDGE.

These appeals question the propriety of dismissing a personal injury diversity action at pre-trial because the district court concluded that it appeared "to a legal certainty" that the claims were "really for less than the jurisdictional amount"[1] of $10,000.

Appellants concede that the court had the power to determine the facts requisite to jurisdiction, Wetmore v. Rymer, 169 U.S. 115 (1898), but contend that the cause should not have been terminated at pre-trial because of the possibility of adducing proof later as to the extent of the injuries.

Thus posited, the issue is whether the facts alleged at pre-trial supporting the complaint were legally insufficient to give rise to a $10,000 claim. St. Paul Mercury Indemnity Co. v. Red Cab Co., supra; Gray v. Occidental Life Insurance Co. of California, 387 F.2d 935 (3d Cir.1968); Jaconski v. Avisun Corp., 359 F.2d 931 (3d Cir.1966); Wade v. Rogala, 270 F.2d 280 (3d Cir.1959). It is appropriate to emphasize that "this court has taken the lead in recognizing diversity jurisdiction over an entire lawsuit in tort cases presenting closely related claims based, in principal part at least, on the same operative facts and normally litigated together, even though one of the claims, if litigated alone, would not satisfy a requirement of diversity jurisdiction." Thus, if any of the three plaintiffs meets the jurisdictional amount, we will extend hospitality to the other claims.

In their combined pre-trial statement, appellants allege that, as a result of an automobile accident caused by defendant's negligence, the minor son sustained a thoracic lumbar sprain, and, as of August 20, 1968—three years after the August 21, 1965 injury—he had incurred a physician's bill of $95.50, hospital expenses of $15.00, and a $25.78 bill for a back brace. Reports of physicians indicate that he was seen by them on four occasions: August 21, 1965, September 1, 1965, November 29, 1965, and February 6, 1968. X-rays taken on August 24, 1965, and November 26, 1965, were negative.

The wife-plaintiff was diagnosed as having sustained a hematoma of the skull, neck lash, and contusions of the right shoulder and right ribs. She was seen by her physician on August 23, 1965, and had an x-ray taken on August 25, 1965, which proved negative. The physician issued a report on October 31, 1966, revealing treatment on August 23, 1965, for which he submitted a bill for $163.00. The bill for the x-rays at St.

---

1. St. Paul Mercury Indemnity Co. v.
Red Cab Co., 303 U.S. 283, 289 (1938).

Luke's Hospital amounted to $65.00, and there was an additional Mercer College Hospital bill for $30.00.

The husband-father supported his claim with the following:

Dr. Brown $322.75

St. Luke's Hospital 262.75

Drugs 18.00

Property Damage 727.69

Dr. Brown's report of October 31, 1966, indicated that Nelson's first treatment was on August 24, 1965, that the diagnosis was "neck lash, bruise left shoulder, pain over lumbar region with tenderness over spleen" and that Nelson "still has pain in neck and shoulder." It is significant that in the 1966 report, Dr. Brown made no attempt to relate the accident to Nelson's hospitalization from August 25 to 28, 1965, which apparently was treatment for "[d]iarrhea, undetermined etiology," including x-rays showing duodenal ulcer symptomatology. In analyzing Nelson's medical expenses, the trial court characterized the bills of the physician and hospital as "of doubtful relation of entire bill to the accident because the hospital treatment and Dr. Brown's records deal mostly with his treatment for diarrhea and pre-existing hemorrhoids." Indeed, in answers to interrogatories, Nelson stated "no loss of compensation (from employment) is being claimed," and to the question: "How much time in weeks and days did you lose from work as a result of the injuries sustained in the accident," he responded, "Not applicable."

Before we apply these facts to the appropriate law, it becomes necessary to observe that other circuits have attributed more sweep to the rule of Wade v. Rogala, than is set forth in the holding of the case.

We did not there say that in all cases where there were intangible factors such as pain, suffering and inconvenience, the cause was required to be submitted to a jury. We did say that "[t]he necessary choice, except in the flagrant case, where the jurisdictional issue cannot be decided without the ruling constituting at the same time a ruling on the merits, is to permit the cause to proceed to trial."

It is our intention to require removal from the trial list of those "flagrant" cases where it can be determined in advance "with legal certainty" that the congressional mandate of a $10,000 minimum was not satisfied. Although adhering to Wade v. Rogala, we have subsequently stated:

> There is small difficulty in applying this rule when the damages claimed are liquidated, but when the damages are unliquidated, as in the instant case, there is no exact yardstick to measure recovery even when most, if not all the operative facts are known. One of the tools developed for determining the intangible factors relating to the amount in controversy is the requirement that a plaintiff must claim the necessary amount in "good faith". * * *

Test

* * * [T]he basic criterion for determining "good faith" is that "[i]t must appear to a legal certainty that the claim is really for less than the jurisdictional amount to justify dismissal." St. Paul Mercury Indemnity Co. v. Red Cab Co., 303 U.S. [283] 288–289 (1938). See also Horton v. Liberty Mutual Insurance Co., 367 U.S. 348 (1961); Brough v. Strathmann Supply Co., Inc., 358 F.2d 374 (3 Cir.1966). The test then is not what amount the plaintiff claims in the *ad damnum* clause of his complaint, but rather, whether it appears to a "legal certainty" that he cannot recover an amount above the jurisdictional minimum. Cumberland v. Household Research Corp. of America, 145 F.Supp. 782 (D.Mass.1956); Cohen v. Proctor & Gamble Distributing Co., 16 F.R.D. 128 (D.Del.1954). It follows, therefore, that in order to find a plaintiff's claim lacking in "good faith", the court must be able to conclude from the record before him that the plaintiff cannot recover a sum by way of damages above the $10,000 jurisdictional floor.

Jaconski v. Avisun Corp., 359 F.2d at 934, 935.[6]

We are not persuaded by the argument that a termination prior to trial deprives a "plaintiff of his present statutory right to a jury trial." See Deutsch v. Hewes Street Realty Corp., 359 F.2d at 100. Indeed, such an argument begs the question, for the precise issue is whether plaintiff has a statutory right to enter the courtroom for any trial, jury or otherwise. The corollary suggestion that the remedy lies with Congress is similarly specious,[7] for the reality is that Congress *did* act in 1958 in raising the amount in controversy from $3,000 to $10,000.

The stated purpose of the 1958 amendment as urged by the Judicial Conference of the United States was to:

> make jurisdiction available in all *substantial* controversies where other elements of Federal jurisdiction are present. The jurisdictional amount should not be so high to convert the Federal courts into courts of big business nor so low as to fritter away their time in the trial of petty controversies.

U.S.Code Cong. and Admin.News, Senate Report No. 1830, 85th Cong., 2d Sess., p. 3101 (1958) (emphasis added).

* * *

can't just state enough state actual damages

Nor can we bring ourselves to believe that the congressional mandate can be thwarted by the simple expedient of inflating the complaint's *ad damnum* clause. It is a phenomenon of both state and federal trial

---

6. As the Seventh Circuit recently noted, "it is not incumbent upon a plaintiff to show to an absolute certainty that he will obtain a verdict in excess of $10,000. Instead, before a suit will be dismissed for lack of jurisdiction, it must appear to a legal certainty that he will *not* recover that amount." Jeffries v. Silvercup Bakers, Inc., 434 F.2d 310, 311–312 (7th Cir.1970).

7. "If access to federal district courts is to be further limited it should be done by statute and not by court decisions that permit a district court judge to prejudge the monetary value of an unliquidated claim." Deutsch, 359 F.2d at 100.

courts that the majority of actual recoveries by verdict and settlement are less than the jurisdictional amount. * * *

We are quick to recognize that the "inability of plaintiff to recover an amount adequate to give the court jurisdiction does not show his bad faith or oust the jurisdiction." St. Paul Mercury Indemnity Co. v. Red Cab Co., supra, 303 U.S. at 289. Furthermore, we acknowledge readily the danger of depriving a plaintiff of a possible right to a jury trial. But the day has long gone in this circuit when a jury has had the last word on the size of personal injury awards. "This court has succinctly and frequently stated that the question of excessiveness of a verdict is primarily a matter to be addressed to the sound discretion of the trial court." Russell v. Monongahela Ry. Co., 262 F.2d 349, 352 (3d Cir.1958). Moreover, we have indicated that the trial court should not permit a jury verdict to stand where there has been a "showing that the jury was biased or acted capriciously or unreasonably." Derewecki v. Pennsylvania R. Co., 353 F.2d 436, 444 (3d Cir.1965). Nor is the court of appeals without responsibility in reviewing the verdict. In Grunenthal v. Long Island R. Co., 393 U.S. 156, 159 (1968), the Supreme Court discussed the Second Circuit's standard of review announced in Dagnello v. Long Island R. Co., 289 F.2d 797, 806 (2d Cir.1961):

> "[W]e appellate judges [are] not to decide whether we would have set aside the verdict if we were presiding at the trial, but whether the amount is so high that it would be a denial of justice to permit it to stand. We must give the benefit of every doubt to the judgment of the trial judge; but surely there must be an upper limit, and whether that has been surpassed is not a question of fact with respect to which reasonable men may differ, but a question of law."

> We read *Dagnello*, however, as requiring the Court of Appeals in applying this standard to make a detailed appraisal of the evidence bearing on damages.

The Court stated that this standard has been variously phrased as " 'grossly excessive,' 'inordinate,' 'shocking to the judicial conscience,' 'outrageously excessive,' 'so large as to shock the conscience of the court,' 'monstrous.' " 393 U.S. 159, n. 4.

Analogizing the authority of the court to reject a jury's verdict through the time-honored practice of remittitur, we have no difficulty in recognizing a corollary power in that same court to evaluate a case prior to trial where sufficient information has been made available through pre-trial discovery and comprehensive pre-trial narrative statements which disclose medical reports. Assuming that claimed tangible items of damage legally related to the cause of action will be taken as true, the court should be able to determine what the *Dagnello* court perceived to be the "upper limit" of a permissible award that includes tangible recoverable items such as medical special and lost wages damage items as well as the intangibles of pain, suffering, and inconvenience. If this "upper limit" does not bear a reasonable relation to the minimum jurisdictional floor, utilizing the test of St. *Paul Mercury Indemnity Co.*, we perceive no legal obstacle to a pre-trial determination that a personal injury action does not satisfy federal jurisdictional requirements.

* * *

Our scope of review under these circumstances is similar to that which is utilized in review of a trial court's determination that a verdict is "excessive" or "capricious." Accordingly, although we must "give the benefit of every doubt to the judgment of the trial judge," we must "make a detailed appraisal of the evidence bearing on damages." Having done so, we find that the district court gave plaintiffs ample opportunity, at the pre-trial stage, to justify their jurisdictional claim. Convinced to a legal certainty that the evidence would not permit it to sustain a verdict for plaintiffs of $10,000 or more, the district court did not—and indeed could not—allow the case to proceed to trial.

Cognizant of the competing arguments heretofore rehearsed, we hold that the district court did not err in concluding that the statutory jurisdictional minimum could not be gleaned from the facts averred in support of the complaint. And since plaintiffs' legally recoverable ceiling did not at its apex reach the federal jurisdictional floor, the judgment of the district court will be affirmed.

Notes

1. A history of the amount in controversy requirement in the federal courts appears in Baker, *The History and Tradition of the Amount in Controversy Requirement: A Proposal to "Up the Ante" in Diversity Jurisdiction,* 102 F.R.D. 299 (1985). The Judiciary Act of 1789 set the requirement, for cases in which it was demanded, at $500. By 1958 the amount had been raised to $10,000, the figure noted in Nelson v. Keefer and most of the cases in this chapter. The Judicial Improvements and Access to Judgments Act of 1988, however, raised the amount in controversy requirement to $50,000 in diversity cases. In 1996, Congress once again raised the jurisdictional amount in controversy, this time to $75,000. Federal Courts Improvement Act of 1996, Pub.J. 104–317, 110 Stat. 3847 (1996). From 1875 until 1980 an amount in controversy requirement applied to general federal question cases as well. In 1980, however, the requirement was deleted from 28 U.S.C. § 1331. Determination of the value of the matter in controversy for purposes of federal jurisdiction is determined by application of federal standards. Horton v. Liberty Mutual Insurance Co., 367 U.S. 348 (1961).

2. In the *St. Paul Mercury* case, discussed in *Nelson,* the Supreme Court stated that "the sum claimed by the plaintiff controls if the claim is apparently made in good faith. It must appear to a legal certainty that the claim is really for less than the jurisdictional amount to justify dismissal." 303 U.S. at 288, 289. By this statement, do you think the Court intended to establish two alternative tests—"good faith" and "legal certainty"—or were the two phrases merely variants of each other? Professor Wright adopts the latter view, "for unless it appears to a legal certainty that plaintiff cannot recover the sum for which he prays, how can it be held that his claim for that sum is not in good faith." C. Wright, The Law of Federal Courts 184

(4th Ed. 1983). Do you agree? Is the judicial inquiry likely to be the same under the two versions of the test?

3. Under the *St. Paul Mercury* test, which party should bear the burden of proof on the jurisdictional amount issue? Cf. Liamuiga Tours v. Travel Impressions, Ltd., 617 F.Supp. 920, 928 (E.D.N.Y.1985): "The courts have differed in their application of the rule in the *St. Paul Mercury Indemnity* case. Some courts have applied it so as to require that a challenge to the sum claimed puts the burden on the plaintiff to show that the claim survives the legal certainty test. Other courts have apparently left the burden on the defendant to show that it is a legal certainty that the claim cannot amount to the jurisdictional minimum or was made in bad faith." An illustration of the former category of cases is Burns v. Massachusetts Mutual Life Insurance Co., 820 F.2d 246, 248 (8th Cir.1987) ("While a plaintiff's good faith allegation is to be taken as true unless challenged, a plaintiff who has been challenged as to the amount in controversy has the burden of showing that the diversity jurisdiction requirements have been met.") For the opposite view, see Adolph Coors Co. v. Movement Against Racism and the Klan, 777 F.2d 1538 (11th Cir.1985). Is the *St. Paul Mercury* test neutral on the burden-of-proof issue, or is one of the two approaches inherently incompatible with the test?

4. The clearest example of a case in which a damage claim fails to meet the "legal certainty" test is one in which allowable damages are capped by law at an amount below the jurisdictional minimum. Such legal limitations may derive either from statute or contractual provision. See, e.g., Pratt Central Park Ltd. v. Dames & Moore, 60 F.3d 350 (7th Cir.1995). Under the logic of the "legal certainty" test, can any case other than those capped by law be found to fail to meet the jurisdictional minimum?

5. Note that claims for punitive damages are included in the calculus determining whether the jurisdictional minimum has been met. See, e.g., Watson v. Shell Oil Co., 979 F.2d 1014 (5th Cir.1992). Does this follow from the logic of the "legal certainty" test?

6. See generally, Barron, *The "Amount in Controversy" Controversy: Using Interest, Costs and Attorney Fees in Computing Its Value*, 41 Okla. L.Rev. 257 (1988).

SNYDER v. HARRIS

Supreme Court of the United States, 1969.
394 U.S. 332.

Mr. Justice Black delivered the opinion of the Court.

Title 28 U.S.C. § 1332 grants jurisdiction to United States district courts of suits between citizens of different States where "the matter in controversy exceeds the sum or value of $10,000...." The issue presented by these two cases is whether separate and distinct claims presented by and for various claimants in a class action may be added together to provide the $10,000 jurisdictional amount in controversy.

Each of these cases involves a single plaintiff suing on behalf of himself and "all others similarly situated." In No. 109, Mrs. Margaret E.

Snyder, a shareholder of Missouri Fidelity Union Trust Life Insurance Company, brought suit against members of the company's board of directors alleging that they had sold their shares of the company's stock for an amount far in excess of its fair market value, that this excess represented payment to these particular directors to obtain complete control of the company, and that under Missouri law the excess should properly be distributed among all the shareholders of the company and not merely to a few of them. The suit was brought in the United States District Court for the Eastern District of Missouri, diversity of citizenship being alleged as the basis for federal jurisdiction. Since petitioner's allegations showed that she sought for herself only $8,740 in damages, respondent moved to dismiss on the grounds that the matter in controversy did not exceed $10,000. Petitioner contended, however, that her claim should be aggregated with those of the other members of her class, approximately 4,000 shareholders of the company stock. If all 4,000 potential claims were aggregated, the amount in controversy would be approximately $1,200,000. The District Court held that the claims could not thus be aggregated to meet the statutory test of jurisdiction and the Court of Appeals for the Eighth Circuit, following a somewhat similar decision by the Court of Appeals for the Fifth Circuit in Alvarez v. Pan American Life Insurance Co., 375 F.2d 992, cert. denied, 389 U.S. 827, affirmed, 390 F.2d 204 (1968).

In No. 117, Otto R. Coburn, a resident of Kansas, brought suit in the United States District Court for the District of Kansas against the Gas Service Company, a corporation marketing natural gas in Kansas. Jurisdiction was predicated upon diversity of citizenship. The complaint alleged that the Gas Service Company had billed and illegally collected a city franchise tax from Coburn and others living outside city limits. Coburn alleged damages to himself of only $7.81. Styling his complaint as a class action, however, Coburn sought relief on behalf of approximately 18,000 other Gas Service Company customers living outside of cities. The amount by which other members of the class had been overcharged was, and is, unknown, but the complaint alleged that the aggregation of all these claims would in any event exceed $10,000. The District Court overruled the Gas Company's motion to dismiss for failure to satisfy the jurisdictional amount and, on interlocutory appeal, the Court of Appeals for the Tenth Circuit affirmed, holding that because of a 1966 amendment to Rule 23 of the Federal Rules of Civil Procedure relating to class actions, separate and distinct claims brought together in a class action could now be aggregated for the purpose of establishing the jurisdictional amount in diversity cases. We granted certiorari to resolve the conflict between the position of the Courts of Appeals for the Fifth and the Eighth Circuits and that of the Court of Appeals for the Tenth Circuit.

The first congressional grant to district courts to take suits between citizens of different States fixed the requirement for the jurisdictional amount in controversy at $500. In 1887 this jurisdictional amount was increased to $2,000; in 1911 to $3,000; and in 1958 to $10,000. The traditional judicial interpretation under all of these statutes has been from the beginning that the separate and distinct claims of two or more plaintiffs cannot be aggregated in order to satisfy the jurisdictional amount requirement. Aggregation has been permitted only (1) in cases in which a single plaintiff seeks to aggregate two or more of his own claims against a single defendant and (2) in cases in which two or more plaintiffs unite to enforce a single title or right in which they have a common and undivided interest. It is contended, however, that the adoption of a 1966 amendment to Rule 23 effectuated a change in this jurisdictional doctrine. Under old Rule 23, class actions were divided into three categories which came to be known as "true," "hybrid," and "spurious." True class actions were those in which the rights of the different class members were common and undivided; in such cases aggregation was permitted. Spurious class actions, on the other hand, were in essence merely a form of permissive joinder in which parties with separate and distinct claims were allowed to litigate those claims in a single suit simply because the different claims involved common questions of law or fact. In such cases aggregation was not permitted: each plaintiff had to show that his individual claim exceeded the jurisdictional amount. The 1966 amendment to Rule 23 replaced the old categories with a functional approach to class actions. The new Rule establishes guidelines for the appropriateness of class actions, makes provision for giving notice to absent members, allows members of the class to remove themselves from the litigation and provides that the judgment will include all members of the class who have not requested exclusion. In No. 117, Gas Service Company, the Court of Appeals for the Tenth Circuit held that these changes in Rule 23 changed the jurisdictional amount doctrine as well. The court noted that: "Because the claims of the individuals constituting the class in the case at bar are neither 'joint' nor 'common' this action under Rule 23 before amendment would not have been classified as a 'true' class action and aggregation of claims would not have been permitted." The Court of Appeals held, however, that a different result was compelled now that the amendment to Rule 23 abolished the distinctions between true and spurious class actions. The court held that because aggregation was permitted in some class actions, it must now be permitted in all class actions under the new Rule. We disagree and conclude, as did the Courts of Appeal for the Fifth and Eighth Circuits, that the adoption of amended Rule 23 did not and could not have brought about this change in the scope of the congressionally enacted grant of jurisdiction to the district courts.

The doctrine that separate and distinct claims could not be aggregated was never, and is not now, based upon the categories of old Rule 23 or of any rule of procedure. That doctrine is based rather upon this Court's interpretation of the statutory phrase "matter in controversy." The interpretation of this phrase as precluding aggregation substantially predates the 1938 Federal Rules of Civil Procedure. In 1911 this Court said in Troy Bank v. Whitehead & Co.:

"When two or more plaintiffs, having separate and distinct demands, unite for convenience and economy in a single suit, it is essential that the demand of each be of the requisite jurisdictional amount...." 222 U.S. 39, 40.

By 1916 this Court was able to say in Pinel v. Pinel, 240 U.S. 594, that it was "settled doctrine" that separate and distinct claims could not be aggregated to meet the required jurisdictional amount. In Clark v. Paul Gray, Inc., 306 U.S. 583 (1939), this doctrine, which had first been declared in cases involving joinder of parties, was applied to class actions under the then recently passed Federal Rules. In that case numerous individuals, partnerships, and corporations joined in bringing a suit challenging the validity of a California statute which exacted fees of $15 on each automobile driven into the State. Raising the jurisdictional amount question *sua sponte*, this Court held that the claims of the various fee payers could not be aggregated "where there are numerous plaintiffs having no joint or common interest or title in the subject matter of the suit." 306 U.S., at 588. Nothing in the amended Rule 23 changes this doctrine. The class action plaintiffs in the two cases before us argue that since the new Rule will include in the judgment all members of the class who do not ask to be out by a certain date, the "matter in controversy" now encompasses all the claims of the entire class. But it is equally true that where two or more plaintiffs join their claims under the joinder provisions of Rule 20, each and every joined plaintiff is bound by the judgment. And it was in joinder cases of this very kind that the doctrine that distinct claims could not be aggregated was originally enunciated. Troy Bank v. G. A. Whitehead & Co., 222 U.S. 39 (1911); Pinel v. Pinel, 240 U.S. 594 (1916). The fact that judgments under class actions formerly classified as spurious may now have the same effect as claims brought under the joinder provisions is certainly no reason to treat them *differently* from joined actions for purposes of aggregation.

Any change in the Rules that did purport to effect a change in the definition of "matter in controversy" would clearly conflict with the command of Rule 82 that "[t]hese rules shall not be construed to extend or limit the jurisdiction of the United States district courts * * *." In Sibbach v. Wilson & Co., this Court held that the rule-making authority was limited by "the inability of a court, by rule, to extend or restrict the jurisdiction conferred by a statute." 312 U.S. 1, 10 (1941). We have consistently interpreted the jurisdictional statute passed by Congress as not conferring jurisdiction where the required amount in controversy can be reached only by aggregating separate and distinct claims. The interpretation of that statute cannot be changed by a change in the Rules.

For the reasons set out above, we think that it is unmistakably clear that the 1966 changes in Rule 23 did not and could not have changed the interpretation of the statutory phrase "matter in controversy." It is urged, however, that this Court should now overrule its established statutory interpretation and hold that "matter in controversy" encompasses the aggregation of all claims that can be brought together in a single suit, regardless of whether any single plaintiff has a claim that exceeds the required jurisdictional amount. It is argued in behalf of this position that (1) the determination of whether claims are "separate and distinct" is a troublesome question that breeds uncertainty and needless litigation, and (2) the inability of parties to aggregate numerous small claims will prevent some important questions from being litigated in federal courts. And both of these factors, it is argued, will tend to undercut the attempt of the Judicial Conference to promulgate efficient and modernized class action procedures. We think that whatever the merit of these contentions, they are not sufficient to justify our abandonment of a judicial interpretation of congressional language that has stood for more than a century and a half.

It is linguistically possible, of course, to interpret the old congressional phrase "matter in controversy" as including all claims that can be joined or brought in a single suit through the class action device. But, beginning with the first Judiciary Act in 1789 Congress has placed a jurisdictional amount requirement on access to the federal courts in certain classes of cases, including diversity actions. The initial requirement was $500 and a series of increases have, as pointed out above, finally placed the amount at $10,000. Congress has thus consistently amended the amount-in-controversy section and re-enacted the "matter-in-controversy" language without change of its jurisdictional effect against a background of judicial interpretation that has consistently interpreted that congressionally enacted phrase as not encompassing the aggregation of separate and distinct claims. This judicial interpretation has been uniform since at least the 1832 decision of this Court in Oliver v. Alexander, 6 Pet. 143. There are no doubt hazards and pitfalls involved in assuming that re-enactment of certain language by Congress always freezes the existing judicial interpretation of the statutes involved. Here, however, the settled judicial interpretation of "amount in controversy" was implicitly taken into account by the relevant congressional committees in determining, in 1958, the extent to which the jurisdictional amount should be raised. It is quite possible, if not probable, that Congress chose the increase to $10,000 rather than the proposed increases to $7,500 or $15,000 on the basis of workload estimates which clearly relied on the settled doctrine that separate and distinct claims could not be aggregated. Where Congress has consistently re-enacted its prior statutory language for more than a century and a half in the face of a settled interpretation of that language, it is perhaps not entirely realistic to designate the resulting rule a "judge-made formula."

To overrule the aggregation doctrine at this late date would run counter to the congressional purpose in steadily increasing through the years the jurisdictional amount requirement. That purpose was to check, to some degree, the rising caseload of the federal courts, especially with regard to the federal courts' diversity of citizenship jurisdiction. Any change in the doctrine of aggregation in class action cases under Rule 23 would inescapably have to be applied as well to the liberal joinder provisions of Rule 20 and to the joinder of claims provisions of Rule 18. The result would be to allow aggregation of practically any claims of any parties that for any reason happen to be brought together in a single action. This would seriously undercut the purpose of the jurisdictional amount requirement. The expansion of the federal caseload could be most noticeable in class actions brought on the basis of diversity of citizenship. Under current doctrine, if one member of a class is of diverse citizenship from the class' opponent, and no nondiverse members are named parties, the suit may be brought in federal court even though all other members of the class are citizens of the same State as the defendant and have nothing to fear from trying the lawsuit in the courts of their own State. See Supreme Tribe of Ben–Hur v. Cauble, 255 U.S. 356 (1921). To allow aggregation of claims where only one member of the entire class is of diverse citizenship could transfer into the federal courts numerous local controversies involving exclusively questions of state law. In Healy v. Ratta, 292 U.S. 263 (1934), this Court noted that by successively raising the jurisdictional amount, Congress had determined that cases involving lesser amounts should be left to be dealt with by the state courts and said:

> "The policy of the statute calls for its strict construction.... Due regard for the rightful independence of state governments, which should actuate federal courts, requires that they scrupulously confine their own jurisdiction to the precise limits which the statute has defined."

Finally, it has been argued that unless the established aggregation principles are overturned, the functional advantages alleged to inhere in the new class action Rule will be undercut by resort to the old forms. But the disadvantageous results are overemphasized, we think, since lower courts have developed largely workable standards for determining when claims are joint and common, and therefore entitled to be aggregated, and when they are separate and distinct and therefore not aggregable. Moreover, while the class action device serves a useful function across the entire range of legal questions, the jurisdictional amount requirement applies almost exclusively to controversies based upon diversity of citizenship. A large part of those matters involving federal questions can be brought, by way of class actions or otherwise, without regard to the amount in controversy. Suits involving issues of state law and brought on the basis of diversity of citizenship can often be most appropriately tried in state courts. The underlying claims in the two cases before us, for example, will be determined exclusively on the basis of Missouri and Kansas law, respectively. In No. 109, a separate suit litigating the underlying issues has already been filed in a Missouri state court. In No. 117, the residents of Kansas who contend that certain gas service charges are not authorized by Kansas law can bring a class action under Kansas procedures that are patterned on former Federal Rule 23. There is no compelling reason for this Court to overturn a settled interpretation of an important congressional statute in order to add to the burdens of an already overloaded federal court system. Nor can we overlook the fact that the Congress that permitted the Federal Rules to go into effect was assured before doing so that none of the Rules would either expand or contract the jurisdiction of federal courts. If there is a present need to expand the jurisdiction of those courts we cannot overlook the fact that the Constitution specifically vests that power in the Congress, not in the courts.

* * *

MR. JUSTICE FORTAS, with whom MR. JUSTICE DOUGLAS joins, dissenting.

The Court today refuses to conform the judge-made formula for computing the amount in controversy in class actions with the 1966 amendment to Rule 23 of the Federal Rules of Civil Procedure. The effect of this refusal is substantially to undermine a generally welcomed and long-needed reform in federal procedure.

Its impact will be noticeable not only in diversity of citizenship cases but also in important classes of federal question cases in which federal jurisdiction must be based on 28 U.S.C. § 1331, the general federal question provision, rather than on one of the specific grants of federal jurisdiction.

The artificial, awkward, and unworkable distinctions between "joint," "common," and "several" claims and between "true," "hybrid," and "spurious" class actions which the amendment of Rule 23 sought to terminate is now re-established in federal procedural law. Litigants, lawyers, and federal courts must now continue to be ensnared in their complexities in all cases where one or more of the coplaintiffs have a claim of less than the jurisdictional amount, usually $10,000.

It was precisely this morass that the 1966 amendment to Rule 23 sought to avoid. The amendment had as its purpose to give the Federal District Courts wider discretion as to the type of claims that could be joined in litigation. That amendment replaced the metaphysics of conceptual analysis of the "character of the right sought to be enforced" by a pragmatic, workable definition of when class actions might be maintained, that is, when claims of various claimants might be aggregated in a class action, and it carefully provided procedures and safeguards to avoid unfairness.

The amendment was formulated with care by an able committee and recommended to this Court by the Judicial Conference of the United States pursuant to 28 U.S.C. § 331. It was accepted and promulgated by this Court, and, with congressional acquiescence, became the law of the land on July 1, 1966. 28 U.S.C. § 2072 (1964 ed., Supp. III). Now the Court, for reasons which in my opinion will not stand analysis, defeats the purpose of the amendment as applied to cases like those before us here and insists upon a perpetuation of distinctions which the profession had hoped would become only curiosities of the past.

The Court is led to this unfortunate result by its insistence upon regarding the method of computing the amount in controversy as embodied in an Act of Congress, as unaffected by the subsequent amendment of Rule 23, and as immune from judicial re-examination because any change would be an impermissible expansion of the jurisdiction of the courts. None of these premises is correct.

I.

Since the first Judiciary Act, Congress has included in certain grants of jurisdiction to the federal courts—notably the grants of jurisdiction based on diversity of citizenship and the later-established grant of a general jurisdiction to consider cases raising federal questions—a requirement that the "matter in controversy" exceed a stated amount of money. Congress has never expanded or explained the bare words of these successive jurisdictional amount statutes. Over the years the courts themselves have developed a detailed and complex set of rules for determining when the jurisdictional amount requirements are met.

Among these rules is the proposition that multiple parties cannot aggregate their "separate and distinct" claims to reach the jurisdictional amount. E.g., Troy Bank v. G. A. Whitehead & Co., 222 U.S. 39, 40 (1911); Oliver v. Alexander, 6 Pet. 143, 147 (1832). Applying that general principle to traditional property law concepts, the courts developed the more specialized rule that multiple parties who asserted very similar legal claims could not aggregate them to make up the jurisdictional amount if their interests, however similar in fact, were in legal theory "several," e.g., Pinel v. Pinel, 240 U.S. 594 (1916), but that such aggregation was permissible where the parties claimed undivided interests in a single "joint" right. E.g., Texas & Pacific R. Co. v. Gentry, 163 U.S. 353 (1896); Shields v. Thomas, 17 How. 3 (1855).

This general aggregation rule, and its much later application to class actions, rest entirely on judicial decisions, not on any Act of Congress. There is certainly no reason the specific application of this body of federal decisional law to class actions should be immune from re-evaluation after a fundamental change in the structure of federal class actions has made its continuing application wholly anomalous.

The majority rather half-heartedly suggests that this judicial interpretation of the jurisdictional amount statute is not subject to judicial re-evaluation because Congress by re-enacting the jurisdictional amount statute from time to time has somehow expressed an intent to freeze once and for all the judicial interpretation of the statute. As the majority frankly acknowledges, there are "hazards and pitfalls involved in assuming that reenactment of certain language by Congress always freezes the existing judicial interpretation of the statutes involved."

* * *

II.

Whatever the pre–1966 status of the aggregation doctrines in class action cases, the amendment of the Rules in that year permits and even requires a re-examination of the application of the doctrines to such cases. The fundamental change in the law of class actions effected by the new Rule 23 requires that prior subsidiary judicial doctrines developed for application to the old Rule be harmonized with the new procedural law. By Act of Congress, the Rules of Procedure, when promulgated according to the statutorily defined process, have the effect of law and supersede all prior laws in conflict with them. 28 U.S.C. § 2072 (1964 ed., Supp. III). Thus, even if the old aggregation doctrines were embodied in statute—as they are not—they could not stand if they conflicted with the new Rule.

Under the pre–1966 version of Rule 23 the very availability of the class action device depended on the "joint" or "common" "character of the right sought to be enforced."[13] If the right were merely "several," only a "spurious" class action could be maintained and only those members of the class who actually appeared as parties were bound by the judgment.[14] It was in this context of a law of class actions already heavily dependent on categorization of interests as "joint" or "several" that the traditional aggregation doctrines were originally applied to class actions under the Federal Rules. In such a context those aggregation doctrines which the majority now perpetuates in the quite different context of the new Rule, whatever their other defects, were at least not anomalous and eccentric.

Scholarly and professional criticism of the "character of interest" classification scheme was vigorous and distinguished. Courts as well found the old Rule 23 categories confusing and unhelpful in making practical decisions. Not only was the categorization difficult, but dividing group interests according to whether they were "joint" or "several" did not isolate those cases in which a class action was appropriate from those in which it was not. In proposing amendment of Rule 23, the Advisory Committee summed up experience under the old Rule by saying:

> "In practice the terms 'joint,' 'common,' etc., which were used as the basis of the Rule 23 classification proved obscure and uncertain." 39 F.R.D. 98.

In response to the demonstrated inappropriateness of the "character of interest" categorization, the Rule dealing with class actions was fundamentally amended, effective in July 1966. Under the new Rule the focus shifts from the abstract character of the right asserted to explicit analysis of the suitability of the particular claim to resolution in a class action. The decision that a class action is appropriate is not to be taken

---

13. A "true" class action could also be maintained to enforce a right "secondary in the sense that the owner of a primary right refuses to enforce that right and a member of the class thereby becomes entitled to enforce it." Stockholders' derivative actions were the most significant type of suit within this group. They are now separately dealt with under Rule 23.1 in addition. Under the former Rule 23(a)(2), if the right was "several" in character, "and the object of the action is the adjudication of claims which do or may affect specific property involved in the action," a "hybrid" class action could be maintained which would determine the interests of each member of the class in the particular property.

14. See, e.g., All Amer. Airways, Inc. v. Elderd, 209 F.2d 247 (C.A. 2d Cir. 1954). Thus, under the prior Rule, the "spurious" class action was in effect little more than a permissive joinder device. The pre-amendment categorization and its consequences are explicated in detail in 3A J. Moore, Federal Practice ¶¶ 23.08–23.14.

lightly; the district court must consider the full range of relevant factors specified in the Rule. However, whether a claim is, in traditional terms, "joint" or "several" no longer has any necessary relevance to whether a class action is proper. Thus, the amended Rule 23, which in the area of its operation has the effect of a statute, states a new method for determining when the common interests of many individuals can be asserted and resolved in a single litigation.

The jurisdictional amount statutes require placing a value on the "matter in controversy" in a civil action. Once it is decided under the new Rule that an action may be maintained as a class action, it is the claim of the whole class and not the individual economic stakes of the separate members of the class which is the "matter in controversy." That this is so is perhaps most clearly indicated by the fact that the judgment in a class action, properly maintained as such, includes all members of the class. Rule 23(c)(3). This effect of the new Rule in broadening the scope of the "controversy" in a class action to include the combined interests of all the members of the class is illustrated by the facts of No. 117. That class action, if allowed to proceed, would, under the Rule, determine not merely whether the gas company wrongfully collected $7.81 for taxes from Mr. Coburn. It would also result in a judgment which, subject to the limits of due process,[18] would determine—authoritatively and not merely as a matter of precedent—the status of the taxes collected from the 18,000 other people allegedly in the class Coburn seeks to represent.[19] That being the case, it is hard to understand why the fact that the alleged claims are, in terms of the old Rule categories, "several" rather than "joint," means that the "matter in controversy" for jurisdictional amount purposes must be regarded as the $7.81 Mr. Coburn claims instead of the thousands of dollars of alleged overcharges of the whole class, the status of all of which would be determined by the judgment.

In past development of rules concerning the jurisdictional amount requirement, the courts have, properly, responded to changes in the procedural and substantive law. Now, confronted by an issue of the meaning of the jurisdictional amount requirement arising in the context of a new procedural law of class actions, we should continue to take account of such changes. We should not allow the judicial interpretation of the jurisdictional amount requirement to become petrified into forms which are products of, and appropriate to, another time. To do this would vitiate a significant part of the reform intended to be accomplished by the amendment of Rule 23. For the majority result will continue to make determinative of the maintainability of a class action just that obsolete conceptualism the amended Rule sought to make irrelevant. In this sense, continued adherence to the old aggregation

18. See Hansberry v. Lee, 311 U.S. 32, 42–43 (1940).

19. If members of the class elected to exercise the right, which might be extended them under Rule 23(b)(3), to exclude themselves from the litigation, they would not be included in the judgment in the class action.

doctrines conflicts with the new Rule and is improper under 28 U.S.C. § 2072 (1964 ed., Supp. III).

III.

Permitting aggregation in class action cases does not involve any violation of the principle, expressed in Rule 82 and inherent in the whole procedure for the promulgation and amendment of the Federal Rules, that the courts cannot by rule expand their own jurisdictions. While the Rules cannot change subject-matter jurisdiction, changes in the forms and practices of the federal courts through changes in the Rules frequently and necessarily will affect the occasions on which subject-matter jurisdiction is exercised, because they will in some cases make a difference in what cases the federal courts will hear and who will be authoritatively bound by the judgment. For example, the development of the law of joinder and ancillary jurisdiction under the Federal Rules has influenced the "jurisdiction" of the federal courts in this broader sense. Indeed, the promulgation of the old Rule 23 provided a new means for resolving in a single federal litigation, based on diversity jurisdiction, the claims of all members of a class, even though some in the class were not of diverse citizenship from parties on the other side. Similarly, the creation in a Rule having statutory effect of a new type of class action— one meeting the requirements of the new Rule as to suitability for class-wide resolution, although involving "several" interests of the members of the class—has changed the procedural context in which the subject-matter-jurisdiction statutes, like those referring to jurisdictional amount, are to be applied. Making judicial rules for calculating jurisdictional amount responsive to the new structure of class actions is not an extension of the jurisdiction of the federal courts, but a recognition that the procedural framework in which the courts operate has been changed by a provision having the effect of law.

In a larger sense as well, abandonment of the old aggregation rules for class actions would fulfill rather than contradict the command that courts adhere to the jurisdictional boundaries established by Congress. * * *

The new Rule 23, by redefining the law of class actions, has, with the effect of statute, provided for a decision by the district courts that the nominally separate and legally "several" claims of individuals may be so much alike that they can be tried all at once, as if there were just one claim, in a single proceeding in which most members of the class asserting the claim will not be personally present at all. When that determination has been made, in accordance with the painstaking demands of Rule 23, there is authorized to be brought in the federal courts a single litigation, in which, both practically and in legal theory, the thing at stake, the "matter in controversy," is the total, combined, aggregated claim of the whole class. When that happens the courts do not obey, but violate, the jurisdictional statutes if they continue to impose ancient and artificial judicial doctrines to fragment what is in every other respect a single claim, which the courts are commanded to stand ready to hear.

For these reasons, I would measure the value of the "matter in controversy" in a class action found otherwise proper under the amended Rule 23 by the monetary value of the claim of the whole class.

Notes

1. Can you articulate the difference in focus between the opinions of Justices Black and Fortas? On what basis does Justice Black disregard the 1966 change in Rule 23? Do you think his grounds are valid? Consider the following facts: According to one of the architects of the 1966 revision, the Advisory Committee "perceived as lawyers had for a long time, that some litigious situations affecting numerous persons 'naturally' or 'necessarily' called for unitary adjudication. The problem was how to elaborate this insight while avoiding the pitfalls of abstract classification on the style of 1938." Kaplan, *Continuing Work of the Civil Committee: 1966 Amendments of the Federal Rules of Civil Procedure (I)*, 81 Harv.L.Rev. 356, 386 (1967). Also, in Dolgow v. Anderson, 43 F.R.D. 472, 484–85 (E.D.N.Y.1968) the court stated:

> The class action is particularly appropriate where those who have allegedly been injured "are in a poor position to seek legal redress, either because they do not know enough or because such redress is disproportionately expensive." Kalven and Rosenfield, The Contemporary Function of the Class Suit, 8 U.Chi.L.Rev. 684, 686 (1941). Its "historic mission" has been to "[t]ake care of the smaller guy." Statement of Professor Ben Kaplan, Reporter of the new Rules, quoted in Frankel, *Amended Rule 23 From A Judge's Point of View,* 32 Antitrust L.J. 295, 299 (1966).

What is likely to be the impact of the holding in *Snyder* on attainment of the goals of the class action device in general and of the 1966 amendments in particular? Should it make a difference? *Can* it, as a legal matter, make a difference? Congress modified *Snyder* somewhat in the Class Action Fairness Act of 2003, providing that for certain large class actions, the claims of individual class members should be aggregated. See 28 U.S.C. § 1332(d)(6).

2. Note that in his dissent in *Snyder*, Justice Fortas cited the special danger of the non-aggregation rule in federal question cases. This is no longer a problem. In 1976, Congress repealed the jurisdictional amount requirement in suits against federal officers acting in their official capacity. Pub.L. 94–574, 90 Stat. 2721 (1976). Four years later, Congress eliminated the jurisdictional amount requirement in all federal question cases. Pub.L. 96–486, 94 Stat. 2369 (1980). Can you imagine why the jurisdictional amount requirement might have presented significant problems in a suit to enjoin a federal officer for violation of, for example, the first amendment right of free speech? See, e.g., Giancana v. Johnson, 335 F.2d 366 (7th Cir.1964), cert. denied, 379 U.S. 1001 (1965); Cortright v. Resor, 325 F.Supp. 797 (E.D.N.Y.), rev'd on other grounds, 447 F.2d 245 (2d Cir.1971), cert. denied, 405 U.S. 965 (1972). What is the rationale for the elimination of the jurisdictional amount requirement in all federal question cases?

3. Lower courts have generally held that "punitive damages may not ordinarily be aggregated and attributed in total to each member of a putative class for purposes of satisfying diversity jurisdiction." Martin v. Franklin Capital Corp., 251 F.3d 1284, 1292 (10th Cir.2001). See also Ayres v. General Motors Corp., 234 F.3d 514 (11th Cir.2000).

4. **The "Viewpoint" Issues.** A question that has long pervaded jurisdictional amount analysis concerns the relevant viewpoint for determining whether the minimum has been met. Under a strict "plaintiff viewpoint" approach, the only relevant concern is whether the plaintiff has a claim in excess of the minimum in controversy. Thus, under this approach, if a plaintiff is suing to enjoin a power plant as a nuisance, unless the plaintiff can establish that he or she stands to gain or lose in excess of $10,000 as a result of the suit, the minimum will not have been met. This is so, even though the defendant stands to lose far in excess of $10,000 if his plant is shut down. This approach was urged by Judge Dobie in his article, *Jurisdictional Amount in The United States District Court*, 38 Harv.L.Rev. 733 (1925), and has been employed by various lower federal courts. E.g., Central Mexico Light & Power Co. v. Munch, 116 F.2d 85, 87 (2d Cir.1940). See also Burns v. Massachusetts Mutual Life Insurance Co., 820 F.2d 246, 248 (8th Cir.1987): "The amount in controversy in a suit for injunctive relief is measured by the value to the plaintiff of the right sought to be enforced." It is also sometimes thought that the principle was adopted by the Supreme Court in Glenwood Light & Water Co. v. Mutual Light, Heat & Power Co., 239 U.S. 121 (1915), although this conclusion is far from clear. Other lower courts, however, have adopted a different rule: "In determining the matter in controversy, we may look to the object sought to be accomplished by the plaintiffs' complaint; the test for determining the amount in controversy is the pecuniary result to either party which the judgment would directly produce." Ronzio v. Denver & Rio Grande Western Railroad Co., 116 F.2d 604, 606 (10th Cir.1940). This rule has been called by a leading commentator "the desirable rule." C. Wright, Law of Federal Courts 193 (4th ed. 1983). What do you suppose are the purposes of requiring a jurisdictional minimum in the first place? In light of these purposes, which of the approaches seems preferable? See generally Casazza, *Valuation of Diversity Jurisdiction Claims in the Federal Courts*, 104 Colum.L.Rev. 1280 (2004); Hininger, *Two Heads are Better than One: Making a Case for the Either Party Viewpoint for Removal*, 69 Mo.L.Rev. 275 (2004).

5. What impact, if any, should *Snyder* have on the viewpoint issue? See, e.g., Snow v. Ford Motor Co., 561 F.2d 787 (9th Cir.1977), holding that, in a class action suit, use of the plaintiff-or-defendant viewpoint would result in a circumvention of *Snyder*. Why would it have that effect? Cf. Massachusetts State Pharmaceutical Association v. Federal Prescription Service, Inc., 431 F.2d 130 (8th Cir.1970). Should the impact of *Snyder* be limited to the class action context? In a leading non-class action case, the Seventh Circuit concluded that "the interests of equity and fairness, as well as the purposes behind the removal statute, would here be well served by allowing the plaintiff's claim to be evaluated for jurisdictional purposes by applying the either viewpoint rule." McCarty v. Amoco Pipeline Co., 595 F.2d 389, 395 (7th Cir.1979). Can the impact of *Snyder* on the viewpoint issue logically be limited to the class action context? Cf. Lonnquist v. J. C. Penney Co., 421

F.2d 597 (10th Cir.1970) (aggregation issue in class action context must be considered prior to reaching viewpoint issue). But see Ferris v. General Dynamics Corp., 645 F.Supp. 1354 (D.R.I.1986) (Defendant's opposition to use of strict plaintiff viewpoint rule disregards fact that class action is involved).

6. It is important to recall that while *Snyder* drastically limits the availability of aggregation in class actions, it does not preclude the possibility. The Court in *Snyder* simply adheres to the pre–1966 practice of allowing aggregation *only* in those cases in which the rights asserted can be characterized as "common" or "undivided." Cf. Eagle v. American Tel. and Tel. Co., 769 F.2d 541 (9th Cir.1985), cert. denied, 475 U.S. 1084 (1986) (*Snyder* does not prevent aggregation, because rights in question are commonly held). How easy is it to apply this concept? Should the Court in *Snyder* have taken into account the fact that one of the major motivations behind the 1966 amendment to Rule 23 of the Federal Rules of Civil Procedure was the desire to avoid the great difficulty of distinguishing between "joint" or "common" rights on the one hand and "several" or "individual" rights on the other hand?

7. *Snyder* was relied upon by the Supreme Court in Zahn v. International Paper Co., 414 U.S. 291 (1973), where it held that absent class members in a diversity class action who failed to meet the jurisdictional minimum could not append their claims, by means of ancillary jurisdiction, to the claim of a named plaintiff which did satisfy that minimum. *Zahn* is discussed further in Chapter Fifteen, infra p. 848. Does the holding in *Zahn* flow logically from *Snyder*?

8. A number of years ago, Professor Meador suggested that perhaps all personal injury cases arising under state law should be statutorily excluded from the diversity jurisdiction. Meador, *A New Approach to Limiting Diversity Jurisdiction*, 46 A.B.A.J. § 83 (1960). In addition to the significant burdens these cases place on the federal courts, he noted that "[o]f all disputes now being handled on diversity grounds, tort actions for personal injury are perhaps the most 'local' in nature and have the least national or interstate impact." Id. at 384. Is this a persuasive ground for narrowing the diversity jurisdiction? Does Meador's reasoning perhaps prove too much?

§ 6. MANUFACTURED DIVERSITY

KRAMER v. CARIBBEAN MILLS, INC.
Supreme Court of the United States, 1969.
394 U.S. 823.

Mr. Justice Harlan delivered the opinion of the Court.

The sole question presented by this case is whether the Federal District Court in which it was brought had jurisdiction over the cause, or whether that court was deprived of jurisdiction by 28 U.S.C. § 1359. That section provides:

> "A district court shall not have jurisdiction of a civil action in which any party, by assignment or otherwise, has been improperly or collusively made or joined to invoke the jurisdiction of such court."

The facts were these. Respondent Caribbean Mills, Inc. (Caribbean) is a Haitian corporation. In May 1959 it entered into a contract with an individual named Kelly and the Panama and Venezuela Finance Company (Panama), a Panamanian corporation. The agreement provided that Caribbean would purchase from Panama 125 shares of corporate stock, in return for payment of $85,000 down and an additional $165,000 in 12 annual installments.

No installment payments ever were made, despite requests for payment by Panama. In 1964 Panama assigned its entire interest in the 1959 contract to petitioner Kramer, an attorney in Wichita Falls, Texas. The stated consideration was $1. By a separate agreement dated the same day, Kramer promised to pay back to Panama 95% of any net recovery on the assigned cause of action,[1] "solely as a Bonus."

Kramer soon thereafter brought suit against Caribbean for $165,000 in the United States District Court for the Northern District of Texas, alleging diversity of citizenship between himself and Caribbean.[2] The District Court denied Caribbean's motion to dismiss for want of jurisdiction. The case proceeded to trial, and a jury returned a $165,000 verdict in favor of Kramer.

On appeal, the Court of Appeals for the Fifth Circuit reversed, holding that the assignment was "improperly or collusively made" within the meaning of 28 U.S.C. § 1359, and that in consequence the District Court lacked jurisdiction. We granted certiorari, 393 U.S. 819 (1968). For reasons which follow, we affirm the judgment of the Court of Appeals.

I.

The issue before us is whether Kramer was "improperly or collusively made" a party "to invoke the jurisdiction" of the District Court, within the meaning of 28 U.S.C. § 1359. We look first to the legislative background.

Section 1359 has existed in its present form only since the 1948 revision of the Judicial Code. Prior to that time, the use of devices to create diversity was regulated by two federal statutes. The first, known as the "assignee clause," provided that, with certain exceptions not here relevant:

> "No district court shall have cognizance of any suit ... to recover upon any promissory note or other chose in action in favor of any assignee, ... unless such suit might have been prosecuted in such court ... if no assignment had been made."[3]

---

1. That is, Kramer would receive 5%, and Panama 95%, of the net proceeds remaining after payment of attorneys' fees and expenses of litigation.

2. Title 28 U.S.C. § 1332(a)(2) grants district courts original jurisdiction of civil actions in which the matter in controversy exceeds $10,000 and is between "citizens of a State, and foreign states or citizens or

subjects thereof * * *." The District Court would have had no jurisdiction of a suit brought by Panama against Caribbean, since both were alien corporations.

3. 28 U.S.C. § 41(1) (1940 ed.). The clause first appeared as § 11 of the Judiciary Act of 1789, 1 Stat. 79.

The second pre–1948 statute, 28 U.S.C. § 80 (1940 ed.),[4] stated that a district court should dismiss an action whenever:

"it shall appear to the satisfaction of the ... court ... that such suit does not really and substantially involve a dispute or controversy properly within the jurisdiction of [the] court, or that the parties to said suit have been improperly or collusively made or joined ... for the purpose of creating [federal jurisdiction]."

As part of the 1948 revision, § 80 was amended to produce the present § 1359. The assignee clause was simultaneously repealed. The Reviser's Note describes the amended assignee clause as a " 'jumble of legislative jargon,' "and states that "[t]he revised section changes this clause by confining its application to cases wherein the assignment is improperly or collusively made.... Furthermore, ... the original purpose of [the assignee] clause is better served by substantially following section 80." That purpose was said to be "to prevent the manufacture of Federal jurisdiction by the device of assignment." Ibid.

II.

Only a small number of cases decided under § 1359 have involved diversity jurisdiction based on assignments, and this Court has not considered the matter since the 1948 revision. Because the approach of the former assignee clause was to forbid the grounding of jurisdiction upon *any* assignment, regardless of its circumstances or purpose, decisions under that clause are of little assistance. However, decisions of this Court under the other predecessor statute, 28 U.S.C. § 80 (1940 ed.), seem squarely in point. These decisions, together with the evident purpose of § 1359, lead us to conclude that the Court of Appeals was correct in finding that the assignment in question was "improperly or collusively made."

The most compelling precedent is Farmington v. Pillsbury, 114 U.S. 138 (1885). There Maine holders of bonds issued by a Maine village desired to test the bonds' validity in the federal courts. In an effort to accomplish this, they cut the coupons from their bonds and transferred them to a citizen of Massachusetts, who gave in return a non-negotiable two-year note for $500 and a promise to pay back 50% of the net amount recovered above $500. The jurisdictional question was certified to this Court, which held that there was no federal jurisdiction because the plaintiff had been "improperly or collusively" made a party within the meaning of the predecessor statute to 28 U.S.C. § 80 (1940 ed.). The Court pointed out that the plaintiff could easily have been released from his non-negotiable note, and found that apart from the hoped-for creation of federal jurisdiction the only real consequence of the transfer was to enable the Massachusetts plaintiff to "retain one-half of what he collects for the use of his name and his trouble in collecting." 114 U.S., at 146. The Court concluded that "the transfer of the coupons was 'a

4. This statute was first enacted in 1875. See 18 Stat. 470.

mere contrivance, a pretence, the result of a collusive arrangement to create' " federal jurisdiction. Ibid.

We find the case before us indistinguishable from *Farmington* and other decisions of like tenor. When the assignment to Kramer is considered together with his total lack of previous connection with the matter and his simultaneous reassignment of a 95% interest back to Panama, there can be little doubt that the assignment was for purposes of collection, with Kramer to retain 5% of the net proceeds "for the use of his name and his trouble in collecting."[9] If the suit had been unsuccessful, Kramer would have been out only $1, plus costs. Moreover, Kramer candidly admits that the "assignment was in substantial part motivated by a desire by [Panama's] counsel to make diversity jurisdiction available...."

[handwritten margin note: Factors show "collusive" assignment]

The conclusion that this assignment was "improperly or collusively made" within the meaning of § 1359 is supported not only by precedent but also by consideration of the statute's purpose. If federal jurisdiction could be created by assignments of this kind, which are easy to arrange and involve few disadvantages for the assignor, then a vast quantity of ordinary contract and tort litigation could be channeled into the federal courts at the will of one of the parties. Such "manufacture of Federal jurisdiction" was the very thing which Congress intended to prevent when it enacted § 1359 and its predecessors.

III.

Kramer nevertheless argues that the assignment to him was not "improperly or collusively made" within the meaning of § 1359, for two main reasons. First, he suggests that the undisputed legality of the assignment under Texas law necessarily rendered it valid for purposes of federal jurisdiction. We cannot accept this contention. The existence of federal jurisdiction is a matter of federal, not state, law. * * * Moreover, to accept this argument would render § 1359 largely incapable of accomplishing its purpose; this very case demonstrates the ease with which a

---

9. Hence, we have no occasion to reexamine the cases in which this Court has held that where the transfer of a claim is absolute, with the transferor retaining no interest in the subject matter, then the transfer is not "improperly or collusively made," regardless of the transferor's motive. See, e.g., Cross v. Allen, 141 U.S. 528 (1891); South Dakota v. North Carolina, 192 U.S. 286 (1904); Black & White Taxicab Co. v. Brown & Yellow Taxicab Co., 276 U.S. 518 (1928); cf. Williamson v. Osenton, 232 U.S. 619 (1914).

Nor is it necessary to consider whether, in cases in which suit is required to be brought by an administrator or guardian, a motive to create diversity jurisdiction renders the appointment of an out-of-state representative "improper" or "collusive." See, e.g., McSparran v. Weist, 402 F.2d 867 (3

Cir.1968); Lang v. Elm City Constr. Co., 324 F.2d 235 (2 Cir.1963); County of Todd v. Loegering, 297 F.2d 470 (8 Cir.1961); cf. Mecom v. Fitzsimmons Drilling Co., 284 U.S. 183 (1931). Cases involving representatives vary in several respects from those in which jurisdiction is based on assignments: (1) in the former situation, some representative must be appointed before suit can be brought, while in the latter the assignor normally is himself capable of suing in state court; (2) under state law, different kinds of guardians and administrators may possess discrete sorts of powers; and (3) all such representatives owe their appointment to the decree of a state court, rather than solely to an action of the parties. It is not necessary to decide whether these distinctions amount to a difference for purposes of § 1359.

party may "manufacture" federal jurisdiction by an assignment which meets the requirements of state law.

Second, Kramer urges that this case is significantly distinguishable from earlier decisions because it involves diversity jurisdiction under 28 U.S.C. § 1332(a)(2), arising from the alienage of one of the parties, rather than the more common diversity jurisdiction based upon the parties' residence in different States. We can perceive no substance in this argument: by its terms, § 1359 applies equally to both types of diversity jurisdiction, and there is no indication that Congress intended them to be treated differently.

* * *

MR. JUSTICE FORTAS took no part in the consideration or decision of this case.

Notes

1. Why do you suppose there is a need for section 1359? Why should the parties not be allowed to manufacture diversity?

2. Note that the Court in *Kramer* indicates that it need not reconsider the cases holding that if an assignor retains no interest, jurisdiction will not be deemed collusive, regardless of the assignor's motives. Do you think the rule is a wise one?

3. As to the state of the post-*Kramer* law in the lower courts, see Attorneys Trust v. Videotape Computer Products, Inc., 93 F.3d 593, 595–96 (9th Cir.1996): "Since *Kramer*, courts have set out a number of factors which are to be considered in deciding whether an assignment is improper or collusive. Among them are: were there good business reasons for the assignment; did the assignee have a prior interest in the item or was the assignment timed to coincide with commencement of litigation; was any consideration given by the assignee; was the assignment partial or complete; and was there an admission that the motive was to create jurisdiction."

4. To what extent should a court, in applying section 1359, take into account the existence of a motivation to manufacture diversity jurisdiction? See Attorneys Trust v. Videotape Computer Products, 93 F.3d 593 (9th Cir.1996) (doubt exists that the subjective motive element is entitled to great weight). But see Grassi v. Ciba–Geigy, Ltd., 894 F.2d 181 (5th Cir.1990) (prior to *Kramer*, district courts almost uniformly refused to inquire into motives behind assignments; after *Kramer*, the court noted, the opposite appears to be true). See also Attorneys Trust v. Videotape Computer Products, Inc., 93 F.3d 593, 596 (9th Cir.1996) ("While motive can often be important, if the assignment is truly absolute and complete, motive often recedes into almost nothing").

Assignments between parent corporations and their subsidiaries are generally subjected to heightened scrutiny under section 1359. See, e.g., Prudential Oil Corp. v. Phillips Petroleum Co., 546 F.2d 469 (2d Cir.1976). See also Toste Farm Corp. v. Hadbury, Inc., 70 F.3d 640, 643–44 (1st

Cir.1995)("Courts have applied elevated scrutiny to assignments between affiliated parties.") Why do you think this is so?

5. Note that the Court in *Kramer* expressly declined to consider the applicability of section 1359 to appointments of administrators and executors, and suggested several possible distinctions between those situations and collusive assignments. Both before and after *Kramer*, the lower courts struggled with the applicability of section 1359 to such appointments. See, for example, Betar v. De Havilland Aircraft of Canada, 603 F.2d 30 (7th Cir.1979); Trager v. New Rochelle Hospital Medical Center, 453 F.Supp. 516 (S.D.N.Y.1978); Martinez v. United States Olympic Committee, 802 F.2d 1275 (10th Cir.1986); and Hackney v. Newman Memorial Hospital, 621 F.2d 1069 (10th Cir.), cert. denied, 449 U.S. 982 (1980). The 1988 amendments to the diversity statute, however, indicate that "the legal representative of the estate of a decedent shall be deemed to be a citizen only of the same state as the decedent, and the legal representative of an infant or incompetent shall be deemed to be a citizen only of the same State as the infant or incompetent." 28 U.S.C. § 1332(c).

6. Should section 1359 be deemed applicable to attempts to defeat, as well as to create, federal jurisdiction? Compare Picquet v. Amoco Production Co., 513 F.Supp. 938, 943 (M.D.La.1981) ("despite the absence of a statute specifically granting district courts the authority to inquire into assignments made for the purpose of defeating federal jurisdiction, the existence of diversity jurisdiction and the removal statute * * * grant the Court the power to protect its own jurisdiction") with Betar v. De Havilland Aircraft of Canada, Limited, note 5, supra, 603 F.2d at 33 ("Devices to create federal jurisdiction have historically been limited by statute; devices to defeat jurisdiction have not"). See also Herrick v. Pioneer Gas Products Co., 429 F.Supp. 80 (W.D.Okl.1976). Cf. 15 Moore's Federal Practice 3d § 102.19[5] (1997) ("the modern trend is toward applying parallel logic [to the limits on the collusive creation of diversity] to reject the collusive destruction of diversity"). Whether or not section 1359 can be properly read to apply to devices used to defeat federal jurisdiction, *should* such devices be deemed improper?

Chapter 15

SUPPLEMENTAL JURISDICTION

§ 1. CONCEPTS AND HISTORICAL DEVELOPMENT

M. REDISH, 16 MOORE'S FEDERAL PRACTICE 3d ¶ 106.02–.03 (1997): Supplemental jurisdiction has proven to be an important component of federal jurisdiction because it allows federal courts to entertain claims over which they have no independent basis of subject matter jurisdiction. When those claims are sufficiently tied to suits properly in federal court, supplemental jurisdiction fosters the interests of efficient judicial administration. And if the initial basis for federal jurisdiction is the presence of a federal question, supplemental jurisdiction removes artificial deterrents to litigants in their desire to have their federal claims adjudicated in federal court.

However, because of concerns over the need both to obey constitutional dictates and to avoid undue encroachment on the scope of state judicial authority, both Congress and the Supreme Court have imposed limits on the concept's reach that have often given rise to substantial confusion.

Originally a judge-made doctrine, Congress [in 1990] codified supplemental jurisdiction in 28 U.S.C. § 1367.

The statute has been subject to significant criticism from commentators, primarily because of both simple errors in drafting and a failure to resolve the numerous doctrinal problems and ambiguities that had evolved from judicial interpretation of the doctrine in its judge-made form. With certain major exceptions, the statute apparently intended simply to codify much of the preexisting judicial doctrine—ambiguities, inconsistencies, and all. The federal courts are now having to wrestle with the newly-created problems identified by critics of the statute, as well as with the many preexisting doctrinal ambiguities that Congress failed to resolve.

* * *

Supplemental jurisdiction is a statutory term that is generally viewed by the courts and commentators as encompassing both what courts previously referred to as "pendent" jurisdiction and "ancillary" jurisdiction.

The term "supplemental jurisdiction" now encompasses three separate though historically and conceptually related concepts: pendent claim jurisdiction, pendent party jurisdiction, and ancillary jurisdiction. Supplemental jurisdiction under the statute thus addresses both the assertion of claims for which there is no independent basis for federal jurisdiction and disputes involving parties who are not otherwise before the court.

There is some suggestion in the courts, possibly including the Supreme Court, that statutory supplemental jurisdiction may not encompass all previous instances of ancillary jurisdiction. [Kokkonen v. Guardian Life Ins. Co., 511 U.S. 375 (1994).]

* * *

The term, "pendent jurisdiction" traditionally described the basis for a court's exercise of jurisdiction to hear a claim for which there is no independent basis for federal jurisdiction, but that arises out of a "common nucleus of operative fact" with a properly asserted claim that does fall within the federal court's subject matter jurisdiction.

For example, an alleged incident of unlawful arrest might give rise simultaneously to claims against the same individual for violation of federally protected civil rights and under state tort law for battery and false imprisonment.

Although there may have been no independent federal jurisdictional basis on which to adjudicate the state tort claims, those claims could be joined and heard with the § 1983 claim because they were within the pendent jurisdiction of the federal court. Such claims were sometimes referred to as "pendent state claims."

The mere fact that a federal court had *power* to assert pendent claim jurisdiction, however, did not mean that it was required to exercise it. The Supreme Court recognized several factors that could justify a district court's exercise of its discretion not to assert pendent jurisdiction.

* * *

Pendent claim jurisdiction presupposed one plaintiff and one defendant, with an independent jurisdictional basis existing for one of the claims but not for the other. Pendent party jurisdiction, on the other hand, constitutes the extension of pendent jurisdiction over parties who are not named in any claim that is independently cognizable by the federal court.

The Supreme Court, in rejecting the concept of pendent party jurisdiction, failed adequately to distinguish the concept of ancillary jurisdiction.

Whether the concept of pendent party jurisdiction is viable has proven to be one of the most contentious elements of the historical development of supplemental jurisdiction.

* * *

The term "ancillary jurisdiction" traditionally described the assertion of jurisdiction over claims or parties over whom the federal court lacked independent subject matter jurisdiction, but that arose out of the same conduct, transaction or occurrence as the plaintiff's original claim, to which federal subject matter jurisdiction extended.

The Supreme Court has noted that ancillary jurisdiction has been asserted for two separate, though sometimes related, purposes: (1) To permit disposition, by a single court, of claims that are, in varying respects and degrees, factually interdependent; and (2) to enable a court to manage its proceedings, vindicate its authority, and effectuate its decrees.

* * *

The Federal Rules of Civil Procedure do not, in and of themselves, create an independent basis for federal jurisdiction.

Though the Rules may provide for the introduction of new parties through impleader (Rule 14), joinder (Rules 19, 20), and intervention (Rule 24), those rules presuppose some basis for jurisdiction. Thus, in order to be heard in federal court, claims against parties joined under those rules must find some distinct basis for federal jurisdiction, such as diversity of citizenship or federal question jurisdiction. If no other jurisdictional basis existed, ancillary jurisdiction historically authorized adjudication of these claims if they arose out of the same transaction or occurrence as the main claim. Usually, though not always, ancillary jurisdiction applied if the joined claims were asserted by a party other than the plaintiff.

* * *

Ancillary jurisdiction was first recognized by the Supreme Court in the 1800 case of *Freeman v. Howe* [65 U.S. (24 How.) 450 (1861)], although it was not so labeled. There the Court held that mortgagees of a piece of property that was the subject of litigation in federal court could intervene in the suit even though they were not diverse from the original parties to the action.

The Supreme Court further expounded the doctrine 66 years later in *Moore v. New York Cotton Exchange* [270 U.S. 593 (1926)], in which the plaintiff had filed a federal antitrust claim against a defendant, who in turn filed a counterclaim against the plaintiff based on state law. The Court held that the district court could exercise jurisdiction over the counterclaim because it arose out of the same transaction as the original claim. In so holding, it defined "transaction" as "a word of flexible meaning. It may comprehend a series of many occurrences, depending not so much upon the immediateness of their connection as upon their logical relationship."

Over the years, especially after the enactment of the liberal joinder devices of the Federal Rules in 1938, federal courts continued to expand the concept of ancillary jurisdiction to include not only compulsory counterclaims, but also cross-claims under Federal Rule of Civil Procedure 13(g), third-party impleader claims under Rule 14(a).

* * *

The doctrine of pendent claim jurisdiction had its early roots in the Supreme Court's decision in *Osborn v. Bank of United States*. In defining the outer limits of Congress's power to vest the federal courts with federal question jurisdiction, Chief Justice Marshall there recognized that "there is scarcely any case, every part of which depends on the constitution, laws, or treaties of the United States." The Court therefore held that when a case involves a federal question, Congress has the power to confer jurisdiction on the district courts, even though other questions of fact or law may be involved.

Although this decision did not directly concern the exercise or creation of pendent claim jurisdiction, the Court in *Osborn* did recognize the possibility that Congress could at some point confer jurisdiction on the federal courts to hear state law claims when the case as a whole involved a federal question and those state law claims were part of the same "case" for purposes of Article III.

* * *

§ 2.   THE CONCEPT OF "COMMON NUCLEUS OF OPERATIVE FACT"

UNITED MINE WORKERS OF AMERICA v. GIBBS

Supreme Court of the United States, 1966.
383 U.S. 715.

Mr. Justice Brennan delivered the opinion of the Court.

Respondent Paul Gibbs was awarded compensatory and punitive damages in this action against petitioner United Mine Workers of America (UMW) for alleged violations of § 303 of the Labor Management Relations Act, 1947, 61 Stat. 158, as amended, and of the common law of Tennessee. The case grew out of the rivalry between the United Mine Workers and the Southern Labor Union over representation of workers in the southern Appalachian coal fields. Tennessee Consolidated Coal Company, not a party here, laid off 100 miners of the UMW's Local 5881 when it closed one of its mines in southern Tennessee during the spring of 1960. Late that summer, Grundy Company, a wholly owned subsidiary of Consolidated, hired respondent as mine superintendent to attempt to open a new mine on Consolidated's property at nearby Gray's Creek through use of members of the Southern Labor Union. As part of the arrangement, Grundy also gave respondent a contract to haul the mine's coal to the nearest railroad loading point.

On August 15 and 16, 1960, armed members of Local 5881 forcibly prevented the opening of the mine, threatening respondent and beating an organizer for the rival union. The members of the local believed Consolidated had promised them the jobs at the new mine; they insisted that if anyone would do the work, they would. At this time, no representative of the UMW, their international union, was present. George Gilbert, the UMW's field representative for the area including Local 5881, was away at Middlesboro, Kentucky, attending an Executive Board meeting when the members of the local discovered Grundy's plan; he did not return to the area until late in the day of August 16. There was uncontradicted testimony that he first learned of the violence while at the meeting, and returned with explicit instructions from his international union superiors to establish a limited picket line, to prevent any further violence, and to see to it that the strike did not spread to neighboring mines. There was no further violence at the mine site; a picket line was maintained there for nine months; and no further attempts were made to open the mine during that period.

Respondent lost his job as superintendent, and never entered into performance of his haulage contract. He testified that he soon began to lose other trucking contracts and mine leases he held in nearby areas. Claiming these effects to be the result of a concerted union plan against him, he sought recovery not against Local 5881 or its members, but only against petitioner, the international union. The suit was brought in the United States District Court for the Eastern District of Tennessee, and jurisdiction was premised on allegations of secondary boycotts under § 303. The state law claim, for which jurisdiction was based upon the doctrine of pendent jurisdiction, asserted "an unlawful conspiracy and an unlawful boycott aimed at him and [Grundy] to maliciously, wantonly and willfully interfere with his contract of employment and with his contract of haulage."

The trial judge refused to submit to the jury the claims of pressure intended to cause mining firms other than Grundy to cease doing business with Gibbs; he found those claims unsupported by the evidence. The jury's verdict was that the UMW had violated both § 303 and state law. Gibbs was awarded $60,000 as damages under the employment contract and $14,500 under the haulage contract; he was also awarded $100,000 punitive damages. On motion, the trial court set aside the award of damages with respect to the haulage contract on the ground that damage was unproved. It also held that union pressure on Grundy to discharge respondent as supervisor would constitute only a primary dispute with Grundy, as respondent's employer, and hence was not cognizable as a claim under § 303. Interference with the employment relationship was cognizable as a state claim, however, and a remitted award was sustained on the state law claim. The Court of Appeals for the Sixth Circuit affirmed. We granted certiorari. We reverse.

I.

A threshold question is whether the District Court properly entertained jurisdiction of the claim based on Tennessee law. There was no need to decide a like question in Teamsters Union v. Morton, 377 U.S. 252, since the pertinent state claim there was based on peaceful secondary activities and we held that state law based on such activities had been pre-empted by § 303. But here respondent's claim is based in part on proofs of violence and intimidation. "[W]e have allowed the States to grant compensation for the consequences, as defined by the traditional law of torts, of conduct marked by violence and imminent threats to the public order. United Automobile Workers v. Russell, 356 U.S. 634; United Construction Workers v. Laburnum Corp., 347 U.S. 656. * * * State jurisdiction has prevailed in these situations because the compelling state interest, in the scheme of our federalism, in the maintenance of domestic peace is not overridden in the absence of clearly expressed congressional direction." San Diego Building Trades Council v. Garmon, 359 U.S. 236, 247.

The fact that state remedies were not entirely preempted does not, however, answer the question whether the state claim was properly adjudicated in the District Court absent diversity jurisdiction. The Court held in Hurn v. Oursler, 289 U.S. 238, that state law claims are appropriate for federal court determination if they form a separate but parallel ground for relief also sought in a substantial claim based on federal law. The Court distinguished permissible from nonpermissible exercises of federal judicial power over state law claims by contrasting "a case where two distinct grounds in support of a single cause of action are alleged, one only of which presents a federal question, and a case where two separate and distinct causes of action are alleged, one only of which is federal in character. In the former, where the federal question averred is not plainly wanting in substance, the federal court, even though the federal ground be not established, may nevertheless retain and dispose of the case upon the non-federal *ground;* in the latter it may not do so upon the non-federal *cause of action.*" 289 U.S., at 246. The question is into which category the present action fell.

Hurn was decided in 1933 before the unification of law and equity by the Federal Rules of Civil Procedure. At the time, the meaning of "cause of action" was a subject of serious dispute; the phrase might "mean one thing for one purpose and something different for another." United States v. Memphis Cotton Oil Co., 288 U.S. 62, 67–68. The Court in *Hurn* identified what it meant by the term by citation of Baltimore S. S. Co. v. Phillips, 274 U.S. 316, a case in which "cause of action" had been used to identify the operative scope of the doctrine of *res judicata.* In that case the Court had noted that " 'the whole tendency of our decisions is to require a plaintiff to try his whole cause of action and his whole case at one time.' " * * * Had the Court found a jurisdictional bar to reaching the state claim in *Hurn,* we assume that the doctrine of *res judicata* would not have been applicable in any subsequent state suit. But the citation of *Baltimore S. S. Co.* shows that the Court found that the weighty policies of judicial economy and fairness to parties reflected in *res judicata* doctrine were in themselves strong counsel for the adoption of a rule which would permit federal courts to dispose of the state as well as the federal claims.

With the adoption of the Federal Rules of Civil Procedure and the unified form of action, Fed.Rule Civ.Proc. 2, much of the controversy over "cause of action" abated. The phrase remained as the keystone of the *Hurn* test, however, and, as commentators have noted, has been the source of considerable confusion. Under the Rules, the impulse is toward entertaining the broadest possible scope of action consistent with fairness to the parties; joinder of claims, parties and remedies is strongly encouraged. Yet because the *Hurn* question involves issues of jurisdiction as well as convenience, there has been some tendency to limit its application to cases in which the state and federal claims are, as in *Hurn*, "little more than the equivalent of different epithets to characterize the same group of circumstances." 289 U.S., at 246.

This limited approach is unnecessarily grudging. Pendent jurisdiction, in the sense of judicial *power*, exists whenever there is a claim "arising under [the] Constitution, the Laws of the United States, and Treaties made, or which shall be made, under their Authority ...," U.S.Const., Art. III, § 2, and the relationship between that claim and the state claim permits the conclusion that the entire action before the court comprises but one constitutional "case." The federal claim must have substance sufficient to confer subject matter jurisdiction on the court. Levering & Garrigues Co. v. Morrin, 289 U.S. 103. The state and federal claims must derive from a common nucleus of operative fact. But if, considered without regard to their federal or state character, a plaintiff's claims are such that he would ordinarily be expected to try them all in one judicial proceeding, then, assuming substantiality of the federal issues, there is *power* in federal courts to hear the whole.

That power need not be exercised in every case in which it is found to exist. It has consistently been recognized that pendent jurisdiction is a doctrine of discretion, not of plaintiff's right. Its justification lies in considerations of judicial economy, convenience and fairness to litigants; if these are not present a federal court should hesitate to exercise jurisdiction over state claims, even though bound to apply state law to them, Erie R. Co. v. Tompkins, 304 U.S. 64. Needless decisions of state law should be avoided both as a matter of comity and to promote justice between the parties, by procuring for them a surer-footed reading of applicable law. Certainly, if the federal claims are dismissed before trial, even though not insubstantial in a jurisdictional sense, the state claims should be dismissed as well. Similarly, if it appears that the state issues substantially predominate, whether in terms of proof, of the scope of the issues raised, or of the comprehensiveness of the remedy sought, the state claims may be dismissed without prejudice and left for resolution to state tribunals. There may, on the other hand, be situations in which the state claim is so closely tied to questions of federal policy that the argument for exercise of pendent jurisdiction is particularly strong. In the present case, for example, the allowable scope of the state claim implicates the federal doctrine of pre-emption; while this interrelationship does not create statutory federal question jurisdiction, Louisville & N. R. Co. v. Mottley, 211 U.S. 149, its existence is relevant to the exercise of discretion. Finally, there may be reasons independent of jurisdictional considerations, such as the likelihood of jury confusion in treating divergent legal theories of relief, that would justify separating state and federal claims for trial, Fed.Rule Civ.Proc. 42(b). If so, jurisdiction should ordinarily be refused.

The question of power will ordinarily be resolved on the pleadings. But the issue whether pendent jurisdiction has been properly assumed is one which remains open throughout the litigation. Pretrial procedures or even the trial itself may reveal a substantial hegemony of state law claims, or likelihood of jury confusion, which could not have been anticipated at the pleading stage. Although it will of course be appropriate to take account in this circumstance of the already completed course of the litigation, dismissal of the state claim might even then be merited. For example, it may appear that the plaintiff was well aware of the nature of his proofs and the relative importance of his claims; recognition of a federal court's wide latitude to decide ancillary questions of state law does not imply that it must tolerate a litigant's effort to impose upon it what is in effect only a state law case. Once it appears that a state claim constitutes the real body of a case, to which the federal claim is only an appendage, the state claim may fairly be dismissed.

We are not prepared to say that in the present case the District Court exceeded its discretion in proceeding to judgment on the state claim. We may assume for purposes of decision that the District Court was correct in its holding that the claim of pressure on Grundy to terminate the employment contract was outside the purview of § 303. Even so, the § 303 claims based on secondary pressures on Grundy relative to the haulage contract and on other coal operators generally were substantial. Although § 303 limited recovery to compensatory damages based on secondary pressures * * * and state law allowed both compensatory and punitive damages, and allowed such damages as to both secondary and primary activity, the state and federal claims arose from the same nucleus of operative fact and reflected alternative remedies. Indeed, the verdict sheet sent in to the jury authorized only one award of damages, so that recovery could not be given separately on the federal and state claims.

It is true that the § 303 claims ultimately failed and that the only recovery allowed respondent was on the state claim. We cannot confidently say, however, that the federal issues were so remote or played such a minor role at the trial that in effect the state claim only was tried. Although the District Court dismissed as unproved the § 303 claims that petitioner's secondary activities included attempts to induce coal operators other than Grundy to cease doing business with respondent, the court submitted the § 303 claims relating to Grundy to the jury. The jury returned verdicts against petitioner on those § 303 claims, and it was only on petitioner's motion for a directed verdict and a judgment *n.o.v.* that the verdicts on those claims were set aside. The District Judge considered the claim as to the haulage contract proved as to liability, and held it failed only for lack of proof of damages. Although there was some risk of confusing the jury in joining the state and federal claims— especially since * * * differing standards of proof of UMW involvement applied—the possibility of confusion could be lessened by employing a special verdict form, as the District Court did. Moreover, the question whether the permissible scope of the state claim was limited by the doctrine of preemption afforded a special reason for the exercise of pendent jurisdiction; the federal courts are particularly appropriate bodies for the application of preemption principles. We thus conclude that although it may be that the District Court might, in its sound discretion, have dismissed the state claim, the circumstances show no error in refusing to do so.

* * *

THE CHIEF JUSTICE took no part in the decision of this case.

* * *

[The concurring opinion of JUSTICE HARLAN, joined by JUSTICE CLARK, is omitted].

Note

What purpose or purposes does the supplemental jurisdiction doctrine serve? In *Gibbs*, the Court refers to such factors as economy and convenience. In what way does the doctrine foster those interests? Are those the *only* interests furthered by use of supplemental jurisdiction? See Schenkier, *Ensuring Access to Federal Courts: A Revised Rationale for Pendent Jurisdiction*, 75 Nw.U.L.Rev. 245 (1980), arguing that if economy and convenience were the only goals of pendent jurisdiction, there would generally be no need for the doctrine, since those goals can be as easily achieved by combining the state and federal issues in a state court suit, as well as in a federal court suit. Schenkier argues that a more appropriate rationale for the pendent jurisdiction doctrine "may be found in a desire to eliminate the bias that would otherwise confront plaintiffs seeking to utilize the federal courts to litigate state and federal claims arising from the same transaction or course of events." Id. at 247. What do you suppose he means by this? Recall that, with relatively rare exceptions, state courts have both the authority and the duty to adjudicate suits brought pursuant to federal law.

§ 3.   THE SUPPLEMENTAL JURISDICTION ACT

In Finley v. United States, 490 U.S. 545 (1989), the Supreme Court held that the judge-made concept of pendent claim jurisdiction did not extend to pendent parties, even where the federal court's jurisdiction over the primary claim was exclusive. Towards the close of the Court's opinion, Justice Scalia wrote: "Whatever we say regarding the scope of jurisdiction conferred by a particular statute can of course be changed by

Congress. What is of paramount importance is that Congress can be able to legislate against a background of clear interpretive rules, so that it may know the effect of the language it adopts." Id. at 556.

The year prior to *Finley*, Chief Justice Rehnquist had, pursuant to the Judicial Improvements and Access to Justice Act, Pub. L. 100–702, 102 Stat. 4642 (1988), created the Federal Courts Study Committee in order to recommend reforms to the federal judicial system. After *Finley*, a subcommittee of the Committee initially suggested codification of the judge-made doctrines of pendent and ancillary jurisdiction. After consideration of various alternatives, Congress enacted 28 U.S.C. § 1367 [contained in Appendix B], based on a proposal made by three academics, Stephen Burbank, Thomas Mengler and Thomas Rowe.

The statute overrules *Finley*, expressly authorizing the use of pendent party jurisdiction. See 28 U.S.C. § 1367 (a) ("Such supplemental jurisdiction shall include claims that involve the joinder or intervention of additional parties"). Other than that change, the Act appears largely to have been intended to codify the preexisting judge-made doctrines of pendent and ancillary jurisdiction.

Nevertheless, a number of significant interpretive ambiguities and controversies have developed. Compare Freer, *Compounding Confusion and Hampering Diversity: Life After* Finley *and the Supplemental Jurisdiction Act*, 40 Emory L.J. 445 (1991) (attacking statute) with Rowe, Burbank & Mengler, *Compounding a Creating Confusion About Supplemental Jurisdiction? A Reply to Professor Freer*, 40 Emory L.J. 943 (1991) (defending statute). See also Arthur & Freer, *Grasping Burnt Straws: The Disaster of the Supplemental Jurisdiction Statute*, 40 Emory L.J. 963 (1991). The Supreme Court has has resolved one ambiguity, holding that the statutory phrase, "so related to claims in the action * * * that they form part of the same case or controversy under Article III" is the same as the test of "common nucleus of operative fact" in *Gibbs*. Chicago v. International College of Surgeons, 522 U.S. 156 (1997).

Another interpretive controversy has concerned the application of supplemental jurisdiction to the claims of additional plaintiffs in two types of diversity cases. First, the Court had previously held, in Clark v. Paul Gray, Inc., 306 U.S. 583 (1939), that if two plaintiffs join together under Rule 20, each must independently meet the minimum amount in controversy; a plaintiff lacking the minimum amount cannot use supplemental jurisdiction even if another plaintiff with a related claim satisfies the jurisdictional minimum. (*Clark* itself was brought under federal question jurisdiction, which at the time contained an amount-in-controversy requirement, but it also applies to diversity cases.) A similar question arises in the case of absent class members in a class action brought pursuant to Rule 23, when the basis for jurisdiction is diversity of citizenship. In Supreme Tribe of Ben–Hur v. Cauble, 255 U.S. 356 (1921), the Court held that ancillary jurisdiction would allow absent plaintiff class members from the same state as the defendant to join a federal class action when the named plaintiff was from a different state as the defendant. The Court so held, despite the existence of the complete diversity requirement [see supra p. 785]. However, more than fifty years later, the Court held in Zahn v. International Paper Co., 414 U.S. 291 (1973), that absent diversity plaintiffs who failed to meet the jurisdictional minimum could not append their claims to that of a named plaintiff who did meet the minimum. At no point did the Court in *Zahn* attempt to explain the differences, if any, between its own facts and those of *Ben-Hur*. Do you see any basis for the distinction? Whether or not such a distinction can be rationalized, lower courts following *Zahn* adhered to it. Examine the text of 28 U.S.C. § 1367(b). What, if anything, can one reasonably infer from this provision concerning the continued vitality of *Zahn* and *Clark* following the enactment of the Supplemental Jurisdiction Act? On that question, consider the following case.

EXXON MOBIL CORP. v. ALLAPATTAH SERVICES, INC.

Supreme Court of the United States, 2005.
545 U.S. 546.

JUSTICE KENNEDY delivered the opinion of the Court.

These consolidated cases* present the question whether a federal court in a diversity action may exercise supplemental jurisdiction over additional plaintiffs whose claims do not satisfy the minimum amount-in-controversy requirement, provided the claims are part of the same case or controversy as the claims of plaintiffs who do allege a sufficient amount in controversy. Our decision turns on the correct interpretation of 28 U.S.C. § 1367. The question has divided the Courts of Appeals, and we granted certiorari to resolve the conflict.

We hold that, where the other elements of jurisdiction are present and at least one named plaintiff in the action satisfies the amount-in-controversy requirement, § 1367 does authorize supplemental jurisdiction over the claims of other plaintiffs in the same Article III case or controversy, even if those claims are for less than the jurisdictional amount specified in the statute setting forth the requirements for diversity jurisdiction. We affirm the judgment of the Court of Appeals for the Eleventh Circuit in [*Allapattah*], and we reverse the judgment of the Court of Appeals for the First Circuit in [*Rosario Ortega*].

I

In 1991, about 10,000 Exxon dealers filed a class-action suit against the Exxon Corporation in the United States District Court for the Northern District of Florida. The dealers alleged an intentional and systematic scheme by Exxon under which they were overcharged for fuel purchased from Exxon. The plaintiffs invoked the District Court's

___

* Exxon Mobil Corp. v. Allapattah Services Inc. was consolidated with Rosario   Ortega v. Star–Kist Foods, Inc., and this opinion decides both cases.—ED.

§ 1332(a) diversity jurisdiction. After a unanimous jury verdict in favor of the plaintiffs, the District Court certified the case for interlocutory review, asking whether it had properly exercised § 1367 supplemental jurisdiction over the claims of class members who did not meet the jurisdictional minimum amount in controversy.

The Court of Appeals for the Eleventh Circuit upheld the District Court's extension of supplemental jurisdiction to these class members. Allapattah Services, Inc. v. Exxon Corp., 333 F.3d 1248 (2003). "[W]e find," the court held, "that § 1367 clearly and unambiguously provides district courts with the authority in diversity class actions to exercise supplemental jurisdiction over the claims of class members who do not meet the minimum amount in controversy as long as the district court has original jurisdiction over the claims of at least one of the class representatives." Id., at 1256. This decision accords with the views of the Courts of Appeals for the Fourth, Sixth, and Seventh Circuits. See Rosmer v. Pfizer, Inc., 263 F.3d 110 (CA4 2001); Olden v. LaFarge Corp., 383 F.3d 495 (CA6 2004); Stromberg Metal Works, Inc. v. Press Mechanical, Inc., 77 F.3d 928 (CA7 1996); In re Brand Name Prescription Drugs Antitrust Litigation, 123 F.3d 599 (CA7 1997). The Courts of Appeals for the Fifth and Ninth Circuits, adopting a similar analysis of the statute, have held that in a diversity class action the unnamed class members need not meet the amount-in-controversy requirement, provided the named class members do. These decisions, however, are unclear on whether all the named plaintiffs must satisfy this requirement. In re Abbott Labs., 51 F.3d 524 (CA5 1995); Gibson v. Chrysler Corp., 261 F.3d 927 (CA9 2001).

In the other case now before us the Court of Appeals for the First Circuit took a different position on the meaning of § 1367(a). 370 F.3d 124 (2004). In that case, a 9–year-old girl sued Star–Kist in a diversity action in the United States District Court for the District of Puerto Rico, seeking damages for unusually severe injuries she received when she sliced her finger on a tuna can. Her family joined in the suit, seeking damages for emotional distress and certain medical expenses. The District Court granted summary judgment to Star–Kist, finding that none of the plaintiffs met the minimum amount-in-controversy requirement. The Court of Appeals for the First Circuit, however, ruled that the injured girl, but not her family members, had made allegations of damages in the requisite amount.

The Court of Appeals then addressed whether, in light of the fact that one plaintiff met the requirements for original jurisdiction, supplemental jurisdiction over the remaining plaintiffs' claims was proper under § 1367. The court held that § 1367 authorizes supplemental jurisdiction only when the district court has original jurisdiction over the action, and that in a diversity case original jurisdiction is lacking if one plaintiff fails to satisfy the amount-in-controversy requirement. Although the Court of Appeals claimed to "express no view" on whether the result would be the same in a class action, id., at 143, n. 19, its analysis is inconsistent with that of the Court of Appeals for the

Eleventh Circuit. The Court of Appeals for the First Circuit's view of § 1367 is, however, shared by the Courts of Appeal for the Third, Eighth, and Tenth Circuits, and the latter two Courts of Appeals have expressly applied this rule to class actions. See Meritcare, Inc. v. St. Paul Mercury Ins. Co., 166 F.3d 214 (CA3 1999); Trimble v. Asarco, Inc., 232 F.3d 946 (CA8 2000); Leonhardt v. Western Sugar Co., 160 F.3d 631 (CA10 1998).

II

A

The district courts of the United States, as we have said many times, are "courts of limited jurisdiction. They possess only that power authorized by Constitution and statute," * * * In order to provide a federal forum for plaintiffs who seek to vindicate federal rights, Congress has conferred on the district courts original jurisdiction in federal-question cases—civil actions that arise under the Constitution, laws, or treaties of the United States. 28 U.S.C. § 1331. In order to provide a neutral forum for what have come to be known as diversity cases, Congress also has granted district courts original jurisdiction in civil actions between citizens of different States, between U.S. citizens and foreign citizens, or by foreign states against U.S. citizens. § 1332. To ensure that diversity jurisdiction does not flood the federal courts with minor disputes, § 1332(a) requires that the matter in controversy in a diversity case exceed a specified amount, currently $75,000. § 1332(a).

Although the district courts may not exercise jurisdiction absent a statutory basis, it is well established—in certain classes of cases—that, once a court has original jurisdiction over some claims in the action, it may exercise supplemental jurisdiction over additional claims that are part of the same case or controversy. The leading modern case for this principle is Mine Workers v. Gibbs, 383 U.S. 715 (1966). In *Gibbs*, the plaintiff alleged the defendant's conduct violated both federal and state law. The District Court, *Gibbs* held, had original jurisdiction over the action based on the federal claims. *Gibbs* confirmed that the District Court had the additional power (though not the obligation) to exercise supplemental jurisdiction over related state claims that arose from the same Article III case or controversy. Id., at 725 ("The federal claim must have substance sufficient to confer subject matter jurisdiction on the court.... [A]ssuming substantiality of the federal issues, there is *power* in federal courts to hear the whole").

As we later noted, the decision allowing jurisdiction over pendent state claims in *Gibbs* did not mention, let alone come to grips with, the text of the jurisdictional statutes and the bedrock principle that federal courts have no jurisdiction without statutory authorization. Finley v. United States, 490 U.S. 545, 548 (1989). In *Finley*, we nonetheless reaffirmed and rationalized *Gibbs* and its progeny by inferring from it the interpretive principle that, in cases involving supplemental jurisdiction over additional claims between parties properly in federal court, the jurisdictional statutes should be read broadly, on the assumption that in this context Congress intended to authorize courts to exercise their full Article III power to dispose of an " 'entire action before the court [which] comprises but one constitutional "case." ' " 490 U.S., at 549 (quoting *Gibbs*, supra, at 725).

We have not, however, applied *Gibbs*' expansive interpretive approach to other aspects of the jurisdictional statutes. For instance, we have consistently interpreted § 1332 as requiring complete diversity: In a case with multiple plaintiffs and multiple defendants, the presence in the action of a single plaintiff from the same State as a single defendant deprives the district court of original diversity jurisdiction over the entire action. Strawbridge v. Curtiss, 3 Cranch 267 (1806) * * *. The complete diversity requirement is not mandated by the Constitution, State Farm Fire & Casualty Co. v. Tashire, 386 U.S. 523, 530–531 (1967), or by the plain text of § 1332(a). The Court, nonetheless, has adhered to the complete diversity rule in light of the purpose of the diversity requirement, which is to provide a federal forum for important disputes where state courts might favor, or be perceived as favoring, home-state litigants. The presence of parties from the same State on both sides of a case dispels this concern, eliminating a principal reason for conferring § 1332 jurisdiction over any of the claims in the action. * * * The specific purpose of the complete diversity rule explains both why we have not adopted *Gibbs*' expansive interpretive approach to this aspect of the jurisdictional statute and why *Gibbs* does not undermine the complete diversity rule. In order for a federal court to invoke supplemental jurisdiction under *Gibbs*, it must first have original jurisdiction over at least one claim in the action. Incomplete diversity destroys original jurisdiction with respect to all claims, so there is nothing to which supplemental jurisdiction can adhere.

In contrast to the diversity requirement, most of the other statutory prerequisites for federal jurisdiction, including the federal-question and amount-in-controversy requirements, can be analyzed claim by claim. True, it does not follow by necessity from this that a district court has authority to exercise supplemental jurisdiction over all claims provided there is original jurisdiction over just one. Before the enactment of § 1367, the Court declined in contexts other than the pendent-claim instance to follow *Gibbs*' expansive approach to interpretation of the jurisdictional statutes. The Court took a more restrictive view of the proper interpretation of these statutes in so-called pendent-party cases involving supplemental jurisdiction over claims involving additional parties—plaintiffs or defendants—where the district courts would lack original jurisdiction over claims by each of the parties standing alone.

Thus, with respect to plaintiff-specific jurisdictional requirements, the Court held in Clark v. Paul Gray, Inc., 306 U.S. 583 (1939), that every plaintiff must separately satisfy the amount-in-controversy requirement. Though *Clark* was a federal-question case, at that time federal-question jurisdiction had an amount-in-controversy requirement analogous to the amount-in-controversy requirement for diversity cases.

"Proper practice," *Clark* held, "requires that where each of several plaintiffs is bound to establish the jurisdictional amount with respect to his own claim, the suit should be dismissed as to those who fail to show that the requisite amount is involved." Id., at 590. The Court reaffirmed this rule, in the context of a class action brought invoking § 1332(a) diversity jurisdiction, in Zahn v. International Paper Co., 414 U.S. 291 (1973). It follows "inescapably" from *Clark*, the Court held in *Zahn*, that "any plaintiff without the jurisdictional amount must be dismissed from the case, even though others allege jurisdictionally sufficient claims." 414 U.S., at 300.

* * *

In Finley v. United States, 490 U.S. 545 (1989), we confronted a similar issue in a different statutory context. The plaintiff in *Finley* brought a Federal Tort Claims Act negligence suit against the Federal Aviation Administration in District Court, which had original jurisdiction under § 1346(b). The plaintiff tried to add related claims against other defendants, invoking the District Court's supplemental jurisdiction over so-called pendent parties. We held that the District Court lacked a sufficient statutory basis for exercising supplemental jurisdiction over these claims. * * * [W]e held in *Finley* that "a grant of jurisdiction over claims involving particular parties does not itself confer jurisdiction over additional claims by or against different parties." 490 U.S., at 556. While *Finley* did not "limit or impair" *Gibbs'* liberal approach to interpreting the jurisdictional statutes in the context of supplemental jurisdiction over additional claims involving the same parties, 490 U.S., at 556, *Finley* nevertheless declined to extend that interpretive assumption to claims involving additional parties. *Finley* held that in the context of parties, in contrast to claims, "we will not assume that the full constitutional power has been congressionally authorized, and will not read jurisdictional statutes broadly." Id., at 549.

As the jurisdictional statutes existed in 1989, then, here is how matters stood: First, the diversity requirement in § 1332(a) required complete diversity; absent complete diversity, the district court lacked original jurisdiction over all of the claims in the action. *Strawbridge*, 3 Cranch, at 267–268 * * *. Second, if the district court had original jurisdiction over at least one claim, the jurisdictional statutes implicitly authorized supplemental jurisdiction over all other claims between the same parties arising out of the same Article III case or controversy. *Gibbs*, 383 U.S., at 725. Third, even when the district court had original jurisdiction over one or more claims between particular parties, the jurisdictional statutes did not authorize supplemental jurisdiction over additional claims involving other parties. *Clark*, supra, at 590; *Zahn*, supra, at 300–301; *Finley*, supra, at 556.

B

In *Finley* we emphasized that "[w]hatever we say regarding the scope of jurisdiction conferred by a particular statute can of course be changed by Congress." 490 U.S., at 556. In 1990, Congress accepted the invitation. It passed the Judicial Improvements Act, 104 Stat. 5089, which enacted § 1367, the provision which controls these cases.

* * *

All parties to this litigation and all courts to consider the question agree that § 1367 overturned the result in *Finley*. There is no warrant, however, for assuming that § 1367 did no more than to overrule *Finley* and otherwise to codify the existing state of the law of supplemental jurisdiction. We must not give jurisdictional statutes a more expansive interpretation than their text warrants, 490 U.S., at 549, 556; but it is just as important not to adopt an artificial construction that is narrower than what the text provides. No sound canon of interpretation requires Congress to speak with extraordinary clarity in order to modify the rules of federal jurisdiction within appropriate constitutional bounds. Ordinary principles of statutory construction apply. In order to determine the scope of supplemental jurisdiction authorized by § 1367, then, we must examine the statute's text in light of context, structure, and related statutory provisions.

Section 1367(a) is a broad grant of supplemental jurisdiction over other claims within the same case or controversy, as long as the action is one in which the district courts would have original jurisdiction. The last sentence of § 1367(a) makes it clear that the grant of supplemental jurisdiction extends to claims involving joinder or intervention of additional parties. The single question before us, therefore, is whether a diversity case in which the claims of some plaintiffs satisfy the amount-in-controversy requirement, but the claims of others plaintiffs do not, presents a "civil action of which the district courts have original jurisdiction." If the answer is yes, § 1367(a) confers supplemental jurisdiction over all claims, including those that do not independently satisfy the amount-in-controversy requirement, if the claims are part of the same Article III case or controversy. If the answer is no, § 1367(a) is inapplicable and, in light of our holdings in *Clark* and *Zahn*, the district court has no statutory basis for exercising supplemental jurisdiction over the additional claims.

We now conclude the answer must be yes. When the well-pleaded complaint contains at least one claim that satisfies the amount-in-controversy requirement, and there are no other relevant jurisdictional defects, the district court, beyond all question, has original jurisdiction over that claim. The presence of other claims in the complaint, over which the district court may lack original jurisdiction, is of no moment. If the court has original jurisdiction over a single claim in the complaint, it has original jurisdiction over a "civil action" within the meaning of § 1367(a), even if the civil action over which it has jurisdiction comprises fewer claims than were included in the complaint. Once the court determines it has original jurisdiction over the civil action, it can turn to the question whether it has a constitutional and statutory basis for exercising supplemental jurisdiction over the other claims in the action.

Section 1367(a) commences with the direction that §§ 1367(b) and (c), or other relevant statutes, may provide specific exceptions, but otherwise § 1367(a) is a broad jurisdictional grant, with no distinction drawn between pendent-claim and pendent-party cases. In fact, the last sentence of § 1367(a) makes clear that the provision grants supplemental jurisdiction over claims involving joinder or intervention of additional parties. The terms of § 1367 do not acknowledge any distinction between pendent jurisdiction and the doctrine of so-called ancillary jurisdiction. Though the doctrines of pendent and ancillary jurisdiction developed separately as a historical matter, the Court has recognized that the doctrines are "two species of the same generic problem," * * *. Nothing in § 1367 indicates a congressional intent to recognize, preserve, or create some meaningful, substantive distinction between the jurisdictional categories we have historically labeled pendent and ancillary.

If § 1367(a) were the sum total of the relevant statutory language, our holding would rest on that language alone. The statute, of course, instructs us to examine § 1367(b) to determine if any of its exceptions apply, so we proceed to that section. While § 1367(b) qualifies the broad rule of § 1367(a), it does not withdraw supplemental jurisdiction over the claims of the additional parties at issue here. The specific exceptions to § 1367(a) contained in § 1367(b), moreover, provide additional support for our conclusion that § 1367(a) confers supplemental jurisdiction over these claims. Section 1367(b), which applies only to diversity cases, withholds supplemental jurisdiction over the claims of plaintiffs proposed to be joined as indispensable parties under Federal Rule of Civil Procedure 19, or who seek to intervene pursuant to Rule 24. Nothing in the text of § 1367(b), however, withholds supplemental jurisdiction over the claims of plaintiffs permissively joined under Rule 20 (like the additional plaintiffs in [Rosario Ortega]) or certified as class-action members pursuant to Rule 23 (like the additional plaintiffs in [Allapattah]). The natural, indeed the necessary, inference is that § 1367 confers supplemental jurisdiction over claims by Rule 20 and Rule 23 plaintiffs. This inference, at least with respect to Rule 20 plaintiffs, is strengthened by the fact that § 1367(b) explicitly excludes supplemental jurisdiction over claims against defendants joined under Rule 20.

We cannot accept the view, urged by some of the parties, commentators, and Courts of Appeals, that a district court lacks original jurisdiction over a civil action unless the court has original jurisdiction over every claim in the complaint. As we understand this position, it requires assuming either that all claims in the complaint must stand or fall as a single, indivisible "civil action" as a matter of definitional necessity—what we will refer to as the "indivisibility theory"—or else that the inclusion of a claim or party falling outside the district court's original jurisdiction somehow contaminates every other claim in the complaint, depriving the court of original jurisdiction over any of these claims—what we will refer to as the "contamination theory."

The indivisibility theory is easily dismissed, as it is inconsistent with the whole notion of supplemental jurisdiction. If a district court must have original jurisdiction over every claim in the complaint in order to have "original jurisdiction" over a "civil action," then in *Gibbs* there was no civil action of which the district court could assume original jurisdiction under § 1331, and so no basis for exercising supplemental jurisdiction over any of the claims. The indivisibility theory is further belied by our practice—in both federal-question and diversity cases—of allowing federal courts to cure jurisdictional defects by dismissing the offending parties rather than dismissing the entire action. *Clark*, for example, makes clear that claims that are jurisdictionally defective as to amount in controversy do not destroy original jurisdiction over other claims. 306 U.S., at 590 (dismissing parties who failed to meet the amount-in-controversy requirement but retaining jurisdiction over the remaining party). If the presence of jurisdictionally problematic claims in the complaint meant the district court was without original jurisdiction over the single, indivisible civil action before it, then the district court would have to dismiss the whole action rather than particular parties.

"Indivisibility rejected" [handwritten margin note]

* * *

The contamination theory, as we have noted, can make some sense in the special context of the complete diversity requirement because the presence of nondiverse parties on both sides of a lawsuit eliminates the justification for providing a federal forum. The theory, however, makes little sense with respect to the amount-in-controversy requirement, which is meant to ensure that a dispute is sufficiently important to warrant federal-court attention. The presence of a single nondiverse party may eliminate the fear of bias with respect to all claims, but the presence of a claim that falls short of the minimum amount in controversy does nothing to reduce the importance of the claims that do meet this requirement.

"Contamination rejected for amt. in controv. cases" [handwritten margin note]

It is fallacious to suppose, simply from the proposition that § 1332 imposes both the diversity requirement and the amount-in-controversy requirement, that the contamination theory germane to the former is also relevant to the latter. There is no inherent logical connection between the amount-in-controversy requirement and § 1332 diversity jurisdiction. After all, federal-question jurisdiction once had an amount-in-controversy requirement as well. If such a requirement were revived under § 1331, it is clear beyond peradventure that § 1367(a) provides supplemental jurisdiction over federal-question cases where some, but not all, of the federal-law claims involve a sufficient amount in controversy. In other words, § 1367(a) unambiguously overrules the holding and the result in *Clark*. If that is so, however, it would be quite extraordinary to say that § 1367 did not also overrule *Zahn*, a case that was premised in substantial part on the holding in *Clark*.

* * *

We also reject the argument * * * that while the presence of additional claims over which the district court lacks jurisdiction does not mean the civil action is outside the purview of § 1367(a), the presence of

"party vs. claim counterargument rejected" [handwritten margin note]

additional parties does. The basis for this distinction is not altogether clear, and it is in considerable tension with statutory text. Section 1367(a) applies by its terms to any civil action of which the district courts have original jurisdiction, and the last sentence of § 1367(a) expressly contemplates that the court may have supplemental jurisdiction over additional parties. So it cannot be the case that the presence of those parties destroys the court's original jurisdiction, within the meaning of § 1367(a), over a civil action otherwise properly before it. Also, § 1367(b) expressly withholds supplemental jurisdiction in diversity cases over claims by plaintiffs joined as indispensable parties under Rule 19. If joinder of such parties were sufficient to deprive the district court of original jurisdiction over the civil action within the meaning of § 1367(a), this specific limitation on supplemental jurisdiction in § 1367(b) would be superfluous. The argument that the presence of additional parties removes the civil action from the scope of § 1367(a) also would mean that § 1367 left the *Finley* result undisturbed. *Finley*, after all, involved a Federal Tort Claims Act suit against a federal defendant and state-law claims against additional defendants not otherwise subject to federal jurisdiction. Yet all concede that one purpose of § 1367 was to change the result reached in *Finley*.

Finally, it is suggested that our interpretation of § 1367(a) creates an anomaly regarding the exceptions listed in § 1367(b): It is not immediately obvious why Congress would withhold supplemental jurisdiction over plaintiffs joined as parties "needed for just adjudication" under Rule 19 but would allow supplemental jurisdiction over plaintiffs permissively joined under Rule 20. The omission of Rule 20 plaintiffs from the list of exceptions in § 1367(b) may have been an "unintentional drafting gap," *Meritcare*, 166 F.3d, at 221 and n. 6. If that is the case, it is up to Congress rather than the courts to fix it. The omission may seem odd, but it is not absurd. An alternative explanation for the different treatment of Rule 19 and Rule 20 is that Congress was concerned that extending supplemental jurisdiction to Rule 19 plaintiffs would allow circumvention of the complete diversity rule: A nondiverse plaintiff might be omitted intentionally from the original action, but joined later under Rule 19 as a necessary party. See *Stromberg Metal Works*, 77 F.3d, at 932. The contamination theory described above, if applicable, means this ruse would fail, but Congress may have wanted to make assurance double sure. More generally, Congress may have concluded that federal jurisdiction is only appropriate if the district court would have original jurisdiction over the claims of all those plaintiffs who are so essential to the action that they could be joined under Rule 19.

To the extent that the omission of Rule 20 plaintiffs from the list of § 1367(b) exceptions is anomalous, moreover, it is no more anomalous than the inclusion of Rule 19 plaintiffs in that list would be if the alternative view of § 1367(a) were to prevail. If the district court lacks original jurisdiction over a civil diversity action where any plaintiff's claims fail to comply with all the requirements of § 1332, there is no need for a special § 1367(b) exception for Rule 19 plaintiffs who do not meet these requirements. Though the omission of Rule 20 plaintiffs from § 1367(b) presents something of a puzzle on our view of the statute, the inclusion of Rule 19 plaintiffs in this section is at least as difficult to explain under the alternative view.

And so we circle back to the original question. When the well-pleaded complaint in district court includes multiple claims, all part of the same case or controversy, and some, but not all, of the claims are within the court's original jurisdiction, does the court have before it "any civil action of which the district courts have original jurisdiction"? It does. Under § 1367, the court has original jurisdiction over the civil action comprising the claims for which there is no jurisdictional defect. No other reading of § 1367 is plausible in light of the text and structure of the jurisdictional statute. Though the special nature and purpose of the diversity requirement mean that a single nondiverse party can contaminate every other claim in the lawsuit, the contamination does not occur with respect to jurisdictional defects that go only to the substantive importance of individual claims.

It follows from this conclusion that the threshold requirement of § 1367(a) is satisfied in cases, like those now before us, where some, but not all, of the plaintiffs in a diversity action allege a sufficient amount in controversy. We hold that § 1367 by its plain text overruled *Clark* and *Zahn* and authorized supplemental jurisdiction over all claims by diverse parties arising out of the same Article III case or controversy, subject only to enumerated exceptions not applicable in the cases now before us.

C

The proponents of the alternative view of § 1367 insist that the statute is at least ambiguous and that we should look to other interpretive tools, including the legislative history of § 1367, which supposedly demonstrate Congress did not intend § 1367 to overrule *Zahn*. We can reject this argument at the very outset simply because § 1367 is not ambiguous. For the reasons elaborated above, interpreting § 1367 to foreclose supplemental jurisdiction over plaintiffs in diversity cases who do not meet the minimum amount in controversy is inconsistent with the text, read in light of other statutory provisions and our established jurisprudence. Even if we were to stipulate, however, that the reading these proponents urge upon us is textually plausible, the legislative history cited to support it would not alter our view as to the best interpretation of § 1367.

Those who urge that the legislative history refutes our interpretation rely primarily on the House Judiciary Committee Report on the Judicial Improvements Act. H.R. Rep. No. 101–734 (1990) (House Report or Report). This Report explained that § 1367 would "authorize jurisdiction in a case like *Finley*, as well as essentially restore the pre-*Finley* understandings of the authorization for and limits on other forms of supplemental jurisdiction." House Report, at 28. * * * The Report then remarked that § 1367(b) "is not intended to affect the jurisdictional

requirements of [§ 1332] in diversity-only class actions, as those requirements were interpreted prior to *Finley*," citing, without further elaboration, *Zahn* and *Supreme Tribe of Ben–Hur v. Cauble*, 255 U.S. 356
(1921). House Report, at 29, and n. 17. * * *

As we have repeatedly held, the authoritative statement is the
statutory text, not the legislative history or any other extrinsic material.
Extrinsic materials have a role in statutory interpretation only to the
extent they shed a reliable light on the enacting Legislature's understanding of otherwise ambiguous terms. Not all extrinsic materials are
reliable sources of insight into legislative understandings, however, and
legislative history in particular is vulnerable to two serious criticisms.
First, legislative history is itself often murky, ambiguous, and contradictory. Judicial investigation of legislative history has a tendency to
become, to borrow Judge Leventhal's memorable phrase, an exercise in
" 'looking over a crowd and picking out your friends.' " * * * Second,
judicial reliance on legislative materials like committee reports, which
are not themselves subject to the requirements of Article I, may give
unrepresentative committee members—or, worse yet, unelected staffers
and lobbyists—both the power and the incentive to attempt strategic
manipulations of legislative history to secure results they were unable to
achieve through the statutory text. We need not comment here on
whether these problems are sufficiently prevalent to render legislative
history inherently unreliable in all circumstances, a point on which
Members of this Court have disagreed. It is clear, however, that in this
instance both criticisms are right on the mark.

First of all, the legislative history of § 1367 is far murkier than
selective quotation from the House Report would suggest. The text of
§ 1367 is based substantially on a draft proposal contained in a Federal
Court Study Committee working paper, which was drafted by a Subcommittee chaired by Judge Posner. Report of the Subcommittee on the
Role of the Federal Courts and Their Relationship to the States 567–
568 (Mar. 12, 1990), reprinted in Judicial Conference of the United
States, 1 Federal Courts Study Committee, Working Papers and Subcommittee Reports (July 1, 1990). * * * While the Subcommittee explained, in language echoed by the House Report, that its proposal
"basically restores the law as it existed prior to *Finley*," Subcommittee
Working Paper, at 561, it observed in a footnote that its proposal would
overrule *Zahn* and that this would be a good idea, Subcommittee
Working Paper, at 561, n. 33. Although the Federal Courts Study
Committee did not expressly adopt the Subcommittee's specific reference to *Zahn*, it neither explicitly disagreed with the Subcommittee's
conclusion that this was the best reading of the proposed text nor
substantially modified the proposal to avoid this result. Study Committee Report, at 47–48. Therefore, even if the House Report could fairly
be read to reflect an understanding that the text of § 1367 did not
overrule *Zahn*, the Subcommittee Working Paper on which § 1367 was
based reflected the opposite understanding. The House Report is no
more authoritative than the Subcommittee Working Paper. The utility

of either can extend no further than the light it sheds on how the enacting Legislature understood the statutory text. Trying to figure out how to square the Subcommittee Working Paper's understanding with the House Report's understanding, or which is more reflective of the understanding of the enacting legislators, is a hopeless task.

Second, the worst fears of critics who argue legislative history will be used to circumvent the Article I process were realized in this case. The telltale evidence is the statement, by three law professors who participated in drafting § 1367 * * * that § 1367 "on its face" permits "supplemental jurisdiction over claims of class members that do not satisfy section 1332's jurisdictional amount requirement, which would overrule [*Zahn*]. [There is] a disclaimer of intent to accomplish this result in the legislative history.... It would have been better had the statute dealt explicitly with this problem, and the legislative history was an attempt to correct the oversight." Rowe, Burbank, & Mengler, *Compounding or Creating Confusion About Supplemental Jurisdiction? A Reply to Professor Freer*, 40 Emory LJ. 943, 960, n. 90 (1991). The professors were frank to concede that if one refuses to consider the legislative history, one has no choice but to "conclude that section 1367 has wiped *Zahn* off the books." Ibid. So there exists an acknowledgment, by parties who have detailed, specific knowledge of the statute and the drafting process, both that the plain text of § 1367 overruled *Zahn* and that language to the contrary in the House Report was a *post hoc* attempt to alter that result. One need not subscribe to the wholesale condemnation of legislative history to refuse to give any effect to such a deliberate effort to amend a statute through a committee report.

* * *

The judgment of the Court of Appeals for the Eleventh Circuit is affirmed. The judgment of the Court of Appeals for the First Circuit is reversed, and the case is remanded for proceedings consistent with this opinion.

It is so ordered.

[The dissenting opinion of JUSTICE STEVENS, joined by JUSTICE BREYER, is omitted.]

JUSTICE GINSBURG, with whom JUSTICE STEVENS, JUSTICE O'CONNOR, and JUSTICE BREYER join, dissenting.

* * *

The Court adopts a plausibly broad reading of § 1367, a measure that is hardly a model of the careful drafter's art. There is another plausible reading, however, one less disruptive of our jurisprudence regarding supplemental jurisdiction. If one reads § 1367(a) to instruct, as the statute's text suggests, that the district court must first have "original jurisdiction" over a "civil action" before supplemental jurisdiction can attach, then *Clark* and *Zahn* are preserved, and supplemental jurisdiction does not open the way for joinder of plaintiffs, or inclusion of class members, who do not independently meet the amount-in-controversy requirement. For the reasons that follow, I conclude that this narrower construction is the better reading of § 1367.

* * *

II

A

Section 1367, by its terms, operates only in civil actions "of which the district courts have original jurisdiction." The "original jurisdiction" relevant here is diversity-of-citizenship jurisdiction, conferred by § 1332. The character of that jurisdiction is the essential backdrop for comprehension of § 1367.

The Constitution broadly provides for federal-court jurisdiction in controversies "between Citizens of different States." Art. III, § 2, cl. 1. This Court has read that provision to demand no more than "minimal diversity," *i.e.*, so long as one party on the plaintiffs' side and one party on the defendants' side are of diverse citizenship, Congress may authorize federal courts to exercise diversity jurisdiction. * * * Further, the Constitution includes no amount-in-controversy limitation on the exercise of federal jurisdiction. But from the start, Congress, as its measures have been construed by this Court, has limited federal court exercise of diversity jurisdiction in two principal ways. First, unless Congress specifies otherwise, diversity must be "complete," *i.e.*, all parties on plaintiffs' side must be diverse from all parties on defendants' side. Strawbridge v. Curtiss, 3 Cranch 267 (1806) * * *. Second, each plaintiff's stake must independently meet the amount-in-controversy specification: "When two or more plaintiffs, having separate and distinct demands, unite for convenience and economy in a single suit, it is essential that the demand of each be of the requisite jurisdictional amount." * * *

The statute today governing federal court exercise of diversity jurisdiction in the generality of cases, § 1332, like all its predecessors, incorporates both a diverse-citizenship requirement and an amount-in-controversy specification.[5] * * *

* * * The rule that each plaintiff must independently satisfy the amount-in-controversy requirement, unless Congress expressly orders otherwise, was thus the solidly established reading of § 1332 when

---

5. Endeavoring to preserve the "complete diversity" rule first stated in *Strawbridge v. Curtiss*, 3 Cranch 267 (1806), the Court's opinion drives a wedge between the two components of 28 U. S. C. § 1332, treating the diversity-of-citizenship requirement as essential, the amount-in-controversy requirement as more readily disposable. * * * Section 1332 itself, however, does not rank order the two requirements. What "[o]rdinary principl[e] of statutory construction" or "sound canon of interpreta-

tion," * * * allows the Court to slice up § 1332 this way? In partial explanation, the Court asserts that amount in controversy can be analyzed claim-by-claim, but the diversity requirement cannot. * * * It is not altogether clear why that should be so. The cure for improper joinder of a nondiverse party is the same as the cure for improper joinder of a plaintiff who does not satisfy the jurisdictional amount. In both cases, original jurisdiction can be preserved by dismissing the nonqualifying party. * * *

Congress enacted the Judicial Improvements Act of 1990, which added § 1367 to Title 28.

B

These cases present the question whether Congress abrogated the nonaggregation rule long tied to § 1332 when it enacted § 1367. In answering that question, "context [should provide] a crucial guide." * * * The Court should assume, as it ordinarily does, that Congress legislated against a background of law already in place and the historical development of that law. * * * Here, that background is the statutory grant of diversity jurisdiction, the amount-in-controversy condition that Congress, from the start, has tied to the grant, and the nonaggregation rule this Court has long applied to the determination of the "matter in controversy."

* * * The Court is unanimous in reading § 1367(a) to permit pendent-party jurisdiction in federal-question cases, and thus, to over-rule *Finley.* * * *

The Court divides, however, on the impact of § 1367(a) on diversity cases controlled by § 1332. Under the majority's reading, § 1367(a) permits the joinder of related claims cut loose from the nonaggregation rule that has long attended actions under § 1332. Only the claims specified in § 1367(b) would be excluded from § 1367(a)'s expansion of § 1332's grant of diversity jurisdiction. And because § 1367(b) contains no exception for joinder of plaintiffs under Rule 20 or class actions under Rule 23, the Court concludes, *Clark* and *Zahn* have been overruled.

The Court's reading is surely plausible, especially if one detaches § 1367(a) from its context and attempts no reconciliation with prior interpretations of § 1332's amount-in-controversy requirement. But § 1367(a)'s text, as the First Circuit held, can be read another way, one that would involve no rejection of *Clark* and *Zahn.*

As explained by the First Circuit in *Ortega*, and applied to class actions by the Tenth Circuit in *Leonhardt*, * * *, § 1367(a) addresses "civil action[s] of which the district courts have original jurisdiction," a formulation that, in diversity cases, is sensibly read to incorporate the rules on joinder and aggregation tightly tied to § 1332 at the time of § 1367's enactment. On this reading, a complaint must first meet that "original jurisdiction" measurement. If it does not, no supplemental jurisdiction is authorized. If it does, § 1367(a) authorizes "supplemental jurisdiction" over related claims. In other words, § 1367(a) would pre-serve undiminished, as part and parcel of § 1332 "original jurisdiction" determinations, both the "complete diversity" rule and the decisions restricting aggregation to arrive at the amount in controversy. * * * See Pfander, *Supplemental Jurisdiction and Section 1367: The Case for a Sympathetic Textualism*, 148 U.Pa.L.Rev. 109, 114 (1999) * * *. In contrast to the Court's construction of § 1367, which draws a sharp line between the diversity and amount-in-controversy components of § 1332,

* * * the interpretation presented here does not sever the two jurisdictional requirements.

The more restrained reading of § 1367 just outlined would yield affirmance of the First Circuit's judgment in *Ortega*, and reversal of the Eleventh Circuit's judgment in *Exxon*. It would not discard entirely, as the Court does, the judicially developed doctrines of pendent and ancillary jurisdiction as they existed when *Finley* was decided. Instead, it would recognize § 1367 essentially as a codification of those doctrines, placing them under a single heading, but largely retaining their substance, with overriding *Finley* the only basic change: Supplemental jurisdiction, once the district court has original jurisdiction, would now include "claims that involve the joinder or intervention of additional parties." § 1367(a).

* * *

The less disruptive view I take of § 1367 also accounts for the omission of Rule 20 plaintiffs and Rule 23 class actions in § 1367(b)'s text. If one reads § 1367(a) as a plenary grant of supplemental jurisdiction to federal courts sitting in diversity, one would indeed look for exceptions in § 1367(b). Finding none for permissive joinder of parties or class actions, one would conclude that Congress effectively, even if unintentionally, overruled *Clark* and *Zahn*. But if one recognizes that the nonaggregation rule delineated in *Clark* and *Zahn* forms part of the determination whether "original jurisdiction" exists in a diversity case, * * * then plaintiffs who do not meet the amount-in-controversy requirement would fail at the § 1367(a) threshold. Congress would have no reason to resort to a § 1367(b) exception to turn such plaintiffs away from federal court, given that their claims, from the start, would fall outside the court's § 1332 jurisdiction. * * *

* * *

What is the utility of § 1367(b) under my reading of § 1367(a)? Section 1367(a) allows parties other than the plaintiff to assert *reactive* claims once entertained under the heading ancillary jurisdiction. See supra * * * (listing claims, including compulsory counterclaims and impleader claims, over which federal courts routinely exercised ancillary jurisdiction). As earlier observed, * * * § 1367(b) stops plaintiffs from circumventing § 1332's jurisdictional requirements by using another's claim as a hook to add a claim that the plaintiff could not have brought in the first instance. * * *

While § 1367's enigmatic text defies flawless interpretation, * * * the precedent-preservative reading, I am persuaded, better accords with the historical and legal context of Congress' enactment of the supplemental jurisdiction statute, * * * and the established limits on pendent and ancillary jurisdiction * * *. It does not attribute to Congress a jurisdictional enlargement broader than the one to which the legislators adverted, * * * and it follows the sound counsel that "close questions of [statutory] construction should be resolved in favor of continuity and against change." Shapiro, *Continuity and Change in Statutory Interpretation*, 67 N.Y.U.L.Rev. 921, 925 (1992).

For the reasons stated, I would hold that § 1367 does not overrule *Clark* and *Zahn*. I would therefore affirm the judgment of the Court of Appeals for the First Circuit and reverse the judgment of the Court of Appeals for the Eleventh Circuit.

Notes

1. Does the majority or the dissent have the better interpretation of the phrase "original jurisdiction"? If a court has to look at the entire case—rather than at individual claims—to determine whether it has jurisdiction, does the notion of supplemental jurisdiction have any meaning? For an excellent pre-*Allapattah* scholarly discussion of the issues that divide the majority and the dissent, compare Freer, *The Cauldron Boils: Supplemental Jurisdiction, Amount in Controversy, and Diversity of Citizenship Class Actions*, 53 Emory L.J. 55 (2004) with Pfander, *The Simmering Debate over Supplemental Jurisdiction*, 2002 U.Ill.L.Rev. 1209 (2002).

2. Note the distinction drawn by the majority, and rejected by the dissent, between the amount-in-controversy requirement and the complete diversity requirement. The majority bases the distinction on its premise that a district court has no jurisdiction of any sort over a § 1332 case in which there is incomplete diversity. If one claim fails to meet the amount-in-controversy requirement, a district court may dismiss that claim. Under the majority's theory, however, what does § 1332 require of a district court in a case in which one plaintiff is diverse from the defendant and another plaintiff is not? What does Justice Ginsburg conclude in footnote 5? In Newman–Green, Inc. v. Alfonzo–Larrain, 490 U.S. 826 (1989), the Court held—over a dissent by Justices Kennedy and Scalia—that Fed.R.Civ.P. 21 "invests district courts with authority to allow a dispensable nondiverse party to be dropped at any time." Id. at 832. Does *Allapattah* overrule *Newman-Green* (which none of the opinions mentions)?

3. Assume that Congress did not intend to overrule *Zahn* or *Clark*. Rewrite the statute to reflect that intent unambiguously. See Redish, 16 Moore's Federal Practice 3d § 106.24 (1997) ("The 'common nucleus of operative fact' standard resisted consistent definition in the lower courts before the enactment of the supplemental jurisdiction statute. An examination of the post-enactment cases reveals that many of the same interpretive ambiguities and inconsistencies continue to exist."); see also Oakley, *Integrating Supplemental Jurisdiction and Diversity Jurisdiction: A Progress Report on the Work of the American Law Institute*, 74 Ind.L.J. 25 (1998) (reprinting and discussing ALI proposal to revise section 1367)

4. Imagine that two plaintiffs sue two defendants on claims arising from a common nucleus of fact. There is no federal question, but there is complete diversity. One plaintiff seeks $100,000 from each defendant. The other plaintiff seeks $25,000 from each defendant. Does the Court have jurisdiction? Read section 1367(b) carefully before you answer, and remember that Fed.R.Civ.P. 20 allows the joinder of multiple defendants as well as the joinder of multiple plaintiffs.

5. Does the distinction between permissive counterclaims, which need an independent jurisdictional basis, and compulsory counterclaims, which do not, survive section 1367? See Channell v. Citicorp National Services, Inc., 89 F.3d 379 (7th Cir.1996) (holding that because section 1367(a) expands jurisdiction to the constitutional limits, permissive counterclaims that are even loosely related to the original claim are within the court's jurisdiction). Most courts disagree with *Channell*. See, e.g., Iglesias v. Mutual Life Ins. Co., 156 F.3d 237 (1st Cir.1998). For a defense of *Channell*, see Simon, *Defining the Limits of Supplemental Jurisdiction Under 28 U.S.C. § 1367: A Hearty Welcome to Permissive Counterclaims*, 9 Lewis & Clark L.Rev. 295 (2005).

6. Why do you suppose section 1367(b) expressly excludes supplemental jurisdiction in most diversity cases? Reconsider the arguments for and against the continuation of the diversity jurisdiction [supra pp. 786–89]. Could the Act be considered a type of "guerilla warfare" against the diversity jurisdiction?

Consider the Supreme Court's pre-section 1367 decision in Owen Equipment & Erection Co. v. Kroger, 437 U.S. 365 (1978). The Court phrased the issue in the following manner: "In an action in which federal jurisdiction is based on diversity of citizenship, may the plaintiff assert a claim against a third-party defendant when there is no independent basis for federal jurisdiction over the claim?" The Court answered that question in the negative: The exercise of supplemental jurisdiction would allow a plaintiff to "defeat the statutory requirement of complete diversity by the simple expedient of suing only those defendants who were of diverse citizenship and waiting for them to implead nondiverse defendants." Note, however, that traditionally, ancillary (now supplemental) jurisdiction *would* apply where complete diversity existed between plaintiff and defendant, and defendant, pursuant to Rule 14, had impleaded a third party defendant from the same state as himself? In *Owen,* the Court made clear that it in no way intended to alter this traditional approach. Can a principled distinction between the use of ancillary jurisdiction by a defendant over a third party defendant under Rule 14 (where it has been permitted) and its use—as in *Owen*—by a plaintiff over a nondiverse third party defendant who had been impleaded? Could it be that in the former case it is the defendant—who we can assume did not invoke the diversity jurisdiction—taking advantage of ancillary jurisdiction while in the latter it is the diversity plaintiff who is seeking to do so? If so, is that a principled basis for the different treatment? Also, what about diversity cases which have been removed to federal court by the defendant? Under *Owen*, the defendant could still take advantage of ancillary jurisdiction by impleading a nondiverse defendant. Examine section 1367(b). Does that provision continue the distinction recognized in *Owen*? For a thorough discussion of whether the *Kroger* rule should be retained, see Hartnett, *Would the* Kroger *Rule Survive the ALI's Proposed Revision of § 1367?*, 51 Duke L.J. 647 (2001); Oakley, Kroger *Redux*, 51 Duke L.J. 663 (2001); Hartnett, *§ 1367 Producamus*, 51 Duke L.J. 687 (2001); Oakley, *Fiat Lux*, 51 Duke L.J. 699 (2001).

7. The Court limited the reach of ancillary jurisdiction in Kokkonen v. Guardian Life Ins. Co. of Am., 511 U.S. 375 (1994). Kokkonen had sued Guardian in state court; the case was then removed to federal court under diversity jurisdiction. After the parties settled, the district court dismissed the suit with prejudice, without any reference to the settlement agreement. When a dispute arose about Kokkonen's obligations under the settlement agreement Guardian went back to federal court to have the agreement enforced. The district court entered an enforcement order, asserting jurisdiction under its "inherent power." The Court of Appeals affirmed. The Supreme Court reversed, holding that the district court lacked jurisdiction in the enforcement action. Justice Scalia, writing for a unanimous Court, held that the district court was not vindicating its authority or effectuating its decree when it enforced the settlement: "the only order here was that the suit be dismissed, a disposition that is in no way flouted or imperiled by the alleged breach of the settlement agreement." Id. at 381. He also noted that "[t]he situation would be quite different if the parties' obligation to comply with the terms of the settlement agreement had been made part of the order of dismissal." Id. See also Peacock v. Thomas, 516 U.S. 349 (1996)(no ancillary jurisdiction over subsequent lawsuit). For a proposal to amend § 1367 to clarify the federal courts' ancillary power in cases like *Kokkonen*, see Parness and Sennott, *Expanded Recognition in Written Laws of Ancillary Federal Court Powers: Supplementing the Supplemental Jurisdiction Statute*, 64 U.Pitt.L.Rev. 303 (2003).

8. The literature on the subject of supplemental jurisdiction is extensive. In addition to the sources already cited, see Symposium: *A Reappraisal of the Supplemental Jurisdiction Statute*, 74 Ind.L.J. 1 (1998); Underwood, *Supplemental Serendipity: Congress' Accidental Improvement of Supplemental Jurisdiction*, 37 Akron L.Rev. 653 (2004); Fairman, *Abdication to Academia: The Case of the Supplemental Jurisdiction Statute*, 28 U.S.C.A. § 1367, 19 Seton Hall Legis.J. 157 (1994); Gold, *Supplemental Jurisdiction Over Claims by Plaintiffs in Diversity Cases: Making Sense of 28 U.S.C.A. § 1367 (b)*, 93 Mich.L.Rev. 2133 (1995); Colloquy, *Perspectives on Supplemental Jurisdiction*, 41 Emory L.J. 1 (1992); McLaughlin, *The Federal Supplemental Jurisdiction Statute—A Constitutional and Statutory Analysis*, 24 Ariz.St. L.J. 849 (1992), and Oakley, *Recent Statutory Changes in the Law of Federal Jurisdiction and Venue: The Judicial Improvements Acts of 1988 and 1990*, 24 U.C. Davis L.Rev. 735 (1991).

Chapter 16

REMOVAL JURISDICTION
AND PROCEDURE

§ 1. FEDERAL QUESTION REMOVAL

Read 28 U.S.C.A. § 1441 in Appendix B.

The basic rule is that a defendant may remove a case from state to federal court if and only if it could have been filed in federal court originally. Under the "well-pleaded complaint" doctrine of Louisville & Nashville R.R. v. Mottley, 211 U.S. 149 (1908) [supra p. 763], this means that a state law claim with a federal defense is not removable.

The Supreme Court, however, has long allowed an exception to the basic rule under the doctrine of "artful pleading." In Avco Corp. v. Aero Lodge No. 735, 390 U.S. 557 (1968), the Court held that where a plaintiff's claim is entirely pre-empted by federal law—and federal law provides the only relief—a court should not allow the plaintiff to defeat federal jurisdiction by "artfully pleading" under state law a claim that is in reality federal. Such a case is therefore removable to federal court. Over a vigorous dissent by Justice Scalia, who argued that the "artful pleading" doctrine of Avco has no statutory or constitutional foundation, the Supreme Court recently applied the doctrine to find state law usury suits against national banks entirely pre-empted by federal legislation and therefore removable to federal court. Beneficial National Bank v. Anderson, 539 U.S. 1 (2003). Even Justice Scalia agreed, however, when the Court unanimously held that state causes of action that are entirely pre-empted by the ERISA can be removed to federal court under *Beneficial National Bank*. Aetna Health Inc. v. Davila, 542 U.S. 200 (2004).

In 1981, the Court, in an apparently offhand footnote, expanded the potential application of the "artful pleading" doctrine. Federated Department Stores, Inc. v. Moitie, 452 U.S. 394 (1981), involved seven parallel civil antitrust suits brought in federal court against Federated by Moitie and others. After the federal district court dismissed all seven actions, five of the plaintiffs appealed. Moitie and another plaintiff, however, chose not to appeal and instead filed state-law claims against

Federated in state court. The allegations were similar to those made in all of the prior complaints.

Federated removed the two new state cases to federal court, and then moved to have them dismissed on the ground of res judicata. The district court denied Moitie's motion to remand to state court, holding "that the complaints, though artfully couched in terms of state law, were 'in many respects identical' with prior complaints, and were thus properly removed to federal court because they raised 'essentially federal law claims.'" 452 U.S. at 396 (quoting district court). It then held the new claims to be barred by res judicata. Though the bulk of the subsequent decisions in both the court of appeals and the Supreme Court dealt with the res judicata issue, both courts affirmed the district court's conclusion that the case was properly removed to federal court.

In a footnote, the Supreme Court stated:

We agree that at least some of the claims had a sufficient federal character to support removal. As one treatise puts it, courts "will not permit plaintiff to use artful pleading to close off defendant's right to a federal forum ... [and] occasionally the removal court will seek to determine whether the real nature of the claim is federal, regardless of plaintiff's characterization." 14 C. Wright, A. Miller, & E. Cooper, Federal Practice and Procedure, § 3722 (1976). The District Court applied that settled principle to the facts of this case. After "an extensive review and analysis of the origins and substance of" the two *Brown* complaints, it found, and the Court of Appeals expressly agreed, that respondents had attempted to avoid removal jurisdiction by "artful[ly]" casting their "essentially federal law claims" as state-law claims. We will not question that factual finding. 452 U.S. at 398 n.2.

Notes

1. How broadly should *Moitie* be read? Several lower courts extended *Moitie* to allow removal of cases in which the state law claims would be barred by the res judicata effect of a prior federal judgment. See Sullivan v. First Affiliated Securities, Inc., 813 F.2d 1368 (9th Cir.), cert. denied, 484 U.S. 850 (1987). Travelers Indemnity Co. v. Sarkisian, 794 F.2d 754 (2d Cir.), cert. denied, 479 U.S. 885 (1986).

The Supreme court put an end to this "res judicata removal" in Rivet v. Regions Bank, 522 U.S. 470 (1998). The Court called the *Moitie* footnote a "marginal comment" that "will not bear the heavy weight lower courts have placed on it." Id. at 477.

Recall that under the relitigation exception to the Anti–Injunction Act [see supra p. 489], a federal court might enjoin the state proceeding. Does it make sense to allow the injunction but not the removal? See NAACP v. Metropolitan Council, 125 F.3d 1171 (8th Cir.1997), rev'd and remanded, 522 U.S. 1145 (1998), reinstated, 144 F.3d 1168 (8th Cir.1998) (removal preferable because it "better preserves state-federal relations").

2.   Both before and after *Rivet*, some courts used the All Writs Act, 28 U.S.C. § 1651(a) [in Appendix B] to remove otherwise unremovable cases that allegedly interfered with a prior federal judgment. In Syngenta Crop Protection, Inc. v. Henson, 537 U.S. 28 (2002), the Supreme Court held that the All Writs Act is not a substitute for meeting the requirements of § 1441. Will this holding increase the number of injunctions issued against state courts under the relitigation exception to the Anti–Injunction Act? See generally Steinman, *The Newest Frontier of Judicial Activism: Removal Under the All Writs Act*, 80 B.U.L.Rev. 773 (2000); Hoffman, *Removal Jurisdiction and the All Writs Act*, 148 U.Pa.L.Rev. 401 (1999).

3.   Note again that section 1441(a) limits removal jurisdiction to "any civil action brought in a State court of which the district courts of the United States have original jurisdiction * * *." Assuming the wisdom of the "well-pleaded complaint" rule in original jurisdiction, does it make sense to extend it to removal jurisdiction? Cf. Rothfeld, *Rationalizing Removal*, 1990 B.Y.U. L.Rev. 221, 228: "[I]t is difficult to imagine a ground of principle on which a system that allows defendants to remove a plaintiff's federal claims would not also permit defendants to remove cases in which they have federal defenses." But see id. at 231: "[T]he caseload impact of federal defense removal would surely be significant." Should this fact make a difference? Cf. Redish, *Reassessing the Allocation of Judicial Business Between State and Federal Courts: Federal Jurisdiction and "The Martian Chronicles,"* 78 Va.L.Rev. 1769, 1798 (1992): "Even if one were to accept the controversial assertion that interests of docket control should be paramount, it is by no means clear that it is federal question jurisdiction that should suffer." This issue is examined more fully in the materials concerning the "well-pleaded complaint" rule [supra pp. 763–84].

4.   Note also that section 1441(a) is prefaced by the words, "[e]xcept as otherwise expressly provided by Act of Congress". An example of such a law denying a defendant's right to remove is the Federal Employers' Liability Act, 45 U.S.C. § 51, authorizing railroad employee negligence suits against employers. Plaintiffs are allowed to sue in either federal or state court, but if plaintiff sues in state court defendant is not authorized to remove the case to federal court. See 28 U.S.C. § 1445(a). Can you imagine why Congress might choose to deny the right of removal in such suits? The Supreme Court has recently reiterated that Congress must make its desire to preclude removal explicit. In Breuer v. Jim's Concrete of Brevard, Inc., 538 U.S. 691 (2003), the Court held that suits under the Fair Labor Standards Act, which provides that an action "may be maintained" in any state or federal court, are removable. The plaintiff unsuccessfully argued that "maintained" must mean that a suit brought in state court must continue there until judgment.

5.   **The Interplay Between Removal Jurisdiction and Supplemental Jurisdiction.** Notice that section 1441(c) allows the removal of the "entire case," at the discretion of the district court, if a removable cause of action is joined with a non-removable cause of action. There is some debate about whether this provision is constitutional. See, e.g., Cohen, *Problems in the Removal of a "Separate and Independent Claim or Cause of Action,"* 46 Minn.L.Rev. 1, 25–26 (1961); Matasar, *Rediscovering "One Constitutional Case": Procedural Rules and the Rejection of the* Gibbs *Test for Supplemental Jurisdiction*, 71 Cal.L.Rev. 1401 (1983); Steinman, *Removal, Remand,*

and Review in Pendent Claim and Pendent Party Cases, 41 Vand.L.Rev. 923, 935 n.72 (1988); McFarland, *The Unconstitutional Stub of Section 1441(c),* 54 Ohio St.L.J. 1059 (1993); Hartnett, *A New Trick From an Old and Abused Dog: Section 1441(c) Lives and Now Permits the Remand of Federal Question Cases,* 63 Fordham L.Rev. 1099 (1995).

Even assuming that section 1441(c) is constitutional, is it still meaningful after the enactment of the Supplemental Jurisdiction Act, 28 U.S.C. § 1367 [discussed supra pp. 846–65]. Is there any cause of action that can be removed under section 1441(c) that could not be brought into federal court under section 1367? If you propose that section1441(c) allows the removal of "separate and independent" state causes of action, is that consistent with Article III limitations on the jurisdiction of the federal courts? Professors McFarland and Hartnett are carrying on this debate in their articles. See also Steinman, *Crosscurrents: Supplemental Jurisdiction, Removal, and the ALI Revision Project,* 74 Ind.L.J. 75 (1998); Steinman, *Supplemental Jurisdiction in § 1441 Removed Cases: An Unsurveyed Frontier of Congress' Handiwork,* 35 Ariz.L.Rev. 305 (1993).

§ 2. FEDERAL OFFICER REMOVAL

Read 28 U.S.C. § 1442 in Appendix B.

TENNESSEE v. DAVIS

Supreme Court of the United States, 1879.
100 U.S. (10 Otto) 257.

The record having been returned, in compliance with the writ, a motion was made to remand the case to the State court; and, on the hearing of the motion, the judges were divided in opinion upon the following questions, which are certified here:—

First, Whether an indictment of a revenue officer (of the United States) for murder, found in a State court, under the facts alleged in the petition for removal in this case, is removable to the Circuit Court of the United States, under sect. 643 of the Revised Statutes.

Second, Whether, if removable from the State court, there is any mode and manner of procedure in the trial prescribed by the act of Congress.

Third, Whether, if not, a trial of the guilt or innocence of the defendant can be had in the United States Circuit Court.

Mr. Justice Strong delivered the opinion of the court.

The first of the questions certified is one of great importance, bringing as it does into consideration the relation of the general government to the government of the States, and bringing also into view not merely the construction of an act of Congress, but its constitutionality. That in this case the defendant's petition for removal of the cause was in the form prescribed by the act of Congress admits of no doubt. It represented that he had been indicted for murder in the Circuit Court of Grundy County, and that the indictment and criminal prosecution were still pending. It represented further, that no murder was committed, but that, on the other hand, the killing was committed in the petitioner's own necessary self-defence, to save his own life; that at the time when the alleged act for which he was indicted was committed he was, and still is, an officer of the United States, to wit, a deputy collector of internal revenue, and that the act for which he was indicted was performed in his own necessary self-defence while engaged in the discharge of his duties as deputy collector; that he was acting by and under the authority of the internal-revenue laws of the United States; that what he did was done under and by right of his office, to wit, as deputy collector of internal revenue; that it was his duty to seize illicit distilleries and the apparatus that is used for the illicit and unlawful distillation of spirits; and that while so attempting to enforce the revenue laws of the United States, as deputy collector as aforesaid, he was assaulted and fired upon by a number of armed men, and that in defence of his life he returned the fire. The petition was verified by oath, and the certificate required by the act of Congress to be given by the petitioner's legal counsel was appended thereto. There is, therefore, no room for reasonable doubt that a case was made for the removal of the indictment into the Circuit Court of the United States, if sect. 643 of the Revised Statutes embraces criminal prosecutions in a State court, and makes them removable, and if that act of Congress was not unauthorized by the Constitution. The language of the statute (so far as it is necessary at present to refer to it) is as follows: "When any civil suit or criminal prosecution is commenced in any court of a State against any officer appointed under, or acting by authority of, any revenue law of the United States, now or hereafter enacted, or against any person acting by or under authority of any such officer, on account of any act done under color of his office or of any such law, or on account of any right, title, or authority claimed by such officer or other person under any such law," the case may be removed into the Federal court. Now, certainly the petition for the removal represented that the act for which the defendant was indicted was done not merely under color of his office as a revenue collector, or under color of the revenue laws, not merely while he was engaged in performing his duties as a revenue officer, but that it was done under and by right of his office, and while he was resisted by an armed force in his attempts to discharge his official duty. This is more than a claim of right and authority under the law of the United States for the act for which he has been indicted. It is a positive assertion of the existence of such authority. But the act of Congress authorizes the removal of any cause, when the acts of the defendant complained of were done, or claimed to have been done, in the discharge of his duty as a Federal officer. It makes such a claim a basis for the assumption of Federal jurisdiction of the case, and for retaining it, at least until the claim proves unfounded.

That the act of Congress does provide for the removal of criminal prosecutions for offences against the State laws, when there arises in them the claim of the Federal right or authority, is too plain to admit of denial. Such is its positive language, and it is not to be argued away by presenting the supposed incongruity of administering State criminal laws by other courts than those established by the State. It has been strenuously urged that murder within a State is not made a crime by any act of Congress, and that it is an offence against the peace and dignity of the State alone. Hence it is inferred that its trial and punishment can be conducted only in State tribunals, and it is argued that the act of Congress cannot mean what it says, but that it must intend only such prosecutions in State courts as are for offences against the United States,—offences against the revenue laws. But there can be no criminal prosecution initiated in any State court for that which is merely an offence against the general government. If, therefore, the statute is to be allowed any meaning, when it speaks of criminal prosecutions in State courts, it must intend those that are instituted for alleged violations of State laws, in which defences are set up or claimed under United States laws or authority.

We come, then, to the inquiry, most discussed during the argument, whether sect. 643 is a constitutional exercise of the power vested in Congress. Has the Constitution conferred upon Congress the power to authorize the removal, from a State court to a Federal court, of an indictment against a revenue officer for an alleged crime against the State, and to order its removal before trial, when it appears that a Federal question or a claim to a Federal right is raised in the case, and must be decided therein? A more important question can hardly be imagined. Upon its answer may depend the possibility of the general government's preserving its own existence. As was said in Martin v. Hunter (1 Wheat. 363), "the general government must cease to exist whenever it loses the power of protecting itself in the exercise of its constitutional powers." It can act only through its officers and agents, and they must act within the States. If, when thus acting, and within the scope of their authority, those officers can be arrested and brought to trial in a State court, for an alleged offence against the law of the State, yet warranted by the Federal authority they possess, and if the general government is powerless to interfere at once for their protection,—if their protection must be left to the action of the State court,—the operations of the general government may at any time be arrested at the will of one of its members. The legislation of a State may be unfriendly. It may affix penalties to acts done under the immediate direction of the national government, and in obedience to its laws. It may deny the authority conferred by those laws. The State court may administer not only the laws of the State, but equally Federal law, in such a manner as to paralyze the operations of the government. And even if, after trial and final judgment in the State court, the case can be brought into the United States court for review, the officer is withdrawn from the discharge of his duty during the pendency of the prosecution, and the exercise of acknowledged Federal power arrested.

We do not think such an element of weakness is to be found in the Constitution. The United States is a government with authority extending over the whole territory of the Union, acting upon the States and upon the people of the States. While it is limited in the number of its powers, so far as its sovereignty extends it is supreme. * * *

By the last clause of the eighth section of the first article of the Constitution, Congress is invested with power to make all laws necessary and proper for carrying into execution not only all the powers previously specified, but also all other powers vested by the Constitution in the government of the United States, or in any department or officer thereof. Among these is the judicial power of the government. That is declared by the second section of the third article to "extend to all cases in law and equity arising under the Constitution, the laws of the United States, and treaties made or which shall be made under their authority," & c. This provision embraces alike civil and criminal cases arising under the Constitution and laws. Both are equally within the domain of the judicial powers of the United States, and there is nothing in the grant to justify an assertion that whatever power may be exerted over a civil case may not be exerted as fully over a criminal one. And a case arising under the Constitution and laws of the United States may as well arise in a criminal prosecution as in a civil suit. What constitutes a case thus arising was early defined * * *. It is not merely one where a party comes into court to demand something conferred upon him by the Constitution or by a law or treaty. A case consists of the right of one party as well as the other, and may truly be said to arise under the Constitution or a law or a treaty of the United States whenever its correct decision depends upon the construction of either. Cases arising under the laws of the United States are such as grow out of the legislation of Congress, whether they constitute the right or privilege, or claim or protection, or defence of the party, in whole or in part, by whom they are asserted. Story on the Constitution, sect. 1647; 6 Wheat. 379. It was said in Osborne v. The Bank of the United States (9 Wheat. 738), "When a question to which the judicial power of the Union is extended by the Constitution forms an ingredient of the original cause, it is in the power of Congress to give the circuit courts jurisdiction of that cause, although other questions of fact or of law may be involved in it." And a case arises under the laws of the United States, when it arises out of the implication of the law. Mr. Chief Justice Marshall said, in the case last cited: "It is not unusual for a legislative act to involve consequences which are not expressed. An officer, for example, is ordered to arrest an individual. It is not necessary, nor is it usual, to say that he shall not be punished for obeying this order. His security is implied in the order itself. It is no unusual thing for an act of Congress to imply, without expressing, this very exemption from State control." . . . "The collectors of the revenue, the carriers of the mail, the mint establishment, and all those institutions which are public in their nature, are examples in point. It has never been doubted that all who are employed in them are protected while in the line of their duty; and yet this protection is not expressed in any act of Congress. It is incidental to, and is implied in, the several acts by which those institutions are created; and is secured to the individuals employed in them by the judicial power alone; that is, the judicial power is the instrument employed by the government in administering this security."

The constitutional right of Congress to authorize the removal before trial of civil cases arising under the laws of the United States has long since passed beyond doubt. It was exercised almost contemporaneously with the adoption of the Constitution, and the power has been in constant use ever since. * * *

The argument so much pressed upon us, that it is an invasion of the sovereignty of a State to withdraw from its courts into the courts of the general government the trial of prosecutions for alleged offences against the criminal laws of a State, even though the defence presents a case arising out of an act of Congress, ignores entirely the dual character of our government. It assumes that the States are completely and in all respects sovereign. But when the national government was formed, some of the attributes of State sovereignty were partially, and others wholly, surrendered and vested in the United States. Over the subjects thus surrendered the sovereignty of the States ceased to extend. Before the adoption of the Constitution, each State had complete and exclusive authority to administer by its courts all the law, civil and criminal, which existed within its borders. Its judicial power extended over every legal question that could arise. But when the Constitution was adopted, a portion of that judicial power became vested in the new government created, and so far as thus vested it was withdrawn from the sovereignty of the State. * * *

* * *

It ought, therefore, to be considered as settled that the constitutional powers of Congress to authorize the removal of criminal cases for alleged offences against State laws from State courts to the circuit courts of the United States, when there arises a Federal question in them, is as ample as its power to authorize the removal of a civil case. Many of the cases referred to, and others, set out with great force the indispensability of such a power to the enforcement of Federal law.

It follows that the first question certified to us from the Circuit Court of Tennessee must be answered in the affirmative.

* * *

[The dissenting opinion of JUSTICE CLIFFORD, joined by JUSTICE FIELD, is omitted.]

Notes

1. Does federal officer removal necessarily fall within the "arising under" jurisdiction of Article III, section 2? Recall the tests of the *Osborn* decision [supra p. 712], and the analysis in *Mesa* [supra p. 733]. Does the decision in *Davis* answer this question? What about a case in which a federal officer is prosecuted in state court for murder, and his defense is not that the killing was justified as part of his duties, but rather simply that he did not

commit the act, and that he is being prosecuted solely because of hostility towards him as a federal officer? Does the concept of "protective jurisdiction" [supra, p. 723], justify federal officer removal in such a case? Does section 1442 even reach this situation? Reconsider this issue in light of *Mesa*.

2. Note that the issue of federal officer removal is also examined in conjunction with the rule in Tarble's Case [supra p. 148].

3. Section 1442(a)(1) allows removal by "any officer (or any person acting under that officer) of the United States." Does this definition include companies that engage in business in an industry that is subject to pervasive federal regulation, such as tobacco companies? See Watson v. Philip Morris Cos., Inc., 420 F.3d 852 (8th Cir.2005).

§ 3. PROCEDURE ON REMOVAL

28 U.S.C. § 1446 requires a state defendant who wishes to remove the action to federal court to file a notice of removal containing "a short and plain statement of the grounds for removal" in the federal district court for the district and division within which the state action is pending. He must also include "a copy of all process, pleadings and orders served upon such defendant or defendants in such action." The notice of removal must be signed in accordance with Rule 11 of the Federal Rules of Civil Procedure.

Removal in Civil Cases. The notice of removal for a civil action must be filed within thirty days after the defendant's receipt of the initial pleading. The thirty days does not begin to run until the defendant is actually served with a summons and also receives a complaint "through service or otherwise;" defendant's receipt of a "courtesy copy" of the complaint, prior to service of a summons, does not trigger the thirty-day period. Murphy Bros., Inc. v. Michetti Pipe Stringing, Inc., 526 U.S. 344, 119 S.Ct. 1322, 143 L.Ed.2d 448 (1999). If the case in its initial form is not removable, it may be removed within thirty days of receipt of an amended complaint rendering the case removable. Under no circumstances, however, may a diversity case be removed more than one year after it is filed in state court. See 28 U.S.C. § 1446(b).

28 U.S.C. § 1446(d) provides that in a civil action once the defendant provides written notice of the filing of the removal petition to all adverse parties and files a copy of the petition with the clerk of the state court, "the State court shall proceed no further unless and until the case is remanded." This provision has been interpreted as a congressional exception to the Anti–Injunction Statute, 28 U.S.C. § 2283 [see Chapter Nine], allowing a federal court to enjoin the plaintiff from proceeding further in the state action if the state court does not itself decline to continue with its proceedings. In addition, the Reviser's Note to section 2283 indicates that the explicit exception in aid of the federal court's jurisdiction was added to cover such removal cases.

Removal in Criminal Cases. The notice of removal in a criminal case must be filed within thirty days after arraignment in state court, or at any time prior to trial, whichever is earlier. However, for good cause shown the district court may grant permission to file the petition at a later time. In a criminal prosecution, 28 U.S.C. § 1446(c)(3) provides that the filing of the removal petition "shall not prevent the State court in which such prosecution is pending from proceeding further, except that a judgment of conviction shall not be entered unless the prosecution is first remanded." If the federal court does not summarily order remand, it must order a prompt evidentiary hearing.

Remands to State Court: There are four circumstances under which the statutory framework permits a federal district court to remand a removed case to the state court. Under 28 U.S.C. § 1447(c), the district court *must* remand the case to state court "[i]f at any time before final judgment it appears that the district court lacks subject matter jurisdiction," and it may remand on the basis of a defect in the removal procedure. Section 1447(e) provides that "[i]f after removal the plaintiff seeks to join additional defendants whose joinder would destroy subject matter jurisdiction, the court may deny joinder, or permit joinder and remand the action to the State court." Finally, under 28 U.S.C. § 1441(c), the district court may also, in its discretion, remand "all matters in which State law predominates." The Supreme Court has also indicated that federal courts may remand for other reasons, but did not specify the contours of the doctrine of extra-statutory remand. Carnegie–Mellon University v. Cohill, 484 U.S. 343 (1988).

Does 28 U.S.C. § 1441(c) permit remand of the entire case, including the federal questions? See Hartnett, *A New Trick From an Old and Abused Dog: Section 1441(c) Lives and Now Permits the Remand of Federal Question Cases*, 63 Fordham L.Rev. 1099, 1159–1181 (1995)(describing cases permitting remand of entire case); In re City of Mobile, 75 F.3d 605 (11th Cir.1996)(reversing remand of entire case). What happens if the federal court lacks jurisdiction altogether over one of the plaintiff's claims, as in suits against a state? Must the federal court force the parties into bifurcated litigation by remanding only that claim and retaining jurisdiction over the rest of the case? See Berman, *Removal and the Eleventh Amendment: The Case for District Court Remand Discretion To Avoid a Bifurcated Suit*, 92 Mich.L.Rev. 683 (1993). May the court do so? See Eastus v. Blue Bell Creameries, 97 F.3d 100 (5th Cir.1996). In Wisconsin Department of Corrections v. Schacht, 524 U.S. 381 (1998), the Supreme Court held unanimously that a case raising federal claims can be removed to federal court even if some of the claims are barred by the Eleventh Amendment.

A decision to remand for the reasons specified in section 1447(c) is not reviewable, except in the case of civil rights removal. However, mandamus is occasionally employed to obtain appellate review. See Thermtron Products, Inc. v. Hermansdorfer, 423 U.S. 336 (1976). There is also some uncertainty about the extent to which extra-statutory remands under *Cohill* are reviewable. See Things Remembered, Inc. v. Petrarca, 516 U.S. 124 (1995); Kircher v. Putnam Funds Trust, 547 U.S. ___, 126 S.Ct. 2145 (2006). Several commentators have criticized the rules on reviewability. See Solimine, *Removal, Remands, and Reforming Federal Appellate Review*, 58 Mo.L.Rev. 287 (1993); Wasserman, *Re-*

thinking Review of Remands: Proposed Amendments to the Federal Removal Statute, 43 Emory L.J. 83 (1994); Hrdlick, *Appellate Review of Remand Orders in Removed Cases: Are They Losing a Certain Appeal?* 82 Marq.L.Rev. 535 (1999).

A decision *not* to remand is, of course, reviewable if the plaintiff claims that the federal court lacked jurisdiction over the case. The Supreme Court has recently held a federal verdict should not be reversed as long as the federal court had jurisdiction at the time the trial began, even if it did not have jurisdiction at the time it refused to remand. Caterpillar, Inc. v. Lewis, 519 U.S. 61 (1996). The Court reasoned:

> In this case * * * no jurisdictional defect lingered through judgment in the District Court. To wipe out the adjudication post-judgment, and return to state court a case now satisfying all federal jurisdictional requirements, would impose an exorbitant cost on our dual court system, a cost incompatible with the fair and unprotracted administration of justice. 519 U.S. at 77.

The case raises interesting questions about the point at which jurisdiction should be measured. Would the result have been the same if the jurisdictional defect had remained throughout the trial but had been cured just before judgment? If it had been cured during the appeals process?

Caterpillar applies only when the jurisdictional defect incurred by the dismissal of the diversity-destroying party, and not when the diversity-destroying party changes domicile after filing. Grupo Dataflux v. Atlas Global Group, L.P., 541 U.S. 567 (2004).

Chapter 17

FEDERAL COMMON LAW

§ 1. FEDERAL PROPRIETARY INTERESTS AND THE SOURCES OF FEDERAL COMMON LAW

In Erie Railroad Co. v. Tompkins, 304 U.S. 64 (1938), Justice Brandeis wrote that "[t]here is no federal general common law." However, the very same day the Supreme Court held that federal common law controlled the issue of the apportionment of an interstate stream in Hinderlider v. La Plata River & Cherry Creek Ditch Co., 304 U.S. 92 (1938). In Clearfield Trust Co. v. United States, 318 U.S. 363 (1943), the Court held that federal common law controlled the rights and duties of the United States on commercial paper. In another decision, Justice Jackson explained the distinction between the form of federal common law rejected in *Erie* and that which continued to exist:

> The federal courts have no *general* common law, as in a sense they have no general or comprehensive jurisprudence of any kind, because many subjects of private law which bulk large in the traditional common law are ordinarily within the province of the states and not of the federal government. But this is not to say that wherever we have occasion to decide a federal question which cannot be answered from federal statutes alone we may not resort to all of the source materials of the common law, or that when we have fashioned an answer it does not become a part of the federal non-statutory or common law.

D'Oench, Duhme & Co. v. FDIC, 315 U.S. 447, 469 (1942) (Jackson, J., concurring). Do you understand the distinction Justice Jackson attempts to draw?

In *Erie*, the Court held that the creation of a general federal common law was prohibited by the Rules of Decision Act, 28 U.S.C. § 1652, which provides: "The laws of the several states, except where the Constitution or treatise of the United States or Acts of Congress otherwise require or provide, shall be regarded as rules of decision in civil actions in the courts of the United States, in cases where they apply." By its terms, does this Act authorize the creation of *any* federal common law, "general" or otherwise? Can you fashion any arguments

877

which would allow you to construe the Rules of Decision Act to authorize the creation of any federal common law? Does the Court's opinion in *Clearfield Trust* give any indication of how the federal common law recognized there can be reconciled with the terms of the Rules of Decision Act? Consider the wisdom of the argument that the Rules of Decision Act presents no barrier to creation of federal common law because

> [t]he difference between "common law" and "statutory interpretation" is a difference in emphasis rather than a difference in kind. The more definite and explicit the prevailing legislative policy, the more likely a court will describe its lawmaking as statutory interpretation; the less precise and less explicit the perceived legislative policy the more likely a court will speak of common law. The distinction, however, is entirely one of degree.

Westen & Lehman, *Is There Life for* Erie *After the Death of Diversity?*, 78 Mich.L.Rev. 311, 332 (1980). Cf. Merrill, *The Common Law Powers of Federal Courts,* 52 U.Chi.L.Rev. 1, 32 (1985), suggesting that such an analysis "involves a highly questionable view of what can legitimately be described as textual 'interpretation.'" If one accepts the view that "the Rules of Decision Act presents no barrier to federal common law because any federal common law rule can be described as a form of textual 'interpretation'" [Merrill, 52 U.Chi.L.Rev. at 32, summarizing the position of Westen and Lehman], what limiting force would the Rules of Decision Act have on the power of the federal courts to fashion substantive federal common law? If *all* common-law making is tantamount to a form of textual interpretation—either of a constitutional provision or a federal statute—what would have been the point of enacting the Rules of Decision Act in the first place? See generally Redish, *Continuing the Erie Debate: A Response to Westen and Lehman,* 78 Mich.L.Rev. 959 (1980).

On the legitimacy of federal common law, consider the following commentary: "In a democratic society, the unrepresentative federal judiciary is not automatically authorized to make subconstitutional policy choices on the basis of its social and moral dictates * * * no matter how correct one believes those policy choices to be * * *. The Rules of Decision Act dictates that if not the product of a legitimate interpretive process of a governing federal statute, the substantive law to be applied in a federal court is the state's. Any change from that directive must emanate from the same source that produced it in the first place." "[T]he Rules of Decision Act does not authorize a federal court to fashion a common law rule simply on the basis of a finding of an overriding federal interest. On the contrary, it quite explicitly prohibits the federal courts from creating their own free-standing substantive common law principles." Redish, *Federal Common Law, Political Legitimacy, and the Interpretive Process: An "Institutionalist" Perspective,* 83 Nw.U.L.Rev. 761, 800, 801 (1989). On the relevance of the Rules of Decision Act to the legitimacy of federal common law, see J. Pfander, Principles of Federal Jurisdiction 141 (2006). See also Musson Theatrical, Inc. v. Federal Express Corp., 89 F.3d 1244, 1250 (6th Cir.1996):

"When a federal court creates a federal common law rule, it risks violating both of the two fundamental limits on the judicial branch: federalism and the separation of powers."

But see Weinberg, *The Curious Notion that the Rules of Decision Act Blocks Supreme Federal Common Law,* 83 Nw.U.L.Rev. 860, 866 (1989), arguing that "[i]t is time to face up to the fact that the [Rules of Decision] Act comes down to us as a relic of prepositivist, prerealist time, with scant relevance for us today." Assuming this to be true, does that justify—as a matter of democratic theory—the federal courts' effective repeal of the Act?

For an interesting comment on this debate, see Brown, *Federal Common Law and the Role of the Federal Courts in Private Law Adjudication—A (New)* Erie *Problem?,* 12 Pace L.Rev. 229 (1992). Professor Brown rejects what he calls these "polar" positions in favor of a "middle ground" approach, which authorizes federal common law "in a limited number of enclaves, or in areas of 'uniquely federal interest.'" Id. at 252. Is the text of the Rules of Decision Act capable of receiving such a construction? See also Merrill, *The Judicial Prerogative,* 12 Pace L.Rev. 327, 356 (1992), advocating a position that "start[s] with the legitimacy perspective [on the judicial power to create federal common law], and * * * builds some flexibility into it." While such an approach would "inevitably sacrifice utility in some cases * * * at least it promises to resume a fair amount of what has been called federal common law * * *."

Another commentator has suggested that many modern federal common law rules "can be justified in terms of the constitutional structure because they govern matters beyond the legislative competence of the states and implement various aspects of the constitutional scheme. Recognizing the structural foundations of various rules currently thought to be 'federal judge-made law' suggests that many of these rules have been essentially mischaracterized. Recasting federal common law rules by reference to the constitutional structure places them on a firmer constitutional footing and dispels the suggestion that judicial application of such rules either usurps the constitutional authority of the states or invades the province of the political branches." Clarke, *Federal Common Law: A Structural Reinterpretation,* 144 U. Pa. L. Rev. 1245, 1375–76 (1996). In addition, on the general subject, see also Weinberg, *Federal Common Law,* 83 Nw.U.L.Rev. 805 (1989); Doernberg, *Juridical Chameleons in the "new* Erie" *Canal,* 1990 Utah L.Rev. 759; and M. Redish, The Federal Courts in The Political Order 29–46 (1991).

If one is to assume the legitimacy of the generic concept of federal common law, the Court must still develop substantive guidelines that determine exactly when federal common law is to be deemed to supplement otherwise applicable state law. According to one scholar, the Supreme Court's decisions in the area "do not form a predictable pattern but have something of an episodic quality; federal common law arises here and there for reasons that one can rationalize in retrospect but cannot often predict in advance." J. Pfander, Principles of Federal Jurisdiction 140 (2006). See also Tidmarsh & Murray, *A Theory of Federal Common Law*, 100 Nw.U.L.Rev. 585, 587 (2006), noting the difficulty in attempting "to craft a theory that both justifies courts' power to create federal law and guides the discretionary refusal to exercise this power." Tidmarsh and Murray suggest that such a theory should be premised on the assertion "that in certain areas, states have such a strong self-interest in a controversy or have erected such high barriers to political participation by some groups that state law cannot be expected to provide a sufficiently detached, reliable, and neutral rule of decision for a controversy." Id. at 588.

Note that when federal common law is deemed applicable, it controls in state courts, as well as federal courts. See Bellia, *State Courts and the Making of Federal Common Law*, 153 U.Pa.L.Rev. 825 (2005).

UNITED STATES v. KIMBELL FOODS, INC.

Supreme Court of the United States, 1979.
440 U.S. 715.

MR. JUSTICE MARSHALL delivered the opinion of the Court.

We granted certiorari in these cases to determine whether contractual liens arising from certain federal loan programs take precedence over private liens, in the absence of a federal statute setting priorities. To resolve this question, we must decide first whether federal or state law governs the controversies; and second, if federal law applies, whether this Court should fashion a uniform priority rule or incorporate state commercial law. We conclude that the source of law is federal, but that a national rule is unnecessary to protect the federal interests underlying the loan programs. Accordingly, we adopt state law as the appropriate federal rule for establishing the relative priority of these competing federal and private liens.

I

A

No. 77–1359 involves two contractual security interests in the personal property of O. K. Super Markets, Inc. Both interests were perfected pursuant to Texas' Uniform Commercial Code (UCC). The United States' lien secures a loan guaranteed by the Small Business Administration (SBA). The private lien, which arises from security agreements that preceded the federal guarantee, secures advances respondent made after the federal guarantee.

In 1968, O. K. Super Markets borrowed $27,000 from Kimbell Foods, Inc. (Kimbell), a grocery wholesaler. Two security agreements identified the supermarket's equipment and merchandise as collateral. The agreements also contained a standard "dragnet" clause providing that this collateral would secure future advances from Kimbell to O. K. Super Markets. Kimbell properly perfected its security interests by filing financing statements with the Texas Secretary of State according to Texas law.

In February 1969, O. K. Super Markets obtained a $300,000 loan from Republic National Bank of Dallas (Republic). The bank accepted as security the same property specified in Kimbell's 1968 agreements, and filed a financing statement with the Texas Secretary of State to perfect its security interest. The SBA guaranteed 90% of this loan under the Small Business Act, which authorizes such assistance but, with one exception, does not specify priority rules to govern the SBA's security interests.

O. K. Super Markets used the Republic loan proceeds to satisfy the remainder of the 1968 obligation and to discharge an indebtedness for inventory purchased from Kimbell on open account. Kimbell continued credit sales to O. K. Super Markets until the balance due reached $18,258.57 on January 15, 1971. Thereupon, Kimbell initiated state proceedings against O. K. Super Markets to recover this inventory debt.

Shortly before Kimbell filed suit, O. K. Super Markets had defaulted on the SBA-guaranteed loan. Republic assigned its security interest to the SBA in late December 1970, and recorded the assignment with Texas authorities on January 21, 1971. The United States then honored its guarantee and paid Republic $252,331.93 (90% of the outstanding indebtedness) on February 3, 1971. That same day, O. K. Super Markets, with the approval of its creditors, sold its equipment and inventory and placed the proceeds in escrow pending resolution of the competing claims to the funds. Approximately one year later, the state court entered judgment against O. K. Super Markets, and awarded Kimbell $24,445.37, representing the inventory debt, plus interest and attorney's fees.

Kimbell thereafter brought the instant action to foreclose on its lien, claiming that its security interest in the escrow fund was superior to the SBA's. The District Court held for the Government. On determining that federal law controlled the controversy, the court applied principles developed by this Court to afford federal statutory tax liens special priority over state and private liens where the governing statute does not specify priorities. * * * Under these rules, the lien "first in time" is "first in right." However, to be considered first in time, the nonfederal lien must be "choate," that is, sufficiently specific, when the federal lien arises. A state-created lien is not choate until the "identity of the lienor, the property subject to the lien, and the amount of the lien are established." United States v. New Britain, 347 U.S. 81, 84 (1954). * * * Failure to meet any one of these conditions forecloses priority over the federal lien, even if under state law the nonfederal lien was enforceable for all purposes when the federal lien arose.

Because Kimbell did not reduce its lien to judgment until February 1972, and the federal lien had been created either in 1969, when Republic filed its financing statement, or in 1971, when Republic recorded its assignment, the District Court concluded that respondent's lien was inchoate when the federal lien arose. * * * Alternatively, the court held that even under state law, the SBA lien was superior to Kimbell's claim because the future advance clauses in the 1968 agreements were not intended to secure the debts arising from O. K. Super Market's subsequent inventory purchases. * * *

The Court of Appeals reversed. * * * It agreed that federal law governs the rights of the United States under its SBA loan program, * * * and that the "first in time, first in right" priority principle should control the competing claims. * * * However, the court refused to extend the choateness rule to situations in which the Federal Government was not an involuntary creditor of tax delinquents, but rather a voluntary commercial lender. * * * Instead, it fashioned a new federal rule for determining which lien was first in time, and concluded that "in the context of competing state security interests arising under the U. C. C.," the first to meet UCC perfection requirements achieved priority. * * *

The Court of Appeals then considered which lien qualified as first perfected. Disagreeing with the District Court, the court determined that, under Texas law, the 1968 security agreements covered Kimbell's future advances, and that the liens securing those advances dated from the filing of the security agreements before the federal lien arose. * * * But the Court of Appeals did not adopt Texas law. Rather, it proceeded to decide whether the future advances should receive the same treatment under federal common law. After surveying three possible approaches, the court held that Kimbell's future advances dated back to the 1968 agreements, and therefore took precedence over Republic's 1969 loan. * * *

B

At issue in No. 77–1644 is whether a federal contractual security interest in a tractor is superior to a subsequent repairman's lien in the same property. * * *

The Court of Appeals * * * first ruled that "the rights and liabilities of the parties to a suit arising from FHA loan transactions must, under the rationale of the *Clearfield Trust* doctrine, be determined with reference to federal law." * * * In fashioning a federal rule for assessing the sufficiency of the FHA's financing statement, the court elected to follow the Model UCC rather than to incorporate [state] law. * * *

The Court of Appeals then addressed the priority question and concluded that neither state law nor the first-in-time, first-in-right and choateness doctrines were appropriate to resolve the conflicting claims. * * * In their place, the court devised a special "federal commercial law rule," using the Model UCC and the Tax Lien Act of 1966 as guides. * * * This rule would give priority to repairman's liens over the Government's previously perfected consensual security interests when the repairman continuously possesses the property from the time his lien arises. * * *

II

This Court has consistently held that federal law governs questions involving the rights of the United States arising under nationwide federal programs. * * *

Guided by these principles, we think it clear that the priority of liens stemming from federal lending programs must be determined with reference to federal law. The SBA and FHA unquestionably perform federal functions within the meaning of *Clearfield*. Since the agencies derive their authority to effectuate loan transactions from specific Acts of Congress passed in the exercise of a "constitutional function or power," Clearfield Trust Co. v. United States, supra, at 366, their rights, as well, should derive from a federal source. When Government activities "aris[e] from and bea[r] heavily upon a federal ... program," the Constitution and Acts of Congress " 'require' otherwise than that state law govern of its own force." United States v. Little Lake Misere Land Co., 412 U.S. 580, 592 (1973). In such contexts, federal interests are sufficiently implicated to warrant the protection of federal law.

That the statutes authorizing these federal lending programs do not specify the appropriate rule of decision in no way limits the reach of federal law. It is precisely when Congress has not spoken " 'in an area comprising issues substantially related to an established program of government operation,' " id., at 593, * * * that *Clearfield* directs federal courts to fill the interstices of federal legislation "according to their own standards." * * *

Federal law therefore controls the Government's priority rights. The more difficult task, to which we turn, is giving content to this federal rule.

III

Controversies directly affecting the operations of federal programs, although governed by federal law, do not inevitably require resort to uniform federal rules. * * * Whether to adopt state law or to fashion a nationwide federal rule is a matter of judicial policy "dependent upon a variety of considerations always relevant to the nature of the specific governmental interests and to the effects upon them of applying state law." United States v. Standard Oil Co., 332 U.S. 301, 310 (1947).

Undoubtedly, federal programs that "by their nature are and must be uniform in character throughout the Nation" necessitate formulation of controlling federal rules. United States v. Yazell, 382 U.S. 341, 354 (1966); see Clearfield Trust Co. v. United States, supra, 318 U.S., at 367; United States v. Standard Oil Co., supra, 332 U.S., at 311; Illinois v. Milwaukee, 406 U.S. 91, 105 n. 6 (1972). Conversely, when there is little need for a nationally uniform body of law, state law may be incorporated as the federal rule of decision. Apart from considerations of uniformity, we must also determine whether application of state law would frustrate specific objectives of the federal programs. If so, we must fashion special rules solicitous of those federal interests. Finally, our choice-of-law inquiry must consider the extent to which application of a federal rule would disrupt commercial relationships predicated on state law.⏋

The Government argues that effective administration of its lending programs requires uniform federal rules of priority. It contends further that resort to any rules other than first in time, first in right and choateness would conflict with protectionist fiscal policies underlying the programs. We are unpersuaded that, in the circumstances presented here, nationwide standards favoring claims of the United States are necessary to ease program administration or to safeguard the Federal Treasury from defaulting debtors. Because the state commercial codes "furnish convenient solutions in no way inconsistent with adequate protection of the federal interest[s]," United States v. Standard Oil Co., supra, 332 U.S., at 309, we decline to override intricate state laws of general applicability on which private creditors base their daily commercial transactions.

A

Incorporating state law to determine the rights of the United States as against private creditors would in no way hinder administration of the SBA and FHA loan programs. In United States v. Yazell, supra, this Court rejected the argument, similar to the Government's here, that a need for uniformity precluded application of state coverture rules to an SBA loan contract. Because SBA operations were "specifically and in great detail adapted to state law," 382 U.S., at 357, the federal interest in supplanting "important and carefully evolved state arrangements designed to serve multiple purposes" was minimal. Id., at 353. Our conclusion that compliance with state law would produce no hardship on the agency was also based on the SBA's practice of "individually negotiat[ing] in painfully particularized detail" each loan transaction. Id., at 345–346. These observations apply with equal force here and compel us again to reject generalized pleas for uniformity as substitutes for concrete evidence that adopting state law would adversely affect administration of the federal programs.

Although the SBA Financial Assistance Manual on which this Court relied in *Yazell* is no longer "replete with admonitions to follow state law carefully," id., at 357 n. 35; SBA employees are still instructed to, and indeed do, follow state law. In fact, a fair reading of the SBA Financial Assistance Manual, SOP 50–10 (SBA Manual), indicates that the agency assumes its security interests are controlled to a large extent by the commercial law of each State. Similarly, FHA regulations expressly incorporate state law. They mandate compliance with state procedures for perfecting and maintaining valid security interests, and highlight those rules that differ from State to State. * * *

Thus, the agencies' own operating practices belie their assertion that a federal rule of priority is needed to avoid the administrative burdens created by disparate state commercial rules. The programs already conform to each State's commercial standards. By using local lending offices and employees who are familiar with the law of their respective localities, the agencies function effectively without uniform procedures and legal rules.

Nevertheless, the Government maintains that requiring the agencies to assess security arrangements under local law would dictate close scrutiny of each transaction and thereby impede expeditious processing of loans. We disagree. Choosing responsible debtors necessarily requires individualized selection procedures, which the agencies have already implemented in considerable detail. Each applicant's financial condition is evaluated under rigorous standards in a lengthy process. Agency employees negotiate personally with borrowers, investigate property offered as collateral for encumbrances, and obtain local legal advice on the adequacy of proposed security arrangements. In addition, they adapt the terms of every loan to the parties' needs and capabilities. Because each application currently receives individual scrutiny, the agencies can readily adjust loan transactions to reflect state priority rules, just as they consider other factual and legal matters before disbursing Government funds. * * * Since there is no indication that variant state priority schemes would burden current methods of loan processing, we conclude that considerations of administrative convenience do not warrant adoption of a uniform federal law.

* * *

C

In structuring financial transactions, businessmen depend on state commercial law to provide the stability essential for reliable evaluation of the risks involved. * * *

Because the ultimate consequences of altering settled commercial practices are so difficult to foresee, we hesitate to create new uncertainties, in the absence of careful legislative deliberation. Of course, formulating special rules to govern the priority of the federal consensual liens in issue here would be justified if necessary to vindicate important national interests. But neither the Government nor the Court of Appeals advanced any concrete reasons for rejecting well-established commercial rules which have proven workable over time. Thus, the prudent course is to adopt the readymade body of state law as the federal rule of decision until Congress strikes a different accommodation.

IV

Accordingly, we hold that, absent a congressional directive, the relative priority of private liens and consensual liens arising from these Government lending programs is to be determined under nondiscriminatory state laws. * * *

———

WEST VIRGINIA v. UNITED STATES, 479 U.S. 305 (1987):

The issue in this case is whether the State of West Virginia is liable for prejudgment interest on a debt arising from a contractual obligation to reimburse the United States for services rendered by the Army Corps of Engineers.

On February 26, 1972, heavy rains and resulting floods caused collapse of a coal waste dam on Buffalo Creek in southwestern West Virginia. * * * In August of that year, a series of storms caused widespread flooding and mudslides in the same region of the state. * * *

The President declared both events 'major disasters,' qualifying the affected area for federal relief under The Disaster Relief Act of 1970, 42 U.S.C. § 4401 et seq. * * *

In the aftermath of both disasters, the state * * * asked the Army Corps of Engineers to [prepare sites for mobile homes authorized by the federal statute], and the Corps agreed. In late 1972, and early 1973, the Corps billed the state for its site preparation services. The State * * * failed to make any payment. * * * [T]he United States brought suit against West Virginia in 1978, seeking to recover $4.2 million in site preparation costs plus prejudgment interest. * * * The District Court * * * found that the State was contractually obligated to the Corps for site preparation services. The United States then moved for an order of prejudgment interest on the outstanding debt. * * * We granted certiorari, limited to the question whether West Virginia was properly required to pay prejudgment interest.

* * *

* * * While there are instances in which state law may be adopted as the federal rule of decision, see *United States v. Yazell,* this case presents no compelling reason for doing so. A single nationwide rule would be preferable to one turning on state law, and the incorporation of state law would not give due regard to the federal interest in maintaining the apportionment of responsibility Congress devised in the [Disaster Relief Act]. Finally, application of a federal rule would not 'disrupt commercial relationships predicated on state law,' *United States v. Kimbell Foods, Inc.,* since state law would not of its own force govern contracts between a state and the Federal Government.

Given that state law may neither govern of its own force nor be adopted as the federal rule of decision, it remains for us to apply the federal rule." [The Court then held "that prejudgment interest should be required."]

Notes

1. For lower court applications of the *Kimbell Foods* test, see Redwing Carriers, Inc. v. Saraland Apartments, 94 F.3d 1489 (11th Cir.1996); Davidson v. FDIC, 44 F.3d 246 (5th Cir.1995); United States v. Ward, 985 F.2d 500 (10th Cir.1993); United States v. Irby, 618 F.2d 352 (5th Cir.1980); United States v. S.K.A. Associates, Inc., 600 F.2d 513 (5th Cir.1979); United States v. Dansby, 509 F.Supp. 188 (N.D.Ohio 1981). In *S.K.A.*, the court noted that the "very detailed opinion for a unanimous Court in *Kimbell* sought to carefully instruct Government agencies that in their commercial lending activities they are subject to 'customary commercial practices' * * * and should fair no better, and no worse, than a private lender." 600 F.2d at 516. See also United States v. Walter Dunlap & Sons, Inc., 800 F.2d 1232 (3d Cir.1986) (relies on *Kimbell Foods* for proposition that uniform nationwide standards are unnecessary for federal lending programs); Johnson v. United States Dept. of Agriculture, 734 F.2d 774 (11th Cir.1984) (under *Kimbell Foods*, state law determines the method of foreclosure on housing laws issued by the Farmers Home Administration).

2. Can the holding in *West Virginia* be reconciled with *Kimbell Foods?* Is the *West Virginia* Court's attempted reconciliation persuasive?

Even prior to the Supreme Court's decision in *West Virginia,* lower courts, applying the *Kimbell Foods* test, had on occasion chosen to employ a distinct federal standard. See, e.g., United States v. Carr, 608 F.2d 886 (1st Cir.1979) ("the federal law of bail bond contracts should consist of uniform federal rules rather than state rules adopted as federal law."); United States v. Larson, 632 F.Supp. 1565 (D.N.D.1986) (federal law governs priority of SBA liens: "To the extent the objectives of SBA's lending program include the government's recoupment of monies loaned, application of the state law would frustrate objectives of the SBA program."); FDIC v. Blue Rock Shopping Center, Inc., 766 F.2d 744 (3d Cir.1985) (federal common law applies when the court is attempting to determine whether the co-maker of a negotiable instrument may assert the defense of unjustifiable impairment of collateral against the holder of the note, when the holder of the note is the FDIC). See also United States v. Landmark Park & Associates, 795 F.2d 683 (8th Cir.1986); FDIC v. Gulf Life Insurance Co., 737 F.2d 1513 (11th Cir.1984).

3. As the cases cited in note 2 indicate, courts have generally treated a litigation in which a federal agency is a party, for purposes of the *Kimbell Foods* doctrine, fungibly with cases in which the United States is itself a party. However, in O'Melveny & Myers v. FDIC, 512 U.S. 79 (1994), the Supreme Court responded to the argument that federal law should control where the FDIC is a litigant by noting that "the FDIC is not the United States * * *."

4. In *O'Melveny*, supra, the Court suggested a restrictive approach to the use of a distinct federal common law standard in suits involving federal agencies, at least where the day-to-day activities of the agency are not directly implicated. The hesitancy to develop an independent federal common law standard had special relevance, the Court indicated, when there

already existed a "comprehensive and detailed" federal statutory scheme. Decisions such as *O'Melveny* have led one commentator to assert that "the Supreme Court has altered dramatically the balance between state and federal power during the 1990s by restricting the federal common law making powers of the federal courts." Lund, *The Decline of Federal Common Law*, 76 B.U. L. Rev. 895, 899 (1996). See also United States v. Yazell, 382 U.S. 341 (1966), where the Supreme Court chose to apply state law, rather than to devise a federal common law standard, to the interpretation of a contract between the Small Business Administration and private parties. The SBA had made a disaster loan to Yazell and his wife. After the Yazells defaulted on the note and the SBA foreclosed on their mortgage, the government brought suit against the Yazells for the deficiency. Mrs. Yazell argued that under the doctrine of "coverture," recognized at the time by Texas law, she lacked the capacity to bind herself contractually, and therefore the contract could not be enforced against her separately held property. The United States argued that absent an applicable federal statute, questions of contractual capacity should be governed by federal common law, and that under federal law the doctrine of coverture should not be recognized.

The Court chose to apply Texas law. Contrasting the case with *Clearfield*, the Court emphasized that "this was a custom-made, hand-tailored, specifically negotiated transaction. It was not a nationwide act of the Federal Government, emanating in a single form from a single source." An additional distinction between *Clearfield* and the other cases applying federal common law and *Yazell*, said the Court, was that the applicable legal principles in *Yazell* concerned "the peculiarly state province of family or family-property arrangements," an area in which federal courts are traditionally reluctant to interfere. The Court rejected the government's arguments for uniformity, noting that the forms used had been "specifically adapted to this transaction and to Texas Law." The Court's emphasis on the individually-negotiated nature of the contract has been relied upon by lower courts as a basis for adopting state law as the federal standard, as has the Court's recognition of the need to avoid interference with matters of peculiarly local concern. But *Yazell* failed to provide a detailed analytical framework for deciding under what circumstances federal common law would adopt state law as its standard.

5. Texas Industries, Inc. v. Radcliff Materials, Inc., 451 U.S. 630 (1981): The Supreme Court held that the federal antitrust laws do not allow a defendant against whom civil damages have been awarded to obtain contribution from other participants in the unlawful conspiracy, and that federal courts are not empowered to fashion a federal common law rule of contribution. The Court acknowledged that "[f]ederal common law * * * may come into play when Congress has vested jurisdiction in the federal courts and empowered them to create governing rules of law", citing, *inter alia*, Textile Workers Union v. Lincoln Mills, 353 U.S. 448 (1957), discussed in Chapter Six, where the Court held that § 301(a) of the Labor Management Relations Act, 29 U.S.C. § 185(a), vests in the federal courts authority to create a federal common law of labor-management relations. The Court further recognized that by their nature, sections 1 and 2 of the Sherman Act (forbidding "every contract, combination * * *, or conspiracy, in restraint of trade" and "monopoliz[ing], or attempt[ing] to monopolize, * * * any part of

the trade or commerce * * *.") gave the federal courts broad power to develop the substantive rules of antitrust law. "It does not necessarily follow, however, that Congress intended to give courts as wide discretion in formulating remedies to enforce the provisions of the Sherman Act or the kind of relief sought through contribution. The intent to allow courts to develop governing principles of law, so unmistakingly clear with regard to substantive violations, does not appear in debates on the treble-damage action created in § 7 of the original Act * * *." The Court noted that "[i]n contrast to the sweeping language of §§ 1 and 2 of the Sherman Act, the remedial provisions defined in the antitrust laws are detailed and specific * * *." 451 U.S. at 643, 644.

6. *Kimbell Foods* was followed by the Supreme Court in Wilson v. Omaha Indian Tribe, 442 U.S. 653 (1979). The issue was whether state or federal law should provide the basis for decision in a boundary dispute, caused by changes in a river's course, between Indians living on a reservation and non-Indian owners of neighboring land. The Court held that state law would apply:

> United States v. Kimbell Foods, Inc. * * * advises that * * * we should consider whether there is need for a nationally uniform body of law to apply in situations comparable to this, whether application of state law would frustrate federal policy or functions and the impact a federal rule might have on existing relationships under state law. An application of these factors suggests to us that state law should be borrowed as the federal rule of decision here. Id. at 673.

"It is true", said the Court, "that States may differ among themselves with respect to the rules that will identify and distinguish between avulsions and accretions, but as long as the applicable standard is applied evenhandedly to particular disputes, we discern no imperative need to develop a general body of federal common law to decide cases such as this, where an interstate boundary is not in dispute." Id. The Court added that "[t]his is also an area in which the States have substantial interests in having their own law resolve controversies such as these. Private landowners rely on state real property law when purchasing real property * * *. There is considerable merit in not having the reasonable expectations of these private landowners upset by the vagaries of being located adjacent to or across from Indian reservations or other property in which the United States has a substantial interest. Borrowing state law will also avoid arriving at one answer to the avulsive-accretion riddle in disputes involving Indians on one side and possibly quite different answers with respect to neighboring land where non-Indians are the disputants." Id. at 674.

Consider the Court's argument about "the reasonable expectations" of private landowners. Might the argument be deemed question-begging, in that if they are told that disputes over land in which there is a strong and obvious federal interest will be controlled by federal law, their "reasonable expectations" would have to be different? Would it be significantly burdensome on owners of land contiguous to land controlled by the federal government to require that they be aware that land disputes will be regulated by federal law? Consider also the Court's concern that, under a separate federal standard, different substantive law will apply to disputes when Indians are involved and when they are not involved. Is that necessarily a bad thing? Might it be argued that, in light of the strong federal interest in assuring proper treatment of and recompense to the Indians, special rules favoring their interests be applied in cases involving them?

BOYLE v. UNITED TECHNOLOGIES CORP.

Supreme Court of the United States, 1988.
487 U.S. 500.

JUSTICE SCALIA delivered the opinion of the Court.

This case requires us to decide when a contractor providing military equipment to the Federal Government can be held liable under state tort law for injury caused by a design defect.

I

On April 27, 1983, David A. Boyle, a United States Marine helicopter copilot, was killed when the CH–53D helicopter in which he was flying crashed off the coast of Virginia Beach, Virginia, during a training exercise. Although Boyle survived the impact of the crash, he was unable to escape from the helicopter and drowned. Boyle's father, petitioner here, brought this diversity action in Federal District Court against the Sikorsky Division of United Technologies Corporation (Sikorsky), which built the helicopter for the United States.

At trial, petitioner presented two theories of liability under Virginia tort law that were submitted to the jury. First, petitioner alleged that Sikorsky had defectively repaired a device called the servo in the helicopter's automatic flight control system, which allegedly malfunctioned and caused the crash. Second, petitioner alleged that Sikorsky had defectively designed the copilot's emergency escape system: the escape hatch opened out instead of in (and was therefore ineffective in a submerged craft because of water pressure), and access to the escape hatch handle was obstructed by other equipment. The jury returned a general verdict in favor of petitioner and awarded him $725,000.

The Court of Appeals reversed and remanded with directions that judgment be entered for Sikorsky. It found, as a matter of Virginia law, that Boyle had failed to meet his burden of demonstrating that the repair work performed by Sikorsky, as opposed to work that had been done by the Navy, was responsible for the alleged malfunction of the flight control system. It also found, as a matter of federal law, that Sikorsky could not be held liable for the allegedly defective design of the escape hatch because, on the evidence presented, it satisfied the requirements of the "military contractor defense," which the court had recognized the same day in *Tozer v. LTV Corp.*, 792 F.2d 403 (C.A.4 1986).

* * *

II

Petitioner's broadest contention is that, in the absence of legislation specifically immunizing Government contractors from liability for design defects, there is no basis for judicial recognition of such a defense. We disagree. In most fields of activity, to be sure, this court has refused to find federal pre-emption of state law in the absence of either a clear statutory prescription, or a direct conflict between federal and state law. But we have held that a few areas, involving "uniquely federal interests," *Texas Industries, Inc. v. Radcliff Materials, Inc.,* 451 U.S. 630, 640 (1981), are so committed by the Constitution and laws of the United States to federal control that state law is preempted and replaced, where necessary, by federal law of a content prescribed (absent explicit statutory directive) by the courts—so-called "federal common law."

The dispute in the present case borders upon two areas that we have found to involve such "uniquely federal interests." We have held that obligations to and rights of the United States under its contracts are governed exclusively by federal law. See, *Clearfield Trust.* The present case does not involve an obligation to the United States under its contract, but rather liability to third persons. That liability may be styled one in tort, but it arises out of performance of the contract—and traditionally has been regarded as sufficiently related to the contract that until 1962 Virginia would generally allow design defect suits only by the purchaser and those in privity with the seller.

Another area that we have found to be of peculiarly federal concern, warranting the displacement of state law, is the civil liability of federal officials for actions taken in the course of their duty. We have held in many contexts that the scope of that liability is controlled by federal law. The present case involves an independent contractor performing its obligation under a procurement contract, rather than an official performing his duty as a federal employee, but there is obviously implicated the same interest in getting the Government's work done.

We think the reasons for considering these closely related areas to be of "uniquely federal" interest apply as well to the civil liabilities arising out of the performance of federal procurement contracts. We have come close to holding as much. In *Yearsley v. W.A. Ross Construction Co.,* 309 U.S. 18 (1940), we rejected an attempt by a landowner to hold a construction contractor liable under state law for the erosion of 95 acres caused by the contractor's work in constructing dikes for the Government. We said that "if [the] authority to carry out the project was validly conferred, that is, if what was done was within the constitutional power of Congress, there is no liability on the part of the contractor for executing its will." The federal interest justifying this holding surely exists as much in procurement contracts as in performance contracts; we see no basis for a distinction.

Moreover, it is plain that the Federal Government's interest in the procurement of equipment is implicated by suits such as the present one—even though the dispute is one between private parties. It is true that where "litigation is purely between private parties and does not touch the rights and duties of the United States," *Bank of America Nat. Trust & Sav. Assn. v. Parnell,* 352 U.S. 29, 33 (1956), federal law does not govern. Thus, for example, in *Miree v. DeKalb County,* 433 U.S. 25, 30 (1977), which involved the question whether certain private parties could sue as third-party beneficiaries to an agreement between a municipality and the Federal Aviation Administration, we found that state law was not displaced because "the operations of the United States in connection with FAA grants such as these ... would [not] be burdened" by allowing state law to determine whether third-party beneficiaries could sue, and because "any federal interest in the outcome of the [dispute] before us '[was] far too speculative, far too remote a possibility to justify the application of federal law to transactions essentially of local concern.' " But the same is not true here. The imposition of liability on Government contractors will directly affect the terms of Government contracts: either the contractor will decline to manufacture the design specified by the Government, or it will raise its price. Either way, the interests of the United States will be directly affected.

That the procurement of equipment by the United States is an area of uniquely federal interest does not, however, end the inquiry. That merely establishes a necessary, not a sufficient, condition for the displacement of state law. Displacement will occur only where, as we have variously described, a "significant conflict" exists between an identifiable "federal policy or interest and the [operation] of state law," or the application of state law would "frustrate specific objectives" of federal legislation. The conflict with federal policy need not be as sharp as that which must exist for ordinary pre-emption when Congress legislates "in a field which the States have traditionally occupied." *Rice v. Santa Fe Elevator Corp.,* 331 U.S., at 230. Or to put the point differently, the fact that the area in question *is* one of unique federal concern changes what would otherwise be a conflict that cannot produce preemption into one that can. But conflict there must be. In some cases, for example where the federal interest requires a uniform rule, the entire body of state law applicable to the area conflicts and is replaced by federal rules. See, *e.g., Clearfield Trust,* 318 U.S., at 366–367. In others, the conflict is more narrow, and only particular elements of state law are superseded. See, *e.g., Little Lake Misere Land Co.,* 412 U.S., at 595.

In *Miree, supra,* the suit was not seeking to impose upon the person contracting with the Government a duty contrary to the duty imposed by the Government contract. Rather, it was the contractual duty *itself* that the private plaintiff (as third party beneficiary) sought to enforce. Between *Miree* and the present case, it is easy to conceive of an intermediate situation, in which the duty sought to be imposed on the contractor is not identical to one assumed under the contract, but is also not contrary to any assumed. If, for example, the United States contracts for the purchase and installation of an air conditioning unit specifying the cooling capacity but not the precise manner of construction, a state law imposing upon the manufacturer of such units a duty of care to include a certain safety feature would not be a duty identical to anything promised the Government, but neither would it be contrary. The contractor could comply with both its contractual obligations and the state-prescribed duty of care. No one suggests that state law would generally be pre-empted in this context.

The present case, however, is at the opposite extreme from *Miree*. Here the state-imposed duty of care that is the asserted basis of the contractor's liability (specifically, the duty to equip helicopters with the sort of escape-hatch mechanism petitioner claims was necessary) is precisely contrary to the duty imposed by the Government contract (the duty to manufacture and deliver helicopters with the sort of escape-hatch mechanism shown by the specifications). Even in this sort of situation, it would be unreasonable to say that there is always a "significant conflict" between the state law and a federal policy or interest. If, for example, a federal procurement officer orders, by model number, a quantity of stock helicopters that happen to be equipped with escape hatches opening outward, it is impossible to say that the Government has a significant interest in that particular feature. That would be scarcely more reasonable than saying that a private individual who orders such a craft by model number cannot sue for the manufacturer's negligence because he got precisely what he ordered.

* * *

There is * * * a statutory provision that demonstrates the potential for, and suggests the outlines of, "significant conflict" between federal interests and state law in the context of government procurement. In the Federal Tort Claims Act (FTCA), Congress authorized damages to be recovered against the United States for harm caused by the negligent or wrongful conduct of Government employees, to the extent that a private person would be liable under the law of the place where the conduct occurred. 28 U.S.C. § 1346(b). It excepted from this consent to suit, however,

> "[a]ny claim * * * based upon the exercise or performance or the failure to exercise or perform a discretionary function or duty on the part of a federal agency or an employee of the Government, whether or not the discretion involved be abused." 28 U.S.C. § 2680(a).

We think that the selection of the appropriate design for military equipment to be used by our Armed Forces is assuredly a discretionary function within the meaning of this provision. It often involves not merely engineering analysis but judgment as to the balancing of many technical, military, and even social considerations, including specifically the trade-off between greater safety and greater combat effectiveness. And we are further of the view that permitting "second-guessing" of these judgments through state tort suits against contractors would produce the same effect sought to be avoided by the FTCA exemption. The financial burden of judgments against the contractors would ultimately be passed through, substantially if not totally, to the United States itself, since defense contractors will predictably raise their prices to cover, or to insure against, contingent liability for the Government-ordered designs. To put the point differently: It makes little sense to insulate the Government against financial liability for the judgment that a particular feature of military equipment is necessary when the Government produces the equipment itself, but not when it contracts for the production. In sum, we are of the view that state law which holds Government contractors liable for design defects in military equipment does in some circumstances present a "significant conflict" with federal policy and must be displaced.

We agree with the scope of displacement adopted by the Fourth Circuit here, which is also that adopted by the Ninth Circuit. Liability for design defects in military equipment cannot be imposed, pursuant to state law, when (1) the United States approved reasonably precise specifications; (2) the equipment conformed to those specifications; and (3) the supplier warned the United States about the dangers in the use of the equipment that were known to the supplier but not to the United States. The first two of these conditions assure that the suit is within the area where the policy of the "discretionary function" would be frustrated—i.e., they assure that the design feature in question was considered by a Government officer, and not merely by the contractor itself. The third condition is necessary because, in its absence, the displacement of state tort law would create some incentive for the manufacturer to withhold knowledge of risks, since conveying that knowledge might disrupt the contract but withholding it would produce no liability. We adopt this provision lest our effort to protect discretionary functions perversely impede them by cutting off information highly relevant to the discretionary decision.

We have considered the alternative formulation of the Government contractor defense, urged upon us by petitioner. That would preclude suit only if (1) the contractor did not participate, or participated only minimally, in the design of the defective equipment; or (2) the contractor timely warned the Government of the risks of the design and notified it of alternative designs reasonably known by it, and the Government, although forewarned, clearly authorized the contractor to proceed with the dangerous design. While this formulation may represent a perfectly reasonable tort rule, it is not a rule designed to protect the federal interest embodied in the "discretionary function" exemption. The design ultimately selected may well reflect a significant policy judgment by Government officials whether or not the contractor rather than those officials developed the design. In addition, it does not seem to us sound policy to penalize, and thus deter, active contractor participation in the design process, placing the contractor at risk unless it identifies all design defects.

[The Court remanded the case to the Court of Appeals to determine whether there was sufficient evidence to submit the case to the jury under the contractor's defense.]

Accordingly, the judgment is vacated and the case is remanded.

JUSTICE BRENNAN, with whom JUSTICE MARSHALL and JUSTICE BLACKMUN join, dissenting.

Lieutenant David A. Boyle died when the CH–53D helicopter he was copiloting spun out of control and plunged into the ocean. We may assume, for purposes of this case, that Lt. Boyle was trapped under water and drowned because respondent United Technologies negligently designed the helicopter's escape hatch. We may further assume that any competent engineer would have discovered and cured the defects, but that they inexplicably escaped respondent's notice. Had respondent designed such a death trap for a commercial firm, Lt. Boyle's family could sue under Virginia tort law and be compensated for his tragic and unnecessary death. But respondent designed the helicopter for the Federal Government, and that, the Court tells us today, makes all the difference: Respondent is immune from liability so long as it obtained approval of "reasonably precise specifications"—perhaps no more than a rubberstamp from a federal procurement officer who might or might not have noticed or cared about the defects, or even had the expertise to discover them.

If respondent's immunity "bore the legitimacy of having been prescribed by the people's elected representatives," we would be duty bound to implement their will, whether or not we approved. Congress, however, has remained silent—and conspicuously so, having resisted a sustained campaign by Government contractors to legislate for them some defense. The Court—unelected and unaccountable to the people—has unabashedly stepped into the breach to legislate a rule denying Lt. Boyle's family the compensation that state law assures them. This time the injustice is of this Court's own making.

Worse yet, the injustice will extend far beyond the facts of this case, for the Court's newly discovered Government contractor defense is breathtakingly sweeping. It applies not only to military equipment like the CH–53D helicopter, but (so far as I can tell) to any made-to-order gadget that the Federal Government might purchase after previewing plans—from NASA's Challenger space shuttle to the Postal Service's old mail cars. The contractor may invoke the defense in suits brought not only by military personnel like Lt. Boyle, or Government employees, but by anyone injured by a Government contractor's negligent design, including, for example, the children who might have died had respondent's helicopter crashed on the beach. It applies even if the Government has not intentionally sacrificed safety for other interests like speed or efficiency, and, indeed, even if the equipment is not of a type that is typically considered dangerous; thus, the contractor who designs a Government building can invoke the defense when the elevator cable snaps or the walls collapse. And the defense is invocable regardless of how blatant or easily remedied the defect, so long as the contractor missed it and the specifications approved by the Government, however unreasonably dangerous, were "reasonably precise."

In my view, this Court lacks both authority and expertise to fashion such a rule, whether to protect the Treasury of the United States or the coffers of industry. Because I would leave that exercise of legislative power to Congress, where our Constitution places it, I would reverse the Court of Appeals and reinstate petitioner's jury award.

I

Before our decision in *Erie R. Co. v. Tompkins,* federal courts sitting in diversity were generally free, in the absence of a controlling state statute, to fashion rules of "general" federal common law. *Erie* renounced the prevailing scheme: "Except in matters governed by the Federal Constitution or by Acts of Congress, the law to be applied in any case is the law of the State." The Court explained that the expansive power that federal courts had theretofore exercised was an unconstitutional " 'invasion of the authority of the State and, to that extent, a denial of its independence.' " Thus, *Erie* was deeply rooted in notions of federalism, and is most seriously implicated when, as here, federal judges displace the state law that would ordinarily govern with their own rules of federal common law.

In pronouncing that "[t]here is no federal general common law," 304 U.S., at 78, *Erie* put to rest the notion that the grant of diversity jurisdiction to federal courts is itself authority to fashion rules of substantive law. As the author of today's opinion for the Court pronounced for a unanimous Court just two months ago, "we start with the assumption that the historic police powers of the States were not to be superseded * * * unless that was the clear and manifest purpose of Congress." *Puerto Rico Dept. of Consumer Affairs v. Isla Petroleum Corp.,* 485 U.S. 495, 499 (1988). Just as "[t]here is no federal preemption *in vacuo,* without a constitutional text or a federal statute to assert it," federal common law cannot supersede state law *in vacuo* out of no more than an idiosyncratic determination by five Justices that a particular area is "uniquely federal."

Accordingly, we have emphasized that federal common law can displace state law in "few and restricted" instances. *Wheeldin v. Wheeler,* 373 U.S. 647, 651 (1963). "[A]bsent some congressional authorization to formulate substantive rules of decision, federal common law exists only in such narrow areas as those concerned with the rights and obligations of the United States, interstate and international disputes implicating conflicting rights of States or our relations with foreign nations, and admiralty cases." *Texas Industries, Inc. v. Radcliff Materials, Inc.,* 451 U.S. 630, 641 (1981). "The enactment of a federal rule in an area of national concern, and the decision whether to displace state law in doing so, is generally made not by the federal judiciary, purposefully insulated from democratic pressures, but by the people through their elected representatives in Congress." *Milwaukee v. Illinois,* 451 U.S. 304, 312–313 (1981). State laws "should be overridden by the federal courts only where clear and substantial interests of the National Government, which cannot be served consistently with respect for such state interests, will suffer major damage if the state law is applied." *United States v. Yazell,* 382 U.S. 341, 352 (1966).

II

Congress has not decided to supersede state law here (if anything, it has decided not to * * *) and the Court does not pretend that its newly manufactured "Government contractor defense" fits within any of the handful of "narrow areas," of "uniquely federal interests" in which we have heretofore done so. Rather, the Court creates a new category of "uniquely federal interests" out of a synthesis of two whose origins predate *Erie* itself: the interest in administering the "obligations to and rights of the United States under its contracts," and the interest in regulating the "civil liability of federal officials for actions taken in the course of their duty." This case is, however, simply a suit between two private parties. We have steadfastly declined to impose federal contract law on relationships that are collateral to a federal contract, or to extend the federal employee's immunity beyond federal employees. And the Court's ability to list two, or ten, inapplicable areas of "uniquely federal interest" does not support its conclusion that the liability of Government contractors is so "clear and substantial" an interest that this Court must step in lest state law does "major damage." *Yazell, supra,* 382 U.S., at 352.

A

The proposition that federal common law continues to govern the "obligations to and rights of the United States under its contracts" is nearly as old as *Erie* itself. Federal law typically controls when the Federal Government is a party to a suit involving its rights or obligations under a contract, whether the contract entails procurement, loan, a conveyance of property, or a commercial instrument issued by the Government. Any such transaction necessarily "radiate[s] interests in transactions between private parties." *Bank of America Nat. Trust & Sav. Assn. v. Parnell,* 352 U.S. 29, 33 (1956). But it is by now established that our power to create federal common law controlling the *Federal Government's* contractual rights and obligations does not translate into a power to prescribe rules that cover all transactions or contractual relationships collateral to Government contracts.

In *Miree v. DeKalb County,* for example, the county was contractually obligated under a grant agreement with the Federal Aviation Administration (FAA) to " 'restrict the use of land adjacent to * * * the Airport to activities and purposes compatible with normal airport operations including landing and takeoff of aircraft.' " At issue was whether the county breached its contractual obligation by operating a garbage dump adjacent to the airport, which allegedly attracted the swarm of birds that caused a plane crash. Federal common law would undoubtedly have controlled in any suit by the Federal Government to enforce the provision against the county or to collect damages for its violation. The diversity suit, however, was brought not by the Government, but by assorted private parties injured in some way by the accident. We observed that "the operations of the United States in connection with FAA grants such as these are undoubtedly of considerable magnitude," and that "the United States has a substantial interest in regulating aircraft travel and promoting air travel safety." Nevertheless, we held that state law should govern the claim because "only the rights of private litigants are at issue here," and the claim against the county "will have *no direct effect upon the United States or its Treasury.*"

Miree relied heavily on *Parnell, supra,* and Wallis [v. Pan American Petroleum Corp., 384 U.S. 63, 68 (1966)], the former involving commercial paper issued by the United States and the latter involving property rights in federal land. In the former case, Parnell cashed certain government bonds that had been stolen from their owner, a bank. It is beyond dispute that federal law would have governed the United States' duty to pay the value bonds upon presentation; we held as much in *Clearfield Trust, supra.* But the central issue in *Parnell,* a diversity suit, was whether the victim of the theft could recover the money paid to Parnell. That issue, we held, was governed by state law, because the "litigation [was] purely between private parties and [did] *not touch the rights and duties of the United States.*"

The same was true in *Wallis,* which also involved a Government contract—a lease issued by the United States to a private party under the Mineral Leasing Act of 1920, 30 U.S.C. § 181 *et seq.* (1982 ed. and Supp. III)—governed entirely by federal law. Again, the relationship at issue in this diversity case was collateral to the Government contract: It involved the validity of contractual arrangements between the lessee and other private parties, not between the lessee and the Federal Government. Even though a federal statute authorized certain assignments of lease rights, and imposed certain conditions on their validity, we held that state law, not federal common law, governed their validity because application of state law would present "no significant threat to any identifiable federal policy or interest."

Here, as in *Miree, Parnell,* and *Wallis,* a Government contract governed by federal common law looms in the background. But here, too, the United States is not a party to the suit and the suit neither "touch[es] the rights and duties of the United States," *Parnell, supra,* 352 U.S., at 33, nor has a "direct effect upon the United States or its Treasury." The relationship at issue is at best collateral to the Government contract. We have no greater power to displace state law governing the collateral relationship in the Government procurement realm than we had to dictate federal rules governing equally collateral relationships in the areas of aviation, Government-issued commercial paper, or federal lands.

That the Government might have to pay higher prices for what it orders if delivery in accordance with the contract exposes the seller to potential liability does not distinguish this case. Each of the cases just discussed declined to extend the reach of federal common law despite the assertion of comparable interests that would have affected the terms of the Government contract—whether its price or its substance—just as "directly" (or indirectly). Third-party beneficiaries can sue under a county's contract with the FAA, for example, even though—as the Court's focus on the absence of *"direct* effect on the United States or its Treasury," suggests—counties will likely pass on the costs to the Government in future contract negotiations. Similarly, we held that state law may govern the circumstances under which stolen federal bonds can be recovered, notwithstanding Parnell's argument that "the value of bonds to the first purchaser and hence their salability by the Government would be materially affected." As in each of the cases declining to extend the traditional reach of federal law of contracts beyond the rights and duties of the *Federal Government,* "any federal interest in the outcome of the question before us 'is far too speculative, far too remote a possibility to justify the application of federal law to transactions essentially of local concern.' "

B

Our "uniquely federal interest" in the tort liability of affiliates of the Federal Government is equally narrow. The immunity we have recognized has extended no further than a subset of "officials of the Federal Government" and has covered only "discretionary" functions within the scope of their legal authority. Never before have we so much as intimated that the immunity (or the "uniquely federal interest" that justifies it) might extend beyond that narrow class to cover also nongovernment employees whose authority to act is independent of any source of federal law and that are as far removed from the "functioning of the Federal Government" as is a Government contractor, Howard [v. Lyons, 360 U.S. 593, 597 (1959)].

The historical narrowness of the federal interest and the immunity is hardly accidental. A federal officer exercises statutory authority, which not only provides the necessary basis for the immunity in positive law, but also permits us confidently to presume that interference with the exercise of discretion undermines congressional will. In contrast, a Government contractor acts independently of any congressional enactment. Thus, immunity for a contractor lacks both the positive law basis and the presumption that it furthers congressional will.

Moreover, even within the category of congressionally authorized tasks, we have deliberately restricted the scope of immunity to circumstances in which "the contributions of immunity to effective government in particular contexts outweigh the perhaps recurring harm to individual citizens," *Doe v. McMillan,* 412 U.S. 306, 320 (1973), because immunity "contravenes the basic tenet that individuals be held accountable for their wrongful conduct," Westfall [v. Erwin, 484 U.S. 292 (1988)]. The extension of immunity to Government contractors skews the balance we have historically struck. On the one hand, whatever marginal effect contractor immunity might have on the "effective administration of policies of government," its "harm to individual citizens" is more severe than in the Government-employee context. Our observation that "there are * * * other sanctions than civil tort suits available to deter the executive official who may be prone to exercise his functions in an unworthy and irresponsible manner," Barr [v. Matteo, 360 U.S. 564, 576 (1959) (plurality opinion)], offers little deterrence to the Government contractor. On the other hand, a grant of immunity to Government contractors could not advance "the fearless, vigorous, and effective administration of policies of government" nearly as much as does the current immunity for Government employees. In the first place, the threat of a tort suit is less likely to influence the conduct of an industrial giant than that of a lone civil servant, particularly since the work of a civil servant is significantly less profitable, and significantly more likely to be the subject of a vindictive lawsuit. In fact, were we to take seriously the Court's assertion that contractors pass their costs—including presumably litigation costs—through, "substantially if not totally, to the United States," the threat of a tort suit should have only marginal impact on the conduct of Government contractors. More importantly, inhibition of the Government official who actually sets Government policy presents a greater threat to the "administration of policies of government," than does inhibition of a private contractor, whose role is devoted largely to assessing the technological feasibility and cost of satisfying the Government's predetermined needs. Similarly, unlike tort suits against Government officials, tort suits against Government contractors would rarely "consume time and energies" that "would otherwise be devoted to governmental service." 360 U.S., at 571.

In short, because the essential justifications for official immunity do not support an extension to the Government contractor, it is no surprise that we have never extended it that far.

* * *

III

* * * [T]he Court invokes the discretionary function exception of the Federal Tort Claims Act (FTCA), 28 U.S.C. § 2680(a). The Court does not suggest that the exception has any direct bearing here, for petitioner has sued a private manufacturer (not the Federal Government) under Virginia law (not the FTCA). Perhaps that is why respondent has three times disavowed any reliance on the discretionary function exception, even after coaching by the Court, as has the Government.

Notwithstanding these disclaimers, the Court invokes the exception, reasoning that federal common law must immunize Government contractors from state tort law to prevent erosion of the discretionary function exception's *policy* of foreclosing judicial " 'second-guessing' " of discretionary governmental decisions. The erosion the Court fears apparently is rooted not in a concern that suits against Government contractors will prevent them from designing, or the Government from commissioning the design of, precisely the product the Government wants, but in the concern that such suits might preclude the Government from purchasing the desired product at the price it wants: "The financial burden of judgments against the contractors," the Court fears, "would ultimately be passed through, substantially if not totally, to the United States itself."

Even granting the Court's factual premise, which is by no means self-evident, the Court cites no authority for the proposition that burdens imposed on Government contractors, but passed on to the Government, burden the Government in a way that justifies extension of its immunity. However substantial such indirect burdens may be, we have held in other contexts that they are legally irrelevant.

Moreover, the statutory basis on which the Court's rule of federal common law totters is more unstable than any we have ever adopted. In the first place, we rejected an analytically similar attempt to construct federal common law out of the FTCA when we held that the Government's waiver of sovereign immunity for the torts of its employees does not give the Government an implied right of indemnity from them, even though the "[t]he financial burden placed on the United States by the Tort Claims Act [could conceivably be] so great that government employees should be required to carry part of the burden." *United States v. Gilman,* 347 U.S. 507, 510 (1954). So too here, the FTCA's retention of sovereign immunity for the Government's discretionary acts does not imply a defense for the benefit of contractors who participate in those acts, even though they might pass on the financial burden to the United States. In either case, the most that can be said is that the position "asserted, though the product of a law Congress passed, is a matter on which Congress has not taken a position."

Here, even that much is an overstatement, for the Government's immunity for discretionary functions is not even "a product of" the FTCA. Before Congress enacted the FTCA (when sovereign immunity barred any tort suit against the Federal Government) we perceived no need for a rule of federal common law to reinforce the Government's immunity by shielding also parties who might contractually pass costs on to it. Nor did we (or any other court of which I am aware) identify a special category of "discretionary" functions for which sovereign immunity was so crucial that a government contractor who exercised discretion should share the Government's immunity from state tort law.

Now, as before the FTCA's enactment, the Federal Government is immune from "[a]ny claim * * * based upon the exercise or performance [of] a discretionary function," including presumably any claim that petitioner might have brought against the Federal Government based upon respondent's negligent design of the helicopter in which Lt. Boyle died. There is no more reason for federal common law to shield contractors now that the Government is liable for some torts than there was when the Government was liable for none. The discretionary function exception does not support an immunity for the discretionary acts of Government *contractors* any more than the exception for "[a]ny claim [against the Government] arising out of assault," § 2680(h), supports a personal immunity for Government employees who commit assaults. Cf. *Sheridan v. United States,* 487 U.S. 392, 396 (1988). In short, while the

Court purports to divine whether Congress would object to this suit, it inexplicably begins and ends its sortilege with an exception to a statute that is itself inapplicable and whose repeal would leave unchanged every relationship remotely relevant to the accident underlying this suit.

* * *

IV

At bottom, the Court's analysis is premised on the proposition that any tort liability indirectly absorbed by the Government so burdens governmental functions as to compel us to act when Congress has not. That proposition is by no means uncontroversial. The tort system is premised on the assumption that the imposition of liability encourages actors to prevent any injury whose expected cost exceeds the cost of prevention. If the system is working as it should, Government contractors will design equipment to avoid certain injuries (like the deaths of soldiers or Government employees), which would be certain to burden the Government. The Court therefore has no basis for its assumption that tort liability will result in a net burden on the Government (let alone a clearly excessive net burden) rather than a net gain.

Perhaps tort liability is an inefficient means of ensuring the quality of design efforts, but "[w]hatever the merits of the policy" the Court wishes to implement, "its conversion into law is a proper subject for congressional action, not for any creative power of ours." [United States v. Standard Oil Co., 332 U.S. 301, 314–315 (1947).] It is, after all, "Congress, not this Court or the other federal courts, [that] is the custodian of the national purse. By the same token [Congress] is the primary and most often the exclusive arbiter of federal fiscal affairs. And these comprehend, as we have said, securing the treasury or the Government against financial losses *however inflicted.* * * * " If Congress shared the Court's assumptions and conclusion it could readily enact "A BILL To place limitations on the civil liability of government contractors to ensure that such liability does not impede the ability of the United States to procure necessary goods and services," H.R. 4765, 99th Cong.2d Sess. (1986). It has not.

Were I a legislator, I would probably vote against any law absolving multibillion dollar private enterprises from answering for their tragic mistakes, at least if that law were justified by no more than the unsupported speculation that their liability might ultimately burden the United States Treasury. Some of my colleagues here would evidently vote otherwise (as they have here), but that should not matter here. We are judges not legislators, and the vote is not ours to cast.

I respectfully dissent.

JUSTICE STEVENS, dissenting.

When judges are asked to embark on a lawmaking venture, I believe they should carefully consider whether they, or a legislative body, are better equipped to perform the task at hand. There are instances of so-called interstitial lawmaking that inevitably become part of the judicial process. But when we are asked to create an entirely new doctrine—to answer "questions of policy on which Congress has not spoken," *United States v. Gilman,* 347 U.S. 507, 511 (1954)—we have a special duty to identify the proper decisionmaker before trying to make the proper decision.

When the novel question of policy involves a balancing of the conflicting interests in the efficient operation of a massive governmental program and the protection of the rights of the individual—whether in the social welfare context, the civil service context, or the military procurement context—I feel very deeply that we should defer to the expertise of the Congress. That is the central message of the unanimous decision in *Bush v. Lucas,* that is why I joined the majority in *Schweiker v. Chilicky,* 487 U.S. 412 (1988), a case decided only three days ago; and that is why I am so distressed by the majority's decision today. For in this case, as in *United States v. Gilman, supra:* "The selection of that policy which is most advantageous to the whole involves a host of considerations that must be weighed and appraised. That function is more appropriately for those who write the laws, rather than for those who interpret them."

I respectfully dissent.

Notes

1. The Supreme Court applied *Boyle* and found jurisdiction lacking in Empire Healthchoice Assurance, Inc. v. McVeigh, 547 U.S. ___, 126 S.Ct. 2121 (2006). In *Empire,* an insurer who contracted with the federal government to cover federal employees sought to recover previously disbursed benefits, which it alleged had been recovered by the beneficiary in a state court tort suit. While a federal statute governed the relationship between the insurer and the government, and also pre-empted state law on coverage and benefits, the statute said nothing about subrogation and did not confer federal jurisdiction. Among other arguments, the insurer contended that its suit "implicated 'uniquely federal interest[s],' because (1) reimbursement directly affects the United States Treasury and the cost of providing health benefits to federal employees; and (2) Congress had expressed its interest in maintaining uniformity among the States on matters relating to federal health-plan benefits." The Court rejected these arguments, summarizing *Boyle* and its antecedents:

> *Clearfield* is indeed a pathmarking precedent on the authority of federal courts to fashion uniform federal common law on issues of national concern. See Friendly, In Praise of *Erie*—and of the New Federal Common Law, 39 N.Y.U.L.Rev. 383, 409–410 (1964). But the dissent is mistaken in supposing that the *Clearfield* doctrine covers this case. *Clearfield* was a suit by the United States to recover from a bank the amount paid on a Government check on which the payee's name had been forged. 318 U.S., at 365. Because the United States was the plaintiff, federal-court jurisdiction was solidly grounded. See *ibid.* ("This suit was instituted ... by the United States ..., the jurisdiction of the

federal District Court being invoked pursuant to the provisions of § 24(1) of the Judicial Code, 28 U.S.C. § 41(1)," now contained in 28 U.S.C. §§ 1332, 1345, 1359). The case presented a vertical choice-of-law issue: Did state law under *Erie R. Co. v. Tompkins,* 304 U.S. 64 (1938), or a court-fashioned federal rule of decision (federal common law) determine the merits of the controversy? The Court held that "[t]he rights and duties of the United States on commercial paper which it issues are governed by federal rather than [state] law." 318 U.S., at 366.

* * *

Later, in *Boyle,* the Court telescoped the appropriate inquiry, focusing it on the straightforward question whether the relevant federal interest warrants displacement of state law. See 487 U.S., at 507, n. 3. Referring simply to "the displacement of state law," the Court recognized that prior cases had treated discretely (1) the competence of federal courts to formulate a federal rule of decision, and (2) the appropriateness of declaring a federal rule rather than borrowing, incorporating, or adopting state law in point. The Court preferred "the more modest terminology," questioning whether "the distinction between displacement of state law and displacement of federal law's incorporation of state law ever makes a practical difference." *Ibid. Boyle* made two further observations here significant. First, *Boyle* explained, the involvement of "an area of uniquely federal interest ... establishes a necessary, not a sufficient, condition for the displacement of state law." *Id.,* at 507. Second, in some cases, an "entire body of state law" may conflict with the federal interest and therefore require replacement. *Id.,* at 508. But in others, the conflict is confined, and "only particular elements of state law are superseded." *Ibid.*

The dissent describes this case as pervasively federal, and "the provisions ... here [as] just a few scattered islands in a sea of federal contractual provisions." But there is nothing "scattered" about the provisions on reimbursement and subrogation in the [federal] master contract. Those provisions are linked together and depend upon a recovery from a third party under terms and conditions ordinarily governed by state law. The Court of Appeals, whose decision we review, trained on the matter of reimbursement, not, as the dissent does, on [federally-authorized] contracts at large. So focused, the appeals court determined that Empire has not demonstrated a "significant conflict ... between an identifiable federal policy or interest and the operation of state law." 396 F.3d, at 150 (Sack, J., concurring, quoting *Boyle,* 487 U.S., at 507). Unless and until that showing is made, there is no cause to displace state law, much less to lodge this case in federal court.

2.   In Kamen v. Kemper Financial Services, Inc., 500 U.S. 90 (1991), the Supreme Court held that in a derivative action for securities fraud under the Investment Company Act of 1940, 15 U.S.C.A. § 80a–1(a) et seq. [ICA], the Court entertaining such an action must apply the so-called "demand futility" exception, which allows a plaintiff to decline to make a precomplaint demand of the defendant on the grounds that such an effort would be futile. The Court indicated "that the contours of the demand requirement in a derivative action founded on the ICA are governed by *federal* law." The

Court reasoned that "[b]ecause the ICA is a federal statute, any common law rule necessary to effectuate a private cause of action under that statute is necessarily federal in character." The Court added, however, that it does not follow

> that the content of such a rule must be wholly the product of a federal court's own devising. Our cases indicate that a court should endeavor to fill the interstices of federal remedial schemes with uniform federal rules only when the scheme in question evidences a distinct need for nationwide legal standards * * *, or when express provisions in analogous statutory schemes embody congressional policy choices readily applicable to the matter at hand * * *. * * * The presumption that state law should be incorporated into federal common law is particularly strong in areas in which private parties have entered legal relationships with the expectation that their rights and obligations would be governed by state-law standards.
>
> 　　* * * Corporation law is one such area. * * * Consequently, we [have] concluded that gaps in these statutes bearing on the allocation of governing power within the corporation should be filled with state law "unless the state la[w] permit[s] action prohibited by the Acts, or unless '[its] application would be inconsistent with the federal policy underlying the cause of action.... ' "

500 U.S. at 98–99 (quoting Burks v. Lasker, 441 U.S. 471 (1979)). However, in O'Melveny & Myers v. FDIC, 512 U.S. 79 (1994), the Court held that state law, rather than federal law, governs the issue of the imputation of corporate officers' knowledge of fraud to a corporation asserting a federal cause of action. "[T]he remote possibility that corporations may go into federal receivership," the Court stated, "is no conceivable basis for adopting a special federal common-law rule divesting States of authority over the entire law of imputation." See also Atherton v. FDIC, 519 U.S. 213 (1997), holding that federal common law did not control the issue of the standard of care for officers and directors of federally issued savings institution, because application of state law standards of care to such institutions would not conflict with or threaten federal policies or interests.

　　3.　To what extent does *Boyle* represent an expansion over previous standards for the determination of whether a distinct federal common law standard will be employed? Is the decision in any way inconsistent with *Kimbell Foods*?

　　4.　Under Justice Brennan's analysis, should there be *any* room for federal common law?

　　5.　How relevant to the finding of federal common law in *Boyle* should be the fact that Congress had previously considered and rejected proposed legislation to achieve the same result as the one attained by the federal common law rule? See J. Pfander, Principles of Federal Jurisdiction 145–46 (2006): "[T]here's no obvious defect in the legislative process that would preclude the federal military and its contractors from obtaining a fair hearing on the need for such a defense. Yet it can be difficult to ascribe interpretive significance to a legislative failure to act; Congress has a variety of competing issues to address, and limited time and energy to work on specific bills. If the absence of explicit legislative authority were a compelling argument against federal common law, very little such law (which almost by definition lacks an explicit statutory predicate) would be adopted." How persuasive is this argument in the context of *Boyle*? In general?

§ 2. FOREIGN RELATIONS

BANCO NACIONAL DE CUBA v. SABBATINO

Supreme Court of the United States, 1964.
376 U.S. 398.

MR. JUSTICE HARLAN delivered the opinion of the Court.

The question which brought this case here, and is now found to be the dispositive issue, is whether the so-called act of state doctrine serves to sustain petitioner's claims in this litigation. Such claims are ultimately founded on a decree of the Government of Cuba expropriating certain property, the right to the proceeds of which is here in controversy. The act of state doctrine in its traditional formulation precludes the courts of this country from inquiring into the validity of the public acts a recognized foreign sovereign power committed within its own territory.

I.

In February and July of 1960, respondent Farr, Whitlock & Co., an American commodity broker, contracted to purchase Cuban sugar, free alongside the steamer, from a wholly owned subsidiary of Compania Azucarera Vertientes–Camaguey de Cuba (C. A. V.), a corporation organized under Cuban law whose capital stock was owned principally by United States residents. Farr, Whitlock agreed to pay for the sugar in New York upon presentation of the shipping documents and a sight draft.

On July 6, 1960, the Congress of the United States amended the Sugar Act of 1948 to permit a presidentially directed reduction of the sugar quota for Cuba. On the same day President Eisenhower exercised the granted power. The day of the congressional enactment, the Cuban Council of Ministers adopted "Law No. 851," which characterized this reduction in the Cuban sugar quota as an act of "aggression, for political purposes" on the part of the United States, justifying the taking of countermeasures by Cuba. The law gave the Cuban President and Prime Minister discretionary power to nationalize by forced expropriation property or enterprises in which American nationals had an interest. Although a system of compensation was formally provided, the possibility of payment under it may well be deemed illusory. Our State Department has described the Cuban law as "manifestly in violation of those principles of international law which have long been accepted by the free countries of the West. It is in its essence discriminatory, arbitrary and confiscatory."

Between August 6 and August 9, 1960, the sugar covered by the contract between Farr, Whitlock and C. A. V. was loaded, destined for Morocco, onto the S.S. *Hornfels*, which was standing offshore at the

Cuban port of Jucaro (Santa Maria). On the day loading commenced, the Cuban President and Prime Minister, acting pursuant to Law No. 851, issued Executive Power Resolution No. 1. It provided for the compulsory expropriation of all property and enterprises, and of rights and interests arising therefrom, of certain listed companies, including C. A. V., wholly or principally owned by American nationals. The preamble reiterated the alleged injustice of the American reduction of the Cuban sugar quota and emphasized the importance of Cuba's serving as an example for other countries to follow "in their struggle to free themselves from the brutal claws of Imperialism." In consequence of the resolution, the consent of the Cuban Government was necessary before a ship carrying sugar of a named company could leave Cuban waters. In order to obtain this consent, Farr, Whitlock, on August 11, entered into contracts, identical to those it had made with C. A. V., with the Banco Para el Comercio Exterior de Cuba, an instrumentality of the Cuban Government. The S.S. *Hornfels* sailed for Morocco on August 12.

Banco Exterior assigned the bills of lading to petitioner, also an instrumentality of the Cuban Government, which instructed its agent in New York, Societe Generale, to deliver the bills and a sight draft in the sum of $175,250.69 to Farr, Whitlock in return for payment. Societe Generale's initial tender of the documents was refused by Farr, Whitlock, which on the same day was notified of C. A. V.'s claim that as rightful owner of the sugar it was entitled to the proceeds. In return for a promise not to turn the funds over to petitioner or its agent, C. A. V. agreed to indemnify Farr, Whitlock for any loss. Farr, Whitlock subsequently accepted the shipping documents, negotiated the bills of lading to its customer, and received payment for the sugar. It refused, however, to hand over the proceeds to Societe Generale. Shortly thereafter, Farr, Whitlock was served with an order of the New York Supreme Court, which had appointed Sabbatino as Temporary Receiver of C. A. V.'s New York assets, enjoining it from taking any action in regard to the money claimed by C. A. V. that might result in its removal from the State. Following this, Farr, Whitlock, pursuant to court order, transferred the funds to Sabbatino, to abide the event of a judicial determination as to their ownership.

Petitioner then instituted this action in the Federal District Court for the Southern District of New York. Alleging conversion of the bills of lading, it sought to recover the proceeds thereof from Farr, Whitlock and to enjoin the receiver from exercising any dominion over such proceeds. Upon motions to dismiss and for summary judgment, the District Court, 193 F.Supp. 375, sustained federal *in personam* jurisdiction despite state control of the funds. * * * The court then dealt with the question of Cuba's title to the sugar, on which rested petitioner's claim of conversion. While acknowledging the continuing vitality of the act of state doctrine, the court believed it inapplicable when the questioned foreign act is in violation of international law. Proceeding on the basis that a taking invalid under international law does not convey good title, the District Court found the Cuban expropriation decree to violate such law in three separate respects: it was motivated by a retaliatory and not a public purpose; it discriminated against American nationals; and it failed to provide adequate compensation. Summary judgment against petitioner was accordingly granted.

The Court of Appeals, affirming the decision on similar grounds, relied on two letters (not before the District Court) written by State Department officers which it took as evidence that the Executive Branch had no objection to a judicial testing of the Cuban decree's validity. The court was unwilling to declare that any one of the infirmities found by the District Court rendered the taking invalid under international law, but was satisfied that in combination they had that effect. We granted certiorari because the issues involved bear importantly on the conduct of the country's foreign relations and more particularly on the proper role of the Judicial Branch in this sensitive area. For reasons to follow we decide that the judgment below must be reversed.

* * *

III.

Respondents claimed in the lower courts that Cuba had expropriated merely contractual rights the situs of which was in New York, and that the propriety of the taking was, therefore, governed by New York law. The District Court rejected this contention on the basis of the right of ownership possessed by C. A. V. against Farr, Whitlock prior to payment for the sugar. That the sugar itself was expropriated rather than a contractual claim is further supported by Cuba's refusal to let the S.S. *Hornfels* sail until a new contract had been signed. Had the Cuban decree represented only an attempt to expropriate a contractual right of C. A. V., the forced delay of shipment and Farr, Whitlock's subsequent contract with petitioner's assignor would have been meaningless. Neither the District Court's finding concerning the location of the S.S. *Hornfels* nor its conclusion that Cuba had territorial jurisdiction to expropriate the sugar, acquiesced in by the Court of Appeals, is seriously challenged here. Respondents' limited view of the expropriation must be rejected.

Respondents further contend that if the expropriation was of the sugar itself, this suit then becomes one to enforce the public law of a foreign state and as such is not cognizable in the courts of this country. They rely on the principle enunciated in federal and state cases that a court need not give effect to the penal or revenue laws of foreign countries or sister states. * * *

The extent to which this doctrine may apply to other kinds of public laws, though perhaps still an open question, need not be decided in this case. For we have been referred to no authority which suggests that the doctrine reaches a public law which, as here, has been fully executed within the foreign state. Cuba's restraint of the S.S. *Hornfels* must be regarded for these purposes to have constituted an effective taking of the sugar, vesting in Cuba C. A. V.'s property right in it. Farr, Whitlock's contract with the Cuban bank, however compelled to sign Farr, Whitlock may have felt, represented indeed a recognition of Cuba's dominion over the property.

In these circumstances the question whether the rights acquired by Cuba are enforceable in our courts depends not upon the doctrine here invoked but upon the act of state doctrine discussed in the succeeding sections of this opinion.

IV.

The classic American statement of the act of state doctrine, which appears to have taken root in England as early as 1674, Blad v. Bamfield, 3 Swans. 604, 36 Eng.Rep. 992, and began to emerge in the jurisprudence of this country in the late eighteenth and early nineteenth centuries, see, e.g., Ware v. Hylton, 3 Dall. 199, 230; Hudson v. Guestier, 4 Cranch 293, 294; The Schooner Exchange v. M'Faddon, 7 Cranch 116, 135, 136; L'Invincible, 1 Wheat. 238, 253; The Santissima Trinidad, 7 Wheat. 283, 336, is found in Underhill v. Hernandez, 168 U.S. 250, p. 252, where Chief Justice Fuller said for a unanimous Court:

"Every sovereign State is bound to respect the independence of every other sovereign State, and the courts of one country will not sit in judgment on the acts of the government of another done within its own territory. Redress of grievances by reason of such acts must be obtained through the means open to be availed of by sovereign powers as between themselves."

Following this precept the Court in that case refused to inquire into acts of Hernandez, a revolutionary Venezuelan military commander whose government had been later recognized by the United States, which were made the basis of a damage action in this country by Underhill, an American citizen, who claimed that he had been unlawfully assaulted, coerced, and detained in Venezuela by Hernandez.

None of this Court's subsequent cases in which the act of state doctrine was directly or peripherally involved manifest any retreat from *Underhill.* * * *

* * *

V.

Preliminarily, we discuss the foundations on which we deem the act of state doctrine to rest, and more particularly the question of whether state or federal law governs its application in a federal diversity case.[20]

* * *

20. Although the complaint in this case alleged both diversity and federal question jurisdiction, the Court of Appeals reached jurisdiction only on the former ground. We need not decide, for reasons appearing hereafter, whether federal question jurisdiction also existed.

Despite the broad statement in Oetjen [v. Central Leather Co.] that "The conduct of the foreign relations of our Government is committed by the Constitution to the Executive and Legislative * * * Departments," 246 U.S., at 302, it cannot of course be thought that "every case or controversy which touches foreign relations lies beyond judicial cognizance." Baker v. Carr, 369 U.S. 186, 211. The text of the Constitution does not require the act of state doctrine; it does not irrevocably remove from the judiciary the capacity to review the validity of foreign acts of state.

The act of state doctrine does, however, have "constitutional" underpinnings. It arises out of the basic relationships between branches of government in a system of separation of powers. It concerns the competency of dissimilar institutions to make and implement particular kinds of decisions in the area of international relations. The doctrine as formulated in past decisions expresses the strong sense of the Judicial Branch that its engagement in the task of passing on the validity of foreign acts of state may hinder rather than further this country's pursuit of goals both for itself and for the community of nations as a whole in the international sphere. Many commentators disagree with this view;[22] they have striven by means of distinguishing and limiting past decisions and by advancing various considerations of policy to stimulate a narrowing of the apparent scope of the rule. Whatever considerations are thought to predominate, it is plain that the problems involved are uniquely federal in nature. If federal authority, in this instance this Court, orders the field of judicial competence in this area for the federal courts, and the state courts are left free to formulate their own rules, the purposes behind the doctrine could be as effectively undermined as if there had been no federal pronouncement on the subject.

We could perhaps in this diversity action avoid the question of deciding whether federal or state law is applicable to this aspect of the litigation. New York has enunciated the act of state doctrine in terms that echo those of federal decisions decided during the reign of Swift v. Tyson, 16 Pet. 1. * * *

However, we are constrained to make it clear that an issue concerned with a basic choice regarding the competence and function of the Judiciary and the National Executive in ordering our relationships with other members of the international community must be treated exclusively as an aspect of federal law.[23] It seems fair to assume that the

---

22. See, e.g., Association of the Bar of the City of New York, Committee on International Law, A Reconsideration of the Act of State Doctrine in United States Courts (1959); * * * Mann, International Delinquencies Before Municipal Courts, 70 L.Q. Rev. 181 (1954); Zander, The Act of State Doctrine, 53 Am.J.Int'l L. 826 (1959). But see, e.g., Falk, Toward a Theory of the Participation of Domestic Courts in the In-

ternational Legal Order: A Critique of Banco Nacional de Cuba v. Sabbatino, 16 Rutgers L.Rev. 1 (1961); Reeves, Act of State Doctrine and the Rule of Law–A Reply, 54 Am.J.Int'l L. 141 (1960).

23. At least this is true when the Court limits the scope of judicial inquiry. We need not now consider whether a state court might, in certain circumstances, adhere to a

Court did not have rules like the act of state doctrine in mind when it decided Erie R. Co. v. Tompkins. Soon thereafter, Professor Philip C. Jessup, now a judge of the International Court of Justice, recognized the potential dangers were *Erie* extended to legal problems affecting international relations.[24] He cautioned that rules of international law should not be left to divergent and perhaps parochial state interpretations. His basic rationale is equally applicable to the act of state doctrine.

The Court in the pre-*Erie* act of state cases, although not burdened by the problem of the source of applicable law, used language sufficiently strong and broad-sweeping to suggest that state courts were not left free to develop their own doctrines (as they would have been had this Court merely been interpreting common law under Swift v. Tyson, supra). * * *

In Hinderlider v. La Plata River Co., 304 U.S. 92, 110, in an opinion handed down the same day as *Erie* and by the same author, Mr. Justice Brandeis, the Court declared, "For whether the water of an interstate stream must be apportioned between the two States is a question of 'federal common law' upon which neither the statutes nor the decisions of either State can be conclusive." Although the suit was between two private litigants and the relevant States could not be made parties, the Court considered itself free to determine the effect of an interstate compact regulating water apportionment. The decision implies that no State can undermine the federal interest in equitably apportioned interstate waters even if it deals with private parties. This would not mean that, absent a compact, the apportionment scheme could not be changed judicially or by Congress, but only that apportionment is a matter of federal law. Cf. Arizona v. California, 373 U.S. 546, 597–598. The problems surrounding the act of state doctrine are, albeit for different reasons, as intrinsically federal as are those involved in water apportionment or boundary disputes. The considerations supporting exclusion of state authority here are much like those which led the Court in United States v. California, 332 U.S. 19, to hold that the Federal Government possessed paramount rights in submerged lands though within the three-mile limit of coastal States. We conclude that the scope of the act of state doctrine must be determined according to federal law.[25]

VI.

If the act of state doctrine is a principle of decision binding on federal and state courts alike but compelled by neither international law

---

more restrictive view concerning the scope of examination of foreign acts than that required by this Court.

24. The Doctrine of Erie Railroad v. Tompkins Applied to International Law, 33 Am.J.Int'l L. 740 (1939).

25. Various constitutional and statutory provisions indirectly support this determination, see U.S.Const., Art. I, § 8, cls. 3, 10; Art. II, §§ 2, 3; Art. III, § 2; 28 U.S.C.

§§ 1251(a)(2), (b)(1), (b)(3), 1332(a)(2), 1333, 1350–1351, by reflecting a concern for uniformity in this country's dealings with foreign nations and indicating a desire to give matters of international significance to the jurisdiction of federal institutions. See Comment, The Act of State Doctrine—Its Relation to Private and Public International Law, 62 Col.L.Rev. 1278, 1297, n. 123 * * * nor the Constitution, its continuing vitality depends on its capacity to reflect the proper distribution of functions between the judicial and political branches of the Government on matters bearing upon foreign affairs. It should be apparent that the greater the degree of codification or consensus concerning a particular area of international law, the more appropriate it is for the judiciary to render decisions regarding it, since the courts can then focus on the application of an agreed principle to circumstances of fact rather than on the sensitive task of establishing a principle not inconsistent with the national interest or with international justice. It is also evident that some aspects of international law touch much more sharply on national nerves than do others; the less important the implications of an issue are for our foreign relations, the weaker the justification for exclusivity in the political branches. * * * Therefore, rather than laying down or reaffirming an inflexible and all-encompassing rule in this case, we decide only that the Judicial Branch will not examine the validity of a taking of property within its own territory by a foreign sovereign government, extant and recognized by this country at the time of suit, in the absence of a treaty or other unambiguous agreement regarding controlling legal principles, even if the complaint alleges that the taking violates customary international law.

There are few if any issues in international law today on which opinion seems to be so divided as the limitations on a state's power to expropriate the property of aliens. There is, of course, authority, in international judicial and arbitral decisions, in the expressions of national governments, and among commentators for the view that a taking is improper under international law if it is not for a public purpose, is discriminatory, or is without provision for prompt, adequate, and effective compensation. However, Communist countries, although they have in fact provided a degree of compensation after diplomatic efforts, commonly recognize no obligation on the part of the taking country. Certain representatives of the newly independent and underdeveloped countries have questioned whether rules of state responsibility toward aliens can bind nations that have not consented to them and it is argued that the traditionally articulated standards governing expropriation of property reflect "imperialist" interests and are inappropriate to the circumstances of emergent states.

The disagreement as to relevant international law standards reflects an even more basic divergence between the national interests of capital importing and capital exporting nations and between the social ideologies of those countries that favor state control of a considerable portion of the means of production and those that adhere to a free enterprise system. It is difficult to imagine the courts of this country embarking on adjudication in an area which touches more sensitively the practical and ideological goals of the various members of the community of nations.

When we consider the prospect of the courts characterizing foreign expropriations, however justifiably, as invalid under international law and ineffective to pass title, the wisdom of the precedents is confirmed. While each of the leading cases in this Court may be argued to be distinguishable on its facts from this one * * * the plain implication of all these opinions, * * * is that the act of state doctrine is applicable even if international law has been violated. * * *

* * *

The judgment of the Court of Appeals is reversed and the case is remanded to the District Court for proceedings consistent with this opinion.

[The dissenting opinion of JUSTICE WHITE is omitted.]

Notes

1. Why is there a need for federal common law in the area of foreign relations? Is the justification for the creation of federal common law in this area stronger, weaker or the same as in the area covered by *Clearfield Trust*? See generally Moore, *Federalism and Foreign Relations*, 1965 Duke L.J. 248.

2. Consider the following argument: The use of federal common law in *Sabbatino* constituted a significant extension of its use in cases such as *Clearfield Trust*, because in the former, unlike the latter, federal common law was created without authorization, direct or indirect, from the political branches of government. Cf. Henkin, *The Foreign Affairs Power of the Federal Courts*: Sabbatino, 64 Colum.L.Rev. 805, 814–17 (1964).

3. According to Professor Hill:

[A] wide variety of state conduct may affect and even exacerbate our relations with foreign nations, and be subject on that account to federal political controls. But local competence is not necessarily ousted in all areas where there is a potential for preemptive action by the federal political branches. The obvious analogy is the commerce clause. Until Congress acts the states may engage in multifarious practices affecting commerce; other practices affecting commerce are forbidden to them whether or not Congress has acted.

Hill, *The Law–Making Power of the Federal Courts: Constitutional Preemption*, 67 Colum.L.Rev. 1024, 1057 (1967).

4. In Sosa v. Alvarez–Machain, 542 U.S. 692 (2004), a case that involved the reach of the Alien Tort Statute, 28 U.S.C. § 1350, the Court held that federal common law includes a narrow group of long established claims under customary international law. In doing so the Court acknowledged that the Alien Tort Statute is solely jurisdictional. The decision is criticized in Note, *An Objection to Sosa—And to the New Federal Common Law*, 119 Harv.L.Rev. 2077 (2006), where it is argued that *Sosa*'s common law is inconsistent with the traditional taxonomy of federal common law. Id. at 2078. The commentator notes that "the federal common law created in *Sosa* cannot be justified as either congressionally authorized or falling within a constitutional enclave." Id. at 2098. Assuming these assertions are accurate, do they in any way distinguish international federal common law from any other area of federal common law?

According to one commentator, in *Sosa* the Court actually "narrowed the scope of the judicial role" that had been developed in such earlier lower court decisions as Filartiga v. Pena–Irala, 630 F.2d 876 (2nd Cir.1980). See J. Pfander, Principles of Federal Jurisdiction 151 (2006).

5. Professors Bradley and Goldsmith have argued that while "the proposition that [customary international law] is federal common law is today a well-settled principle of U.S. foreign relations law," "substantial reasons exist to question the validity of the modern position." Bradley & Goldsmith, *Customary International Law As Federal Common Law: A Critique of the Modern Position*, 110 Harv.L.Rev. 815, 822, 876 (1997). They note that "[n]othing on the face of the Constitution or any federal statute authorizes such a practice. Article III of the Constitution does not even list [customary international law] as a basis for the exercise of federal judicial power, much less authorize federal courts to incorporate [it] wholesale into federal law. Nor does Article VI list [it] as a source of supreme federal law. Article I does authorize Congress to define and punish offenses against the law of nations, and Congress has exercised this and related powers to incorporate select [customary international law] principles into federal statutes. But Congress has never purported to incorporate all [customary international law] into federal law." Id. at 856–57.

6. In First National City Bank v. Banco Nacional de Cuba, 406 U.S. 759 (1972), Justice Rehnquist, speaking for three Justices, concluded that when the executive branch objects to invocation of the act-of-state doctrine, the Court will abandon its use. Is this decision consistent with *Sabbatino*? See also Alfred Dunhill of London, Inc. v. Republic of Cuba, 425 U.S. 682 (1976).

§ 3. INTERSTATE POLLUTION

ILLINOIS v. CITY OF MILWAUKEE, WIS., 406 U.S. 91 (1972). The State of Illinois sought to invoke the original jurisdiction of the United States Supreme Court to hear a suit against several Wisconsin cities and local commissions to halt their pollution of Lake Michigan. The Court rejected the claim that its original jurisdiction should be exercised, but found that the suit "arose" under federal common law and therefore fell within the "federal question" jurisdiction of the district court. In reaching the conclusion that federal common law controlled this interstate pollution suit, Justice Douglas, speaking for the Court, recognized that "Congress has enacted numerous laws touching interstate waters," id. at 101, which expressed federal concern with the need to reduce pollution. Though the precise remedy sought by Illinois was not authorized by federal statute, the Court noted that "[i]t is not uncommon for federal courts to fashion federal law where federal rights are concerned," quoting Textile Workers v. Lincoln Mills, 353 U.S. 448, 457.

"When we deal with air and water in their ambient or interstate aspects, there is a federal common law * * *" Id. at 103. The Court added that "[t]he application of federal common law to abate a public nuisance in interstate or navigable waters is not inconsistent with the Water Pollution Control Act. Congress provided in § 10(b) of that Act that, save as a court may decree otherwise in an enforcement action, '[s]tate and interstate action to abate pollution of interstate or navigable waters shall be encouraged and shall not * * * be displaced by Federal enforcement action.' " Id. at 104. The Court relied as well on the cases applying federal common law to disputes over rights in interstate streams. Finally, the Court stated: "It may happen that new federal laws and new federal regulations may in time pre-empt the field of federal common law of nuisance. But until that comes to pass, federal courts will be empowered to appraise the equities of the suits alleging creation of a public nuisance by water pollution." Id. at 107.

Notes

1. The *Milwaukee* decision has been heavily criticized. See, e.g., Note, *Federal Common Law and Interstate Pollution*, 85 Harv.L.Rev. 1439 (1972). Professor Currie has suggested that "the Court's approach leads one to fear that henceforth further inroads may be made upon the clear provisions of the Rules of Decision Act on vague grounds of federal interest." D. Currie, Federal Jurisdiction in a Nutshell 244 (2d Ed. 1981). Do you think that the justification asserted for the creation of federal common law in *Milwaukee* amounts to no more than "vague grounds of federal interest"?

2. Should the creation of federal common law for interstate pollution disputes under *Milwaukee* be limited to cases in which the litigants are states or different governmental subdivisions? Cf. Committee for the Consideration of the Jones Falls Sewage System v. Train, 539 F.2d 1006, 1009 (4th Cir.1976). What about a pollution dispute between a state or political subdivision on the one hand and a private individual or entity from another state? Cf. Illinois v. Outboard Marine Corp., 619 F.2d 623 (7th Cir.1980), vacated and remanded 453 U.S. 917 (1981).

3. Does the recognition of a federal common law remedy such as that recognized in *Milwaukee* necessarily preempt alternative state law remedies? Is there any difference between federal preemption through an act of Congress on the one hand and through the recognition of a federal common law remedy on the other?

4. City of Milwaukee v. Illinois and Michigan, 451 U.S. 304 (1981) (*Milwaukee II*): Following the Supreme Court's refusal to exercise original jurisdiction, Illinois filed a complaint in federal district court. The District Court for the Northern District of Illinois entered judgment for the state and the city appealed. The Court of Appeals for the Seventh Circuit affirmed in part and reversed in part, and the Supreme Court granted certiorari. In an opinion by Justice Rehnquist, the Court held that the Federal Water Pollution Act Amendments of 1972 displaced federal common law as to the state's claims, and that federal common law could not be created to impose standards more stringent than those imposed by the Act. In reaching this conclusion, the Court explained congressional intent as manifested in the legislative history of the 1972 Amendments: "Congress' intent in enacting the amendments was clearly to establish an all-encompassing program of water pollution regulation * * *. No Congressman's remarks on the legislation were complete without reference to the 'comprehensive' nature of the Amendments * * *. The establishment of such a self-consciously comprehensive program by Congress, which certainly did not exist when Illinois v.

Milwaukee was decided, strongly suggests that there is no room for courts to attempt to improve on that program with federal common law." 451 U.S. at 318, 319. The Court added that "[t]he statutory scheme established by Congress provides a forum for the pursuit of such claims before expert agencies by means of the permit-granting process. It would be quite inconsistent with this scheme if federal courts were in effect to 'write their own ticket' under the guise of federal common law after permits have already been issued and permittees have been planning and operating in reliance on them." Id. at 326. Justice Blackmun, joined by Justices Marshall and Stevens, dissented:

> The Court's analysis of federal common-law displacement rests, I am convinced, on a faulty assumption. In contrasting congressional displacement of the common law with federal pre-emption of state law, the Court assumes that as soon as Congress "addresses a question previously governed" by federal common law, "the need of such an unusual exercise of lawmaking by federal courts disappears." * * * This "automatic displacement" approach is inadequate in two respects. It fails to reflect the unique role federal common law plays in resolving disputes between one State and the citizens or government of another. In addition, it ignores this Court's frequent recognition that federal common law may complement congressional action in the fulfillment of federal policies. Id. at 333–34.

Is the majority's decision justified by considerations of separation of powers, federalism, both, or neither? At no point did the 1972 Amendments explicitly preclude the federal common law remedy recognized in *Milwaukee I*. Should such express congressional preclusion be deemed required before a previously-recognized federal common law remedy will be preempted?

5. Middlesex County Sewerage Authority v. National Sea Clammers Association, 453 U.S. 1 (1981): Individual fisherman and an association of shell fishermen brought a class action against federal, state and local officials for violation of various federal statutes and constitutional provisions, as well as the federal common law of nuisance. The Supreme Court, in an opinion by Justice Powell, first refused to find any implied right of action in either the Federal Water Pollution Control Act or the Marine Protection, Research, and Sanctuaries Act of 1972, and then concluded that the federal common law of nuisance was preempted by these laws. Because of this latter conclusion, the Court believed it "need not discuss the question whether the federal common law of nuisance could ever be the basis of a suit for damages by a private party." Id. at 11.

6. On *Milwaukee I* and the general issue of federal common law of interstate pollution, see Note, Illinois v. City of Milwaukee: *What Price Federal Common Law?*, 4 Harv.J.L.Pub.Pol. 323 (1981).

§ 4. CONSTITUTIONAL COMMON LAW

BIVENS v. SIX UNKNOWN NAMED AGENTS OF FEDERAL BUREAU OF NARCOTICS

Supreme Court of the United States, 1971.
403 U.S. 388.

Mr. Justice Brennan delivered the opinion of the Court.

The Fourth Amendment provides that:

"The right of the people to be secure in their persons, houses, papers, and effects, against unreasonable searches and seizures, shall not be violated. . . ."

In Bell v. Hood, 327 U.S. 678 (1946), we reserved the question whether violation of that command by a federal agent acting under color of his authority gives rise to a cause of action for damages consequent upon his unconstitutional conduct. Today we hold that it does.

This case has its origin in an arrest and search carried out on the morning of November 26, 1965. Petitioner's complaint alleged that on that day respondents, agents of the Federal Bureau of Narcotics acting under claim of federal authority, entered his apartment and arrested him for alleged narcotics violations. The agents manacled petitioner in front of his wife and children, and threatened to arrest the entire family. They searched the apartment from stem to stern. Thereafter, petitioner was taken to the federal courthouse in Brooklyn, where he was interrogated, booked, and subjected to a visual strip search.

On July 7, 1967, petitioner brought suit in Federal District Court. In addition to the allegations above, his complaint asserted that the arrest and search were effected without a warrant, and that unreasonable force was employed in making the arrest; fairly read, it alleges as well that the arrest was made without probable cause.[1] Petitioner claimed to have suffered great humiliation, embarrassment, and mental suffering as a result of the agents' unlawful conduct, and sought $15,000 damages from each of them. The District Court, on respondents' motion, dismissed the complaint on the ground, *inter alia*, that it failed to state a cause of action.[2] The Court of Appeals, one judge concurring specially, affirmed on that basis. We granted certiorari. We reverse.

I

Respondents do not argue that petitioner should be entirely without remedy for an unconstitutional invasion of his rights by federal agents.

---

1. Petitioner's complaint does not explicitly state that the agents had no probable cause for his arrest, but it does allege that the arrest was "done unlawfully, unreasonably and contrary to law." Petitioner's affidavit in support of his motion for summary judgment swears that the search was "without cause, consent or warrant," and that the arrest was "without cause, reason or warrant."

2. The agents were not named in petitioner's complaint, and the District Court ordered that the complaint be served upon "those federal agents who it is indicated by the records of the United States Attorney participated in the November 25, 1965, arrest of the [petitioner]." Five agents were ultimately served.

In respondents' view, however, the rights that petitioner asserts—primarily rights of privacy—are creations of state and not of federal law. Accordingly, they argue, petitioner may obtain money damages to redress invasion of these rights only by an action in tort, under state law, in the state courts. In this scheme the Fourth Amendment would serve merely to limit the extent to which the agents could defend the state law tort suit by asserting that their actions were a valid exercise of federal power: if the agents were shown to have violated the Fourth Amendment, such a defense would be lost to them and they would stand before the state law merely as private individuals. Candidly admitting that it is the policy of the Department of Justice to remove all such suits from the state to the federal courts for decision, respondents nevertheless urge that we uphold dismissal of petitioner's complaint in federal court, and remit him to filing an action in the state courts in order that the case may properly be removed to the federal court for decision on the basis of state law.

We think that respondents' thesis rests upon an unduly restrictive view of the Fourth Amendment's protection against unreasonable searches and seizures by federal agents, a view that has consistently been rejected by this Court. Respondents seek to treat the relationship between a citizen and a federal agent unconstitutionally exercising his authority as no different from the relationship between two private citizens. In so doing, they ignore the fact that power, once granted, does not disappear like a magic gift when it is wrongfully used. An agent acting—albeit unconstitutionally—in the name of the United States possesses a far greater capacity for harm than an individual trespasser exercising no authority other than his own. * * * Accordingly, as our cases make clear, the Fourth Amendment operates as a limitation upon the exercise of federal power regardless of whether the State in whose jurisdiction that power is exercised would prohibit or penalize the identical act if engaged in by a private citizen. It guarantees to citizens of the United States the absolute right to be free from unreasonable searches and seizures carried out by virtue of federal authority. And "where federally protected rights have been invaded, it has been the rule from the beginning that courts will be alert to adjust their remedies so as to grant the necessary relief." Bell v. Hood, 327 U.S., at 684 (footnote omitted) * * *.

First. Our cases have long since rejected the notion that the Fourth Amendment proscribes only such conduct as would, if engaged in by private persons, be condemned by state law. * * *

* * *

Third. That damages may be obtained for injuries consequent upon a violation of the Fourth Amendment by federal officials should hardly seem a surprising proposition. Historically, damages have been regarded as the ordinary remedy for an invasion of personal interests in liberty. See Nixon v. Condon, 286 U.S. 73 (1932) * * *. Of course, the Fourth Amendment does not in so many words provide for its enforcement by an award of money damages for the consequences of its violation. But "it is . . . well settled that where legal rights have been invaded, and a federal statute provides for a general right to sue for such invasion, federal courts may use any available remedy to make good the wrong done." Bell v. Hood, 327 U.S., at 684 (footnote omitted). The present case involves no special factors counselling hesitation in the absence of affirmative action by Congress. We are not dealing with a question of "federal fiscal policy," as in United States v. Standard Oil Co., 332 U.S. 301, 311 (1947). In that case we refused to infer from the Government-soldier relationship that the United States could recover damages from one who negligently injured a soldier and thereby caused the Government to pay his medical expenses and lose his services during the course of his hospitalization. Noting that Congress was normally quite solicitous where the federal purse was involved, we pointed out that "the United States [was] the party plaintiff to the suit. And the United States has power at any time to create the liability." Id., at 316; see United States v. Gilman, 347 U.S. 507 (1954). Nor are we asked in this case to impose liability upon a congressional employee for actions contrary to no constitutional prohibition, but merely said to be in excess of the authority delegated to him by the Congress. Wheeldin v. Wheeler, 373 U.S. 647 (1963). Finally, we cannot accept respondents' formulation of the question as whether the availability of money damages is necessary to enforce the Fourth Amendment. For we have here no explicit congressional declaration that persons injured by a federal officer's violation of the Fourth Amendment may not recover money damages from the agents, but must instead be remitted to another remedy, equally effective in the view of Congress. The question is merely whether petitioner, if he can demonstrate an injury consequent upon the violation by federal agents of his Fourth Amendment rights, is entitled to redress his injury through a particular remedial mechanism normally available in the federal courts. Cf. J. I. Case Co. v. Borak, 377 U.S. 426, 433 (1964); Jacobs v. United States, 290 U.S. 13, 16 (1933). "The very essence of civil liberty certainly consists in the right of every individual to claim the protection of the laws, whenever he receives an injury." Marbury v. Madison, 5 U.S. (1 Cranch) 137, 163 (1803). Having concluded that petitioner's complaint states a cause of action under the Fourth Amendment, * * * we hold that petitioner is entitled to recover money damages for any injuries he has suffered as a result of the agents' violation of the Amendment.

II

In addition to holding that petitioner's complaint had failed to state facts making out a cause of action, the District Court ruled that in any event respondents were immune from liability by virtue of their official position. This question was not passed upon by the Court of Appeals, and accordingly we do not consider it here. The judgment of the Court of Appeals is reversed and the case is remanded for further proceedings consistent with this opinion.

Mr. Justice Harlan, concurring in the judgment.

My initial view of this case was that the Court of Appeals was correct in dismissing the complaint, but for reasons stated in this opinion I am now persuaded to the contrary. Accordingly, I join in the judgment of reversal.

* * *

For the reasons set forth below, I am of the opinion that federal courts do have the power to award damages for violation of "constitutionally protected interests" and I agree with the Court that a traditional judicial remedy such as damages is appropriate to the vindication of the personal interests protected by the Fourth Amendment.

I

I turn first to the contention that the constitutional power of federal courts to accord Bivens damages for his claim depends on the passage of a statute creating a "federal cause of action." Although the point is not entirely free of ambiguity, I do not understand either the Government or my dissenting Brothers to maintain that Bivens' contention that he is entitled to be free from the type of official conduct prohibited by the Fourth Amendment depends on a decision by the State in which he resides to accord him a remedy. Such a position would be incompatible with the presumed availability of federal equitable relief, if a proper showing can be made in terms of the ordinary principles governing equitable remedies. See Bell v. Hood, 327 U.S. 678, 684 (1946). However broad a federal court's discretion concerning equitable remedies, it is absolutely clear—at least after Erie R. Co. v. Tompkins, 304 U.S. 64 (1938)—that in a nondiversity suit a federal court's power to grant even equitable relief depends on the presence of a substantive right derived from federal law. * * *

Thus the interest which Bivens claims—to be free from official conduct in contravention of the Fourth Amendment—is a federally protected interest. * * * Therefore, the question of judicial *power* to grant Bivens damages is not a problem of the "source" of the "right"; instead, the question is whether the power to authorize damages as a judicial remedy for the vindication of a federal constitutional right is placed by the Constitution itself exclusively in Congress' hands.

II

The contention that the federal courts are powerless to accord a litigant damages for a claimed invasion of his federal constitutional rights until Congress explicitly authorizes the remedy cannot rest on the notion that the decision to grant compensatory relief involves a resolution of policy considerations not susceptible of judicial discernment. Thus, in suits for damages based on violations of federal statutes lacking any express authorization of a damage remedy, this Court has authorized such relief where, in its view, damages are necessary to effectuate the congressional policy underpinning the substantive provisions of the statute. J. I. Case Co. v. Borak, 377 U.S. 426 (1964); Tunstall v.

Brotherhood of Locomotive Firemen & Enginemen, 323 U.S. 210, 213 (1944). Cf. Wyandotte Transportation Co. v. United States, 389 U.S. 191, 201–204, (1967).

If it is not the nature of the remedy which is thought to render a judgment as to the appropriateness of damages inherently "legislative," then it must be the nature of the legal interest offered as an occasion for invoking otherwise appropriate judicial relief. But I do not think that the fact that the interest is protected by the Constitution rather than statute or common law justifies the assertion that federal courts are powerless to grant damages in the absence of explicit congressional action authorizing the remedy. Initially, I note that it would be at least anomalous to conclude that the federal judiciary—while competent to choose among the range of traditional judicial remedies to implement statutory and common-law policies, and even to generate substantive rules governing primary behavior in furtherance of broadly formulated policies articulated by statute or Constitution, see Textile Workers v. Lincoln Mills, 353 U.S. 448 (1957); United States v. Standard Oil Co., 332 U.S. 301, 304–311 (1947); Clearfield Trust Co. v. United States, 318 U.S. 363 (1943)—is powerless to accord a damages remedy to vindicate social policies which, by virtue of their inclusion in the Constitution, are aimed predominantly at restraining the Government as an instrument of the popular will.

More importantly, the presumed availability of federal equitable relief against threatened invasions of constitutional interests appears entirely to negate the contention that the status of an interest as constitutionally protected divests federal courts of the power to grant damages absent express congressional authorization. Congress provided specially for the exercise of equitable remedial powers by federal courts, see Act of May 8, 1792, § 2, 1 Stat. 276; C. Wright, Law of Federal Courts 257 (2d ed., 1970), in part because of the limited availability of equitable remedies in state courts in the early days of the Republic. See Guaranty Trust Co. v. York, 326 U.S. 99, 104–105 (1945). And this Court's decisions make clear that, at least absent congressional restrictions, the scope of equitable remedial discretion is to be determined according to the distinctive historical traditions of equity as an institution, Holmberg v. Armbrecht, 327 U.S. 392, 395–396 (1946); Sprague v. Ticonic National Bank, 307 U.S. 161, 165–166 (1939). The reach of a federal district court's "inherent equitable powers," Textile Workers v. Lincoln Mills, 353 U.S. 448, 460 (Burton, J., concurring in result), is broad indeed, e.g., Swann v. Charlotte–Mecklenburg Board of Education, 402 U.S. 1 (1971); nonetheless, the federal judiciary is not empowered to grant equitable relief in the absence of congressional action extending jurisdiction over the subject matter of the suit. See Textile Workers v. Lincoln Mills, supra, at 460 (Burton, J., concurring in result); Katz, 117 U.Pa.L.Rev., at 43.[5]

5. With regard to a court's authority to grant an equitable remedy, the line between "subject matter" jurisdiction and remedial powers has undoubtedly been obscured by the fact that historically the "system of equity 'derived its doctrines, as well as its powers, from its mode of giving relief.'" See Guaranty Trust Co. v. York, supra, 326

If explicit congressional authorization is an absolute prerequisite to the power of a federal court to accord compensatory relief regardless of the necessity or appropriateness of damages as a remedy simply because of the status of a legal interest as constitutionally protected, then it seems to me that explicit congressional authorization is similarly prerequisite to the exercise of equitable remedial discretion in favor of constitutionally protected interests. Conversely, if a general grant of jurisdiction to the federal courts by Congress is thought adequate to empower a federal court to grant equitable relief for all areas of subject-matter jurisdiction enumerated therein, see 28 U.S.C. § 1331(a), then it seems to me that the same statute is sufficient to empower a federal court to grant a traditional remedy at law. Of course, the special historical traditions governing the federal equity system, see Sprague v. Ticonic National Bank, 307 U.S. 161 (1939), might still bear on the comparative appropriateness of granting equitable relief as opposed to money damages. That possibility, however, relates, not to whether the federal courts have the power to afford one type of remedy as opposed to the other, but rather to the criteria which should govern the exercise of our power. To that question, I now pass.

III

The major thrust of the Government's position is that, where Congress has not expressly authorized a particular remedy, a federal court should exercise its power to accord a traditional form of judicial relief at the behest of a litigant, who claims a constitutionally protected interest has been invaded, only where the remedy is "essential," or "indispensable for vindicating constitutional rights." While this "essentiality" test is most clearly articulated with respect to damages remedies, apparently the Government believes the same test explains the exercise of equitable remedial powers. It is argued that historically the Court has rarely exercised the power to accord such relief in the absence of an express congressional authorization and that "[i]f Congress had thought that federal officers should be subject to a law different than state law, it would have had no difficulty in saying so, as it did with respect to state officers * * *." See 42 U.S.C. § 1983. Although conceding that the standard of determining whether a damage remedy should be utilized to effectuate statutory policies is one of "necessity" or "appropriateness," see J. I. Case Co. v. Borak, 377 U.S. 426, 432 (1964); United States v. Standard Oil Co., 332 U.S. 301, 307 (1947), the Government contends that questions concerning congressional discretion to modify judicial remedies relating to constitutionally protected interests warrant a more stringent constraint on the exercise of judicial power with respect to this class of legally protected interests.

U.S., at 105, quoting C. Langdell, Summary of Equity Pleading xxvii (1877). Perhaps this fact alone accounts for the suggestion sometimes made that a court's power to enjoin invasion of constitutionally protected interests derives directly from the Constitution. See Bell v. Hood, 71 F.Supp. 813, 819 (S.D.Cal.1947).

These arguments for a more stringent test to govern the grant of damages in constitutional cases[7] seem to be adequately answered by the point that the judiciary has a particular responsibility to assure the vindication of constitutional interests such as those embraced by the Fourth Amendment. To be sure, "it must be remembered that legislatures are ultimate guardians of the liberties and welfare of the people in quite as great a degree as the courts." Missouri, Kansas & Texas R. Co. v. May, 194 U.S. 267, 270 (1904). But it must also be recognized that the Bill of Rights is particularly intended to vindicate the interests of the individual in the face of the popular will as expressed in legislative majorities; at the very least, it strikes me as no more appropriate to await express congressional authorization of traditional judicial relief with regard to these legal interests than with respect to interests protected by federal statutes.

The question then, is, as I see it, whether compensatory relief is "necessary" or "appropriate" to the vindication of the interest asserted. Cf. J. I. Case Co. v. Borak, supra, 377 U.S., at 432; United States v. Standard Oil Co., supra, 332 U.S., at 307; Hill, Constitutional Remedies, 69 Col.L.Rev. 1109, 1155 (1969); Katz, 117 U.Pa.L.Rev., at 72. In resolving that question, it seems to me that the range of policy considerations we may take into account is at least as broad as the range of those a legislature would consider with respect to an express statutory authorization of a traditional remedy. In this regard I agree with the Court that the appropriateness of according Bivens compensatory relief does not turn simply on the deterrent effect liability will have on federal official conduct.[8] Damages as a traditional form of compensation for invasion of a legally protected interest may be entirely appropriate even if no substantial deterrent effects on future official lawlessness might be thought to result. Bivens, after all, has invoked judicial processes claiming entitlement to compensation for injuries resulting from allegedly lawless official behavior, if those injuries are properly compensable in money damages. I do not think a court of law—vested with the power to accord a remedy—should deny him his relief simply because he cannot show that future lawless conduct will thereby be deterred.

7. I express no view on the Government's suggestion that congressional authority to simply discard the remedy the Court today authorizes might be in doubt; nor do I understand the Court's opinion today to express any view on that particular question.

8. And I think it follows from this point that today's decision has little, if indeed any, bearing on the question whether a federal court may properly devise remedies—other than traditionally available forms of judicial relief—for the purpose of enforcing substantive social policies embodied in constitutional or statutory policies. Compare today's decision with Mapp v. Ohio, 367 U.S. 643 (1961), and Weeks v. United States, 232 U.S. 383 (1914). The Court today simply recognizes what has long been implicit in our decisions concerning equitable relief and remedies implied from statutory schemes; i.e., that a court of law vested with jurisdiction over the subject matter of a suit has the power—and therefore the duty—to make principled choices among traditional judicial remedies. Whether special prophylactic measures—which at least arguably the exclusionary rule exemplifies, see Hill, The Bill of Rights and the Supervisory Power, 69 Col.L.Rev. 181, 182–185 (1969)—are supportable on grounds other than a court's competence to select among traditional judicial remedies to make good the wrong done, cf. Bell v. Hood, supra, 327 U.S. at 684, is a separate question.

And I think it is clear that Bivens advances a claim of the sort that if proved, would be properly compensable in damages. * * *

* * *

MR. CHIEF JUSTICE BURGER, dissenting.

I dissent from today's holding which judicially creates a damage remedy not provided for by the Constitution and not enacted by Congress. We would more surely preserve the important values of the doctrine of separation of powers—and perhaps get a better result—by recommending a solution to the Congress as the branch of government in which the Constitution has vested the legislative power. Legislation is the business of the Congress, and it has the facilities and competence for that task—as we do not. * * *

* * *

MR. JUSTICE BLACK, dissenting.

In my opinion for the Court in Bell v. Hood, 327 U.S. 678 (1946), we did as the Court states, reserve the question whether an unreasonable search made by a federal officer in violation of the Fourth Amendment gives the subject of the search a federal cause of action for damages against the officers making the search. There can be no doubt that Congress could create a federal cause of action for damages for an unreasonable search in violation of the Fourth Amendment. Although Congress has created such a federal cause of action against *state* officials acting under color of state law, it has never created such a cause of action against federal officials. If it wanted to do so, Congress could, of course, create a remedy against federal officials who violate the Fourth Amendment in the performance of their duties. But the point of this case and the fatal weakness in the Court's judgment is that neither Congress nor the State of New York has enacted legislation creating such a right of action. For us to do so is, in my judgment, an exercise of power that the Constitution does not give us.

Even if we had the legislative power to create a remedy, there are many reasons why we should decline to create a cause of action where none has existed since the formation of our Government. The courts of the United States as well as those of the States are choked with lawsuits. The number of cases on the docket of this Court have reached an unprecedented volume in recent years. A majority of these cases are brought by citizens with substantial complaints—persons who are physically or economically injured by torts or frauds or governmental infringement of their rights; persons who have been unjustly deprived of their liberty or their property; and persons who have not yet received the equal opportunity in education, employment, and pursuit of happiness that was the dream of our forefathers. Unfortunately, there have also been a growing number of frivolous lawsuits, particularly actions for damages against law enforcement officers whose conduct has been judicially sanctioned by state trial and appellate courts and in many instances even by this Court. My fellow Justices on this Court and our brethren throughout the federal judiciary know only too well the time-consuming task of conscientiously poring over hundreds of thousands of pages of factual allegations of misconduct by police, judicial, and corrections officials. Of course, there are instances of legitimate grievances, but legislators might well desire to devote judicial resources to other problems of a more serious nature.

Jud shau devote ~~~~ resour to other issues

* * *

[The dissenting opinion of JUSTICE BLACKMUN is omitted.]

Notes

1.   Does *Bivens* involve the creation of federal common law, or does it represent simply constitutional interpretation? See Monaghan, *The Supreme Court 1974 Term—Foreword: Constitutional Common Law*, 89 Harv.L.Rev. 1, 24 (1975): " * * * [U]nless the Court views a damage action as an indispensable remedial dimension of the underlying guarantee, it is not constitutional interpretation, but the common law. The latter position commends itself, since this would be entirely analogous to the long recognized federal common law process of articulating the remedial implications of federal statutory rights." Professor Monaghan believes that the Court did not view the damage remedy "as an indispensable remedial dimension of the underlying guarantee * * *." Id. at 24 n. 124. Do you agree? Is Monaghan's approach to the issue correct? What consequences, if any, turn on whether *Bivens* involved constitutional interpretation or the creation of federal common law? Contrast with Monaghan's article Schrock & Welsh, *Reconsidering the Constitutional Common Law*, 91 Harv.L.Rev. 1117, 1135–36 (1978): "We believe the mistake in understanding *Bivens* is Monaghan's, not the Court's, and that properly understood *Bivens* is a constitutional (not common law) decision. It is a constitutional decision, we believe, because it prevents the fourth amendment from being rendered a 'mere form of words' *in the relevant sense of that phrase*. That sense is appreciated when one notes * * * that although the fourth amendment could be given some indeterminate generalized force (say through the deterrent effect of the exclusionary rule) without a cause of action for money damages, it would remain the merest 'form of words' for persons like Webster Bivens."

2.   Does the Court adequately explain the principle it used to rationalize the recognition of a damage remedy for fourth amendment violations? Cf. Dellinger, *Of Rights and Remedies: The Constitution as a Sword*, 85 Harv. L.Rev. 1532, 1544 (1972): "The closest the Court came to articulating a principle to justify its creation of a compensatory remedy for fourth amendment violations was its statement that '[h]istorically, damages have been regarded as the ordinary remedy for an invasion of personal interests in liberty.' This assertion may be meant to suggest that the Court's remedial power over constitutionally based claims will be exercised only when the remedy sought has traditionally been available in the federal courts for other constitutionally based actions. However, with respect to the independent *judicial* creation of remedies for invasions of 'personal interests in liberty,' what emerges from the cases is a sense that the exercise of remedial power to create a damage action directly from the Constitution is virtually unprece-

dented." Do you think that the portion quoted by Professor Dellinger from the *Bivens* opinion explains the Court's rationale? If not, what is the Court's rationale? Does the Court's opinion, either implicitly or explicitly, suggest that the recognition of a damage remedy for a constitutional violation is limited to cases involving the fourth amendment? Does it suggest, either implicitly or explicitly, that a damage remedy will be recognized for *any* constitutional violation? *Should* it logically be extended to all constitutional violations?

3. In *Bivens*, the government argued "that where a constitutional provision rather than a federal statute was offered as the basis for a cause of action, the Court should be considerably more hesitant to supply a [private] remedy." Dellinger, supra, 85 Harv.L.Rev. at 1545. On what basis do you suppose this argument was made? Is it persuasive?

4. Carlson v. Green, 446 U.S. 14 (1980): Suit was brought in federal district court on behalf of plaintiff's deceased son, alleging that while a federal prisoner, her son suffered personal injuries from which he died because prison officials violated his eighth amendment right against cruel and unusual punishment by failing to give him proper medical attention. The district court held that the allegations gave rise to a cause of action under *Bivens*, but dismissed the complaint because the victim had died and damages were therefore limited to those provided by state survivorship and wrongful-death laws, and those amounts did not equal the $10,000 federal jurisdictional minimum. The Court of Appeals held that whenever a state survivorship statute would abate a *Bivens* action, federal common law allows survival of the action.

The Supreme Court, in an opinion by Justice Brennan, affirmed the Court of Appeals' decision:

> [A *Bivens*] cause of action may be defeated in a particular case * * * in two situations. The first is when defendants demonstrate 'special factors counseling hesitation in the absence of affirmative action by Congress.' * * * The second is when defendants show that Congress has provided an alternative remedy which it explicitly declared to be a *substitute* for recovery directly under the Constitution and viewed as equally effective * * *.

Neither situation obtains in this case. 446 U.S. at 18, 19.

The Court held that there is "nothing in the Federal Tort Claims Act (FTCA) or its legislative history to show that Congress meant to pre-empt a *Bivens* remedy or to create an equally effective remedy for constitutional violations." Id. The Court also cited factors "suggesting that the *Bivens* remedy is more effective than the FTCA remedy * * *," Id. at 20, concluding that "[p]lainly FTCA is not a sufficient protector of the citizens' constitutional rights, and without a clear congressional mandate we cannot hold that Congress relegated respondent exclusively to the FTCA remedy." Id. at 23.

Finally, the Court held that "*Bivens* actions are a creation of federal law and, therefore, the question whether respondent's action survived [her son's] death is a question of federal law." The Court rejected the incorporation of the state law of survivorship as the federal standard: "Whatever difficulty we might have resolving the question were the federal involvement less clear, we hold that only a uniform federal rule of survivorship will suffice to redress the constitutional deprivation here alleged and to protect against repetition of such conduct." Id.

Justice Powell, with whom Justice Stewart joined, concurred separately:

The Court now volunteers the view that a defendant cannot defeat a *Bivens* action simply by showing that there are adequate alternative avenues of relief * * *. The Court cites no authority and advances no policy reason—indeed no reason at all—for imposing this threshold burden upon the defendant in an implied remedy case. Id. at 26, 27.

Justice Powell "agree[d] that the relevant policies require the application of federal common law to allow survival in this case."

It is not 'obvious' to me, however, that 'the liability of federal officials for violations of citizens' constitutional rights should be governed by uniform rules' in every case * * *. On the contrary, federal courts routinely refer to state law to fill the procedural gaps in national remedial schemes. Id. at 29.

Justice Rehnquist and Chief Justice Burger dissented in separate opinions.

5. According to one commentator, on the basis of recent trends, it appears clear that "the Court will think long and hard before expanding the range of constitutional provisions that individuals may enforce with a *Bivens* claim." J. Pfander, Principles of Federal Jurisdiction 161 (2006). On the general issue, see Hill, *Constitutional Remedies*, 69 Colum.L.Rev. 1109 (1969); Katz, *The Jurisprudence of Remedies: Constitutional Legality and the Law of Torts* in Bell v. Hood, 117 U.Pa.L.Rev. 1 (1968).

See also Jeffries, *Compensation for Constitutional Torts: Reflections on the Significance of Fault,* 88 Mich.L.Rev. 82 (1989) ("The assumption of compensation as a universal desideratum of the law governing official misconduct seems to me misguided"); and the analogous issues discussed in Symposium, *Section 1983: The Constitution and the Courts,* 77 Geo.L.Rev. 1437 (1989).

BUSH v. LUCAS

Supreme Court of the United States, 1983.
462 U.S. 367.

JUSTICE STEVENS delivered the opinion of the Court.

Petitioner asks us to authorize a new nonstatutory damages remedy for federal employees whose First Amendment rights are violated by their superiors. Because such claims arise out of an employment relationship that is governed by comprehensive procedural and substantive provisions giving meaningful remedies against the United States, we conclude that it would be inappropriate for us to supplement that regulatory scheme with a new judicial remedy.

Petitioner Bush is an aerospace engineer employed at the George C. Marshall Space Flight Center, a major facility operated by the National

Aeronautics and Space Administration in Alabama. Respondent Lucas is the Director of the Center. In 1974 the facility was reorganized and petitioner was twice reassigned to new positions. He objected to both reassignments and sought formal review by the Civil Service Commission. In May and June 1975, while some of his administrative appeals were pending, he made a number of public statements, including two televised interviews, that were highly critical of the agency. The news media quoted him as saying that he did not have enough meaningful work to keep him busy, that his job was "a travesty and worthless," and that the taxpayers' money was being spent fraudulently and wastefully at the Center. His statements were reported on local television, in the local newspaper, and in a national press release that appeared in newspapers in at least three other States.

In June 1975 respondent, in response to a reporter's inquiry, stated that he had conducted an investigation and that petitioner's statements regarding his job had "no basis in fact." * * * In August 1975 an adverse personnel action was initiated to remove petitioner from his position. Petitioner was charged with "publicly mak[ing] intemperate remarks which were misleading and often false, evidencing a malicious attitude towards Management and generating an environment of sensationalism demeaning to the Government, the National Aeronautics and Space Administration and the personnel of the George C. Marshall Space Flight Center, thereby impeding Government efficiency and economy and adversely affecting public confidence in the Government service." He was also informed that his conduct had undermined morale at the Center and caused disharmony and disaffection among his fellow employees. Petitioner had the opportunity to file a written response and to make an oral presentation to agency officials. Respondent then determined that petitioner's statements were false and misleading and that his conduct would justify removal, but that the lesser penalty of demotion was appropriate for a "first offense." * * * He approved a reduction in grade from GS–14 to GS–12, which decreased petitioner's annual salary by approximately $9,716.

Petitioner exercised his right to appeal to the Federal Employee Appeals Authority. After a three-day public hearing, the Authority upheld some of the charges and concluded that the demotion was justified. It specifically determined that a number of petitioner's public statements were misleading and that, for three reasons, they "exceeded the bounds of expression protected by the First Amendment." First, petitioner's statements did not stem from public interest, but from his desire to have his position abolished so that he could take early retirement and go to law school. Second, the statements conveyed the erroneous impression that the agency was deliberately wasting public funds, thus discrediting the agency and its employees. Third, there was no legitimate public interest to be served by abolishing petitioner's position.

Two years after the Appeals Authority's decision, petitioner requested the Civil Service Commission's Appeals Review Board to reopen the proceeding. The Board reexamined petitioner's First Amendment claim and, after making a detailed review of the record and the applicable authorities, applied the balancing test articulated in Pickering v. Board of Education, 391 U.S. 563 (1968). On the one hand, it acknowledged the evidence tending to show that petitioner's motive might have been personal gain, and the evidence that his statements caused some disruption of the agency's day-to-day routine. On the other hand, it noted that society as well as the individual had an interest in free speech, including "a right to disclosure of information about how tax dollars are spent and about the functioning of government apparatus, an interest in the promotion of the efficiency of the government, and in the maintenance of an atmosphere of freedom of expression by the scientists and engineers who are responsible for the planning and implementation of the nation's space program." Because petitioner's statements, though somewhat exaggerated, "were not wholly without truth, they properly stimulated public debate." Thus the nature and extent of proven disruption to the agency's operations did not "justify abrogation of the exercise of free speech." The Board recommended that petitioner be restored to his former position, retroactively to November 30, 1975, and that he receive back pay. That recommendation was accepted. Petitioner received approximately $30,000 in back pay.

While his administrative appeal was pending, petitioner filed an action against respondent in state court in Alabama seeking to recover damages for defamation and violation of his constitutional rights. Respondent removed the lawsuit to the United States District Court for the Northern District of Alabama, which granted respondent's motion for summary judgment. It held, first, that the defamation claim could not be maintained because, under Barr v. Matteo, 360 U.S. 564 (1959), respondent was absolutely immune from liability for damages for defamation; and second, that petitioner's demotion was not a constitutional deprivation for which a damages action could be maintained. The United States Court of Appeals for the Fifth Circuit affirmed. We vacated that court's judgment, and directed that it reconsider the case in the light of our intervening decision in Carlson v. Green, 446 U.S. 14 (1980). The Court of Appeals again affirmed the judgment against petitioner. It adhered to its previous conclusion "that plaintiff had no cause of action for damages under the First Amendment for retaliatory demotion in view of the available remedies under the Civil Service Commission regulations." It explained that the relationship between the Federal Government and its civil service employees was a special factor counselling against the judicial recognition of a damages remedy under the Constitution in this context.

We assume for purposes of decision that petitioner's First Amendment rights were violated by the adverse personnel action. We also assume that, as petitioner asserts civil service remedies were not as effective as an individual damages remedy[8] and did not fully compensate

---

8. See Carlson v. Green, 446 U.S. 14, 20–23 (1980) (factors making Federal Tort Claims Act recovery less "effective" than an action under the Constitution to recover

him for the harm he suffered. Two further propositions are undisputed. Congress has not expressly authorized the damages remedy that petitioner asks us to provide. On the other hand, Congress has not expressly precluded the creation of such a remedy by declaring that existing statutes provide the exclusive mode of redress.

Thus, we assume, a federal right has been violated and Congress has provided a less than complete remedy for the wrong. If we were writing on a clean slate, we might answer the question whether to supplement the statutory scheme in either of two quite simple ways. We might adopt the common-law approach to the judicial recognition of new causes of action and hold that it is the province of the judiciary to fashion an adequate remedy for every wrong that can be proved in a case over which a court has jurisdiction.[10] Or we might start from the premise that federal courts are courts of limited jurisdiction whose remedial powers do not extend beyond the granting of relief expressly authorized by Congress.[11] Under the former approach, petitioner would obviously prevail; under the latter, it would be equally clear that he would lose.

Our prior cases, although sometimes emphasizing one approach and sometimes the other, have unequivocally rejected both extremes. They establish our power to grant relief that is not expressly authorized by statute, but they also remind us that such power is to be exercised in the light of relevant policy determinations made by the Congress. We therefore first review some of the cases establishing our power to remedy violations of the Constitution and then consider the bearing of the existing statutory scheme on the precise issue presented by this case.

I

The federal courts' power to grant relief not expressly authorized by Congress is firmly established. Under 28 U.S.C. § 1331, the federal courts have jurisdiction to decide all cases "aris[ing] under the Constitution, laws, or treaties of the United States." This jurisdictional grant provides not only the authority to decide whether a cause of action is stated by a plaintiff's claim that he has been injured by a violation of the Constitution, Bell v. Hood, 327 U.S. 678, 684 (1946), but also the authority to choose among available judicial remedies in order to vindicate constitutional rights. This Court has fashioned a wide variety of nonstatutory remedies for violations of the Constitution by federal and state officials. The cases most relevant to the problem before us are

damages against the individual official). Petitioner contends that, unlike a damages remedy against respondent individually, civil service remedies against the Government do not provide for punitive damages or a jury trial and do not adequately deter.

10. In Marbury v. Madison, 1 Cranch 137, 162–163 (1803), Chief Justice Marshall invoked the authority of Blackstone's *Commentaries* in support of this proposition. Blackstone had written, "it is a general and indisputable rule, that where there is a

legal right, there is also a legal remedy by suit, or action at law, whenever that right is invaded ... [I]t is a settled and invariable principle in the laws of England, that every right, when withheld, must have a remedy, and every injury its proper redress." 3 Commentaries 23, 109.

11. See Bivens v. Six Unknown Fed. Narcotics Agents, 403 U.S. 388, 428 (1971) (Black, J., dissenting).

those in which the Court has held that the Constitution itself supports a private cause of action for damages against a federal official. Bivens v. Six Unknown Fed. Narcotics Agents, 403 U.S. 388 (1971); Davis v. Passman, 442 U.S. 228 (1979); Carlson v. Green, 446 U.S. 14 (1980).

* * *

This much is established by our prior cases. The federal courts' statutory jurisdiction to decide federal questions confers adequate power to award damages to the victim of a constitutional violation. When Congress provides an alternative remedy, it may, of course, indicate its intent, by statutory language, by clear legislative history, or perhaps even by the statutory remedy itself, that the Court's power should not be exercised. In the absence of such a congressional directive, the federal courts must make the kind of remedial determination that is appropriate for a common-law tribunal, paying particular heed, however, to any special factors counselling hesitation before authorizing a new kind of federal litigation.

Congress has not resolved the question presented by this case by expressly denying petitioner the judicial remedy he seeks or by providing him with an equally effective substitute.[14] There is, however, a good deal of history that is relevant to the question whether a federal employee's attempt to recover damages from his superior for violation of his First Amendment rights involves any "special factors counselling hesitation." When those words were first used in *Bivens,* 403 U.S., at 396, we illustrated our meaning by referring to United States v. Standard Oil Co., 332 U.S. 301, 311, 316 (1947), and United States v. Gilman, 347 U.S. 507 (1954).

In the *Standard Oil* case the Court had been asked to authorize a new damages remedy for the Government against a tortfeasor who had injured a soldier, imposing hospital expenses on the Government and depriving it of his services. Although, as Justice Jackson properly noted in dissent, the allowance of recovery would not have involved any usurpation of legislative power, the Court nevertheless concluded that Congress as "the custodian of the national purse" should make the necessary determination of federal fiscal policy.[15] The Court refused to

---

14. We need not reach the question whether the Constitution itself requires a judicially-fashioned damages remedy in the absence of any other remedy to vindicate the underlying right, unless there is an express textual command to the contrary. Cf. Davis v. Passman, supra, 442 U.S., at 246. The existing civil service remedies for a demotion in retaliation for protected speech are clearly constitutionally adequate. * * *

15. "Whatever the merits of the policy, its conversion into law is a proper subject for congressional action, not for any creative power of ours. Congress, not this Court or the other federal courts, is the custodian

of the national purse. By the same token it is the primary and most often the exclusive arbiter of federal fiscal affairs. And these comprehend, as we have said, securing the treasury or the government against financial losses however inflicted, including requiring reimbursement for injuries creating them, as well as filling the treasury itself."

The Court further noted that the type of harm for which the Executive sought judicial redress was not new, and that Congress presumably knew of it but had not exercised its undoubted power to authorize a damages action.

create a damages remedy, which would be "the instrument for determining and establishing the federal fiscal and regulatory policies which the Government's executive arm thinks should prevail in a situation not covered by traditionally established liabilities."

Similarly, in *Gilman,* the Court applied the *Standard Oil* rationale to reject the Government's attempt to recover indemnity from one of its employees after having been held liable under the FTCA for the employee's negligence. As the Court noted, "The relations between the United States and its employees have presented a myriad of problems with which the Congress over the years has dealt.... Government employment gives rise to policy questions of great import, both to the employees and to the Executive and Legislative Branches." The decision regarding indemnity involved questions of employee discipline and morale, fiscal policy, and the efficiency of the federal service. Hence, the Court wrote, the reasons for deferring to Congressional policy determinations were even more compelling than in *Standard Oil.*

> "Here a complex of relations between federal agencies and their staffs is involved. Moreover, the claim now asserted, though the product of a law Congress passed, is a matter on which Congress has not taken a position. It presents questions of policy on which Congress has not spoken. The selection of that policy which is most advantageous to the whole involves a host of considerations that must be weighed and appraised. That function is more appropriately for those who write the laws, rather than for those who interpret them." Id. at 511–13.

The special factors counselling hesitation in the creation of a new remedy in *Standard Oil* and *Gilman* did not concern the merits of the particular remedy that was sought. Rather, they related to the question of who should decide whether such a remedy should be provided. We should therefore begin by considering whether there are reasons for allowing Congress to prescribe the scope of relief that is made available to federal employees whose First Amendment rights have been violated by their supervisors.

II

Unlike *Standard Oil* and *Gilman,* this case concerns a claim that a constitutional right has been violated. Nevertheless, just as those cases involved "federal fiscal policy" and the relations between the Government and its employees, the ultimate question on the merits in this case may appropriately be characterized as one of "federal personnel policy." When a federal civil servant is the victim of a retaliatory demotion or discharge because he has exercised his First Amendment rights, what legal remedies are available to him?

The answer to that question has changed dramatically over the years. Originally the answer was entirely a matter of Executive discretion. During the era of the patronage system that prevailed in the federal government prior to the enactment of the Pendleton Act in 1883, 22

Stat. 403, the federal employee had no legal protection against political retaliation. Indeed, the exercise of the First Amendment right to support a political candidate opposing the party in office would routinely have provided an accepted basis for discharge. During the past century, however, the job security of federal employees has steadily increased.

In the Pendleton Act Congress created the Civil Service Commission and provided for the selection of federal civil servants on a merit basis by competitive examination. Although the statute did not address the question of removals in general, it provided that no employee in the public service could be required to contribute to any political fund or fired for refusing to do so, and it prohibited officers from attempting to influence or coerce the political actions of others.

* * *

* * * Federal civil servants are now protected by an elaborate, comprehensive scheme that encompasses substantive provisions forbidding arbitrary action by supervisors and procedures—administrative and judicial—by which improper action may be redressed. They apply to a multitude of personnel decisions that are made daily by federal agencies. Constitutional challenges to agency action, such as the First Amendment claims raised by petitioner, are fully cognizable within this system. As the record in this case demonstrates, the Government's comprehensive scheme is costly to administer, but it provides meaningful remedies for employees who may have been unfairly disciplined for making critical comments about their agencies.

A federal employee in the competitive service may be removed or demoted "only for such cause as will promote the efficiency of the service." The regulations applicable at the time of petitioner's demotion in 1975, which are substantially similar to those now in effect, required that an employee be given 30 days' written notice of a proposed discharge, suspension, or demotion, accompanied by the agency's reasons and a copy of the charges. The employee then had the right to examine all disclosable materials that formed the basis of the proposed action, 5 CFR § 752.202(a) (1975), the right to answer the charges with a statement and supporting affidavits, and the right to make an oral nonevidentiary presentation to an agency official. § 752.202(b). The regulations required that the final agency decision be made by an official higher in rank than the official who proposed the adverse action, § 752.202(f). The employee was entitled to notification in writing stating which of the initial reasons had been sustained. 5 U.S.C. § 7501(b)(4) (1976).

The next step was a right to appeal to the Civil Service Commission's Federal Employee Appeals Authority. 5 CFR §§ 752.203, 772.101 (1975). The Appeals Authority was required to hold a trial-type hearing at which the employee could present witnesses, cross-examine the agency's witnesses, and secure the attendance of agency officials, § 772.307(c), and then to render a written decision, § 772.309(a). An adverse decision by the FEAA was judicially reviewable in either federal district court or the Court of Claims. In addition, the employee had the right to ask the Commission's Appeals Review Board to reopen an adverse decision by the FEAA. § 772.310.

If the employee prevailed in the administrative process or upon judicial review, he was entitled to reinstatement with retroactive seniority. § 752.402. He also had a right to full back pay, including credit for periodic within-grade or step increases and general pay raises during the relevant period, allowances, differentials, and accumulated leave. § 550.803. Congress intended that these remedies would put the employee "in the same position he would have been in had the unjustified or erroneous personnel action not taken place."

Given the history of the development of civil service remedies and the comprehensive nature of the remedies currently available, it is clear that the question we confront today is quite different from the typical remedial issue confronted by a common-law court. The question is not what remedy the court should provide for a wrong that would otherwise go unredressed. It is whether an elaborate remedial system that has been constructed step by step, with careful attention to conflicting policy considerations, should be augmented by the creation of a new judicial remedy for the constitutional violation at issue. That question obviously cannot be answered simply by noting that existing remedies do not provide complete relief for the plaintiff. The policy judgment should be informed by a thorough understanding of the existing regulatory structure and the respective costs and benefits that would result from the addition of another remedy for violations of employees' First Amendment rights.

The costs associated with the review of disciplinary decisions are already significant—not only in monetary terms, but also in the time and energy of managerial personnel who must defend their decisions. The Government argues that supervisory personnel are already more hesitant than they should be in administering discipline, because the review that ensues inevitably makes the performance of their regular duties more difficult. Whether or not this assessment is accurate, it is quite probable that if management personnel face the added risk of personal liability for decisions that they believe to be a correct response to improper criticism of the agency, they would be deterred from imposing discipline in future cases. In all events, Congress is in a far better position than a court to evaluate the impact of a new species of litigation between federal employees on the efficiency of the civil service. Not only has Congress developed considerable familiarity with balancing governmental efficiency and the rights of employees, but it also may inform itself through factfinding procedures such as hearings that are not available to the courts.

Nor is there any reason to discount Congress' ability to make an evenhanded assessment of the desirability of creating a new remedy for federal employees who have been demoted or discharged for expressing controversial views. Congress has a special interest in informing itself about the efficiency and morale of the Executive Branch. In the past it has demonstrated its awareness that lower-level government employees are a valuable source of information, and that supervisors might improperly attempt to curtail their subordinates' freedom of expression.

Thus, we do not decide whether or not it would be good policy to permit a federal employee to recover damages from a supervisor who has improperly disciplined him for exercising his First Amendment rights. As we did in *Standard Oil,* we decline "to create a new substantive legal liability without legislative aid and as at the common law", because we are convinced that Congress is in a better position to decide whether or not the public interest would be served by creating it.

The judgment of the Court of Appeals is affirmed.

JUSTICE MARSHALL, with whom JUSTICE BLACKMUN joins, concurring.

I join the Court's opinion because I agree that there are "special factors counselling hesitation in the absence of affirmative action by Congress." Bivens v. Six Unknown Fed. Narcotics Agents, 403 U.S. 388, 396 (1971). I write separately only to emphasize that in my view a different case would be presented if Congress had not created a comprehensive scheme that was specifically designed to provide full compensation to civil service employees who are discharged or disciplined in violation of their First Amendment rights, cf. Carlson v. Green, 446 U.S. 14, 23 (1980); Sonntag v. Dooley, 650 F.2d 904, 907 (C.A.7 1981), and that affords a remedy that is substantially as effective as a damage action.

Although petitioner may be correct that the administrative procedure created by Congress, unlike a *Bivens* action, does not permit recovery for loss due to emotional distress and mental anguish, Congress plainly intended to provide what it regarded as full compensatory relief when it enacted the Back Pay Act of 1966, 5 U.S.C. (Supp. V) § 5596. * * * Moreover, there is nothing in today's decision to foreclose a federal employee from pursuing a *Bivens* remedy where his injury is not attributable to personnel actions which may be remedied under the federal statutory scheme.

I cannot agree with petitioner's assertion that civil service remedies are substantially less effective than an individual damages remedy. * * *

As the Court emphasizes, "[t]he question is not what remedy the court should provide for a wrong that would otherwise go unredressed." * * * The question is whether an alternative remedy should be provided when the wrong may already be redressed under "an elaborate remedial system that has been constructed step by step, with careful attention to conflicting policy considerations." * * * I agree that a *Bivens* remedy is unnecessary in this case.

Notes

1.   The Court in *Bush* defers to Congress largely because "Congress is in a far better position than a court to evaluate the impact of a new species of litigation between federal employees on the efficiency of the civil service." Is the Court ignoring the fact that enforcement of a *constitutional* right, rather than a statutory right, is at stake?

2.   Consider also the Court's reliance on the *Standard Oil* analysis. Is that case a legitimate precedent for *Bush?*

3.   The Court claimed to follow *Bush* in Schweiker v. Chilicky, 487 U.S. 412 (1988). *Chilicky* involved a challenge, based on the due process clause of the Fifth Amendment, to the denial of certain social security disability benefits. The thrust of the plaintiffs' argument was that government officials had, primarily through the use of impermissible quotas, intentionally deprived certain recipients of fair treatment in the determination of their benefits claims. The complaint sought equitable relief, damages for emotional distress and for the loss of food, shelter and other necessities caused consequentially by the denial of benefits. [Full retroactive benefits had already been restored for the wrongful denials.] The Court held, in response, that no *Bivens* remedy will be recognized for the denial of fair treatment in the social security disability context. 487 U.S. at 414.

The majority, in an opinion by Justice O'Connor, ruled that the case could not "reasonably be distinguished from *Bush v. Lucas.*" The intricate scheme of administrative and judicial review provided for under the Social Security Act limits relief to restoration of benefits. As in *Bush,* however:

> Congress has failed to provide for "complete relief": respondents have not been given a remedy for emotional distress or for other hardships suffered because of delays in their receipt of * * * benefits * * *. Congress, however, has not failed to provide meaningful safeguards or remedies for protecting their rights is, if anything, considerably more elaborate than the civil service system considered in *Bush.* 487 U.S. at 423.

Justice O'Connor's opinion concluded that "Congress is in a better position to decide whether or not the public interest would be served by creating [a new substantive legal liability]", quoting *Bush.*

Was not "Congress in a better position" to decide the liability issues raised in *Boyle v. United Technologies Corp.* [supra p. 890]? Should it make a difference that the Court in *Bush* deferred to an intricate congressional scheme which not only provided relief for the First Amendment claim made, but was ruled by the Court "clearly constitutionally adequate"? 462 U.S. at 378 n. 14. The damage action sought by the *Chilicky* plaintiffs—based on intentional manipulation of the review process itself—could not be maintained under the Social Security Act.

See, for example, the D.C. Circuit's decision in Spagnola v. Mathis, 859 F.2d 223 (D.C.Cir.1988), where the court dismissed a variety of constitutional damage claims filed by federal civil servants. Alternative remedies under the Civil Service Reform Act were characterized as clearly inadequate. Citing

Chilicky, however, the court found the existence of special factors indicating that the focus is "appropriately the comprehensiveness of the statutory scheme involved, not the 'adequacy' of specific remedies extended." Id. at 227. Accordingly it was thought unimportant, consistent with *Chilicky,* whether or not the litigants had a meaningful opportunity to present their constitutional claims.

Chilicky has received criticism from commentators. See Nichol, *Bivens, Chilicky, and Constitutional Damages Claims,* 75 Va.L.Rev. 1117, 1154 (1989): "*Bush v. Lucas* and *Schweiker v. Chilicky* have dislodged the 'special factors' exception from any justifiable foundations to which the concept might previously have been tied. The judiciary's obligation—whether federal or state—to decide cases arising under the Constitution embraces and demands the implementation of effective remedies. That obligation does not disappear merely because Congress may be in a better position than the Supreme Court to ascertain the public good. The recent, and dramatic, expansion of the special factors analysis has demonstrated that the concept, at its core, is inconsistent with the demands of constitutional interpretation." See also Brown, *Letting Statutory Tails Wag Constitutional Dogs— Have the Bivens Dissenters Prevailed?,* 64 Ind.L.J. 263 (1989) (criticizing recent *Bivens* rulings and questioning Court's under-estimation of judicial competence to fashion damage remedies); Rosen, *The* Bivens *Constitutional Tort: An Unfulfilled Promise,* 67 N.C.L.Rev. 337 (1989); and Note, Bivens *Doctrine in Flux: Statutory Preclusion of a Constitutional Cause of Action,* 101 Harv.L.Rev. 1251 (1988).

Professors Fallon and Meltzer offer a helpful perspective on constitutional remedies law in their article, *New Law, Non–Retroactivity, and Constitutional Remedies,* 104 Harv.L.Rev. 1733 (1991). They argue that "two principles, each capable of accommodating competing values in its own way, underlie the law of constitutional remedies. The first principle, which is strong but not always unyielding, calls for effective redress to individual victims of constitutional violations. The second, more absolute principle demands a general structure of constitutional remedies adequate to keep government within the bounds of law. Under these two principles, the Constitution typically allows the substitution of one remedy for another, and sometimes tolerates situations in which individual victims receive no effective redress." 104 Harv.L.Rev. at 1736.

In *McCarthy v. Madigan,* 503 U.S. 140 (1992), the Court distinguished *Chilicky* in holding that exhaustion of the Bureau of Prisons' administrative procedure is not required before a federal prisoner can initiate a *Bivens* action solely for money damages. In *Chilicky,* said the Court, "Congress had legislated an elaborate and comprehensive remedial scheme. * * * Here, Congress has enacted nothing." Id. at 152.

4. Some courts of appeals have held that even where employees may not sue for damages under *Bivens* because they are protected by remedial administrative schemes, they may nevertheless sue for equitable relief. See, e.g., Mitchum v. Hurt, 73 F.3d 30 (3d Cir.1995); Hubbard v. EPA, 809 F.2d 1 (D.C.Cir.1986). In *Mitchum,* the court reasoned: "It is reasonable to assume that Congress legislates with the understanding that this form of judicial relief is generally available to protect constitutional rights. While Congress

may restrict the availability of injunctive relief * * * we believe that we should be very hesitant before concluding that Congress has impliedly imposed such a restriction on the authority to award injunctive relief to vindicate constitutional rights." Several other courts of appeals have concluded that a federal employee who has available meaningful administrative remedies under a congressional scheme should not be permitted to bypass that scheme by bringing an action under the general federal question statute seeking declaratory or injunctive relief. See, e.g., Saul v. United States, 928 F.2d 829 (9th Cir.1991); Stephens v. Department of Health and Human Services, 901 F.2d 1571 (11th Cir.1990).

5. *Bush* and *Chilicky* are illustrative of the Court's approach to *Bivens* since 1980. As the Court notes in its most recent case, it has "consistently refused to extend *Bivens* liability to any new context or new category of defendants." Correctional Services Corp. v. Malesko, 534 U.S. 61 (2001). In *Malesko*, the Court held that a prisoner had no cause of action against a private corporation operating a federal halfway house. Chief Justice Rehnquist's opinion for a five-Justice majority distinguished *Bivens* on several grounds, including the availability of alternative remedies and the fact that the prisoner was suing the corporation rather than the individual. Justice Scalia (with Justice Thomas) joined the majority opinion but wrote separately to emphasize his disagreement with *Bivens* itself:

> *Bivens* is a relic of the heady days in which this Court assumed common-law powers to create causes of action–decreeing them to be "implied" by the mere existence of a statutory or constitutional prohibition. As the Court points out, we have abandoned that power to invent "implications" in the statutory field, * * * since an "implication" imagined in the Constitution can presumably not even be repudiated by Congress. I would limit *Bivens* and its two follow-on cases (*Davis v. Passman* and *Carlson v. Green*) to the precise circumstances that they involved.

Id. at 75.

§ 5. IMPLIED STATUTORY REMEDIES

J.I. CASE CO. v. BORAK, 377 U.S. 426 (1964): Respondent Borak, a stockholder of J.I. Case, filed a civil action in federal court for deprivation of his and other stockholders' preemptive rights as a result of a merger allegedly accomplished by means of a false and misleading proxy statement. One of the counts in the complaint alleged a violation of section 14(a) of the Securities Exchange Act of 1934, 15 U.S.C. § 78n(a), which provides:

> It shall be unlawful for any person, by the use of the mails or by any means or instrumentality of interstate commerce or of any facility of any national securities exchange or otherwise to solicit or to permit the use of his name to solicit any proxy or consent or authorization in respect of any security * * * registered on any national securities exchange in contravention of such rules and regulations as the [Securities and Exchange] Commission may prescribe as necessary or appropriate in the public interest or for the protection of investors.

Section 27 of the Act provides exclusive federal jurisdiction over violations of any other provision of the Act, "and of all suits in equity and actions at law brought to enforce any liability or duty created by this title or the rules and regulations thereunder."

The district court held that under section 27 it had jurisdiction to issue only declaratory relief, rather than remedial relief. The court of appeals reversed.

The Supreme Court considered whether section 27 "authorizes a federal cause of action for recission or damages to a corporate stockholder with respect to a consummated merger which was authorized pursuant to the use of a proxy statement alleged to contain false and misleading statements violative of section 14(a) of the Act." In an opinion by Justice Clark, the Court held that such relief was, in fact, authorized:

> The purpose of § 14(a) is to prevent management or others from obtaining authorization for corporate action by means of deceptive or inadequate disclosure in proxy solicitation. * * * These broad remedial purposes are evidenced in the language of the section which makes it "unlawful for any person ... to solicit or to permit the use of his name to solicit any proxy or consent or authorization in respect of any security ... registered on any national securities exchange in contravention of such rules and regulations as the Commission may prescribe as necessary or appropriate in the public interest *or for the protection of investors*." (Italics supplied). While this language makes no specific reference to a private right of action, among its chief purposes is "the protection of investors," which certainly implies the availability of judicial relief where necessary to achieve that result.
>
> * * * Private enforcement of the proxy rules provides a necessary supplement to Commission action. As in antitrust treble damage litigation, the possibility of civil damages or injunctive relief serves as a most effective weapon in the enforcement of proxy requirements. * * * Time does not permit an independent examination [by the Commission] of the facts set out in the proxy material and this results in the Commission's acceptance of the representations contained therein at their face value, unless contrary to other material on file with it. * * *
>
> We, therefore, believe that under the circumstances here it is the duty of the courts to be alert to provide such remedies as are necessary to make effective the congressional purpose.
>
> * * *
>
> [I]f federal jurisdiction were limited to the granting of declaratory relief, victims of deceptive proxy statements would be obliged to go into state courts for remedial relief. Id. at 431–35.

CORT v. ASH, 422 U.S. 66 (1975): A stockholder filed a derivative action in federal court alleging that the corporate directors had authorized expenditures from general corporate funds, claimed to be in violation of 18 U.S.C.A. § 610, prohibiting corporations from making contributions or expenditures in connection with specified federal elections. Respondent sought to assert a private claim for relief under section 610, even though the Act failed expressly to provide such a remedy. Rather, the Act's express enforcement mechanism was in the form of criminal penalties.

The Supreme Court, in an opinion by Justice Brennan, held that no such private remedy could be implied:

> In determining whether a private remedy is implicit in a statute not expressly providing one, several factors are relevant. First, is the plaintiff "one of the class for whose *especial* benefit the statute was enacted,"—that is, does the statute create a federal right in favor of the plaintiff? Second, is there any indication of legislative intent, explicit or implicit, either to create such a remedy or to deny one? Third, is it consistent with the underlying purposes of the legislative scheme to imply such a remedy for the plaintiff? And finally, is the cause of action one traditionally relegated to state law, in an area basically the concern of the States, so that it would be inappropriate to infer a cause of action based solely on federal law?

* * *

> Clearly, provision of a criminal penalty does not necessarily *preclude* implication of a private cause of action for damages. * * * Here, [however,] there was nothing more than a bare criminal statute, with absolutely no indication that civil enforcement of any kind was available to anyone.

> We need not, however, go so far as to say that in this circumstance a bare criminal statute can *never* be deemed sufficiently protective of some special group so as to give rise to a private cause of action by a member of that group. For the intent to protect corporate shareholders particularly was at best a subsidiary purpose of § 610, and the other relevant factors all either are not helpful or militate against implying a private cause of action.

* * *

> [T]here is no indication whatever in the legislative history of § 610 which suggests a congressional intention to vest in corporate shareholders a federal right to damages for violation of § 610. True, in situations in which it is clear that federal law has granted a class of persons certain rights, it is not necessary to show an intention to *create* a private cause of action, although an explicit purpose to *deny* such cause of action would be controlling. But where, as here, it is at

least dubious whether Congress intended to vest in the plaintiff class rights broader than those provided by state regulation of corporations, the fact that there is no suggestion at all that § 610 may give rise to a suit for damages or, indeed, to any civil cause of action, reinforces the conclusions that the expectation, if any, was that the relationship between corporations and their stockholders would continue to be entrusted entirely to state law.

* * *

[I]n this instance the remedy sought would not aid the primary congressional goal. Recovery of derivative damages by the corporations for violation of § 610 would not cure the influence which the use of corporate funds in the first instance may have had on a federal election. Rather, such a remedy would only permit directors in effect to "borrow" corporate funds for a time; the later compelled repayment might well not deter the initial violation * * *. 422 U.S. at 84.

CANNON v. UNIVERSITY OF CHICAGO, 441 U.S. 677 (1979): Petitioner Cannon filed suit in federal court, alleging that she had been excluded from participation in the medical education programs of defendant private universities, recipients of federal financial assistance, because of her gender, in violation of Title IX of the Education Amendments of 1972, which provides that "[n]o person in the United States shall, on the basis of sex, be excluded from participation in, be denied the benefits of, or be subjected to discrimination under any education or activity receiving Federal financial assistance." The district court granted defendants' motions to dismiss because Title IX does not expressly authorize a private right of action for a violation and the court decided that no private remedy should be inferred. The court of appeals affirmed.

The Supreme Court, in an opinion by Justice Stevens, reversed:

As our recent cases—particularly *Cort v. Ash*—demonstrate, the fact that a federal statute has been violated and some person harmed does not automatically give rise to a private cause of action in favor of that person. Instead, before concluding that Congress intended to make a remedy available to a special class of litigants, a court must carefully analyze the four factors that *Cort* identifies as indicative of such an intent. Our review of those factors persuades us, however, that the Court of Appeals reached the wrong conclusion and that petitioner does have a statutory right to pursue her claim that respondents rejected her application on the basis of her sex.

* * *

First, the threshold question under *Cort* is whether the statute was enacted for the benefit of a special class of which the plaintiff is a member. That question is answered by looking to the language of the statute itself.

* * *

Second, the *Cort* analysis requires consideration of legislative history. We must recognize, however, that the legislative history of a statute that does not expressly create or deny a private remedy will typically be equally silent or ambiguous on the question. Therefore, in situations such as the present one "in which it is clear that federal law has granted a class of persons certain rights, it is not necessary to show an intention to *create* a private cause of action, although an explicit purpose to *deny* such cause of action would be controlling." [quoting *Cort.*] But this is not the typical case. Far from evidencing any purpose to *deny* a private cause of action, the history of Title IX rather plainly indicates that Congress intended to create such a remedy.

Title IX was patterned after Title VI of the Civil Rights Act of 1964. Except for the substitution of the word "sex" in Title IX to replace the words "race, color, or national origin" in Title VI, the two statutes use identical language to describe the benefited class. * * * Neither statute expressly mentions a private remedy for the person excluded from participation in a federally funded program. The drafters of Title IX explicitly assumed that it would be interpreted and applied as Title VI had been * * *.

In 1972 when Title IX was enacted, the critical language in Title VI had already been construed as creating a private remedy. * * * It is always appropriate to assume that our elected representatives, like other citizens, know the law * * *.

* * *

Third, under *Cort,* a private remedy should not be implied if it would frustrate the underlying purpose of the legislative scheme. On the other hand, when that remedy is necessary or at least helpful to the accomplishment of the statutory purpose, the Court is decidedly receptive to its implication under the statute.

Title IX * * * sought to accomplish two related, but nevertheless somewhat different, objectives. First, Congress wanted to avoid the use of federal resources to support discriminatory practices; second, it wanted to provide individual citizens effective protection against those practices. * * *

The first purpose is generally served by the statutory procedure for the termination of federal financial support for institutions engaged in discriminatory practices. That remedy is, however, severe and often may not provide an appropriate means of accomplishing the second purpose if merely an isolated violation has occurred. * * * The award of individual relief to a private litigant who has prosecuted her own suit is not only sensible but is also fully consistent with—and in some cases even necessary to—the orderly enforcement of the statute.

* * *

Fourth, the final inquiry suggested by *Cort* is whether implying a federal remedy is inappropriate because the subject matter involves an area basically of concern to the States. No such problem is raised by a prohibition against insidious discrimination of any sort, including that on the basis of sex.

Justice Rehnquist, joined by Justice Stewart, concurred separately. Justice White, joined by Justice Blackmun, dissented:

Because in my view the legislative history and statutory scheme show that Congress intended not to provide a new private cause of action, and because under our previous decisions such intent is controlling, I dissent.

* * *

Congress decided in Title IX, as it had in Title VI, to prohibit certain forms of discrimination by recipients of federal funds. * * * But, excepting post–Civil War Enactments dealing with racial discrimination in specified situations, these forms of discrimination by private entities had not previously been subject to individual redress under federal law, and Congress decided to reach such discrimination not by creating a new remedy for individuals, but by relying on the authority of the Federal Government to enforce the terms under which federal assistance would be provided. Whatever may be the wisdom of this approach to the problem of private discrimination, it was Congress' choice, not to be overridden by this Court.

Justice Powell also dissented:

I agree with Justice White that even under the standards articulated in our prior decisions, it is clear that no private action should be implied here. * * * But * * * the mode of analysis we have applied in the recent past cannot be squared with the doctrine of separation of powers. * * *

As the Legislative Branch, Congress * * * should determine when private parties are to be given causes of action under legislation it adopts. As countless statutes demonstrate, * * * Congress recognizes that the creation of private actions is a legislative function and frequently exercises it. When Congress chooses to provide a private civil remedy, federal courts should not assume the legislative role of creating such a remedy and thereby enlarge their jurisdiction.

In Franklin v. Gwinnett County Public Schools, 503 U.S. 60 (1992), the Court reaffirmed its conclusion in *Cannon* that an implied right of action existed under Title IX, and that the available remedies for violation of Title IX included an award of damages.

THOMPSON v. THOMPSON

Supreme Court of the United States, 1988.
484 U.S. 174.

JUSTICE MARSHALL delivered the opinion of the Court.

We granted certiorari in this case to determine whether the Parental Kidnaping Prevention Act of 1980, 28 U.S.C. § 1738A, furnishes an implied cause of action in federal court to determine which of two conflicting state custody decisions is valid.

I

The Parental Kidnaping Prevention Act (PKPA or Act) imposes a duty on the States to enforce a child custody determination entered by a court of a sister State if the determination is consistent with the provisions of the Act.[1] In order for a state court's custody decree to be consistent with the provisions of the Act, the State must have jurisdic-

---

1. Section 1738A reads in relevant part:

"(a) The appropriate authorities of every State shall enforce according to its terms, and shall not modify except as provided in subsection (f) of this section, any child custody determination made consistently with the provisions of this section by a court of another State.

. . .

"(c) A child custody determination made by a court of a State is consistent with the provisions of this section only if—

"(1) such court has jurisdiction under the law of such state; and

"(2) one of the following conditions is met:

"(A) such State (i) is the home State of the child on the date of the commencement of the proceeding, or (ii) had been the child's home State within six months before the date of the commencement of the proceeding and the child is absent from such State because of his removal or retention by a contestant or for other reasons, and a contestant continues to live in such State;

"(B)(i) it appears that no other State would have jurisdiction under subparagraph (A), and (ii) it is in the best interest of the child that a court of such State assume jurisdiction because (I) the child and his parents, or the child and at least one contestant, have a significant connection with such State other than mere physical presence in such State, and (II) there is available in such State substantial evidence concerning the child's present or future care, protection, training, and personal relationships;

"(C) the child is physically present in such State and (i) the child has been abandoned, or (ii) it is necessary in an emergency to protect the child because he has been subjected to or threatened with mistreatment or abuse;

"(D)(i) it appears that no other State would have jurisdiction under subparagraph (A), (B), (C), or (E), or another State has declined to exercise jurisdiction on the ground that the State whose jurisdiction is in issue is the more appropriate forum to determine the custody of the child, and (ii) it is in the best interest of the child that such court assume jurisdiction; or

"(E) the court has continuing jurisdiction pursuant to subsection (d) of this section.

"(d) The jurisdiction of a court of a State which has made a child custody determination consistently with the provisions of this section continues as long as the requirement of subsection (c)(1) of this section continues to be met and such State remains the residence of the child or of any contestant.

. . .

"(f) A court of a State may modify a determination of the custody of the same child made by a court of another State, if—

"(1) it has jurisdiction to make such a child custody determination; and

"(2) the court of the other State no longer has jurisdiction, or it has declined to exercise such jurisdiction to modify such determination.

"(g) A court of a State shall not exercise jurisdiction in any proceeding for a custo-

tion under its own local law and one of five conditions set out in § 1738A(c)(2) must be met. Briefly put, these conditions authorize the state court to enter a custody decree if the child's home is or recently has been in the State, if the child has no home State and it would be in the child's best interest for the State to assume jurisdiction, or if the child is present in the State and has been abandoned or abused. Once a State exercises jurisdiction consistently with the provisions of the Act, no other State may exercise concurrent jurisdiction over the custody dispute, § 1738A(g), even if it would have been empowered to take jurisdiction in the first instance,[2] and all States must accord full faith and credit to the first State's ensuing custody decree.

As the legislative scheme suggests, and as Congress explicitly specified, one of the chief purposes of the PKPA is to "avoid jurisdictional competition and conflict between State courts." This case arises out of a jurisdictional stalemate that came to pass notwithstanding the strictures of the Act. In July 1978, respondent Susan Clay (then Susan Thompson) filed a petition in Los Angeles Superior Court asking the court to dissolve her marriage to petitioner David Thompson and seeking custody of the couple's infant son, Matthew. The court initially awarded the parents joint custody of Matthew, but that arrangement became infeasible when respondent decided to move from California to Louisiana to take a job. The court then entered an order providing that respondent would have sole custody of Matthew once she left for Louisiana. This state of affairs was to remain in effect until the court investigator submitted a report on custody, after which the court intended to make a more studied custody determination.

Respondent and Matthew moved to Louisiana in December of 1980. Three months later, respondent filed a petition in Louisiana state court for enforcement of the California custody decree, judgment of custody, and modification of petitioner's visitation privileges. By order dated April 7, 1981, the Louisiana court granted the petition and awarded sole custody of Matthew to respondent. Two months later, however, the California court, having received and reviewed its investigator's report, entered an order awarding sole custody of Matthew to petitioner. Thus arose the current impasse.

In August 1983, petitioner brought this action in the District Court for the Central District of California. Petitioner requested an order declaring the Louisiana decree invalid and the California decree valid, and enjoining the enforcement of the Louisiana decree. Petitioner did not attempt to enforce the California decree in a Louisiana state court before he filed suit in federal court. The District Court granted respondent's motion to dismiss the complaint for lack of subject matter and

dy determination commenced during the pendency of a proceeding in a court of another State where such court of that other State is exercising jurisdiction consistently with the provisions of this section to make a custody determination."

2. The sole exception to this constraint occurs where the first State either has lost jurisdiction or has declined to exercise continuing jurisdiction. See § 1738A(f).

personal jurisdiction. The Court of Appeals for the Ninth Circuit affirmed. Although it disagreed with the District Court's jurisdictional analyses, the Court of Appeals affirmed the dismissal of the complaint on the ground that petitioner had failed to state a claim upon which relief could be granted. Canvassing the background, language, and legislative history of the PKPA, the Court of Appeals held that the Act does not create a private right of action in federal court to determine the validity of two conflicting custody decrees. We granted certiorari, and we now affirm.

II

In determining whether to infer a private cause of action from a federal statute, our focal point is Congress' intent in enacting the statute. As guides to discerning that intent, we have relied on the four factors set out in Cort v. Ash, see 422 U.S. 66, 78 (1975), along with other tools of statutory construction. Our focus on congressional intent does not mean that we require evidence that Members of Congress, in enacting the statute, actually had in mind the creation of a private cause of action. The implied cause of action doctrine would be a virtual dead letter were it limited to correcting drafting errors when Congress simply forgot to codify its evident intention to provide a cause of action. Rather, as an *implied* cause of action doctrine suggests, "the legislative history of a statute that does not expressly create or deny a private remedy will typically be equally silent or ambiguous on the question." Cannon v. University of Chicago, 441 U.S. 677, 694 (1979). We therefore have recognized that Congress' "intent may appear implicitly in the language or structure of the statute, or in the circumstances of its enactment." Transamerica Mortgage Advisors, Inc. v. Lewis, 444 U.S. 11, 18, (1979). The intent of Congress remains the ultimate issue, however, and "unless this congressional intent can be inferred from the language of the statute, the statutory structure, or some other source, the essential predicate for implication of a private remedy simply does not exist." Northwest Airlines, Inc. v. Transport Workers Union, 451 U.S. 77, 94 (1981). In this case, the essential predicate for implication of a private remedy plainly does not exist. None of the factors that have guided our inquiry in this difficult area points in favor of inferring a private cause of action. Indeed, the context, language, and legislative history of the PKPA all point sharply away from the remedy petitioner urges us to infer.

We examine initially the context of the PKPA with an eye toward determining Congress' perception of the law that it was shaping or reshaping. At the time Congress passed the PKPA, custody orders held a peculiar status under the full faith and credit doctrine, which requires each State to give effect to the judicial proceedings of other States, see U.S. Const., Art. IV, § 1; 28 U.S.C. § 1738. The anomaly traces to the fact that custody orders characteristically are subject to modification as required by the best interests of the child. As a consequence, some courts doubted whether custody orders were sufficiently "final" to trigger full faith and credit requirements and this Court had declined expressly to settle the question. Even if custody orders were subject to full faith and credit requirements, the Full Faith and Credit Clause obliges States only to accord the same force to judgments as would be accorded by the courts of the State in which the judgment was entered. Because courts entering custody orders generally retain the power to modify them, courts in other States were no less entitled to change the terms of custody according to their own views of the child's best interest. For these reasons, a parent who lost a custody battle in one State had an incentive to kidnap the child and move to another State to relitigate the issue. This circumstance contributed to widespread jurisdictional deadlocks like this one, and more importantly, to a national epidemic of parental kidnaping. * * *

A number of States joined in an effort to avoid these jurisdictional conflicts by adopting the Uniform Child Custody Jurisdiction Act (UCCJA), 9 U.L.A. §§ 1–28 (1979). The UCCJA prescribed uniform standards for deciding which State could make a custody determination and obligated enacting States to enforce the determination made by the State with proper jurisdiction. The project foundered, however, because a number of States refused to enact the UCCJA while others enacted it with modifications. In the absence of uniform national standards for allocating and enforcing custody determinations, noncustodial parents still had reason to snatch their children and petition the courts of any of a number of haven States for sole custody.

The context of the PKPA therefore suggests that the principal problem Congress was seeking to remedy was the inapplicability of full faith and credit requirements to custody determinations. Statements made when the Act was introduced in Congress forcefully confirm that suggestion. The sponsors and supporters of the Act continually indicated that the purpose of the PKPA was to provide for nationwide enforcement of custody orders made in accordance with the terms of the UCCJA. * * *

The significance of Congress' full faith and credit approach to the problem of child snatching is that the Full Faith and Credit Clause, in either its constitutional or statutory incarnations, does not give rise to an implied federal cause of action. Rather, the clause "only prescribes a rule by which courts, Federal and state, are to be guided when a question arises in the progress of a pending suit as to the faith and credit to be given by the court to the public acts, records, and judicial proceedings of a State other than that in which the court is sitting." Minnesota v. Northern Securities, 194 U.S. 48, 72 (1904). Because Congress' chief aim in enacting the PKPA was to extend the requirements of the Full Faith and Credit Clause to custody determinations, the Act is most naturally construed to furnish a rule of decision for courts to use in adjudicating custody disputes and not to create an entirely new cause of action. It thus is not compatible with the purpose and context of the legislative scheme to infer a private cause of action.

The language and placement of the statute reinforce this conclusion. The PKPA, 28 U.S.C. § 1738A, is an addendum to the full faith and credit statute, 28 U.S.C. § 1738. This fact alone is strong proof that the Act is intended to have the same operative effect as the full faith and credit statute. Similarly instructive is the heading to the PKPA: "Full faith and credit given to child custody determinations." As for the language of the Act, it is addressed entirely to States and state courts. Unlike statutes that explicitly confer a right on a specified class of persons, the PKPA is a mandate directed to state courts to respect the custody decrees of sister States. We agree with the Court of Appeals that "[i]t seems highly unlikely Congress would follow the pattern of the Full Faith and Credit Clause and section 1738 by structuring section 1738A as a command to state courts to give full faith and credit to the child custody decrees of other states, and yet, without comment, depart from the enforcement practice followed under the Clause and section 1738."

Finally, the legislative history of the PKPA provides unusually clear indication that Congress did not intend the federal courts to play the enforcement role that petitioner urges. Two passages are particularly revealing. The first of these is a colloquy between Congressmen Conyers and Fish. Congressman Fish had been the sponsor of a competing legislative proposal—ultimately rejected by Congress—that would have extended the District Courts' diversity jurisdiction to encompass actions for enforcement of state custody orders. In the following exchange, Congressman Conyers questioned Congressman Fish about the differences between his proposal and "the Bennett proposal," which was a precursor to the PKPA.

"Mr. Conyers: Could I just interject, the difference between the Bennett proposal and yours: You would have, enforcing the full faith and credit provision, the parties removed to a Federal court. Under the Bennett provision, his bill would impose the full faith and credit enforcement on the State court.

"It seems to me that that is a very important difference. The Federal jurisdiction, could it not, Mr. Fish, result in the Federal court litigating between two State court decrees; whereas, in an alternate method previously suggested, we would be imposing the responsibility of the enforcement upon the State court, and thereby reducing, it seems to me, the amount of litigation.

"Do you see any possible merit in leaving the enforcement at the State level, rather than introducing the Federal judiciary?

"Mr. Fish: Well, I really think that it is easier on the parent that has custody of the child to go to the nearest Federal district court. . . .

"Mr. Conyers: Of course you know that the Federal courts have no experience in these kinds of matters, and they would be moving into this other area. I am just thinking of the fact that they have [many areas of federal concern and] on the average of a 21–month docket, you would now be imposing custody matters which it seems

might be handled in the courts that normally handle that.... "
Parental Kidnaping: Hearing on H.R. 1290 Before the Subcommittee
on Crime of the House Committee on the Judiciary, 96th Cong., 2d
Sess., 14 (1980).

This exchange suggests that Congress considered and rejected an approach to the problem that would have resulted in a "[f]ederal court
litigating between two State court decrees."

The second noteworthy entry in the legislative history is a letter
from then Assistant Attorney General Patricia Wald to the Chairman of
the House Judiciary Committee, which was referred to extensively
during the debate on the PKPA. The letter outlined a variety of solutions
to the child-snatching problem. It specifically compared proposals that
would "grant jurisdiction to the federal courts to enforce state custody
decrees" with an approach, such as was proposed in the PKPA, that
would "impose on states a federal duty, under enumerated standards
derived generally from the UCCJA, to give full faith and credit to the
custody decrees of other states." Addendum to Joint Hearing 103. The
letter endorsed the full faith and credit approach that eventually was
codified in the PKPA. More importantly, it "strongly oppose[d] ... the
creation of a federal forum for resolving custody disputes." Like Congressman Conyers, the Justice Department reasoned that federal enforcement of state custody decrees would increase the workload of the
federal courts and entangle the federal judiciary in domestic relations
disputes with which they have little experience and which traditionally
have been the province of the States. That the views of the Justice
Department and Congressman Conyers prevailed, and that Congress
explicitly opted for a full faith and credit approach over reliance on
enforcement by the federal courts, provide strong evidence against
inferring a federal cause of action.

Petitioner discounts these portions of the legislative history. He
argues that the cause of action that he asks us to infer arises only in
cases of an actual conflict between two state custody decrees, and thus is
substantially narrower than the cause of action proposed by Congressman Fish and rejected by Congress. The Fish bill would have extended
federal-diversity jurisdiction to permit federal courts to enforce custody
orders in the first instance, before a second State had created a conflict
by refusing to do so. This cause of action admittedly is farther reaching
than that which we reject today. But the considerations that prompted
Congress to reject the Fish bill also militate against the more circumscribed role for the federal courts that petitioner proposes. Instructing
the federal courts to play Solomon where two state courts have issued
conflicting custody orders would entangle them in traditional state-law

questions that they have little expertise to resolve.[4] This is a cost that Congress made clear it did not want the PKPA to carry.[5]

In sum, the context, language, and history of the PKPA together make out a conclusive case against inferring a cause of action in federal court to determine which of two conflicting state custody decrees is valid. Against this impressive evidence, petitioner relies primarily on the argument that failure to infer a cause of action would render the PKPA nugatory. We note, as a preliminary response, that ultimate review remains available in this Court for truly intractable jurisdictional deadlocks. In addition, the unspoken presumption in petitioner's argument is that the States are either unable or unwilling to enforce the provisions of the Act. This is a presumption we are not prepared, and more importantly, Congress was not prepared, to indulge. State courts faithfully administer the Full Faith and Credit Clause every day; now that Congress has extended full faith and credit requirements to child custody orders, we can think of no reason why the courts' administration of federal law in custody disputes will be any less vigilant. Should state courts prove as obstinate as petitioner predicts, Congress may choose to revisit the issue. But any more radical approach to the problem will have to await further legislative action; we "will not engraft a remedy on a statute, no matter how salutary, that Congress did not intend to provide." California v. Sierra Club, 451 U.S. 287, 297 (1981). The judgment of the Court of Appeals is affirmed.

JUSTICE O'CONNOR, concurring in part and concurring in the judgment.

For the reasons expressed by JUSTICE SCALIA in Part I of his opinion in this case, I join all but the first full paragraph of Part II of the Court's opinion and judgment.

JUSTICE SCALIA, concurring in the judgment.

I write separately because in my view the Court is not being faithful to current doctrine in its dictum denying the necessity of an actual congressional intent to create a private right of action, and in referring

---

4. Petitioner argues that determining which of two conflicting custody decrees should be given effect under the PKPA would not require the federal courts to resolve the merits of custody disputes and thus would not offend the longstanding tradition of reserving domestic-relations matters to the States. Petitioner contends that the cause of action he champions would require federal courts only to analyze which of two States is given exclusive jurisdiction under a federal statute, a task for which the federal courts are well-qualified. We cannot agree with petitioner that making a jurisdictional determination under the PKPA would not involve the federal courts in substantive domestic-relations determinations. Under the Act, jurisdiction can turn on the child's "best interest" or on proof that the child has been abandoned or abused. See

§§ 1738A(c)(2)(B), (C), and (D). In fact, it would seem that the jurisdictional disputes that are sufficiently complicated as to have provoked conflicting state-court holdings are the most likely to require resolution of these traditional domestic-relations inquiries.

5. Moreover, petitioner's argument serves to underscore the extraordinary nature of the cause of action he urges us to infer. Petitioner essentially asks that federal district courts exercise appellate review of state-court judgments. This is an unusual cause of action for Congress to grant, either expressly or by implication. Petitioner's proposal is all the more remarkable in the present case, in which he seeks to have a California District Court enjoin enforcement of a Louisiana state-court judgment

to *Cort v. Ash,* as though its analysis had not been effectively overruled by our later opinions. I take the opportunity to suggest, at the same time, why in my view the law revision that the Court's dicta would undertake moves in precisely the wrong direction.

I

I agree that the Parental Kidnapping Prevention Act, does not create a private right of action in federal court to determine which of two conflicting child custody decrees is valid. I disagree, however, with the portion of the Court's analysis that flows from the following statement:

> "Our focus on congressional intent does not mean that we require evidence that members of Congress, in enacting the statute, actually had in mind the creation of a private cause of action."

disagreement

I am at a loss to imagine what congressional intent to create a private right of action might mean, if it does not mean that Congress had in mind the creation of a private right of action. Our precedents, moreover, give no indication of a secret meaning, but to the contrary seem to use "intent" to mean "intent." * * * We have said, to be sure, that the existence of intent may be inferred from various indicia; but that is worlds apart from today's delphic pronouncement that intent is required but need not really exist.

I also find misleading the Court's statement that, in determining the existence of a private right of action, "we have relied on the four factors set out in *Cort v. Ash,* . . . along with other tools of statutory construction." That is not an accurate description of what we have done. It could not be plainer that we effectively overruled the *Cort v. Ash* analysis in Touche Ross & Co. v. Redington, 442 U.S. 560, 575–76 (1979) and Transamerica Mortgage Advisors, Inc. v. Lewis, 444 U.S. 11, 18 (1979), converting one of its four factors (congressional intent) into *the determinative factor*, with the other three merely indicative of its presence or absence.

Finally, the Court's opinion conveys a misleading impression of current law when it proceeds to examine the "context" of the legislation for indication of intent to create a private right of action, after having found no such indication in either text or legislative history. In my view that examination is entirely superfluous, since context alone cannot suffice. We have held context to be relevant to our determination in only two cases—both of which involved statutory language that, in the judicial interpretation of related legislation prior to the subject statute's enactment, or of the same legislation prior to its reenactment, had been held to create private rights of action. Since this is not a case where such textual support exists, or even where there is any support in legislative history, the "context" of the enactment is immaterial.

Contrary to what the language of today's opinion suggests, this Court has long since abandoned its hospitable attitude towards implied rights of action. In the 23 years since Justice Clark's opinion for the court in J.I. Case Co. v. Borak, 377 U.S. 426 (1964), we have *twice* narrowed the test for implying a private right, first in *Cort v. Ash,* itself,

before the intermediate and supreme courts
of Louisiana even have had an opportunity
to review that judgment.

and then again in *Touche Ross & Co. v. Redington,* and *Transamerica Mortgage Advisers, Inc. v. Lewis,* supra. *See also Cannon v. University of Chicago,* 441 U.S. 677, 730 (1979) (Powell, J. dissenting) and *California v. Sierra Club,* 451 U.S. 287, 301 (1981) (REHNQUIST, J., joined by Burger, C.J., and Stewart and Powell, JJ., concurring). The recent history of our holdings is one of repeated rejection of claims of an implied right. This has been true in nine of eleven recent private right of action cases heard by this Court, including the instant case. The Court's opinion exaggerates the difficulty of establishing an implied right when it surmises that "[t]he implied cause of action doctrine would be a virtual dead letter were it limited to correcting drafting errors when Congress simply forgot to codify its evident intention to provide a cause of action." That statement rests upon the erroneous premise that one never implies anything except when he forgets to say it expressly. It is true, however, that the congressional intent test for implying private rights of action as it has evolved since the repudiation of *Cort v. Ash* is much more stringent than the Court's dicta in the present case suggest.

II

I have found the Court's dicta in the present case particularly provocative of response because it is my view that, if the current state of the law were to be changed, it should be moved in precisely the opposite direction—away from our current congressional intent test to the categorical position that federal private rights of action will not be implied.

As JUSTICE POWELL observed in his dissent in *Cannon,* supra 441 U.S., at 730–731:

> "Under Art. III, Congress alone has the responsibility for determining the jurisdiction of the lower federal courts. As the Legislative Branch, Congress also should determine when private parties are to be given causes of action under legislation it adopts. As countless statutes demonstrate, including Titles of the Civil Rights Act of 1964, Congress recognizes that the creation of private actions is a legislative function and frequently exercises it. When Congress chooses not to provide a private civil remedy, federal courts should not assume the legislative role of creating such a remedy and thereby enlarge their jurisdiction."

It is, to be sure, not beyond imagination that in a particular case Congress may intend to create a private right of action, but choose to do so by implication. One must wonder, however, whether the good produced by a judicial rule that accommodates this remote possibility is outweighed by its adverse effects. An enactment by implication cannot realistically be regarded as the product of the difficult lawmaking process our Constitution has prescribed. Committee reports, floor speeches, and even colloquies between congressmen, are frail substitute for bicameral vote upon the text of a law and its presentment to the President. See generally INS v. Chadha, 462 U.S. 919 (1983). It is at best dangerous to assume that all the necessary participants in the law-enactment process are acting upon the same unexpressed assumptions. And likewise dangerous to assume that, even with the utmost self-discipline, judges can prevent the implications they see from mirroring the policies they favor.

I suppose all this could be said, to a greater or lesser degree, of *all* implications that courts derive from statutory language, which are assuredly numerous as the stars. But as the likelihood that Congress would leave the matter to implication decreases, so does the justification for bearing the risk of distorting the constitutional process. A legislative act so significant, and so separable from the remainder of the statute, as the creation of a private right of action seems to me so implausibly left to implication that the risk should not be endured.

If we were to announce a flat rule that private rights of action will not be implied in statutes hereafter enacted, the risk that that course would occasionally frustrate genuine legislative intent would decrease from its current level of minimal to virtually zero. It would then be true that the opportunity for frustration of intent "would be a virtual dead letter[,] . . . limited to . . . drafting errors when Congress simply forgot to codify its * * * intention to provide a cause of action." I believe, moreover, that Congress would welcome the certainty that such a rule would produce. Surely conscientious legislators cannot relish the current situation, in which the existence or nonexistence of a private right of action depends upon which of the opposing legislative forces may have guessed right as to the implications the statute will be found to contain.

If a change is to be made, we should get out of the business of implied private rights of action altogether.

Notes

1. A unanimous Court in Karahalios v. National Federation of Federal Employees, 489 U.S. 527 (1989), rejected a claim that Title VII of the Civil Service Reform Act of 1978 confers an implied cause of action for breach of a duty of fair representation. Quoting *Thompson,* the Court concluded that unless "congressional intent can be inferred from the language of the statute, the statutory structure, or some other source, the essential predicate for implication of a private remedy does not exist." Id., at 532.

2. One post-*Thompson* court of appeals decision described the state of the law in the following manner: "Generally, federal courts should presume that Congress did not intend to replace viable state law with federal law.* * * Congress can overcome this presumption with a clear statement. And a compelling federal interest or need for uniformity can overcome the presumption even if Congress was silent." Kelvin Publishing Inc. v. Avon Printing Co., Inc., 72 F.3d 129 (6th Cir.1995). So described, can the doctrine of implied causes of action be reconciled with the principles of separation of powers?

3. According to one commentator, prior to Bush v. Lucas "[a] significant feature of the implied-remedies cases [was] the Court's disparate treatment of constitutional and statutory rights." Merrill, *The Common Law Powers of Federal Courts,* 52 U.Chi.L.Rev. 1, 48–49 (1985). Professor Merrill describes the pre-*Bush* differences in the following manner:

With respect to constitutional rights, the Court has declared that federal courts can decide whether or not to create an implied remedy in the manner of "a common law tribunal." * * * Thus, there seems to be a presumption in favor of an implied remedy, and the burden is on Congress to negate such a presumption.

With respect to statutory rights, however, the Court has recently formulated a quite different standard. * * * [T]he Court has now determined that the "central inquiry" in every case is whether "Congress intended to create, either expressly or by implication, a private cause of action." [quoting Touche Ross & Co. v. Redington, 442 U.S. 560, 575 (1979)]. Id. at 49.

Professor Merrill speculates, however, that the decision in *Bush* may "mark the beginning of a convergence in the Court's doctrine regarding constitutional and statutory remedies," because there "[t]he Court declined to recognize a *Bivens* remedy where Congress had erected an 'elaborate, comprehensive scheme' of administrative remedies. * * * In the context of statutory remedies, the Court has similarly relied on the existence of 'elaborate' congressional legislation to infer the absence of congressional intent to create an implied damages remedy." Id. at 49, n. 209.

4.   Assuming Professor Merrill's speculation is accurate, do you think it is a good idea for the Court to treat implied *constitutional* remedies and implied *statutory* remedies under the same standards? Merrill contends that "[t]he Court has not satisfactorily explained * * * why its power to create constitutional remedies ought to differ so drastically from its power to create statutory remedies." 52 U.Chi.L.Rev. at 49–50. Can you think of any satisfactory explanations for drawing the distinction?

Consider the following argument: There exist significant differences, in terms of judicial legitimacy, between recognition of an implied *constitutional* remedy on the one hand and an implied *statutory* remedy on the other. Under our accepted traditions and governing political theory, the judicial branch has the final say as to the meaning of the Constitution, and it is therefore appropriate for the Supreme Court to develop the remedies which, in its opinion, most effectively enforce the constraints of the Constitution. This is especially true in cases—such as *Bush*—in which individual liberties constitutionally insulated from majoritarian encroachment are at stake. The situation is totally different, however, when statutory rights are involved: in such cases, the Constitution has vested final decisionmaking authority in the democratically elected Congress, and the judiciary's legitimate role is therefore limited to ascertaining congressional intent. Thus, while it may make perfect sense for the Court, in deciding whether Congress intended an implied statutory cause of action, to take into account the existence of a congressionally-created "elaborate, comprehensive scheme" of administrative remedies, it is illogical for the existence of such a scheme to influence a judicial finding concerning the existence of an implied constitutional remedy.

Consider the following possible response to this argument: Such a view "would appear to beg the question: even if Congress does not 'create' constitutional rights and obligations, it doesn't necessarily follow that federal courts, rather than Congress, should be the primary agency to determine 'who may enforce them and in what manner.'" Merrill, supra, 52 U.Chi.

L.Rev. at 50, n. 213. Is this persuasive? What about the argument that, at least in cases, like *Bush,* in which individual liberty is sought to be protected against majoritarian incursion, it would make little sense to entrust the final say as to the method of enforcement of a constitutional right to a majoritarian branch of government?

To what extent is your view on this issue determined by your view of judicial review in constitutional cases? In other words, if one believes in a strict "originalist" view of the Constitution, meaning that the Constitution can legitimately be interpreted only in the exact manner in which the framers intended, is one more likely to accept Professor Merrill's view of implied constitutional remedies than if one believes that the Constitution must be freely interpreted in order to make it effective for modern conditions?

5. Consider the merits of the following argument: The entire concept of implied statutory rights constitutes a judicial violation of the separation-of-powers principle, because if and when Congress wishes to provide a private cause of action in a federal statute, it does so. Hence absence of an *explicit* private cause of action in the statute's text unambiguously establishes congressional intent *not* to provide such a remedy. Is this argument persuasive?

Consider also the following argument, made in M. Redish, The Federal Courts in the Political Order 39 (1991): "The facts that the damage remedy may be thought to foster the beneficial purposes served by the statute or that the legislature may not have foreseen the severity of the problem matter little because the damage remedy was not subjected to the formal requirements of the legislative process * * *."

See the counter-position articulated in Stewart & Sunstein, *Public Programs and Private Rights,* 95 Harv.L.Rev. 1193, 1229 (1982), characterizing such an argument as "[t]he formalist thesis", and describing it as "both incomplete and inconsistent," They argue:

> It is a commonplace that a lawmaker cannot anticipate all of the situations to which a law may be applied; as a result, he cannot specify in advance the legal consequences of all future events. Moreover, statutory language cannot be intelligently interpreted in isolation from the background understandings from which it arises. * * * Because the [formalist] thesis is inescapably agnostic with respect to the existence or possible content of a text's underlying purposes, the gaps cannot be filled by reasoned elaboration of any such purposes. The text must be taken to be an arbitrary expression of sovereign will. The thesis is therefore fatally incomplete, for it cannot generate solutions to unforeseen cases. Id. at 1229–30.

Does this reasoning adequately respond to the initial argument? Might one recognize the need for courts to fill in statutory gaps for specific situations not contemplated by Congress, yet nevertheless still deny judicial authority to infer private causes of action? Is it reasonable to characterize the arguable need for a private cause of action as a situation which a lawmaker cannot anticipate?

Stewart and Sunstein attempt to circumvent the separation-of-powers difficulty by contending: "When courts apply or interpret a statute, they must look to general background understandings as a basis for identifying the norms—sometimes hypostatized as 'legislative intent'—that underlie the statute." Id. at 1231. Professor Thomas Merrill responds, however: "The problem here is that the language and legislative history of a text are usually consistent with more than one asserted 'background understanding.' In selecting one 'background understanding' out of several possible candidates, the court may thus be substituting its own conception of public policy for that of the enacting body." Merrill, *The Common Law Powers of Federal Courts,* 52 U.Chi.L.Rev. 1, 38–39 (1985).

6. Professor Merrill, however, suggests that the Supreme Court has been "too restrictive with respect to judicially created remedies for statutory violations." Id. at 53. He contends that "if state-created remedies, together with whatever federal remedies are specified by Congress, are insufficient to preserve a specifically intended federal right, then it is appropriate for federal courts to create additional remedies that will preserve that right." Id. at 51. But in enacting the federal statute in the first place, wasn't it open to Congress to decide whether existing remedies are "adequate"? Isn't it always open to Congress to reconsider that issue if remedies once deemed adequate may no longer be so? In any event, isn't the key question, *who* determines adequacy? Is it appropriate for the judiciary to make a finding of inadequacy, when the legislative history demonstrates that Congress concluded that existing remedies were, in fact, adequate? Does the fact that Congress never considered the issue of adequacy necessarily increase the legitimacy of the judiciary's making of such a finding? Might one reasonably conclude that, if not a single member of Congress raised so obvious a possible need as the provision for a private cause of action, Congress did not deem existing remedies inadequate?

7. Is it accurate to characterize a statute that fails to provide a private cause of action as "silent" on the issue of the existence of a private remedy? Is it likely that if Congress decides not to provide such a remedy, it would place an explicit *prohibition* on the creation of such a remedy in the text of the statute?

8. Richard Posner has argued that "the elements of a positive economic theory of legislation are now in place," and that "[s]uch a theory would appear to have implications for how judges do, and perhaps for how they should, interpret legislative provisions * * *." Posner, *Economics, Politics, and the Reading of Statutes and the Constitution,* 49 U.Chi.L.Rev. 263 (1982).

Posner describes two major theories of the determination of the content of legislation: the "public interest" theory and the "interest group" theory. The "public interest" theory "conceives both the ideal and the actual function of legislation to be to increase economic welfare by correcting market failures such as crime and pollution." Id. at 265. The "interest group" theory "asserts that legislation is a good demanded and supplied much as other goods, so that legislative protection flows to those groups that derive the greatest value from it, regardless of overall social welfare, whether 'welfare' is defined as wealth, utility, or some other version of equity or justice."

Posner sees implications of these theories for the recognition of implied private rights of action:

> In deciding whether a statute creates a private cause of action for those injured by its violation, courts frequently ask whether the statute creates an adequate set of public remedies for its violation, so that implied private remedies are not needed to enforce it effectively. If courts find the statutory remedial scheme so incomplete or defective that private remedies are necessary to make it enforceable they are more likely to imply a private remedy. This result is defensible only under the public interest theory of legislation. The absence of effective remedies implies to the interest group theorist that the group that procured the legislation lacked the political muscle to get an effective statute, and it is not the business of the courts to give an interest group a benefit that was devised by the legislature. Under this view, to imply a private right of action is to intervene in the legislative struggle on the side of one interest group, overriding opposing groups that had managed to thwart the enactment of an effective statute. Id. at 278–79.

Do you agree that judicial implication of a private cause of action is legitimate under the "public interest" theory? In a democracy, which organ of government is supposed to make such determinations?

9. Is it correct to view judicial implication of private remedies for statutory violations as a form of federal common law? See Brown, *Of Activism and* Erie—*The Implication Doctrine's Implications for the Nature and Role of the Federal Courts,* 69 Iowa L.Rev. 617, 628 (1984), arguing that "[n]ot only does it make sense to view implication analysis and federal common-law analysis as one question, treating them as two can lead to anomalies." If implication analysis is so viewed, is it more legitimate, less legitimate, or equally as legitimate as the federal common law derived from *Clearfield Trust* [supra p. 877]?

10. Professor Brown asserts that "[i]t seems unlikely that the 'law of separation of powers' gives any clear answer to the question of the validity of implied rights of action", in part because of the absence of a specific constitutional prohibition. Brown, supra, 69 Iowa L.Rev. at 648. Assuming the absence of *specific* textual prohibition, does it necessarily follow that judicial implications are not inconsistent with the concept of separation of powers? Professor Brown finally concludes, however, that "[f]or those who take the separation of powers doctrine seriously, Justices Powell and Rehnquist have chosen the correct course." Id. at 654. Do you agree?

11. To what extent, if at all, does the approach to a finding of an implied cause of action in *Thompson* differ from the approach used in *Borak?* Would the Court that decided *Thompson* have decided *Borak* the way it was actually decided?

12. Do you think the Court in *Thompson* is strictly adhering to the test adopted in *Cort,* or is it modifying it? Could you fashion a persuasive argument that the Court is actually abandoning the *Cort* analysis? In light of

the Court's analysis in *Thompson,* how likely is it that private statutory remedies will be implied in the future?

13. 42 U.S.C. § 1983 creates a cause of action for damages against "every person" who "under color of" state or local law subjects "any citizen * * * to the deprivation of any rights, privileges or immunities, secured by the Constitution *and laws*" of the United States. In Maine v. Thiboutot, 448 U.S. 1 (1980), the Supreme Court ruled that section 1983 meant what it said and, therefore, provides a cause of action for violations of federal statutes as well as the Constitution. The Court in Wright v. Roanoke Redevelopment and Housing Authority, 479 U.S. 418, 423 (1987), ruled that a plaintiff alleging a violation of a federal statute will be permitted to sue under section 1983 unless (1) "the statute does not create enforceable rights, privileges, or immunities within the meaning of section 1983," or (2) "Congress has foreclosed such enforcement of the statute in the enactment itself." If a state actor is the defendant, then, section 1983 alters the determination of whether a cause of action exists for the violation of a federal statute.

In Wilder v. Virginia Hospital Association, 496 U.S. 498 (1990), the Court held that a group of health care providers could sue a Virginia agency under section 1983, for an alleged violation of the Medicaid Act. [42 U.S.C. § 1396]. The Medicaid statute regulates reimbursement rates for medical care provided to the financially needy. Writing for a bare majority, Justice Brennan indicated:

> This is a different inquiry than that involved in determining whether a private right of action can be implied from a particular statute. See, Cort v. Ash * * *. In the implied right of action cases, we employ the four-factor Cort test to determine "whether Congress intended to create the private remedy asserted" for the violation of the statutory rights. The test reflects a concern, grounded in separation of powers, that Congress rather than the courts controls the availability of remedies for violations of statutes. Because sec. 1983 provides an "alternative source of express congressional authorization of private suits", these separation of powers concerns are not present in a sec. 1983 case. Consistent with this view, we recognize an exception to the general rule that sec. 1983 provides a remedy for violation of federal statutory rights only when Congress has affirmatively withdrawn the remedy. Id. at 509.

14. The literature on the subject of implication analysis is extensive. In addition to the sources already cited, see generally Creswell, *The Separation of Powers Implications of Implied Rights of Action,* 34 Mercer L.Rev. 973 (1983); Frankel, *Implied Rights of Action,* 67 Va.L.Rev. 553 (1981); Greene, *Judicial Implication of Remedies for Federal Statutory Violations: The Separation of Powers Concerns,* 53 Temp.L.Q. 469 (1980); Hazen, *Implied Private Remedies Under Federal Statutes: Neither a Death Knell nor a Moratorium—Civil Rights, Securities Regulation, and Beyond,* 33 Vand. L.Rev. 1333 (1980); Pillai, *Negative Implication: The Demise of Private Rights of Action in the Federal Courts,* 47 U.Chi.L.Rev. 1 (1978); Steinberg, *Implied Rights of Action Under Federal Law,* 55 N.D.L.Rev. 33 (1979).

§ 6. ADMIRALTY

KOSSICK v. UNITED FRUIT CO.

Supreme Court of the United States, 1961.
365 U.S. 731.

MR. JUSTICE HARLAN delivered the opinion of the Court.

This case calls in question the propriety of a dismissal before trial of the first cause of action in a seaman's diversity complaint. Dismissal was on the ground that the allegations of the complaint are deficient by reason of the New York Statute of Frauds.

The allegations of the complaint, which for present purposes must be taken as true, are in substance as follows: Petitioner, while employed as chief steward on one of the vessels of respondent, United Fruit Company, suffered a thyroid ailment, not attributable to any fault of the respondent, but with respect to which it concededly had a legal duty to provide him with maintenance and cure. The Osceola, 189 U.S. 158. Respondent insisted that petitioner undergo treatment at a United States Public Health Service Hospital. Petitioner, however, considering on the basis of past experience that such treatment would prove unsatisfactory and inadequate, notified respondent that he wished to be treated by a private physician who had agreed to take care of him for $350, which amount petitioner insisted would be payable by the respondent in fulfillment of its obligation for maintenance and cure.

Respondent, the complaint continues, declined to accede to this course, but agreed that if petitioner would enter a Public Health Service Hospital (where he would receive free care) it would assume responsibility for all consequences of improper or inadequate treatment. Relying on that undertaking, and being unable himself to defray the cost of private treatment, petitioner underwent treatment at a Public Health Service Hospital. The Public Health Service Hospital and private physician alluded to were both located in New York.

Finally, it is alleged that by reason of the improper treatment received at such hospital, petitioner suffered grievous unwonted bodily injury, for which the respondent, because of its undertaking, is liable to the petitioner for damages in the amount of $250,000.

The District Court dismissed the complaint, considering that the agreement sued on was void under the New York Statute of Frauds. N.Y. Personal Property Law, § 31, par. 2, there being no allegation that such agreement was evidenced by any writing, 166 F.Supp. 571. The Court of Appeals affirmed. * * *

At the outset, we think it clear that the lower courts were correct in regarding the sufficiency of this complaint as depending entirely upon its averments respecting respondent's alleged agreement with petitioner. Liability here certainly cannot be founded on principles of *respondeat superior*. Nor is there anything in the authorities relating to a shipowner's duty to provide maintenance and cure which suggests that respondent was obliged, as a matter of law, to honor petitioner's preference for private treatment, or that it was responsible for the quality of petitioner's treatment at other hands which, for all that appears, may reasonably have been assumed to be well trained and careful.

With respect to respondent's alleged agreed undertaking, as the case comes to us, petitioner, on the one hand, does not deny the contract's invalidity under the New York Statute of Frauds, if state law controls, nor, on the other hand, can its validity well be doubted, though the alleged agreement was not reduced to writing, if maritime law controls. For it is an established rule of ancient respectability that oral contracts are generally regarded as valid by maritime law. In this posture of things two questions must be decided: *First*, was this alleged contract a maritime one? *Second*, if so, was it nevertheless of such a "local" nature that its validity should be judged by state law?

I.

The boundaries of admiralty jurisdiction over contracts—as opposed to torts or crimes—being conceptual rather than spatial, have always been difficult to draw. Precedent and usage are helpful insofar as they exclude or include certain common types of contract: a contract to repair, Endner v. Greco, D.C., 3 F. 411, or to insure a ship, Insurance Co. v. Dunham, 11 Wall. 1, is maritime but a contract to build a ship is not. People's Ferry Co. v. Beers, 20 How. 393. Without doubt a contract for hire either of a ship or of the sailors and officers to man her is within the admiralty jurisdiction. 1 Benedict, Admiralty, 366. A suit on a bond covering cargo on general average is governed by admiralty law, Cie Francaise de Navigation v. Bonnasse, 2 Cir., 19 F.2d 777, while an agreement to pay damages for another's breach of a maritime charter is not, Pacific Surety Co. v. Leatham & Smith T. & W. Co., 7 Cir., 151 F. 440. The closest analogy we have found to the case at hand is a contract for hospital services rendered an injured seaman in satisfaction of a shipowner's liability for maintenance and cure, which has been held to be a maritime contract. Methodist Episcopal Hospital v. Pacific Transport Co., D.C., 3 F.2d 508. The principle by reference to which the cases are supposed to fall on one side of the line or the other is an exceedingly broad one. "The only question is whether the transaction relates to ships and vessels, masters and mariners, as the agents of commerce * * *." I Benedict, Admiralty, 131.

* * * The Court of Appeals and respondent are certainly correct in considering that a shipowner's duty to provide maintenance and cure may ordinarily be discharged by the issuing of a master's certificate carrying admittance to a public hospital, and that a seaman who refuses such a certificate or the free treatment to which it entitles him without just cause, cannot further hold the shipowner to his duty to provide maintenance and cure. * * * But without countenancing petitioner's intemperate aspersions against Public Health Service Hospitals, and rejecting as we have the noncontractual grounds upon which he seeks to predicate liability here, we nevertheless are clear that the duty to afford

maintenance and cure is not simply and as a matter of law an obligation to provide for entrance to a public hospital. * * * Presumably if a seaman refuses to enter a public hospital or, having entered, if he leaves to undergo treatment elsewhere, he may recover the cost of such other treatment upon proof that "proper and adequate" cure was not available at such hospital. * * *

No matter how skeptical one may be that such a burden of proof could be sustained, or that an indigent seaman would be likely to risk losing his rights to free treatment on the chance of sustaining that burden, since we should not exclude that possibility as a matter of law as the Court of Appeals apparently did, it must follow that the contract here alleged should be regarded as an agreement on the part of petitioner to forego a course of treatment which might have involved respondent in some additional expense, in return for respondent's promise to make petitioner whole for any consequences of what appeared to it at the time as the cheaper alternative. * * * So viewed, we think that the alleged agreement was sufficiently related to peculiarly maritime concerns as not to put it, without more, beyond the pale of admiralty law.

This brings us, then, to the remaining, and what we believe is the controlling, question: whether the alleged contract, though maritime, is "maritime and local," Western Fuel Co. v. Garcia, 257 U.S. 233, 242, in the sense that the application of state law would not disturb the uniformity of maritime law, Southern Pacific Co. v. Jensen, 244 U.S. 205.

II.

Although the doctrines of the uniformity and supremacy of the maritime law have been vigorously criticized—see Southern Pacific Co. v. Jensen, supra, 244 U.S. at page 218 (dissenting opinion); Standard Dredging Corp. v. Murphy, 319 U.S. 306, 309—the qualifications and exceptions which this Court has built up to that imperative doctrine have not been considered notably more adequate. See Gilmore and Black, Admiralty, *passim*; Currie, Federalism and the Admiralty: "The Devil's Own Mess," 1960, The Supreme Court Review, 158; The Application of State Survival Statutes in Maritime Causes, 60 Col.L.Rev. 534. Perhaps the most often heard criticism of the supremacy doctrine is this: the fact that maritime law is—in a special sense at least, Romero v. International Terminal Co., 358 U.S. 354—federal law and therefore supreme by virtue of Article VI of the Constitution, carries with it the implication that wherever a maritime interest is involved, no matter how slight or marginal, it must displace a local interest, no matter how pressing and significant. But the process is surely rather one of accommodation, entirely familiar in many areas of overlapping state and federal concern, or a process somewhat analogous to the normal conflict of laws situation where two sovereignties assert divergent interests in a transaction as to which both have some concern. Surely the claim of federal supremacy is adequately served by the availability of a federal forum in the first instance and of review in this Court to provide assurance that the federal interest is correctly assessed and accorded due weight.

Thus, for instance, it blinks at reality to assert that because a longshoreman, living ashore and employed ashore by shoreside employers, performs seaman's work, the State with these contacts must lose all concern for the longshoreman's status and well-being. In allowing state wrongful death statutes, The Tungus v. Skovgaard, 358 U.S. 588; The Hamilton, 207 U.S. 398, and state survival of actions statutes, Just v. Chambers, 312 U.S. 383, respectively, to grant and to preserve a cause of action based ultimately on a wrong committed within the admiralty jurisdiction and defined by admiralty law, this Court has attempted an accommodation between a liability dependent primarily upon the breach of a maritime duty and state rules governing the extent of recovery for such breach. Since the chance of death foreclosing recovery is necessarily a fortuitous matter, and since the recovery afforded the disabled victim of an accident need be no less than that afforded to his family should he die, the intrusion of these state remedial systems need not bring with it any undesirable disuniformity in the scheme of maritime law.

* * *

Turning to the present case, we think that several considerations point to an accommodation favoring the application of maritime law. It must be remembered that we are dealing here with a contract, and therefore with obligations, by hypothesis, voluntarily undertaken, and not, as in the case of tort liability or public regulations, obligations imposed simply by virtue of the authority of the State or Federal Government. This fact in itself creates some presumption in favor of applying that law tending toward the validation of the alleged contract. * * * As we have already said, it is difficult to deny the essentially maritime character of this contract without either indulging in fine-spun distinctions in terms of what the transaction was *really* about, or simply denying the alleged agreement that characterization by reason of its novelty. Considering that sailors of any nationality may join a ship in any port, and that it is the clear duty of the ship to put into the first available port if this be necessary to provide prompt and adequate maintenance and cure to a seaman who falls ill during the voyage, The Iroquois, 194 U.S. 240, it seems to us that this is such a contract as may well have been made anywhere in the world, and that the validity of it should be judged by one law wherever it was made. On the other hand we are hard put to perceive how this contract was "peculiarly a matter of state and local concern," * * * unless it be New York's interest in not lending her courts to the accomplishment of fraud, something which appears to us insufficient to overcome the countervailing considerations. Finally, since the effect of the application of New York law here would be to invalidate the contract, this case can hardly be analogized to cases * * * where state law had the effect of supplementing the remedies available in admiralty for the vindication of maritime rights. Nor is Wilburn Boat Co. v. Fireman's Ins. Co., 348 U.S. 310, apposite. The application of state law in that case was justified by the Court on the basis of a lack of any provision of maritime law governing the matter there presented. A concurring opinion, id., 348 U.S. at page 321, and some commentators have preferred to refer the decision to the absurdity of applying maritime law to a contract of insurance on a houseboat established in the waters of a small artificial lake between Texas and Oklahoma. See Gilmore and Black, Admiralty 44–45. Needless to say the situation presented here has a more genuinely salty flavor than that.

In sum, were contracts of the kind alleged in this complaint known to be a normal phenomenon in maritime affairs, we think that there would be little room for argument in favor of allowing local law to control their validity. A different conclusion should not be reached either because such a contract may be thought to be a rarity, or because of any suspicion that this complaint may have been contrived to serve ulterior purposes. Without remotely intimating any view upon the merits of petitioner's claim, we conclude that it was error to apply the New York Statute of Frauds to bar proof of the agreement alleged in the complaint.

MR. JUSTICE FRANKFURTER, whom MR. JUSTICE STEWART joins, dissenting.

Certainly no decision in the Court's history has been the progenitor of more lasting dissatisfaction and disharmony within a particular area of the law than Southern Pacific Co. v. Jensen, 244 U.S. 205. The mischief it has caused was due to the uncritical application of the loose doctrine of observing "the very uniformity in respect to maritime matters which the Constitution was designed to establish." Southern Pacific Co. v. Jensen, supra, 244 U.S. at page 217. The looser a legal doctrine, like that of the duty to observe "the uniformity of maritime law," the more incumbent it is upon the judiciary to apply it with well-defined concreteness. It can fairly be said that the *Jensen* decision has not been treated as a favored doctrine. Quite the contrary. It has been steadily narrowed in application, as is strikingly illustrated by such a *tour de force* as our decision in Davis v. Department of Labor, 317 U.S. 249.

The Court today, relying as it does on *Jensen*, reinvigorates that "ill-starred decision." Davis v. Department of Labor, supra, 317 U.S. at page 259 (concurring opinion). The notion that if such a limited and essentially local transaction as the contract here in issue were allowed to be governed by a local statute of frauds it would "disturb the uniformity of maritime law" is, I respectfully submit, too abstract and doctrinaire a view of the true demands of maritime law. I would affirm the judgment below.

MR. JUSTICE WHITTAKER, dissenting.

Like the Court of Appeals, I think the oral contract here claimed by petitioner was not a maritime but a New York contract and barred by its statute of frauds. New York Personal Property Law, § 31, par. 2. I therefore dissent.

Notes

1. "It is a common notion that admiralty law is a special enclave of federal judge-made law. Under this view, federal courts create admiralty law without any authorization in statute. Although Congress may revise the courts' efforts, statutory enactments are often regarded as interstitial to the corpus of judge-made admiralty law. This federal common law sometimes displaces state law, usually in an unpredictable fashion because it is inherently difficult to determine the exact contours of federal judge-made law." Theis, *United States Admiralty Law as an Enclave of Federal Common Law*, 23 Tul. Mar. L. J. 73 (1998). A number of scholars have attacked the federal common law of admiralty as a violation of the *Erie* doctrine and the Rules of Decision Act. See, e.g., Martin H. Redish, Federal Jurisdiction: Tensions in the Allocation of Judicial Power 147 (2d ed. 1990); Young, *Preemption at Sea*, 67 Geo. Wash. L. Rev. 273 (1999). One commentator, while conceding that "the judge-made law of admiralty may appear strange and has few active supporters in practice on the academy," argues that its problems have been seriously exaggerated. Gutoff, *Federal Common Law and Congressional Delegation: A Reconceptualization of Admiralty*, 61 U. Pitt. L. Rev. 367 (2000).

2. In Southern Pacific Co. v. Jensen, 244 U.S. 205 (1917), the Court invalidated a New York State workmen's compensation award to the dependents of a deceased stevedore. In doing so, it held that "no such legislation is valid if it * * * works material prejudice to the characteristic features of the general maritime law or interferes with the proper harmony and uniformity of that law in its international and interstate relations." 244 U.S. at 216. See also Knickerbocker Ice Co. v. Stewart, 253 U.S. 149 (1920) (Congress may not delegate to the states power to create workmen's compensation for maritime workers). Note Justice Frankfurter's stinging attack on the *Jensen* decision in his *Kossick* dissent. The primary problem with the decision was that while it appeared to establish an unduly rigid pro-federal rule, to the extent it left room for exceptions to its rigid rule, it gave no guidance as to when such exceptions were to be drawn.

3. Compare *Kossick* to Wilburn Boat Co. v. Fireman's Fund Insurance Co., 348 U.S. 310 (1955), discussed in *Kossick*. The owners of a houseboat sued their insurer to recover for damage caused by fire incurred while the boat was situated on an inland lake between Texas and Oklahoma. While holding that the case fell within the federal maritime jurisdiction, the Court also noted that "[T]he National Government has left much regulatory power to the states." 348 U.S. at 313. Finding no applicable federal maritime principle, the Court chose to apply state law.

Do you agree with commentators who suggest that *Wilburn* "seems to make serious inroads on the uniformity of maritime law"? G. Gilmore & C. Black, The Law of Admiralty 49 (1975). Can a satisfactory distinction be drawn between *Kossick* and *Wilburn Boat*? How relevant is the fact that *Wilburn Boat* involved insurance, the regulation of which "has been primarily a state function since the States came into being"? 348 U.S. at 316. What other distinctions does the *Kossick* Court draw?

4. In Exxon Corp. v. Central Gulf Lines, Inc., 500 U.S. 603 (1991), the Supreme Court reversed its prior holding that recognized a *per se* exclusion of agency contracts from admiralty jurisdiction. "Rather than apply a rule excluding all or certain agency contracts from the realm of admiralty," the Court stated, "lower courts should look to the subject matter of the agency contract and determine whether the services performed under the contract were maritime in nature," citing *Kossick*. 500 U.S. at 612.

5. Should there be a federal common law of admiralty at all? What justifications are there for its existence? What costs are incurred because of it? In *Erie*, the Supreme Court made clear that, in most cases, no legitimate basis existed for the creation of substantive federal common law to regulate land-based commerce. Can regulation or private maritime commerce be distinguished? On the similarilty of admiralty to pre-*Erie* federal common law, see J. Pfander, Principles of Federal Jurisdiction 146 (2006). How relevant is the fact that Article III, Section 2 of the Constitution specifically includes within the federal judicial power cases in admiralty? The origins of this constitutional provision are generally thought to be unclear. See G. Gilmore & C. Black, supra at 18 n. 52; Stolz, *Pleasure Boating and Admiralty*: Erie *at Sea*, 51 Calif.L.Rev. 661, 669 (1963). But see D. Robertson, Admiralty and Federalism 18–27 (1970).

6. In *Jensen* the Court acknowledged as an exception to its principle of federal supremacy in admiralty the authority of the states to add to the federal maritime law a remedy for wrongful death. In The Harrisburg, 119 U.S. 199 (1886), the Court had denied the existence of such a federal remedy. However, in Moragne v. States Marine Lines, Inc., 398 U.S. 375 (1970), the Court overruled The Harrisburg, noting that "the rule against recovery for wrongful death is sharply out of keeping with the policies of modern American maritime law." 398 U.S. at 388.

7. Congress had already repudiated The Harrisburg for deaths occurring beyond the territorial waters of any state in 1920 when it enacted the Death on the High Seas Act, 46 U.S.C. § 761 (DOSHA). *Moragne*, however, involved an occurrence which took place within territorial waters, and DOSHA was therefore inapplicable. In reaching its decision the *Moragne* Court rejected the argument that by limiting DOSHA to the high seas, Congress had evidenced an intent to preclude judicial creation of federal remedies in territorial waters, reasoning that Congress' decision was based on the need to avoid abrogating state remedies which were then available in state waters. In Sea–Land Services, Inc. v. Gaudet, 414 U.S. 573 (1974), the Court held that awards under the *Moragne* remedy could include compensation for loss of support and services, funeral expenses and loss of society, but not for mental anguish. DOSHA did not allow a remedy for loss of society, but, like *Moragne*, *Gaudet* involved activity in territorial waters.

In Mobil Oil Corp. v. Higginbotham, 436 U.S. 618 (1978), involving an action for wrongful death on the high seas, the Court held that DOSHA preempted creation of any federal judicial remedy for loss of society in such an action. " * * * [W]e need not pause to evaluate the opposing policy arguments," said the Court. "Congress has struck the balance for us. It has limited survivors to recovery of their pecuniary losses." 436 U.S. at 623.

Chapter 18

SUPREME COURT APPELLATE
JURISDICTION

§ 1. METHOD OF OBTAINING APPELLATE REVIEW

Historically, the appellate jurisdiction of the United States Supreme Court has been divided between review by appeal and by writ of certiorari. At least for most of the twentieth century, final judgments from a state court were reviewable on appeal if the state court decision invalidated a federal statute or upheld a state statute against a federal constitutional challenge. Final judgments of a federal court could be appealed if the court invalidated a state statute or declared a federal statute unconstitutional in a civil action in which the federal government was a party. Otherwise, cases came to the United States Supreme Court by writ of certiorari. The principal distinction between the two bases for review is that appeal is had as a matter of right while certiorari lies purely within the Court's discretion. See generally R. Stern et al., Supreme Court Practice 54–55 (8th ed. 2002). One scholar has suggested that the Court's certiorari jurisdiction may give it too much discretion. Hartnett, *Questioning Certiorari: Some Reflections Seventy–Five Years After the Judges' Bill*, 100 Colum. L. Rev. 1643 (2000).

As a practical matter, however, the Court frequently treated even its appellate jurisdiction as discretionary. For example, appeals could be dismissed on the judgment below or summarily affirmed without full briefing or oral argument. See, e.g. Zucht v. King, 260 U.S. 174 (1922); and Report of the Study Group on the Caseload of the Supreme Court, 57 F.R.D. 573, 595–96 (1972) ("the discretionary-mandatory distinction between certiorari and appeal has been largely eroded.") A summary affirmance is of limited precedential value. The Supreme Court has held that "although summary dispositions are decisions on the merits, the decisions extend only to 'the precise issues presented and necessarily decided by those actions.'" Metromedia, Inc. v. City of San Diego, 453 U.S. 490 (1981) (quoting Mandel v. Bradley, 432 U.S. 173, 176 (1977)).

In 1988 Congress amended the statutes governing Supreme Court review to virtually eliminate mandatory appellate jurisdiction. 28 U.S.C.

§ 1257 was changed to make all state court judgments reviewable only by certiorari. Section 1254(2), which had permitted appeals as of right from federal court decisions holding state statutes unconstitutional, was altered to allow review only by certiorari. And section 1252 of Title 28, which had authorized some appeals from federal cases in which the United States was a party, was repealed. Appellate jurisdiction remains from the narrow category of cases heard by three-judge courts under 28 U.S.C. § 1253. [See Appendix B.] See also Boskey & Gressman, The Supreme Court Bids Farewell to Mandatory Appeals, 21 F.R.D. 81 (1988). Congress has also occasionally provided for mandatory appellate jurisdiction in specific statutes. See, e.g., 2 U.S.C. § 692(b) (providing for direct, expedited appeal to the Supreme Court for challenges to the constitutionality of the line-item veto).

§ 2. REVIEW OF "FINAL JUDGMENTS OR DECREES"

Read 28 U.S.C. § 1257 in Appendix B.

RADIO STATION WOW v. JOHNSON

Supreme Court of the United States, 1945.
326 U.S. 120.

MR. JUSTICE FRANKFURTER delivered the opinion of the Court.

This case concerns the relation of the Federal Communications Act, 48 Stat. 1064, 47 U.S.C. § 151 *et seq.*, to the power of a State to adjudicate conflicting claims to the property used by a licensed radio station. At the outset, however, our right to review the decision below is seriously challenged.

The facts relevant to the jurisdictional problem as well as to the main issues are these, summarized as briefly as accuracy permits. Petitioner, Woodmen of the World Life Insurance Society, a fraternal benefit association of Nebraska, owns radio station WOW. The Society leased this station for fifteen years to petitioner, Radio Station WOW, Inc., a Nebraska corporation formed to operate the station as lessee. After the Society and the lessee had jointly applied to the Federal Communications Commission for consent to transfer the station license, Johnson, the respondent, a member of the Society, filed this suit to have the lease and the assignment of the license set aside for fraud. While this suit was pending, the Federal Communications Commission consented to assignment of the license, and the Society transferred both the station properties and the license to the lessee. Thereafter the Society answered that "the Federal Communications Commission ... has and concedes that it has no jurisdiction over the subject matter of plaintiff's action, except jurisdiction to determine the transfer of the license to operate said radio station, which jurisdiction after full and complete showing and notwithstanding objections filed thereto, was exercised in the approval of the transfer of said license to the defendant Radio Station WOW, Inc. and further order to the Society to execute and perform the provisions of said lease by virtue of which the possession of said lease property has now been delivered to the lessee, all as more particularly herein found.'' Respondent's reply admitted "that the Federal Communications Commission has and concedes that it has no jurisdiction over the subject matter of plaintiff's action except jurisdiction to determine the transfer of the license to operate said radio station." The trial court found no fraud and dismissed the suit.

The Supreme Court of Nebraska, three Judges dissenting, reversed and entered judgment for respondent, directing that the lease and license be set aside and that the original position of the parties be restored as nearly as possible. The judgment further ordered that an accounting be had of the operation of the station by the lessee since it came into its possession and that the income less operating expenses be returned to the Society.[1] On motions for rehearing, the petitioners asserted that only the Federal Communications Commission and the federal courts had jurisdiction over the subject matter, not the Nebraska courts. These motions were denied in an opinion in which the Nebraska Supreme Court stated, "We conclude at the outset that the power to license a radio station, or to transfer, assign or annul such a license, is within the exclusive jurisdiction of the Federal Communications Commission.... The effect of our former opinion was to vacate the lease of the radio station and to order a return of the property to its former status, the question of the federal license being a question solely for the Federal Communications Commission. Our former opinion should be so construed." The claim that the Nebraska courts had no jurisdiction over the subject matter of the action was thus dealt with: "The fact that the property involved was used in a licensed business was an incident to the suit only. The answer of the defendants, heretofore quoted, squarely contradicts the position they now endeavor to assume. Their position is unsound on its merits and, in addition thereto, it was eliminated from the case by the pleadings they filed in their own behalf." Because of the importance of the contention that the State court's decision had invaded the domain of the Federal Communications Commission, we granted certiorari. In the order allowing certiorari we directed attention to the questions whether the judgment is a final one and whether the federal

1. The judgment directed "that said judgment of the district court be, and hereby, is, reversed and cause is remanded, with directions that the lease to the station, the lease to the space occupied by the station and the transfer of the license to operate the station be vacated and set aside; that the $25,000 of accounts turned over by the society to lessee be returned; that an accounting be had of the operation of the station by lessee since it took possession thereof on January 14, 1943, and that the income thereof less operating expenses be returned to the society; that the license to operate the station be returned and that lessee be directed to do all things necessary for that purpose; that generally everything be done to restore the parties to their original position prior to the entering into the lease; that all expenses had by the society in connection with the transfer of the station and license to the lessee and the expense had in connection with returning the same to the society pursuant hereto are to be paid by the lessee. It is further ordered and adjudged that all costs, both in this court and in the district court shall be paid by the defendants, except the Woodmen of the World Life Insurance Society, costs in this court being taxed at $ ___; for all of which execution is hereby awarded, and that a mandate issue accordingly."

questions raised by the petition for certiorari are properly presented by the record.

Since its establishment, it has been a marked characteristic of the federal judicial system not to permit an appeal until a litigation has been concluded in the court of first instance. See Heike v. United States, 217 U.S. 423; Cobbledick v. United States, 309 U.S. 323; Catlin v. United States, 324 U.S. 229. This requirement has the support of considerations generally applicable to good judicial administration. It avoids the mischief of economic waste and of delayed justice. Only in very few situations, where intermediate rulings may carry serious public consequences, has there been a departure from this requirement of finality for federal appellate jurisdiction. This prerequisite to review derives added force when the jurisdiction of this Court is invoked to upset the decision of a State court. Here we are in the realm of potential conflict between the courts of two different governments. And so, ever since 1789, Congress has granted this Court the power to intervene in State litigation only after "the highest court of a State in which a decision in the suit could be had" has rendered a "final judgment or decree." * * * This requirement is not one of those technicalities to be easily scorned. It is an important factor in the smooth working of our federal system.

But even so circumscribed a legal concept as appealable finality has a penumbral area. The problem of determining when a litigation is concluded so as to be "final" to permit review here arises in this case because, as has been indicated, the Nebraska Supreme Court not only directed a transfer of property, but also ordered an accounting of profits from such property. Considerations of English usage as well as those of judicial policy would readily justify an interpretation of "final judgment" so as to preclude reviewability here where anything further remains to be determined by a State court, no matter how dissociated from the only federal issue that has finally been adjudicated by the highest court of the State. Specifically, it might well be held that, even though definitive rulings on questions otherwise reviewable here have been made below, such rulings cannot be brought here for review if the State court calls for the ascertainment by a master or a lower State court of an account upon which a further decree is to be entered. See California National Bank v. Stateler, 171 U.S. 447, 449; Boskey, *Finality of State Court Judgments under the Federal Judicial Code* (1943) 43 Col.L.Rev. 1002, 1009; Robertson and Kirkham, Jurisdiction of the Supreme Court (1936) p. 58.

Unfortunately, however, the course of our jurisdictional history has not run as smoothly as such a mechanical rule would make it. To enforce it now, or to pronounce it for the future, would involve disregard of at least two controlling precedents, both of them expressing the views of unanimous courts and one of which has stood on our books for nearly a hundred years in an opinion carrying the authority, especially weighty in such matters, of Chief Justice Taney. Leaving to a footnote the details of a somewhat sinuous story,[2] it suffices to say that Forgay v. Conrad, 6

2. Most of the cases cited which involve an accounting have come from federal courts. In this category are Forgay v. Conrad, 6 How. 201; Thomson v. Dean, 7 Wall.

How. 201, and Carondelet Canal Co. v. Louisiana, 233 U.S. 362, found the requirement of finality to be satisfied by judgments the characteristics of which cannot be distinguished from those presented by the Nebraska decree. In short, the rationale of those cases is that a judgment directing immediate delivery of physical property is reviewable and is to be deemed dissociated from a provision for an accounting even though that is decreed in the same order. In effect, such a controversy is a multiple litigation allowing review of the adjudication which is concluded because it is independent of, and unaffected by, another litigation with which it happens to be entangled.

The presupposition in allowing such review is that the federal questions that could come here have been adjudicated by the State court, and that the accounting which remains to be taken could not remotely give rise to a federal question. * * * Since, by awarding an execution, the Nebraska Supreme Court directed immediate possession of the property to be transferred, the case comes squarely within Forgay v. Conrad, * * * and the challenge to our jurisdiction cannot be sustained.

* * *

[The opinions of JUSTICE DOUGLAS, concurring in the result, and JUSTICE JACKSON, dissenting on other grounds, are omitted. JUSTICE BLACK did not participate.]

Notes

1. What are the purposes behind the statutory requirement that the Supreme Court review only *final* decisions of the state's highest court? There is a similar statutorily imposed requirement of finality in 28 U.S.C. § 1291, governing appeals from the federal district court to the federal court of appeals. Generally, cases construing the two finality requirements are cited interchangeably. See Frank, *Requiem for the Final Judgment Rule*, 45 Tex.L.Rev. 292, 295 (1966); Note, *The Requirement of a Final Judgment or Decree for Supreme Court Review of State Courts*, 73 Yale L.J. 515 (1964). *Should* the two requirements be deemed identical, or should one be construed more narrowly than the other? Note that under 28 U.S.C. § 1292(b), courts of appeals may, in their discretion, review non-final orders of the district court when the district judge certifies "that such order involves a controlling question of law as to which there is substantial ground for

342; Winthrop Iron Co. v. Meeker, 109 U.S. 180; Keystone Manganese & Iron Co. v. Martin, 132 U.S. 91; McGourkey v. Toledo & Ohio Railway, 146 U.S. 536; Gulf Refining Co. v. United States, 269 U.S. 125.

In the *Forgay* case the court below set aside a conveyance of land and slaves and ordered a master to take an accounting of the rents and profits. This Court held the decree to be appealable since immediate delivery of the property was ordered although the decree was "not final, in the strict, technical sense of that term." The Court said of the lower court judgment that "the bill is retained merely for the purpose of adjusting the accounts referred to the master. In all other respects, the whole of the matters brought into controversy by the bill are finally disposed of as to all of the defendants." 6 How. 201, 203, 204. It was suggested that if appellants had to wait, they would be subjected to irremediable injury, for execution had been awarded. * * *

difference of opinion and that an immediate appeal from the order may materially advance the ultimate termination of the litigation * * *." No such statutory safety valve from the finality requirement exists for Supreme Court review of state court decisions. Does this fact influence your conclusion as to whether one of the two finality requirements should be interpreted more narrowly than the other? See Redish, *The Pragmatic Approach to Appealability in the Federal Courts*, 75 Colum.L.Rev. 89, 91–92 n. 19 (1975).

2. What was the Court's rationale for allowing Supreme Court review in *Radio Station WOW*? Does the decision represent an *interpretation* of the finality requirement, or an *exception* to it? If the latter, is it appropriate for the Supreme Court to create such exceptions? In answering, you should be aware that the Supreme Court had previously defined "final" judgments as those which "end * * * the litigation on the merits and leave * * * nothing for the lower court to do but execute the judgment." Catlin v. United States, 324 U.S. 229, 233 (1945). Whether an interpretation or an exception, does allowance of Supreme Court review in *Radio Station WOW* make sense, in light of the purposes of the finality requirement in section 1257?

3. The Court in *Radio Station WOW* relied on the well-known decision in Forgay v. Conrad, 47 U.S. (6 How.) 201 (1848). How does the Court in *Radio Station WOW* characterize the principle of that case? The Court has generally refused to apply the *Forgay* principle to condemnation proceedings, where only the amount of compensation remains to be determined. E.g., Washington ex rel. Grays Harbor Logging Co. v. Coats–Fordney Logging Co., 243 U.S. 251 (1917). Is there a logical basis for not allowing appeal to the Supreme Court until the damages are determined in such a proceeding?

4. The issue of finality is a federal question, to be determined by federal law. Therefore a state court's characterization of an order as final or not final is not binding on the Supreme Court. Department of Banking, State of Nebraska v. Pink, 317 U.S. 264 (1942). The same result holds in diversity cases. See, Budinich v. Becton Dickinson & Co., 486 U.S. 196 (1988).

COX BROADCASTING CORP. v. COHN

Supreme Court of the United States, 1975.
420 U.S. 469.

MR. JUSTICE WHITE delivered the opinion of the Court.

The issue before us in this case is whether, consistently with the First and Fourteenth Amendments, a State may extend a cause of action for damages for invasion of privacy caused by the publication of the name of a deceased rape victim which was publicly revealed in connection with the prosecution of the crime.

I

In August 1971, appellee's 17–year-old daughter was the victim of a rape and did not survive the incident. Six youths were soon indicted for murder and rape. Although there was substantial press coverage of the crime and of subsequent developments, the identity of the victim was not

disclosed pending trial, perhaps because of Ga.Code Ann. § 26–9901
(1972), which makes it a misdemeanor to publish or broadcast the name
or identity of a rape victim. In April 1972, some eight months later, the
six defendants appeared in court. Five pleaded guilty to rape or attempted rape, the charge of murder having been dropped. The guilty pleas
were accepted by the court, and the trial of the defendant pleading not
guilty was set for a later date.

In the course of the proceedings that day, appellant Wassell, a
reporter covering the incident for his employer, learned the name of the
victim from an examination of the indictments which were made available for his inspection in the courtroom. That the name of the victim
appears in the indictments and that the indictments were public records
available for inspection are not disputed. Later that day, Wassell broadcast over the facilities of station WSB–TV, a television station owned by
appellant Cox Broadcasting Corp., a news report concerning the court
proceedings. The report named the victim of the crime and was repeated
the following day.

In May 1972, appellee brought an action for money damages against
appellants, relying on § 26–9901 and claiming that his right to privacy
had been invaded by the television broadcasts giving the name of his
deceased daughter. Appellants admitted the broadcasts but claimed that
they were privileged under both state law and the First and Fourteenth
Amendments. The trial court, rejecting appellants' constitutional claims
and holding that the Georgia statute gave a civil remedy to those injured
by its violation, granted summary judgment to appellee as to liability,
with the determination of damages to await trial by jury.

On appeal, the Georgia Supreme Court, in its initial opinion, held
that the trial court had erred in construing § 26–9901 to extend a civil
cause of action for invasion of privacy and thus found it unnecessary to
consider the constitutionality of the statute. The court went on to rule,
however, that the complaint stated a cause of action "for the invasion of
the appellee's right of privacy, or for the tort of public disclosure"—a
"common law tort exist[ing] in this jurisdiction without the help of the
statute that the trial judge in this case relied on." Although the privacy
invaded was not that of the deceased victim, the father was held to have
stated a claim for invasion of his own privacy by reason of the publication of his daughter's name. The court explained, however, that liability
did not follow as a matter of law and that summary judgment was
improper; whether the public disclosure of the name actually invaded
appellee's "zone of privacy," and if so, to what extent, were issues to be
determined by the trier of fact. Also, "in formulating such an issue for
determination by the fact-finder, it is reasonable to require the appellee
to prove that the appellants invaded his privacy with wilful or negligent
disregard for the fact that reasonable men would find the invasion highly
offensive." The Georgia Supreme Court did agree with the trial court,
however, that the First and Fourteenth Amendments did not, as a
matter of law, require judgment for appellants. The court concurred with
the statement in Briscoe v. Reader's Digest Assn., Inc., 4 Cal.3d 529, 541

(1971), that "the rights guaranteed by the First Amendment do not require total abrogation of the right to privacy. The goals sought by each may be achieved with a minimum of intrusion upon the other."

Upon motion for rehearing the Georgia court countered the argument that the victim's name was a matter of public interest and could be published with impunity by relying on § 26–9901 as an authoritative declaration of state policy that the name of a rape victim was not a matter of public concern. This time the court felt compelled to determine the constitutionality of the statute and sustained it as a "legitimate limitation on the right of freedom of expression contained in the First Amendment." The court could discern "no public interest or general concern about the identity of the victim of such a crime as will make the right to disclose the identity of the victim rise to the level of First Amendment protection."

We conclude that the Court has jurisdiction, and reverse the judgment of the Georgia Supreme Court.

II

Appellants invoke the appellate jurisdiction of this Court under 28 U.S.C. § 1257(2) and, if that jurisdictional basis is found to be absent, through a petition for certiorari under 28 U.S.C. § 2103. Two questions concerning our jurisdiction must be resolved: (1) whether the constitutional validity of § 26–9901 was "drawn in question," with the Georgia Supreme Court upholding its validity, and (2) whether the decision from which this appeal has been taken is a "[f]inal judgment or decree."

* * *

B

Since 1789, Congress has granted this Court appellate jurisdiction with respect to state litigation only after the highest state court in which judgment could be had has rendered a "[f]inal judgment or decree." Title 28 U.S.C. § 1257 retains this limitation on our power to review cases coming from state courts. The Court has noted that "[c]onsiderations of English usage as well as those of judicial policy" would justify an interpretation of the final-judgment rule to preclude review "where anything further remains to be determined by a State court, no matter how dissociated from the only federal issue that has finally been adjudicated by the highest court of the State." Radio Station WOW, Inc. v. Johnson, 326 U.S. 120, 124 (1945). But the Court there observed that the rule had not been administered in such a mechanical fashion and that there were circumstances in which there has been "a departure from this requirement of finality for federal appellate jurisdiction." Ibid.

These circumstances were said to be "very few," ibid.; but as the cases have unfolded, the Court has recurringly encountered situations in which the highest court of a State has finally determined the federal issue present in a particular case, but in which there are further proceedings in the lower state courts to come. There are now at least four categories of such cases in which the Court has treated the decision on the federal issue as a final judgment for the purposes of 28 U.S.C. § 1257 and has taken jurisdiction without awaiting the completion of the additional proceedings anticipated in the lower state courts. In most, if not all, of the cases in these categories, these additional proceedings would not require the decision of other federal questions that might also require review by the Court at a later date,[6] and immediate rather than delayed review would be the best way to avoid "the mischief of economic waste and of delayed justice," Radio Station WOW, Inc. v. Johnson, supra, at 124, as well as precipitate interference with state litigation.[7] In the cases in the first two categories considered below, the federal issue would not be mooted or otherwise affected by the proceedings yet to be had because those proceedings have little substance, their outcome is certain, or they are wholly unrelated to the federal question. In the other two categories, however, the federal issue would be mooted if the petitioner or appellant seeking to bring the action here prevailed on the merits in the later state-court proceedings, but there is nevertheless sufficient justification for immediate review of the federal question finally determined in the state courts.

In the first category are those cases in which there are further proceedings—even entire trials—yet to occur in the state courts but where for one reason or another the federal issue is conclusive or the outcome of further proceedings preordained. In these circumstances, because the case is for all practical purposes concluded, the judgment of the state court on the federal issue is deemed final. In Mills v. Alabama, 384 U.S. 214 (1966), for example, a demurrer to a criminal complaint was sustained on federal constitutional grounds by a state trial court. The State Supreme Court reversed, remanding for jury trial. This Court

6. Eminent domain proceedings are of the type that may involve an interlocutory decision as to a federal question with another federal question to be decided later. "For in those cases the federal constitutional question embraces not only a taking, but a taking on payment of just compensation. A state judgment is not final unless it covers both aspects of that integral problem." North Dakota State Board of Pharmacy v. Snyder's Drug Stores, Inc., 414 U.S. 156, 163 (1973). See also Grays Harbor Co. v. Coats–Fordney Co., 243 U.S. 251, 256 (1917); Radio Station WOW, Inc. v. Johnson, 326 U.S. 120, 127 (1945).

7. Gillespie v. United States Steel Corp., 379 U.S. 148 (1964), arose in the federal courts and involved the requirement of 28 U.S.C. § 1291 that judgments of district courts be final if they are to be appealed to the courts of appeals. In the course of deciding that the judgment of the District Court in the case had been final, the Court indicated its approach to finality requirements:

"And our cases long have recognized that whether a ruling is 'final' within the meaning of § 1291 is frequently so close a question that decision of that issue either way can be supported with equally forceful arguments, and that it is impossible to devise a formula to resolve all marginal cases coming within what might well be called the 'twilight zone' of finality. Because of this difficulty this Court has held that the requirement of finality is to be given a 'practical rather than a technical construction.' Cohen v. Beneficial Industrial Loan Corp., [337 U.S. 541, 546]. See also Brown Shoe Co. v. United States, 370 U.S. 294, 306; Bronson v. Railroad Co., 2 Black 524, 531; Forgay v. Conrad, 6 How. 201, 203. Dickinson v. Petroleum Conversion Corp., 338 U.S. 507, 511, pointed out that in deciding the question of finality the most important competing considerations are 'the inconvenience and costs of piecemeal review on the one hand and the danger of denying justice by delay on the other.'" 379 U.S., at 152–153.

took jurisdiction on the reasoning that the appellant had no defense other than his federal claim and could not prevail at trial on the facts or any nonfederal ground. To dismiss the appeal "would not only be an inexcusable delay of the benefits Congress intended to grant by providing for appeal to this Court, but it would also result in a completely unnecessary waste of time and energy in judicial systems already troubled by delays due to congested dockets." Id., at 217–218 (footnote omitted).[8]

Second, there are cases such as *Radio Station WOW,* supra, and *Brady v. Maryland,* 373 U.S. 83 (1963), in which the federal issue, finally decided by the highest court in the State, will survive and require decision regardless of the outcome of future state-court proceedings. In *Radio Station WOW,* the Nebraska Supreme Court directed the transfer of the properties of a federally licensed radio station and ordered an accounting, rejecting the claim that the transfer order would interfere with the federal license. The federal issue was held reviewable here despite the pending accounting on the "presupposition ... that the federal questions that could come here have been adjudicated by the State court, and that the accounting which remains to be taken could not remotely give rise to a federal question ... that may later come here...." 326 U.S., at 127. The judgment rejecting the federal claim and directing the transfer was deemed "dissociated from a provision for an accounting even though that is decreed in the same order." Id., at 126. Nothing that could happen in the course of the accounting, short of settlement of the case, would foreclose or make unnecessary decision on the federal question. Older cases in the Court had reached the same result on similar facts. Carondelet Canal & Nav. Co. v. Louisiana, 233 U.S. 362 (1914); Forgay v. Conrad, 6 How. 201 (1848). In the latter case, the Court, in an opinion by Mr. Chief Justice Taney, stated that the Court had not understood the final-judgment rule "in this strict and technical sense, but has given [it] a more liberal, and, as we think, a more reasonable construction, and one more consonant to the intention of the legislature." Id., at 203.

In the third category are those situations where the federal claim has been finally decided, with further proceedings on the merits in the state courts to come, but in which later review of the federal issue cannot be had, whatever the ultimate outcome of the case. Thus, in these cases, if the party seeking interim review ultimately prevails on the merits, the federal issue will be mooted; if he were to lose on the merits, however, the governing state law would not permit him again to present his federal claims for review. The Court has taken jurisdiction in these circumstances prior to completion of the case in the state courts. * * *

8. Other cases from state courts where this Court's jurisdiction was sustained for similar reasons include: Organization for a Better Austin v. Keefe, 402 U.S. 415, 418 n., (1971); Construction Laborers v. Curry, 371 U.S. 542, 550–551 (1963); Pope v. Atlantic C.L.R. Co., 345 U.S. 379, 382 (1953); Richfield Oil Corp. v. State Board, 329 U.S. 69, 73–74 (1946). * * *

A recent decision in this category is North Dakota State Board of Pharmacy v. Snyder's Drug Stores, Inc., 414 U.S. 156 (1973), in which the Pharmacy Board rejected an application for a pharmacy operating permit relying on a state statute specifying ownership requirements which the applicant did not meet. The State Supreme Court held the statute unconstitutional and remanded the matter to the Board for further consideration of the application, freed from the constraints of the ownership statute. The Board brought the case here, claiming that the statute was constitutionally acceptable under modern cases. After reviewing the various circumstances under which the finality requirement has been deemed satisfied despite the fact that litigation had not terminated in the state courts, we entertained the case over claims that we had no jurisdiction. The federal issue would not survive the remand, whatever the result of the state administrative proceedings. The Board might deny the license on state-law grounds, thus foreclosing the federal issue, and the Court also ascertained that under state law the Board could not bring the federal issue here in the event the applicant satisfied the requirements of state law except for the invalidated ownership statute. Under these circumstances, the issue was ripe for review.[10]

Lastly, there are those situations where the federal issue has been finally decided in the state courts with further proceedings pending in which the party seeking review here might prevail on the merits on nonfederal grounds, thus rendering unnecessary review of the federal issue by this Court, and where reversal of the state court on the federal issue would be preclusive of any further litigation on the relevant cause of action rather than merely controlling the nature and character of, or determining the admissibility of evidence in, the state proceedings still to come. In these circumstances, if a refusal immediately to review the state-court decision might seriously erode federal policy, the Court has entertained and decided the federal issue, which itself has been finally determined by the state courts for purposes of the state litigation.

In Construction Laborers v. Curry, 371 U.S. 542 (1963), the state courts temporarily enjoined labor union picketing over claims that the National Labor Relations Board had exclusive jurisdiction of the controversy. The Court took jurisdiction for two independent reasons. First, the power of the state court to proceed in the face of the preemption claim was deemed an issue separable from the merits and ripe for review in this Court, particularly "when postponing review would seriously erode the national labor policy requiring the subject matter of respondents' cause to be heard by the ... Board, not by the state courts." Id.,

---

10. Cohen v. Beneficial Industrial Loan Corp., 337 U.S. 541 (1949), was a diversity action in the federal courts in the course of which there arose the question of the validity of a state statute requiring plaintiffs in stockholder suits to post security for costs as a prerequisite to bringing the action. The District Court held the state law inapplicable, the Court of Appeals reversed, and this Court, after granting certiorari, held that the issue of security for costs was separable from and independent of the merits and that if review were to be postponed until the termination of the litigation, "it will be too late effectively to review the present order, and the rights conferred by the statute, if it is applicable, will have been lost, probably irreparably." Id., at 546.

at 550. Second, the Court was convinced that in any event the union had no defense to the entry of a permanent injunction other than the preemption claim that had already been ruled on in the state courts. Hence the case was for all practical purposes concluded in the state tribunals.

In Mercantile National Bank v. Langdeau, 371 U.S. 555 (1963), two national banks were sued, along with others, in the courts of Travis County, Tex. The claim asserted was conspiracy to defraud an insurance company. The banks as a preliminary matter asserted that a special federal venue statute immunized them from suit in Travis County and that they could properly be sued only in another county. Although trial was still to be had and the banks might well prevail on the merits, the Court, relying on *Curry,* entertained the issue as a "separate and independent matter, anterior to the merits and not enmeshed in the factual and legal issues comprising the plaintiff's cause of action." Id., at 558. Moreover, it would serve the policy of the federal statute "to determine now in which state court appellants may be tried rather than to subject them ... to long and complex litigation which may all be for naught if consideration of the preliminary question of venue is postponed until the conclusion of the proceedings." Ibid.

Miami Herald Publishing Co. v. Tornillo, 418 U.S. 241 (1974), is the latest case in this category. There a candidate for public office sued a newspaper for refusing, allegedly contrary to a state statute, to carry his reply to the paper's editorial critical of his qualifications. The trial court held the act unconstitutional, denying both injunctive relief and damages. The State Supreme Court reversed, sustaining the statute against the challenge based upon the First and Fourteenth Amendments and remanding the case for a trial and appropriate relief, including damages. The newspaper brought the case here. We sustained our jurisdiction, relying on the principles elaborated in the *North Dakota* case and observing:

> "Whichever way we were to decide on the merits, it would be intolerable to leave unanswered under these circumstances, an important question of freedom of the press under the First Amendment; an uneasy and unsettled constitutional posture of § 104.38 could only further harm the operation of a free press. Mills v. Alabama, 384 U.S. 214, 221–222 (1966) (Douglas, J., concurring). See also Organization for a Better Austin v. Keefe, 402 U.S. 415, 418 n. (1971)." 418 U.S., at 247 n. 6.

In light of the prior cases, we conclude that we have jurisdiction to review the judgment of the Georgia Supreme Court rejecting the challenge under the First and Fourteenth Amendments to the state law authorizing damage suits against the press for publishing the name of a rape victim whose identity is revealed in the course of a public prosecution. The Georgia Supreme Court's judgment is plainly final on the federal issue and is not subject to further review in the state courts. Appellants will be liable for damages if the elements of the state cause of action are proved. They may prevail at trial on nonfederal grounds, it is true, but if the Georgia court erroneously upheld the statute, there should be no trial at all. Moreover, even if appellants prevailed at trial and made unnecessary further consideration of the constitutional question, there would remain in effect the unreviewed decision of the State Supreme Court that a civil action for publishing the name of a rape victim disclosed in a public judicial proceeding may go forward despite the First and Fourteenth Amendments. Delaying final decision of the First Amendment claim until after trial will "leave unanswered ... an important question of freedom of the press under the First Amendment," "an uneasy and unsettled constitutional posture [that] could only further harm the operation of a free press." *Tornillo,* supra, at 247 n. 6. On the other hand, if we now hold that the First and Fourteenth Amendments bar civil liability for broadcasting the victim's name, this litigation ends. Given these factors—that the litigation could be terminated by our decision on the merits and that a failure to decide the question now will leave the press in Georgia operating in the shadow of the civil and criminal sanctions of a rule of law and a statute the constitutionality of which is in serious doubt—we find that reaching the merits is consistent with the pragmatic approach that we have followed in the past in determining finality.

* * *

Mr. Justice Rehnquist, dissenting.

Because I am of the opinion that the decision which is the subject of this appeal is not a "final" judgment or decree, as that term is used in 28 U.S.C. § 1257, I would dismiss this appeal for want of jurisdiction.

* * *

I

The Court has taken what it terms a "pragmatic" approach to the finality problem presented in this case. In so doing, it has relied heavily on Gillespie v. United States Steel Corp., 379 U.S. 148 (1964). As the Court acknowledges, *Gillespie* involved 28 U.S.C. § 1291, which restricts the appellate jurisdiction of the federal courts of appeals to "final decisions of the district courts." Although acknowledging this distinction, the Court accords it no importance and adopts *Gillespie*'s approach without any consideration of whether the finality requirement for this Court's jurisdiction over a "judgment or decree" of a state court is grounded on more serious concerns than is the limitation of court of appeals jurisdiction to final "decisions" of the district courts. I believe that the underlying concerns are different, and that the difference counsels a more restrictive approach when § 1257 finality is at issue.

* * *

II

But quite apart from the considerations of federalism which counsel against an expansive reading of our jurisdiction under § 1257, the

Court's holding today enunciates a virtually formless exception to the finality requirement, one which differs in kind from those previously carved out. By contrast, Construction Laborers v. Curry, and Mercantile National Bank v. Langdeau, are based on the understandable principle that where the proper forum for trying the issue joined in the state courts depends on the resolution of the federal question raised on appeal, sound judicial administration requires that such a question be decided by this Court, if it is to be decided at all, sooner rather than later in the course of the litigation. Organization for a Better Austin v. Keefe, 402 U.S. 415 (1971), and Mills v. Alabama, 384 U.S. 214 (1966), rest on the premise that where as a practical matter the state litigation has been concluded by the decision of the State's highest court, the fact that in terms of state procedure the ruling is interlocutory should not bar a determination by this Court of the merits of the federal question.

Still other exceptions, as noted in the Court's opinion, have been made where the federal question decided by the highest court of the State is bound to survive and be presented for decision here regardless of the outcome of future state-court proceedings, *Radio Station WOW*, supra; Brady v. Maryland, 373 U.S. 83 (1963), and for the situation in which later review of the federal issue cannot be had, whatever the ultimate outcome of the subsequent proceedings directed by the highest court of the State, California v. Stewart, 384 U.S. 436 (1966) (decided with Miranda v. Arizona); North Dakota State Board of Pharmacy v. Snyder's Drug Stores, Inc., 414 U.S. 156 (1973). While the totality of these exceptions certainly indicates that the Court has been willing to impart to the language "final judgment or decree" a great deal of flexibility, each of them is arguably consistent with the intent of Congress in enacting § 1257, if not with the language it used, and each of them is relatively workable in practice.

To those established exceptions is now added one so formless that it cannot be paraphrased, but instead must be quoted:

> "Given these factors—that the litigation could be terminated by our decision on the merits and that a failure to decide the question now will leave the press in Georgia operating in the shadow of the civil and criminal sanctions of a rule of law and a statute the constitutionality of which is in serious doubt—we find that reaching the merits is consistent with the pragmatic approach that we have followed in the past in determining finality."

There are a number of difficulties with this test. One of them is the Court's willingness to look to the merits. It is not clear from the Court's opinion, however, exactly how great a look at the merits we are to take. On the one hand, the Court emphasizes that if we reverse the Supreme Court of Georgia the litigation will end, and it refers to cases in which the federal issue has been decided "arguably wrongly." On the other hand, it claims to look to the merits "only to the extent of determining that the issue is substantial." * * * If the latter is all the Court means, then the inquiry is no more extensive than is involved when we determine whether a case is appropriate for plenary consideration; but if no more is meant, our decision is just as likely to be a costly intermediate step in the litigation as it is to be the concluding event. If, on the other hand, the Court really intends its doctrine to reach only so far as cases in which our decision in all probability will terminate the litigation, then the Court is reversing the traditional sequence of judicial decisionmaking. Heretofore, it has generally been thought that a court first assumed jurisdiction of a case, and then went on to decide the merits of the questions it presented. But henceforth in determining our own jurisdiction we may be obliged to determine whether or not we agree with the merits of the decision of the highest court of a State.

* * *

But the greatest difficulty with the test enunciated today is that it totally abandons the principle that constitutional issues are too important to be decided save when absolutely necessary, and are to be avoided if there are grounds for decision of lesser dimension. The long line of cases which established this rule makes clear that it is a principle primarily designed, not to benefit the lower courts, or state-federal relations, but rather to safeguard this Court's own process of constitutional adjudication. * * * In this case there has yet to be an adjudication of liability against appellants, and unlike the appellant in Mills v. Alabama, they do not concede that they have no nonfederal defenses. Nonetheless, the Court rules on their constitutional defense. Far from eschewing a constitutional holding in advance of the necessity for one, the Court construes § 1257 so that it may virtually rush out and meet the prospective constitutional litigant as he approaches our doors.

[The separate concurring opinions of JUSTICES POWELL and DOUGLAS are omitted.]

Notes

1. Consider separately each of the four categories of appealability described in *Cox*. Are they interpretations of the finality requirement, or exceptions to it? Are they consistent with the policies behind the finality requirement in section 1257? Examine in particular the Court's fourth category. What limitations does the Court impose on use of that category? What is the purpose of those limitations?

2. Which of the four categories was the Court relying on in *Cox*? Do you think allowance of appeal in *Cox* represents an appropriate construction of section 1257's finality requirement?

3. How would *Cox* apply to the following factual situation: Defendants were prosecuted in state court on obscenity charges. The trial court dismissed the charges on the ground that the defendants had been discriminatorily prosecuted. The appellate court reversed and remanded for trial, and the state supreme court affirmed the appellate court's decision. The defendants seek review in the United States Supreme Court. If the Supreme Court decided to reverse the state court decision, there would of course be no

further prosecution. If, however, the Supreme Court were to affirm, then the defendants would have to be tried, at which time they could raise first amendment defenses to the obscenity charges. Is the state court's decision "final" under any of the categories recognized in *Cox*? See Flynt v. Ohio, 451 U.S. 619 (1981) (per curiam).

4. The Supreme Court interpreted the fourth *Cox* category broadly in Fort Wayne Books, Inc. v. Indiana, 489 U.S. 46 (1989). There the Court chose to review two cases from the Indiana state court system involving challenges to the use of a state Racketeering Influenced and Corrupt Organizations Activity [RICO] statute to prosecute "adult bookstores". In both cases, state appellate courts had reinstated the actions after lower courts held that the prosecutions would have violated the federal Constitution. The Supreme Court reviewed the cases on the merits even though there had yet to be a state conviction. Justice White's opinion for the majority addressed the finality question as follows:

> Before we address the merits of petitioner's claims, we must first consider our jurisdiction to hear this case. The relevant statute, 28 U.S.C.A. § 1257, limits our review to "[f]inal judgments or decrees" of the state courts. The general rule is that finality in the context of a criminal prosecution is defined by a judgment of conviction and the imposition of a sentence. Since neither is present here, we would usually conclude that the judgment below is not final and is hence unreviewable.
>
> There are, however, exceptions to the general rule. See Cox Broadcasting Corp. v. Cohn, 420 U.S. 469 (1975). *Cox* identified four categories of cases in which a judgment is final even though further proceedings are pending in the state courts. This case fits within the fourth category of cases described in *Cox:*
>
>> "[W]here the federal issue has been finally decided in the state courts with further proceedings pending in which the party seeking review here might prevail on the merits on nonfederal grounds, thus rendering unnecessary review of the federal issue by this Court, and where reversal of the state court on the federal issue would be preclusive of any further litigation on the relevant cause of action ... in the state court proceedings still to come. In these circumstances, if a refusal immediately to review the state-court decision might seriously erode federal policy, the Court has entertained and decided the federal issue, which itself has been finally determined by the state courts for the purposes of the state litigation."

This case clearly satisfies the first sentence of the above-cited passage: petitioner could well prevail on nonfederal grounds at a subsequent trial, and reversal of the Indiana Court of Appeals' holding would bar further prosecution on the RICO counts at issue here. Thus, the only debatable question is whether a refusal to grant immediate review of petitioner's claims "might seriously erode federal policy."

Adjudicating the proper scope of First Amendment protections has often been recognized by this Court as a "federal policy" that merits application of an exception to the general finality rule. See, e.g., National Socialist Party of America v. Skokie, 432 U.S. 43, 44 (1977) (*per curiam*); Miami Herald Publishing Co. v. Tornillo, 418 U.S. 241, 246–247 (1974). Petitioner's challenge to the constitutionality of the use of RICO statutes to criminalize patterns of obscenity offenses calls into question the legitimacy of the law enforcement practices of several States, as well as the Federal Government. Resolution of this important issue of the possible limits the First Amendment places on state and federal efforts to control organized crime should not remain in doubt. "Whichever way we were to decide on the merits, it would be intolerable to leave unanswered, under these circumstances, an important question of freedom of the press under the First Amendment; an uneasy and unsettled constitutional posture [of the state statute in question] could only further harm the operation of a free press." *Tornillo,* supra, at 247, n. 6.

Justice O'Connor contends that a contrary result is counseled here by our decision in Flynt v. Ohio, 451 U.S. 619 (1981) (*per curiam*). But as the Court understood it, "[t]he question presented for review [in *Flynt* was] whether on [that] record the decision to prosecute petitioners was selective or discriminatory *in violation of the Equal Protection Clause.*" *Flynt,* supra, at 622 (emphasis added). The claim before us in *Flynt* was not a First Amendment claim, but rather an equal protection claim (albeit one in the context of a trial raising First Amendment issues). As a result, *Cox's* fourth exception was held to be inapplicable in that case. Though the dissenters in *Flynt* disagreed with the premise of the Court's holding, and contended that that case was a First Amendment dispute that demanded immediate attention under *Cox's* fourth exception, the fact is that no Member of the Court concluded in *Flynt*— as Justice O'Connor does today—that where an important First Amendment claim *is* before us, the Court should refuse to invoke *Cox's* fourth exception and hold that we have no authority to address the issue.

Consequently, we conclude that this case, which clearly involves a First Amendment challenge to the facial validity of the Indiana RICO statute, merits review under the fourth exception recognized by *Cox* to the finality rule. Id. at 54–59.

5. For other cases applying and refining *Cox,* see National Socialist Party of America v. Village of Skokie, 432 U.S. 43 (1977); Southland Corp. v. Keating, 465 U.S. 1 (1984); Pennsylvania v. Ritchie, 480 U.S. 39 (1987); Florida v. Thomas, 532 U.S. 774 (2001); Johnson v. California, 541 U.S. 428 (2004); Kansas v. Marsh, 548 U.S. ___, 126 S.Ct 2516 (2006).

7. **Appeal From the State's Highest Court.** What do you suppose is the rationale for the requirement in section 1257 that appeal be from the highest state court? What if the losing party in the state trial or intermediate court has failed to invoke the jurisdiction of the highest state court prior to seeking review in the United States Supreme Court? Should it matter whether review in the highest court is as a matter of right or is discretionary with that court? What if the state's highest court refuses to review because of the losing party's failure to comply with applicable State procedural rules? Should it matter whether those procedural requirements are "reasonable" or not? What if the losing party in the intermediate court has unsuccessfully

sought discretionary review in the state's highest court? See generally R. Stern, et al., Supreme Court Practice 163–68 (8th ed. 2002).

8. **The Supreme Court's Original Jurisdiction.** The finality problem involved in *Cox* is of course irrelevant to the Supreme Court's original jurisdiction. This jurisdiction is defined in Article III, section 2, and 28 U.S.C.A. § 1251, both set out in Appendix B. Examine the constitutional language regarding the Court's original jurisdiction. Is it clear on its face the extent to which the Court's original and appellate jurisdictions are mutually exclusive? In other words, does the Constitution imply that the Court's original jurisdiction is to be *limited* to the types of cases enumerated there, or that the Court's original jurisdiction include *at least* those cases? Moreover, is the Constitution clear as to whether the Court's appellate jurisdiction may not extend also to the types of cases included within the Court's original jurisdiction? See Illinois v. City of Milwaukee, 406 U.S. 91 (1972), where the Court held that a case falling within its original jurisdiction could more appropriately be litigated in a district court. The Court cited its earlier statement that " 'our original jurisdiction should be invoked sparingly.' " Utah v. United States, 394 U.S. 89, 95 (1969), quoted in 406 U.S. at 93. "We incline to a sparing use of our original jurisdiction", the Court added, "so that our increasing duties with the appellate docket will not suffer." 406 U.S. at 93–94.

Look at 28 U.S.C. § 1251(a)(1). Note that Congress has chosen to render the Court's original jurisdiction exclusive under the circumstances so described. What do you suppose is the reason for this? In the *Milwaukee* case, the Court held that "the term 'States' as used in 28 U.S.C. § 1251(a)(1) should not be read to include their political subdivisions." 406 U.S. at 98. This was so, even though "there is no doubt that the actions of public entities might, under appropriate pleadings, be attributed to a State so as to warrant a joinder of the State as a party defendant." Id. at 94. Do you agree with the Court's exclusion of political subdivisions from the scope of section 1251(a)(1)? What are the competing considerations? If the Court excludes political subdivisions from the scope of section 1251(a)(1), and does not allow joinder of the state of Wisconsin as a defendant in the suit by Illinois (which it did not), how can the Court find that the suit against the political subdivision nevertheless falls within its *discretionary* original jurisdiction?

§ 3. THE "ADEQUATE AND INDEPENDENT STATE GROUND" DOCTRINE

MURDOCK v. CITY OF MEMPHIS, 87 U.S. (20 Wall.) 590 (1874): In the Act of February 5, 1867, 14 Stat. 385–387, Congress amended the Judiciary Act of 1789, 1 Stat. 73–95. One of those amendments eliminated from section 25 of that Act, dealing with Supreme Court review of state court final judgments, the section's last sentence which, following a description of the grounds on which review could be obtained, provided: "But no other error shall be assigned or regarded as a ground of reversal in any such case as aforesaid, than such as appears on the face of the record, and immediately respects the before mentioned questions of validity or construction of the said constitution, treaties, statutes, commissions, or authorities in dispute." It was argued that elimination of this sentence dictated that the Supreme Court "must, when it obtains jurisdiction of a case decided in a State court, by reason of one of the questions stated in the act, proceed to decide every other question which the case presents which may be found necessary to final judgment on the whole merits." The logic of the argument, described in the opinion for the Court by Justice Miller, was as follows:

*case =
"all of
the case"*

> 1.   That the Constitution declares that the judicial power of the United States shall extend to *cases* of a character which includes the questions described in the section, and that by the word *case*, is to be understood all of the case in which such a question arises.

> 2.   That by the fair construction of the act of 1789 in regard to removing those cases to this court, the power and the duty of re-examining the whole case would have been devolved on the court, but for the restriction of the clause omitted in the act of 1867; and that the same language is used in the latter act regulating the removal, but omitting the restrictive clause. And,

> 3.   That by re-enacting the statute in the same terms as to the removal of cases from the State courts, without the restrictive clause, Congress is to be understood as conferring the power which that clause prohibited. 87 U.S. at 618.

The Court concluded, however, that "[t]here is * * * no sufficient reason for holding that Congress, by repealing or omitting this restrictive clause, intended to enact affirmatively the thing which that clause had prohibited." Id. at 619. The Court noted that "if when we once get jurisdiction, everything in the case is open to re-examination, it follows that every case tried in any State court, from that of a justice of the peace to the highest court of the State, may be brought to this court for final decision on all the points involved in it." Id. at 628. "It is impossible to believe," Justice Miller added, "that Congress intended this result, and equally impossible that they did not see that it would follow if they intended to open the cases that are brought here under this section to re-examination on all the points involved in them and necessary to a final judgment on the merits." Id. at 629. After holding that the 1867 act did not accomplish this end, the Court found that "[t]his renders unnecessary a decision of the question whether, if Congress had conferred such authority, the act would have been constitutional." Id. at 633.

The Court then considered how to deal with state court decisions that turned on both federal and state grounds:

> But when it appears that the Federal question was decided erroneously against the plaintiff in error, we must then reverse the case undoubtedly, if there are no other issues decided in it than that. It often has occurred, however, and will occur again, that there are other points in the case than those of Federal cognizance, on which the judgment of the court below may stand; those points being of themselves sufficient to control the case.

Or it may be, that there are other issues in the case, but they are not of such controlling influence on the whole case that they are alone sufficient to support the judgment.

It may also be found that notwithstanding there are many other questions in the record of the case, the issue raised by the Federal question is such that its decision must dispose of the whole case.

In the two latter instances there can be no doubt that the judgment of the State court must be reversed, and under the new act this court can either render the final judgment or decree here, or remand the case to the State court for that purpose.

But in the other cases supposed, why should a judgment be reversed for an error in deciding the Federal question, if the same judgment must be rendered on the other points in the case? And why should this court reverse a judgment which is right on the whole record presented to us; or where the same judgment will be rendered by the court below, after they have corrected the error in the Federal question?

We have already laid down the rule that we are not authorized to examine these other questions for the purpose of deciding whether the State court ruled correctly on them or not. We are of opinion that on these subjects not embraced in the class of questions stated in the statute, we must receive the decision of the State courts as conclusive.

But when we find that the State court has decided the Federal question erroneously, then to prevent a useless and profitless reversal, which can do the plaintiff in error no good, and can only embarrass and delay the defendant, we must so far look into the remainder of the record as to see whether the decision of the Federal question alone is sufficient to dispose of the case, or to require its reversal; or on the other hand, whether there exist other matters in the record actually decided by the State court which are sufficient to maintain the judgment of that court, notwithstanding the error in deciding the Federal question. In the latter case the court would not be justified in reversing the judgment of the State court. Id. at 634–35.

In summary, the Court stated that "if it be found that the issue raised by the question of Federal law is of such controlling character that its correct decision is necessary to any final judgment in the case, or that there has been no decision by the State court of any other matter or issue which is sufficient to maintain the judgment of that court without regard to the Federal question, then this court will reverse the judgment of the State court, and will either render such judgment here as the State court should have rendered, or remand the case to that court, as the circumstances of the case may require." Id. at 636. A more recent Supreme Court decision characterized the doctrine in this manner: "where the judgment of a state court rests upon two grounds, one of which is federal and the other non-federal in character, our jurisdiction

o fed
ur if
un-fed?
dispositive. //

fails if the non-federal ground is independent of the federal ground and adequate to support the judgment." Fox Film Corp. v. Muller, 296 U.S. 207, 210 (1935).

HENRY v. MISSISSIPPI

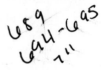

Supreme Court of the United States, 1965.
379 U.S. 443.

MR. JUSTICE BRENNAN delivered the opinion of the Court.

Petitioner was convicted of disturbing the peace, by indecent proposals to and offensive contact with an 18–year-old hitchhiker to whom he is said to have given a ride in his car. The trial judge charged the jury that "you cannot find the defendant guilty on the unsupported and uncorroborated testimony of the complainant alone." The petitioner's federal claim derives from the admission of a police officer's testimony, introduced to corroborate the hitchhiker's testimony. The Mississippi Supreme Court held that the officer's testimony was improperly admitted as the fruit of "an unlawful search and was in violation of § 23, Miss. Constitution 1890." The tainted evidence tended to substantiate the hitchhiker's testimony by showing its accuracy in a detail which could have been seen only by one inside the car. In particular, it showed that the right-hand ashtray of the car in which the incident took place was full of Dentyne chewing gum wrappers, and that the cigarette lighter did not function. The police officer testified that after petitioner's arrest he had returned to the petitioner's home and obtained the permission of petitioner's wife to look in petitioner's car. The wife provided the officer with the keys, with which the officer opened the car. He testified that he tried the lighter and it would not work, and also that the ashtray "was filled with red dentyne chewing gum wrappers."

The Mississippi Supreme Court first filed an opinion which reversed petitioner's conviction and remanded for a new trial. The court held that the wife's consent to the search of the car did not waive petitioner's constitutional rights, and noted that the "[t]estimony of the State's witness ... is, in effect, uncorroborated without the evidence disclosed by the inspection of defendant's automobile." Acting in the belief that petitioner had been represented by nonresident counsel unfamiliar with local procedure, the court reversed despite petitioner's failure to comply with the Mississippi requirement that an objection to illegal evidence be made at the time it is introduced. The court noted that petitioner had moved for a directed verdict at the close of the State's case, assigning as one ground the use of illegally obtained evidence; it did not mention petitioner's renewal of his motion at the close of all evidence.

testimony
uncorroborated
w/o search
of the car

After the first opinion was handed down, the State filed a Suggestion of Error, pointing out that petitioner was in fact represented at his trial by competent local counsel, as well as by out-of-state lawyers. Thereupon the Mississippi Supreme Court withdrew its first opinion and filed a new opinion in support of a judgment affirming petitioner's conviction. The new opinion is identical with the first save for the result, the statement that petitioner had local counsel, and the discussion of the effect of failure for whatever reason to make timely objection to the evidence. "In such circumstances, even if honest mistakes of counsel in respect to policy or strategy or otherwise occur, they are binding upon the client as a part of the hazards of courtroom battle." * * * We vacate the judgment of conviction and remand for a hearing on the question whether the petitioner is to be deemed to have knowingly waived decision of his federal claim when timely objection was not made to the admission of the illegally seized evidence.

It is, of course, a familiar principle that this Court will decline to review state court judgments which rest on independent and adequate state grounds, even where those judgments also decide federal questions. The principle applies not only in cases involving state substantive grounds, Murdock v. City of Memphis, 20 Wall. 590, but also in cases involving state procedural grounds. Compare Herb v. Pitcairn, 324 U.S. 117, 125–126, with Davis v. Wechsler, 263 U.S. 22. But it is important to distinguish between state substantive grounds and state procedural grounds. Where the ground involved is substantive, the determination of the federal question cannot affect the disposition if the state court decision on the state law question is allowed to stand. Under the view taken in *Murdock* of the statutes conferring appellate jurisdiction on this Court, we have no power to revise judgments on questions of state law. Thus, the adequate nonfederal ground doctrine is necessary to avoid advisory opinions.

These justifications have no application where the state ground is purely procedural. A procedural default which is held to bar challenge to a conviction in state courts, even on federal constitutional grounds, prevents implementation of the federal right. Accordingly, we have consistently held that the question of when and how defaults in compliance with state procedural rules can preclude our consideration of a federal question is itself a federal question. Cf. Lovell v. City of Griffin, 303 U.S. 444, 450. As Mr. Justice Holmes said:

> "When as here there is a plain assertion of federal rights in the lower court, local rules as to how far it shall be reviewed on appeal do not necessarily prevail.... Whether the right was denied or not given due recognition by the [state court] ... is a question as to which the plaintiffs are entitled to invoke our judgment." Love v. Griffith, 266 U.S. 32, 33–34.

* * * These cases settle the proposition that a litigant's procedural defaults in state proceedings do not prevent vindication of his federal rights unless the State's insistence on compliance with its procedural rule serves a legitimate state interest. In every case we must inquire whether the enforcement of a procedural forfeiture serves such a state interest. If it does not, the state procedural rule ought not be permitted to bar vindication of important federal rights.[3]

---

3. This will not lead inevitably to a plethora of attacks on the application of state procedural rules; where the state rule is a reasonable one and clearly announced to

The Mississippi rule requiring contemporaneous objection to the introduction of illegal evidence clearly does serve a legitimate state interest. By immediately apprising the trial judge of the objection, counsel gives the court the opportunity to conduct the trial without using the tainted evidence. If the objection is well taken the fruits of the illegal search may be excluded from jury consideration, and a reversal and new trial avoided. But on the record before us it appears that this purpose of the contemporaneous-objection rule may have been substantially served by petitioner's motion at the close of the State's evidence asking for a directed verdict because of the erroneous admission of the officer's testimony. For at this stage the trial judge could have called for elaboration of the search and seizure argument and, if persuaded, could have stricken the tainted testimony or have taken other appropriate corrective action. For example, if there was sufficient competent evidence without this testimony to go to the jury, the motion for a directed verdict might have been denied, and the case submitted to the jury with a properly worded appropriate cautionary instruction.[4] In these circumstances, the delay until the close of the State's case in presenting the objection cannot be said to have frustrated the State's interest in avoiding delay and waste of time in the disposition of the case. If this is so, and enforcement of the rule here would serve no substantial state interest, then settled principles would preclude treating the state ground as adequate; giving effect to the contemporaneous-objection rule for its own sake "would be to force resort to an arid ritual of meaningless form." Staub v. City of Baxley, 355 U.S. 313, 320; see also Wright v. Georgia, 373 U.S. 284, 289–291.[5]

We have no reason, however, to decide that question now or to express any view on the merits of petitioner's substantial constitutional claim. For even assuming that the making of the objection on the motion for a directed verdict satisfied the state interest served by the contemporaneous-objection rule, the record suggests a possibility that petitioner's counsel deliberately bypassed the opportunity to make timely objection

---

defendant and counsel, application of the waiver doctrine will yield the same result as that of the adequate nonfederal ground doctrine in the vast majority of cases.

4. The view of the Mississippi court in its first opinion seems to have been that there was insufficient evidence apart from the tainted testimony to support the conviction. Hence, appropriate corrective action as a matter of state law might have included granting petitioner's motion. We have not overlooked the fact that the first opinion remanded for a new trial, although the usual practice of the Mississippi Supreme Court where a motion for directed verdict, renewed at the close of all the evidence, is improperly denied is to dismiss the prosecution. The opinion offers no explanation of

the mandate; the answer is probably that the court refers only to the motion at the end of the State's case, and overlooks the fact that it was renewed at the close of all the evidence, just as it overlooks the presence of local counsel. If the motion were not renewed, the appellate court could not dismiss the prosecution. See Smith v. State, supra.

5. We do not rely on the principle that our review is not precluded when the state court has failed to exercise discretion to disregard the procedural default. See Williams v. Georgia, 349 U.S. 375. We read the second Mississippi Supreme Court opinion as holding that there is no such discretion where it appears that petitioner was represented by competent local counsel familiar with local procedure.

in the state court, and thus that the petitioner should be deemed to have forfeited his state court remedies. Although the Mississippi Supreme Court characterized the failure to object as an "honest mistake," * * * the State, in the brief in support of its Suggestion of Error in the Supreme Court of Mississippi asserted its willingness to agree that its Suggestion of Error "should not be sustained if either of the three counsel [for petitioner] participating in this trial would respond hereto with an affidavit that he did not know that at some point in a trial in criminal court in Mississippi that an objection to such testimony must have been made." * * * Another indication of possible waiver appears in an affidavit attached to the State's brief in this Court; there, the respondent asserted that one of petitioner's lawyers stood up as if to object to the officer's tainted testimony, and was pulled down by co-counsel. Again, this furnishes an insufficient basis for decision of the waiver questions at this time. But, together with the proposal in the Suggestion of Error, it is enough to justify an evidentiary hearing to determine whether petitioner "after consultation with competent counsel or otherwise, understandingly and knowingly forewent the privilege of seeking to vindicate his federal claims in the state courts, whether for strategic, tactical, or any other reasons that can fairly be described as the deliberate by-passing of state procedures. . . ." Fay v. Noia, 372 U.S. 391, 439.

The evidence suggests reasons for a strategic move. * * * [C]ounsel's deliberate choice of the strategy would amount to a waiver binding on petitioner and would preclude him from a decision on the merits of his federal claim either in the state courts or here. Although trial strategy adopted by counsel without prior consultation with an accused will not, where the circumstances are exceptional, preclude the accused from asserting constitutional claims, see Whitus v. Balkcom, 333 F.2d 496 (C.A. 5th Cir. 1964), we think that the deliberate bypassing by counsel of the contemporaneous-objection rule as a part of trial strategy would have that effect in this case.

Only evidence extrinsic to the record before us can establish the fact of waiver, and the State should have an opportunity to establish that fact. In comparable cases arising in federal courts we have vacated the judgments of conviction and remanded for a hearing, suspending the determination of the validity of the conviction pending the outcome of the hearing. See United States v. Shotwell Mfg. Co., 355 U.S. 233; Campbell v. United States, 365 U.S. 85. * * * We think a similar course is particularly desirable here, since a dismissal on the basis of an adequate state ground would not end this case; petitioner might still pursue vindication of his federal claim in a federal habeas corpus proceeding in which the procedural default will not alone preclude consideration of his claim, at least unless it is shown that petitioner deliberately bypassed the orderly procedure of the state courts. Fay v. Noia, supra, 372 U.S. at 438.

Of course, in so remanding we neither hold nor even remotely imply that the State must forgo insistence on its procedural requirements if it finds no waiver. Such a finding would only mean that petitioner could have a federal court apply settled principles to test the effectiveness of the procedural default to foreclose consideration of his constitutional claim. If it finds the procedural default ineffective, the federal court will itself decide the merits of his federal claim, at least so long as the state court does not wish to do so. By permitting the Mississippi courts to make an initial determination of waiver, we serve the causes of efficient administration of criminal justice, and of harmonious federal-state judicial relations. Such a disposition may make unnecessary the processing of the case through federal courts already laboring under congested dockets, or it may make unnecessary the relitigation in a federal forum of certain issues. See Townsend v. Sain, 372 U.S. 293, 312–319. The Court is not blind to the fact that the federal habeas corpus jurisdiction has been a source of irritation between the federal and state judiciaries. It has been suggested that this friction might be ameliorated if the States would look upon our decisions in Fay v. Noia, supra, and Townsend v. Sain, supra, as affording them an opportunity to provide state procedures, direct or collateral, for a full airing of federal claims. That prospect is better served by a remand than by relegating petitioner to his federal habeas remedy. Therefore, the judgment is vacated and the case if remanded to the Mississippi Supreme Court for further proceedings not inconsistent with this opinion.

Mr. Justice Harlan, with whom Mr. Justice Clark and Mr. Justice Stewart join, dissenting.

Flying banners of federalism, the Court's opinion actually raises storm signals of a most disquieting nature. While purporting to recognize the traditional principle that an adequate procedural, as well as substantive, state ground of decision bars direct review here of any federal claim asserted in the state litigation, the Court, unless I wholly misconceive what is lurking in today's opinion, portends a severe dilution, if not complete abolition, of the concept of "adequacy" as pertaining to state procedural grounds.

In making these preliminary observations I do not believe I am seeing ghosts. For I cannot account for the remand of this case in the face of what is a demonstrably adequate state procedural ground of decision by the Mississippi Supreme Court except as an early step toward extending in one way or another the doctrine of Fay v. Noia, 372 U.S. 391, to direct review. In that case, decided only two Terms ago, the Court turned its back on history (see dissenting opinion of this writer, at 448 *et seq.*), and did away with the adequate state ground doctrine in federal habeas corpus proceedings.

Believing that any step toward extending *Noia* to direct review should be flushed out and challenged at its earliest appearance in an opinion of this Court, I respectfully dissent.

I

The Mississippi Supreme Court did not base its ultimate decision upon petitioner's federal claim that his wife's consent could not validate an otherwise improper police search of the family car, but on the procedural ground that petitioner (who was represented by three experienced lawyers) had not objected at the time the fruits of this search were received in evidence. This Court now strongly implies, but does not decide (in view of its remand on the "waiver" issue) that enforcement of the State's "contemporaneous-objection" rule was inadequate as a state ground of decision because the petitioner's motion for a directed verdict of acquittal afforded the trial judge a satisfactory opportunity to take "appropriate corrective action" with reference to the allegedly inadmissible evidence. * * *

From the standpoint of the realities of the courtroom, I can only regard the Court's analysis as little short of fanciful. The petitioner's motion for a verdict could have provoked one of three courses of action by the trial judge, none of which can reasonably be considered as depriving the State's contemporaneous-objection rule of its capacity to serve as an adequate state ground.

1. The trial judge might have granted the directed verdict. But had this action been appropriate, the Supreme Court of Mississippi, in its first opinion, would have ordered the prosecution dismissed. Since it did not, and the matter is entirely one of state law, further speculation by this Court should be foreclosed.

2. The trial judge might have directed a mistrial. The State's interest in preventing mistrials through the contemporaneous-objection requirement is obvious.

3. The remaining course of action is the example given by the Court; the trial judge could have denied the motion for a directed verdict, but, *sua sponte*, called for elaboration of the argument, determined that the search of the automobile was unconstitutional, and given cautionary instructions to the jury to disregard the inadmissible evidence when the case was submitted to it.

The practical difficulties with this approach are manifestly sufficient to show a substantial state interest in their avoidance, and thus to show an "adequate" basis for the State's adherence to the contemporaneous-objection rule. * * *

As every trial lawyer of any experience knows, motions for directed verdicts are generally made as a matter of course at the close of the prosecution's case, and are generally denied without close consideration unless the case is clearly borderline. It is simply unrealistic in this context to have expected the trial judge to pick out the single vague sentence from the directed verdict motion and to have acted upon it with the refined imagination the Court would require of him. Henry's three lawyers apparently regarded the search and seizure claim as makeweight. They had not mentioned it earlier in the trial and gave no explanation for their laxity in raising it. And when they did mention it, they did so in a cursory and conclusional sentence placed in a secondary position in a directed verdict motion. The theory underlying the search and seizure argument—that a wife's freely given permission to search the family car is invalid—is subtle to say the very least, and as the matter was presented to the trial judge it would have been extraordinary had he caught it, or even realized that there was a serious problem to catch. But this is not all the Court would require of him. He must, in addition, realize that despite the inappropriateness of granting the directed verdict requested of him, he could partially serve the cause of the defense by taking it upon himself to frame and give cautionary instructions to the jury to disregard the evidence obtained as fruits of the search.[2]

Contrast with this the situation presented by a contemporaneous objection. The objection must necessarily be directed to the single question of admissibility; the judge must inevitably focus on it; there would be no doubt as to the appropriate form of relief, and the effect of the trial judge's decision would be immediate rather than remote. Usually the proper timing of an objection will force an elaboration of it. Had objection been made in this case during the officer's testimony about the search, it would have called forth of its own force the specific answer that the wife had given her permission and, in turn, the assertion that the permission was ineffective. The issue, in short, would have been advertently faced by the trial judge and the likelihood of achieving a correct result maximized.

Thus the state interest which so powerfully supports the contemporaneous-objection rule is that of maximizing correct decisions and concomitantly minimizing errors requiring mistrials and retrials. The alternative for the State is to reverse a trial judge who, from a long motion, fails to pick out and act with remarkable imagination upon a single vague sentence relating to admissibility of evidence long since admitted. * * *

There was no "appropriate corrective action" that could have realistically satisfied the purposes of the contemporaneous-objection rule. Without question the State had an interest in maintaining the integrity of its procedure, and thus without doubt reliance on the rule in question is "adequate" to bar direct review of petitioner's federal claim by this Court.

* * *

[The dissenting opinion of Justice Black is omitted.]

Notes

1. What is the rationale for the independent and adequate state ground doctrine? Consider the opinion of Justice Jackson in Herb v. Pitcairn, 324

---

2. Furthermore, even if counsel had fully elaborated the argument and had made it in the context of a motion to strike rather than a motion for directed verdict, the trial judge could properly have exercised his discretion (as the Mississippi Supreme Court did) and denied any relief. This power is recognized in trial judges in the federal system in order to prevent the "ambushing" of a trial through the withholding of an objection that should have been made when questionable evidence was first introduced. Federalism is turned upside down if it is denied to judges in the state systems. * * *

U.S. 117, 126 (1945): "We are not permitted to render an advisory opinion, and if the same judgment would be rendered by the state court after we corrected its views of federal laws, our review could amount to nothing more than an advisory opinion." Is this a proper justification for the doctrine? In what sense would a decision of the federal issue in such a situation constitute an advisory opinion? If this rationale is accepted, does it follow that the doctrine is constitutionally compelled? *Should* the doctrine be deemed to be required by the Constitution? Cf. Sandalow, Henry v. Mississippi *and the Adequate State Ground: Proposals for a Revised Doctrine*, 1965 Sup.Ct.Rev. 187, 201. For an argument that the adequate state ground doctrine is not constitutionally dictated, see Matasar & Bruch, *Procedural Common Law, Federal Jurisdictional Policy, and Abandonment of the Adequate and Independent State Grounds Doctrine*, 86 Colum.L.Rev. 1291, 1295–1315 (1986). For an argument that it *is* constitutionally mandated, see Fountaine, *Article III and the Adequate and Independent State Grounds Doctrine*, 48 Am.U.L.Rev. 1053 (1999).

The "advisory opinion" rationale has been criticized by commentators. See, e.g., Bice, Anderson *and the Adequate State Ground*, 45 S.Cal.L.Rev. 750, 765 (1972). See also Matasar & Bruch, supra, 86 Colum.L.Rev. at 1302–03: "Article III's core 'case or controversy' requirement of an actual dispute presented in an adverserial fashion is fully satisfied in federal appellate review of state court decisions containing adequate state grounds. This is so even if there is some likelihood that the judgment in the case might be unaffected by a reversal of the federal issues in the case. * * * [P]arties in this situation do not argue hypothetically on an appeal * * *." After *Henry*, what is the continued viability of this rationale? If the "advisory opinion" rationale is rejected, what other justification can be used to support the doctrine?

2.   The independent and adequate state ground doctrine is sometimes used in situations in which a state court cites two grounds to support its decision, one state and one federal, and sometimes used when the state court refuses to rule upon a claim under federal law because the litigant has failed to comply with applicable state procedural requirements. Which of these two categories describes the situation in *Henry*? Could the "advisory opinion" rationale be relied upon to justify the procedural form of the doctrine? Is it legitimate, as either a conceptual or practical matter, to draw a distinction between substantive and procedural forms of the doctrine? See Sandalow, supra, 1965, Sup.Ct.Rev. at 197; Wechsler, *The Appellate Jurisdiction of the Supreme Court: Reflections on the Law and the Logistics of Direct Review*, 34 Wash. & Lee L.Rev. 1043, 1054 (1977) (suggesting that *Henry* "suffers * * * from a patent analytical defect in the significance that it attaches to the distinction between substance and procedure. State court rulings on substantive state questions obviously may prevent 'the implementation' of a federal right no less than state procedural determinations * * *."). Professor Kermit Roosevelt argues that Supreme Court review is *more* justifiable in procedural cases such as *Henry*, because the limitations on review of state procedural rulings stem from § 1257 while the Court's inability to review state substantive law is a constitutional bar. Roosevelt, *Light from Dead Stars: The Procedural Adequate and Independent State Ground Reconsidered*, 103 Colum.L.Rev.1888 (2003).

3. Prior to the Supreme Court's decision in *Henry*, the Court had recognized several specific sub-categories of the adequate state ground doctrine. The classic illustration of an inadequate state ground is one that "is so certainly unfounded that it properly may be regarded as essentially arbitrary or a mere device to prevent a review of the decision upon the federal question." Enterprise Irrigation District v. Farmers' Mutual Canal Co., 243 U.S. 157, 164 (1917). By its terms, this test seems to suggest that a relevant inquiry is the possibility of an ulterior state court motive to avoid adjudication of the federal issue. Is this likely to be a workable test? What, if any, are the dangers in the use of such a standard? The Supreme Court has also recognized an exception to the adequate state ground doctrine when the state court's findings on the issue of state law lack "fair or substantial support". Is this inquiry different from the inquiry into the state court's motives? If so, is it preferable to it? Can it achieve much the same goal? Cf. NAACP v. Alabama ex rel. Flowers, 377 U.S. 288 (1964).

4. The Supreme Court has on occasion suggested that the adequate state ground doctrine will not apply when the state court has applied a "novel" state procedural rule. E.g., NAACP v. Alabama ex rel. Patterson, 357 U.S. 449, 457–458 (1958); Wright v. Georgia, 373 U.S. 284, 291 (1963). What do you suppose is the rationale for this exception? Is the exception wise?

5. It has also been suggested that an exception exists for state procedural rules which impose a heavy burden on the party attempting to exercise a federal right. See Brown v. Western Railway, 338 U.S. 294 (1949). But see Hill, *The Inadequate State Ground*, 65 Colum.L.Rev. 943, 952 (1965), suggesting that "what was said on the subject in *Brown* was unnecessary to the decision, and no holding before or after *Brown* supports the proposition." Whether or not this is so, *should* such an exception be recognized? What are the arguments for and against?

6. In addition, the Court has held that "where a State allows [constitutional challenges] to be raised at a late stage and be determined by its courts as a matter of discretion, we are not concluded from assuming jurisdiction and deciding whether the state court action in the particular circumstances is, in effect, an avoidance of the federal right." Williams v. Georgia, 349 U.S. 375, 383 (1955). Cf. Sullivan v. Little Hunting Park, Inc., 396 U.S. 229 (1969). Is this a valid exception to the adequate state ground doctrine? What do you think of the following argument as a justification for the exception: "[T]he existence of the [discretionary] power suggests that no vital state interest is at stake. If some deviations from regular procedure can be tolerated, a few more can hardly be seriously disruptive." Sandalow, supra, 1965 Sup.Ct.Rev. at 225.

7. How persuasive is Justice Harlan's response to Justice Brennan's intimation that the directed verdict procedure adequately served the same interest served by the contemporaneous objection rule?

8. Note that Justice Brennan in *Henry* does not actually determine whether failure to comply with the state's contemporaneous objection rule is an adequate state ground in this case. Instead, he remands for a finding as to whether there had been a knowing waiver by defense counsel. If, as Justice Brennan intimates, the state rule is—as a general matter—not an

adequate ground for refusal to hear the constitutional challenge to admission of evidence because the state's interest is adequately served by other means, why should it matter whether or not counsel knowingly waived his or her right to raise the objection contemporaneously?

9. Consider how the adequate state ground issues in the following cases should be decided in light of *Henry*:

(a) Defense counsel made an initial objection, on constitutional grounds, to the prosecutor's mode of questioning, repeated it immediately and reasserted it at the close of the questioning. The state court holds that there had been a waiver because counsel had stopped objecting during the bulk of the questioning, though the state law had at no time imposed such a requirement. See Douglas v. Alabama, 380 U.S. 415 (1965).

(b) A criminal defendant raises for the first time on appeal constitutional objection to the prosecutor's summation, though state law requires it to be made at trial. See Camp v. Arkansas, 404 U.S. 69, 92 S.Ct. 307 (1971) (per curiam).

(c) The state supreme court dismisses defendant's criminal appeal, because it was filed after the judgment had been pronounced orally but before the written judgment had been entered. See Monger v. Florida, 405 U.S. 958 (1972).

10. Is *Henry* still good law after Wainwright v. Sykes, 433 U.S. 72 (1977) [supra p. 637]? Recall that *Sykes* dealt with procedural forfeit in habeas cases. Under *Sykes*, federal courts cannot hear claims raised on habeas if a state court has found the claims barred by a procedural default. *Sykes* abandoned the earlier rule, announced in Fay v. Noia, 372 U.S. 391 (1963), that a procedural forfeit barred habeas review only if the petitioner had knowingly waived his right to present the claim to the state courts. Thus *Henry* applied on direct review the same rule that *Fay* applied to habeas review. Should *Sykes*'s abandonment of *Fay* be extended to *Henry*? See Lambrix v. Singletary, 520 U.S. 518 (1997) (noting similarities and differences between the adequate and independent grounds doctrine and the procedural forfeit rules).

11. *Henry* was cited in Michigan v. Tyler, 436 U.S. 499, 512 n. 7 (1978). The state argued that one of the defendants lacked standing to raise a fourth amendment challenge to certain searches and seizures. The state supreme court refused to consider the argument because the prosecutor failed to raise the objection at either the trial or appellate court stages. In accepting the state supreme court's refusal, the Court stated: "Failure to present a federal question in conformance with state procedure constitutes an adequate and independent ground of decision barring review in this Court, so long as the State has a legitimate interest in enforcing its procedural rule [citing *Henry*]. The petitioner does not claim that Michigan's procedural rule serves no legitimate purpose. Accordingly, we do not entertain the petitioner's standing claim which the state court refused to consider because of procedural default." What, if anything, does this decision suggest about the current viability of *Henry*? See Hill, *The Forfeiture of Constitutional Rights in Criminal Cases*, 78 Colum.L.Rev. 1050, 1052 (1978), referring to "[t]he seeming decay of the *Henry* doctrine". According to Hill, "[w]hile *Henry* was

invoked in a few early cases to strike down state procedural defaults, for the most part the case has been ignored, sometimes in situations where the *Henry* approach would probably have led to disallowance of the default. *Henry* has never been overruled, but seems relatively moribund." Another commentator has suggested that the Court may be treating *Henry* with "intelligent neglect." Wechsler, *The Appellate Jurisdiction of the Supreme Court: Reflections on the Law and the Logistics of Direct Review*, supra, 34 Wash. & Lee L.Rev. 1043, 1055 (1977). More recently, in Lee v. Kemna, 534 U.S. 362 (2002), a divided Court allowed a habeas petitioner to bring a procedurally defaulted claim, because the petitioner had "substantially, if imperfectly" complied with the state procedural rule. The majority explicitly eschewed reliance on *Henry*, but Justice Kennedy's dissent—joined by Justices Scalia and Thomas—accused the Court of applying "the flawed analytical approach" of *Henry*. Do you think the Court *should* disregard *Henry*? Are there differences between direct review by the Supreme Court and collateral review by lower federal courts that might justify different rules for procedural default? See Struve, *Direct and Collateral Federal Court Review of the Adequacy of State Procedural Rules*, 103 Colum.L.Rev. 243 (2003) (suggesting a more searching examination of state procedural rules on habeas than on direct review).

12. The Court dealt with the adequate state ground doctrine in Hathorn v. Lovorn, 457 U.S. 255 (1982). The case concerned the issue of "whether a state court may order implementation of a change in election procedure over objections that the change is subject to preclearance under § 5 of the Voting Rights Act of 1965." In the United States Supreme Court, it was argued that the decision of the Mississippi Supreme Court upholding most of the state statute altering election procedures was based on two independent and adequate state grounds: first, that the challenge based on the federal legislation was "law of the case", because it had been decided at an earlier stage of the same proceedings, and second, "that the Mississippi Supreme Court pretermitted consideration of the Voting Rights Act because petitioners' reliance upon the issue in a petition for rehearing was untimely." The Court rejected both contentions. In rejecting the first asserted ground, the Court reasoned that "[b]ecause we cannot review a state court judgment until it is final, a contrary rule [i.e., a rule recognizing the law-of-the-case doctrine as an adequate state ground] would insulate interlocutory state court rulings on important federal questions from our consideration." In regard to the second ground, the Court stated: "We have recognized that the failure to comply with a state procedural rule may constitute an independent and adequate state ground barring our review of a federal question. Our decisions, however, stress that a state procedural ground is not 'adequate' unless the procedural rule is 'strictly or regularly followed.' Barr v. City of Columbia, 378 U.S. 146, 149 (1964). State courts may not avoid deciding federal issues by invoking procedural rules that they do not apply evenhandedly to all similar claims. Even if we construe the Mississippi Supreme Court's denial of petitioners' petition for rehearing as the silent application of a procedural bar, we cannot conclude that the state court consistently relies upon this rule."

13. Does the adequate state ground doctrine apply in cases brought to the Supreme Court from the lower federal courts, as well as from the state

courts? Consider City of Mesquite v. Aladdin's Castle, Inc., 455 U.S. 283 (1982). The United States Court of Appeals for the Fifth Circuit had declared unconstitutional two sections of a licensing ordinance governing coin-operated amusement establishments. The court's first holding rested squarely on the due process clause of the fourteenth amendment. The court stated that its second holding rested on two provisions of the Texas Constitution, as well as the fourteenth amendment. The Supreme Court held that "[b]ecause Congress has limited our jurisdiction to review questions of state law, and because there is ambiguity in the Court of Appeals' second holding, we conclude that a remand for clarification of that holding is necessary."

14.   In a provocative article, two commentators referred to the adequate state ground doctrine as "a continuous pattern of unnecessary self-restraint". Matasar & Bruch, *Procedural Common Law, Federal Jurisdictional Policy, and Abandonment of the Adequate and Independent State Grounds Doctrine,* 86 Colum.L.Rev. 1291, 1292 (1986). Characterizing the doctrine as "judge-made common law, developed from erroneous constitutional jurisprudence, misconstructions of federal statutes, and historical happenstance", they assert that

> [t]he doctrine is fundamentally inconsistent with other common law jurisdictional doctrines, all of which insure Supreme Court review. That review is the safety net permitting the Court to make procedural common law without falling into unprincipled judicial usurpation of the legislative function.

* * *

The adequate and independent state grounds doctrine should be abandoned to insure federal court power to hear and decide all federal cases without concurrently diminishing the power of the states. Abandonment of the doctrine would reinforce state court autonomy to make state law, free state political processes from federal interference, and insure a continuing dialogue between state and federal courts that would promote cooperative federalism.

MICHIGAN v. LONG

Supreme Court of the United States, 1983.
463 U.S. 1032.

Justice O'Connor delivered the opinion of the Court.

In Terry v. Ohio, 392 U.S. 1 (1968), we upheld the validity of a protective search for weapons in the absence of probable cause to arrest because it is unreasonable to deny a police officer the right "to neutralize the threat of physical harm," when he possesses an articulable suspicion that an individual is armed and dangerous. We did not, however, expressly address whether such a protective search for weapons could extend to an area beyond the person in the absence of probable cause to arrest. In the present case, respondent David Long was convicted for possession of marijuana found by police in the passenger compartment and trunk of the automobile that he was driving. The police searched the passenger compartment because they had reason to believe that the vehicle contained weapons potentially dangerous to the officers. We hold that the protective search of the passenger compartment was reasonable under the principles articulated in *Terry* and other decisions of this Court. We also examine Long's argument that the decision below rests upon an adequate and independent state ground, and we decide in favor of our jurisdiction.

* * *

Before reaching the merits, we must consider Long's argument that we are without jurisdiction to decide this case because the decision below rests on an adequate and independent state ground. The court below referred twice to the state constitution in its opinion, but otherwise relied exclusively on federal law.[3] Long argues that the Michigan courts have provided greater protection from searches and seizures under the state constitution than is afforded under the Fourth Amendment, and the references to the state constitution therefore establish an adequate and independent ground for the decision below.

It is, of course, "incumbent upon this Court ... to ascertain for itself ... whether the asserted non-federal ground independently and adequately supports the judgment." Abie State Bank v. Bryan, 282 U.S. 765, 773 (1931). Although we have announced a number of principles in order to help us determine whether various forms of references to state law constitute adequate and independent state grounds,[4] we openly admit that we have thus far not developed a satisfying and consistent approach for resolving this vexing issue. In some instances, we have taken the strict view that if the ground of decision was at all unclear, we would dismiss the case. See, e.g., Lynch v. New York, 293 U.S. 52 (1934). In other instances, we have vacated, see, e.g., Minnesota v. National Tea Co., 309 U.S. 551 (1940), or continued a case, see e.g., Herb v. Pitcairn, 324 U.S. 117 (1945), in order to obtain clarification about the nature of a state court decision. See also California v. Krivda, 409 U.S. 33 (1972). In

---

3. On the first occasion, the court merely cited in a footnote both the state and federal constitutions. On the second occasion, at the conclusion of the opinion, the court stated: "We hold, therefore, that the deputies' search of the vehicle was proscribed by the Fourth Amendment to the United States Constitution and art. 1, § 11 of the Michigan Constitution."

4. For example, we have long recognized that "where the judgment of a state court rests upon two grounds, one of which is federal and the other non-federal in character, our jurisdiction fails if the non-federal ground is independent of the federal ground and adequate to support the judgment." Fox Film Corp. v. Muller, 296 U.S. 207, 210 (1935). We may review a state case decided on a federal ground even if it is clear that there was an available state ground for decision on which the state court could

properly have relied. Beecher v. Alabama, 389 U.S. 35, 37, n. 3 (1967). Also, if, in our view, the state court " 'felt compelled by what it understood to be federal constitutional considerations to construe ... its own law in the manner that it did,' " then we will not treat a normally adequate state ground as independent, and there will be no question about our jurisdiction. Delaware v. Prouse, 440 U.S. 648, 653 (1979) (quoting Zacchini v. Scripps–Howard Broadcasting Co., 433 U.S. 562, 568 (1977)). Finally, "where the non-federal ground is so interwoven with the [federal ground] as not to be an independent matter, or is not of sufficient breadth to sustain the judgment without any decision of the other, our jurisdiction is plain." Enterprise Irrigation District v. Farmers' Mutual Canal Company, 243 U.S. 157, 164 (1917).

more recent cases, we have ourselves examined state law to determine whether state courts have used federal law to guide their application of state law or to provide the actual basis for the decision that was reached. In Oregon v. Kennedy, 456 U.S. 667, 670–671 (1982), we rejected an invitation to remand to the state court for clarification even when the decision rested in part on a case from the state court, because we determined that the state case itself rested upon federal grounds. We added that "[e]ven if the case admitted of more doubt as to whether federal and state grounds for decision were intermixed, the fact that the state court relied to the extent it did on federal grounds requires us to reach the merits."

This ad hoc method of dealing with cases that involve possible adequate and independent state grounds is antithetical to the doctrinal consistency that is required when sensitive issues of federal-state relations are involved. Moreover, none of the various methods of disposition that we have employed thus far recommends itself as the preferred method that we should apply to the exclusion of others, and we therefore determine that it is appropriate to reexamine our treatment of this jurisdictional issue in order to achieve the consistency that is necessary.

The process of examining state law is unsatisfactory because it requires us to interpret state laws with which we are generally unfamiliar, and which often, as in this case, have not been discussed at length by the parties. Vacation and continuance for clarification have also been unsatisfactory both because of the delay and decrease in efficiency of judicial administration, see Dixon v. Duffy, 344 U.S. 143 (1952),[5] and, more important, because these methods of disposition place significant burdens on state courts to demonstrate the presence or absence of our jurisdiction. Finally, outright dismissal of cases is clearly not a panacea because it cannot be doubted that there is an important need for uniformity in federal law, and that this need goes unsatisfied when we fail to review an opinion that rests primarily upon federal grounds and where the *independence* of an alleged state ground is not apparent from the four corners of the opinion. We have long recognized that dismissal is inappropriate "where there is strong indication ... that the federal constitution as judicially construed controlled the decision below." National Tea Co., supra, 309 U.S., at 556 (1940).

Respect for the independence of state courts, as well as avoidance of rendering advisory opinions, have been the cornerstones of this Court's refusal to decide cases where there is an adequate and independent state ground. It is precisely because of this respect for state courts, and this desire to avoid advisory opinions, that we do not wish to continue to

---

5. Indeed, Dixon v. Duffy is also illustrative of another difficulty involved in our requiring state courts to reconsider their decisions for purposes of clarification. In *Dixon,* we continued the case on two occasions in order to obtain clarification, but none was forthcoming:

"[T]he California court advised petitioner's counsel informally that it doubted its jurisdiction to render such a determination." We then vacated the judgment of the state court, and remanded.

decide issues of state law that go beyond the opinion that we review, or to require state courts to reconsider cases to clarify the grounds of their decisions. Accordingly, when, as in this case, a state court decision fairly appears to rest primarily on federal law, or to be interwoven with the federal law, and when the adequacy and independence of any possible state law ground is not clear from the face of the opinion, we will accept as the most reasonable explanation that the state court decided the case the way it did because it believed that federal law required it to do so. If a state court chooses merely to rely on federal precedents as it would on the precedents of all other jurisdictions, then it need only make clear by a plain statement in its judgment or opinion that the federal cases are being used only for the purpose of guidance, and do not themselves compel the result that the court has reached. In this way, both justice and judicial administration will be greatly improved. If the state court decision indicates clearly and expressly that it is alternatively based on bona fide separate, adequate, and independent grounds, we, of course, will not undertake to review the decision.

This approach obviates in most instances the need to examine state law in order to decide the nature of the state court decision, and will at the same time avoid the danger of our rendering advisory opinions.[6] It also avoids the unsatisfactory and intrusive practice of requiring state courts to clarify their decisions to the satisfaction of this Court. We believe that such an approach will provide state judges with a clearer opportunity to develop state jurisprudence unimpeded by federal interference, and yet will preserve the integrity of federal law. "It is fundamental that state courts be left free and unfettered by us in interpreting their state constitutions. But it is equally important that ambiguous or obscure adjudications by state courts do not stand as barriers to a determination by this Court of the validity under the federal constitution of state action." *National Tea Co.,* supra, 309 U.S., at 557.

The principle that we will not review judgments of state courts that rest on adequate and independent state grounds is based, in part, on "the limitations of our own jurisdiction." Herb v. Pitcairn, 324 U.S. 117, 125 (1945).[7] The jurisdictional concern is that we not "render an advisory opinion, and if the same judgment would be rendered by the state court after we corrected its views of federal laws, our review could amount to nothing more than an advisory opinion." Id., at 126. Our requirement of a "plain statement" that a decision rests upon adequate

6. There may be certain circumstances in which clarification is necessary or desirable, and we will not be foreclosed from taking the appropriate action.

7. In Herb v. Pitcairn the Court also wrote that it was desirable that state courts "be asked rather than told what they have intended." It is clear that we have already departed from that view in those cases in which we have examined state law to determine whether a particular result was guided or compelled by federal law. Our decision

today departs further from *Herb* insofar as we disfavor further requests to state courts for clarification, and we require a clear and express statement that a decision rests on adequate and independent state grounds. However, the "plain statement" rule protects the integrity of state courts for the reasons discussed above. The preference for clarification expressed in *Herb* has failed to be a completely satisfactory means of protecting the state and federal interests that are involved.

and independent state grounds does not in any way authorize the rendering of advisory opinions. Rather, in determining, as we must, whether we have jurisdiction to review a case that is alleged to rest on adequate and independent state grounds, see Abie State Bank v. Bryan, 282 U.S., at 773, we merely assume that there are no such grounds when it is not clear from the opinion itself that the state court relied upon an adequate and independent state ground and when it fairly appears that the state court rested its decision primarily on federal law.[8]

Our review of the decision below under this framework leaves us unconvinced that it rests upon an independent state ground. Apart from its two citations to the state constitution, the court below relied *exclusively* on its understanding of *Terry* and other federal cases. Not a single state case was cited to support the state court's holding that the search of the passenger compartment was unconstitutional.[9] Indeed, the court declared that the search in this case was unconstitutional because "[t]he Court of Appeals erroneously applied the principles of Terry v. Ohio . . . to the search of the interior of the vehicle in this case." The references to the state constitution in no way indicate that the decision below rested on grounds in any way *independent* from the state court's interpretation of federal law. Even if we accept that the Michigan constitution has been interpreted to provide independent protection for certain rights also secured under the Fourth Amendment, it fairly appears in this case that the Michigan Supreme Court rested its decision primarily on federal law.

8. It is not unusual for us to employ certain presumptions in deciding jurisdictional issues. For instance, although the petitioner bears the burden of establishing our jurisdiction, Durley v. Mayo, 351 U.S. 277, 285 (1956), we have held that the party who alleges that a controversy before us has become moot has the "heavy burden" of establishing that we lack jurisdiction. County of Los Angeles v. Davis, 440 U.S. 625, 631 (1979). That is, we presume in those circumstances that we have jurisdiction until some party establishes that we do not for reasons of mootness.

We also note that the rule that we announce today was foreshadowed by our opinions in Delaware v. Prouse, supra, and Zacchini v. Scripps–Howard Broadcasting Co. In these cases, the state courts relied on both state and federal law. We determined that we had jurisdiction to decide the cases because our reading of the opinions led us to conclude that each court "felt compelled by what it understood to be federal constitutional considerations to construe and apply its own law in the manner it did." *Zacchini*, 433 U.S., at 568. In *Delaware,* we referred to prior state decisions that confirmed our understanding of the opinion in that case, but our primary focus was on the face of the opinion. In *Zacchini,* we relied

entirely on the syllabus and opinion of the state court.

In dissent, Justice Stevens proposes the novel view that this Court should never review a state court decision unless the Court wishes to vindicate a federal right that has been endangered. The rationale of the dissent is not restricted to cases where the decision is arguably supported by adequate and independent state grounds. Rather, Justice Stevens appears to believe that even if the decision below rests exclusively on federal grounds, this Court should not review the decision as long as there is no federal right that is endangered. * * *

9. At oral argument, Long argued that the state court relied on its decision in People v. Reed, 224 N.W.2d 867, cert. denied, 422 U.S. 1044 (1975). However, the court cited that case only in the context of a statement that the State did not seek to justify the search in this case "by reference to other exceptions to the warrant requirement." The court then noted that *Reed* held that " 'A warrantless search and seizure is unreasonable per se and violates the Fourth Amendment of the United States Constitution and art. 1, § 11 of the state constitution unless shown to be within one of the exceptions to the rule.' "

Rather than dismissing the case, or requiring that the state court reconsider its decision on our behalf solely because of a mere possibility that an adequate and independent ground supports the judgment, we find that we have jurisdiction in the absence of a plain statement that the decision below rested on an adequate and independent state ground. It appears to us that the state court "felt compelled by what it understood to be federal constitutional considerations to construe ... its own law in the manner it did." Zacchini v. Scripps–Howard Broadcasting Co., 433 U.S. 562, 568 (1977).[10]

* * *

The decision of the Michigan Supreme Court is reversed, and the case is remanded for further proceedings not inconsistent with this opinion.

* * *

JUSTICE BLACKMUN, concurring in part and concurring in the judgment.

* * * While I am satisfied that the Court has jurisdiction in this particular case, I do not join the Court * * * in fashioning a new presumption of jurisdiction over cases coming here from state courts. Although I agree with the Court that uniformity in federal criminal law

---

10. There is nothing unfair about requiring a plain statement of an independent state ground in this case. Even if we were to rest our decision on an evaluation of the state law relevant to Long's claim, as we have sometimes done in the past, our understanding of Michigan law would also result in our finding that we have jurisdiction to decide this case. Under state search and seizure law, a "higher standard" is imposed under art. 1, § 11 of the 1963 Michigan Constitution. See People v. Secrest, 321 N.W.2d 368, 369 (Mich. 1982). If, however, the item seized is, *inter alia*, a "narcotic drug ... seized by a peace officer outside the curtilage of any dwelling house in this state," art. 1, § 11 of the 1963 Michigan Constitution, then the seizure is governed by a standard identical to that imposed by the Fourth Amendment. See People v. Moore, 216 N.W.2d 770, 775 (Mich. 1974).

Long argues that under the current Michigan Public Health Code § 333.7107, the definition of a "narcotic" does not include marijuana. The difficulty with this argument is that Long fails to cite any authority for the proposition that the term "narcotic" as used in the Michigan constitution is dependent on current statutory definitions of that term. Indeed, it appears that just the opposite is true. The Michigan Supreme Court has held that constitutional provi-

sions are presumed "to be interpreted in accordance with existing laws and legal usages of the time" of the passage of the provision. Bacon v. Kent–Ottawa Authority, 92 N.W.2d 492, 497 (Mich. 1958). If the state legislature were able to change the interpretation of a constitutional provision by statute, then the legislature would have "the power of outright repeal of a duly-voted constitutional provision." Applying these principles, the Michigan courts have held that a statute passed subsequent to the applicable state constitutional provision is not relevant for interpreting its constitution, and that a definition in a legislative act pertains only to that act. At the time that the 1963 Michigan Constitution was enacted, it is clear that marijuana was considered a narcotic drug. Indeed, it appears that marijuana was considered a narcotic drug in Michigan until 1978, when it was removed from the narcotic classification. We would conclude that the seizure of marijuana in Michigan is not subject to analysis under any "higher standard" that may be imposed on the seizure of other items. In the light of our holding in Delaware v. Prouse, that an interpretation of state law in our view compelled by federal constitutional considerations is not an independent state ground, we would have jurisdiction to decide the case.

is desirable, I see little efficiency and an increased danger of advisory opinions in the Court's new approach.

* * *

JUSTICE STEVENS, dissenting.

The jurisprudential questions presented in this case are far more important than the question whether the Michigan police officer's search of respondent's car violated the Fourth Amendment. The case raises profoundly significant questions concerning the relationship between two sovereigns—the State of Michigan and the United States of America.

The Supreme Court of the State of Michigan expressly held "that the deputies' search of the vehicle was proscribed by the Fourth Amendment of the United States Constitution and *art. 1, § 11 of the Michigan Constitution.*" The state law ground is clearly adequate to support the judgment, but the question whether it is independent of the Michigan Supreme Court's understanding of federal law is more difficult. Four possible ways of resolving that question present themselves: (1) asking the Michigan Supreme Court directly, (2) attempting to infer from all possible sources of state law what the Michigan Supreme Court meant, (3) presuming that adequate state grounds are independent unless it clearly appears otherwise, or (4) presuming that adequate state grounds are *not* independent unless it clearly appears otherwise. This Court has, on different occasions, employed each of the first three approaches; never until today has it even hinted at the fourth. In order to "achieve the consistency that is necessary," the Court today undertakes a reexamination of all the possibilities. It rejects the first approach as inefficient and unduly burdensome for state courts, and rejects the second approach as an inappropriate expenditure of our resources. Ibid. Although I find both of those decisions defensible in themselves, I cannot accept the Court's decision to choose the fourth approach over the third—to presume that adequate state grounds are intended to be dependent on federal law unless the record plainly shows otherwise. I must therefore dissent.

If we reject the intermediate approaches, we are left with a choice between two presumptions: one in favor of our taking jurisdiction, and one against it. Historically, the latter presumption has always prevailed. See, e.g., Durley v. Mayo, 351 U.S. 277, 285 (1956); Stembridge v. Georgia, 343 U.S. 541, 547 (1952); Lynch v. New York, 293 U.S. 52 (1934). * * * The Court today points out that in several cases we have weakened the traditional presumption by using the other two intermediate approaches identified above. Since those two approaches are now to be rejected, however, I would think that *stare decisis* would call for a return to historical principle. Instead, the Court seems to conclude that because some precedents are to be rejected, we must overrule them all.

Even if I agreed with the Court that we are free to consider as a fresh proposition whether we may take presumptive jurisdiction over the decisions of sovereign states, I could not agree that an expansive attitude makes good sense. It appears to be common ground that any rule we adopt should show "respect for state courts, and [a] desire to avoid advisory opinions." And I am confident that all members of this Court agree that there is a vital interest in the sound management of scarce federal judicial resources. All of those policies counsel against the exercise of federal jurisdiction. They are fortified by my belief that a policy of judicial restraint—one that allows other decisional bodies to have the last word in legal interpretation until it is truly necessary for this Court to intervene—enables this Court to make its most effective contribution to our federal system of government.

The nature of the case before us hardly compels a departure from tradition. These are not cases in which an American citizen has been deprived of a right secured by the United States Constitution or a federal statute. Rather, they are cases in which a state court has upheld a citizen's assertion of a right, finding the citizen to be protected under both federal and state law. The complaining party is an officer of the state itself, who asks us to rule that the state court interpreted federal rights too broadly and "overprotected" the citizen.

Such cases should not be of inherent concern to this Court. The reason may be illuminated by assuming that the events underlying this case had arisen in another country, perhaps the Republic of Finland. If the Finnish police had arrested a Finnish citizen for possession of marijuana, and the Finnish courts had turned him loose, no American would have standing to object. If instead they had arrested an American citizen and acquitted him, we might have been concerned about the arrest but we surely could not have complained about the acquittal, even if the Finnish Court had based its decision on its understanding of the United States Constitution. That would be true even if we had a treaty with Finland requiring it to respect the rights of American citizens under the United States Constitution. We would only be motivated to intervene if an American citizen were unfairly arrested, tried, and convicted by the foreign tribunal.

In this case the State of Michigan has arrested one of its citizens and the Michigan Supreme Court has decided to turn him loose. The respondent is a United States citizen as well as a Michigan citizen, but since there is no claim that he has been mistreated by the State of Michigan, the final outcome of the state processes offended no federal interest whatever. Michigan simply provided greater protection to one of its citizens than some other State might provide or, indeed, than this Court might require throughout the country.

I believe that in reviewing the decisions of state courts, the primary role of this Court is to make sure that persons who seek to *vindicate* federal rights have been fairly heard. That belief resonates with statements in many of our prior cases. In Abie State Bank v. Bryan, 282 U.S. 765 (1931), the Supreme Court of Nebraska had rejected a federal constitutional claim, relying in part on the state law doctrine of laches. Writing for the Court in response to the Nebraska governor's argument that the Court should not accept jurisdiction because laches provided an independent ground for decision, Chief Justice Hughes concluded that this Court must ascertain for itself whether the asserted nonfederal ground independently and adequately supported the judgment "in order that constitutional guarantees may appropriately be enforced." Id., at 773. He relied on our earlier opinion in Union Pacific Railroad Co. v. Public Service Commission of Missouri, 248 U.S. 67 (1918), in which Justice Holmes had made it clear that the Court engaged in such an inquiry so that it would not "be possible for a State to impose an unconstitutional burden" on a private party. Id., at 70. And both *Abie* and *Union Pacific* rely on Creswill v. Knights of Pythias, 225 U.S. 246, 261 (1912), in which the Court explained its duty to review the findings of fact of a state court "where a Federal right has been denied."

Until recently we had virtually no interest in cases of this type. * * * Some time during the past decade, perhaps about the time of the 5–to–4 decision in Zacchini v. Scripps–Howard Broadcasting Co., 433 U.S. 562 (1977), our priorities shifted. The result is a docket swollen with requests by states to reverse judgments that their courts have rendered in favor of their citizens. I am confident that a future Court will recognize the error of this allocation of resources. When that day comes, I think it likely that the Court will also reconsider the propriety of today's expansion of our jurisdiction.

The Court offers only one reason for asserting authority over cases such as the one presented today: "an important need for uniformity in federal law [that] goes unsatisfied when we fail to review an opinion that rests primarily upon federal grounds and where the independence of an alleged state ground is not apparent from the four corners of the opinion." Of course, the supposed need to "review an opinion" clashes directly with our oft-repeated reminder that "our power is to correct wrong judgments, not to revise opinions." Herb v. Pitcairn, 324 U.S. 117 (1945). The clash is not merely one of form: the "need for uniformity in federal law" is truly an ungovernable engine. That same need is no less present when it is perfectly clear that a state ground is both independent and adequate. In fact, it is equally present if a state prosecutor announces that he believes a certain policy of nonenforcement is commanded by federal law. Yet we have never claimed jurisdiction to correct such errors, no matter how egregious they may be, and no matter how much they may thwart the desires of the state electorate. We do not sit to expound our understanding of the Constitution to interested listeners in the legal community; we sit to resolve disputes. If it is not apparent that our views would affect the outcome of a particular case, we cannot presume to interfere.[4]

4. In this regard, one of the cases overruled today deserves comment. In Minnesota v. National Tea Co., 309 U.S. 551 (1940), the Court considered a case much like this one—the Minnesota Supreme Court had concluded that both the Fourteenth Amendment to the United States Constitution and Article 9, § 1, of the Minnesota Constitution prohibited a graduated income tax on chain store income. The state court stated that "the[ ] provisions of the Federal and State Constitutions impose identical restric-

Finally, I am thoroughly baffled by the Court's suggestion that it must stretch its jurisdiction and reverse the judgment of the Michigan Supreme Court in order to show "[r]espect for the independence of state courts." Would we show respect for the Republic of Finland by convening a special sitting for the sole purpose of declaring that its decision to release an American citizen was based upon a misunderstanding of American law?

I respectfully dissent.

[The dissenting opinion of JUSTICE BRENNAN, joined by JUSTICE MARSHALL, is omitted.]

Notes

1.   Could the approach adopted in *Long* be deemed unduly invasive of state court prerogatives to rely on state, rather than federal law? Consider the argument in Redish, *Supreme Court Review of State Court "Federal" Decisions: A Study in Interactive Federalism,* 19 Ga.L.Rev. 861, 864–65 (1985):

> Recognition of the fundamentally interactive, synergistic nature of American federalism leads to the conclusion that the Supreme Court's willingness in Michigan v. Long to exercise review power over state court decisions constitutes a perfectly legitimate application of these theoretical perspectives. Ultimately, the Supreme Court cannot force a state court to rely on principles of federal, rather than state law, at least as long as the state law has not been preempted by federal doctrine.

tions upon the legislative power of the state in respect to classification for purposes of taxation," and "then adverted briefly to three of its former decisions which had interpreted" the state provision. It then proceeded to conduct a careful analysis of the federal constitution. It could justly be said that the decision rested primarily on federal law. The majority of the Court reasoned as follows:

> "Enough has been said to demonstrate that there is considerable uncertainty as to the precise grounds for the decision. That is sufficient reason for us to decline at this time to review the federal question asserted to be present, Honeyman v. Hanan, 300 U.S. 14, consistently with the policy of not passing upon questions of a constitutional nature which are not clearly necessary to a decision of the case."

The Court therefore remanded to the state court for clarification.

Today's Court rejects that approach as intruding unduly on the state judicial process. One might therefore expect it to turn to Chief Justice Hughes's dissenting opinion in *National Tea.* In a careful statement of the applicable principles, he made an observation that I find unanswerable:

> "The fact that provisions of the state and federal constitutions may be similar or even identical does not justify us in disturbing a judgment of a state court which adequately rests upon its application of the provisions of its own constitution. That the state court may be influenced by the reasoning of our opinions makes no difference. The state court may be persuaded by majority opinions in this Court or it may prefer the reasoning of dissenting judges, but the judgment of the state court upon the application of its own constitution remains a judgment which we are without jurisdiction to review. Whether in this case we thought that the state tax was repugnant to the federal constitution or consistent with it, the judgment of the state court that the tax violated the state constitution would still stand. It cannot be supposed that the Supreme Court of Minnesota is not fully conscious of its independent authority to construe the constitution of the State, whatever reasons it may adduce in so doing."

Thus, *Long* is not "invasive" of state court prerogatives in the true sense of the term; if the state court makes clear that the state ground independently supports its decision, *Long* has no effect. Indeed, once the state court fully understands the status of federal law as construed by the Supreme Court, it may, in the next case, choose to fashion parallel state law in an entirely divergent manner. However, *Long* does allow a state court interested in understanding federal legal principles in order to inform the development of its own law by example, to gain the benefit of the Supreme Court's input on the meaning of relevant federal law. In this manner, the interactive dialogue between representatives of the state and federal judicial systems can enrich the substantive development of the law of both jurisdictions.

2.   Does the *Long* approach misconceive the basis of judicial federalism? Consider Welsh, *Reconsidering the Constitutional Relationship Between State and Federal Courts: A Critique of* Michigan v. Long, 59 Notre Dame L.Rev. 1118, 1120 (1984):

The positions expressed by Justices O'Connor and Stevens rest on two different models of federal/state relations. * * * Justice O'Connor subscribes to "the interstitial model," which holds that the dominance of federal civil liberties law has resulted in state bills of rights being assigned the narrow function of "filling the gaps." In contrast, Justice Stevens' position follows the "classical model," which envisions a state court as primarily enforcing state law, including state constitutional law. Recourse to federal law is only necessary if state law fails to afford the desired relief. Under this model, federal law assumes the limited "gap-filling" role.

Is it accurate to describe Justice O'Connor's approach as equivalent to the "interstitial" model and Justice Stevens' analysis to the "classical" model? Which of the two models described by Professor Welsh better describes American judicial federalism? In responding, reconsider the materials in Chapters Two and Five. Professor Welsh contends that "[t]he Convention * * * limited the tribunals that could exercise federal judicial power to those 'ordain[ed] and establish[ed]' by Congress. This definition excluded state courts which were already established under state law." Id. at 1135. He further argues that "much of the evidence suggests that article III was written to *preclude* reliance on state courts altogether." Id. at 1137 (emphasis in original). Is this view of the history consistent with the descriptions contained in Chapters Two and Five?

Does the dichotomy described by Professor Welsh accurately describe the appropriate alternatives? *See* Redish, supra, 19 Ga.L.Rev. at 872–73:

Professor Welsh describes two versions of an "all-or-nothing" federalism: either federal law is considered dominant, in which event both state law and state courts are relegated to the menial tasks of gap-filling, or state and federal governmental bodies are thought to function in totally distinct universes, each involved predominantly with the laws and concerns of its own governmental system. Nowhere in Professor Welsh's dichotomy is there room for recognition of the interactive, cooperative functioning of the state and federal systems for the purpose of achieving the mutually shared goal of the maximization of societal welfare. * * *

[T]he concept of cooperative federalism simultaneously recognizes the vitality and integrity of both governmental systems, the significant overlap of their functioning, and the benefits that derive from their mutual involvement and interchange.

Consider Justice Stevens' analogy to Finland. Is that a fair comparison?

3. In cases such as *Long*, the state executive is asking the Supreme Court to review a ruling against it by the state supreme court. Should the Supreme Court even be deciding disputes between the state judiciary and the state executive? Before 1914, the Supreme Court lacked jurisdiction over cases in which a state court *upheld* a federal defense. Why do you think 28 U.S.C. § 1257 [in Appendix B] was amended in 1914 to allow Supreme Court review of such cases? See Hartnett, *Why Is the Supreme Court of the United States Protecting State Judges from Popular Democracy?*, 75 Tex.L.Rev. 907, 913 (1997). Justice Stevens renewed his objection to deciding such cases in his dissent in Kansas v. Marsh, 548 U.S. ___, 126 S.Ct. 2516 (2006):

In this case * * * the State of Kansas petitioned us to review a ruling of its own Supreme Court on the grounds that the Kansas court had granted more protection to a Kansas litigant than the Federal Constitution required. A policy of judicial restraint would allow the highest court of the State to be the final decisionmaker in a case of this kind.

Quoting his own dissent in a case decided the same day as *Long*, he argued that " '[n]othing more than an interest in facilitating the imposition of the death penalty in [Kansas] justified this Court's exercise of its discretion to review the judgment of the [Kansas] Supreme Court.' " See also Washington v. Recuenco, 548 U.S. ___, 126 S.Ct. 2546 (2006) (Stevens, J., dissenting); Brigham City v. Stuart, 547 U.S. ___, 126 S.Ct. 1943 (2006) (Stevens, J., concurring).

Justice Scalia joined the majority opinion in *Marsh*—which upheld the imposition of the death penalty, reversing the Kansas Supreme Court—but wrote separately to respond to Justice Stevens:

Our principal responsibility under current practice * * * is to ensure the integrity and uniformity of federal law. * * *

* * * When state courts erroneously invalidate actions taken by the people of a State (through initiative or through normal operation of the political branches of their state government) on *state-law* grounds, it is generally none of our business; and our displacing of those judgments would indeed be an intrusion upon state autonomy. But when state courts erroneously invalidate such actions because they believe federal law requires it—and *especially* when they do so because they believe the Federal *Constitution* requires it—review by this Court, far from *undermining* state autonomy, is the only possible way to *vindicate* it. When a federal constitutional interdict against the duly expressed will of the people of a State is erroneously pronounced by a State's highest court, no authority in the State—not even a referendum agreed to by all its citizens—can undo the error. * * * When we correct a state court's federal errors, *we return power to the State, and to its people*.

Who has the better of the argument? Does it depend on one's view of the primary purposes of judicial review?

4. One argument in favor of generous Supreme Court review of state decisions upholding constitutional rights in state criminal prosecutions is that otherwise state courts are immune from democratic accountability. It has been suggested that prior to *Long*, certain state supreme courts, particularly California's, had been simultaneously premising their decisions on both the state and federal constitutions in order to insulate their constitutional decisions from any form of review:

> By invoking the state constitution the court insulates its decisions from federal judicial review; by simultaneously invoking the Federal Constitution, the court effectively blocks popular review through the initiative process. In a sense, this dual reliance makes the people of California the prisoners of the privileges conferred by their own state constitution.

Deukmejian & Thompson, *All Sail and No Anchor—Judicial Review Under the California Constitution*, 6 Hast. Const.L.Q. 975, 996–97 (1979).

Do you agree that a state supreme court's dual reliance on state and federal constitutions is a problem? What effect, if any, should *Long* have on this practice? Two recent studies suggest that state courts still generally fail to include a plain statement of reliance on state law. Gardner, *The Failed Discourse of State Constitutionalism*, 90 Mich.L.Rev. 761 (1992); O'Neill, *"Stop Me Before I Get Reversed Again": The Failure of Illinois Appellate Courts to Protect Their Criminal Decisions from United States Supreme Court Review*, 36 Loy.U.Chi.L.J. 893 (2005). Why do you think state courts have, by and large, failed to follow the *Long* directive? Consider the following argument:

> When state courts issue decisions that are unreviewable by the United States Supreme Court, they must be prepared to take all of the heat; when they issue decisions reviewable by the Supreme Court, they can partially insulate themselves from that heat. Faced with a choice between insulating their judgments from Supreme Court review or partially insulating themselves from internal political pressure, it is hardly surprising that most of the time state judges opt for the latter.

Hartnett, *Why Is the Supreme Court of the United States Protecting State Judges from Popular Democracy?*, 75 Tex.L.Rev. 907, 983 (1997). Does Professor Hartnett's argument support or undermine the soundness of the Supreme Court's decision in *Long*?

5. In response to *Long*, a number of state supreme court opinions have included explicit—and rather irritated—language stating that their decisions are founded on adequate and independent state grounds. See, e.g., Charter Township of Delta v. Dinolfo, 351 N.W.2d 831, 843 n. 7 (Mich.1984) ("For the benefit of the parties to this case and for any future review, we offer the following 'plain statement.' As should be clear from our outright rejection of [a Supreme Court case], our decision here is based solely on the Due Process Clause of the Michigan Constitution, * * * notwithstanding the use of a standard originally developed in the federal system"); State v. Kennedy, 666 P.2d 1316, 1321 (Or.1983) ("Lest there be any doubt about it, when this court cites federal opinions in interpreting a provision of Oregon law, it does so because it finds the views there expressed persuasive, not because it considers itself bound to do so by its understanding of federal doctrines").

Justice O'Connor justified the rule of *Long* on federalism grounds. Do you think the Michigan and Oregon state supreme courts approve of *Long*?

6. Florida has taken a different approach. Florida voters recently approved an amendment to article one, section twelve of the Florida constitution, which protects against unreasonable searches and seizures. The new language reads:

> This right shall be construed in conformity with the 4th Amendment to the United States Constitution, as interpreted by the United States Supreme Court. Articles or information obtained in violation of this right shall not be admissible in evidence if such articles or information would be inadmissible under the decisions of the United States Supreme Court construing the 4th Amendment to the United States Constitution.

Does the United States Supreme Court have jurisdiction to review a holding by the Florida Supreme Court that a particular search is in violation of the Florida constitution? See Delaware v. Prouse, 440 U.S. 648 (1979) (finding jurisdiction in analogous circumstances).

7. Note that the *Long* presumption of jurisdiction (on direct review) only has an effect in cases in which the Supreme Court takes a more restrictive view of criminal defendants' rights than the state court does. Where the Supreme Court and the state court agree on the scope of defendants' rights, it will not matter whether the presumption is in favor of or against taking jurisdiction. Where the Supreme Court reads the federal Constitution to provide *greater* protection to criminal defendants, that interpretation will trump any less generous state ruling anyway, under the supremacy clause. It is only where the state court protects rights that the United States Supreme Court would not protect, that it matters which presumption the Court adopts. See Sherry, *Issue Manipulation by the Burger Court: Saving the Community from Itself*, 70 Minn.L.Rev. 611, 638–39 (1986).

8. The Supreme Court has extended the *Long* doctrine to the one situation in which it works to the advantage of criminal defendants: federal habeas corpus review of defaulted claims. [See Chapter Twelve]. In Harris v. Reed, 489 U.S. 255 (1989), the Court confronted the question of habeas review of a state court which had denied a prisoner's appeal because of a procedural default, but had nevertheless gone on to reach the substantive federal merits. The Court in *Harris* held that a state court that reaches the merits should be presumed to have forgiven the procedural default unless it makes a plain statement to the contrary. Thus, in the absence of a plain statement, the procedural default will not bar habeas review.

9. What should the Court do when a state court decision rests on no federal ground at all but contains ambiguities about the state ground, ambiguities which might affect a federal question on appeal? Consider Bush v. Palm Beach County Canvassing Bd., 531 U.S. 70 (2000). In that case, the Florida Supreme Court had interpreted Florida statutes to require the secretary of state to accept late election returns from counties undergoing a recount process. Candidate George W. Bush appealed to the U.S. Supreme Court, arguing that the state court interpretation of state law violated Art. II, § 1, cl. 2 of the federal Constitution by judicially varying the *legislative* directions for conducting elections. (Art. II, § 1, cl. 2 provides that each state

shall appoint electors "in such manner as the legislature thereof may direct.") Bush contended that to the extent that the Florida court relied on the Florida Constitution—and not just the language of the state statutes—it was acting illegitimately.

Bush also argued that the Florida court, in its interpretation of the state statute, ignored a federal statute governing presidential elections. That federal statute, 3 U.S.C. § 5, provides that if states resolve election disputes by a certain date, Congress will consider that resolution conclusive when it eventually counts electoral votes. Bush contended that had the Florida court considered § 5, it might have concluded that the state legislature wished to take advantage of this "safe harbor" and therefore prohibited late returns that might jeopardize the finality of the state's resolution.

The Supreme Court vacated the Florida decision and remanded for clarification on both issues:

> After reviewing the opinion of the Florida Supreme Court, we find "that there is considerable uncertainty as to the precise grounds for the decision." Minnesota v. National Tea Co., 309 U.S. 551 (1940). This is sufficient reason for us to decline at this time to review the federal questions asserted to be present. See *ibid.*
>
>> "It is fundamental that state courts be left free and unfettered by us in interpreting their state constitutions. But it is equally important that ambiguous or obscure adjudications by state courts do not stand as barriers to a determination by this Court of the validity under the federal constitution of state action. Intelligent exercise of our appellate powers compels us to ask for the elimination of the obscurities and ambiguities from the opinions in such cases." *Id.*, at 557.
>
> Specifically, we are unclear as to the extent to which the Florida Supreme Court saw the Florida Constitution as circumscribing the legislature's authority under Art. II, § 1, cl. 2. We are also unclear as to the consideration the Florida Supreme Court accorded to 3 U.S.C. § 5. The judgment of the Supreme Court of Florida is therefore vacated, and the case is remanded for further proceedings not inconsistent with this opinion.

Does the remand for consideration of the § 5 question violate the basic principles of judicial federalism discussed in the cases throughout this book? Certainly, if the interpretation of Florida law violates the federal Constitution, there is a role for the U.S. Supreme Court. But was the Florida court *federally required* to interpret state election law in light of the "safe harbor" provision of § 5? Should federal courts be involved in dictating to state courts which sources they should consider in interpreting state laws?

In any case, was vacatur the appropriate response in this case? What should a federal court do when ambiguities in state law prevent it from addressing a federal question? Recall Railroad Commission v. Pullman, [supra p. 446] and its progeny: is the result in *Palm Beach County Canvassing Board* the Supreme Court's version of *Pullman* abstention? Is it justified? Instead of vacating the opinion below, should the Court have certified the question to the state Supreme Court? See *Fiore v. White*, 528 U.S. 23 (1999) (certifying question to Pennsylvania Supreme Court).

Contrast *Palm Beach County Canvassing Board* with Bush v. Gore, 531 U.S. 98 (2000). In Gore v. Harris, 772 So.2d 1243 (Fla.2000), the Florida Supreme Court interpreted Florida law to require a statewide manual recount of certain disputed ballots in the presidential election. Because the Florida court issued its decision only 4 days before the "safe harbor" deadline, it ordered recounts to begin immediately so that they might be completed in time. The United States Supreme Court stayed the recount process the next day. Two hours before the expiration of the "safe harbor" period, the Supreme Court issued a 5 to 4 decision reversing the Florida court and permanently halting the recounts. After concluding that the recount mandated by the state court violated equal protection, the majority opinion reasoned that because the recounts could not be completed in a constitutional fashion by the "safe harbor" deadline, they should not be undertaken. But the Florida Supreme Court had interpreted the state statutes to aim for *two* goals: to make every vote count and to meet the "safe harbor" deadline. When the U.S. Supreme Court's equal protection ruling established that both goals could not be met simultaneously, which court should have identified the more important goal? Perhaps the legislature that enacted the statute would have preferred to give up the safe harbor in exchange for counting every vote. Isn't that solely a question of state law? Following *Palm Beach County Canvassing Board*, what should the Court have done in *Bush v. Gore* once it identified a constitutional violation?

Three Justices—the Chief Justice and Justices Scalia and Thomas—issued a separate concurring opinion in *Bush v. Gore*. In addition to holding that the recount violated equal protection, they would have held that it violated Article II, which provides that "[e]ach State shall appoint, in such manner as the Legislature thereof may direct," electors for president and vice president. The concurring Justices re-examined the Florida statutes relied on by the Florida court, and concluded that the Florida court's interpretation of the statutes "departed from the legislative scheme" and thus usurped the legislature's constitutionally-granted authority to specify how electors should be chosen.

Is the concurrence consistent with the doctrine of adequate and independent state grounds? With the principles of federalism explored in earlier chapters? Consider Justice Ginsburg's dissent in *Bush v. Gore*:

> THE CHIEF JUSTICE acknowledges that provisions of Florida's Election Code "may well admit of more than one interpretation." But instead of respecting the state high court's province to say what the State's Election Code means, THE CHIEF JUSTICE maintains that Florida's Supreme Court has veered so far from the ordinary practice of judicial review that what it did cannot properly be called judging. My colleagues have offered a reasonable construction of Florida's law. Their construction coincides with the view of one of Florida's seven Supreme Court justices. I might join THE CHIEF JUSTICE were it my commission to interpret Florida law. But disagreement with the Florida court's interpretation of its own State's law does not warrant the conclusion that the justices of that court have legislated. There is no cause here to

believe that the members of Florida's high court have done less than "their mortal best to discharge their oath of office," Sumner v. Mata, 449 U.S. 539, 549 (1981), and no cause to upset their reasoned interpretation of Florida law.

This Court more than occasionally affirms statutory, and even constitutional, interpretations with which it disagrees. For example, when reviewing challenges to administrative agencies' interpretations of laws they implement, we defer to the agencies unless their interpretation violates "the unambiguously expressed intent of Congress." Chevron U.S.A., Inc. v. Natural Resources Defense Council, Inc., 467 U.S. 837, 843 (1984). We do so in the face of the declaration in Article I of the United States Constitution that "All legislative Powers herein granted shall be vested in a Congress of the United States." Surely the Constitution does not call upon us to pay more respect to a federal administrative agency's construction of federal law than to a state high court's interpretation of its own state's law. And not uncommonly, we let stand state-court interpretations of *federal* law with which we might disagree. Notably, in the habeas context, the Court adheres to the view that "there is 'no intrinsic reason why the fact that a man is a federal judge should make him more competent, or conscientious, or learned with respect to [federal law] than his neighbor in the state courthouse.'" Stone v. Powell, 428 U.S. 465, 494, n. 35 (1976) (quoting Bator, Finality in Criminal Law and Federal Habeas Corpus For State Prisoners, 76 Harv. L.Rev. 441, 509 (1963)).

* * *

In deferring to state courts on matters of state law, we appropriately recognize that this Court acts as an " 'outside[r]' lacking the common exposure to local law which comes from sitting in the jurisdiction." Lehman Brothers v. Schein, 416 U.S. 386, 391 (1974). That recognition has sometimes prompted us to resolve doubts about the meaning of state law by certifying issues to a State's highest court, even when federal rights are at stake. Notwithstanding our authority to decide issues of state law underlying federal claims, we have used the certification device to afford state high courts an opportunity to inform us on matters of their own State's law because such restraint "helps build a cooperative judicial federalism." Lehman Brothers, 416 U.S., at 391.

* * *

The extraordinary setting of this case has obscured the ordinary principle that dictates its proper resolution: Federal courts defer to state high courts' interpretations of their state's own law. This principle reflects the core of federalism, on which all agree. "The Framers split the atom of sovereignty. It was the genius of their idea that our citizens would have two political capacities, one state and one federal, each protected from incursion by the other." Saenz v. Roe, 526 U.S. 489, 504, n. 17 (1999). THE CHIEF JUSTICE's solicitude for the Florida Legislature comes at the expense of the more fundamental solicitude we owe to the legislature's sovereign. U.S. Const., Art. II, § 1, cl. 2 ("Each *State* shall appoint, in such Manner as the Legislature *thereof* may direct," the electors for President and Vice President) (emphasis added). Were the other members of this Court as mindful as they generally are of our system of dual sovereignty, they would affirm the judgment of the Florida Supreme Court.

Might the Court's review in *Bush v. Gore* be justified by an argument that the state court's ruling on state law prevents any court from reaching the federal question (sometimes called "antecedence-based jurisdiction," because the state decision is "antecedent" to a question of federal law)? For differing answers to this question, compare Fitzgerald, *Suspecting the States: Supreme Court Review of State-Court State-Law Judgments*, 101 Mich.L.Rev. 80 (2002) with Monaghan, *Supreme Court Review of State-Court Determinations of State Law in Constitutional Cases*, 103 Colum.L.Rev. 1919 (2003).

10.   The adequate and independent state grounds doctrine has generated extensive scholarly commentary. In addition to the articles cited in the notes, see generally Althouse, *How to Build a Separate Sphere: Federal Courts and State Power*, 100 Harv.L.Rev. 1485 (1987); Baker, *The* Ambiguous *Independent and Adequate State Ground in Criminal Cases: Federalism Along a Möbius Strip*, 19 Ga.L.Rev. 799 (1985); Seid, *Schizoid Federalism, Supreme Court Power, and Inadequate Adequate State Ground Theory:* Michigan v. Long, 18 Creighton L.Rev. 1 (1984).

Appendix A

THE CONSTITUTION OF THE UNITED STATES OF AMERICA

We the People of the United States, in Order to form a more perfect Union, establish Justice, insure domestic Tranquility, provide for the common defence, promote the general Welfare, and secure the Blessings of Liberty to ourselves and our Posterity, do ordain and establish this Constitution for the United States of America.

ARTICLE I

SECTION 1. All legislative Powers herein granted shall be vested in a Congress of the United States, which shall consist of a Senate and House of Representatives.

SECTION 2. The House of Representatives shall be composed of Members chosen every second Year by the People of the several States, and the Electors in each State shall have the Qualifications requisite for Electors of the most numerous Branch of the State Legislature.

No Person shall be a Representative who shall not have attained to the Age of twenty five Years, and been seven Years a Citizen of the United States, and who shall not, when elected, be an Inhabitant of that State in which he shall be chosen.

Representatives and direct Taxes shall be apportioned among the several States which may be included within this Union, according to their respective Numbers, which shall be determined by adding to the whole Number of free Persons, including those bound to Service for a Term of Years, and excluding Indians not taxed, three fifths of all other Persons. The actual Enumeration shall be made within three Years after the first Meeting of the Congress of the United States, and within every subsequent Term of ten Years, in such Manner as they shall by Law direct. The Number of Representatives shall not exceed one for every thirty Thousand, but each State shall have at Least one Representative; and until such enumeration shall be made, the State of New Hampshire shall be entitled to chuse three, Massachusetts eight, Rhode Island and

Providence Plantations one, Connecticut five, New–York six, New Jersey four, Pennsylvania eight, Delaware one, Maryland six, Virginia ten, North Carolina five, South Carolina five, and Georgia three.

When vacancies happen in the Representation from any State, the Executive Authority thereof shall issue Writs of Election to fill such Vacancies.

The House of Representatives shall chuse their Speaker and other Officers; and shall have the sole Power of Impeachment.

SECTION 3. The Senate of the United States shall be composed of two Senators from each State, chosen by the Legislature thereof, for six Years; and each Senator shall have one Vote.

Immediately after they shall be assembled in Consequence of the first Election, they shall be divided as equally as may be into three Classes. The Seats of the Senators of the first Class shall be vacated at the Expiration of the second Year, of the second Class at the Expiration of the fourth Year, and of the third Class at the Expiration of the sixth Year, so that one third may be chosen every second Year; and if Vacancies happen by Resignation, or otherwise, during the Recess of the Legislature of any State, the Executive thereof may make temporary Appointments until the next Meeting of the Legislature, which shall then fill such Vacancies.

No Person shall be a Senator who shall not have attained to the Age of thirty Years, and been nine Years a Citizen of the United States, and who shall not, when elected, be an Inhabitant of that State for which he shall be chosen.

The Vice President of the United States shall be President of the Senate, but shall have no Vote, unless they be equally divided.

The Senate shall chuse their other Officers, and also a President pro tempore, in the Absence of the Vice President, or when he shall exercise the Office of President of the United States.

The Senate shall have the sole Power to try all Impeachments. When sitting for that Purpose, they shall be on Oath or Affirmation. When the President of the United States is tried, the Chief Justice shall preside: And no Person shall be convicted without the Concurrence of two thirds of the Members present.

Judgment in Cases of Impeachment shall not extend further than to removal from Office, and disqualification to hold and enjoy any Office of honor, Trust or Profit under the United States: but the party convicted shall nevertheless be liable and subject to Indictment, Trial, Judgment and Punishment, according to Law.

SECTION 4. The Times, Places and Manner of holding Elections for Senators and Representatives, shall be prescribed in each State by the Legislature thereof; but the Congress may at any time by Law make or alter such Regulations, except as to the Places of chusing Senators.

The Congress shall assemble at least once in every Year, and such Meeting shall be on the first Monday in December, unless they shall by Law appoint a different Day.

SECTION 5. Each House shall be the Judge of the Elections, Returns and Qualifications of its own Members, and a Majority of each shall constitute a Quorum to do Business; but a smaller Number may adjourn from day to day, and may be authorized to compel the Attendance of absent Members, in such Manner, and under such Penalties as each House may provide.

Each House may determine the Rules of its Proceedings, punish its Members for disorderly Behaviour, and, with the concurrence of two thirds, expel a Member.

Each House shall keep a Journal of its Proceedings, and from time to time publish the same, excepting such Parts as may in their Judgment require Secrecy; and the Yeas and Nays of the Members of either House on any question shall, at the Desire of one fifth of those Present, be entered on the Journal.

Neither House, during the Session of Congress, shall, without the Consent of the other, adjourn for more than three days, nor to any other Place than that in which the two Houses shall be sitting.

SECTION 6. The Senators and Representatives shall receive a Compensation for their Services, to be ascertained by Law, and paid out of the Treasury of the United States. They shall in all Cases, except Treason, Felony and Breach of the Peace, be privileged from Arrest during their Attendance at the Session of their respective Houses, and in going to and returning from the same; and for any Speech or Debate in either House, they shall not be questioned in any other Place.

No Senator or Representative shall, during the Time for which he was elected, be appointed to any civil Office under the Authority of the United States, which shall have been created, or the Emoluments whereof shall have been encreased during such time; and no Person holding any Office under the United States, shall be a Member of either House during his Continuance in Office.

SECTION 7. All Bills for raising Revenue shall originate in the House of Representatives; but the Senate may propose or concur with Amendments as on other Bills.

Every Bill which shall have passed the House of Representatives and the Senate, shall, before it become a Law, be presented to the President of the United States; If he approve he shall sign it, but if not he shall return it, with his Objections to that House in which it shall have originated, who shall enter the Objections at large on their Journal, and proceed to reconsider it. If after such Reconsideration two thirds of that House shall agree to pass the Bill, it shall be sent, together with the Objections, to the other House, by which it shall likewise be reconsidered, and if approved by two thirds of that House, it shall become a Law. But in all such Cases the Votes of both Houses shall be determined by

Yeas and Nays, and the Names of the Persons voting for and against the Bill shall be entered on the Journal of each House respectively. If any Bill shall not be returned by the President within ten Days (Sundays excepted) after it shall have been presented to him, the Same shall be a Law, in like Manner as if he had signed it, unless the Congress by their Adjournment prevent its Return, in which Case it shall not be a Law.

Every Order, Resolution, or Vote to which the Concurrence of the Senate and House of Representatives may be necessary (except on a question of Adjournment) shall be presented to the President of the United States; and before the Same shall take Effect, shall be approved by him, or being disapproved by him, shall be repassed by two thirds of the Senate and House of Representatives, according to the Rules and Limitations prescribed in the Case of a Bill.

SECTION 8. The Congress shall have Power To lay and collect Taxes, Duties, Imposts and Excises, to pay the Debts and provide for the common Defence and general Welfare of the United States; but all Duties, Imposts and Excises shall be uniform throughout the United States;

To borrow Money on the credit of the United States;

To regulate Commerce with foreign Nations, and among the several States, and with the Indian Tribes;

To establish an uniform Rule of Naturalization, and uniform Laws on the subject of Bankruptcies throughout the United States;

To coin Money, regulate the Value thereof, and of foreign Coin, and fix the Standard of Weights and Measures;

To provide for the Punishment of counterfeiting the Securities and current Coin of the United States;

To establish Post Offices and post Roads;

To promote the Progress of Science and useful Arts, by securing for limited Times to Authors and Inventors the exclusive Right to their respective Writings and Discoveries;

To constitute Tribunals inferior to the supreme Court;

To define and punish Piracies and Felonies committed on the high Seas, and Offences against the Law of Nations;

To declare War, grant Letters of Marque and Reprisal, and make Rules concerning Captures on Land and Water;

To raise and support Armies, but no Appropriation of Money to that Use shall be for a longer Term than two Years;

To provide and maintain a Navy;

To make Rules for the Government and Regulation of the land and naval Forces;

To provide for calling forth the Militia to execute the Laws of the Union, suppress Insurrections and repel Invasions;

To provide for organizing, arming, and disciplining, the Militia, and for governing such Part of them as may be employed in the Service of the United States, reserving to the States respectively, the Appointment of the Officers, and the Authority of training the Militia according to the discipline prescribed by Congress;

To exercise exclusive Legislation in all Cases whatsoever, over such District (not exceeding ten Miles square) as may, by Cession of particular States and the Acceptance of Congress, become the Seat of the Government of the United States, and to exercise like Authority over all Places purchased by the Consent of the Legislature of the State in which the Same shall be, for the Erection of Forts, Magazines, Arsenals, dock-Yards, and other needful Buildings;—And

To make all Laws which shall be necessary and proper for carrying into Execution the foregoing Powers, and all other Powers vested by this constitution in the Government of the United States, or in any Department or Officer thereof.

SECTION 9. The Migration or Importation of such Persons as any of the States now existing shall think proper to admit, shall not be prohibited by the Congress prior to the Year one thousand eight hundred and eight, but a Tax or duty may be imposed on such Importation, not exceeding ten dollars for each Person.

The Privilege of the Writ of Habeas Corpus shall not be suspended, unless when in Cases of Rebellion or Invasion the public Safety may require it.

No Bill of Attainder or ex post facto Law shall be passed.

No Capitation, or other direct, Tax shall be laid, unless in Proportion to the Census or Enumeration herein before directed to be taken.

No Tax or Duty shall be laid on Articles exported from any State.

No Preference shall be given by any Regulation of Commerce or Revenue to the Ports of one State over those of another: nor shall Vessels bound to, or from, one State, be obliged to enter, clear, or pay Duties in another.

No Money shall be drawn from the Treasury, but in Consequence of Appropriations made by Law; and a regular Statement and Account of the Receipts and Expenditures of all public Money shall be published from time to time.

No Title of Nobility shall be granted by the United States: And no Person holding any Office of Profit or Trust under them, shall, without the Consent of the Congress, accept of any present, Emolument, Office, or Title, of any kind whatever, from any King, Prince, or foreign State.

SECTION 10. No State shall enter into any Treaty, Alliance, or Confederation; grant Letters of Marque and Reprisal; coin Money; emit Bills of Credit; make any Thing but gold and silver Coin a Tender in Payment of Debts; pass any Bill of Attainder, ex post facto Law, or Law impairing the Obligation of Contracts, or grant any Title of Nobility.

No State shall, without the Consent of the Congress, lay any Imposts or Duties on Imports or Exports, except what may be absolutely necessary for executing its inspection Laws: and the net Produce of all Duties and Imposts, laid by any State on Imports or Exports, shall be for the Use of the Treasury of the United States; and all such Laws shall be subject to the Revision and Controul of the Congress.

No State shall, without the Consent of Congress, lay any Duty of Tonnage, keep Troops, or Ships of War in time of Peace, enter into any Agreement or Compact with another State, or with a foreign Power, or engage in War, unless actually invaded, or in such imminent Danger as will not admit of delay.

ARTICLE II

SECTION 1. The executive Power shall be vested in a President of the United States of America. He shall hold his Office during the Term of four Years, and, together with the Vice President, chosen for the same Term, be elected, as follows

Each State shall appoint, in such Manner as the Legislature thereof may direct, a Number of Electors, equal to the whole Number of Senators and Representatives to which the State may be entitled in the Congress: but no Senator or Representative, or Person holding an Office of Trust or Profit under the United States, shall be appointed an Elector.

The Electors shall meet in their respective States, and vote by Ballot for two Persons, of whom one at least shall not be an Inhabitant of the same State with themselves. And they shall make a List of all the Persons voted for, and of the Number of Votes for each; which List they shall sign and certify, and transmit sealed to the Seat of the Government of the United States, directed to the President of the Senate. The President of the Senate shall, in the Presence of the Senate and House of Representatives, open all the certificates, and the Votes shall then be counted. The Person having the greatest Number of Votes shall be the President, if such Number be a Majority of the whole Number of Electors appointed; and if there be more than one who have such Majority, and have an equal Number of Votes, then the House of Representatives shall immediately chuse by Ballot one of them for President; and if no Person have a Majority, then from the five highest on the List the said House shall in like Manner chuse the President. But in chusing the President, the Votes shall be taken by States, the Representation from each State having one Vote; A quorum for this Purpose shall consist of a Member or Members from two thirds of the States, and a Majority of all the States shall be necessary to a Choice. In every Case, after the Choice of the president, the Person having the greatest Number of Votes of the Electors shall be the Vice President. But if there should remain two or more who have equal Votes, the Senate shall chuse from them by Ballot the Vice President.

The Congress may determine the Time of chusing the Electors, and the Day on which they shall give their Votes; which Day shall be the same throughout the United States.

No Person except a natural born Citizen, or a Citizen of the United States, at the time of the Adoption of this Constitution, shall be eligible to the Office of President; neither shall any Person be eligible to that office who shall not have attained to the Age of thirty-five Years, and been fourteen Years a Resident within the United States.

In Case of the Removal of the President from Office, or of his Death, Resignation, or Inability to discharge the Powers and Duties of the said Office, the Same shall devolve on the Vice President, and the Congress may by Law provide for the Case of Removal, Death, Resignation or Inability, both of the President and Vice President, declaring what Officer shall then act as President, and such Officer shall act accordingly, until the Disability be removed, or a President shall be elected.

The President shall, at stated Times, receive for his Services, a Compensation, which shall neither be encreased nor diminished during the Period for which he shall have been elected, and he shall not receive within that Period any other Emolument from the United States, or any of them.

Before he enter on the Execution of his Office, he shall take the following Oath or Affirmation:—"I do solemnly swear (or affirm) that I will faithfully execute the Office of President of the United States, and will to the best of my ability, preserve, protect and defend the Constitution of the United States."

SECTION 2. The President shall be Commander in Chief of the Army and Navy of the United States, and of the Militia of the several States, when called into the actual Service of the United States; he may require the Opinion, in writing, of the principal Officer in each of the executive Departments, upon any Subject relating to the Duties of their respective Offices, and he shall have Power to grant Reprieves and Pardons for Offences against the United States, except in Cases of Impeachment.

He shall have Power, by and with the Advice and Consent of the Senate, to make Treaties, providing two thirds of the Senators present concur; and he shall nominate, and by and with the Advice and Consent of the Senate, shall appoint Ambassadors, other public Ministers and Consuls, Judges of the supreme Court, and all other Officers of the United States, whose Appointments are not herein otherwise provided for, and which shall be established by Law: but the Congress may by Law vest the Appointment of such inferior Officers, as they think proper, in the President alone, in the Courts of Law, or in the Heads of Departments.

The President shall have Power to fill up all Vacancies that may happen during the Recess of the Senate, by granting Commissions which shall expire at the End of their next Session.

SECTION 3. He shall from time to time give to the Congress Information of the State of the Union, and recommend to their Consideration such Measures as he shall judge necessary and expedient; he may, on extraordinary Occasions, convene both Houses, or either of them, and in Case of Disagreement between them, with Respect to the Time of Adjournment, he may adjourn them to such Time as he shall think proper; he shall receive Ambassadors and other public Ministers; he shall take Care that the Laws be faithfully executed, and shall Commission all the Officers of the United States.

SECTION 4. The President, Vice President and all civil Officers of the United States, shall be removed from Office on Impeachment for, and Conviction of, Treason, Bribery, or other high Crimes and Misdemeanors.

ARTICLE III

SECTION 1. The judicial Power of the United States, shall be vested in one supreme Court, and in such inferior Courts as the Congress may from time to time ordain and establish. The Judges, both of the supreme and inferior Courts, shall hold their Offices during good Behaviour, and shall, at stated Times, receive for their Services, a Compensation, which shall not be diminished during their Continuance in Office.

SECTION 2. The judicial Power shall extend to all Cases, in Law and Equity, arising under this Constitution, the Laws of the United States, and Treaties made, or which shall be made, under their Authority;—to all Cases affecting Ambassadors, other public Ministers and Consuls;—to all Cases of admiralty and maritime Jurisdiction;—to Controversies to which the United States shall be a Party;—to Controversies between two or more States;—between a State and Citizens of another State;—between Citizens of different States;—between Citizens of the same State claiming Lands under Grants of different States, and between a State, or the Citizens thereof, and foreign States, Citizens or Subjects.

In all Cases affecting Ambassadors, other public Ministers and Consuls, and those in which a State shall be Party, the supreme Court shall have original Jurisdiction. In all the other Cases before mentioned, the supreme Court shall have appellate Jurisdiction, both as to Law and Fact, with such Exceptions, and under such Regulations as the Congress shall make.

The Trial of all Crimes, except in Cases of Impeachment, shall be by Jury; and such Trial shall be held in the State where the said Crimes shall have been committed; but when not committed within any State, the Trial shall be at such Place or Places as the Congress may by Law have directed.

SECTION 3. Treason against the United States, shall consist only in levying War against them, or in adhering to their Enemies, giving them Aid and Comfort. No Person shall be convicted of Treason unless on the

Testimony of two Witnesses to the same overt Act, or on Confession in open Court.

The Congress shall have Power to declare the Punishment of Treason, but no Attainder of Treason shall work Corruption of Blood, or Forfeiture except during the Life of the Person attainted.

ARTICLE IV

SECTION 1. Full Faith and Credit shall be given in each State to the public Acts, Records, and judicial Proceedings of every other State. And the Congress may by general Laws prescribe the Manner in which such Acts, Records and Proceedings shall be proved, and the Effect thereof.

SECTION 2. The Citizens of each State shall be entitled to all Privileges and Immunities of Citizens in the several States.

A Person charged in any State with Treason, Felony, or other Crime, who shall flee from Justice, and be found in another State, shall on Demand of the executive Authority of the State from which he fled, be delivered up, to be removed to the State having Jurisdiction of the Crime.

No Person held to Service or Labour in one State, under the Laws thereof, escaping into another, shall, in Consequence of any Law or Regulation therein, be discharged from such Service or Labour, but shall be delivered up on Claim of the party to whom such Service or Labour may be due.

SECTION 3. New States may be admitted by the Congress into this Union; but no new State shall be formed or erected within the Jurisdiction of any other State; nor any State be formed by the Junction of two or more States, or Parts of States, without the Consent of the Legislatures of the States concerned as well as of the Congress.

The Congress shall have Power to dispose of and make all needful Rules and Regulations respecting the Territory or other Property belonging to the United States; and nothing in this Constitution shall be so construed as to Prejudice any Claims of the United States, or of any particular State.

SECTION 4. The United States shall guarantee to every State in this Union a Republican Form of Government, and shall protect each of them against Invasion; and on Application of the Legislature, or of the Executive (when the Legislature cannot be convened) against domestic Violence.

ARTICLE V

The Congress, whenever two thirds of both Houses shall deem it necessary, shall propose Amendments to this Constitution, or, on the

Application of the Legislatures of two thirds of the several States, shall call a Convention for proposing Amendments, which, in either Case, shall be valid to all Intents and Purposes, as part of this Constitution, when ratified by the Legislatures of three fourths of the several States, or by Conventions in three fourths thereof, as the one or the other Mode of Ratification may be proposed by the Congress; Provided that no Amendment which may be made prior to the Year One thousand eight hundred and eight shall in any Manner affect the first and fourth Clauses in the Ninth Section of the first Article; and that no State, without its Consent, shall be deprived of its equal Suffrage in the Senate.

ARTICLE VI

All Debts contracted and Engagements entered into, before the Adoption of this Constitution, shall be as valid against the United States under this Constitution, as under the Confederation.

This Constitution, and the Laws of the United States which shall be made in Pursuance thereof; and all Treaties made, or which shall be made, under the Authority of the United States, shall be the supreme Law of the Land; and the Judges in every State shall be bound thereby, any Thing in the Constitution or Laws of any State to the Contrary notwithstanding.

The Senators and Representatives before mentioned, and the Members of the several State Legislatures, and all executive and judicial Officers, both of the United States and of the several States, shall be bound by Oath or Affirmation, to support this Constitution; but no religious Test shall ever be required as a Qualification to any Office or public Trust under the United States.

ARTICLE VII

The Ratification of the Conventions of nine States, shall be sufficient for the Establishment of this Constitution between the States so ratifying the Same.*

* * *

* On the same day, September 17, 1787, on which the Constitution was completed, the Convention adopted a Resolution directing that the Constitution be laid before the Continental Congress with the view to its being submitted to conventions in the several states for ratification; and that, upon ratification by nine States, Congress should fix the time and place "for commencing proceedings under this Constitution." By July 26, 1788, eleven States had ratified. (The remaining two States, North Carolina and Rhode Island, ratified on November 21, 1789, and May 29, 1790, respectively). On September 13, 1788, Congress passed a resolution to put the new Constitution into operation, and fixed the first Wednesday in March of the following year for the opening session of the new Congress. Congress met on that day—March 4, 1789—but was unable to assemble a quorum until April 1, 1789. It was not until April 30, 1789, that Washington was inaugurated as the first President. The Supreme Court met for the first time on February 1, 1790.

The first ten Amendments—the Bill of Rights—were submitted together in 1789; ratification was completed on December 15, 1791. Ed.

ARTICLES IN ADDITION TO, AND AMENDMENT OF, THE CONSTITUTION OF THE UNITED STATES OF AMERICA, PROPOSED BY CONGRESS, AND RATIFIED BY THE LEGISLATURES OF THE SEVERAL STATES, PURSUANT TO THE FIFTH ARTICLE OF THE ORIGINAL CONSTITUTION.

AMENDMENT I [1791]

Congress shall make no law respecting an establishment of religion, or prohibiting the free exercise thereof; or abridging the freedom of speech, or of the press; or the right of the people peaceably to assemble, and to petition the Government for a redress of grievances.

AMENDMENT II [1791]

A well regulated Militia, being necessary to the security of a free State, the right of the people to keep and bear Arms, shall not be infringed.

AMENDMENT III [1791]

No Soldier shall, in time of peace be quartered in any house, without the consent of the Owner, nor in time of war, but in a manner to be prescribed by law.

AMENDMENT IV [1791]

The right of the people to be secure in their persons, houses, papers, and effects, against unreasonable searches and seizures, shall not be violated, and no Warrants shall issue, but upon probable cause, supported by Oath or affirmation, and particularly describing the place to be searched, and the persons or things to be seized.

AMENDMENT V [1791]

No person shall be held to answer for a capital, or otherwise infamous crime, unless on a presentment or indictment of a Grand Jury, except in cases arising in the land or naval forces, or in the Militia, when in actual service in time of War or public danger; nor shall any person be subject for the same offence to be twice put in jeopardy of life or limb; nor shall be compelled in any criminal case to be a witness against himself, nor be deprived of life, liberty, or property, without due process of law; nor shall private property be taken for public use, without just compensation.

AMENDMENT VI [1791]

In all criminal prosecutions, the accused shall enjoy the right to a speedy and public trial, by an impartial jury of the State and district wherein the crime shall have been committed, which district shall have been previously ascertained by law, and to be informed of the nature and cause of the accusation; to be confronted with the Witnesses against him; to have compulsory process for obtaining witnesses in his favor, and to have the Assistance of Counsel for his defence.

AMENDMENT VII [1791]

In Suits at common law, where the value in controversy shall exceed twenty dollars, the right of trial by jury shall be preserved, and no fact tried by a jury, shall be otherwise re-examined in any Court of the United States, than according to the rules of the common law.

AMENDMENT VIII [1791]

Excessive bail shall not be required, nor excessive fines imposed, nor cruel and unusual punishments inflicted.

AMENDMENT IX [1791]

The enumeration in the Constitution, of certain rights, shall not be construed to deny or disparage others retained by the people.

AMENDMENT X [1791]

The powers not delegated to the United States by the Constitution, nor prohibited by it to the States, are reserved to the States respectively, or to the people.

AMENDMENT XI [1798]

The Judicial power of the United States shall not be construed to extend to any suit in law or equity, commenced or prosecuted against one of the United States by Citizens of another State, or by Citizens or Subjects of any Foreign State.

AMENDMENT XII [1804]

The Electors shall meet in their respective states and vote by ballot for President and Vice–President, one of whom, at least, shall not be an inhabitant of the same state with themselves; they shall name in their ballots the person voted for as President, and in distinct ballots the person voted for as Vice–President, and they shall make distinct lists of all persons voted for as President, and of all persons voted for as Vice–President, and of the number of votes for each, which lists they shall sign and certify, and transmit sealed to the seat of the government of the United States, directed to the President of the Senate;—The President of the Senate shall, in the presence of the Senate and House of Representatives, open all the certificates and the votes shall then be counted;—The person having the greatest number of votes for President, shall be the President, if such number be a majority of the whole number of Electors appointed; and if no person have such majority, then from the persons having the highest numbers not exceeding three on the list of those voted for as President, the House of Representatives shall choose immediately, by ballot, the President. But in choosing the President, the votes shall be taken by states, the representation from each state having one vote; a quorum for this purpose shall consist of a member or members from two-thirds of the states, and a majority of all the states shall be necessary to a choice. And if the House of Representatives shall not choose a President whenever the right of choice shall devolve upon them, before the fourth day of March next following, then the Vice–President shall act as President, as in the case of the death or other constitutional disability of the President. The person having the greatest number of votes as Vice–President, shall be the Vice–President, if such number be a majority of the whole number of Electors appointed, and if no person have a majority, then from the two highest numbers on the list, the Senate shall choose the Vice–President; a quorum for the purpose shall consist of two-thirds of the whole number of Senators, and a majority of the whole number shall be necessary to a choice. But no person constitutionally ineligible to the office of President shall be eligible to that of Vice–President of the United States.

AMENDMENT XIII [1865]

SECTION 1. Neither slavery nor involuntary servitude, except as a punishment for crime whereof the party shall have been duly convicted, shall exist within the United States, or any place subject to their jurisdiction.

SECTION 2. Congress shall have power to enforce this article by appropriate legislation.

AMENDMENT XIV [1868]

SECTION 1. All persons born or naturalized in the United States, and subject to the jurisdiction thereof, are citizens of the United States and of the State wherein they reside. No State shall make or enforce any law which shall abridge the privileges or immunities of citizens of the United States; nor shall any State deprive any person of life, liberty, or property, without due process of law; nor deny to any person within its jurisdiction the equal protection of the laws.

SECTION 2. Representatives shall be apportioned among the several States according to their respective numbers, counting the whole number of persons in each State, excluding Indians not taxed. But when the right to vote at any election for the choice of electors for President and Vice President of the United States, Representatives in Congress, the Executive and Judicial officers of a State, or the members of the Legislature thereof, is denied to any of the male inhabitants of such State, being twenty-one years of age, and citizens of the United States, or in any way abridged, except for participation in rebellion, or other crime, the basis of representation therein shall be reduced in the proportion which the number of such male citizens shall bear to the whole number of male citizens twenty-one years of age in such State.

SECTION 3. No person shall be a Senator or Representative in Congress, or elector of President and Vice President, or hold any office, civil or military, under the United States, or under any State, who, having previously taken an oath, as a member of Congress, or as an officer of the United States, or as a member of any State legislature, or as an executive or judicial officer of any State, to support the Constitution of the United States, shall have engaged in insurrection or rebellion against the same, or given aid or comfort to the enemies thereof. But Congress may by a vote of two-thirds of each House, remove such disability.

SECTION 4. The validity of the public debt of the United States, authorized by law, including debts incurred for payment of pensions and bounties for services in suppressing insurrection or rebellion, shall not be questioned. But neither the United States nor any State shall assume or pay any debt or obligation incurred in aid of insurrection or rebellion against the United States, or any claim for the loss or emancipation of any slave; but all such debts, obligations and claims shall be held illegal and void.

SECTION 5. The Congress shall have power to enforce, by appropriate legislation, the provisions of this article.

AMENDMENT XV [1870]

SECTION 1. The right of citizens of the United States to vote shall not be denied or abridged by the United States or by any State on account of race, color, or previous condition of servitude.

SECTION 2. The Congress shall have power to enforce this article by appropriate legislation.

AMENDMENT XVI [1913]

The Congress shall have power to lay and collect taxes on incomes, from whatever source derived, without apportionment among the several States, and without regard to any census or enumeration.

AMENDMENT XVII [1913]

The Senate of the United States shall be composed of two Senators from each State, elected by the people thereof, for six years; and each Senator shall have one vote. The electors in each State shall have the qualifications requisite for electors of the most numerous branch of the State legislatures.

When vacancies happen in the representation of any State in the Senate, the executive authority of such State shall issue writs of election to fill such vacancies: *Provided*, That the legislature of any State may empower the executive thereof to make temporary appointments until the people fill the vacancies by election as the legislature may direct.

This amendment shall not be so construed as to affect the election or term of any Senator chosen before it becomes valid as part of the Constitution.

AMENDMENT XVIII [1919]

SECTION 1. After one year from the ratification of this article the manufacture, sale, or transportation of intoxicating liquors within, the importation thereof into, or the exportation thereof from the United States and all territory subject to the jurisdiction thereof for beverage purposes is hereby prohibited.

SECTION 2. The Congress and the several States shall have concurrent power to enforce this article by appropriate legislation.

SECTION 3. This article shall be inoperative unless it shall have been ratified as an amendment to the Constitution by the legislatures of the several States, as provided in the Constitution, within seven years from the date of the submission hereof to the States by the Congress.

AMENDMENT XIX [1920]

The right of citizens of the United States to vote shall not be denied or abridged by the United States or by any State on account of sex.

Congress shall have power to enforce this article by appropriate legislation.

AMENDMENT XX [1933]

SECTION 1. The terms of the President and Vice President shall end at noon on the 20th day of January, and the terms of Senators and Representatives at noon on the 3d day of January, of the years in which such terms would have ended if this article had not been ratified; and the terms of their successors shall then begin.

SECTION 2. The Congress shall assemble at least once in every year, and such meeting shall begin at noon on the 3d day of January, unless they shall by law appoint a different day.

SECTION 3. If, at the time fixed for the beginning of the term of the President, the President elect shall have died, the Vice President elect shall become President. If a President shall not have been chosen before the time fixed for the beginning of his term, or if the President elect shall have failed to qualify, then the Vice President elect shall act as President until a President shall have qualified; and the Congress may by law provide for the case wherein neither a President elect nor a Vice President elect shall have qualified, declaring who shall then act as President, or the manner in which one who is to act shall be selected, and such person shall act accordingly until a President or Vice President shall have qualified.

SECTION 4. The Congress may by law provide for the case of the death of any of the persons from whom the House of Representatives may choose a President whenever the right of choice shall have devolved upon them, and for the case of the death of any of the persons from whom the Senate may choose a Vice President whenever the right of choice shall have devolved upon them.

SECTION 5. Sections 1 and 2 shall take effect on the 15th day of October following the ratification of this article.

SECTION 6. This article shall be inoperative unless it shall have been ratified as an amendment to the Constitution by the legislatures of three-fourths of the several States within seven years from the date of its submission.

AMENDMENT XXI [1933]

SECTION 1. The eighteenth article of amendment to the Constitution of the United States is hereby repealed.

SECTION 2. The transportation or importation into any State, Territory, or possession of the United States for delivery or use therein of intoxicating liquors, in violation of the laws thereof, is hereby prohibited.

SECTION 3. This article shall be inoperative unless it shall have been ratified as an amendment to the Constitution by conventions in the several States, as provided in the Constitution, within seven years from the date of the submission hereof to the State by the Congress.

AMENDMENT XXII [1951]

SECTION 1. No person shall be elected to the office of the President more than twice, and no person who has held the office of President, or acted as President, for more than two years of a term to which some other person was elected President shall be elected to the office of the President more than once. But this Article shall not apply to any person holding the office of President when this Article was proposed by the Congress, and shall not prevent any person who may be holding the office of President, or acting as President, during the term within which this Article becomes operative from holding the office of President or acting as President during the remainder of such term.

SECTION 2. This article shall be inoperative unless it shall have been ratified as an amendment to the Constitution by the legislatures of three-fourths of the several States within seven years from the date of its submission to the States by the Congress.

AMENDMENT XXIII [1961]

SECTION 1. The District constituting the seat of Government of the United States shall appoint in such manner as the Congress may direct:

A number of electors of President and Vice President equal to the whole number of Senators and Representatives in Congress to which the District would be entitled if it were a State, but in no event more than the least populous State; they shall be in addition to those appointed by the States, but they shall be considered, for the purposes of the election of President and Vice President, to be electors appointed by a State; and they shall meet in the District and perform such duties as provided by the twelfth article of amendment.

SECTION 2. The Congress shall have power to enforce this article by appropriate legislation.

AMENDMENT XXIV [1964]

SECTION 1. The right of citizens of the United States to vote in any primary or other election for President or Vice President, for electors for President or Vice President, or for Senator or Representative in Congress, shall not be denied or abridged by the United States or any State by reason of failure to pay any poll tax or other tax.

SECTION 2. The Congress shall have power to enforce this article by appropriate legislation.

AMENDMENT XXV [1967]

SECTION 1. In case of the removal of the President from office or of his death or resignation, the Vice President shall become President.

SECTION 2. Whenever there is a vacancy in the office of the Vice President, the President shall nominate a Vice President who shall take office upon confirmation by a majority vote of both Houses of Congress.

SECTION 3. Whenever the President transmits to the President pro tempore of the Senate and the Speaker of the House of Representatives his written declaration that he is unable to discharge the powers and duties of his office, and until he transmits to them a written declaration to the contrary, such powers and duties shall be discharged by the Vice President as Acting President.

SECTION 4. Whenever the Vice President and a majority of either the principal officers of the executive departments or of such other body as Congress may by law provide, transmit to the President pro tempore of the Senate and the Speaker of the House of Representatives their written declaration that the President is unable to discharge the powers and duties of his office, the Vice President shall immediately assume the powers and duties of the office as Acting President.

Thereafter, when the President transmits to the President pro tempore of the Senate and the Speaker of the House of Representatives his written declaration that no inability exists, he shall resume the powers and duties of his office unless the Vice President and a majority of either the principal officers of the executive department or of such other body as Congress may by law provide, transmit within four days to the President pro tempore of the Senate and the Speaker of the House of Representatives their written declaration that the President is unable to discharge the powers and duties of his office. Thereupon Congress shall decide the issue, assembling within forty-eight hours for that purpose if not in session. If the Congress, within twenty-one days after receipt of the latter written declaration, or, if Congress is not in session, within twenty-one days after Congress is required to assemble, determines by two-thirds vote of both Houses that the President is unable to discharge the powers and duties of his office, the Vice President shall continue to discharge the same as Acting President; otherwise, the President shall resume the powers and duties of his office.

AMENDMENT XXVI [1971]

SECTION 1. The right of citizens of the United States, who are eighteen years of age or older, to vote shall not be denied or abridged by the United States or by any State on account of age.

SECTION 2. The Congress shall have power to enforce this article by appropriate legislation.

AMENDMENT XXVII [1992]

No law varying the compensation for the services of the Senators and Representatives shall take effect, until an election of Representatives shall have intervened.

*

Appendix B

Excerpts From 28 U.S.C.A.

CHAPTER 81—SUPREME COURT

§ 1251. Original jurisdiction

(a) The Supreme Court shall have original and exclusive jurisdiction of all controversies between two or more States.

(b) The Supreme Court shall have original but not exclusive jurisdiction of:

(1) All actions or proceedings to which ambassadors, other public ministers, consuls, or vice consuls of foreign states are parties;

(2) All controversies between the United States and a State;

(3) All actions or proceedings by a State against the citizens of another State or against aliens. As amended Sept. 30, 1978, Pub.L. 95–393, § 8(b), 92 Stat. 810.

§ 1253. Direct appeals from decisions of three-judge courts

Except as otherwise provided by law, any party may appeal to the Supreme Court from an order granting or denying, after notice and hearing, an interlocutory or permanent injunction in any civil action, suit or proceeding required by any Act of Congress to be heard and determined by a district court of three judges.

§ 1254. Courts of appeals; certiorari; appeal; certified questions

Cases in the courts of appeals may be reviewed by the Supreme Court by the following methods:

(1) By writ of certiorari granted upon the petition of any party to any civil or criminal case, before or after rendition of judgment or decree;

(2) By certification at any time by a court of appeals of any question of law in any civil or criminal case as to which instructions are desired,

and upon such certification the Supreme Court may give binding instructions or require the entire record to be sent up for decision of the entire matter in controversy.

§ 1257. State courts; certiorari

(a) Final judgments or decrees rendered by the highest court of a State in which a decision could be had, may be reviewed by the Supreme Court by writ of certiorari where the validity of a treaty or statute of the United States is drawn in question or where the validity of a statute of any state is drawn in question on the ground of its being repugnant to the Constitution, treaties or laws of the United States, or where any title, right, privilege, or immunity is specially set up or claimed under the Constitution or the treaties or statutes of, or any commission held or authority exercised under, the United States.

(b) For the purposes of this section, the term "highest court of a State" includes the District of Columbia Court of Appeals.

CHAPTER 83—COURTS OF APPEALS

§ 1291. Final decisions of district courts

The courts of appeals (other than the United States Court of Appeals for the Federal Circuit) shall have jurisdiction of appeals from all final decisions of the district courts of the United States, the United States District Court for the District of the Canal Zone, the District Court of Guam, and the District Court of the Virgin Islands, except where a direct review may be had in the Supreme Court. The jurisdiction of the United States Court of Appeals for the Federal Circuit shall be limited to the jurisdiction described in sections 1292 (c) and (d) and 1295 of this title. As amended Oct. 31, 1951, c. 655, § 48, 65 Stat. 726; July 7, 1958, Pub.L. 85–508, § 12(e), 72 Stat. 348; Apr. 2, 1982, Pub.L. 97–164, Title I, § 124, 96 Stat. 36.

§ 1292. Interlocutory decisions

(a) Except as provided in subsections (c) and (d) of this section, the courts of appeals shall have jurisdiction of appeals from:

(1) Interlocutory orders of the district courts of the United States, the United States District Court for the District of the Canal Zone, the District Court of Guam, and the District Court of the Virgin Islands, or of the judges thereof, granting, continuing, modifying, refusing or dissolving injunctions, or refusing to dissolve or modify injunctions, except where a direct review may be had in the Supreme Court;

(2) Interlocutory orders appointing receivers, or refusing orders to wind up receiverships or to take steps to accomplish the purposes thereof, such as directing sales or other disposals of property;

(3) Interlocutory decrees of such district courts or the judges thereof determining the rights and liabilities of the parties to admiralty cases in which appeals from final decrees are allowed.

(b) When a district judge, in making a civil action an order not otherwise appealable under this section, shall be of the opinion that such order involves a controlling question of law as to which there is substantial ground for difference of opinion and that an immediate appeal from the order may materially advance the ultimate termination of the litigation, he shall so state in writing in such order. The Court of Appeals which would have jurisdiction of an appeal of such action may thereupon, in its discretion, permit an appeal to be taken from such order, if application is made to it within ten days after the entry of the order: *Provided, however,* That application for an appeal hereunder shall not stay proceedings in the district court unless the district judge or the Court of Appeals or a judge thereof shall so order.

(c) The United States Court of Appeals for the Federal Circuit shall have exclusive jurisdiction—

(1) of an appeal from an interlocutory order or decree described in subsection (a) or (b) of this section in any case over which the court would have jurisdiction of an appeal under section 1295 of this title; and

(2) of an appeal from a judgment in a civil action for patent infringement which would otherwise be appealable to the United States Court of Appeals for the Federal Circuit and is final except for an accounting.

(d)(1) When the chief judge of the Court of International Trade issues an order under the provisions of section 256(b) of this title, or when any judge of the Court of International Trade, in issuing any other interlocutory order, includes in the order a statement that a controlling question of law is involved with respect to which there is a substantial ground for difference of opinion and that an immediate appeal from that order may materially advance the ultimate termination of the litigation, the United States Court of Appeals for the Federal Circuit may, in its discretion, permit an appeal to be taken from such order, if application is made to that Court within ten days after the entry of such order.

(2) When the chief judge of the United States Court of Federal Claims issues an order under section 798(b) of this title, or when any judge of the United States Claims Court, in issuing an interlocutory order, includes in the order a statement that a controlling question of law is involved with respect to which there is a substantial ground for difference of opinion and that an immediate appeal from that order may materially advance the ultimate termination of the litigation, the United States Court of Appeals for the Federal Circuit may, in its discretion, permit an appeal to be taken from such order, if application is made to that Court within ten days after the entry of such order.

(3) Neither the application for nor the granting of an appeal under this subsection shall stay proceedings in the Court of International Trade or in the Court of Federal Claims, as the case may be, unless a stay is ordered by a judge of the Court of International Trade or of the Court of Federal Claims or by the United States Court of Appeals for the Federal Circuit or a judge of that court.

(4)(A) The United States Court of Appeals for the Federal Circuit shall have exclusive jurisdiction of an appeal from an interlocutory order of a district court of the United States, the District Court of Guam, the District Court of the Virgin Islands, or the District Court for the Northern Mariana Islands, granting or denying, in whole or in part, a motion to transfer an action to the United States Court of Federal Claims under section 1631 of this title.

(B) When a motion to transfer an action to the Court of Federal Claims is filed in a district court, no further proceedings shall be taken in the district court until 60 days after the court has ruled upon the motion. If an appeal is taken from the district court's grant or denial of the motion, proceedings shall be further stayed until the appeal has been decided by the Court of Appeals for the Federal Circuit. The stay of proceedings in the district court shall not bar the granting of preliminary or injunctive relief, where appropriate and where expedition is reasonably necessary. However, during the period in which proceedings are stayed as provided in this subparagraph, no transfer to the Court of Federal Claims pursuant to the motion shall be carried out.

(e) The Supreme Court may prescribe rules, in accordance with section 2072 of this title, to provide for an appeal of an interlocutory decision to the courts of appeals that is not otherwise provided for under subsection (a), (b), (c), or (d).

§ 1295. Jurisdiction of the United States Court of Appeals for the Federal Circuit

(a) The United States Court of Appeals for the Federal Circuit shall have exclusive jurisdiction—

(1) of an appeal from a final decision of a district court of the United States, the United States District Court for the District of the Canal Zone, the District Court of Guam, the District Court of the Virgin Islands, or the District Court for the Northern Mariana Islands, if the jurisdiction of that court was based, in whole or in part, on section 1338 of this title, except that a case involving a claim arising under any Act of Congress relating to copyrights, exclusive rights in mask works, or trademarks and no other claims under section 1338(a) shall be governed by sections 1291, 1292, and 1294 of this title;

(2) of an appeal from a final decision of a district court of the United States, the United States District Court for the District of the Canal Zone, the District Court of Guam, the District Court of the Virgin Islands, or the District Court for the Northern Mariana

Islands, if the jurisdiction of that court was based, in whole or in part, on section 1346 of this title, except that jurisdiction of an appeal in a case brought in a district court under section 1346(a)(1), 1346(b), 1346(e), or 1346(f) of this title or under section 1346(a)(2) when the claim is founded upon an Act of Congress or a regulation of an executive department providing for internal revenue shall be governed by sections 1291, 1292, and 1294 of this title;

(3) of an appeal from a final decision of the United States Court of Federal Claims;

(4) of an appeal from a decision of—

(A) the Board of Patent Appeals and Interferences of the Patent and Trademark Office with respect to patent applications and interferences, at the instance of an applicant for a patent or any party to a patent interference, and any such appeal shall waive the right of such applicant or party to proceed under section 145 or 146 of title 35;

(B) the Commissioner of Patents and Trademarks or the Trademark Trial and Appeal Board with respect to applications for registration of marks and other proceedings as provided in section 21 of the Trademark Act of 1946 (15 U.S.C. 1071); or

(C) a district court to which a case was directed pursuant to section 145 or 146 of title 35;

(5) of an appeal from a final decision of the United States Court of International Trade;

(6) to review the final determinations of the United States International Trade Commission relating to unfair practices in import trade, made under section 337 of the Tariff Act of 1930 (19 U.S.C. 1337);

(7) to review, by appeal on questions of law only, findings of the Secretary of Commerce under U.S. note 6 to subchapter X of chapter 98 of the Harmonized Tariff Schedule of the United States (relating to importation of instruments or apparatus);

(8) of an appeal under section 71 of the Plant Variety Protection Act (7 U.S.C. 2461);

(9) of an appeal from a final order or final decision of the Merit Systems Protection Board, pursuant to sections 7703(b)(1) and 7703(d) of title 5;

(10) of an appeal from a final decision of an agency board of contract appeals pursuant to section 8(g)(1) of the Contract Disputes Act of 1978 (41 U.S.C. 607(g)(1));

(11) of an appeal under section 211 of the Economic Stabilization Act of 1970;

(12) of an appeal under section 5 of the Emergency Petroleum Allocation Act of 1973;

(13) of an appeal under section 506(c) of the Natural Gas Policy Act of 1978; and

(14) of an appeal under section 523 of the Energy Policy and Conservation Act.

(b) The head of any executive department or agency may, with the approval of the Attorney General, refer to the Court of Appeals for the Federal Circuit for judicial review any final decision rendered by a board of contract appeals pursuant to the terms of any contract with the United States awarded by that department or agency which the head of such department or agency has concluded is not entitled to finality pursuant to the review standards specified in section 10(b) of the Contract Disputes Act of 1978 (41 U.S.C. 609(b)). The head of each executive department or agency shall make any referral under this section within one hundred and twenty days after the receipt of a copy of the final appeal decision.

(c) The Court of Appeals for the Federal Circuit shall review the matter referred in accordance with the standards specified in section 10(b) of the Contract Disputes Act of 1978. The court shall proceed with judicial review on the administrative record made before the board of contract appeals on matters so referred as in other cases pending in such court, shall determine the issue of finality of the appeal decision, and shall, if appropriate, render judgment thereon, or remand the matter to any administrative or executive body or official with such direction as it may deem proper and just.

CHAPTER 85—DISTRICT COURTS; JURISDICTION

§ 1330. Actions against foreign states

(a) The district courts shall have original jurisdiction without regard to amount in controversy of any nonjury civil action against a foreign state as defined in section 1603(a) of this title as to any claim for relief in personam with respect to which the foreign state is not entitled to immunity either under sections 1605–1607 of this title or under any applicable international agreement.

(b) Personal jurisdiction over a foreign state shall exist as to every claim for relief over which the district courts have jurisdiction under subsection (a) where service has been made under section 1608 of this title.

(c) For purposes of subsection (b), an appearance by a foreign state does not confer personal jurisdiction with respect to any claim for relief not arising out of any transaction or occurrence enumerated in sections 1605–1607 of this title.

§ 1331. Federal question

The district courts shall have original jurisdiction of all civil actions arising under the Constitution, laws, or treaties of the United States.

§ 1332. Diversity of citizenship; amount in controversy; costs

(a) The district courts shall have original jurisdiction of all civil actions where the matter in controversy exceeds the sum or value of $75,000, exclusive of interest and costs, and is between—

(1) citizens of different States;

(2) citizens of a State and citizens or subjects of a foreign state;

(3) citizens of different States and in which citizens or subjects of a foreign state are additional parties; and

(4) a foreign state, defined in section 1603(a) of this title, as plaintiff and citizens of a State or of different States.

For the purposes of this section, section 1335, and section 1441, an alien admitted to the United States for permanent residence shall be deemed a citizen of the State in which such alien is domiciled.

(b) Except when express provision therefor is otherwise made in a statute of the United States, where the plaintiff who files the case originally in the Federal courts is finally adjudged to be entitled to recover less than the sum or value of $75,000, computed without regard to any setoff or counterclaim to which the defendant may be adjudged to be entitled, and exclusive of interest and costs, the district court may deny costs to the plaintiff and, in addition, may impose costs on the plaintiff.

(c) For the purposes of this section and section 1441 of this title—

(1) a corporation shall be deemed to be a citizen of any State by which it has been incorporated and of the State where it has its principal place of business, except that in any direct action against the insurer of a policy or contract of liability insurance, whether incorporated or unincorporated, to which action the insured is not joined as a party-defendant, such insurer shall be deemed a citizen of the State of which the insured is a citizen, as well as of any State by which the insurer has been incorporated and of the State where it has its principal place of business; and

(2) the legal representative of the estate of a decedent shall be deemed to be a citizen only of the same State as the decedent, and the legal representative of an infant or incompetent shall be deemed to be a citizen only of the same State as the infant or incompetent.

(d) (1) In this subsection—

(A) the term "class" means all of the class members in a class action;

(B) the term "class action" means any civil action filed under rule 23 of the Federal Rules of Civil Procedure or similar State statute or rule of judicial procedure authorizing an action to be brought by 1 or more representative persons as a class action;

(C) the term "class certification order" means an order issued by a court approving the treatment of some or all aspects of a civil action as a class action; and

(D) the term "class members" means the persons (named or unnamed) who fall within the definition of the proposed or certified class in a class action.

(2) The district courts shall have original jurisdiction of any civil action in which the matter in controversy exceed the sum or value of $5,000,000, exclusive of interest and costs, and is a class action in which—

(A) any member of a class of plaintiffs is a citizen of a State different from any defendant;

(B) any member of a class of plaintiffs is a foreign state or a citizen or subject of a foreign state and any defendant is a citizen of a State; or

(C) any member of a class of plaintiffs is a citizen of a State and any defendant is a foreign state or a citizen or subject of a foreign state.

(3) A district court may, in the interests of justice and looking at the totality of the circumstances, decline to exercise jurisdiction under paragraph (2) over a class action in which greater than one-third but less than two-thirds of the members of all proposed plaintiff classes in the aggregate and the primary defendants are citizen of the State in which the action was originally filed based on consideration of—

(A) whether the claims asserted involve matters of national or interstate interest;

(B) whether the claims asserted will be governed by laws of the State in which the action was originally filed or by the laws of other States;

(C) whether the class action has been pleaded in a manner that seeks to avoid Federal jurisdiction;

(D) whether the action was brought in a forum with a distinct nexus with the class members, the alleged harm, or the defendants;

(E) whether the number of citizens of the State in which the action was originally filed in all proposed plaintiff classes in the aggregate is substantially larger than the number of citizens from any other State, and the citizenship of the other members of the proposed class is dispersed among a substantial number of States; and

(F) whether, during the 3–year period preceding the filing of that class action, 1 or more other class actions asserting the same or similar claims on behalf of the same or other persons have been filed.

(4) A district court shall decline to exercise jurisdiction under paragraph (2)—

(A) (i) over a class action in which—

(I) greater than two-thirds of the members of all proposed plaintiff classes in the aggregate are citizens of the State in which the action was originally filed;

(II) at least 1 defendant is a defendant—

(aa) from whom significant relief is sought by members of the plaintiff class;

(bb) whose alleged conduct forms a significant basis for the claims asserted by the proposed plaintiff class; and

(cc) who is a citizen of the State in which the action was originally filed; and

(III) principal injuries resulting from the alleged conduct or any related conduct of each defendant were incurred in the State in which the action was originally filed; and

(ii) during the 3–year period preceding the filing of that class action, no other class action has been filed asserting the same or similar factual allegations against any of the defendants on behalf of the same or other persons; or

(B) two-thirds or more of the members of all proposed plaintiff classes in the aggregate, and the primary defendants, are citizens of the State in which the action was originally filed.

(5) Paragraphs (2) through (4) shall not apply to any class action in which—

(A) the primary defendants are States, State officials, or other governmental entities against whom the district court may be foreclosed from ordering relief; or

(B) the number of members of all proposed plaintiff classes in the aggregate is less than 100.

(6) In any class action, the claims of individual class members shall be aggregated to determine whether the matter in controversy exceeds the sum or value of $5,000,000, exclusive of interest and costs.

(7) Citizenship of the members of the proposed plaintiff classes shall be determined for purposes of paragraphs (2) through (6) as of the date of filing of the complaint or amended complaint, or if the case stated by the initial pleading is not subject to Federal jurisdiction, as of the date of service by plaintiffs of an amended pleading, motion, or other paper, indicating the existence of Federal jurisdiction.

(8) This subsection shall apply to any class action before or after the entry of a class certification order by the court with respect to that action.

(9) Paragraph (2) shall not apply to any class action that solely involves a claim—

(A) concerning a covered security as defined under 16(f)(3) of the Securities Act of 1933 (15 U.S.C. 78p(f)(3)) and section 28(f)(5)(E) of the Securities Exchange Act of 1934 (15 U.S.C. 78bb(f)(5)(E));

(B) that relates to the internal affairs or governance of a corporation or other form of business enterprise and that arises under or by virtue of the laws of the State in which such corporation or business enterprise is incorporated or organized; or

(C) that relates to the rights, duties (including fiduciary duties), and obligations relating to or created by or pursuant to any security (as defined under section 2(a)(1) of the Securities Act of 1933 (15 U.S.C. 77b(a)(1)) and the regulations issued thereunder).

(10) For purposes of this subsection and section 1453, an unincorporated association shall be deemed to be a citizen of the State where it has its principal place of business and the State under whose laws it is organized.

(11) (A) For purposes of this subsection and section 1453, a mass action shall be deemed to be a class action removable under paragraphs (2) through (10) if it otherwise meets the provisions of those paragraphs.

(B) (i) As used in subparagraph (A), the term "mass action" means any civil action (except a civil action within the scope of section 1711(2)) in which monetary relief claims of 100 or more persons are proposed to be tried jointly on the ground that the plaintiffs' claims involve common questions of law or fact, except that jurisdiction shall exist only over those plaintiffs whose claims in a mass action satisfy the jurisdictional amount requirements under subsection (a).

(ii) As used in subparagraph (A), the term "mass action" shall not include any civil action in which—

(I) all of the claims in the action arise from an event or occurrence in the State in which the action was filed, and that allegedly resulted in injuries in that State or in States contiguous to that State;

(II) the claims are joined upon motion of a defendant;

(III) all of the claims in the action are asserted on behalf of the general public (and not on behalf of individual claimants or members of a purported class) pursuant to a State statute specifically authorizing such action; or

(IV) the claims have been consolidated or coordinated solely for pretrial proceedings.

(C) (i) Any action(s) removed to Federal court pursuant to this subsection shall not thereafter be transferred to any other court pursuant to section 1407, or the rules promulgated thereunder, unless a majority of the plaintiffs in the action request transfer pursuant to section 1407.

(ii) This subparagraph will not apply—

(I) to cases certified pursuant to rule 23 of the Federal Rules of Civil Procedure; or

(II) if plaintiffs propose that the action proceed as a class action pursuant to rule 23 of the Federal Rules of Civil Procedure.

(D) The limitations periods on any claims asserted in a mass action that is removed to Federal court pursuant to this subsection shall be deemed tolled during the period that the action is pending in Federal court.

(e) The word "States", as used in this section, includes the Territories, the District of Columbia, and the Commonwealth of Puerto Rico.

§ 1333. Admiralty, maritime and prize cases

The district courts shall have original jurisdiction, exclusive of the courts of the States, of:

(1) Any civil case of admiralty or maritime jurisdiction, saving to suitors in all cases all other remedies to which they are otherwise entitled.

(2) Any prize brought into the United States and all proceedings for the condemnation of property taken as prize. As amended May 24, 1949, 63 Stat. 101.

§ 1335. Interpleader

(a) The district courts shall have original jurisdiction of any civil action of interpleader or in the nature of interpleader filed by any person, firm, or corporation, association, or society having in his or its custody or possession money or property of the value of $500 or more, or having issued a note, bond, certificate, policy of insurance, or other instrument of value or amount of $500 or more, or providing for the delivery or payment or the loan of money or property of such amount or value, or being under any obligation written or unwritten to the amount of $500 or more, if

(1) Two or more adverse claimants, of diverse citizenship as defined in subsection (a) or (d) of section 1332 of this title, are claiming or

may claim to be entitled to such money or property, or to any one or more of the benefits arising by virtue of any note, bond, certificate, policy or other instrument, or arising by virtue of any such obligation; and if (2) the plaintiff has deposited such money or property or has paid the amount of or the loan or other value of such instrument or the amount due under such obligation into the registry of the court, there to abide the judgment of the court, or has given bond payable to the clerk of the court in such amount and with such surety as the court or judge may deem proper, conditioned upon the compliance by the plaintiff with the future order or judgment of the court with respect to the subject matter of the controversy.

(b) Such an action may be entertained although the titles or claims of the conflicting claimants do not have a common origin, or are not identical, but are adverse to and independent of one another.

§ 1337. Commerce and antitrust regulations; amount in controversy, costs

(a) The district courts shall have original jurisdiction of any civil action or proceeding arising under any Act of Congress regulating commerce or protecting trade and commerce against restraints and monopolies: *Provided, however*, That the district courts shall have original jurisdiction of an action brought under section 11706 or 14706 of title 49, only if the matter in controversy for each receipt or bill of lading exceeds $10,000, exclusive of interest and costs.

(b) Except when express provision therefor is otherwise made in a statute of the United States, where a plaintiff who files the case under section 11706 or 14706 of title 49, originally in the Federal courts is finally adjudged to be entitled to recover less than the sum or value of $10,000, computed without regard to any setoff or counterclaim to which the defendant may be adjudged to be entitled, and exclusive of any interest and costs, the district court may deny costs to the plaintiff and, in addition, may impose costs on the plaintiff.

(c) The district courts shall not have jurisdiction under this section of any matter within the exclusive jurisdiction of the Court of International Trade under chapter 95 of this title.

§ 1338. Patents, plant variety protection, copyrights, trade-marks, mask works, and unfair competition

(a) The district courts shall have original jurisdiction of any civil action arising under any Act of Congress relating to patents, plant variety protection, copyrights and trade-marks. Such jurisdiction shall be exclusive of the courts of the states in patent, plant variety protection and copyright cases.

(b) The district courts shall have original jurisdiction of any civil action asserting a claim of unfair competition when joined with a substantial and related claim under the copyright, patent, plant variety protection, or trade-mark laws.

(c) Subsections (a) and (b) apply to exclusive rights in mask works under chapter 9 of title 17 to the same extent as such subsections apply to copyrights.

§ 1339. Postal matters

The district courts shall have original jurisdiction of any civil action arising under any Act of Congress relating to the postal service.

§ 1340. Internal revenue; customs duties

The district court shall have original jurisdiction of any civil action arising under any Act of Congress providing for internal revenue, or revenue from imports or tonnage except matters within the jurisdiction of the Court of International Trade.

§ 1341. Taxes by States

The district courts shall not enjoin, suspend or restrain the assessment, levy or collection of any tax under State law where a plain, speedy and efficient remedy may be had in the courts of such State.

§ 1342. Rate orders of State agencies

The district courts shall not enjoin, suspend or restrain the operation of, or compliance with, any order affecting rates chargeable by a public utility and made by a State administrative agency or a rate-making body of a State political subdivision, where:

(1) Jurisdiction is based solely on diversity of citizenship or repugnance of the order to the Federal Constitution; and,

(2) The order does not interfere with interstate commerce; and,

(3) The order has been made after reasonable notice and hearing; and,

(4) A plain, speedy and efficient remedy may be had in the courts of such State.

§ 1343. Civil rights and elective franchise

(a) The district courts shall have original jurisdiction of any civil action authorized by law to be commenced by any person:

(1) To recover damages for injury to his person or property, or because of the deprivation of any right or privilege of a citizen of the United States, by any act done in furtherance of any conspiracy mentioned in section 1985 of Title 42;

(2) To recover damages from any person who fails to prevent or to aid in preventing any wrongs mentioned in section 1985 of Title 42 which he had knowledge were about to occur and power to prevent;

(3) To redress the deprivation, under color of any State law, statute, ordinance, regulation, custom or usage, of any right, privilege or immunity secured by the Constitution of the United States or by any Act of Congress providing for equal rights of citizens or of all persons within the jurisdiction of the United States;

(4) To recover damages or to secure equitable or other relief under any Act of Congress providing for the protection of civil rights, including the right to vote.

(b) For purposes of this section—

(1) the District of Columbia shall be considered to be a State; and

(2) any Act of Congress applicable exclusively to the District of Columbia shall be considered to be a statute of the District of Columbia.

§ 1344. Election disputes

The district courts shall have original jurisdiction of any civil action to recover possession of any office, except that of elector of President or Vice President, United States Senator, Representative in or delegate to Congress, or member of a state legislature, authorized by law to be commenced, wherein it appears that the sole question touching the title to office arises out of denial of the right to vote, to any citizen offering to vote, on account of race, color or previous condition of servitude.

The jurisdiction under this section shall extend only so far as to determine the rights of the parties to office by reason of the denial of the right, guaranteed by the Constitution of the United States and secured by any law, to enforce the right of citizens of the United States to vote in all the States.

§ 1345. United States as plaintiff

Except as otherwise provided by Act of Congress, the district courts shall have original jurisdiction of all civil actions, suits or proceedings commenced by the United States, or by any agency or officer thereof expressly authorized to sue by Act of Congress.

§ 1346. United States as defendant

(a) The district courts shall have original jurisdiction, concurrent with the United States Court of Federal Claims, of:

(1) Any civil action against the United States for the recovery of any internal-revenue tax alleged to have been erroneously or illegally assessed or collected, or any penalty claimed to have been collected without authority or any sum alleged to have been excessive or in any manner wrongfully collected under the internal-revenue laws;

(2) Any other civil action or claim against the United States, not exceeding $10,000 in amount, founded either upon the Constitution, or any Act of Congress, or any regulation of an executive

department, or upon any express or implied contract with the United States, or for liquidated or unliquidated damages in cases not sounding in tort, except that the district courts shall not have jurisdiction of any civil action or claim against the United States founded upon any express or implied contract with the United States or for liquidated or unliquidated damages in cases not sounding in tort which are subject to sections 8(g)(1) and 10(a)(1) of the Contract Disputes Act of 1978. For the purpose of this paragraph, an express or implied contract with the Army and Air Force Exchange Service, Navy Exchanges, Marine Corps Exchanges, Coast Guard Exchanges, or Exchange Councils of the National Aeronautics and Space Administration shall be considered an express or implied contract with the United States.

(b)(1) Subject to the provisions of chapter 171 of this title, the district courts, together with the United States District Court for the District of the Canal Zone and the District Court of the Virgin Islands, shall have exclusive jurisdiction of civil actions on claims against the United States, for money damages, accruing on and after January 1, 1945, for injury or loss of property, or personal injury or death caused by the negligent or wrongful act or omission of any employee of the Government while acting within the scope of his office or employment, under circumstances where the United States, if a private person, would be liable to the claimant in accordance with the law of the place where the act or omission occurred.

(2) No person convicted of a felony who is incarcerated while awaiting sentencing or while serving a sentence may bring a civil action against the United States or an agency, officer, or employee of the Government, for mental or emotional injury suffered while in custody without a prior showing of physical injury.

(c) The jurisdiction conferred by this section includes jurisdiction of any set-off, counterclaim, or other claim or demand whatever on the part of the United States against any plaintiff commencing an action under this section.

(d) The district courts shall not have jurisdiction under this section of any civil action or claim for a pension.

(e) The district courts shall have original jurisdiction of any civil action against the United States provided in section 7426 or section 7428 (in the case of the United States district court for the District of Columbia) of the Internal Revenue Code of 1954.

(f) The district courts shall have exclusive original jurisdiction of civil actions under section 2409a to quiet title to an estate or interest in real property in which an interest is claimed by the United States.

(g) Subject to the provisions of chapter 179, the district courts of the United States shall have exclusive jurisdiction over any civil action commenced under section 453(2) of title 3, by a covered employee under chapter 5 of such title.

§ 1348. Banking association as party

The district courts shall have original jurisdiction of any civil action commenced by the United States, or by direction of any officer thereof, against any national banking association, any civil action to wind up the affairs of any such association, and any action by a banking association established in the district for which the court is held, under chapter 2 of Title 12, to enjoin the Comptroller of the Currency, or any receiver acting under his direction, as provided by such chapter.

All national banking associations shall, for the purposes of all other actions by or against them, be deemed citizens of the States in which they are respectively located.

§ 1349. Corporation organized under federal law as party

The district courts shall not have jurisdiction of any civil action by or against any corporation upon the ground that it was incorporated by or under an Act of Congress, unless the United States is the owner of more than one-half of its capital stock.

§ 1350. Alien's action for tort

The district courts shall have original jurisdiction of any civil action by an alien for a tort only, committed in violation of the law of nations or a treaty of the United States.

§ 1351. Consuls, vice consuls, and members of a diplomatic mission as defendant

The district courts shall have original jurisdiction, exclusive of the courts of the States, of all civil actions and proceedings against—

(1) consuls or vice consuls of foreign states; or

(2) members of a mission or members of their families (as such terms are defined in section 2 of the Diplomatic Relations Act).

§ 1354. Land grants from different states

The district courts shall have original jurisdiction of actions between citizens of the same state claiming lands under grants from different states.

§ 1355. Fine, penalty or forfeiture

(a) The district courts shall have original jurisdiction, exclusive of the courts of the States, of any action or proceeding for the recovery or enforcement of any fine, penalty, or forfeiture, pecuniary or otherwise, incurred under any Act of Congress, except matters within the jurisdiction of the Court of International Trade under section 1582 of this title.

(b)(1) A forfeiture action or proceeding may be brought in—

(A) the district court for the district in which any of the acts or omissions giving rise to the forfeiture occurred, or

(B) any other district where venue for the forfeiture action or proceeding is specifically provided for in section 1395 of this title or any other statute.

(2) Whenever property subject to forfeiture under the laws of the United States is located in a foreign country, or has been detained or seized pursuant to legal process or competent authority of a foreign government, an action or proceeding for forfeiture may be brought as provided in paragraph (1), or in the United States District court for the District of Columbia.

(c) In any case in which a final order disposing of property in a civil forfeiture action or proceeding is appealed, removal of the property by the prevailing party shall not deprive the court of jurisdiction. Upon motion of the appealing party, the district court or the court of appeals shall issue any order necessary to preserve the right of the appealing party to the full value of the property at issue, including a stay of the judgment of the district court pending appeal or requiring the prevailing party to post an appeal bond.

(d) Any court with jurisdiction over a forfeiture action pursuant to subsection (b) may issue and cause to be served in any other district such process as may be required to bring before the court the property that is the subject of the forfeiture action.

§ 1356. Seizures not within admiralty and maritime jurisdiction

The district courts shall have original jurisdiction, exclusive of the courts of the States, of any seizure under any law of the United States on land or upon waters not within admiralty and maritime jurisdiction, except matters within the jurisdiction of the Court of International Trade under section 1582 of this title.

§ 1357. Injuries under Federal laws

The district courts shall have original jurisdiction of any civil action commenced by any person to recover damages for any injury to his person or property on account of any act done by him, under any Act of Congress, for the protection or collection of any of the revenues, or to enforce the right of citizens of the United States to vote in any State.

§ 1358. Eminent domain

The district courts shall have original jurisdiction of all proceedings to condemn real estate for the use of the United States or its departments or agencies.

§ 1359. Parties collusively joined or made

A district court shall not have jurisdiction of a civil action in which any party, by assignment or otherwise, has been improperly or collusively made or joined to invoke the jurisdiction of such court.

§ 1360. State civil jurisdiction in actions to which Indians are parties

(a) Each of the States listed in the following table shall have jurisdiction over civil causes of action between Indians or to which Indians are parties which arise in the areas of Indian country listed opposite the name of the State to the same extent that such State has jurisdiction over other civil causes of action, and those civil laws of such State that are of general application to private persons or private property shall have the same force and effect within such Indian country as they have elsewhere within the State:

State of	Indian country affected
Alaska	All Indian country within the State
California	All Indian country within the State
Minnesota	All Indian country within the State, except the Red Lake Reservation
Nebraska	All Indian country within the State
Oregon	All Indian country within the State, except the Warm Springs Reservation
Wisconsin	All Indian country within the State

(b) Nothing in this section shall authorize the alienation, encumbrance, or taxation of any real or personal property, including water rights, belonging to any Indian or any Indian tribe, band, or community that is held in trust by the United States or is subject to a restriction against alienation imposed by the United States; or shall authorize regulation of the use of such property in a manner inconsistent with any Federal treaty, agreement, or statute or with any regulation made pursuant thereto; or shall confer jurisdiction upon the State to adjudicate, in probate proceedings or otherwise, the ownership or right to possession of such property or any interest therein.

(c) Any tribal ordinance or custom heretofore or hereafter adopted by an Indian tribe, band, or community in the exercise of any authority which it may possess shall, if not inconsistent with any applicable civil law of the State, be given full force and effect in the determination of civil causes of action pursuant to this section.

§ 1361. Action to compel an officer of the United States to perform his duty

The district courts shall have original jurisdiction of any action in the nature of mandamus to compel an officer or employee of the United States or any agency thereof to perform a duty owed to the plaintiff.

§ 1362. Indian tribes

The district courts shall have original jurisdiction of all civil actions, brought by any Indian tribe or band with a governing body duly recognized by the Secretary of the Interior, wherein the matter in controversy arises under the Constitution, laws, or treaties of the United States.

§ 1367. Supplemental jurisdiction

(a) Except as provided in subsections (b) and (c) or as expressly provided otherwise by Federal statute, in any civil action of which the district courts have original jurisdiction, the district courts shall have supplemental jurisdiction over all other claims that are so related to claims in the action within such original jurisdiction that they form part of the same case or controversy under Article III of the United States Constitution. Such supplemental jurisdiction shall include claims that involve the joinder or intervention of additional parties.

(b) In any civil action of which the district courts have original jurisdiction founded solely on section 1332 of this title, the district courts shall not have supplemental jurisdiction under subsection (a) over claims by plaintiffs against persons made parties under Rule 14, 19, 20, or 24 of the Federal Rules of Civil Procedure, or over claims by persons proposed to be joined as plaintiffs under Rule 19 of such rules, or seeking to intervene as plaintiffs under Rule 24 of such rules, when exercising supplemental jurisdiction over such claims would be inconsistent with the jurisdictional requirements of section 1332.

(c) The district courts may decline to exercise supplemental jurisdiction over a claim under subsection (a) if—

(1) the claim raises a novel or complex issue of State law,

(2) the claim substantially predominates over the claim or claims over which the district court has original jurisdiction,

(3) the district court has dismissed all claims over which it has original jurisdiction, or

(4) in exceptional circumstances, there are other compelling reasons for declining jurisdiction.

(d) The period of limitations for any claim asserted under subsection (a), and for any other claim in the same action that is voluntarily dismissed at the same time as or after the dismissal of the claim under subsection (a), shall be tolled while the claim is pending and for a period of 30 days after it is dismissed unless State law provides for a longer tolling period.

(e) As used in this section, the term "State" includes the District of Columbia, the Commonwealth of Puerto Rico, and any territory or possession of the United States.

§ 1369. Multiparty, multiforum jurisdiction

(a) **In general.**—The district courts shall have original jurisdiction of any civil action involving minimal diversity between adverse parties that arises from a single accident, where at least 75 natural persons have died in the accident at a discrete location, if—

(1) a defendant resides in a State and a substantial part of the accident took place in another State or other location, regardless of whether that defendant is also a resident of the State where a substantial part of the accident took place;

(2) any two defendants reside in different States, regardless of whether such defendants are also resident of the same State or States; or

(3) substantial parts of the accident took place in different States.

(b) **Limitation of jurisdiction of district courts.**—The district court shall abstain from hearing any civil action described in subsection (a) in which—

(1) the substantial majority of all plaintiffs are citizens of a single State of which the primary defendants are also citizens; and

(2) the claims asserted will be governed primarily by the laws of that State.

(c) **Special rules and definitions.**—For purposes of this section—

(1) minimal diversity exists between adverse parties if any party is a citizen of a State and any adverse party is a citizen of another State, a citizen or subject of a foreign state, or a foreign state as defined in section 1603(a) of this title;

(2) a corporation is deemed to be a citizen of any State, and a citizen or subject of any foreign state, in which it is incorporated or has its principal place of business, and is deemed to be a resident of any State in which it is incorporated or licensed to do business or is doing business;

(3) the term "injury" means—

(A) physical harm to a natural person; and

(B) physical damage to or destruction of tangible property, but only if physical harm described in subparagraph (A) exists;

(4) the term "accident" means a sudden accident, or a natural event culminating in an accident, that results in death incurred at a discrete location by at least 75 natural persons; and

(5) the term "State" includes the District of Columbia, the Commonwealth of Puerto Rico, and any territory or possession of the United States.

(d) **Intervening parties.**—In any action in a district court which is or could have been brought, in whole or in part, under this section, any person with a claim arising from the accident described in subsection (a) shall be permitted to intervene as a party plaintiff in the action, even if that person could not have brought an action in a district court as an original matter.

(e) **Notification of judicial panel on multidistrict litigation.**—A district court in which an action under this section is pending shall promptly notify the judicial panel on multidistrict litigation of the pendency of the action.

CHAPTER 87—DISTRICT COURTS; VENUE

§ 1391. Venue generally

(a) A civil action wherein jurisdiction is founded only on diversity of citizenship may, except as otherwise provided by law, be brought only in (1) a judicial district where any defendant resides, if all defendants reside in the same State, (2) a judicial district in which a substantial part of the events or omissions giving rise to the claim occurred, or a substantial part of property that is the subject of the action is situated, or (3) a judicial district in which any defendant is subject to personal jurisdiction at the time the action is commenced, if there is no district in which the action may otherwise be brought.

(b) A civil action wherein jurisdiction is not founded solely on diversity of citizenship may, except as otherwise provided by law, be brought only in (1) a judicial district where any defendant resides, if all defendants reside in the same State, (2) a judicial district in which a substantial part of the events or omissions giving rise to the claim occurred, or a substantial part of property that is the subject of the action is situated, or (3) a judicial district in which any defendant may be found, if there is no district in which the action may otherwise be brought.

(c) For purposes of venue under this chapter, a defendant that is a corporation shall be deemed to reside in any judicial district in which it is subject to personal jurisdiction at the time the action is commenced. In a State which has more than one judicial district and in which a defendant that is a corporation is subject to personal jurisdiction at the time an action is commenced, such corporation shall be deemed to reside in any district in that State within which its contacts would be sufficient to subject it to personal jurisdiction if that district were a separate State, and, if there is no such district, the corporation shall be deemed to reside in the district within which it has the most significant contacts.

(d) An alien may be sued in any district.

(e) A civil action in which a defendant is an officer or employee of the United States or any agency thereof acting in his official capacity or under color of legal authority, or an agency of the United States, or the United States, may, except as otherwise provided by law, be brought in any judicial district in which (1) a defendant in the action resides, (2) a substantial part of the events or omissions giving rise to the claim occurred, or a substantial part of property that is the subject of the action is situated, or (3) the plaintiff resides if no real property is involved in the action. Additional persons may be joined as parties to any such action in accordance with the Federal Rules of Civil Procedure and with such other venue requirements as would be applicable if the United States or one of its officers, employees, or agencies were not a party.

The summons and complaint in such an action shall be served as provided by the Federal Rules of Civil Procedure except that the delivery of the summons and complaint to the officer or agency as required by the rules may be made by certified mail beyond the territorial limits of the district in which the action is brought.

(f) A civil action against a foreign state as defined in section 1603(a) of this title may be brought—

(1) in any judicial district in which a substantial part of the events or omissions giving rise to the claim occurred, or a substantial part of property that is the subject of the action is situated;

(2) in any judicial district in which the vessel or cargo of a foreign state is situated, if the claim is asserted under section 1605(b) of this title;

(3) in any judicial district in which the agency or instrumentality is licensed to do business or is doing business, if the action is brought against an agency or instrumentality of a foreign state as defined in section 1603(b) of this title; or

(4) in the United States District Court for the District of Columbia if the action is brought against a foreign state or political subdivision thereof.

(g) A civil action in which jurisdiction of the district court is based upon section 1369 of this title may be brought in any district in which any defendant resides or in which a substantial part of the accident giving rise to the action took place.

§ 1392. Defendants or property in different districts in same State

Any civil action, of a local nature, involving property located in different districts in the same State, may be brought in any of such districts.

§ 1394. Banking association's action against Comptroller of Currency

Any civil action by a national banking association to enjoin the Comptroller of the Currency, under the provisions of any Act of Congress relating to such associations, may be prosecuted in the judicial district where such association is located.

§ 1395. Fine, penalty or forfeiture

(a) A civil proceeding for the recovery of a pecuniary fine, penalty or forfeiture may be prosecuted in the district where it accrues or the defendant is found.

(b) A civil proceeding for the forfeiture of property may be prosecuted in any district where such property is found.

(c) A civil proceeding for the forfeiture of property seized outside any judicial district may be prosecuted in any district into which the property is brought.

(d) A proceeding in admiralty for the enforcement of fines, penalties and forfeitures against a vessel may be brought in any district in which the vessel is arrested.

(e) Any proceeding for the forfeiture of a vessel or cargo entering a port of entry closed by the President in pursuance of law, or of goods and chattels coming from a State or section declared by proclamation of the President to be in insurrection, or of any vessel or vehicle conveying persons or property to or from such State or section or belonging in whole or in part to a resident thereof, may be prosecuted in any district into which the property is taken and in which the proceeding is instituted.

§ 1396. Internal revenue taxes

Any civil action for the collection of internal revenue taxes may be brought in the district where the liability for such tax accrues, in the district of the taxpayer's residence, or in the district where the return was filed.

§ 1397. Interpleader

Any civil action of interpleader or in the nature of interpleader under section 1335 of this title may be brought in the judicial district in which one or more of the claimants reside.

§ 1400. Patents and copyrights

(a) Civil actions, suits, or proceedings arising under any Act of Congress relating to copyrights or exclusive rights in mask works may be instituted in the district in which the defendant or his agent resides or may be found.

(b) Any civil action for patent infringement may be brought in the judicial district where the defendant resides, or where the defendant has committed acts of infringement and has a regular and established place of business.

§ 1401. Stockholder's derivative action

Any civil action by a stockholder on behalf of his corporation may be prosecuted in any judicial district where the corporation might have sued the same defendants.

§ 1402. United States as defendant

(a) Any civil action in a district court against the United States under subsection (a) of section 1346 of this title may be prosecuted only:

(1) Except as provided in paragraph (2), in the judicial district where the plaintiff resides;

(2) In the case of a civil action by a corporation under paragraph (1) of subsection (a) of section 1346, in the judicial district in which is located the principal place of business or principal office or agency of the corporation; or if it has no principal place of business or principal office or agency in any judicial district (A) in the judicial district in which is located the office to which was made the return of the tax in respect of which the claim is made, or (B) if no return was made, in the judicial district in which lies the District of Columbia. Notwithstanding the foregoing provisions of this paragraph a district court, for the convenience of the parties and witnesses, in the interest of justice, may transfer any such action to any other district or division.

(b) Any civil action on a tort claim against the United States under subsection (b) of section 1346 of this title may be prosecuted only in the judicial district where the plaintiff resides or wherein the act or omission complained of occurred.

(c) Any civil action against the United States under subsection (e) of section 1346 of this title may be prosecuted only in the judicial district where the property is situated at the time of levy, or if no levy is made, in the judicial district in which the event occurred which gave rise to the cause of action.

(d) Any civil action under section 2409a to quiet title to an estate or interest in real property in which an interest is claimed by the United States shall be brought in the district court of the district where the property is located or, if located in different districts, in any of such districts.

§ 1403. Eminent domain

Proceedings to condemn real estate for the use of the United States or its departments or agencies shall be brought in the district court of the district where the land is located or, if located in different districts in the same State, in any of such districts.

§ 1404. Change of venue

(a) For the convenience of parties and witnesses, in the interest of justice, a district court may transfer any civil action to any other district or division where it might have been brought.

(b) Upon motion, consent or stipulation of all parties, any action, suit or proceeding of a civil nature or any motion or hearing thereof, may be transferred, in the discretion of the court, from the division in which pending to any other division in the same district. Transfer of proceedings in rem brought by or on behalf of the United States may be transferred under this section without the consent of the United States where all other parties request transfer.

(c) A district court may order any civil action to be tried at any place within the division in which it is pending.

(d) As used in this section, "district court" includes the District Court of Guam, the District Court for the Northern Mariana Islands, and the District Court of the Virgin Islands, and the term "district" includes the territorial jurisdiction of each such court.

§ 1405. Creation or alteration of district or division

Actions or proceedings pending at the time of the creation of a new district or division or transfer of a county or territory from one division or district to another may be tried in the district or division as it existed at the institution of the action or proceeding, or in the district or division so created or to which the county or territory is so transferred as the parties shall agree or the court direct.

§ 1406. Cure or waiver of defects

(a) The district court of a district in which is filed a case laying venue in the wrong division or district shall dismiss, or if it be in the interest of justice, transfer such case to any district or division in which it could have been brought.

(b) Nothing in this chapter shall impair the jurisdiction of a district court of any matter involving a party who does not interpose timely and sufficient objection to the venue.

(c) As used in this section, the term "district court" includes the District Court of Guam, the District Court for the Northern Mariana Islands, and the District Court of the Virgin Islands; and the term "district" includes the territorial jurisdiction of each court.

§ 1407. Multidistrict litigation

(a) When civil actions involving one or more common questions of fact are pending in different districts, such actions may be transferred to any district for coordinated or consolidated pretrial proceedings. Such transfers shall be made by the judicial panel on multidistrict litigation authorized by this section upon its determination that transfers for such proceedings will be for the convenience of parties and witnesses and will promote the just and efficient conduct of such actions. Each action so transferred shall be remanded by the panel at or before the conclusion of such pretrial proceedings to the district from which it was transferred unless it shall have been previously terminated: *Provided, however,* That the panel may separate any claim, cross-claim, counter-claim, or third-party claim and remand any of such claims before the remainder of the action is remanded.

(b) Such coordinated or consolidated pretrial proceedings shall be conducted by a judge or judges to whom such actions are assigned by the judicial panel on multidistrict litigation. For this purpose, upon request of the panel, a circuit judge or a district judge may be designated and assigned temporarily for service in the transferee district by the Chief Justice of the United States or the chief judge of the circuit, as may be required, in accordance with the provisions of chapter 13 of this title.

With the consent of the transferee district court, such actions may be assigned by the panel to a judge or judges of such district. The judge or judges to whom such actions are assigned, the members of the judicial panel on multidistrict litigation, and other circuit and district judges designated when needed by the panel may exercise the powers of a district judge in any district for the purpose of conducting pretrial depositions in such coordinated or consolidated pretrial proceedings.

(c) Proceedings for the transfer of an action under this section may be initiated by—

(i) the judicial panel on multidistrict litigation upon its own initiative, or

(ii) motion filed with the panel by a party in any action in which transfer for coordinated or consolidated pretrial proceedings under this section may be appropriate. A copy of such motion shall be filed in the district court in which the moving party's action is pending.

The panel shall give notice to the parties in all actions in which transfers for coordinated or consolidated pretrial proceedings are contemplated, and such notice shall specify the time and place of any hearing to determine whether such transfer shall be made. Orders of the panel to set a hearing and other orders of the panel issued prior to the order either directing or denying transfer shall be filed in the office of the clerk of the district court in which a transfer hearing is to be or has been held. The panel's order of transfer shall be based upon a record of such hearing at which material evidence may be offered by any party to an action pending in any district that would be affected by the proceedings under this section, and shall be supported by findings of fact and conclusions of law based upon such record. Orders of transfer and such other orders as the panel may make thereafter shall be filed in the office of the clerk of the district court of the transferee district and shall be effective when thus filed. The clerk of the transferee district court shall forthwith transmit a certified copy of the panel's order to transfer to the clerk of the district court from which the action is being transferred. An order denying transfer shall be filed in each district wherein there is a case pending in which the motion for transfer has been made.

(d) The judicial panel on multidistrict litigation shall consist of seven circuit and district judges designated from time to time by the Chief Justice of the United States, no two of whom shall be from the same circuit. The concurrence of four members shall be necessary to any action by the panel.

(e) No proceedings for review of any order of the panel may be permitted except by extraordinary writ pursuant to the provisions of title 28, section 1651, United States Code. Petitions for an extraordinary writ to review an order of the panel to set a transfer hearing and other orders of the panel issued prior to the order either directing or denying transfer shall be filed only in the court of appeals having jurisdiction over the district in which a hearing is to be or has been held. Petitions for an extraordinary writ to review an order to transfer or orders subsequent to transfer shall be filed only in the court of appeals having jurisdiction over the transferee district. There shall be no appeal or review of an order of the panel denying a motion to transfer for consolidated or coordinated proceedings.

(f) The panel may prescribe rules for the conduct of its business not inconsistent with Acts of Congress and the Federal Rules of Civil Procedure.

(g) Nothing in this section shall apply to any action in which the United States is a complainant arising under the antitrust laws. "Antitrust laws" as used herein include those acts referred to in the Act of October 15, 1914, as amended (38 Stat. 730; 15 U.S.C. § 12), and also include the Act of June 19, 1936 (49 Stat. 1526; 15 U.S.C. §§ 13, 13a, and 13b) and the Act of September 26, 1914, as added March 21, 1938 (52 Stat. 116, 117; 15 U.S.C. § 56); but shall not include section 4A of the Act of October 15, 1914 as added July 7, 1955 (69 Stat. 282; 15 U.S.C. § 15a).

(h) Notwithstanding the provisions of section 1404 or subsection (f) of this section, the judicial panel on multidistrict litigation may consolidate and transfer with or without the consent of the parties, for both pretrial purposes and for trial, any action brought under section 4C of the Clayton Act.

CHAPTER 89—DISTRICT COURTS; REMOVAL
OF CASES FROM STATE COURTS

§ 1441. Actions removable generally

(a) Except as otherwise expressly provided by Act of Congress, any civil action brought in a State court of which the district courts of the United States have original jurisdiction, may be removed by the defendant or the defendants, to the district court of the United States for the district and division embracing the place where such action is pending. For purposes of removal under this chapter, the citizenship of defendants sued under fictitious names shall be disregarded.

(b) Any civil action of which the district courts have original jurisdiction founded on a claim or right arising under the Constitution, treaties or laws of the United States shall be removable without regard to the citizenship or residence of the parties. Any other such action shall be removable only if none of the parties in interest properly joined and served as defendants is a citizen of the State in which such action is brought.

(c) Whenever a separate and independent claim or cause of action, within the jurisdiction conferred by section 1331 of this title is joined with one or more otherwise non-removable claims or causes of action, the entire case may be removed and the district court may determine all issues therein, or, in its discretion, may remand all matters in which State law predominates.

(d) Any civil action brought in a State court against a foreign state as defined in section 1603(a) of this title may be removed by the foreign state to the district court of the United States for the district and division embracing the place where such action is pending. Upon removal the action shall be tried by the court without jury. Where removal is based upon this subsection, the time limitations of section 1446(b) of this chapter may be enlarged at any time for cause shown.

(e) (1) Notwithstanding the provisions of subsection (b) of this section, a defendant in a civil action in a State court may remove the action to the district court of the United States for the district and division embracing the place where the action is pending if—

(A) the action could have been brought in a United States district court under section 1369 of this title; or

(B) the defendant is a party to an action which is or could have been brought, in whole or in part, under section 1369 in a United States district court and arises from the same accident as the action in State court, even if the action to be removed could not have been brought in a district court as an original matter.

The removal of an action under this subsection shall be made in accordance with section 1446 of this title, except that a notice of removal may also be filed before trial of the action in State court within 30 days after the date on which the defendant first becomes a party to an action under section 1369 in a United States district court that arises from the same accident as the action in State court, or at a later time with leave of the district court.

(2) Whenever an action is removed under this subsection and the district court to which it is removed or transferred under section 1407(j) has made a liability determination requiring further proceedings as to damages, the district court shall remand the action to the State court from which it had been removed for the determination of damages, unless the court finds that, for the convenience of parties and witnesses and in the interest of justice, the action should be retained for the determination of damages.

(3) Any remand under paragraph (2) shall not be effective until 60 days after the district court has issued an order determining liability and has certified its intention to remand the removed action for the determination of damages. An appeal with respect to the liability determination of the district court may be taken during that 60–day period to the court of appeals with appellate jurisdiction over the district court. In the event a party files such an appeal, the remand shall not be effective until the appeal has been finally disposed of. Once the remand has become effective, the liability determination shall not be subject to further review by appeal or otherwise.

(4) Any decision under this subsection concerning remand for the determination of damages shall not be reviewable by appeal or otherwise.

(5) An action removed under this subsection shall be deemed to be an action under section 1369 and an action in which jurisdiction is based on section 1369 of this title for purposes of this section and sections 1407, 1697, and 1785 of this title.

(6) Nothing in this subsection shall restrict the authority of the district court to transfer or dismiss an action on the ground of inconvenient forum.

(f) The court to which a civil action is removed under this section is not precluded from hearing and determining any claim in such civil action because the State court from which such civil action is removed did not have jurisdiction over that claim.

§ 1442. Federal officers or agencies sued or prosecuted

(a) A civil action or criminal prosecution commenced in a State court against any of the following may be removed by them to the district court of the United States for the district and division embracing the place wherein it is pending:

(1) The United States or any agency thereof, or any officer (or any person acting under that officer) of the United States or of any agency thereof, sued in an official or individual capacity for any act under color of such office or on account of any right, title or authority claimed under any Act of Congress for the apprehension or punishment of criminals or the collection of the revenue.

(2) A property holder whose title is derived from any such officer, where such action or prosecution affects the validity of any law of the United States.

(3) Any officer of the courts of the United States, for any Act under color of office or in the performance of his duties;

(4) Any officer of either House of Congress, for any act in the discharge of his official duty under an order of such House.

(b) A personal action commenced in any State court by an alien against any citizen of a State who is, or at the time the alleged action accrued was, a civil officer of the United States and is a nonresident of such State, wherein jurisdiction is obtained by the State court by personal service of process, may be removed by the defendant to the district court of the United States for the district and division in which the defendant was served with process.

§ 1442a. Members of armed forces sued or prosecuted

A civil or criminal prosecution in a court of a State of the United States against a member of the armed forces of the United States on account of an act done under color of his office or status, or in respect to which he claims any right, title, or authority under a law of the United

States respecting the armed forces thereof, or under the law of war, may at any time before the trial or final hearing thereof be removed for trial into the district court of the United States for the district where it is pending in the manner prescribed by law, and it shall thereupon be entered on the docket of the district court, which shall proceed as if the cause had been originally commenced therein and shall have full power to hear and determine the cause.

§ 1443. Civil rights cases

Any of the following civil actions or criminal prosecutions, commenced in a State court may be removed by the defendant to the district court of the United States for the district and division embracing the place wherein it is pending:

(1) Against any person who is denied or cannot enforce in the courts of such State a right under any law providing for the equal civil rights of citizens of the United States, or of all persons within the jurisdiction thereof;

(2) For any act under color of authority derived from any law providing for equal rights, or for refusing to do any act on the ground that it would be inconsistent with such law.

§ 1444. Foreclosure action against United States

Any action brought under section 2410 of this title against the United States in any State court may be removed by the United States to the district court of the United States for the district and division in which the action is pending.

§ 1445. Nonremovable actions

(a) A civil action in any State court against a railroad or its receivers or trustees, arising under sections 1–4 and 5–10 of the Act of April 22, 1908 (45 U.S.C. 51–54, 55–60), may not be removed to any district court of the United States.

(b) A civil action in any State court against a common carrier or its receivers or trustees to recover damages for delay, loss, or injury of shipments, arising under section 11706 or 14706 of title 49, may not be removed to any district court of the United States unless the matter in controversy exceeds $10,000, exclusive of interest and costs.

(c) A civil action in any State court arising under the workmen's compensation laws of such State may not be removed to any district court of the United States.

(d) A civil action in any State court arising under section 40302 of the Violence Against Women Act of 1994 may not be removed to any district court of the United States.

§ 1446. Procedure for removal

(a) A defendant or defendants desiring to remove any civil action or criminal prosecution from a State court shall file in the district court of the United States for the district and division within which such action is pending a notice of removal signed pursuant to Rule 11 of the Federal Rules of Civil Procedure and containing a short and plain statement of the grounds for removal, together with a copy of all process, pleadings, and orders served upon such defendant or defendants in such action.

(b) The notice of removal of a civil action or proceeding shall be filed within thirty days after the receipt by the defendant, through service or otherwise, of a copy of the initial pleading setting forth the claim for relief upon which such action or proceeding is based, or within thirty days after the service of summons upon the defendant if such initial pleading has then been filed in court and is not required to be served on the defendant, whichever period is shorter.

If the case stated by the initial pleading is not removable, a notice of removal may be filed within thirty days after receipt by the defendant, through service or otherwise, of a copy of an amended pleading, motion, order or other paper from which it may first be ascertained that the case is one which is or has become removable except that a case may not be removed on the basis of jurisdiction conferred by section 1332 of this title more than 1 year after commencement of the action.

(c)(1) A notice of removal of a criminal prosecution shall be filed not later than thirty days after the arraignment in the State court, or at any time before trial, whichever is earlier, except that for good cause shown the United States district court may enter an order granting the defendant or defendants leave to file the notice at a later time.

(2) A notice of removal of a criminal prosecution shall include all grounds for such removal. A failure to state grounds which exist at the time of the filing of the notice shall constitute a waiver of such grounds, and a second notice may be filed only on grounds not existing at the time of the original notice. For good cause shown, the United States district court may grant relief from the limitations of this paragraph.

(3) The filing of a notice of removal of a criminal prosecution shall not prevent the State court in which such prosecution is pending from proceeding further, except that a judgment of conviction shall not be entered unless the prosecution is first remanded.

(4) The United States district court in which such notice is filed shall examine the notice promptly. If it clearly appears on the face of the notice and any exhibits annexed thereto that removal shall not be permitted, the court shall make an order for summary remand.

(5) If the United States district court does not order the summary remand of such prosecution, it shall order an evidentiary hearing to be held promptly and after such hearing shall make such disposition of the prosecution as justice shall require. If the United States district court determines that removal shall be permitted, it shall so notify the State court in which prosecution is pending, which shall proceed no further.

(d) Promptly after the filing of such notice of removal of a civil action the defendant or defendants shall give written notice thereof to all adverse parties and shall file a copy of the notice with the clerk of such State court, which shall effect the removal and the State court shall proceed no further unless and until the case is remanded.

(e) If the defendant or defendants are in actual custody on process issued by the State court, the district court shall issue its writ of habeas corpus, and the marshal shall thereupon take such defendant or defendants into his custody and deliver a copy of the writ to the clerk of such State court.

(f) With respect to any counterclaim removed to a district court pursuant to section 337(c) of Tariff Act of 1930, the district court shall resolve such counterclaim in the same manner as an original complaint under the Federal Rules of Civil Procedure, except that the payment of a filing fee shall not be required in such cases and the counterclaim shall relate back to the date of the original complaint in the proceeding before the International Trade Commission under section 337 of the Act.

§ 1447. Procedure after removal generally

(a) In any case removed from a State court, the district court may issue all necessary orders and process to bring before it all proper parties whether served by process issued by the State court or otherwise.

(b) It may require the removing party to file with its clerk copies of all records and proceedings in such State court or may cause the same to be brought before it by writ of certiorari issued to such State court.

(c) A motion to remand the case on the basis of any defect other than lack of subject matter jurisdiction must be made within 30 days after the filing of the notice of removal under section 1446(a). If at any time before final judgment it appears that the district court lacks subject matter jurisdiction, the case shall be remanded. An order remanding the case may require payment of just costs and any actual expenses, including attorney fees, incurred as a result of the removal. A certified copy of the order of remand shall be mailed by the clerk to the clerk of the State court. The State court may thereupon proceed with such case.

(d) An order remanding a case to the State court from which it was removed is not reviewable on appeal or otherwise, except that an order remanding a case to the State court from which it was removed pursuant to section 1443 of this title shall be reviewable by appeal or otherwise.

(e) If after removal the plaintiff seeks to join additional defendants whose joinder would destroy subject matter jurisdiction, the court may deny joinder, or permit joinder and remand the action to the State court.

§ 1448. Process after removal

In all cases removed from any State court to any district court of the United States in which any one or more of the defendants has not been served with process or in which the service has not been perfected prior to removal, or in which process served proves to be defective, such process or service may be completed or new process issued in the same manner as in cases originally filed in such district court.

This section shall not deprive any defendant upon whom process is served after removal of his right to move to remand the case.

§ 1449. State court record supplied

Where a party is entitled to copies of the records and proceedings in any suit or prosecution in a State court, to be used in any district court of the United States, and the clerk of such State court, upon demand, and the payment or tender of the legal fees, fails to deliver certified copies, the district court may, on affidavit reciting such facts, direct such record to be supplied by affidavit or otherwise. Thereupon such proceedings, trial, and judgment may be had in such district court, and all such process awarded, as if certified copies had been filed in the district court.

§ 1450. Attachment or sequestration; securities

Whenever any action is removed from a State court to a district court of the United States, any attachment or sequestration of the goods or estate of the defendant in such action in the State court shall hold the goods or estate to answer the final judgment or decree in the same manner as they would have been held to answer final judgment or decree had it been rendered by the State court.

All bonds, undertakings, or security given by either party in such action prior to its removal shall remain valid and effectual notwithstanding such removal.

All injunctions, orders, and other proceedings had in such action prior to its removal shall remain in full force and effect until dissolved or modified by the district court.

§ 1451. Definitions

For purposes of this chapter—

(1) The term "State court" includes the Superior Court of the District of Columbia.

(2) The term "State" includes the District of Columbia.

§ 1453. Removal of class actions

(a) **Definitions.**—In this section, the terms "class", "class action", "class certification order", and "class member" shall have the meanings given such terms under section 1332(d)(1).

(b) **In general.**—A class action may be removed to a district court of the United States in accordance with section 1446 (except that the 1–year limitation under section 1446(b) shall not apply), without regard to whether any defendant is a citizen of the State in which the action is brought, except that such action may be removed by any defendant without the consent of all defendants.

(c) **Review of remand orders.—**

(1) **In general.**—Section 1447 shall apply to any removal of a case under this section, except that notwithstanding section 1447(d), a court of appeals may accept an appeal from an order of a district court granting or denying a motion to remand a class action to the State court from which it was removed if application is made to the court of appeals not less than 7 days after entry of the order.

(2) **Time period for judgment.**—If the court of appeals accepts an appeal under paragraph (1), the court shall complete all action on such appeal, including rendering judgment, not later than 60 days after the date on which such appeal was filed, unless an extension is granted under paragraph (3).

(3) **Extension of time period.**—The court of appeals may grant an extension of the 60–day time period described in paragraph (2) if–

(A) all parties to the proceeding agree to such an extension, for any period of time; or

(B) such extension is for good cause shown and in the interests of justice, or a period not to exceed 10 days.

(4) **Denial of appeal.**—If a final judgment on the appeal under paragraph (1) is not issued before the end of the period described in paragraph (2), including any extension under paragraph (3), the appeal shall be denied.

(d) **Exception.**—This section shall not apply to any class action that solely involves—

(1) a claim concerning a covered security as defined under section 16(f)(3) of the Securities Act of 1933 (15 U.S.C. 78p(f)(3)) and section 28(f)(5)(E) of the Securities Exchange Act of 1934 (15 U.S.C. 78bb(f)(5)(E));

(2) a claim that relates to the internal affairs or governance of a corporation or other form of business enterprise and arises under or by virtue of the laws of the State in which such corporation or business enterprise is incorporated or organized; or

(3) a claim that relates to the rights, duties (including fiduciary duties), and obligations relating to or created by or pursuant to any security (as defined under section 2(a)(1) of the Securities Act of 1933 (15 U.S.C. 77b(a)(1)) and the regulations issued thereunder).

CHAPTER 111—GENERAL PROVISIONS

§ 1651. Writs

(a) The Supreme Court and all courts established by Act of Congress may issue all writs necessary or appropriate in aid of their respective jurisdictions and agreeable to the usages and principles of law.

(b) An alternative writ or rule nisi may be issued by a justice or judge of a court which has jurisdiction.

§ 1652. State laws as rules of decision

The laws of the several states, except where the Constitution or treaties of the United States or Acts of Congress otherwise require or provide, shall be regarded as rules of decision in civil actions in the courts of the United States, in cases where they apply.

§ 1653. Amendment of pleadings to show jurisdiction

Defective allegations of jurisdiction may be amended, upon terms, in the trial or appellate courts.

§ 1654. Appearance personally or by counsel

In all courts of the United States the parties may plead and conduct their own cases personally or by counsel, as, by the rules of such courts, respectively, are permitted to manage and conduct causes therein.

CHAPTER 113—PROCESS

§ 1697. Service in multiparty, multiforum actions

When the jurisdiction of the district court is based in whole or in part upon section 1369 of this title, process, other than subpoenas, may be served at any place within the United States, or anywhere outside the United States if otherwise permitted by law.

CHAPTER 115—EVIDENCE; DOCUMENTARY

§ 1738. State and Territorial statutes and judicial proceedings; full faith and credit

The Acts of the legislature of any State, Territory, or Possession of the United States, or copies thereof, shall be authenticated by affixing the seal of such State, Territory or Possession thereto.

The records and judicial proceedings of any court of any such State, Territory or Possession, or copies thereof, shall be proved or admitted in other courts within the United States and its Territories and Possessions by the attestation of the clerk and seal of the court annexed, if a seal exists, together with a certificate of a judge of the court that the said attestation is in proper form.

Such Acts, records and judicial proceedings or copies thereof, so authenticated, shall have the same full faith and credit in every court within the United States and its Territories and Possessions as they have by law or usage in the courts of such State, Territory or Possession from which they are taken.

§ 1738A. Full faith and credit given to child custody determinations

(a) The appropriate authorities of every State shall enforce according to its terms, and shall not modify except as provided in subsection (f) of this section, any child custody determination made consistently with the provisions of this section by a court of another State.

(b) As used in this section, the term—

(1) "child" means a person under the age of eighteen;

(2) "contestant" means a person, including a parent, who claims a right to custody or visitation of a child;

(3) "custody determination" means a judgment, decree, or other order of a court providing for the custody or visitation of a child, and includes permanent and temporary orders, and initial orders and modifications;

(4) "home State" means the State in which, immediately preceding the time involved, the child lived with his parents, a parent, or a person acting as parent, for at least six consecutive months, and in the case of a child less than six months old, the State in which the child lived from birth with any of such persons. Periods of temporary absence of any of such persons are counted as part of the six-month or other period;

(5) "modification" and "modify" refer to a custody determination which modifies, replaces, supersedes, or otherwise is made subsequent to, a prior custody determination concerning the same child, whether made by the same court or not;

(6) "person acting as a parent" means a person, other than a parent, who has physical custody of a child and who has either been awarded custody by a court or claims a right to custody;

(7) "physical custody" means actual possession and control of a child; and

(8) "State" means a State of the United States, the District of Columbia, the Commonwealth of Puerto Rico, or a territory or possession of the United States.

(c) A child custody determination made by a court of a State is consistent with the provisions of this section only if—

(1) such court has jurisdiction under the law of such State; and

(2) one of the following conditions is met:

(A) such State (i) is the home State of the child on the date of the commencement of the proceeding, or (ii) had been the child's home State within six months before the date of the commencement of the proceeding and the child is absent from such State because of his removal or retention by a contestant or for other reasons, and a contestant continues to live in such State;

(B)(i) it appears that no other State would have jurisdiction under subparagraph (A), and (ii) it is in the best interest of the child that a court of such State assume jurisdiction because (i) the child and his parents, or the child and at least one contestant, have a significant connection with such State other than mere physical presence in such State, and (ii) there is available in such state substantial evidence concerning the child's present or future care, protection, training, and personal relationships;

(C) the child is physically present in such State and (i) the child has been abandoned, or (ii) it is necessary in an emergency to protect the child because he has been subjected to or threatened with mistreatment or abuse;

(D)(i) it appears that no other state would have jurisdiction under subparagraph (A), (B), (C), or (E), or another State has declined to exercise jurisdiction on the ground that the State whose jurisdiction is in issue is the more appropriate forum to determine the custody of the child, and (ii) it is in the best interest of the child that such court assume jurisdiction; or

(E) the court has continuing jurisdiction pursuant to subsection (d) of this section.

(d) The jurisdiction of a court of a State which has made a child custody determination consistently with the provisions of this section continues as long as the requirement of subsection (c)(1) of this section continues to be met and such State remains the residence of the child or of any contestant.

(e) Before a child custody determination is made, reasonable notice and opportunity to be heard shall be given to the contestants, any parent whose parental rights have not been previously terminated and any person who has physical custody of a child.

(f) A court of a State may modify a determination of the custody of the same child made by a court of another State, if—

(1) it has jurisdiction to make such a child custody determination; and

(2) the court of the other State no longer has jurisdiction, or it has declined to exercise such jurisdiction to modify such determination.

(g) A court of a State shall not exercise jurisdiction in any proceeding for a custody determination commenced during the pendency of a proceeding in a court of another State where such court of that other State is exercising jurisdiction consistently with the provisions of this section to make a custody determination.

(h) A court of a State may not modify a visitation determination made by a court of another State unless the court of the other State no longer has jurisdiction to modify such determination or has declined to exercise jurisdiction to modify such determination.

§ 1739. State and Territorial nonjudicial records; full faith and credit

All nonjudicial records or books kept in any public office of any State, Territory, or Possession of the United States, or copies thereof, shall be proved or admitted in any court or office in any other State, Territory, or Possession by the attestation of the custodian of such records or books, and the seal of his office annexed, if there be a seal, together with a certificate of a judge of a court of record of the county, parish, or district in which such office may be kept, or of the Governor, or secretary of state, the chancellor or keeper of the great seal, of the State, Territory, or Possession that the said attestation is in due form and by the proper officers.

If the certificate is given by a judge, it shall be further authenticated by the clerk or prothonotary of the court, who shall certify, under his hand and the seal of his office, that such judge is duly commissioned and qualified; or, if given by such governor, secretary, chancellor, or keeper of the great seal, it shall be under the great seal of the State, Territory, or Possession in which it is made.

Such records or books, or copies thereof, so authenticated, shall have the same full faith and credit in every court and office within the United States and its Territories and Possessions as they have by law or usage in the courts or offices of the State, Territory, or Possession from which they are taken.

CHAPTER 131—RULES OF COURTS

§ 2071. Rule-making power generally

(a) The Supreme Court and all courts established by Act of Congress may from time to time prescribe rules for the conduct of their business. Such rules shall be consistent with Acts of Congress and rules of practice and procedure prescribed under section 2072 of this title.

(b) Any rule prescribed by a court, other than the Supreme Court, under subsection (a) shall be prescribed only after giving appropriate public notice and an opportunity for comment. Such rule shall take effect upon the date specified by the prescribing court and shall have such effect on pending proceedings as the prescribing court may order.

(c)(1) A rule of a district court prescribed under subsection (a) shall remain in effect unless modified or abrogated by the judicial council of the relevant circuit.

(2) Any other rule prescribed by a court other than the Supreme Court under subsection (a) shall remain in effect unless modified or abrogated by the Judicial Conference.

(d) Copies of rules prescribed under subsection (a) by a district court shall be furnished to the judicial council, and copies of all rules prescribed by a court other than the Supreme Court under subsection (a) shall be furnished to the Director of the Administrative Office of the United States Courts and made available to the public.

(e) If the prescribing court determines that there is an immediate need for a rule, such court may proceed under this section without public notice and opportunity for comment, but such court shall promptly thereafter afford such notice and opportunity for comment.

(f) No rule may be prescribed by a district court other than under this section.

§ 2072. Rules of procedure and evidence; power to prescribe

(a) The Supreme Court shall have the power to prescribe general rules of practice and procedure and rules of evidence for cases in the United States district courts (including proceedings before magistrates thereof) and courts of appeals.

(b) Such rules shall not abridge, enlarge or modify any substantive right. All laws in conflict with such rules shall be of no further force or effect after such rules have taken effect.

(c) Such rules may define when a ruling of a district court is final for the purposes of appeal under section 1291 of this title.

§ 2073. Rules of procedure and evidence; method of prescribing

(a)(1) The Judicial Conference shall prescribe and publish the procedures for the consideration of proposed rules under this section.

(2) The Judicial Conference may authorize the appointment of committees to assist the Conference by recommending rules to be prescribed under section 2072 and 2075 of this title. Each such committee shall consist of members of the bench and the professional bar, and trial and appellate judges.

(b) The Judicial Conference shall authorize the appointment of a standing committee on rules of practice, procedure, and evidence under subsection (a) of this section. Such standing committee shall review each recommendation of any other committees so appointed and recommend to the Judicial Conference rules of practice, procedure, and evidence and such changes in rules proposed by a committee appointed under subsection (a)(2) of this section as may be necessary to maintain consistency and otherwise promote the interest of justice.

(c)(1) Each meeting for the transaction of business under this chapter by any committee appointed under this section shall be open to the public, except when the committee so meeting, in open session and with a majority present, determines that it is in the public interest that all or part of the remainder of the meeting on that day shall be closed to the public, and states the reason for so closing the meeting. Minutes of each meeting for the transaction of business under this chapter shall be maintained by the committee and made available to the public, except that any portion of such minutes, relating to a closed meeting and made available to the public, may contain such deletions as may be necessary to avoid frustrating the purposes of closing the meeting.

(2) Any meeting for the transaction of business under this chapter, by a committee appointed under this section, shall be preceded by sufficient notice to enable all interested persons to attend.

(d) In making a recommendation under this section or under section 2072 or 2075, the body making that recommendation shall provide a proposed rule, an explanatory note on the rule, and a written report explaining the body's action, including any minority or other separate views.

(e) Failure to comply with this section does not invalidate a rule prescribed under section 2072 or 2075 of this title.

§ 2074. Rules of procedure and evidence; submission to Congress; effective date

(a) The Supreme Court shall transmit to the Congress not later than May 1 of the year in which a rule prescribed under section 2072 is to become effective a copy of the proposed rule. Such rule shall take effect no earlier than December 1 of the year in which such rule is so transmitted unless otherwise provided by law. The Supreme Court may fix the extent such rule shall apply to proceedings then pending, except that the Supreme Court shall not require the application of such rule to further proceedings then pending to the extent that, in the opinion of the court in which such proceedings are pending, the application of such rule in such proceedings would not be feasible or would work injustice, in which event the former rule applies.

(b) Any such rule creating, abolishing, or modifying an evidentiary privilege shall have no force or effect unless approved by Act of Congress.

§ 2075. Bankruptcy rules

The Supreme Court shall have the power to prescribe by general rules, the forms of process, writs, pleadings, and motions, and the practice and procedure in cases under title 11.

Such rules shall not abridge, enlarge, or modify any substantive right.

The Supreme Court shall transmit to Congress not later than May 1 of the year in which a rule prescribed under this section is to become effective a copy of the proposed rule. The rule shall take effect no earlier than December 1 of the year in which it is transmitted to Congress unless otherwise prescribed by law.

The bankruptcy rules promulgated under this section shall prescribe a form for the statement required under section 707(b)(2)(C) of title 11 and may provide general rules on the content of such statement.

CHAPTER 133—REVIEW—MISCELLANEOUS PROVISIONS

§ 2101. Supreme Court; time for appeal or certiorari; docketing; stay

(a) A direct appeal to the Supreme Court from any decision under section 1253 of this title, holding unconstitutional in whole or in part, any Act of Congress, shall be taken within thirty days after the entry of the interlocutory or final order, judgment or decree. The record shall be made up and the case docketed within sixty days from the time such appeal is taken under rules prescribed by the Supreme Court.

(b) Any other direct appeal to the Supreme Court which is authorized by law, from a decision of a district court in any civil action, suit or proceeding, shall be taken within thirty days from the judgment, order or decree, appealed from, if interlocutory, and within sixty days if final.

(c) Any other appeal or any writ of certiorari intended to bring any judgment or decree in a civil action, suit or proceeding before the Supreme Court for review shall be taken or applied for within ninety days after the entry of such judgment or decree. A justice of the Supreme Court, for good cause shown, may extend the time for applying for a writ of certiorari for a period not exceeding sixty days.

(d) The time for appeal or application for a writ of certiorari to review the judgment of a State court in a criminal case shall be as prescribed by rules of the Supreme Court.

(e) An application to the Supreme Court for a writ of certiorari to review a case before judgment has been rendered in the court of appeals may be made at any time before judgment.

(f) In any case in which the final judgment or decree of any court is subject to review by the Supreme Court on writ of certiorari, the execution and enforcement of such judgment or decree may be stayed for a reasonable time to enable the party aggrieved to obtain a writ of certiorari from the Supreme Court. The stay may be granted by a judge of the court rendering the judgment or decree or by a justice of the Supreme Court, and may be conditioned on the giving of security, approved by such judge or justice, that if the aggrieved party fails to make application for such writ within the period allotted therefor, or fails to obtain an order granting his application, or fails to make his plea good in the Supreme Court, he shall answer for all damages and costs which the other party may sustain by reason of the stay.

(g) The time for application for a writ of certiorari to review a decision of the United States Court of Appeals for the Armed Forces shall be as prescribed by rules of the Supreme Court.

§ 2102. Priority of criminal case on appeal from State court

Criminal cases on review from State courts shall have priority, on the docket of the Supreme Court, over all cases except cases to which the United States is a party and such other cases as the court may decide to be of public importance.

§ 2104. Review of State court decisions

A review by the Supreme Court of a judgment or decree of a State court shall be conducted in the same manner and under the same regulations, and shall have the same effect, as if the judgment or decree reviewed had been rendered in a court of the United States.

§ 2105. Scope of review; abatement

There shall be no reversal in the Supreme Court or a court of appeals for error in ruling upon matters in abatement which do not involve jurisdiction.

§ 2106. Determination

The Supreme Court or any other court of appellate jurisdiction may affirm, modify, vacate, set aside or reverse any judgment, decree, or order of a court lawfully brought before it for review, and may remand the cause and direct the entry of such appropriate judgment, decree, or order, or require such further proceedings to be had as may be just under the circumstances.

§ 2107. Time for appeal to court of appeals

(a) Except as otherwise provided in this section, no appeal shall bring any judgment, order or decree in an action, suit or proceeding of a civil nature before a court of appeals for review unless notice of appeal is filed, within thirty days after the entry of such judgment, order or decree.

(b) In any such action, suit or proceeding in which the United States or an officer or agency thereof is a party, the time as to all parties shall be sixty days from such entry.

(c) The district court may, upon motion filed not later than 30 days after the expiration of the time otherwise set for bringing appeal, extend the time for appeal upon a showing of excusable neglect or good cause. In addition if the district court finds—

(1) that a party entitled to notice of the entry of a judgment or order did not receive such notice from the clerk or any party within 21 days of its entry, and

(2) that no party would be prejudiced, the district court may, upon motion filed within 180 days after entry of the judgment or order or within 7 days after receipt of such notice, whichever is earlier, reopen the time for appeal for a period of 14 days from the date of entry of the order reopening the time for appeal.

(d) This section shall not apply to bankruptcy matters or other proceedings under Title 11.

§ 2108. Proof of amount in controversy

Where the power of any court of appeals to review a case depends upon the amount or value in controversy, such amount or value, if not otherwise satisfactorily disclosed upon the record, may be shown and ascertained by the oath of a party to the case or by other competent evidence.

§ 2111. Harmless error

On the hearing of any appeal or writ of certiorari in any case, the court shall give judgment after an examination of the record without regard to errors or defects which do not affect the substantial rights of the parties.

CHAPTER 151—DECLARATORY JUDGMENTS

§ 2201. Creation of remedy

(a) In a case of actual controversy within its jurisdiction, except with respect to Federal taxes other than actions brought under section 7428 of the Internal Revenue Code of 1986, a proceeding under section 505 or 1146 of title 11, or in any civil action involving an antidumping or countervailing duty proceeding regarding a class or kind of merchandise of a free trade area country (as defined in section 516A(f)(10) of the Tariff Act of 1930), as determined by the administering authority, any court of the United States, upon the filing of an appropriate pleading, may declare the rights and other legal relations of any interested party seeking such declaration, whether or not further relief is or could be sought. Any such declaration shall have the force and effect of a final judgment or decree and shall be reviewable as such.

(b) For limitations on actions brought with respect to drug patents see section 505 or 512 of the Federal Food, Drug, and Cosmetic Act.

§ 2202. Further relief

Further necessary or proper relief based on a declaratory judgment or decree may be granted, after reasonable notice and hearing, against any adverse party whose rights have been determined by such judgment.

CHAPTER 153—HABEAS CORPUS

§ 2241. Power to grant writ

(a) Writs of habeas corpus may be granted by the Supreme Court, any justice thereof, the district courts and any circuit judge within their respective jurisdictions. The order of a circuit judge shall be entered in the records of the district court of the district wherein the restraint complained of is had.

(b) The Supreme Court, any justice thereof, and any circuit judge may decline to entertain an application for a writ of habeas corpus and may transfer the application for hearing and determination to the district court having jurisdiction to entertain it.

(c) The writ of habeas corpus shall not extend to a prisoner unless—

(1) He is in custody under or by color of the authority of the United States or is committed for trial before some court thereof; or

(2) He is in custody for an act done or omitted in pursuance of an Act of Congress, or an order, process, judgment or decree of a court or judge of the United States; or

(3) He is in custody in violation of the Constitution or laws or treaties of the United States; or

(4) He, being a citizen of a foreign state and domiciled therein is in custody for an act done or omitted under any alleged right, title, authority, privilege, protection, or exemption claimed under the commission, order or sanction of any foreign state, or under color thereof, the validity and effect of which depend upon the law of nations; or

(5) It is necessary to bring him into court to testify or for trial.

(d) Where an application for a writ of habeas corpus is made by a person in custody under the judgment and sentence of a State court of a State which contains two or more Federal judicial districts, the application may be filed in the district court for the district wherein such person is in custody or in the district court for the district within which the State court was held which convicted and sentenced him and each of such district courts shall have concurrent jurisdiction to entertain the application. The district court for the district wherein such an application is filed in the exercise of its discretion and in furtherance of justice may transfer the application to the other district court for hearing and determination.

(e) Except as provided in section 1405* of the Detainee Treatment Act of 2005, no court, justice, or judge shall have jurisdiction to hear or consider—

(1) an application for a writ of habeas corpus filed by or on behalf of an alien detained by the Department of Defense at Guantanamo Bay, Cuba; or

(2) any other action against the United States or its agents relating to any aspect of the detention by the Department of Defense of an alien at Guantanamo Bay, Cuba, who—

(A) is currently in military custody; or

(B) has been determined by the United States Court of Appeals for the District of Columbia Circuit in accordance with the procedures set forth in section 1405(e) of the Detainee Treatment Act of 2005 to have been properly detained as an enemy combatant.

---

* Two versions of § 2241(e) were enacted. They are identical except that one version refers to sections 1005 and 1005(e) of the Detainee Treatment Act of 2005 and the other refers to sections 1405 and 1405(e) of the Detainee Treatment Act of 2005. The correct reference appears to be sections 1405 and 1405(e) of Pub. L. 109–163, 119 Stat. 3476, which is codified only in the Statutory Notes to 10 U.S.C. § 801 (2006 Supp.) and provides for limited judicial review of the status of enemy combatant detainees.

§ 2242. Application

Application for a writ of habeas corpus shall be in writing signed and verified by the person for whose relief it is intended or by someone acting in his behalf.

It shall allege the facts concerning the applicant's commitment or detention, the name of the person who has custody over him and by virtue of what claim or authority, if known.

It may be amended or supplemented as provided in the rules of procedure applicable to civil actions.

If addressed to the Supreme Court, a justice thereof or a circuit judge it shall state the reasons for not making application to the district court of the district in which the applicant is held.

§ 2243. Issuance of writ; return; hearing; decision

A court, justice or judge entertaining an application for a writ of habeas corpus shall forthwith award the writ or issue an order directing the respondent to show cause why the writ should not be granted, unless it appears from the application that the applicant or person detained is not entitled thereto.

The writ, or order to show cause shall be directed to the person having custody of the person detained. It shall be returned within three days unless for good cause additional time, not exceeding twenty days, is allowed.

The person to whom the writ or order is directed shall make a return certifying the true cause of the detention.

When the writ or order is returned a day shall be set for hearing, not more than five days after the return unless for good cause additional time is allowed.

Unless the application for the writ and the return present only issues of law the person to whom the writ is directed shall be required to produce at the hearing the body of the person detained.

The applicant or the person detained may, under oath, deny any of the facts set forth in the return or allege any other material facts.

The return and all suggestions made against it may be amended, by leave of court, before or after being filed.

The court shall summarily hear and determine the facts, and dispose of the matter as law and justice require.

§ 2244. Finality of determination

(a) No circuit or district judge shall be required to entertain an application for a writ of habeas corpus to inquire into the detention of a person pursuant to a judgment of a court of the United States if it appears that the legality of such detention has been determined by a judge or court of the United States on a prior application for a writ of habeas corpus, except as provided by section 2255.

(b)(1) A claim presented in a second or successive habeas corpus application under section 2254 that was presented in a prior application shall be dismissed.

(2) A claim presented in a second or successive habeas corpus application under section 2254 that was not presented in a prior application shall be dismissed unless

(A) the applicant shows that the claim relies on a new rule of constitutional law, made retroactive to cases on collateral review by the Supreme Court, that was previously unavailable; or

(B)(i) the factual predicate for the claim could not have been discovered previously through the exercise of due diligence; and

(ii) the facts underlying the claim, if proven and viewed in light of the evidence as a whole, would be sufficient to establish by clear and convincing evidence that, but for constitutional error, no reasonable factfinder would have found the applicant guilty of the underlying offense.

(3)(A) Before a second or successive application permitted by this section is filed in the district court, the applicant shall move in the appropriate court of appeals for an order authorizing the district court to consider the application.

(B) A motion in the court of appeals for an order authorizing the district court to consider a second or successive application shall be determined by a three-judge panel of the court of appeals.

(C) The court of appeals may authorize the filing of a second or successive application only if it determines that the application makes a prima facie showing that the application satisfies the requirements of this subsection.

(D) The court of appeals shall grant or deny the authorization to file a second or successive application not later than 30 days after the filing of the motion.

(E) The grant or denial of an authorization by a court of appeals to file a second or successive application shall not be appealable and shall not be the subject of a petition for rehearing or for a writ of certiorari.

(4) A district court shall dismiss any claim presented in a second or successive application that the court of appeals has authorized to be filed unless the applicant shows that the claim satisfies the requirements of this section.

(c) In a habeas corpus proceeding brought in behalf of a person in custody pursuant to the judgment of a State court, a prior judgment of the Supreme Court of the United States on an appeal or review by a writ of certiorari at the instance of the prisoner of the decision of such State court, shall be conclusive as to all issues of fact or law with respect to an asserted denial of a Federal right which constitutes ground for discharge in a habeas corpus proceeding, actually adjudicated by the Supreme Court therein, unless the applicant for the writ of habeas corpus shall plead and the court shall find the existence of a material and controlling fact which did not appear in the record of the proceeding in the Supreme Court and the court shall further find that the applicant for the writ of habeas corpus could not have caused such fact to appear in such record by the exercise of reasonable diligence.

(d)(1) A 1–year period of limitation shall apply to an application for a writ of habeas corpus by a person in custody pursuant to the judgment of a State court. The limitation period shall run from the latest of

(A) the date on which the judgment became final by the conclusion of direct review or the expiration of the time for seeking such review;

(B) the date on which the impediment to filing an application created by state action in violation of the Constitution or laws of the United States is removed, if the applicant was prevented from filing by such State action;

(C) the date on which the constitutional right asserted was initially recognized by the Supreme Court, if the right has been newly recognized by the Supreme Court and made retroactively applicable to cases on collateral review; or

(D) the date on which the factual predicate of the claim or claims presented could have been discovered through the exercise of due diligence.

(2) The time during which a properly filed application for State post-conviction or other collateral review with respect to the pertinent judgment or claim is pending shall not be counted toward any period of limitation under this subsection.

§ 2245. Certificate of trial judge admissible in evidence

On the hearing of an application for a writ of habeas corpus to inquire into the legality of the detention of a person pursuant to a judgment the certificate of the judge who presided at the trial resulting in the judgment, setting forth the facts occurring at the trial, shall be admissible in evidence. Copies of the certificate shall be filed with the court in which the application is pending and in the court in which the trial took place.

§ 2246. Evidence; depositions; affidavits

On application for a writ of habeas corpus, evidence may be taken orally or by deposition, or, in the discretion of the judge, by affidavit. If affidavits are admitted any party shall have the right to propound written interrogatories to the affiants, or to file answering affidavits.

§ 2247. Documentary evidence

On application for a writ of habeas corpus documentary evidence, transcripts of proceedings upon arraignment, plea and sentence and a transcript of the oral testimony introduced on any previous similar application by or in behalf of the same petitioner, shall be admissible in evidence.

§ 2248. Return or answer; conclusiveness

The allegations of a return to the writ of habeas corpus or of an answer to an order to show cause in a habeas corpus proceeding, if not traversed, shall be accepted as true except to the extent that the judge finds from the evidence that they are not true.

§ 2249. Certified copies of indictment, plea and judgment; duty of respondent

On application for a writ of habeas corpus to inquire into the detention of any person pursuant to a judgment of a court of the United States, the respondent shall promptly file with the court certified copies of the indictment, plea of petitioner and the judgment, or such of them as may be material to the questions raised, if the petitioner fails to attach them to his petition, and same shall be attached to the return to the writ, or to the answer to the order to show cause.

§ 2250. Indigent petitioner entitled to documents without cost

If on any application for a writ of habeas corpus an order has been made permitting the petitioner to prosecute the application in forma pauperis, the clerk of any court of the United States shall furnish to the petitioner without cost certified copies of such documents or parts of the record on file in his office as may be required by order of the judge before whom the application is pending.

§ 2251. Stay of State court proceedings

(a) In general.—

(1) Pending matters.—A justice or judge of the United States before whom a habeas corpus proceeding is pending, may, before final judgment or after final judgment of discharge, or pending appeal, stay any proceeding against the person detained in any State court or by or under the authority of any State for any matter involved in the habeas corpus proceeding.

(2) Matter not pending.—For purposes of this section, a habeas corpus proceeding is not pending until the application is filed.

(3) Application for appointment of counsel.—If a State prisoner sentenced to death applies for appointment of counsel pursuant to section 3599(a)(2) of title 18 in a court that would have jurisdiction to entertain a habeas corpus application regarding that sentence, that court may stay execution of the sentence of death, but such stay shall terminate not later than 90 days after counsel is appointed or the application for appointment of counsel is withdrawn or denied.

(b) No further proceedings.—After the granting of such a stay, any such proceeding in any State court or by or under the authority of any

State shall be void. If no stay is granted, any such proceeding shall be as valid as if no habeas corpus proceedings or appeal were pending.

§ 2252. Notice

Prior to the hearing of a habeas corpus proceeding in behalf of a person in custody of State officers or by virtue of State laws notice shall be served on the attorney general or other appropriate officer of such State as the justice or judge at the time of issuing the writ shall direct.

§ 2253. Appeal

(a) In a habeas corpus proceeding or a proceeding under section 2255 before a district judge, the final order shall be subject to review, on appeal, by the court of appeals for the circuit in which the proceeding is held.

(b) There shall be no right of appeal from a final order in a proceeding to test the validity of a warrant to remove to another district or place for commitment or trial a person charged with a criminal offense against the United States, or to test the validity of such person's detention pending removal proceedings.

(c)(1) Unless a circuit justice or judge issues a certificate of appealability, an appeal may not be taken to the court of appeals from

(A) the final order in a habeas corpus proceeding in which the detention complained of arises out of process issued by a State court; or

(B) the final order in a proceeding under section 2255.

(2) A certificate of appealability may issue under paragraph (1) only if the applicant has made a substantial showing of the denial of a constitutional right.

(3) The certificate of appealability under paragraph (1) shall indicate which specific issue or issues satisfy the showing required by paragraph (2).

§ 2254. State custody; remedies in Federal courts

(a) The Supreme Court, a Justice thereof, a circuit judge, or a district court shall entertain an application for a writ of habeas corpus in behalf of a person in custody pursuant to the judgment of a State court only on the ground that he is in custody in violation of the Constitution or laws or treaties of the United States.

(b)(1) An application for a writ of habeas corpus on behalf of a person in custody pursuant to the judgment of a State court shall not be granted unless it appears that

(A) the applicant has exhausted the remedies available in the courts of the State; or

(B)(i) there is an absence of available state corrective process; or

(ii) circumstances exist that render such process ineffective to protect the rights of the applicant.

(2) An application for a writ of habeas corpus may be denied on the merits, notwithstanding the failure of the applicant to exhaust the remedies available in the courts of the State.

(3) A State shall not be deemed to have waived the exhaustion requirement or be estopped from reliance upon the requirement unless the State, through counsel, expressly waives the requirement.

(c) An applicant shall not be deemed to have exhausted the remedies available in the courts of the State, within the meaning of this section, if he has the right under the law of the State to raise, by any available procedure, the question presented.

(d) An application for a writ of habeas corpus on behalf of a person in custody pursuant to the judgment of a State court shall not be granted with respect to any claim that was adjudicated on the merits in State court proceedings unless the adjudication of the claim

(1) resulted in a decision that was contrary to, or involved an unreasonable application of, clearly established Federal law, as determined by the Supreme Court of the United States; or

(2) resulted in a decision that was based on an unreasonable determination of the facts in light of the evidence presented in the state court proceeding.

(e)(1) In a proceeding instituted by an application for a writ of habeas corpus by a person in custody pursuant to the judgment of a State court, a determination of a factual issue made by a State court shall be presumed to be correct. The applicant shall have the burden of rebutting the presumption of correctness by clear and convincing evidence.

(2) If the applicant has failed to develop the factual basis of a claim in State court proceedings, the court shall not hold an evidentiary hearing on the claim unless the applicant shows that

(A) the claim relies on

(i) a new rule of constitutional law, made retroactive to cases on collateral review by the Supreme Court, that was previously unavailable; or

(ii) a factual predicate that could not have been previously discovered through the exercise of due diligence; and

(B) the facts underlying the claim would be sufficient to establish by clear and convincing evidence that but for constitutional error, no reasonable factfinder would have found the applicant guilty of the underlying offense.

(f) If the applicant challenges the sufficiency of the evidence adduced in such State court proceeding to support the State court's determination of a factual issue made therein, the applicant, if able, shall produce that part of the record pertinent to a determination of the sufficiency of the evidence to support such determination. If the applicant, because of indigency or other reason is unable to produce such part of the record, then the State shall produce such part of the record and the Federal court shall direct the State to do so by order directed to an appropriate State official. If the State cannot provide such pertinent part of the record, then the court shall determine under the existing facts and circumstances what weight shall be given to the State court's factual determination.

(g) A copy of the official records of the State court, duly certified by the clerk of such court to be a true and correct copy of a finding, judicial opinion, or other reliable written indicia showing such a factual determination by the State court shall be admissible in the Federal Court proceeding.

(h) Except as provided in section 408 of the Controlled Substances Act, in all proceedings brought under this section, and any subsequent proceedings on review, the court may appoint counsel for an applicant who is or becomes financially unable to afford counsel, except as provided by a rule promulgated by the Supreme Court pursuant to statutory authority. Appointment of counsel under this section shall be governed by section 3006A of title 18.

(i) The ineffectiveness or incompetence of counsel during Federal or State collateral post-conviction proceedings shall not be a ground for relief in a proceeding arising under section 2254.

§ 2255. Federal custody; remedies on motion attacking sentence

A prisoner in custody under sentence of a court established by Act of Congress claiming the right to be released upon the ground that the sentence was imposed in violation of the Constitution or laws of the United States, or that the court was without jurisdiction to impose such sentence, or that the sentence was in excess of the maximum authorized by law, or is otherwise subject to collateral attack, may move the court which imposed the sentence to vacate, set aside or correct the sentence.

Unless the motion and the files and records of the case conclusively show that the prisoner is entitled to no relief, the court shall cause notice thereof to be served upon the United States attorney, grant a prompt hearing thereon, determine the issues and make findings of fact and conclusions of law with respect thereto. If the court finds that the judgment was rendered without jurisdiction, or that the sentence imposed was not authorized by law or otherwise open to collateral attack, or that there has been such a denial or infringement of the constitutional rights of the prisoner as to render the judgment vulnerable to collateral attack, the court shall vacate and set the judgment aside and shall discharge the prisoner or resentence him or grant a new trial or correct the sentence as may appear appropriate.

A court may entertain and determine such motion without requiring the production of the prisoner at the hearing.

An appeal may be taken to the court of appeals from the order entered on the motion as from a final judgment on application for a writ of habeas corpus.

An application for a writ of habeas corpus in behalf of a prisoner who is authorized to apply for relief by motion pursuant to this section, shall not be entertained if it appears that the applicant has failed to apply for relief, by motion, to the court which sentenced him, or that such court has denied him relief, unless it also appears that the remedy by motion is inadequate or ineffective to test the legality of his detention.

A 1–year period of limitation shall apply to a motion under this section. The limitation period shall run from the latest of

(1) the date on which the judgment of conviction becomes final;

(2) the date on which the impediment to making a motion created by governmental action in violation of the Constitution or laws of the United States is removed, if the movant was prevented from making a motion by such governmental action;

(3) the date on which the right asserted was initially recognized by the Supreme Court, if that right has been newly recognized by the Supreme Court and made retroactively applicable to cases on collateral review; or

(4) the date on which the facts supporting the claim or claims presented could have been discovered through the exercise of due diligence.

Except as provided in section 408 of the Controlled Substances Act, in all proceedings brought under this section, and any subsequent proceedings on review, the court may appoint counsel, except as provided by a rule promulgated by the Supreme Court pursuant to statutory authority. Appointment of counsel under this section shall be governed by section 3006A of title 18.

A second or successive motion must be certified as provided in section 2244 by a panel of the appropriate court of appeals to contain

(1) newly discovered evidence that, if proven and viewed in light of the evidence as a whole, would be sufficient to establish by clear and convincing evidence that no reasonable factfinder would have found the movant guilty of the offense; or

(2) a new rule of constitutional law, made retroactive to cases on collateral review by the Supreme Court, that was previously unavailable.

CHAPTER 154—SPECIAL HABEAS CORPUS PROCEDURES IN CAPITAL CASES

§ 2261. Prisoners in State custody subject to capital sentence; appointment of counsel; requirement of rule of court or statute; procedures for appointment

(a) This chapter shall apply to cases arising under section 2254 brought by prisoners in State custody who are subject to a capital sentence. It shall apply only if the provisions of subsections (b) and (c) are satisfied.

(b) Counsel.—this chapter is applicable if—

(1) the Attorney General of the United States certifies that a State has established a mechanism for providing counsel in postconviction proceedings as provided in section 2265; and

(2) counsel was appointed pursuant to that mechanism, petitioner validly waived counsel, petitioner retained counsel, or petitioner was found not to be indigent.

(c) Any mechanism for the appointment, compensation, and reimbursement of counsel as provided in subsection (b) must offer counsel to all State prisoners under capital sentence and must provide for the entry of an order by a court of record—

(1) appointing one or more counsels to represent the prisoner upon a finding that the prisoner is indigent and accepted the offer or is unable competently to decide whether to accept or reject the offer;

(2) finding, after a hearing if necessary, that the prisoner rejected the offer of counsel and made the decision with an understanding of its legal consequences; or

(3) denying the appointment of counsel upon a finding that the prisoner is not indigent.

(d) No counsel appointed pursuant to subsections (b) and (c) to represent a State prisoner under capital sentence shall have previously represented the prisoner at trial in the case for which the appointment is made unless the prisoner and counsel expressly request continued representation.

(e) The ineffectiveness or incompetence of counsel during State or Federal post-conviction proceedings in a capital case shall not be a ground for relief in a proceeding arising under section 2254. This limitation shall not preclude the appointment of different counsel, on the court's own motion or at the request of the prisoner, at any phase of State or Federal post-conviction proceedings on the basis of the ineffectiveness or incompetence of counsel in such proceedings.

§ 2262. Mandatory stay of execution; duration; limits on stays of execution; successive petitions

(a) Upon the entry in the appropriate State court of record of an order under section 2261(c), a warrant or order setting an execution date for a State prisoner shall be stayed upon application to any court that would have jurisdiction over any proceedings filed under section 2254. The application shall recite that the State has invoked the post-conviction review procedures of this chapter and that the scheduled execution is subject to stay.

(b) A stay of execution granted pursuant to subsection (a) shall expire if

(1) a state prisoner fails to file a habeas corpus application under section 2254 within the time required in section 2263;

(2) before a court of competent jurisdiction, in the presence of counsel, unless the prisoner has competently and knowingly waived such counsel, and after having been advised of the consequences, a state prisoner under capital sentence waives the right to pursue habeas corpus review under section 2254; or

(3) a State prisoner files a habeas corpus petition under section 2254 within the time required by section 2263 and fails to make a substantial showing of the denial of a Federal right or is denied relief in the district court or at any subsequent stage of review.

(c) If one of the conditions in subsection (b) has occurred, no Federal court thereafter shall have the authority to enter a stay of execution in the case, unless the court of appeals approves the filing of a second or successive application under section 2244(b).

§ 2263. Filing of habeas corpus application; time requirements; tolling rules

(a) Any application under this chapter for habeas corpus relief under section 2254 must be filed in the appropriate district court not later than 180 days after final State court affirmance of the conviction and sentence on direct review or the expiration of the time for seeking such review.

(b) The time requirements established by subsection (a) shall be tolled

(1) from the date that a petition for certiorari is filed in the Supreme Court until the date of final disposition of the petition if a State prisoner files the petition to secure review by the Supreme Court of the affirmance of a capital sentence on direct review by the court of last resort of the State or other final State court decision on direct review;

(2) from the date on which the first petition for post-conviction review or other collateral relief is filed until the final State court disposition of such petition; and

(3) during an additional period not to exceed 30 days, if

(A) a motion for an extension of time is filed in the Federal district court that would have jurisdiction over the case upon the filing of a habeas corpus application under section 2254; and

(B) a showing of good cause is made for the failure to file the habeas corpus application within the time period established by this section.

§ 2264. Scope of Federal review; district court adjudications

(a) Whenever a State prisoner under capital sentence files a petition for habeas corpus relief to which this chapter applies, the district court shall only consider a claim or claims that have been raised and decided on the merits in the State courts, unless the failure to raise the claim properly is

(1) the result of state action in violation of the Constitution or laws of the United States;

(2) the result of the Supreme Court's recognition of a new Federal right that is made retroactively applicable; or

(3) based on a factual predicate that could not have been discovered through the exercise of due diligence in time to present the claim for State or Federal post-conviction review.

(b) Following review subject to subsections (a), (d), and (e) of section 2254, the court shall rule on the claims properly before it.

§ 2265. Certification and judicial review.

(a) Certification—

(1) In general.—If requested by an appropriate State official, the Attorney General of the United States shall determine—

(A) whether the State has established a mechanism for the appointment, compensation, and payment of reasonable litigation expenses of competent counsel in State postconviction proceedings brought by indigent prisoners who have been sentence to death;

(B) the date on which the mechanism described in subparagraph (A) was established; and

(C) whether the State provides standards of competency for the appointment of counsel in proceedings described in subparagraph (a).

(2) Effective date.—The date the mechanism described in paragraph (1)(A) was established shall be the effective date of the certification under this subsection.

(3) Only express requirements.—There are no requirements for certification or for application of this chapter other than those expressly stated in this chapter.

(b) Regulations.—The Attorney General shall promulgate regulations to implement the certification procedure under subsection (a).

(c) Review of certification.—

(1) In general.—The determination by the Attorney General regarding whether to certify a State under this section is subject to review exclusively as provided under chapter 158 of this title.

(2) Venue.—The Court of Appeals for the District of Columbia Circuit shall have exclusive jurisdiction over matters under paragraph (1), subject to review by the Supreme Court under section 2350 of this title.

(3) Standard of review.—The determination by the Attorney General regarding whether to certify a State under this section shall be subject to de novo review.

§ 2266. Limitation periods for determining applications and motions

(a) The adjudication of any application under section 2254 that is subject to this chapter, and the adjudication of any motion under section 2255 by a person under sentence of death, shall be given priority by the district court and by the court of appeals over all noncapital matters.

(b)(1)(A) A district court shall render a final determination and enter a final judgment on any application for a writ of habeas corpus brought under this chapter in a capital case not later than 450 days after the date on which the application is filed, or 60 days after the date on which the case is submitted for decision, whichever is earlier.

(B) A district court shall afford the parties at least 120 days in which to complete all actions, including the preparation of all pleadings and briefs, and if necessary, a hearing, prior to the submission of the case for decision.

(C)(i) A district court may delay for not more than one additional 30–day period beyond the period specified in subparagraph (A), the rendering of a determination of an application for a writ of habeas corpus if the court issues a written order making a finding, and stating the reasons for the finding, that the ends of justice that would be served by allowing the delay outweigh the best interests of the public and the applicant in a speedy disposition of the application.

(ii) The factors, among others, that a court shall consider in determining whether a delay in the disposition of an application is warranted are as follows:

(I) Whether the failure to allow the delay would be likely to result in a miscarriage of justice.

(II) Whether the case is so unusual or so complex, due to the number of defendants, the nature of the prosecution, or the existence of novel questions of fact or law, that it is unreasonable to expect adequate briefing within the time limitations established by subparagraph (A).

(III) Whether the failure to allow a delay in a case that, taken as a whole, is not so unusual or so complex as described in subclause (II), but would otherwise deny the applicant reasonable time to obtain counsel, would unreasonably deny the applicant or the government continuity of counsel, or would deny counsel for the applicant or the government the reasonable time necessary for effective preparation, taking into account the exercise of due diligence.

(iii) No delay in disposition shall be permissible because of general congestion of the court's calendar.

(iv) The court shall transmit a copy of any order issued under clause (i) to the Director of the Administrative Office of the United States Courts for inclusion in the report under paragraph (5).

(2) The time limitations under paragraph (1) shall apply to

(A) an initial application for a writ of habeas corpus;

(B) any second or successive application for a writ of habeas corpus; and

(C) any redetermination of an application for a writ of habeas corpus following a remand by the court of appeals or the Supreme Court for further proceedings, in which case the limitation period shall run from the date the remand is ordered.

(3)(A) The time limitations under this section shall not be construed to entitle an applicant to a stay of execution, to which the applicant would otherwise not be entitled, for the purpose of litigating any application or appeal.

(B) No amendment to an application for a writ of habeas corpus under this chapter shall be permitted after the filing of the answer to the application, except on the grounds specified in section 2244(b).

(4)(A) the failure of a court to meet or comply with a time limitation under this section shall not be a ground for granting relief from a judgment of conviction or sentence.

(B) The State may enforce a time limitation under this section by petitioning for a writ of mandamus to the court of appeals. The court of appeals shall act on the petition for a writ of mandamus not later than 30 days after the filing of the petition.

(5)(A) The Administrative Office of the United States Courts shall submit to Congress an annual report on the compliance by the district courts with the time limitations under this section.

(B) the report described in subparagraph (A) shall include copies of the orders submitted by the district courts under paragraph (1)(B)(iv).

(c)(1)(A) A court of appeals shall hear and render a final determination of any appeal of an order granting or denying, in whole or in part, an application brought under this chapter in a capital case not later than 120 days after the date on which the reply brief is filed, or if no reply brief is filed, not later than 120 days after the date on which the answering brief is filed.

(B)(i) A court of appeals shall decide whether to grant a petition for rehearing or other request for rehearing en banc not later than 30 days after the date on which the petition for rehearing is filed unless a responsive pleading is required, in which case the court shall decide whether to grant the petition not later than 30 days after the date on which the responsive pleading is filed.

(ii) If a petition for rehearing or rehearing en banc is granted, the court of appeals shall hear and render a final determination of the appeal not later than 120 days after the date on which the order granting rehearing or rehearing en banc is entered.

(2) The time limitations under paragraph (1) shall apply to

(A) an initial application for a writ of habeas corpus;

(B) any second or successive application for a writ of habeas corpus; and

(C) any redetermination of an application for a writ of habeas corpus or related appeal following a remand by the court of appeals en banc or the Supreme Court for further proceedings, in which case the limitation period shall run from the date the remand is ordered.

(3) The time limitations under this section shall not be construed to entitle an applicant to a stay of execution, to which the applicant would otherwise not be entitled, for the purpose of litigating any application or appeal.

(4)(A) The failure of a court to meet or comply with a time limitation under this section shall not be a ground for granting relief from a judgment of conviction or sentence.

(B) the State may enforce a time limitation under this section by applying for a writ of mandamus to the Supreme Court.

(5) The Administrative Office of the United States Courts shall submit to Congress an annual report on the compliance by the courts of appeals with the time limitations under this section.

CHAPTER 155—INJUNCTIONS; THREE–JUDGE COURTS

§ 2283. Stay of State court proceedings

A court of the United States may not grant an injunction to stay proceedings in a State court except as expressly authorized by Act of Congress, or where necessary in aid of its jurisdiction, or to protect or effectuate its judgments.

§ 2284. Three-judge court; when required; composition; procedure

(a) A district court of three judges shall be convened when otherwise required by Act of Congress, or when an action is filed challenging the constitutionality of the apportionment of congressional districts or the apportionment of any statewide legislative body.

(b) In any action required to be heard and determined by a district court of three judges under subsection (a) of this section, the composition and procedure of the court shall be as follows:

(1) Upon the filing of a request for three judges, the judge to whom the request is presented shall, unless he determines that three judges are not required, immediately notify the chief judge of the circuit, who shall designate two other judges, at least one of whom shall be a circuit judge. The judges so designated, and the

judge to whom the request was presented, shall serve as members of the court to hear and determine the action or proceeding.

(2) If the action is against a State, or officer or agency thereof, at least five days' notice of hearing of the action shall be given by registered or certified mail to the Governor and attorney general of the State.

(3) A single judge may conduct all proceedings except the trial, and enter all orders permitted by the rules of civil procedure except as provided in this subsection. He may grant a temporary restraining order on a specific finding, based on evidence submitted, that specified irreparable damage will result if the order is not granted, which order, unless previously revoked by the district judge, shall remain in force only until the hearing and determination by the district court of three judges of an application for a preliminary injunction. A single judge shall not appoint a master, or order a reference, or hear and determine any application for a preliminary or permanent injunction or motion to vacate such an injunction, or enter judgment on the merits. Any action of a single judge may be reviewed by the full court at any time before final judgment.

*

Index

References are to Pages